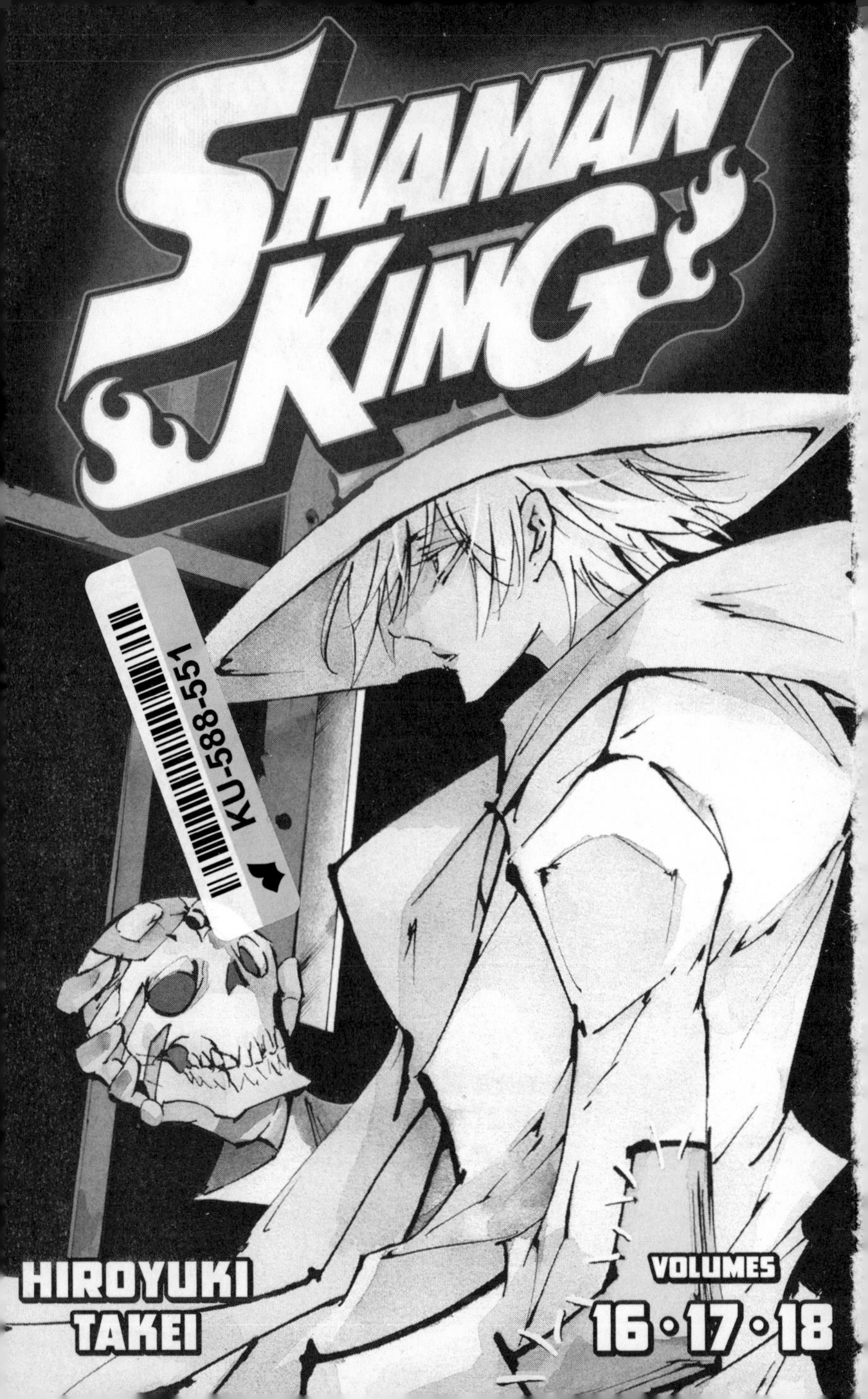
SHAMAN KING
HIROYUKI
TAKEI
VOLUMES
16 • 17 • 18
KU-588-551

VOLUMES
16·17·18

TABLE OF CONTENTS

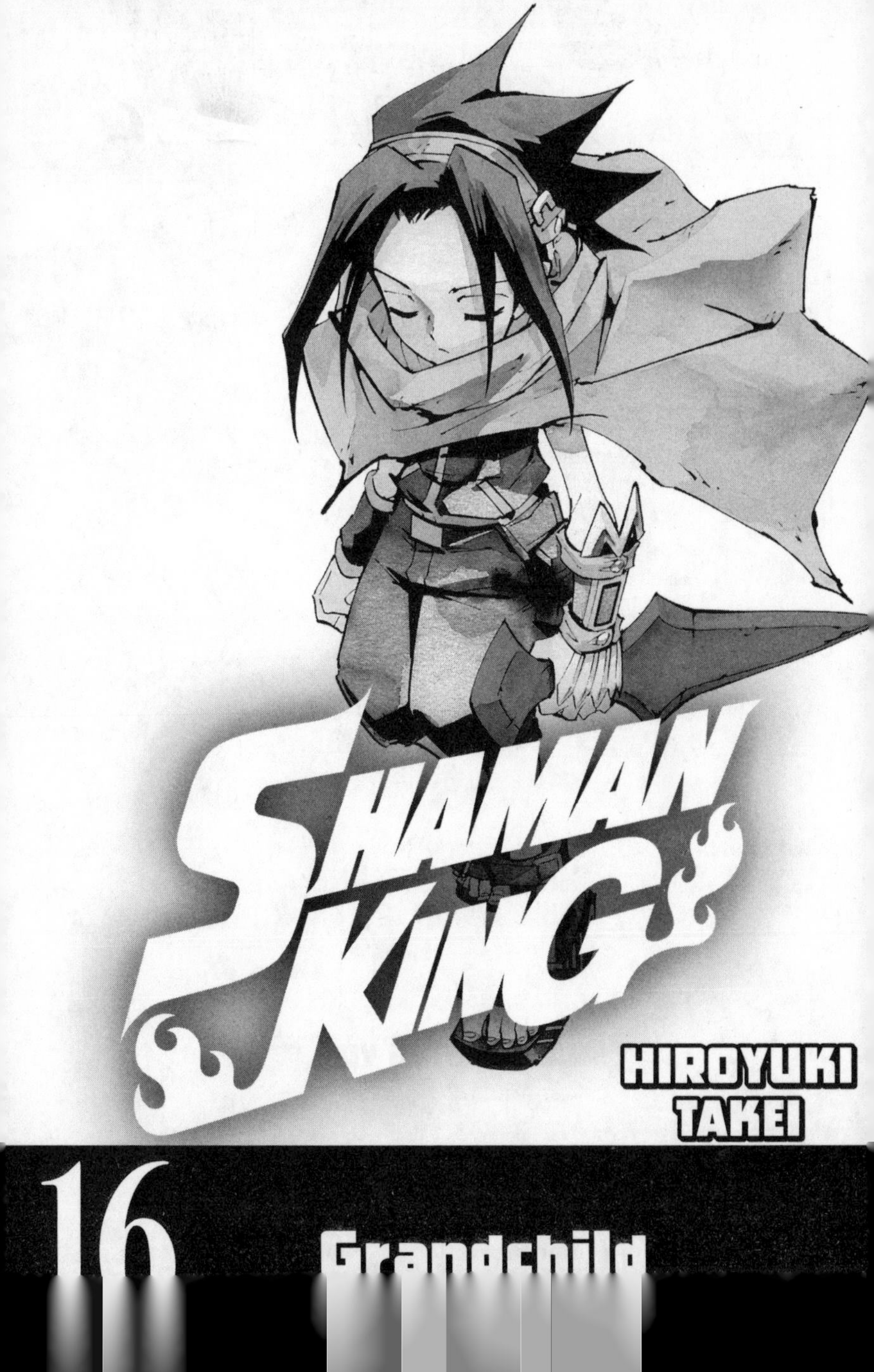

SHAMAN KING

HIROYUKI TAKEI

16

Grandchild

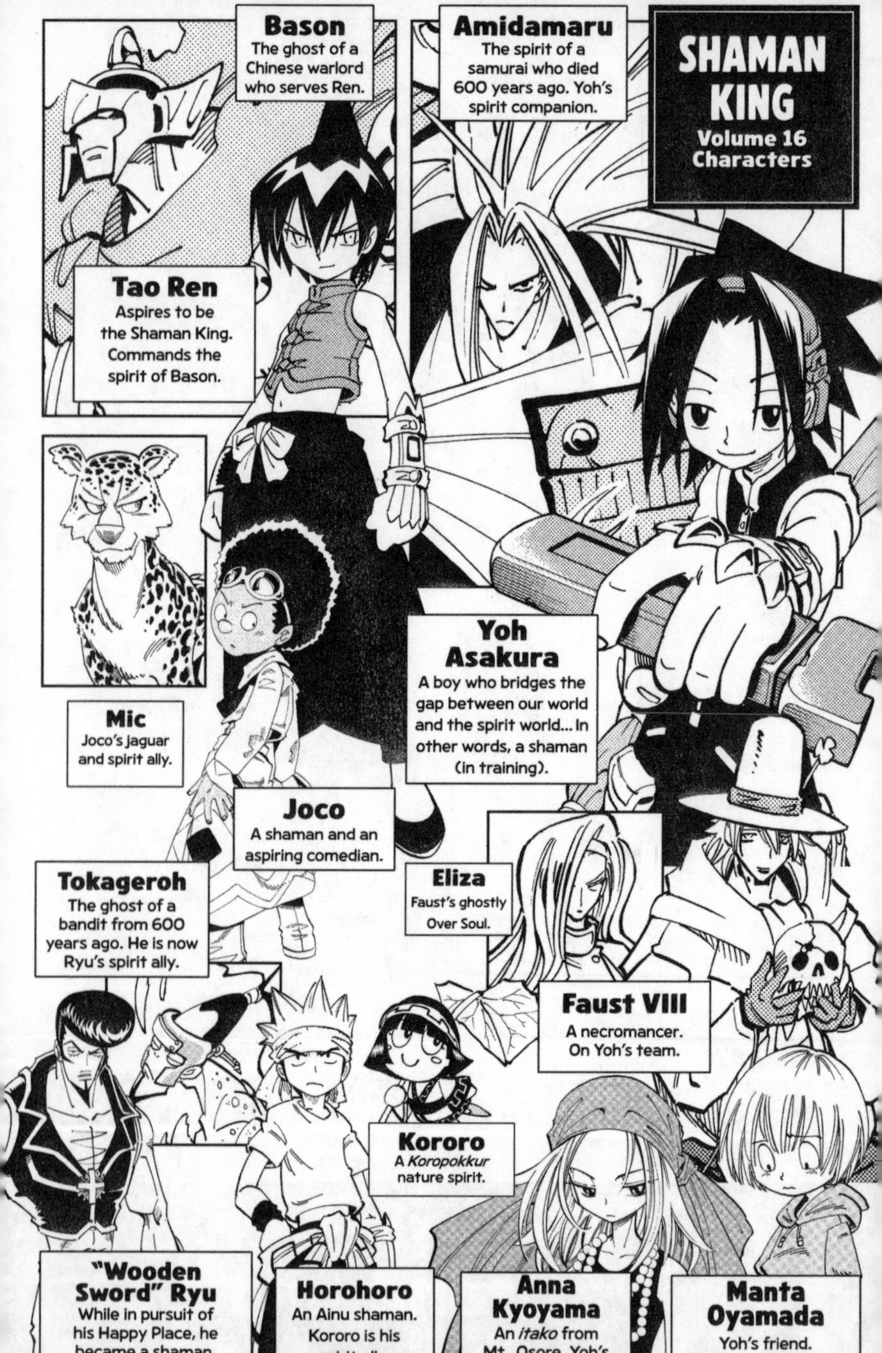
SHAMAN KING
Volume 16 Characters
Amidamaru
The spirit of a samurai who died 600 years ago. Yoh's spirit companion.
Bason
The ghost of a Chinese warlord who serves Ren.
Tao Ren
Aspires to be the Shaman King. Commands the spirit of Bason.
Yoh Asakura
A boy who bridges the gap between our world and the spirit world... In other words, a shaman (in training).
Mic
Joco's jaguar and spirit ally.
Joco
A shaman and an aspiring comedian.
Eliza
Faust's ghostly Over Soul.
Tokageroh
The ghost of a bandit from 600 years ago. He is now Ryu's spirit ally.
Faust VIII
A necromancer. On Yoh's team.
Kororo
A *Koropokkur* nature spirit.
Manta Oyamada
Yoh's friend.
Anna Kyoyama
An *itako* from Mt. Osore. Yoh's arranged fiancée.
Horohoro
An Ainu shaman. Kororo is his spirit ally.
"Wooden Sword" Ryu
While in pursuit of his Happy Place, he became a shaman.

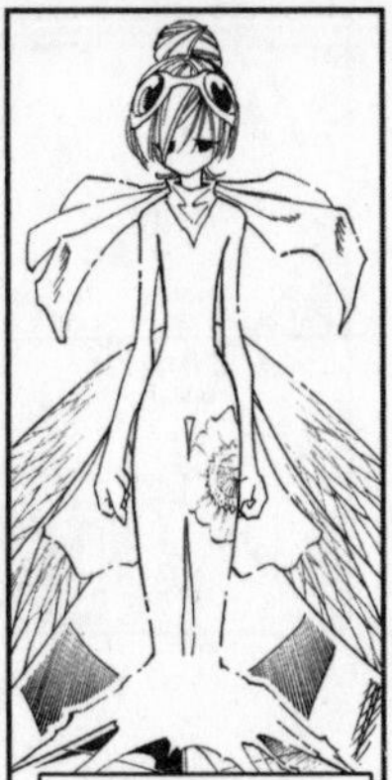

Morphea
Lyserg's spirit ally. A poppy flower fairy.

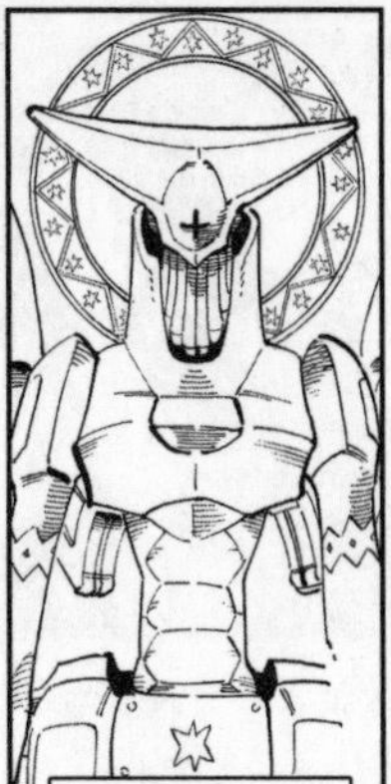

Michael
Marco's spirit ally. An angel.

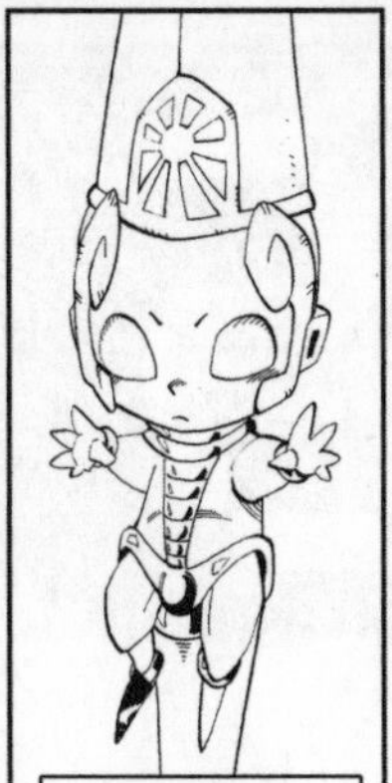

Shamash
Jeanne's spirit ally. *kami* class.

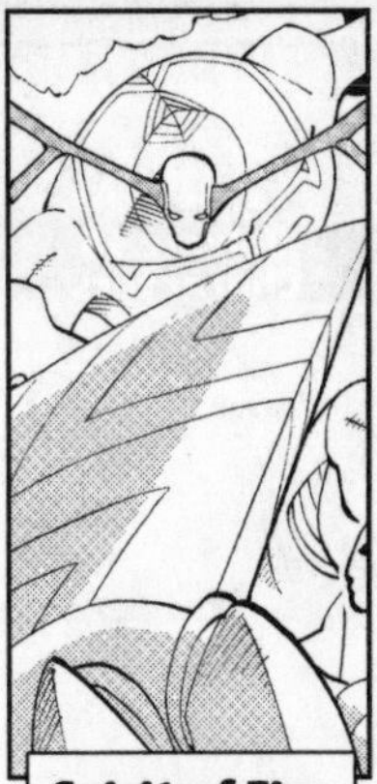

Spirit of Fire
One of the five High Spirits, and Hao's spirit ally.

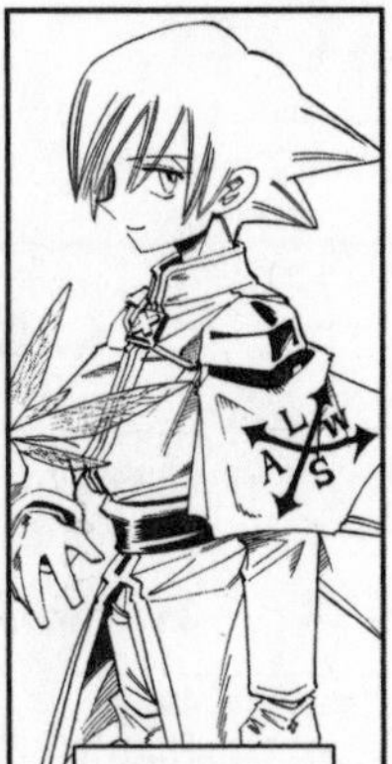

Lyserg
A boy who wants revenge against Hao.

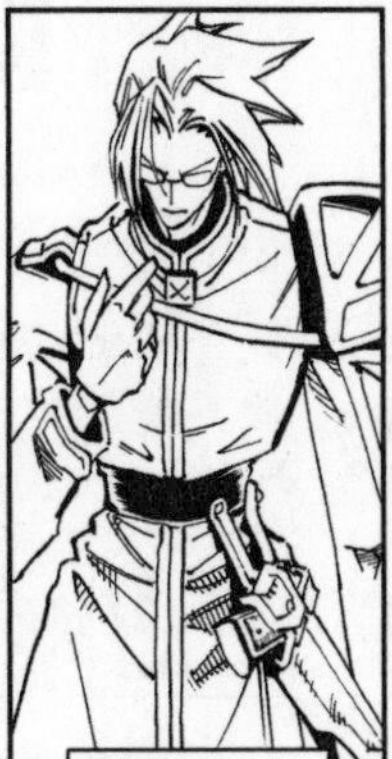

Marco
The leader of the X-Laws.

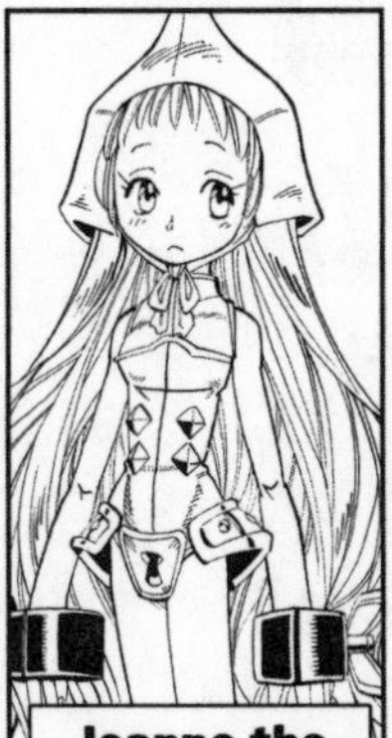

Jeanne the Iron Maiden
The true leader of the X-Laws. Mostly inside an iron maiden.

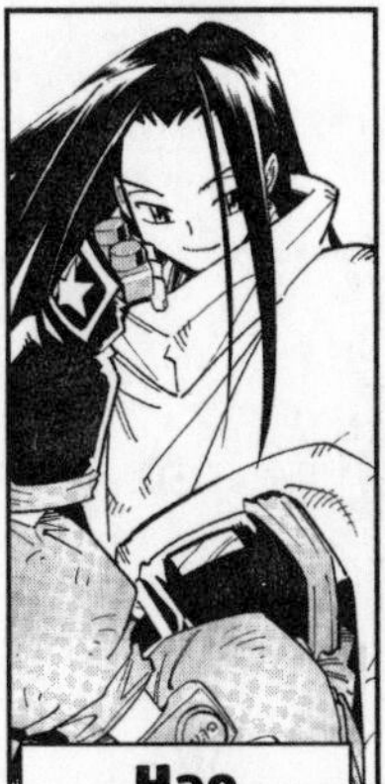

Hao
An enigmatic figure who calls himself the "Future King."

THE STORY SO FAR

This kid named Yoh Asakura-kun transferred to my class from Izumo...and it turns out he's a shaman! The Shaman Fight, which takes place once every 500 years, has begun. Yoh-kun and friends arrived at Patch Village—and experienced the limitless power of the Great Spirit. They formed new teams for the tournament proper. Along with their new ally, Joco, they divided into two teams. Next up was Yoh-kun's team. Empowered by *The Ultra Senji Ryakketsu*, they emerged victorious, but...

SHAMAN KING

Grandchild

16

Chapter 135: Ren's Point

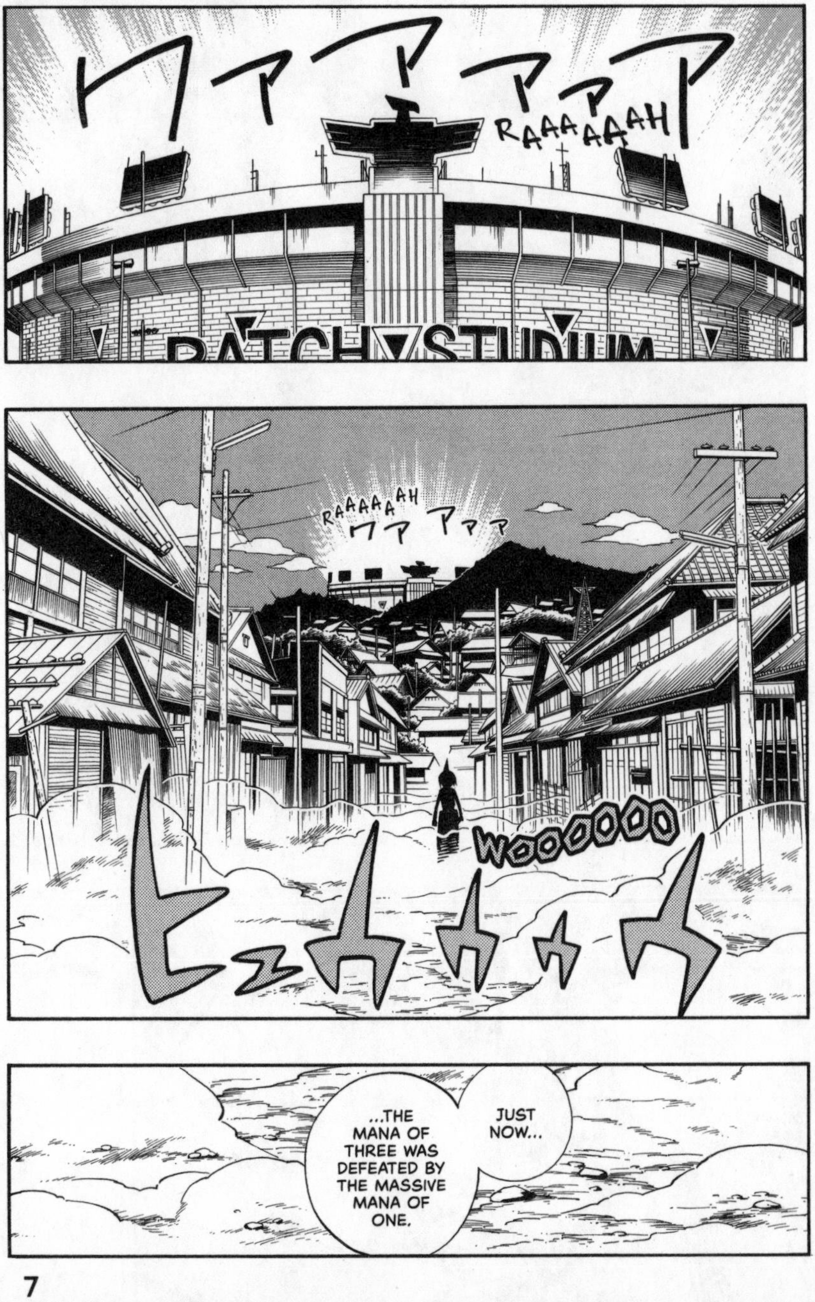
RAAAAAAH
RAAAAAAH
WOOOOOO
JUST NOW...
...THE MANA OF THREE WAS DEFEATED BY THE MASSIVE MANA OF ONE.

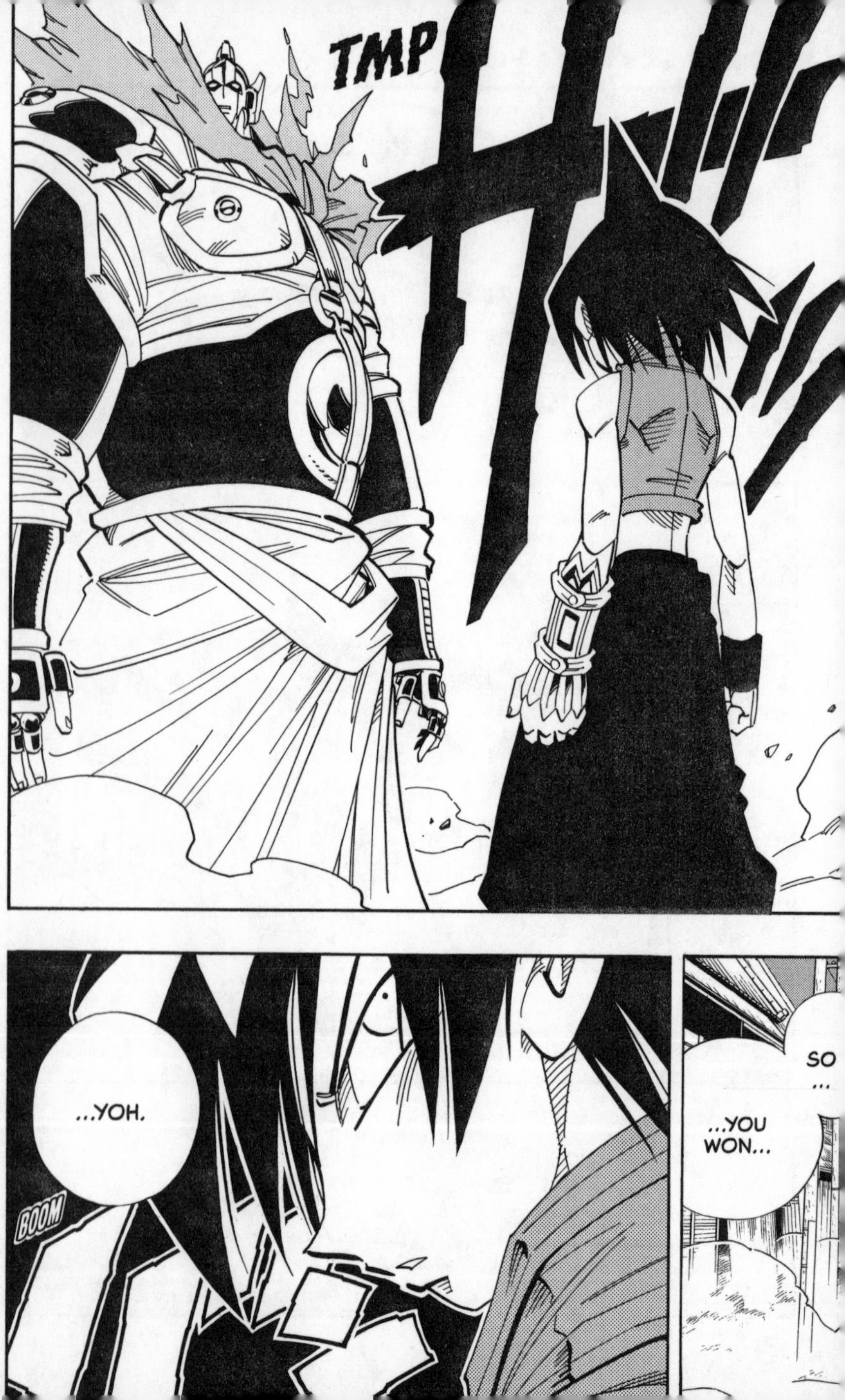
TMP
SO ...
...YOU WON...
...YOH.
BOOM

Chapter 135:

Ren's Point

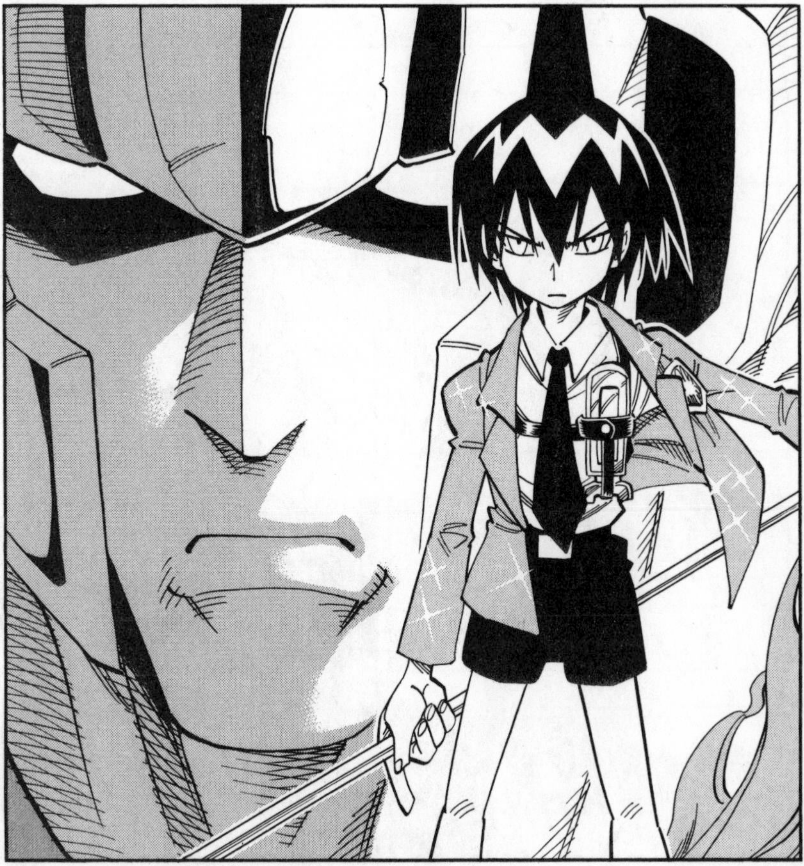

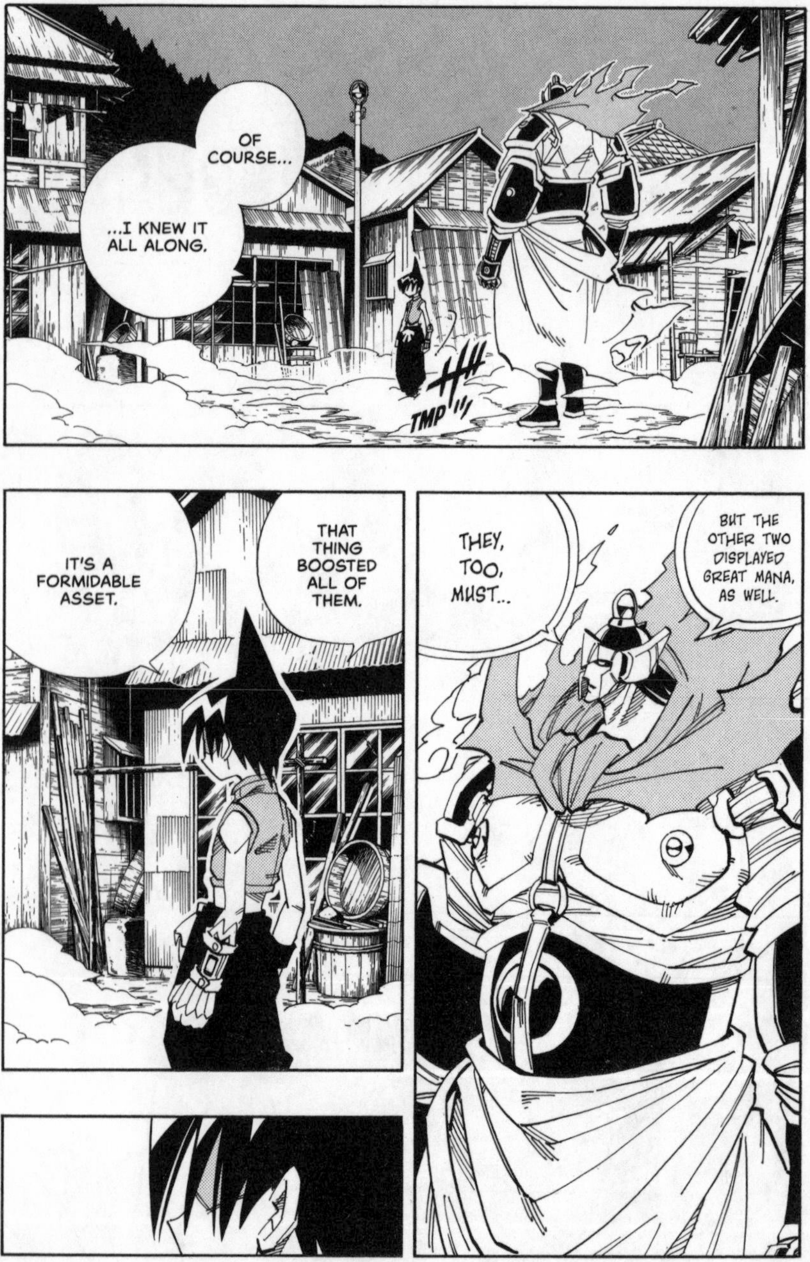
OF COURSE...
...I KNEW IT ALL ALONG.
TMP
BUT THE OTHER TWO DISPLAYED GREAT MANA, AS WELL.
THEY, TOO, MUST...
THAT THING BOOSTED ALL OF THEM.
IT'S A FORMIDABLE ASSET.

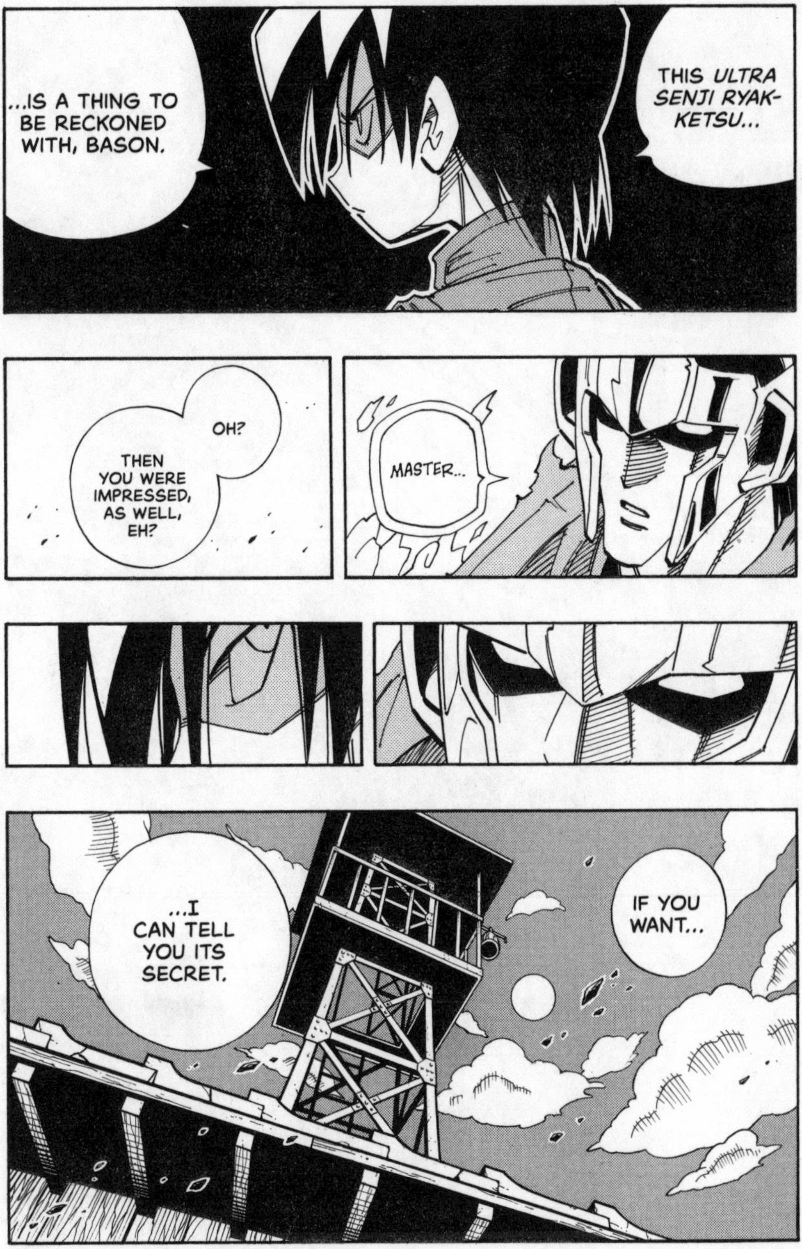
THIS ULTRA SENJI RYAK-KETSU...
...IS A THING TO BE RECKONED WITH, BASON.
MASTER...
OH?
THEN YOU WERE IMPRESSED, AS WELL, EH?
IF YOU WANT...
...I CAN TELL YOU ITS SECRET.

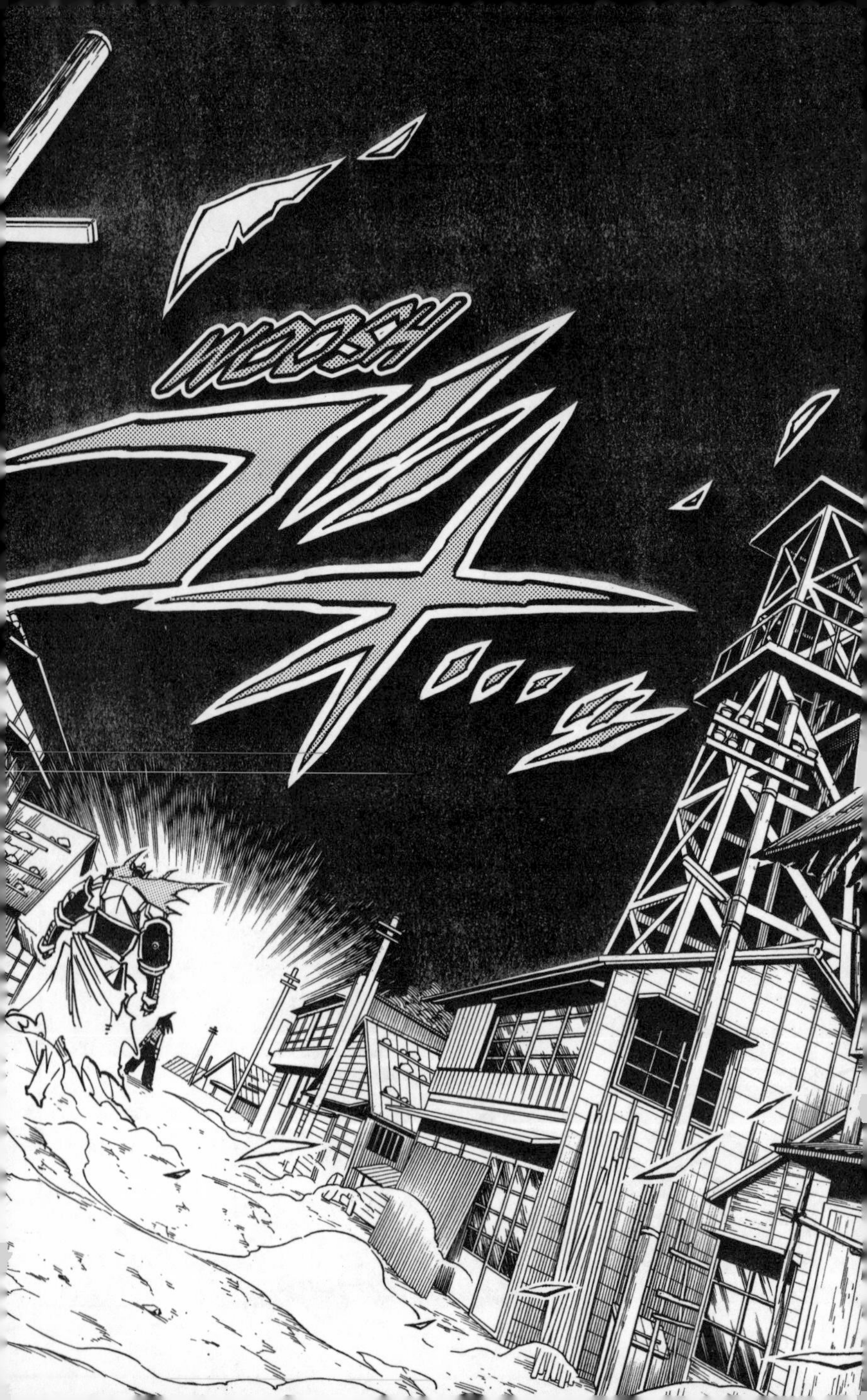
WOOSH

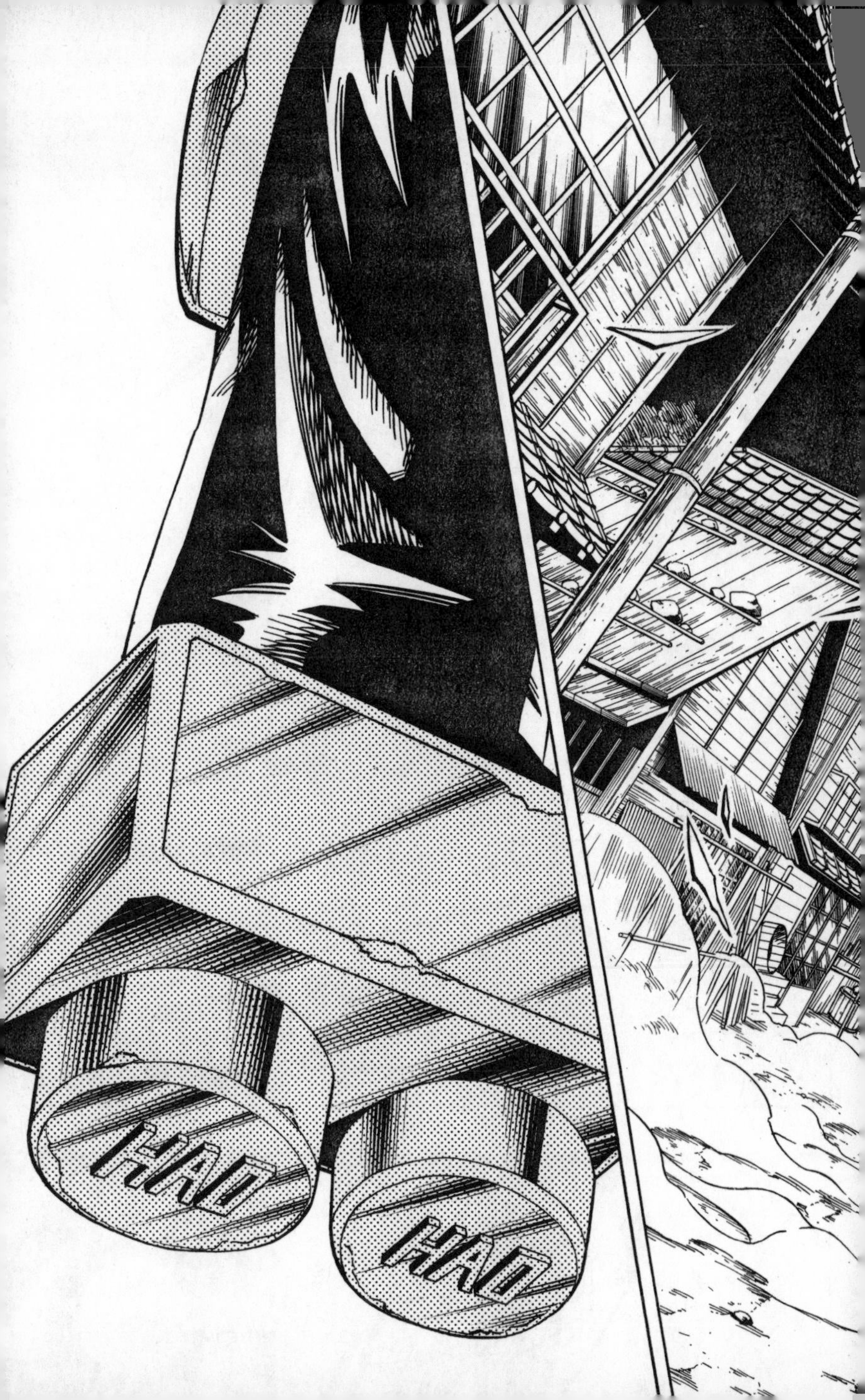
HAO
HAO

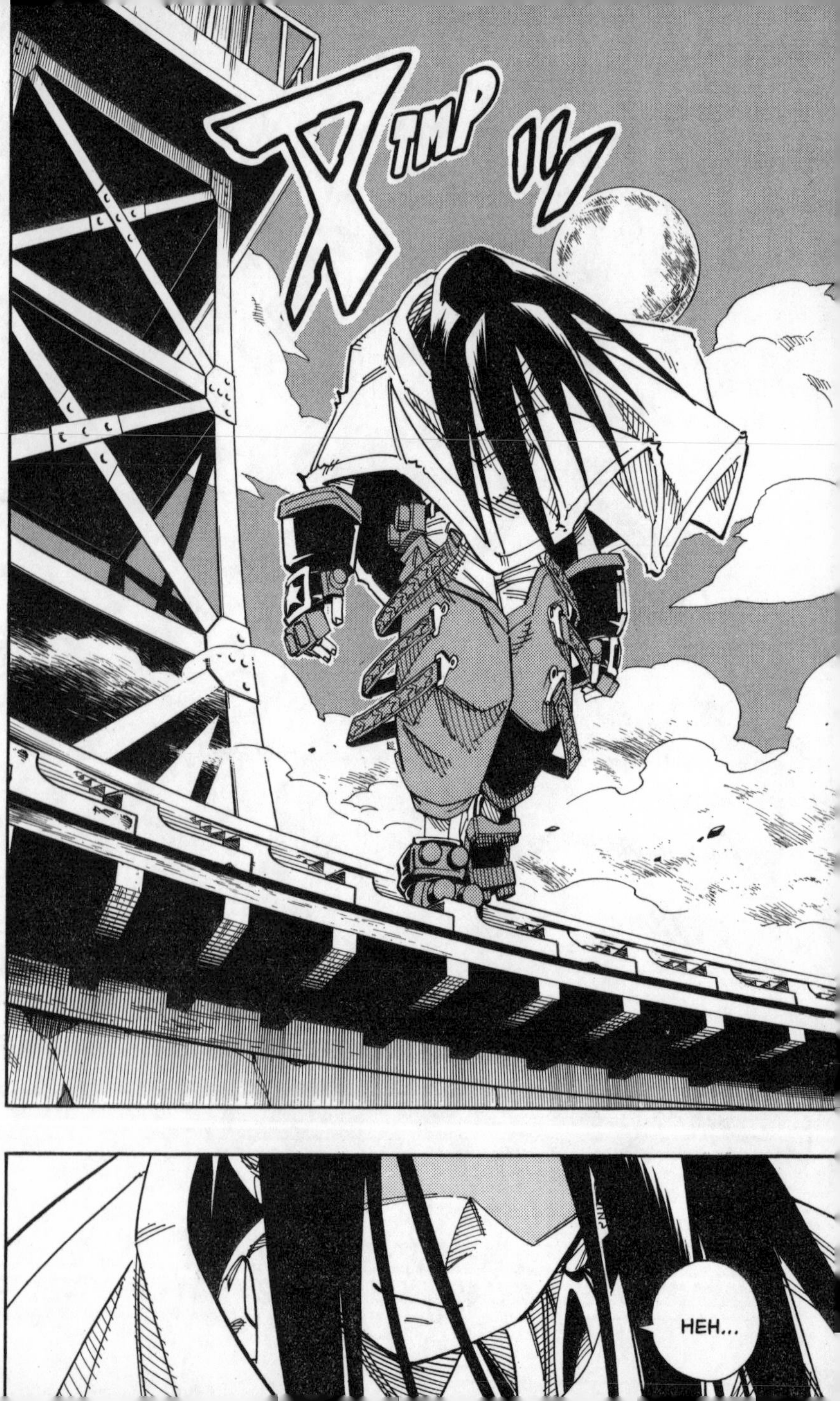
TMP
HEH...

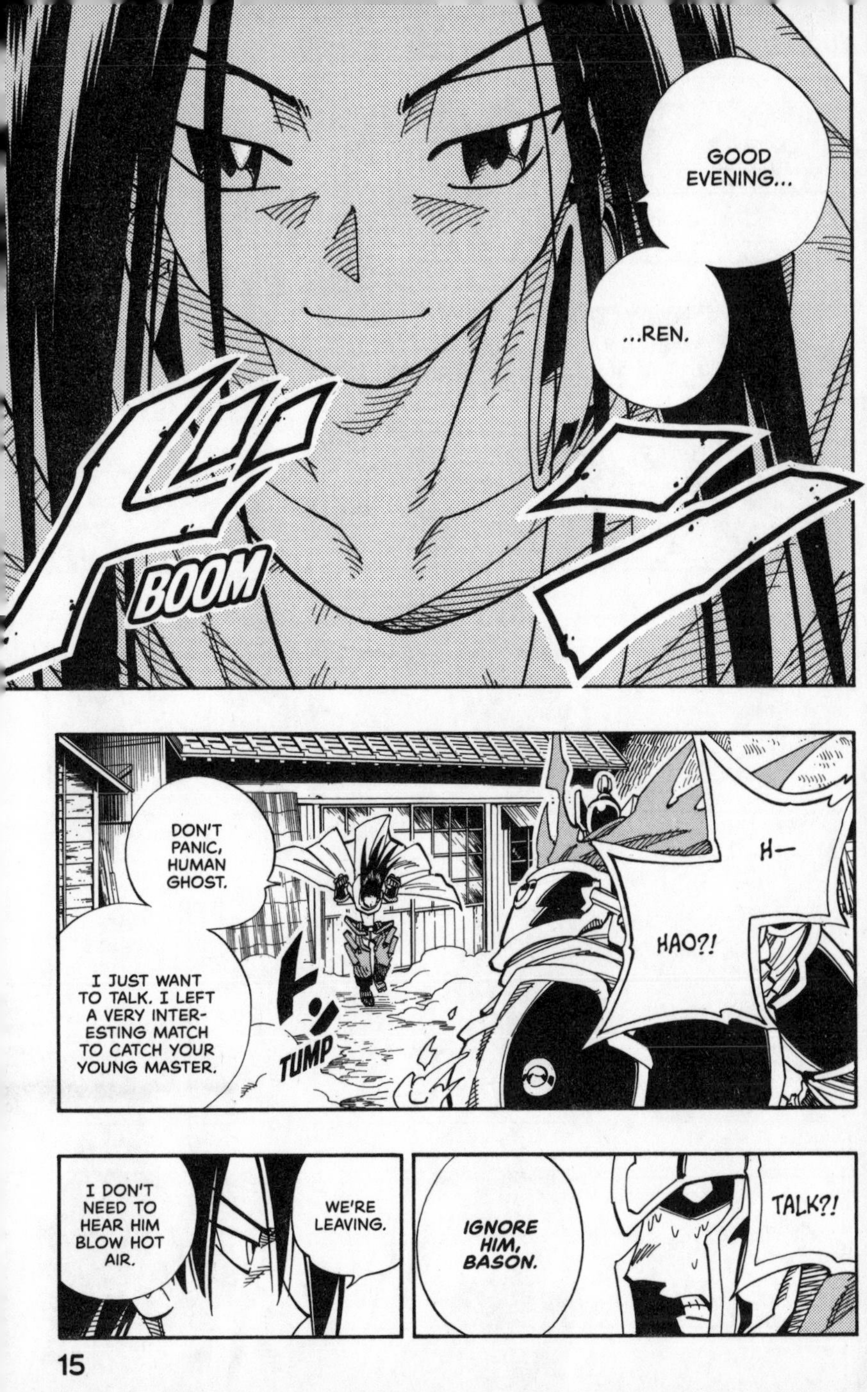
GOOD EVENING...
...REN.
BOOM
H—
HAO?!
DON'T PANIC, HUMAN GHOST.
I JUST WANT TO TALK. I LEFT A VERY INTERESTING MATCH TO CATCH YOUR YOUNG MASTER.
TUMP
TALK?!
IGNORE HIM, BASON.
WE'RE LEAVING.
I DON'T NEED TO HEAR HIM BLOW HOT AIR.

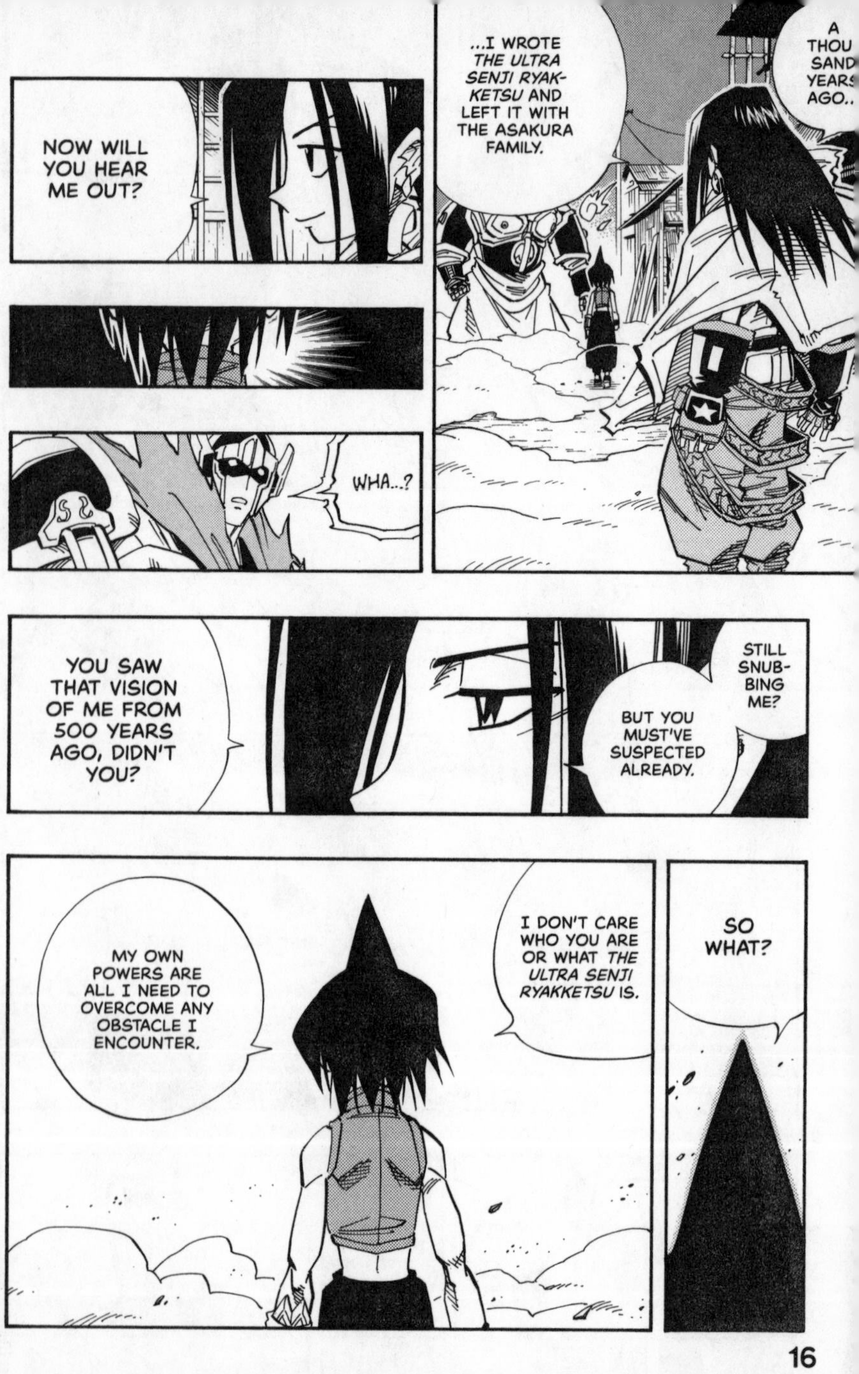

A THOUSAND YEARS AGO..
...I WROTE *THE ULTRA SENJI RYAKKETSU* AND LEFT IT WITH THE ASAKURA FAMILY.
NOW WILL YOU HEAR ME OUT?
WHA...?
STILL SNUBBING ME?
BUT YOU MUST'VE SUSPECTED ALREADY.
YOU SAW THAT VISION OF ME FROM 500 YEARS AGO, DIDN'T YOU?
SO WHAT?
I DON'T CARE WHO YOU ARE OR WHAT *THE ULTRA SENJI RYAKKETSU* IS.
MY OWN POWERS ARE ALL I NEED TO OVERCOME ANY OBSTACLE I ENCOUNTER.

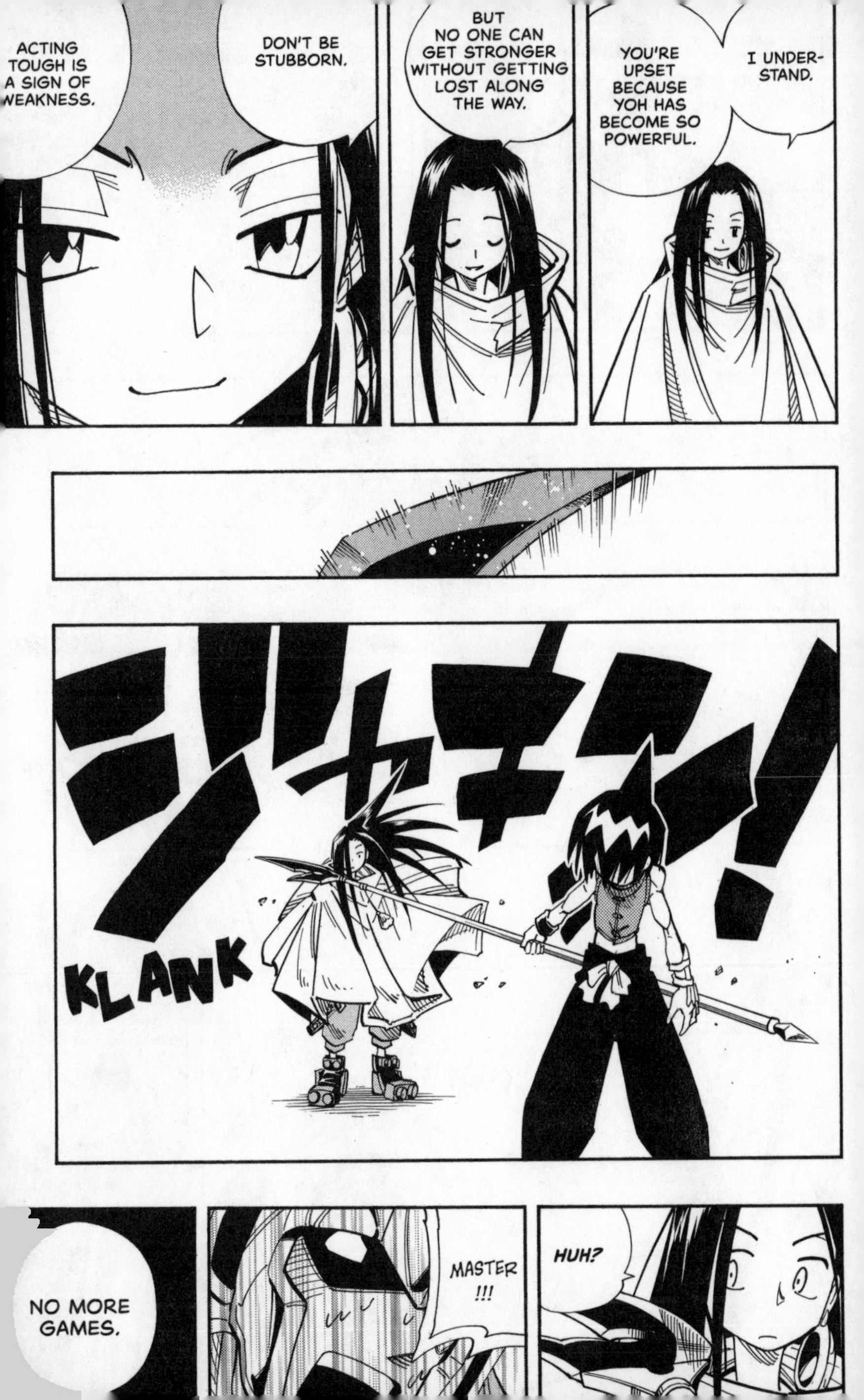
I UNDER-STAND.
YOU'RE UPSET BECAUSE YOH HAS BECOME SO POWERFUL.
BUT NO ONE CAN GET STRONGER WITHOUT GETTING LOST ALONG THE WAY.
DON'T BE STUBBORN.
ACTING TOUGH IS A SIGN OF WEAKNESS.
KLANK
HUH?
MASTER !!!
NO MORE GAMES.

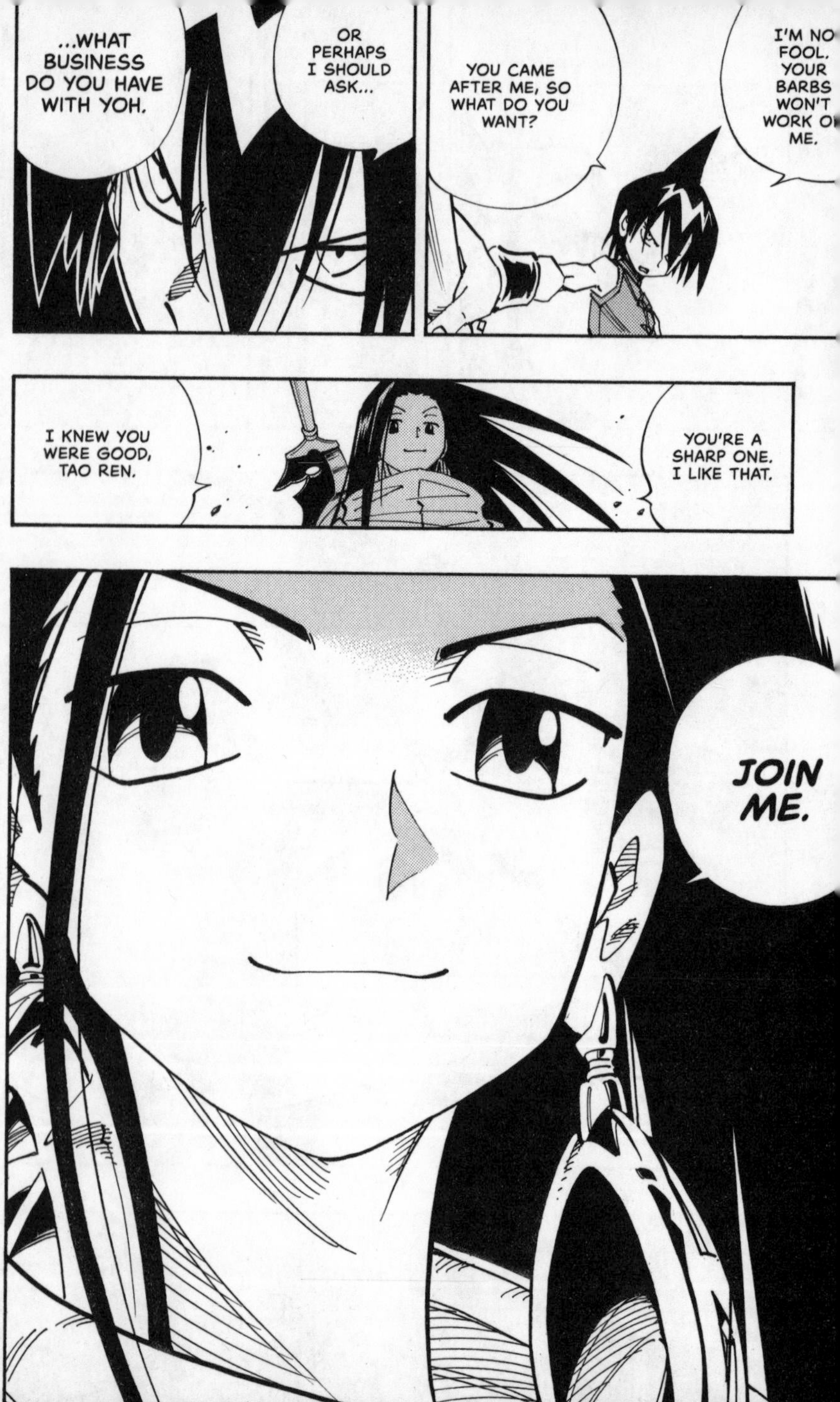
I'M NO FOOL. YOUR BARBS WON'T WORK ON ME.
YOU CAME AFTER ME, SO WHAT DO YOU WANT?
OR PERHAPS I SHOULD ASK...
...WHAT BUSINESS DO YOU HAVE WITH YOH.
YOU'RE A SHARP ONE. I LIKE THAT.
I KNEW YOU WERE GOOD, TAO REN.
JOIN ME.

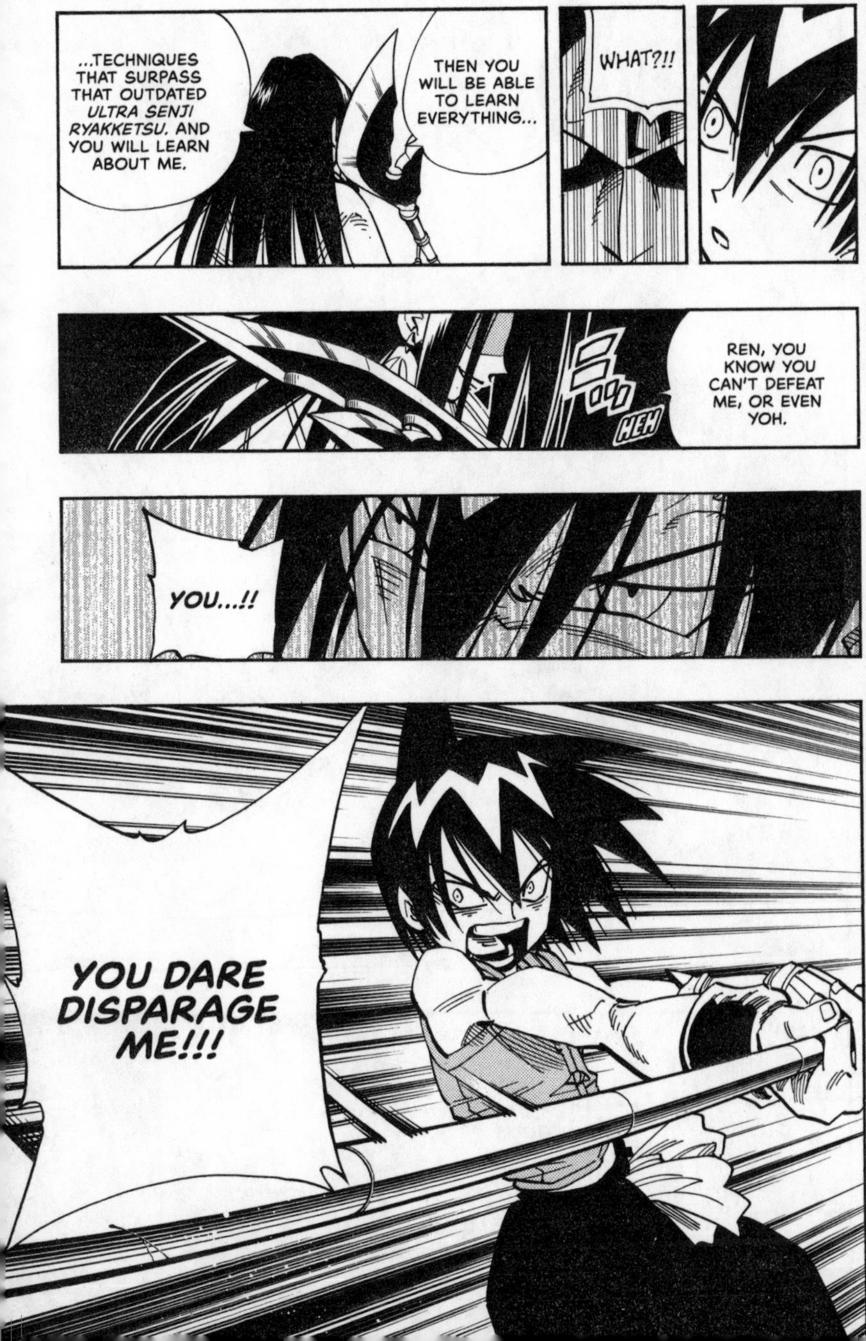

WHAT?!!
THEN YOU WILL BE ABLE TO LEARN EVERYTHING...
...TECHNIQUES THAT SURPASS THAT OUTDATED *ULTRA SENJI RYAKKETSU.* AND YOU WILL LEARN ABOUT ME.
REN, YOU KNOW YOU CAN'T DEFEAT ME, OR EVEN YOH.
HEH
YOU...!!
YOU DARE DISPARAGE ME!!!

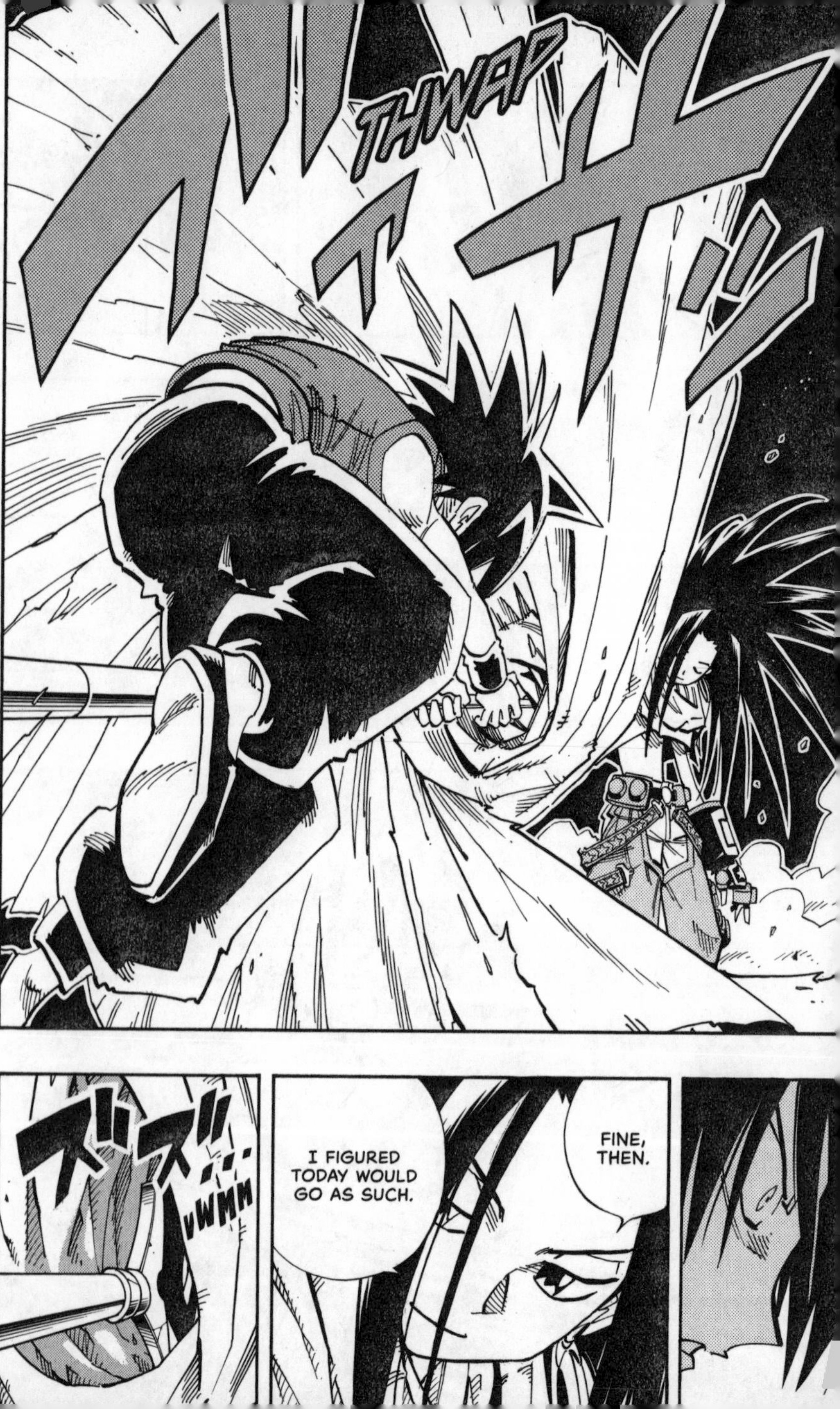
THWAP
FINE, THEN.
I FIGURED TODAY WOULD GO AS SUCH.
VWMM

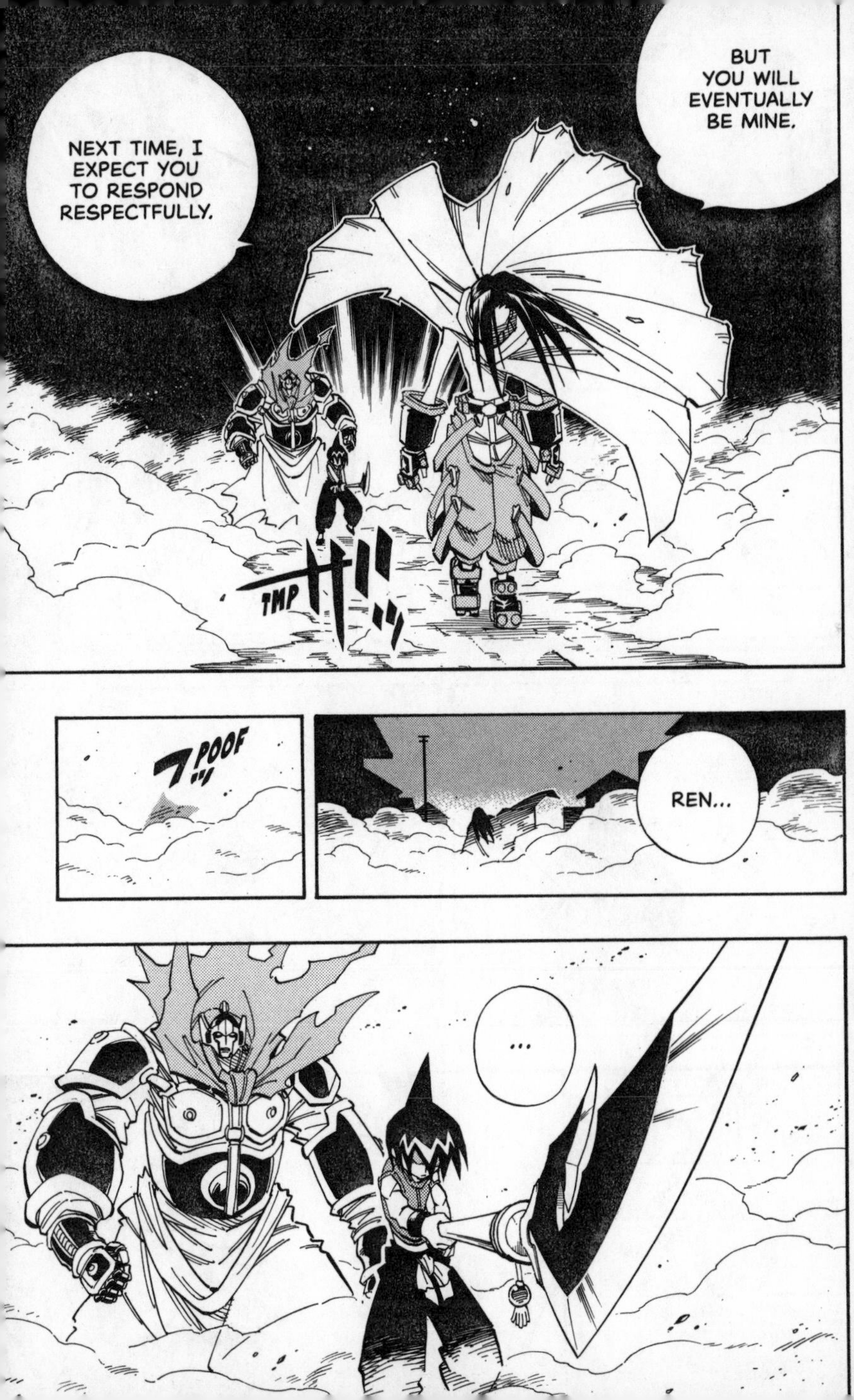
BUT YOU WILL EVENTUALLY BE MINE.
NEXT TIME, I EXPECT YOU TO RESPOND RESPECTFULLY.
TMP
REN...
POOF
...

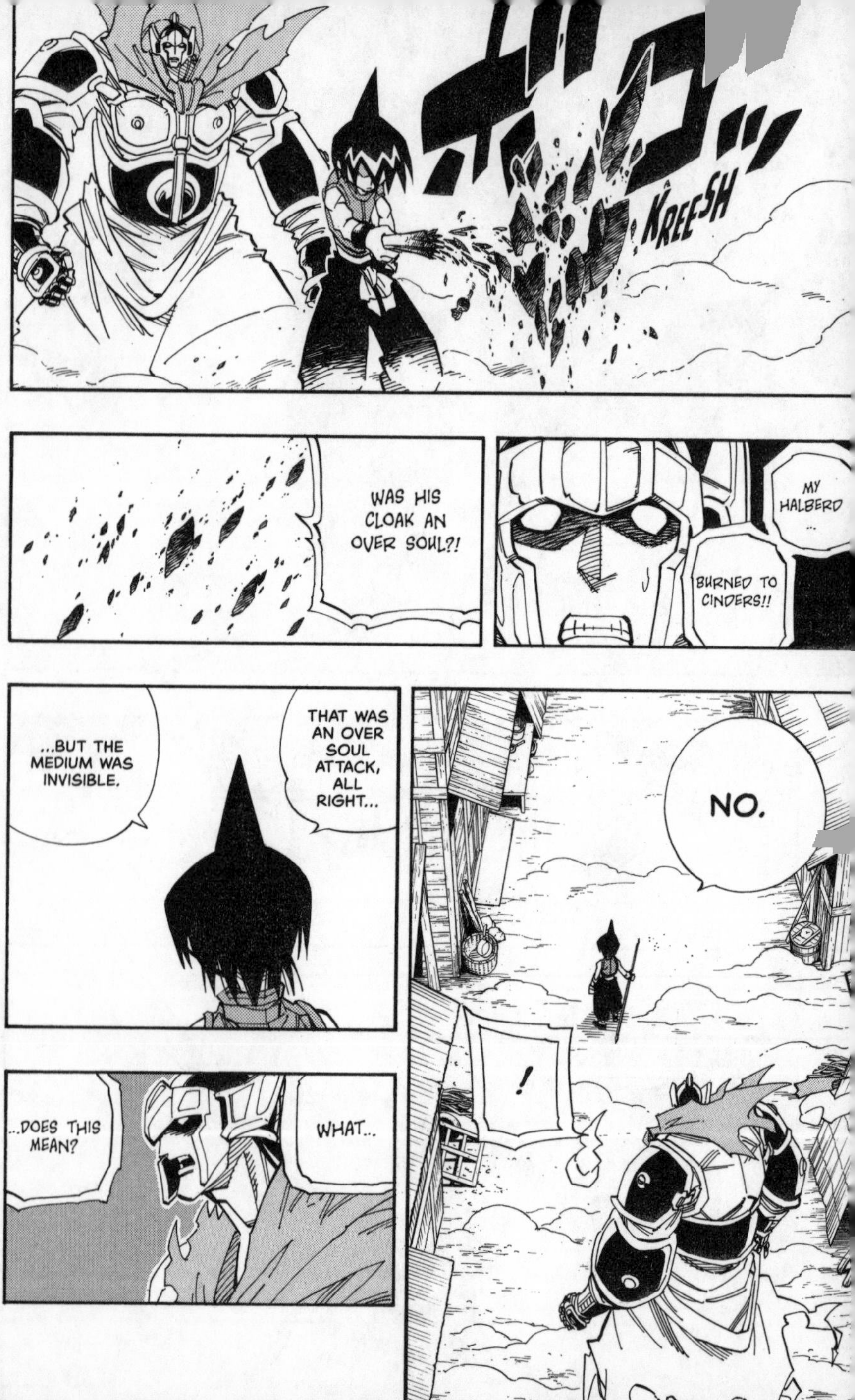
KREESH
MY HALBERD ...
BURNED TO CINDERS!!
WAS HIS CLOAK AN OVER SOUL?!
NO.
!
THAT WAS AN OVER SOUL ATTACK, ALL RIGHT...
...BUT THE MEDIUM WAS INVISIBLE.
WHAT...
...DOES THIS MEAN?

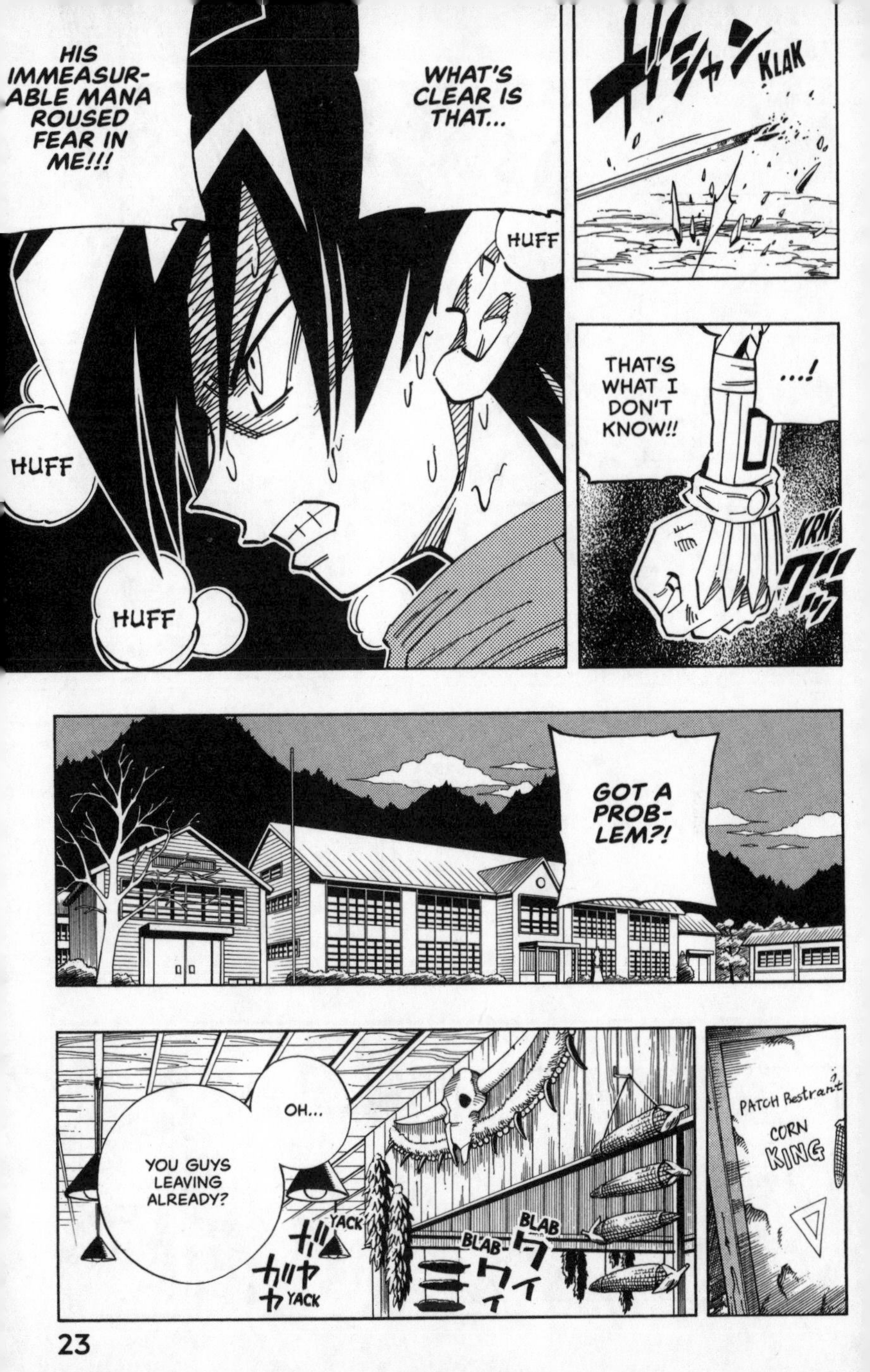
KLAK
THAT'S WHAT I DON'T KNOW!!
...!
KRK
WHAT'S CLEAR IS THAT...
HUFF
HIS IMMEASURABLE MANA ROUSED FEAR IN ME!!!
HUFF
HUFF
GOT A PROBLEM?!
PATCH Restrant
CORN KING
BLAB BLAB-
OH...
YOU GUYS LEAVING ALREADY?
YACK YACK

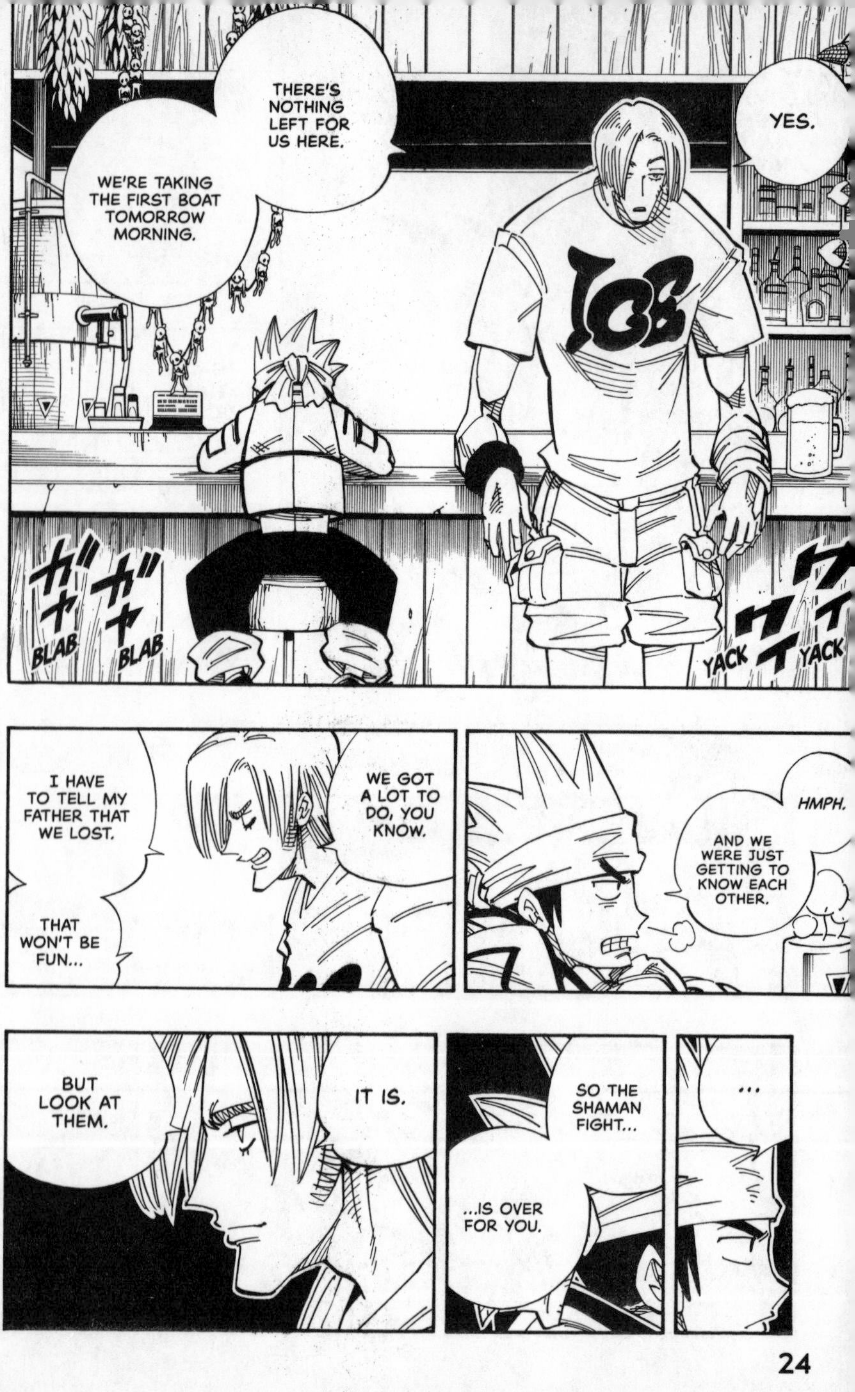
YES.
THERE'S NOTHING LEFT FOR US HERE.
WE'RE TAKING THE FIRST BOAT TOMORROW MORNING.
ワイワイ
YACK YACK
ガヤガヤ
BLAB BLAB
HMPH.
AND WE WERE JUST GETTING TO KNOW EACH OTHER.
WE GOT A LOT TO DO, YOU KNOW.
I HAVE TO TELL MY FATHER THAT WE LOST.
THAT WON'T BE FUN...
...
SO THE SHAMAN FIGHT...
...IS OVER FOR YOU.
IT IS.
BUT LOOK AT THEM.

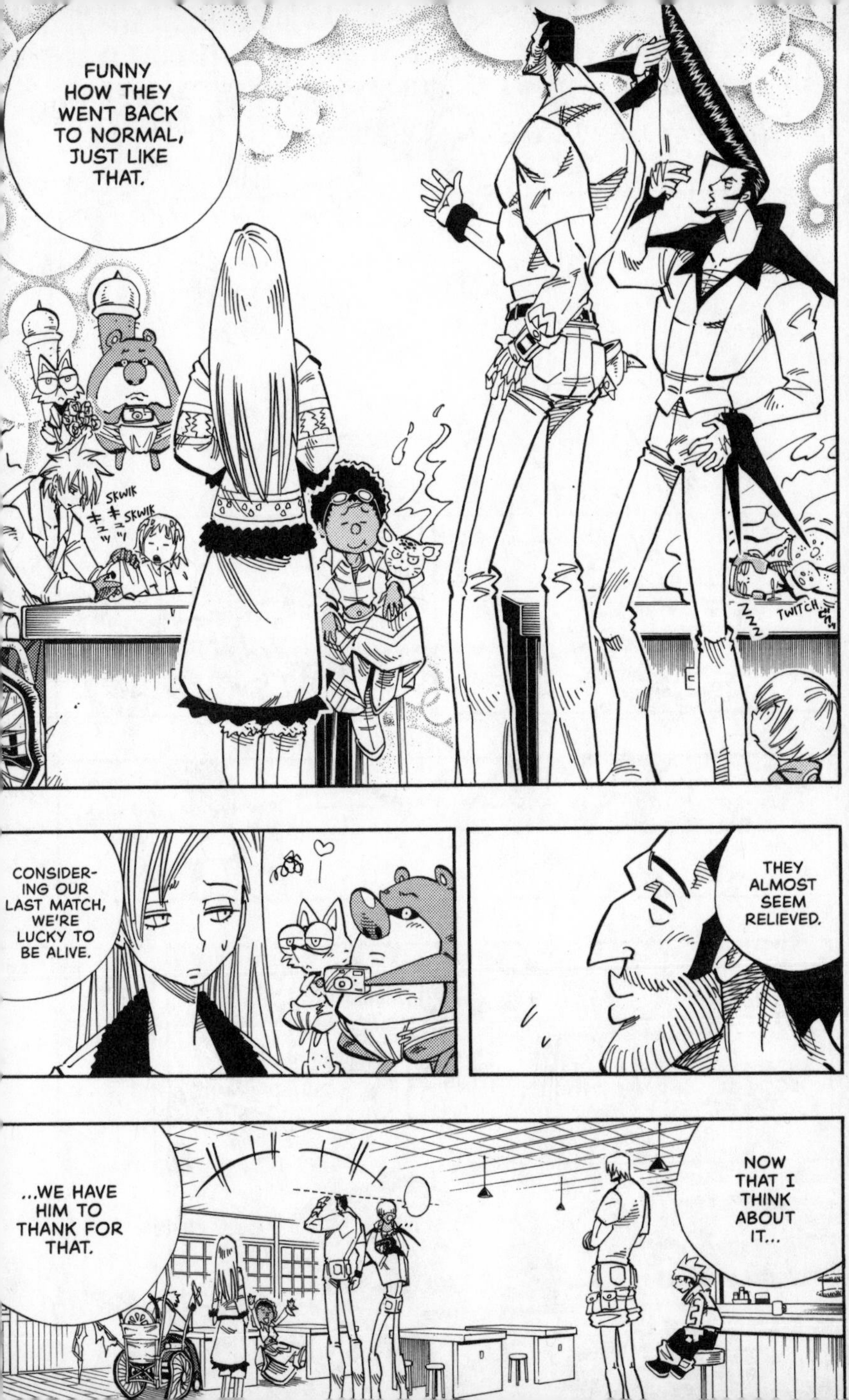
FUNNY HOW THEY WENT BACK TO NORMAL, JUST LIKE THAT.
TWITCH
SKWIK SKWIK
THEY ALMOST SEEM RELIEVED.
CONSIDERING OUR LAST MATCH, WE'RE LUCKY TO BE ALIVE.
NOW THAT I THINK ABOUT IT...
...WE HAVE HIM TO THANK FOR THAT.

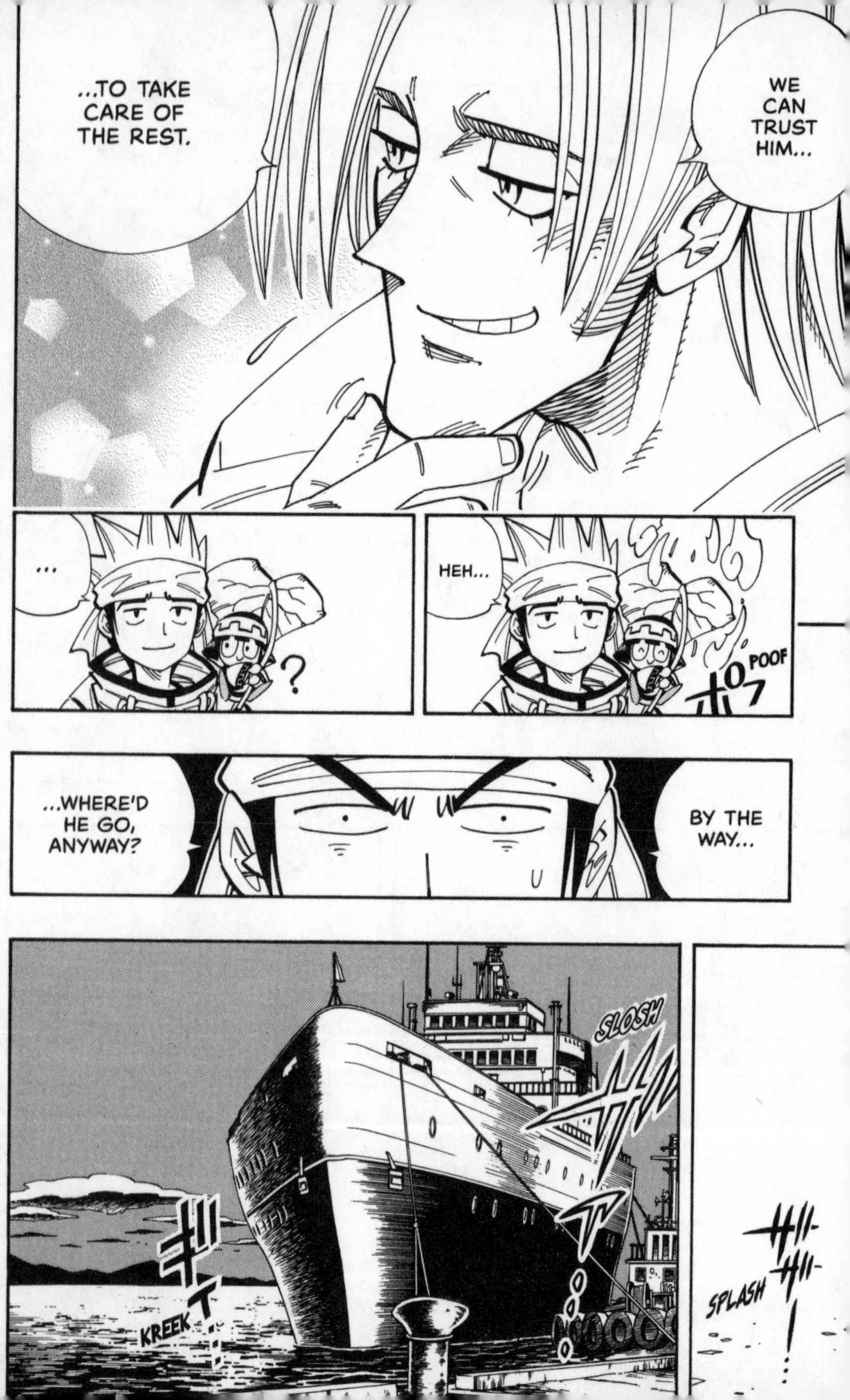
WE CAN TRUST HIM...
...TO TAKE CARE OF THE REST.
HEH...
POOF
...
?
BY THE WAY...
...WHERE'D HE GO, ANYWAY?
SPLASH
SLOSH
KREEK

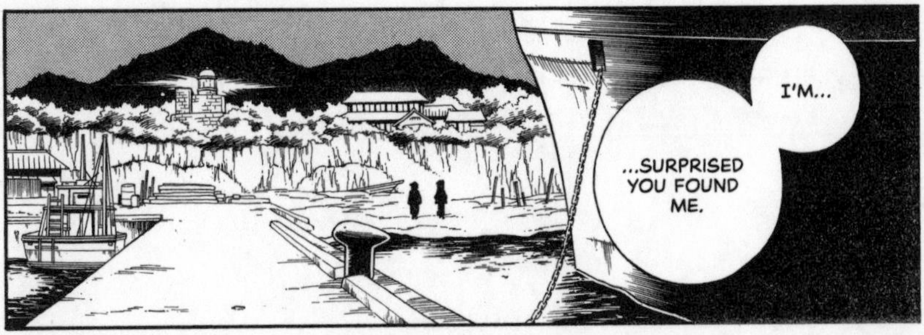
I'M...
...SURPRISED YOU FOUND ME.

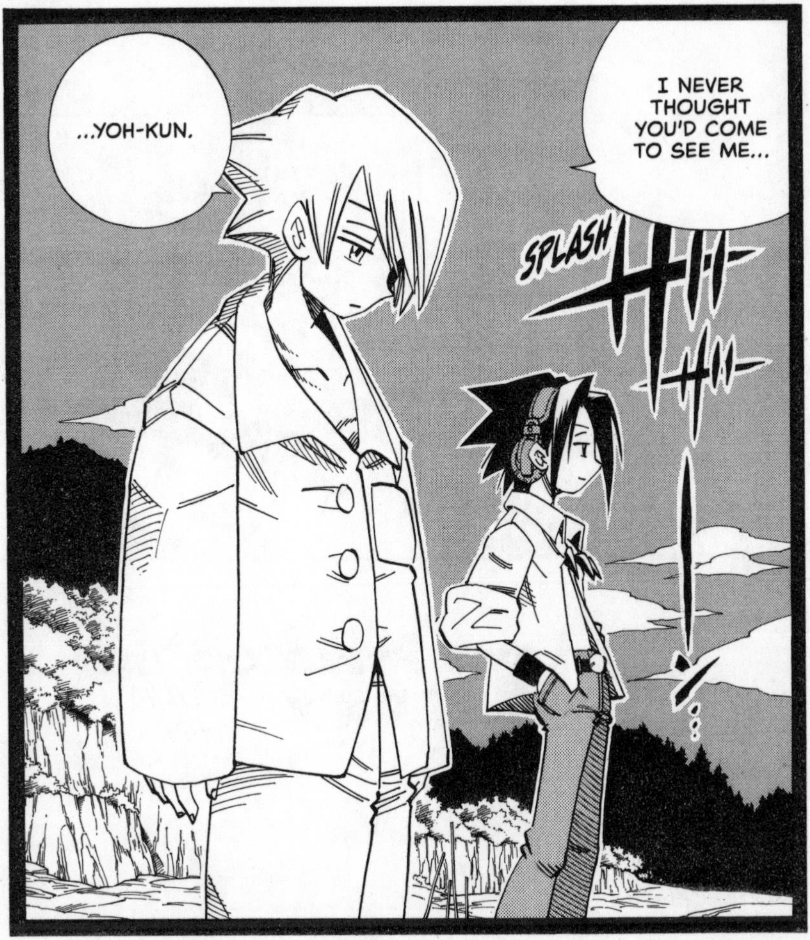
I NEVER THOUGHT YOU'D COME TO SEE ME...
...YOH-KUN.
SPLASH

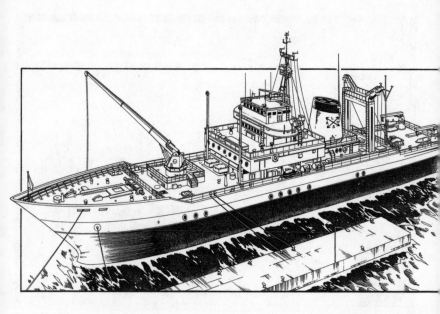

X-Laws Private Ship
ARK X

Chapter 136:

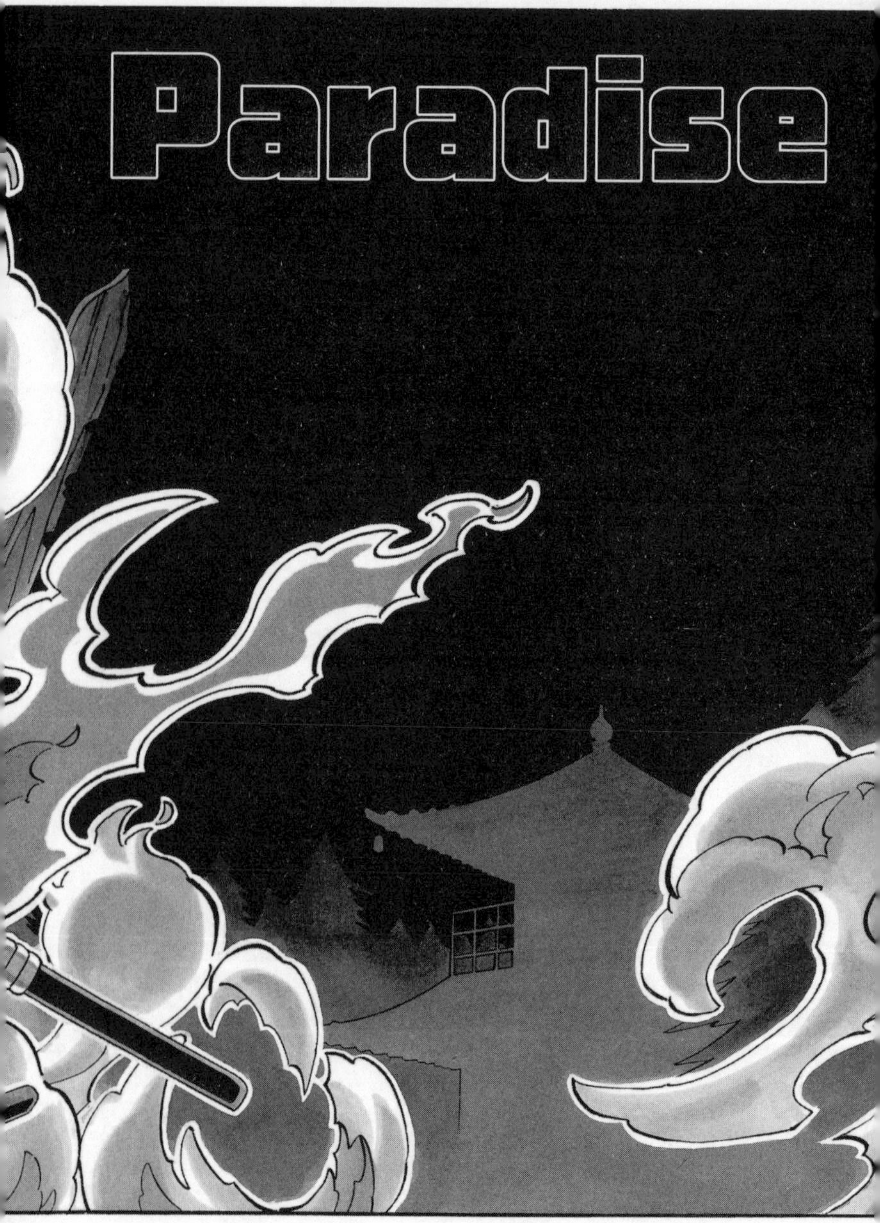
Paradise

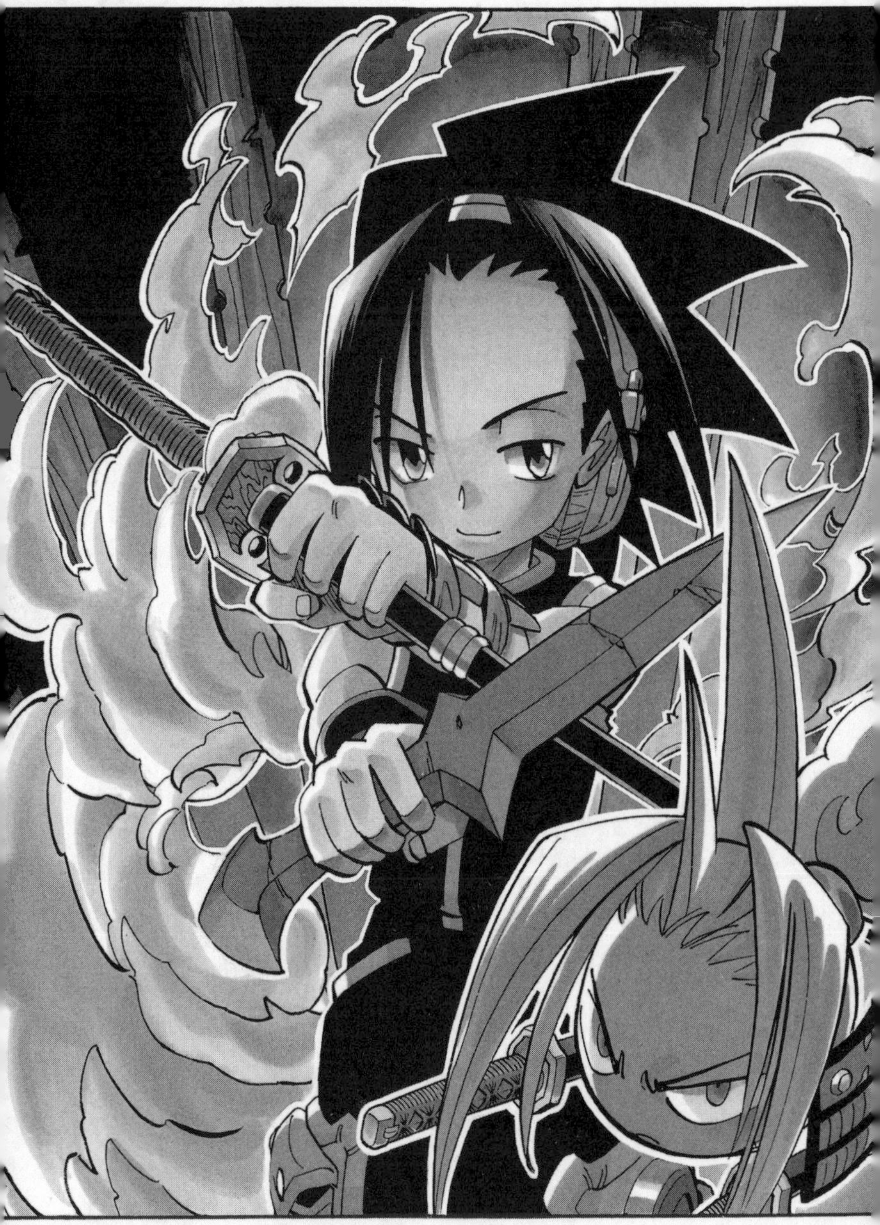

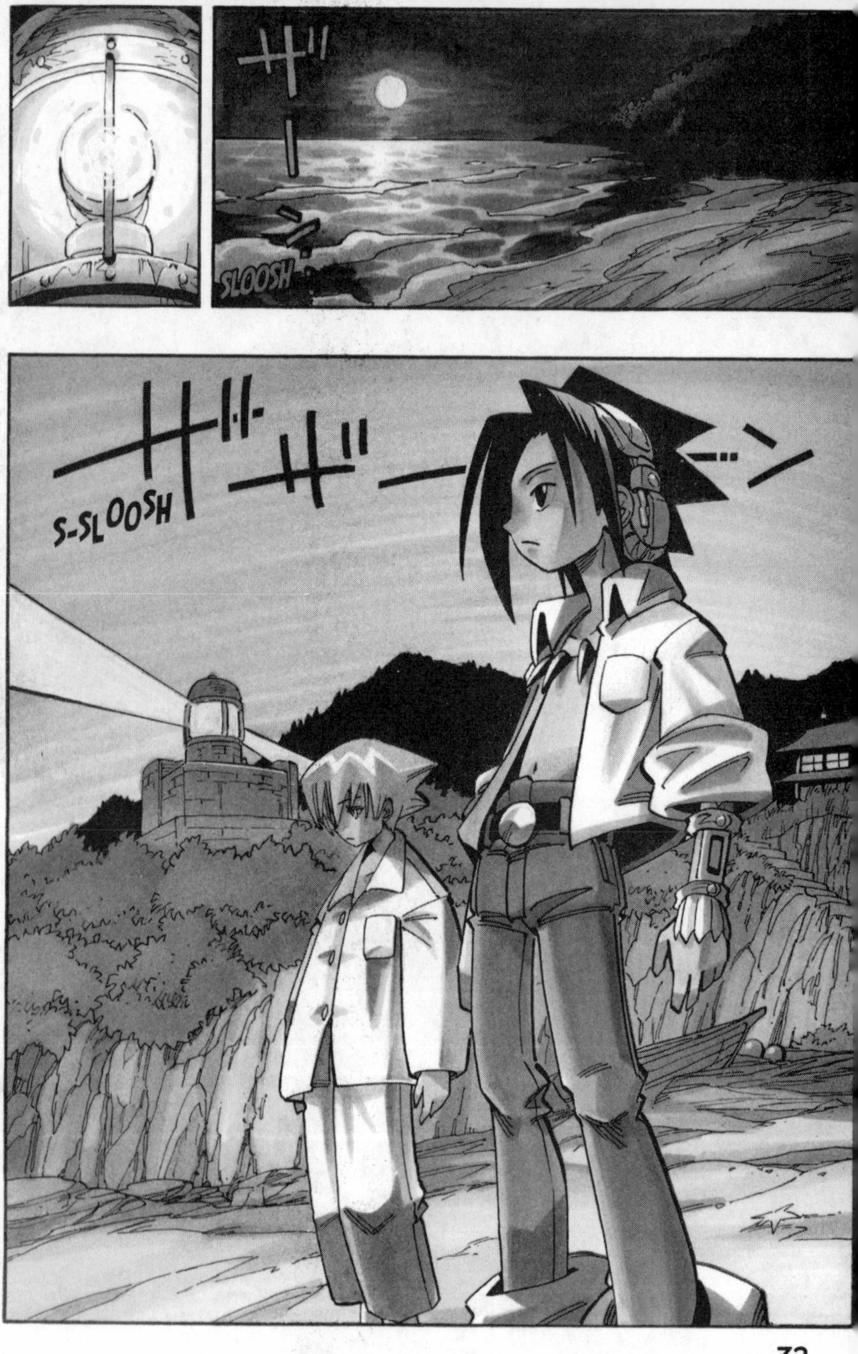
SLOOSH
S-SLOOSH

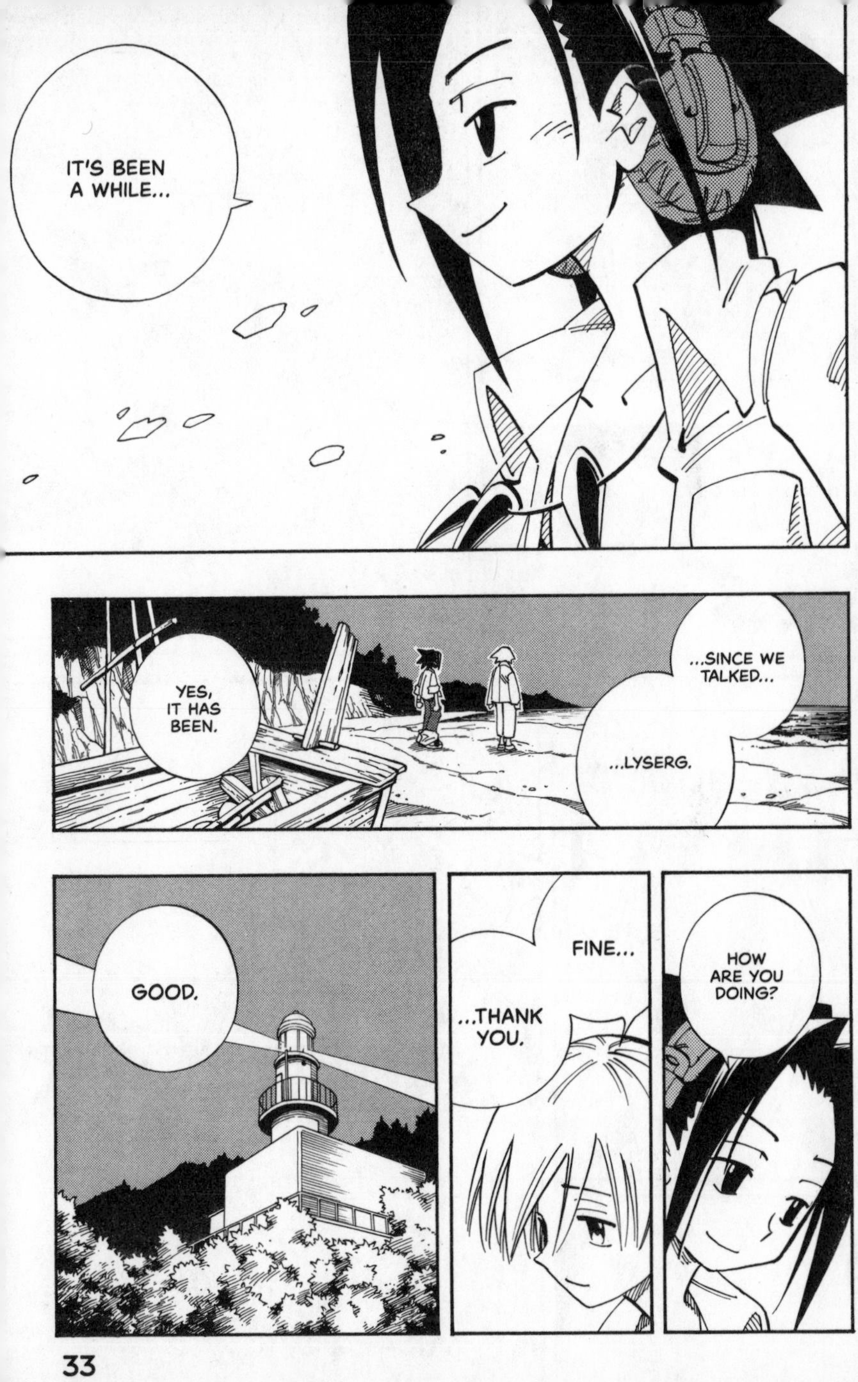
IT'S BEEN A WHILE...
...SINCE WE TALKED...
...LYSERG.
YES, IT HAS BEEN.
HOW ARE YOU DOING?
FINE...
...THANK YOU.
GOOD.

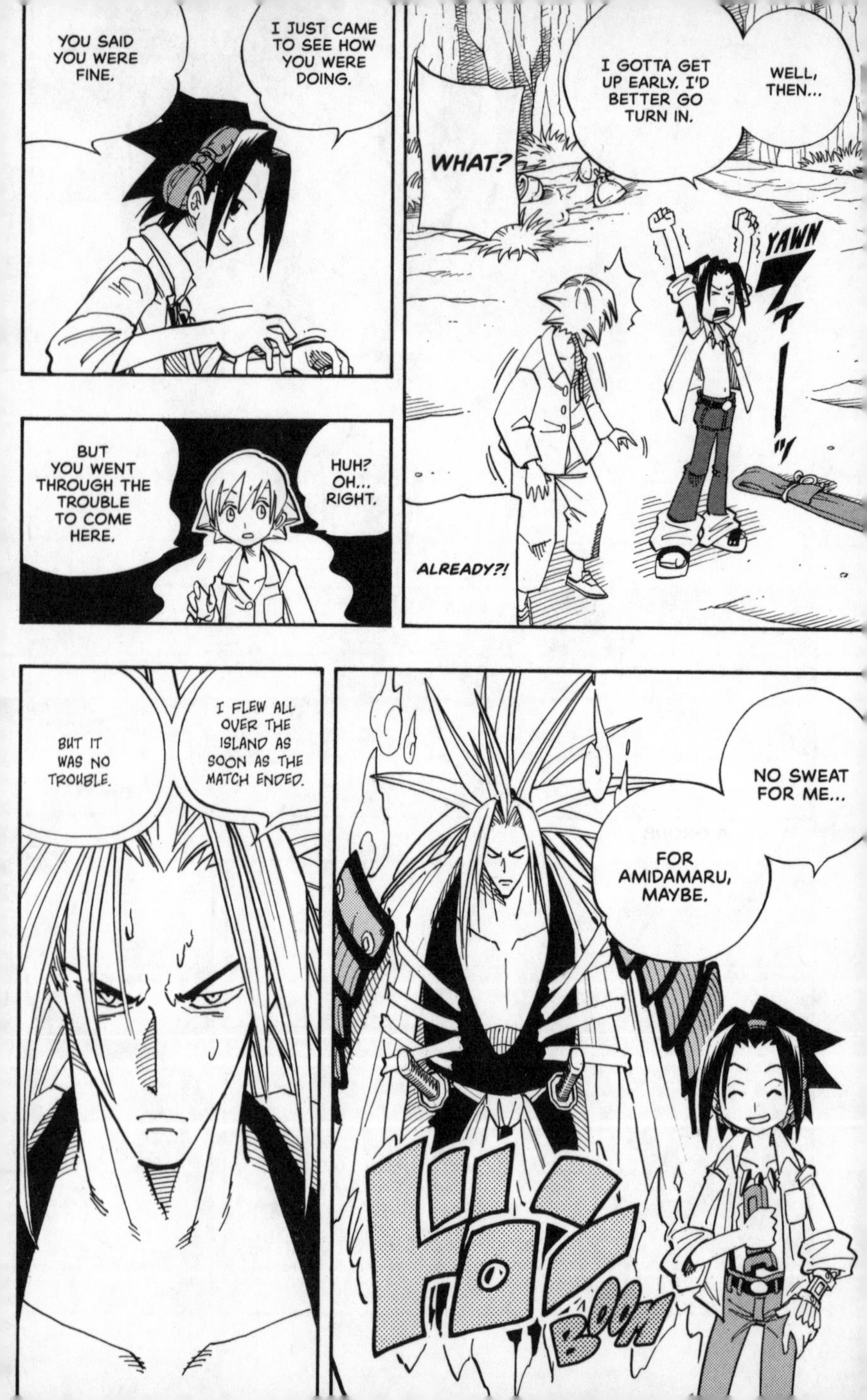
WELL, THEN...
I GOTTA GET UP EARLY. I'D BETTER GO TURN IN.
YAWN
WHAT?
ALREADY?!
I JUST CAME TO SEE HOW YOU WERE DOING.
YOU SAID YOU WERE FINE.
HUH? OH... RIGHT.
BUT YOU WENT THROUGH THE TROUBLE TO COME HERE.
NO SWEAT FOR ME...
FOR AMIDAMARU, MAYBE.
BOOM
I FLEW ALL OVER THE ISLAND AS SOON AS THE MATCH ENDED.
BUT IT WAS NO TROUBLE.

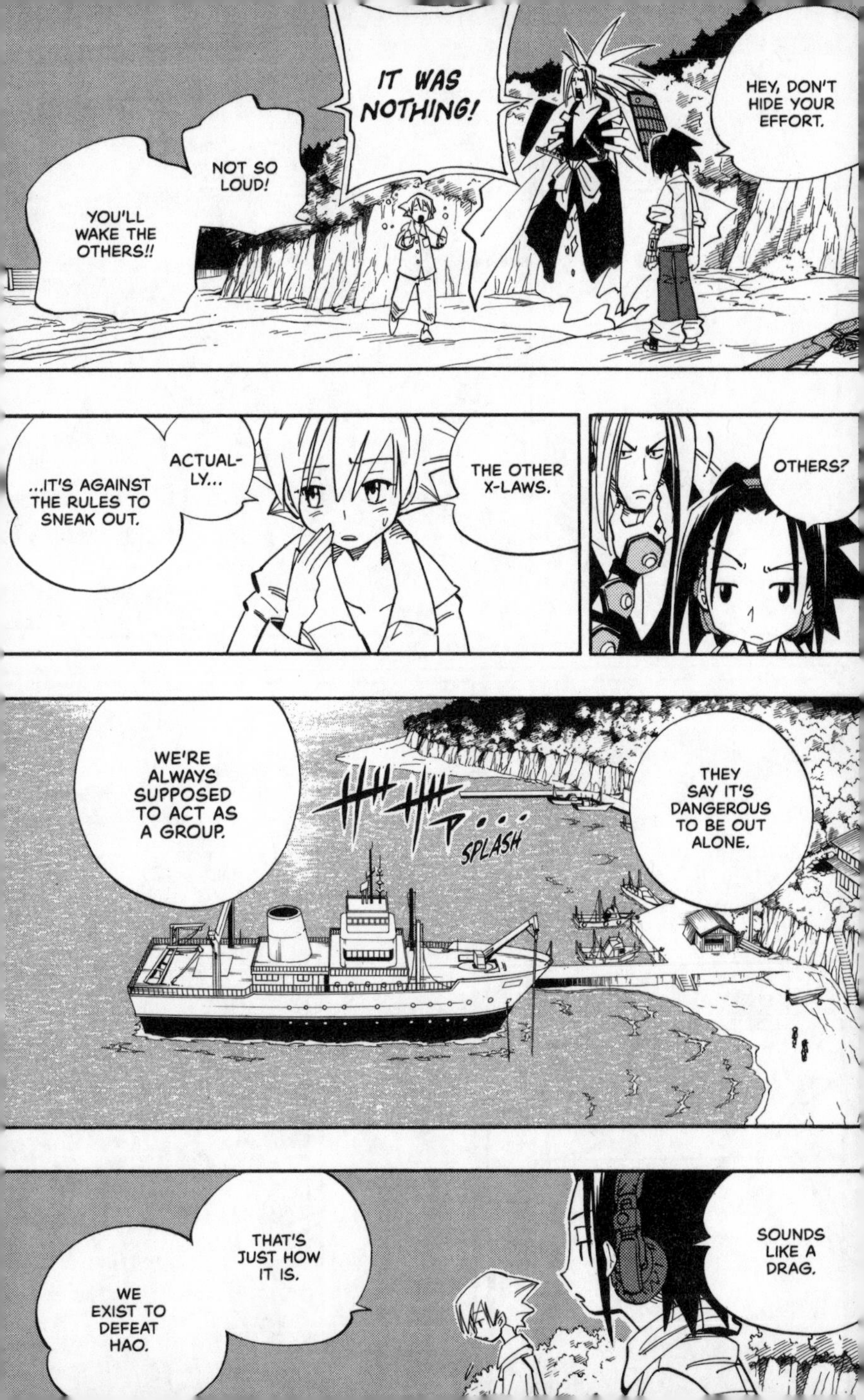
HEY, DON'T HIDE YOUR EFFORT.
IT WAS NOTHING!
NOT SO LOUD!
YOU'LL WAKE THE OTHERS!!
OTHERS?
THE OTHER X-LAWS.
ACTUAL-LY...
...IT'S AGAINST THE RULES TO SNEAK OUT.
THEY SAY IT'S DANGEROUS TO BE OUT ALONE.
SPLASH
WE'RE ALWAYS SUPPOSED TO ACT AS A GROUP.
SOUNDS LIKE A DRAG.
THAT'S JUST HOW IT IS.
WE EXIST TO DEFEAT HAO.

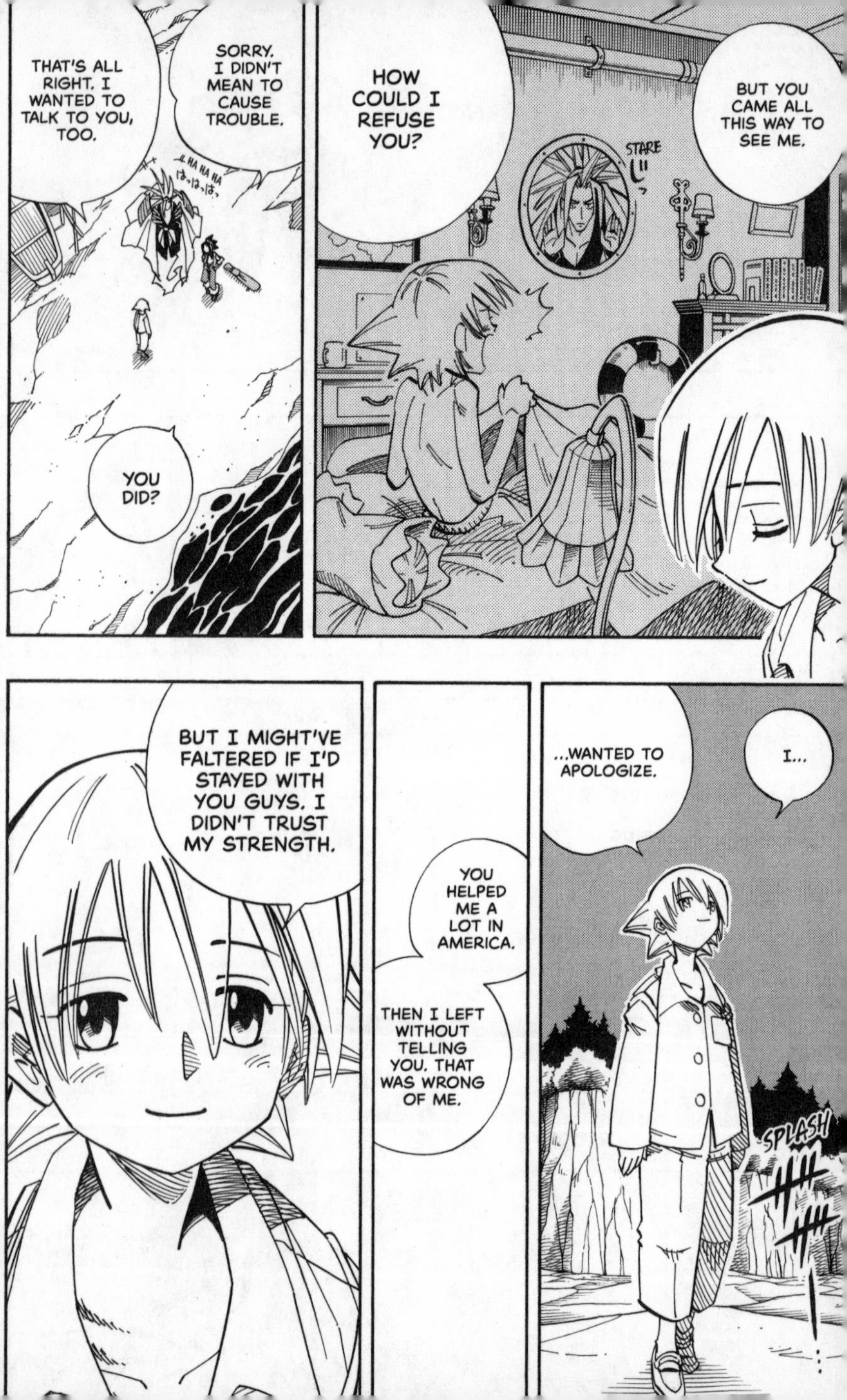
BUT YOU CAME ALL THIS WAY TO SEE ME.
STARE
じーっ
HOW COULD I REFUSE YOU?
SORRY. I DIDN'T MEAN TO CAUSE TROUBLE.
THAT'S ALL RIGHT. I WANTED TO TALK TO YOU, TOO.
HA HA HA
はっはっはっ
YOU DID?
I...
...WANTED TO APOLOGIZE.
SPLASH
YOU HELPED ME A LOT IN AMERICA.
THEN I LEFT WITHOUT TELLING YOU. THAT WAS WRONG OF ME.
BUT I MIGHT'VE FALTERED IF I'D STAYED WITH YOU GUYS. I DIDN'T TRUST MY STRENGTH.

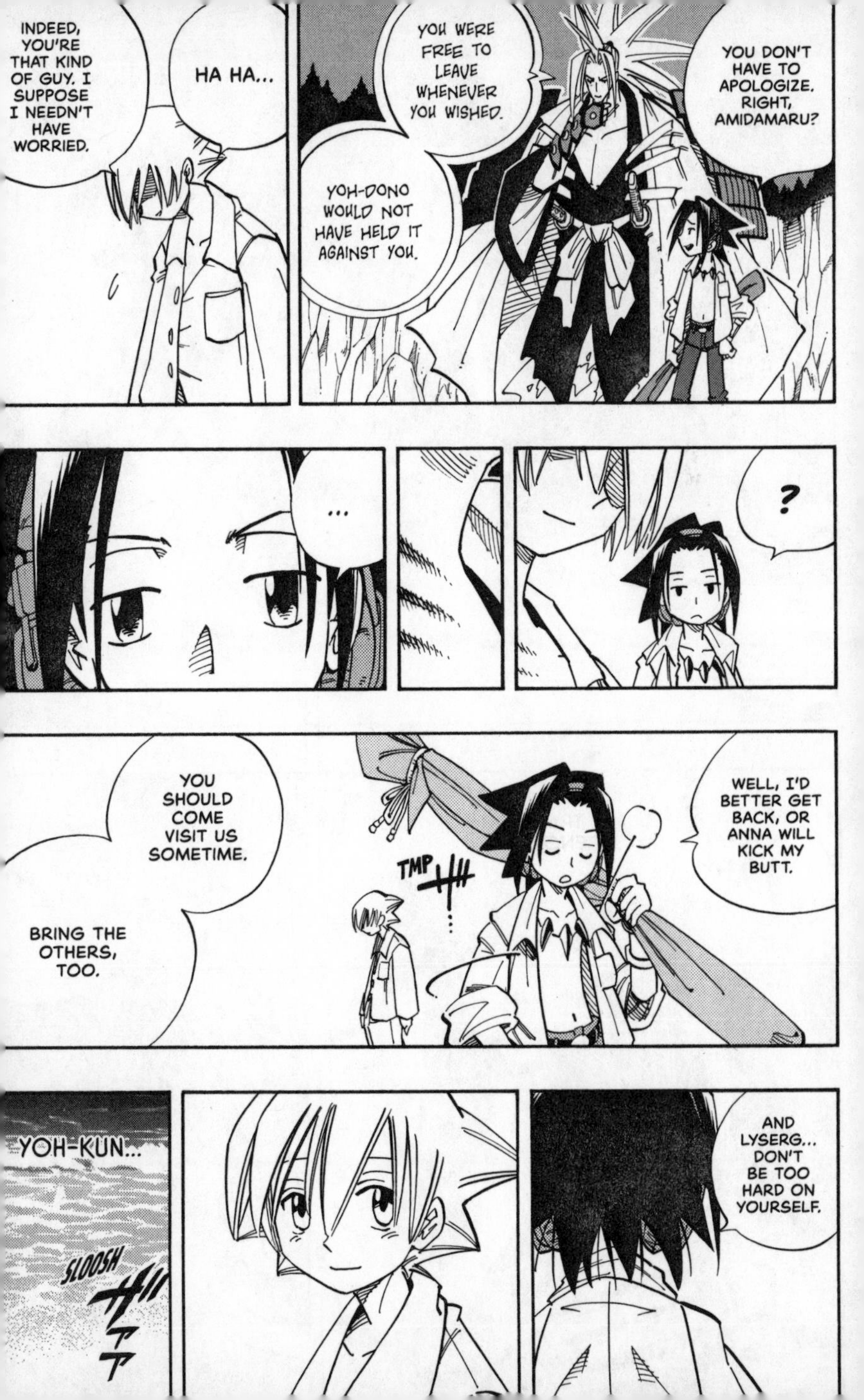
YOU DON'T HAVE TO APOLOGIZE. RIGHT, AMIDAMARU?
YOU WERE FREE TO LEAVE WHENEVER YOU WISHED.
YOH-DONO WOULD NOT HAVE HELD IT AGAINST YOU.
HA HA...
INDEED, YOU'RE THAT KIND OF GUY. I SUPPOSE I NEEDN'T HAVE WORRIED.
?
...
WELL, I'D BETTER GET BACK, OR ANNA WILL KICK MY BUTT.
TMP
YOU SHOULD COME VISIT US SOMETIME.
BRING THE OTHERS, TOO.
AND LYSERG... DON'T BE TOO HARD ON YOURSELF.
YOH-KUN...
SLOOSH

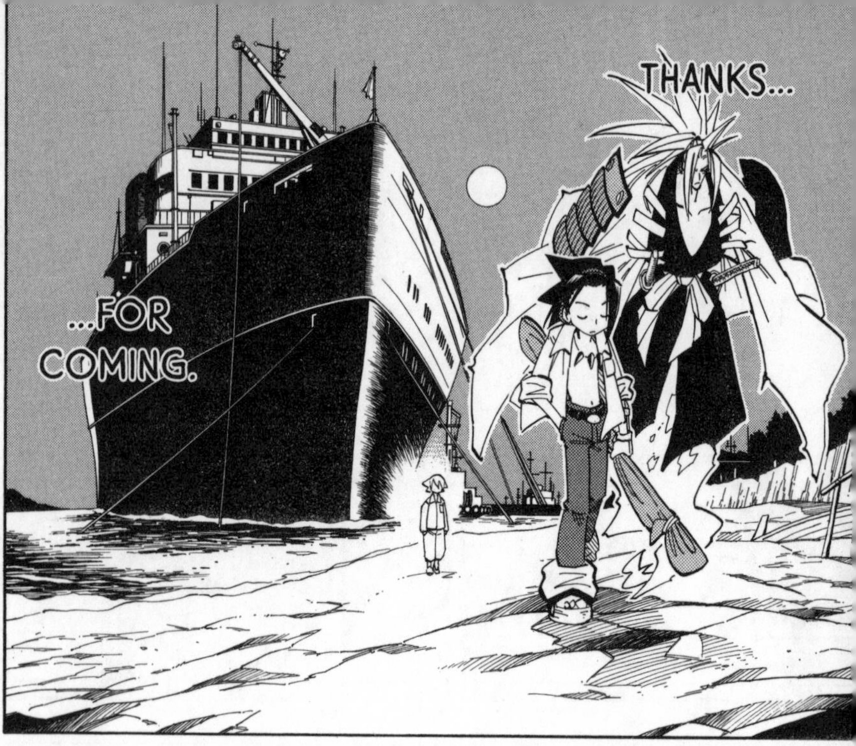
THANKS...
...FOR COMING.
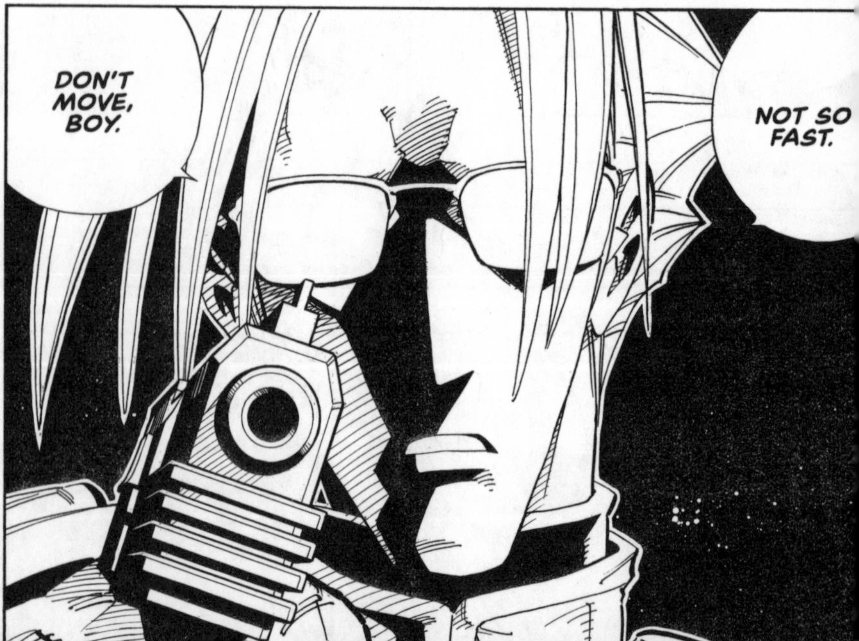
NOT SO FAST.
DON'T MOVE, BOY.

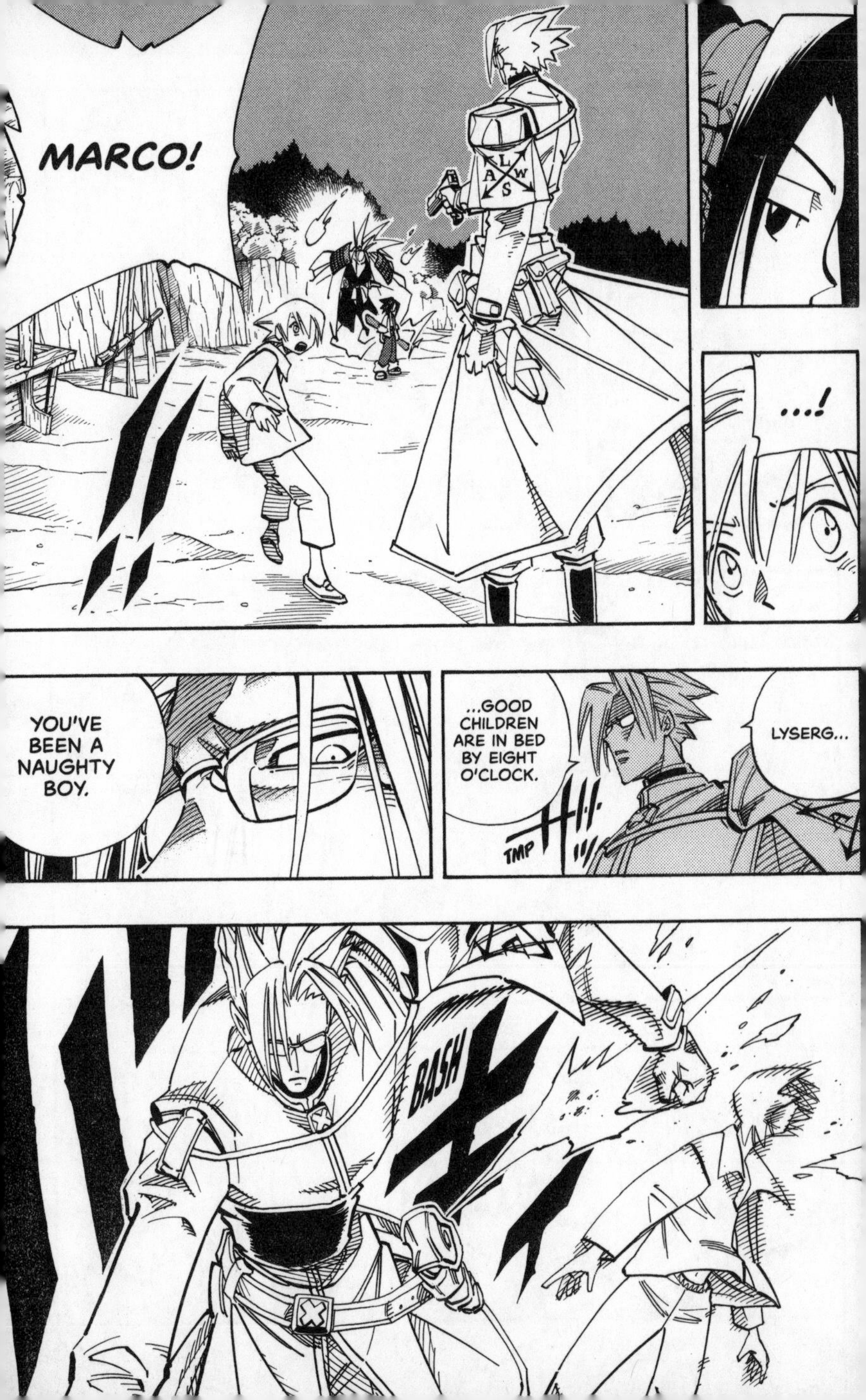

...!
MARCO!
LYSERG...
...GOOD CHILDREN ARE IN BED BY EIGHT O'CLOCK.
TMP
YOU'VE BEEN A NAUGHTY BOY.
BASH

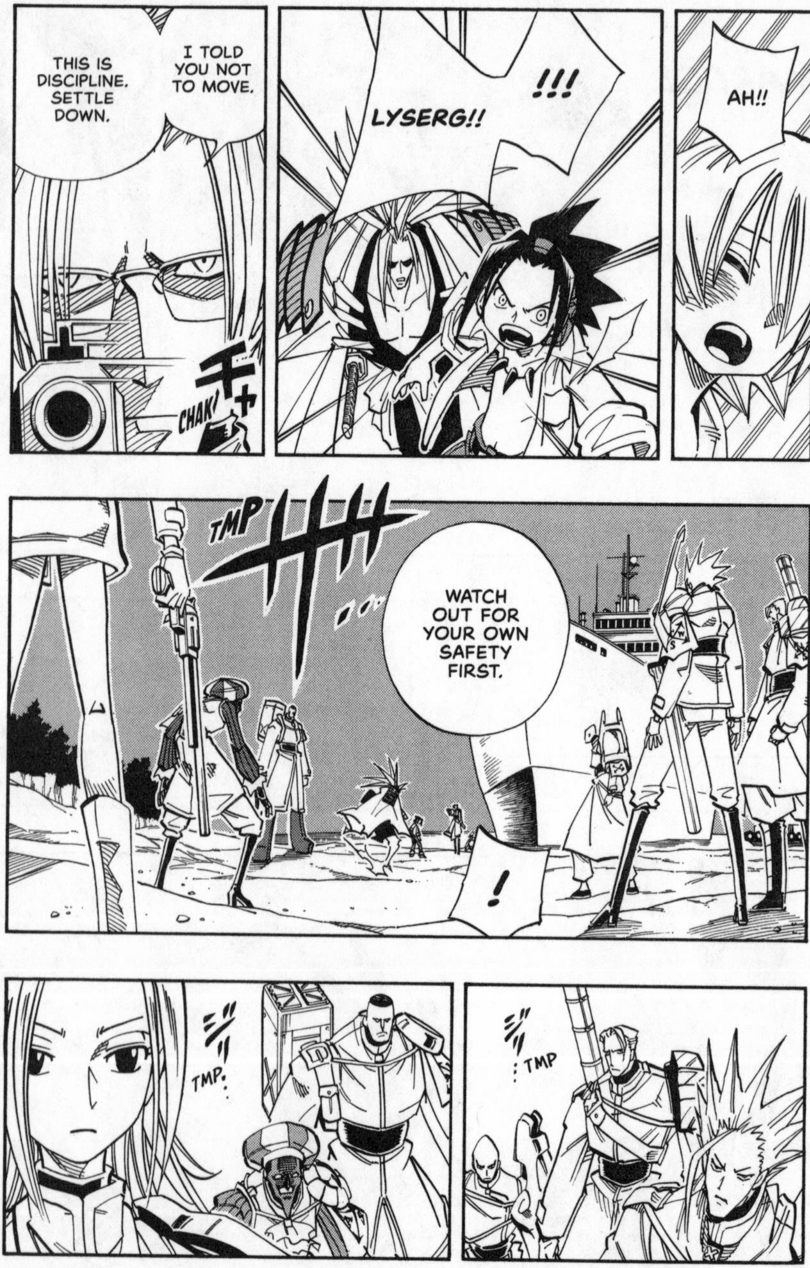
AH!!
!!!
LYSERG!!
I TOLD YOU NOT TO MOVE.
THIS IS DISCIPLINE. SETTLE DOWN.
CHAK
チャ
!
WATCH OUT FOR YOUR OWN SAFETY FIRST.
TMP
TMP
TMP

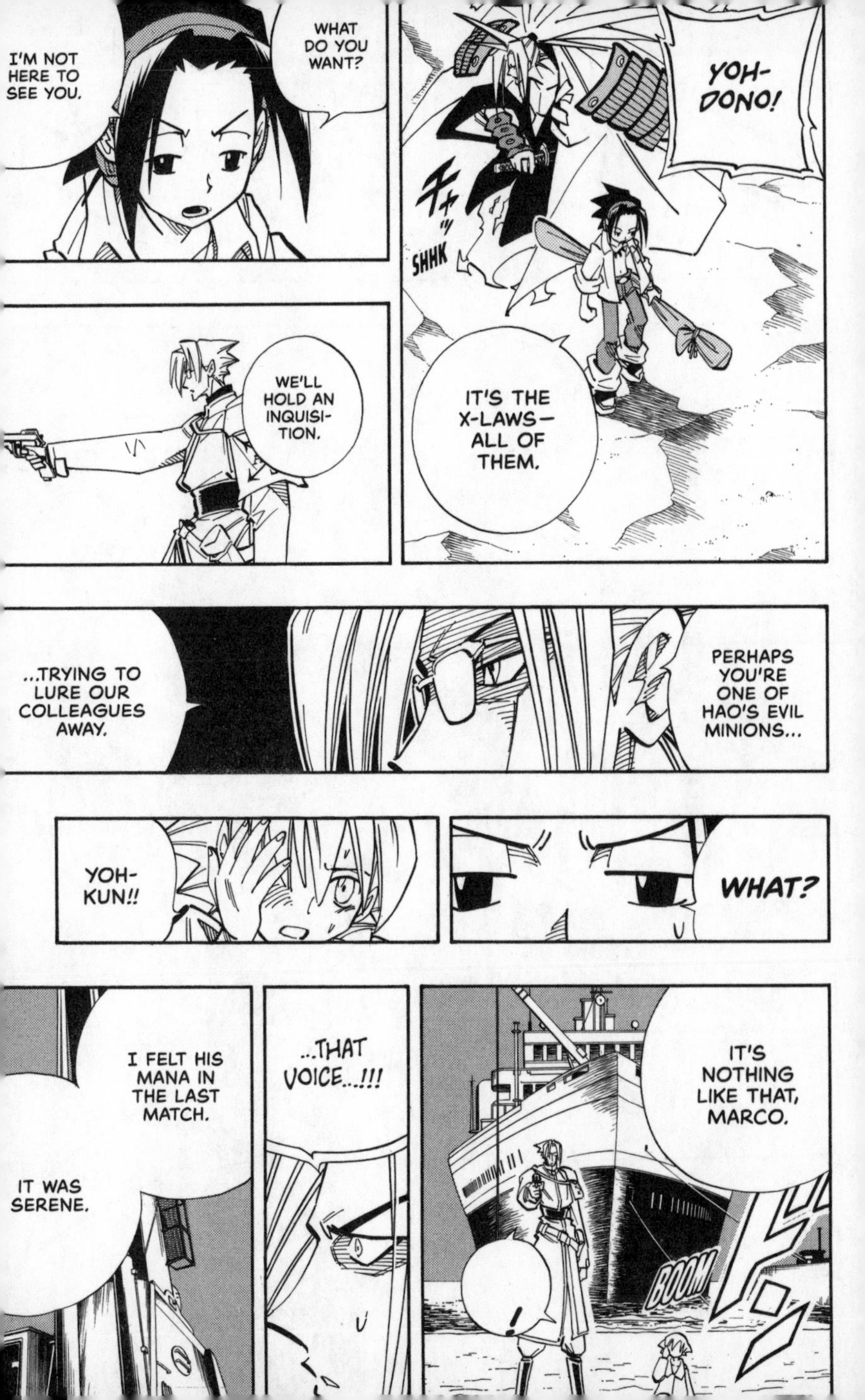
YOH-DONO!
チャッ
SHHK
IT'S THE X-LAWS— ALL OF THEM.
WHAT DO YOU WANT?
I'M NOT HERE TO SEE YOU.
WE'LL HOLD AN INQUISITION.
PERHAPS YOU'RE ONE OF HAO'S EVIL MINIONS...
...TRYING TO LURE OUR COLLEAGUES AWAY.
WHAT?
YOH-KUN!!
IT'S NOTHING LIKE THAT, MARCO.
BOOM
...THAT VOICE...!!!
I FELT HIS MANA IN THE LAST MATCH.
IT WAS SERENE.

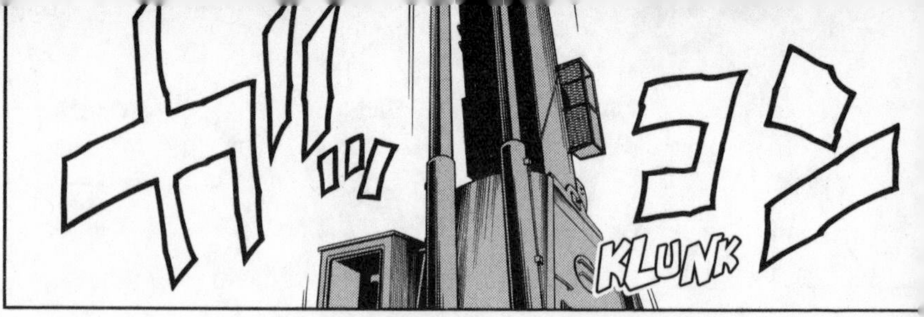
KLUNK

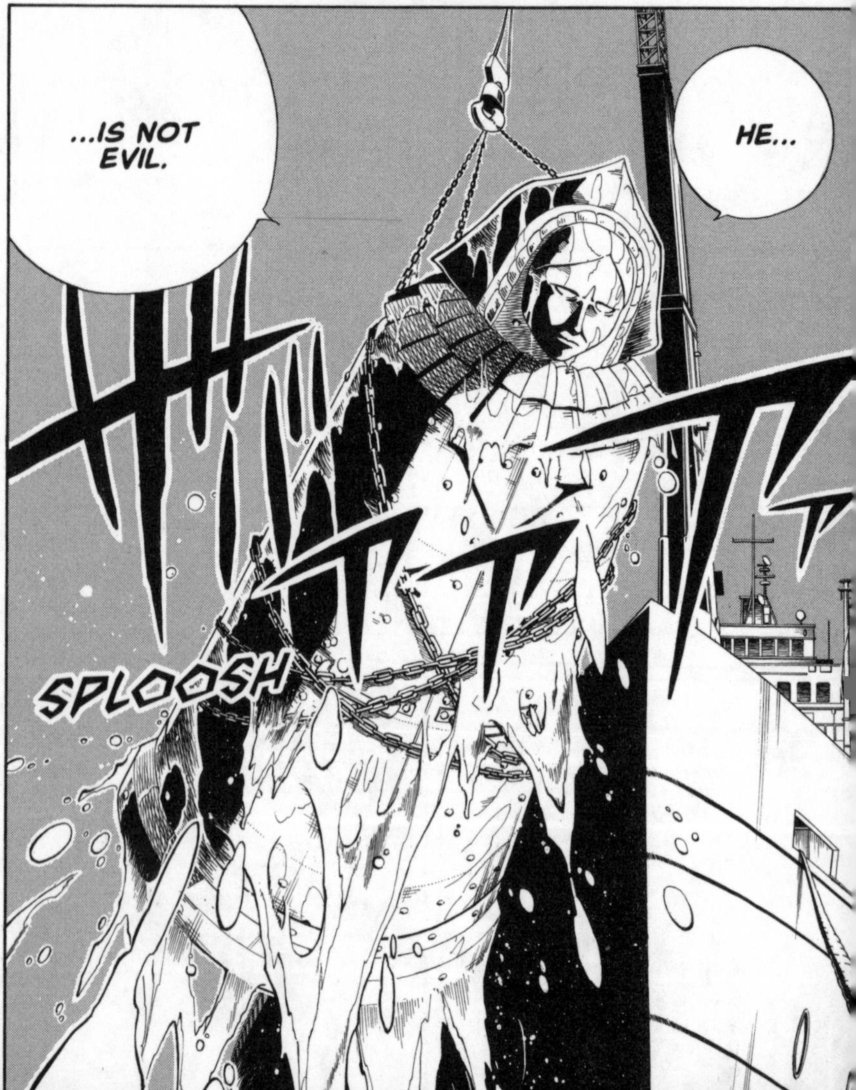
HE...
...IS NOT EVIL.
SPLOOSH

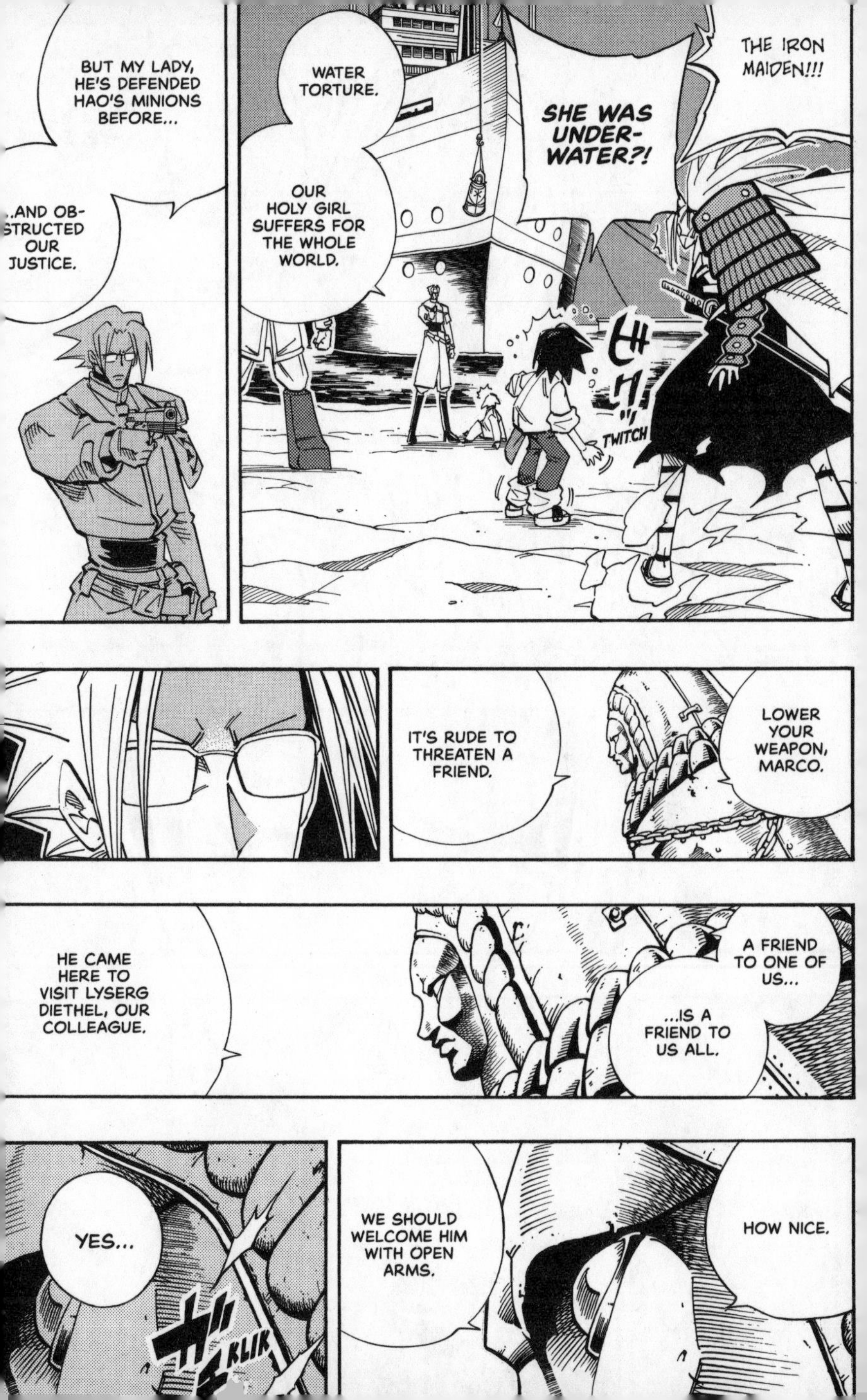
THE IRON MAIDEN!!!
SHE WAS UNDER-WATER?!
WATER TORTURE.
OUR HOLY GIRL SUFFERS FOR THE WHOLE WORLD.
TWITCH
BUT MY LADY, HE'S DEFENDED HAO'S MINIONS BEFORE...
..AND OB-STRUCTED OUR JUSTICE.
LOWER YOUR WEAPON, MARCO.
IT'S RUDE TO THREATEN A FRIEND.
A FRIEND TO ONE OF US...
...IS A FRIEND TO US ALL.
HE CAME HERE TO VISIT LYSERG DIETHEL, OUR COLLEAGUE.
HOW NICE.
WE SHOULD WELCOME HIM WITH OPEN ARMS.
YES...
KLIK

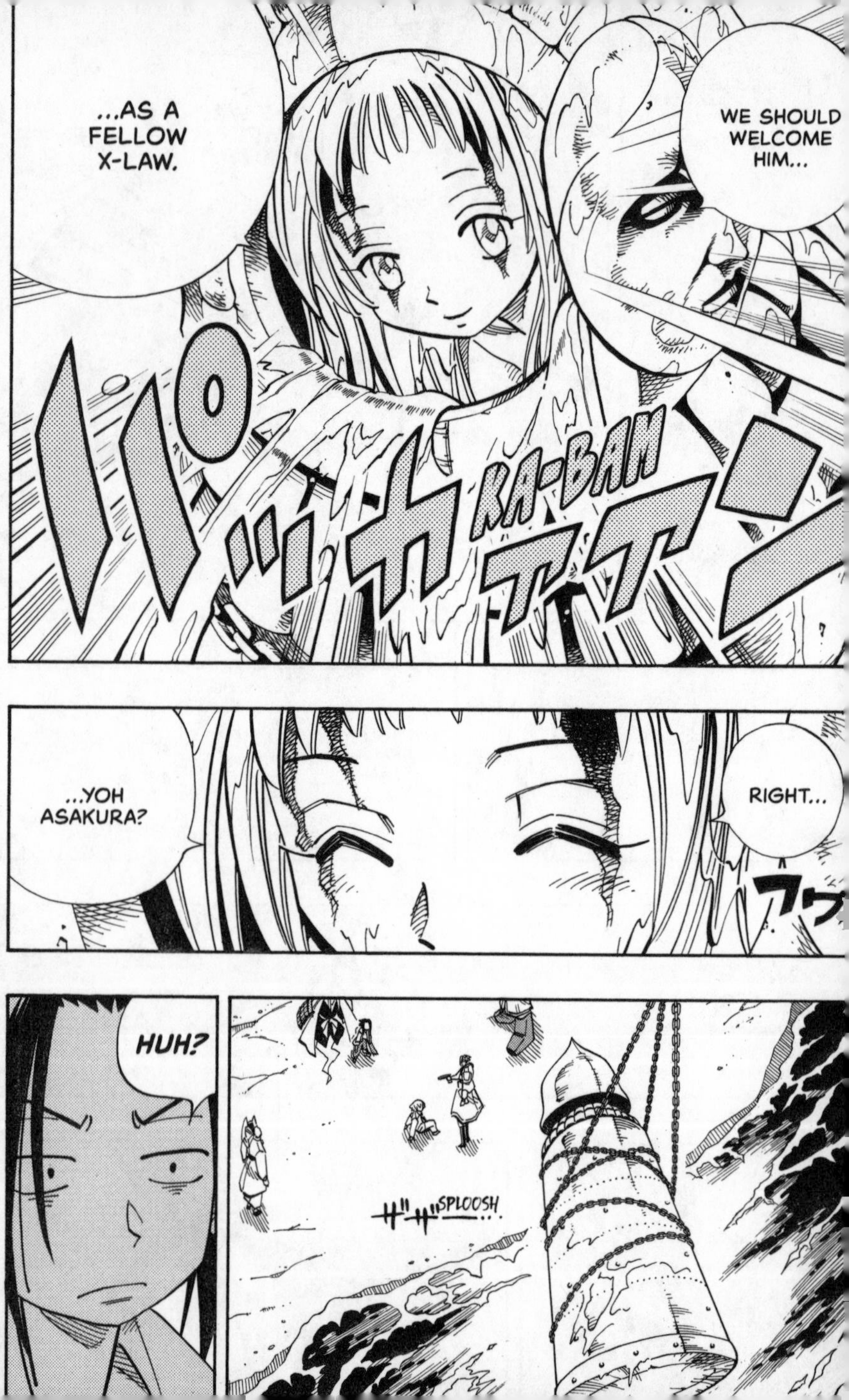
WE SHOULD WELCOME HIM...
...AS A FELLOW X-LAW.
KA-BAM
RIGHT...
...YOH ASAKURA?
SPLOOSH
HUH?

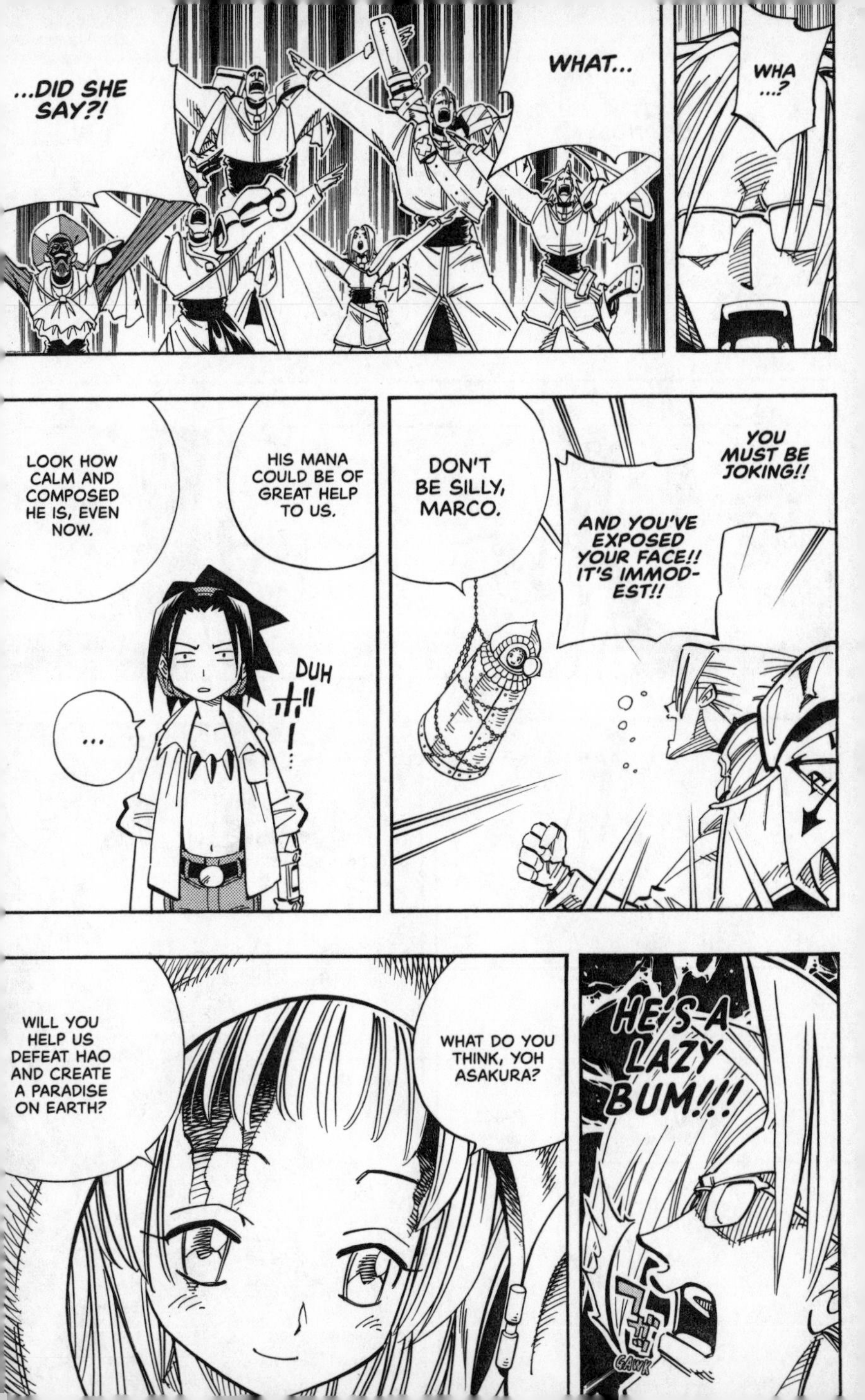
WHA ...?
WHAT...
...DID SHE SAY?!
YOU MUST BE JOKING!!
AND YOU'VE EXPOSED YOUR FACE!! IT'S IMMOD-EST!!
DON'T BE SILLY, MARCO.
HIS MANA COULD BE OF GREAT HELP TO US.
LOOK HOW CALM AND COMPOSED HE IS, EVEN NOW.
DUH
...
HE'S A LAZY BUM!!!
GAWK
WHAT DO YOU THINK, YOH ASAKURA?
WILL YOU HELP US DEFEAT HAO AND CREATE A PARADISE ON EARTH?

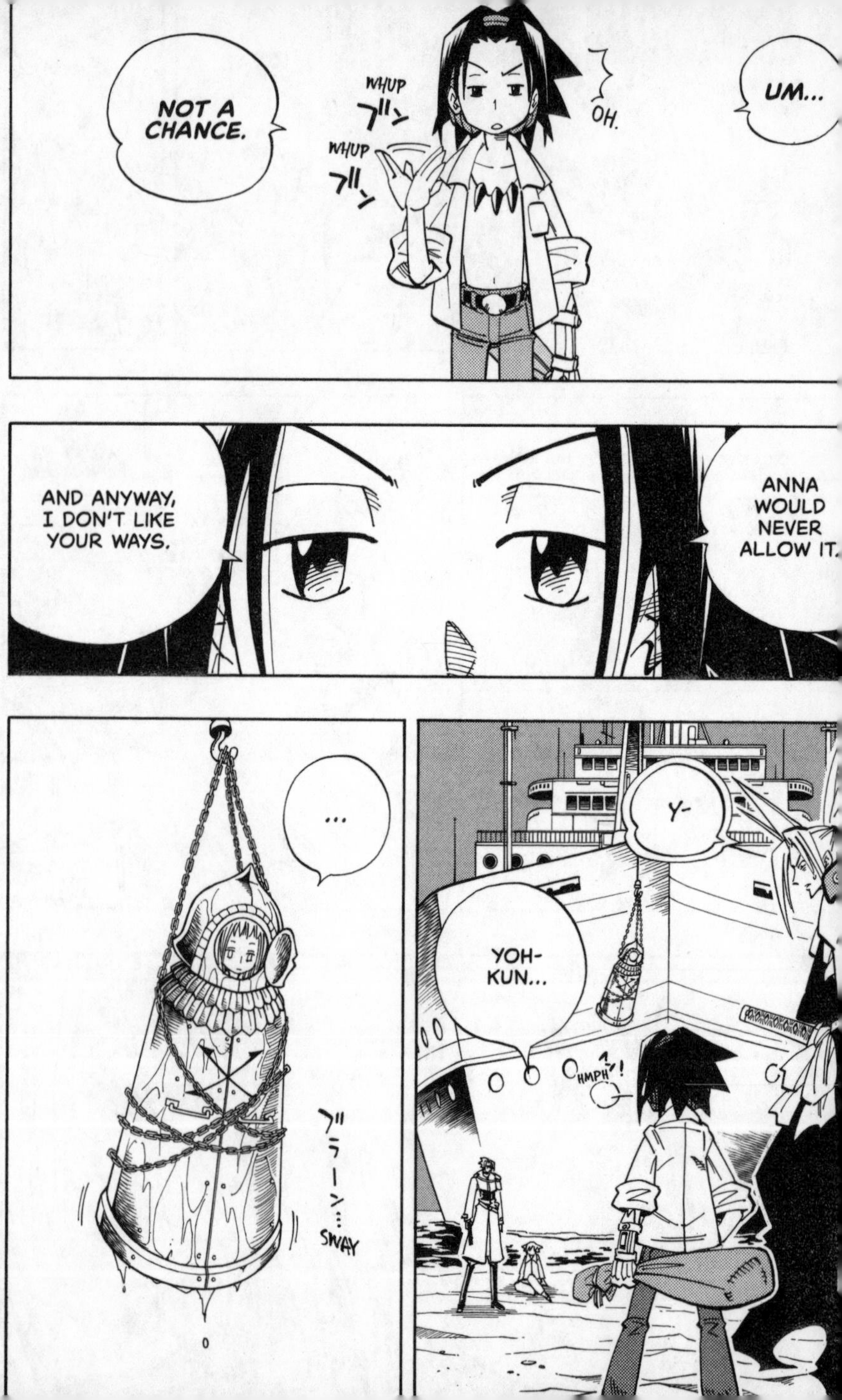
UM...
OH.
WHUP
WHUP
NOT A CHANCE.
ANNA WOULD NEVER ALLOW IT.
AND ANYWAY, I DON'T LIKE YOUR WAYS.
Y-
YOH-KUN...
HMPH!
...
SWAY

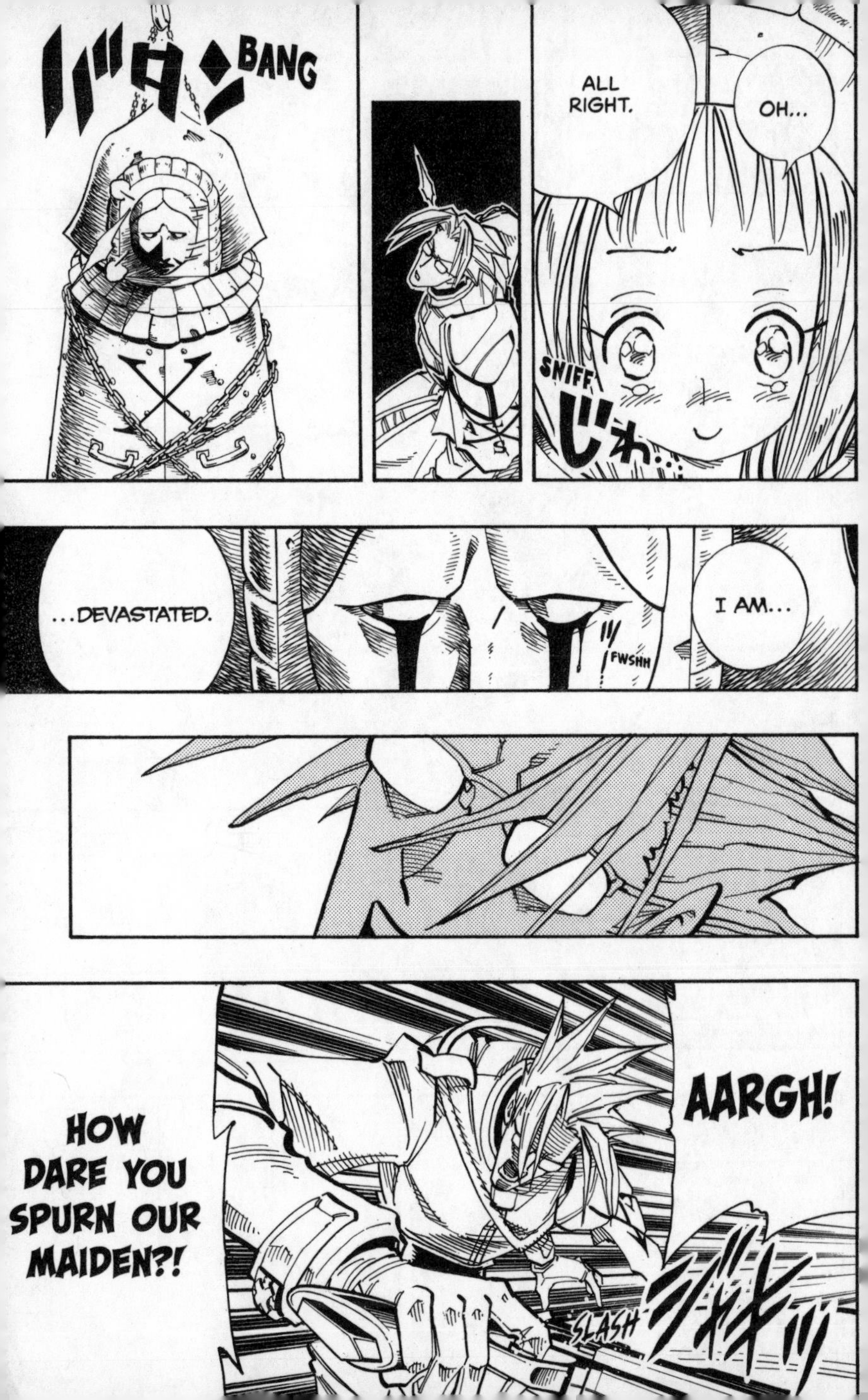
OH...
ALL RIGHT.
SNIFF
じわ
バタン
BANG
I AM...
FWSHH
...DEVASTATED.
AARGH!
HOW DARE YOU SPURN OUR MAIDEN?!
SLASH

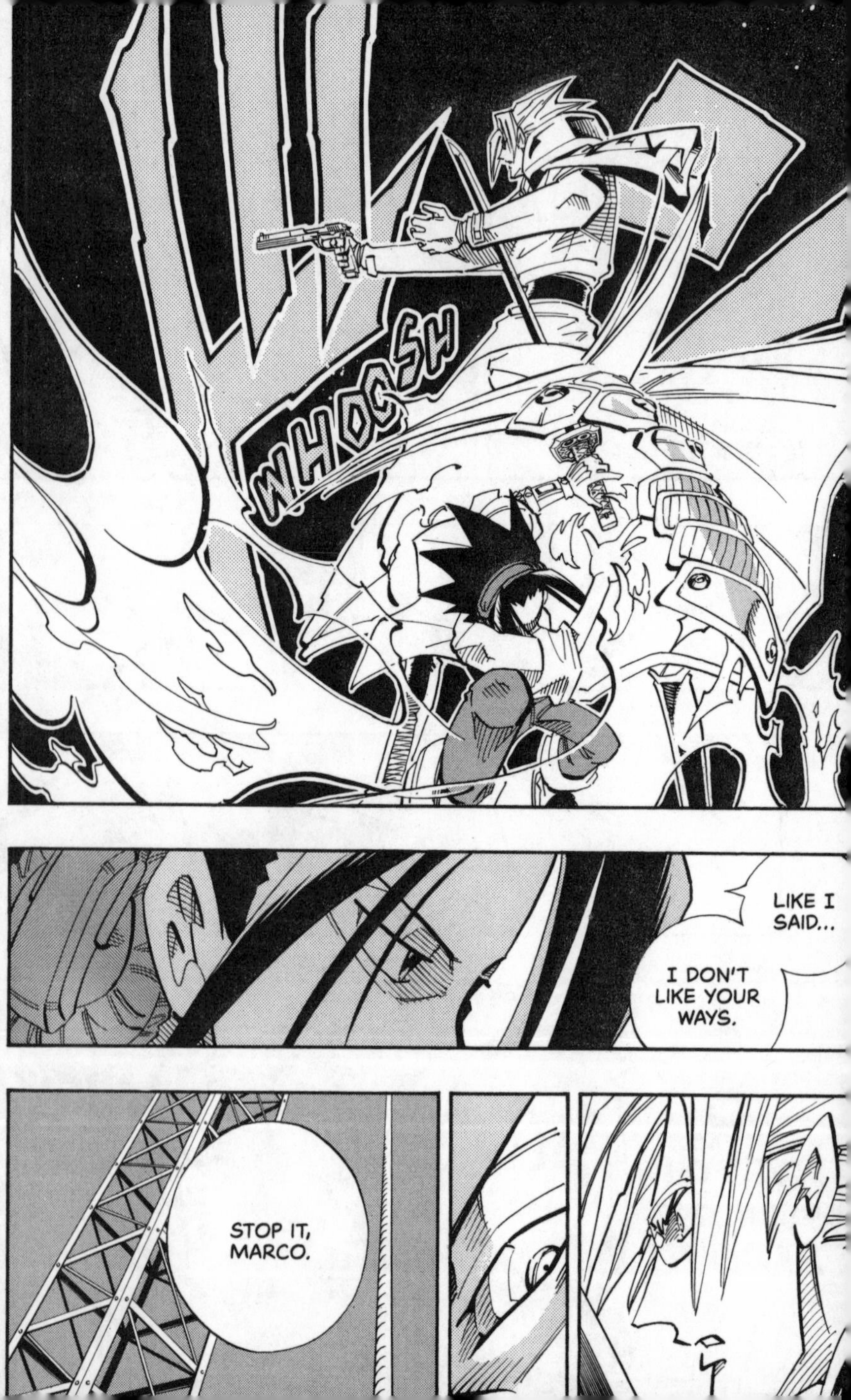
WHOOSH
LIKE I SAID...
I DON'T LIKE YOUR WAYS.
STOP IT, MARCO.

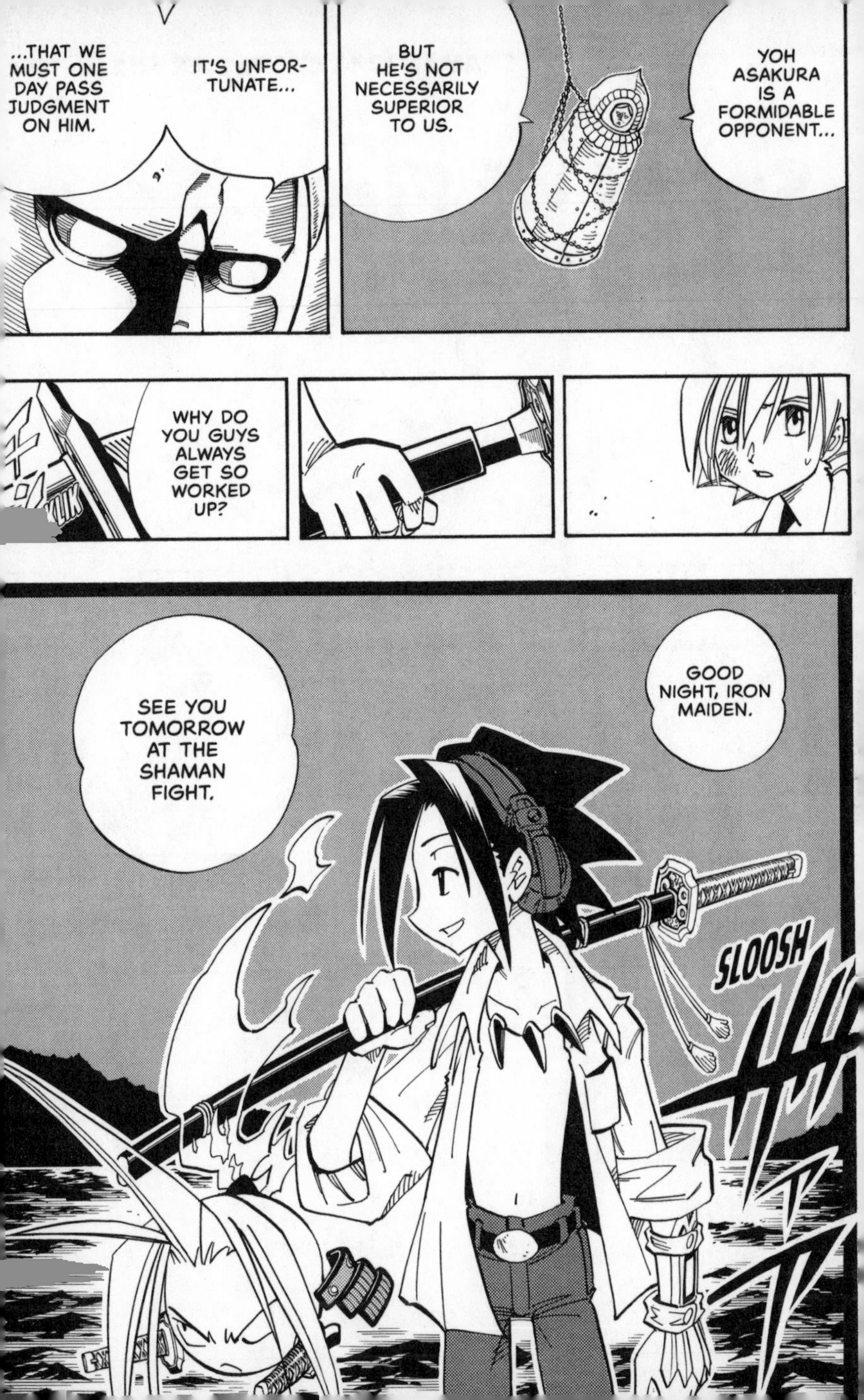
YOH ASAKURA IS A FORMIDABLE OPPONENT...
BUT HE'S NOT NECESSARILY SUPERIOR TO US.
IT'S UNFORTUNATE...
...THAT WE MUST ONE DAY PASS JUDGMENT ON HIM.
KLIK
WHY DO YOU GUYS ALWAYS GET SO WORKED UP?
GOOD NIGHT, IRON MAIDEN.
SEE YOU TOMORROW AT THE SHAMAN FIGHT.
SLOOSH

Spirit of Fire

January 2001

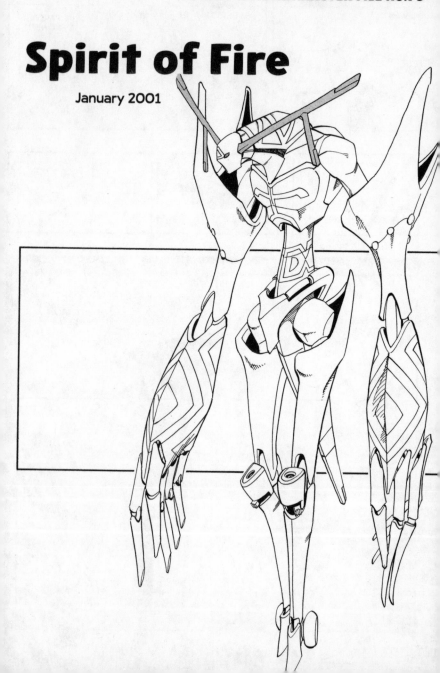

Chapter 137: Burning Angel

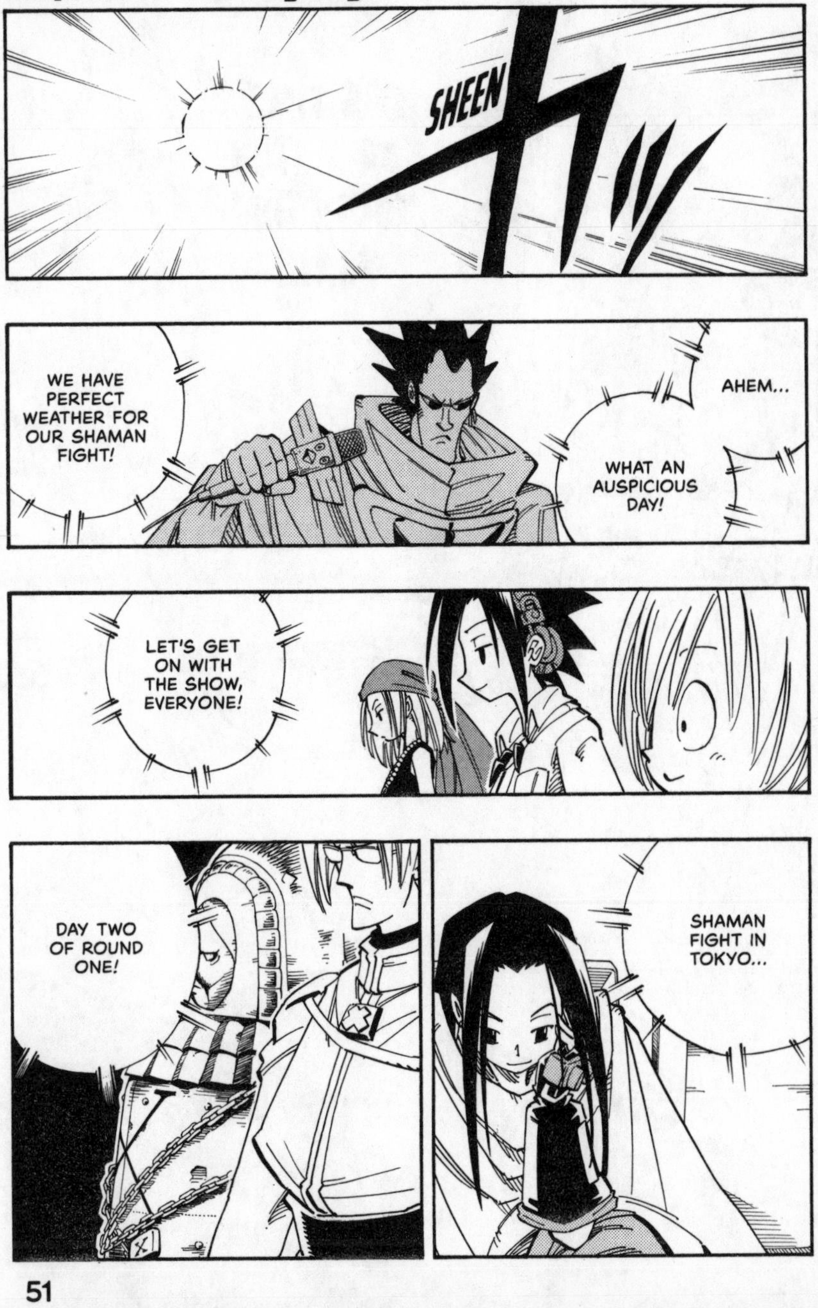
SHEEN
AHEM...
WHAT AN AUSPICIOUS DAY!
WE HAVE PERFECT WEATHER FOR OUR SHAMAN FIGHT!
LET'S GET ON WITH THE SHOW, EVERYONE!
SHAMAN FIGHT IN TOKYO...
DAY TWO OF ROUND ONE!

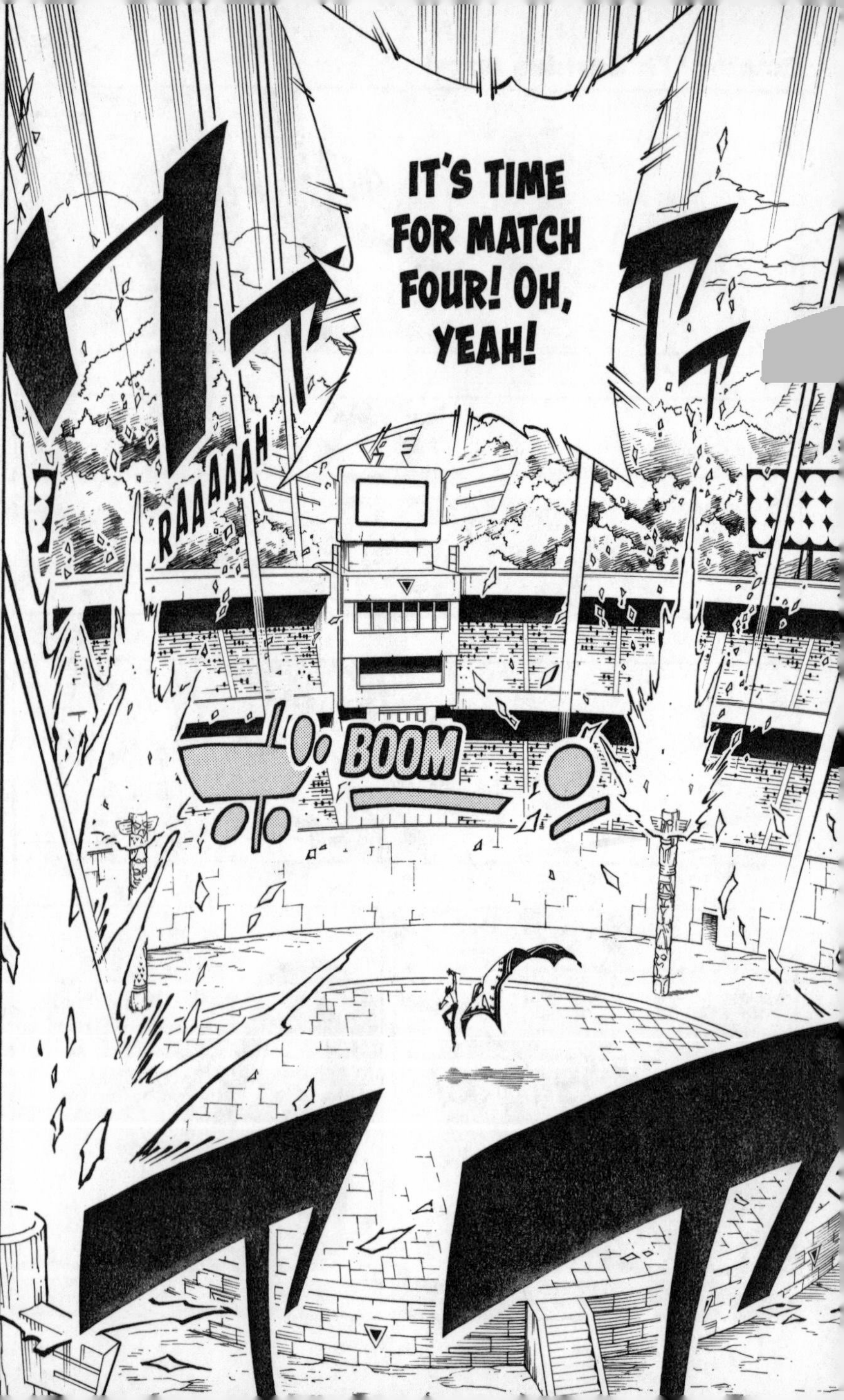
IT'S TIME FOR MATCH FOUR! OH, YEAH!
RAAAAAAH
BOOM

Chapter 137:

Burning Angel

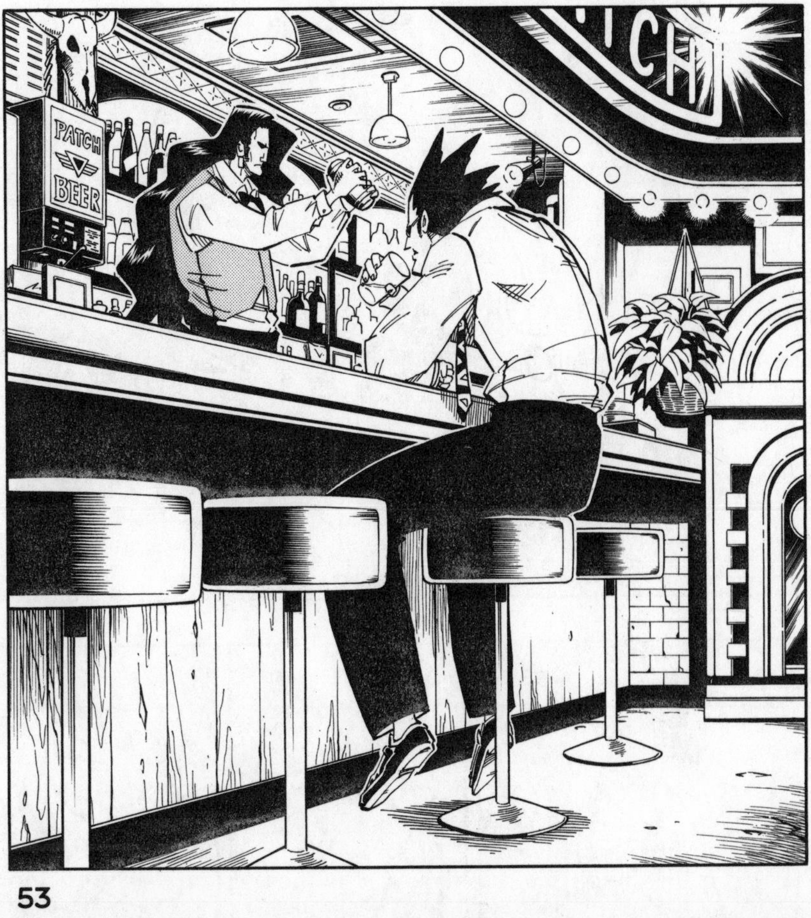

PATCH
BEER

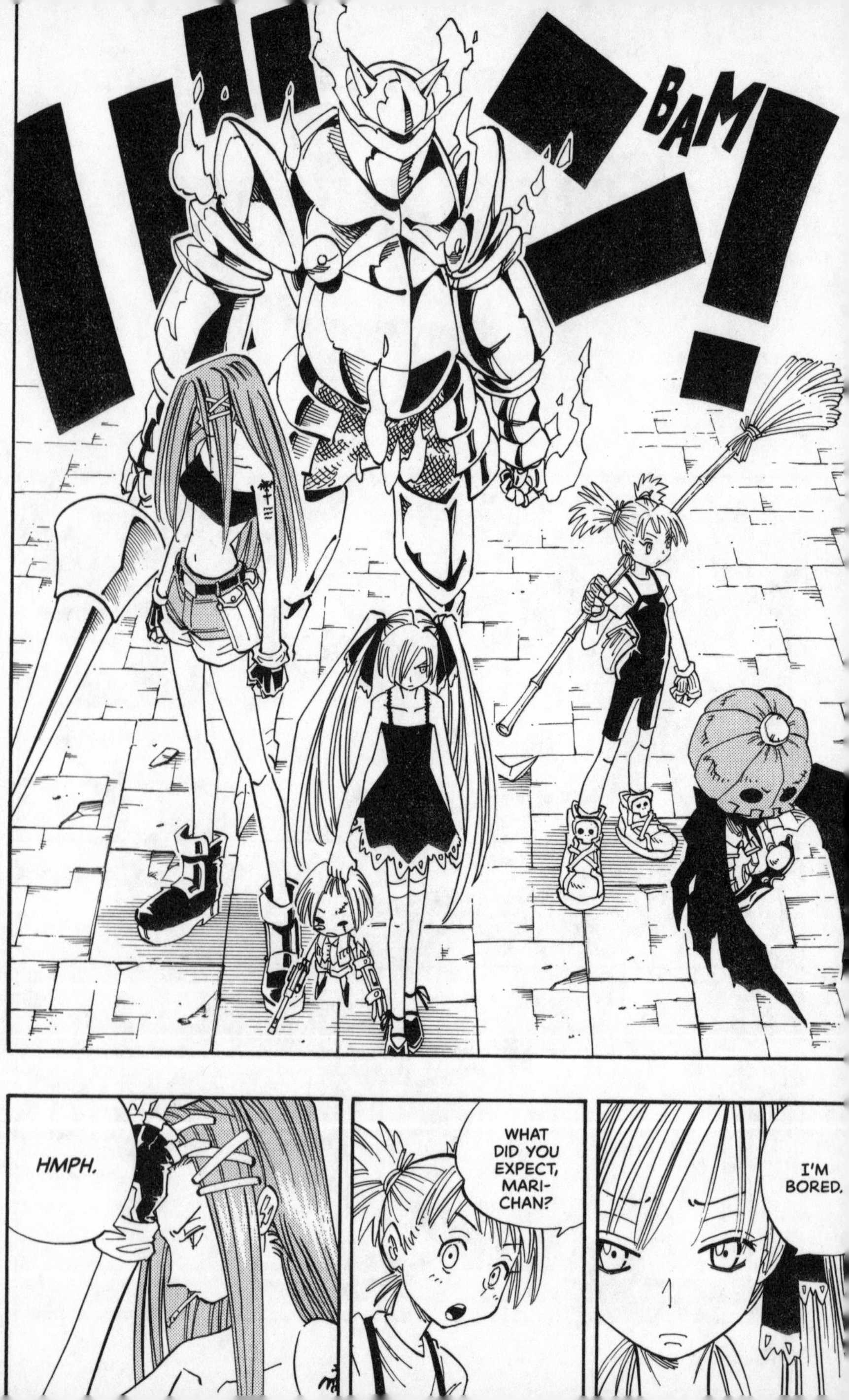
BAM
I'M BORED.
WHAT DID YOU EXPECT, MARI-CHAN?
HMPH.

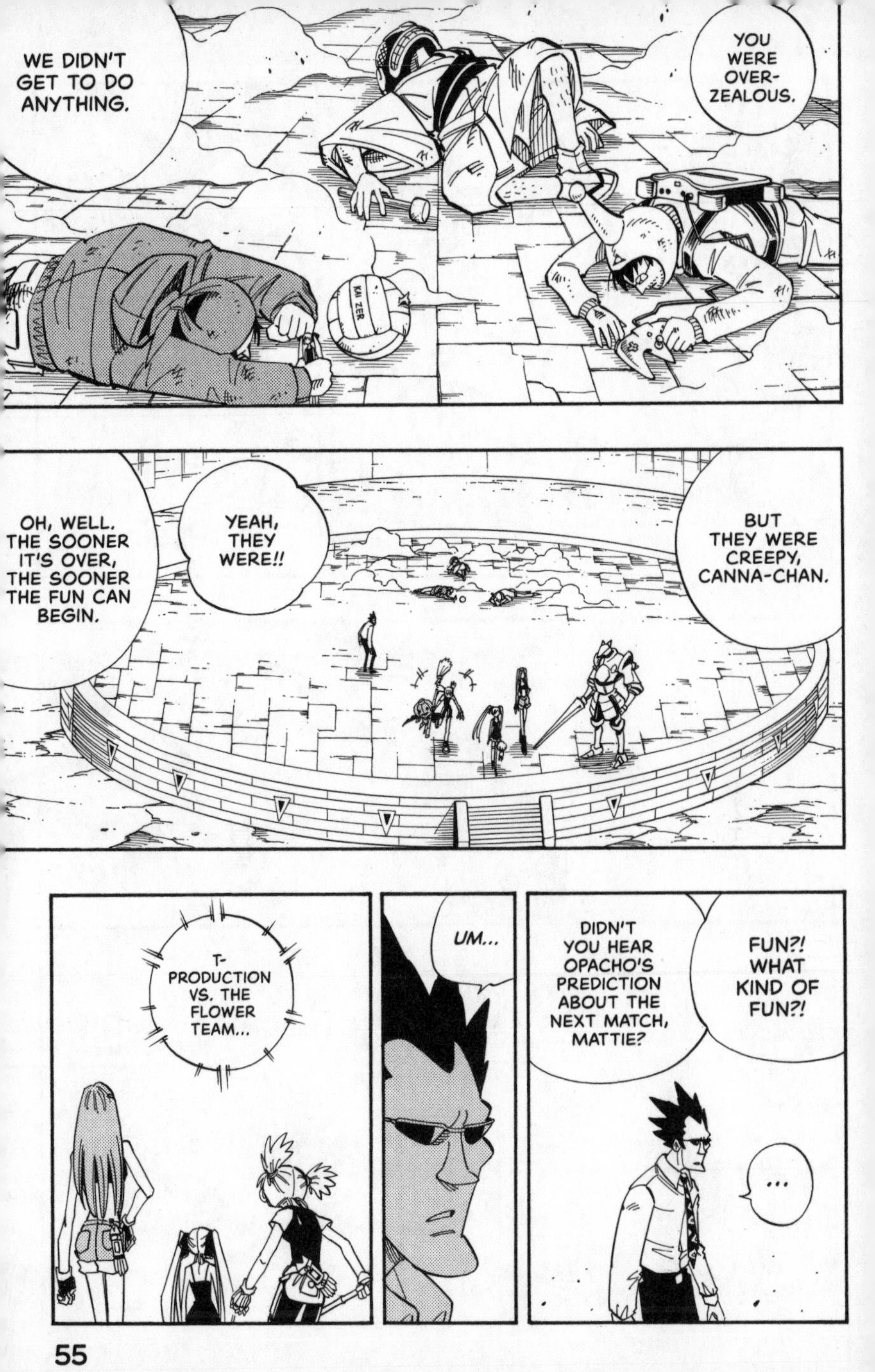
YOU WERE OVER-ZEALOUS.
WE DIDN'T GET TO DO ANYTHING.
KAI ZER
BUT THEY WERE CREEPY, CANNA-CHAN.
YEAH, THEY WERE!!
OH, WELL. THE SOONER IT'S OVER, THE SOONER THE FUN CAN BEGIN.
FUN?! WHAT KIND OF FUN?!
DIDN'T YOU HEAR OPACHO'S PREDICTION ABOUT THE NEXT MATCH, MATTIE?
...
UM...
T-PRODUCTION VS. THE FLOWER TEAM...

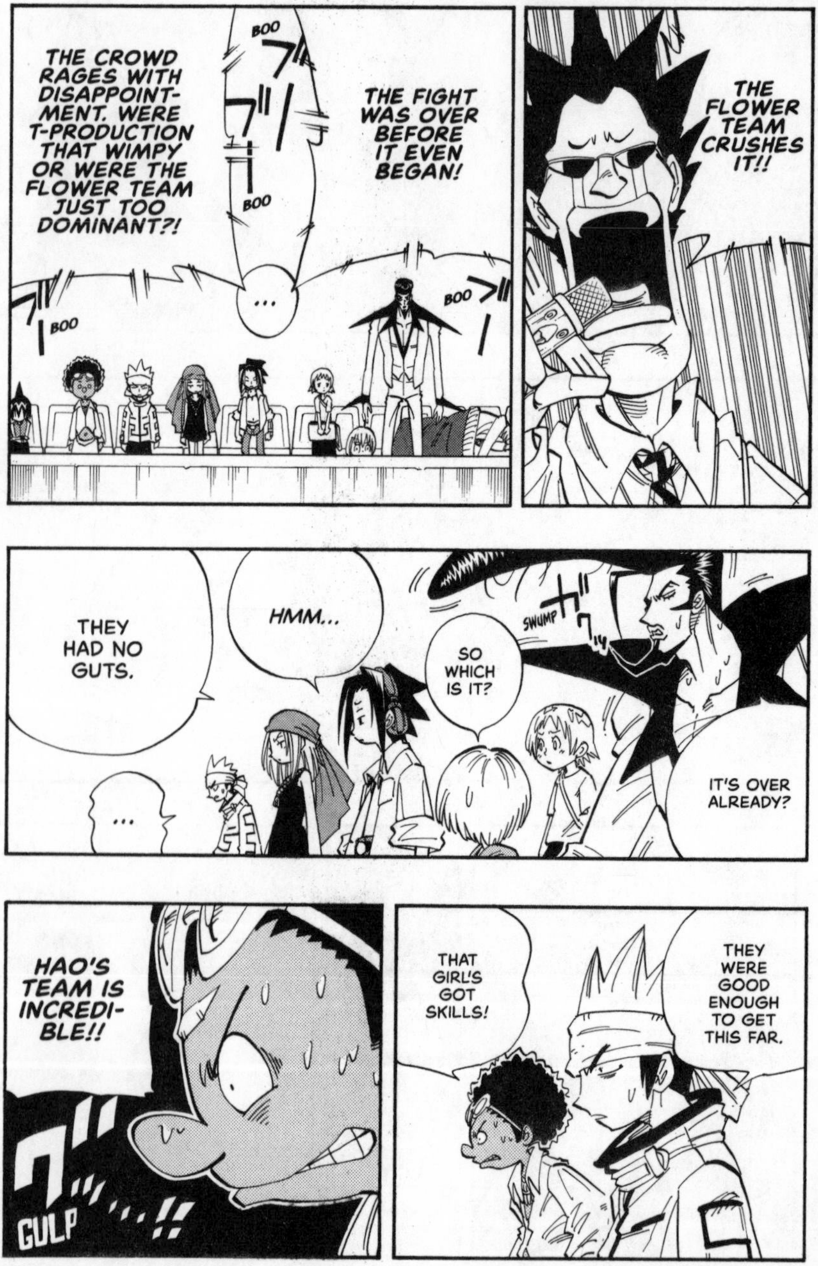
THE FLOWER TEAM CRUSHES IT!!
THE FIGHT WAS OVER BEFORE IT EVEN BEGAN!
BOO
THE CROWD RAGES WITH DISAPPOINTMENT. WERE T-PRODUCTION THAT WIMPY OR WERE THE FLOWER TEAM JUST TOO DOMINANT?!
BOO
BOO
...
BOO
SWUMP
IT'S OVER ALREADY?
SO WHICH IS IT?
HMM...
THEY HAD NO GUTS.
...
THEY WERE GOOD ENOUGH TO GET THIS FAR.
THAT GIRL'S GOT SKILLS!
HAO'S TEAM IS INCREDIBLE!!
GULP

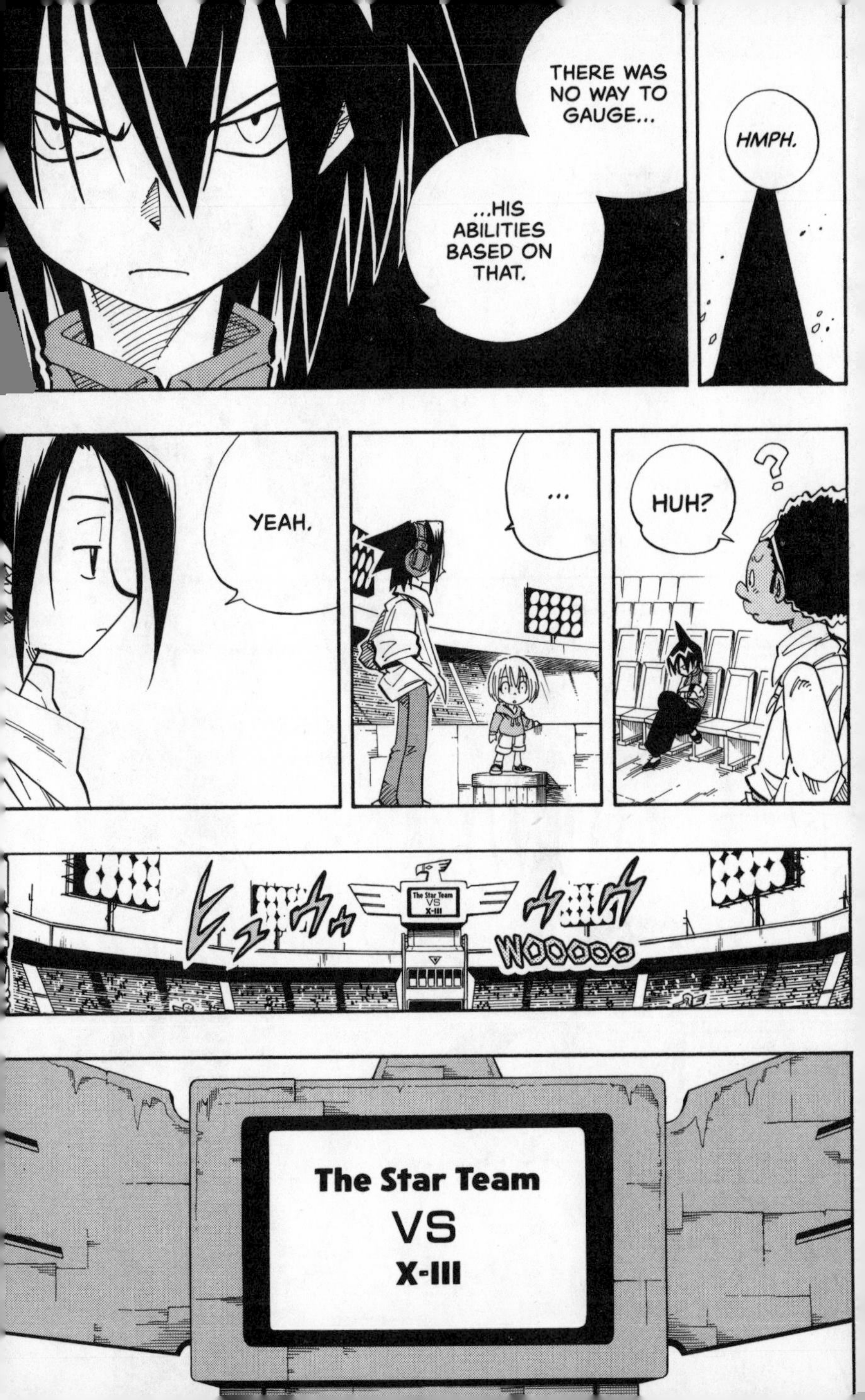
HMPH.
THERE WAS NO WAY TO GAUGE...
...HIS ABILITIES BASED ON THAT.
HUH?
?
...
YEAH.
WOOOOO
The Star Team
VS
X-III
The Star Team
VS
X-III

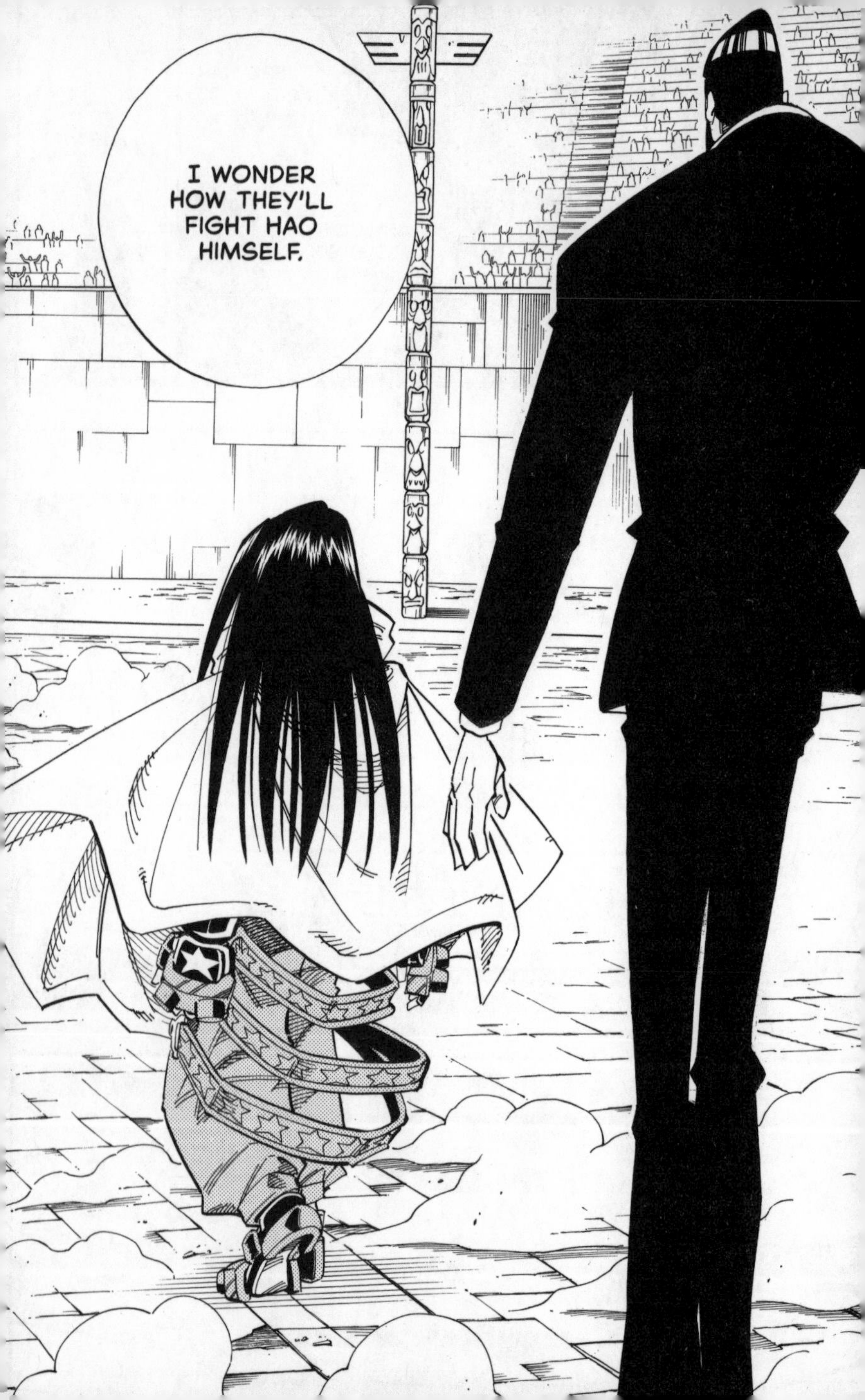
I WONDER HOW THEY'LL FIGHT HAO HIMSELF.

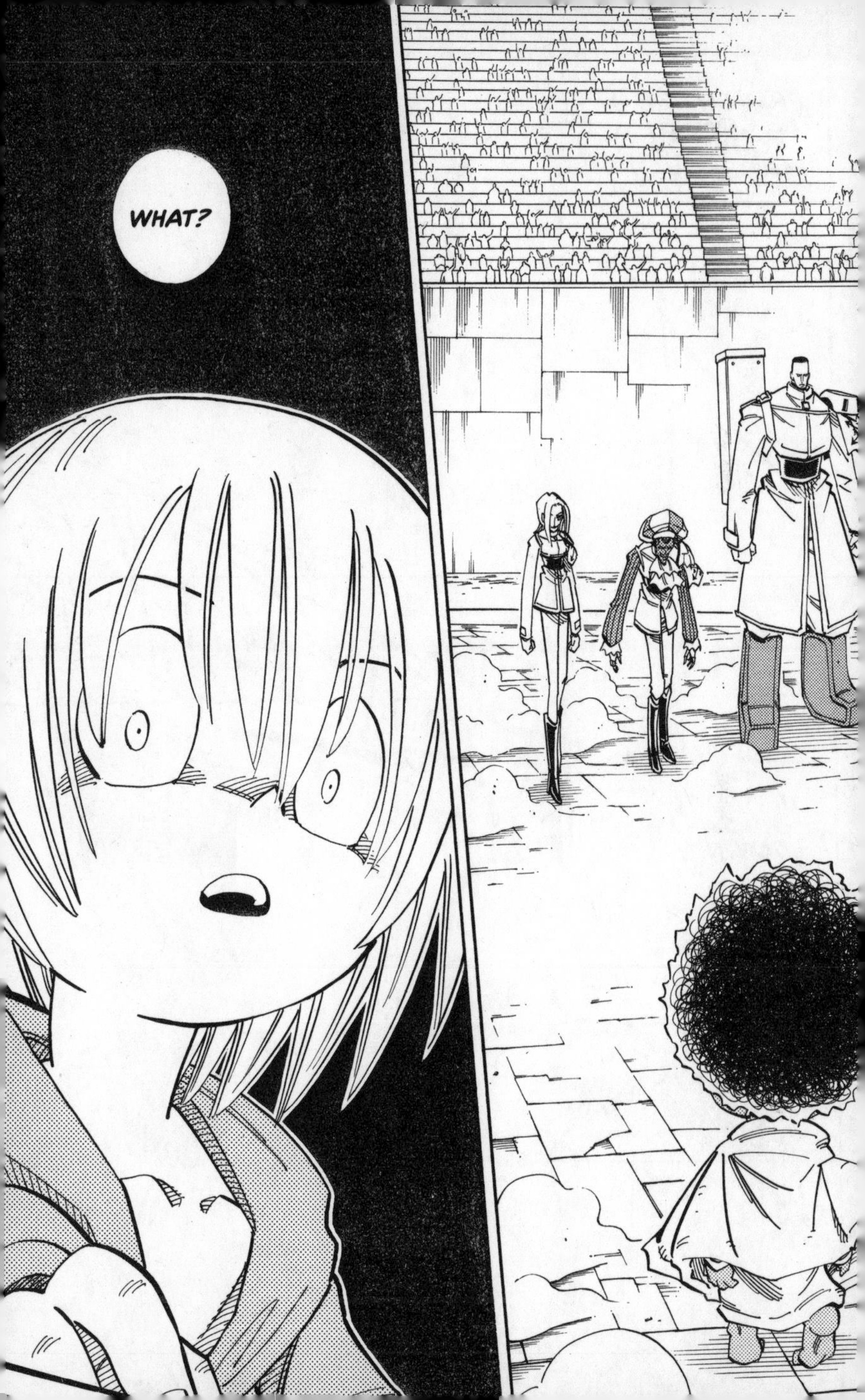
WHAT?

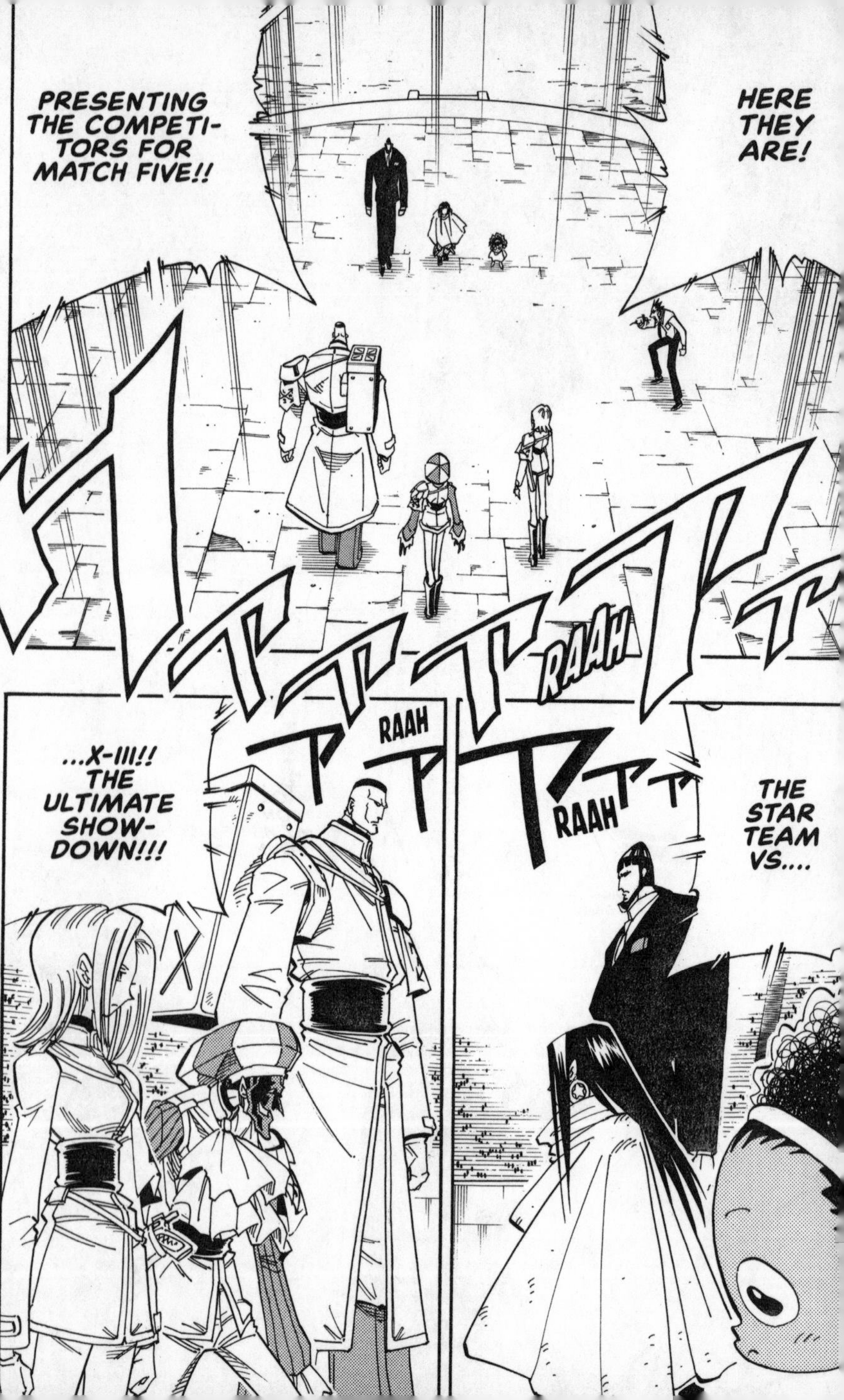
HERE THEY ARE!
PRESENTING THE COMPETITORS FOR MATCH FIVE!!
RAAH
THE STAR TEAM VS....
RAAH
RAAH
...X-III!! THE ULTIMATE SHOW-DOWN!!!

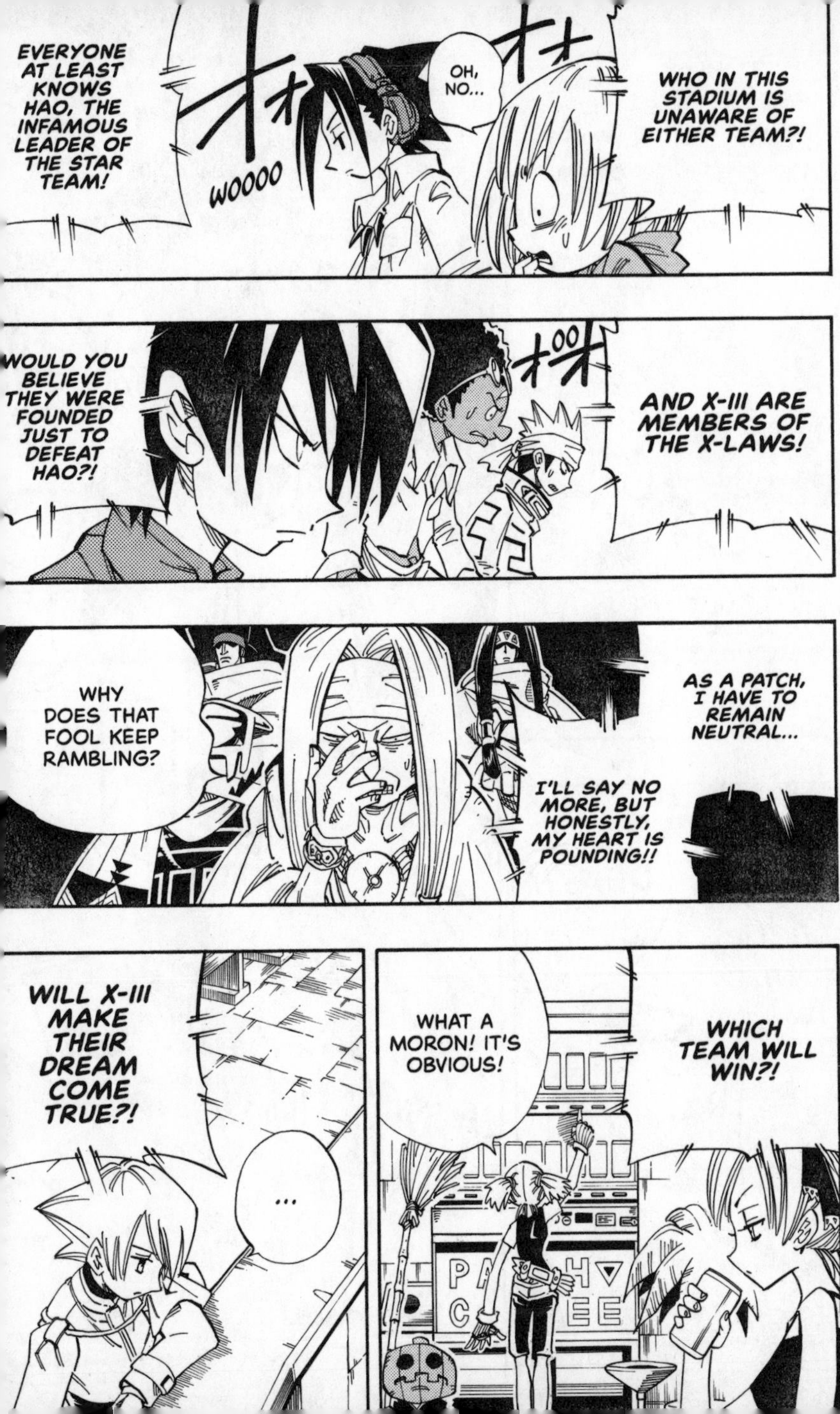
WHO IN THIS STADIUM IS UNAWARE OF EITHER TEAM?!
OH, NO...
WOOOO
EVERYONE AT LEAST KNOWS HAO, THE INFAMOUS LEADER OF THE STAR TEAM!
OO
AND X-III ARE MEMBERS OF THE X-LAWS!
WOULD YOU BELIEVE THEY WERE FOUNDED JUST TO DEFEAT HAO?!
AS A PATCH, I HAVE TO REMAIN NEUTRAL...
I'LL SAY NO MORE, BUT HONESTLY, MY HEART IS POUNDING!!
WHY DOES THAT FOOL KEEP RAMBLING?
WHICH TEAM WILL WIN?!
WHAT A MORON! IT'S OBVIOUS!
WILL X-III MAKE THEIR DREAM COME TRUE?!
...

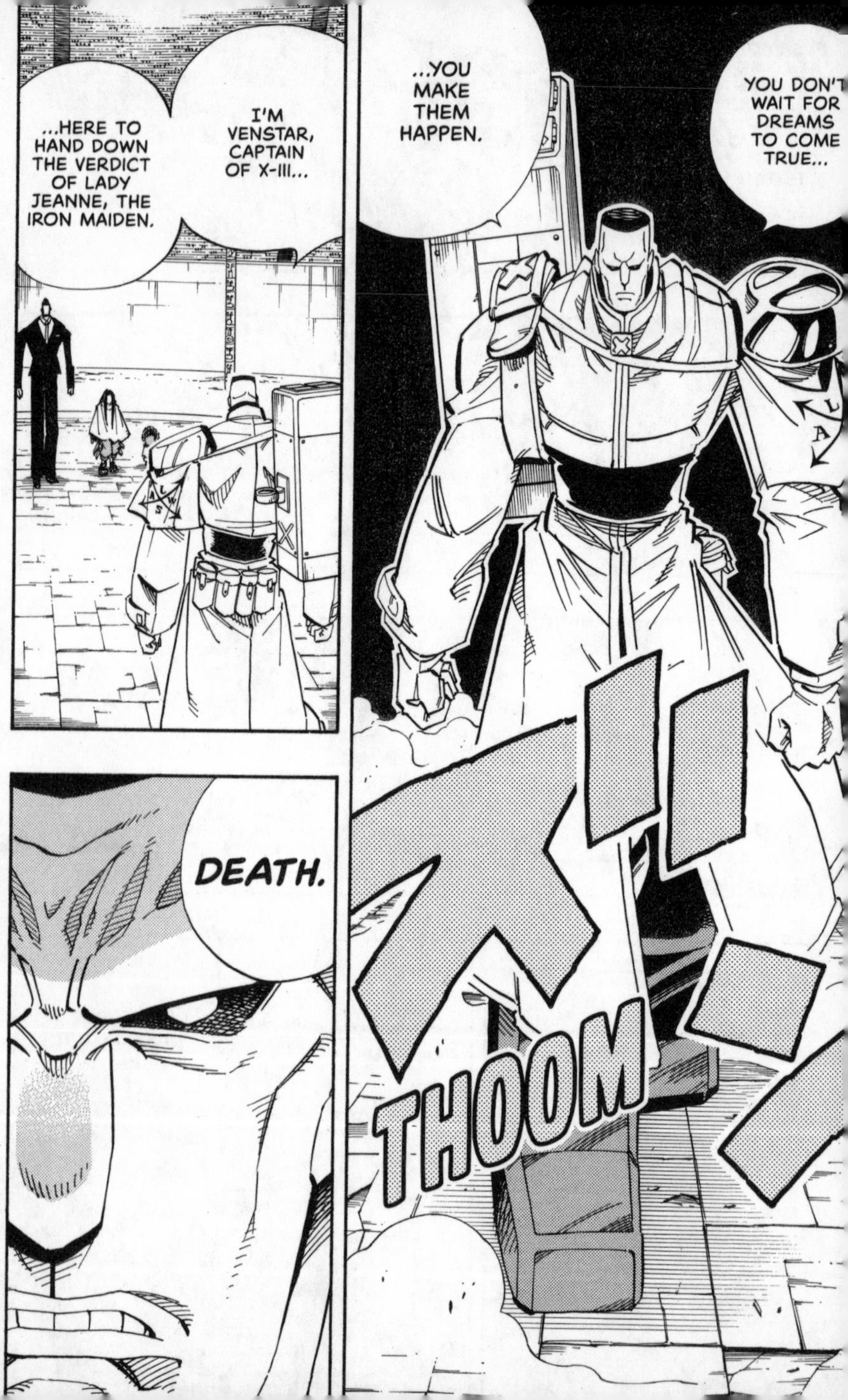
YOU DON'T WAIT FOR DREAMS TO COME TRUE...
...YOU MAKE THEM HAPPEN.
THOOM
I'M VENSTAR, CAPTAIN OF X-III...
...HERE TO HAND DOWN THE VERDICT OF LADY JEANNE, THE IRON MAIDEN.
DEATH.

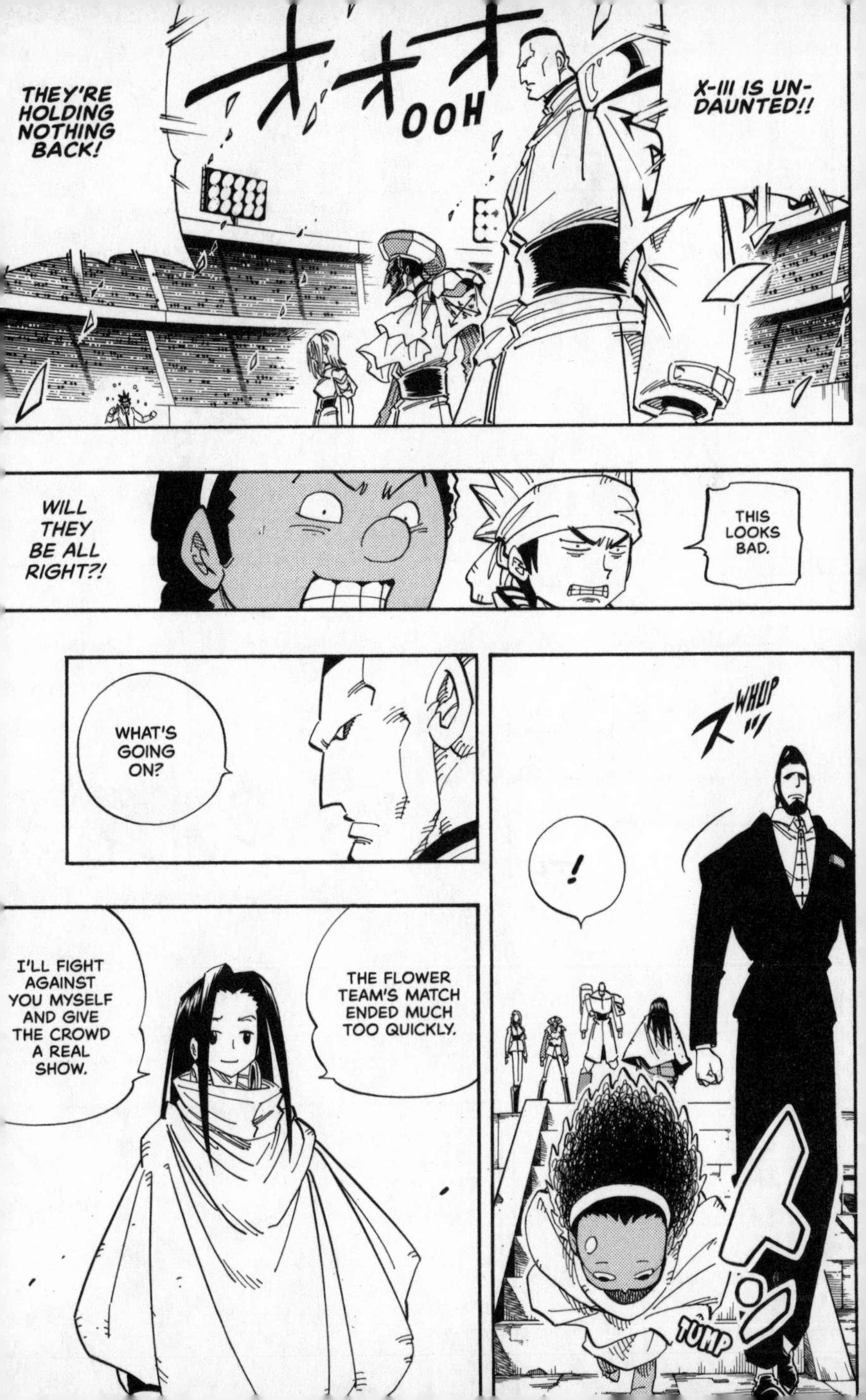
X-III IS UN-DAUNTED!!
オオオ
OOH
THEY'RE HOLDING NOTHING BACK!
THIS LOOKS BAD.
WILL THEY BE ALL RIGHT?!
スッ
WHUP
!
TUMP
WHAT'S GOING ON?
THE FLOWER TEAM'S MATCH ENDED MUCH TOO QUICKLY.
I'LL FIGHT AGAINST YOU MYSELF AND GIVE THE CROWD A REAL SHOW.

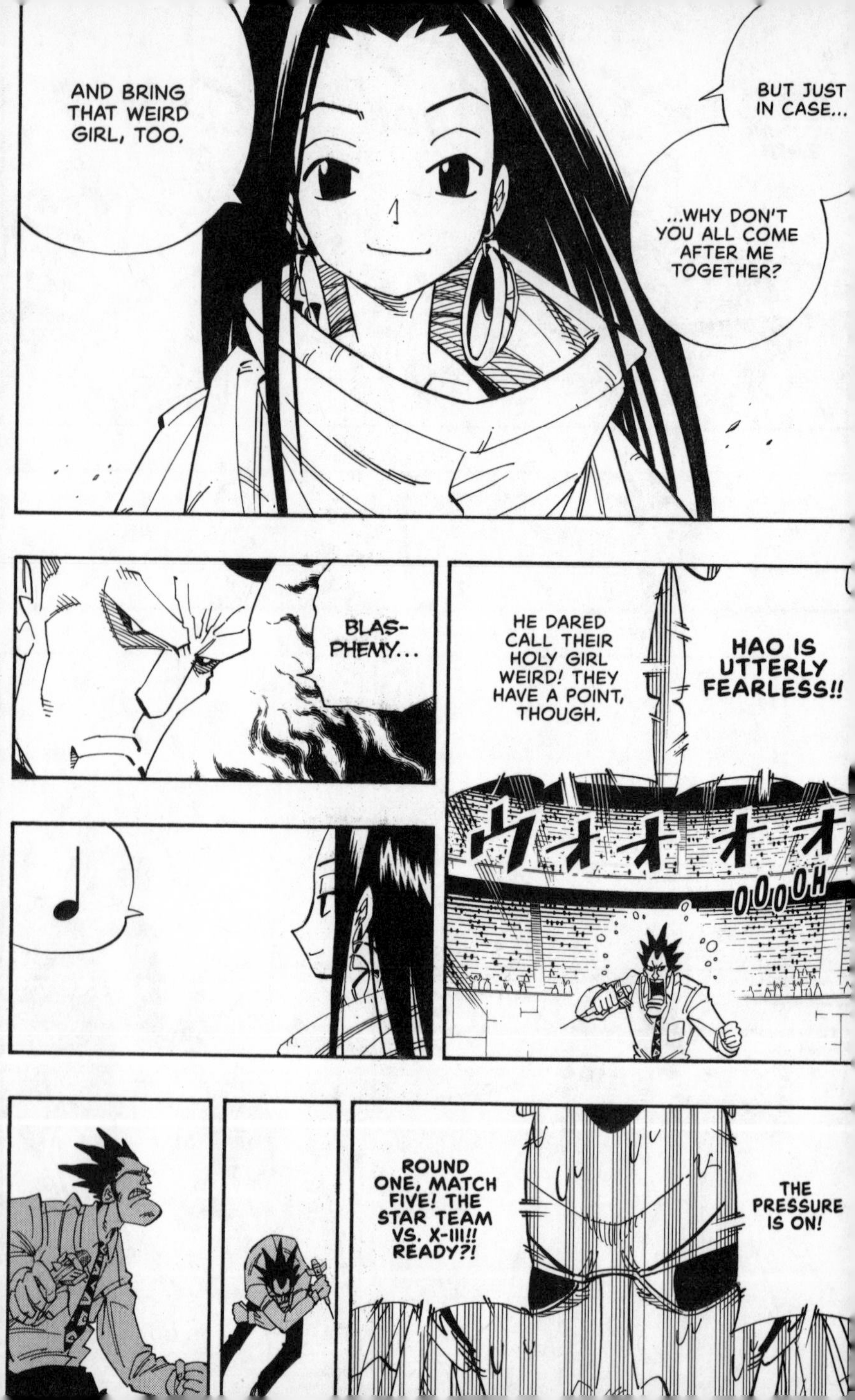
BUT JUST IN CASE...
...WHY DON'T YOU ALL COME AFTER ME TOGETHER?
AND BRING THAT WEIRD GIRL, TOO.
HAO IS UTTERLY FEARLESS!!
HE DARED CALL THEIR HOLY GIRL WEIRD! THEY HAVE A POINT, THOUGH.
ウォオオオ
OOOOH
BLAS-PHEMY...
♪
THE PRESSURE IS ON!
ROUND ONE, MATCH FIVE! THE STAR TEAM VS. X-III!! READY?!

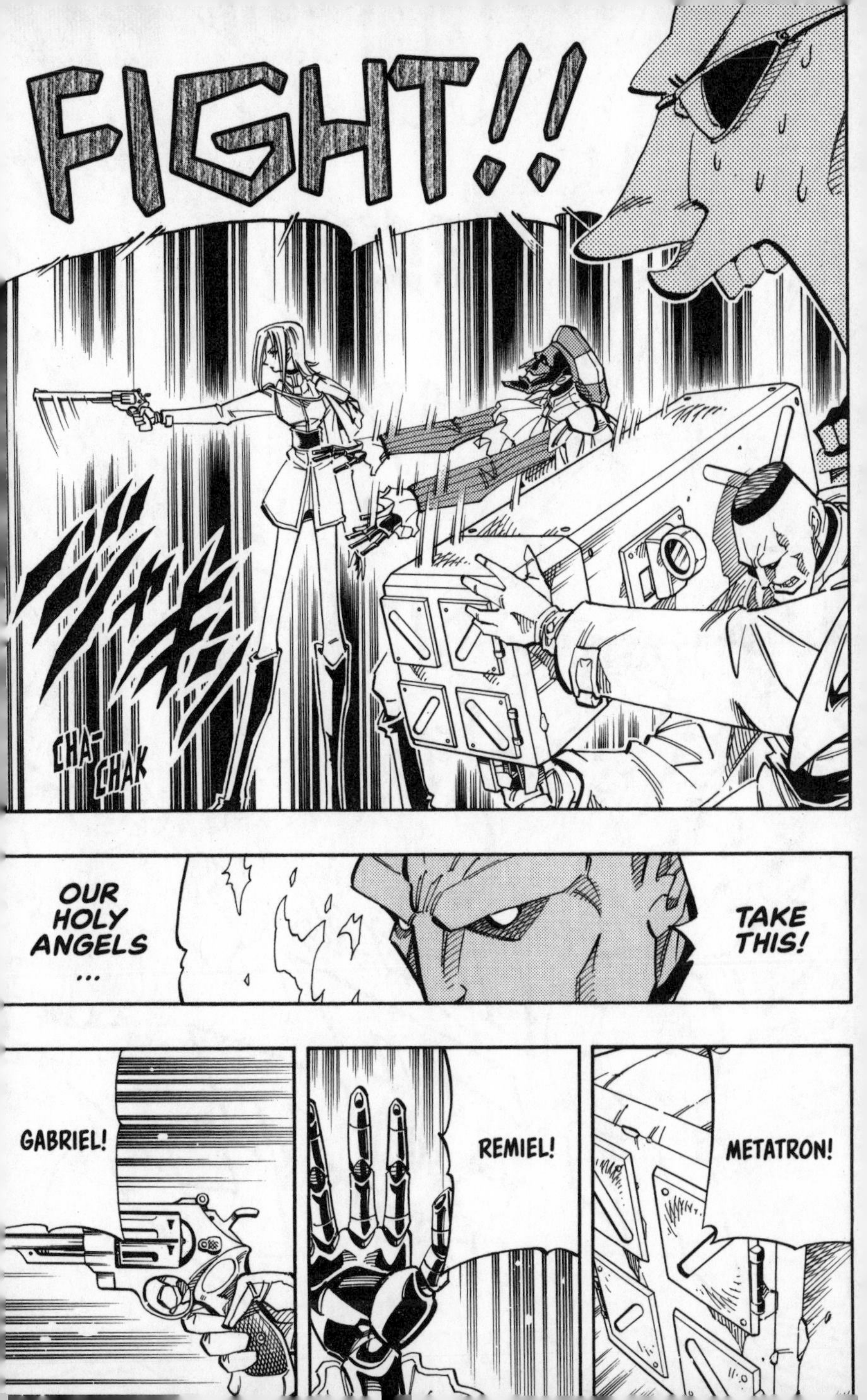
FIGHT!!
CHA-CHAK
TAKE THIS!
OUR HOLY ANGELS ...
METATRON!
REMIEL!
GABRIEL!

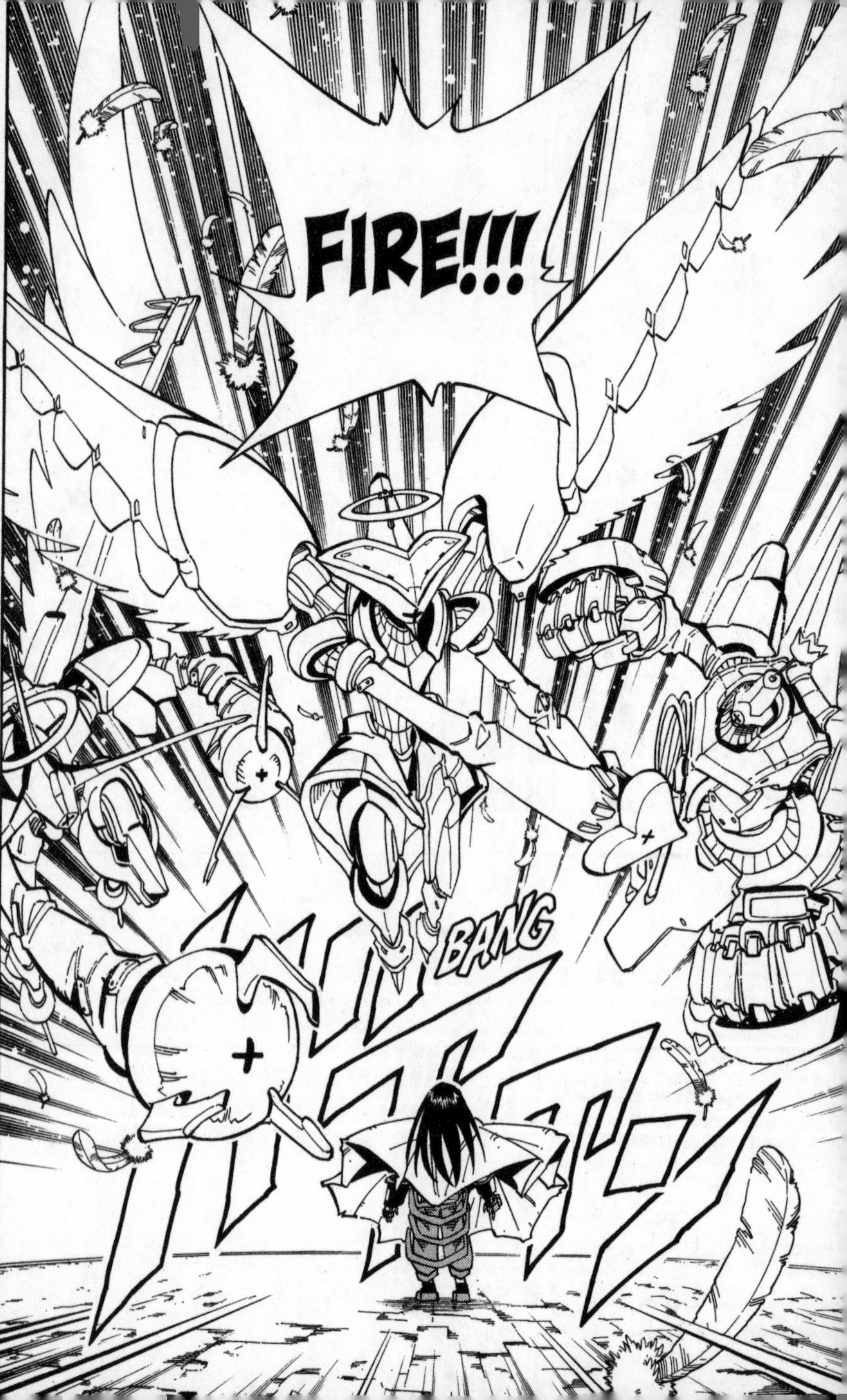
FIRE!!!
BANG

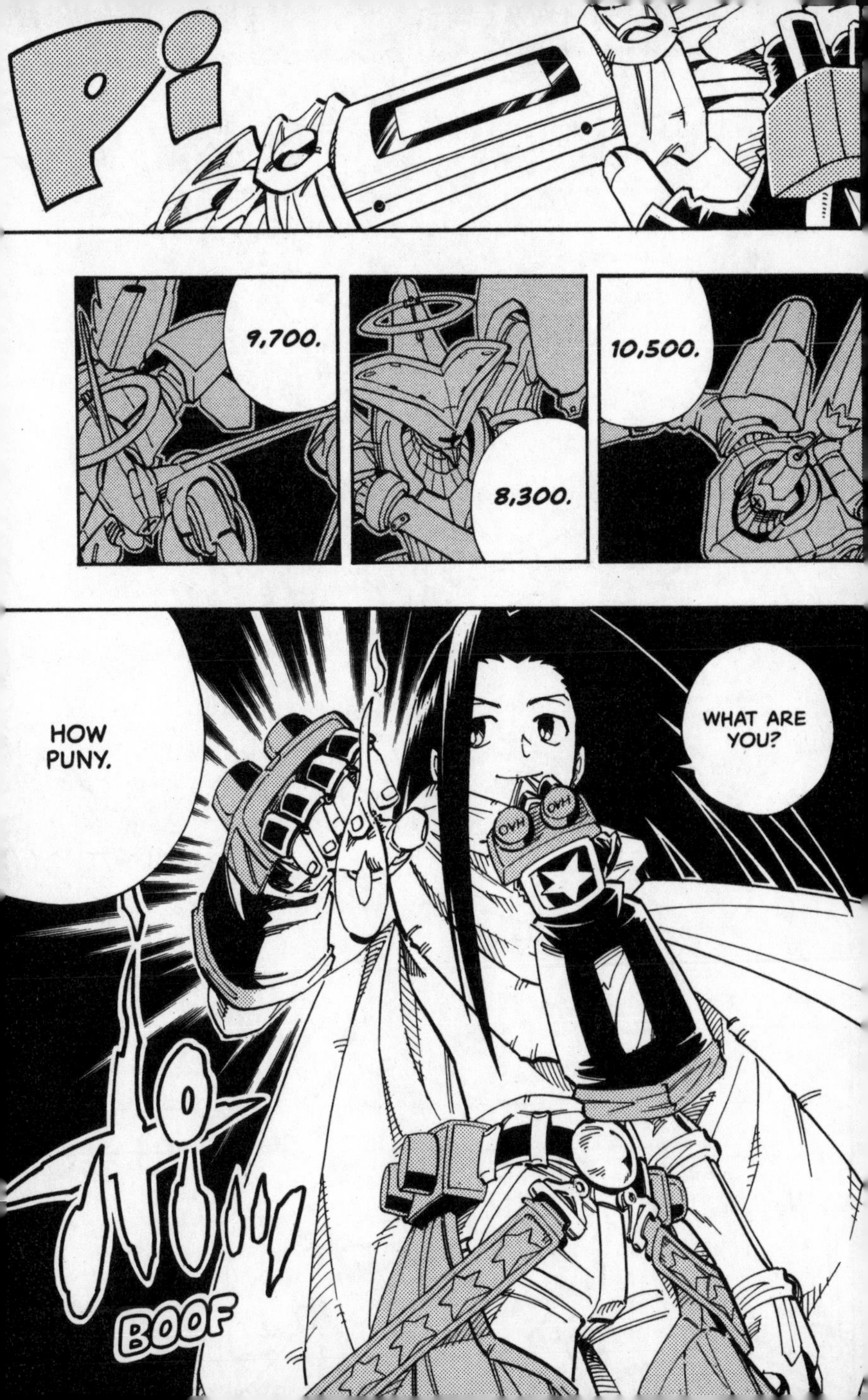
Pi
10,500.
8,300.
9,700.
WHAT ARE YOU?
HOW PUNY.
BOOF

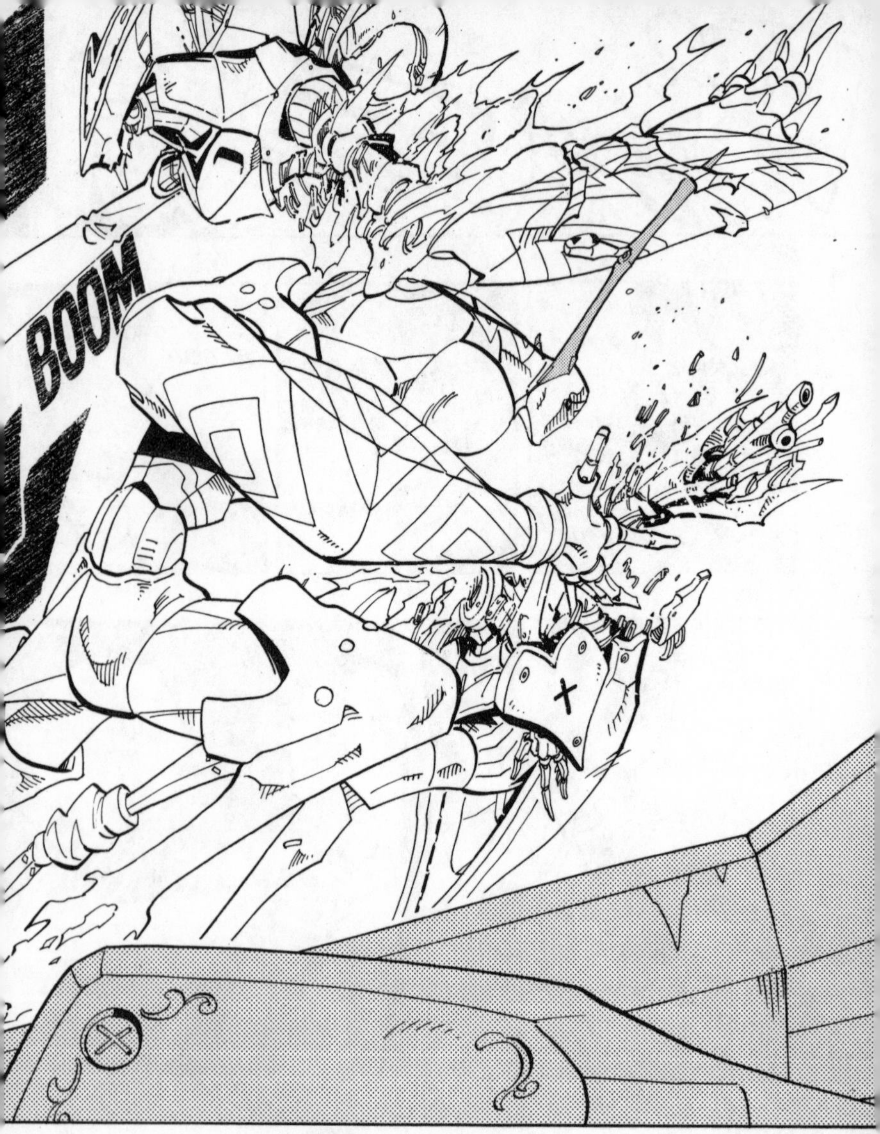
BOOM
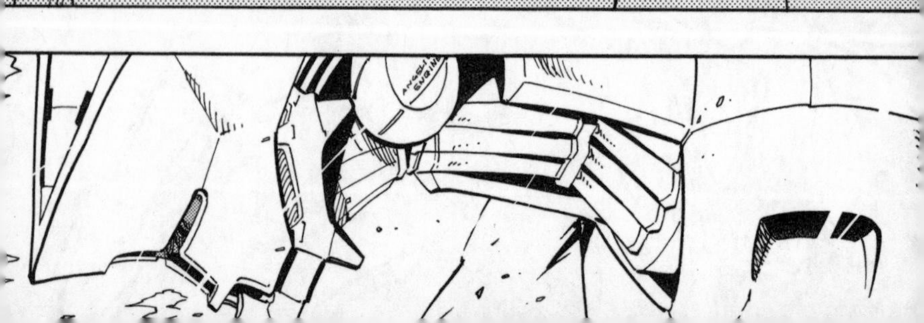
ANGELI ENGINE

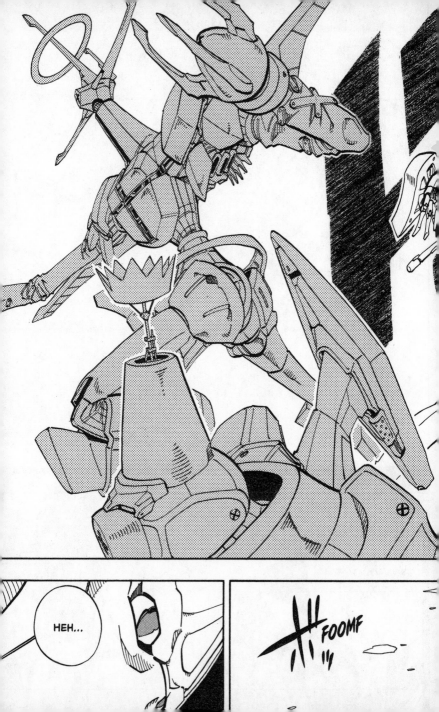

HEH...

FOOMF

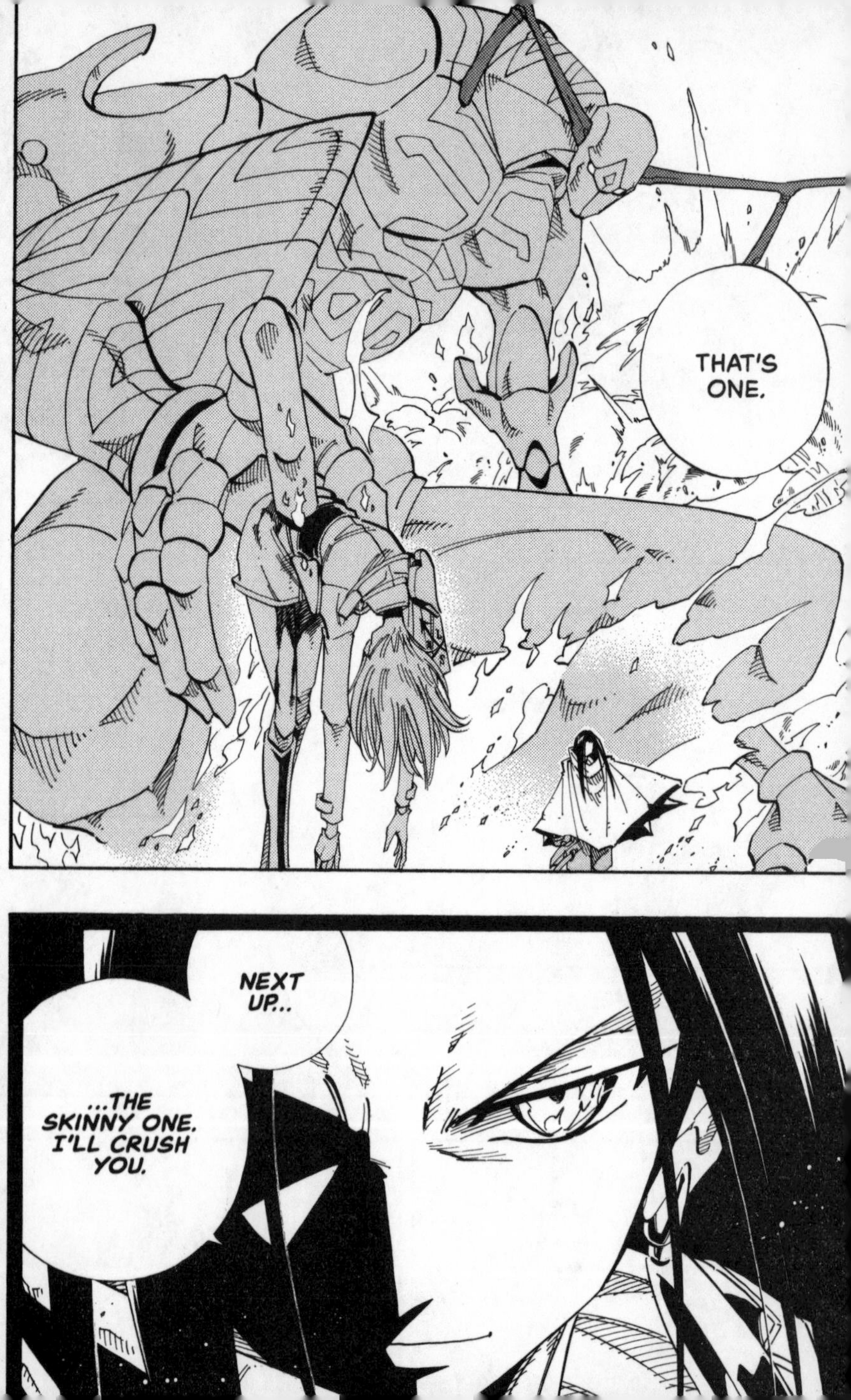
THAT'S ONE.
NEXT UP...
...THE SKINNY ONE. I'LL CRUSH YOU.

Meene

January 2001

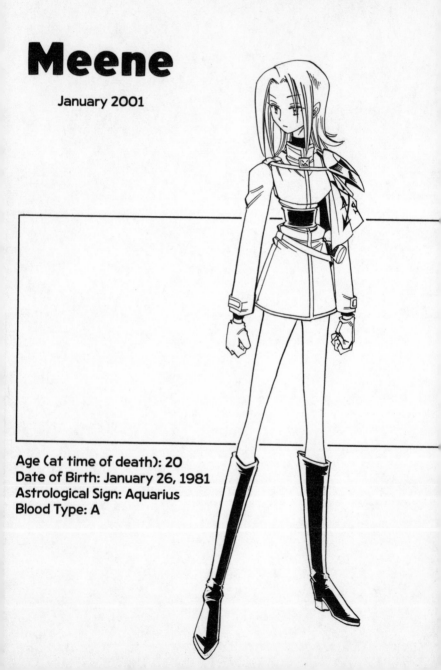

Age (at time of death): 20
Date of Birth: January 26, 1981
Astrological Sign: Aquarius
Blood Type: A

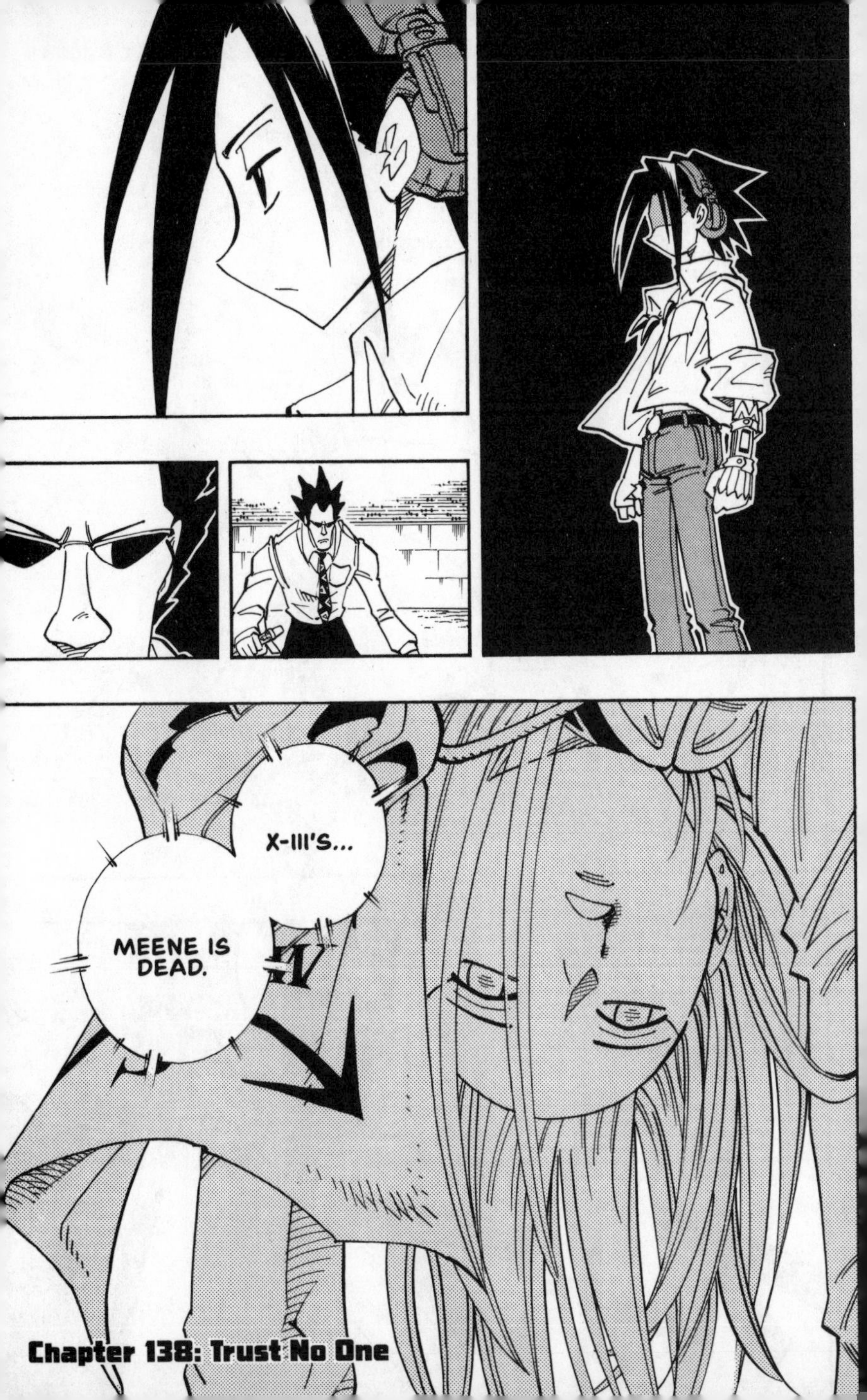
X-III'S...
MEENE IS DEAD.

Chapter 138: Trust No One

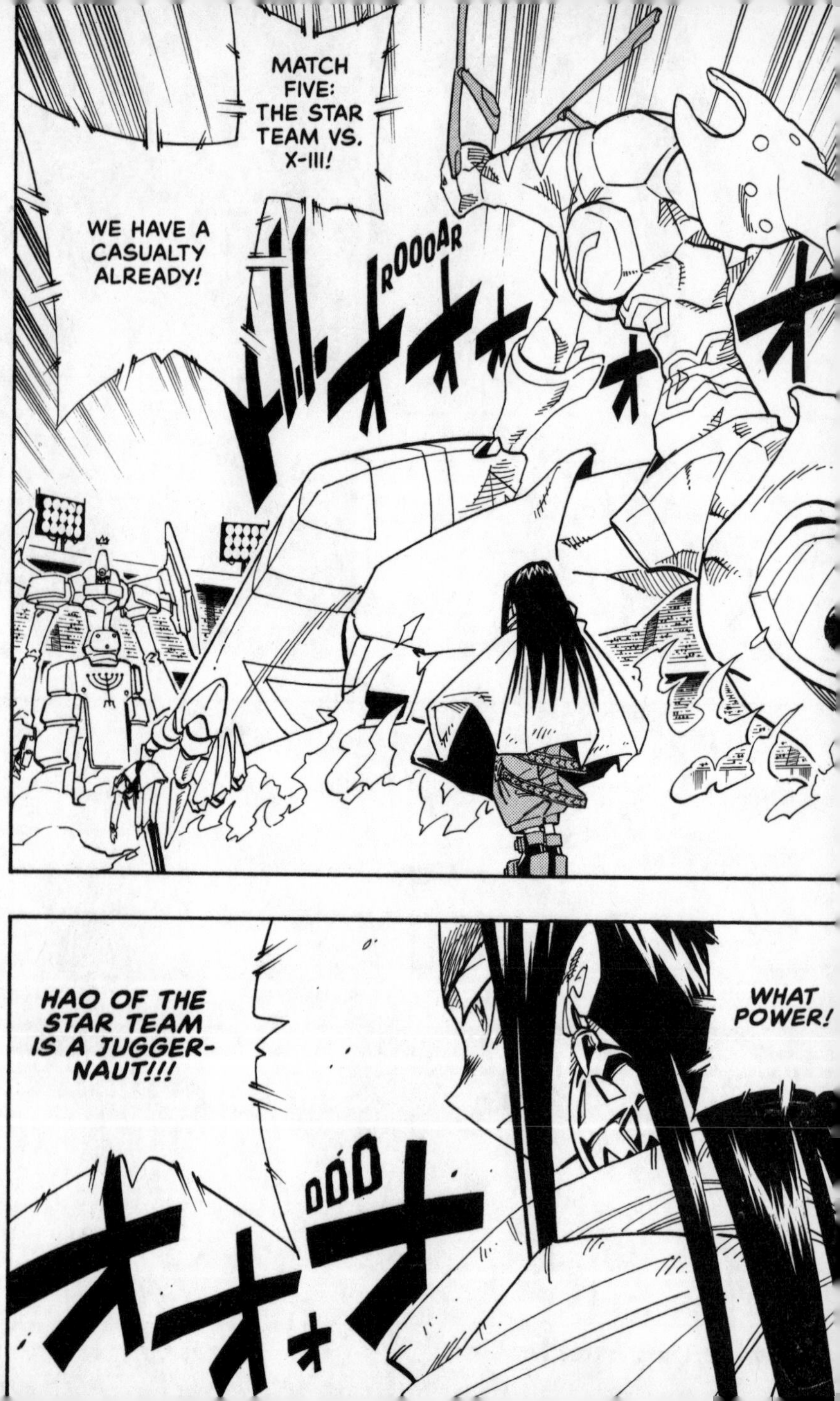
MATCH FIVE: THE STAR TEAM VS. X-III!
WE HAVE A CASUALTY ALREADY!
ROOOAR
WHAT POWER!
HAO OF THE STAR TEAM IS A JUGGER-NAUT!!!
OOO

Chapter 138:

Trust No One

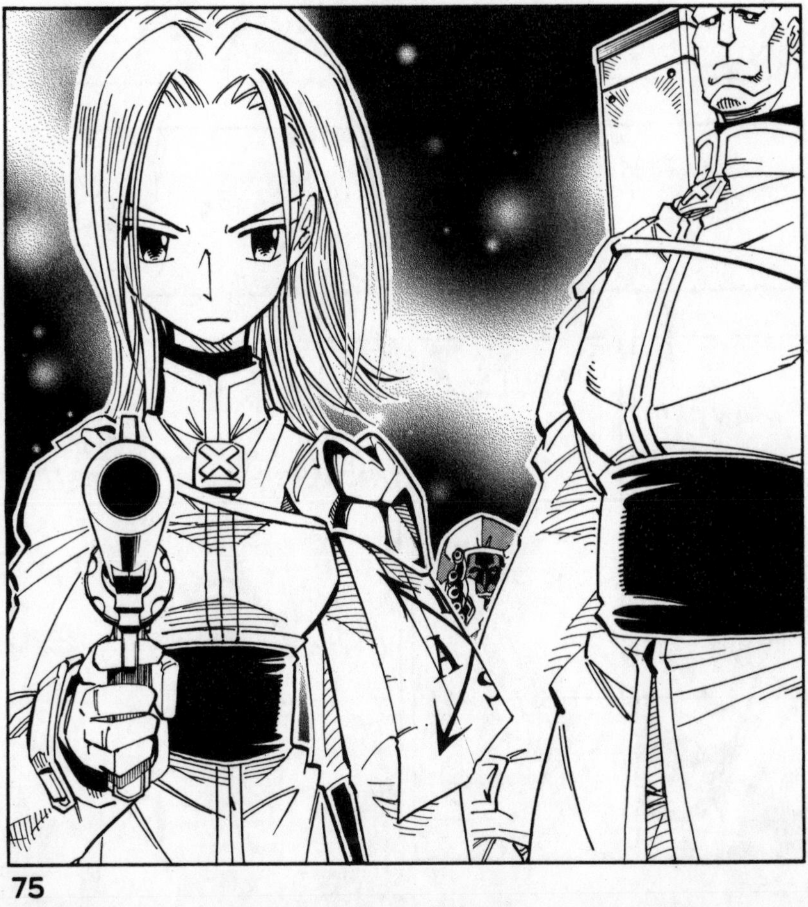

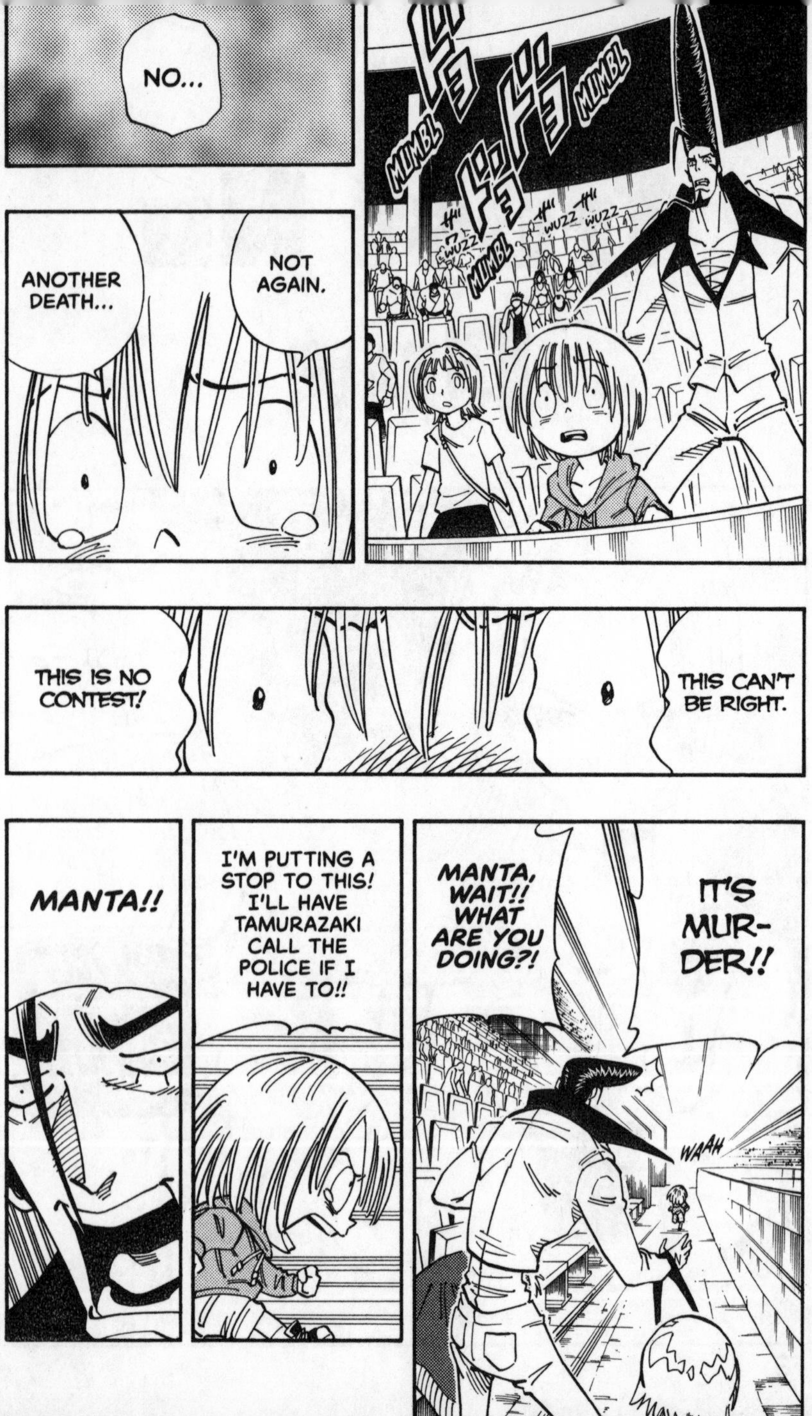
MUMBL
MUMBL
WUZZ
WUZZ
MUMBL
NO...
NOT AGAIN.
ANOTHER DEATH...
THIS CAN'T BE RIGHT.
THIS IS NO CONTEST!
IT'S MUR-DER!!
MANTA, WAIT!! WHAT ARE YOU DOING?!
WAAH
I'M PUTTING A STOP TO THIS! I'LL HAVE TAMURAZAKI CALL THE POLICE IF I HAVE TO!!
MANTA!!

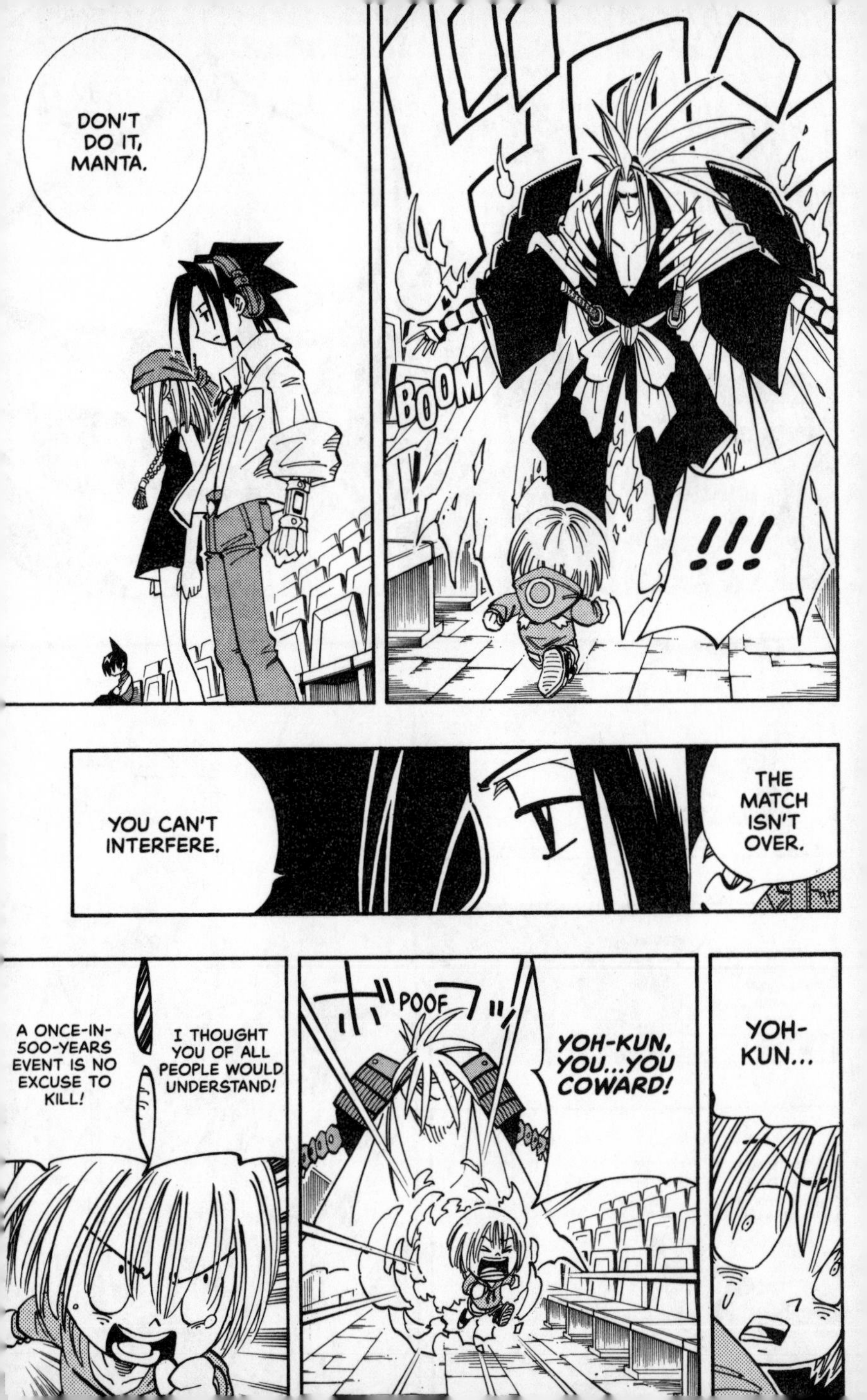
BOOM
!!!
DON'T DO IT, MANTA.
THE MATCH ISN'T OVER.
YOU CAN'T INTERFERE.
YOH-KUN...
POOF
YOH-KUN, YOU...YOU COWARD!
I THOUGHT YOU OF ALL PEOPLE WOULD UNDERSTAND!
A ONCE-IN-500-YEARS EVENT IS NO EXCUSE TO KILL!

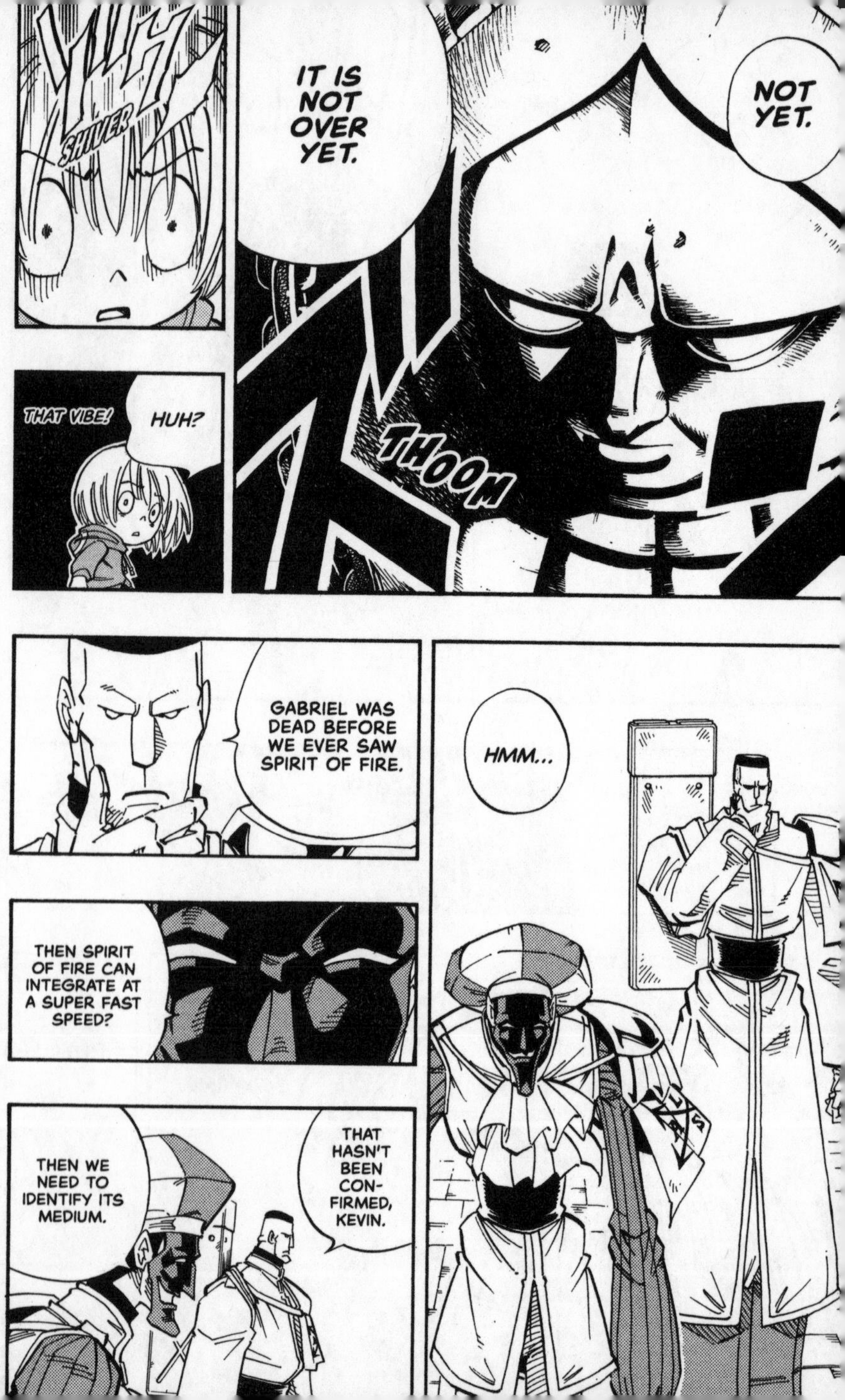
NOT YET.
IT IS NOT OVER YET.
THOOM
SHIVER
HUH?
THAT VIBE!
HMM...
GABRIEL WAS DEAD BEFORE WE EVER SAW SPIRIT OF FIRE.
THEN SPIRIT OF FIRE CAN INTEGRATE AT A SUPER FAST SPEED?
THAT HASN'T BEEN CON-FIRMED, KEVIN.
THEN WE NEED TO IDENTIFY ITS MEDIUM.

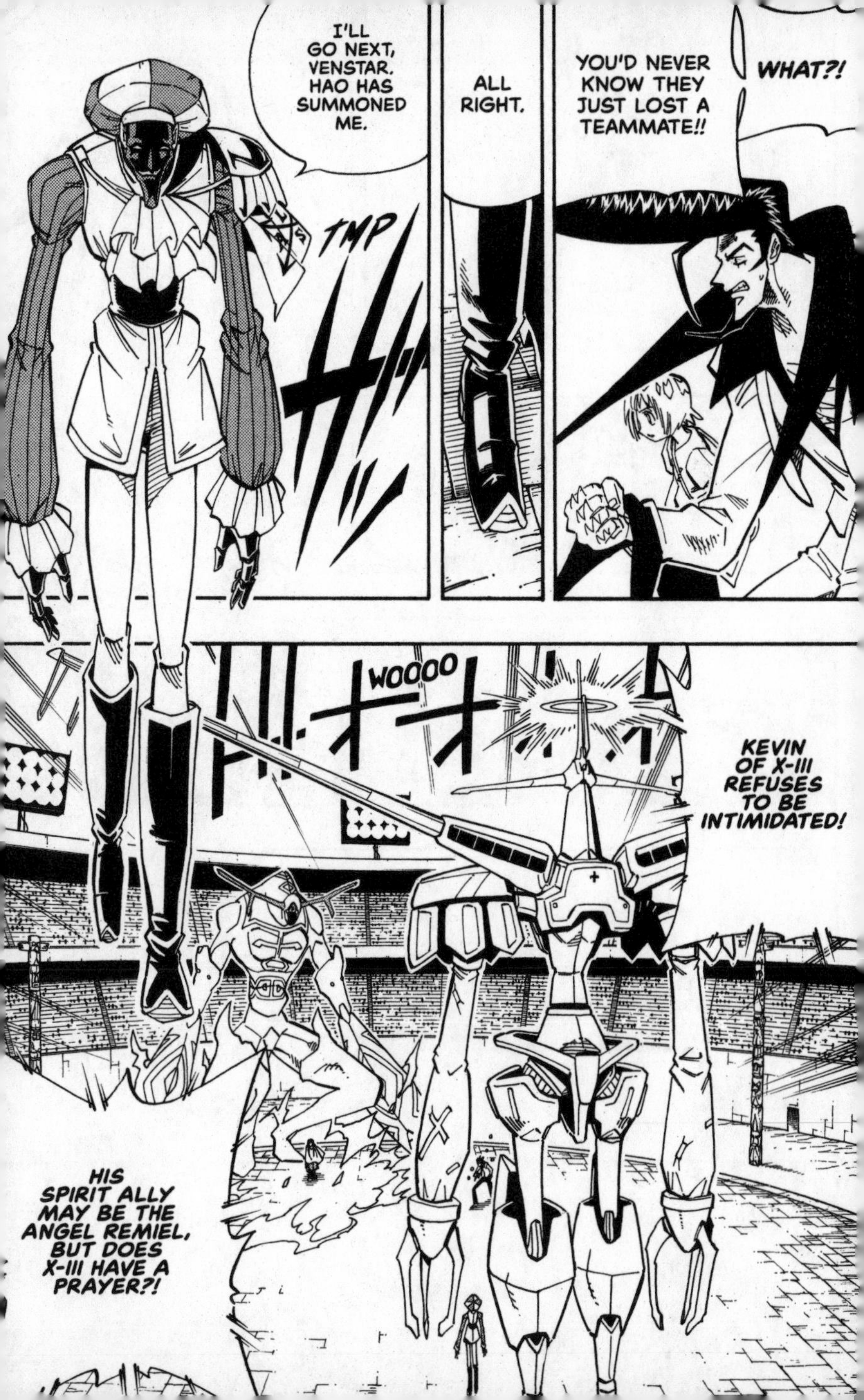
I'LL GO NEXT, VENSTAR. HAO HAS SUMMONED ME.
TMP
ALL RIGHT.
YOU'D NEVER KNOW THEY JUST LOST A TEAMMATE!!
WHAT?!
WOOOO
KEVIN OF X-III REFUSES TO BE INTIMIDATED!
HIS SPIRIT ALLY MAY BE THE ANGEL REMIEL, BUT DOES X-III HAVE A PRAYER?!

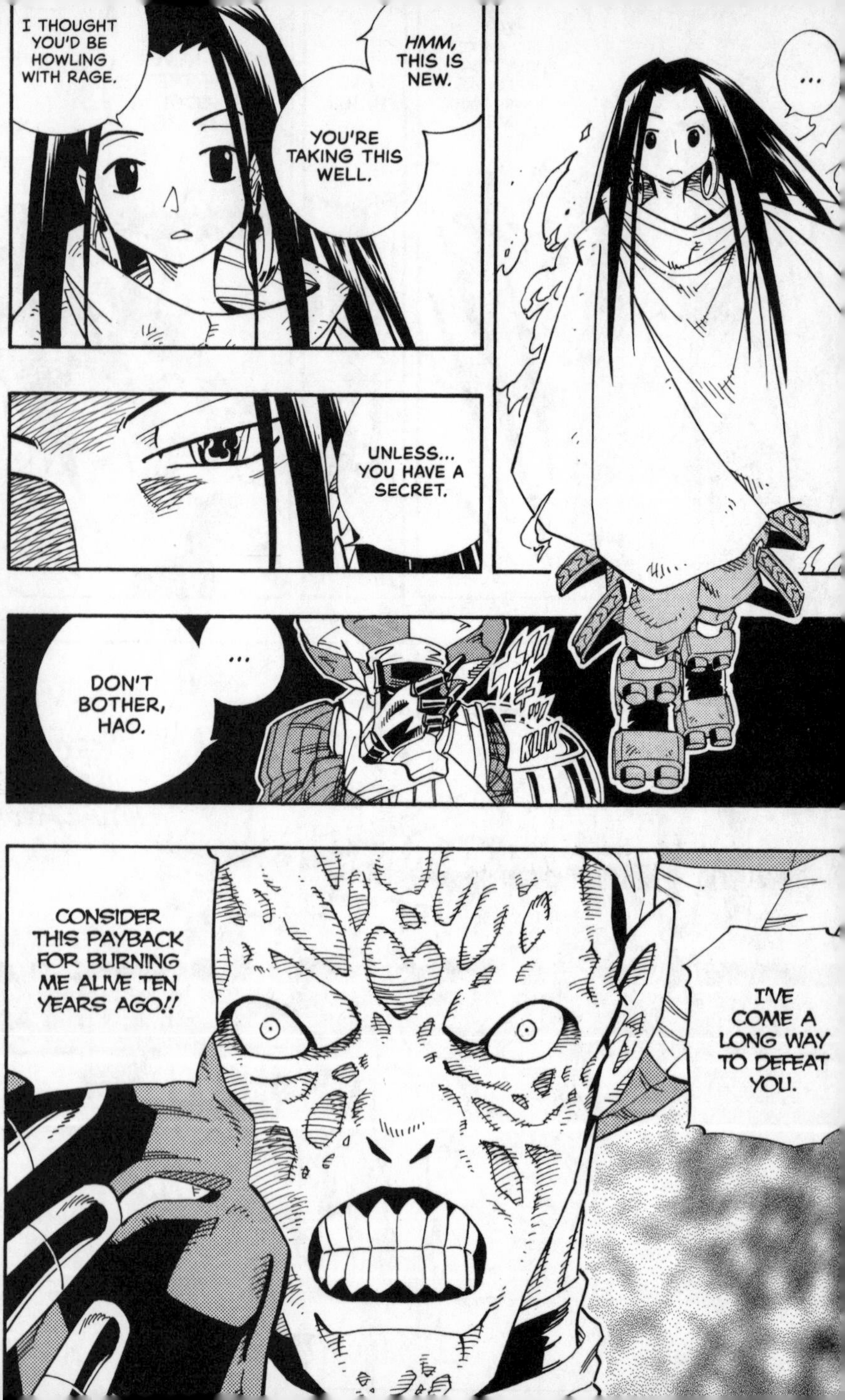
...
HMM, THIS IS NEW.
YOU'RE TAKING THIS WELL.
I THOUGHT YOU'D BE HOWLING WITH RAGE.
UNLESS... YOU HAVE A SECRET.
KLIK
...
DON'T BOTHER, HAO.
I'VE COME A LONG WAY TO DEFEAT YOU.
CONSIDER THIS PAYBACK FOR BURNING ME ALIVE TEN YEARS AGO!!

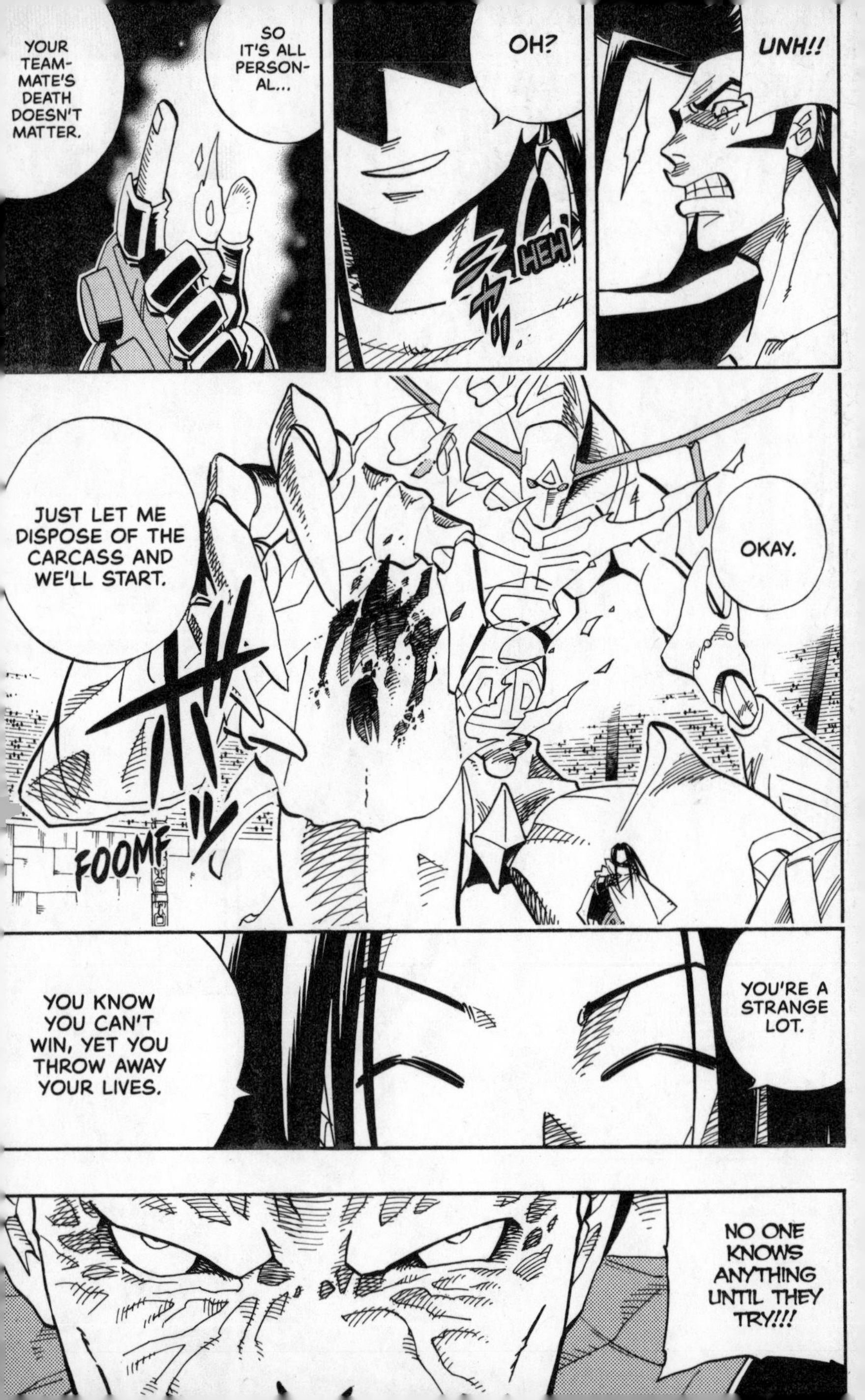
UNH!!
OH?
HEH
SO IT'S ALL PERSON-AL...
YOUR TEAM-MATE'S DEATH DOESN'T MATTER.
JUST LET ME DISPOSE OF THE CARCASS AND WE'LL START.
OKAY.
FOOMF
YOU'RE A STRANGE LOT.
YOU KNOW YOU CAN'T WIN, YET YOU THROW AWAY YOUR LIVES.
NO ONE KNOWS ANYTHING UNTIL THEY TRY!!!

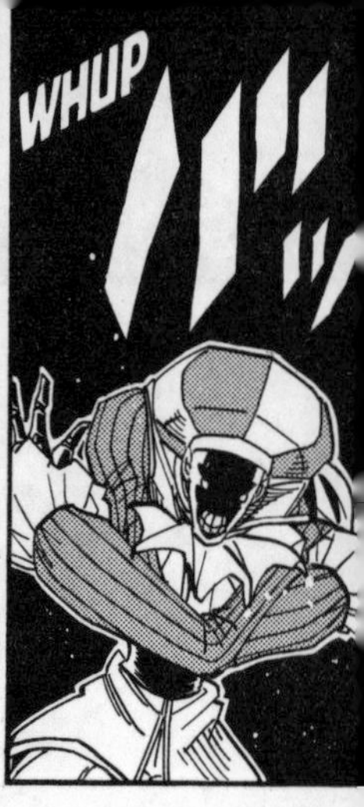
WHUP
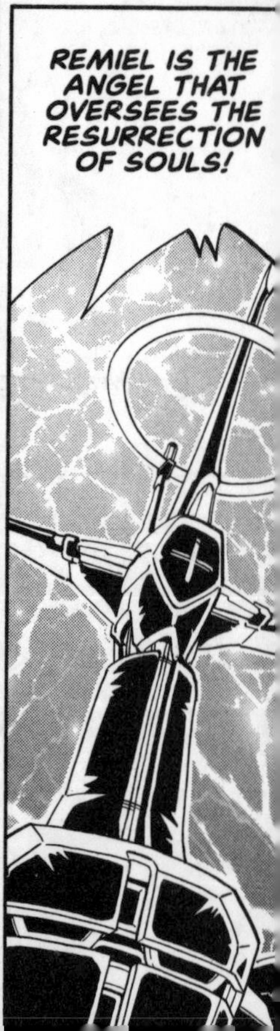
REMIEL IS THE ANGEL THAT OVERSEES THE RESURRECTION OF SOULS!
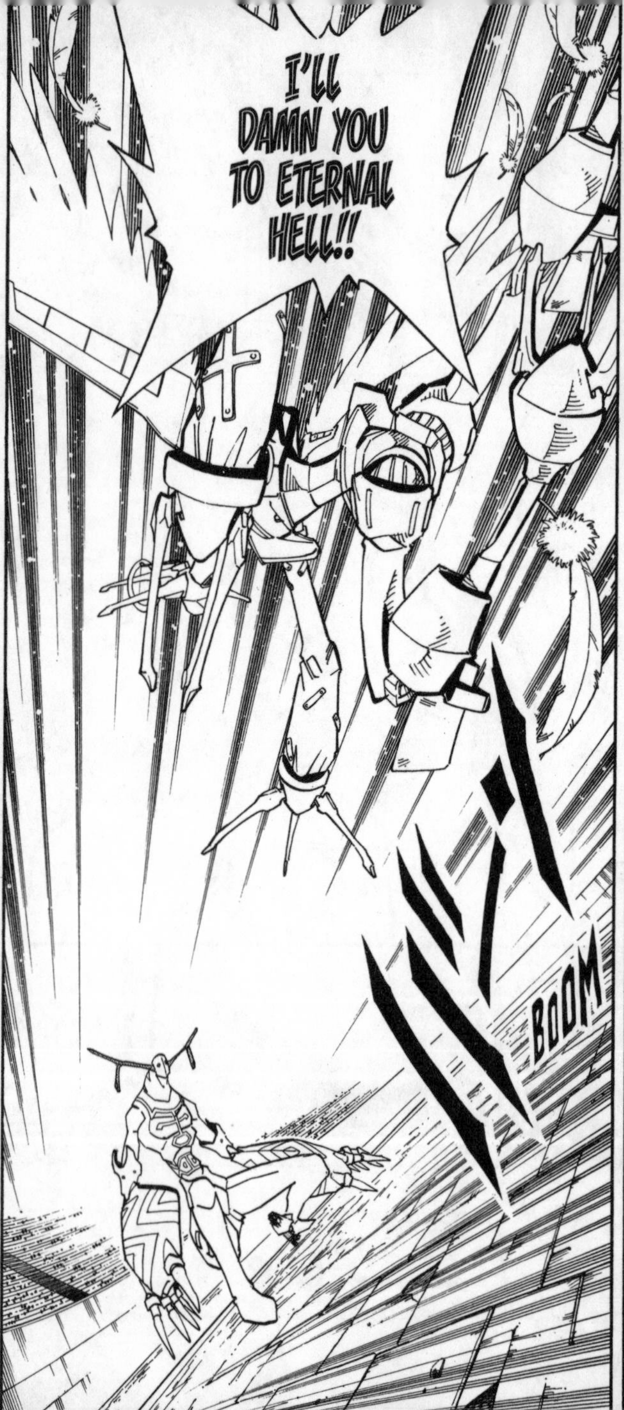
I'LL DAMN YOU TO ETERNAL HELL!!
BOOM

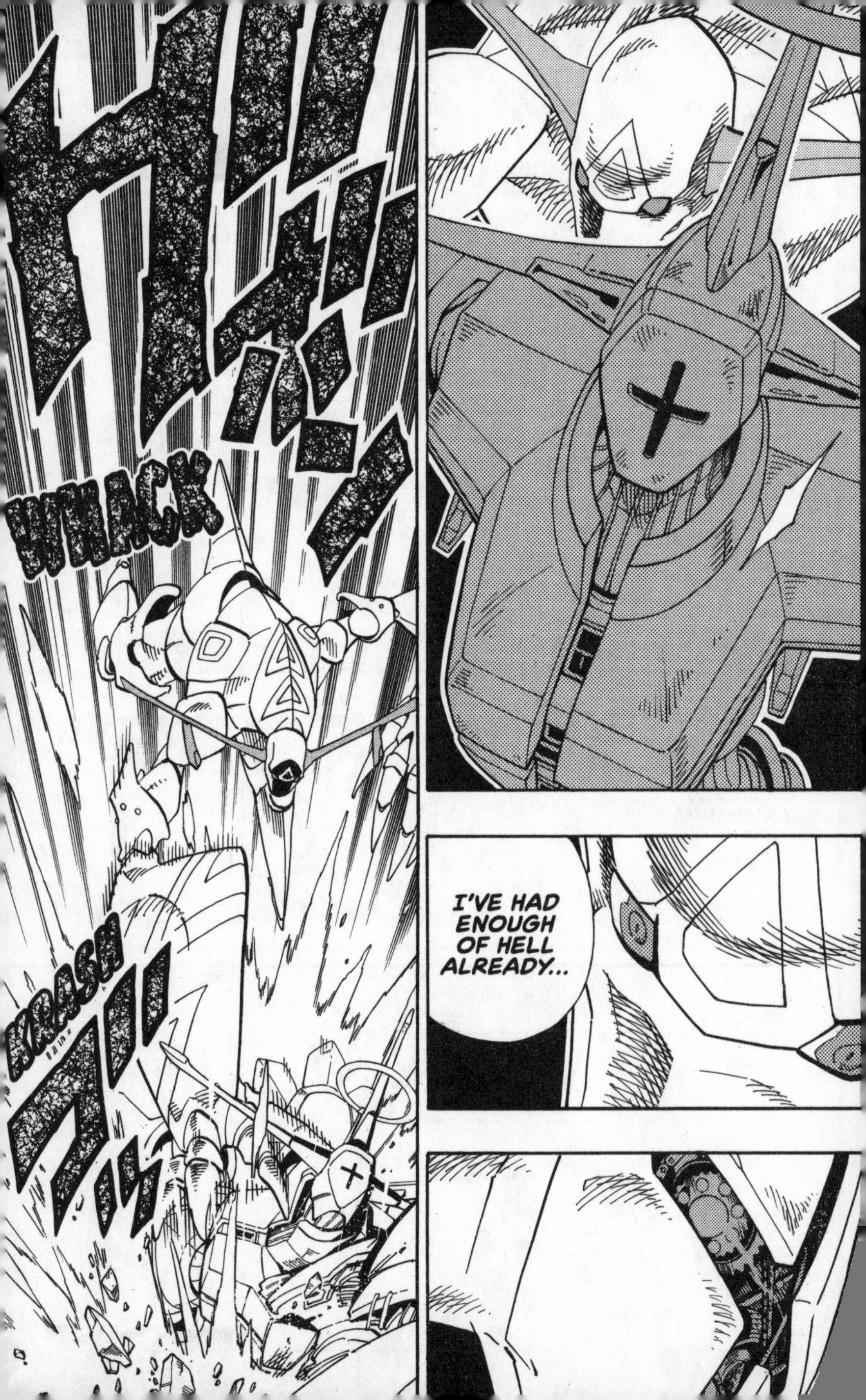
I'VE HAD ENOUGH OF HELL ALREADY...
WHACK
KRASH

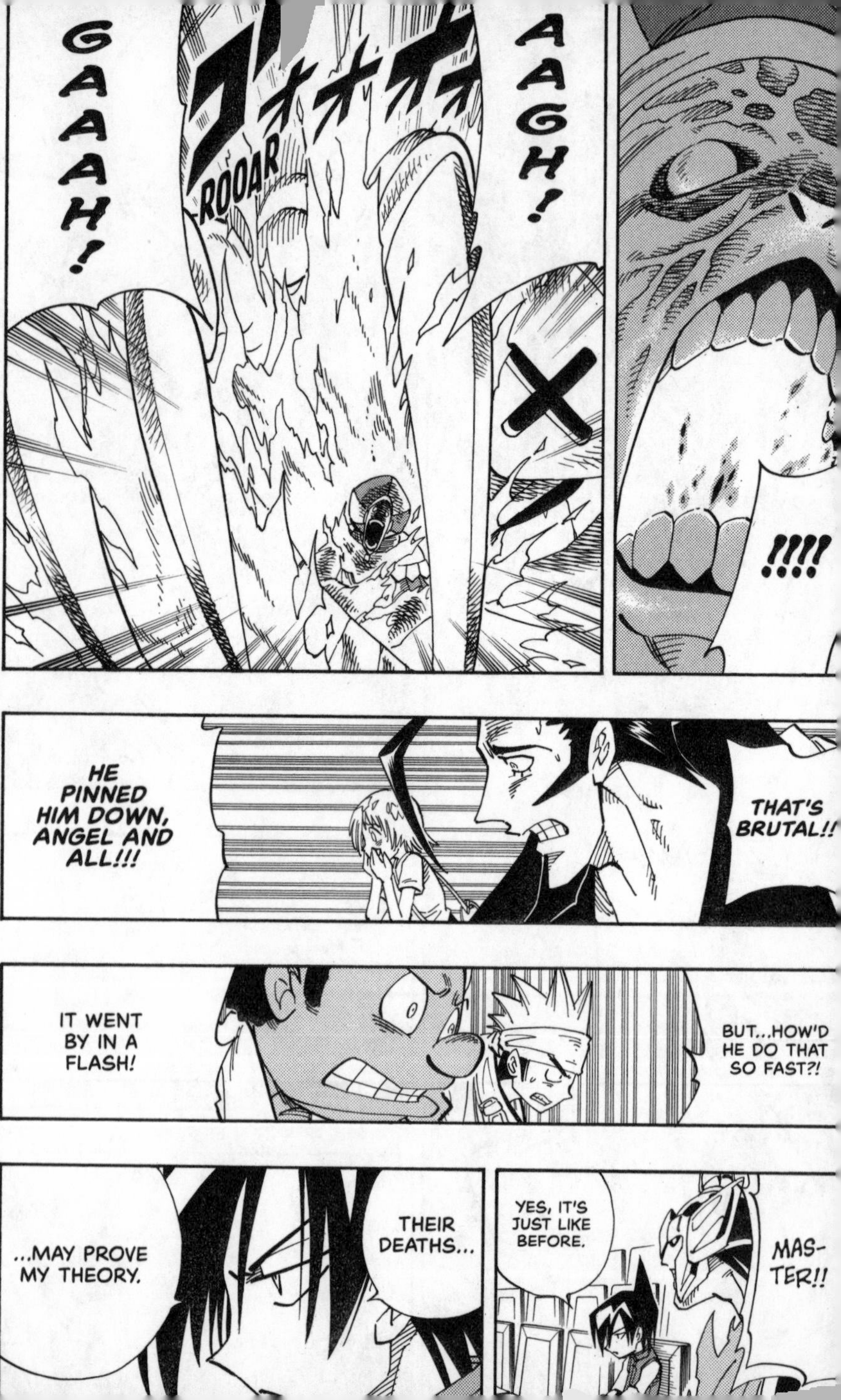
!!!!
AAGH!
グオオオォ
ROOAR
GAAAAH!
THAT'S BRUTAL!!
HE PINNED HIM DOWN, ANGEL AND ALL!!!
BUT...HOW'D HE DO THAT SO FAST?!
IT WENT BY IN A FLASH!
MASTER!!
YES, IT'S JUST LIKE BEFORE.
THEIR DEATHS...
...MAY PROVE MY THEORY.

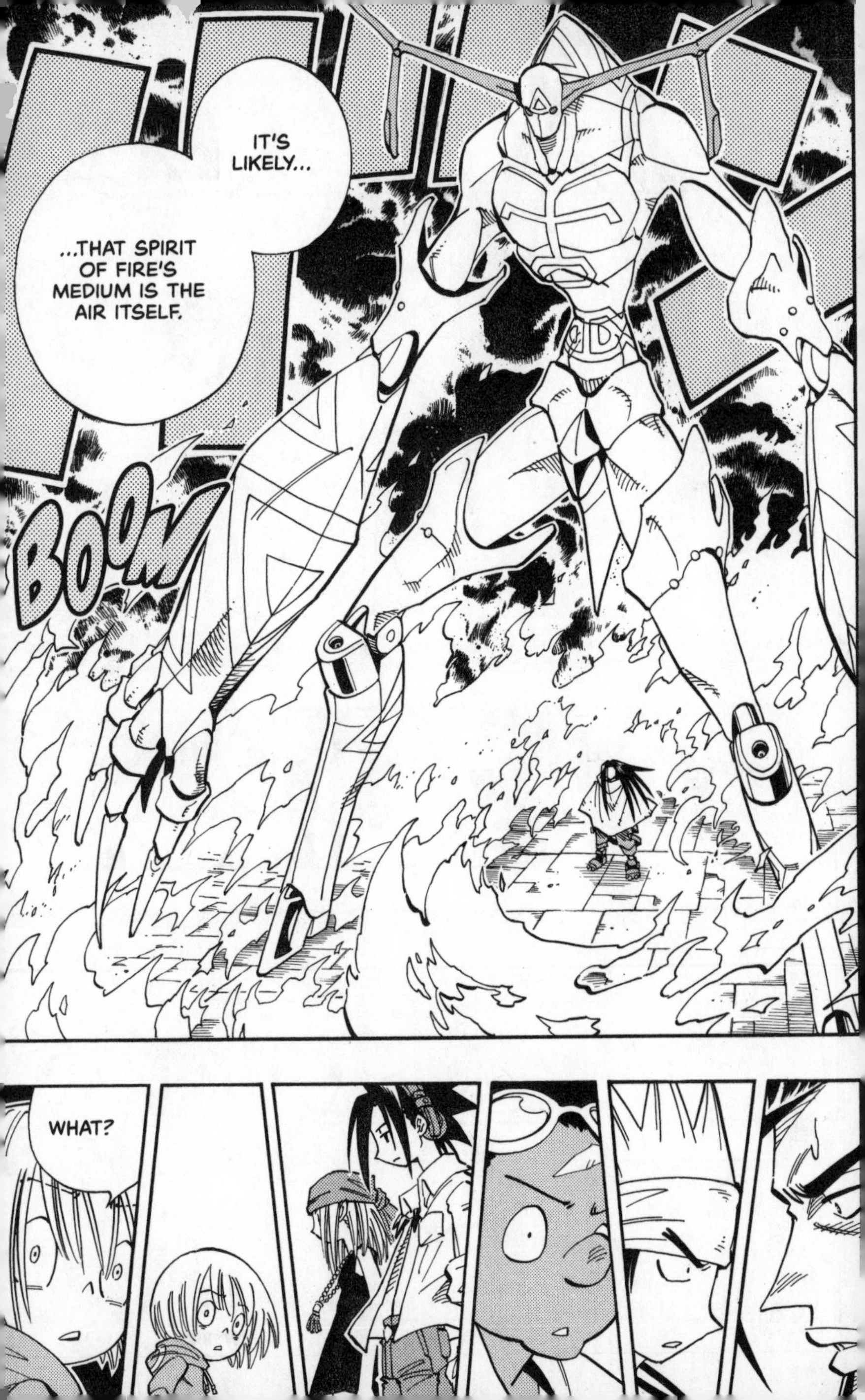
IT'S LIKELY...
...THAT SPIRIT OF FIRE'S MEDIUM IS THE AIR ITSELF.
BOOM
WHAT?

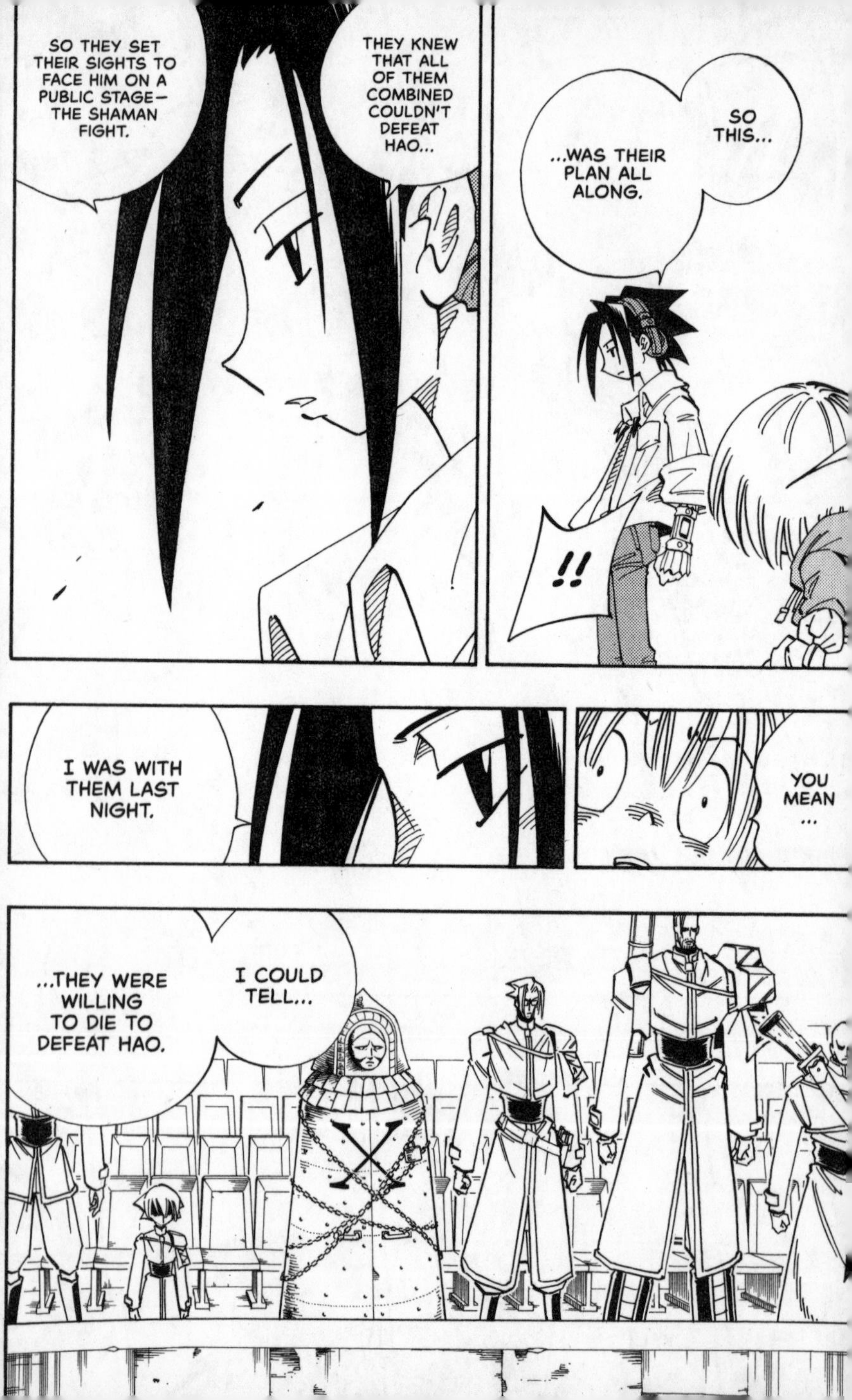
SO THIS...
...WAS THEIR PLAN ALL ALONG.
!!
THEY KNEW THAT ALL OF THEM COMBINED COULDN'T DEFEAT HAO...
SO THEY SET THEIR SIGHTS TO FACE HIM ON A PUBLIC STAGE—THE SHAMAN FIGHT.
YOU MEAN ...
I WAS WITH THEM LAST NIGHT.
I COULD TELL...
...THEY WERE WILLING TO DIE TO DEFEAT HAO.

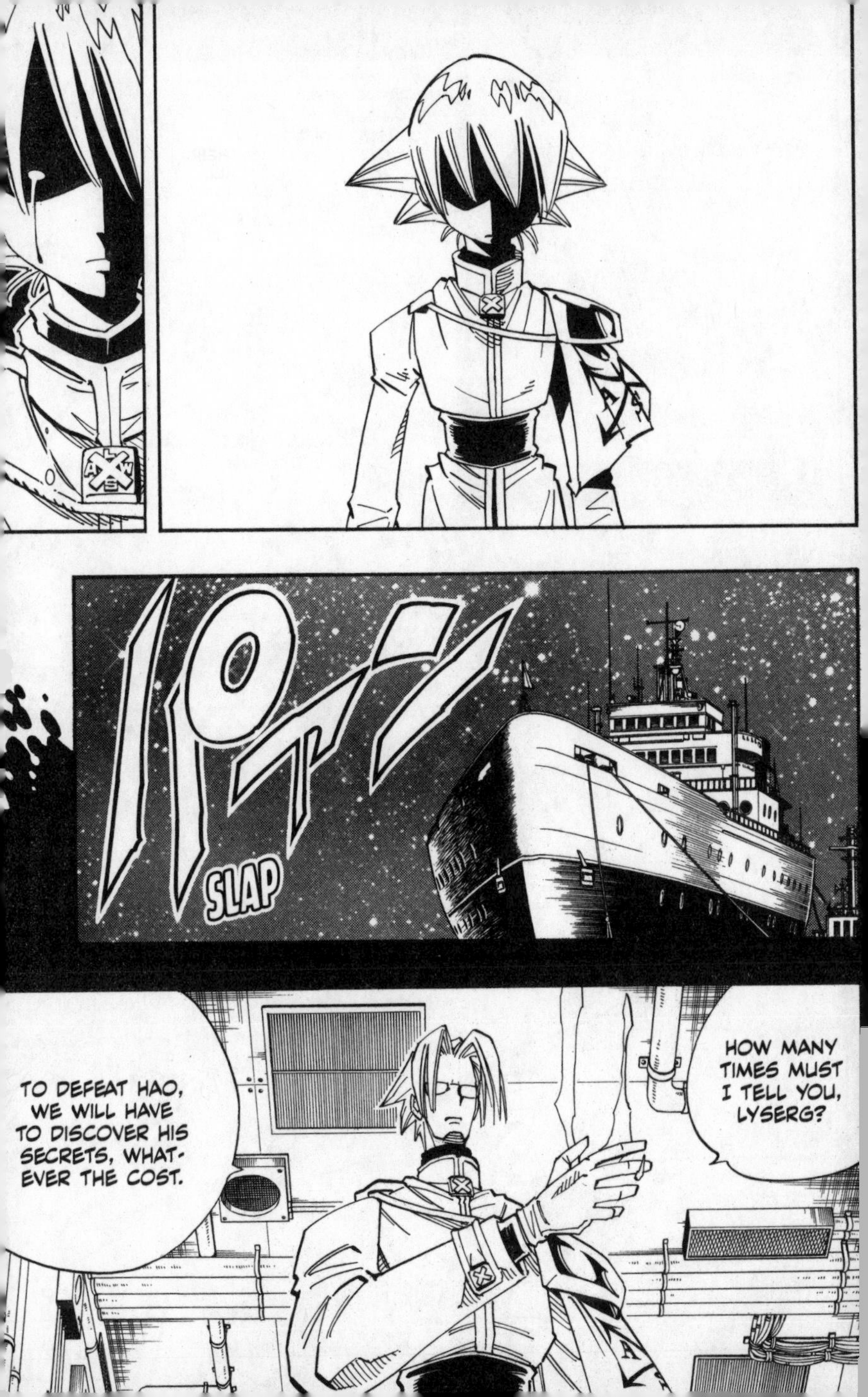
SLAP
HOW MANY TIMES MUST I TELL YOU, LYSERG?
TO DEFEAT HAO, WE WILL HAVE TO DISCOVER HIS SECRETS, WHATEVER THE COST.

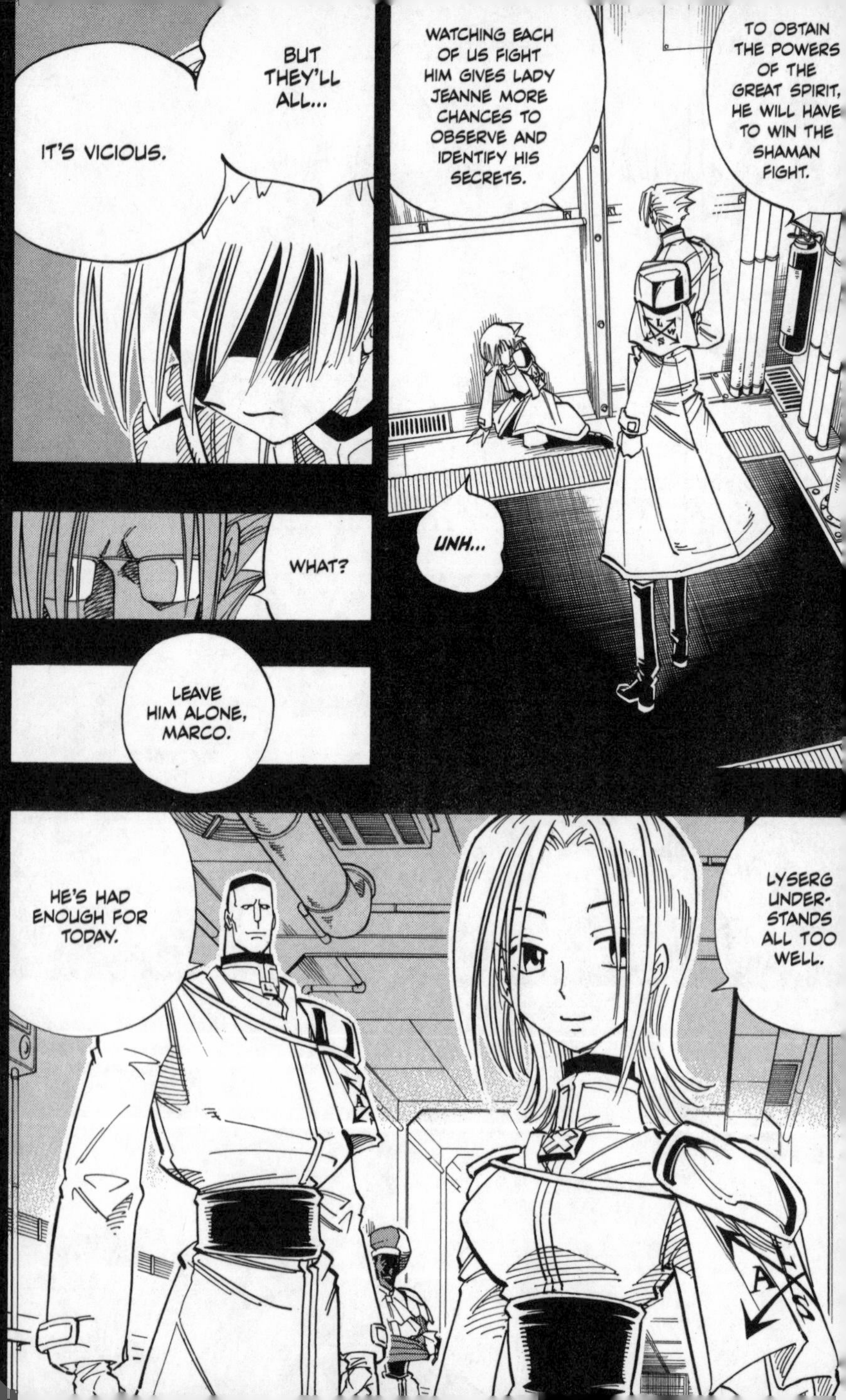
TO OBTAIN THE POWERS OF THE GREAT SPIRIT, HE WILL HAVE TO WIN THE SHAMAN FIGHT.
WATCHING EACH OF US FIGHT HIM GIVES LADY JEANNE MORE CHANCES TO OBSERVE AND IDENTIFY HIS SECRETS.
UNH...
BUT THEY'LL ALL...
IT'S VICIOUS.
WHAT?
LEAVE HIM ALONE, MARCO.
LYSERG UNDERSTANDS ALL TOO WELL.
HE'S HAD ENOUGH FOR TODAY.

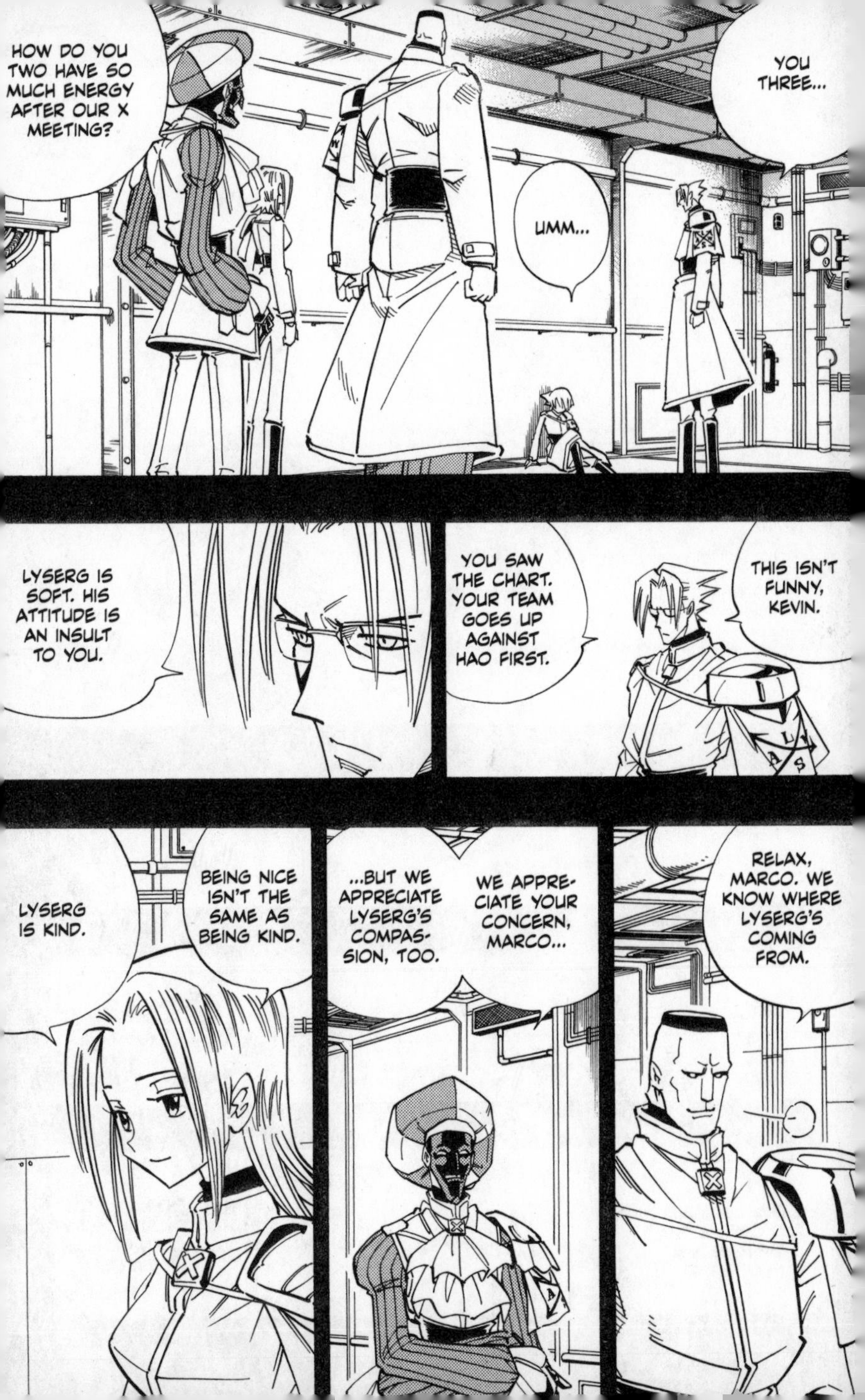
YOU THREE...
UMM...
HOW DO YOU TWO HAVE SO MUCH ENERGY AFTER OUR X MEETING?
THIS ISN'T FUNNY, KEVIN.
YOU SAW THE CHART. YOUR TEAM GOES UP AGAINST HAO FIRST.
LYSERG IS SOFT. HIS ATTITUDE IS AN INSULT TO YOU.
RELAX, MARCO. WE KNOW WHERE LYSERG'S COMING FROM.
WE APPRE-CIATE YOUR CONCERN, MARCO...
...BUT WE APPRECIATE LYSERG'S COMPAS-SION, TOO.
BEING NICE ISN'T THE SAME AS BEING KIND.
LYSERG IS KIND.

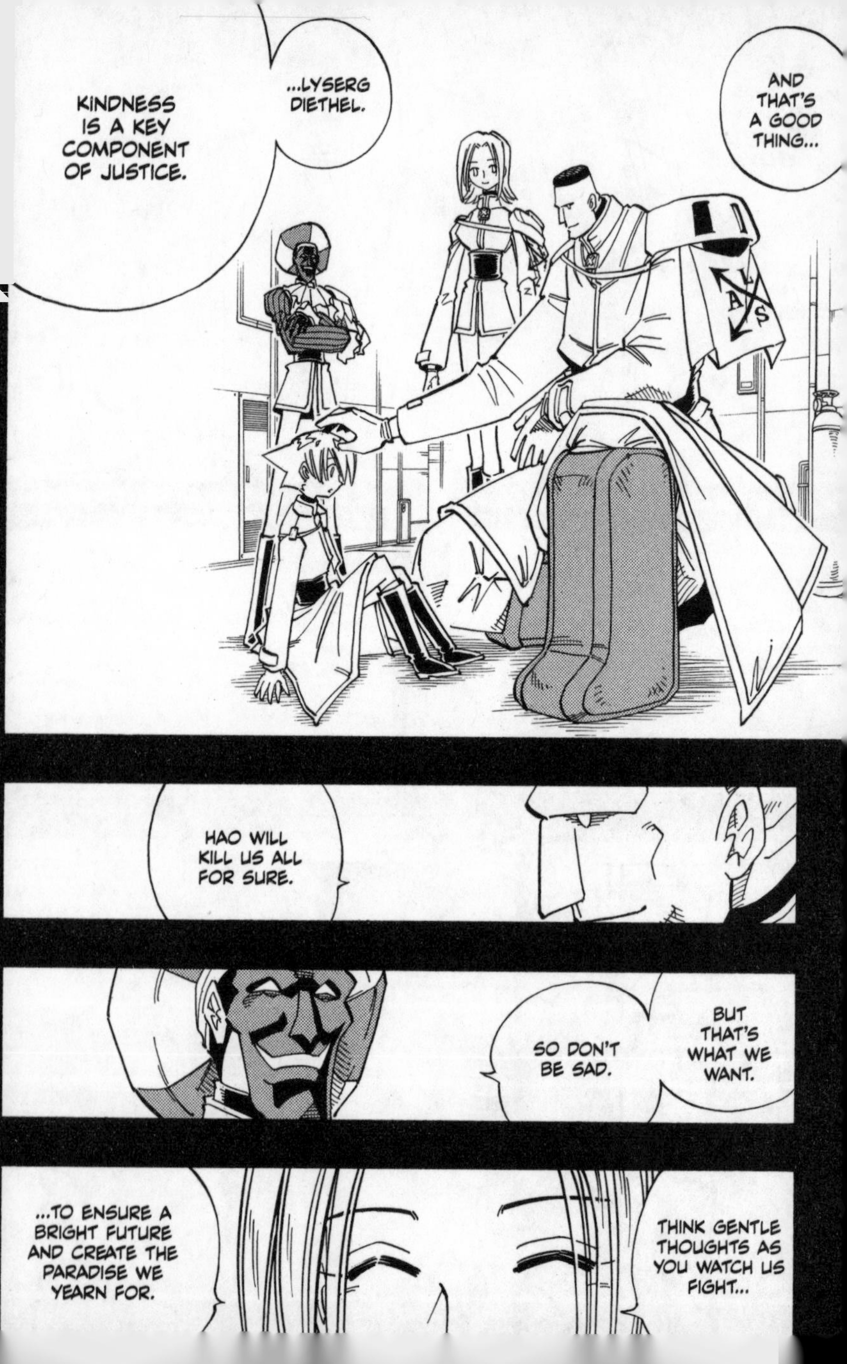
AND THAT'S A GOOD THING...
...LYSERG DIETHEL.
KINDNESS IS A KEY COMPONENT OF JUSTICE.
HAO WILL KILL US ALL FOR SURE.
BUT THAT'S WHAT WE WANT.
SO DON'T BE SAD.
THINK GENTLE THOUGHTS AS YOU WATCH US FIGHT...
...TO ENSURE A BRIGHT FUTURE AND CREATE THE PARADISE WE YEARN FOR.

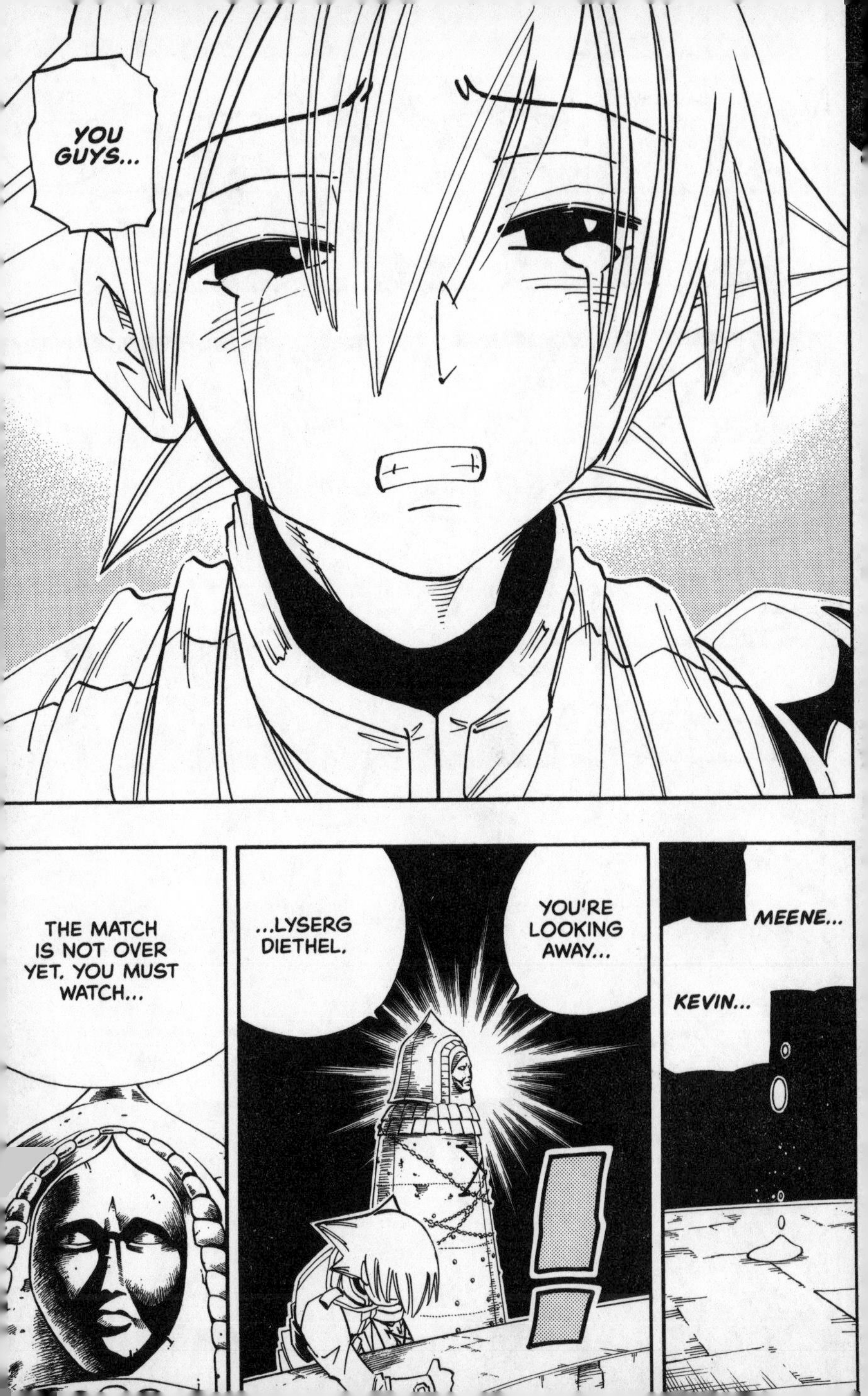
YOU GUYS...
MEENE...
KEVIN...
YOU'RE LOOKING AWAY...
...LYSERG DIETHEL.
THE MATCH IS NOT OVER YET. YOU MUST WATCH...

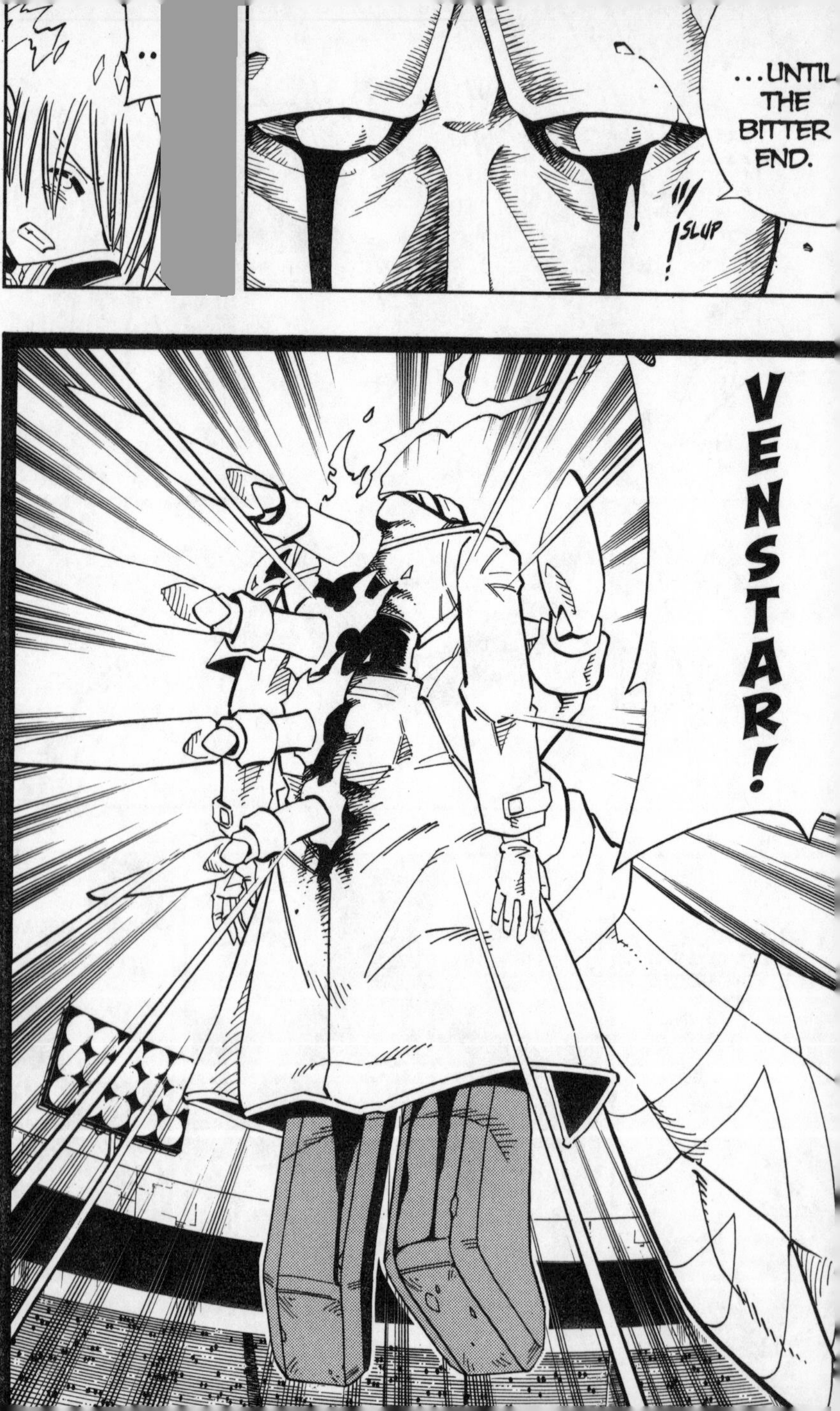
...UNTIL THE BITTER END.
SLUP
..
VENSTAR!

SHAMAN KING CHARACTER FILE No.81

Kevin

January 2001

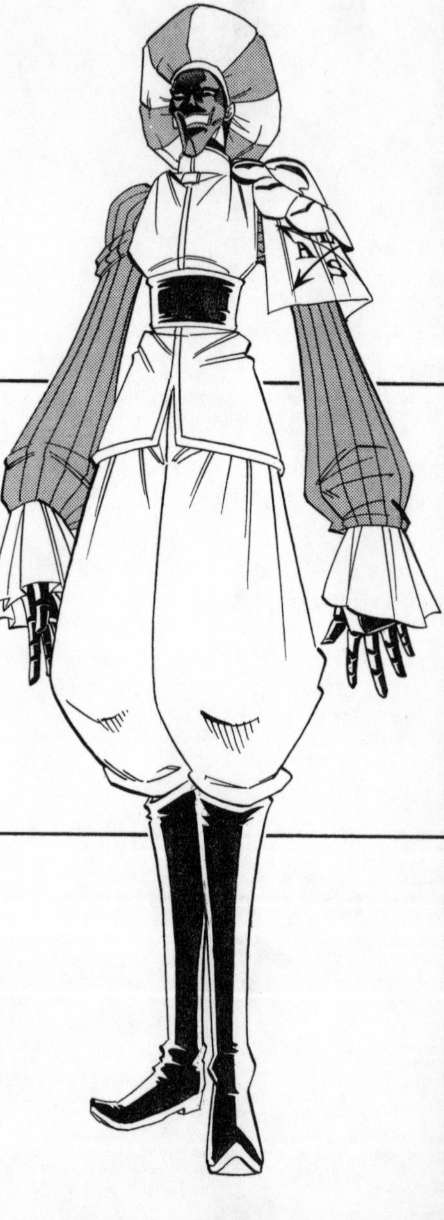

Age (at time of death): 30
Date of Birth: Sept. 18, 1971
Astrological Sign: Virgo
Blood Type: AB

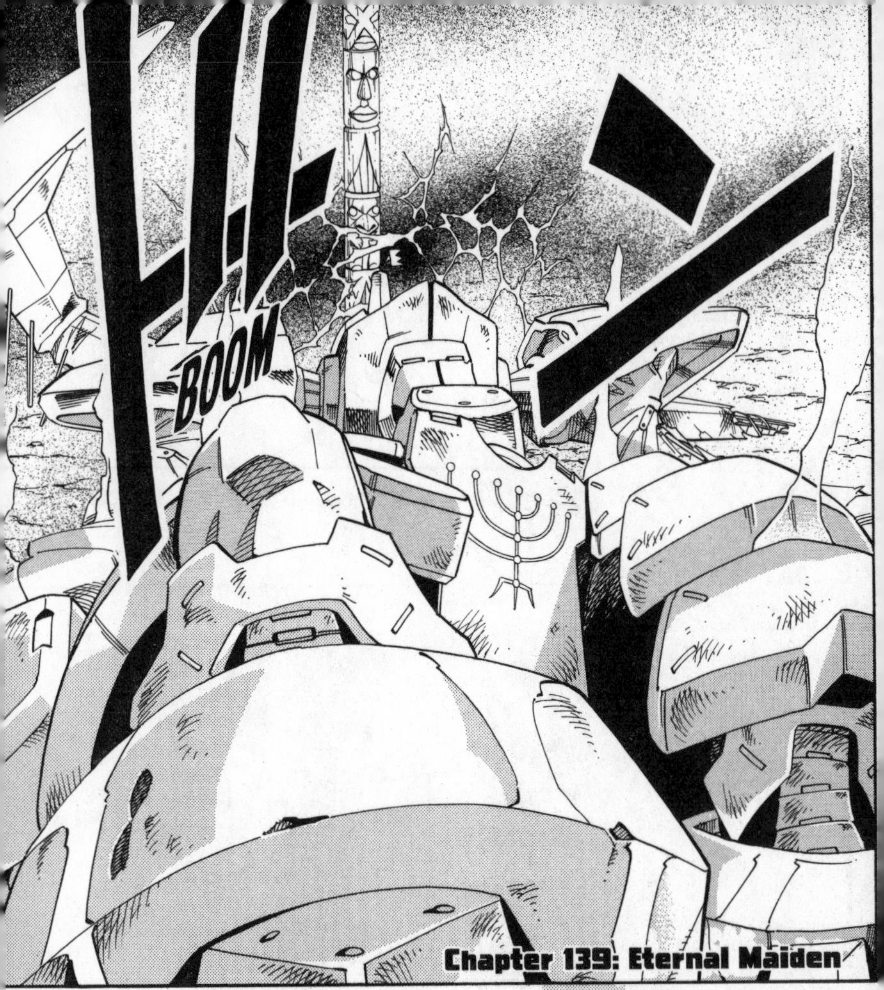
BOOM
Chapter 139: Eternal Maiden
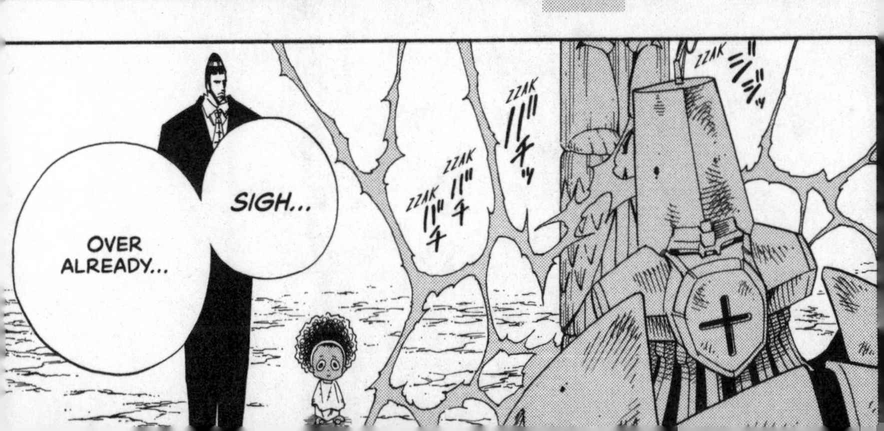
ZZAK
ZZAK
ZZAK
ZZAK
SIGH...
OVER ALREADY...

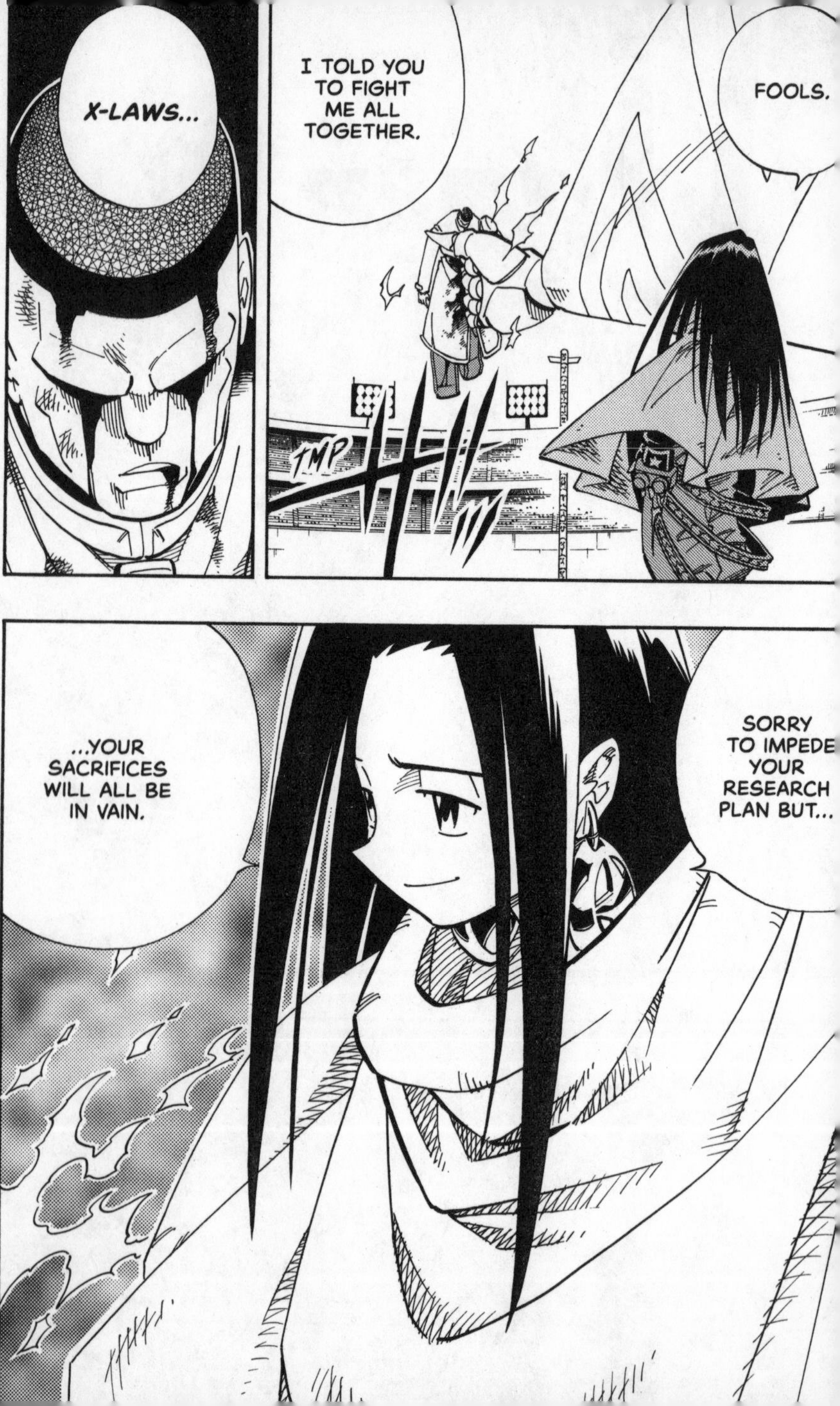
FOOLS.
I TOLD YOU TO FIGHT ME ALL TOGETHER.
TMP
X-LAWS...
SORRY TO IMPEDE YOUR RESEARCH PLAN BUT...
...YOUR SACRIFICES WILL ALL BE IN VAIN.

Chapter 139:

Eternal Maiden

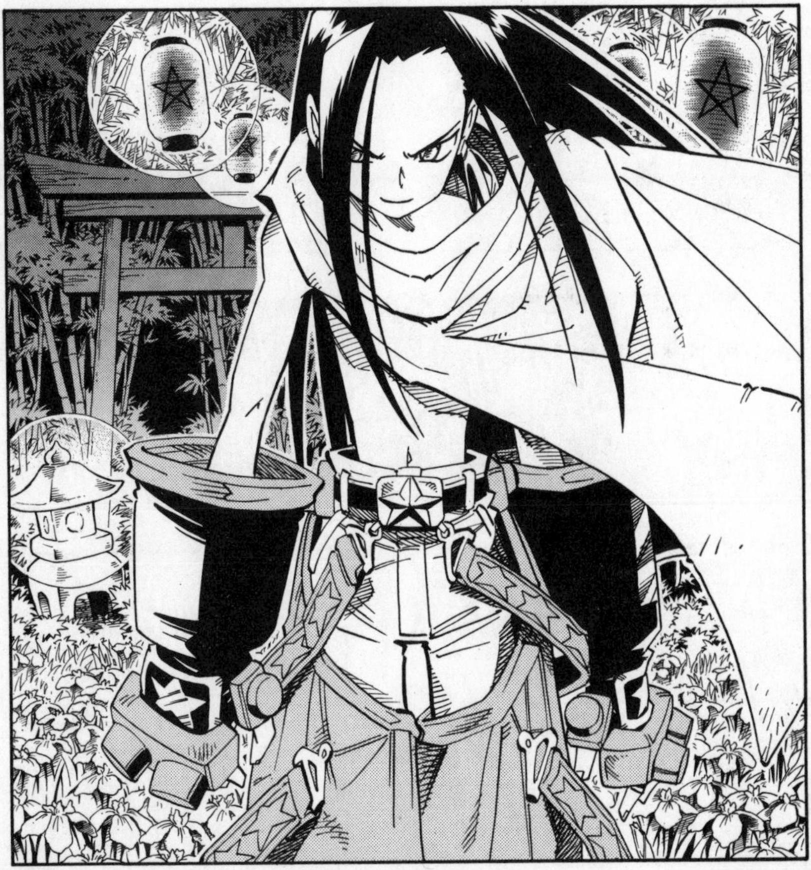

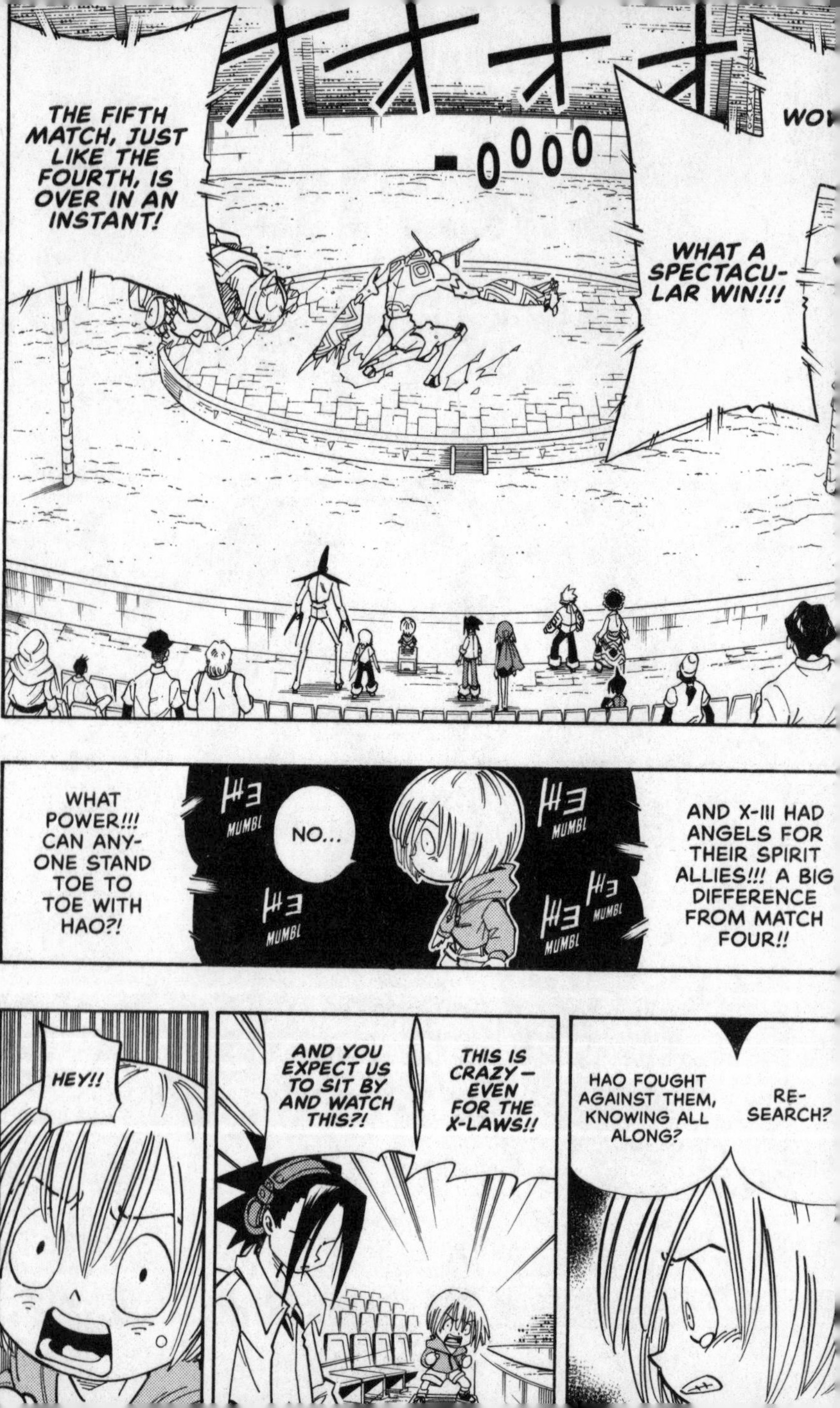

オオオオ
WO
WHAT A SPECTACULAR WIN!!!
...OOOO
THE FIFTH MATCH, JUST LIKE THE FOURTH, IS OVER IN AN INSTANT!
AND X-III HAD ANGELS FOR THEIR SPIRIT ALLIES!!! A BIG DIFFERENCE FROM MATCH FOUR!!
MUMBL
MUMBL
MUMBL
NO...
MUMBL
MUMBL
WHAT POWER!!! CAN ANYONE STAND TOE TO TOE WITH HAO?!
RE-SEARCH?
HAO FOUGHT AGAINST THEM, KNOWING ALL ALONG?
THIS IS CRAZY—EVEN FOR THE X-LAWS!!
AND YOU EXPECT US TO SIT BY AND WATCH THIS?!
HEY!!

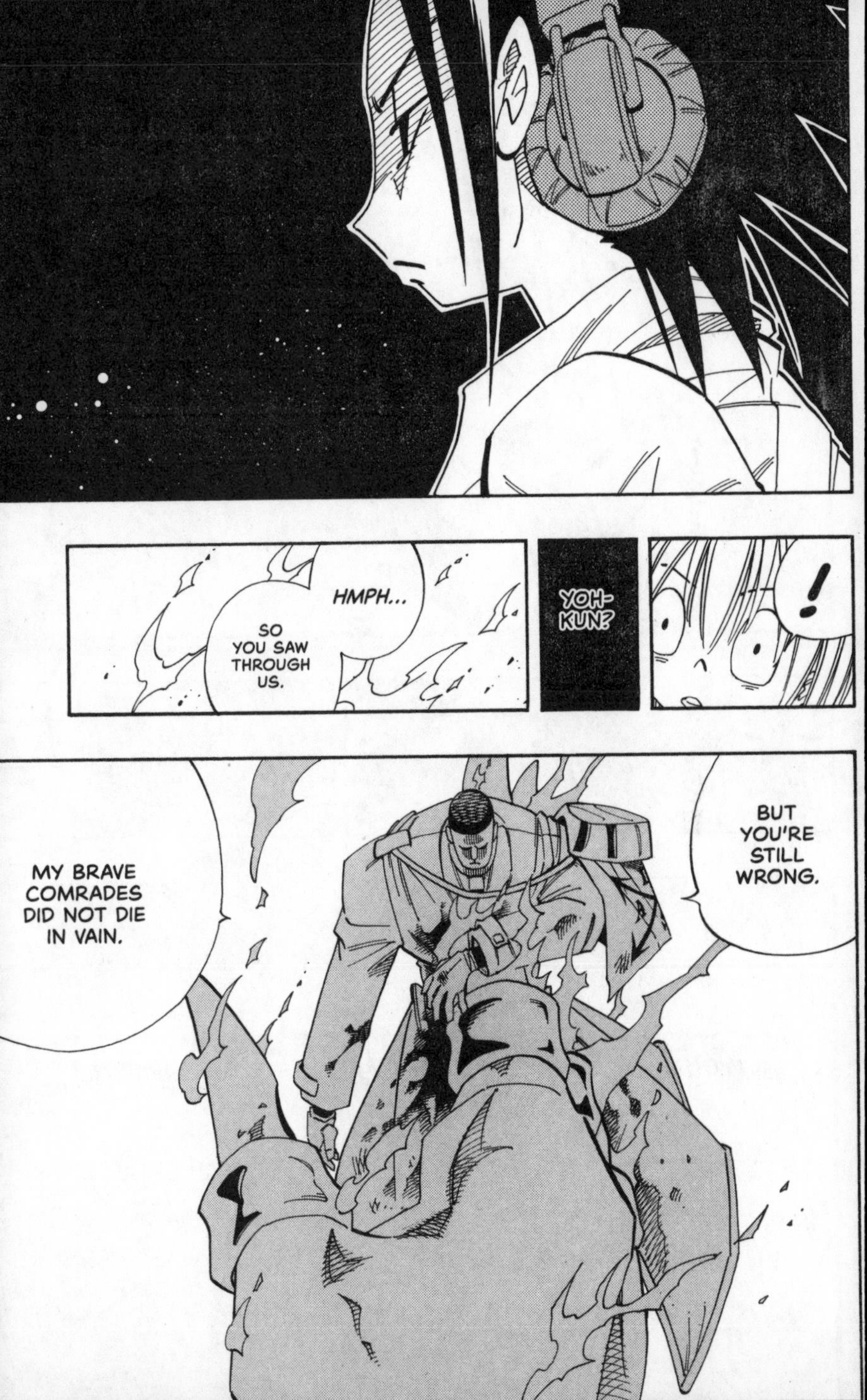
!
YOH-KUN?
HMPH...
SO YOU SAW THROUGH US.
BUT YOU'RE STILL WRONG.
MY BRAVE COMRADES DID NOT DIE IN VAIN.

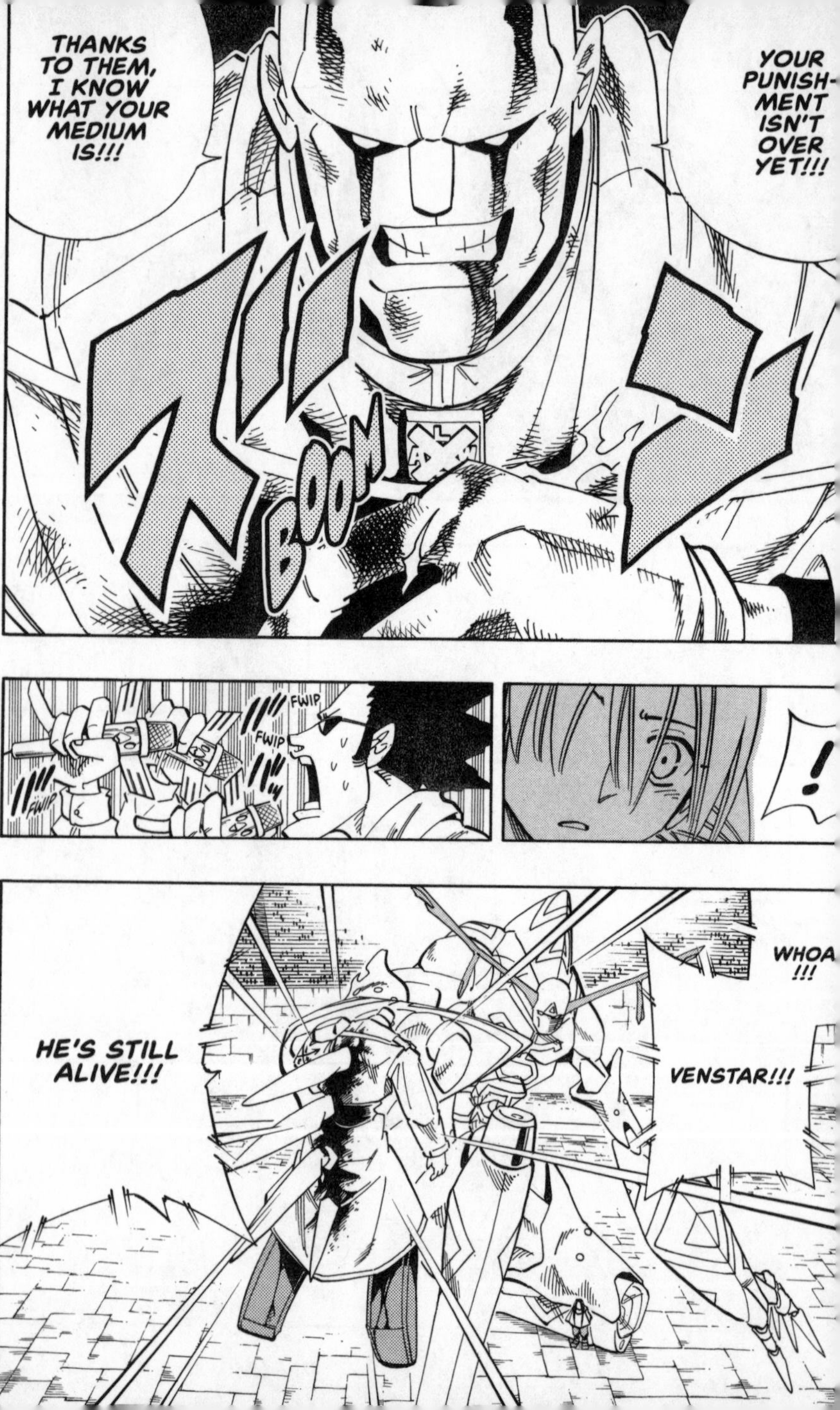
YOUR PUNISHMENT ISN'T OVER YET!!!
THANKS TO THEM, I KNOW WHAT YOUR MEDIUM IS!!!
BOOM
!
FWIP
FWIP
FWIP
WHOA!!!
VENSTAR!!!
HE'S STILL ALIVE!!!

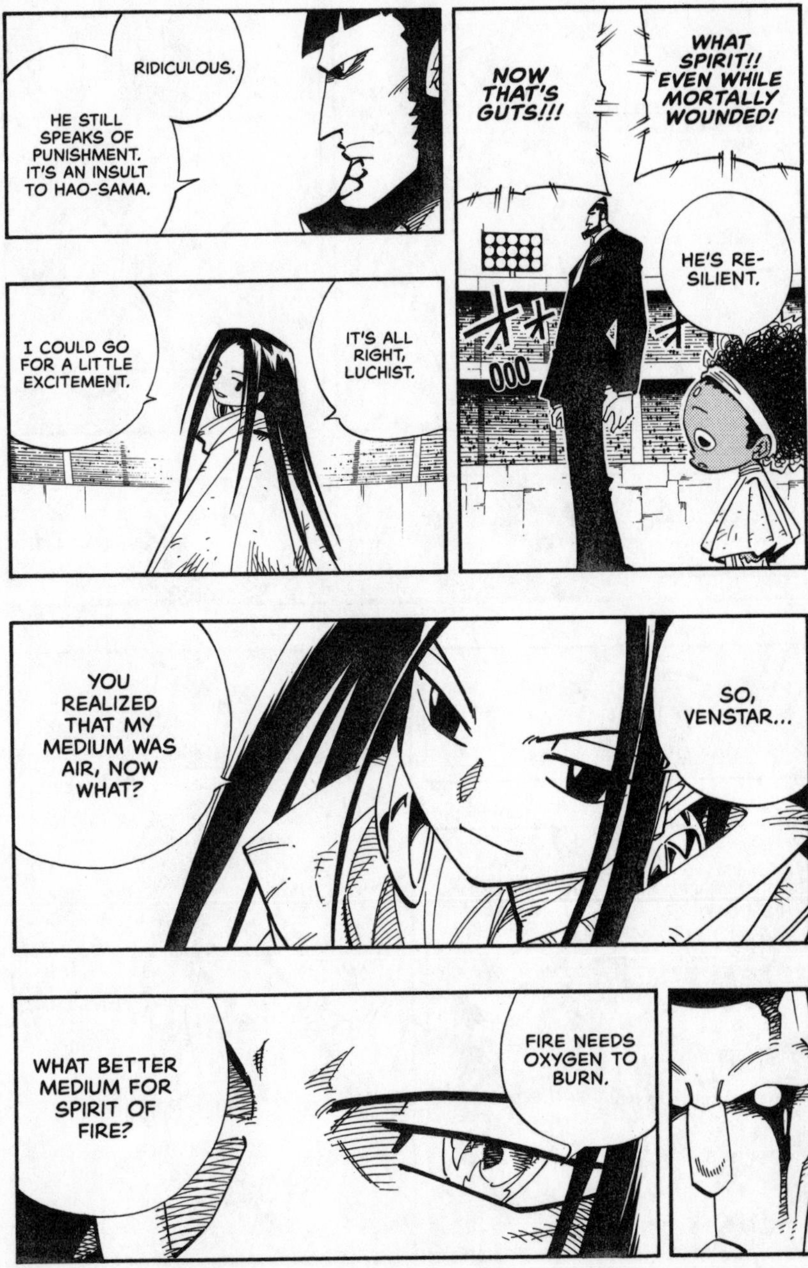
WHAT SPIRIT!! EVEN WHILE MORTALLY WOUNDED!
NOW THAT'S GUTS!!!
HE'S RE-SILIENT.
RIDICULOUS.
HE STILL SPEAKS OF PUNISHMENT. IT'S AN INSULT TO HAO-SAMA.
IT'S ALL RIGHT, LUCHIST.
I COULD GO FOR A LITTLE EXCITEMENT.
SO, VENSTAR...
YOU REALIZED THAT MY MEDIUM WAS AIR, NOW WHAT?
FIRE NEEDS OXYGEN TO BURN.
WHAT BETTER MEDIUM FOR SPIRIT OF FIRE?

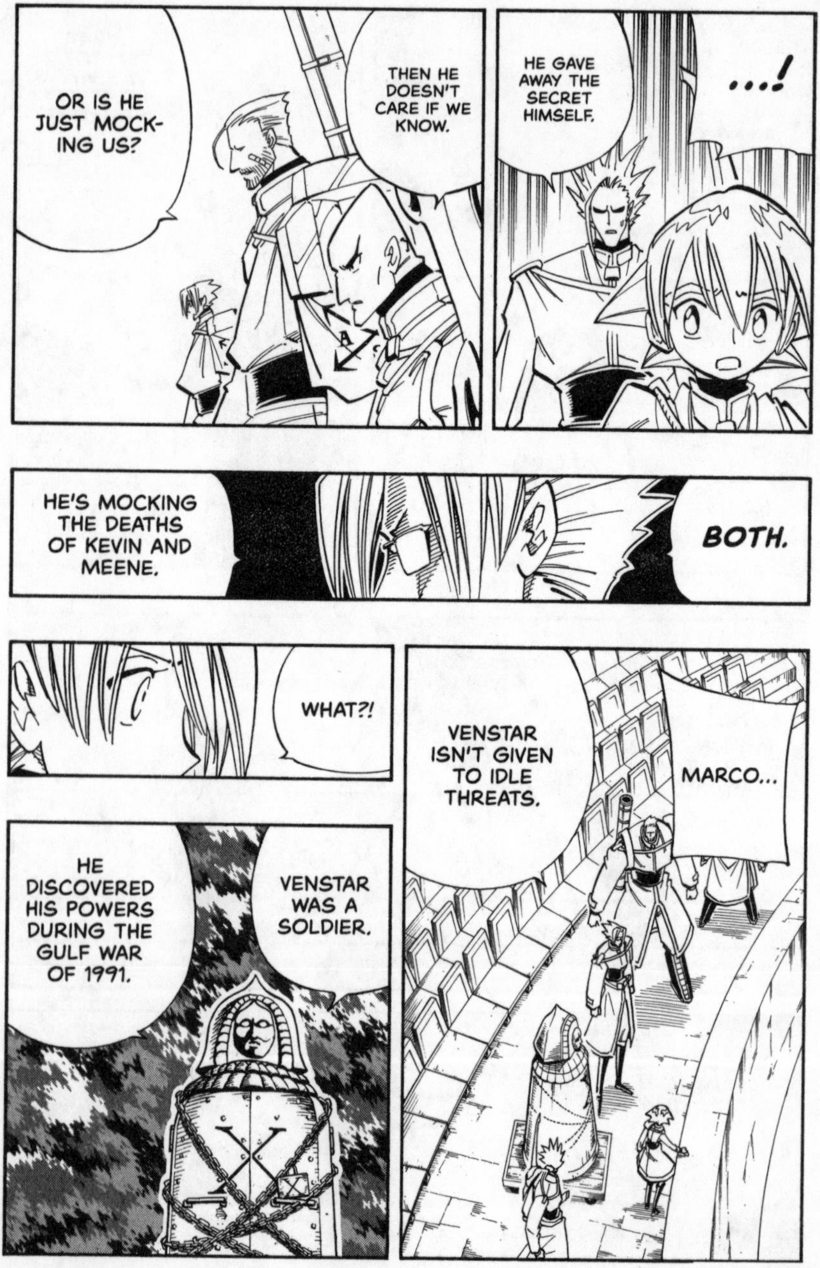
HE GAVE AWAY THE SECRET HIMSELF.
...!
THEN HE DOESN'T CARE IF WE KNOW.
OR IS HE JUST MOCK-ING US?
BOTH.
HE'S MOCKING THE DEATHS OF KEVIN AND MEENE.
MARCO...
VENSTAR ISN'T GIVEN TO IDLE THREATS.
WHAT?!
VENSTAR WAS A SOLDIER.
HE DISCOVERED HIS POWERS DURING THE GULF WAR OF 1991.

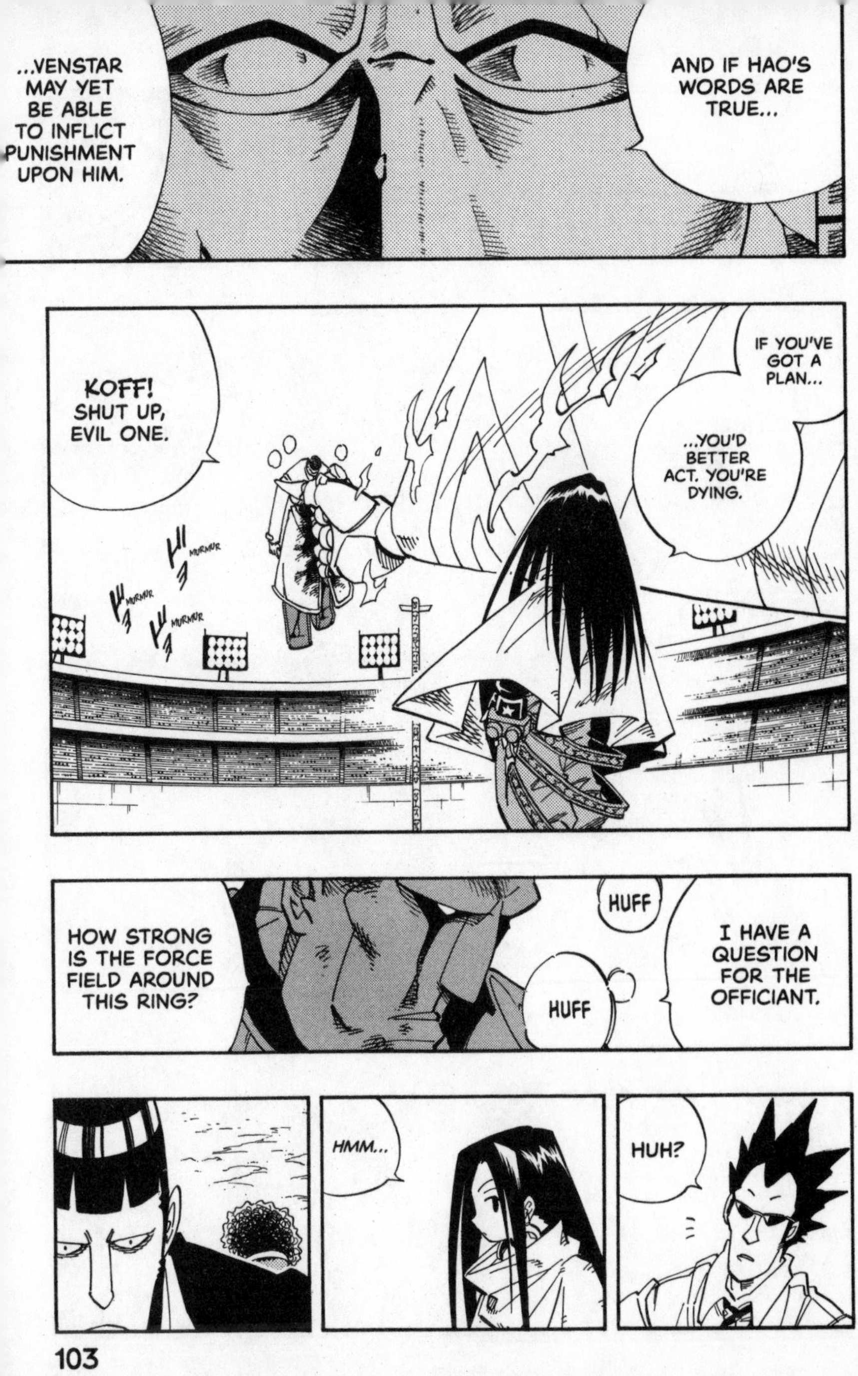
AND IF HAO'S WORDS ARE TRUE...
...VENSTAR MAY YET BE ABLE TO INFLICT PUNISHMENT UPON HIM.
IF YOU'VE GOT A PLAN...
...YOU'D BETTER ACT. YOU'RE DYING.
KOFF! SHUT UP, EVIL ONE.
MURMUR
MURMUR
MURMUR
I HAVE A QUESTION FOR THE OFFICIANT.
HUFF
HUFF
HOW STRONG IS THE FORCE FIELD AROUND THIS RING?
HUH?
HMM...

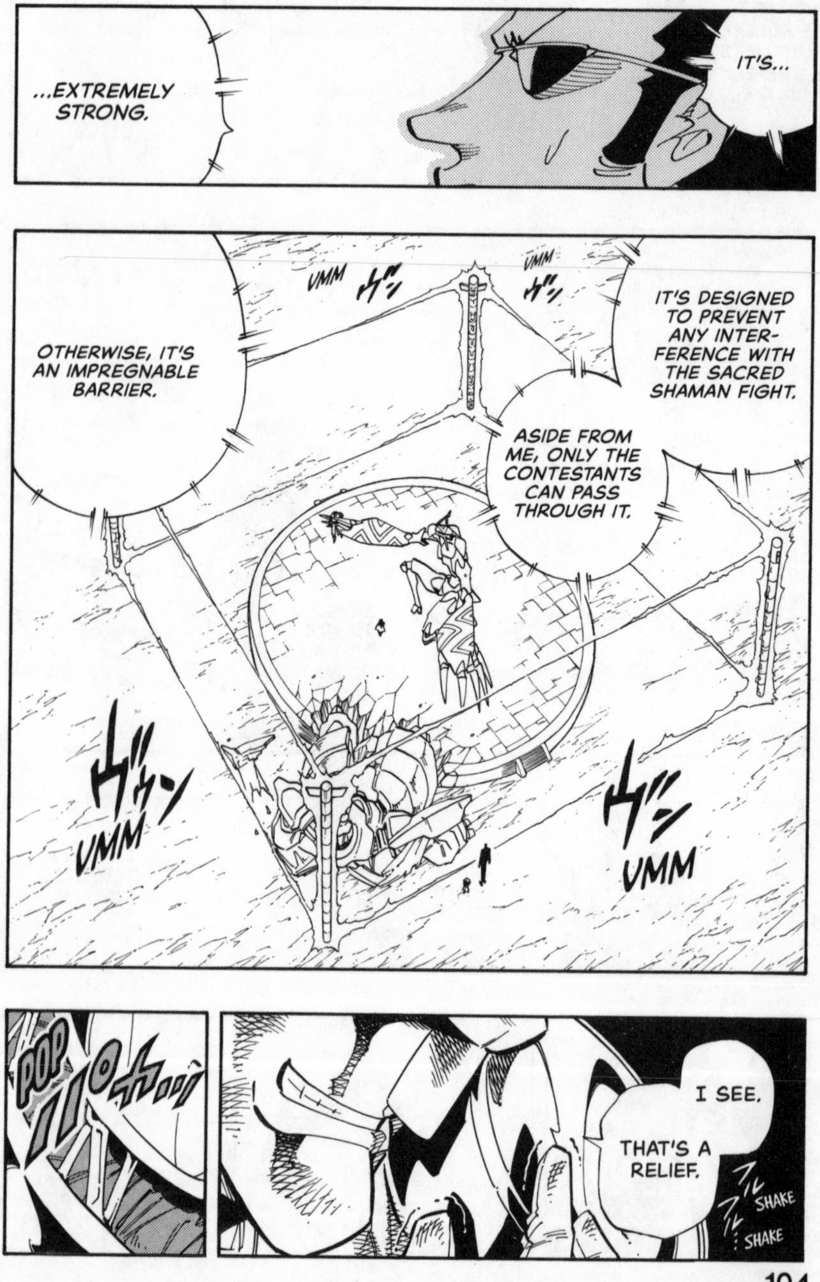
IT'S...
...EXTREMELY STRONG.
UMM
UMM
IT'S DESIGNED TO PREVENT ANY INTERFERENCE WITH THE SACRED SHAMAN FIGHT.
ASIDE FROM ME, ONLY THE CONTESTANTS CAN PASS THROUGH IT.
OTHERWISE, IT'S AN IMPREGNABLE BARRIER.
UMM
UMM
I SEE.
THAT'S A RELIEF.
SHAKE
SHAKE
POP

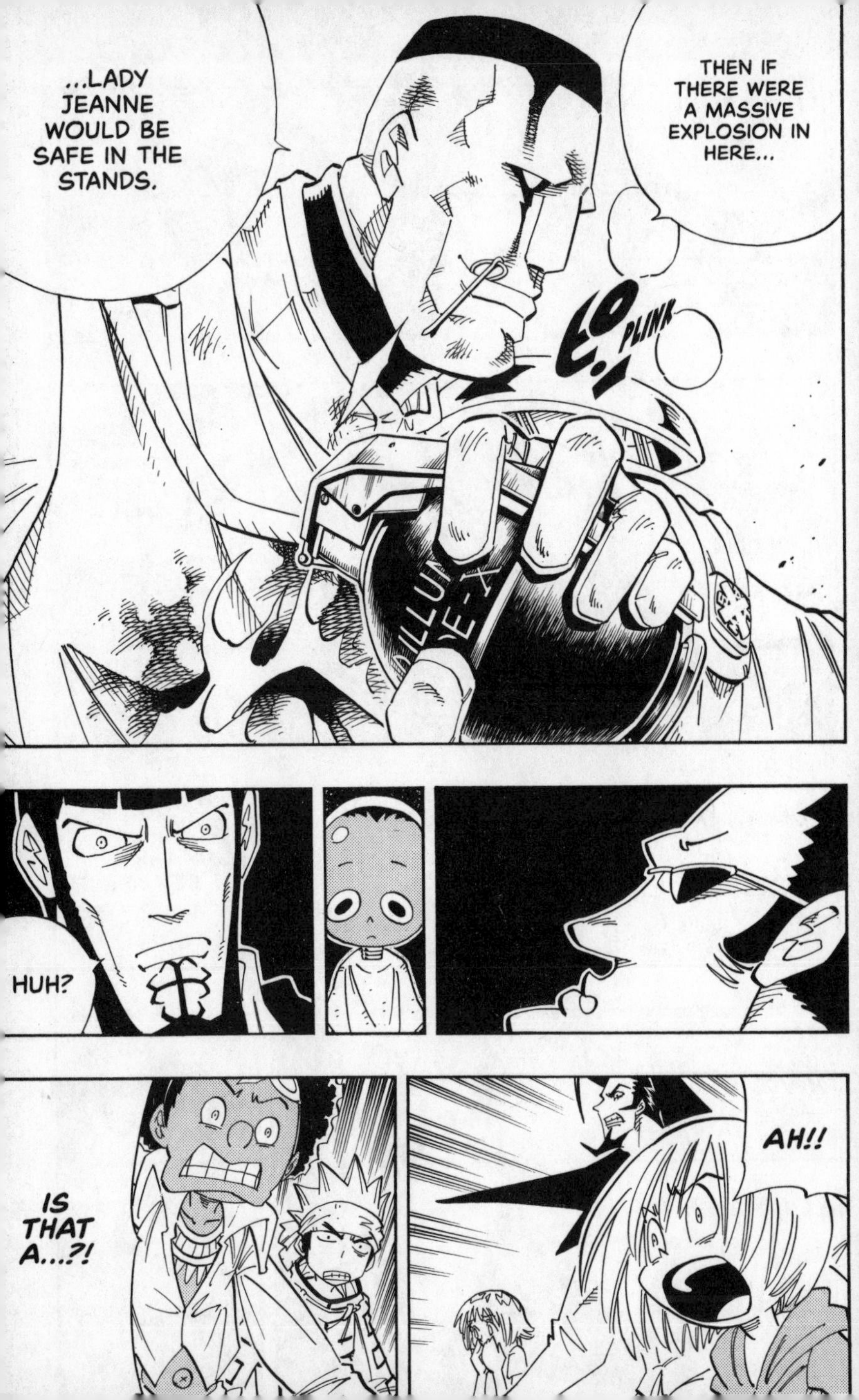
THEN IF THERE WERE A MASSIVE EXPLOSION IN HERE...
...LADY JEANNE WOULD BE SAFE IN THE STANDS.
PLINK
HUH?
AH!!
IS THAT A...?!

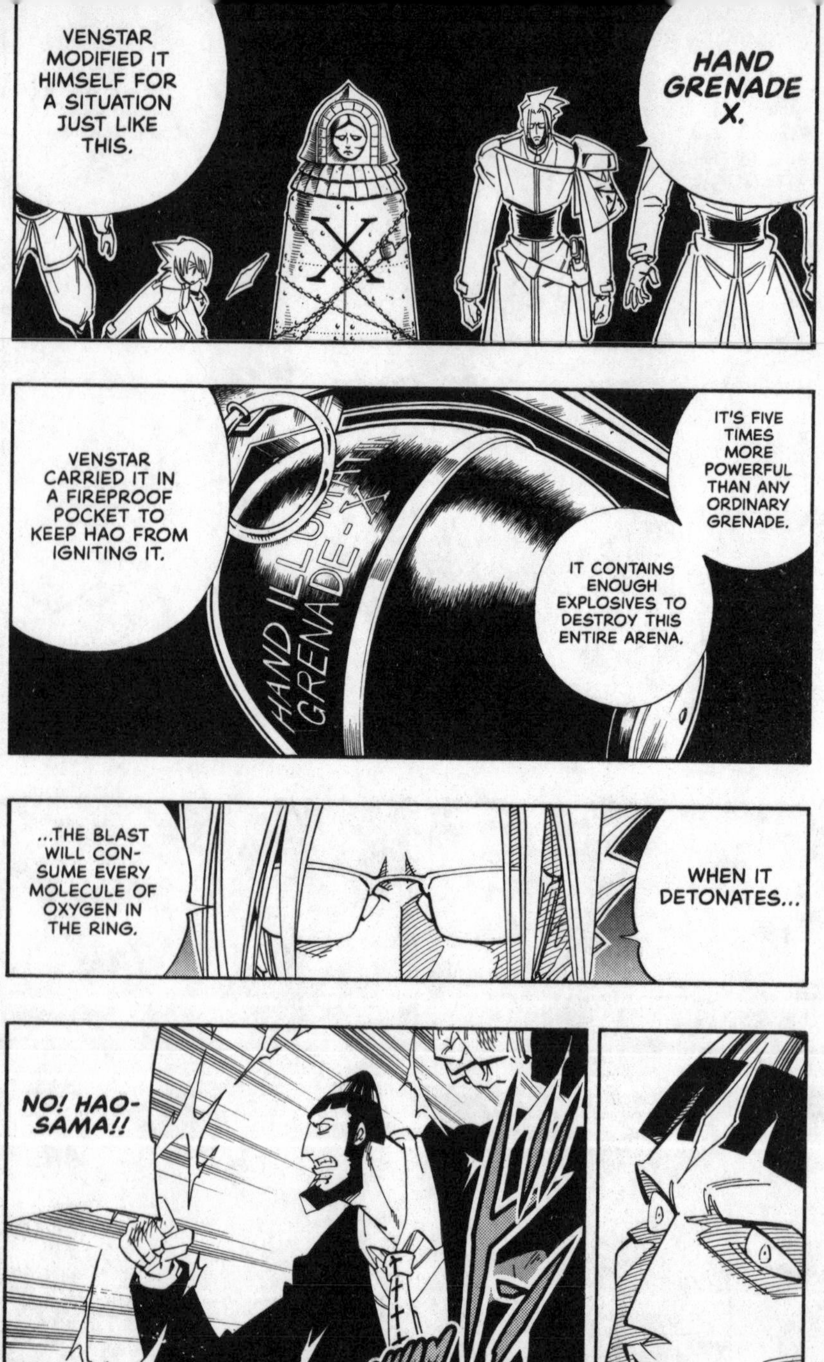
HAND GRENADE X.
VENSTAR MODIFIED IT HIMSELF FOR A SITUATION JUST LIKE THIS.
IT'S FIVE TIMES MORE POWERFUL THAN ANY ORDINARY GRENADE.
IT CONTAINS ENOUGH EXPLOSIVES TO DESTROY THIS ENTIRE ARENA.
VENSTAR CARRIED IT IN A FIREPROOF POCKET TO KEEP HAO FROM IGNITING IT.
WHEN IT DETONATES...
...THE BLAST WILL CON-SUME EVERY MOLECULE OF OXYGEN IN THE RING.
NO! HAO-SAMA!!
WHAM

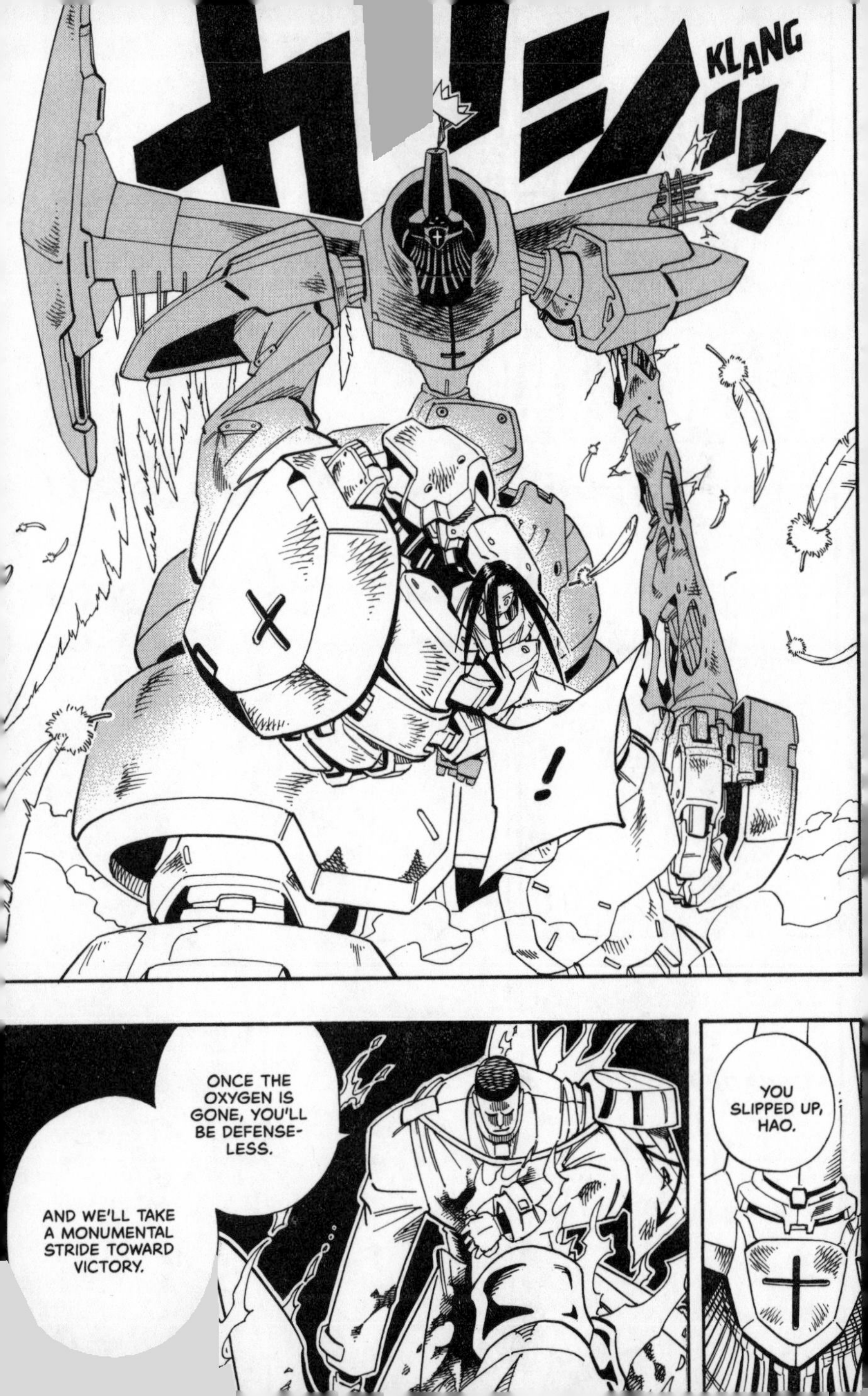
KLANG
!
YOU SLIPPED UP, HAO.
ONCE THE OXYGEN IS GONE, YOU'LL BE DEFENSELESS.
AND WE'LL TAKE A MONUMENTAL STRIDE TOWARD VICTORY.

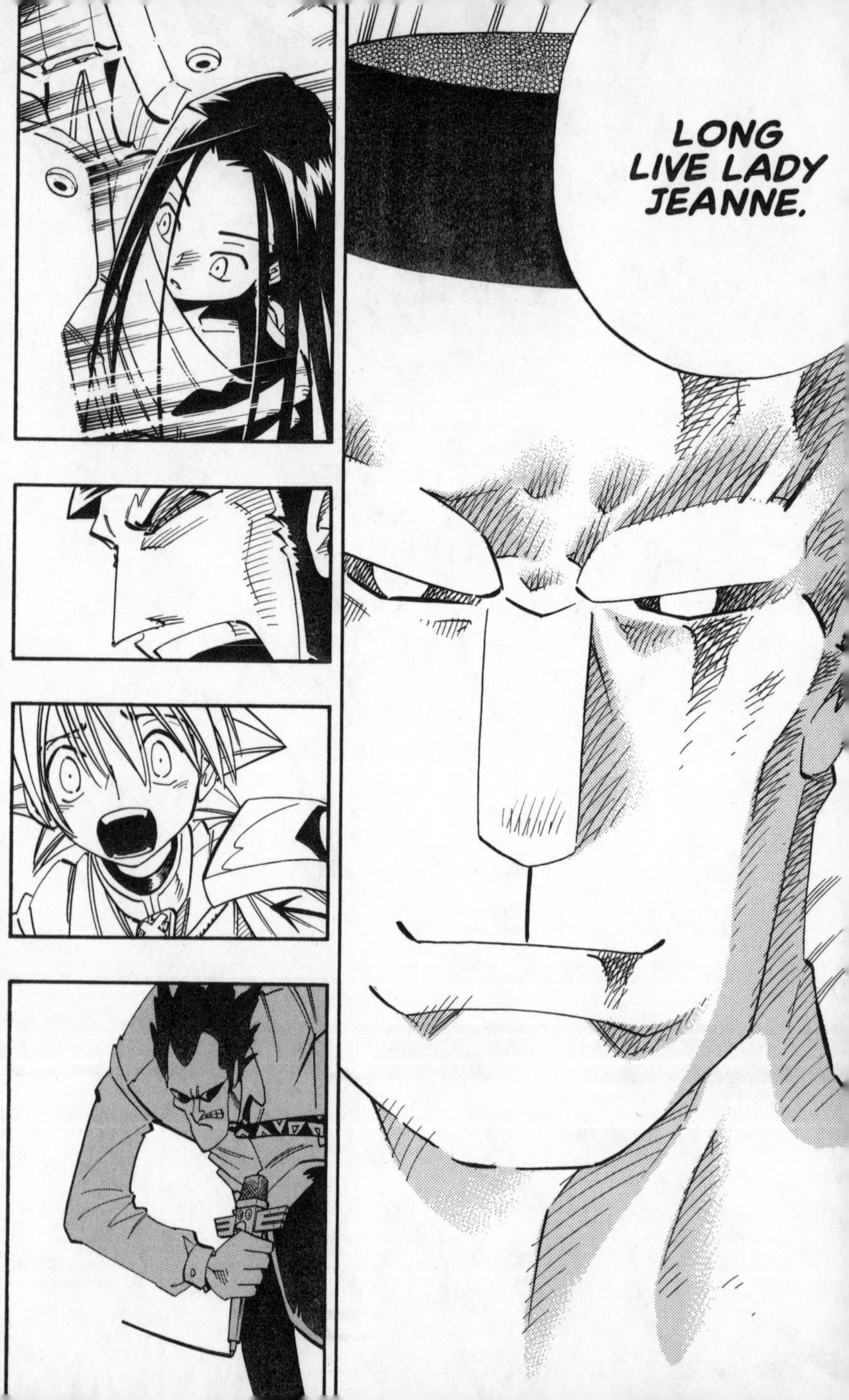
LONG LIVE LADY JEANNE.

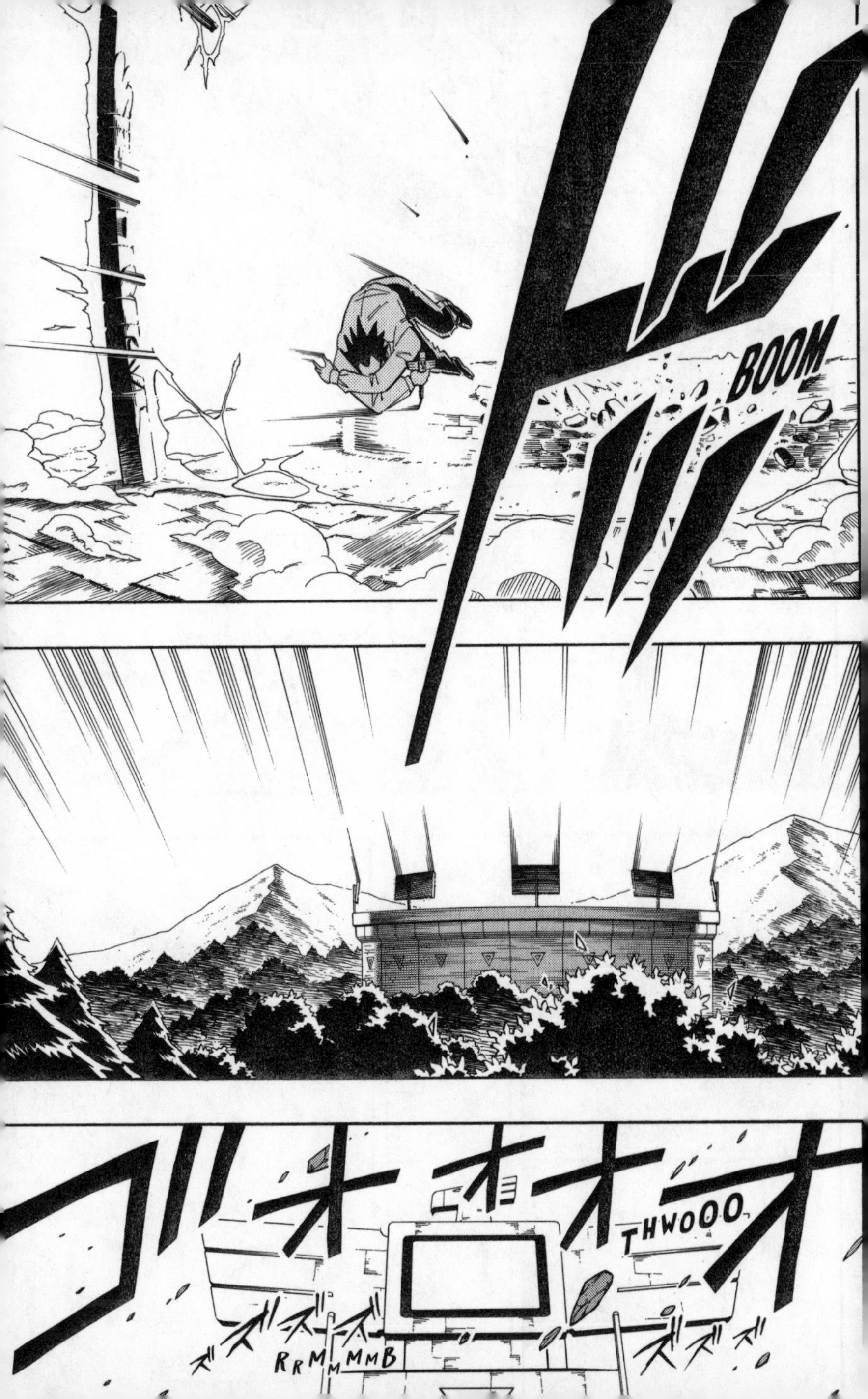
BOOM
THWOOO
RRMMMMB

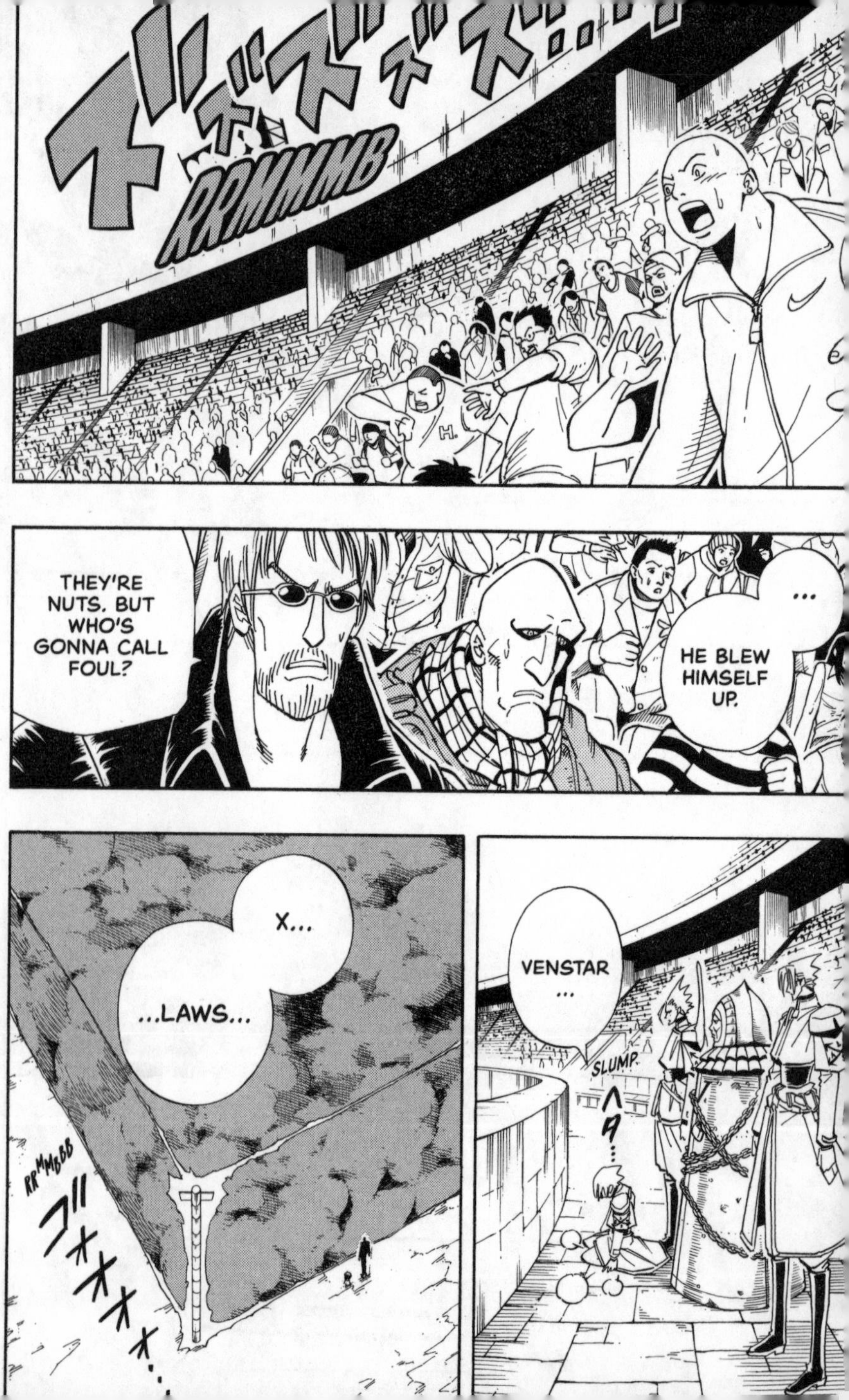
RRMMMB
...
HE BLEW HIMSELF UP.
THEY'RE NUTS. BUT WHO'S GONNA CALL FOUL?
VENSTAR ...
SLUMP
ヘタ...
X...
...LAWS...
RRMMBBB

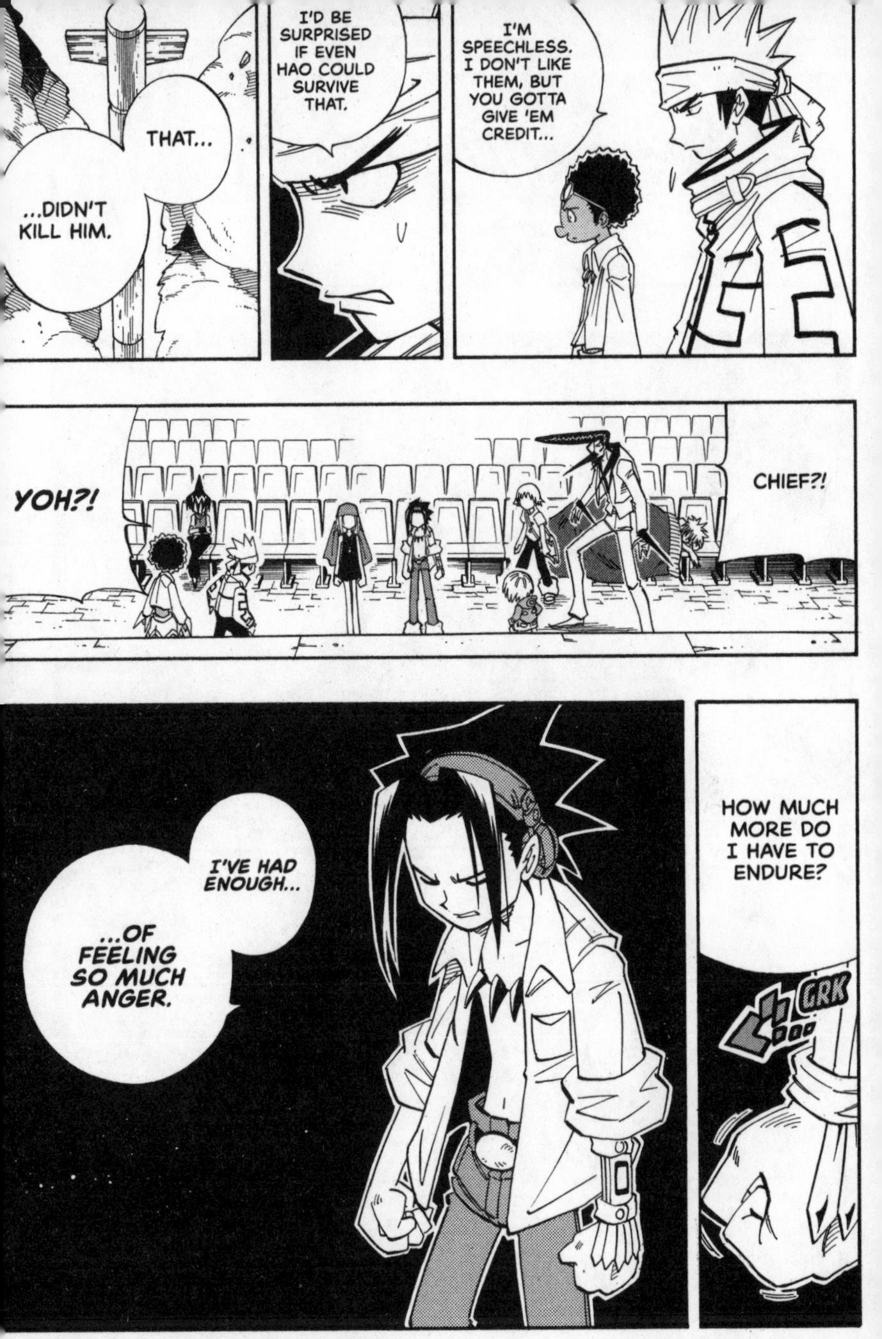
I'M SPEECHLESS. I DON'T LIKE THEM, BUT YOU GOTTA GIVE 'EM CREDIT...
I'D BE SURPRISED IF EVEN HAO COULD SURVIVE THAT.
THAT...
...DIDN'T KILL HIM.
CHIEF?!
YOH?!
HOW MUCH MORE DO I HAVE TO ENDURE?
GRK
I'VE HAD ENOUGH...
...OF FEELING SO MUCH ANGER.

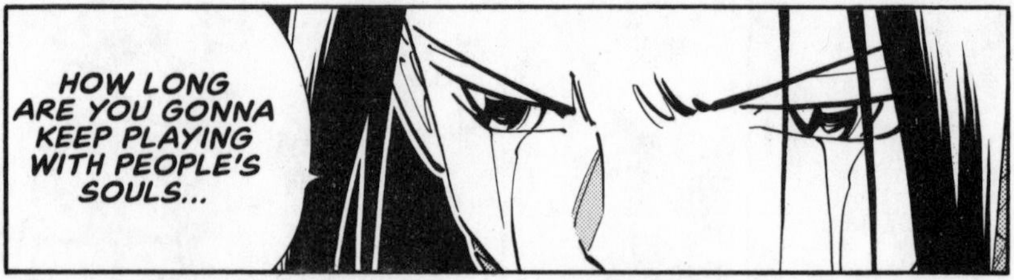
HOW LONG ARE YOU GONNA KEEP PLAYING WITH PEOPLE'S SOULS...
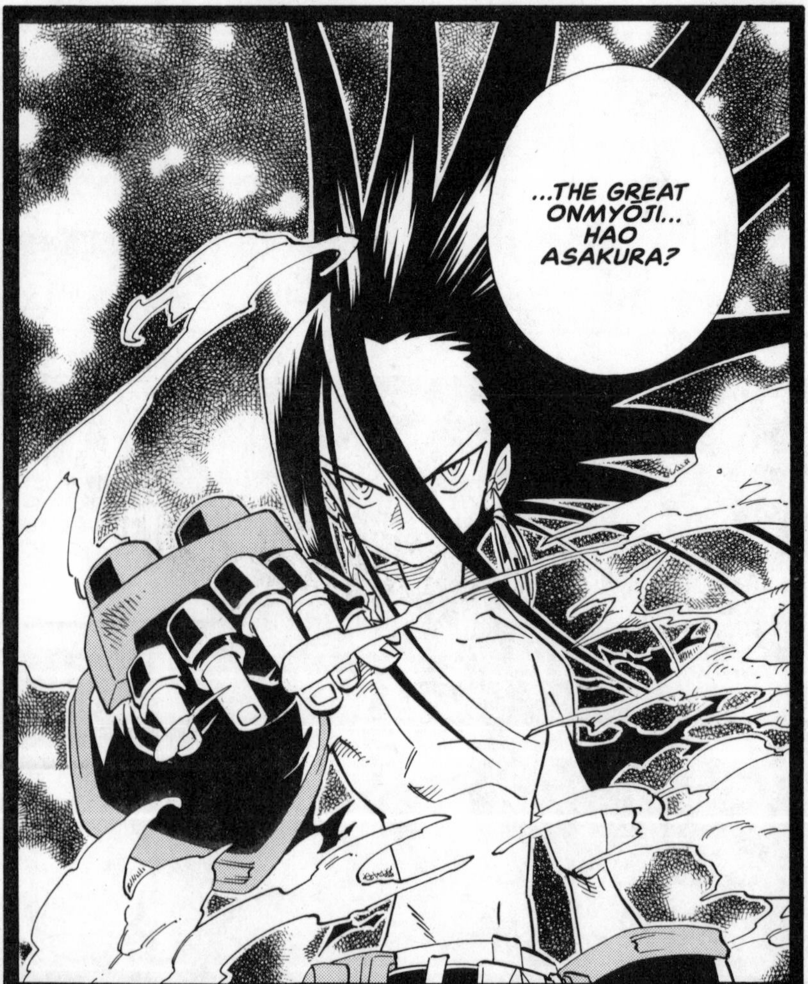
...THE GREAT ONMYŌJI... HAO ASAKURA?

SHAMAN KING CHARACTER FILE No.82

Venstar

January 2001

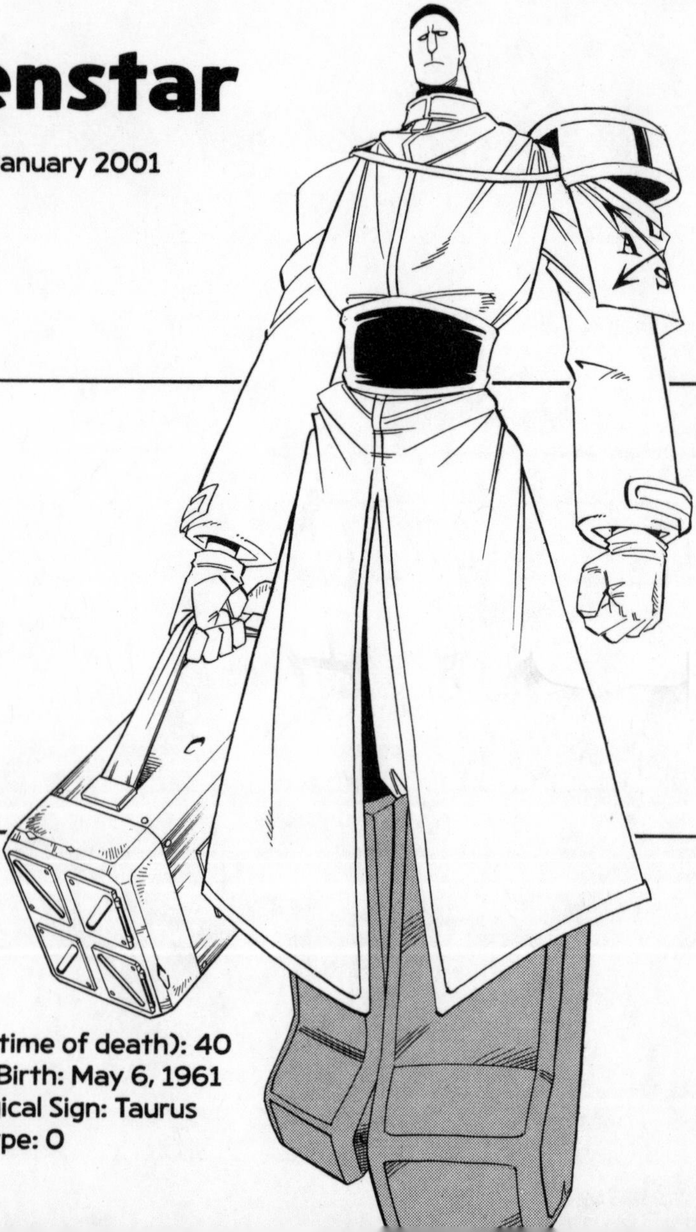

Age (at time of death): 40
Date of Birth: May 6, 1961
Astrological Sign: Taurus
Blood Type: O

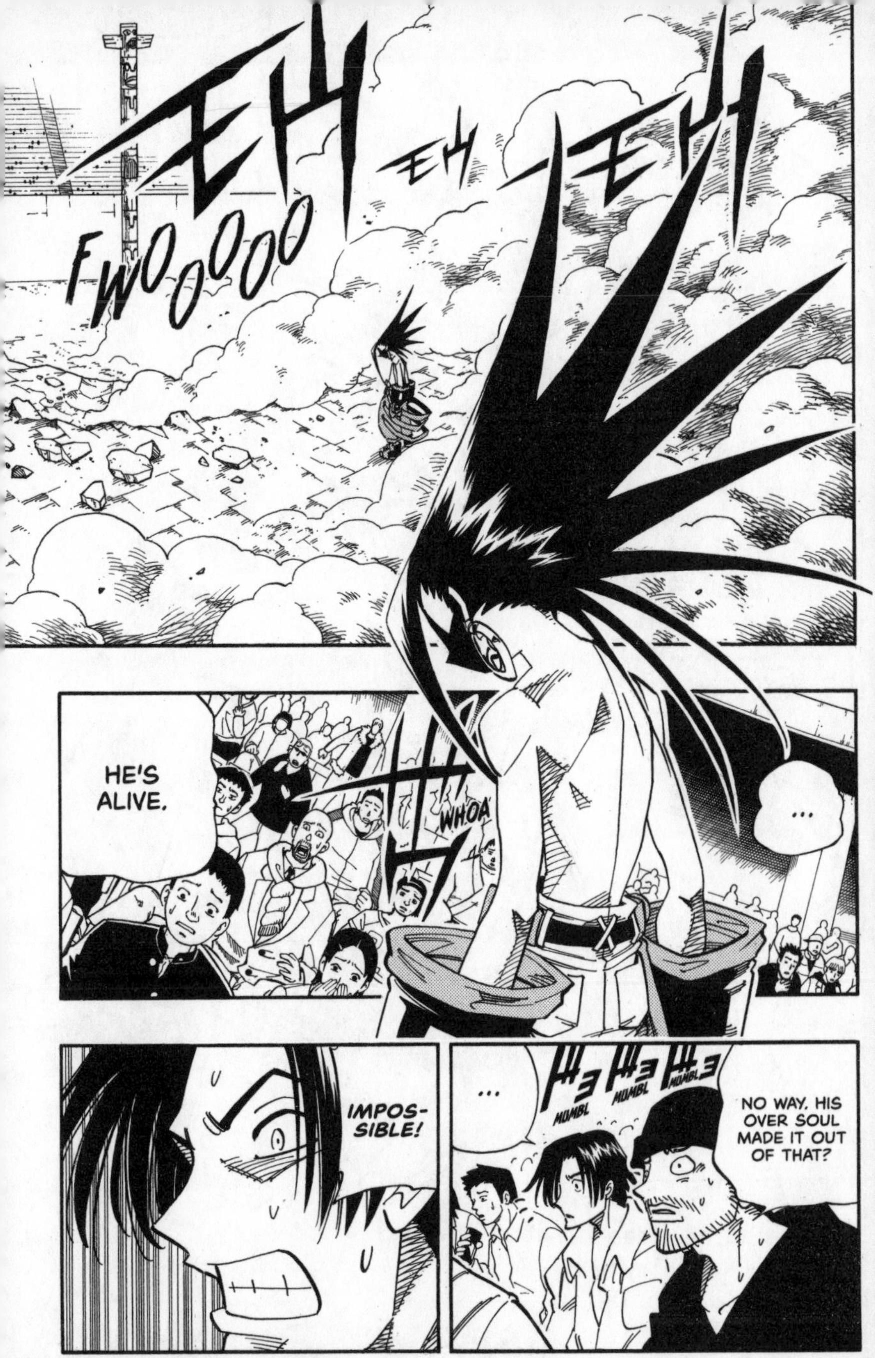
TEH
TEH
TEH
FWOOOOO
...
WHOA
HE'S ALIVE.
NO WAY. HIS OVER SOUL MADE IT OUT OF THAT?
MUMBL
MUMBL
MUMBL
...
IMPOSSIBLE!

Chapter 140: Logic

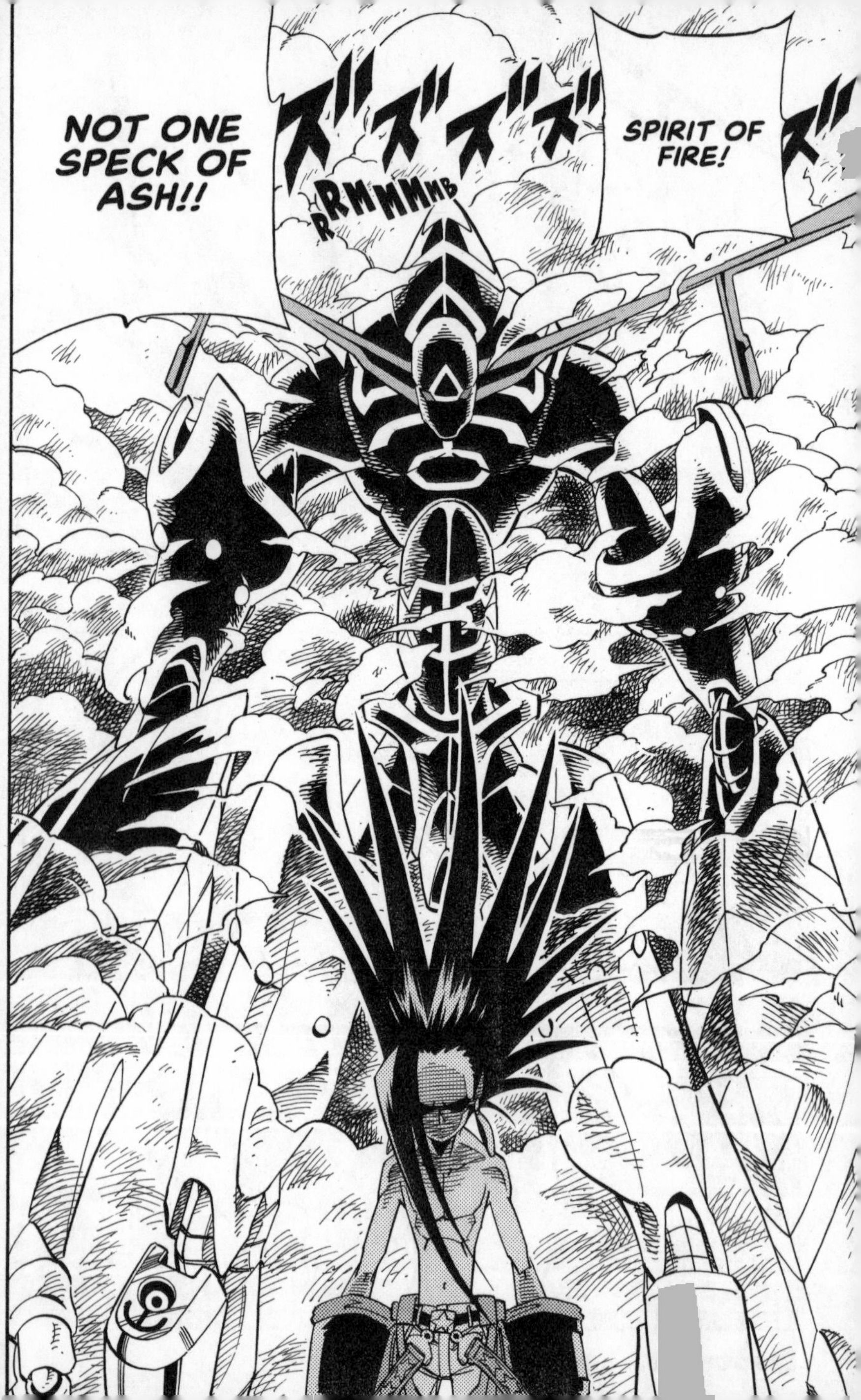
SPIRIT OF FIRE!
ズ
ズズズズ
RRMMMMB
NOT ONE SPECK OF ASH!!

Chapter 140:

Logic

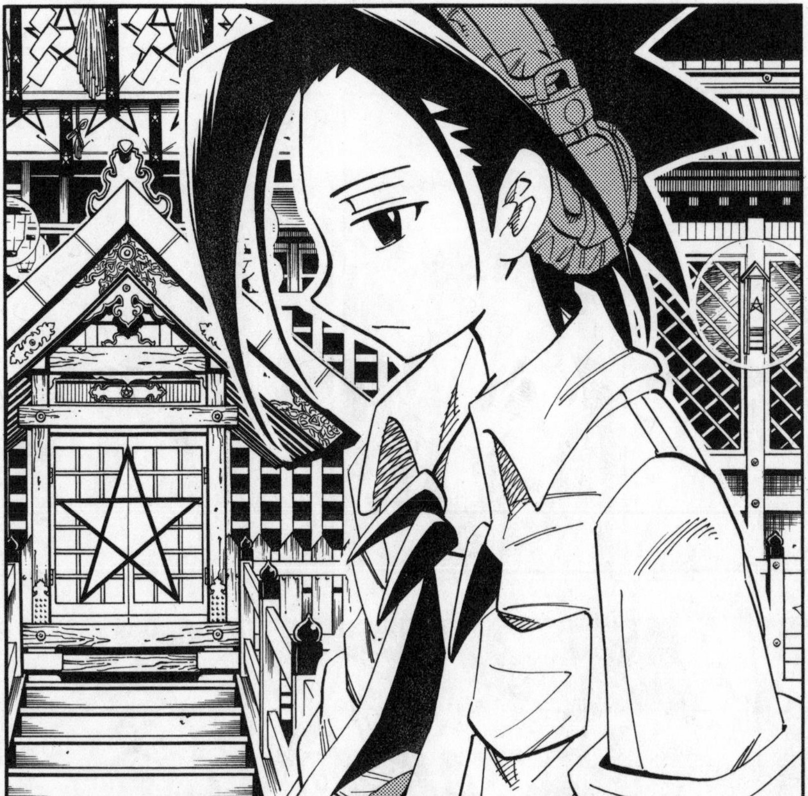

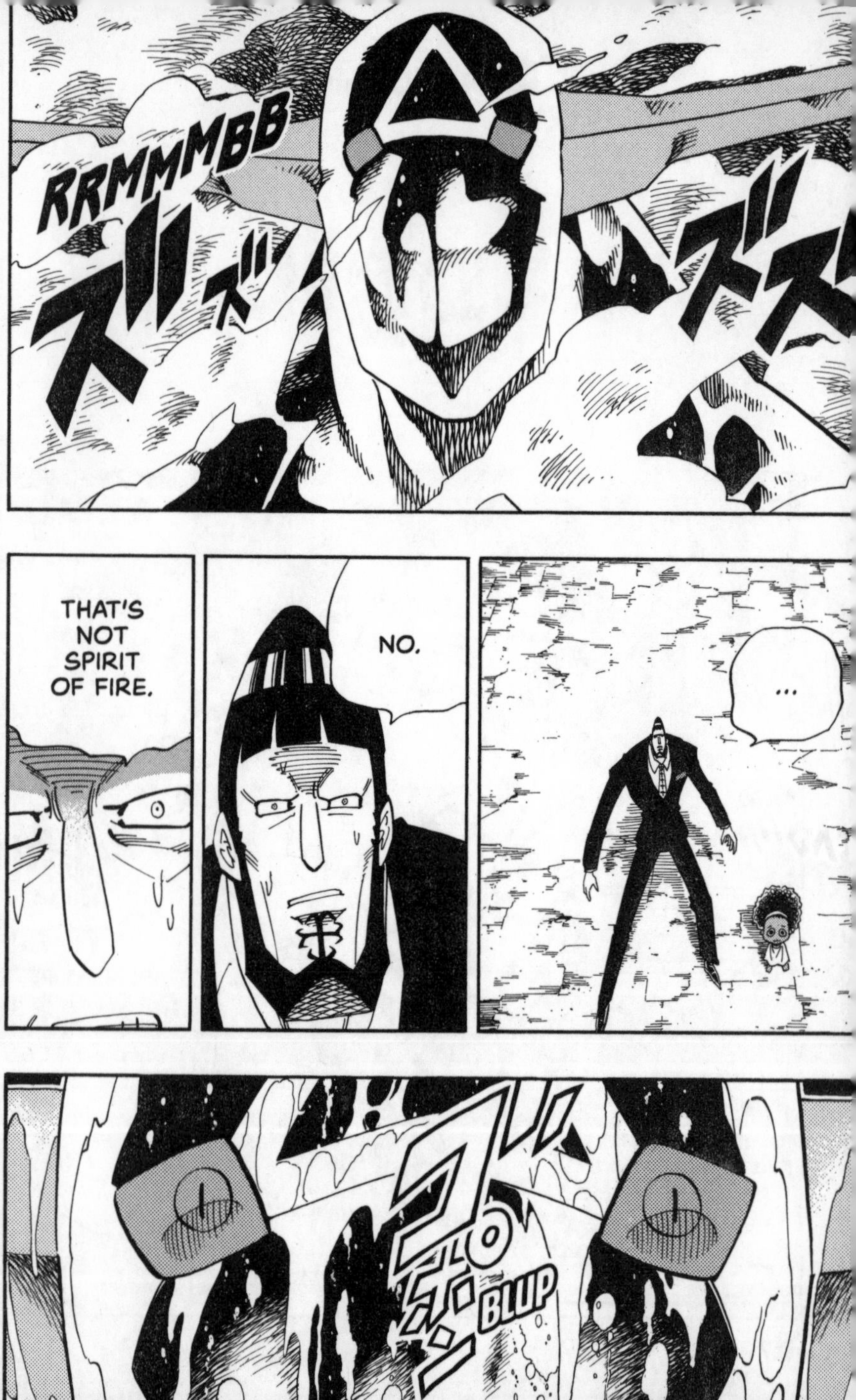

RRMMMBB
...
NO.
THAT'S NOT SPIRIT OF FIRE.
BLUP

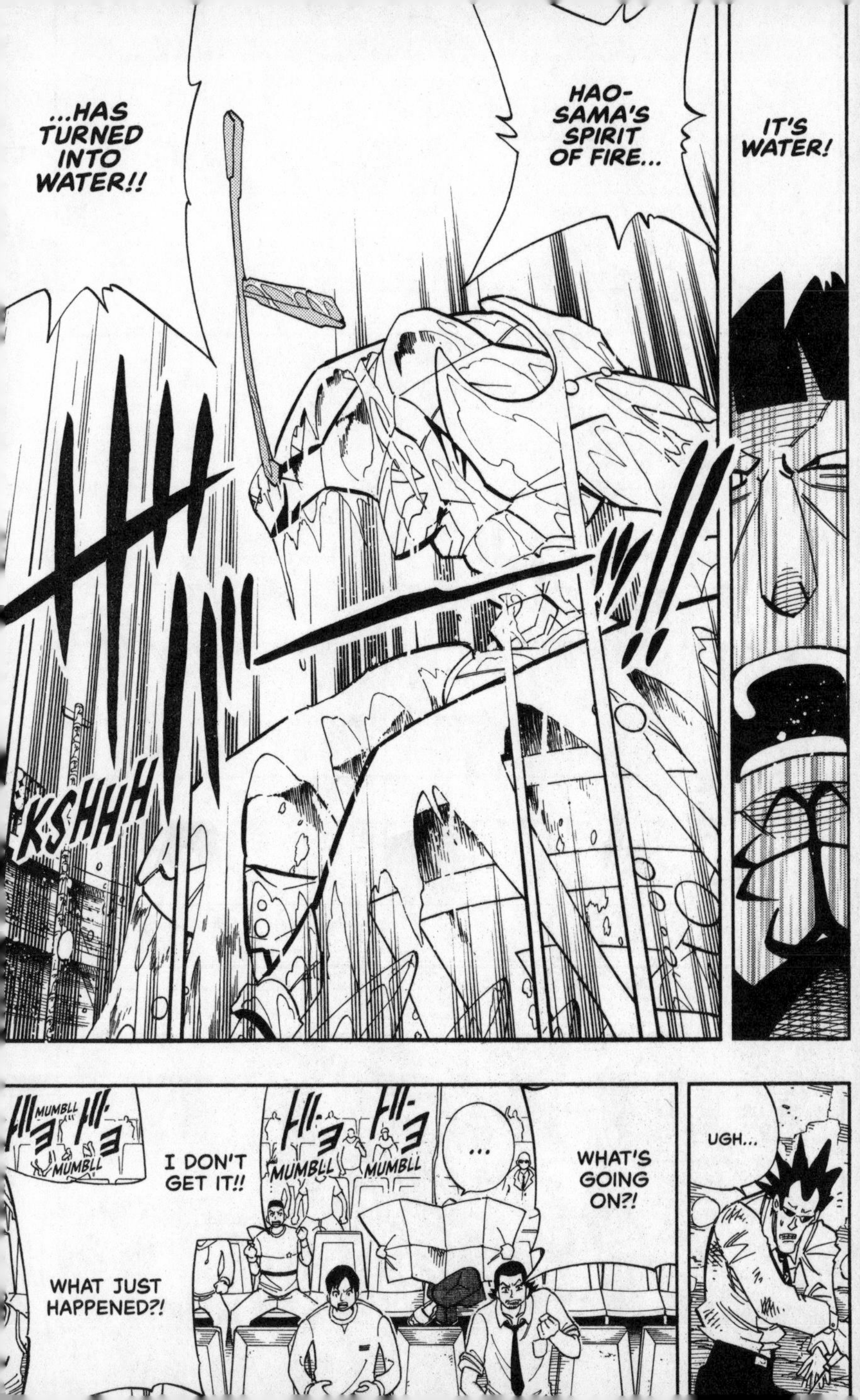
IT'S WATER!
HAO-SAMA'S SPIRIT OF FIRE...
...HAS TURNED INTO WATER!!
KSHHH
UGH...
WHAT'S GOING ON?!
...
MUMBLL
MUMBLL
I DON'T GET IT!!
MUMBLL
MUMBLL
WHAT JUST HAPPENED?!

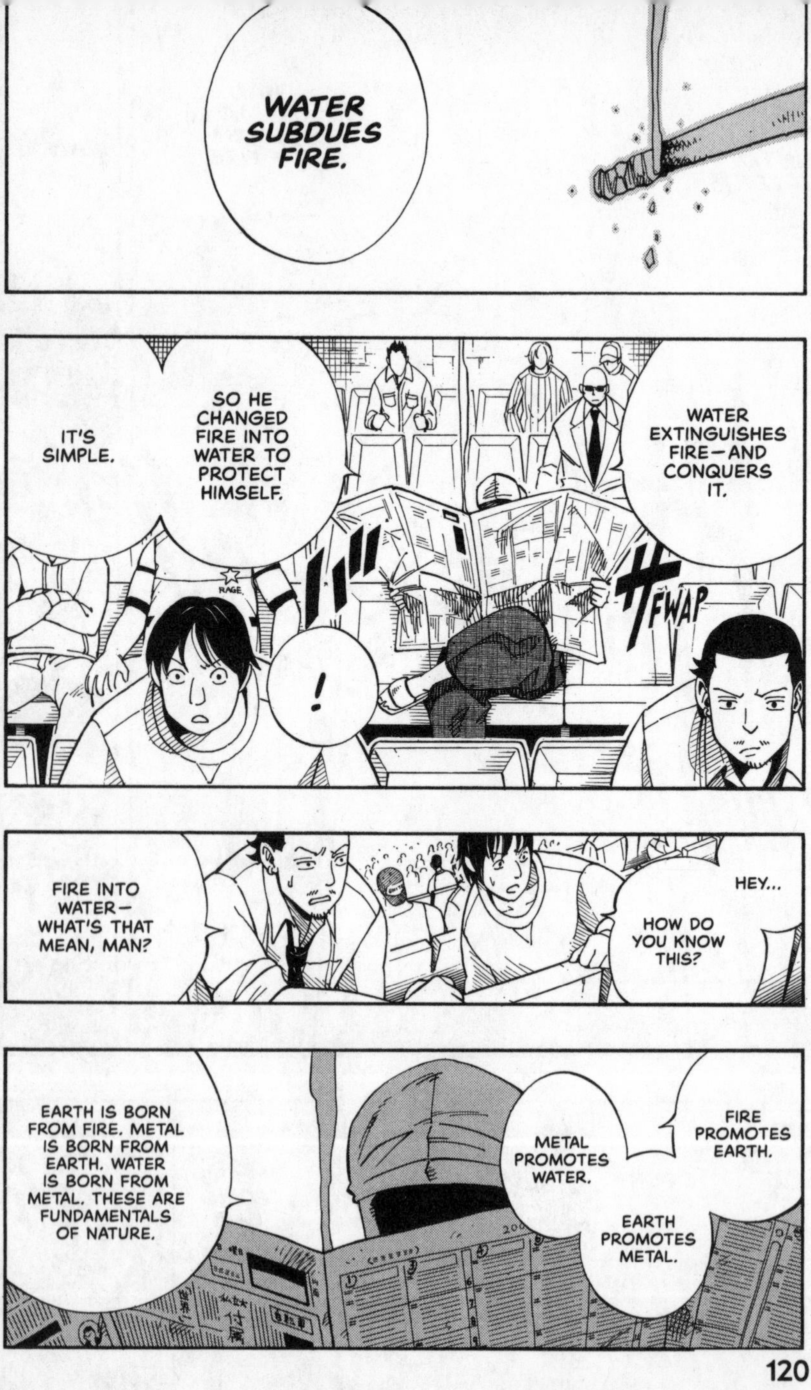

WATER SUBDUES FIRE.
WATER EXTINGUISHES FIRE—AND CONQUERS IT.
SO HE CHANGED FIRE INTO WATER TO PROTECT HIMSELF.
IT'S SIMPLE.
FWAP
!
RAGE
HEY...
HOW DO YOU KNOW THIS?
FIRE INTO WATER—WHAT'S THAT MEAN, MAN?
FIRE PROMOTES EARTH.
METAL PROMOTES WATER.
EARTH PROMOTES METAL.
EARTH IS BORN FROM FIRE. METAL IS BORN FROM EARTH. WATER IS BORN FROM METAL. THESE ARE FUNDAMENTALS OF NATURE.

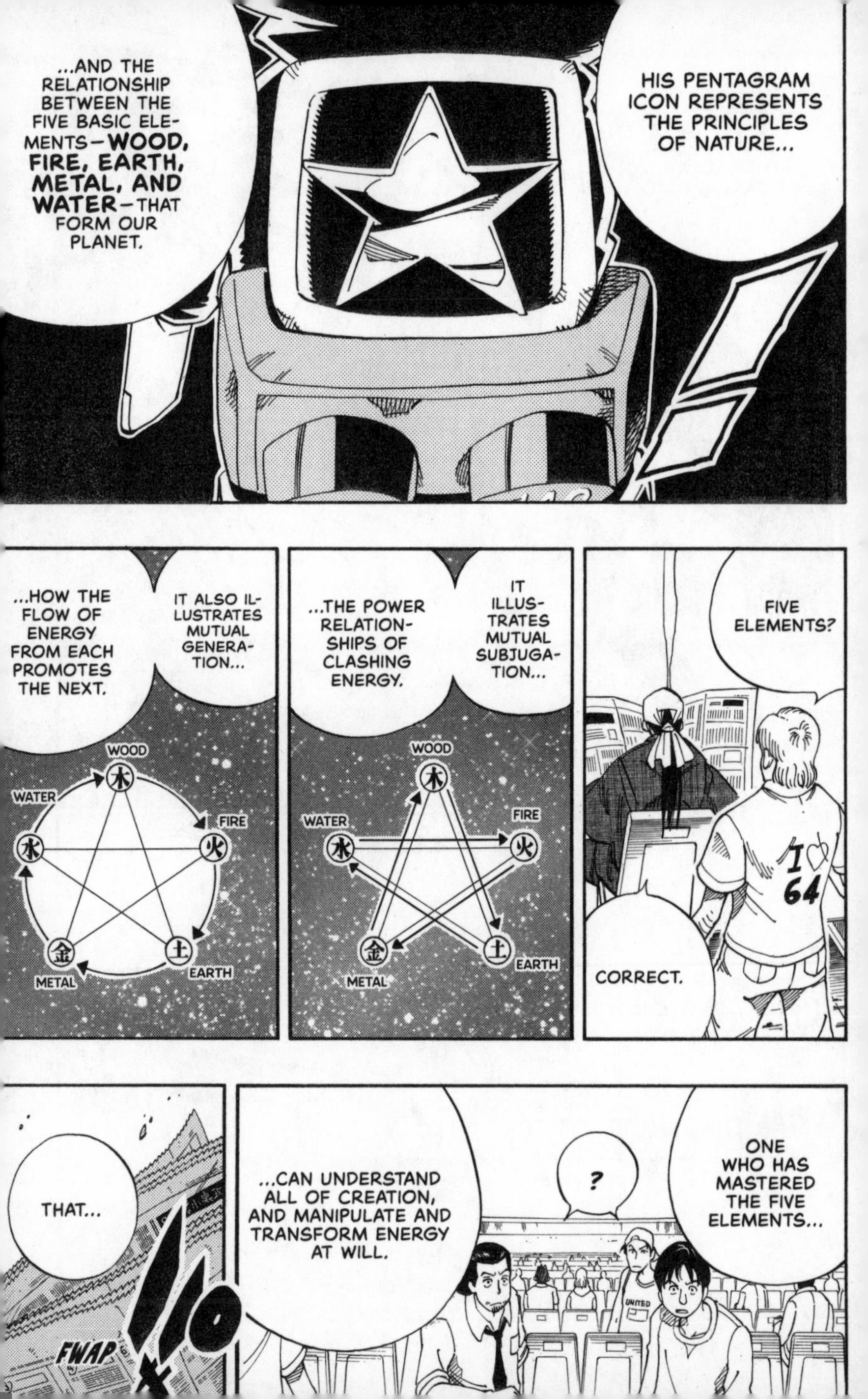

HIS PENTAGRAM ICON REPRESENTS THE PRINCIPLES OF NATURE...
...AND THE RELATIONSHIP BETWEEN THE FIVE BASIC ELEMENTS—**WOOD, FIRE, EARTH, METAL, AND WATER**—THAT FORM OUR PLANET.
FIVE ELEMENTS?
I ♡ 64
CORRECT.
IT ILLUSTRATES MUTUAL SUBJUGATION...
...THE POWER RELATIONSHIPS OF CLASHING ENERGY.
WOOD
木
FIRE
火
WATER
水
EARTH
土
METAL
金
IT ALSO ILLUSTRATES MUTUAL GENERATION...
...HOW THE FLOW OF ENERGY FROM EACH PROMOTES THE NEXT.
WOOD
木
WATER
水
FIRE
火
METAL
金
EARTH
土
ONE WHO HAS MASTERED THE FIVE ELEMENTS...
?
UNITED
...CAN UNDERSTAND ALL OF CREATION, AND MANIPULATE AND TRANSFORM ENERGY AT WILL.
THAT...
FWAP

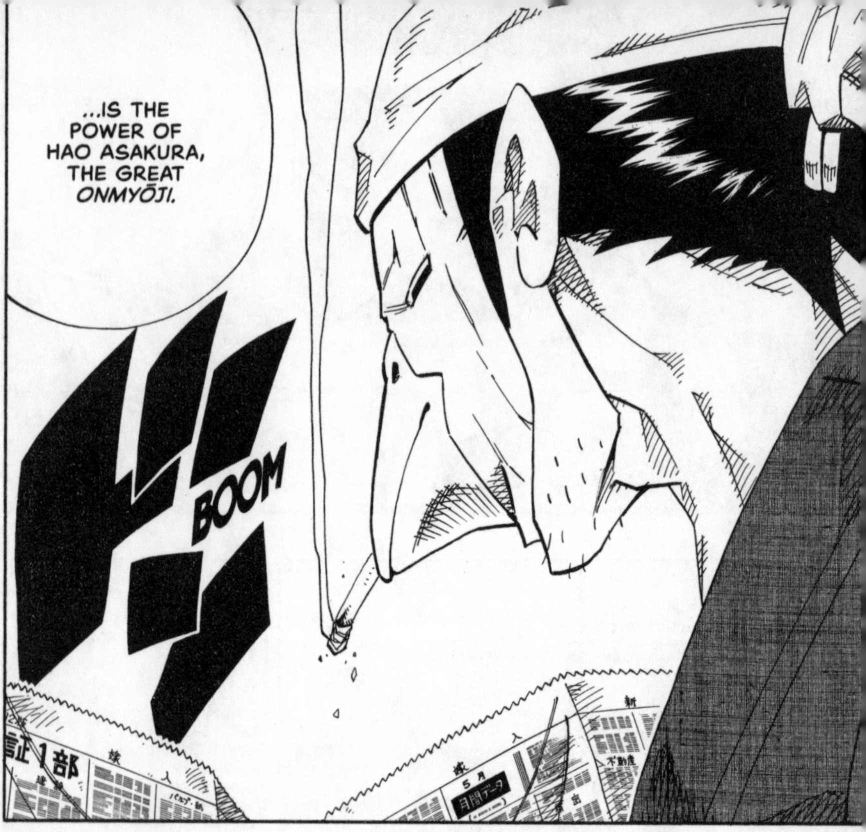
...IS THE POWER OF HAO ASAKURA, THE GREAT *ONMYŌJI.*
BOOM
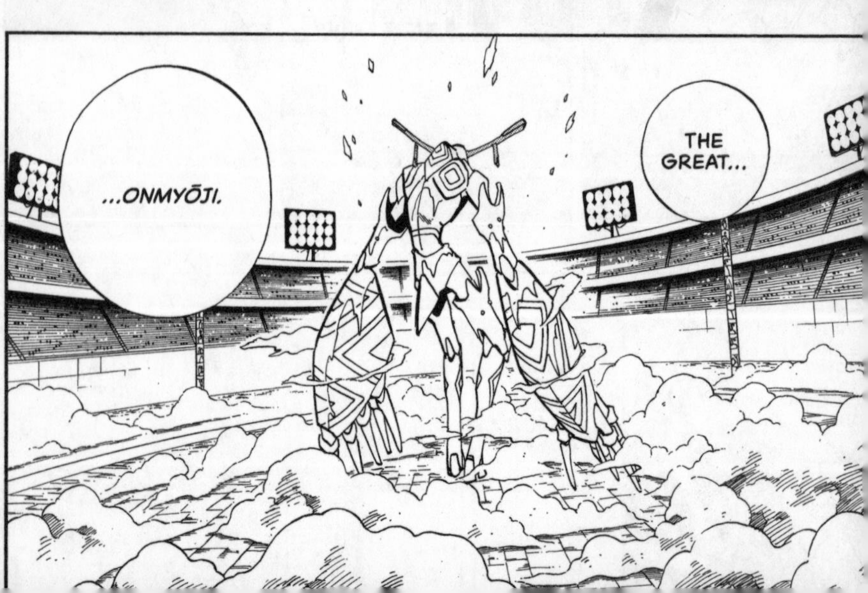
THE GREAT...
...ONMYŌJI.

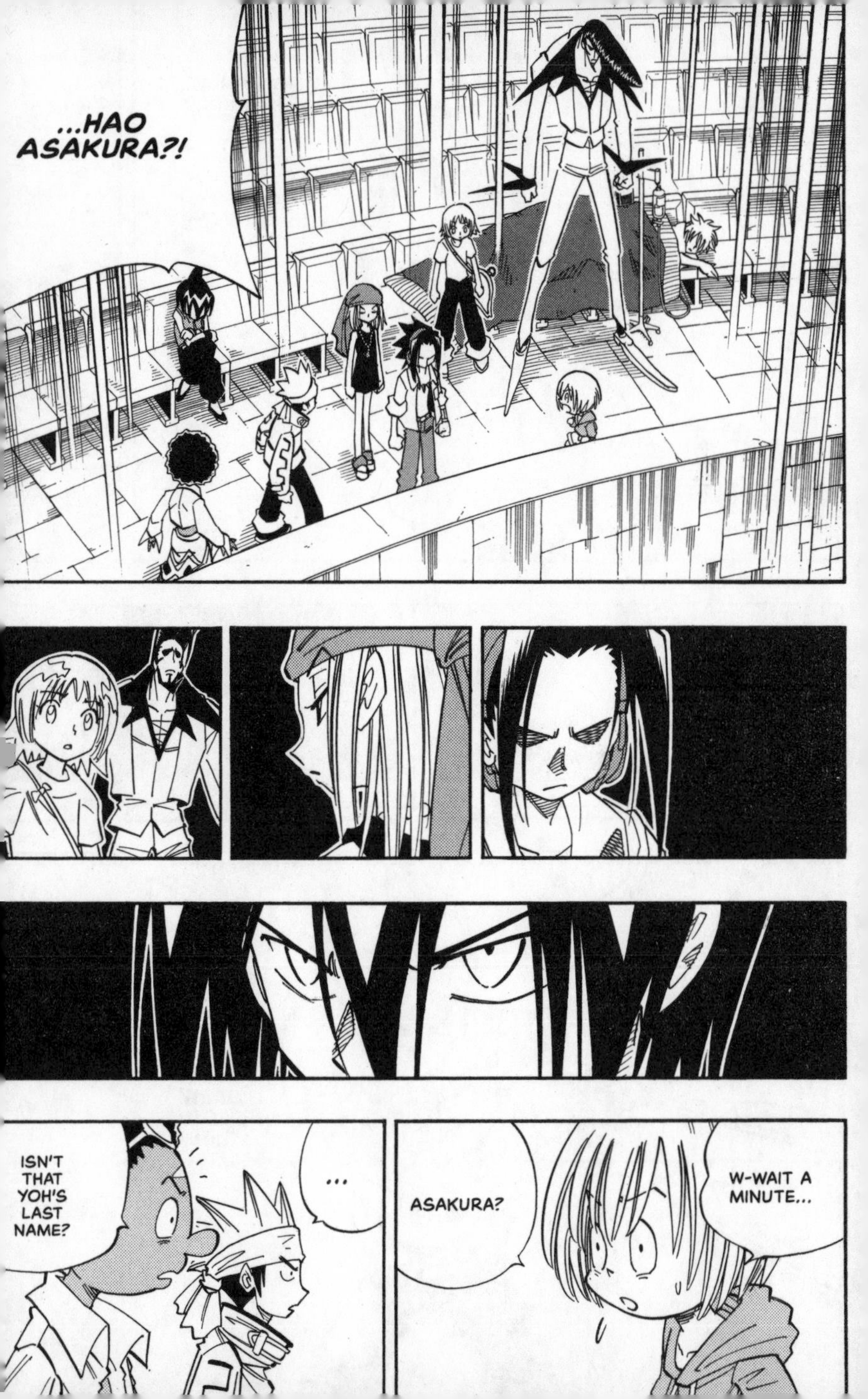
...HAO ASAKURA?!
W-WAIT A MINUTE...
ASAKURA?
...
ISN'T THAT YOH'S LAST NAME?

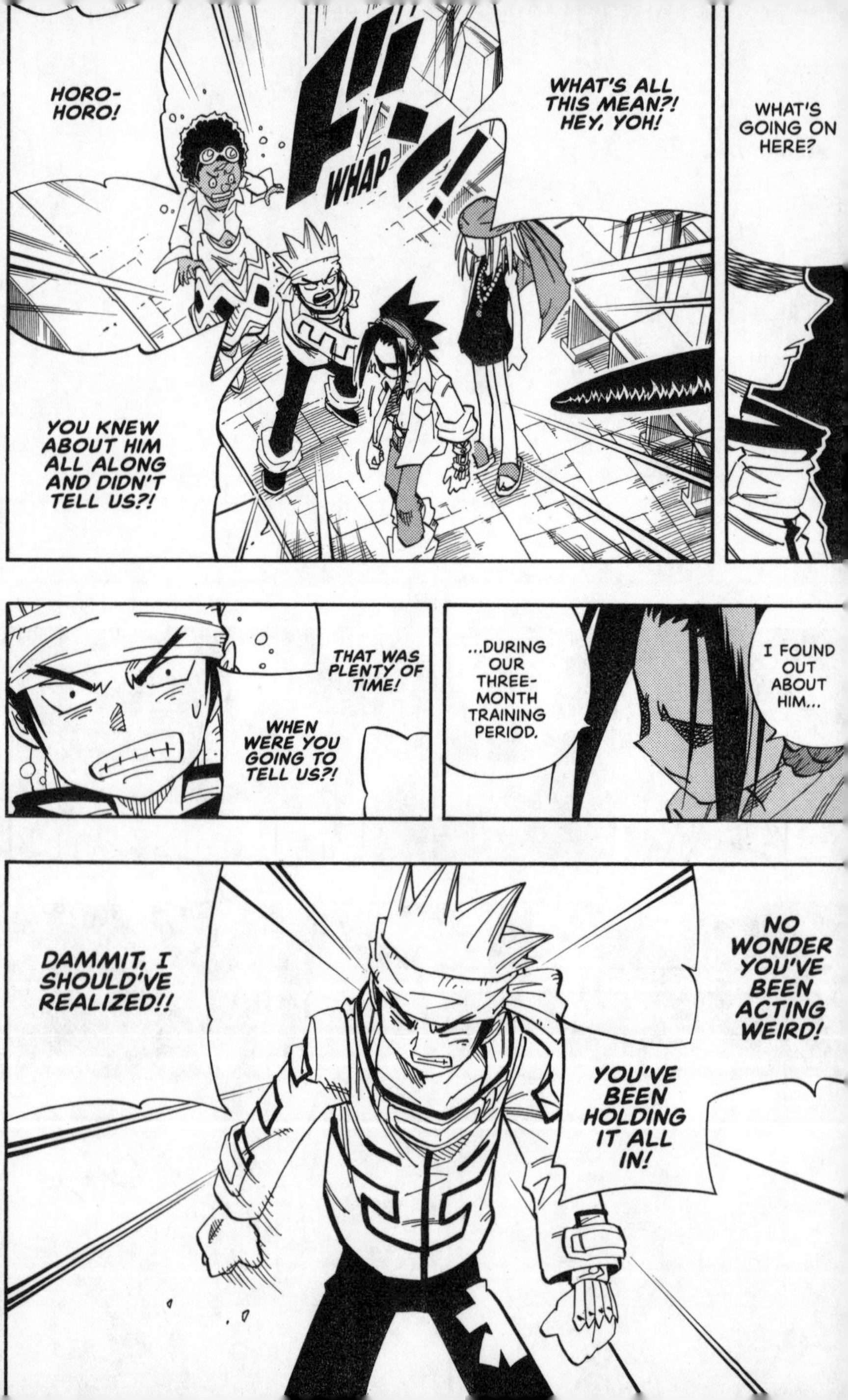
WHAT'S GOING ON HERE?
WHAT'S ALL THIS MEAN?! HEY, YOH!
WHAP
HORO-HORO!
YOU KNEW ABOUT HIM ALL ALONG AND DIDN'T TELL US?!
I FOUND OUT ABOUT HIM...
...DURING OUR THREE-MONTH TRAINING PERIOD.
THAT WAS PLENTY OF TIME!
WHEN WERE YOU GOING TO TELL US?!
NO WONDER YOU'VE BEEN ACTING WEIRD!
YOU'VE BEEN HOLDING IT ALL IN!
DAMMIT, I SHOULD'VE REALIZED!!

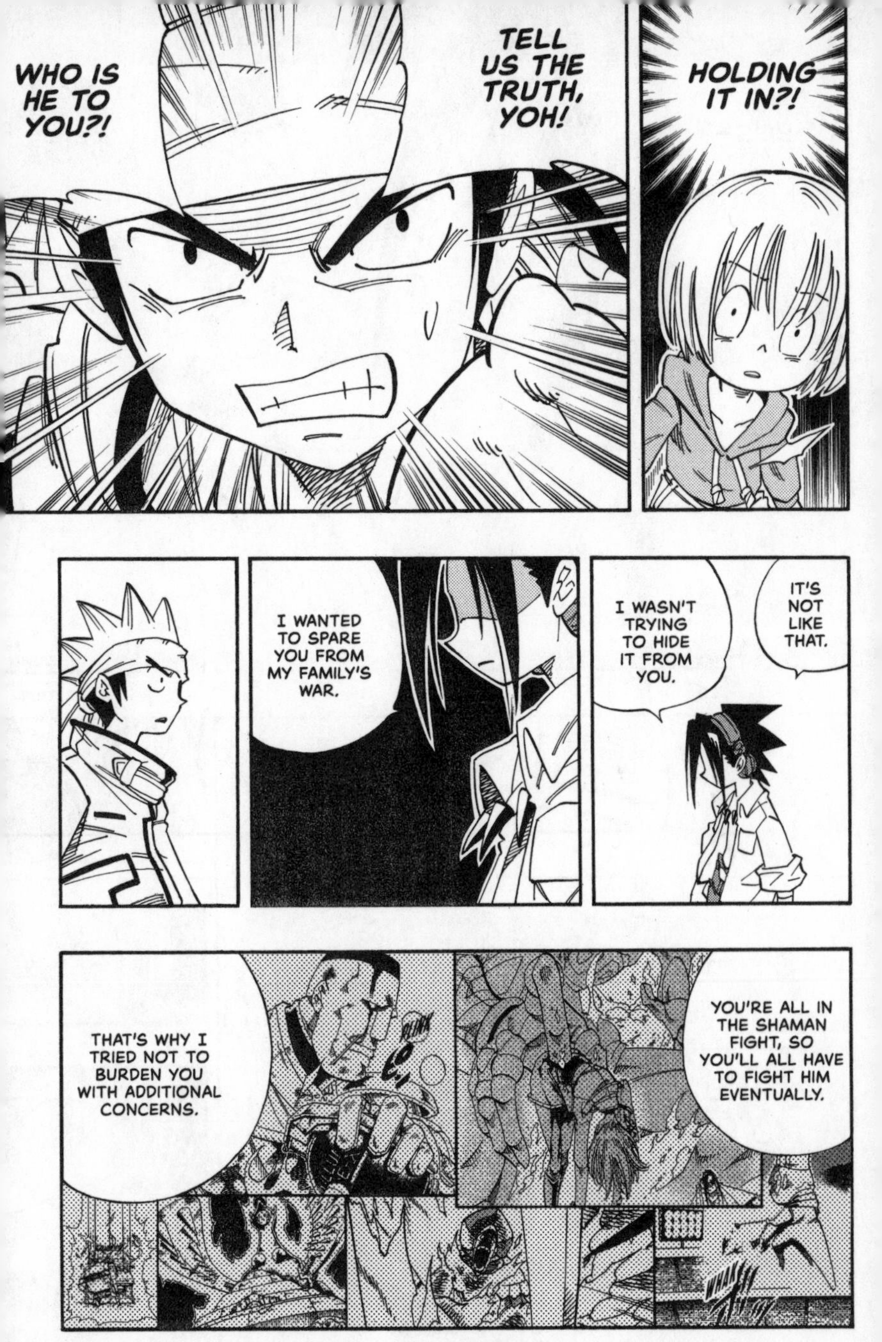
HOLDING IT IN?!
TELL US THE TRUTH, YOH!
WHO IS HE TO YOU?!
IT'S NOT LIKE THAT.
I WASN'T TRYING TO HIDE IT FROM YOU.
I WANTED TO SPARE YOU FROM MY FAMILY'S WAR.
YOU'RE ALL IN THE SHAMAN FIGHT, SO YOU'LL ALL HAVE TO FIGHT HIM EVENTUALLY.
THAT'S WHY I TRIED NOT TO BURDEN YOU WITH ADDITIONAL CONCERNS.

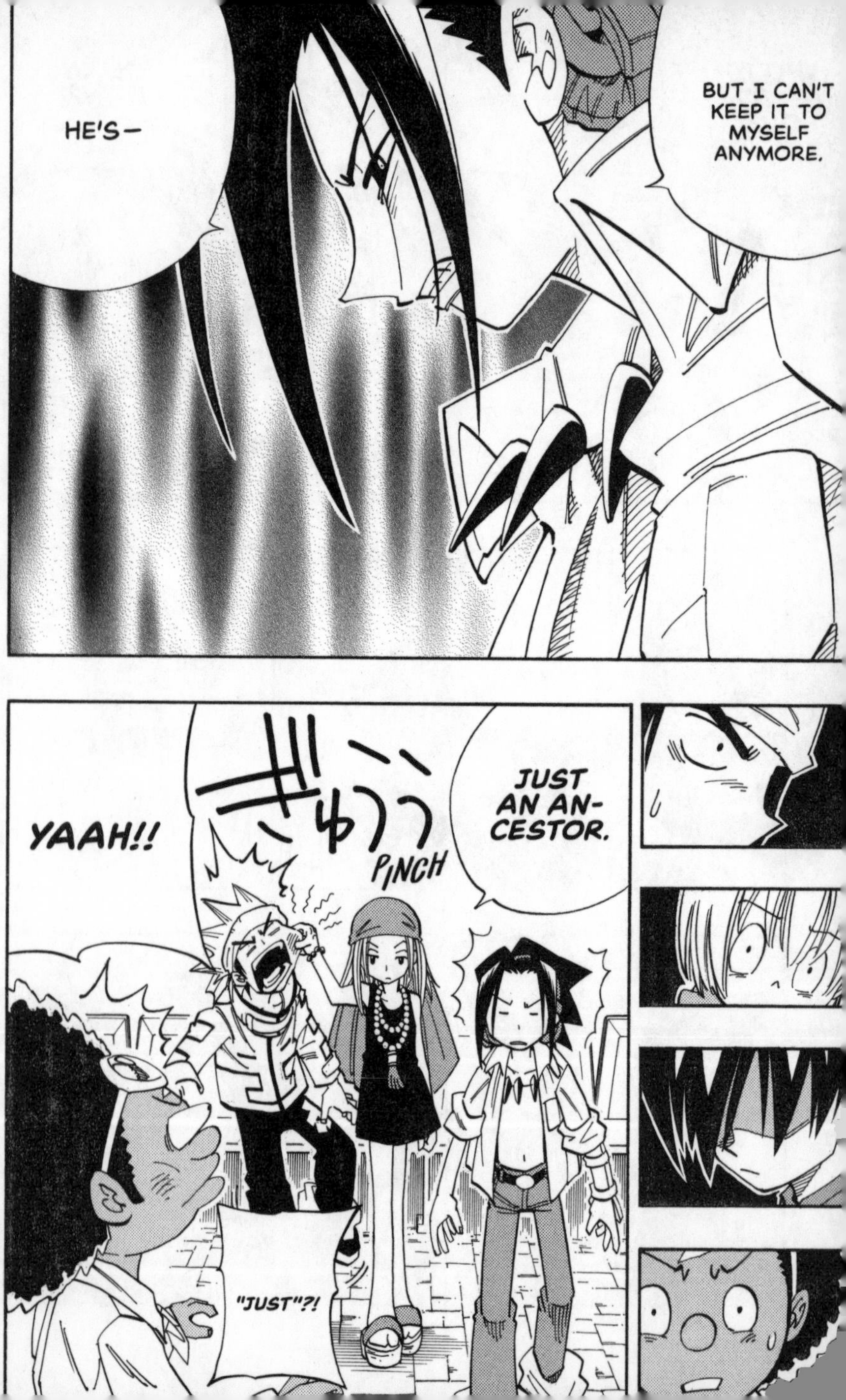
BUT I CAN'T KEEP IT TO MYSELF ANYMORE.
HE'S—
JUST AN AN-CESTOR.
ぎゅうう
PINCH
YAAH!!
"JUST"?!

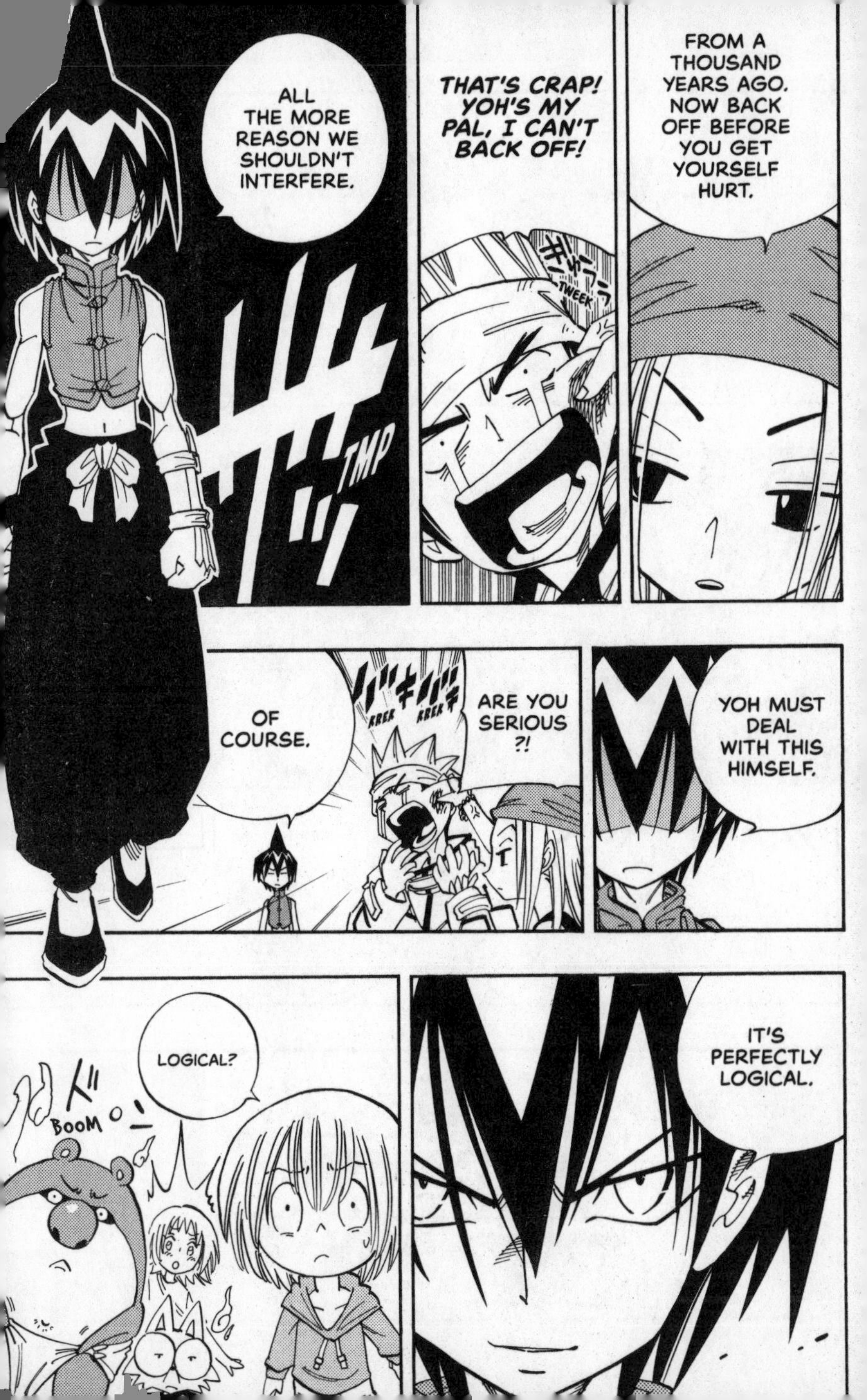
FROM A THOUSAND YEARS AGO. NOW BACK OFF BEFORE YOU GET YOURSELF HURT.
TWEEK
THAT'S CRAP! YOH'S MY PAL, I CAN'T BACK OFF!
ALL THE MORE REASON WE SHOULDN'T INTERFERE.
TMP
YOH MUST DEAL WITH THIS HIMSELF.
KREEK KREEK
ARE YOU SERIOUS ?!
OF COURSE.
IT'S PERFECTLY LOGICAL.
LOGICAL?
BOOM

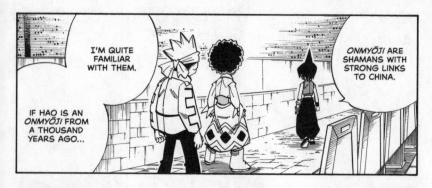

ONMYŌJI ARE SHAMANS WITH STRONG LINKS TO CHINA.
I'M QUITE FAMILIAR WITH THEM.
IF HAO IS AN ONMYŌJI FROM A THOUSAND YEARS AGO...
...THEN THE MAN LILIRARA SHOWED US FROM 500 YEARS AGO...
...WAS HAO, AS WELL.
?
WHAT?!
THIS IS A 1,000-YEAR JOURNEY OF THE SOUL.
NOW HE HAS RETURNED TO EARTH ONCE MORE...
...TO OBTAIN THE MOST POWERFUL SPIRIT ALLY AND BECOME THE SHAMAN KING.

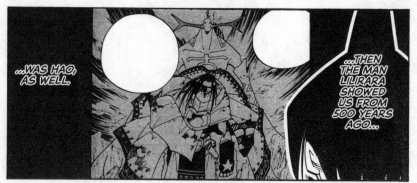

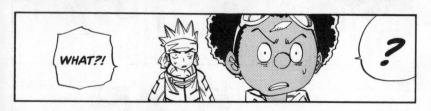

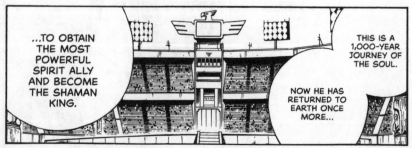

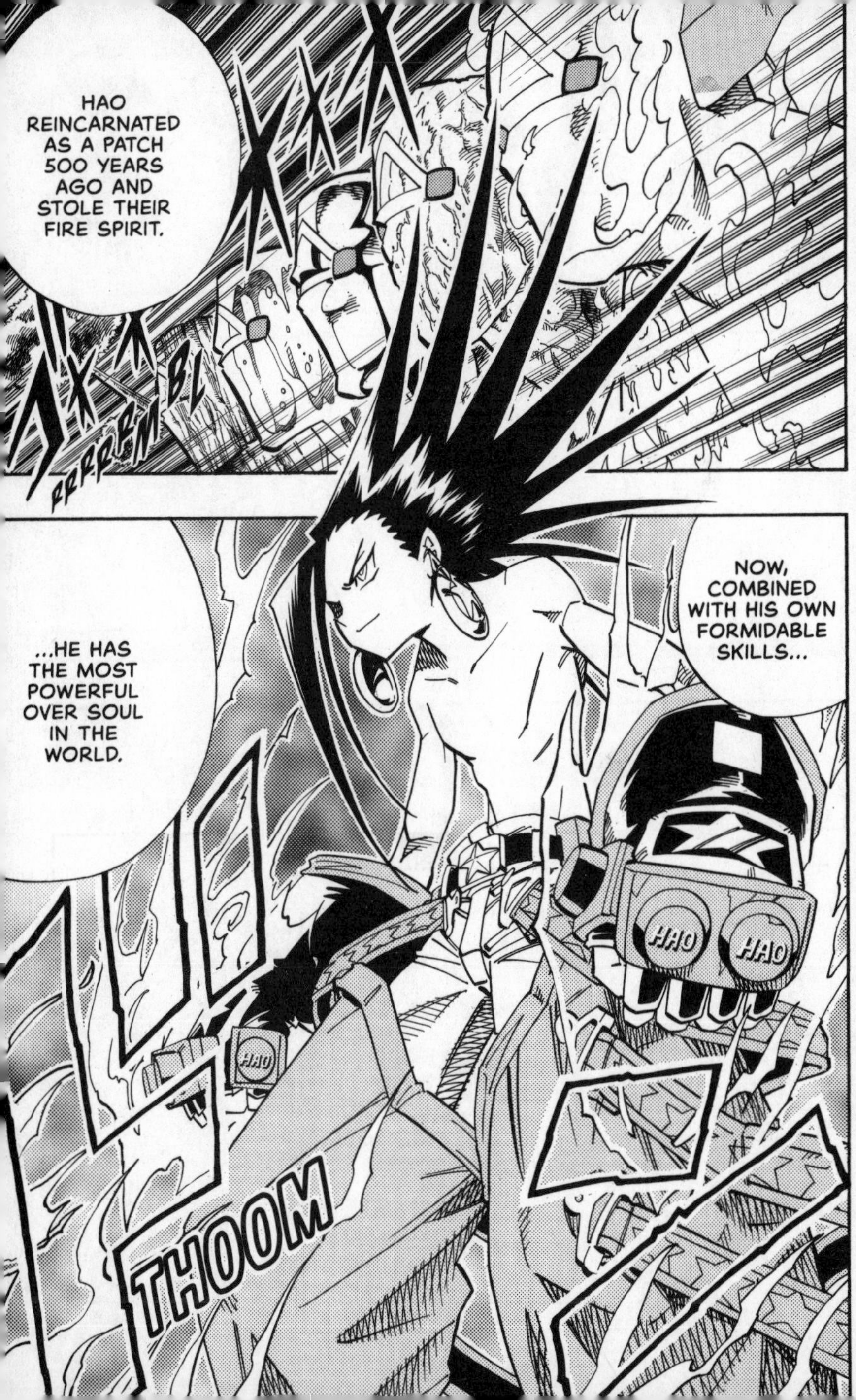
HAO REINCARNATED AS A PATCH 500 YEARS AGO AND STOLE THEIR FIRE SPIRIT.
RRRRRMBL
NOW, COMBINED WITH HIS OWN FORMIDABLE SKILLS...
...HE HAS THE MOST POWERFUL OVER SOUL IN THE WORLD.
HAO
HAO
HAO
THOOM

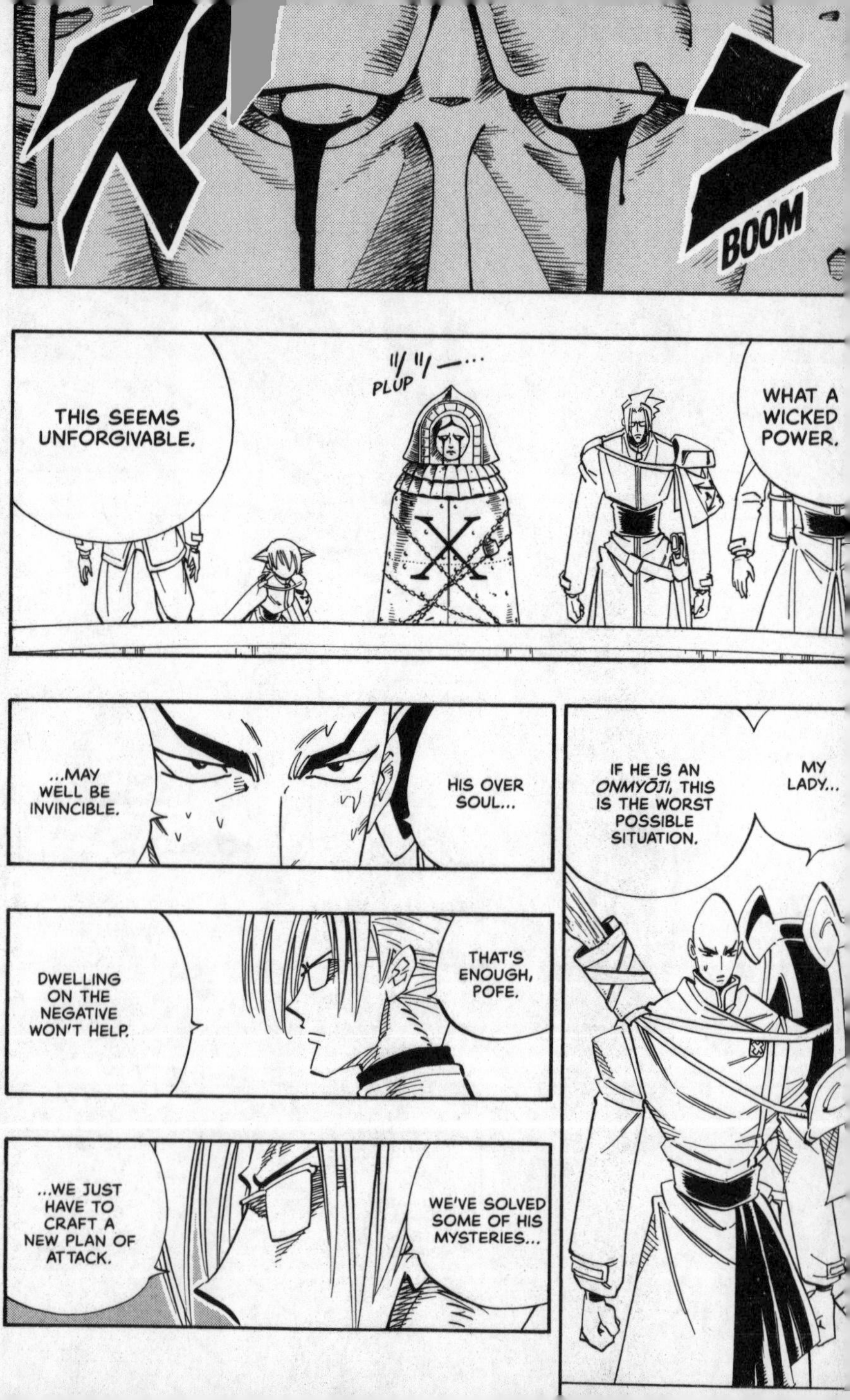
BOOM
WHAT A WICKED POWER.
PLUP
THIS SEEMS UNFORGIVABLE.
MY LADY...
IF HE IS AN ONMYŌJI, THIS IS THE WORST POSSIBLE SITUATION.
HIS OVER SOUL...
...MAY WELL BE INVINCIBLE.
THAT'S ENOUGH, POFE.
DWELLING ON THE NEGATIVE WON'T HELP.
WE'VE SOLVED SOME OF HIS MYSTERIES...
...WE JUST HAVE TO CRAFT A NEW PLAN OF ATTACK.

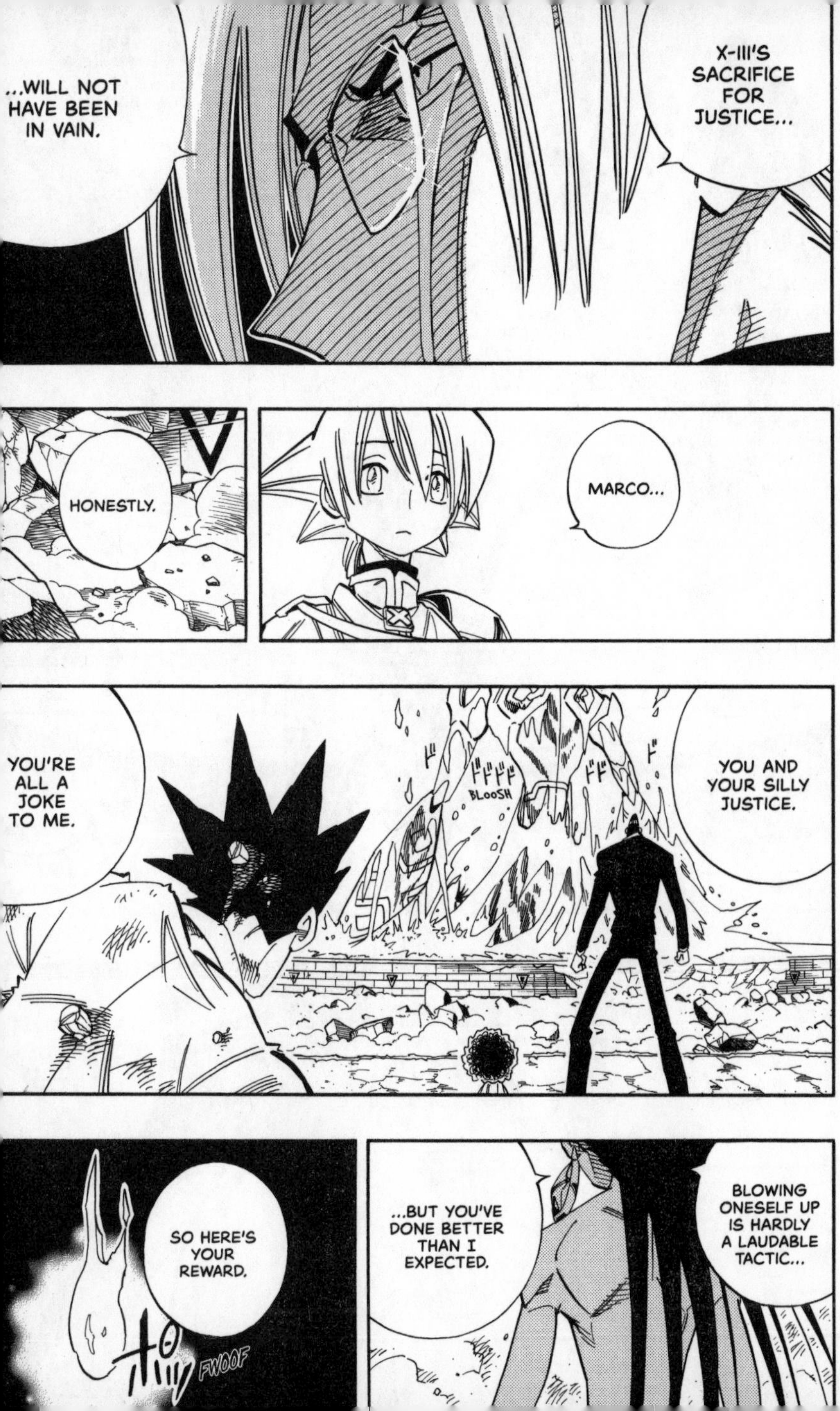
X-III'S SACRIFICE FOR JUSTICE...
...WILL NOT HAVE BEEN IN VAIN.
MARCO...
HONESTLY.
YOU AND YOUR SILLY JUSTICE.
ドドドド
BLOOSH
ドド
ド
YOU'RE ALL A JOKE TO ME.
BLOWING ONESELF UP IS HARDLY A LAUDABLE TACTIC...
...BUT YOU'VE DONE BETTER THAN I EXPECTED.
SO HERE'S YOUR REWARD.
FWOOF

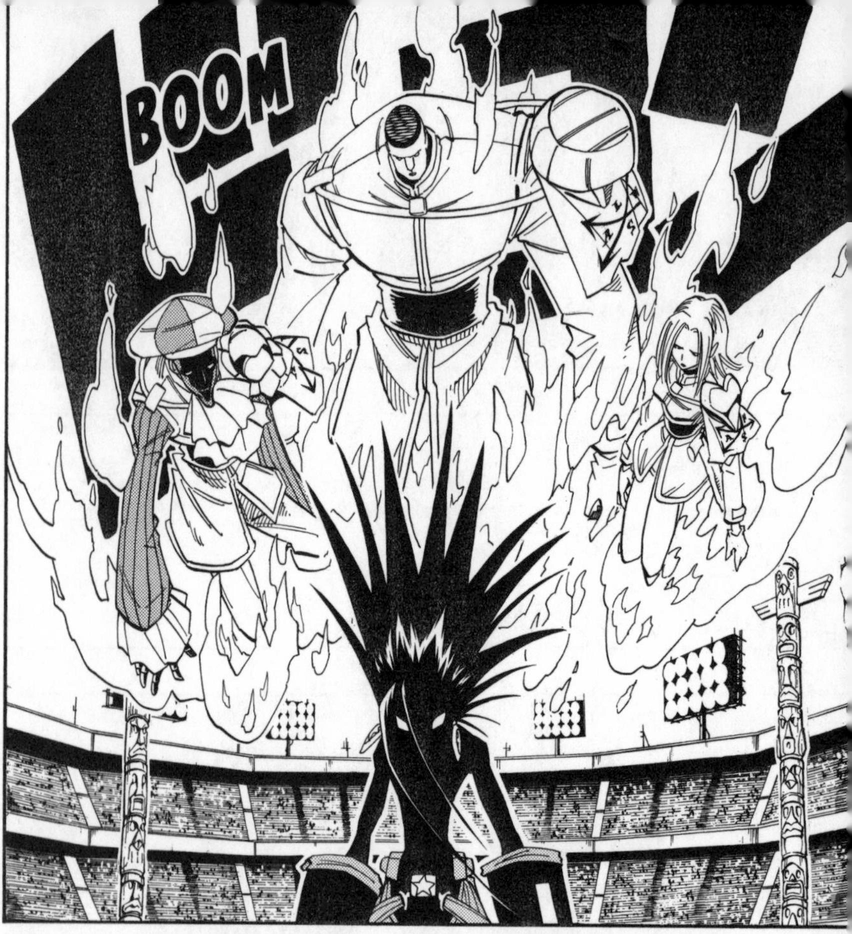
BOOM
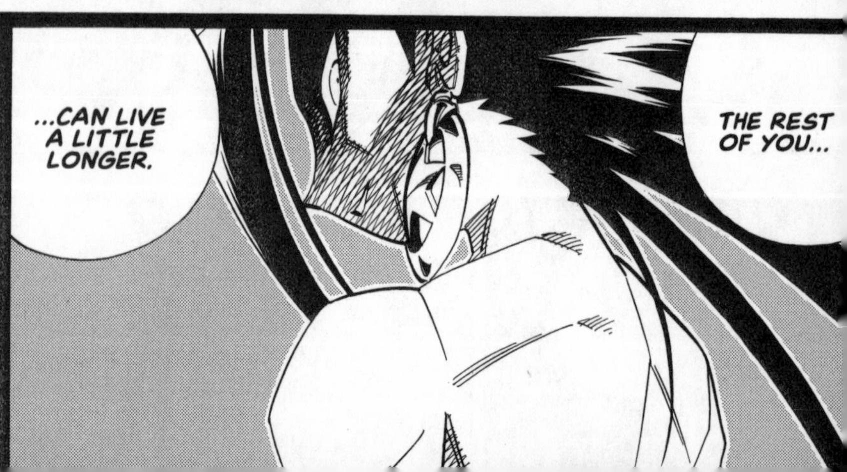
THE REST OF YOU...
...CAN LIVE A LITTLE LONGER.

SHAMAN KING ITEM FILE No.48

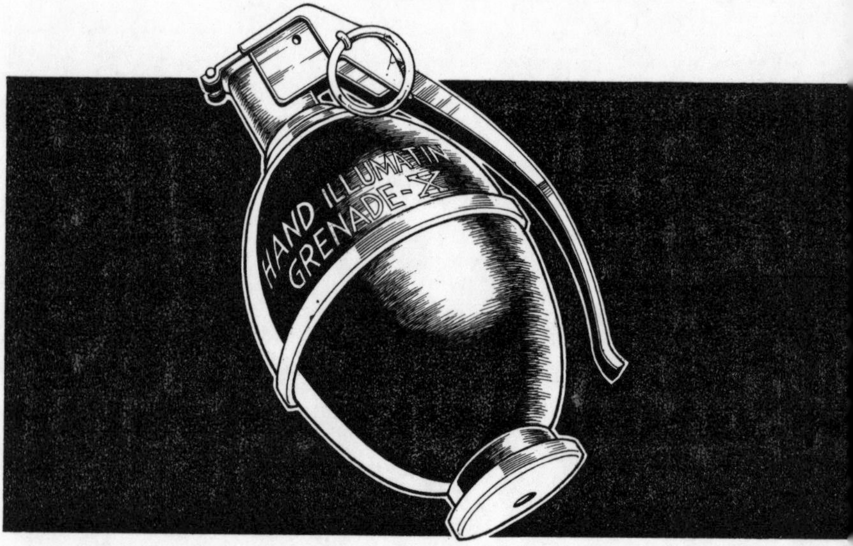
HAND ILLUMATIN
GRENADE-X

Modified Hand Grenade X

Chapter 141: He's My...

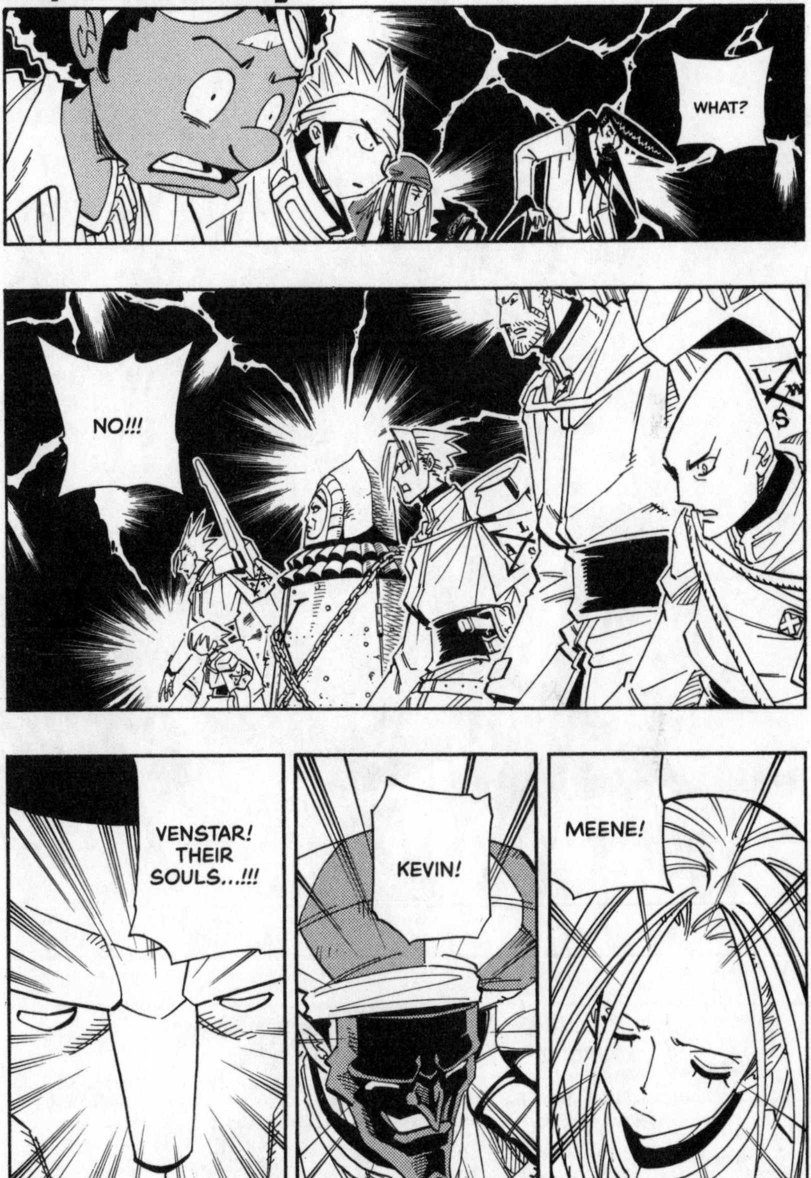

WHAT?
NO!!!
MEENE!
KEVIN!
VENSTAR! THEIR SOULS...!!!

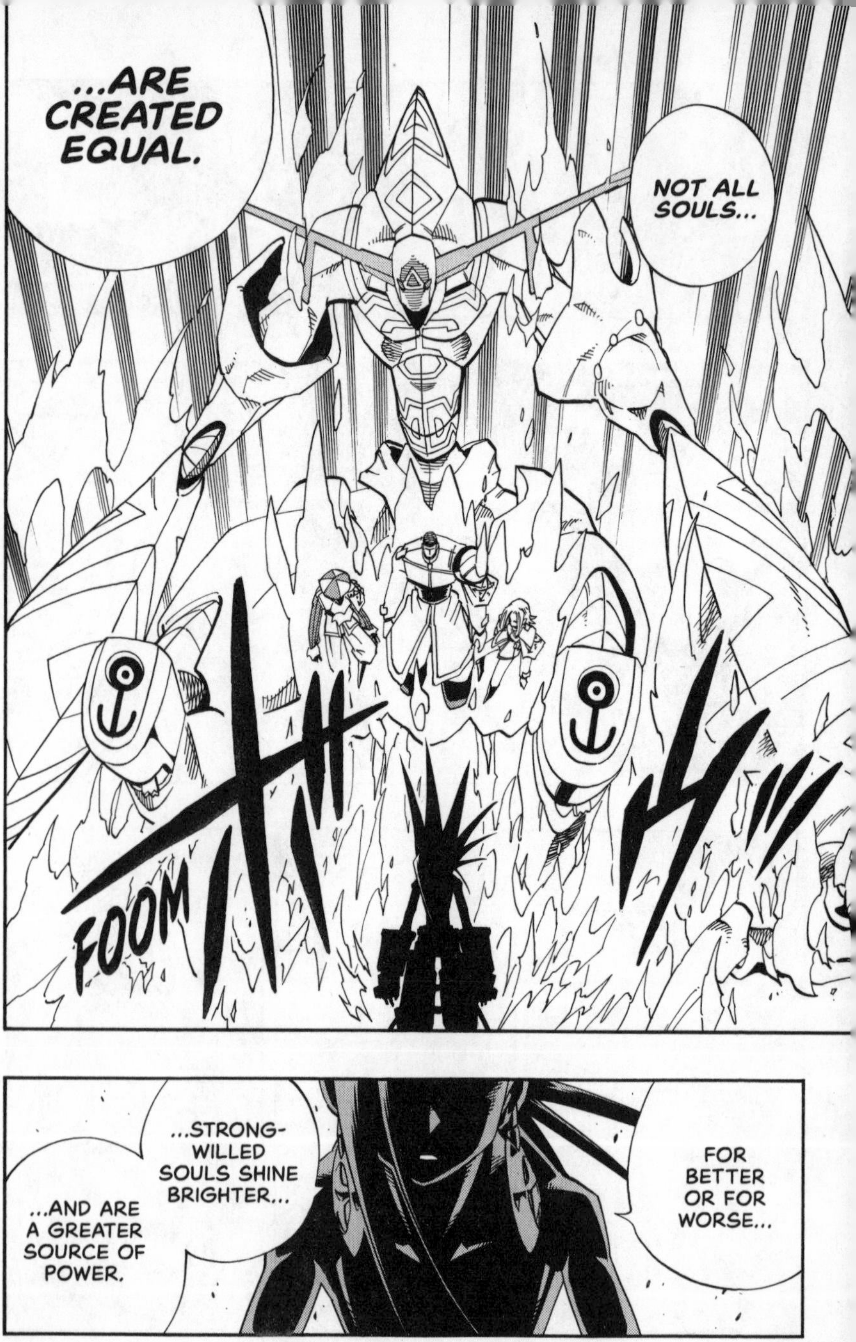
NOT ALL SOULS...
...ARE CREATED EQUAL.
FOOM
FOR BETTER OR FOR WORSE...
...STRONG-WILLED SOULS SHINE BRIGHTER...
...AND ARE A GREATER SOURCE OF POWER.

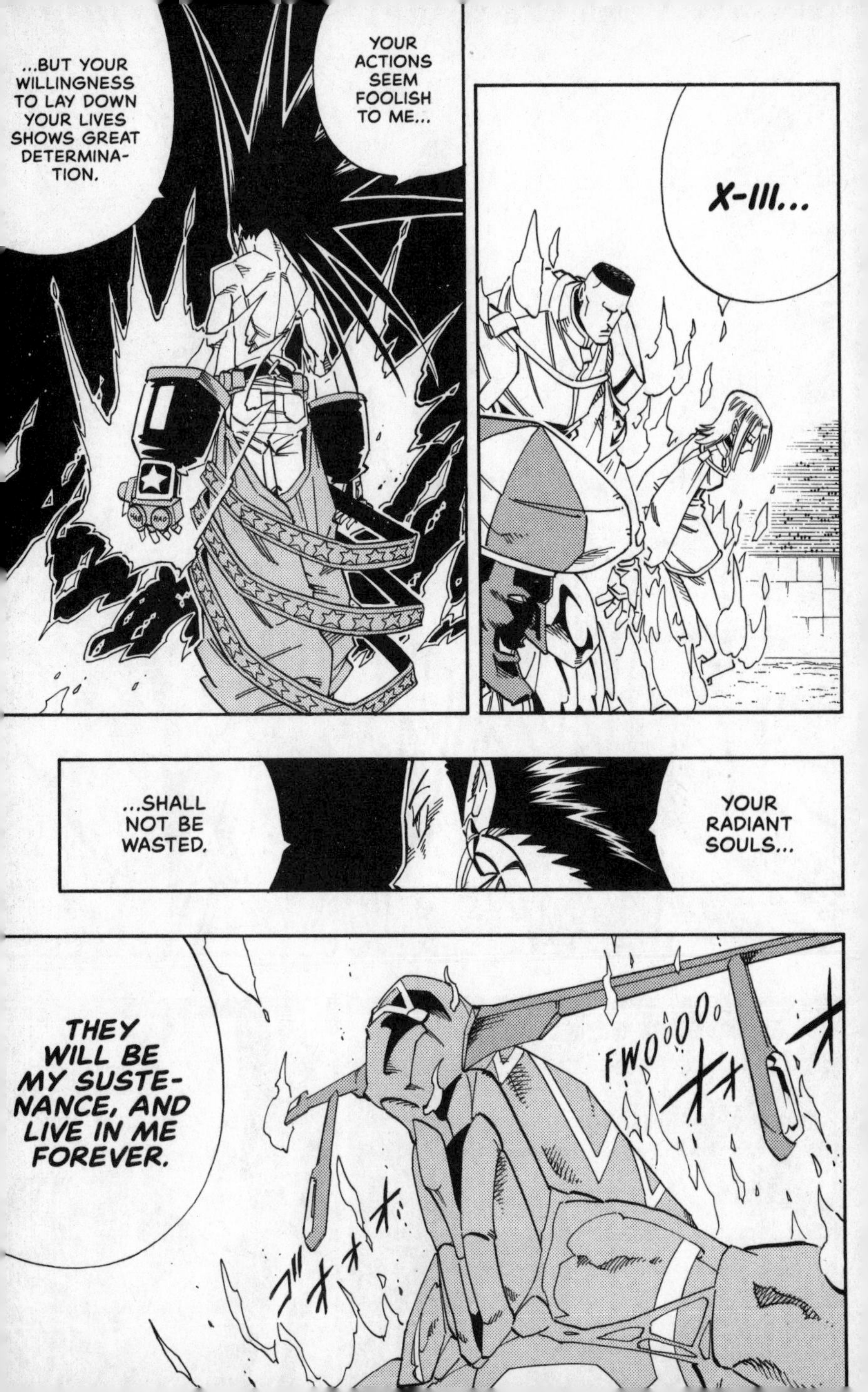
X-III...
YOUR ACTIONS SEEM FOOLISH TO ME...
...BUT YOUR WILLINGNESS TO LAY DOWN YOUR LIVES SHOWS GREAT DETERMINA-TION.
YOUR RADIANT SOULS...
...SHALL NOT BE WASTED.
FWOOOOO
THEY WILL BE MY SUSTE-NANCE, AND LIVE IN ME FOREVER.

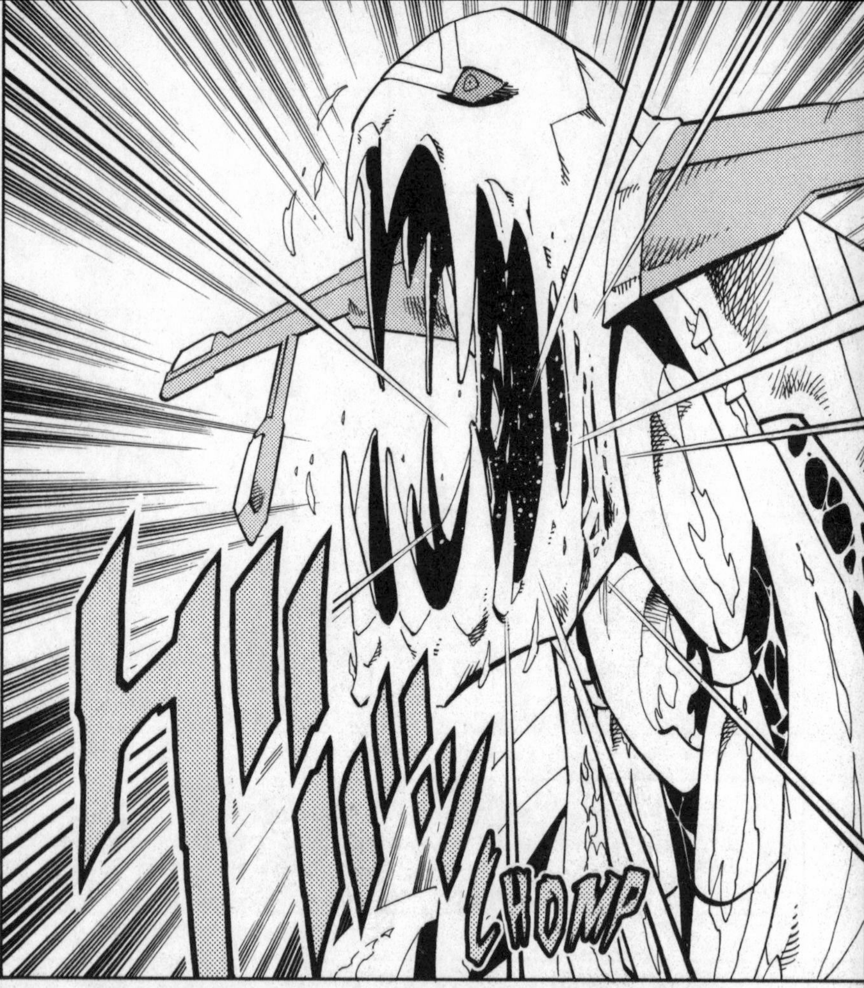
CHOMP
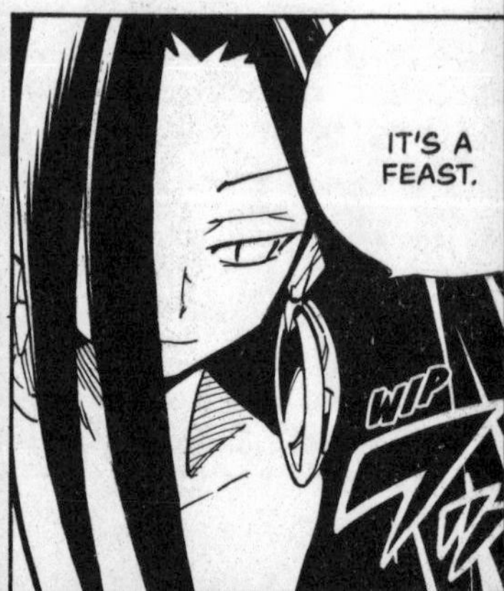
IT'S A FEAST.
WIP
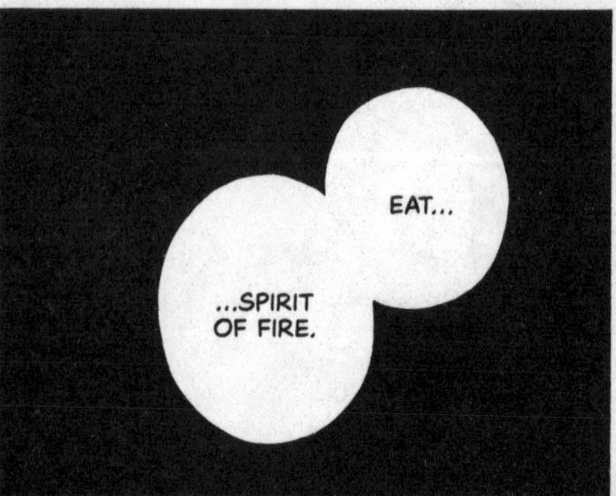
EAT...
...SPIRIT OF FIRE.

Chapter 141:

He's My...

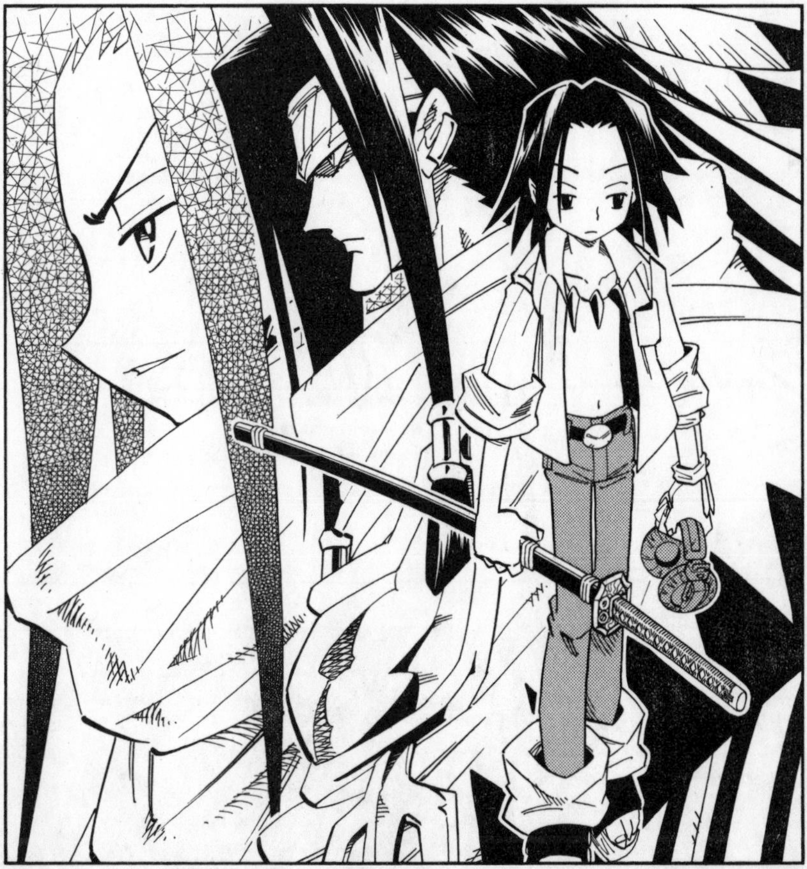

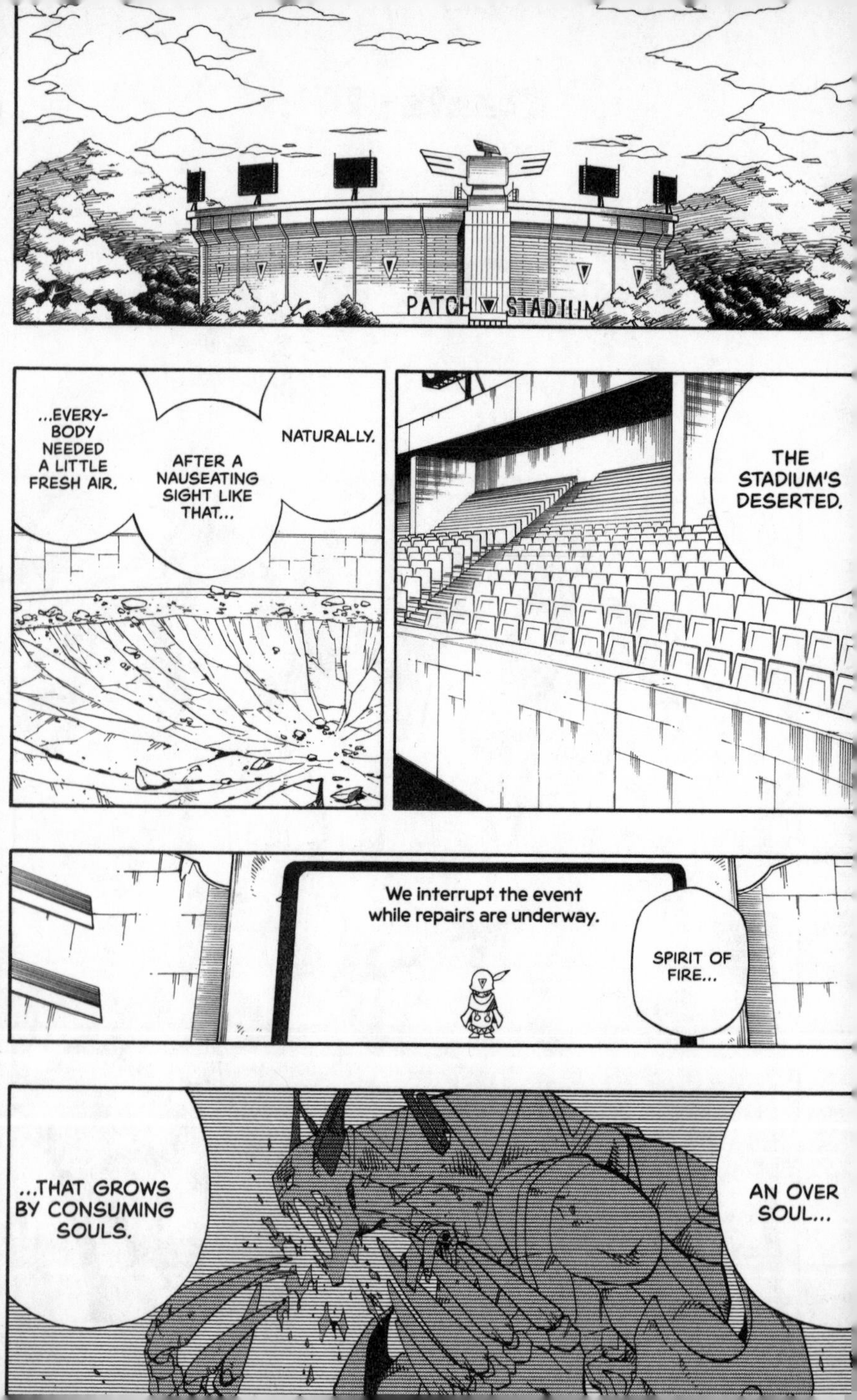
PATCH ▼ STADIUM
THE STADIUM'S DESERTED.
NATURALLY.
AFTER A NAUSEATING SIGHT LIKE THAT...
...EVERY-BODY NEEDED A LITTLE FRESH AIR.
We interrupt the event while repairs are underway.
SPIRIT OF FIRE...
AN OVER SOUL...
...THAT GROWS BY CONSUMING SOULS.

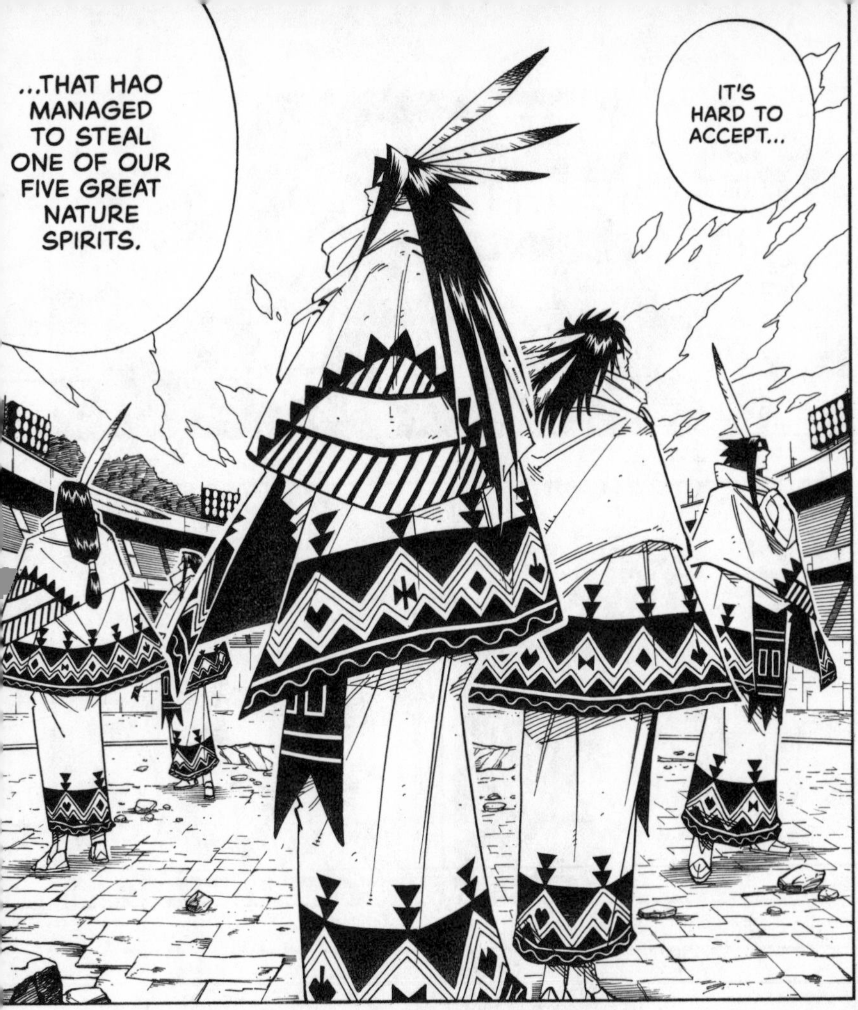
IT'S HARD TO ACCEPT...
...THAT HAO MANAGED TO STEAL ONE OF OUR FIVE GREAT NATURE SPIRITS.

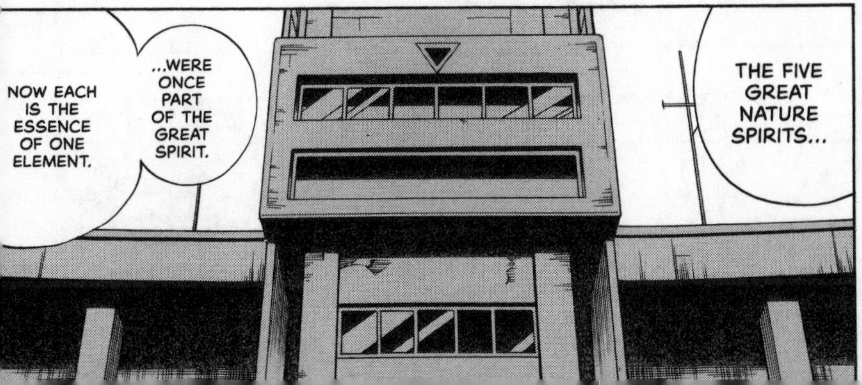
THE FIVE GREAT NATURE SPIRITS...
...WERE ONCE PART OF THE GREAT SPIRIT.
NOW EACH IS THE ESSENCE OF ONE ELEMENT.

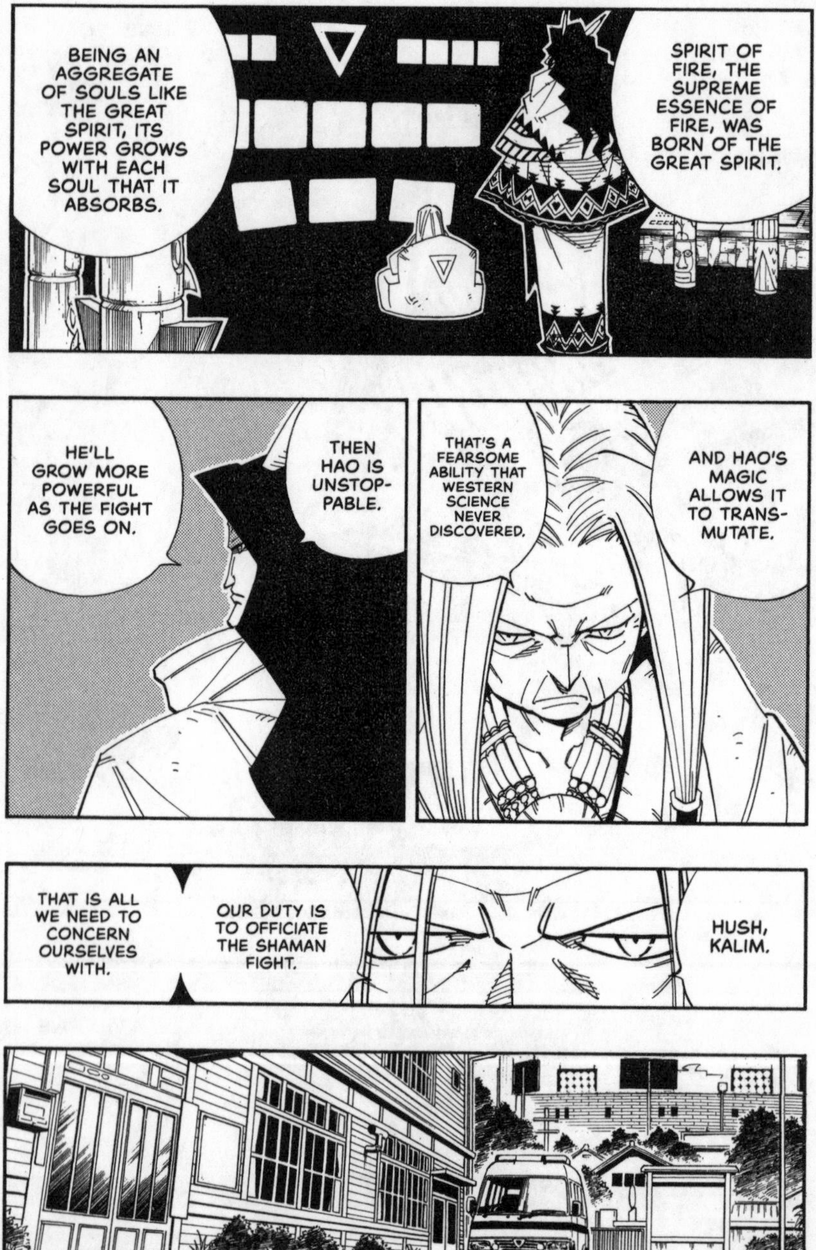
SPIRIT OF FIRE, THE SUPREME ESSENCE OF FIRE, WAS BORN OF THE GREAT SPIRIT.
BEING AN AGGREGATE OF SOULS LIKE THE GREAT SPIRIT, ITS POWER GROWS WITH EACH SOUL THAT IT ABSORBS.
AND HAO'S MAGIC ALLOWS IT TO TRANS-MUTATE.
THAT'S A FEARSOME ABILITY THAT WESTERN SCIENCE NEVER DISCOVERED.
THEN HAO IS UNSTOP-PABLE.
HE'LL GROW MORE POWERFUL AS THE FIGHT GOES ON.
HUSH, KALIM.
OUR DUTY IS TO OFFICIATE THE SHAMAN FIGHT.
THAT IS ALL WE NEED TO CONCERN OURSELVES WITH.

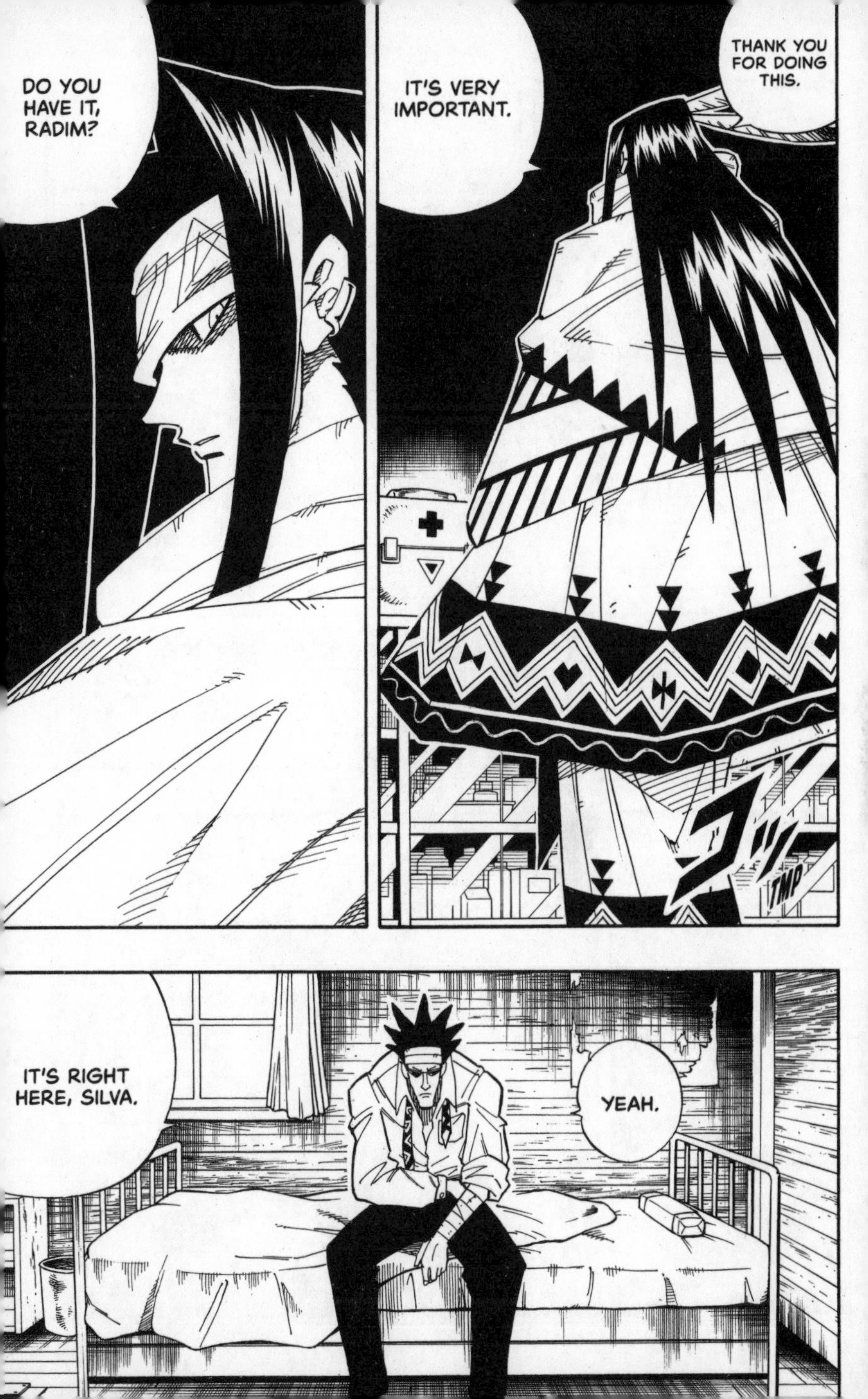
THANK YOU FOR DOING THIS.
IT'S VERY IMPORTANT.
TMP
DO YOU HAVE IT, RADIM?
YEAH.
IT'S RIGHT HERE, SILVA.

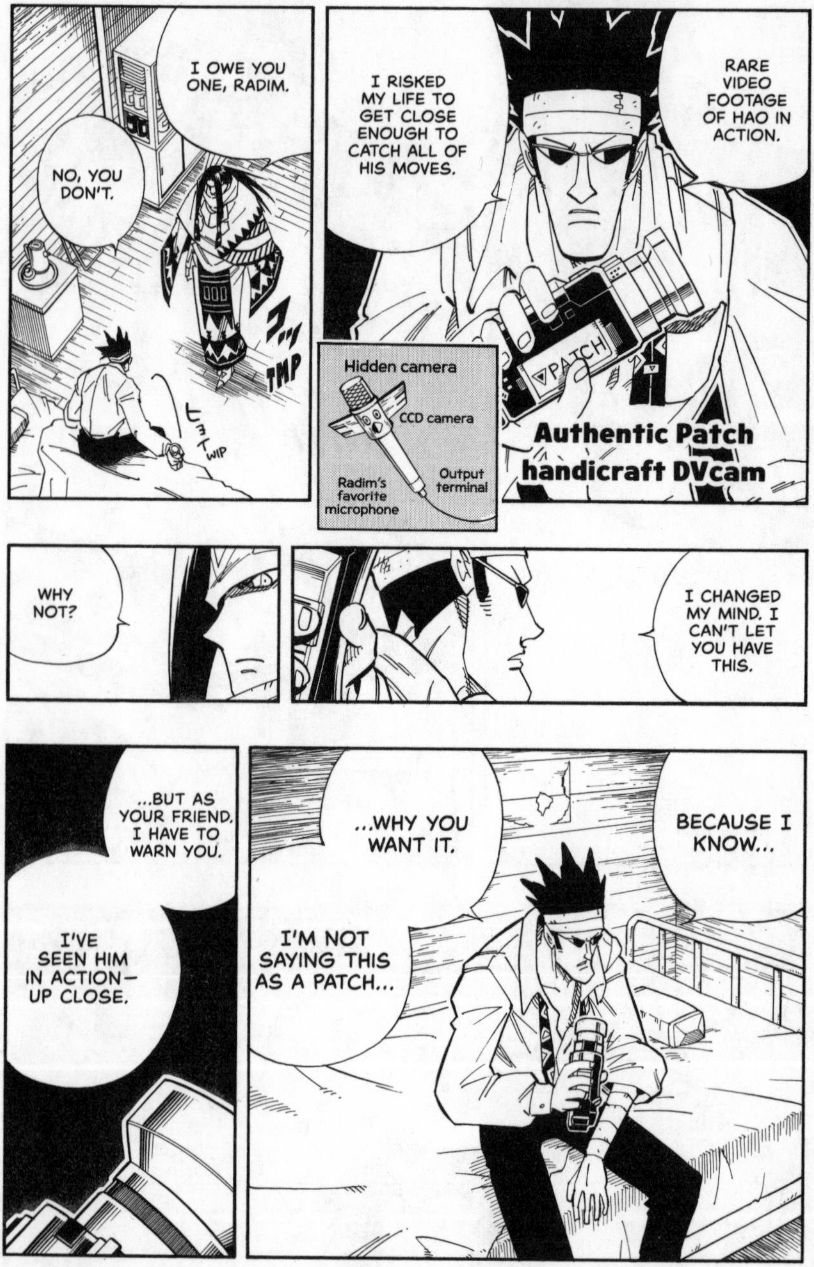
RARE VIDEO FOOTAGE OF HAO IN ACTION.
I RISKED MY LIFE TO GET CLOSE ENOUGH TO CATCH ALL OF HIS MOVES.
PATCH
Authentic Patch handicraft DVcam
Hidden camera
CCD camera
Output terminal
Radim's favorite microphone
I OWE YOU ONE, RADIM.
NO, YOU DON'T.
TMP
WIP
I CHANGED MY MIND. I CAN'T LET YOU HAVE THIS.
WHY NOT?
BECAUSE I KNOW...
...WHY YOU WANT IT.
I'M NOT SAYING THIS AS A PATCH...
...BUT AS YOUR FRIEND, I HAVE TO WARN YOU.
I'VE SEEN HIM IN ACTION— UP CLOSE.

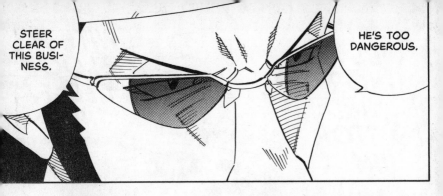

HE'S TOO DANGEROUS.
STEER CLEAR OF THIS BUSINESS.
...
HEH
YOU'RE A GOOD MAN, RADIM.
HUH?
I'M SORRY...
SNATCH
...BUT I HAVE TO SEE THIS THROUGH.
HEY!
THAT'S A CHEAP SHOT!
HAO, AS A PATCH, KILLED OUR PEOPLE 500 YEARS AGO.

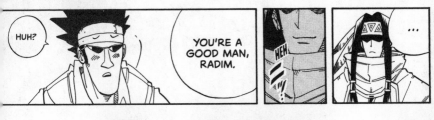

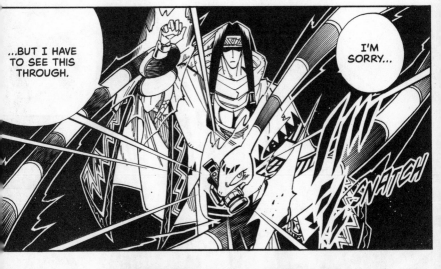

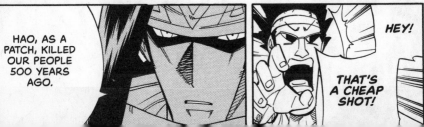

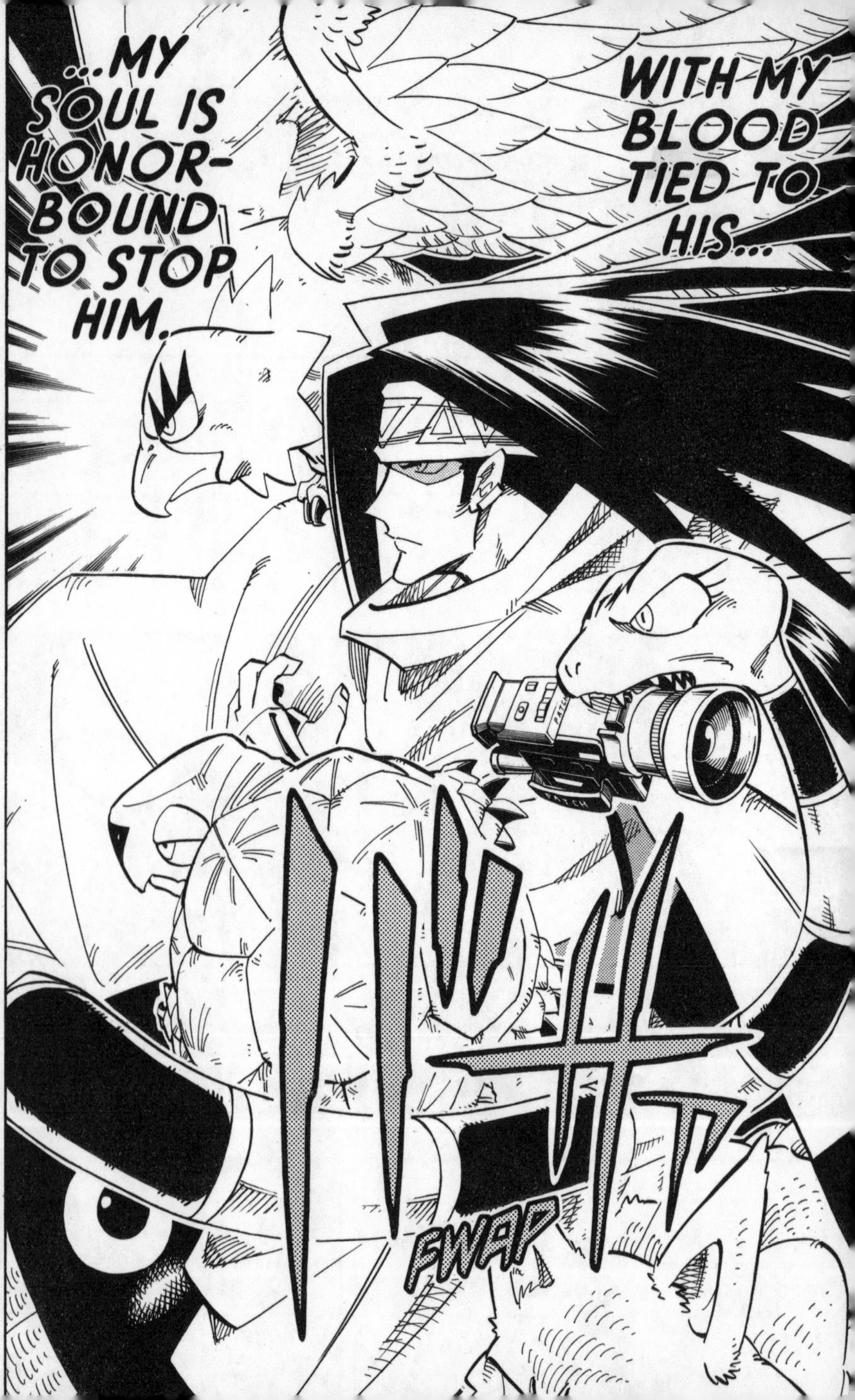
WITH MY BLOOD TIED TO HIS...
...MY SOUL IS HONOR-BOUND TO STOP HIM.
FWAP

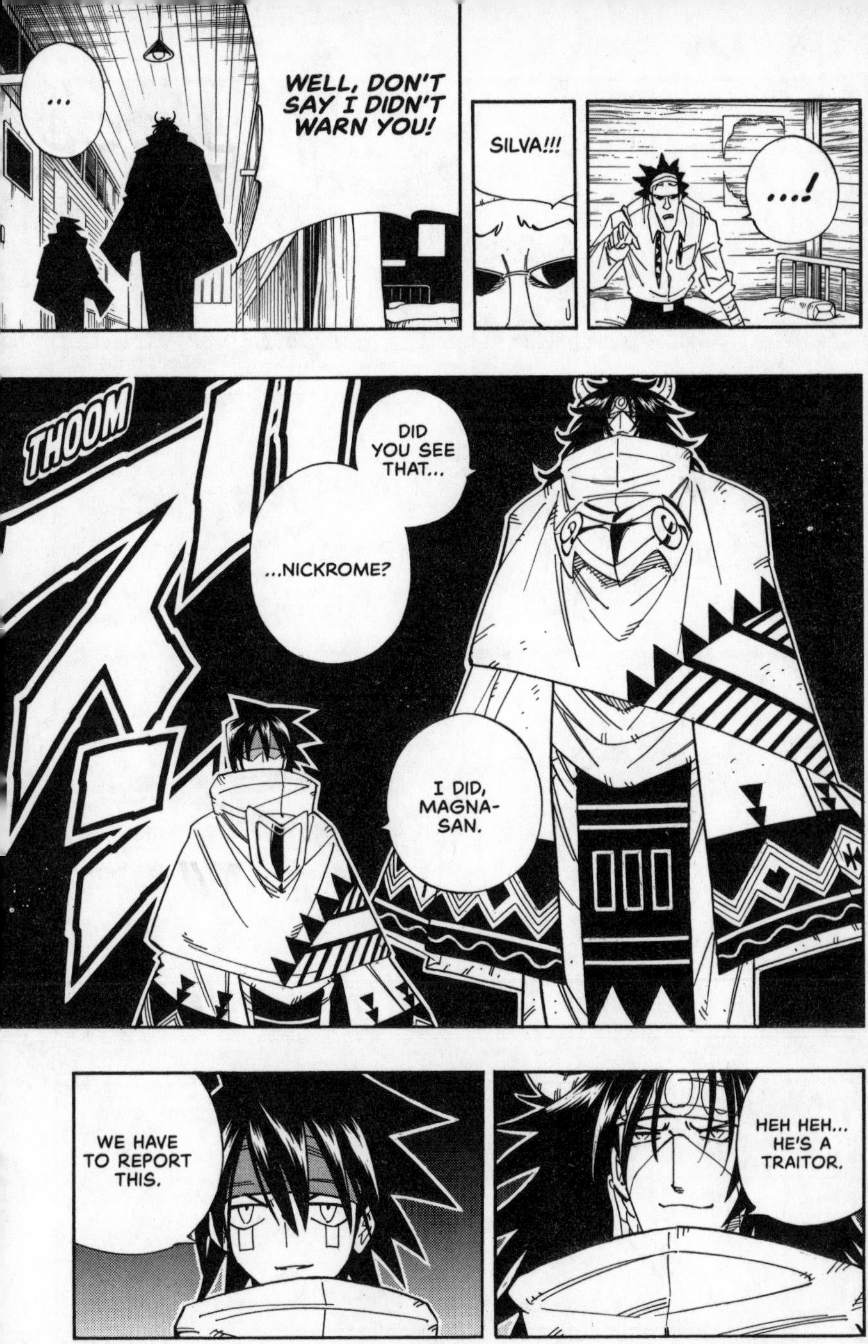
...!
SILVA!!!
WELL, DON'T SAY I DIDN'T WARN YOU!
...
THOOM
DID YOU SEE THAT...
...NICKROME?
I DID, MAGNA-SAN.
HEH HEH... HE'S A TRAITOR.
WE HAVE TO REPORT THIS.

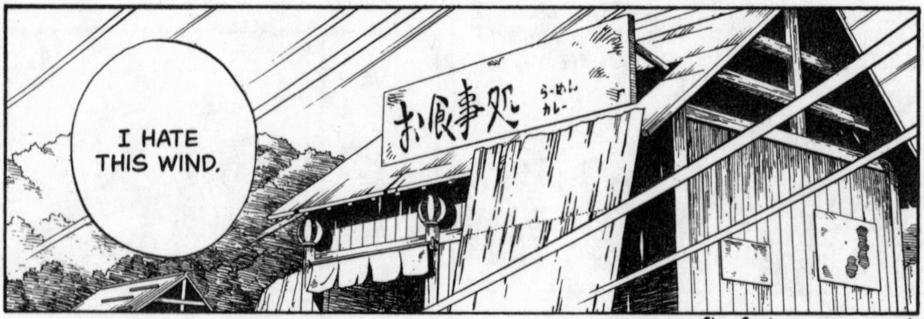
I HATE THIS WIND.
お食事処
らーめん カレー

Sign: Canteen-ramen, curry rice

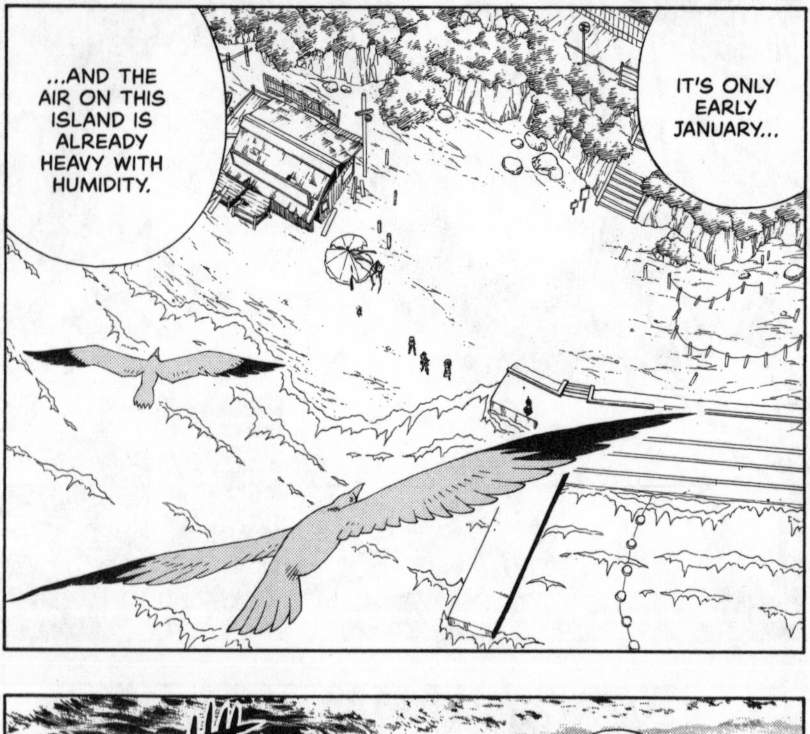
IT'S ONLY EARLY JANUARY...
...AND THE AIR ON THIS ISLAND IS ALREADY HEAVY WITH HUMIDITY.

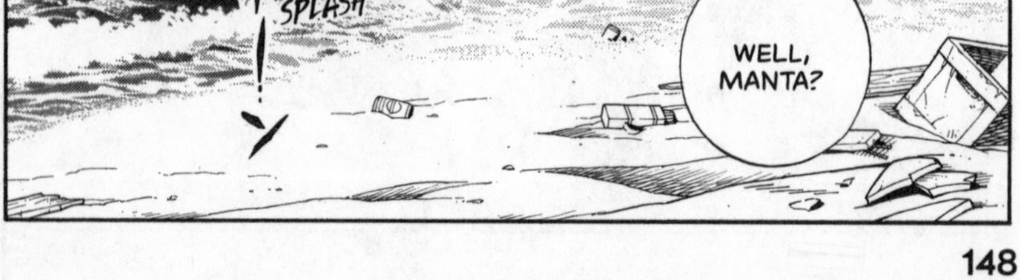
WELL, MANTA?
SPLASH

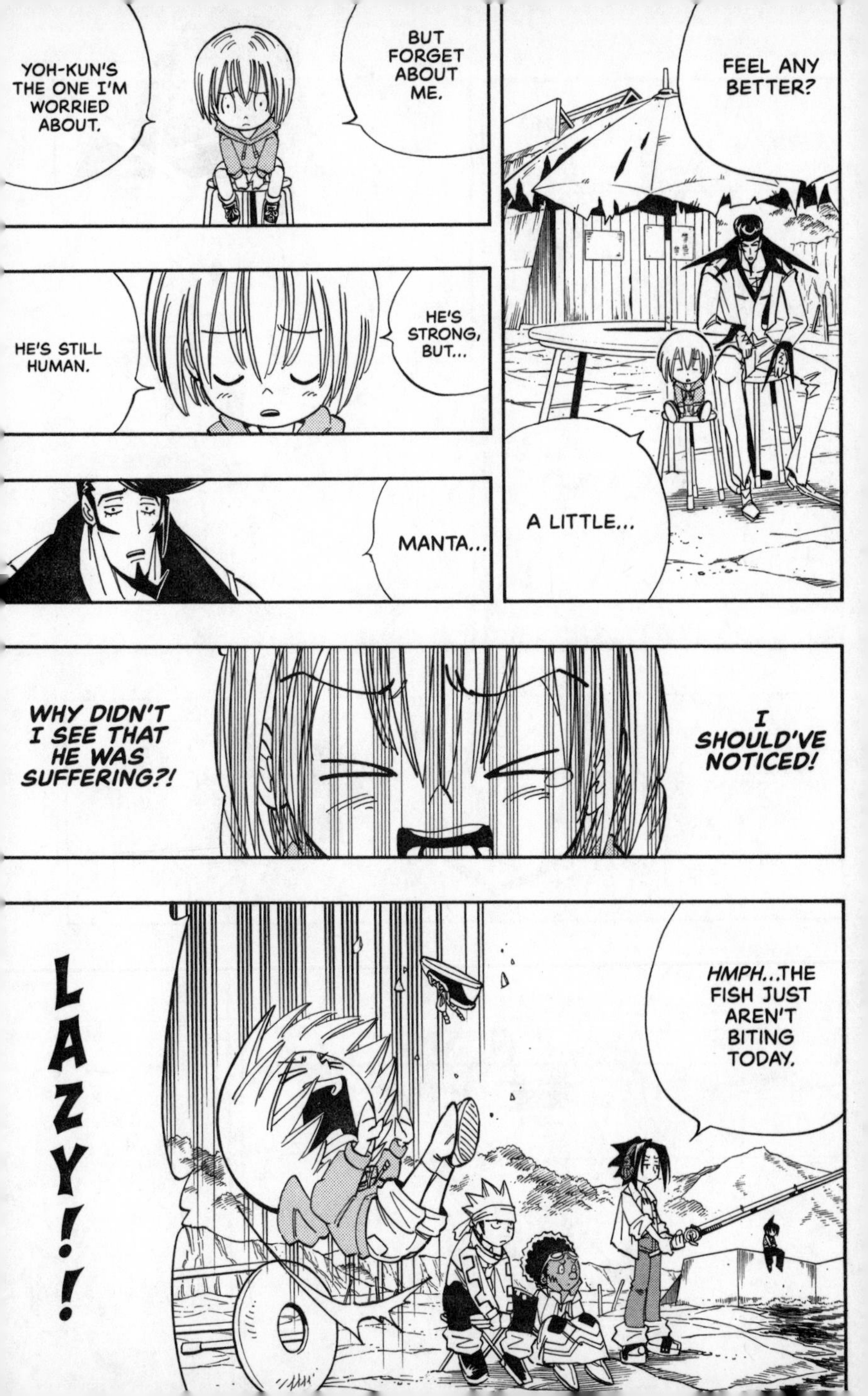
FEEL ANY BETTER?
A LITTLE...
BUT FORGET ABOUT ME.
YOH-KUN'S THE ONE I'M WORRIED ABOUT.
HE'S STRONG, BUT...
HE'S STILL HUMAN.
MANTA...
I SHOULD'VE NOTICED!
WHY DIDN'T I SEE THAT HE WAS SUFFERING?!
HMPH...THE FISH JUST AREN'T BITING TODAY.
LAZY!!!

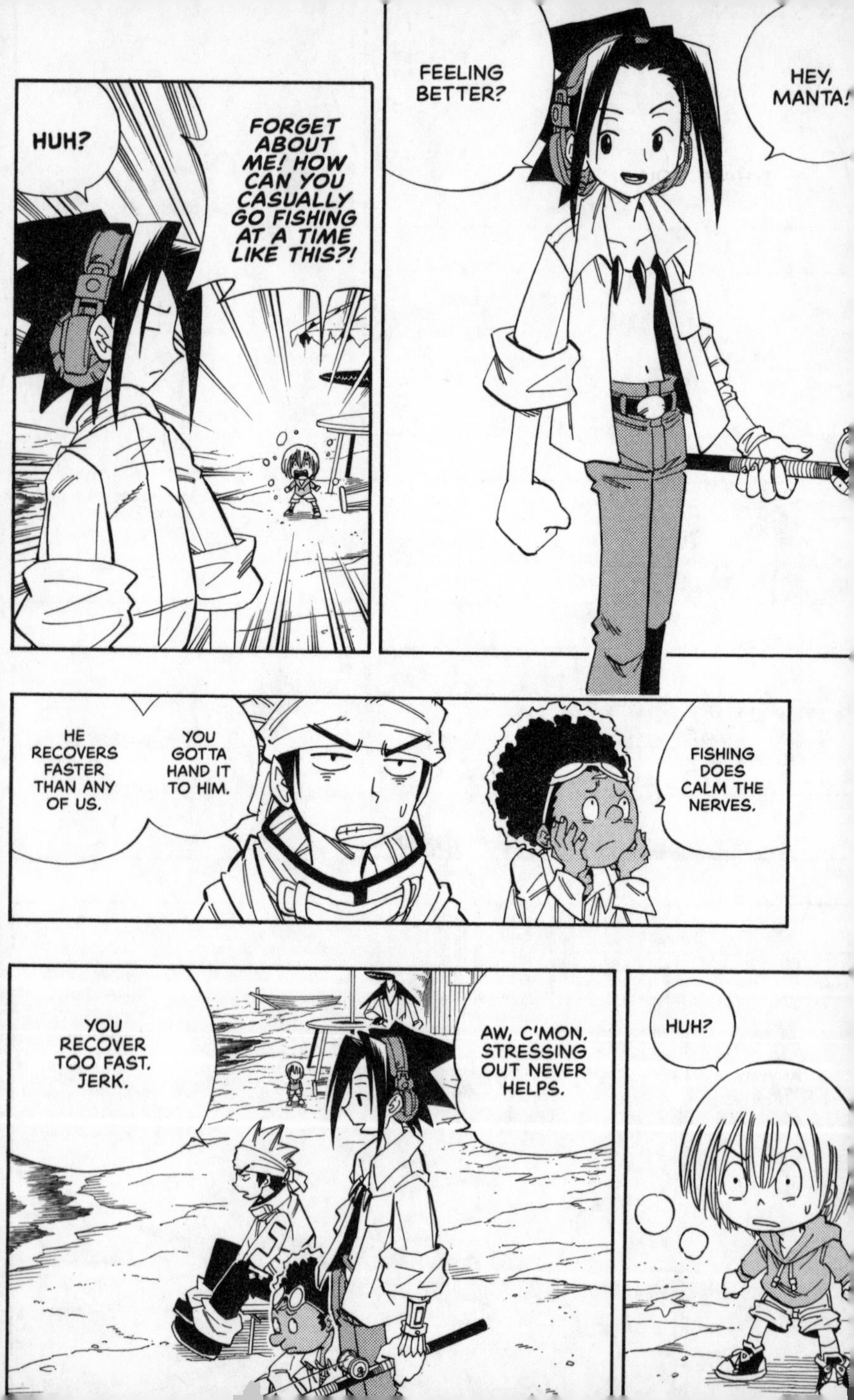
HEY, MANTA!
FEELING BETTER?
FORGET ABOUT ME! HOW CAN YOU CASUALLY GO FISHING AT A TIME LIKE THIS?!
HUH?
FISHING DOES CALM THE NERVES.
YOU GOTTA HAND IT TO HIM.
HE RECOVERS FASTER THAN ANY OF US.
HUH?
AW, C'MON. STRESSING OUT NEVER HELPS.
YOU RECOVER TOO FAST. JERK.

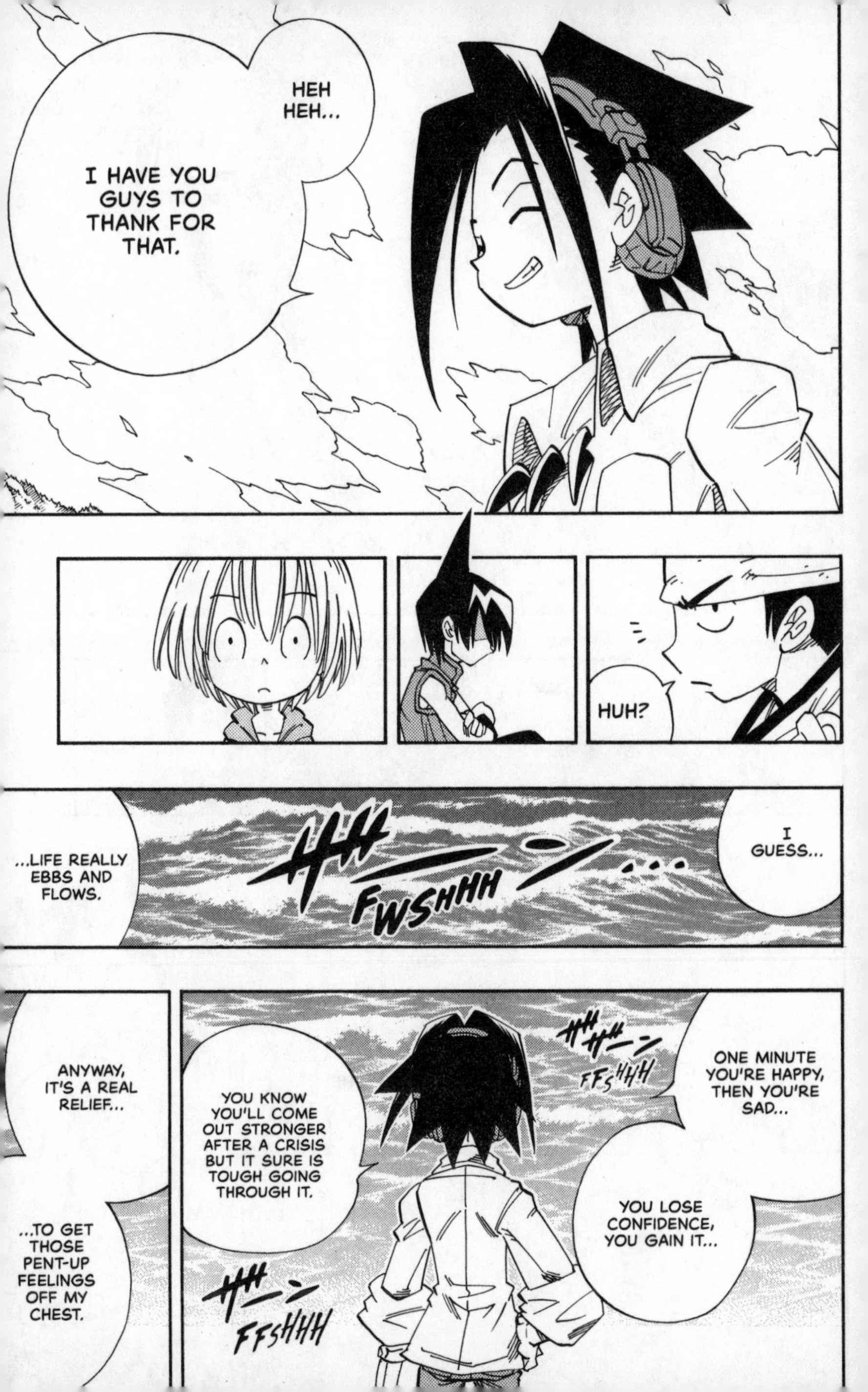
HEH HEH...
I HAVE YOU GUYS TO THANK FOR THAT.
HUH?
I GUESS...
FWSHHH
...LIFE REALLY EBBS AND FLOWS.
ONE MINUTE YOU'RE HAPPY, THEN YOU'RE SAD...
FFSHHH
YOU LOSE CONFIDENCE, YOU GAIN IT...
YOU KNOW YOU'LL COME OUT STRONGER AFTER A CRISIS BUT IT SURE IS TOUGH GOING THROUGH IT.
FFSHHH
ANYWAY, IT'S A REAL RELIEF...
...TO GET THOSE PENT-UP FEELINGS OFF MY CHEST.

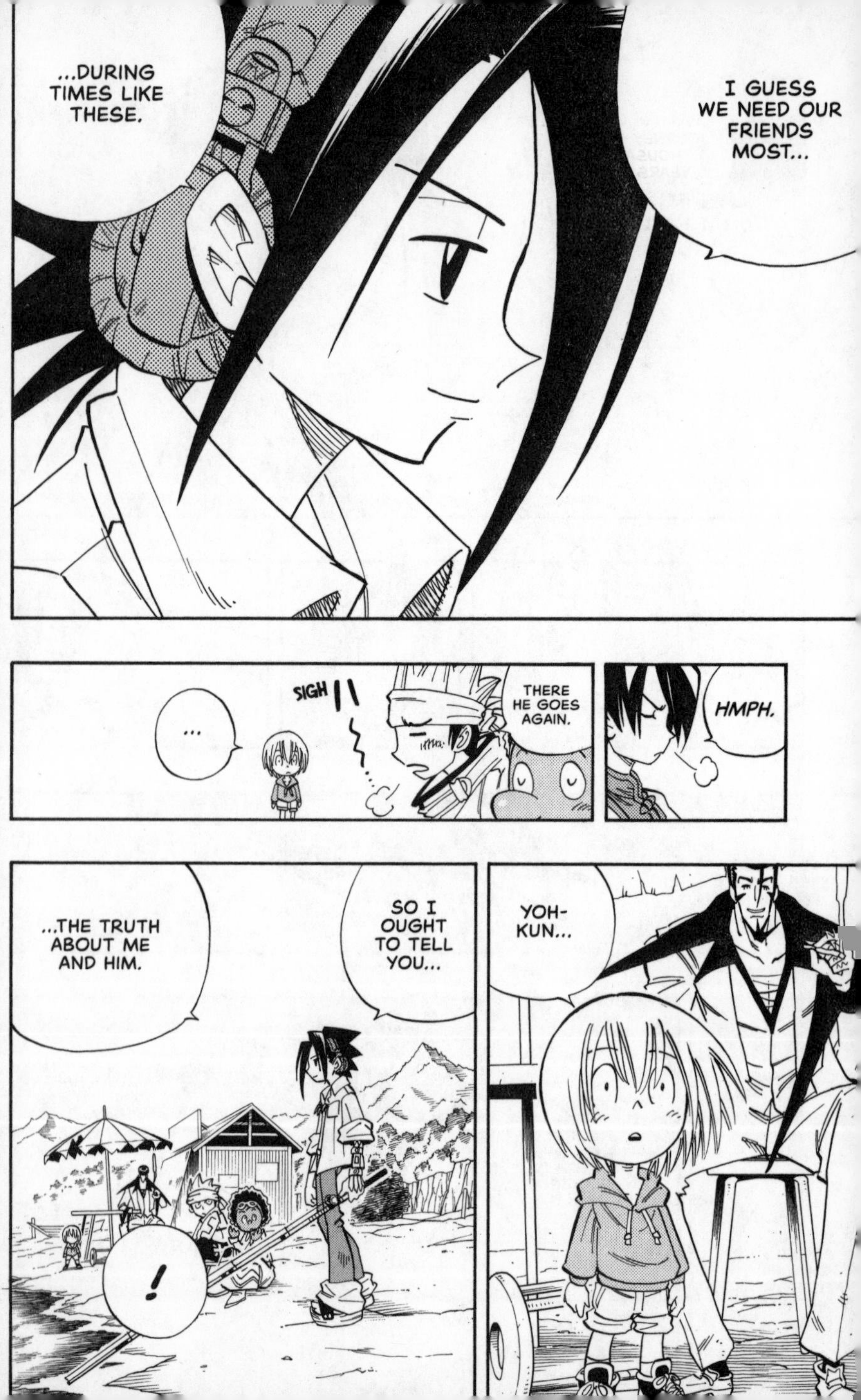
I GUESS WE NEED OUR FRIENDS MOST...
...DURING TIMES LIKE THESE.
HMPH.
THERE HE GOES AGAIN.
SIGH
...
YOH-KUN...
SO I OUGHT TO TELL YOU...
...THE TRUTH ABOUT ME AND HIM.
!

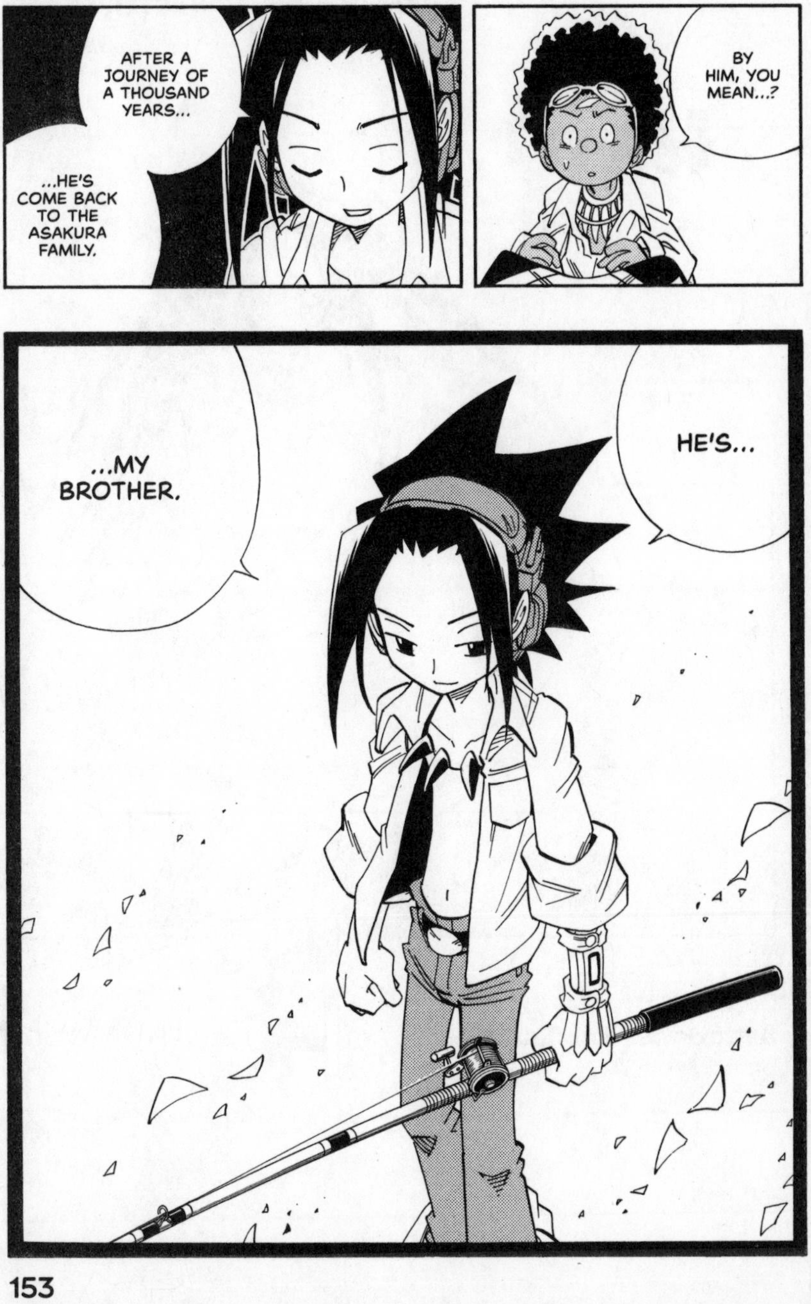
BY HIM, YOU MEAN...?
AFTER A JOURNEY OF A THOUSAND YEARS...
...HE'S COME BACK TO THE ASAKURA FAMILY.
HE'S...
...MY BROTHER.

Hao

January 2001

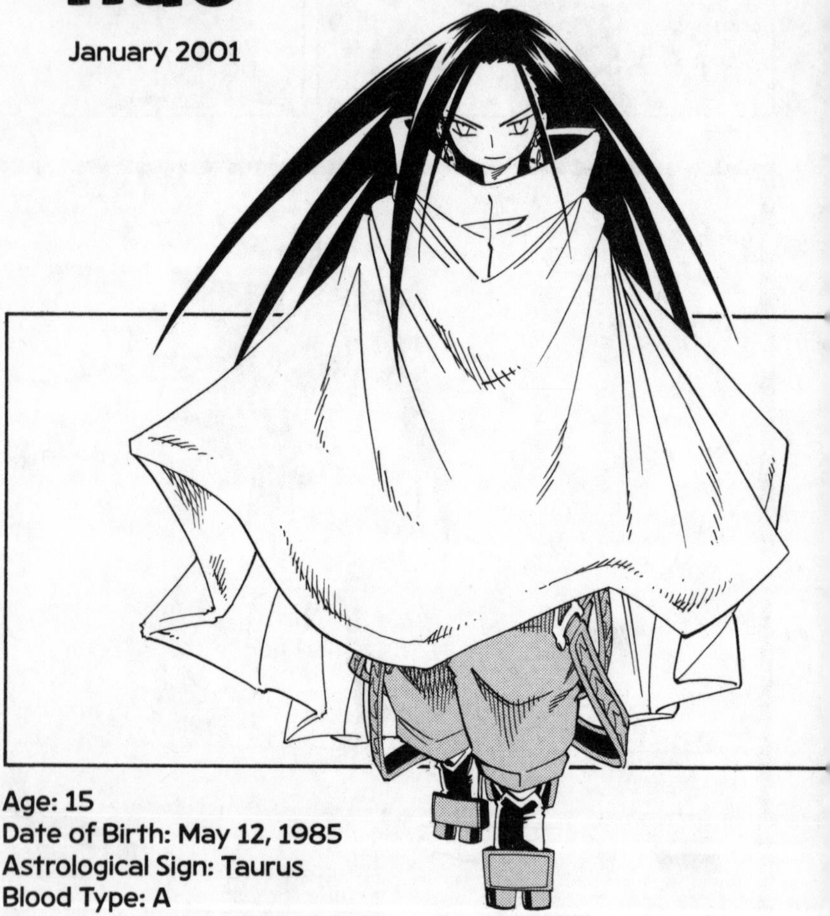

Age: 15
Date of Birth: May 12, 1985
Astrological Sign: Taurus
Blood Type: A

Chapter 142: Oh, Brother

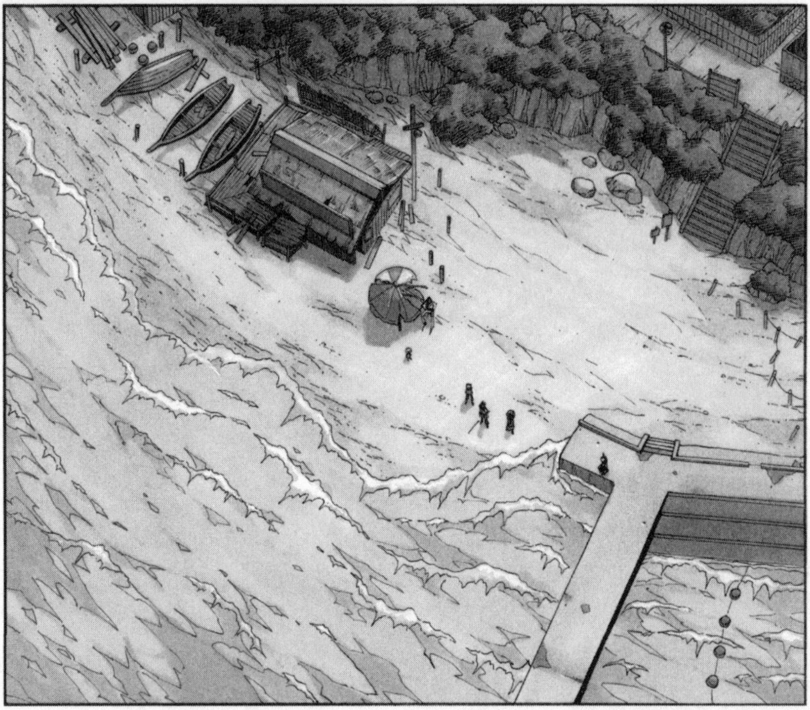

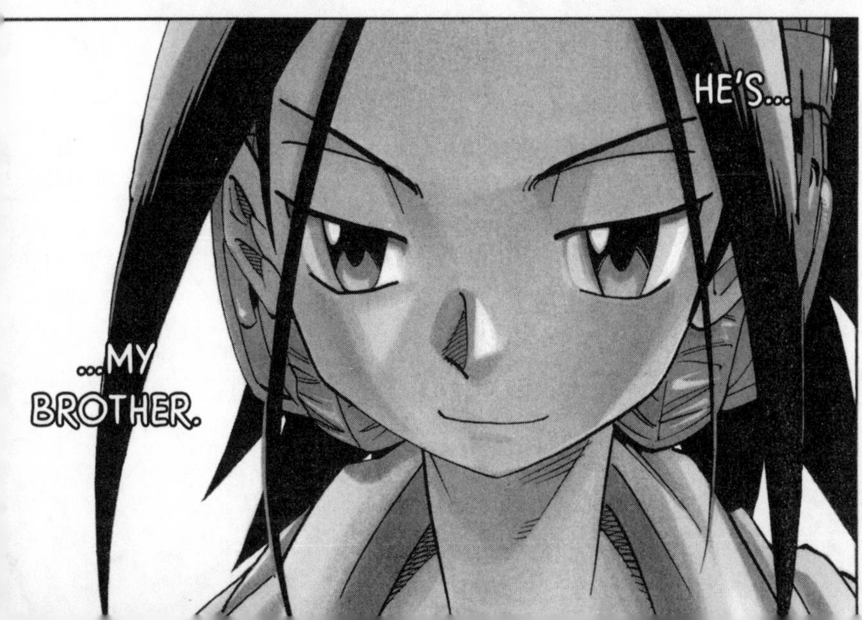
HE'S...
...MY BROTHER.

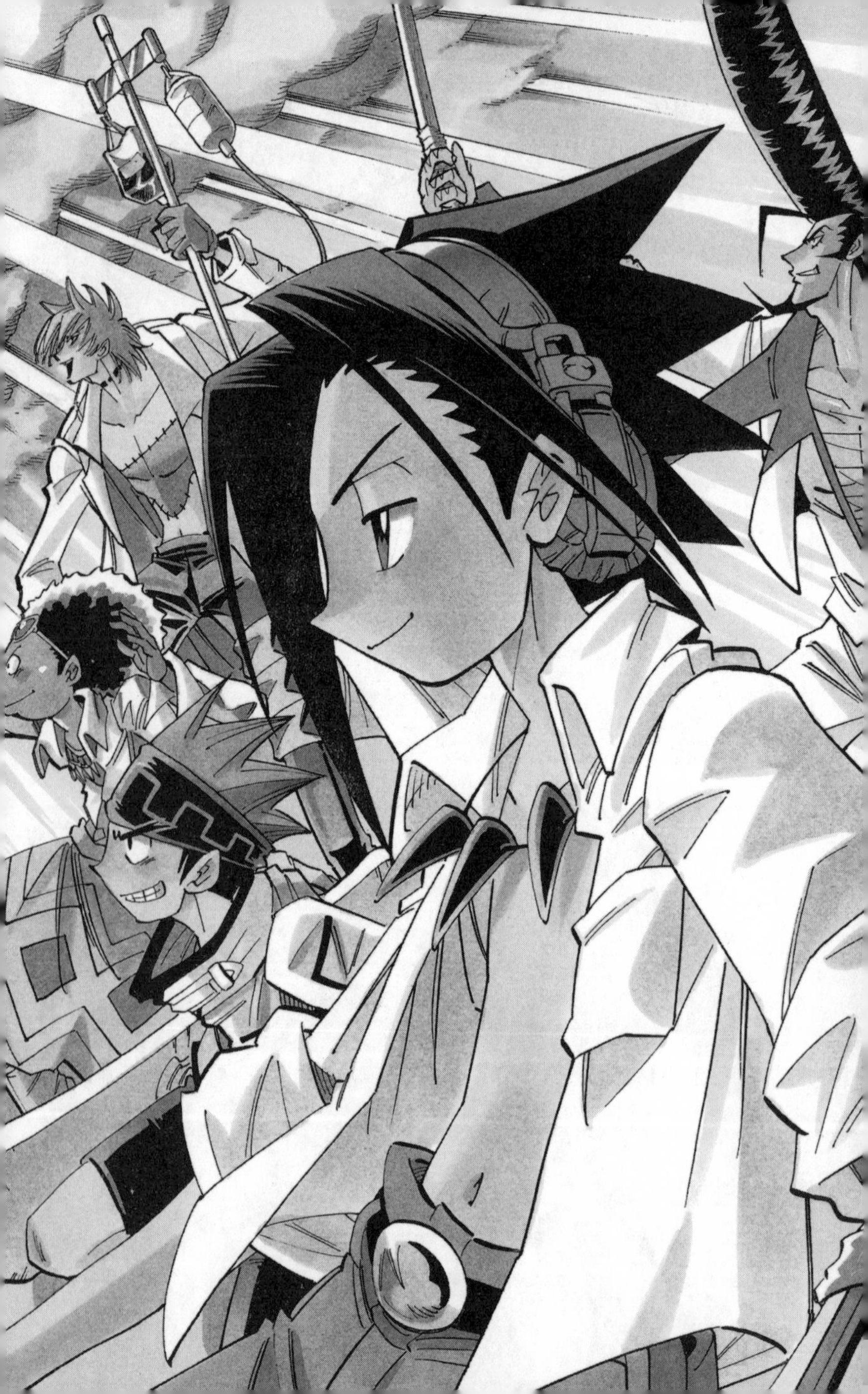

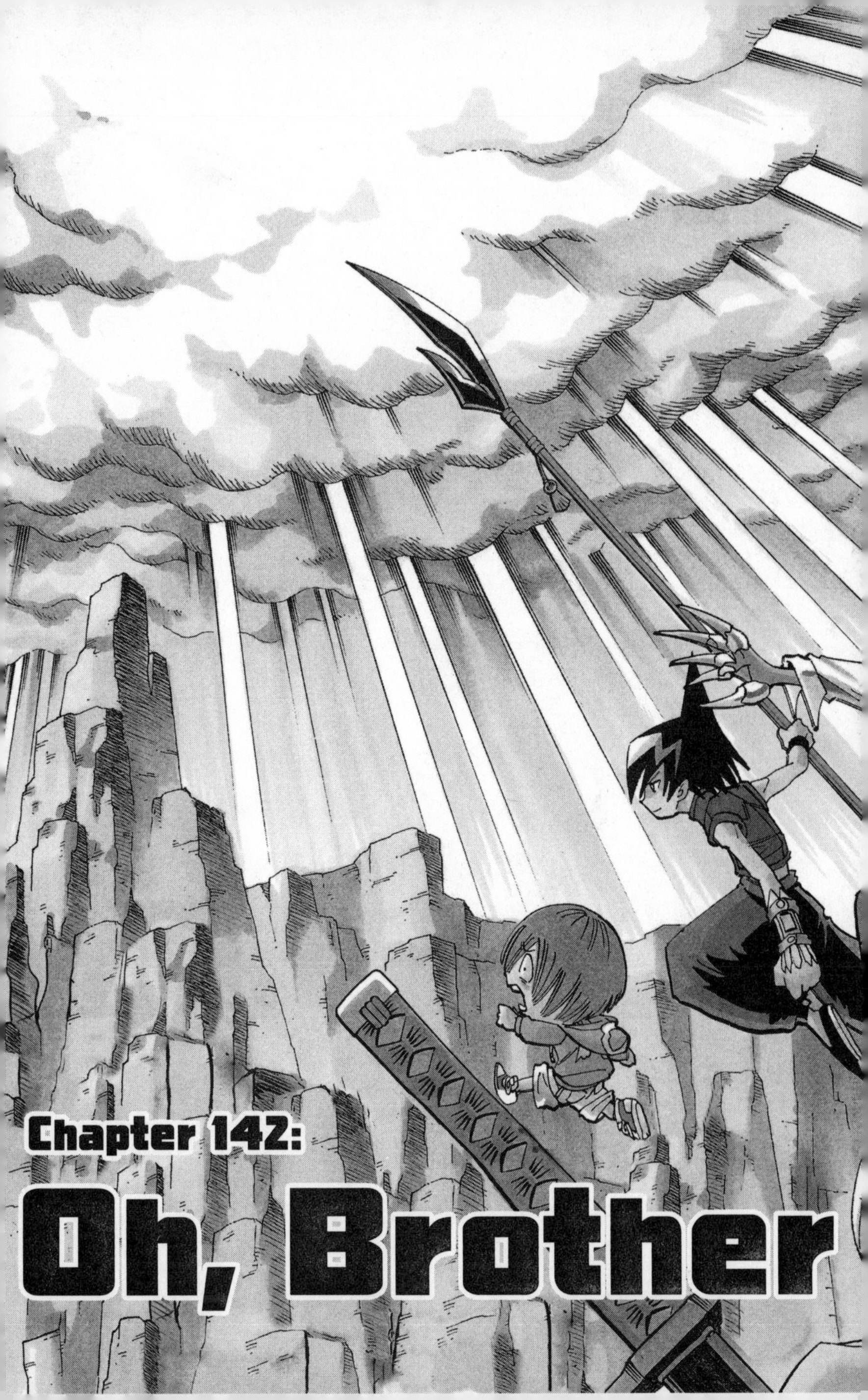
Chapter 142:
Oh, Brother

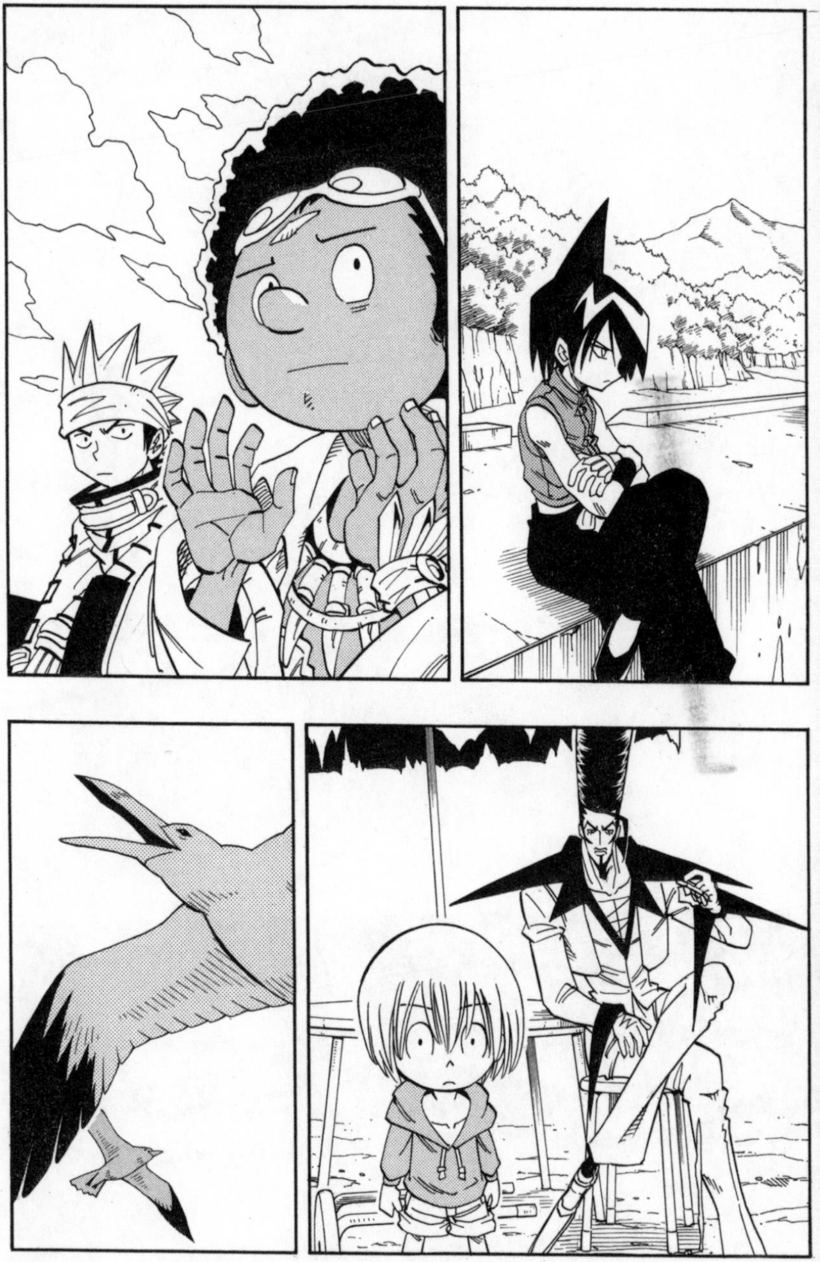

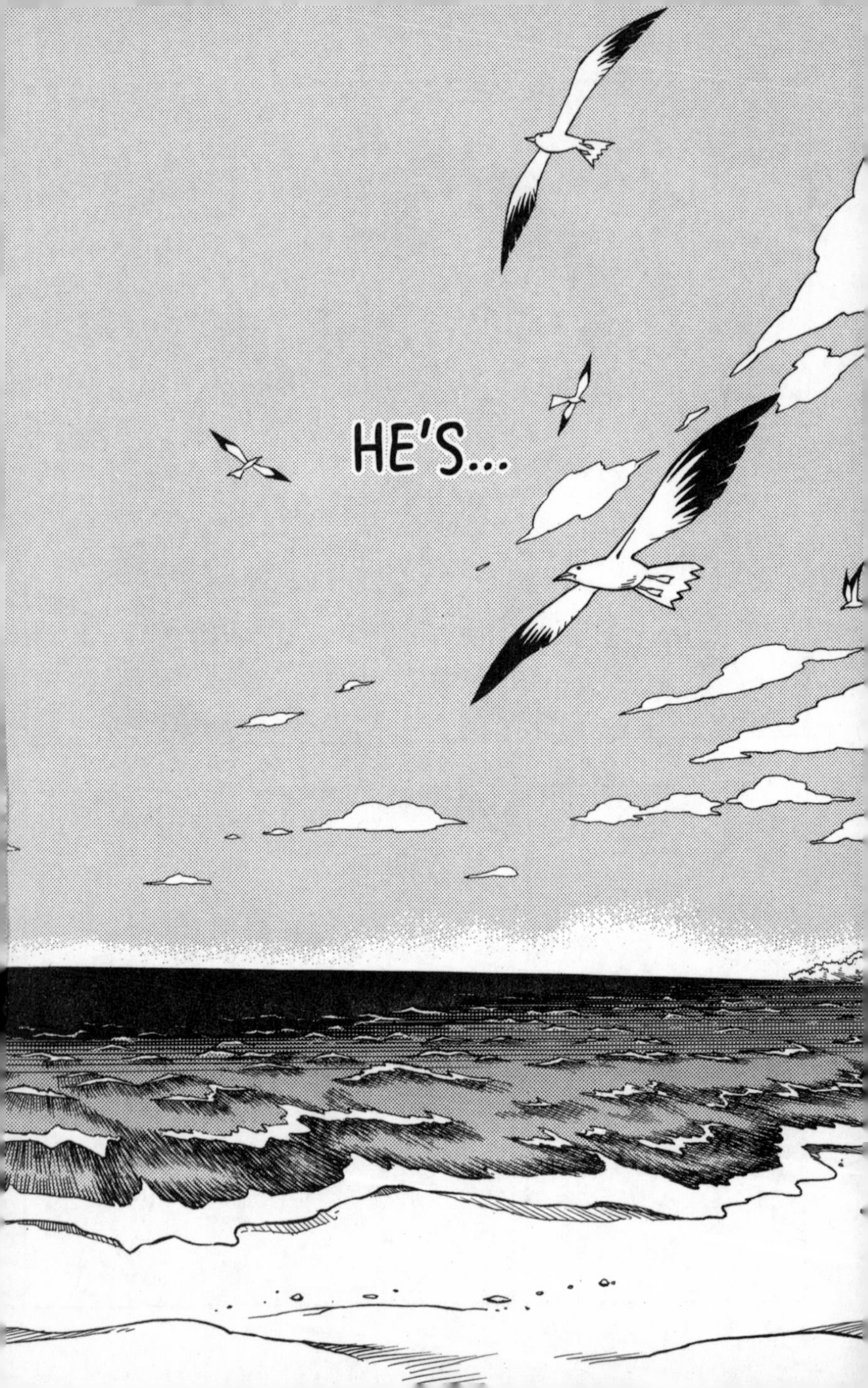
HE'S...

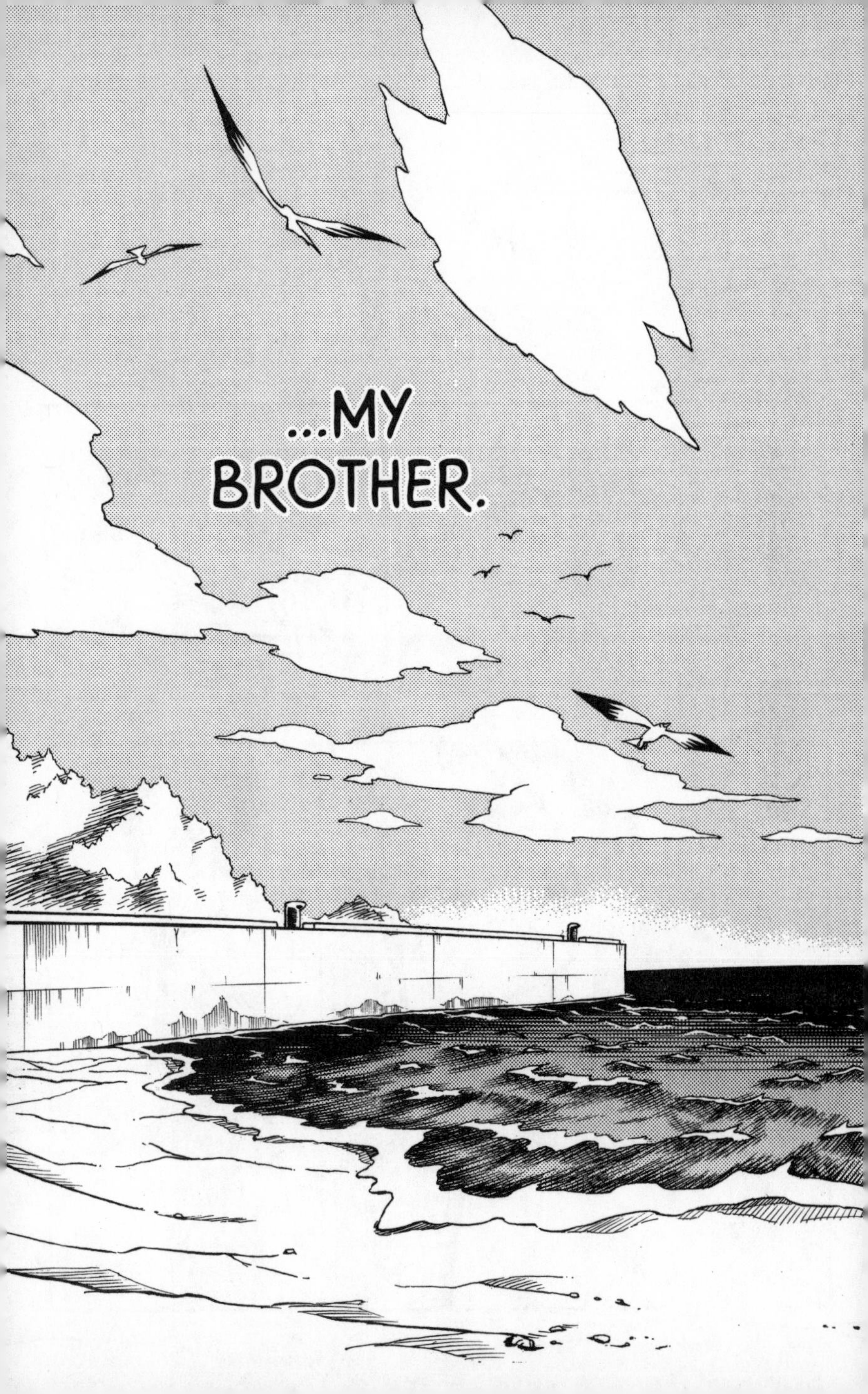
...MY BROTHER.

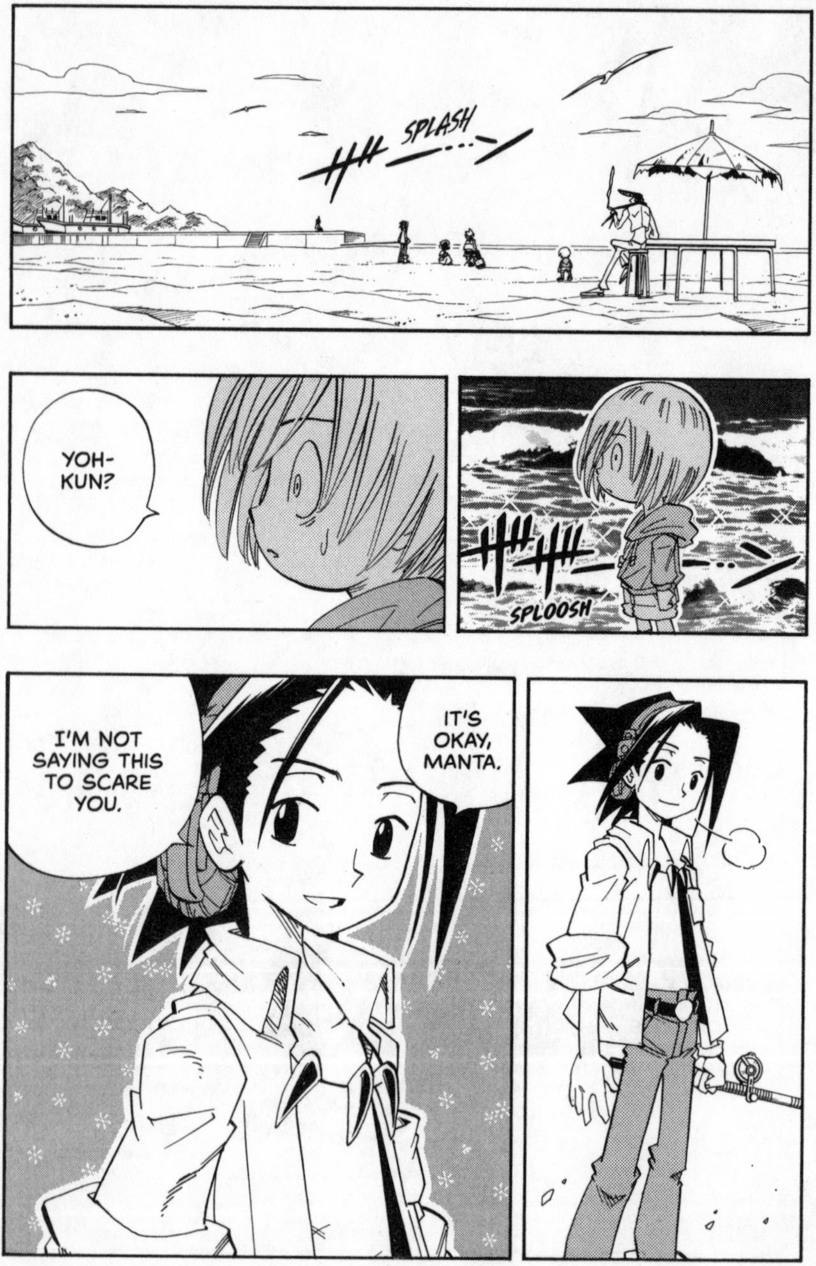
SPLASH
SPLOOSH
YOH-KUN?
IT'S OKAY, MANTA.
I'M NOT SAYING THIS TO SCARE YOU.

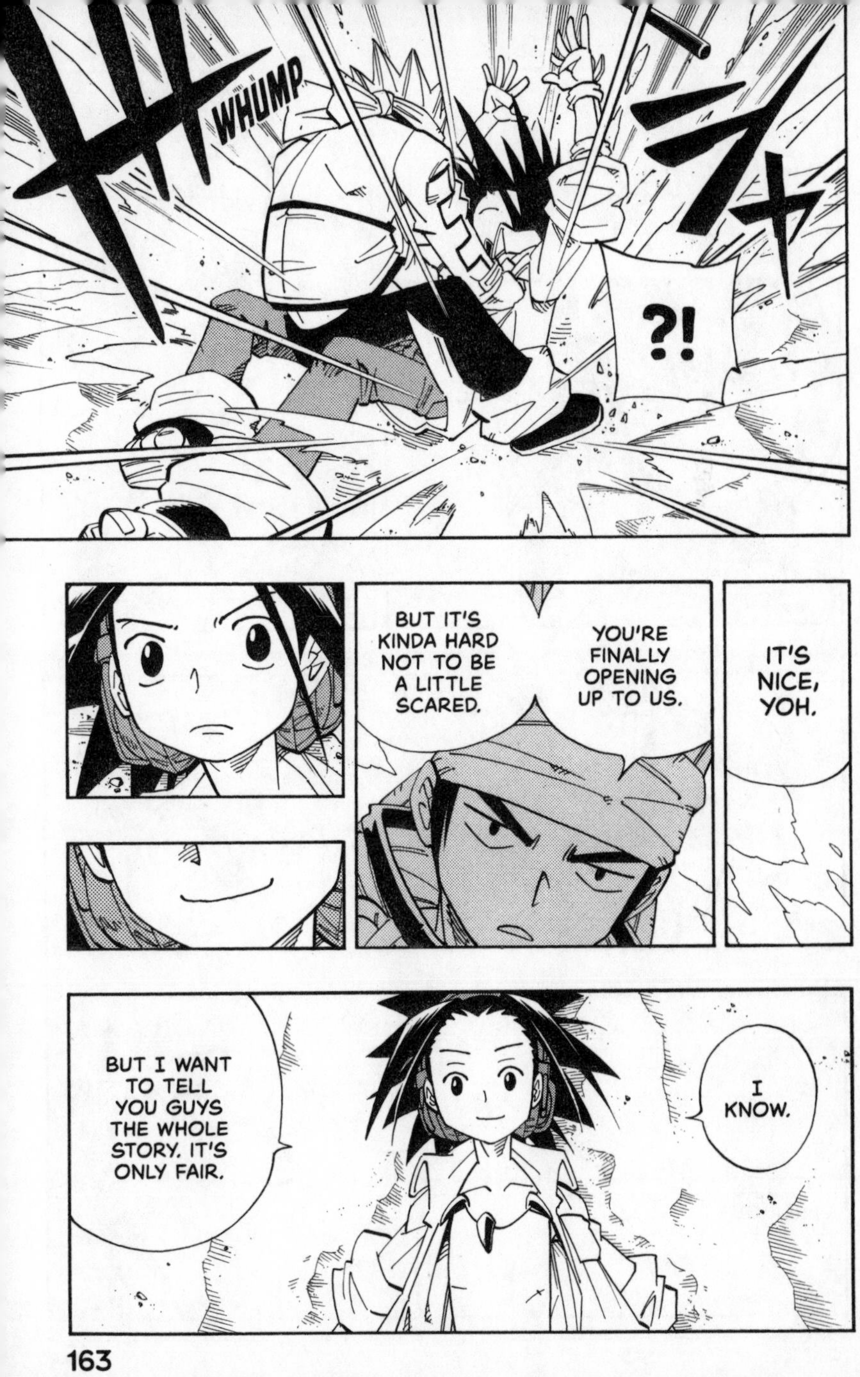
WHUMP
?!
IT'S NICE, YOH.
YOU'RE FINALLY OPENING UP TO US.
BUT IT'S KINDA HARD NOT TO BE A LITTLE SCARED.
I KNOW.
BUT I WANT TO TELL YOU GUYS THE WHOLE STORY. IT'S ONLY FAIR.

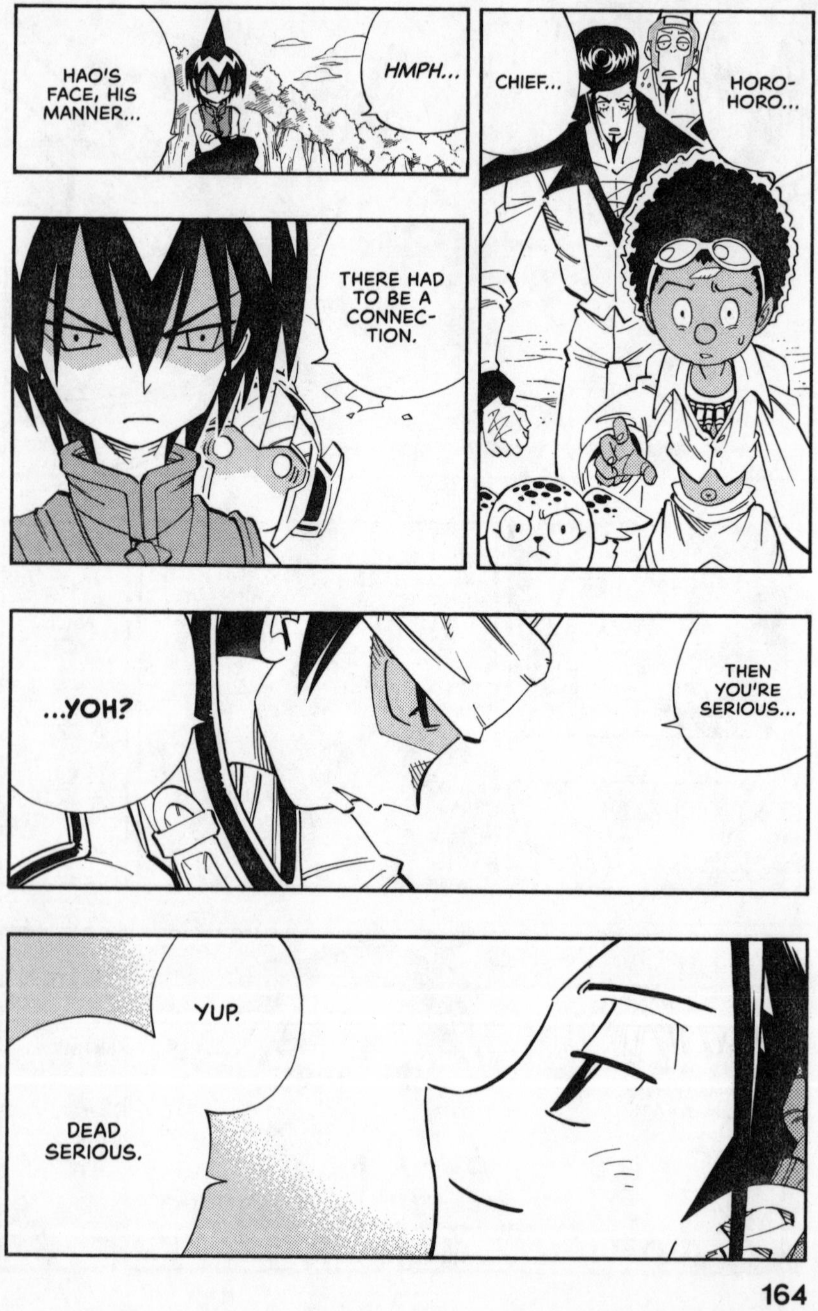
HORO-HORO...
CHIEF...
HMPH...
HAO'S FACE, HIS MANNER...
THERE HAD TO BE A CONNECTION.
THEN YOU'RE SERIOUS...
...YOH?
YUP.
DEAD SERIOUS.

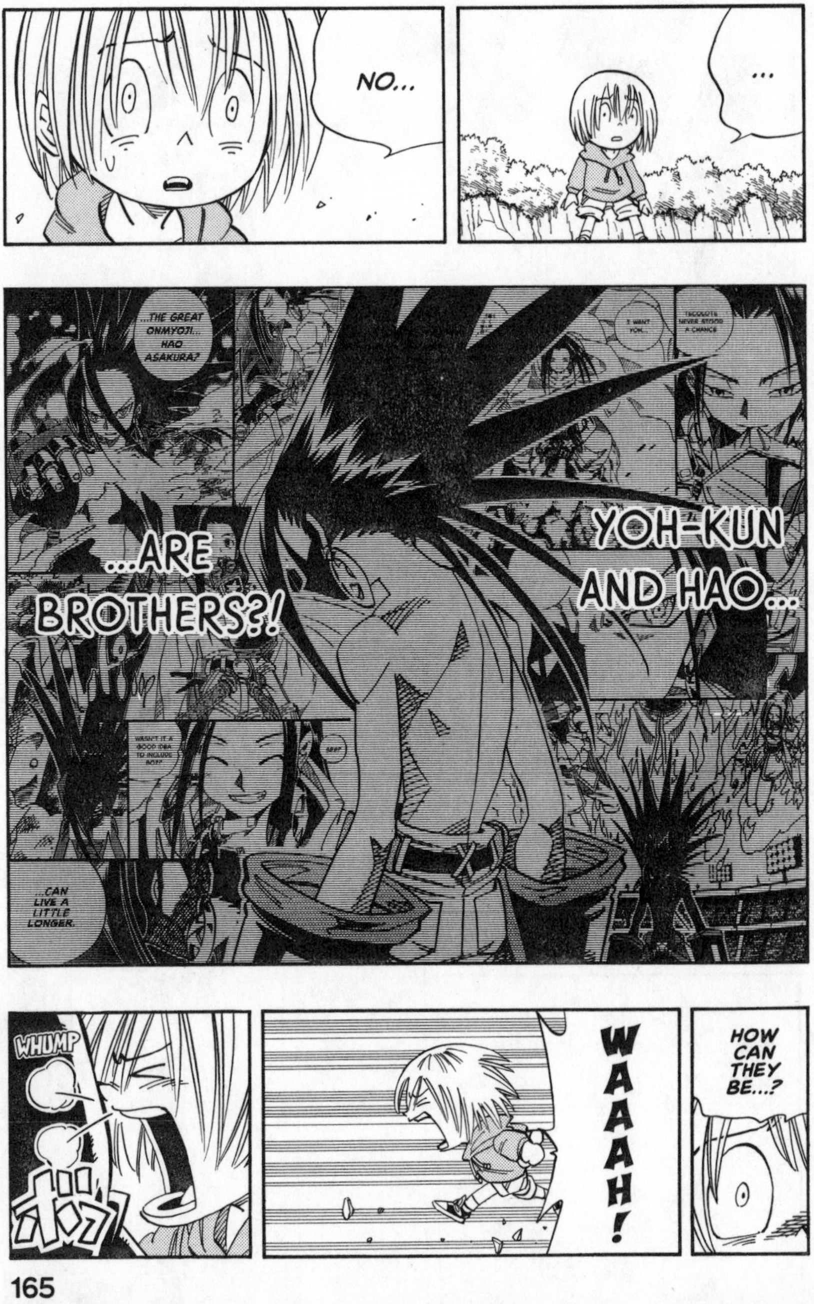
...
NO...
TECOLOTE NEVER STOOD A CHANCE
I WANT YOH...
...THE GREAT ONMYOJI... HAO ASAKURA?
YOH-KUN AND HAO...
...ARE BROTHERS?!
SEE?
...CAN LIVE A LITTLE LONGER.
HOW CAN THEY BE...?
WAAAAH!
WHUMP

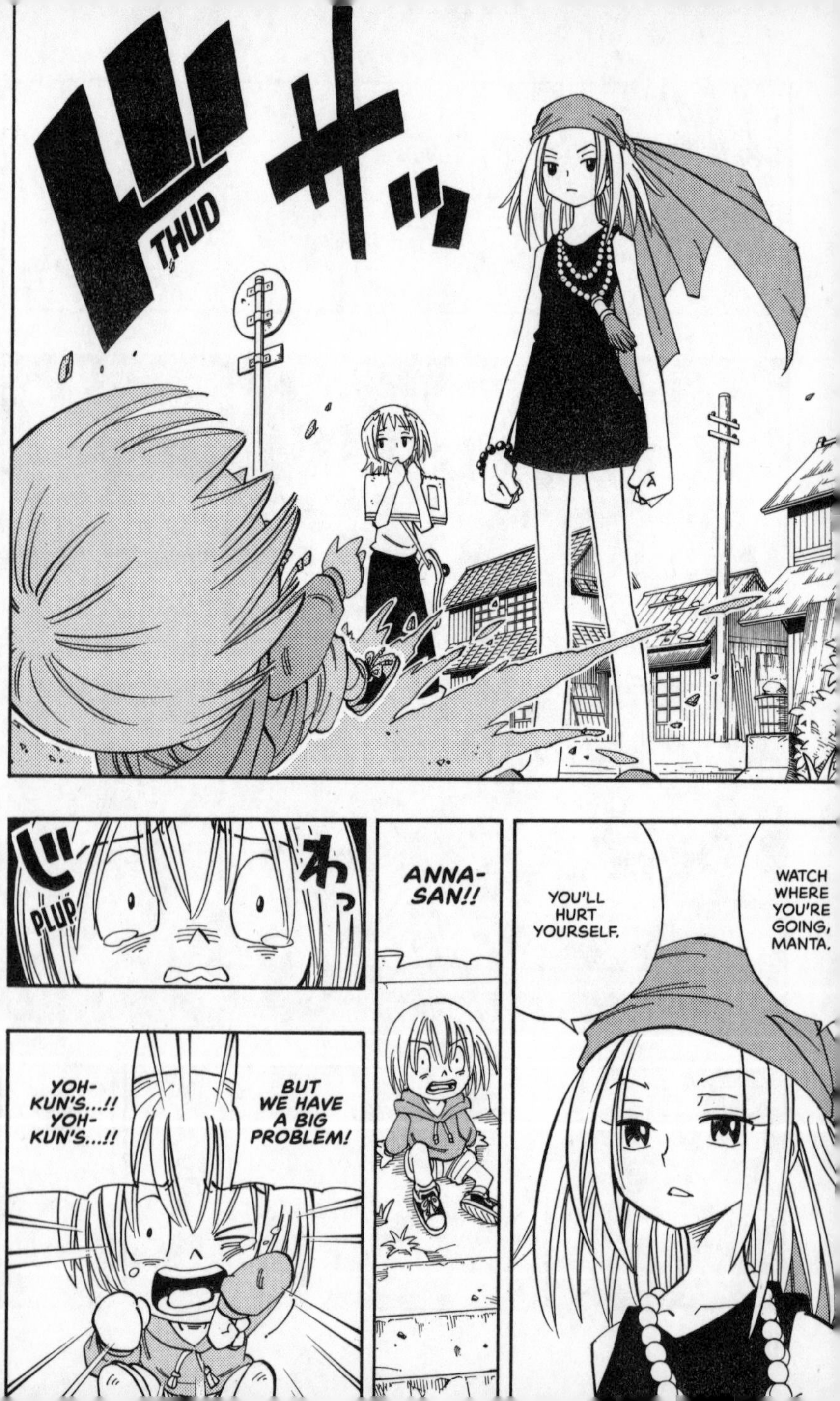
ドサッ
THUD
WATCH WHERE YOU'RE GOING, MANTA.
YOU'LL HURT YOURSELF.
ANNA-SAN!!
わっ
じ
PLUP
BUT WE HAVE A BIG PROBLEM!
YOH-KUN'S...!! YOH-KUN'S...!!

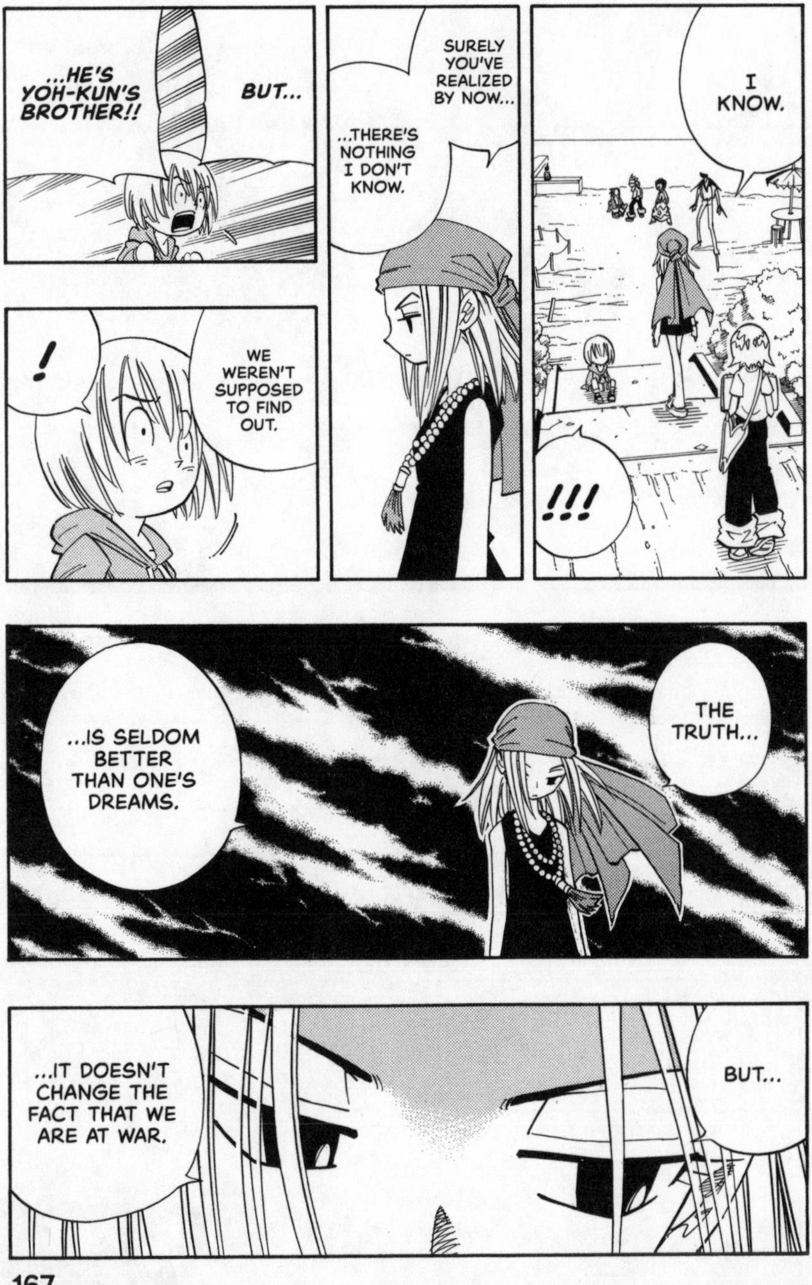
I KNOW.
!!!
SURELY YOU'VE REALIZED BY NOW...
...THERE'S NOTHING I DON'T KNOW.
BUT...
...HE'S YOH-KUN'S BROTHER!!
WE WEREN'T SUPPOSED TO FIND OUT.
!
THE TRUTH...
...IS SELDOM BETTER THAN ONE'S DREAMS.
BUT...
...IT DOESN'T CHANGE THE FACT THAT WE ARE AT WAR.

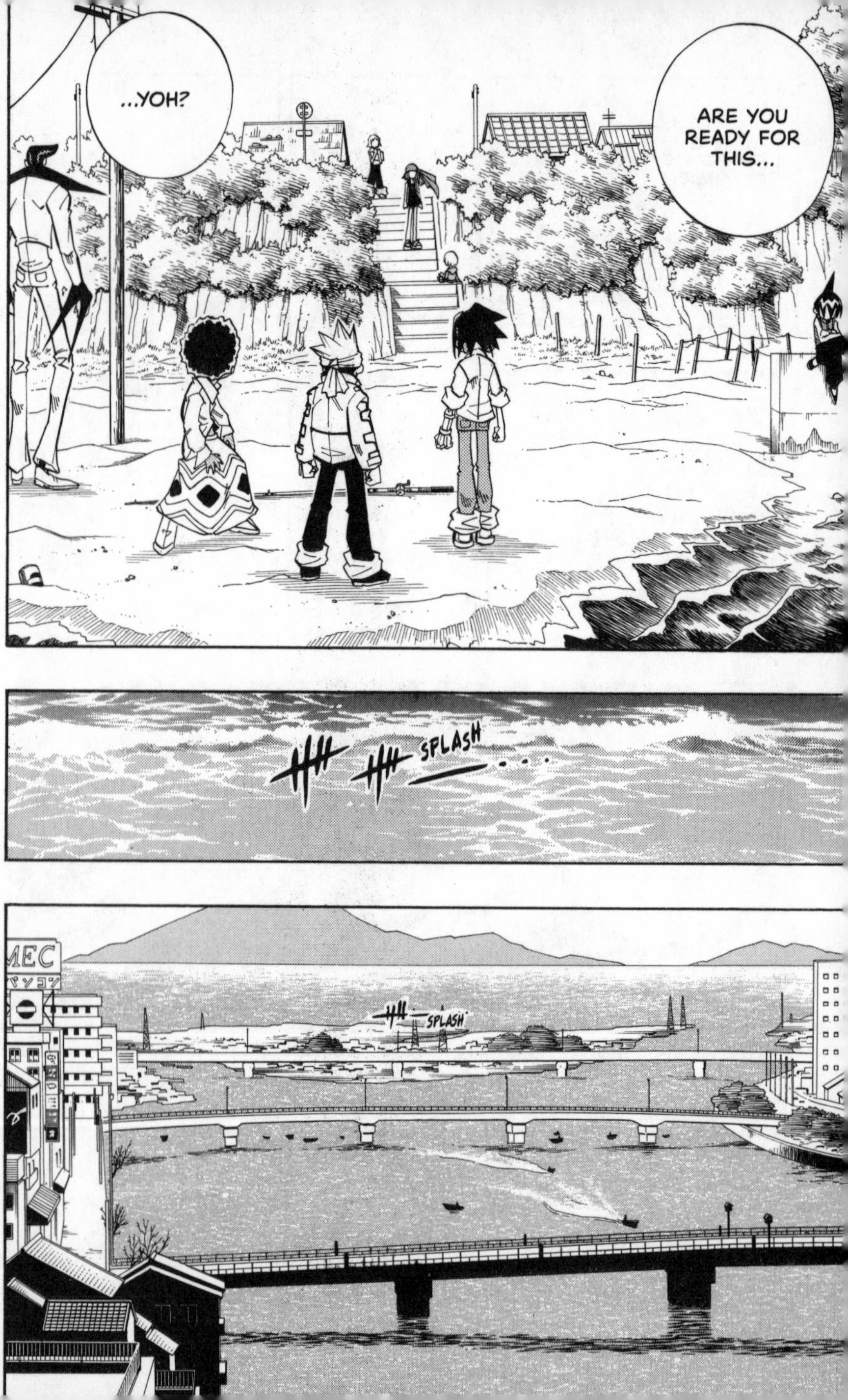
ARE YOU READY FOR THIS...
...YOH?
SPLASH
SPLASH

SO YOU TOLD THEM EVERYTHING.

VROOMM

I SEE.

THIS IS A PATH THEY'LL HAVE TO WALK. I'LL LEAVE THE OTHERS TO YOU.

NO MATTER.

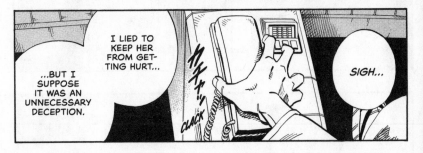

I LIED TO KEEP HER FROM GETTING HURT...

...BUT I SUPPOSE IT WAS AN UNNECESSARY DECEPTION.

CLACK

SIGH...

THEY'RE STRONG CHILDREN.

MATSUE

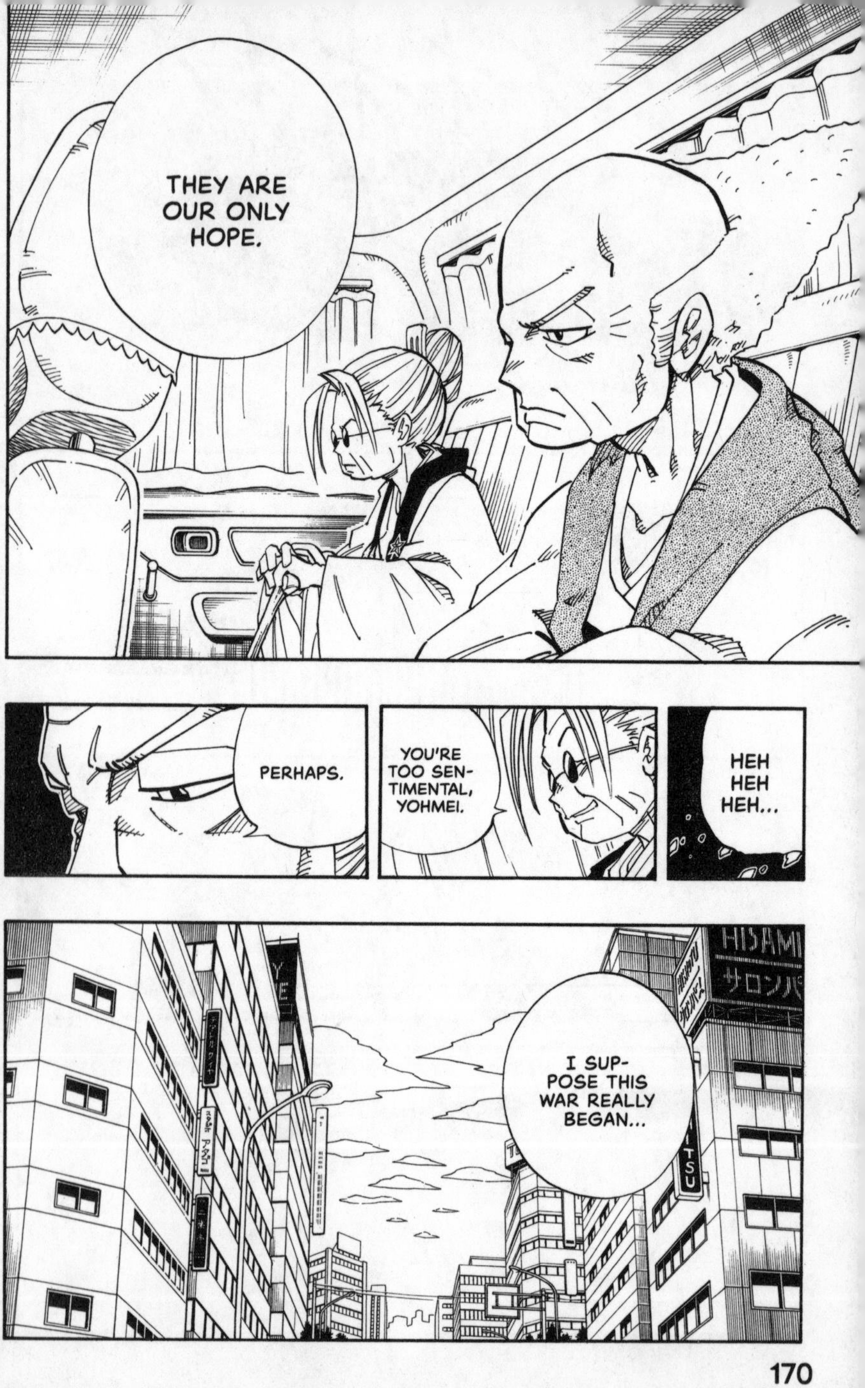
THEY ARE OUR ONLY HOPE.
HEH HEH HEH...
YOU'RE TOO SEN-TIMENTAL, YOHMEI.
PERHAPS.
I SUP-POSE THIS WAR REALLY BEGAN...

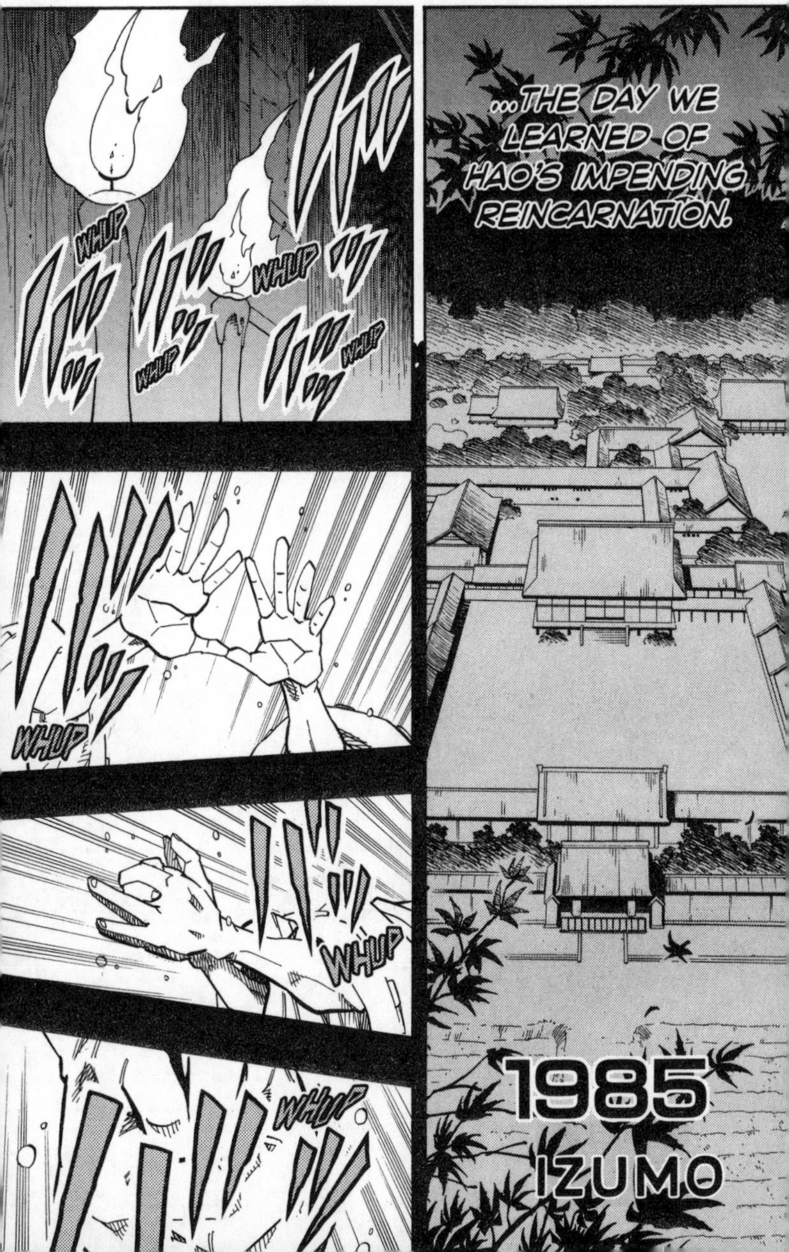
...THE DAY WE LEARNED OF HAO'S IMPENDING REINCARNATION.
1985
IZUMO
WHUP
WHUP
WHUP
WHUP
WHUP
WHUP
WHUP
WHUP

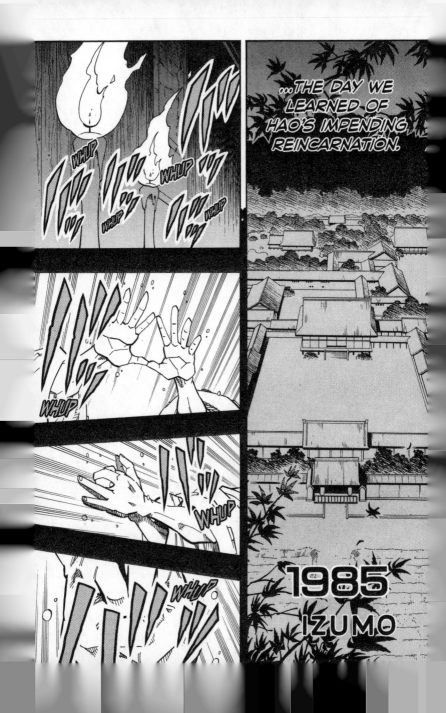

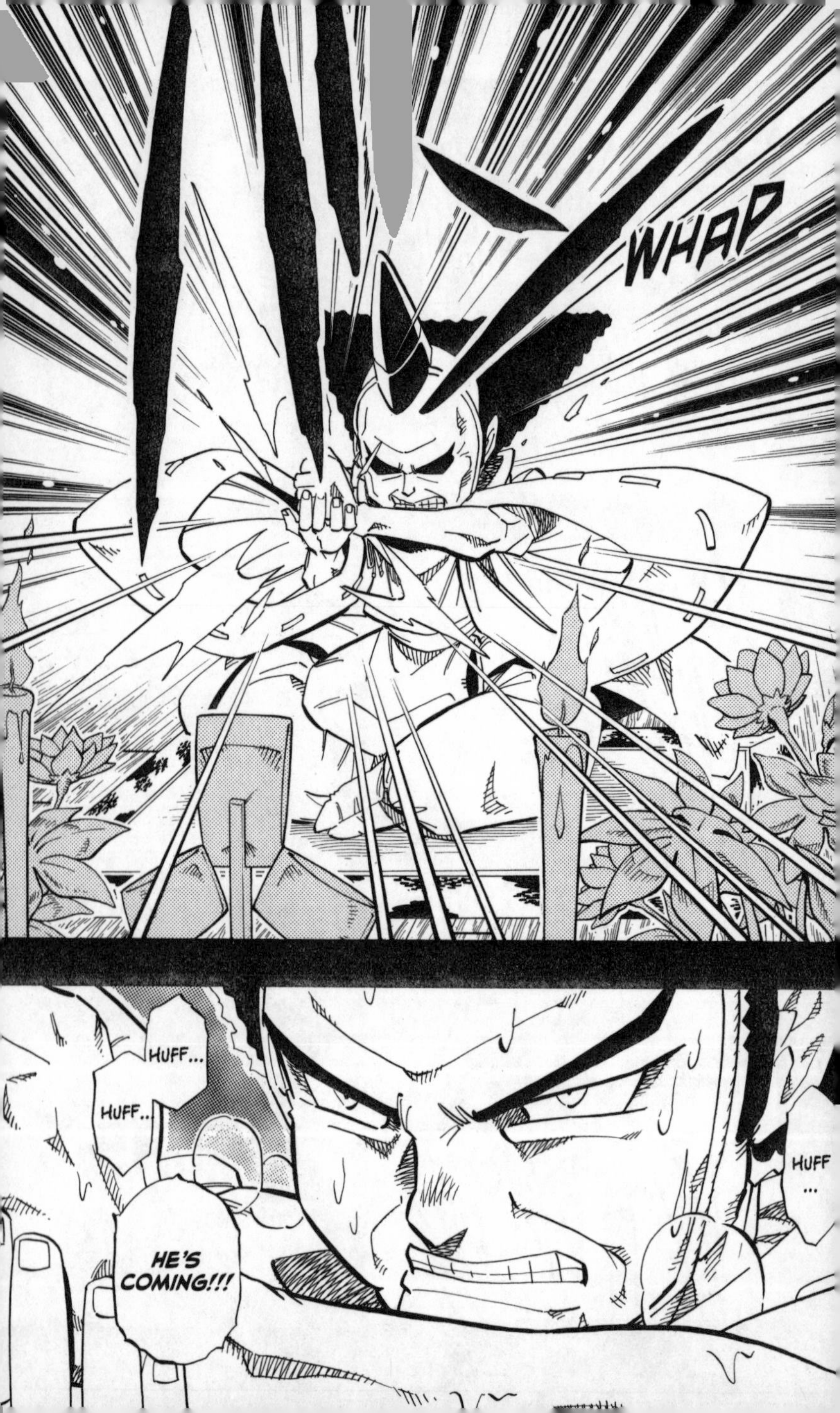
WHAP
HUFF...
HUFF...
HUFF
...
HE'S COMING!!!

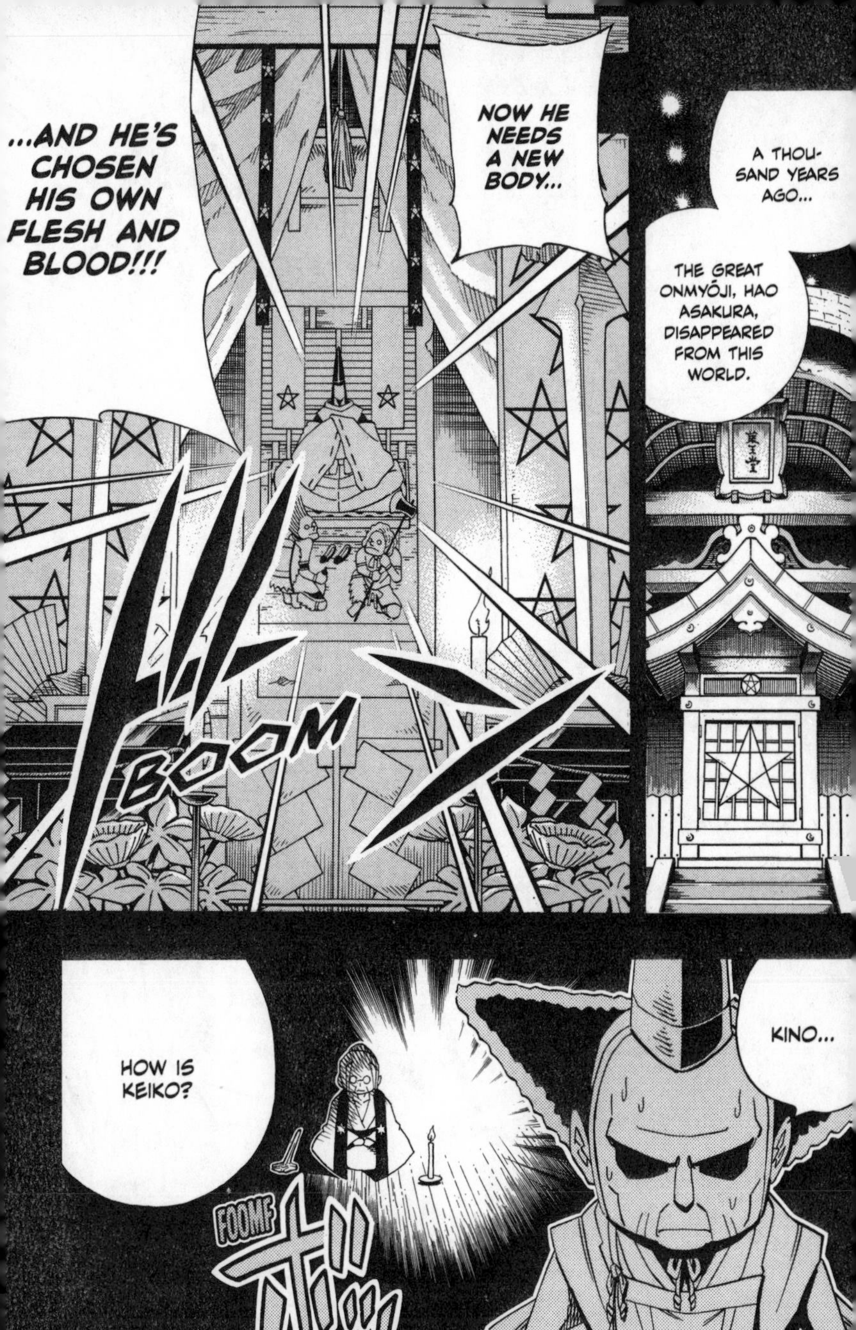
A THOU-SAND YEARS AGO...
THE GREAT ONMYŌJI, HAO ASAKURA, DISAPPEARED FROM THIS WORLD.
NOW HE NEEDS A NEW BODY...
...AND HE'S CHOSEN HIS OWN FLESH AND BLOOD!!!
BOOM
KINO...
HOW IS KEIKO?
FOOMF

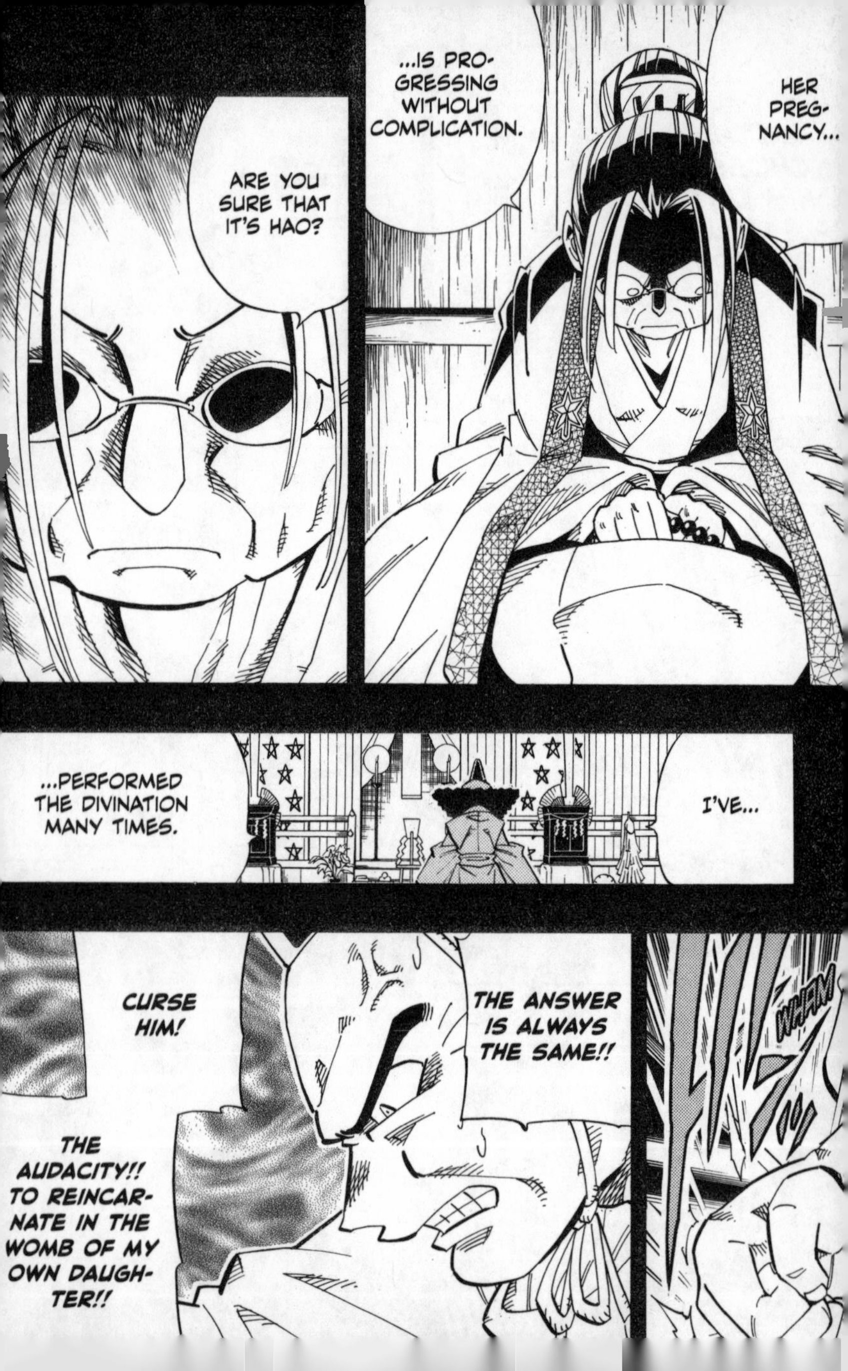
HER PREG-NANCY...
...IS PRO-GRESSING WITHOUT COMPLICATION.
ARE YOU SURE THAT IT'S HAO?
I'VE...
...PERFORMED THE DIVINATION MANY TIMES.
WHAM
THE ANSWER IS ALWAYS THE SAME!!
CURSE HIM!
THE AUDACITY!! TO REINCAR-NATE IN THE WOMB OF MY OWN DAUGH-TER!!

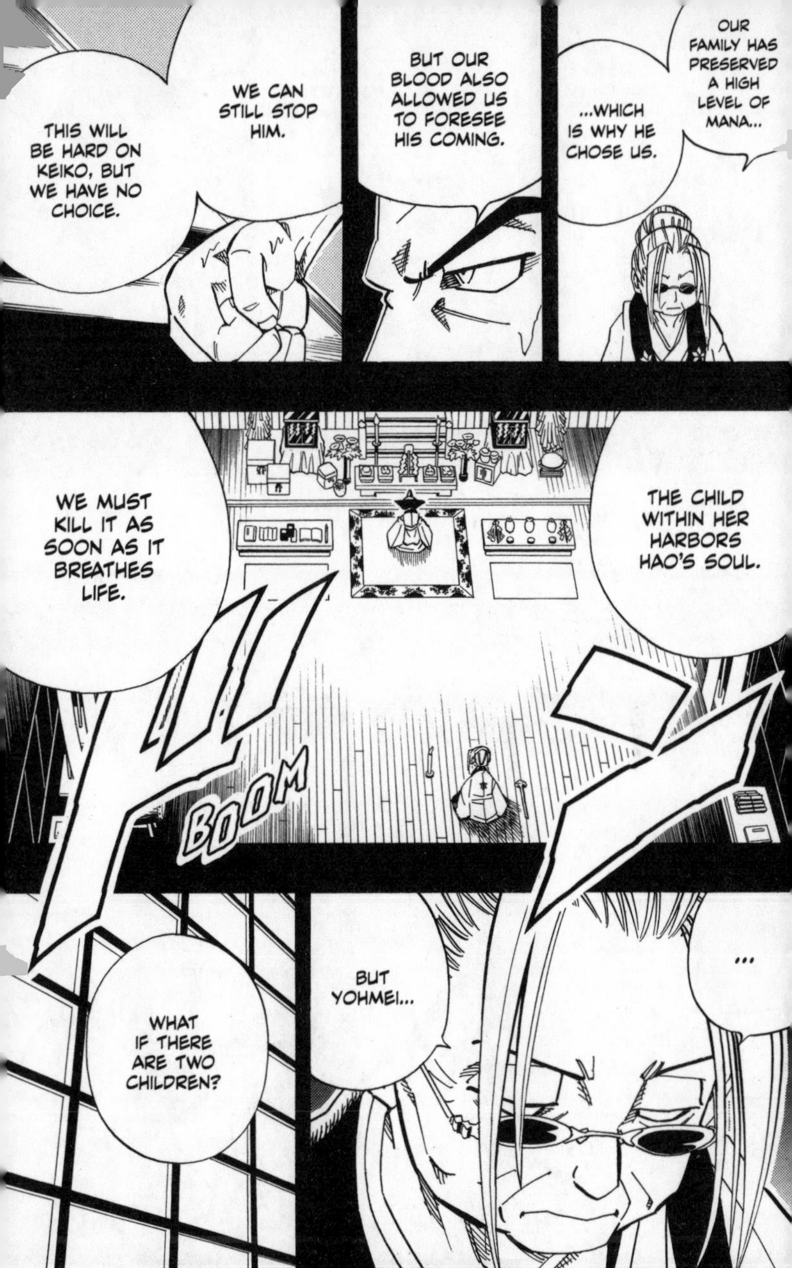
OUR FAMILY HAS PRESERVED A HIGH LEVEL OF MANA...
...WHICH IS WHY HE CHOSE US.
BUT OUR BLOOD ALSO ALLOWED US TO FORESEE HIS COMING.
WE CAN STILL STOP HIM.
THIS WILL BE HARD ON KEIKO, BUT WE HAVE NO CHOICE.
THE CHILD WITHIN HER HARBORS HAO'S SOUL.
WE MUST KILL IT AS SOON AS IT BREATHES LIFE.
BOOM
...
BUT YOHMEI...
WHAT IF THERE ARE TWO CHILDREN?

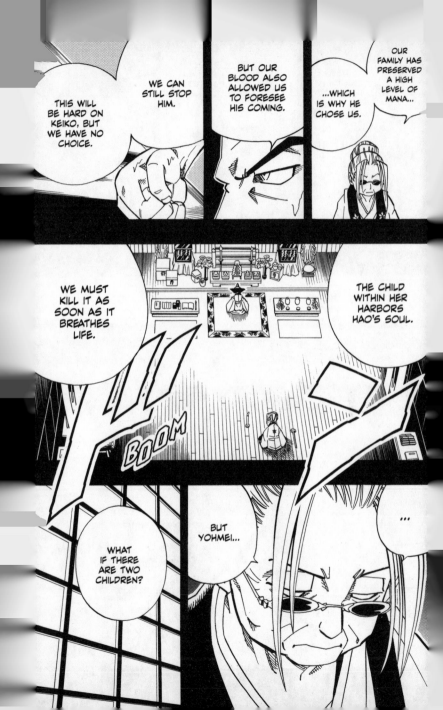

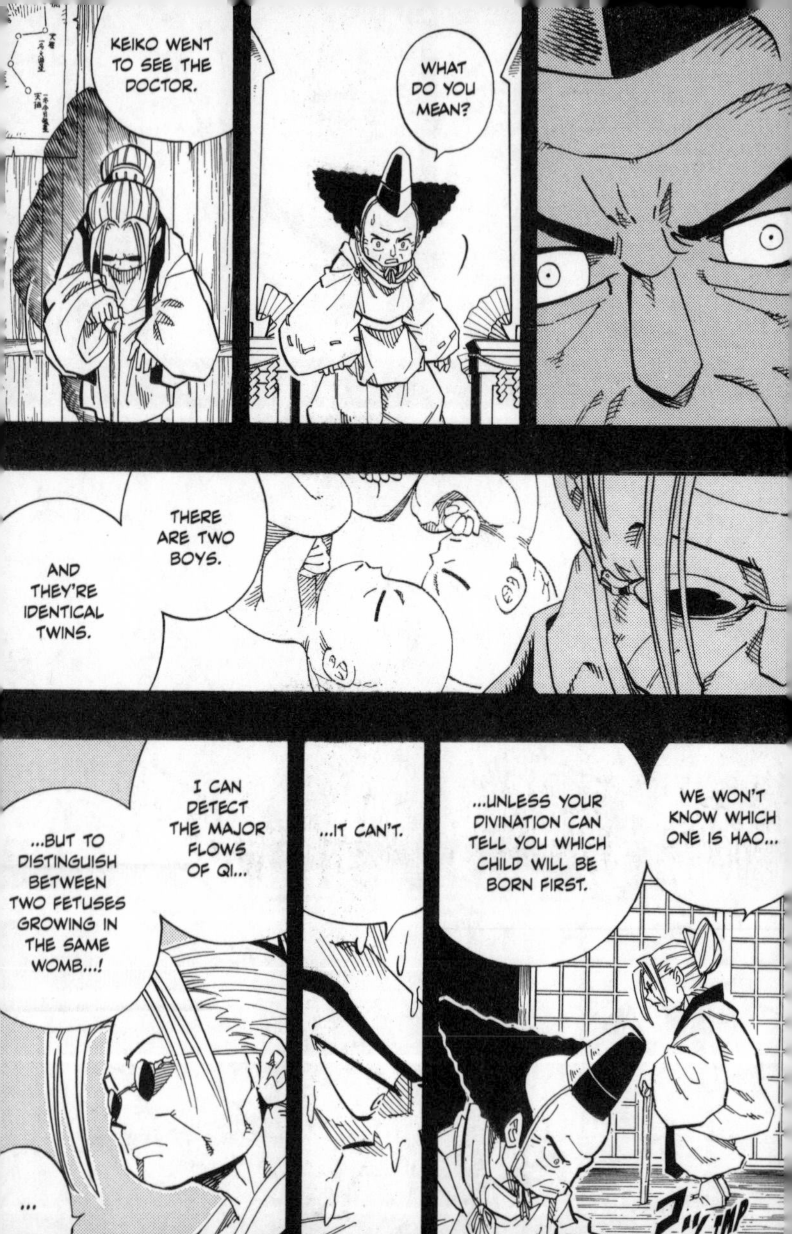
WHAT DO YOU MEAN?
KEIKO WENT TO SEE THE DOCTOR.
THERE ARE TWO BOYS.
AND THEY'RE IDENTICAL TWINS.
WE WON'T KNOW WHICH ONE IS HAO...
...UNLESS YOUR DIVINATION CAN TELL YOU WHICH CHILD WILL BE BORN FIRST.
コッ TMP
...IT CAN'T.
I CAN DETECT THE MAJOR FLOWS OF QI...
...BUT TO DISTINGUISH BETWEEN TWO FETUSES GROWING IN THE SAME WOMB...!
...

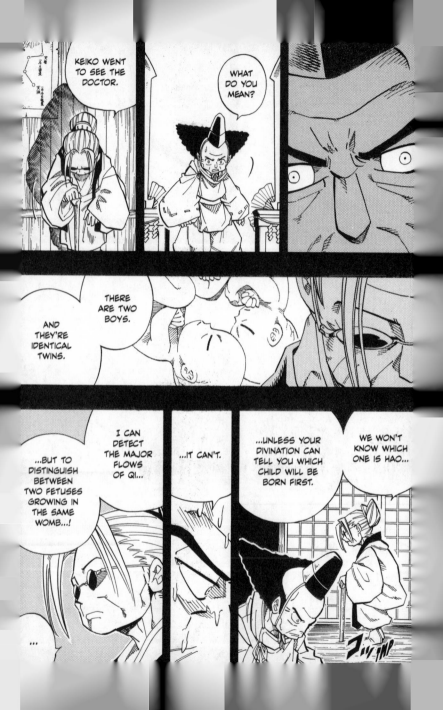

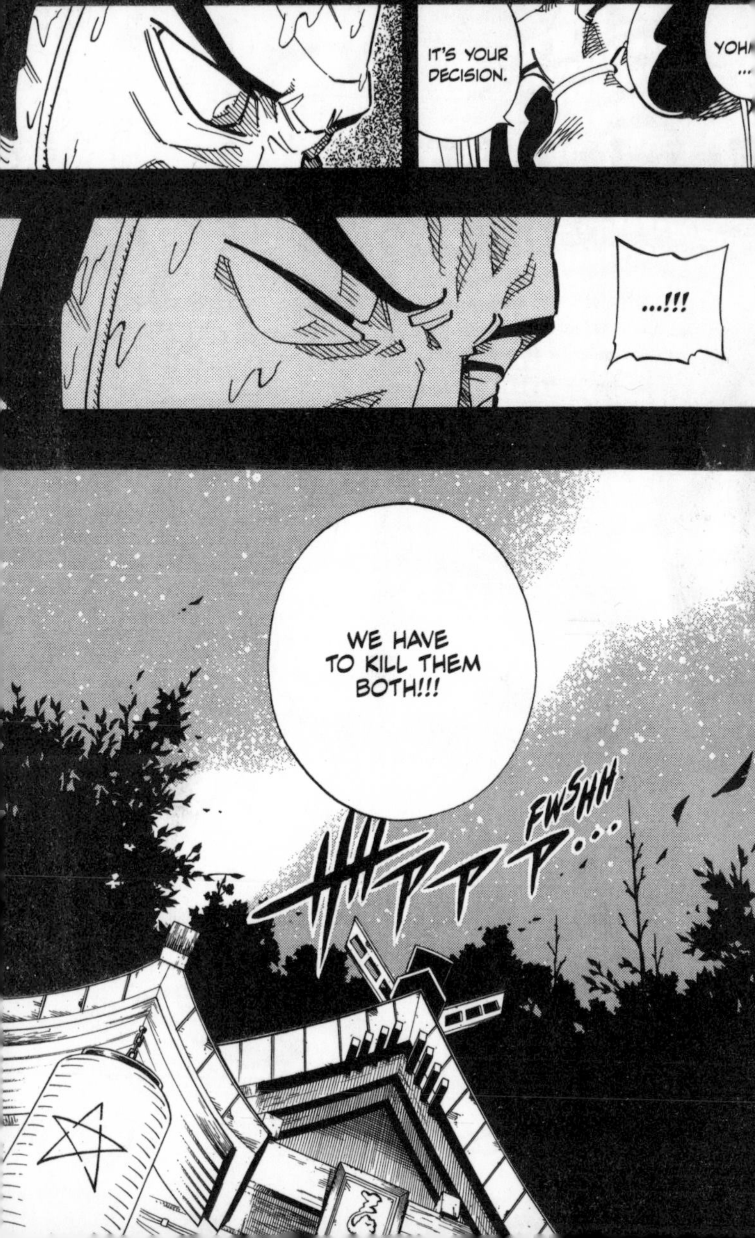
YOH...
IT'S YOUR DECISION.
...!!!
WE HAVE TO KILL THEM BOTH!!!
FWSHH

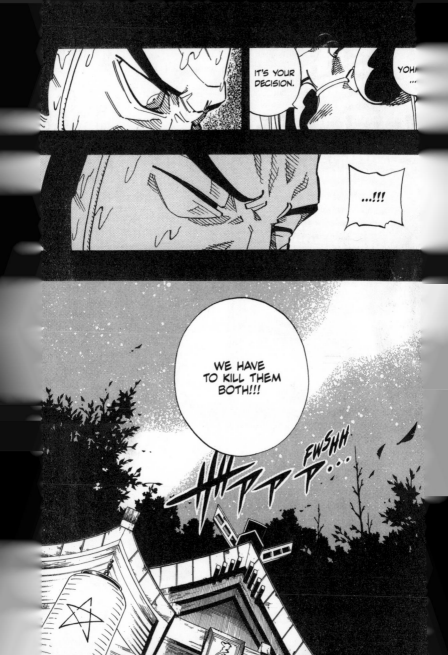

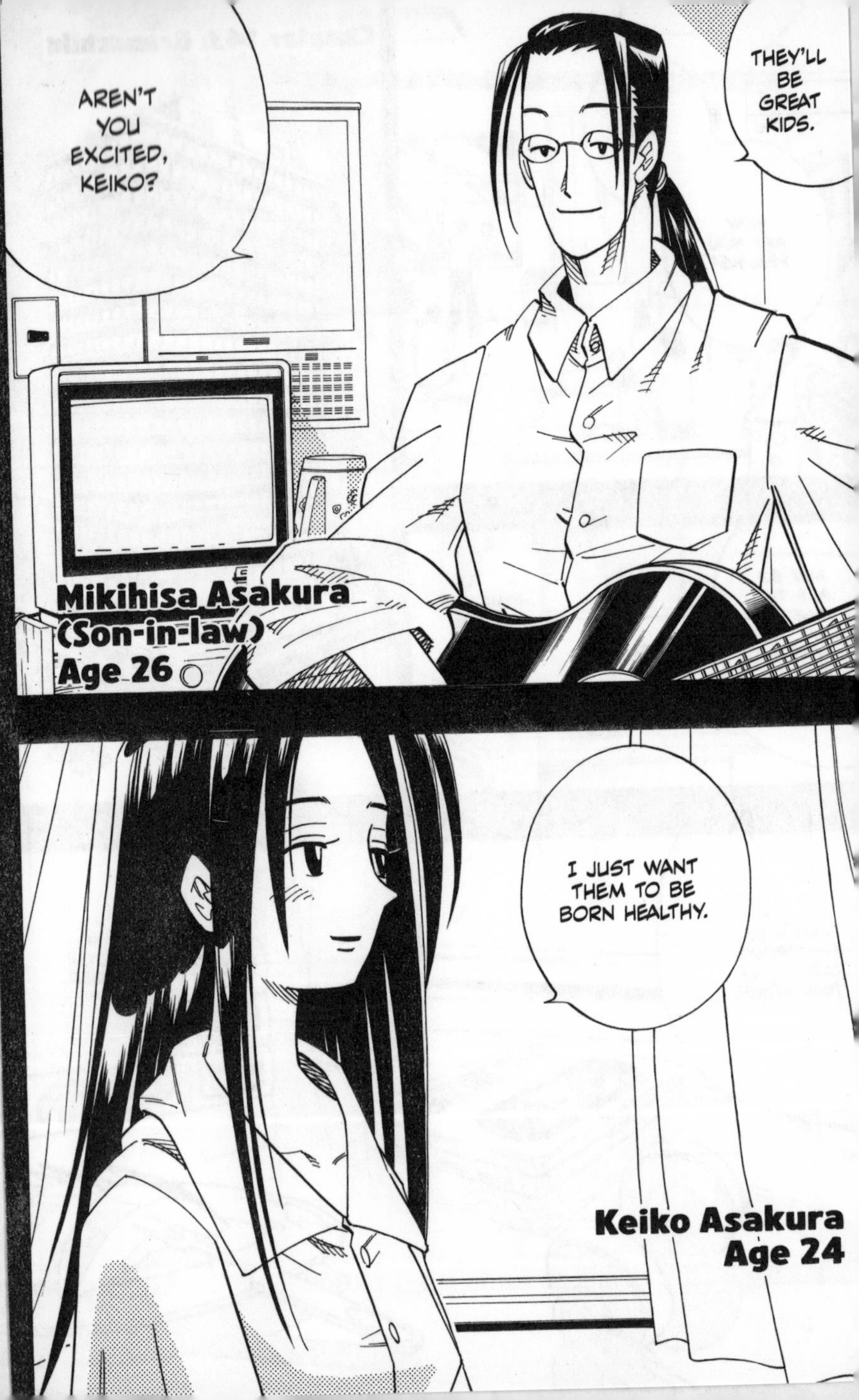
THEY'LL BE GREAT KIDS.
AREN'T YOU EXCITED, KEIKO?
Mikihisa Asakura (Son-in-law) Age 26
I JUST WANT THEM TO BE BORN HEALTHY.
Keiko Asakura Age 24

Chapter 143:

Grandchild

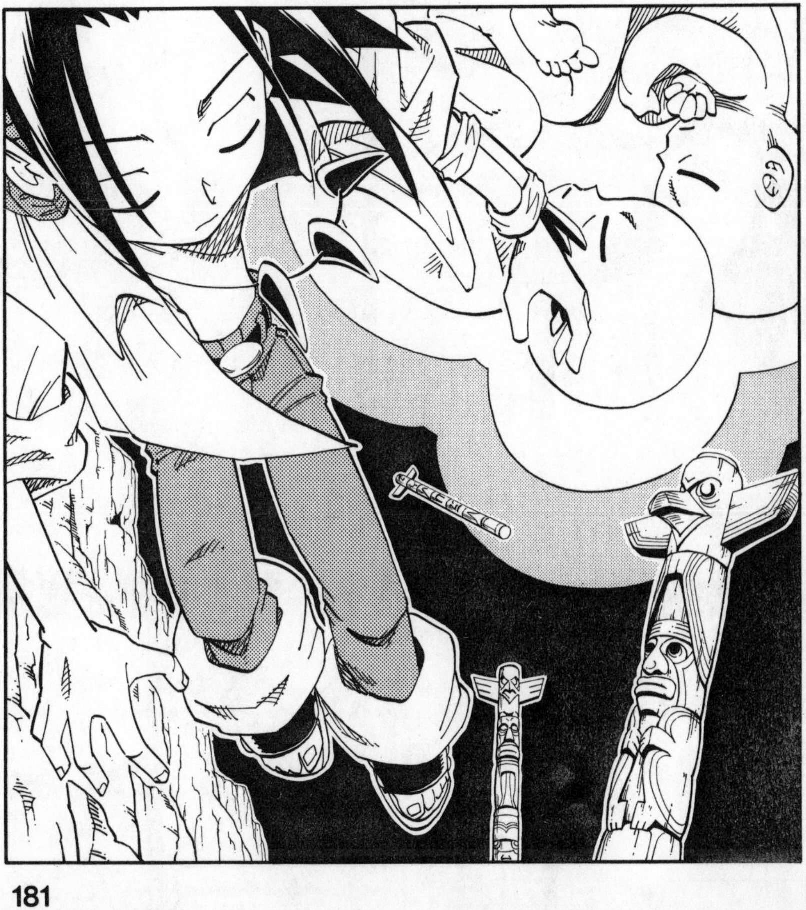

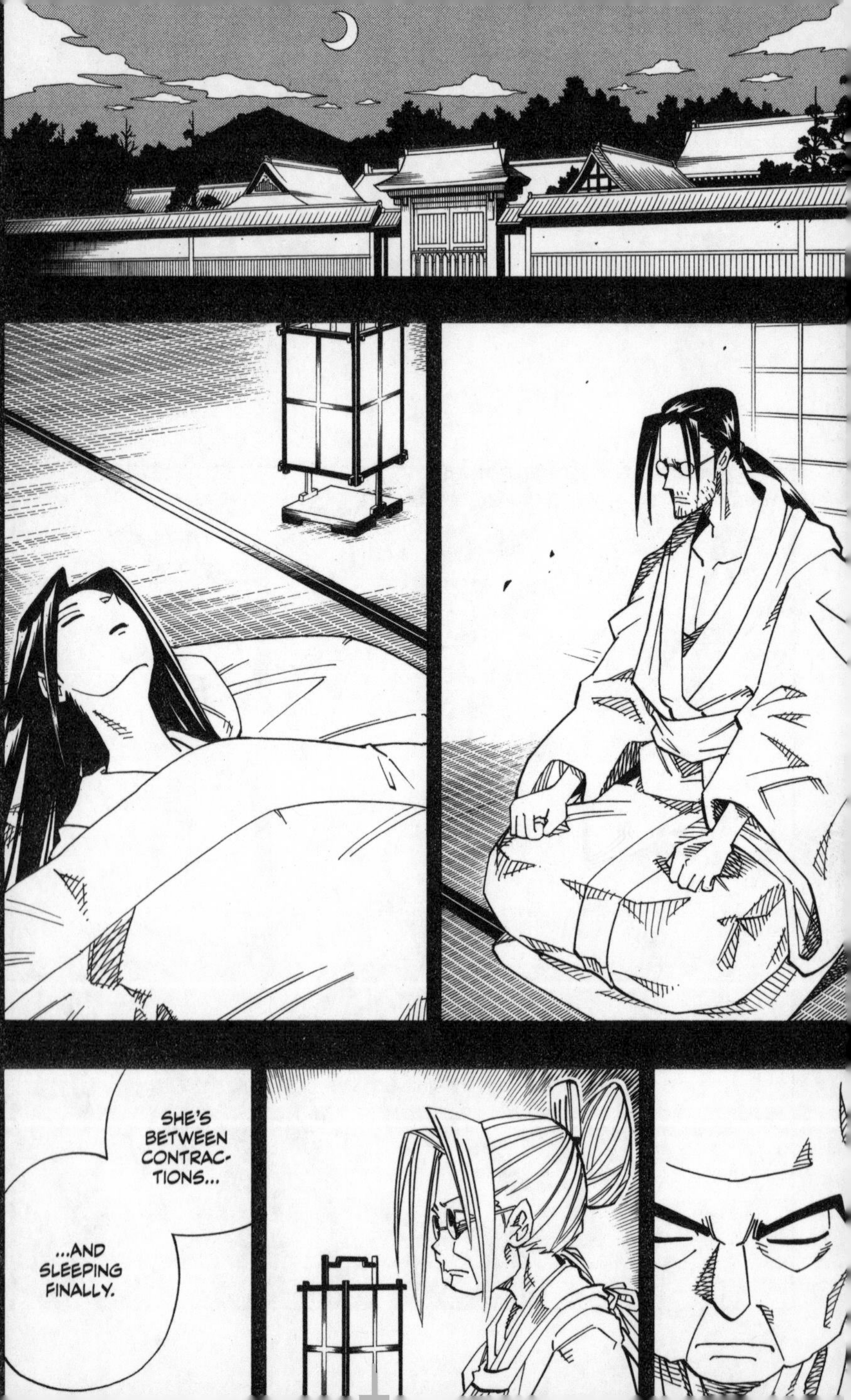
SHE'S BETWEEN CONTRACTIONS...
...AND SLEEPING FINALLY.

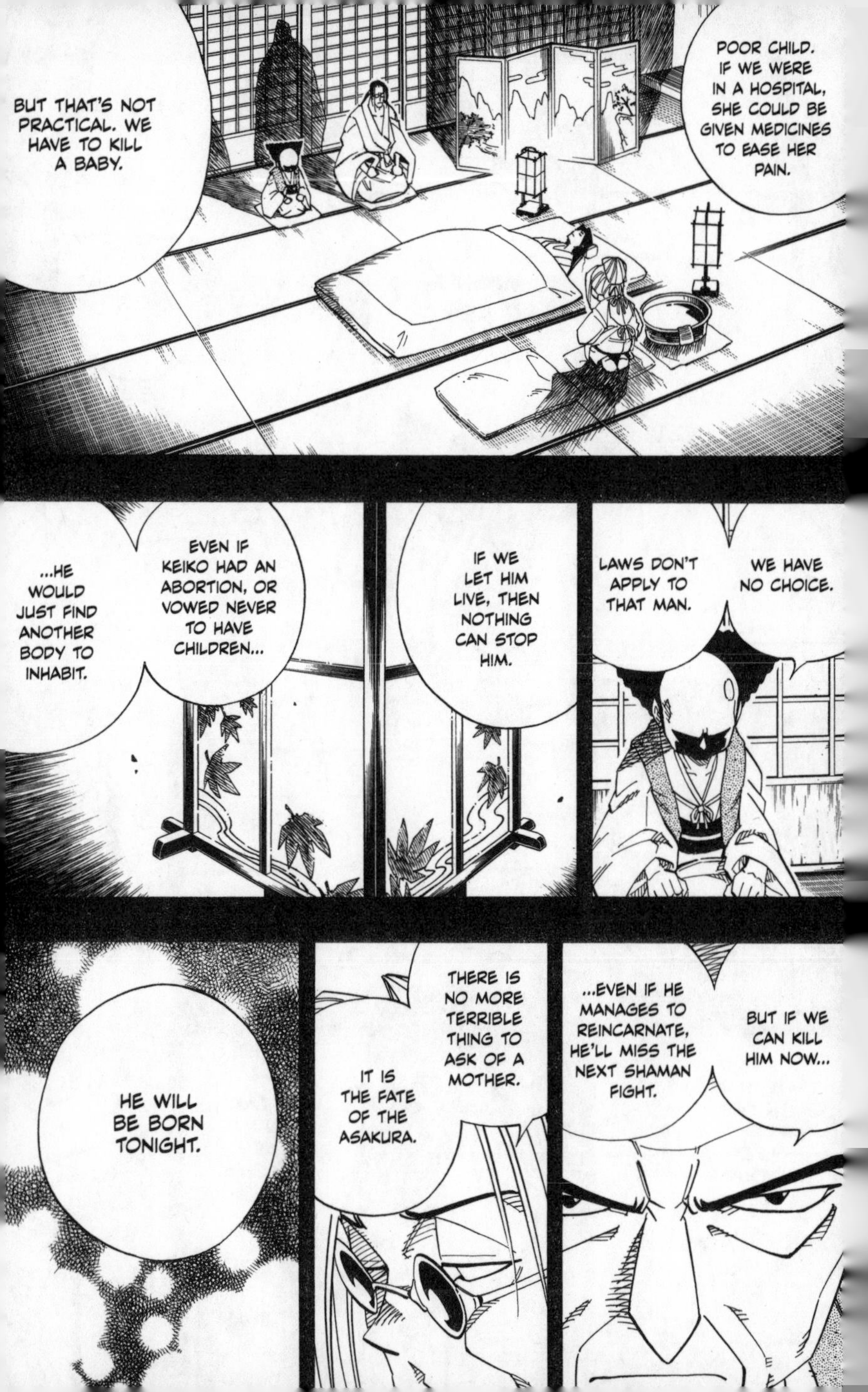
POOR CHILD. IF WE WERE IN A HOSPITAL, SHE COULD BE GIVEN MEDICINES TO EASE HER PAIN.
BUT THAT'S NOT PRACTICAL. WE HAVE TO KILL A BABY.
WE HAVE NO CHOICE.
LAWS DON'T APPLY TO THAT MAN.
IF WE LET HIM LIVE, THEN NOTHING CAN STOP HIM.
EVEN IF KEIKO HAD AN ABORTION, OR VOWED NEVER TO HAVE CHILDREN...
...HE WOULD JUST FIND ANOTHER BODY TO INHABIT.
BUT IF WE CAN KILL HIM NOW...
...EVEN IF HE MANAGES TO REINCARNATE, HE'LL MISS THE NEXT SHAMAN FIGHT.
THERE IS NO MORE TERRIBLE THING TO ASK OF A MOTHER.
IT IS THE FATE OF THE ASAKURA.
HE WILL BE BORN TONIGHT.

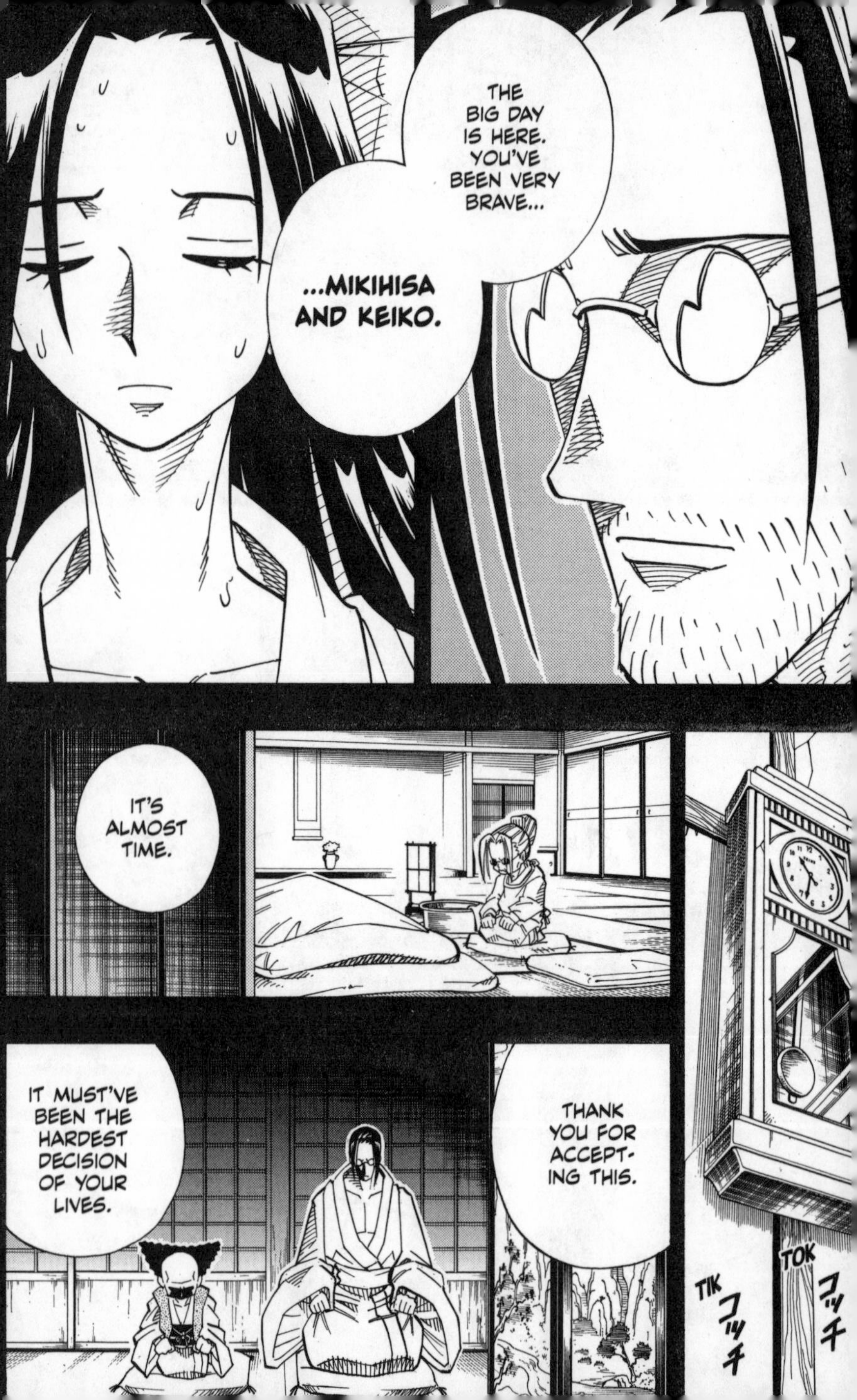
THE BIG DAY IS HERE. YOU'VE BEEN VERY BRAVE...
...MIKIHISA AND KEIKO.
TOK
コッチ
TIK
コッチ
IT'S ALMOST TIME.
THANK YOU FOR ACCEPT-ING THIS.
IT MUST'VE BEEN THE HARDEST DECISION OF YOUR LIVES.

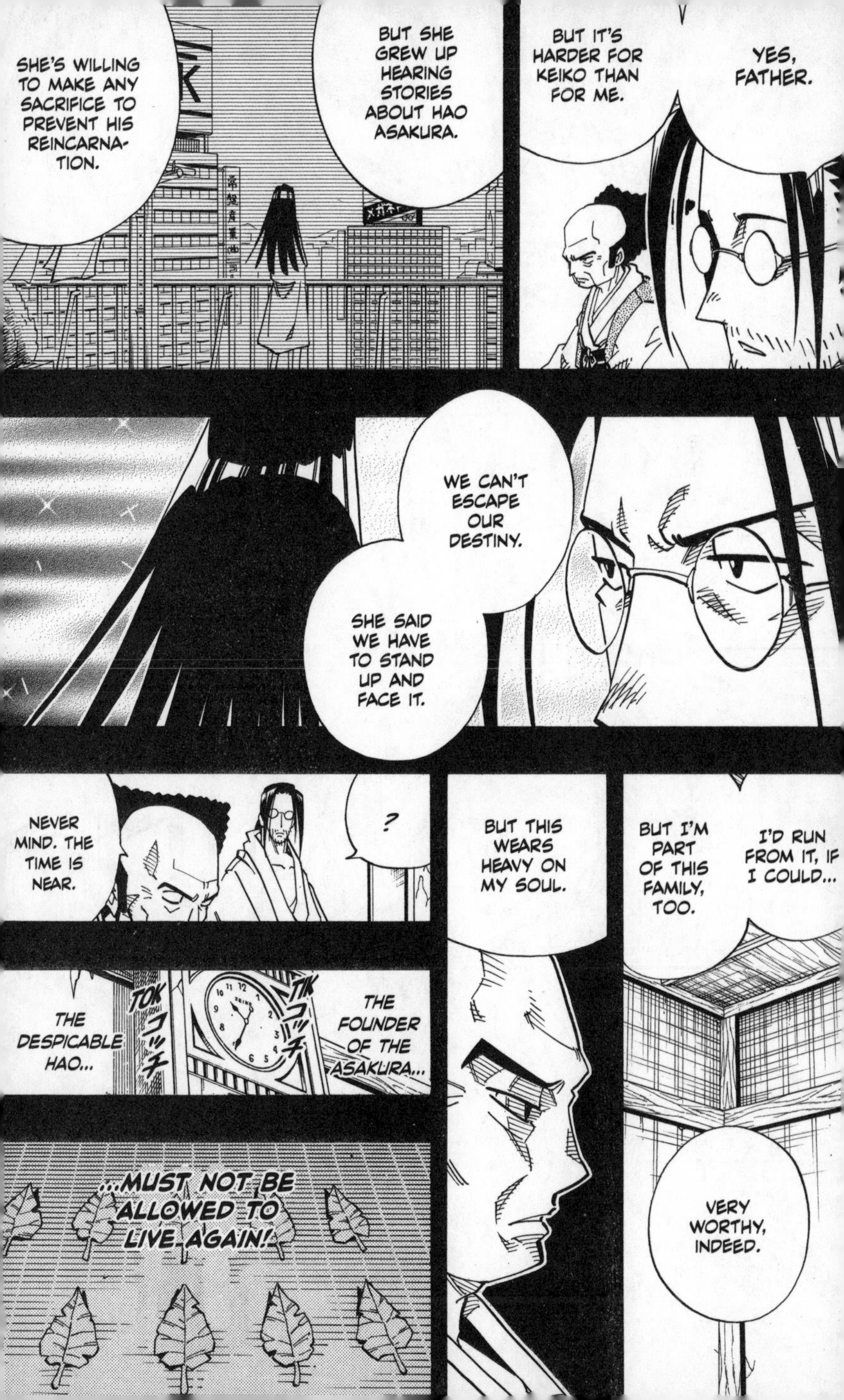
YES, FATHER.
BUT IT'S HARDER FOR KEIKO THAN FOR ME.
BUT SHE GREW UP HEARING STORIES ABOUT HAO ASAKURA.
SHE'S WILLING TO MAKE ANY SACRIFICE TO PREVENT HIS REINCARNATION.
WE CAN'T ESCAPE OUR DESTINY.
SHE SAID WE HAVE TO STAND UP AND FACE IT.
I'D RUN FROM IT, IF I COULD...
BUT I'M PART OF THIS FAMILY, TOO.
VERY WORTHY, INDEED.
BUT THIS WEARS HEAVY ON MY SOUL.
?
NEVER MIND. THE TIME IS NEAR.
THE FOUNDER OF THE ASAKURA...
TIK
TOK
THE DESPICABLE HAO...
...MUST NOT BE ALLOWED TO LIVE AGAIN!

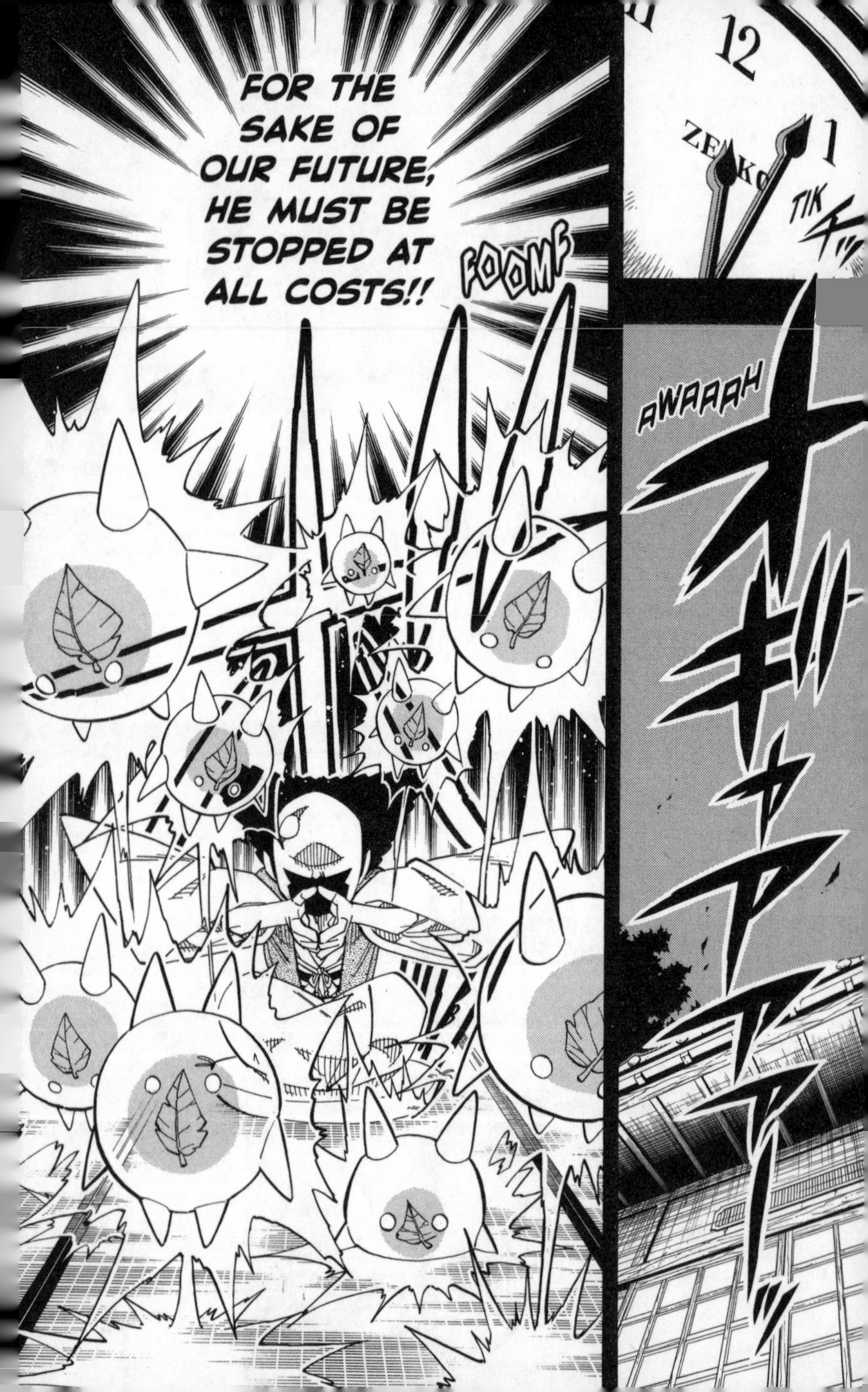
TIK
AWAAAH
FOR THE SAKE OF OUR FUTURE, HE MUST BE STOPPED AT ALL COSTS!!
FOOMF

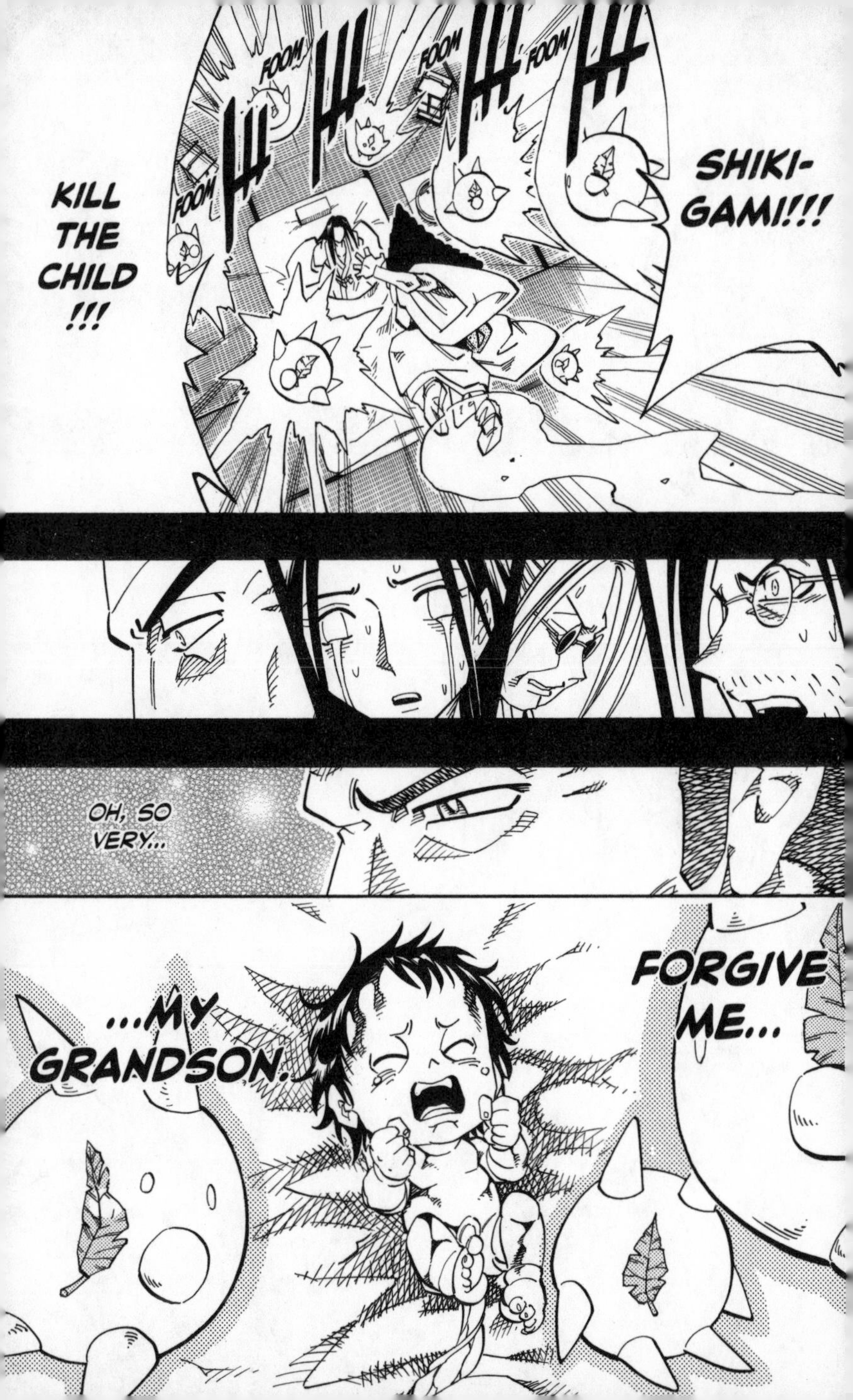
SHIKI-GAMI!!!
FOOM
FOOM
FOOM
FOOM
KILL THE CHILD!!!
OH, SO VERY...
FORGIVE ME...
...MY GRANDSON.

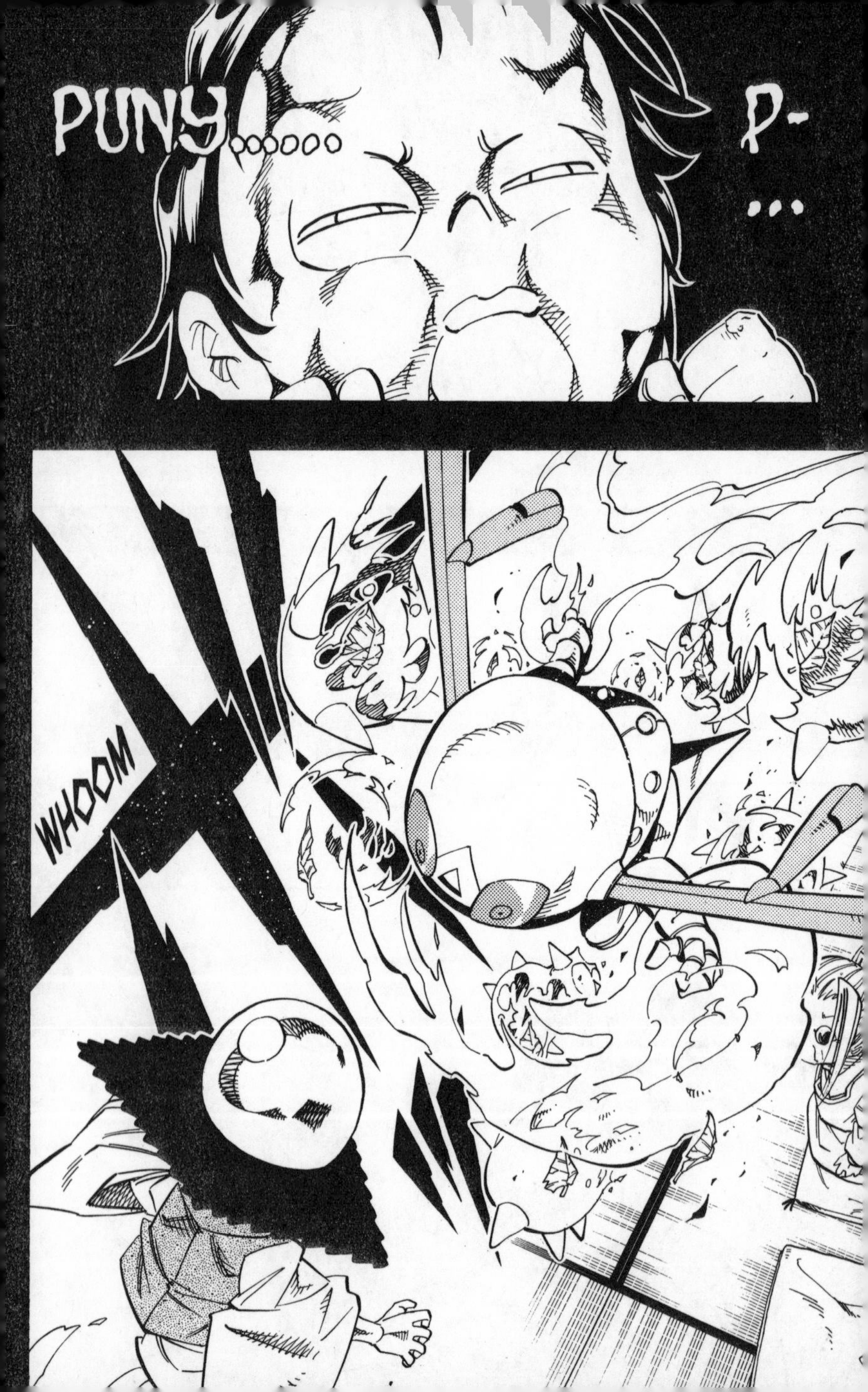
P- ...
PUNY......
WHOOM

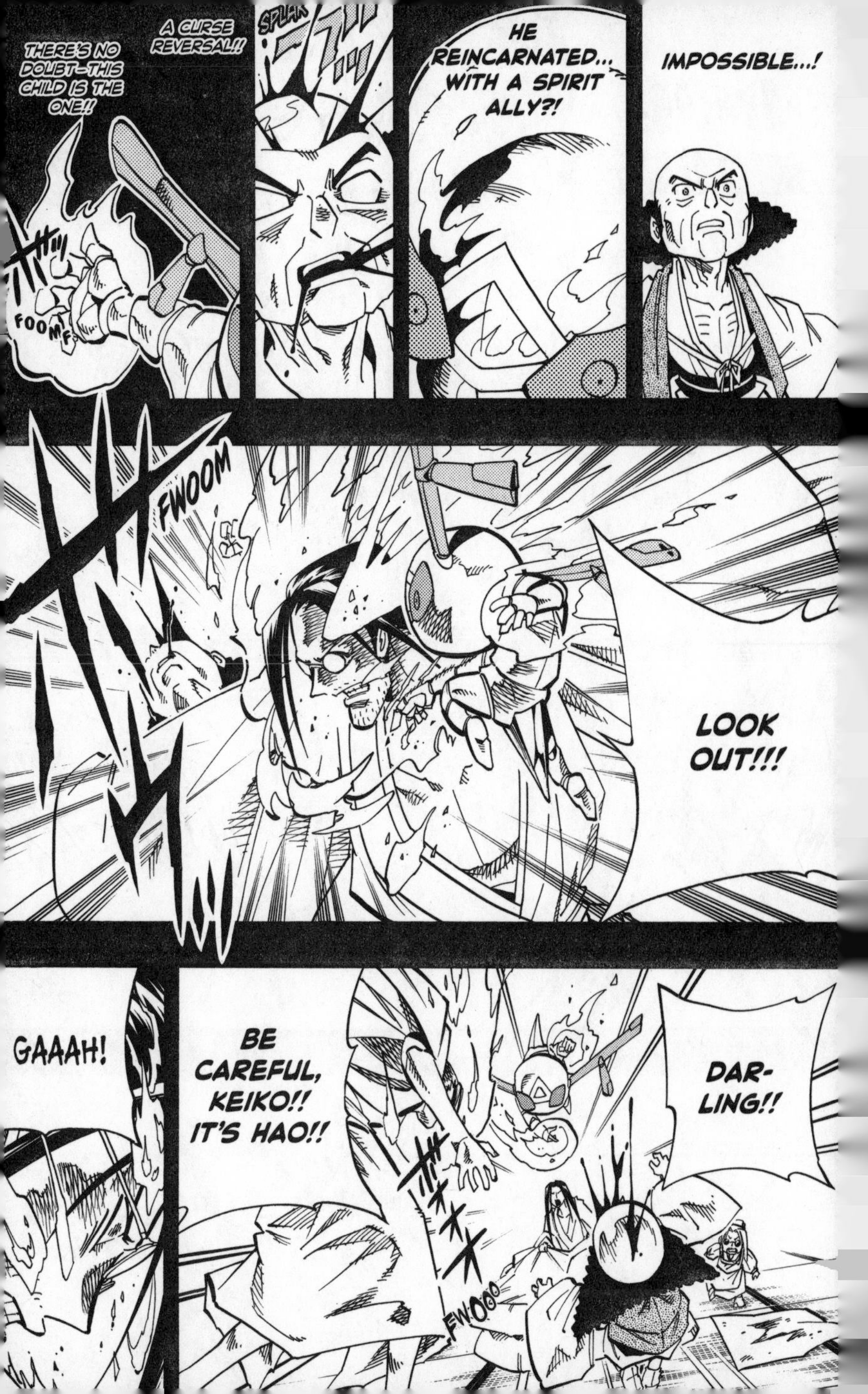

IMPOSSIBLE...!
HE REINCARNATED... WITH A SPIRIT ALLY?!
SPLAK
A CURSE REVERSAL!!
THERE'S NO DOUBT-THIS CHILD IS THE ONE!!
FOOMF
LOOK OUT!!!
FWOOM
DAR-LING!!
BE CAREFUL, KEIKO!! IT'S HAO!!
FWOOO
GAAAH!

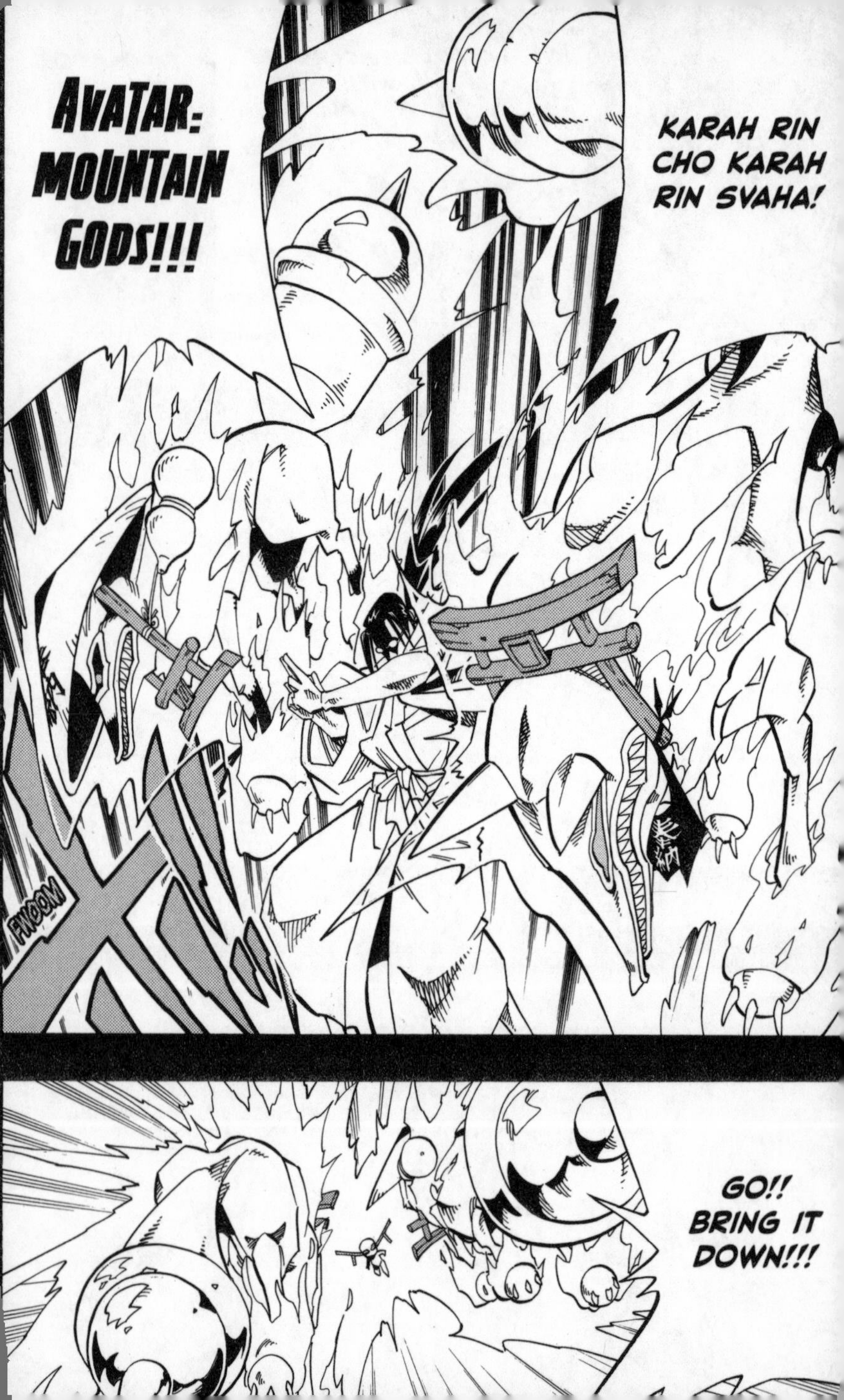
KARAH RIN CHO KARAH RIN SVAHA!
AVATAR: MOUNTAIN GODS!!!
FWOOM
GO!! BRING IT DOWN!!!

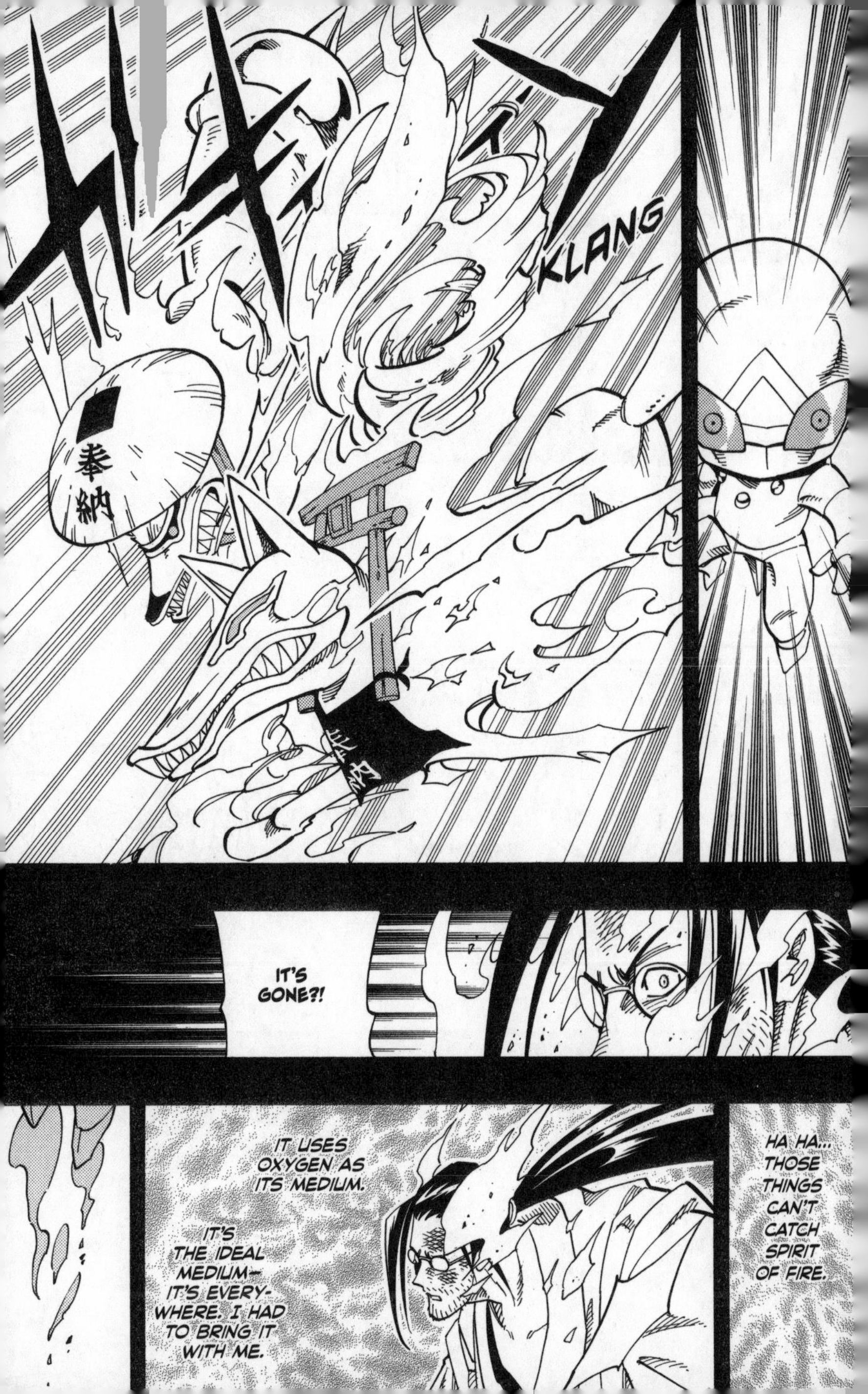
KLANG
奉納
IT'S GONE?!
HA HA... THOSE THINGS CAN'T CATCH SPIRIT OF FIRE.
IT USES OXYGEN AS ITS MEDIUM.
IT'S THE IDEAL MEDIUM—IT'S EVERY-WHERE. I HAD TO BRING IT WITH ME.

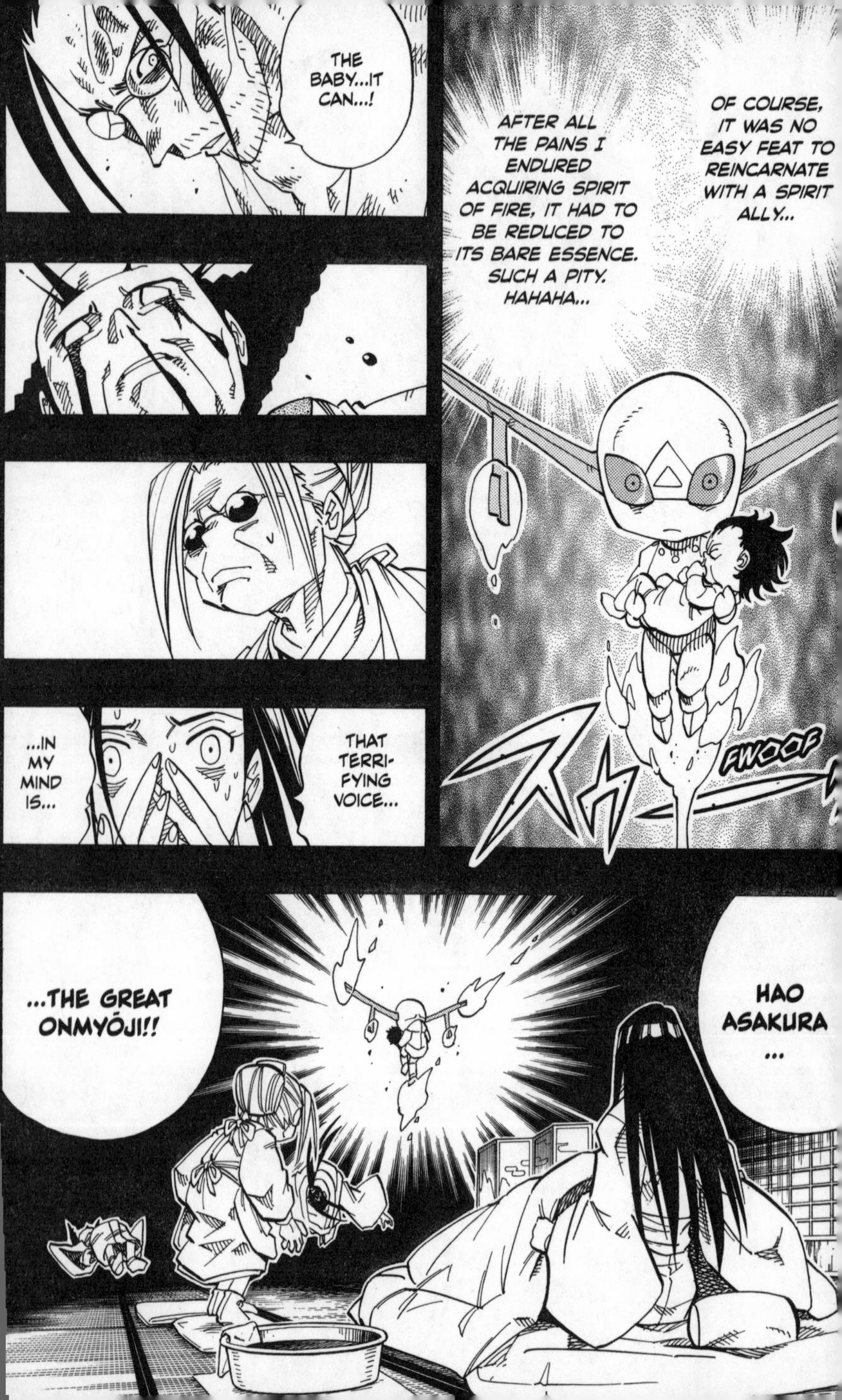
OF COURSE, IT WAS NO EASY FEAT TO REINCARNATE WITH A SPIRIT ALLY...
AFTER ALL THE PAINS I ENDURED ACQUIRING SPIRIT OF FIRE, IT HAD TO BE REDUCED TO ITS BARE ESSENCE. SUCH A PITY. HAHAHA...
FWOOF
THE BABY...IT CAN...!
THAT TERRI-FYING VOICE...
...IN MY MIND IS...
HAO ASAKURA ...
...THE GREAT ONMYŌJI!!

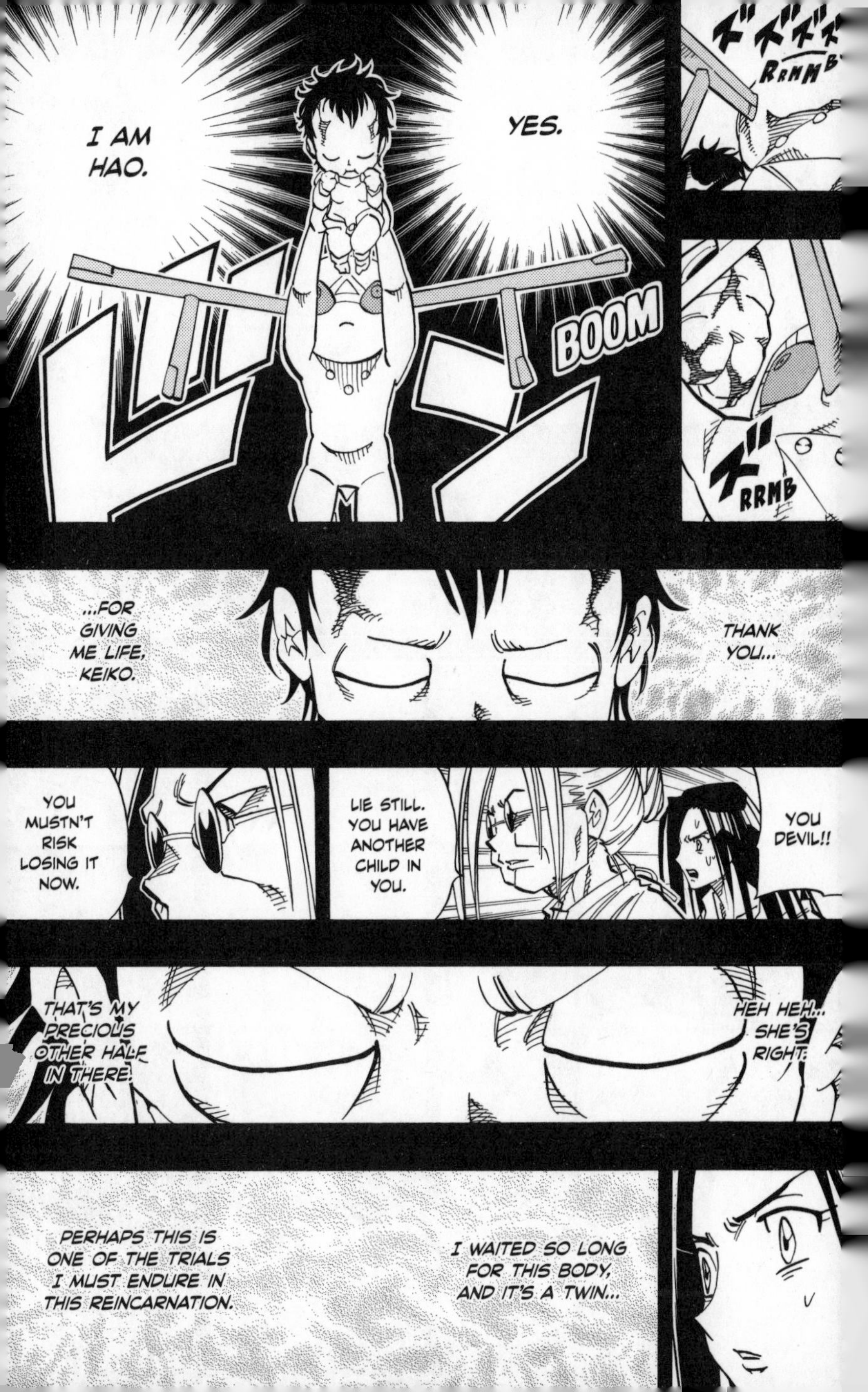
RRMB
RRMB
YES.
I AM HAO.
BOOM
THANK YOU...
...FOR GIVING ME LIFE, KEIKO.
YOU DEVIL!!
LIE STILL. YOU HAVE ANOTHER CHILD IN YOU.
YOU MUSTN'T RISK LOSING IT NOW.
HEH HEH... SHE'S RIGHT.
THAT'S MY PRECIOUS OTHER HALF IN THERE.
I WAITED SO LONG FOR THIS BODY, AND IT'S A TWIN...
PERHAPS THIS IS ONE OF THE TRIALS I MUST ENDURE IN THIS REINCARNATION.

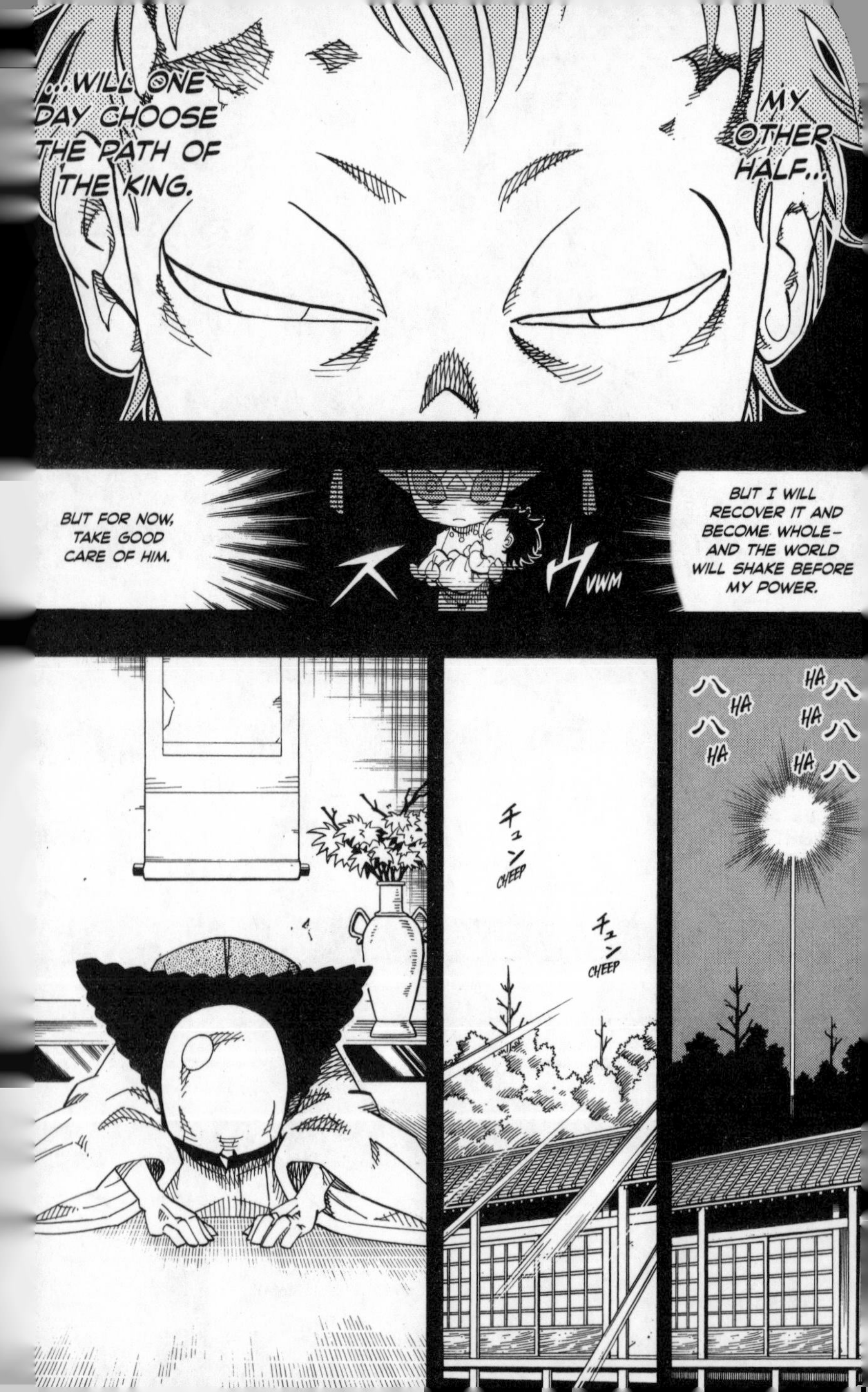
MY OTHER HALF...
...WILL ONE DAY CHOOSE THE PATH OF THE KING.
BUT I WILL RECOVER IT AND BECOME WHOLE— AND THE WORLD WILL SHAKE BEFORE MY POWER.
ヴ VWM
ス
BUT FOR NOW, TAKE GOOD CARE OF HIM.
ハ HA ハ HA ハ HA
ハ HA ハ HA
チュン CHEEP
チュン CHEEP

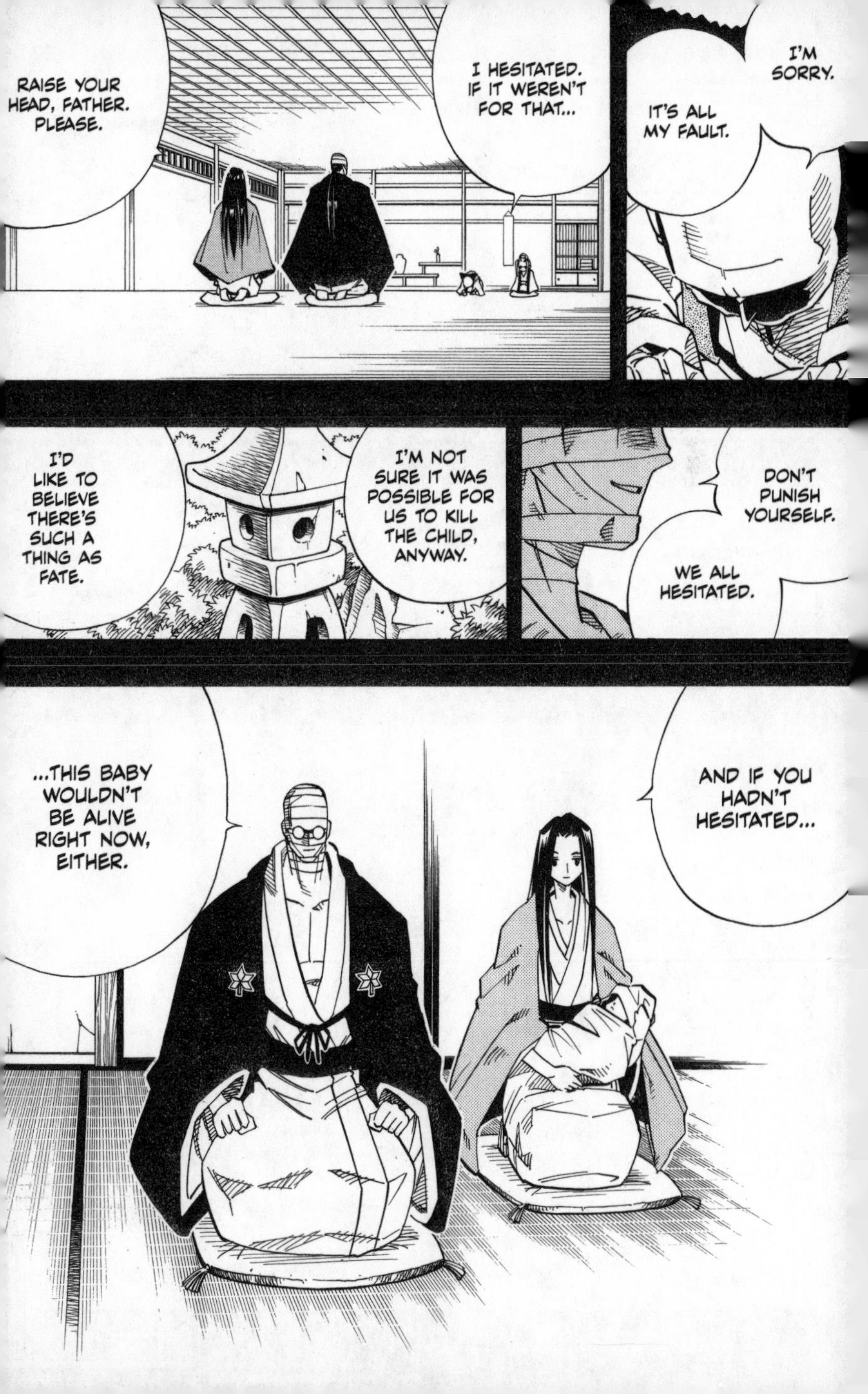
I'M SORRY.
IT'S ALL MY FAULT.
I HESITATED. IF IT WEREN'T FOR THAT...
RAISE YOUR HEAD, FATHER. PLEASE.
DON'T PUNISH YOURSELF.
WE ALL HESITATED.
I'M NOT SURE IT WAS POSSIBLE FOR US TO KILL THE CHILD, ANYWAY.
I'D LIKE TO BELIEVE THERE'S SUCH A THING AS FATE.
AND IF YOU HADN'T HESITATED...
...THIS BABY WOULDN'T BE ALIVE RIGHT NOW, EITHER.

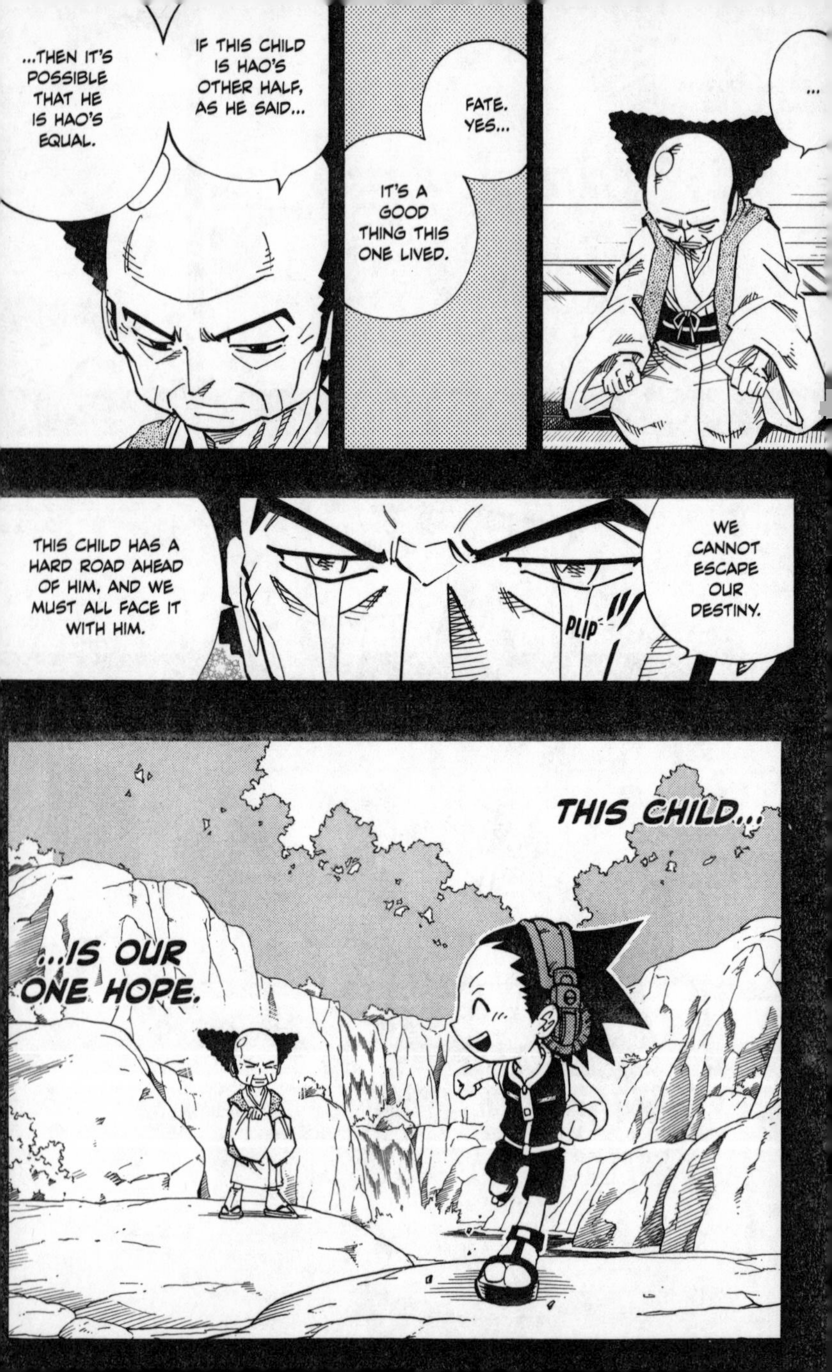
...
FATE. YES...
IT'S A GOOD THING THIS ONE LIVED.
IF THIS CHILD IS HAO'S OTHER HALF, AS HE SAID...
...THEN IT'S POSSIBLE THAT HE IS HAO'S EQUAL.
WE CANNOT ESCAPE OUR DESTINY.
PLIP
THIS CHILD HAS A HARD ROAD AHEAD OF HIM, AND WE MUST ALL FACE IT WITH HIM.
THIS CHILD...
...IS OUR ONE HOPE.

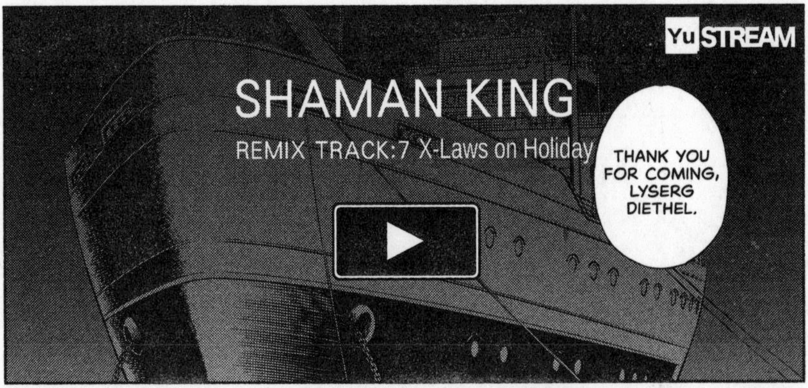
Yu STREAM
SHAMAN KING
REMIX TRACK:7 X-Laws on Holiday
THANK YOU FOR COMING, LYSERG DIETHEL.

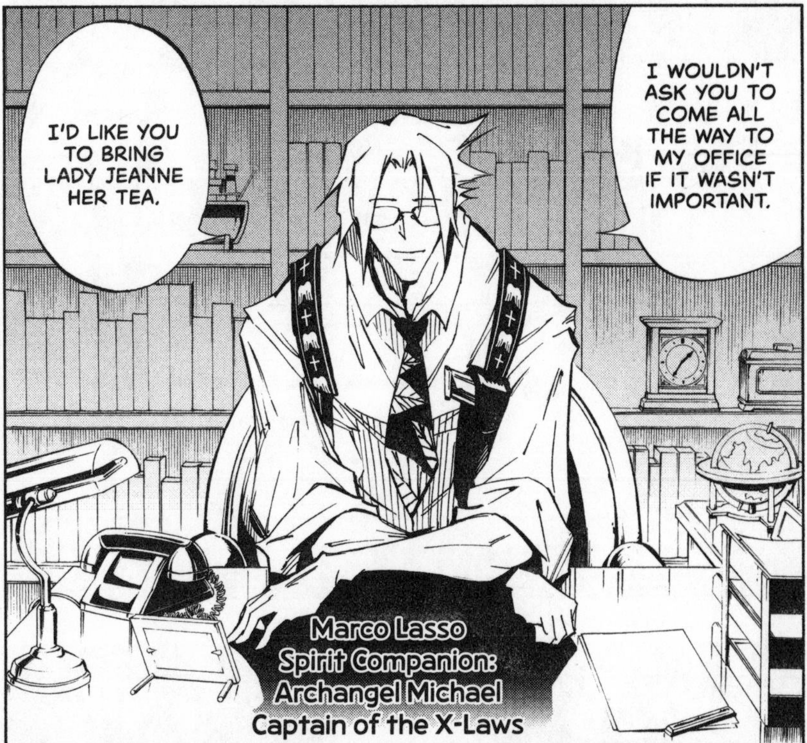
I WOULDN'T ASK YOU TO COME ALL THE WAY TO MY OFFICE IF IT WASN'T IMPORTANT.
I'D LIKE YOU TO BRING LADY JEANNE HER TEA.
Marco Lasso
Spirit Companion: Archangel Michael
Captain of the X-Laws

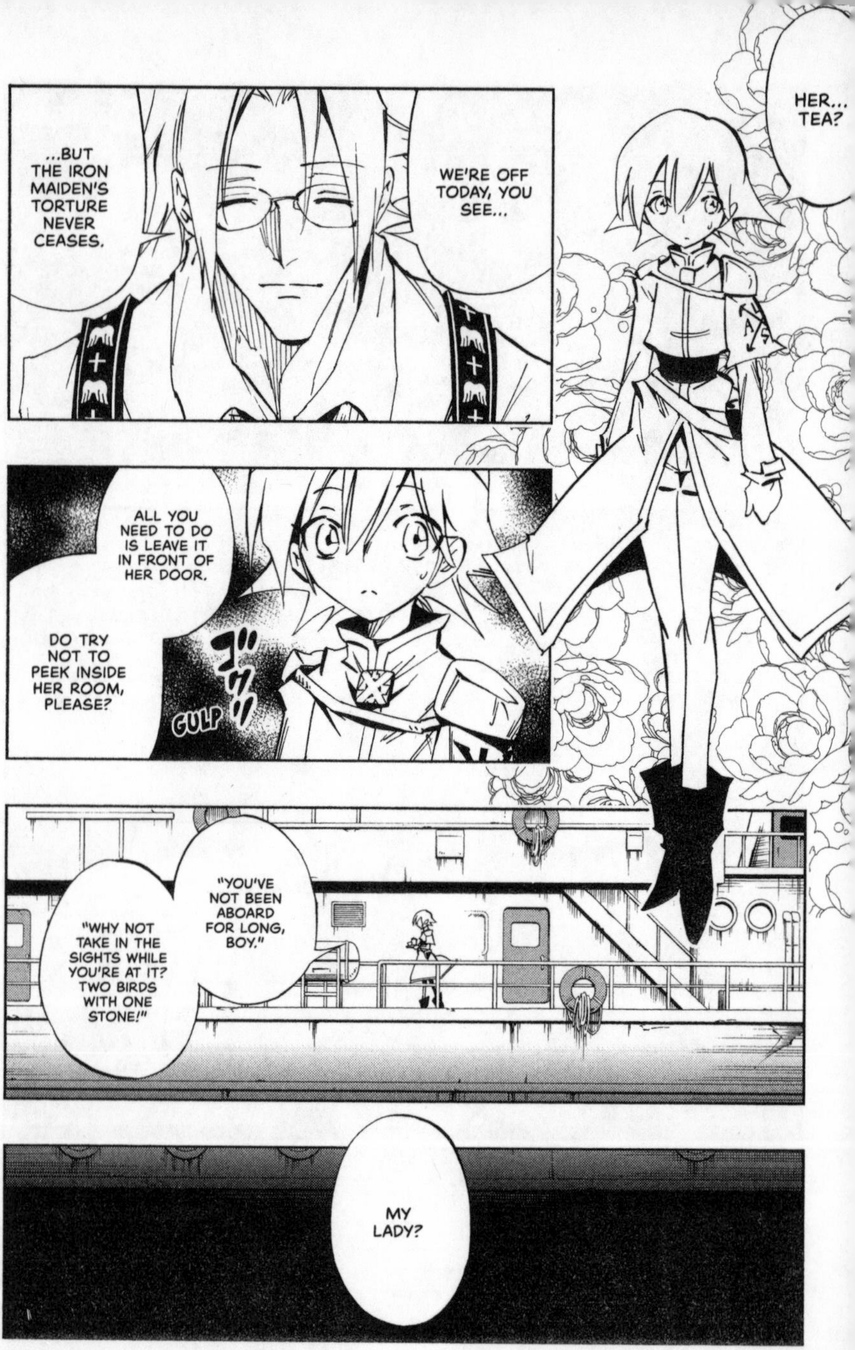
HER... TEA?
WE'RE OFF TODAY, YOU SEE...
...BUT THE IRON MAIDEN'S TORTURE NEVER CEASES.
ALL YOU NEED TO DO IS LEAVE IT IN FRONT OF HER DOOR.
DO TRY NOT TO PEEK INSIDE HER ROOM, PLEASE?
GULP
"YOU'VE NOT BEEN ABOARD FOR LONG, BOY."
"WHY NOT TAKE IN THE SIGHTS WHILE YOU'RE AT IT? TWO BIRDS WITH ONE STONE!"
MY LADY?

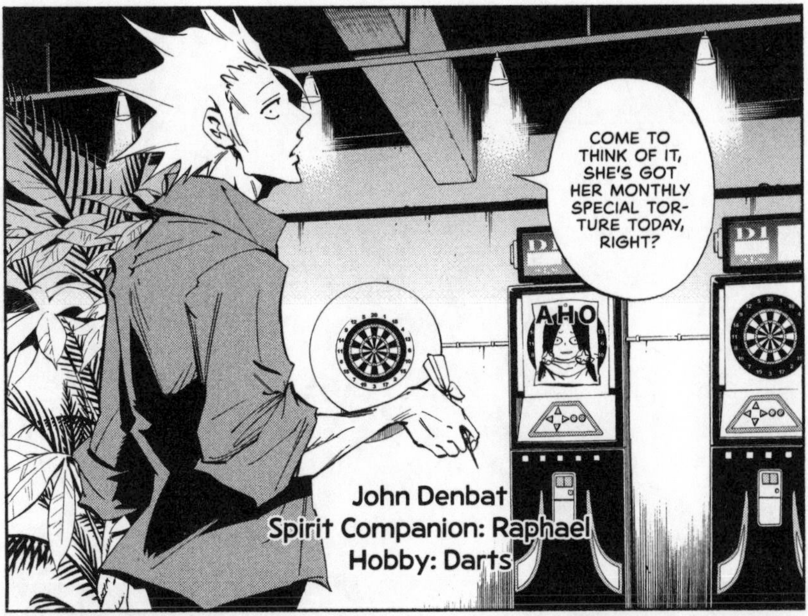
COME TO THINK OF IT, SHE'S GOT HER MONTHLY SPECIAL TORTURE TODAY, RIGHT?
AHO
John Denbat
Spirit Companion: Raphael
Hobby: Darts

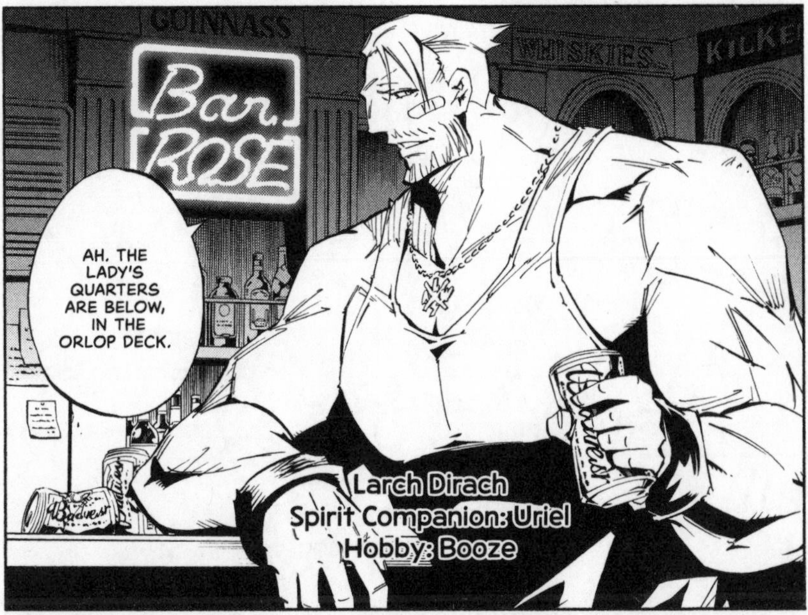
GUINNASS
WHISKIES
Bar. ROSE
AH. THE LADY'S QUARTERS ARE BELOW, IN THE ORLOP DECK.
Larch Dirach
Spirit Companion: Uriel
Hobby: Booze

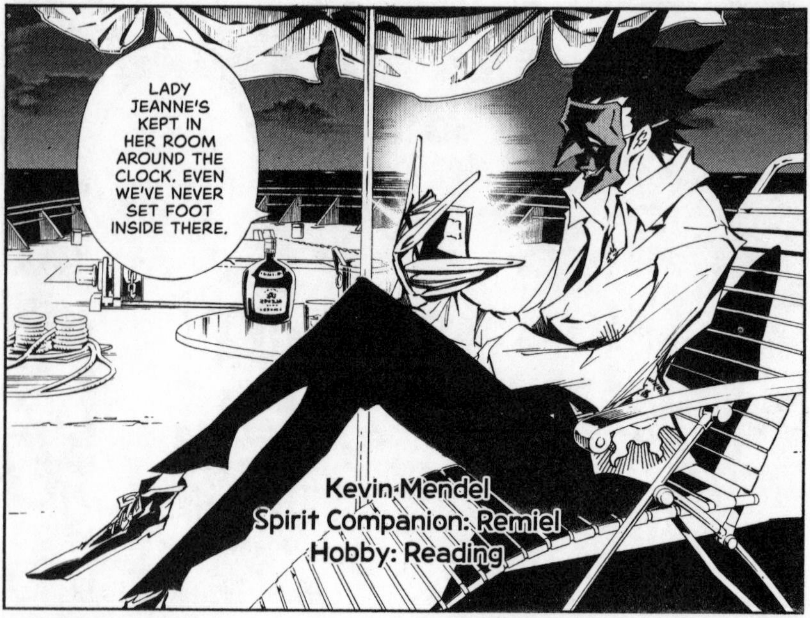
LADY JEANNE'S KEPT IN HER ROOM AROUND THE CLOCK. EVEN WE'VE NEVER SET FOOT INSIDE THERE.
Kevin Mendel
Spirit Companion: Remiel
Hobby: Reading

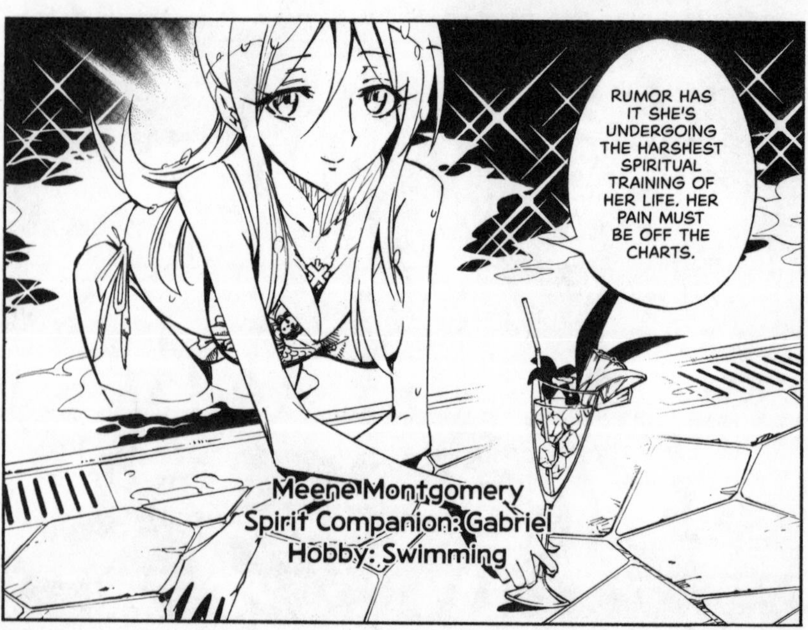
RUMOR HAS IT SHE'S UNDERGOING THE HARSHEST SPIRITUAL TRAINING OF HER LIFE. HER PAIN MUST BE OFF THE CHARTS.
Meene Montgomery
Spirit Companion: Gabriel
Hobby: Swimming

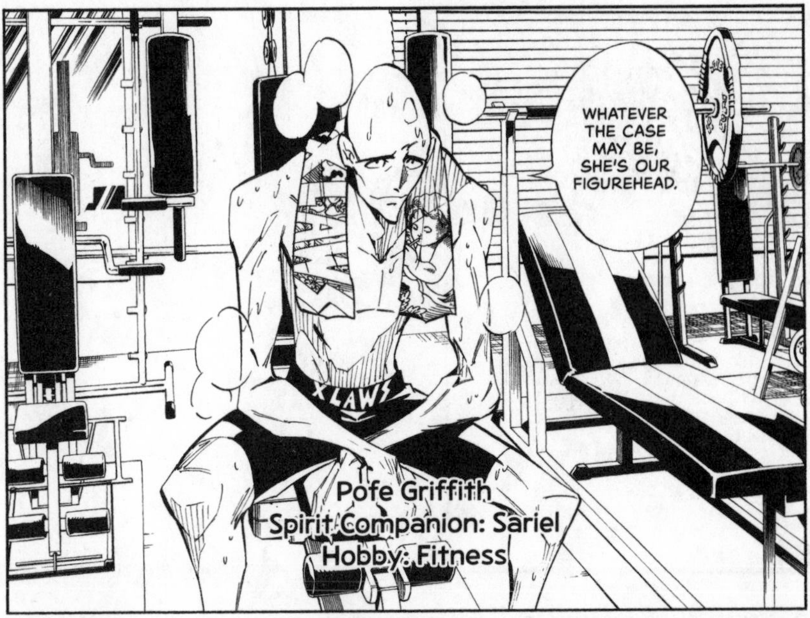
WHATEVER THE CASE MAY BE, SHE'S OUR FIGUREHEAD.
Pofe Griffith
Spirit Companion: Sariel
Hobby: Fitness
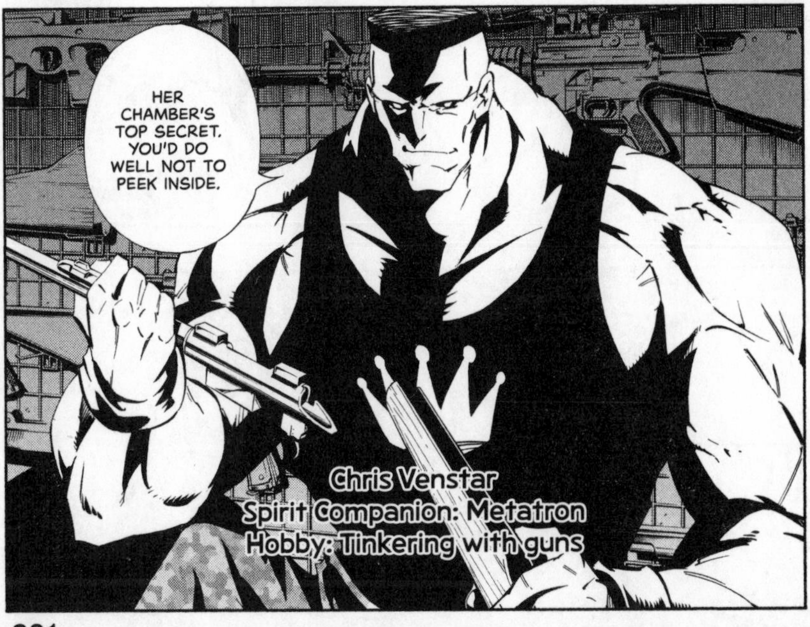
HER CHAMBER'S TOP SECRET. YOU'D DO WELL NOT TO PEEK INSIDE.
Chris Venstar
Spirit Companion: Metatron
Hobby: Tinkering with guns

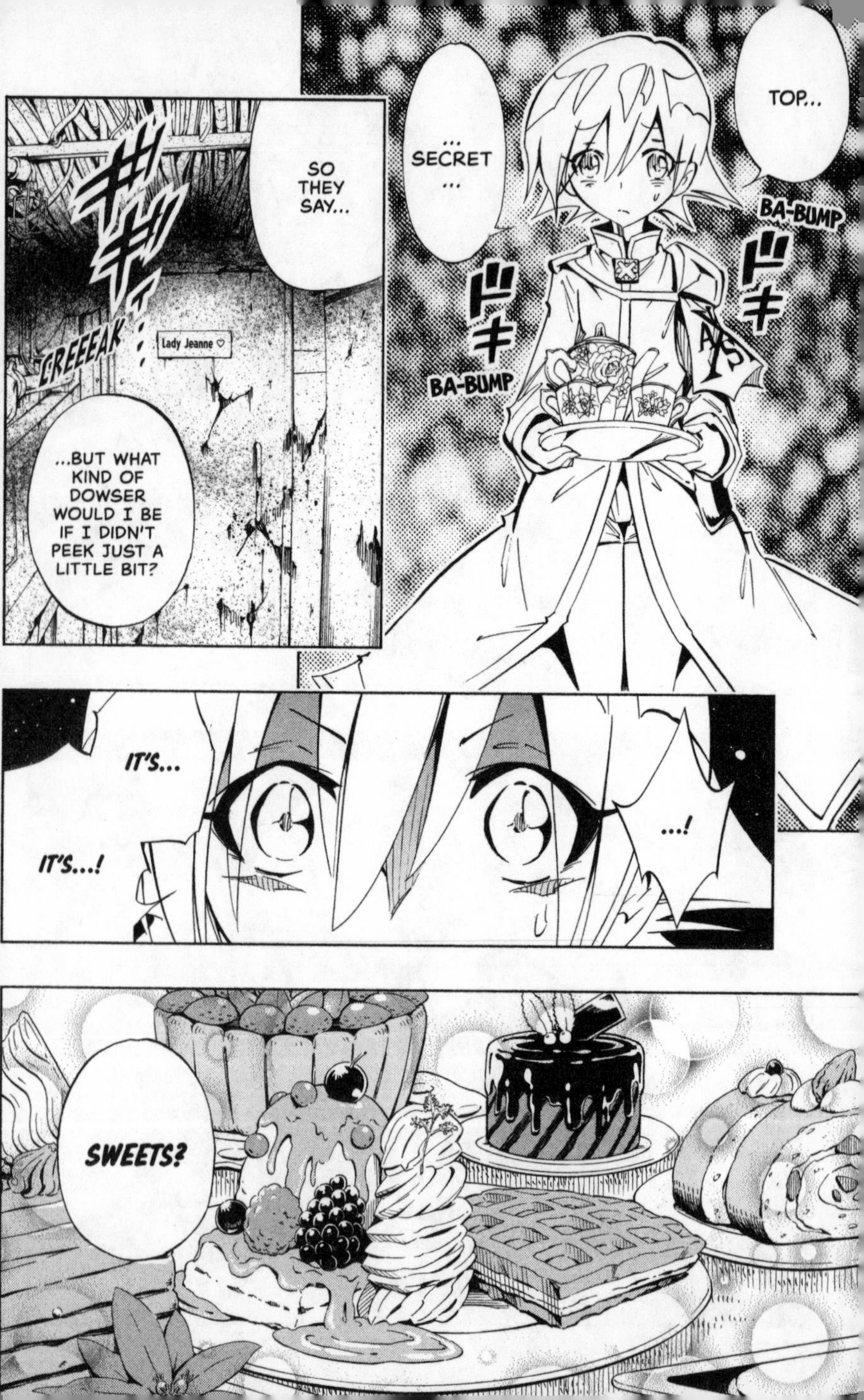
TOP...
... SECRET ...
BA-BUMP
ドキ
BA-BUMP
ドキ
SO THEY SAY...
CREEEAK
Lady Jeanne ♡
...BUT WHAT KIND OF DOWSER WOULD I BE IF I DIDN'T PEEK JUST A LITTLE BIT?
...!
IT'S...
IT'S...!
SWEETS?

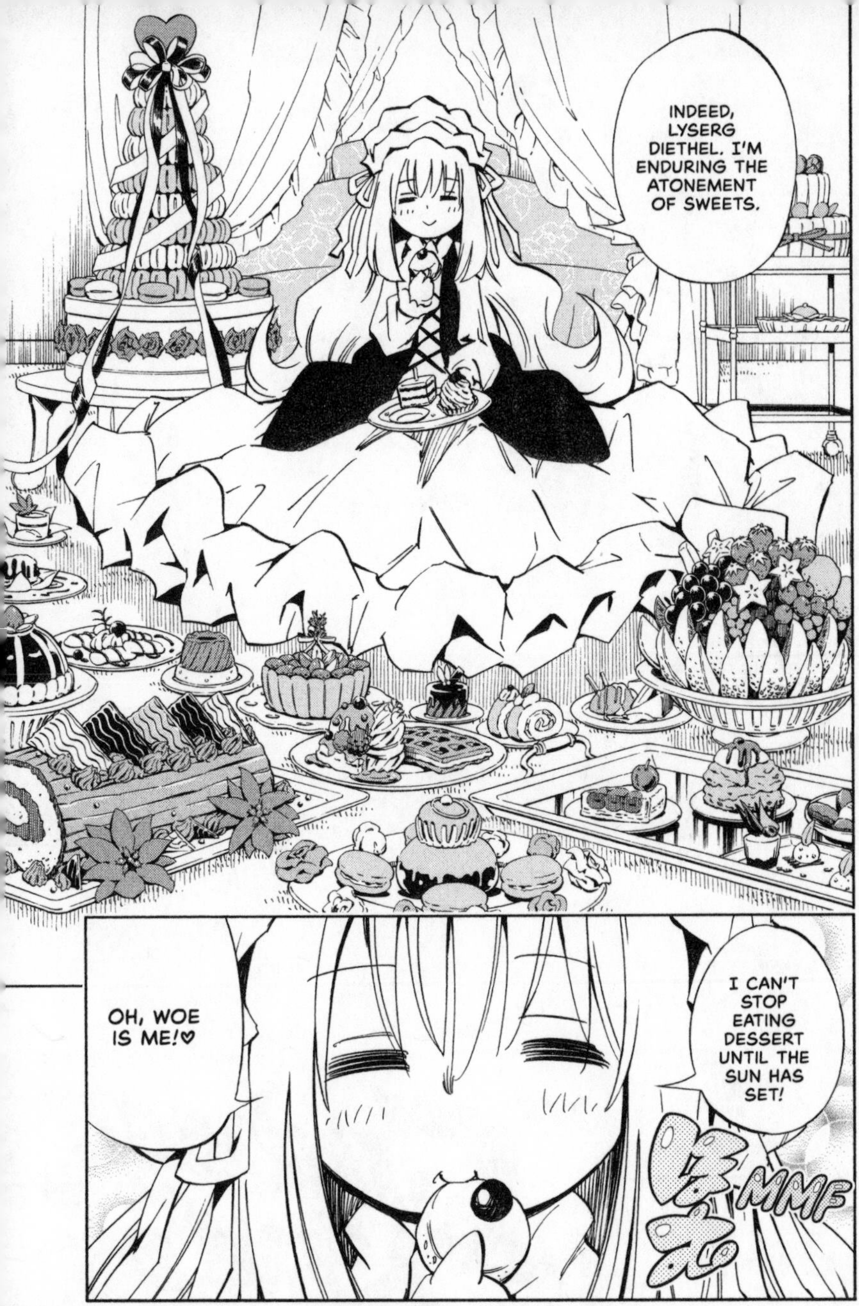
INDEED, LYSERG DIETHEL. I'M ENDURING THE ATONEMENT OF SWEETS.
I CAN'T STOP EATING DESSERT UNTIL THE SUN HAS SET!
OH, WOE IS ME!♡
MMF

SHAMAN KING

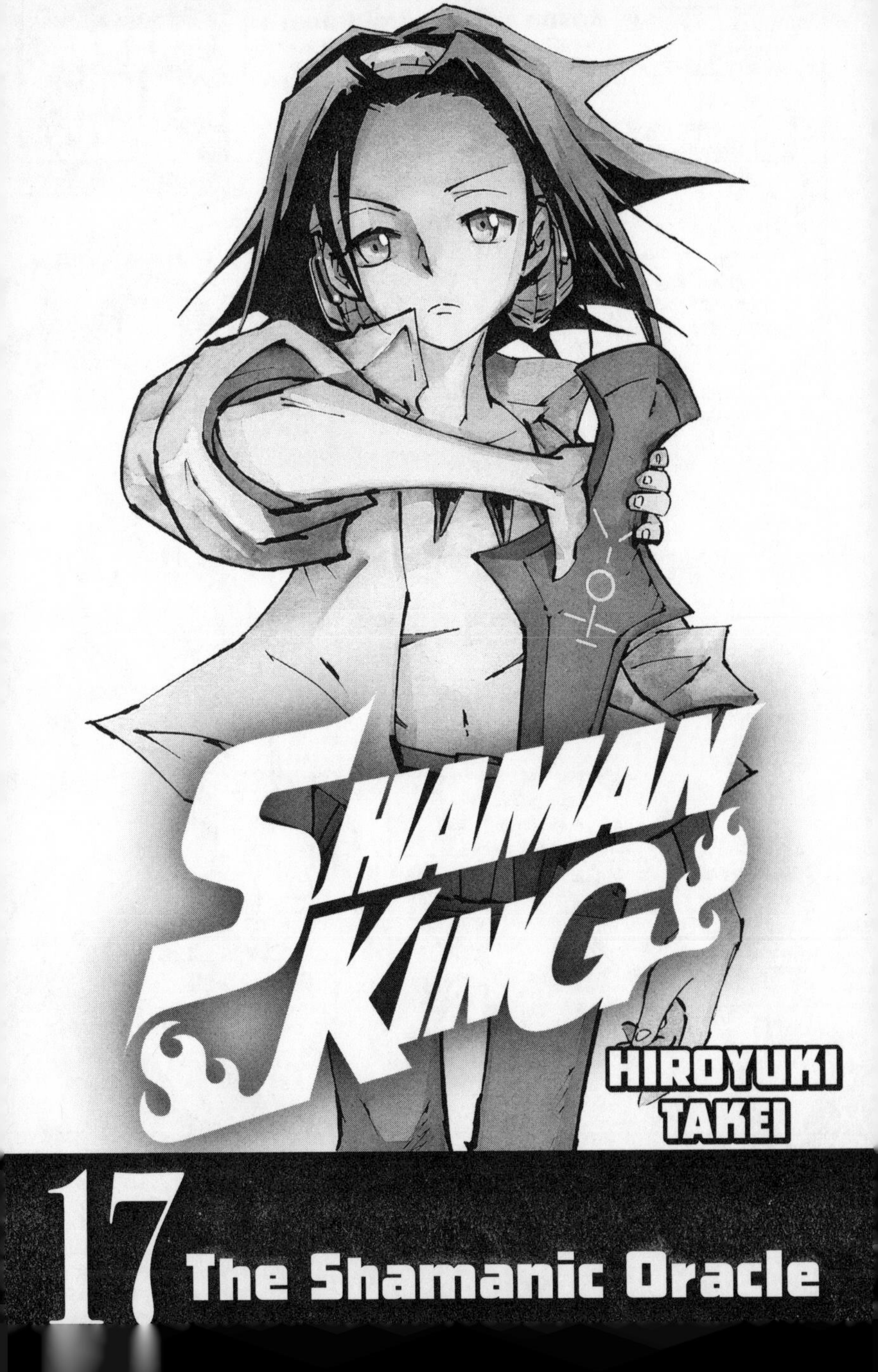

SHAMAN KING

HIROYUKI TAKEI

17 The Shamanic Oracle

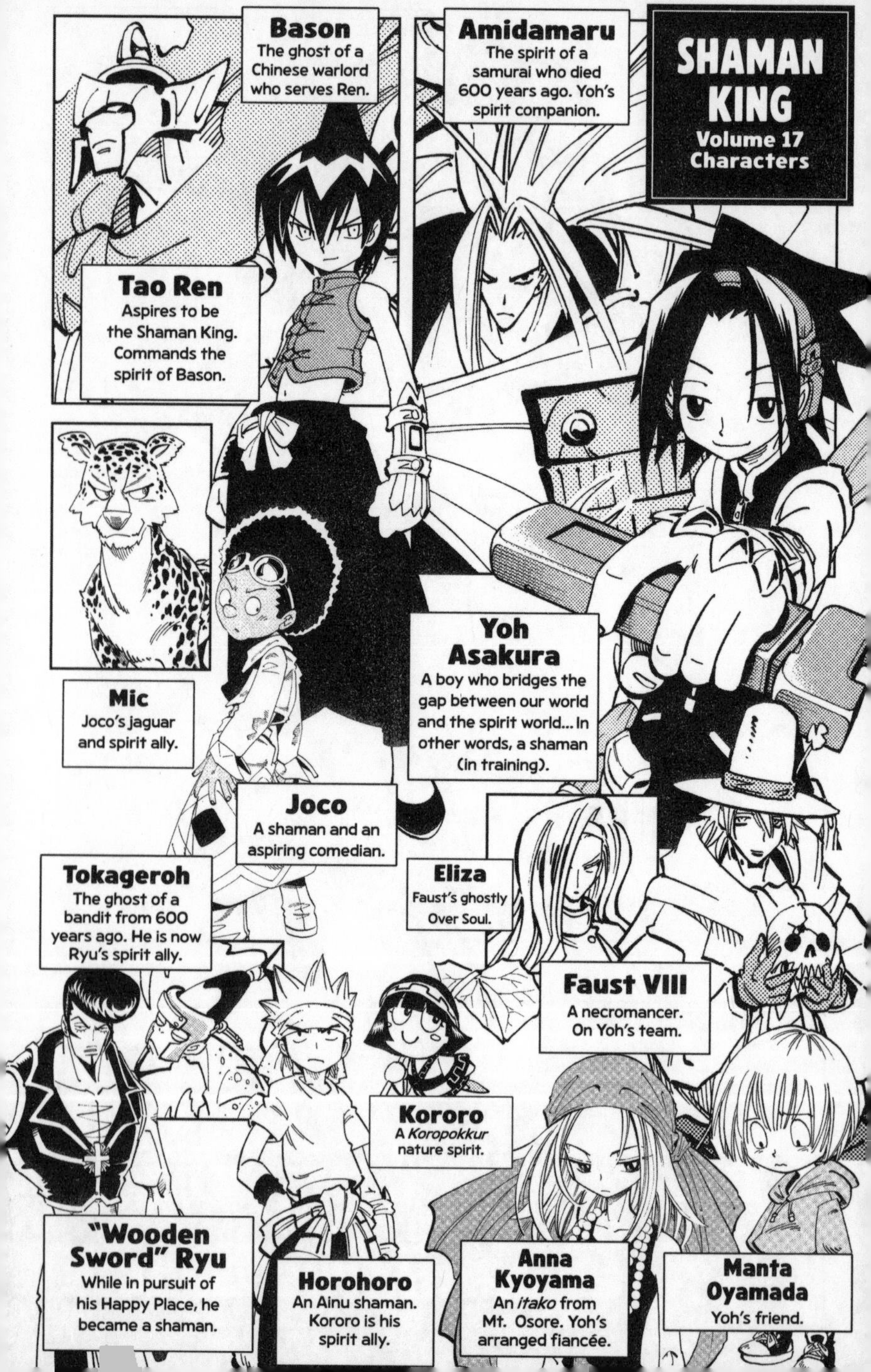
SHAMAN KING
Volume 17 Characters
Amidamaru
The spirit of a samurai who died 600 years ago. Yoh's spirit companion.
Bason
The ghost of a Chinese warlord who serves Ren.
Tao Ren
Aspires to be the Shaman King. Commands the spirit of Bason.
Yoh Asakura
A boy who bridges the gap between our world and the spirit world... In other words, a shaman (in training).
Mic
Joco's jaguar and spirit ally.
Joco
A shaman and an aspiring comedian.
Eliza
Faust's ghostly Over Soul.
Tokageroh
The ghost of a bandit from 600 years ago. He is now Ryu's spirit ally.
Faust VIII
A necromancer. On Yoh's team.
Kororo
A *Koropokkur* nature spirit.
Manta Oyamada
Yoh's friend.
Anna Kyoyama
An *itako* from Mt. Osore. Yoh's arranged fiancée.
Horohoro
An Ainu shaman. Kororo is his spirit ally.
"Wooden Sword" Ryu
While in pursuit of his Happy Place, he became a shaman.

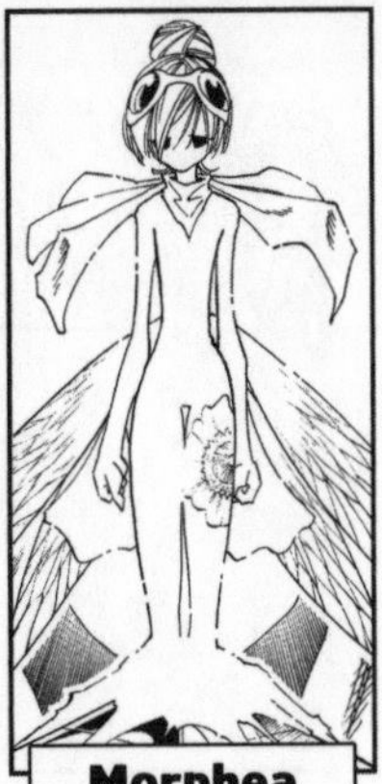

Morphea
Lyserg's spirit ally. A poppy flower fairy.

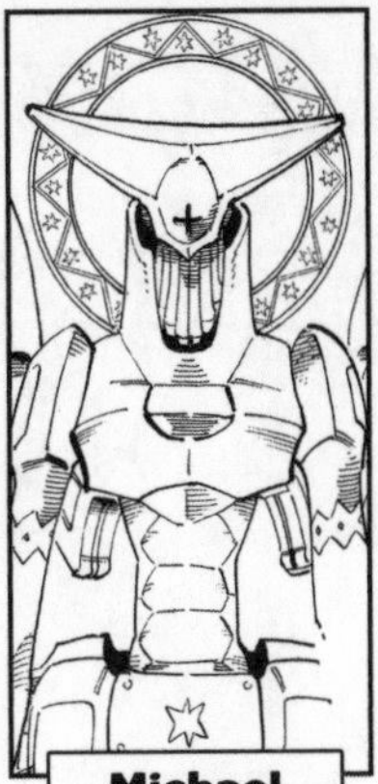

Michael
Marco's spirit ally. An angel.

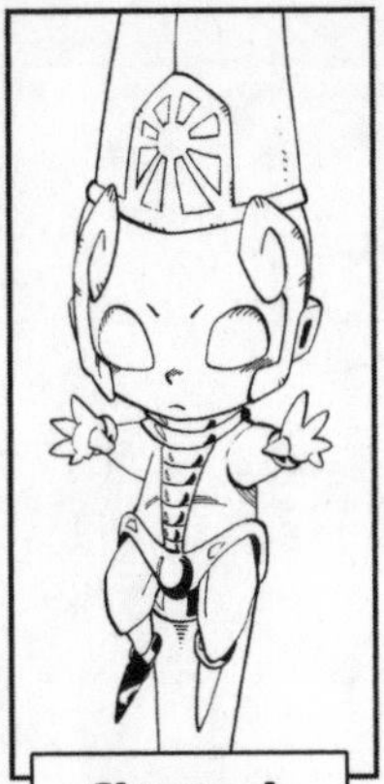

Shamash
Jeanne's spirit ally. *kami* class.

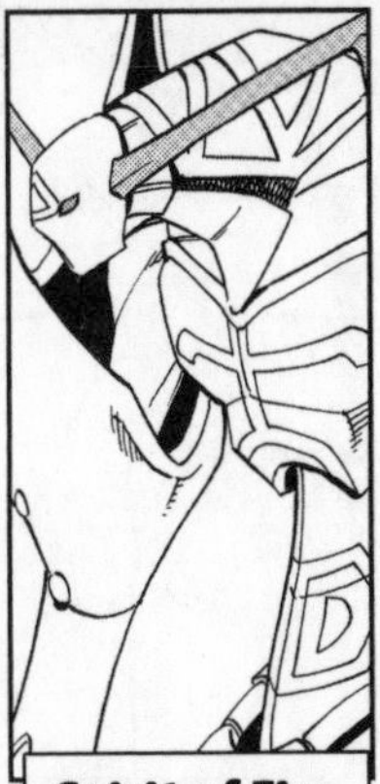

Spirit of Fire
One of the five High Spirits, and Hao's spirit ally.

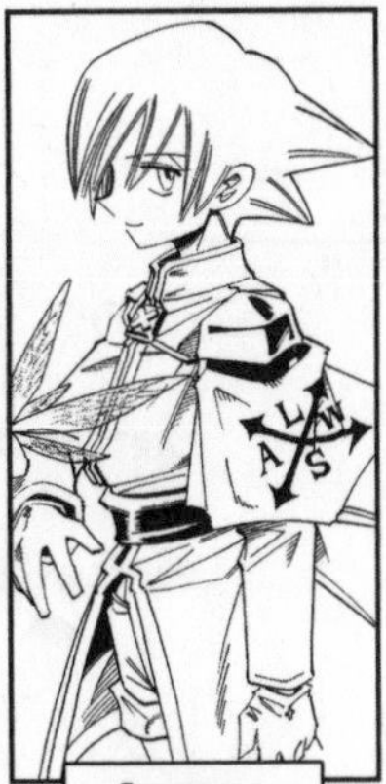

Lyserg
A boy who wants revenge against Hao.

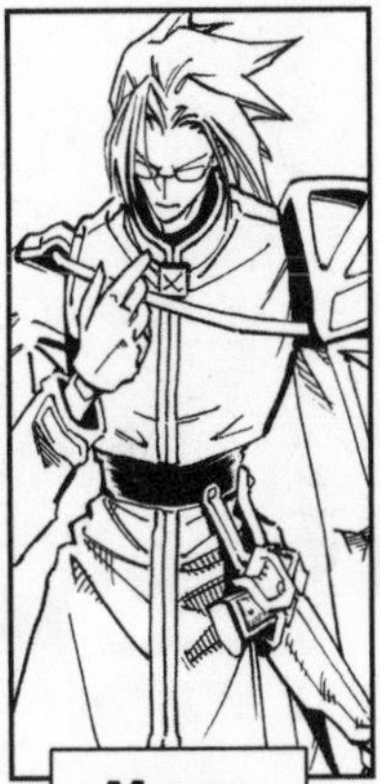

Marco
The leader of the X-Laws.

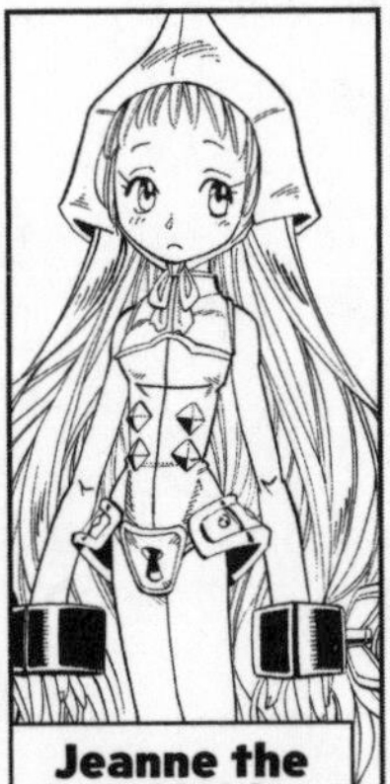

Jeanne the Iron Maiden
The true leader of the X-Laws. Mostly inside an iron maiden.

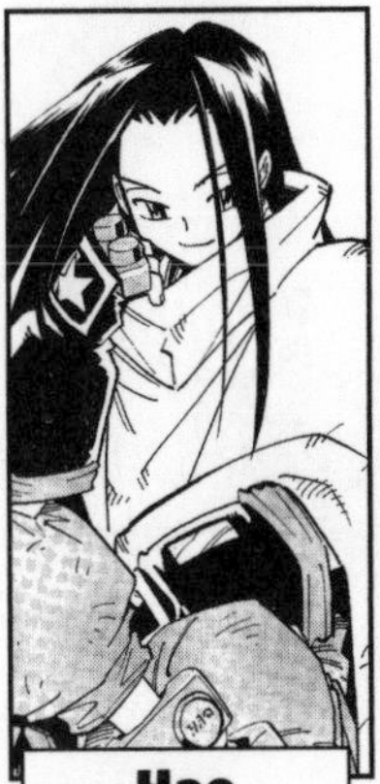

Hao
An enigmatic figure who calls himself the "Future King."

THE STORY SO FAR

This kid named Yoh Asakura-kun transferred to my class from Izumo... and it turns out he's a shaman! The Shaman Fight, which takes place once every 500 years, has begun. Yoh-kun and friends arrived at Patch Village—and experienced the limitless power of the Great Spirit. They formed new teams for the tournament proper. Along with their new ally, Joco, they divided into two teams. As the competition proceeded, Yoh-kun is outraged by Hao's vicious actions. On top of everything, it turns out Yoh and Hao are twin brothers, leaving everyone absolutely stunned...

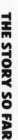

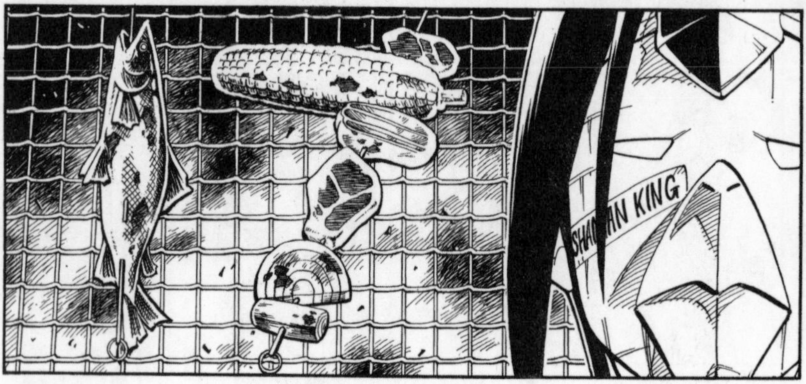
SHAMAN KING

Shamanic Oracle

17

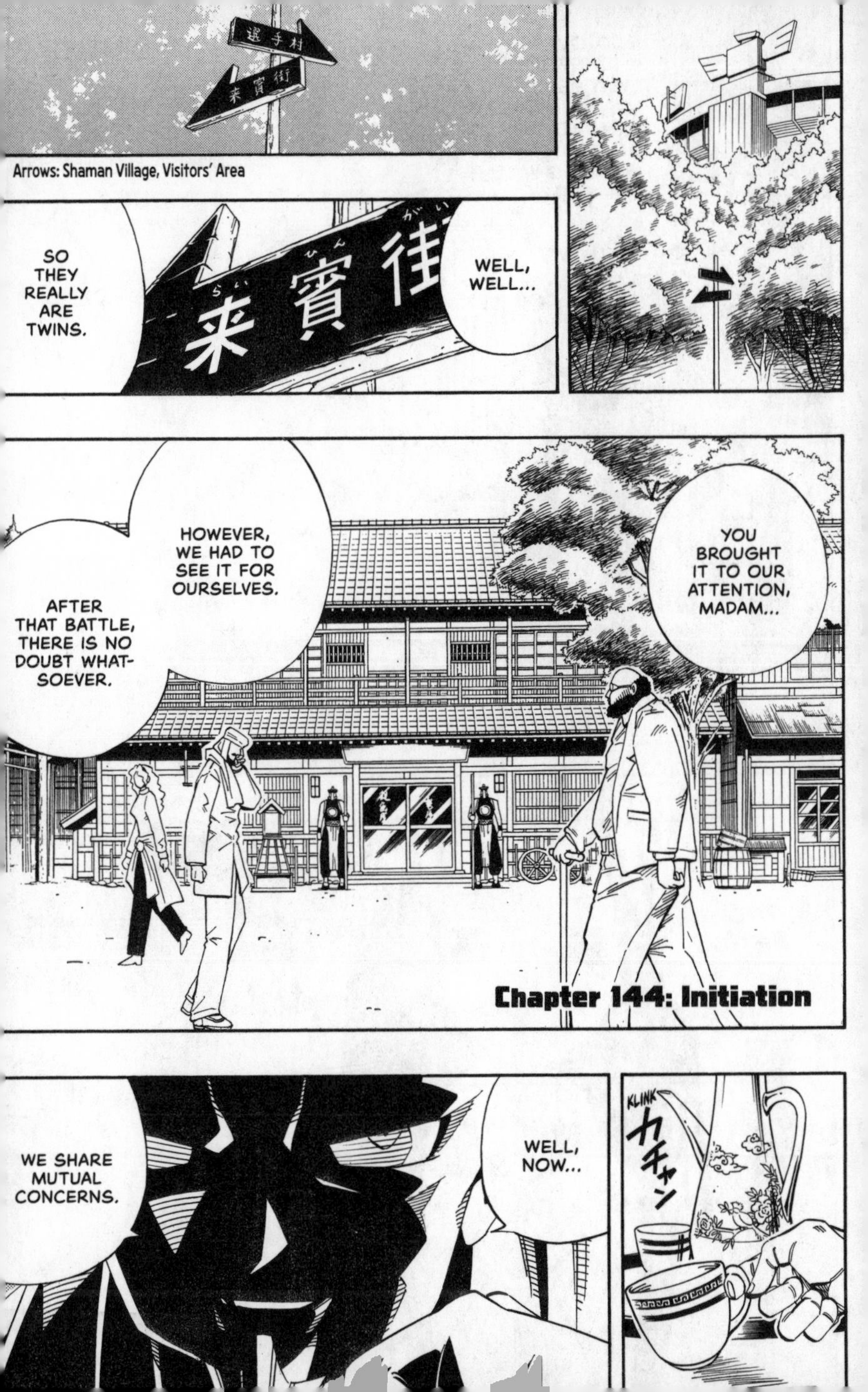

選手村
来賓街
Arrows: Shaman Village, Visitors' Area
来賓街
WELL, WELL...
SO THEY REALLY ARE TWINS.
YOU BROUGHT IT TO OUR ATTENTION, MADAM...
HOWEVER, WE HAD TO SEE IT FOR OURSELVES.
AFTER THAT BATTLE, THERE IS NO DOUBT WHATSOEVER.
Chapter 144: Initiation
KLINK
カチャン
WELL, NOW...
WE SHARE MUTUAL CONCERNS.

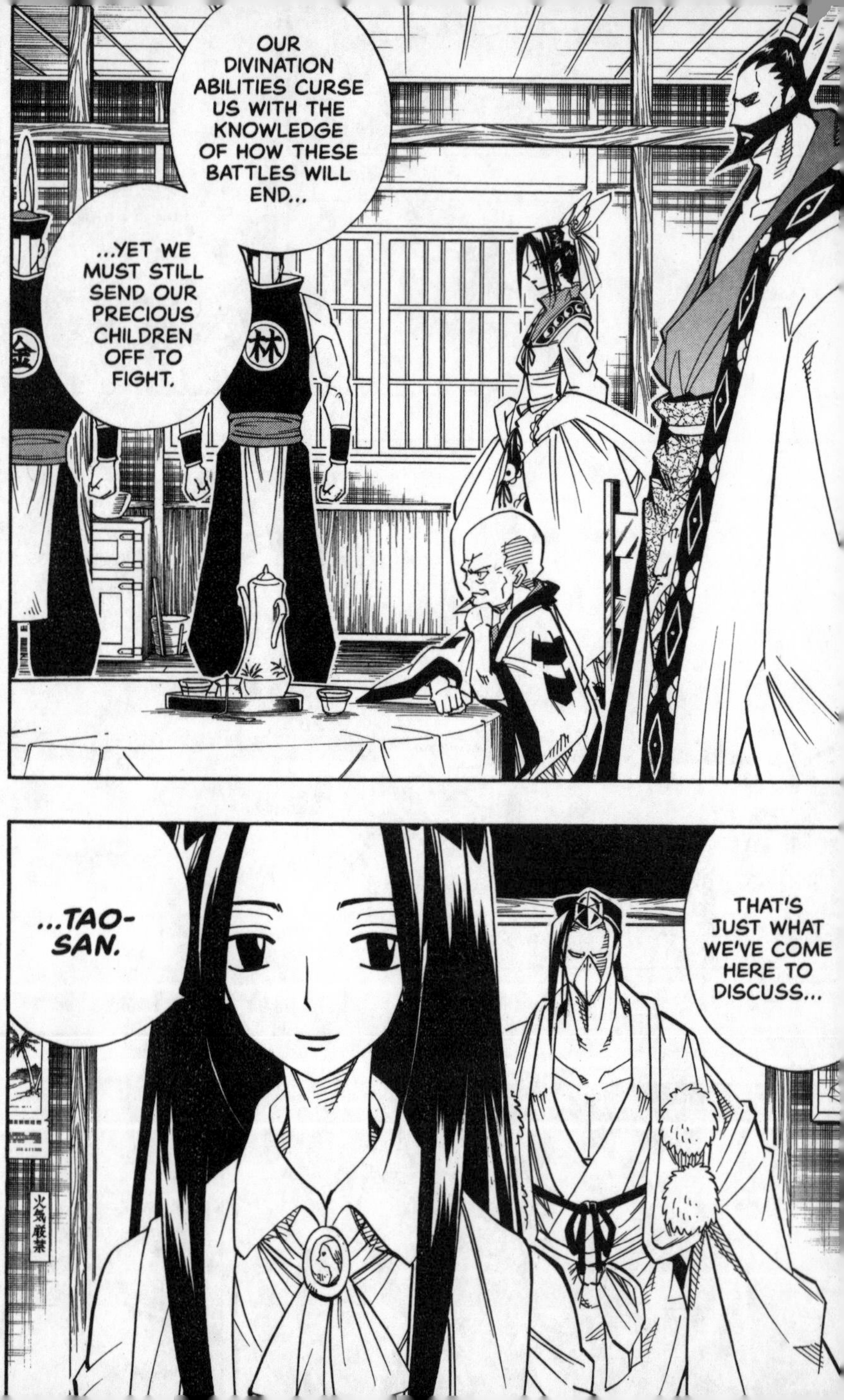
OUR DIVINATION ABILITIES CURSE US WITH THE KNOWLEDGE OF HOW THESE BATTLES WILL END...
...YET WE MUST STILL SEND OUR PRECIOUS CHILDREN OFF TO FIGHT.
THAT'S JUST WHAT WE'VE COME HERE TO DISCUSS...
...TAO-SAN.
火気厳禁

Chapter 144:

Initiation

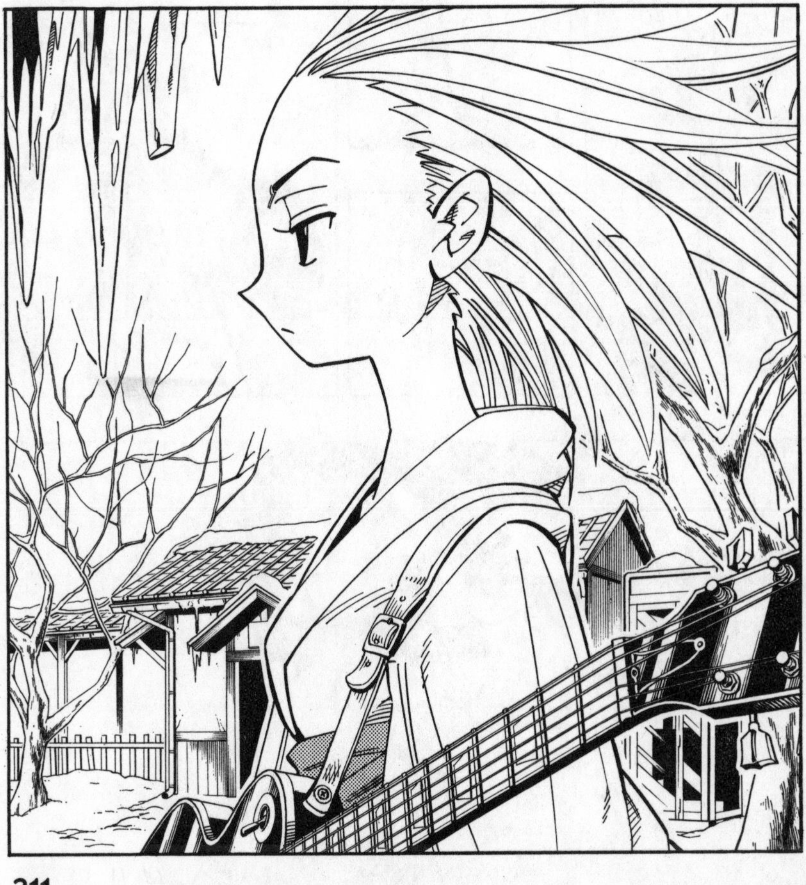

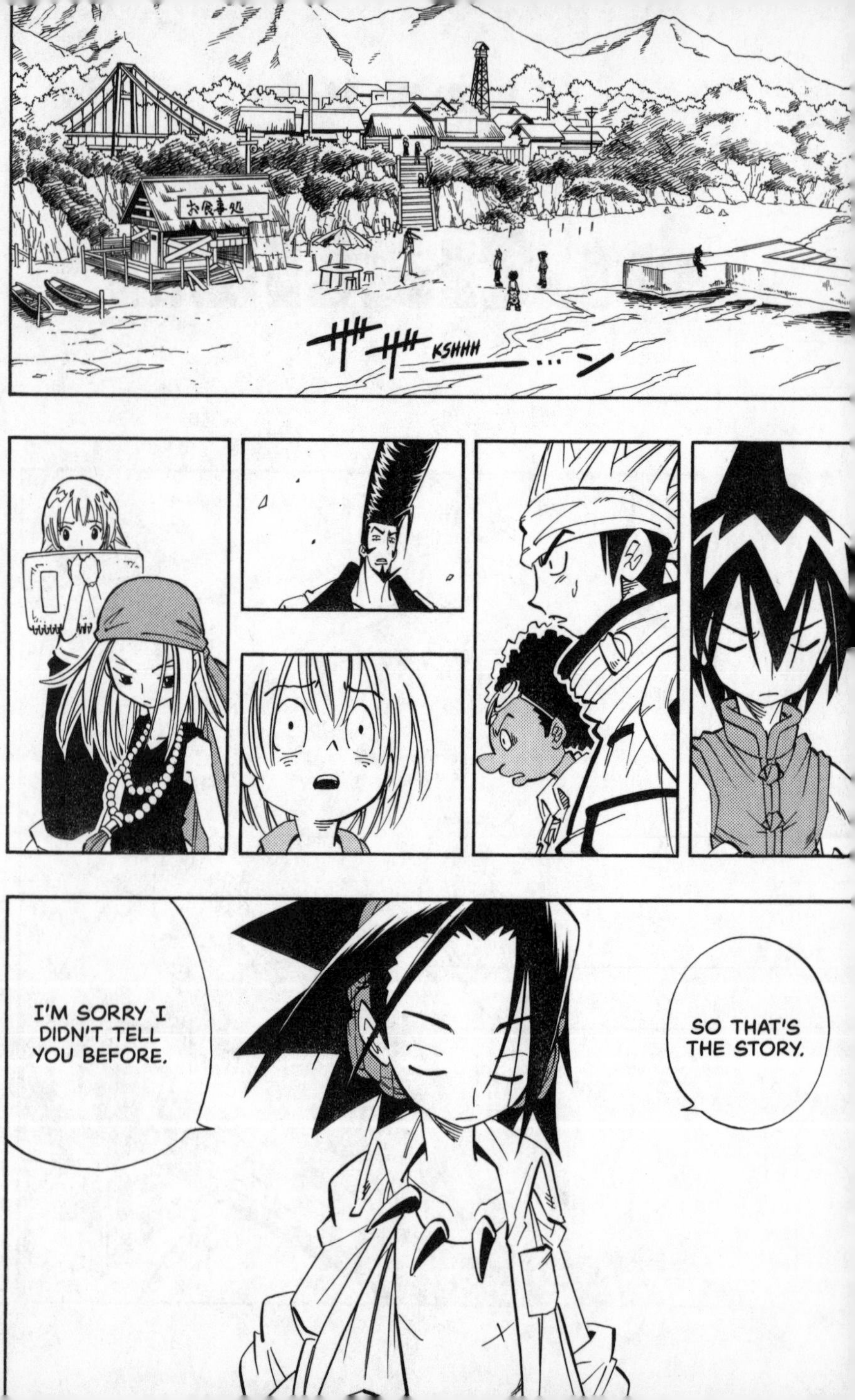

KSHHH
SO THAT'S THE STORY.
I'M SORRY I DIDN'T TELL YOU BEFORE.

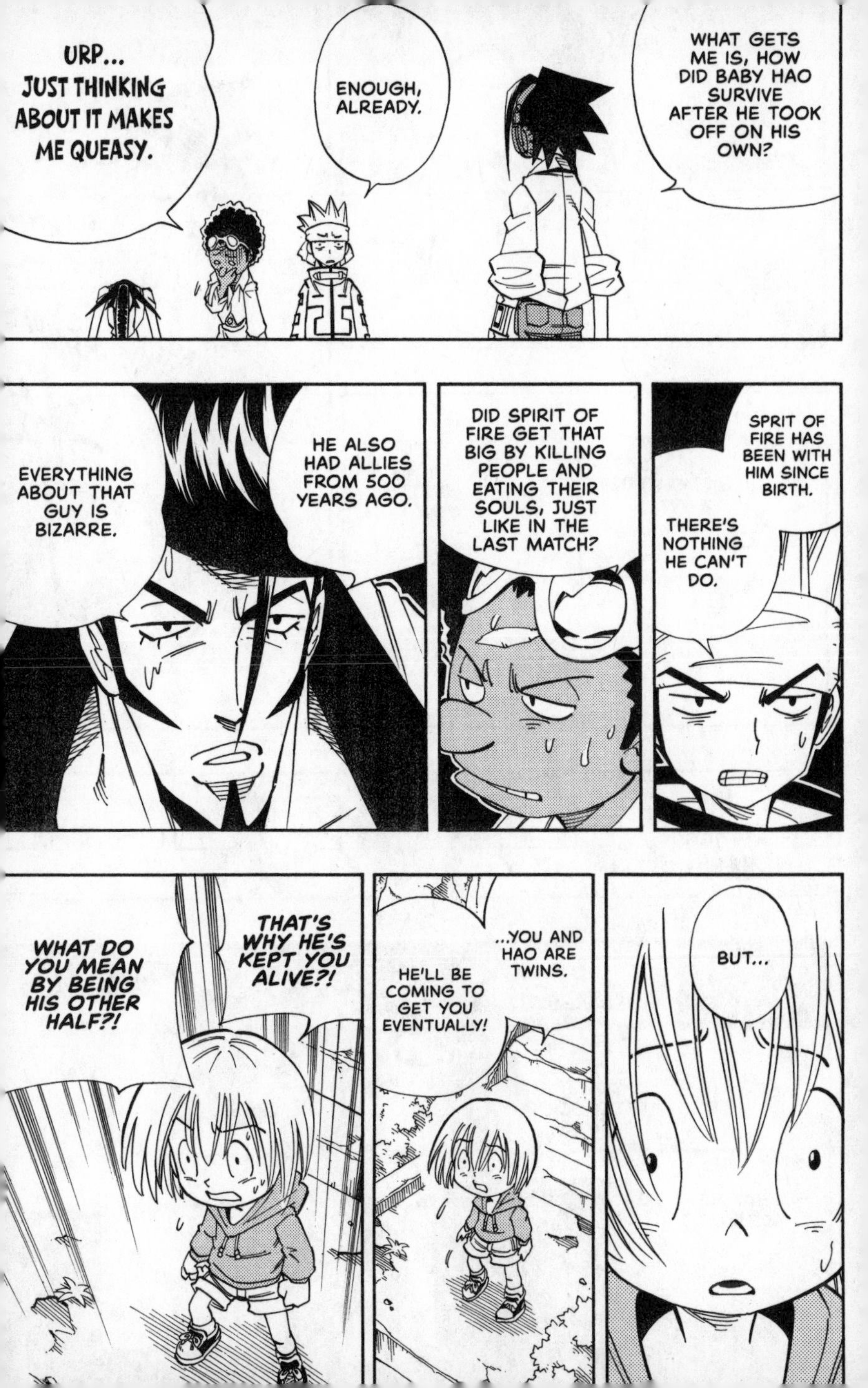
WHAT GETS ME IS, HOW DID BABY HAO SURVIVE AFTER HE TOOK OFF ON HIS OWN?
ENOUGH, ALREADY.
URP... JUST THINKING ABOUT IT MAKES ME QUEASY.
SPRIT OF FIRE HAS BEEN WITH HIM SINCE BIRTH.
THERE'S NOTHING HE CAN'T DO.
DID SPIRIT OF FIRE GET THAT BIG BY KILLING PEOPLE AND EATING THEIR SOULS, JUST LIKE IN THE LAST MATCH?
HE ALSO HAD ALLIES FROM 500 YEARS AGO.
EVERYTHING ABOUT THAT GUY IS BIZARRE.
BUT...
...YOU AND HAO ARE TWINS.
HE'LL BE COMING TO GET YOU EVENTUALLY!
THAT'S WHY HE'S KEPT YOU ALIVE?!
WHAT DO YOU MEAN BY BEING HIS OTHER HALF?!

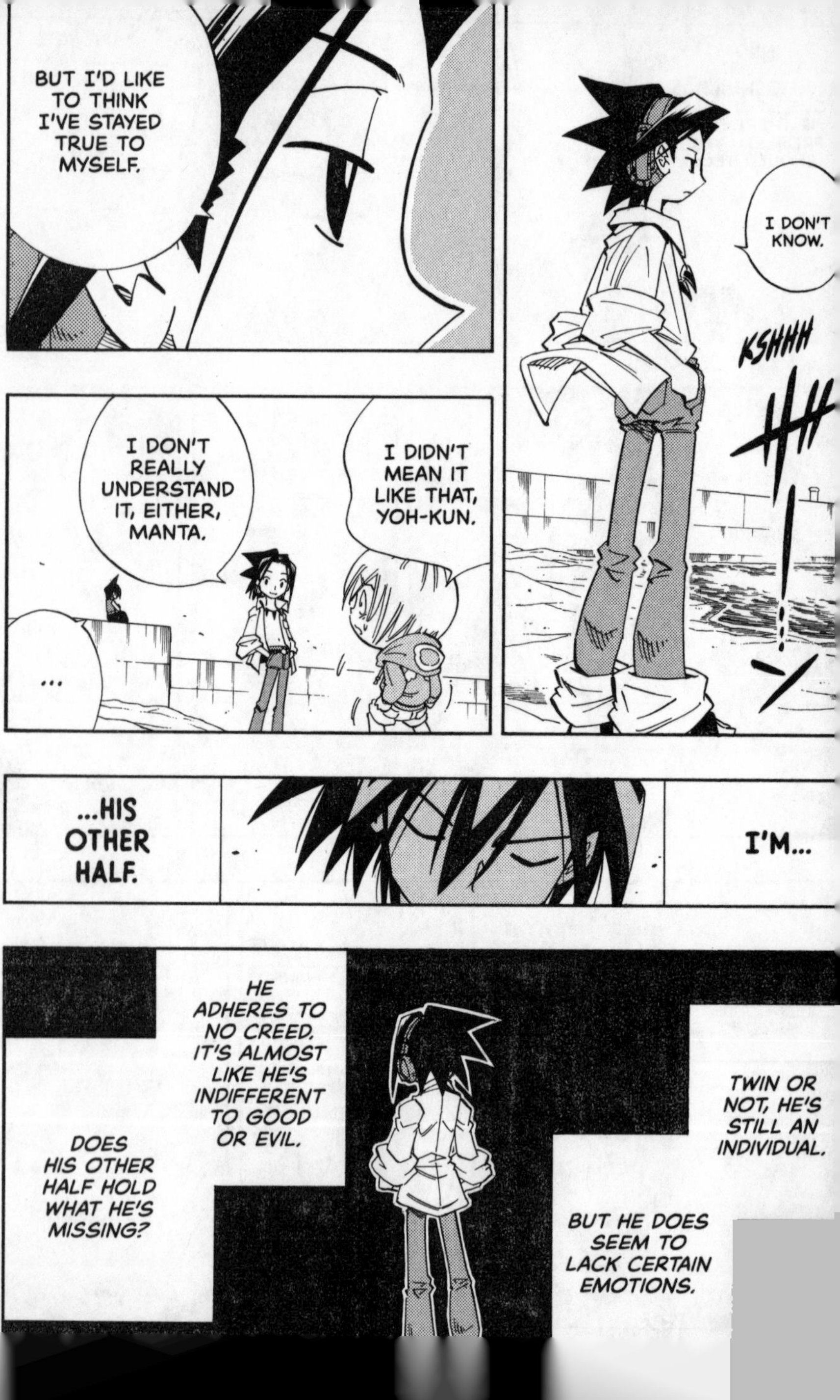
I DON'T KNOW.
KSHHHH
BUT I'D LIKE TO THINK I'VE STAYED TRUE TO MYSELF.
I DIDN'T MEAN IT LIKE THAT, YOH-KUN.
I DON'T REALLY UNDERSTAND IT, EITHER, MANTA.
...
I'M...
...HIS OTHER HALF.
TWIN OR NOT, HE'S STILL AN INDIVIDUAL.
BUT HE DOES SEEM TO LACK CERTAIN EMOTIONS.
HE ADHERES TO NO CREED. IT'S ALMOST LIKE HE'S INDIFFERENT TO GOOD OR EVIL.
DOES HIS OTHER HALF HOLD WHAT HE'S MISSING?

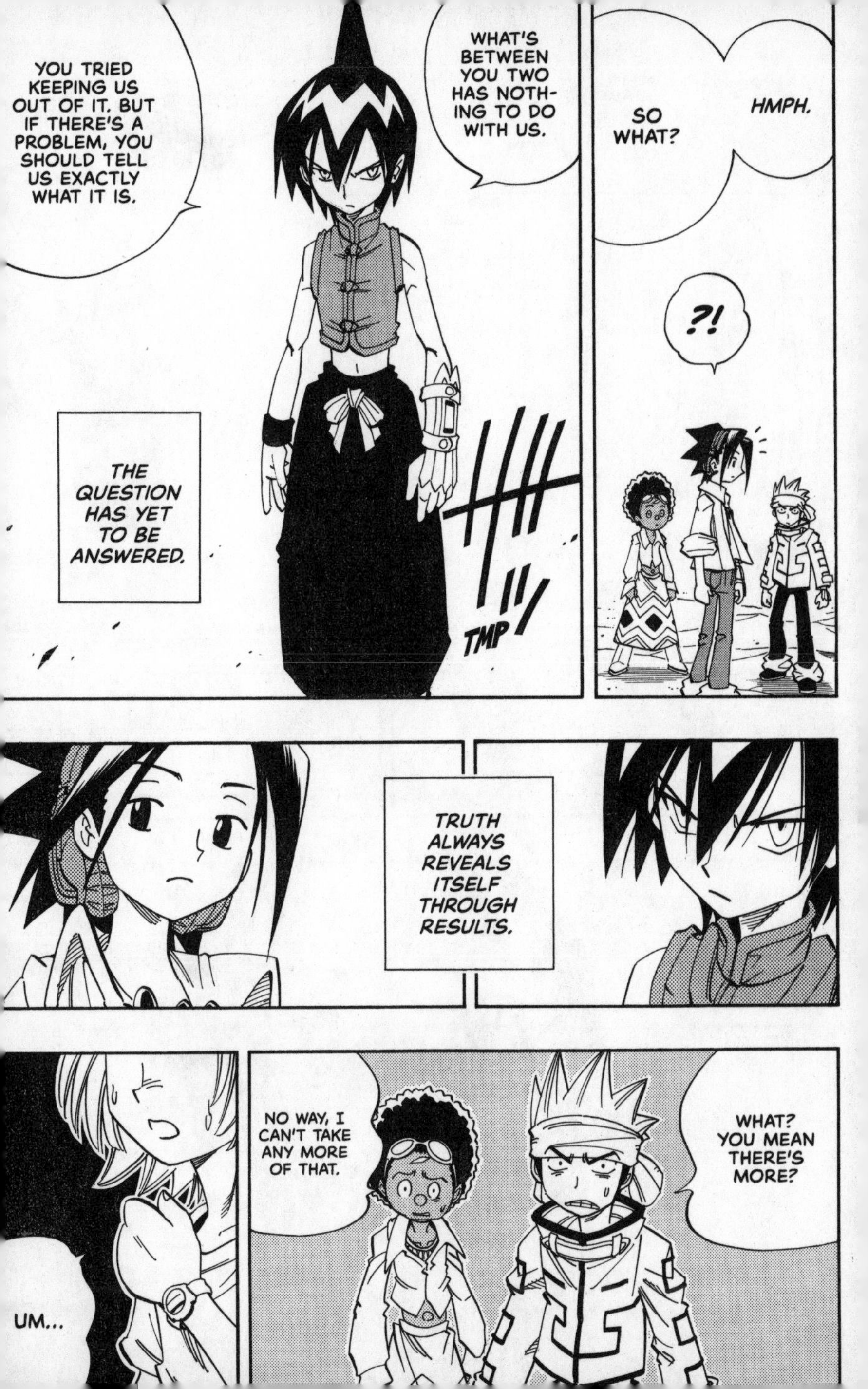
HMPH.
SO WHAT?
?!
WHAT'S BETWEEN YOU TWO HAS NOTHING TO DO WITH US.
YOU TRIED KEEPING US OUT OF IT. BUT IF THERE'S A PROBLEM, YOU SHOULD TELL US EXACTLY WHAT IT IS.
THE QUESTION HAS YET TO BE ANSWERED.
TMP
TRUTH ALWAYS REVEALS ITSELF THROUGH RESULTS.
WHAT? YOU MEAN THERE'S MORE?
NO WAY, I CAN'T TAKE ANY MORE OF THAT.
UM...

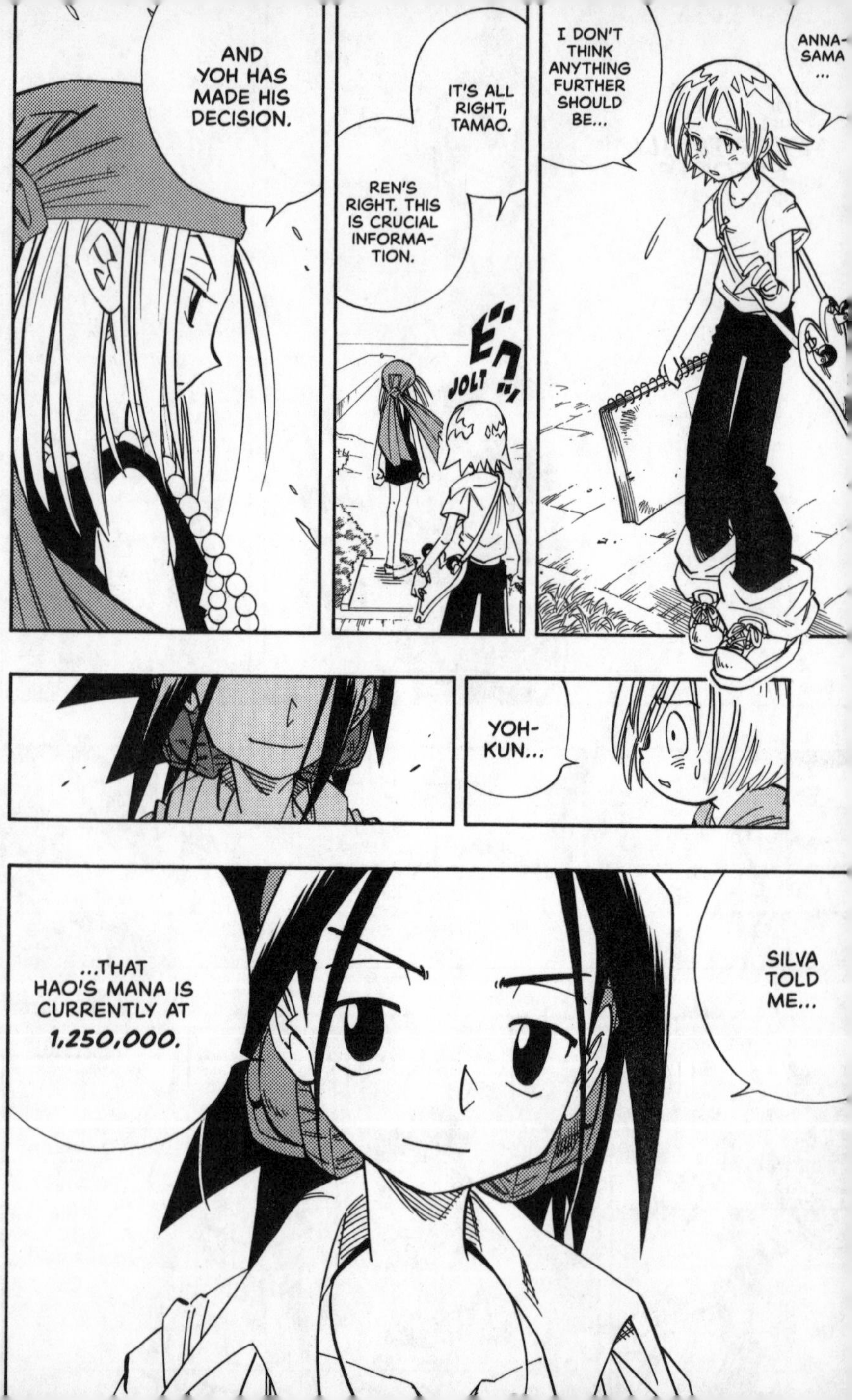
ANNA-SAMA...
I DON'T THINK ANYTHING FURTHER SHOULD BE...
IT'S ALL RIGHT, TAMAO.
REN'S RIGHT. THIS IS CRUCIAL INFORMATION.
JOLT
AND YOH HAS MADE HIS DECISION.
YOH-KUN...
SILVA TOLD ME...
...THAT HAO'S MANA IS CURRENTLY AT 1,250,000.

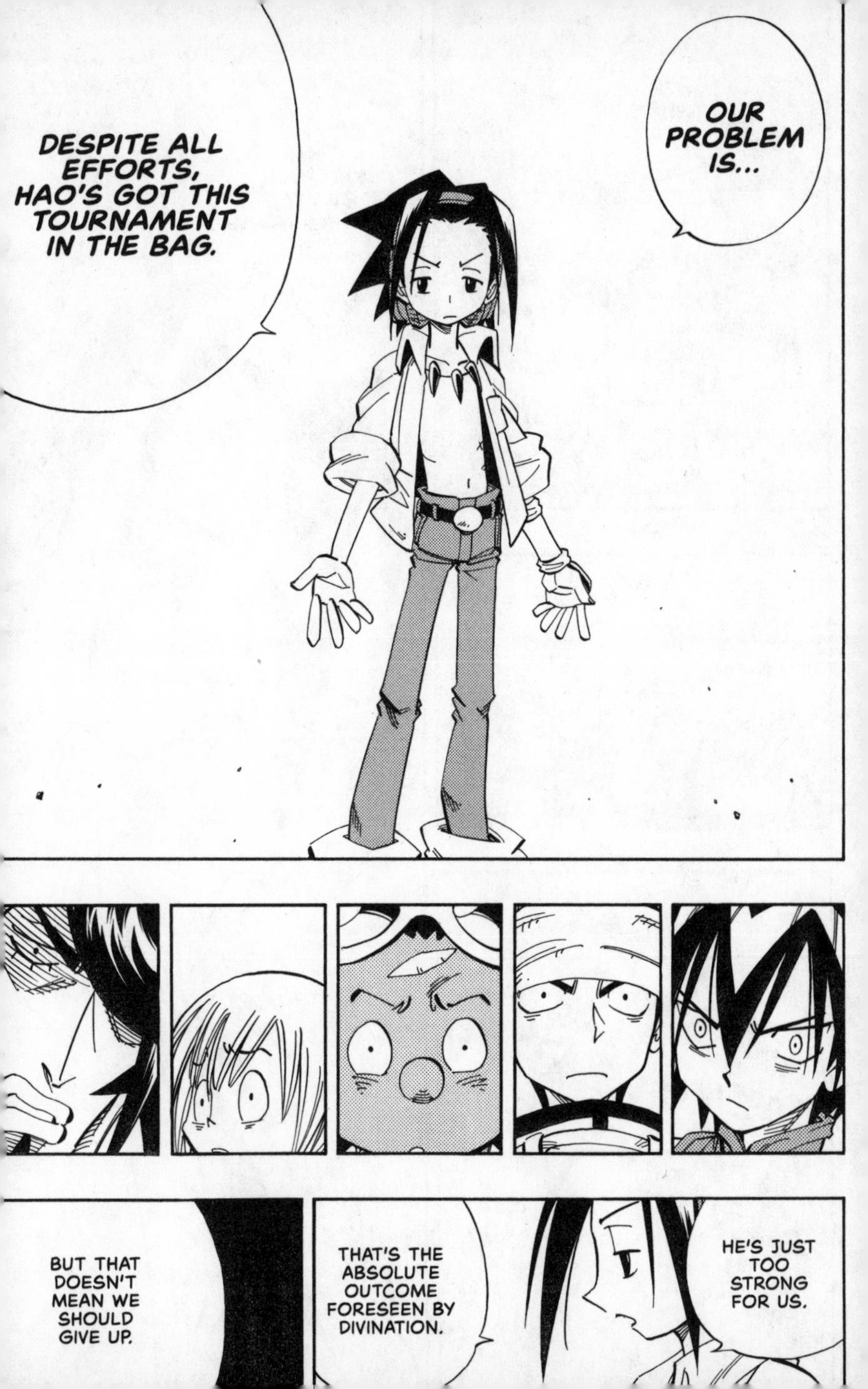
OUR PROBLEM IS...
DESPITE ALL EFFORTS, HAO'S GOT THIS TOURNAMENT IN THE BAG.
HE'S JUST TOO STRONG FOR US.
THAT'S THE ABSOLUTE OUTCOME FORESEEN BY DIVINATION.
BUT THAT DOESN'T MEAN WE SHOULD GIVE UP.

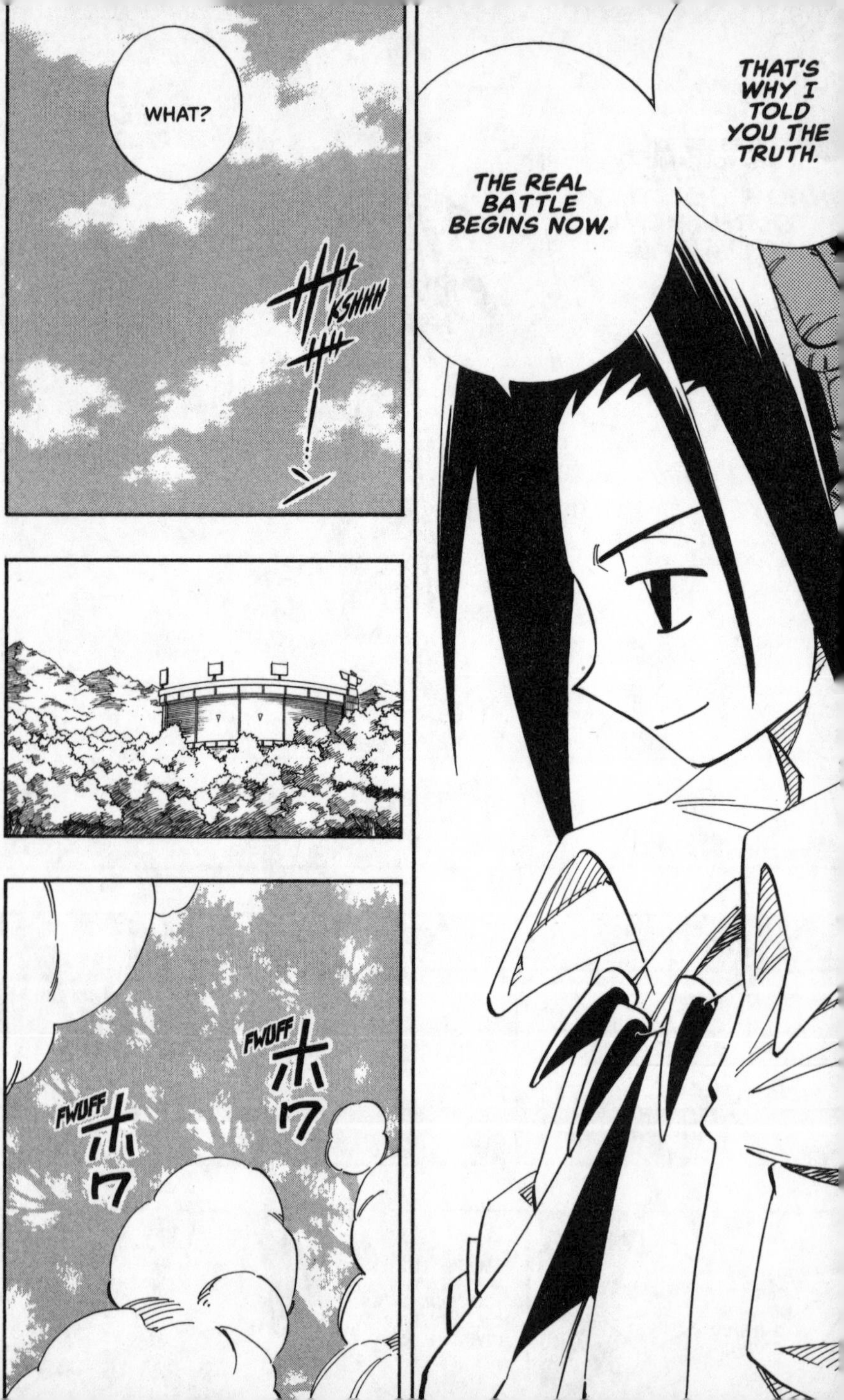
THAT'S WHY I TOLD YOU THE TRUTH.
THE REAL BATTLE BEGINS NOW.
WHAT?
KSHHH
FWUFF
ホワ
FWUFF
ホワ

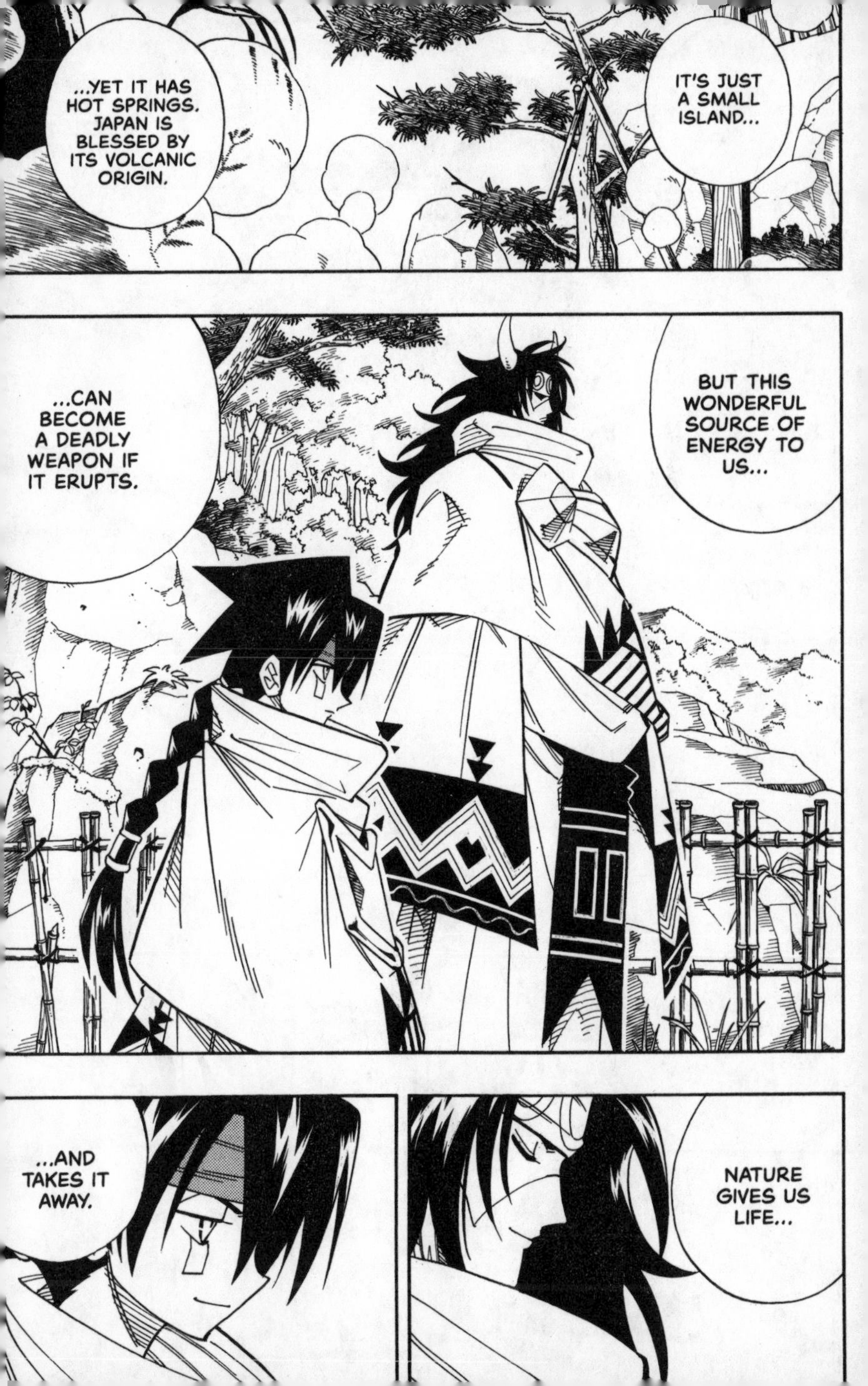
IT'S JUST A SMALL ISLAND...
...YET IT HAS HOT SPRINGS. JAPAN IS BLESSED BY ITS VOLCANIC ORIGIN.
BUT THIS WONDERFUL SOURCE OF ENERGY TO US...
...CAN BECOME A DEADLY WEAPON IF IT ERUPTS.
NATURE GIVES US LIFE...
...AND TAKES IT AWAY.

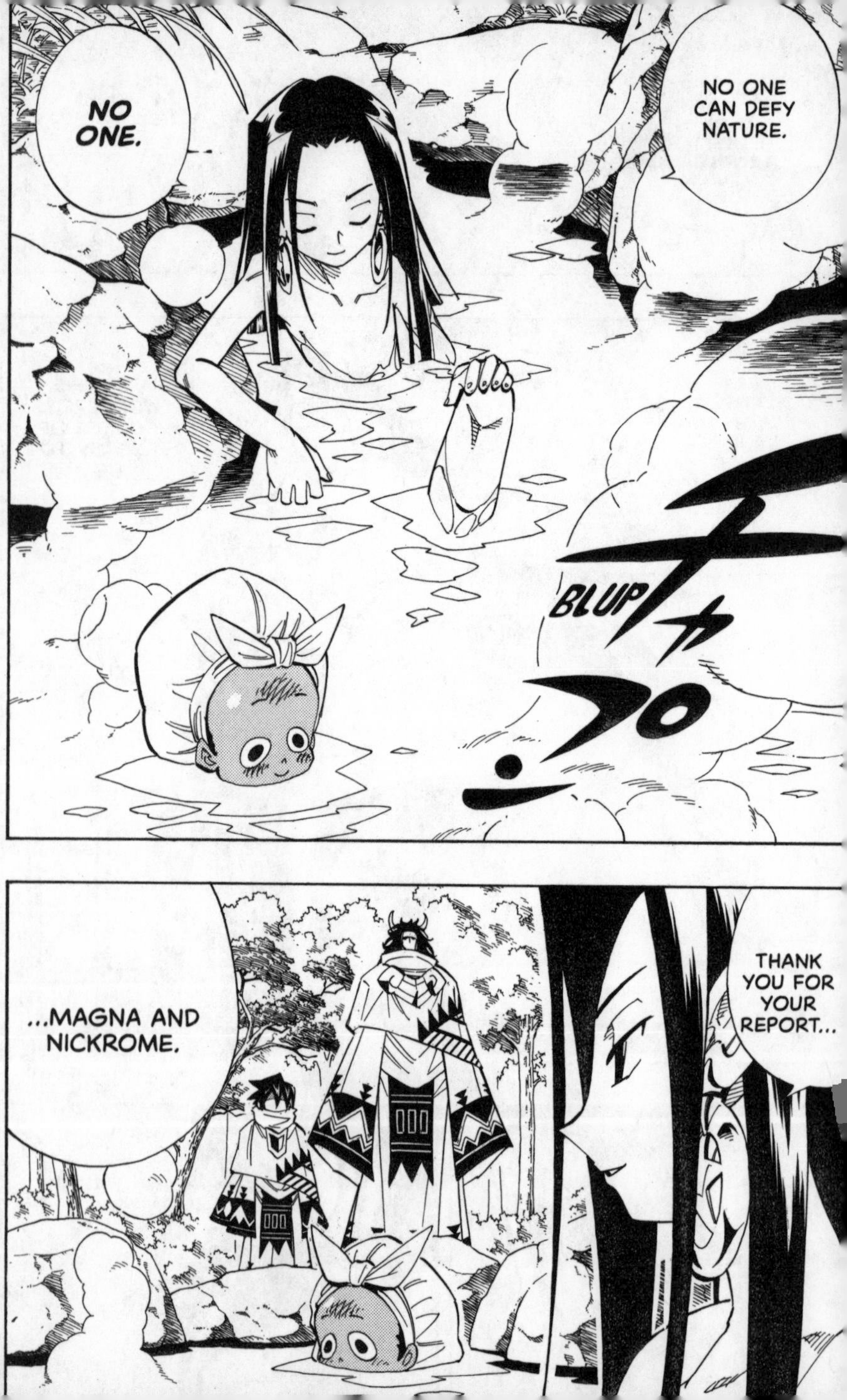
NO ONE CAN DEFY NATURE.
NO ONE.
BLUP
THANK YOU FOR YOUR REPORT...
...MAGNA AND NICKROME.

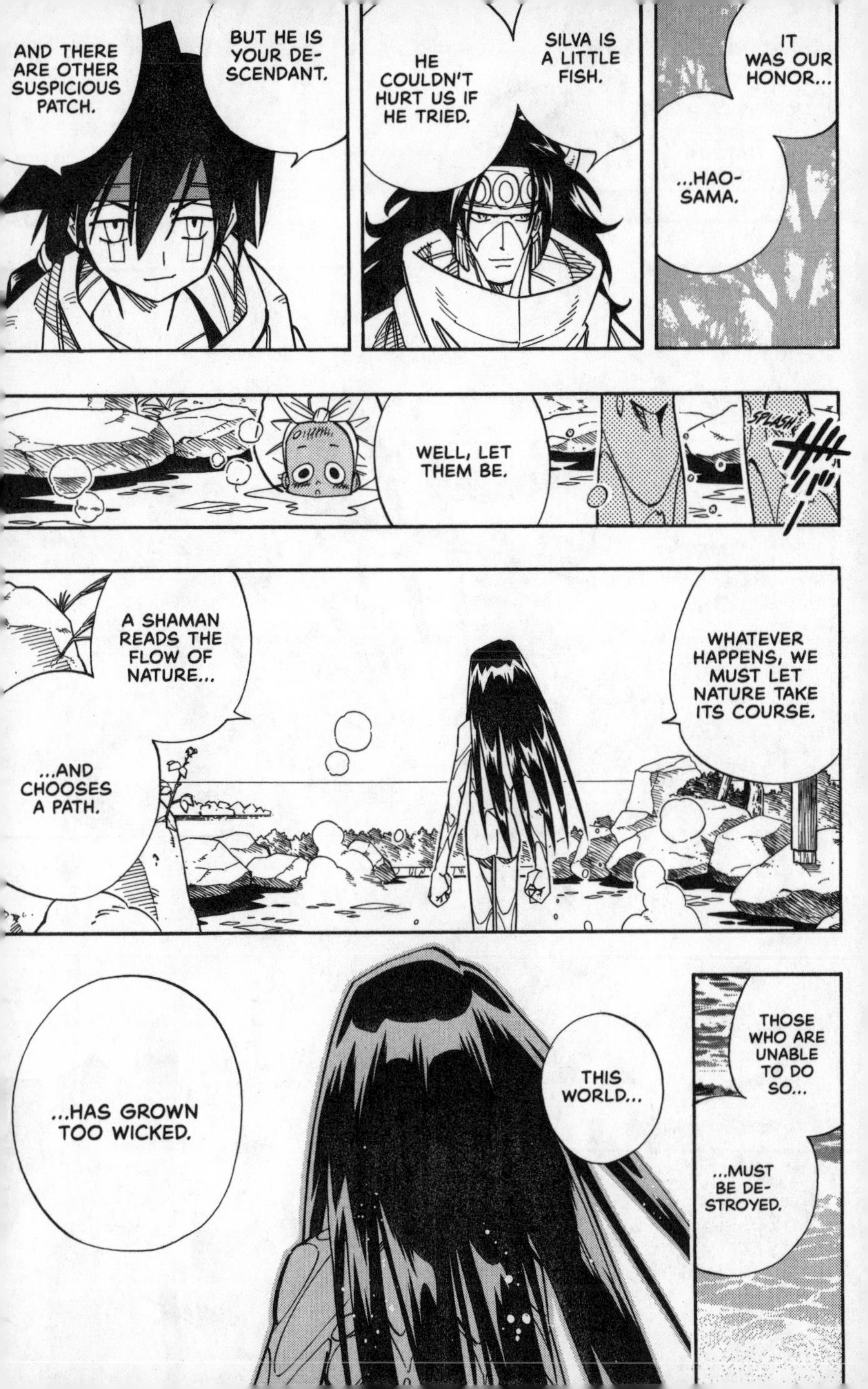
IT WAS OUR HONOR...
...HAO-SAMA.
SILVA IS A LITTLE FISH.
HE COULDN'T HURT US IF HE TRIED.
BUT HE IS YOUR DE-SCENDANT.
AND THERE ARE OTHER SUSPICIOUS PATCH.
SPLASH
WELL, LET THEM BE.
WHATEVER HAPPENS, WE MUST LET NATURE TAKE ITS COURSE.
A SHAMAN READS THE FLOW OF NATURE...
...AND CHOOSES A PATH.
THOSE WHO ARE UNABLE TO DO SO...
...MUST BE DE-STROYED.
THIS WORLD...
...HAS GROWN TOO WICKED.

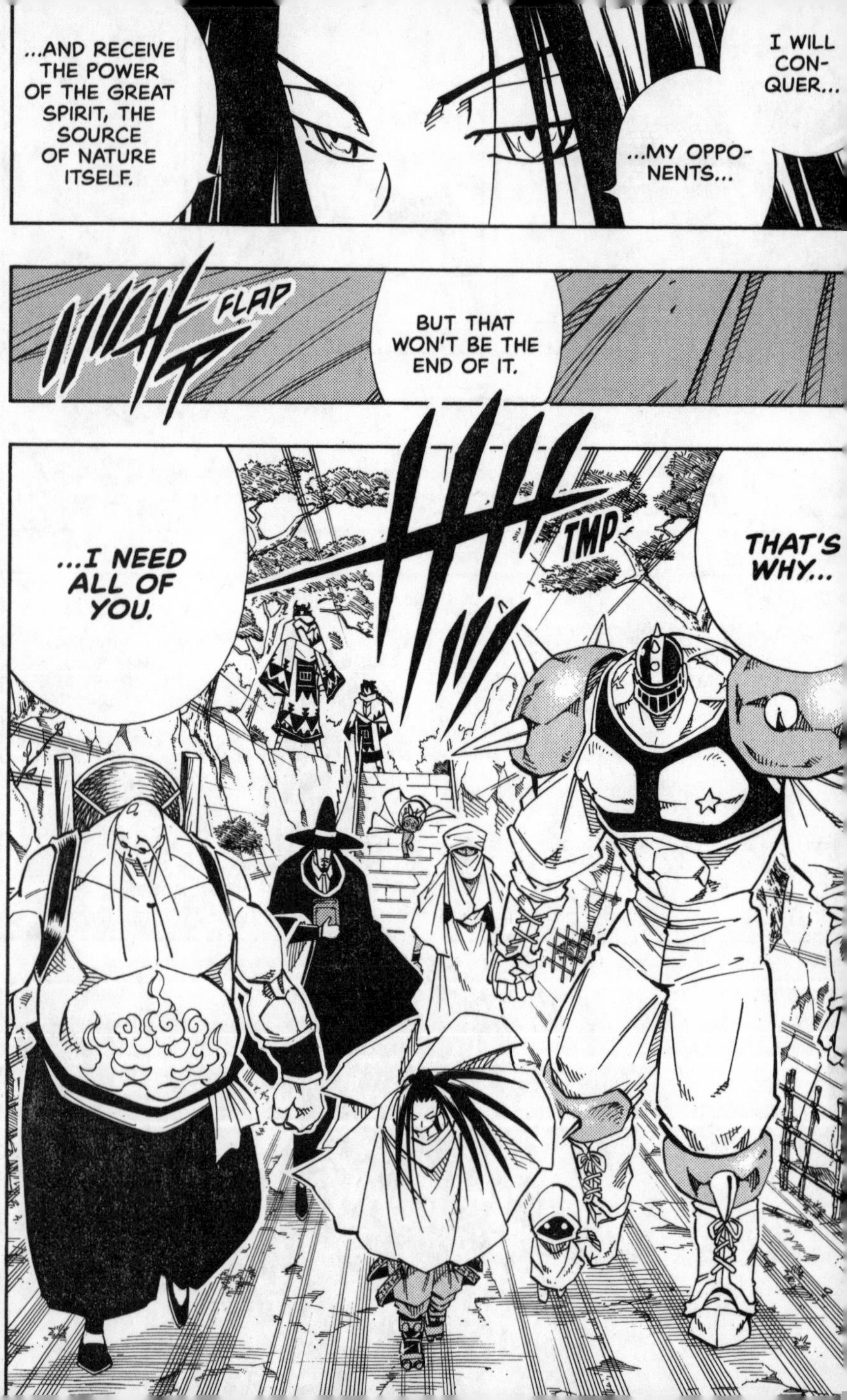
I WILL CON- QUER...
...MY OPPO- NENTS...
...AND RECEIVE THE POWER OF THE GREAT SPIRIT, THE SOURCE OF NATURE ITSELF.
BUT THAT WON'T BE THE END OF IT.
FLAP
THAT'S WHY...
TMP
...I NEED ALL OF YOU.

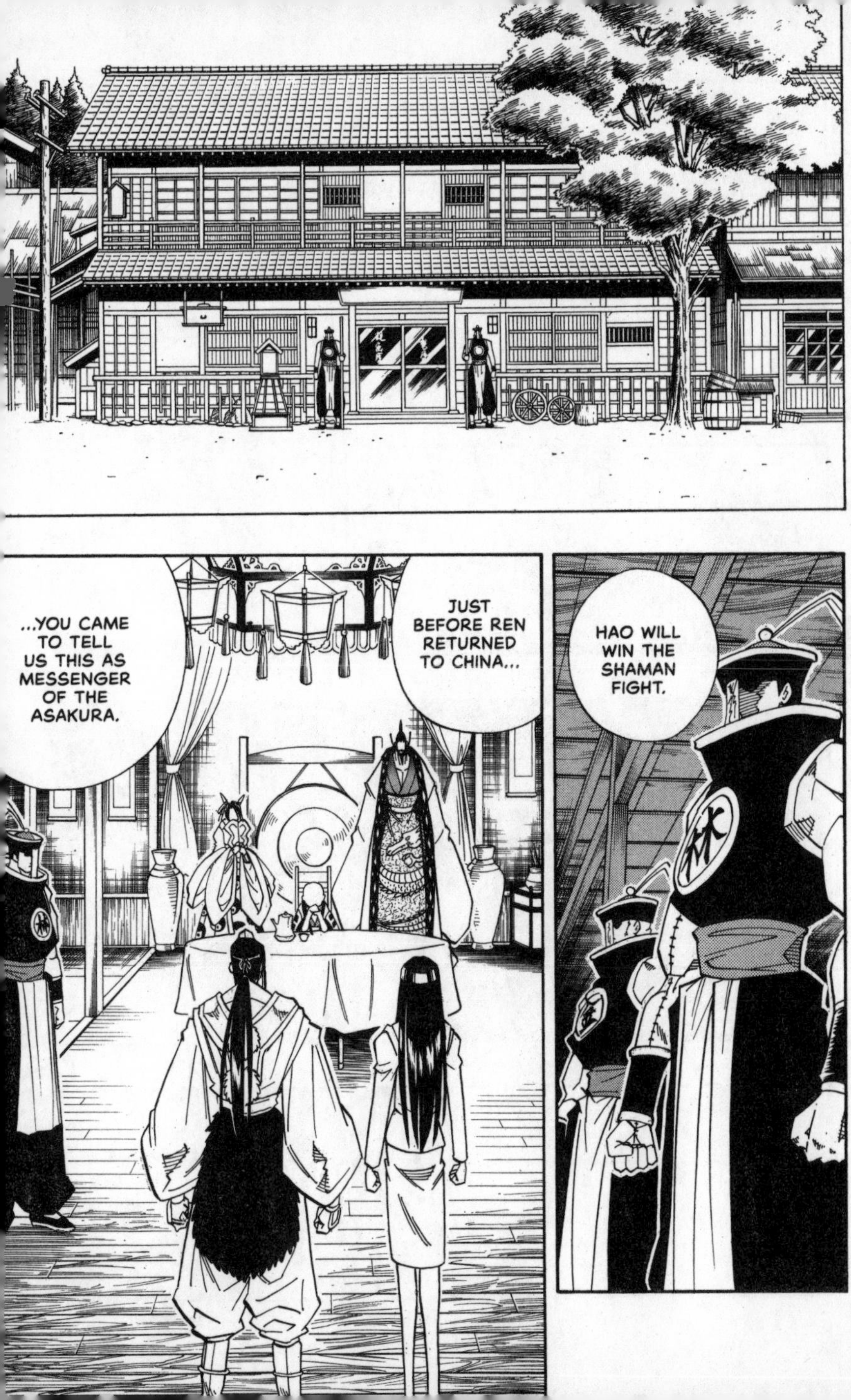
HAO WILL WIN THE SHAMAN FIGHT.
JUST BEFORE REN RETURNED TO CHINA...
...YOU CAME TO TELL US THIS AS MESSENGER OF THE ASAKURA.

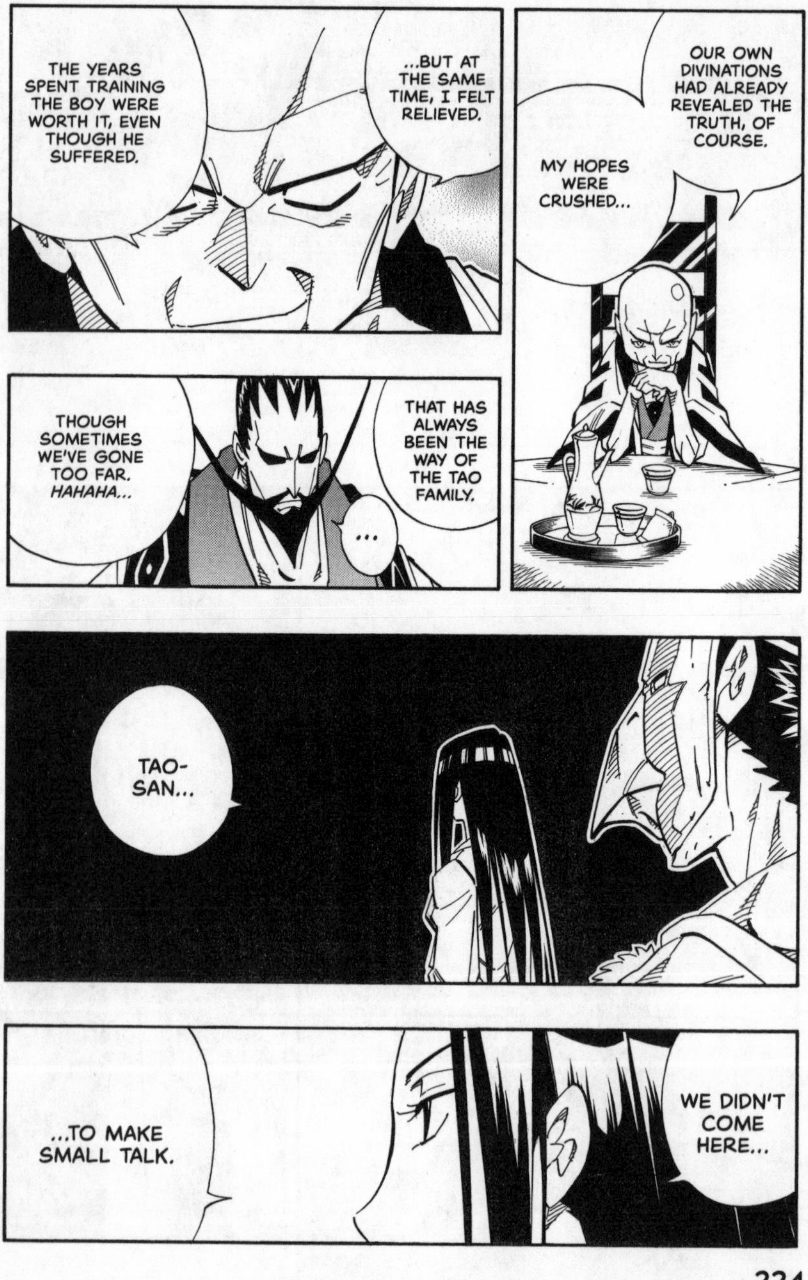
OUR OWN DIVINATIONS HAD ALREADY REVEALED THE TRUTH, OF COURSE.
MY HOPES WERE CRUSHED...
...BUT AT THE SAME TIME, I FELT RELIEVED.
THE YEARS SPENT TRAINING THE BOY WERE WORTH IT, EVEN THOUGH HE SUFFERED.
THAT HAS ALWAYS BEEN THE WAY OF THE TAO FAMILY.
...
THOUGH SOMETIMES WE'VE GONE TOO FAR. *HAHAHA*...
TAO-SAN...
WE DIDN'T COME HERE...
...TO MAKE SMALL TALK.

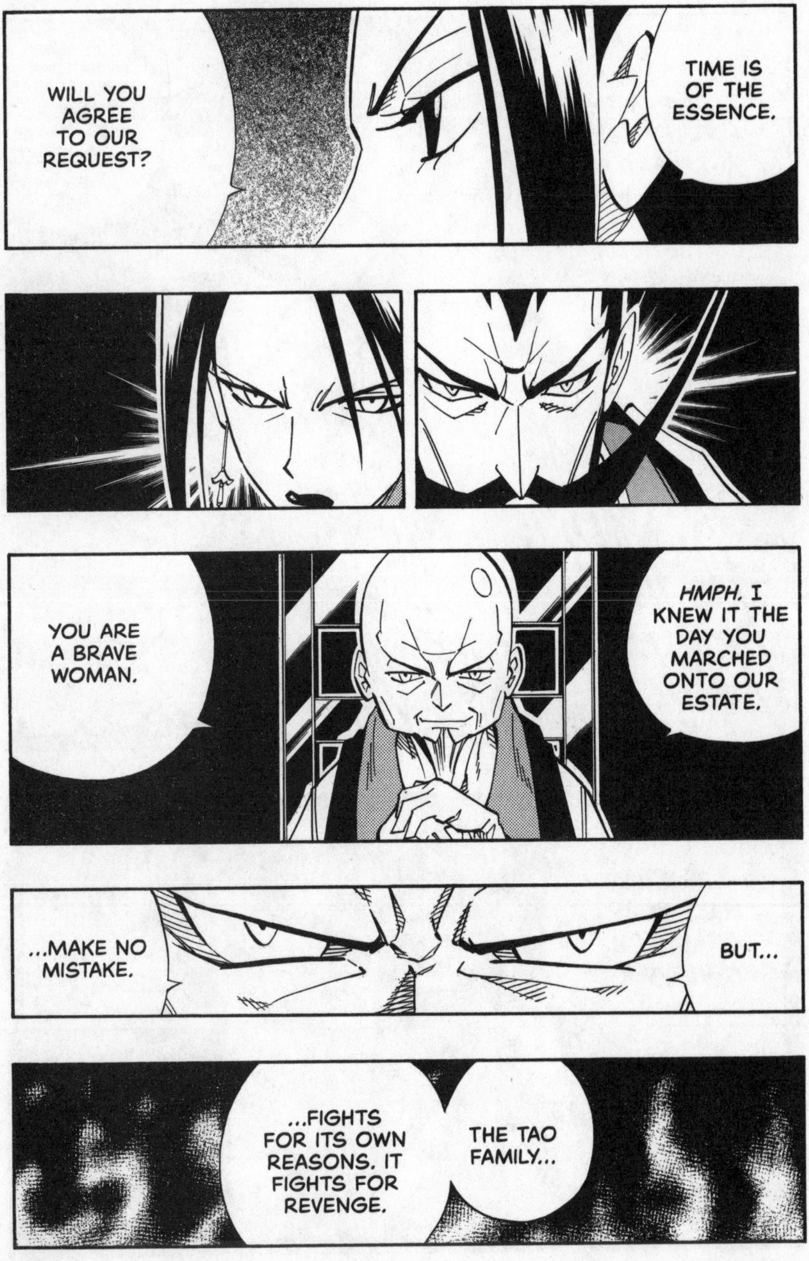
TIME IS OF THE ESSENCE.
WILL YOU AGREE TO OUR REQUEST?
HMPH. I KNEW IT THE DAY YOU MARCHED ONTO OUR ESTATE.
YOU ARE A BRAVE WOMAN.
BUT...
...MAKE NO MISTAKE.
THE TAO FAMILY...
...FIGHTS FOR ITS OWN REASONS. IT FIGHTS FOR REVENGE.

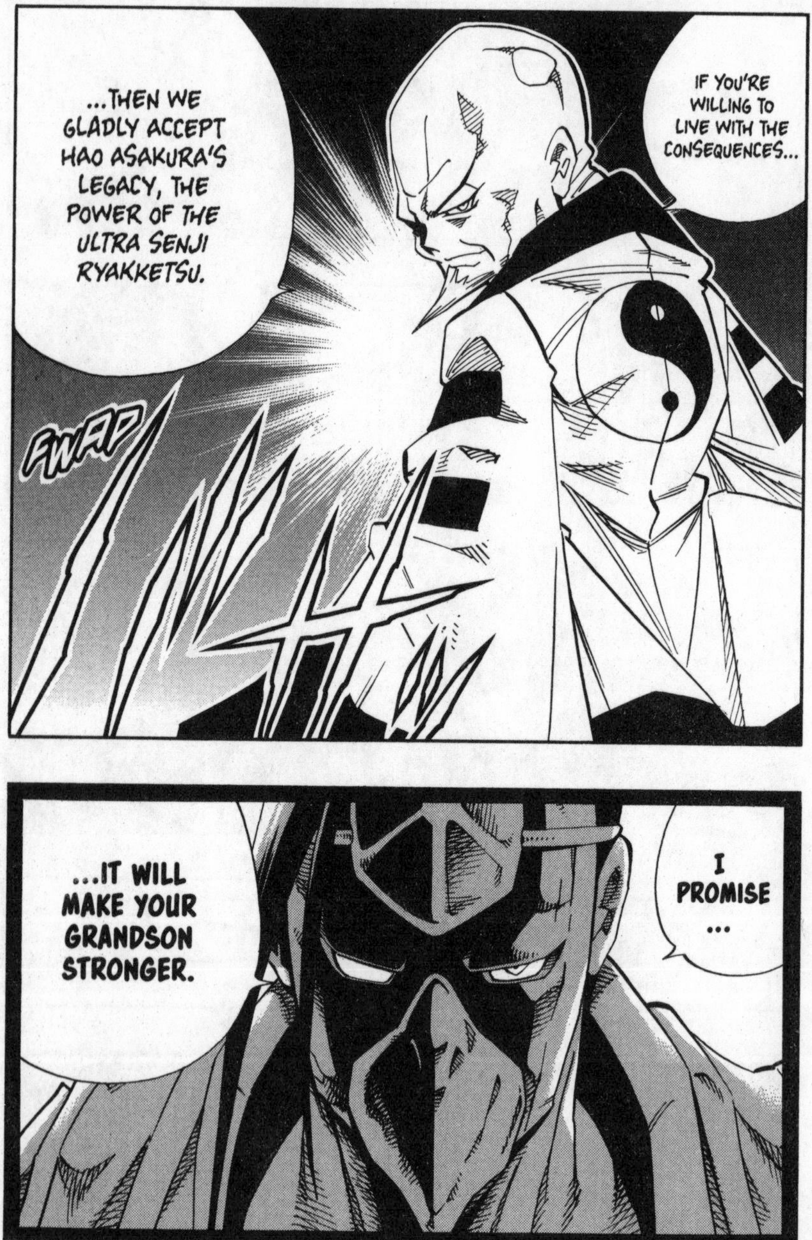
IF YOU'RE WILLING TO LIVE WITH THE CONSEQUENCES...
...THEN WE GLADLY ACCEPT HAO ASAKURA'S LEGACY, THE POWER OF THE ULTRA SENJI RYAKKETSU.
FWAP
I PROMISE ...
...IT WILL MAKE YOUR GRANDSON STRONGER.

Keiko Asakura

May 1985

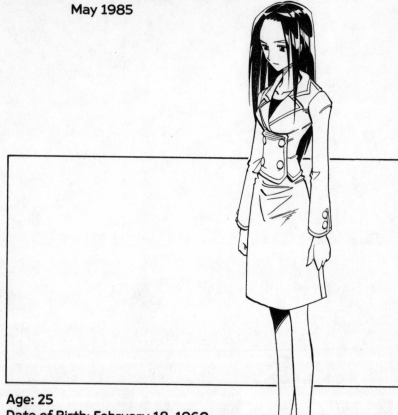

Age: 25
Date of Birth: February 18, 1960
Astrological Sign: Aquarius
Blood Type: A
Occupation: Office Worker

Chapter 145: Typhoon Mikihisa

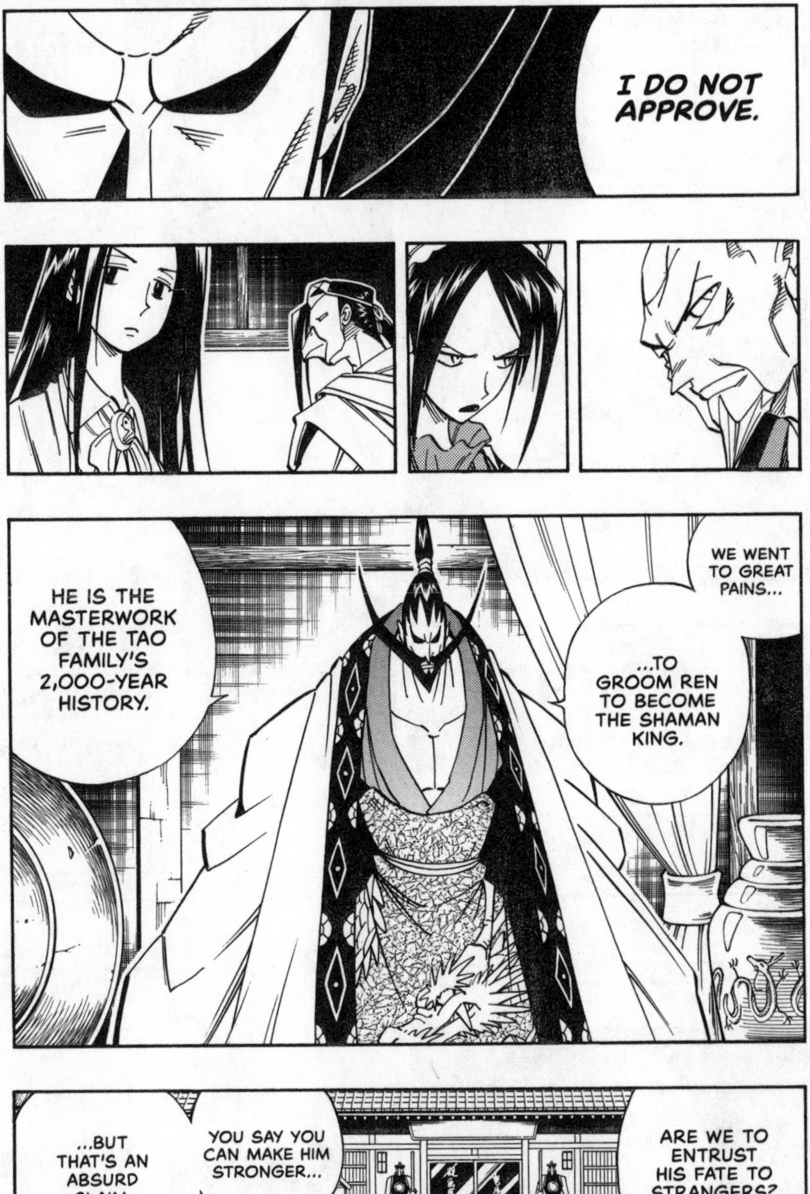
I DO NOT APPROVE.
WE WENT TO GREAT PAINS...
...TO GROOM REN TO BECOME THE SHAMAN KING.
HE IS THE MASTERWORK OF THE TAO FAMILY'S 2,000-YEAR HISTORY.
ARE WE TO ENTRUST HIS FATE TO STRANGERS?
YOU SAY YOU CAN MAKE HIM STRONGER...
...BUT THAT'S AN ABSURD CLAIM.

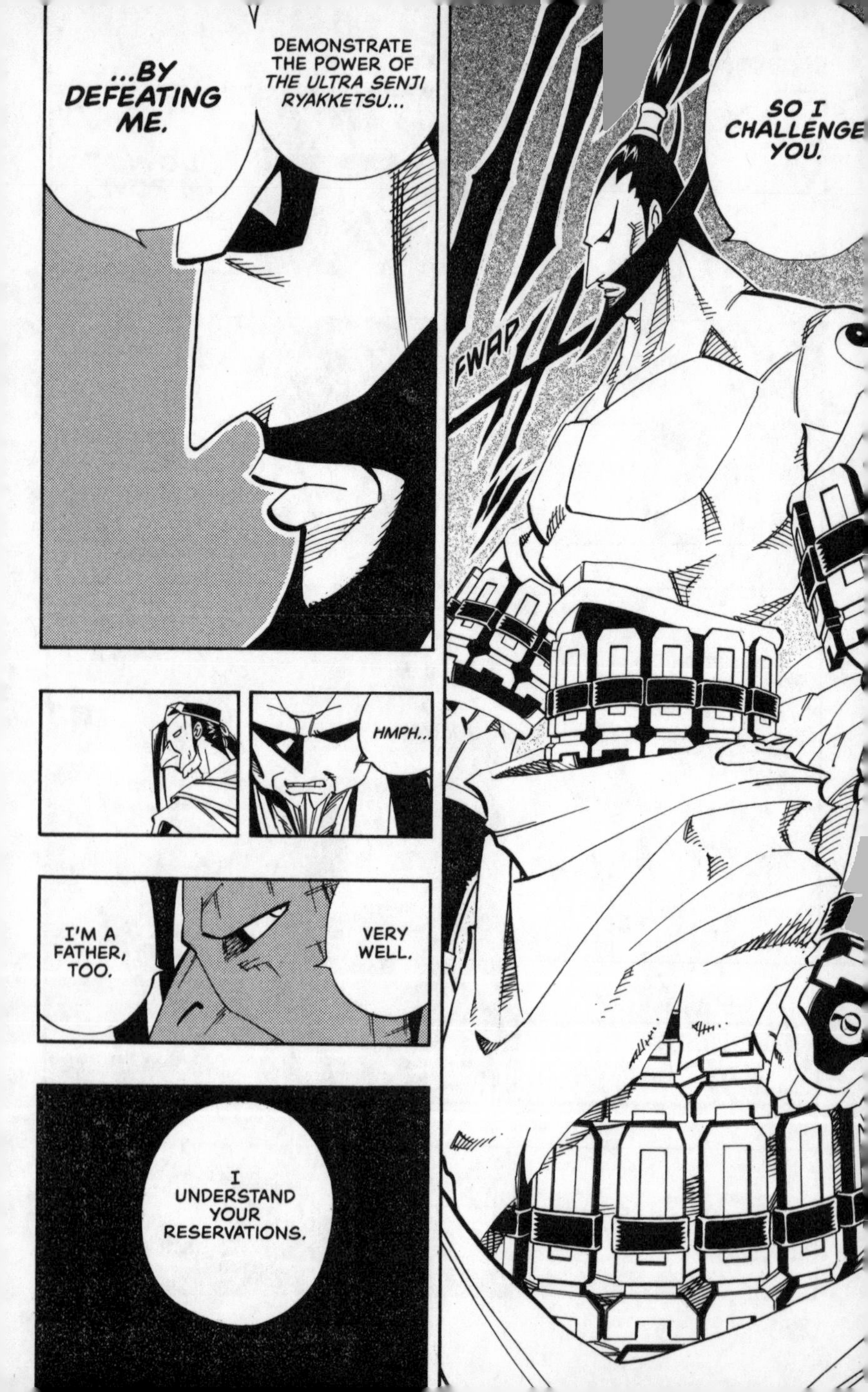
SO I CHALLENGE YOU.
FWAP
DEMONSTRATE THE POWER OF THE ULTRA SENJI RYAKKETSU...
...BY DEFEATING ME.
HMPH...
VERY WELL.
I'M A FATHER, TOO.
I UNDERSTAND YOUR RESERVATIONS.

Chapter 145:

Typhoon Mikihisa

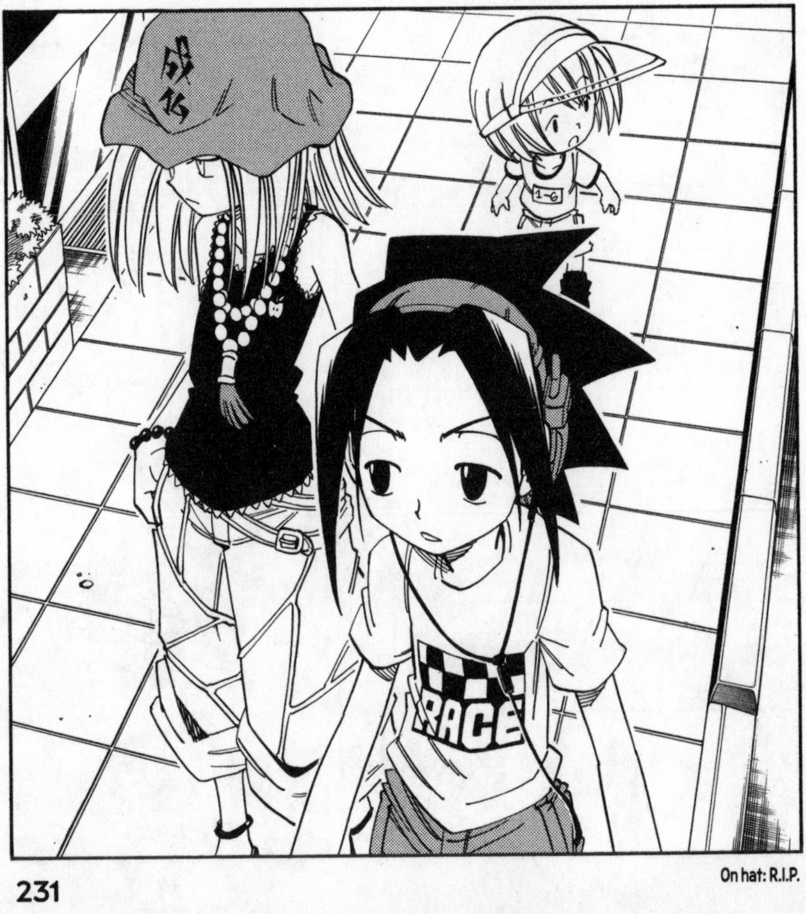
1-6
RACE

On hat: R.I.P.

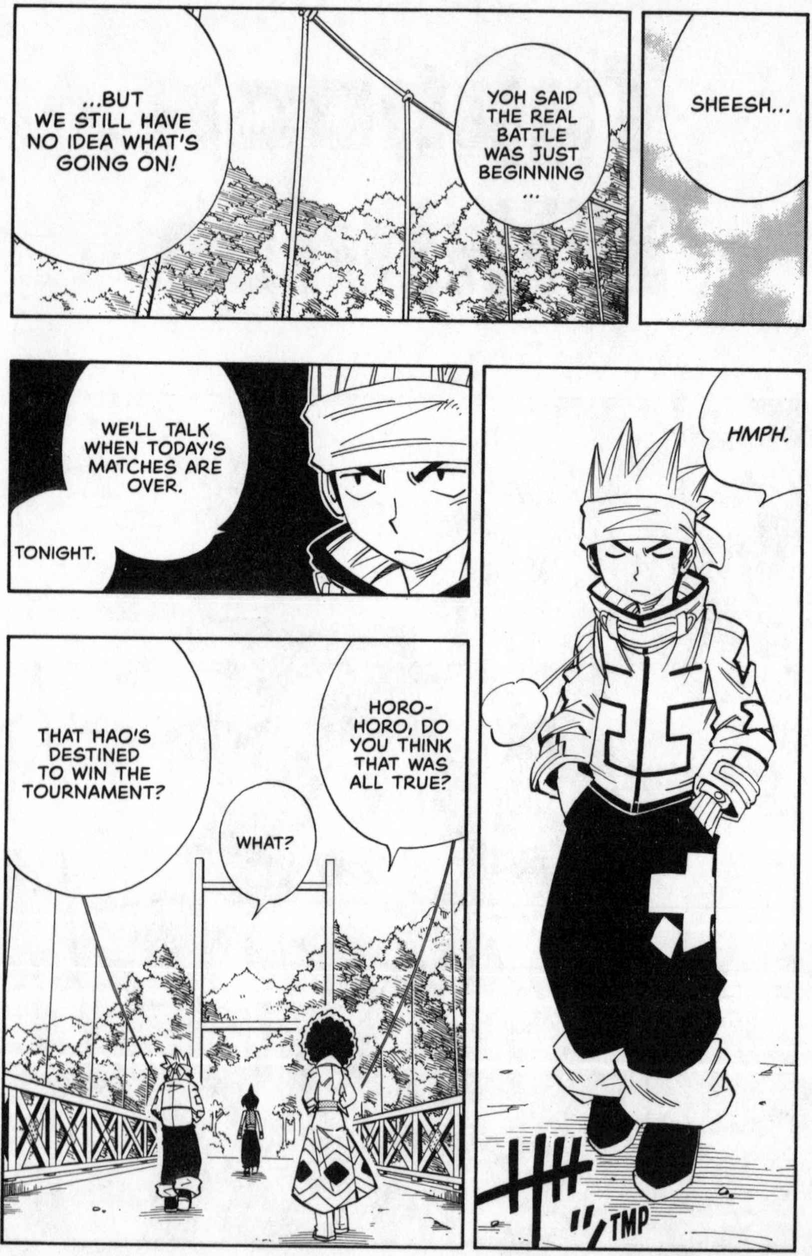
SHEESH...
YOH SAID THE REAL BATTLE WAS JUST BEGINNING...
...BUT WE STILL HAVE NO IDEA WHAT'S GOING ON!
HMPH.
TMP
WE'LL TALK WHEN TODAY'S MATCHES ARE OVER.
TONIGHT.
HORO-HORO, DO YOU THINK THAT WAS ALL TRUE?
WHAT?
THAT HAO'S DESTINED TO WIN THE TOURNAMENT?

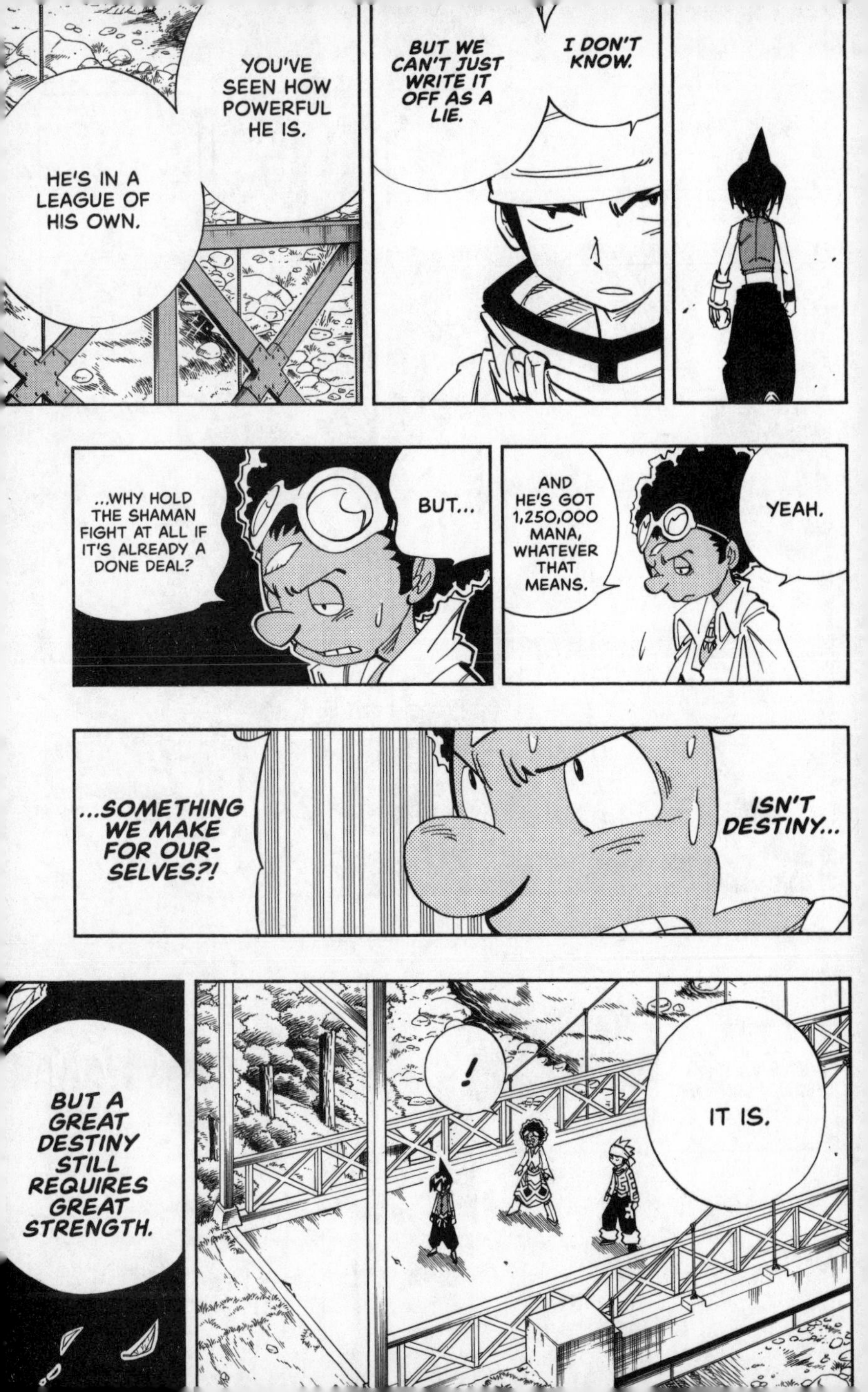
I DON'T KNOW.
BUT WE CAN'T JUST WRITE IT OFF AS A LIE.
YOU'VE SEEN HOW POWERFUL HE IS.
HE'S IN A LEAGUE OF HIS OWN.
YEAH.
AND HE'S GOT 1,250,000 MANA, WHATEVER THAT MEANS.
BUT...
...WHY HOLD THE SHAMAN FIGHT AT ALL IF IT'S ALREADY A DONE DEAL?
ISN'T DESTINY...
...SOMETHING WE MAKE FOR OUR-SELVES?!
IT IS.
!
BUT A GREAT DESTINY STILL REQUIRES GREAT STRENGTH.

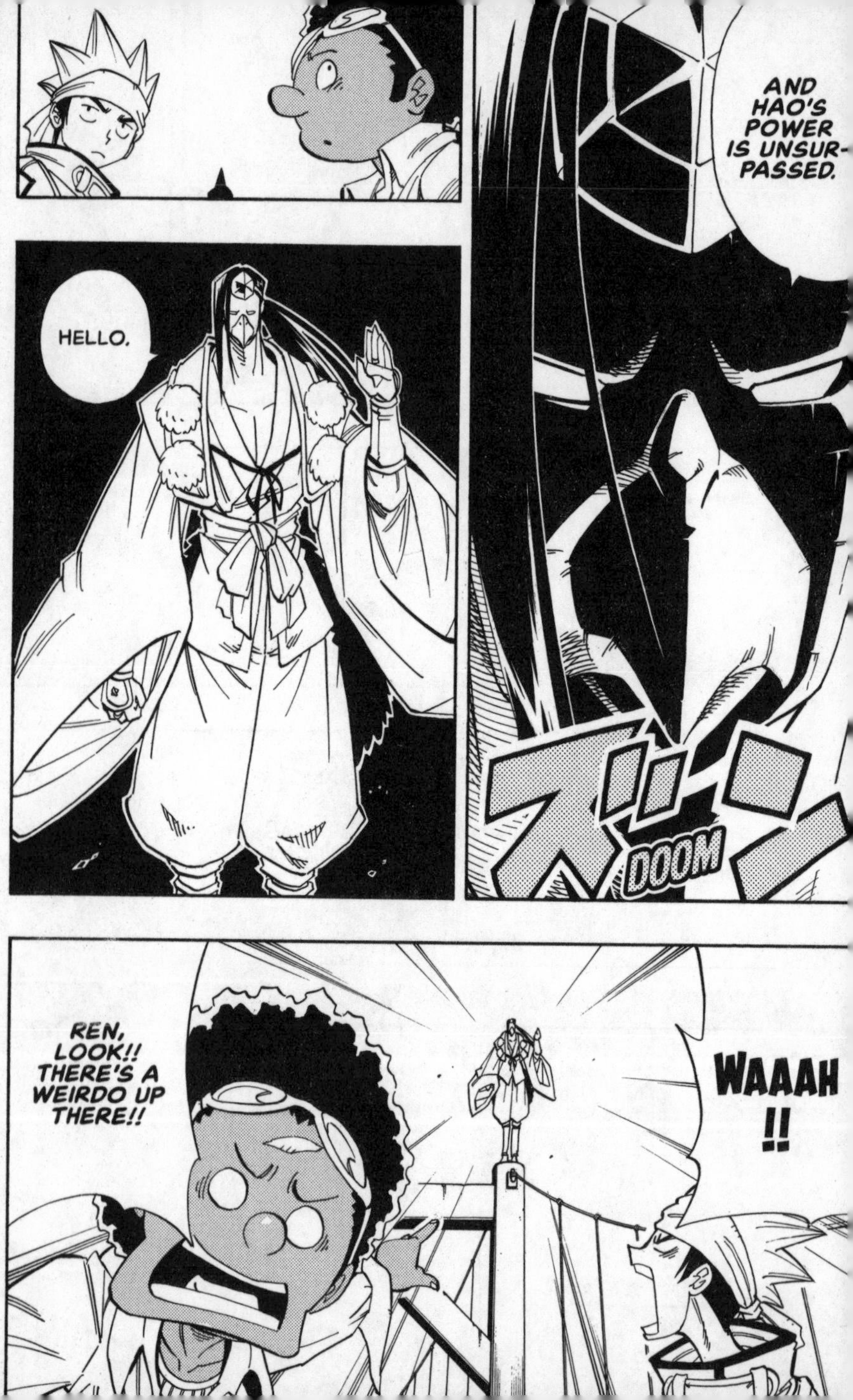
AND HAO'S POWER IS UNSURPASSED.
DOOM
HELLO.
WAAAH!!
REN, LOOK!! THERE'S A WEIRDO UP THERE!!

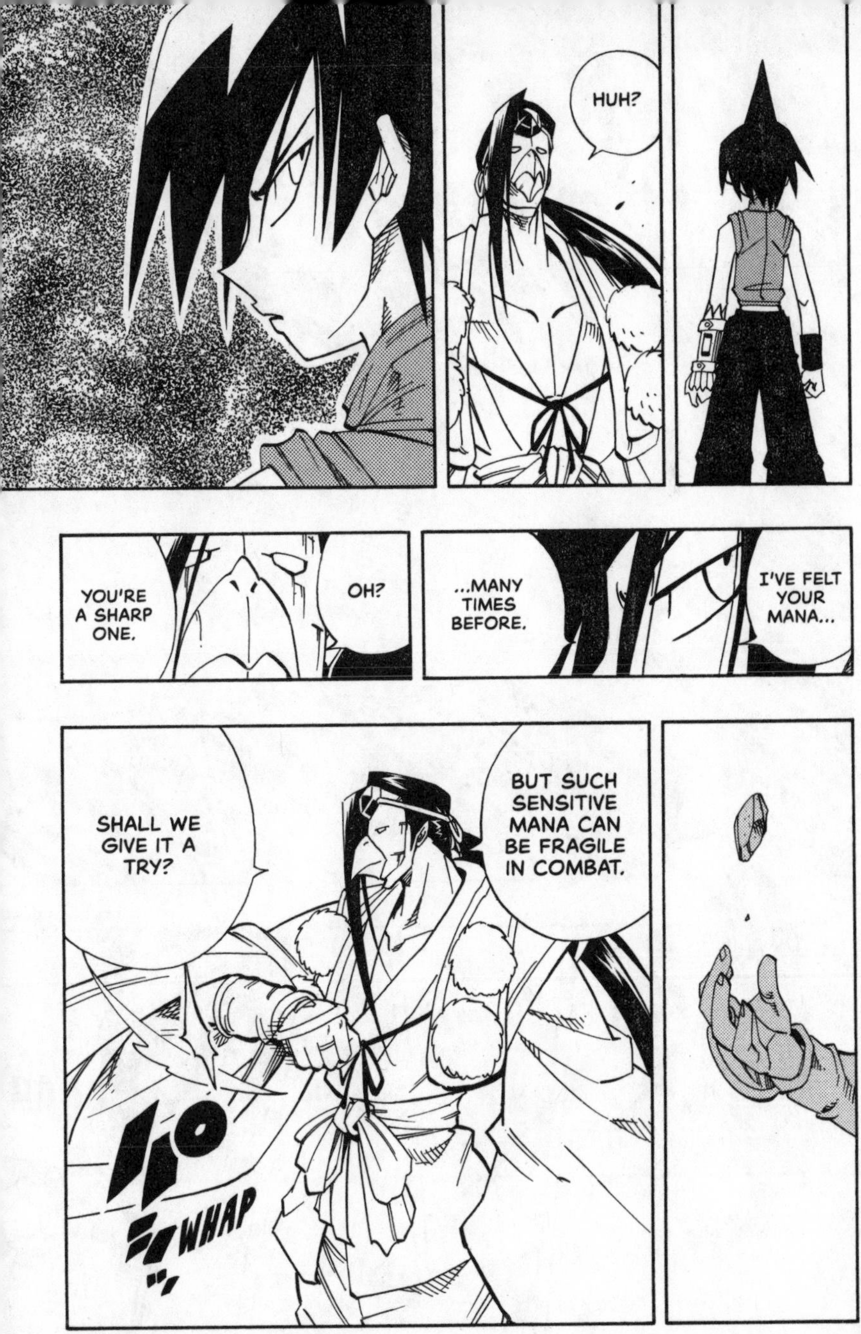
HUH?
I'VE FELT YOUR MANA...
...MANY TIMES BEFORE.
OH?
YOU'RE A SHARP ONE.
BUT SUCH SENSITIVE MANA CAN BE FRAGILE IN COMBAT.
SHALL WE GIVE IT A TRY?
WHAP

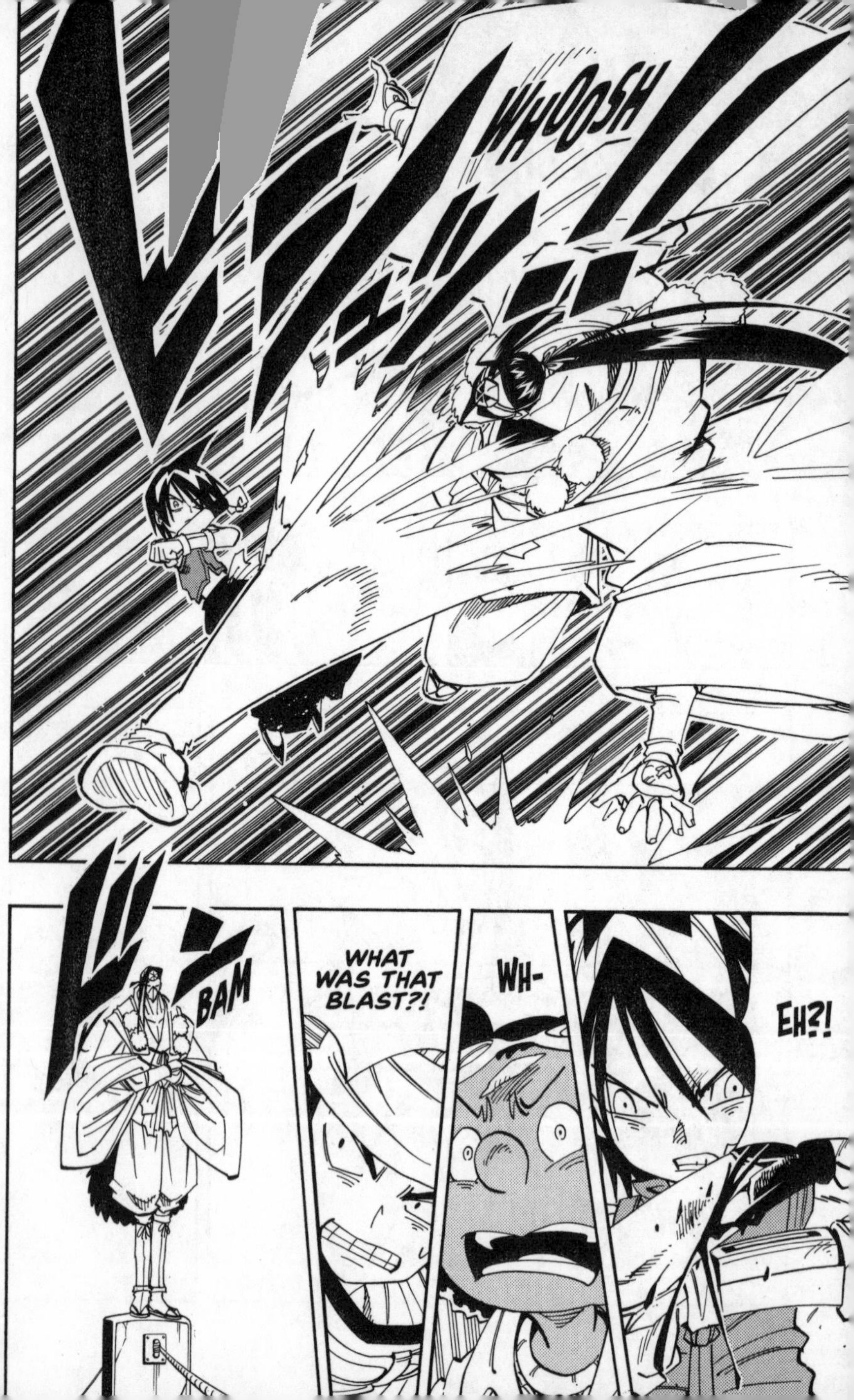
WHOOSH
EH?!
WH-
WHAT WAS THAT BLAST?!
BAM

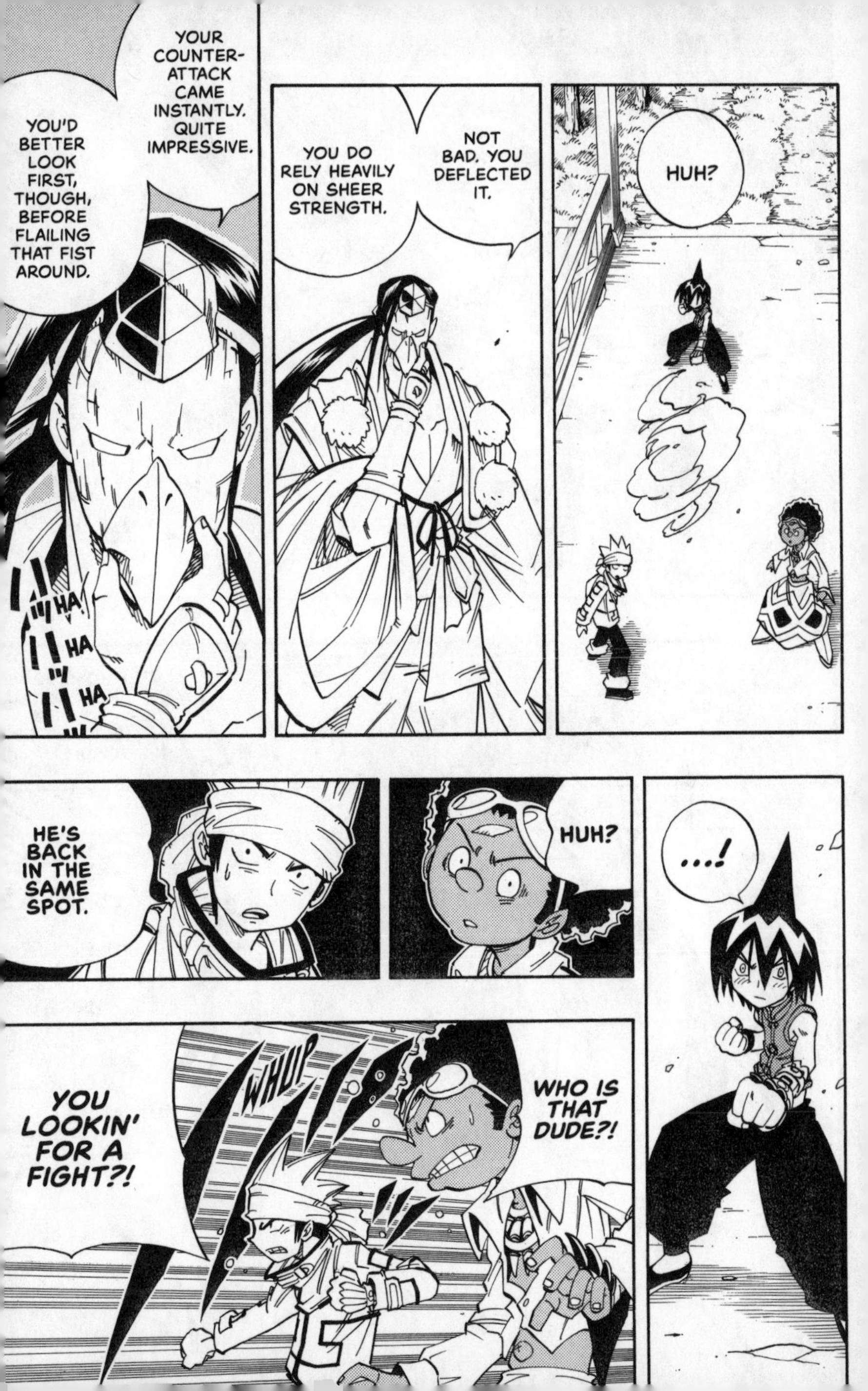
HUH?
NOT BAD. YOU DEFLECTED IT.
YOU DO RELY HEAVILY ON SHEER STRENGTH.
YOUR COUNTER-ATTACK CAME INSTANTLY. QUITE IMPRESSIVE.
YOU'D BETTER LOOK FIRST, THOUGH, BEFORE FLAILING THAT FIST AROUND.
HA HA HA
...!
HUH?
HE'S BACK IN THE SAME SPOT.
WHO IS THAT DUDE?!
WHUP
YOU LOOKIN' FOR A FIGHT?!

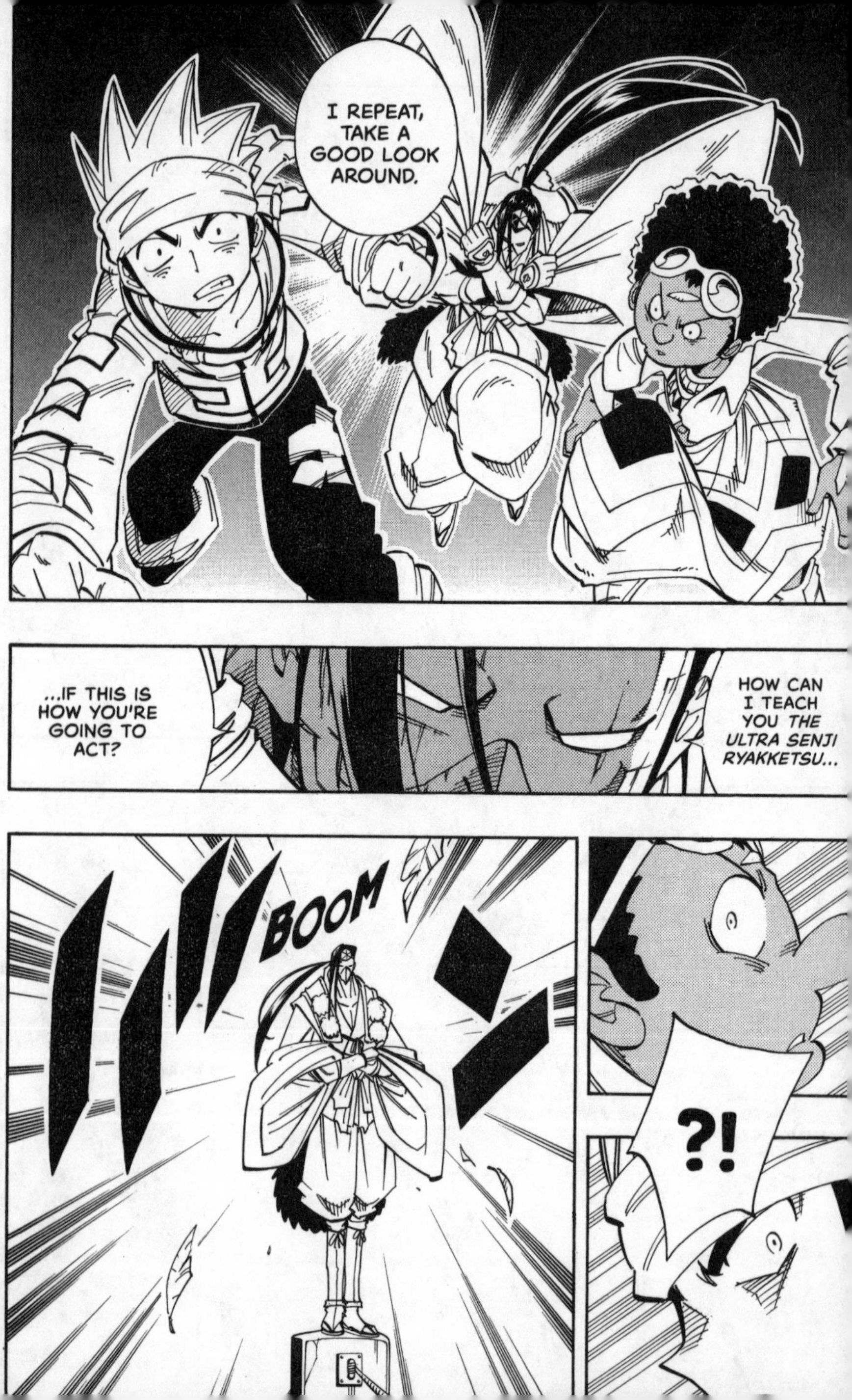
I REPEAT, TAKE A GOOD LOOK AROUND.
HOW CAN I TEACH YOU THE ULTRA SENJI RYAKKETSU...
...IF THIS IS HOW YOU'RE GOING TO ACT?
?!
BOOM

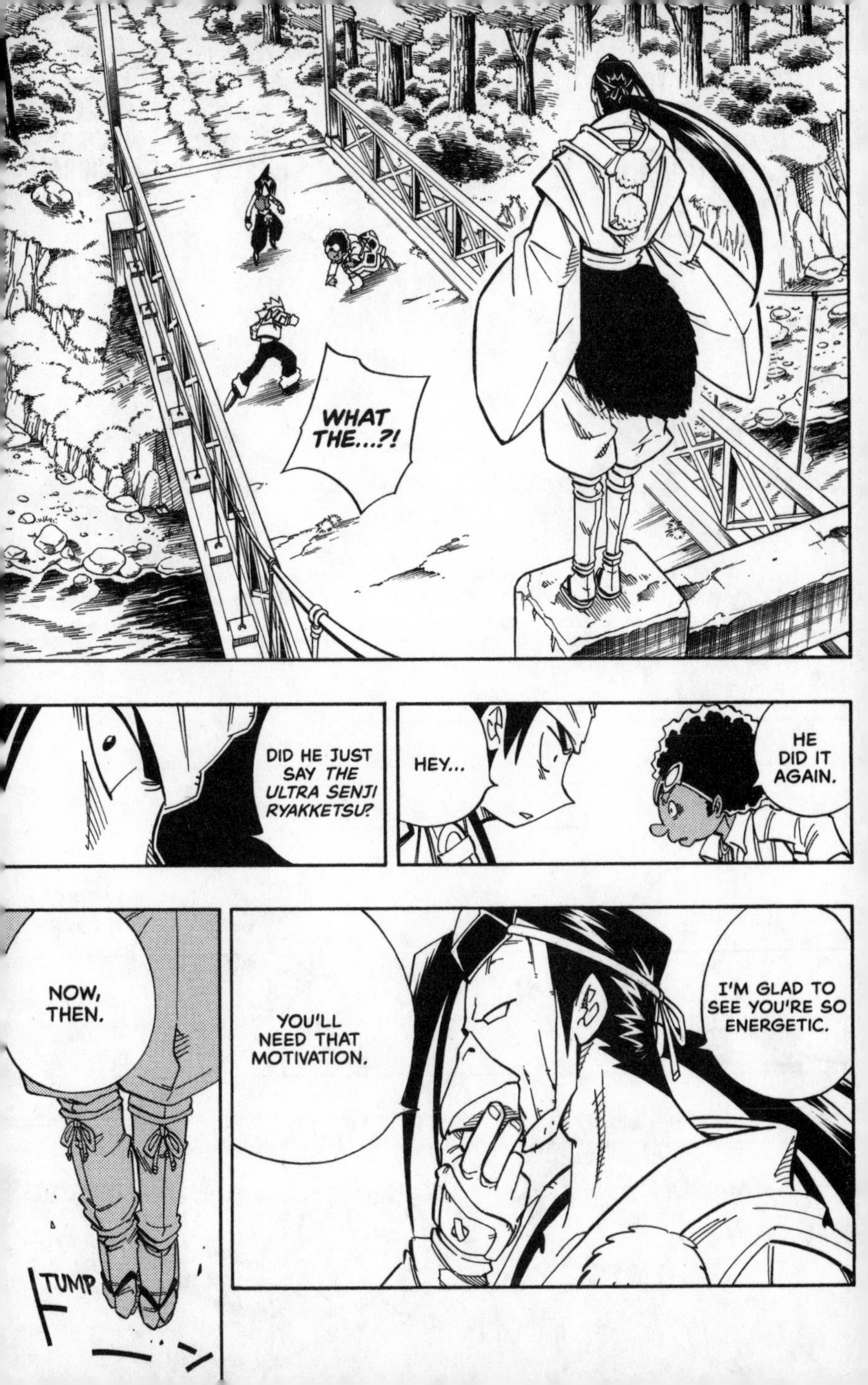
WHAT THE...?!
HE DID IT AGAIN.
HEY...
DID HE JUST SAY THE ULTRA SENJI RYAKKETSU?
I'M GLAD TO SEE YOU'RE SO ENERGETIC.
YOU'LL NEED THAT MOTIVATION.
NOW, THEN.
TUMP

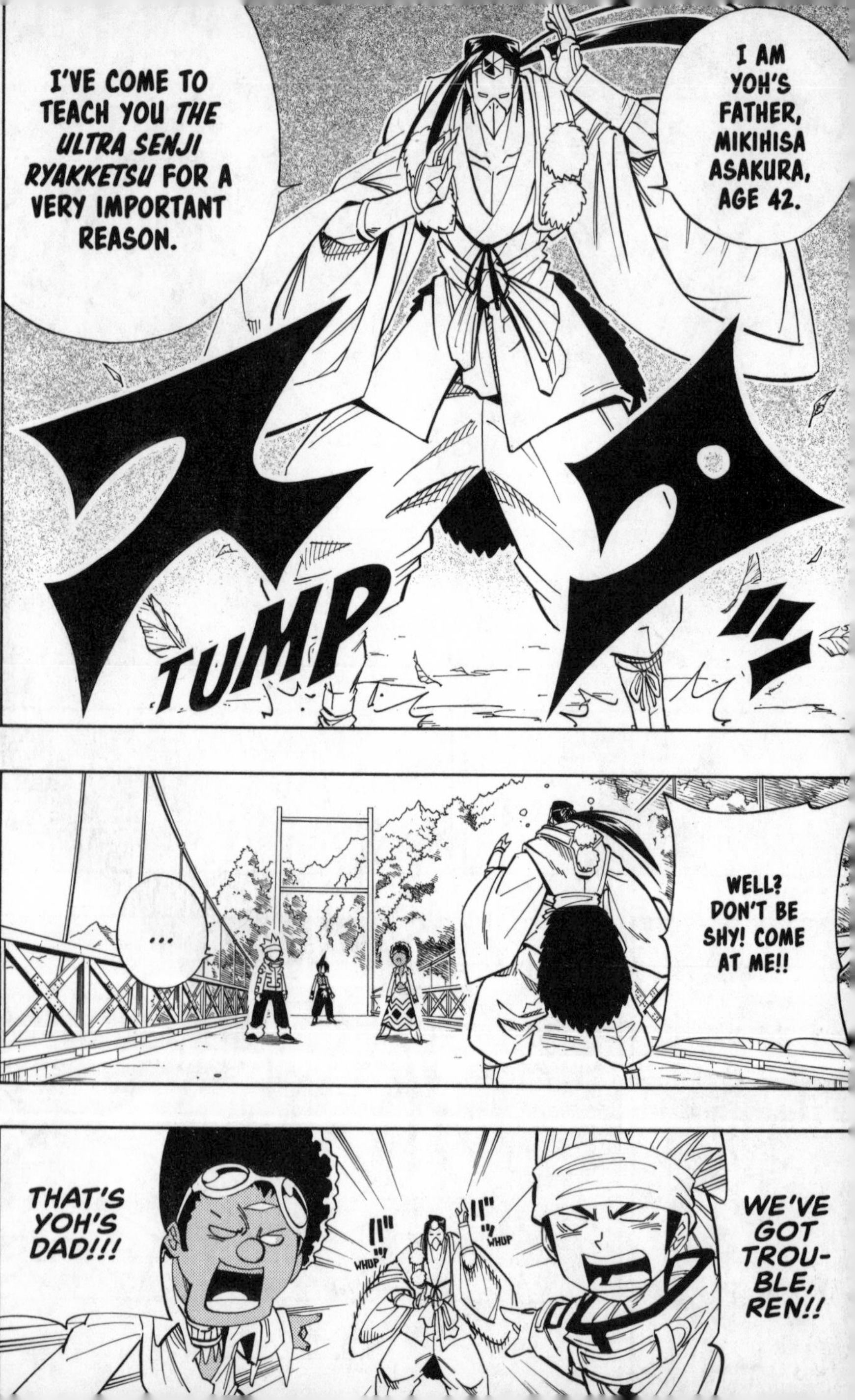
I AM YOH'S FATHER, MIKIHISA ASAKURA, AGE 42.
I'VE COME TO TEACH YOU *THE ULTRA SENJI RYAKKETSU* FOR A VERY IMPORTANT REASON.
TUMP
WELL? DON'T BE SHY! COME AT ME!!
...
WE'VE GOT TROU-BLE, REN!!
WHUP
WHUP
THAT'S YOH'S DAD!!!

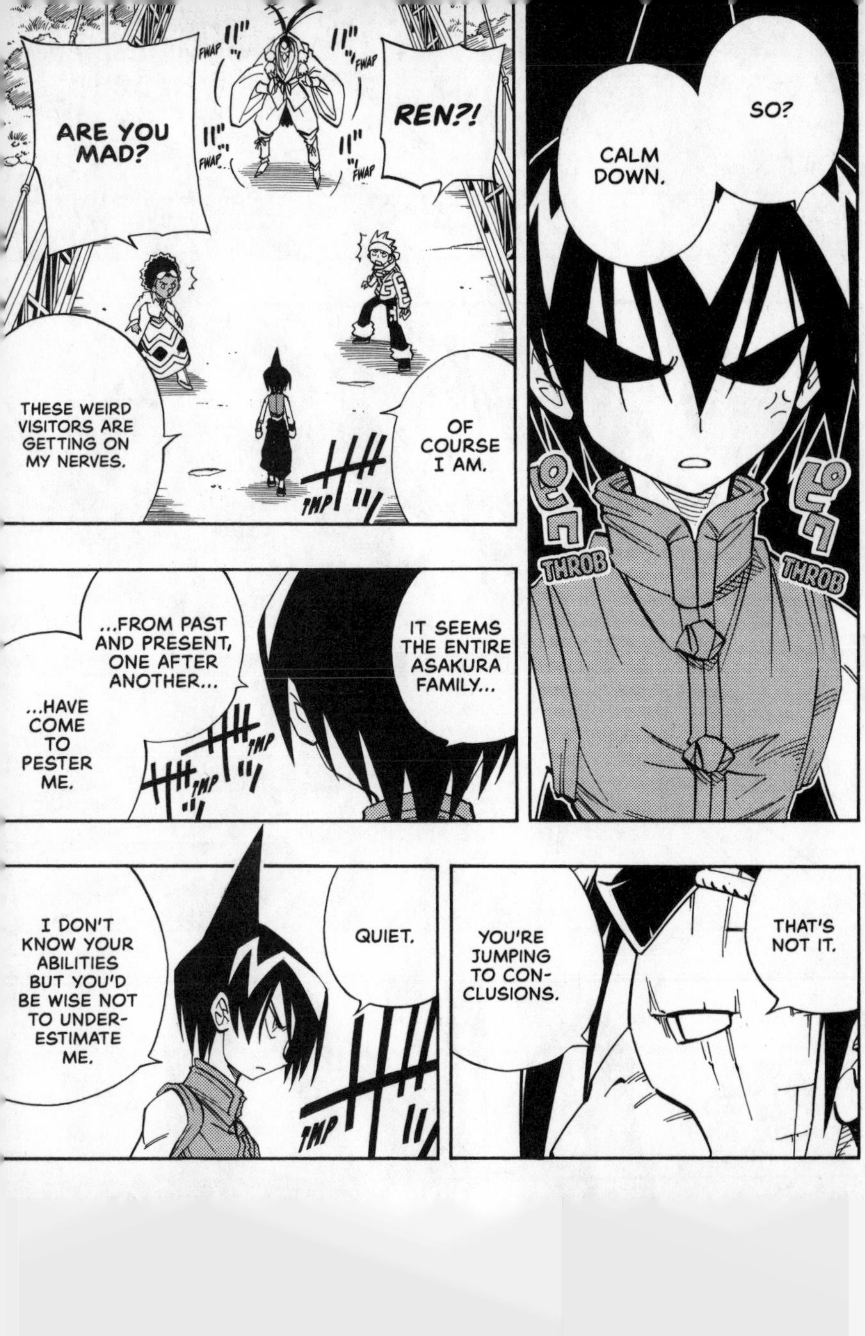
SO?
CALM DOWN.
THROB
THROB
REN?!
FWAP
FWAP
FWAP
FWAP
ARE YOU MAD?
OF COURSE I AM.
TMP
THESE WEIRD VISITORS ARE GETTING ON MY NERVES.
IT SEEMS THE ENTIRE ASAKURA FAMILY...
...FROM PAST AND PRESENT, ONE AFTER ANOTHER...
TMP
TMP
...HAVE COME TO PESTER ME.
THAT'S NOT IT.
YOU'RE JUMPING TO CON- CLUSIONS.
QUIET.
TMP
I DON'T KNOW YOUR ABILITIES BUT YOU'D BE WISE NOT TO UNDER- ESTIMATE ME.

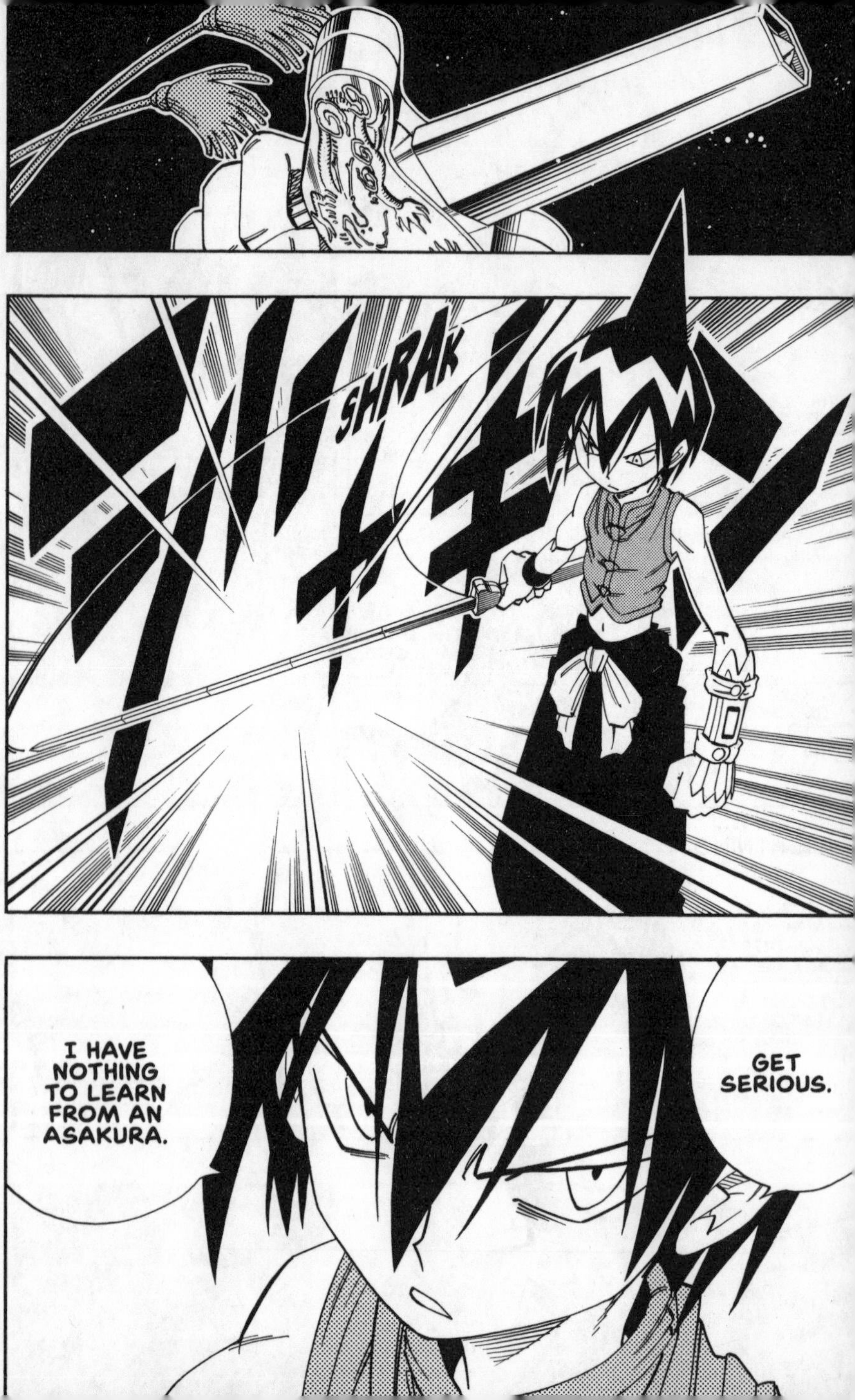
SHRAK
GET SERIOUS.
I HAVE NOTHING TO LEARN FROM AN ASAKURA.

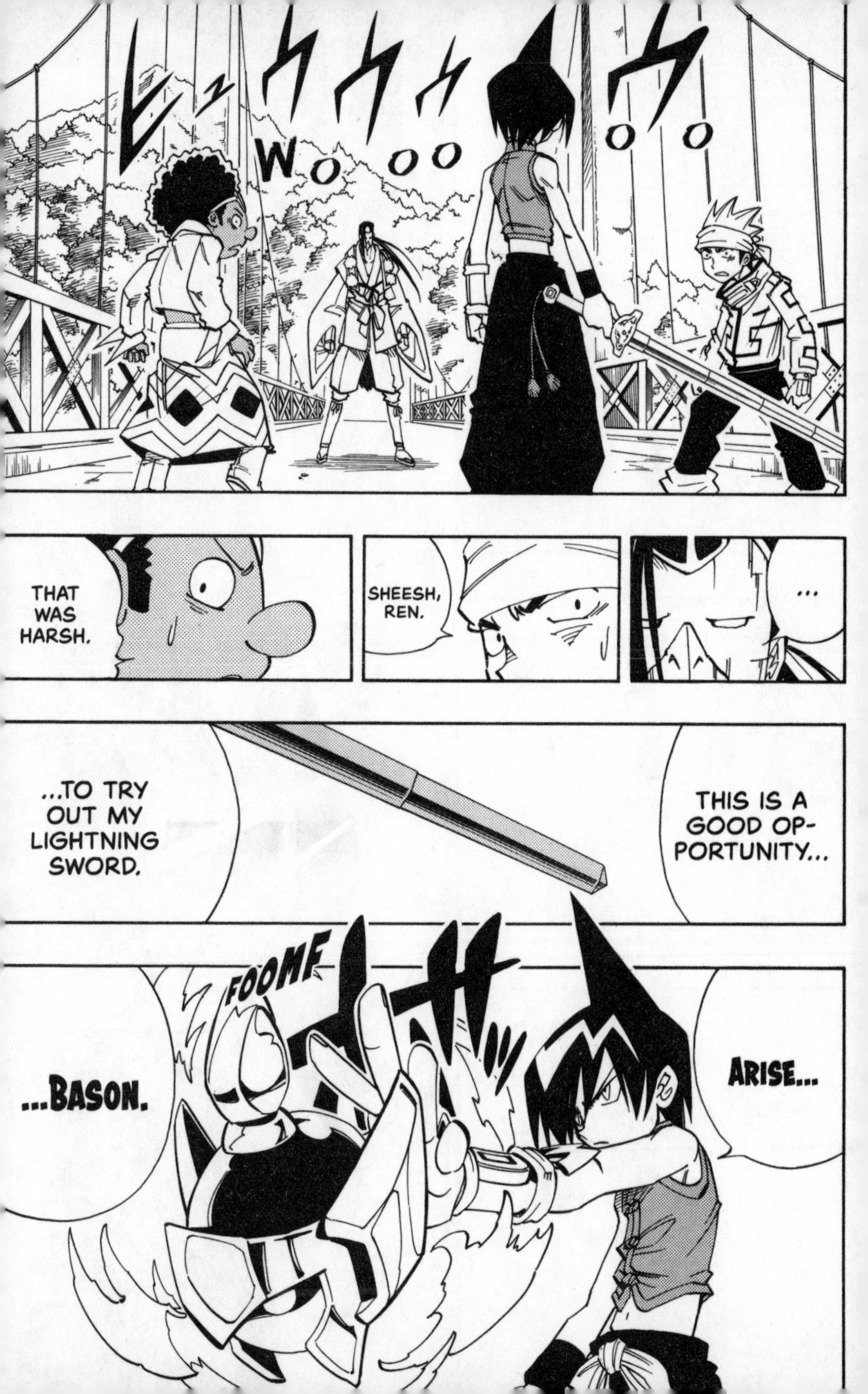
WOOOOO
...
SHEESH, REN.
THAT WAS HARSH.
THIS IS A GOOD OP-PORTUNITY...
...TO TRY OUT MY LIGHTNING SWORD.
ARISE...
FOOMF
...BASON.

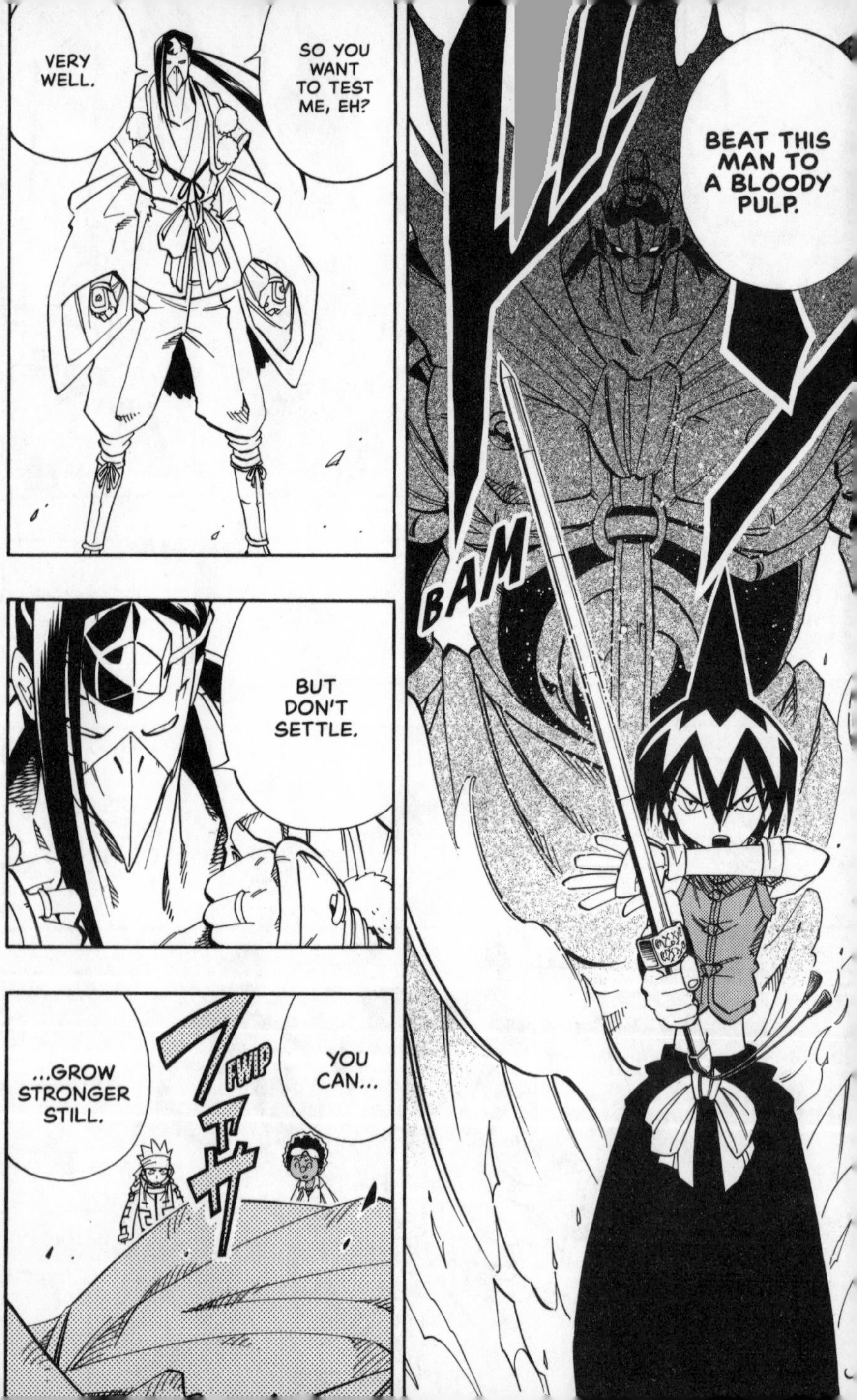
BEAT THIS MAN TO A BLOODY PULP.
BAM
SO YOU WANT TO TEST ME, EH?
VERY WELL.
BUT DON'T SETTLE.
YOU CAN...
FWIP
...GROW STRONGER STILL.

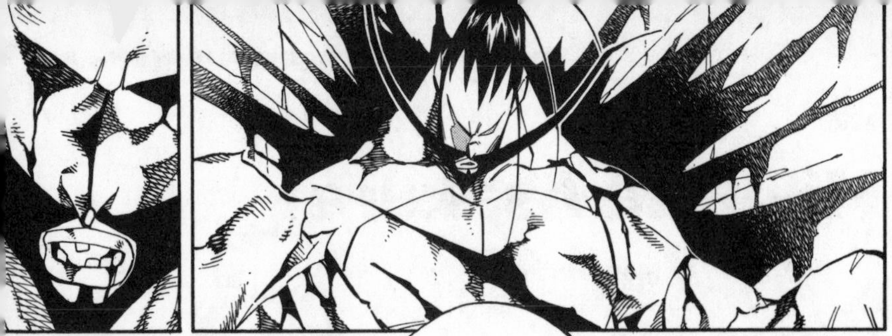

Hat and bib: Offering

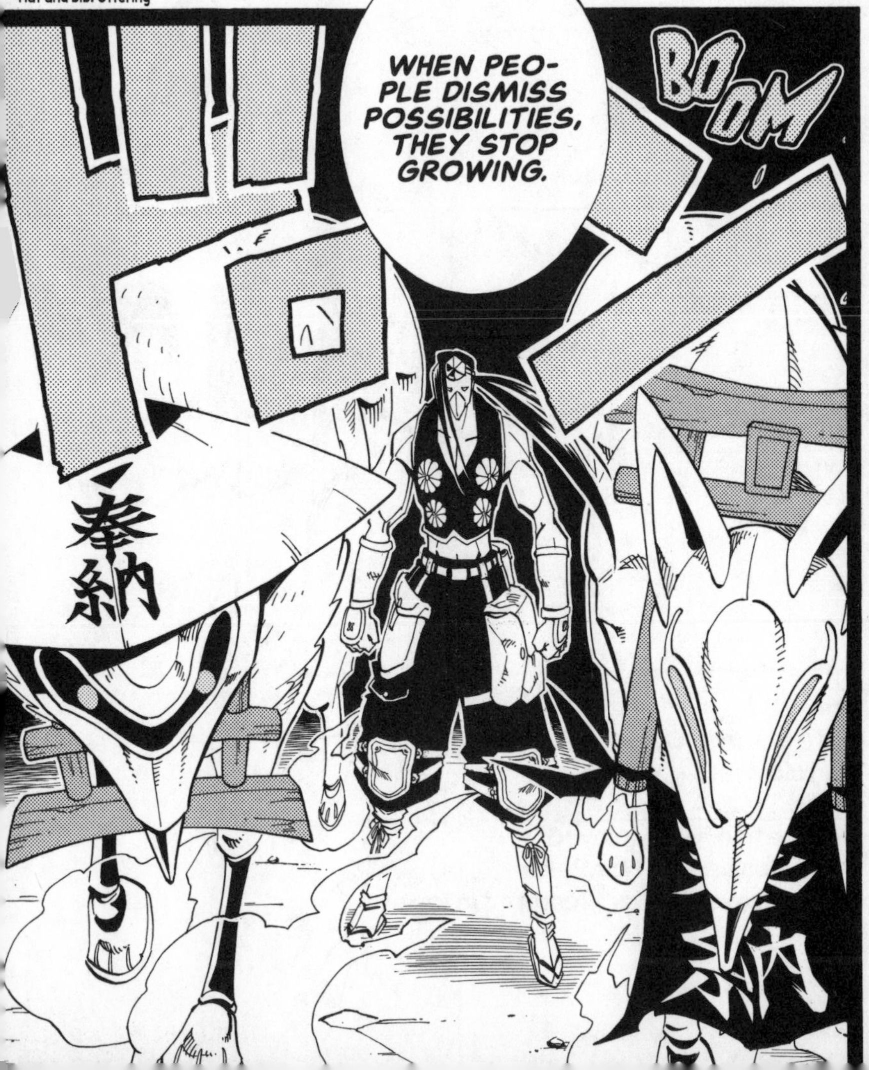
BOOM
WHEN PEOPLE DISMISS POSSIBILITIES, THEY STOP GROWING.
奉納

Mikihisa Asakura

May 1985

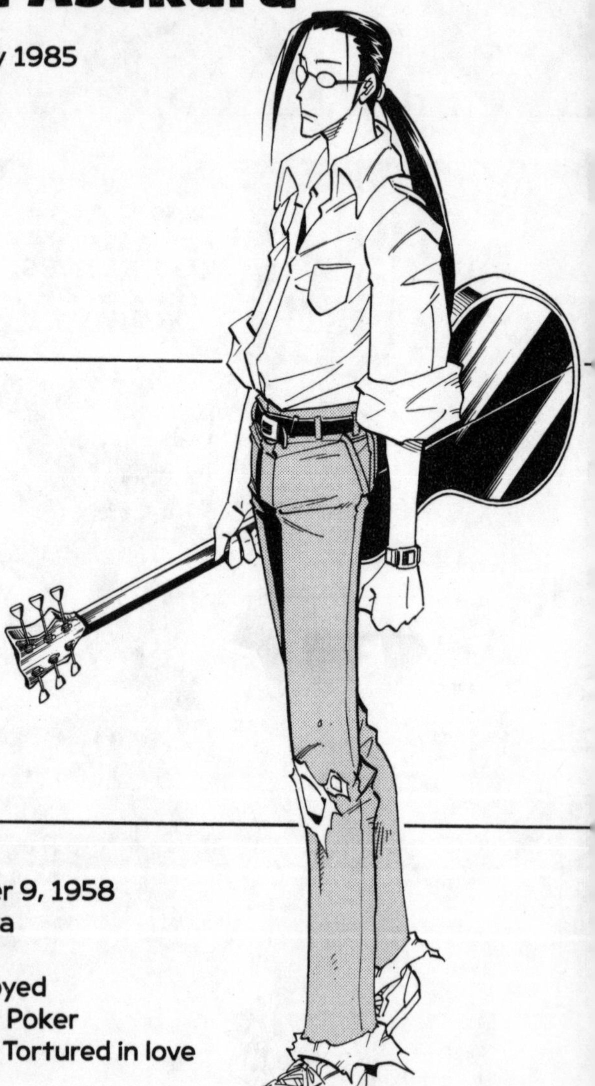

Age: 26
Date of Birth: October 9, 1958
Astrological Sign: Libra
Blood Type: A
Occupation: Unemployed
Birth Flower: Red Hot Poker
Symbolism of Flower: Tortured in love

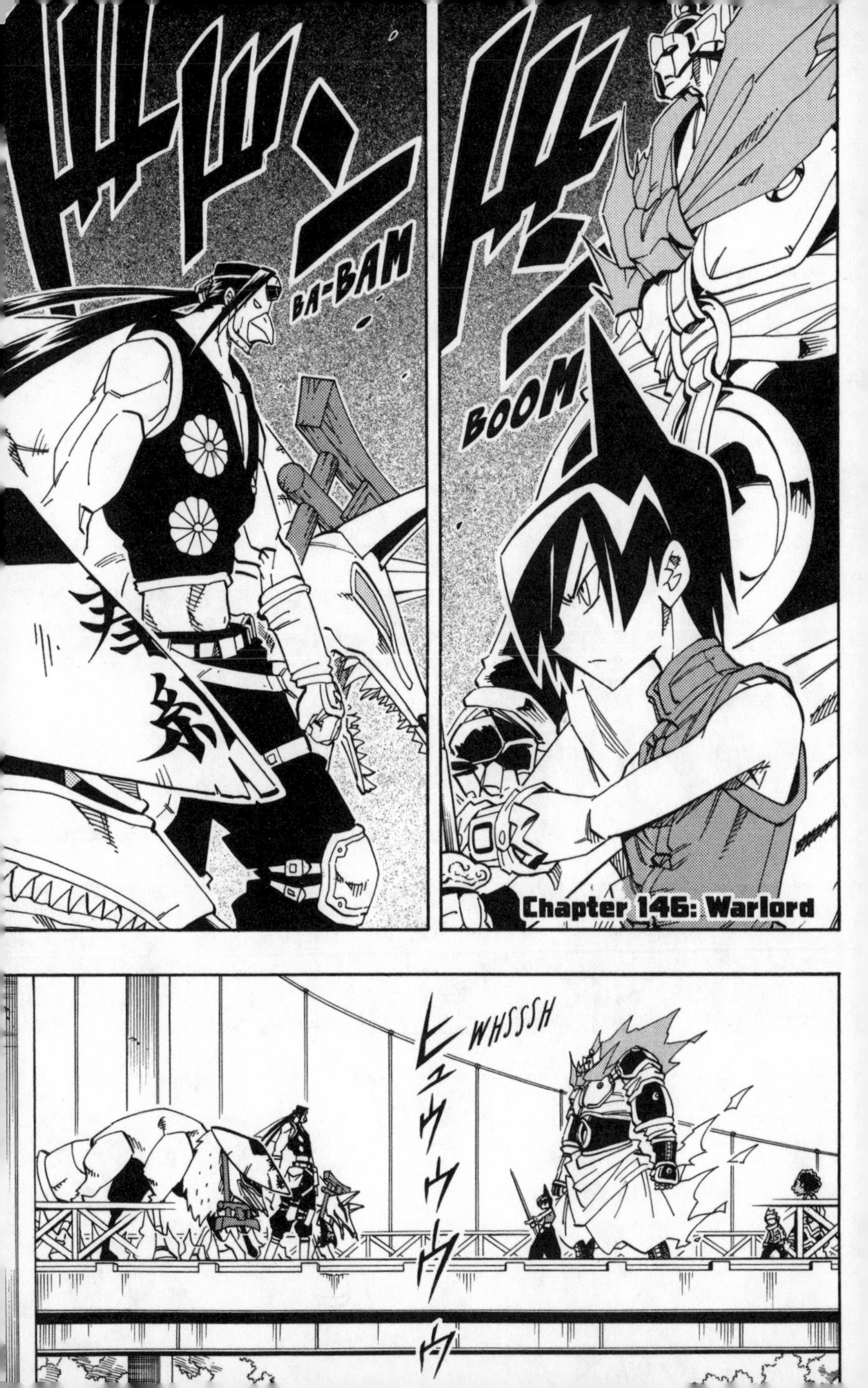
BOOM
Chapter 146: Warlord
BA-BAM
WHSSSH

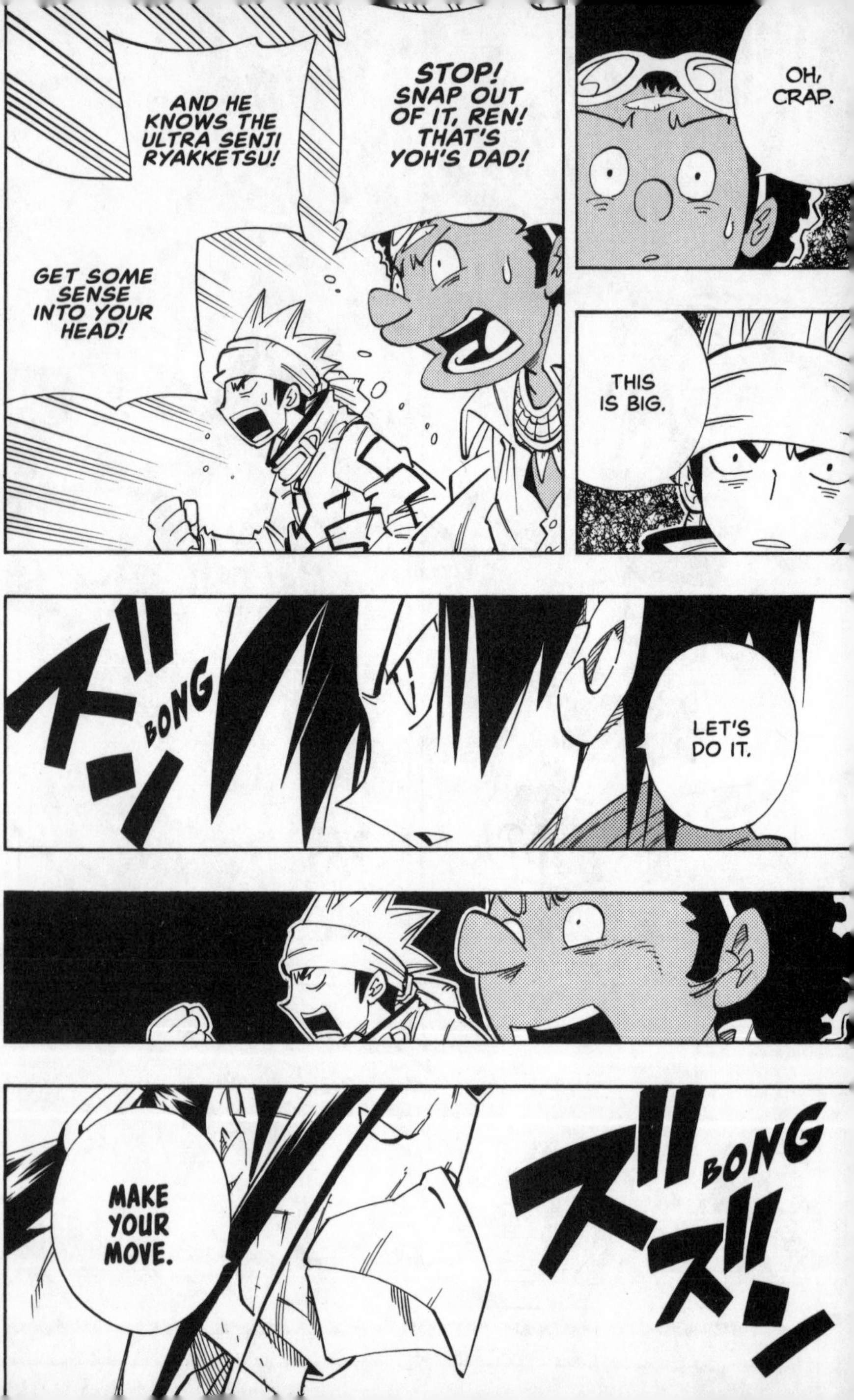
OH, CRAP.
THIS IS BIG.
STOP! SNAP OUT OF IT, REN! THAT'S YOH'S DAD!
AND HE KNOWS THE ULTRA SENJI RYAKKETSU!
GET SOME SENSE INTO YOUR HEAD!
LET'S DO IT.
BONG
BONG
MAKE YOUR MOVE.

Chapter 146:

Warlord

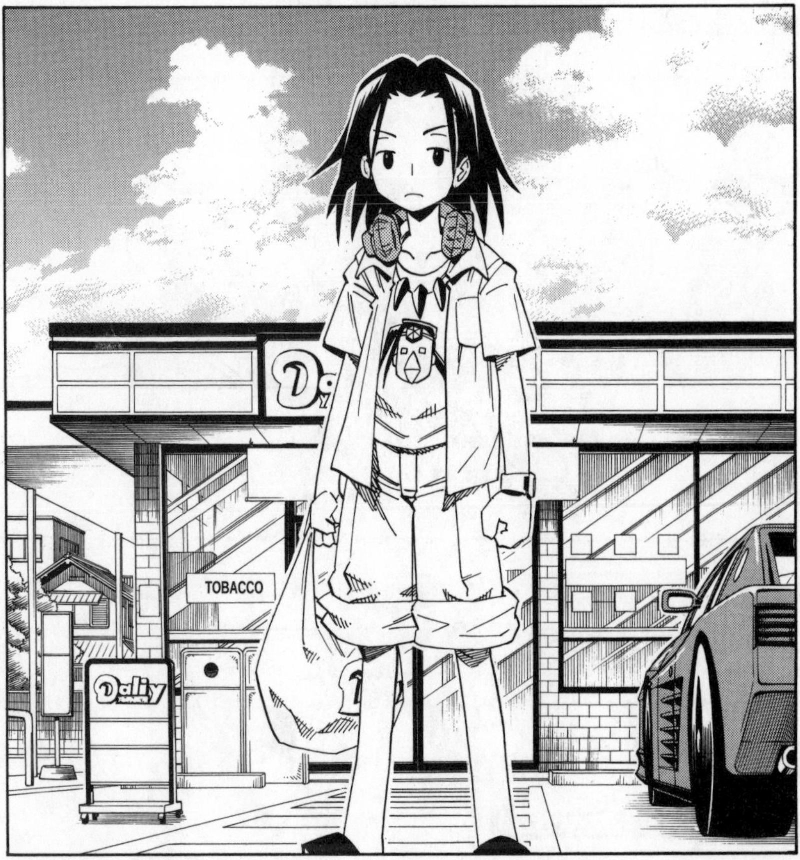
TOBACCO
Daliy

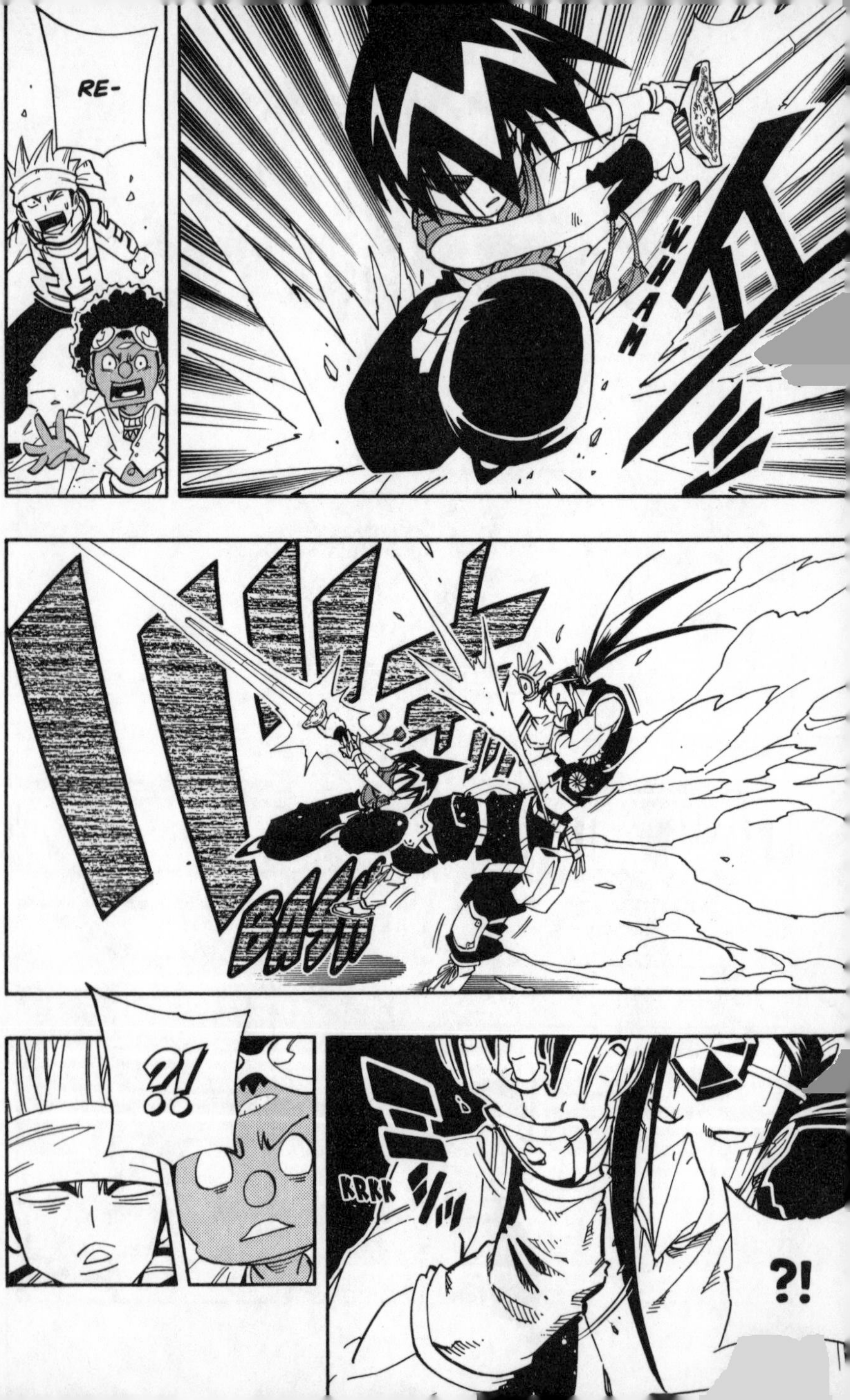
WHAM
RE-
BASH
KRRK
?!
?!

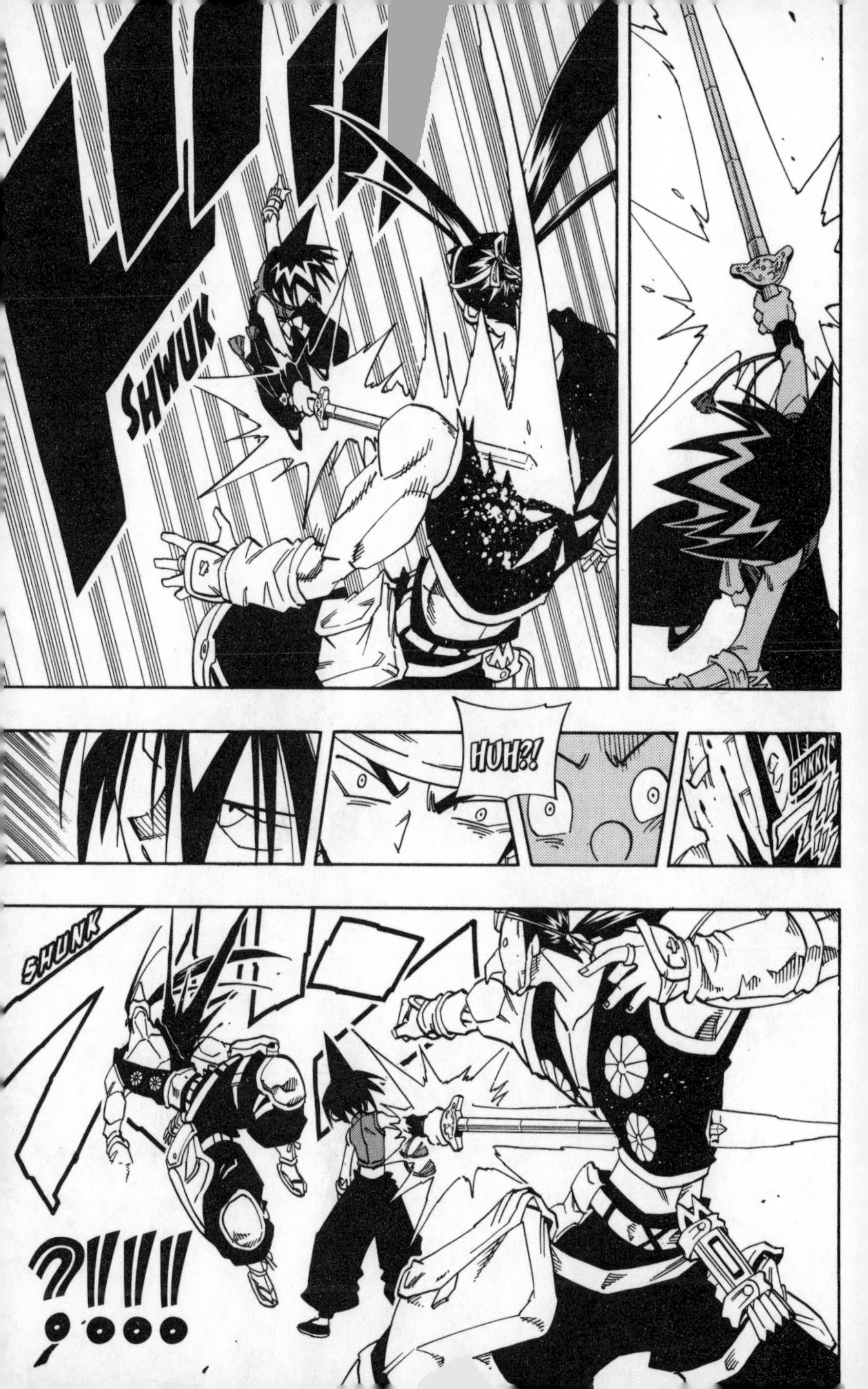
SHWUK
BWKK
HUH?!
SHUNK
?!!!!

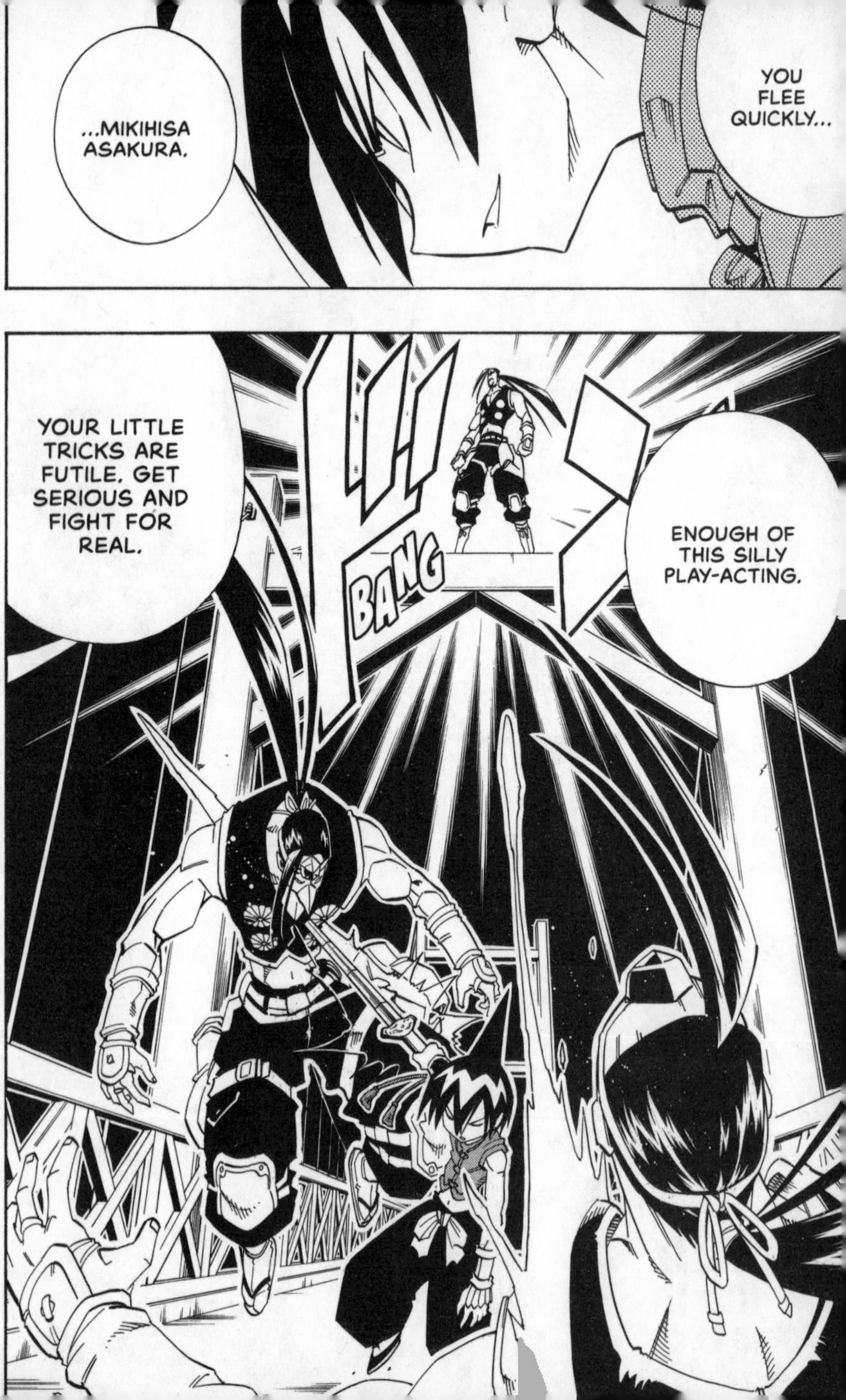
YOU FLEE QUICKLY...
...MIKIHISA ASAKURA.
ENOUGH OF THIS SILLY PLAY-ACTING.
YOUR LITTLE TRICKS ARE FUTILE. GET SERIOUS AND FIGHT FOR REAL.
BANG

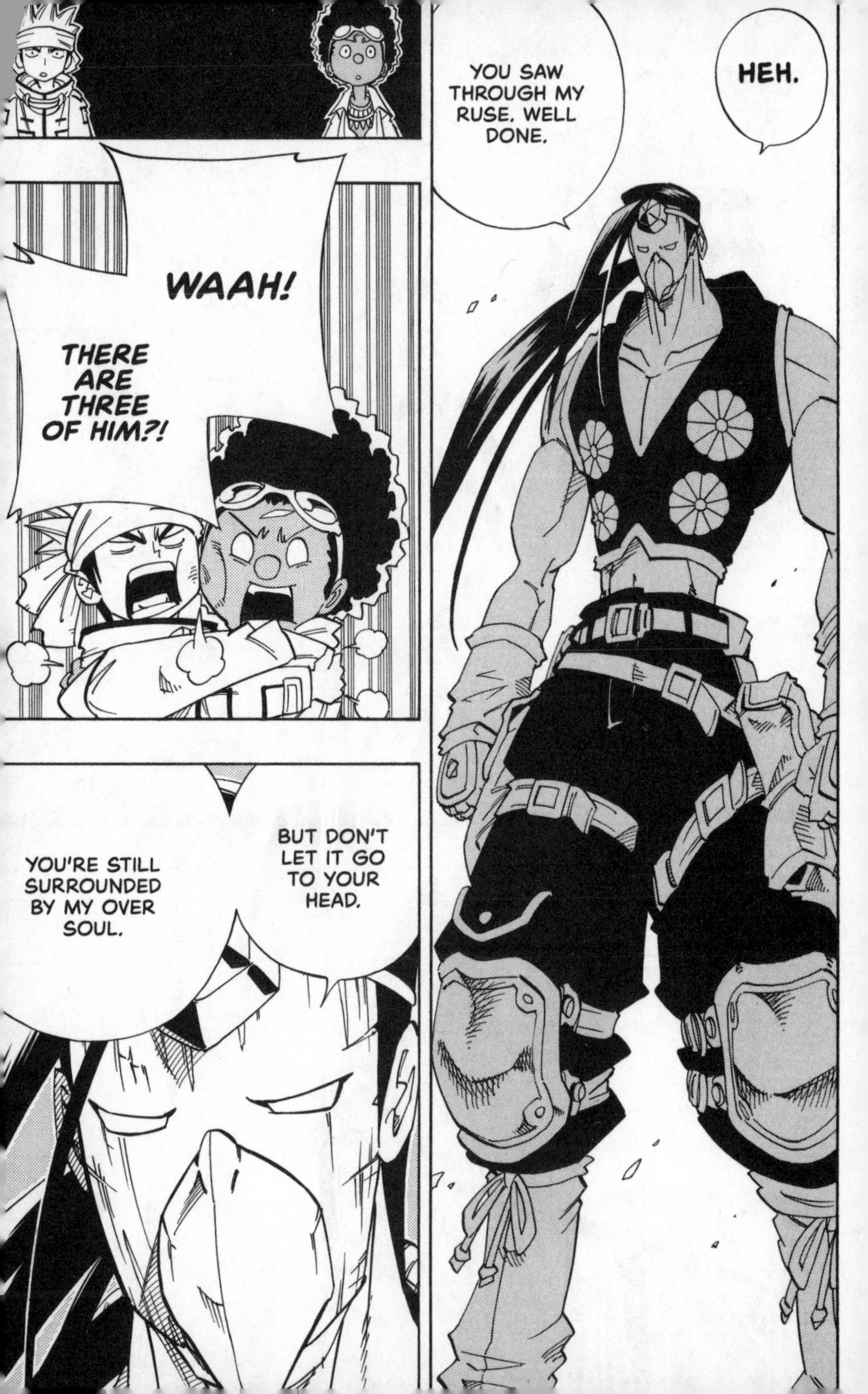
HEH.
YOU SAW THROUGH MY RUSE. WELL DONE.
WAAH!
THERE ARE THREE OF HIM?!
BUT DON'T LET IT GO TO YOUR HEAD.
YOU'RE STILL SURROUNDED BY MY OVER SOUL.

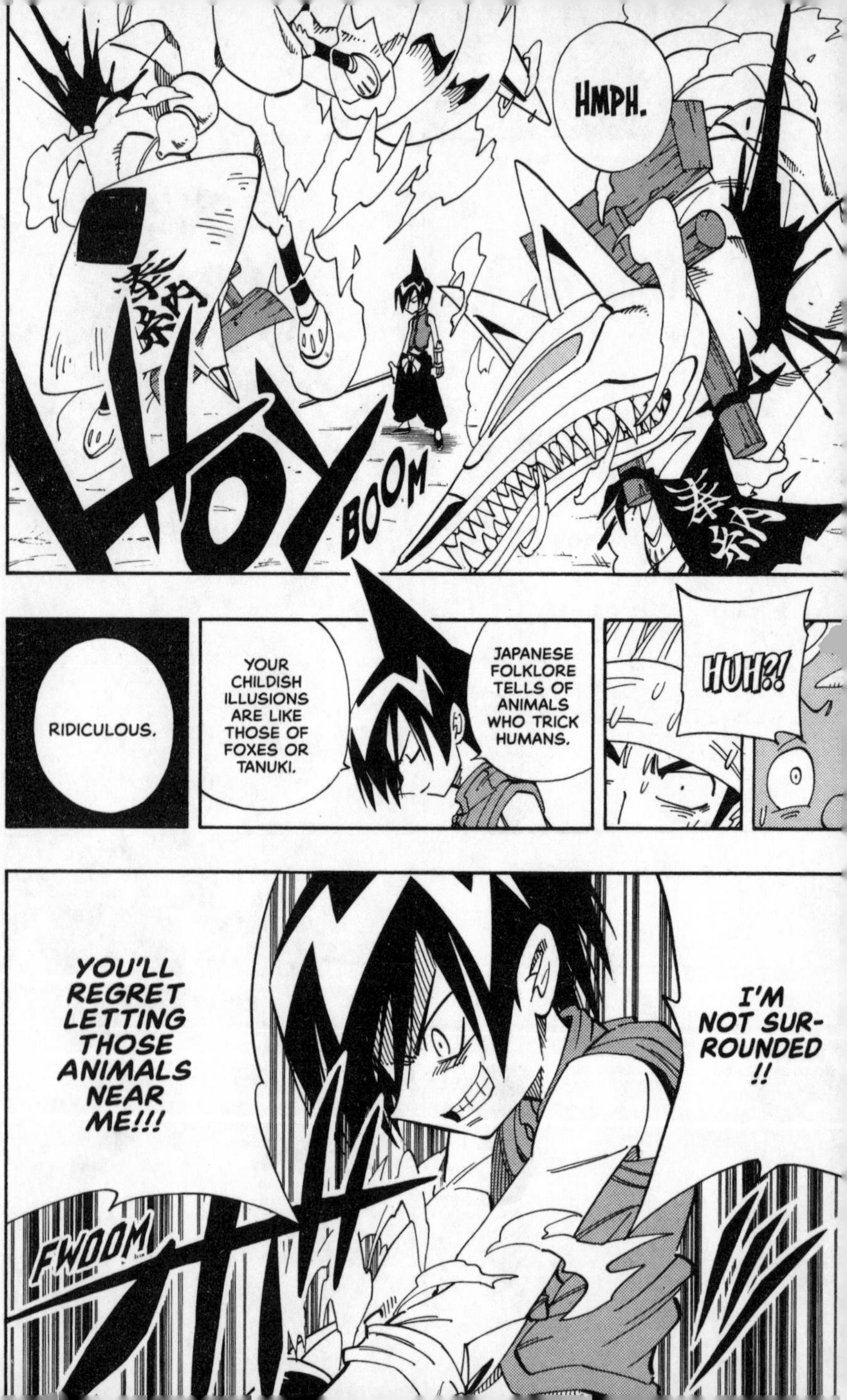
HMPH.
BOOM
HUH?!
JAPANESE FOLKLORE TELLS OF ANIMALS WHO TRICK HUMANS.
YOUR CHILDISH ILLUSIONS ARE LIKE THOSE OF FOXES OR TANUKI.
RIDICULOUS.
I'M NOT SUR-ROUNDED!!
YOU'LL REGRET LETTING THOSE ANIMALS NEAR ME!!!
FWOOM

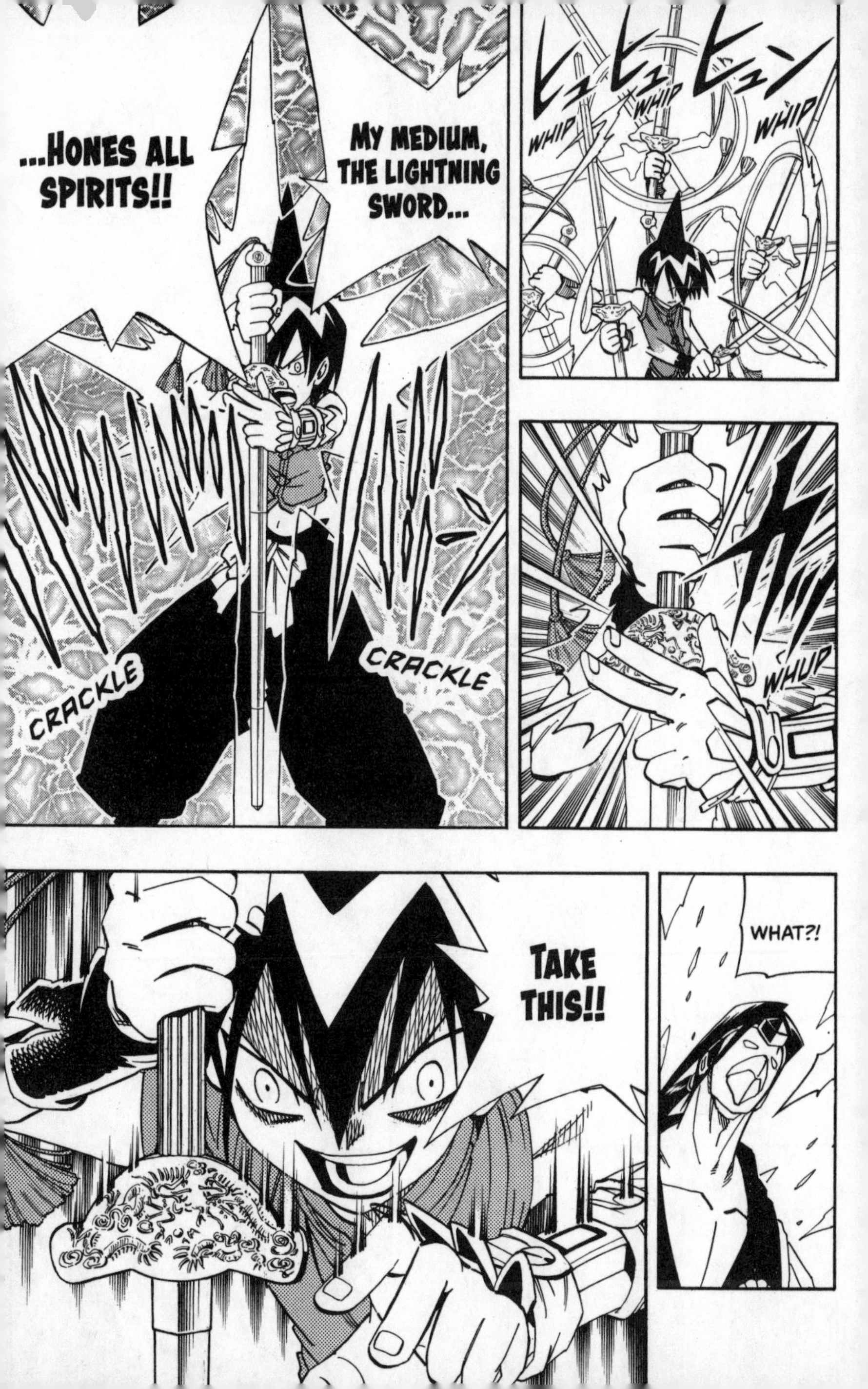

ヒュヒュヒュン
WHIP
WHIP
WHIP
WHUP
MY MEDIUM, THE LIGHTNING SWORD...
...HONES ALL SPIRITS!!
CRACKLE
CRACKLE
WHAT?!
TAKE THIS!!

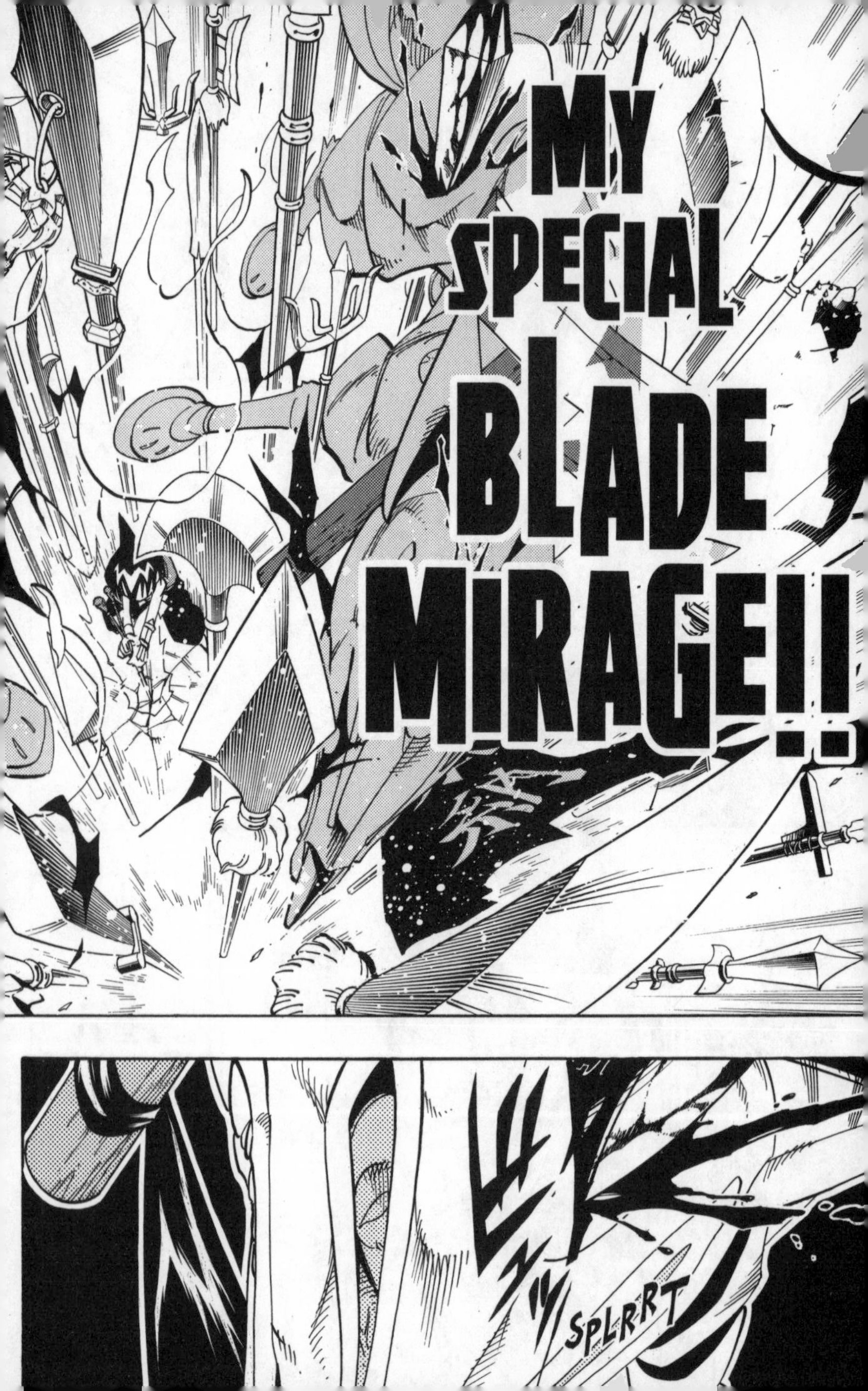
MY SPECIAL BLADE MIRAGE!!
SPLRRT

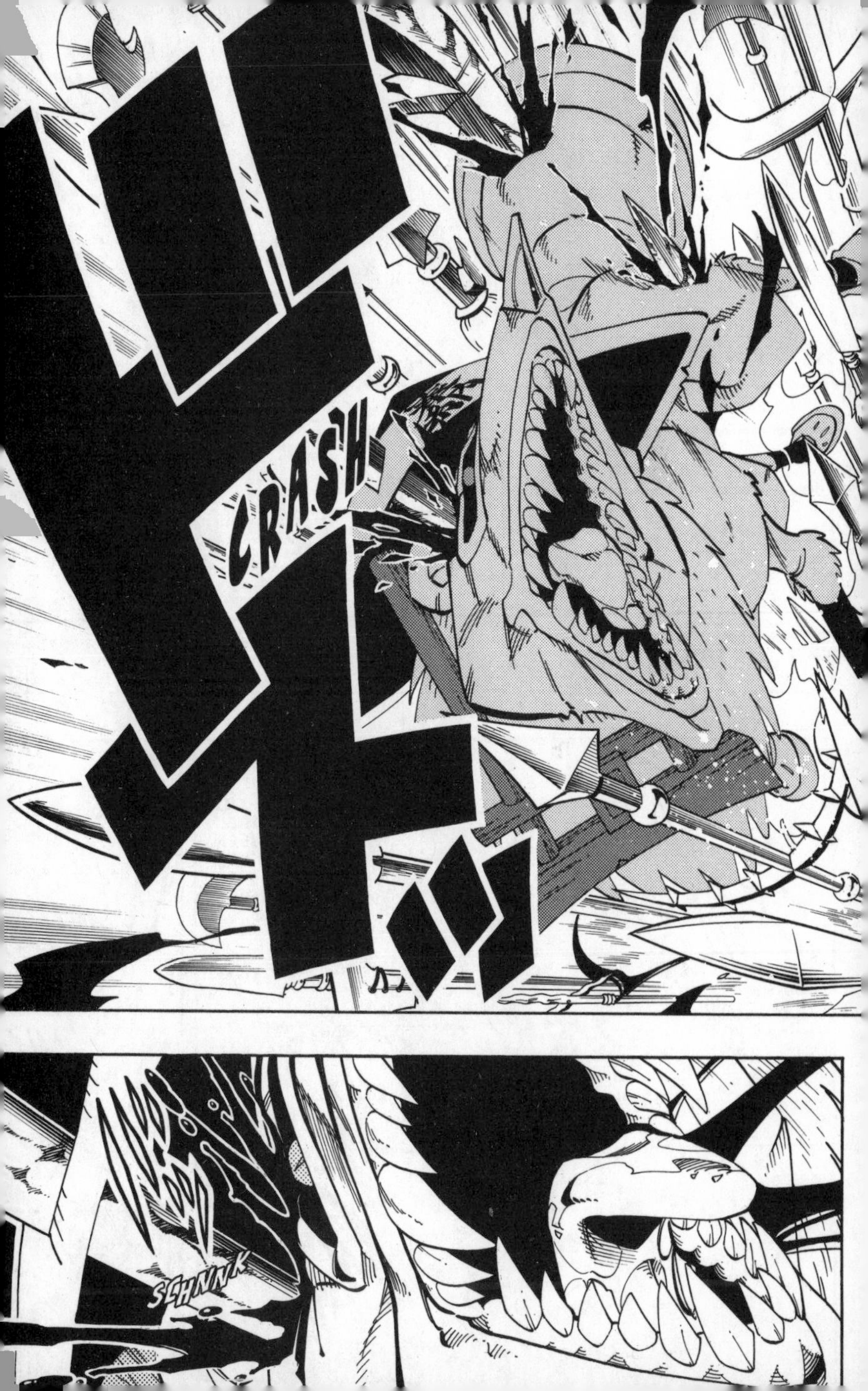
CRASH
SCHNNK

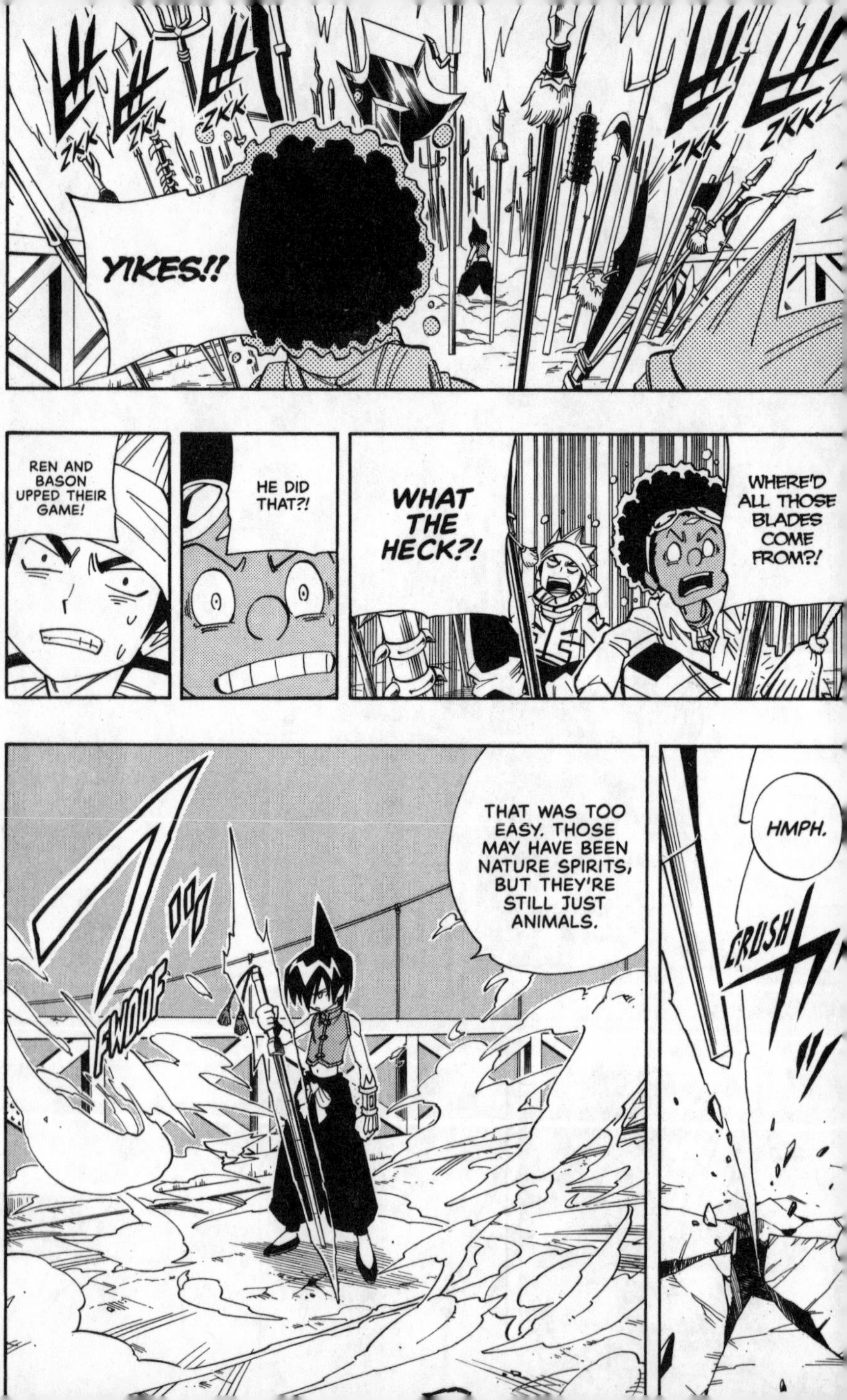
ZKK
ZKK
ZKK
ZKK
ZKK
YIKES!!
WHERE'D ALL THOSE BLADES COME FROM?!
WHAT THE HECK?!
HE DID THAT?!
REN AND BASON UPPED THEIR GAME!
HMPH.
CRUSH
THAT WAS TOO EASY. THOSE MAY HAVE BEEN NATURE SPIRITS, BUT THEY'RE STILL JUST ANIMALS.
FWOOF

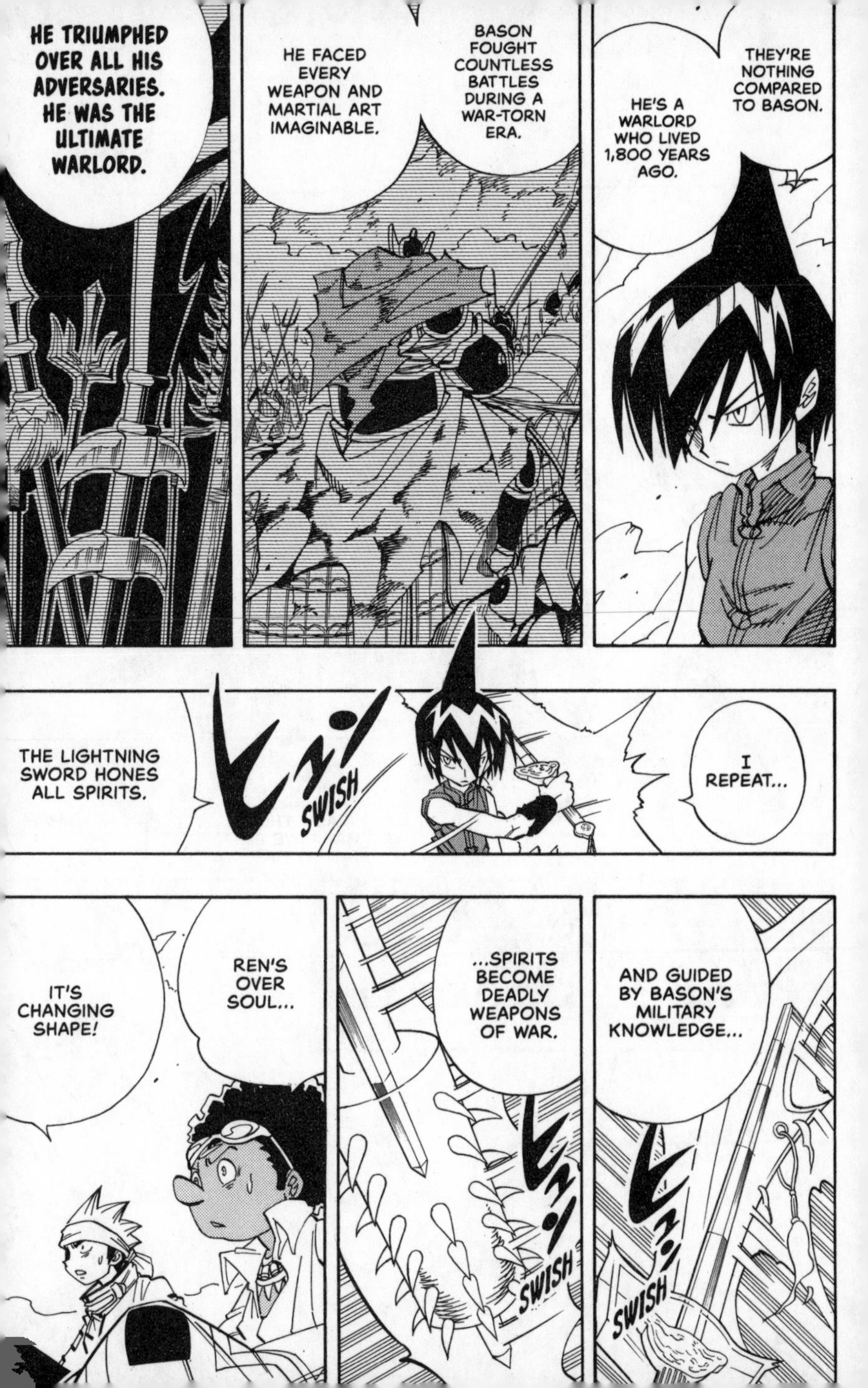
THEY'RE NOTHING COMPARED TO BASON.
HE'S A WARLORD WHO LIVED 1,800 YEARS AGO.
BASON FOUGHT COUNTLESS BATTLES DURING A WAR-TORN ERA.
HE FACED EVERY WEAPON AND MARTIAL ART IMAGINABLE.
HE TRIUMPHED OVER ALL HIS ADVERSARIES. HE WAS THE ULTIMATE WARLORD.
I REPEAT...
SWISH
THE LIGHTNING SWORD HONES ALL SPIRITS.
AND GUIDED BY BASON'S MILITARY KNOWLEDGE...
SWISH
...SPIRITS BECOME DEADLY WEAPONS OF WAR.
SWISH
REN'S OVER SOUL...
IT'S CHANGING SHAPE!

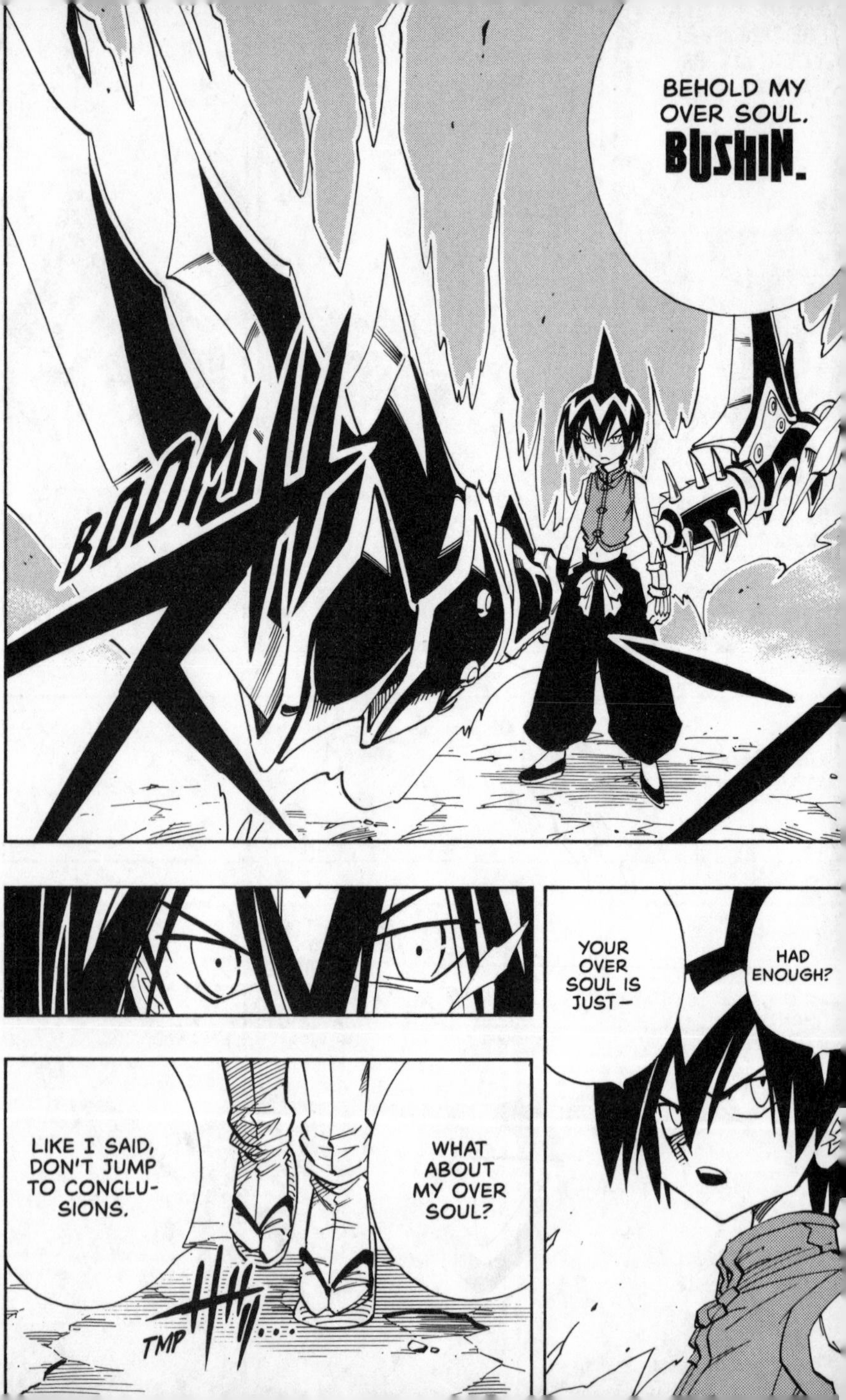
BEHOLD MY OVER SOUL. BUSHIN.
BOOM
HAD ENOUGH?
YOUR OVER SOUL IS JUST—
WHAT ABOUT MY OVER SOUL?
LIKE I SAID, DON'T JUMP TO CONCLU-SIONS.
TMP

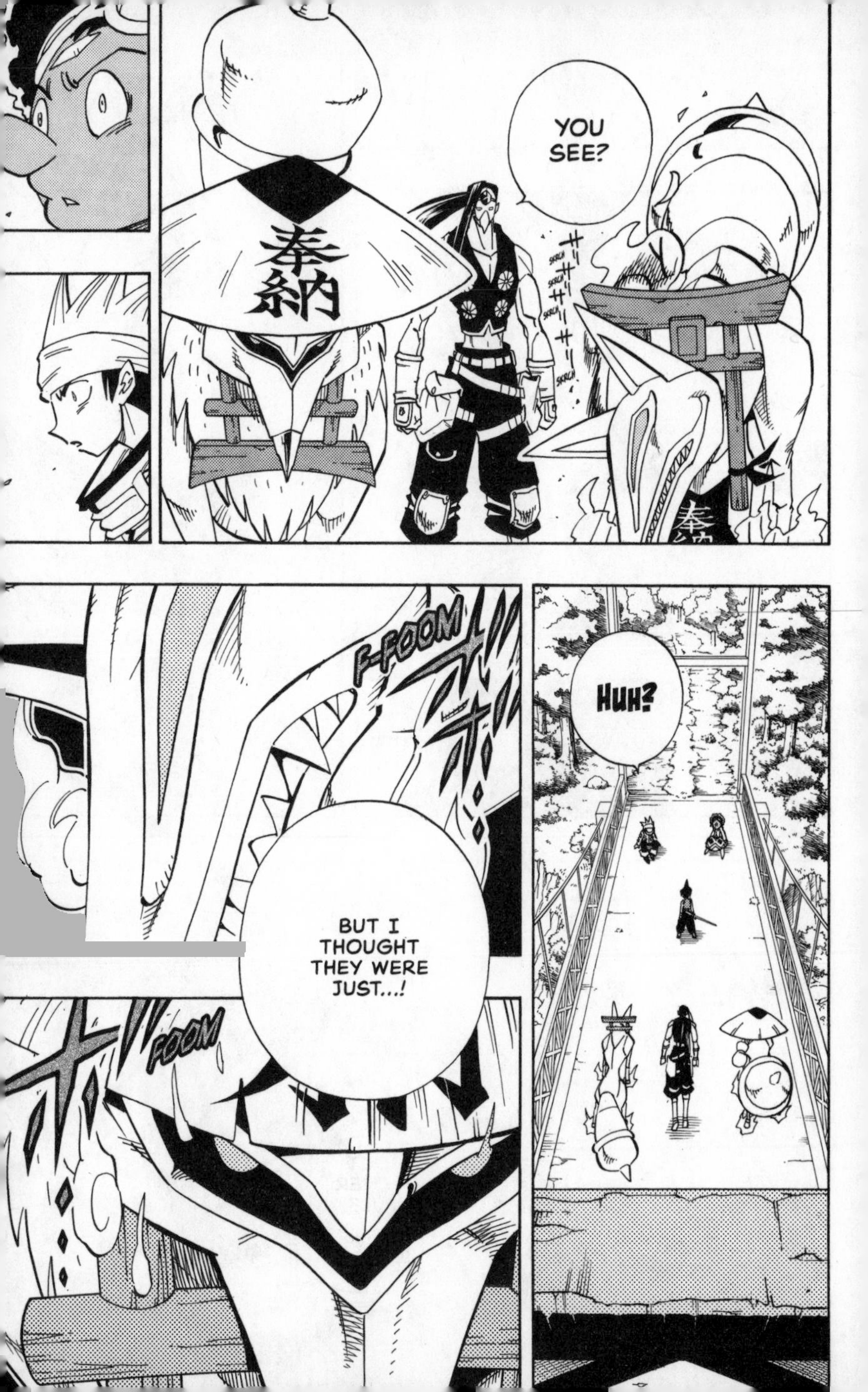
YOU SEE?
SKRCH
SKRCH
SKRCH
SKRCH
奉納
HUH?
F-FOOM
BUT I THOUGHT THEY WERE JUST...!
FOOM

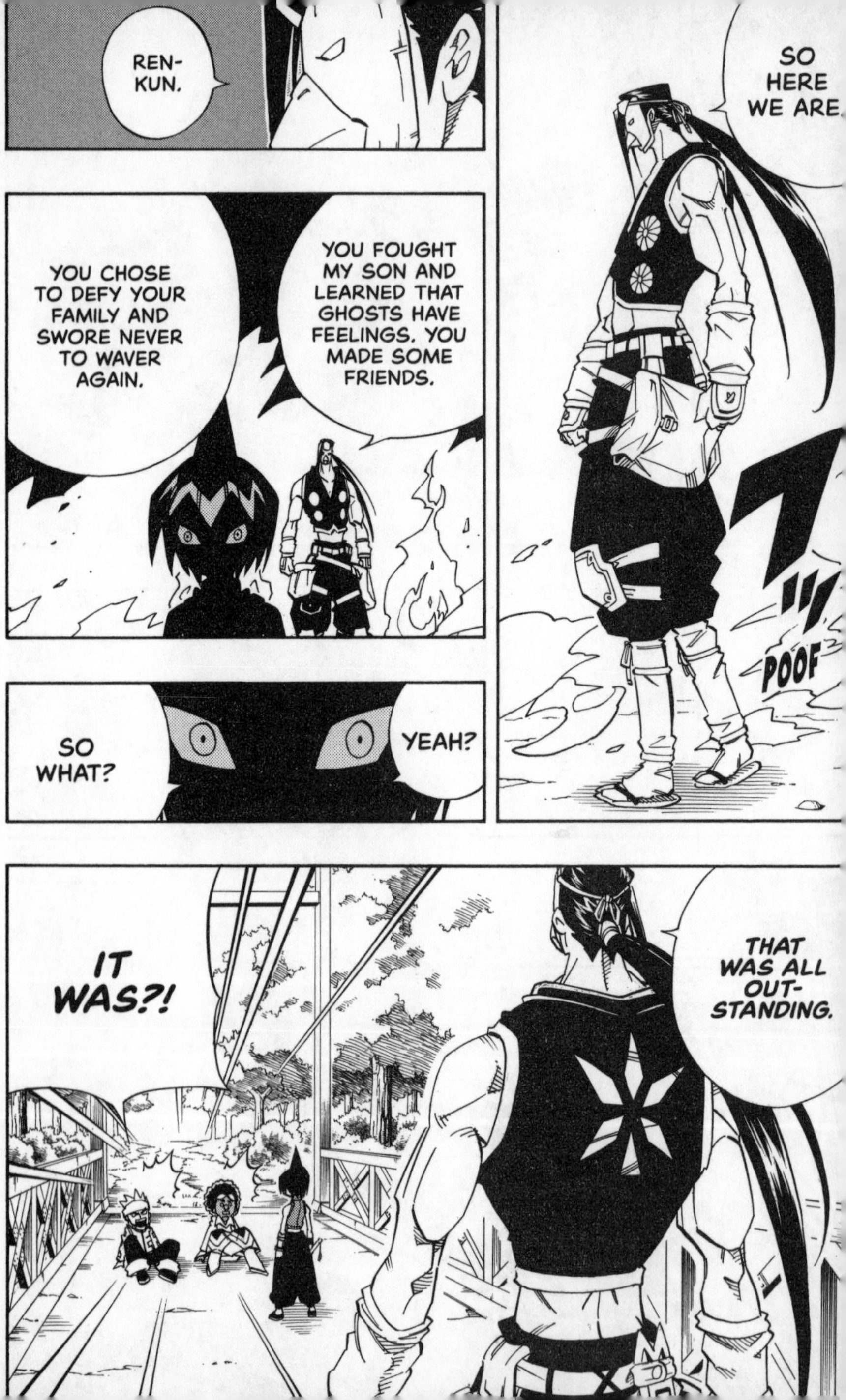
SO HERE WE ARE.
POOF
REN-KUN.
YOU FOUGHT MY SON AND LEARNED THAT GHOSTS HAVE FEELINGS. YOU MADE SOME FRIENDS.
YOU CHOSE TO DEFY YOUR FAMILY AND SWORE NEVER TO WAVER AGAIN.
YEAH?
SO WHAT?
THAT WAS ALL OUT-STANDING.
IT WAS?!

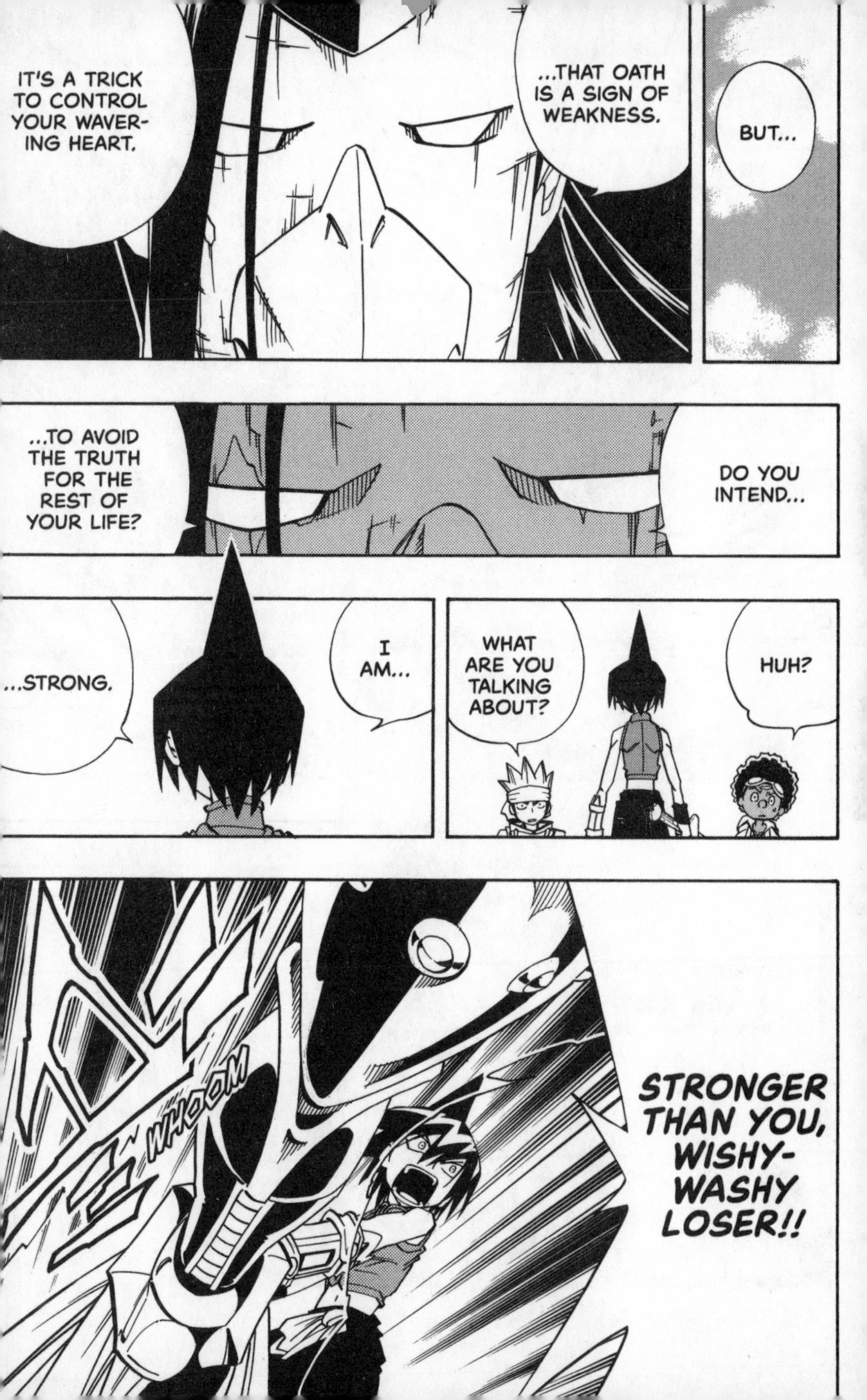
BUT...
...THAT OATH IS A SIGN OF WEAKNESS.
IT'S A TRICK TO CONTROL YOUR WAVERING HEART.
DO YOU INTEND...
...TO AVOID THE TRUTH FOR THE REST OF YOUR LIFE?
HUH?
WHAT ARE YOU TALKING ABOUT?
I AM...
...STRONG.
STRONGER THAN YOU, WISHY-WASHY LOSER!!
WHOOM

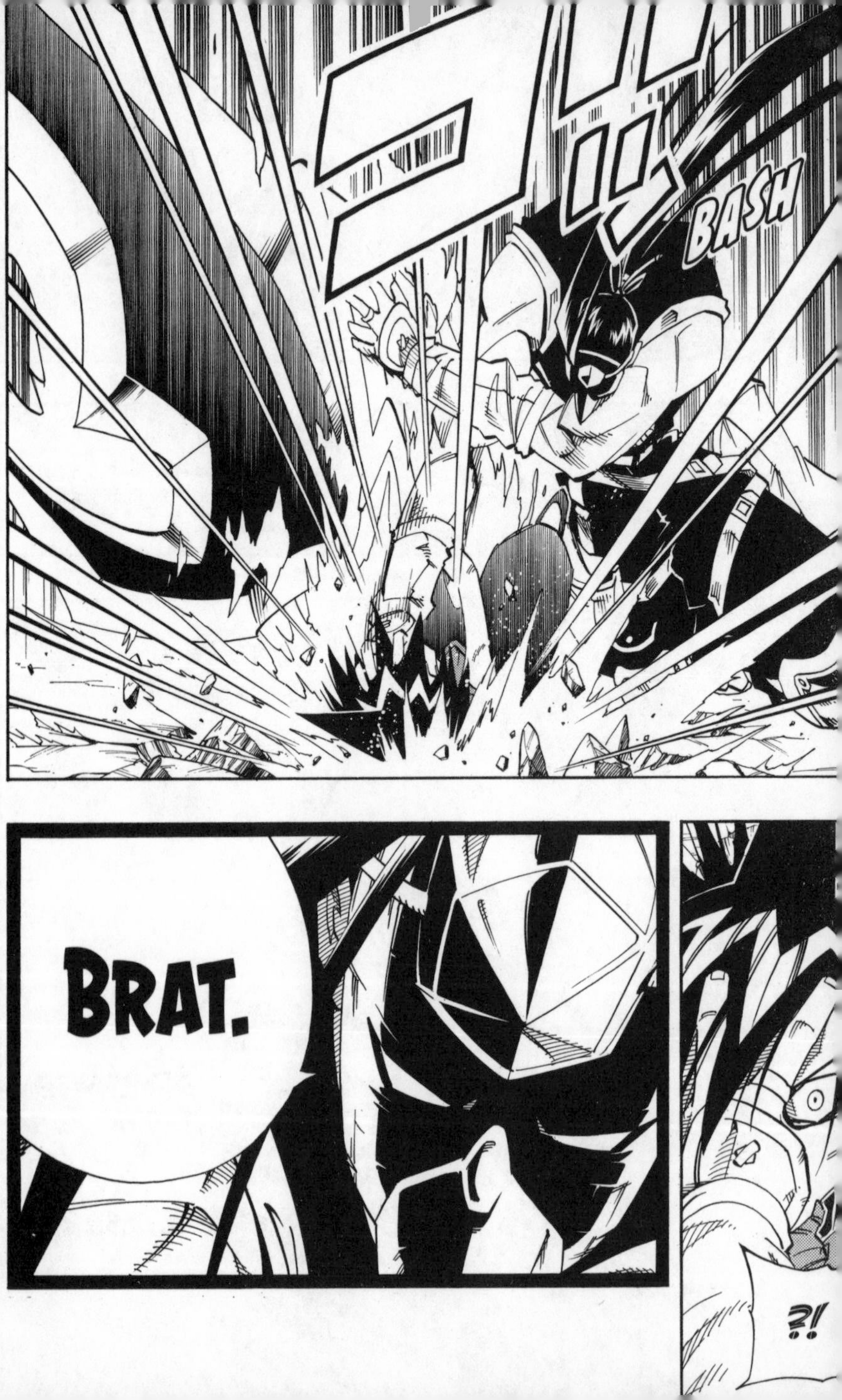
BASH
?!
BRAT.

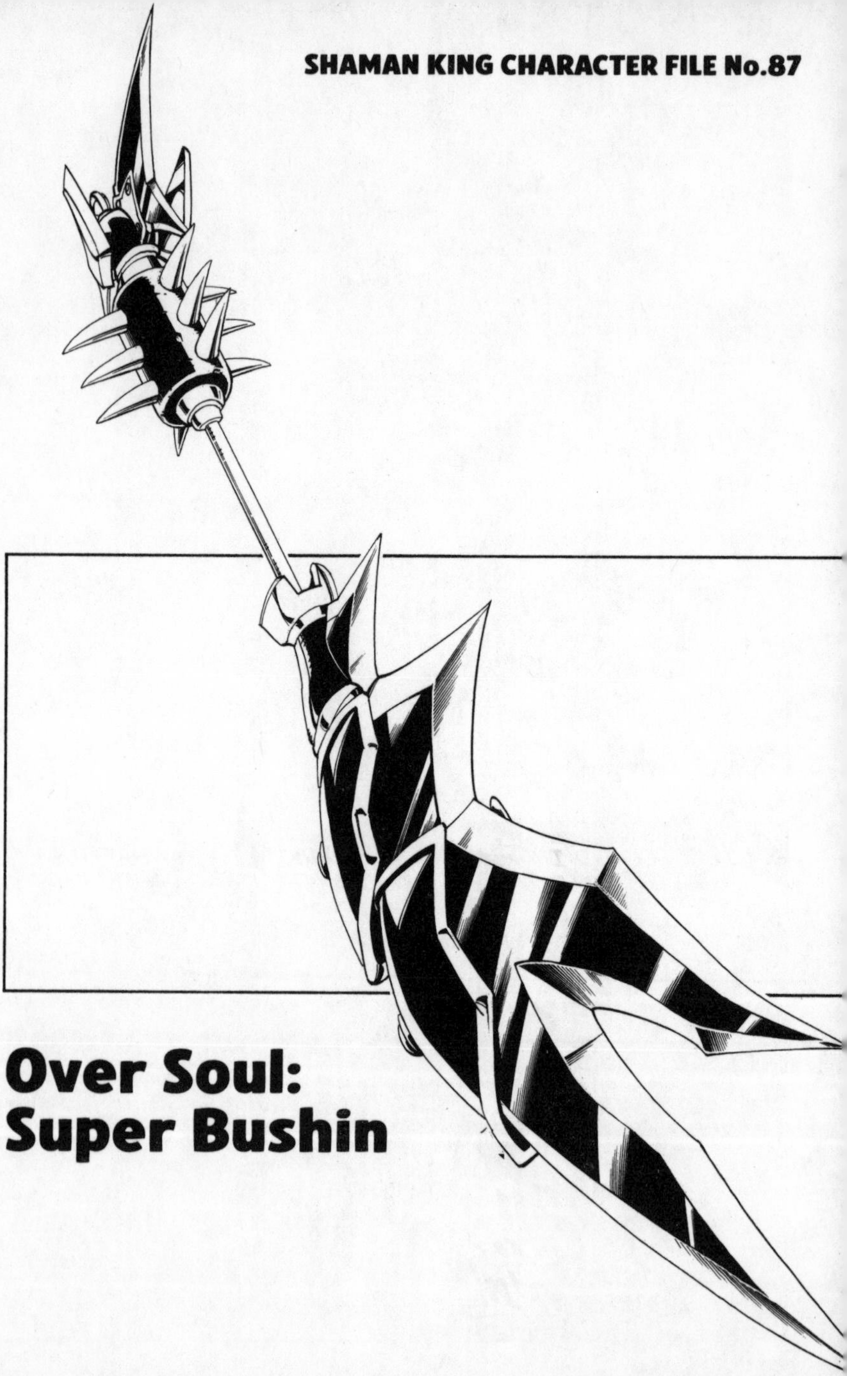

Over Soul:
Super Bushin

Chapter 147: Ascetic

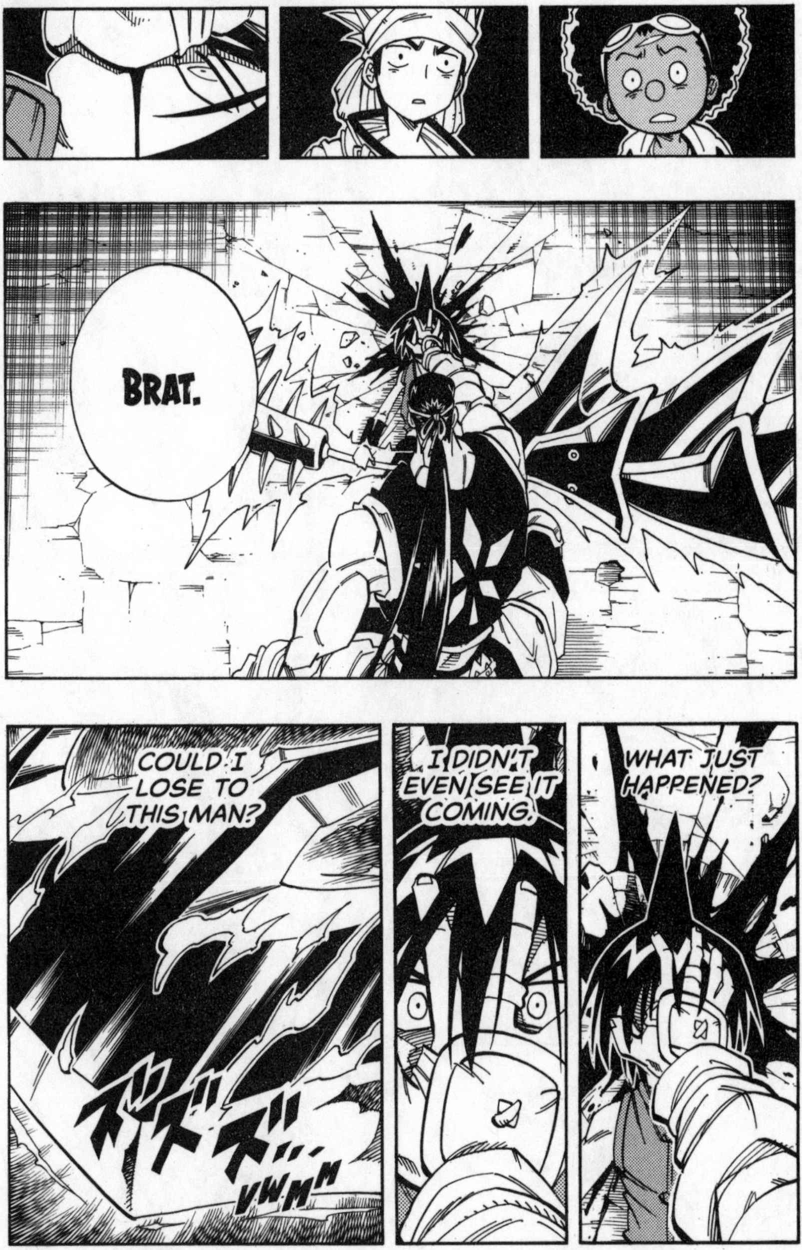
BRAT.
WHAT JUST HAPPENED?
I DIDN'T EVEN SEE IT COMING.
COULD I LOSE TO THIS MAN?
VWMM

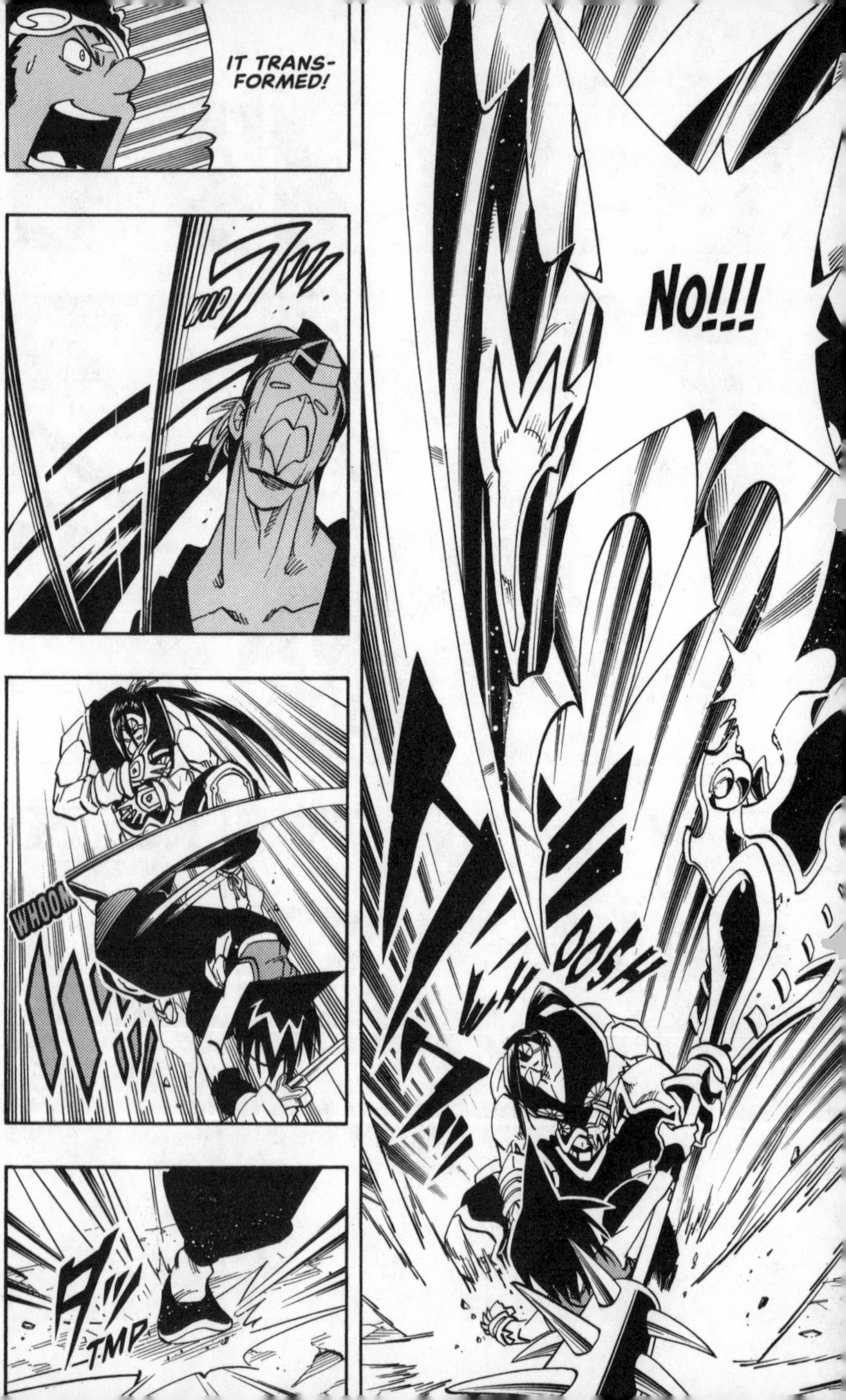
NO!!!
IT TRANS-
FORMED!
WHOOM
TMP

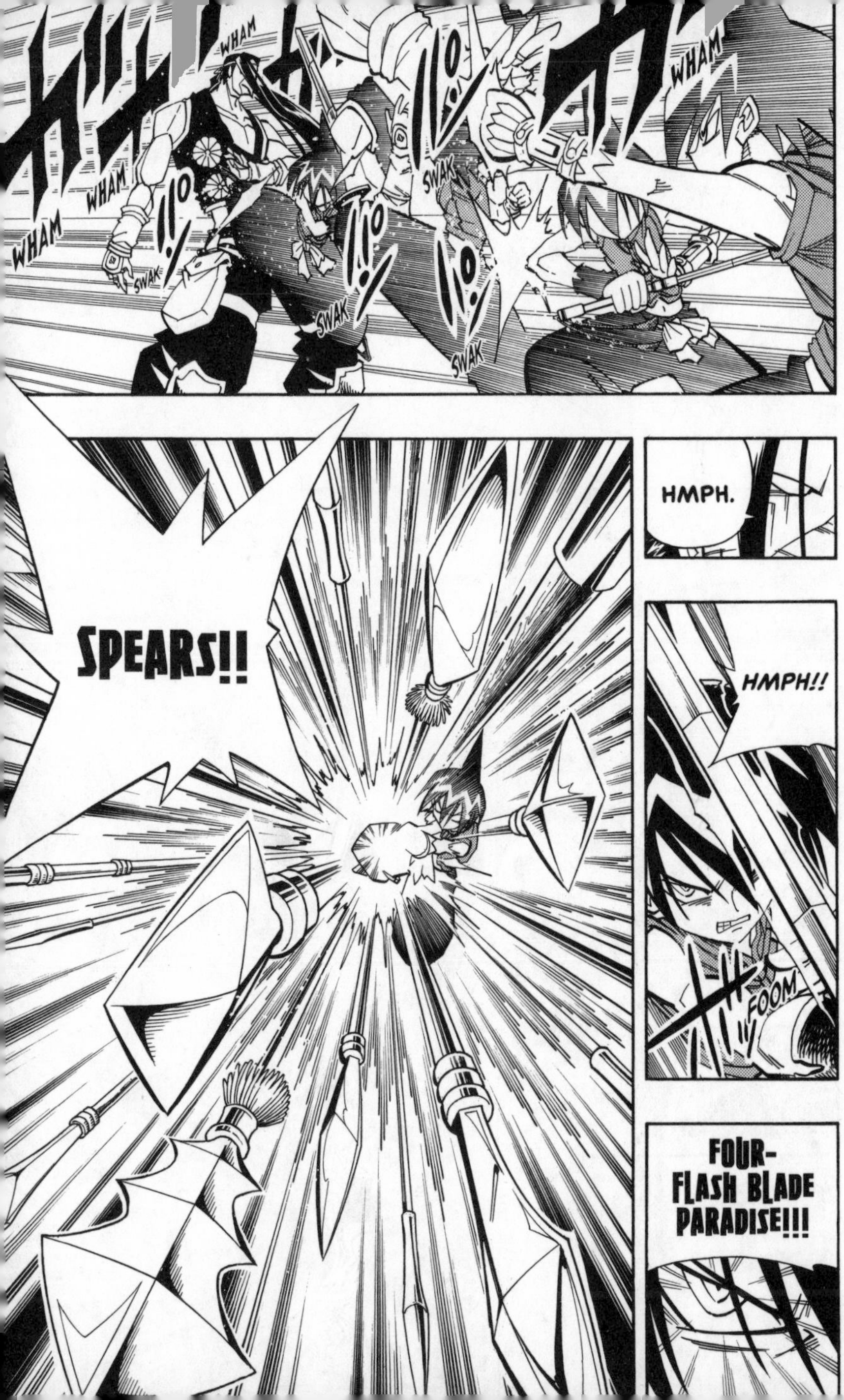
WHAM
SWAK
WHAM
SWAK
WHAM
WHAM
SWAK
SWAK
SWAK
HMPH.
HMPH!!
FOOM
FOUR-FLASH BLADE PARADISE!!!
SPEARS!!

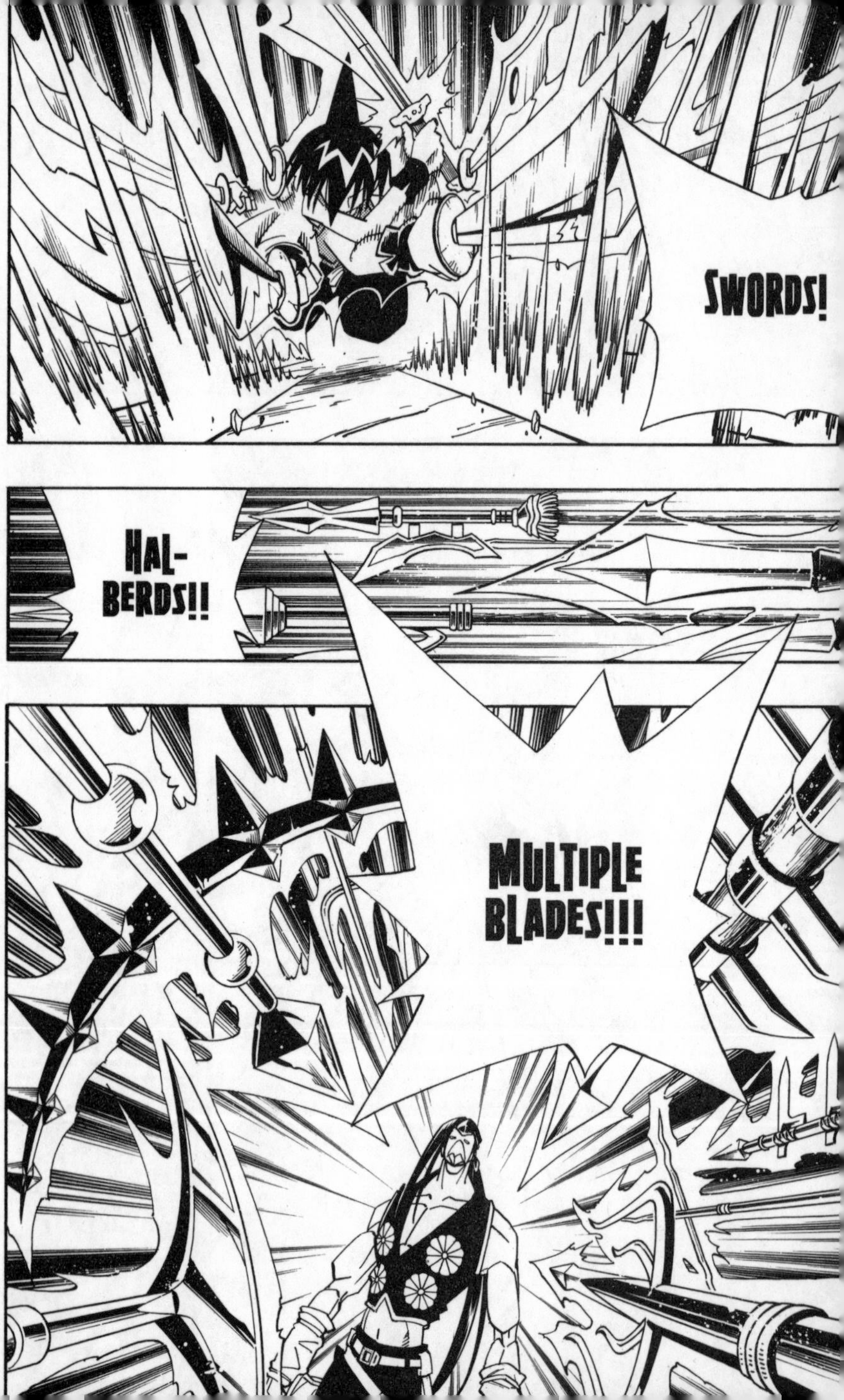
SWORDS!
HAL-BERDS!!
MULTIPLE BLADES!!!

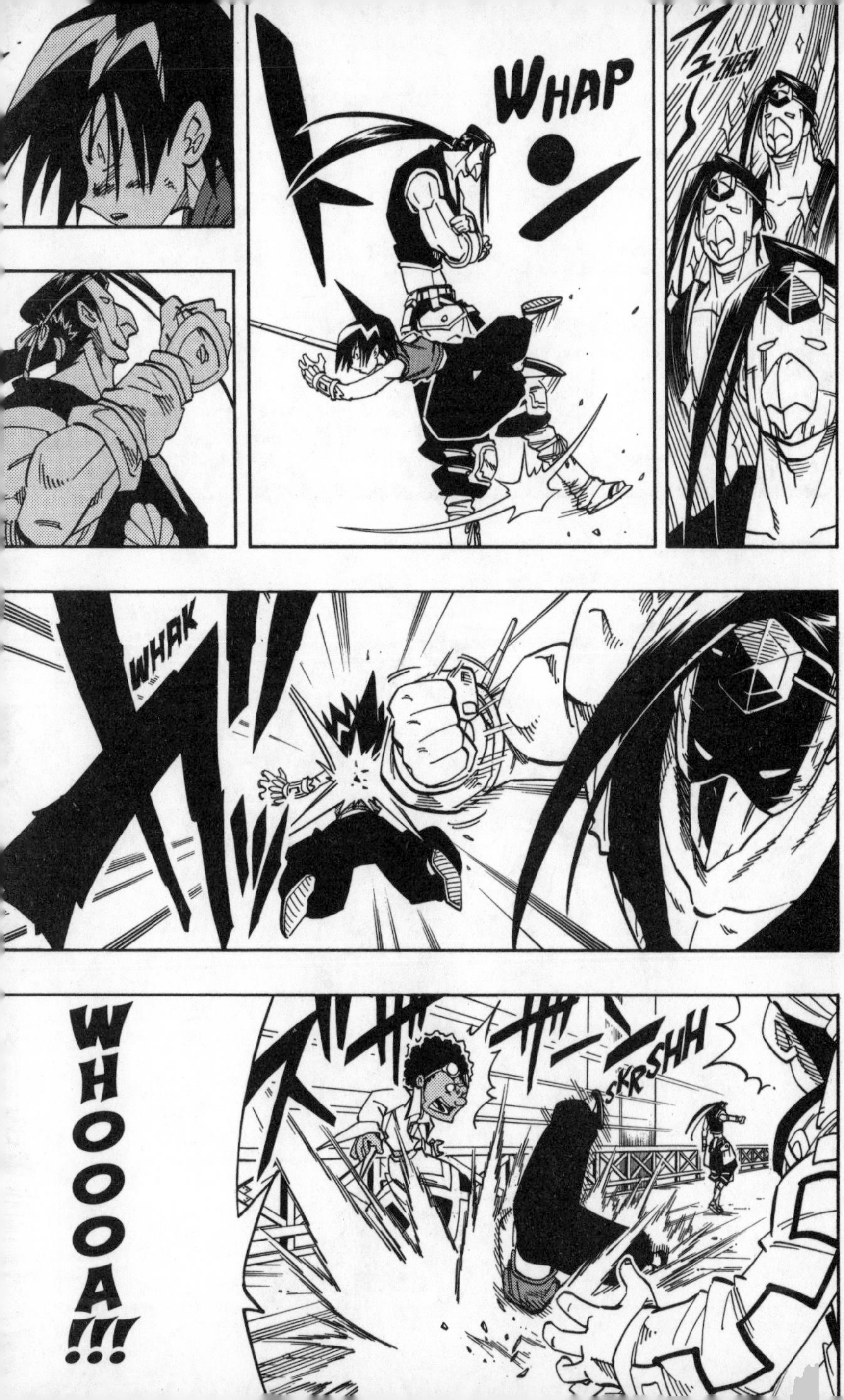
ZHEEN
WHAP
WHAK
SKRSHH
WHOOOA!!!

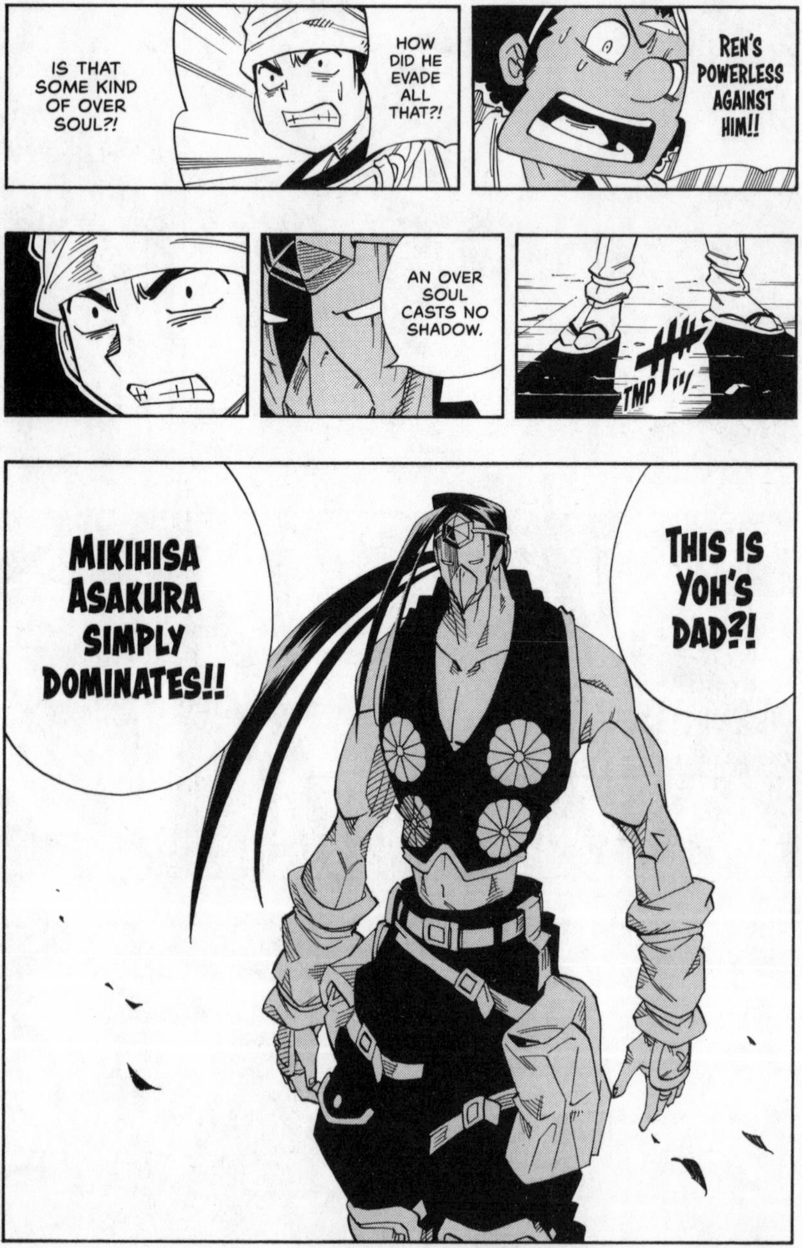
REN'S POWERLESS AGAINST HIM!!
HOW DID HE EVADE ALL THAT?!
IS THAT SOME KIND OF OVER SOUL?!
TMP
AN OVER SOUL CASTS NO SHADOW.
THIS IS YOH'S DAD?!
MIKIHISA ASAKURA SIMPLY DOMINATES!!

Chapter 147:

Ascetic

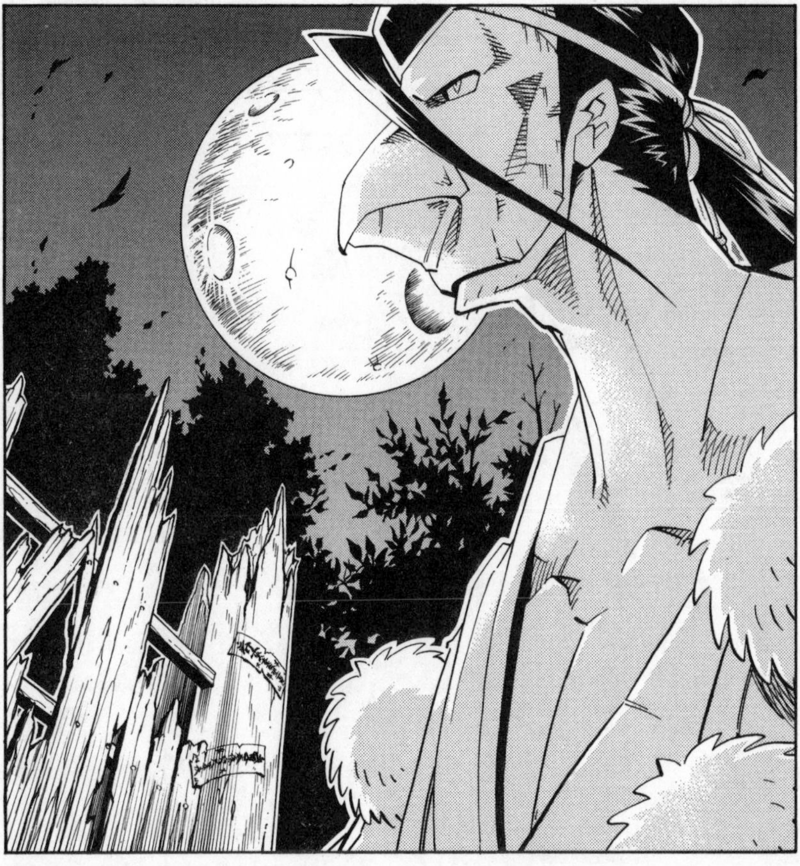

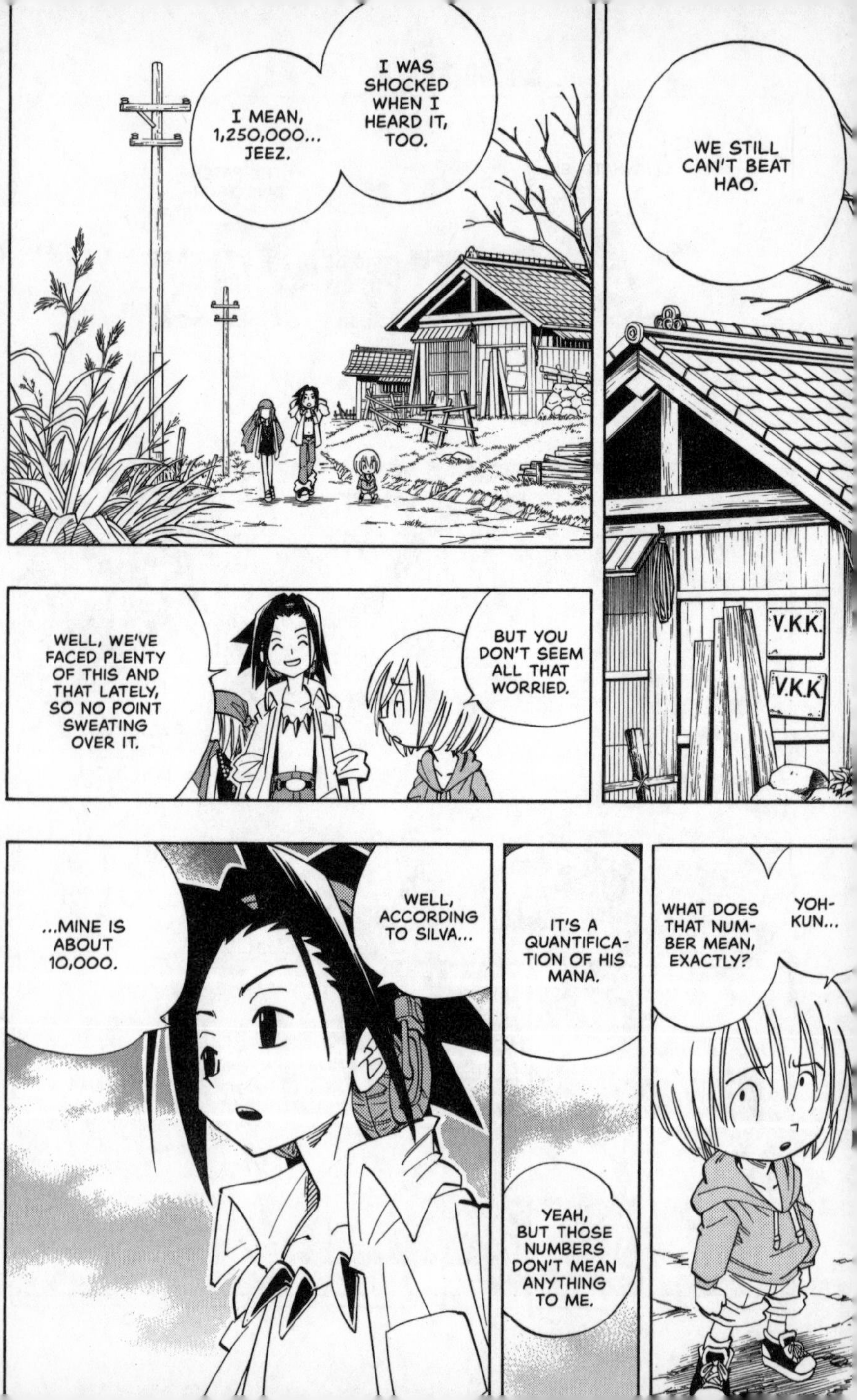
WE STILL CAN'T BEAT HAO.
I WAS SHOCKED WHEN I HEARD IT, TOO.
I MEAN, 1,250,000... JEEZ.
BUT YOU DON'T SEEM ALL THAT WORRIED.
WELL, WE'VE FACED PLENTY OF THIS AND THAT LATELY, SO NO POINT SWEATING OVER IT.
V.K.K.
V.K.K
YOH-KUN...
WHAT DOES THAT NUMBER MEAN, EXACTLY?
IT'S A QUANTIFICATION OF HIS MANA.
YEAH, BUT THOSE NUMBERS DON'T MEAN ANYTHING TO ME.
WELL, ACCORDING TO SILVA...
...MINE IS ABOUT 10,000.

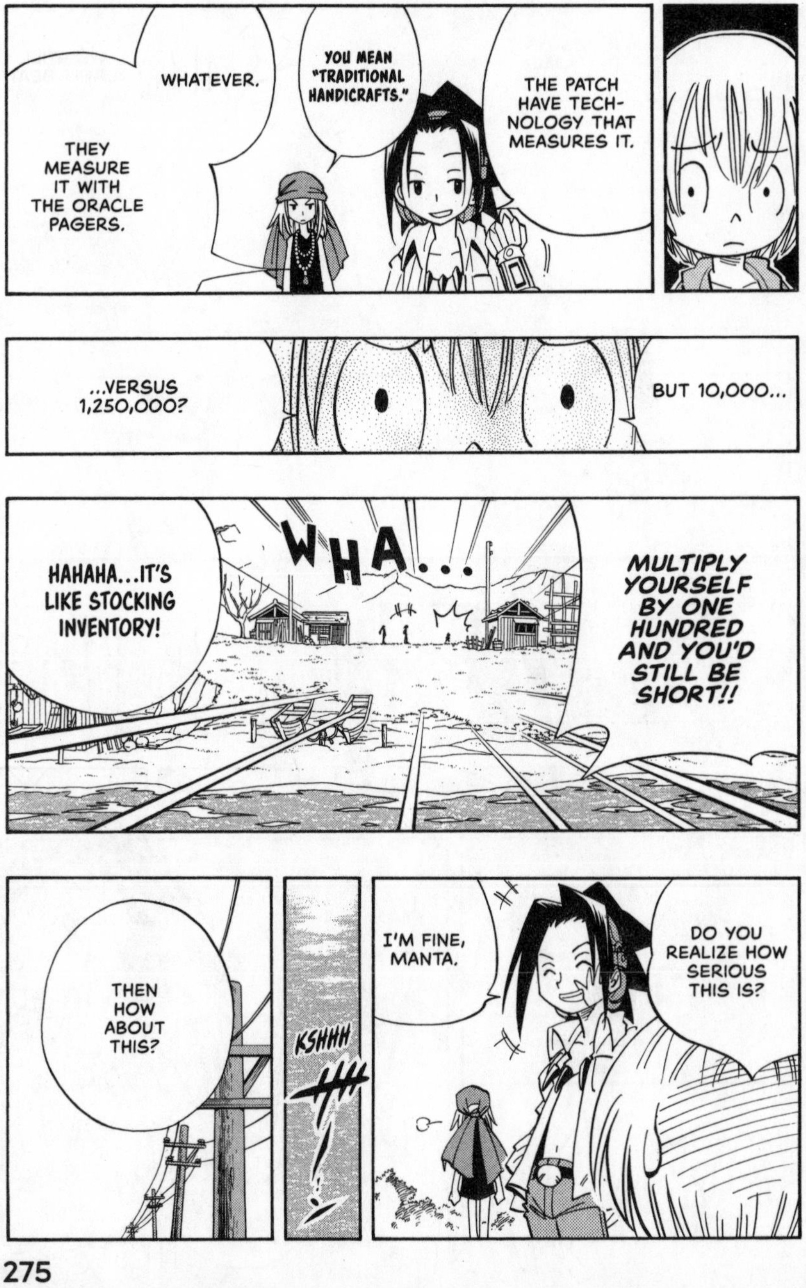
THE PATCH HAVE TECHNOLOGY THAT MEASURES IT.
YOU MEAN "TRADITIONAL HANDICRAFTS."
WHATEVER.
THEY MEASURE IT WITH THE ORACLE PAGERS.
BUT 10,000...
...VERSUS 1,250,000?
MULTIPLY YOURSELF BY ONE HUNDRED AND YOU'D STILL BE SHORT!!
WHA...
HAHAHA...IT'S LIKE STOCKING INVENTORY!
DO YOU REALIZE HOW SERIOUS THIS IS?
I'M FINE, MANTA.
KSHHH
THEN HOW ABOUT THIS?

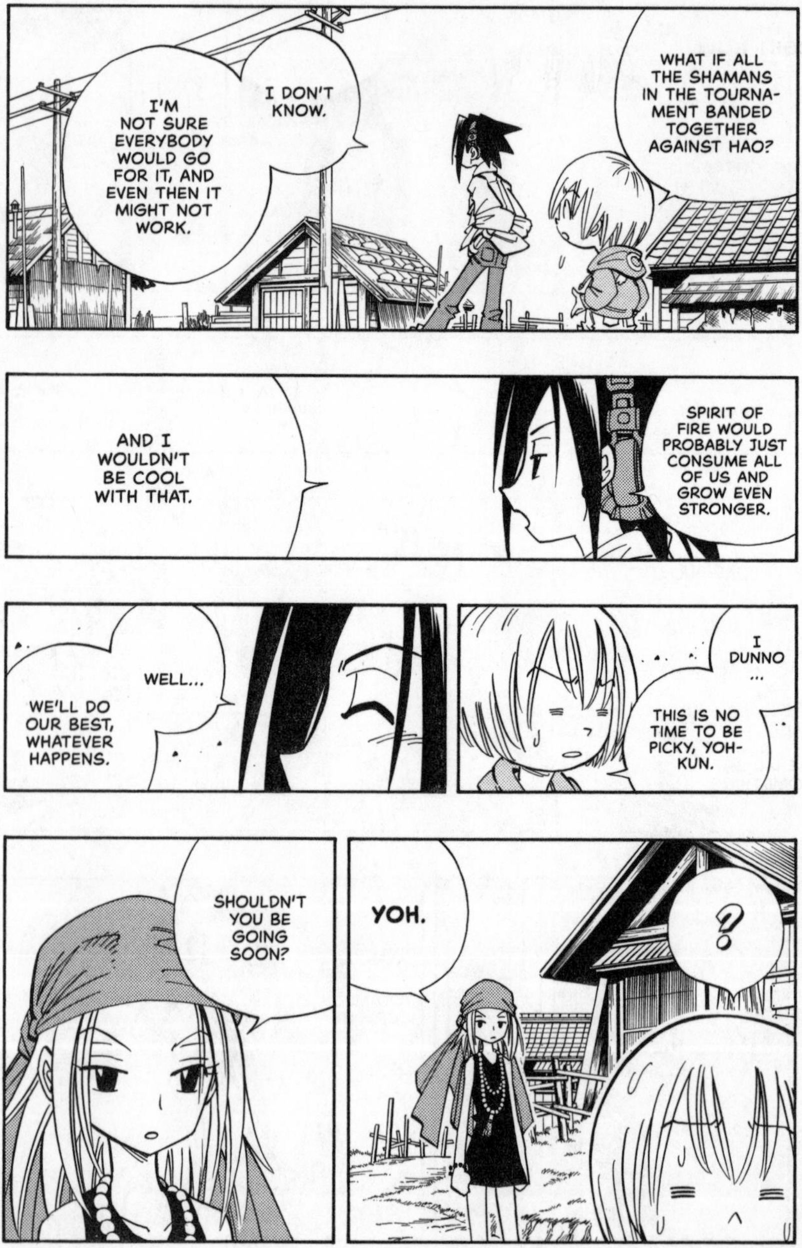
WHAT IF ALL THE SHAMANS IN THE TOURNAMENT BANDED TOGETHER AGAINST HAO?
I DON'T KNOW.
I'M NOT SURE EVERYBODY WOULD GO FOR IT, AND EVEN THEN IT MIGHT NOT WORK.
SPIRIT OF FIRE WOULD PROBABLY JUST CONSUME ALL OF US AND GROW EVEN STRONGER.
AND I WOULDN'T BE COOL WITH THAT.
I DUNNO ...
THIS IS NO TIME TO BE PICKY, YOH-KUN.
WELL...
WE'LL DO OUR BEST, WHATEVER HAPPENS.
?
YOH.
SHOULDN'T YOU BE GOING SOON?

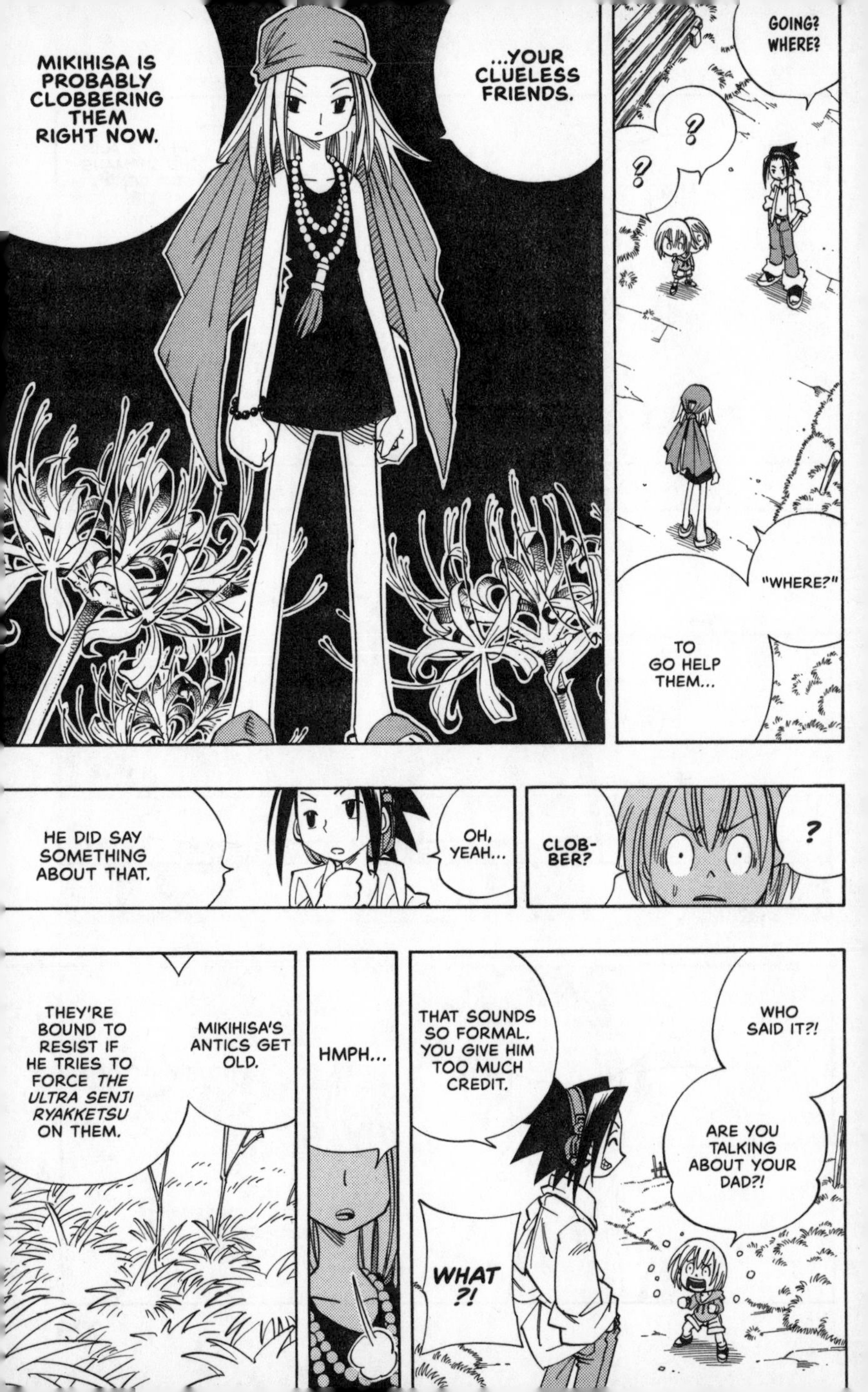
GOING? WHERE?
?
?
"WHERE?"
TO GO HELP THEM...
...YOUR CLUELESS FRIENDS.
MIKIHISA IS PROBABLY CLOBBERING THEM RIGHT NOW.
?
CLOB-BER?
OH, YEAH...
HE DID SAY SOMETHING ABOUT THAT.
WHO SAID IT?!
ARE YOU TALKING ABOUT YOUR DAD?!
THAT SOUNDS SO FORMAL. YOU GIVE HIM TOO MUCH CREDIT.
WHAT ?!
HMPH...
MIKIHISA'S ANTICS GET OLD.
THEY'RE BOUND TO RESIST IF HE TRIES TO FORCE *THE ULTRA SENJI RYAKKETSU* ON THEM.

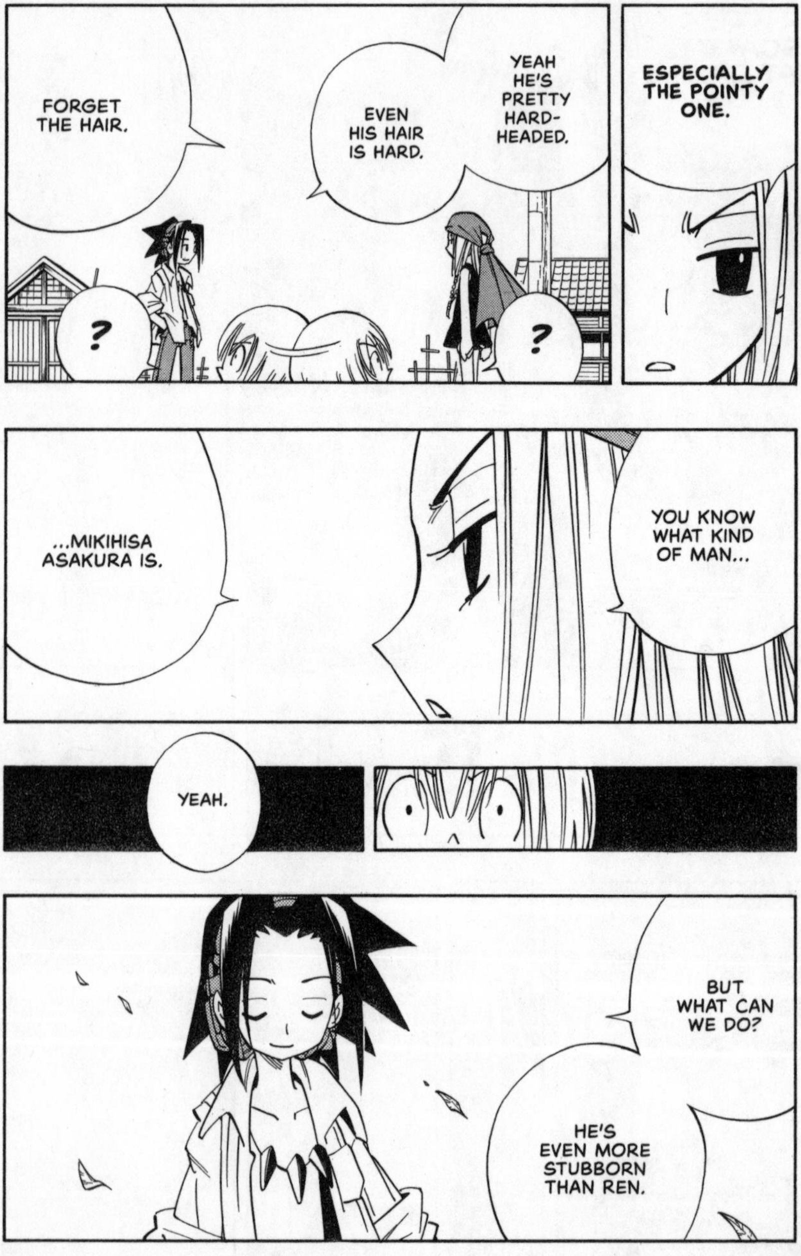
ESPECIALLY THE POINTY ONE.
YEAH HE'S PRETTY HARD-HEADED.
EVEN HIS HAIR IS HARD.
FORGET THE HAIR.
?
?
YOU KNOW WHAT KIND OF MAN...
...MIKIHISA ASAKURA IS.
YEAH.
BUT WHAT CAN WE DO?
HE'S EVEN MORE STUBBORN THAN REN.

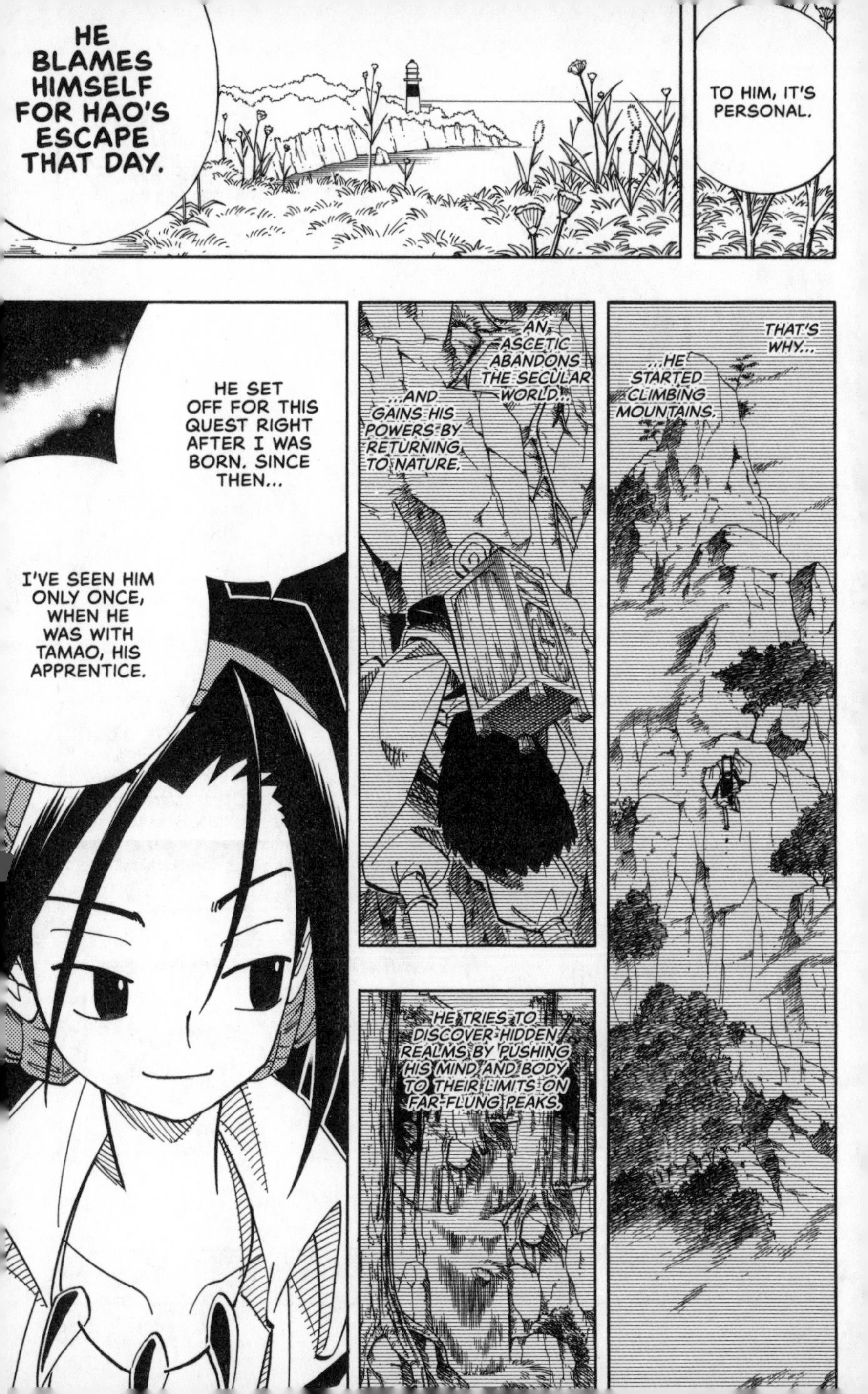
TO HIM, IT'S PERSONAL.
HE BLAMES HIMSELF FOR HAO'S ESCAPE THAT DAY.
THAT'S WHY...
...HE STARTED CLIMBING MOUNTAINS.
AN ASCETIC ABANDONS THE SECULAR WORLD...
...AND GAINS HIS POWERS BY RETURNING TO NATURE.
HE TRIES TO DISCOVER HIDDEN REALMS BY PUSHING HIS MIND AND BODY TO THEIR LIMITS ON FAR-FLUNG PEAKS.
HE SET OFF FOR THIS QUEST RIGHT AFTER I WAS BORN. SINCE THEN...
I'VE SEEN HIM ONLY ONCE, WHEN HE WAS WITH TAMAO, HIS APPRENTICE.

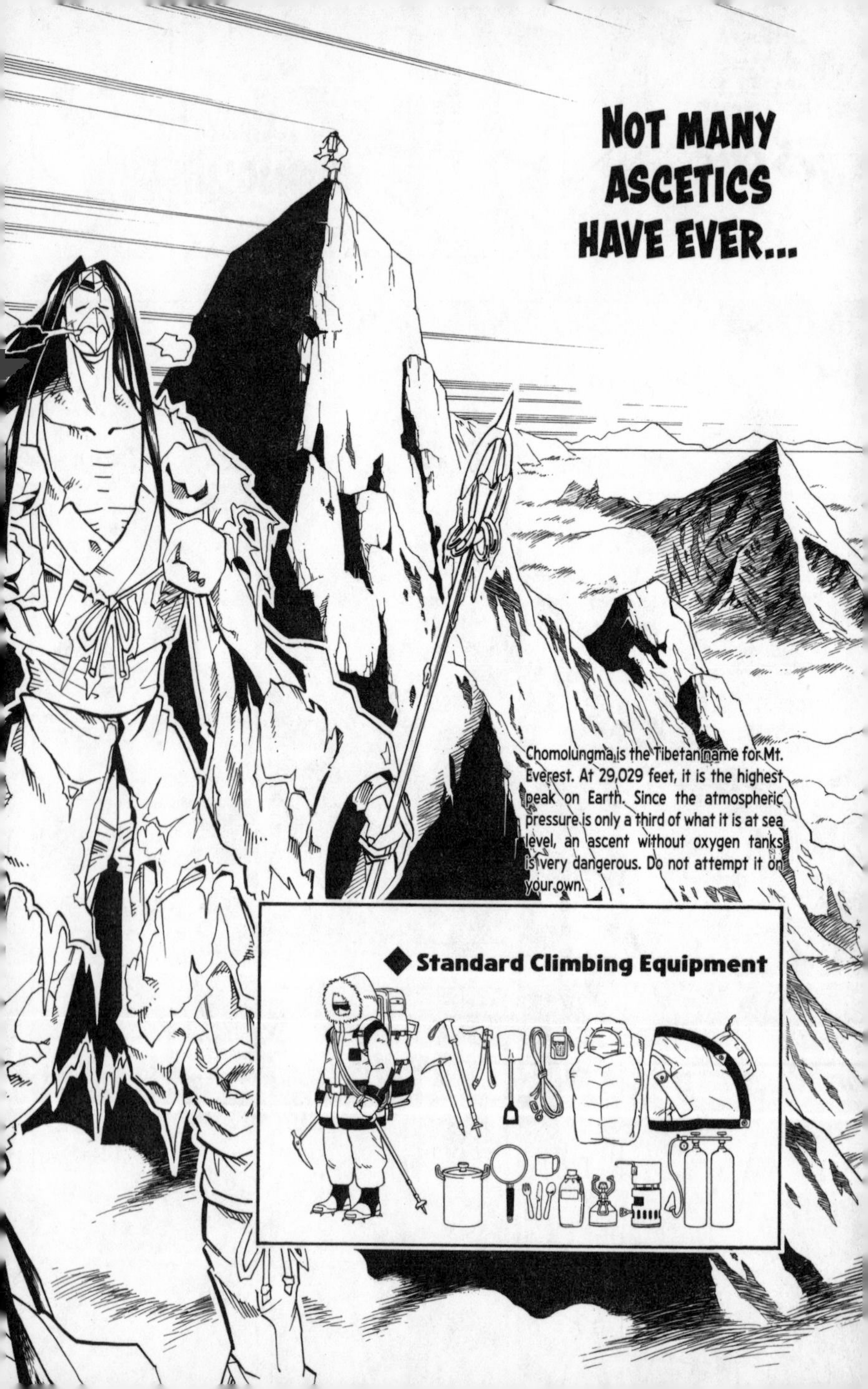
NOT MANY ASCETICS HAVE EVER...
Chomolungma is the Tibetan name for Mt. Everest. At 29,029 feet, it is the highest peak on Earth. Since the atmospheric pressure is only a third of what it is at sea level, an ascent without oxygen tanks is very dangerous. Do not attempt it on your own.
◆Standard Climbing Equipment

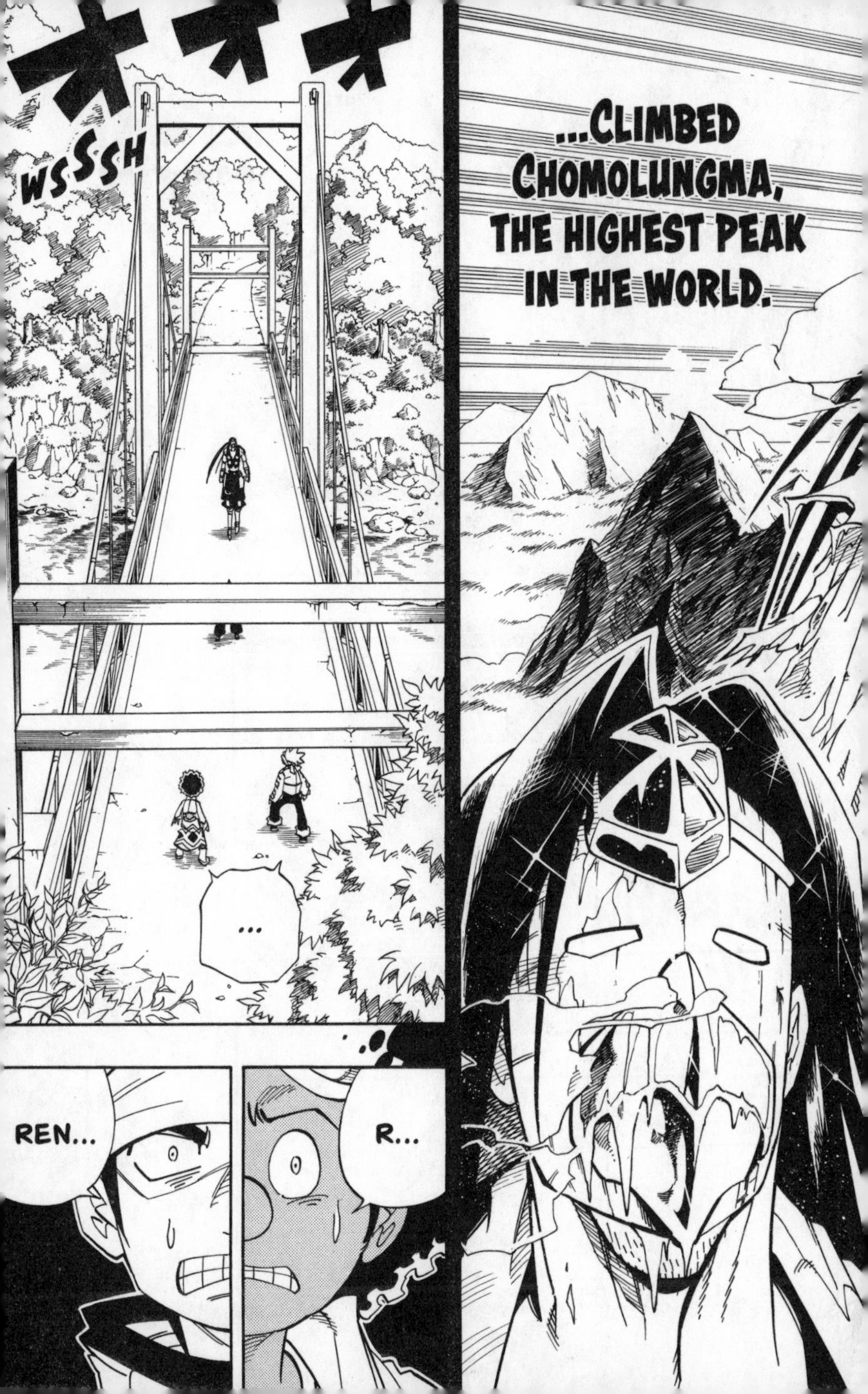
...CLIMBED CHOMOLUNGMA, THE HIGHEST PEAK IN THE WORLD.
オオオ
WSSSH
...
R...
REN...

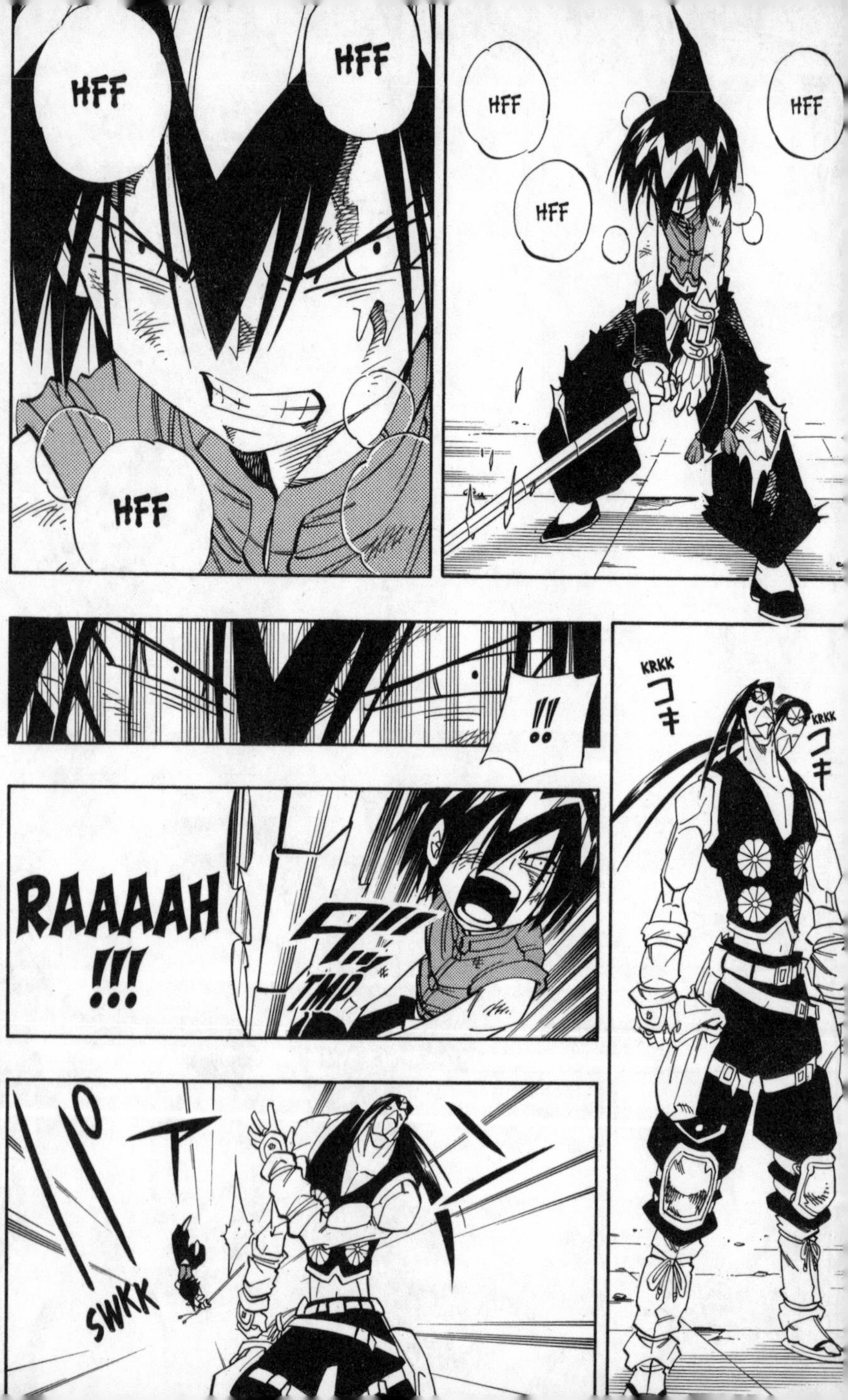

HFF
HFF
HFF
HFF
HFF
HFF
KRKK
コキ
KRKK
コキ
!!
RAAAAH!!!
タッ
TMP
SWKK

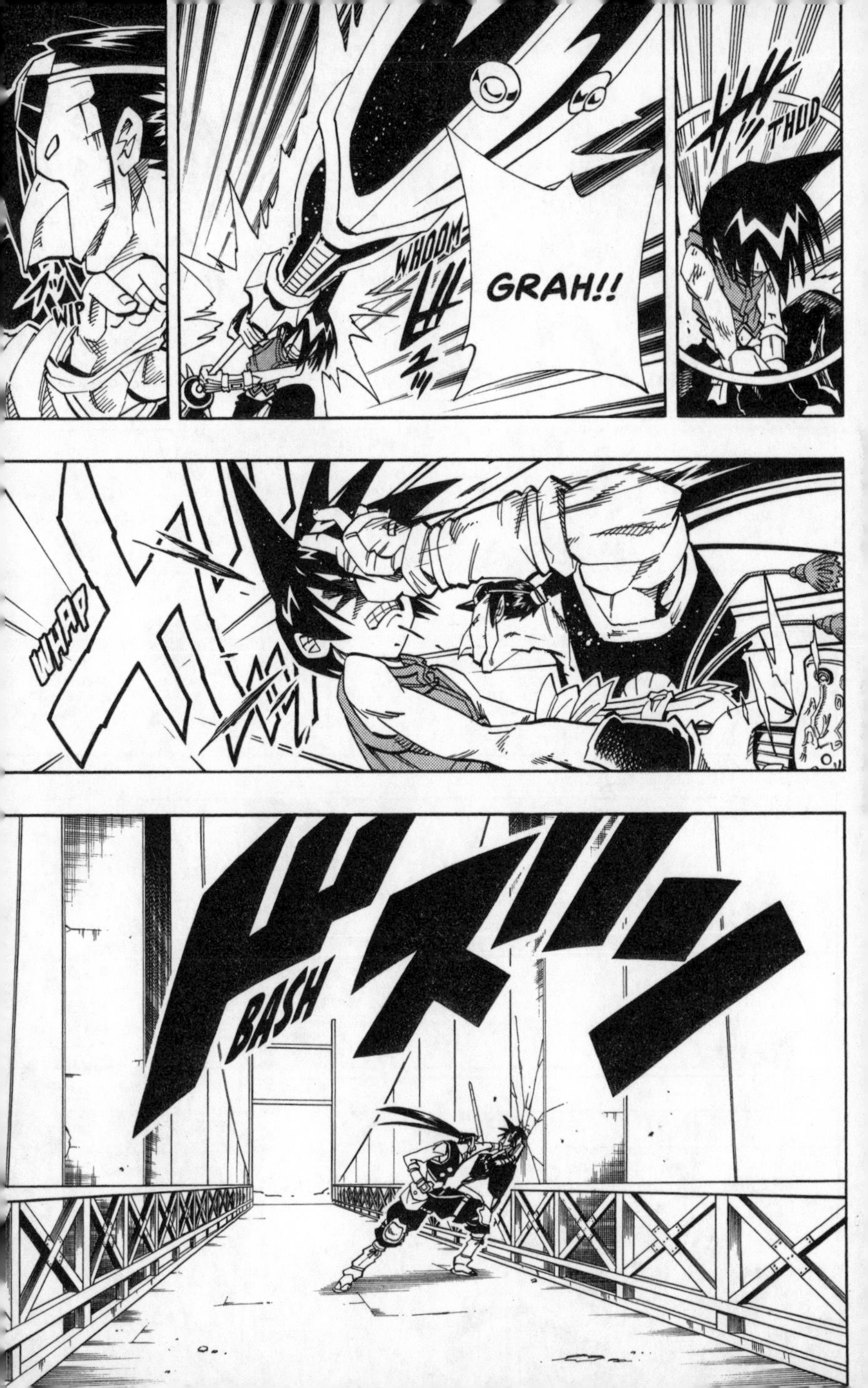
THUD
WHOOM
GRAH!!
WIP
WHAP
BASH

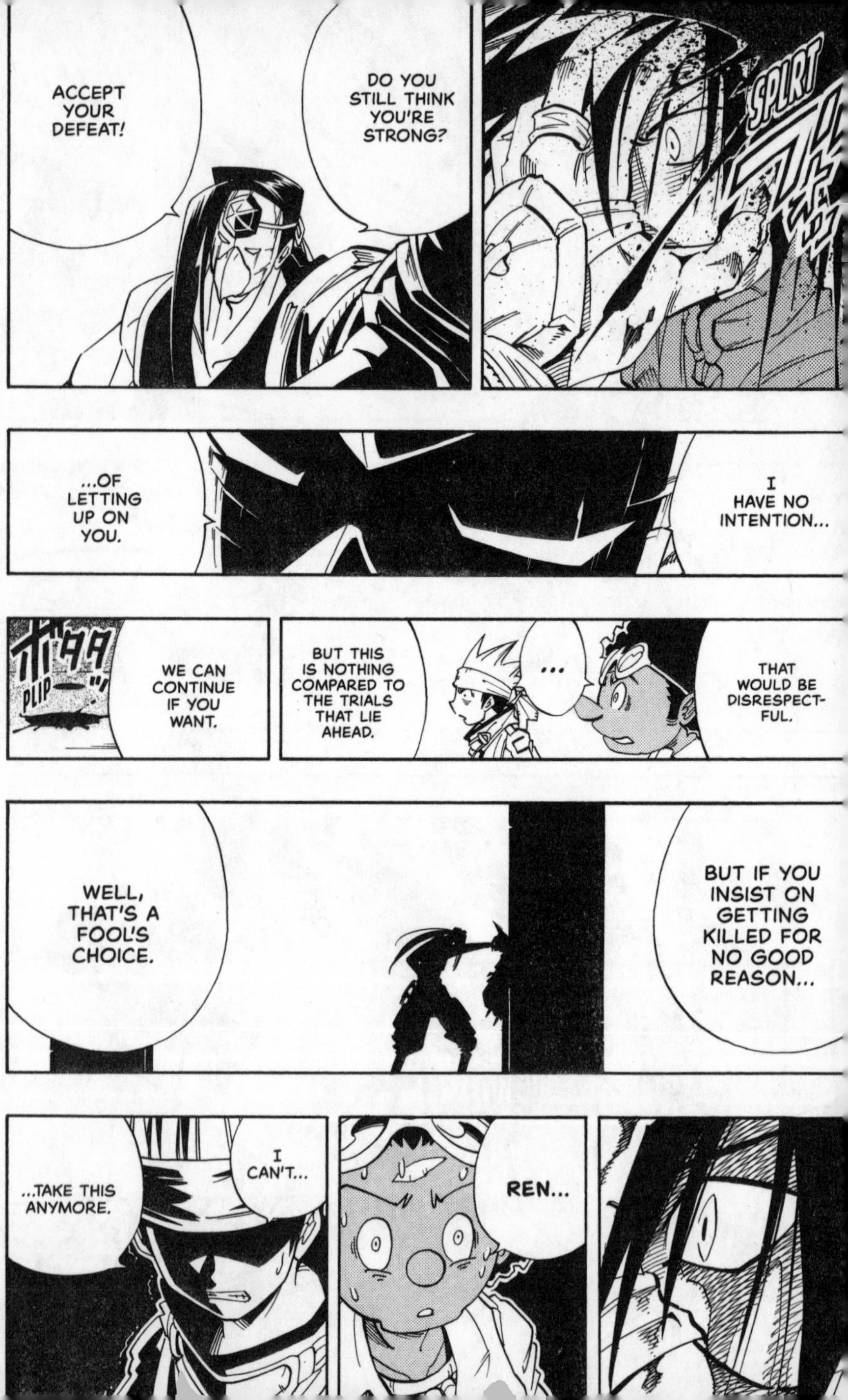
SPLRT
DO YOU STILL THINK YOU'RE STRONG?
ACCEPT YOUR DEFEAT!
I HAVE NO INTENTION...
...OF LETTING UP ON YOU.
THAT WOULD BE DISRESPECT-FUL.
...
BUT THIS IS NOTHING COMPARED TO THE TRIALS THAT LIE AHEAD.
WE CAN CONTINUE IF YOU WANT.
PLIP
BUT IF YOU INSIST ON GETTING KILLED FOR NO GOOD REASON...
WELL, THAT'S A FOOL'S CHOICE.
REN...
I CAN'T...
...TAKE THIS ANYMORE.

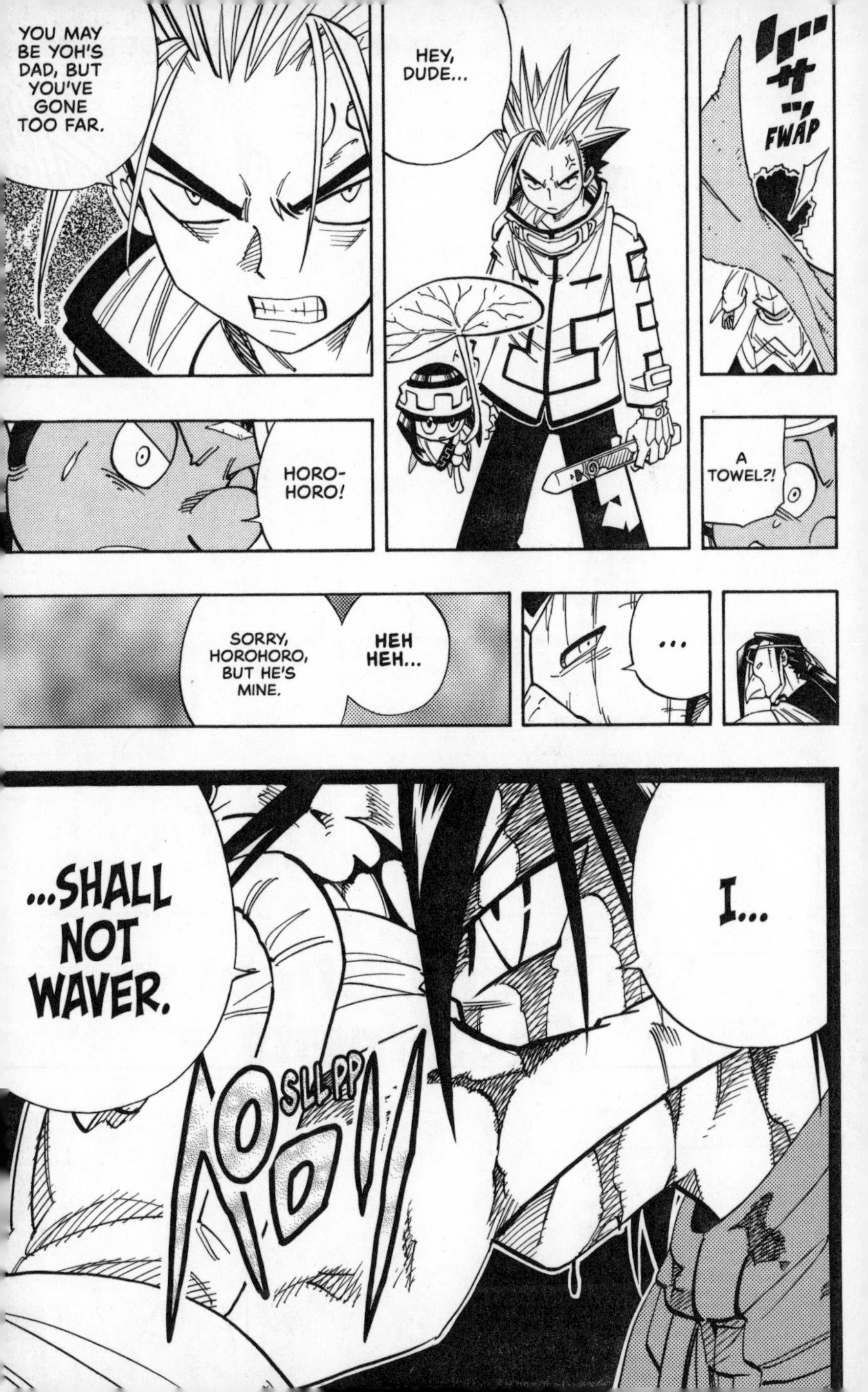
FWAP
A TOWEL?!
HEY, DUDE...
YOU MAY BE YOH'S DAD, BUT YOU'VE GONE TOO FAR.
HORO-HORO!
...
HEH HEH...
SORRY, HOROHORO, BUT HE'S MINE.
I...
...SHALL NOT WAVER.
SLLPP

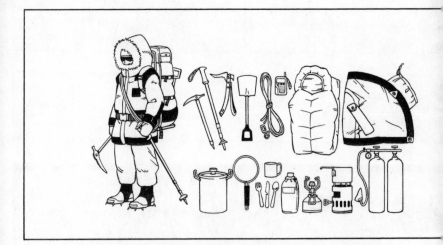

Standard Climbing Equipment

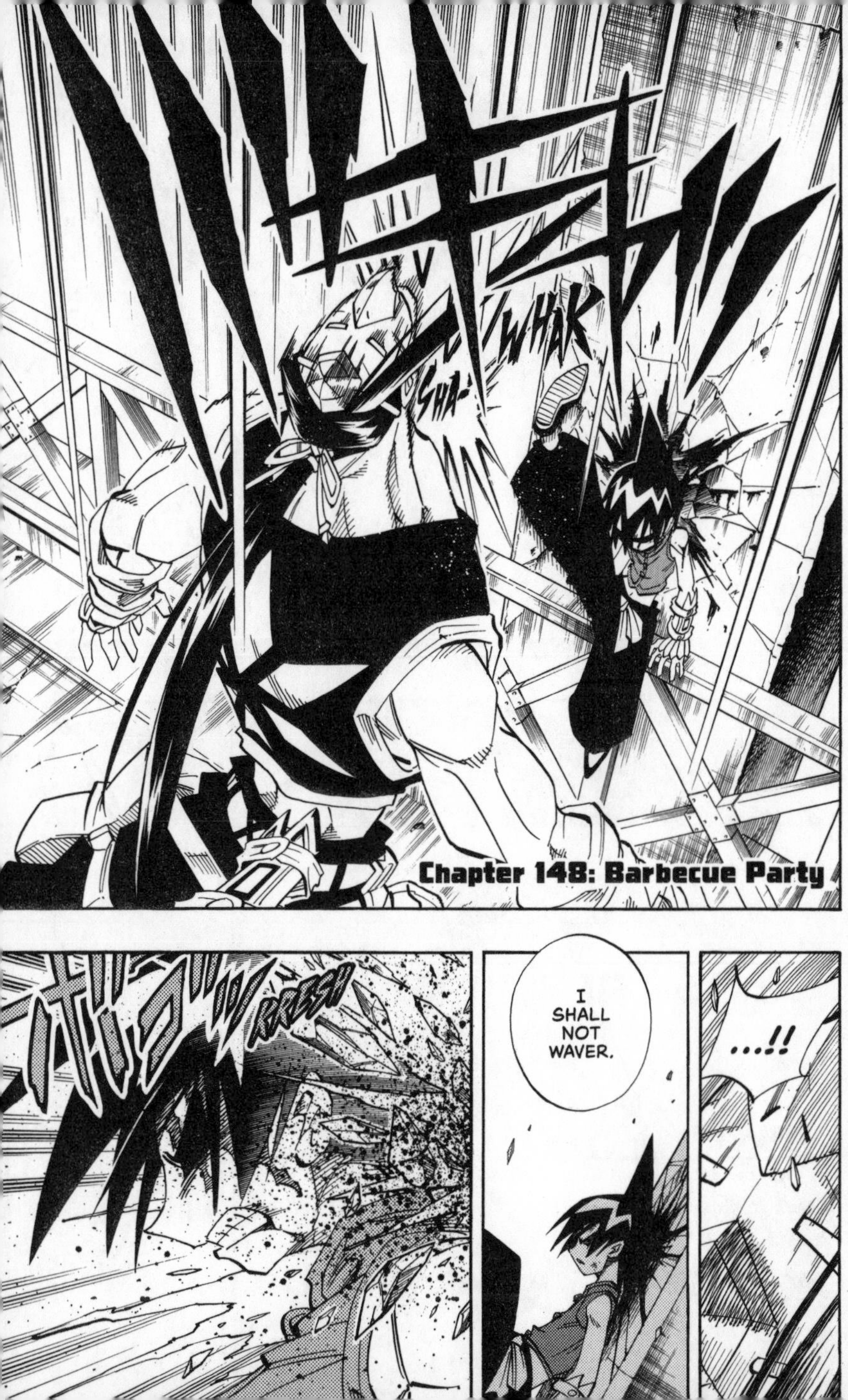
WHAK
SHA-
Chapter 148: Barbecue Party
...!!
I SHALL NOT WAVER.
KRESH

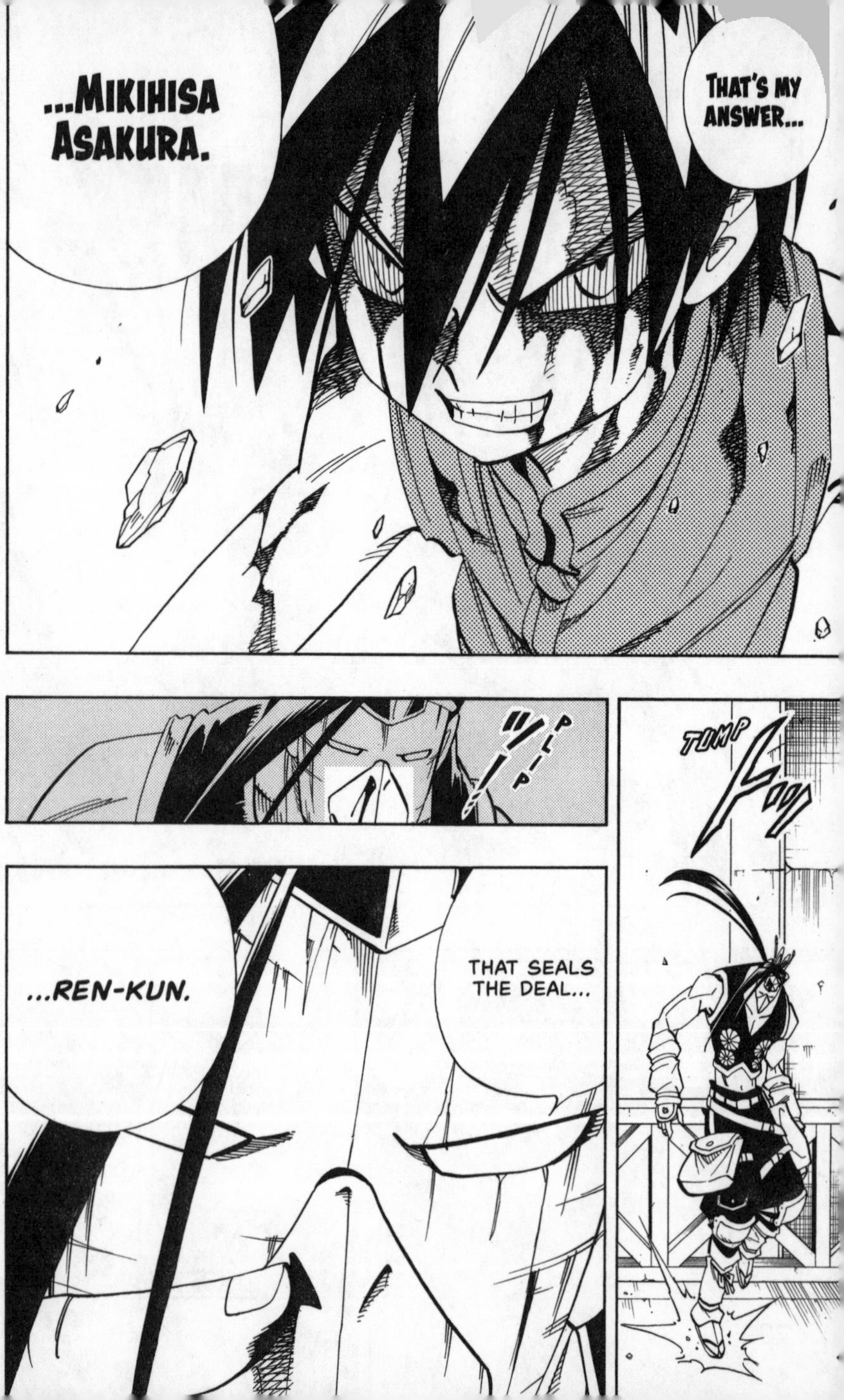
THAT'S MY ANSWER...
...MIKIHISA ASAKURA.
TOMP
PLIP
THAT SEALS THE DEAL...
...REN-KUN.

Chapter 148:

Barbecue Party

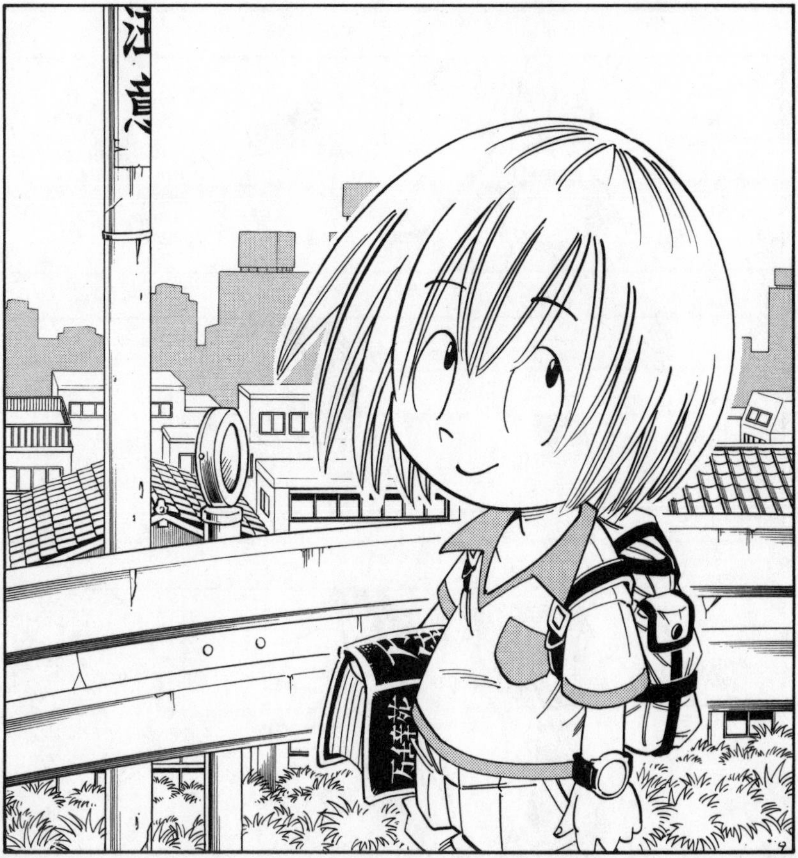

Sign: Caution

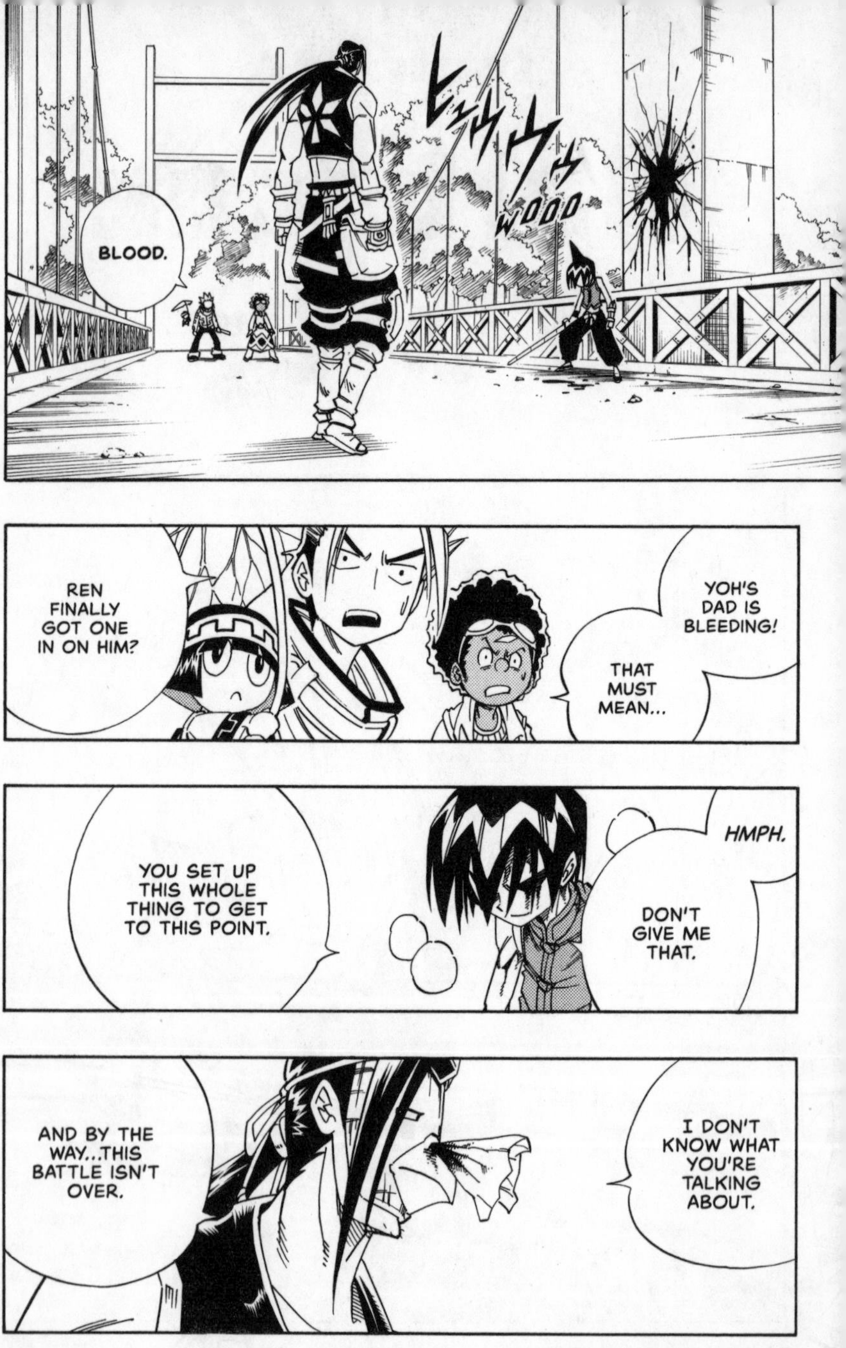
WOOD
BLOOD.
YOH'S DAD IS BLEEDING!
THAT MUST MEAN...
REN FINALLY GOT ONE IN ON HIM?
HMPH.
DON'T GIVE ME THAT.
YOU SET UP THIS WHOLE THING TO GET TO THIS POINT.
I DON'T KNOW WHAT YOU'RE TALKING ABOUT.
AND BY THE WAY...THIS BATTLE ISN'T OVER.

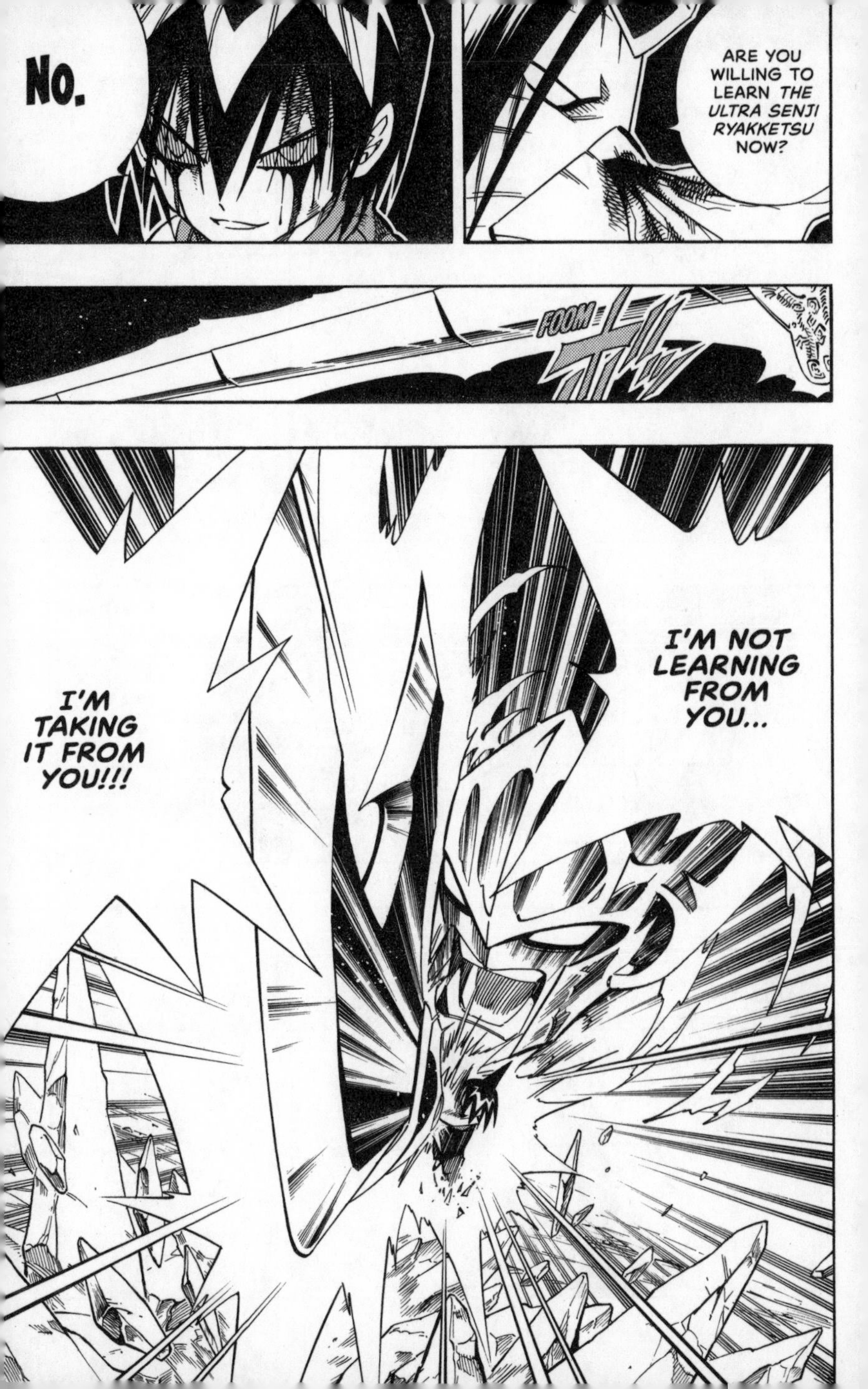
ARE YOU WILLING TO LEARN THE ULTRA SENJI RYAKKETSU NOW?
NO.
FOOM
I'M NOT LEARNING FROM YOU...
I'M TAKING IT FROM YOU!!!

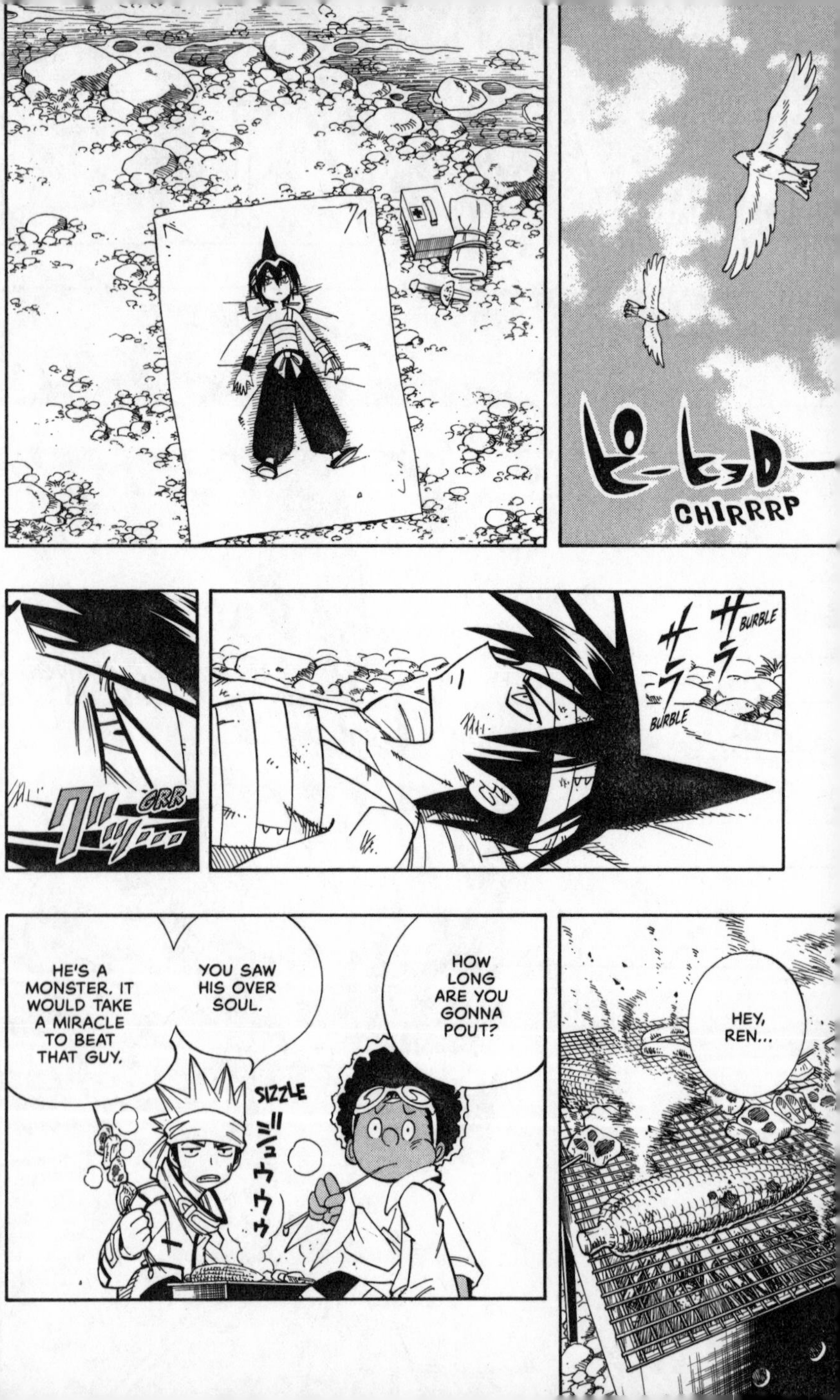
ピーヒョロー
CHIRRRP
サラサラ
BURBLE
BURBLE
GRR
HEY, REN...
HOW LONG ARE YOU GONNA POUT?
YOU SAW HIS OVER SOUL.
HE'S A MONSTER. IT WOULD TAKE A MIRACLE TO BEAT THAT GUY.
SIZZLE
ジュウウウ

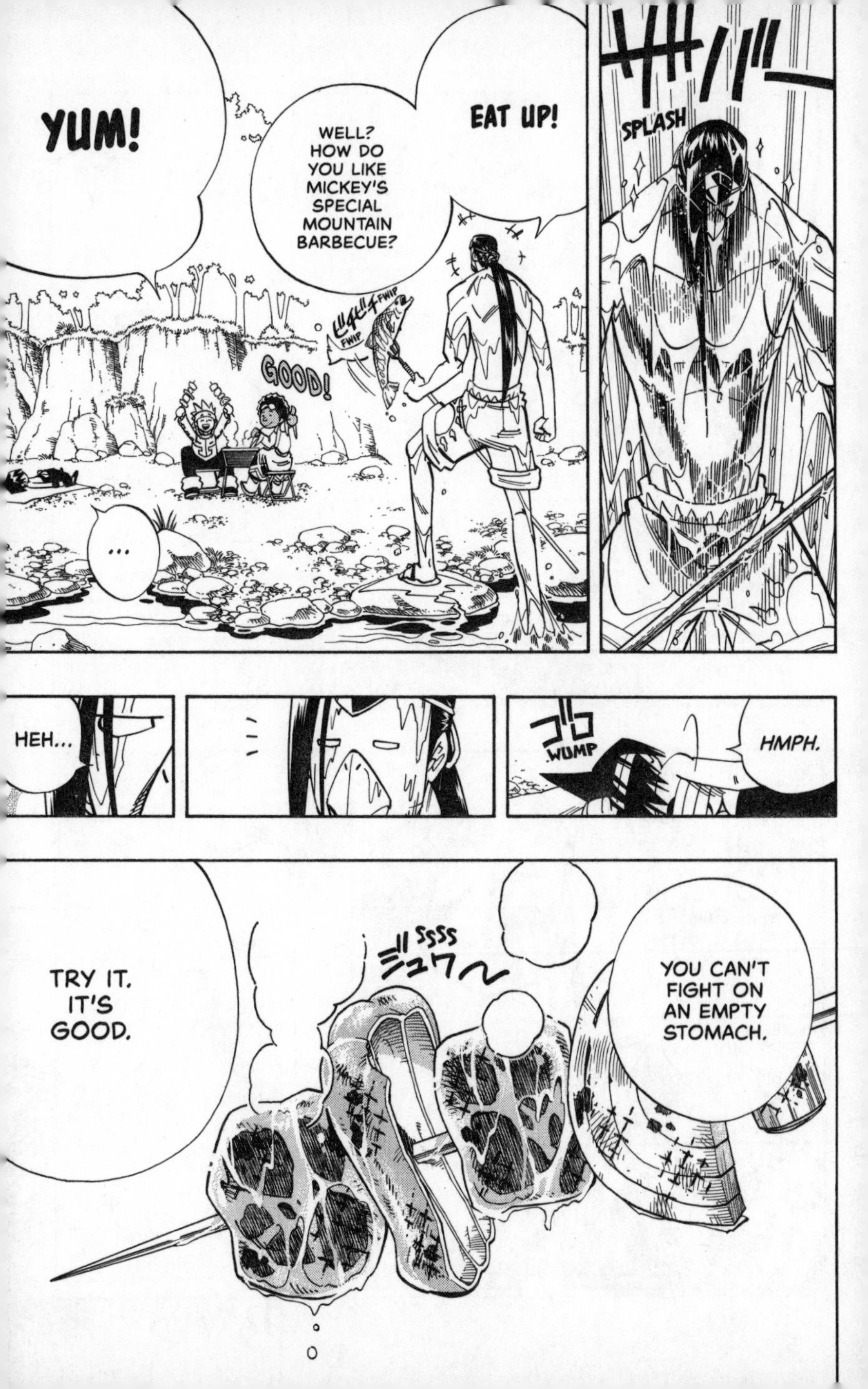
ザバー
SPLASH
EAT UP!
WELL? HOW DO YOU LIKE MICKEY'S SPECIAL MOUNTAIN BARBECUE?
YUM!
ビチビチ
FWIP FWIP
GOOD!
...
WUMP
HMPH.
HEH...
ジュワ～
SSSS
YOU CAN'T FIGHT ON AN EMPTY STOMACH.
TRY IT. IT'S GOOD.

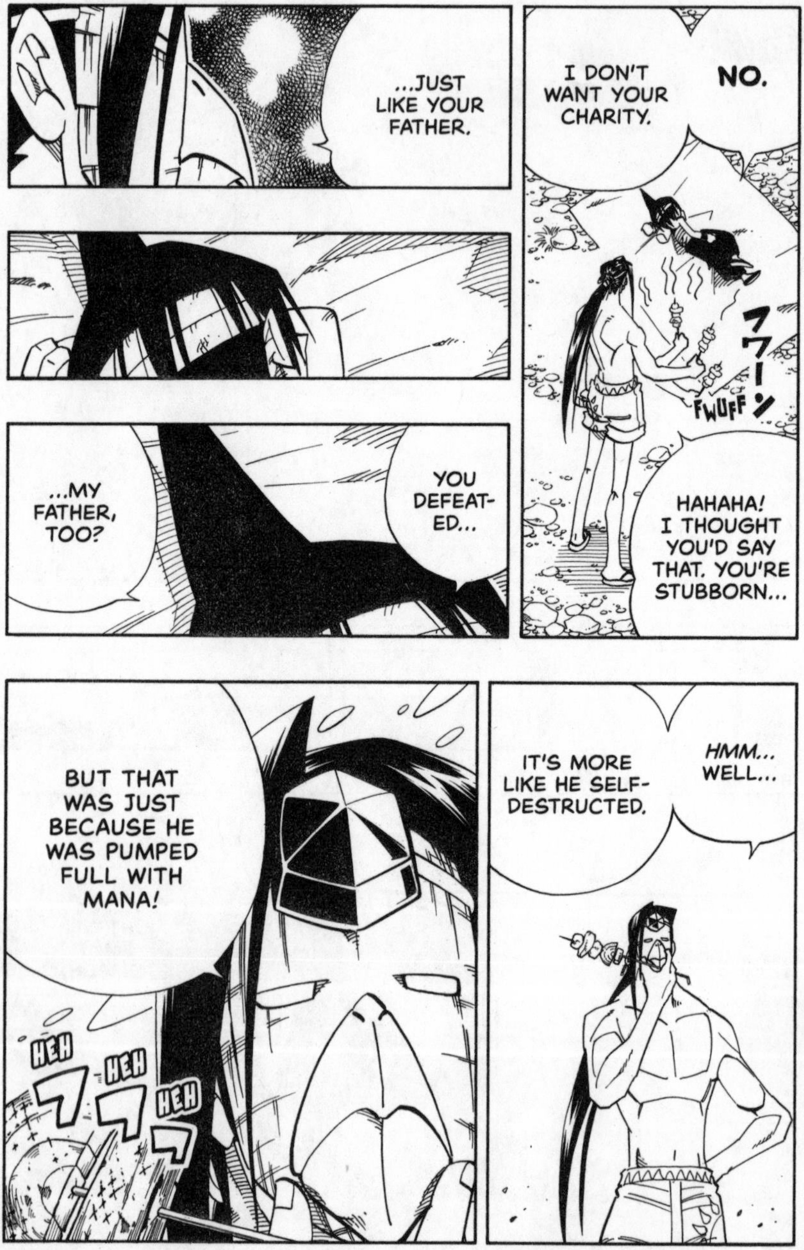
NO.
I DON'T WANT YOUR CHARITY.
フワーン
FWUFF
HAHAHA! I THOUGHT YOU'D SAY THAT. YOU'RE STUBBORN...
...JUST LIKE YOUR FATHER.
YOU DEFEAT-ED...
...MY FATHER, TOO?
HMM... WELL...
IT'S MORE LIKE HE SELF-DESTRUCTED.
BUT THAT WAS JUST BECAUSE HE WAS PUMPED FULL WITH MANA!
HEH
HEH
HEH

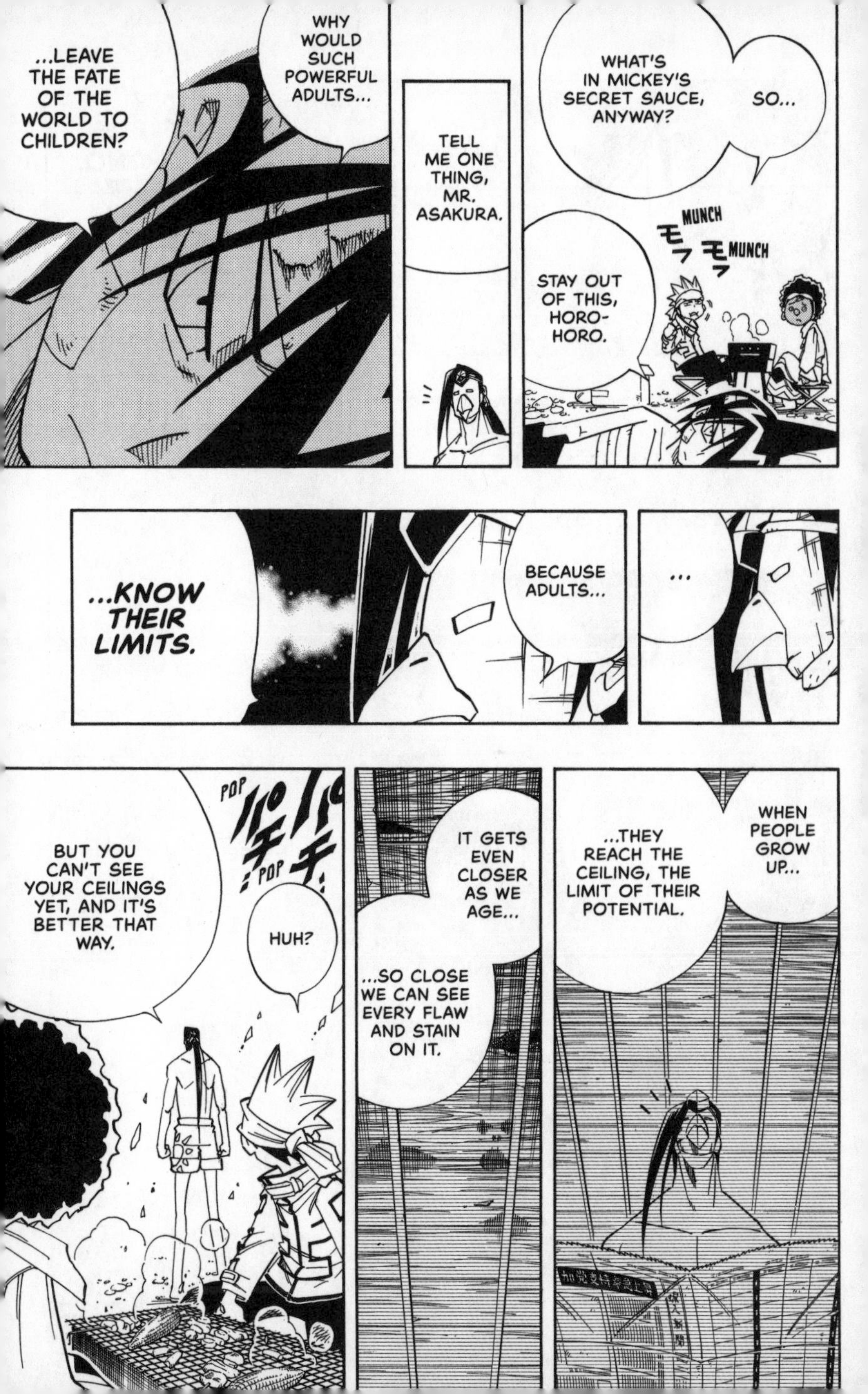

SO...
WHAT'S IN MICKEY'S SECRET SAUCE, ANYWAY?
MUNCH
MUNCH
STAY OUT OF THIS, HORO-HORO.
TELL ME ONE THING, MR. ASAKURA.
WHY WOULD SUCH POWERFUL ADULTS...
...LEAVE THE FATE OF THE WORLD TO CHILDREN?
...
BECAUSE ADULTS...
...KNOW THEIR LIMITS.
WHEN PEOPLE GROW UP...
...THEY REACH THE CEILING, THE LIMIT OF THEIR POTENTIAL.
IT GETS EVEN CLOSER AS WE AGE...
...SO CLOSE WE CAN SEE EVERY FLAW AND STAIN ON IT.
POP
POP
HUH?
BUT YOU CAN'T SEE YOUR CEILINGS YET, AND IT'S BETTER THAT WAY.

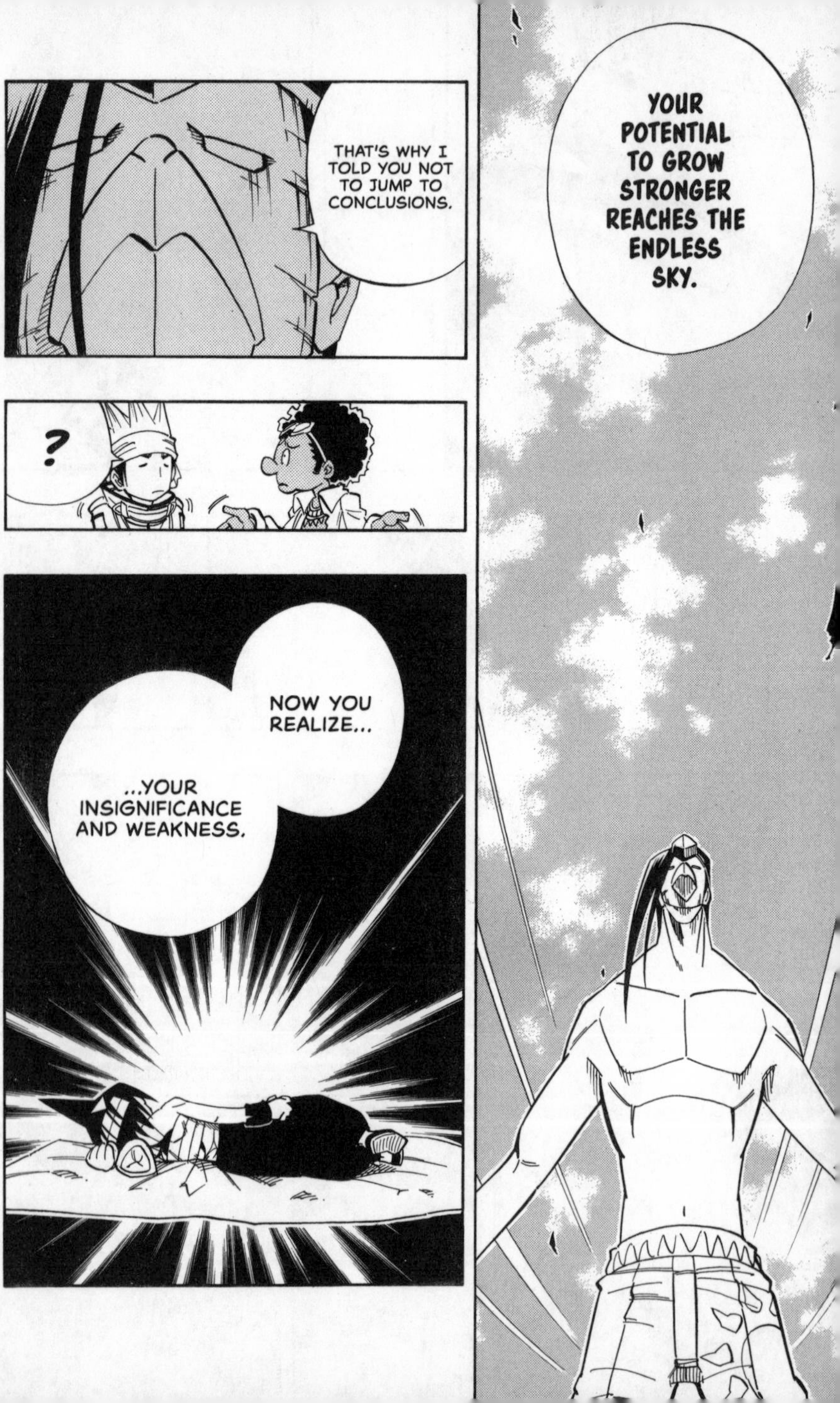
THAT'S WHY I TOLD YOU NOT TO JUMP TO CONCLUSIONS.
?
NOW YOU REALIZE...
...YOUR INSIGNIFICANCE AND WEAKNESS.
YOUR POTENTIAL TO GROW STRONGER REACHES THE ENDLESS SKY.

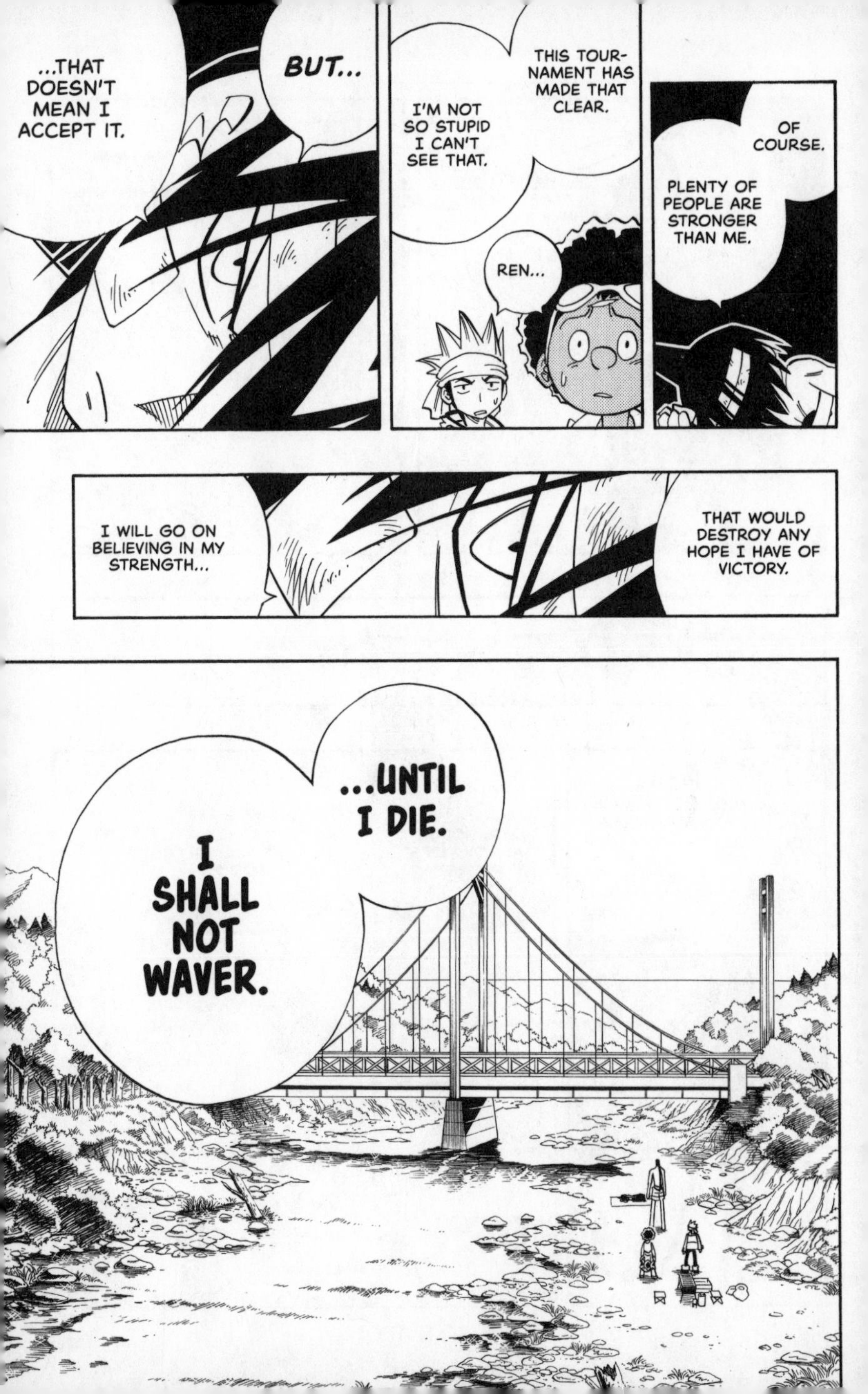

OF COURSE.
PLENTY OF PEOPLE ARE STRONGER THAN ME.
THIS TOURNAMENT HAS MADE THAT CLEAR.
I'M NOT SO STUPID I CAN'T SEE THAT.
REN...
BUT...
...THAT DOESN'T MEAN I ACCEPT IT.
THAT WOULD DESTROY ANY HOPE I HAVE OF VICTORY.
I WILL GO ON BELIEVING IN MY STRENGTH...
...UNTIL I DIE.
I SHALL NOT WAVER.

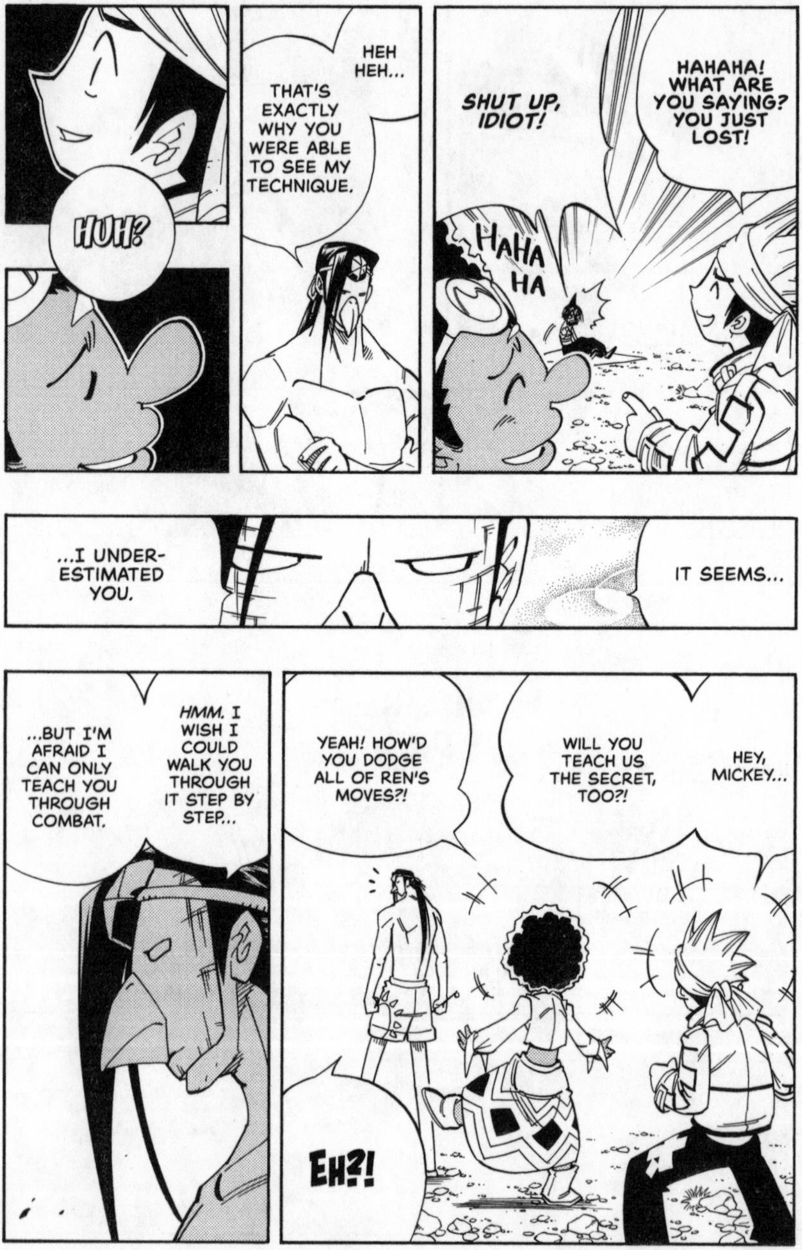
HAHAHA! WHAT ARE YOU SAYING? YOU JUST LOST!
SHUT UP, IDIOT!
HAHA HA
HEH HEH...
THAT'S EXACTLY WHY YOU WERE ABLE TO SEE MY TECHNIQUE.
HUH?
IT SEEMS...
...I UNDER-ESTIMATED YOU.
HEY, MICKEY...
WILL YOU TEACH US THE SECRET, TOO?!
YEAH! HOW'D YOU DODGE ALL OF REN'S MOVES?!
EH?!
HMM. I WISH I COULD WALK YOU THROUGH IT STEP BY STEP...
...BUT I'M AFRAID I CAN ONLY TEACH YOU THROUGH COMBAT.

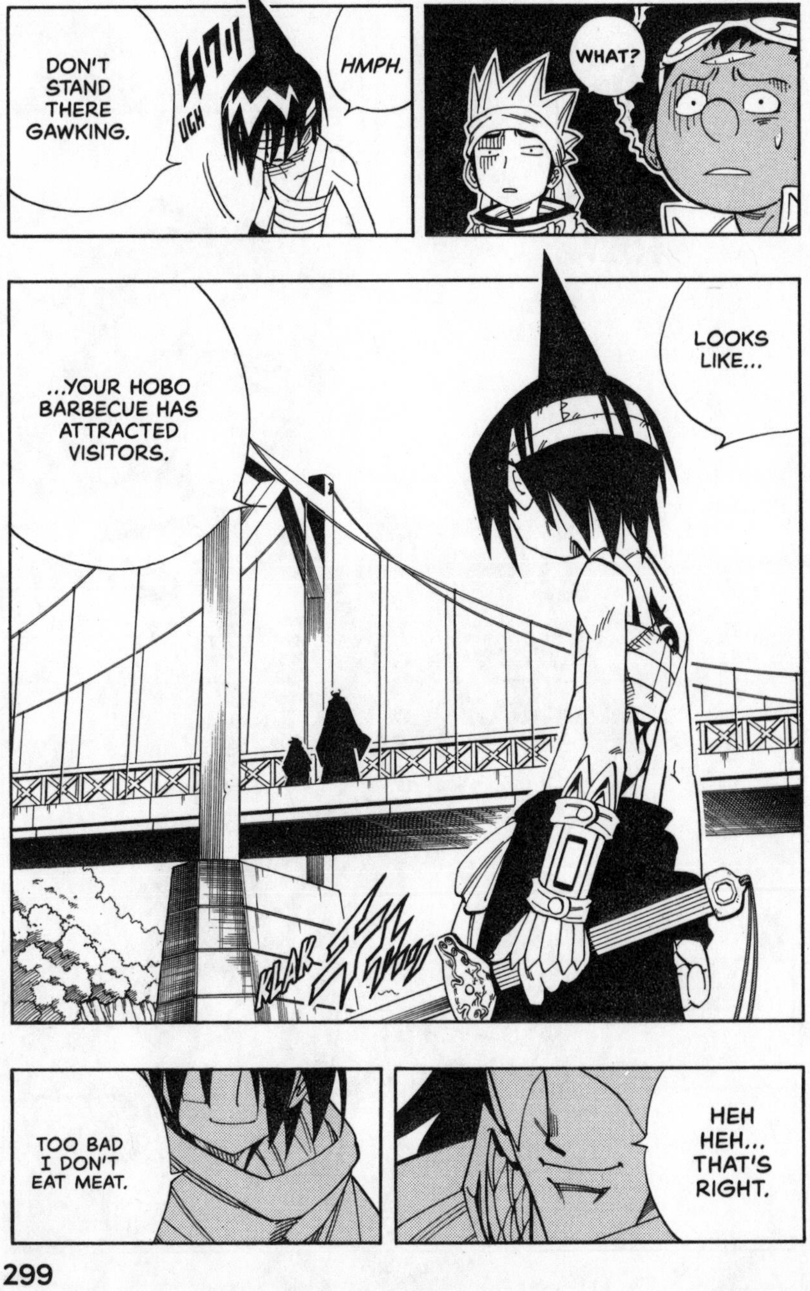
WHAT?
HMPH.
UGH
DON'T STAND THERE GAWKING.
LOOKS LIKE...
...YOUR HOBO BARBECUE HAS ATTRACTED VISITORS.
KLAK
HEH HEH... THAT'S RIGHT.
TOO BAD I DON'T EAT MEAT.

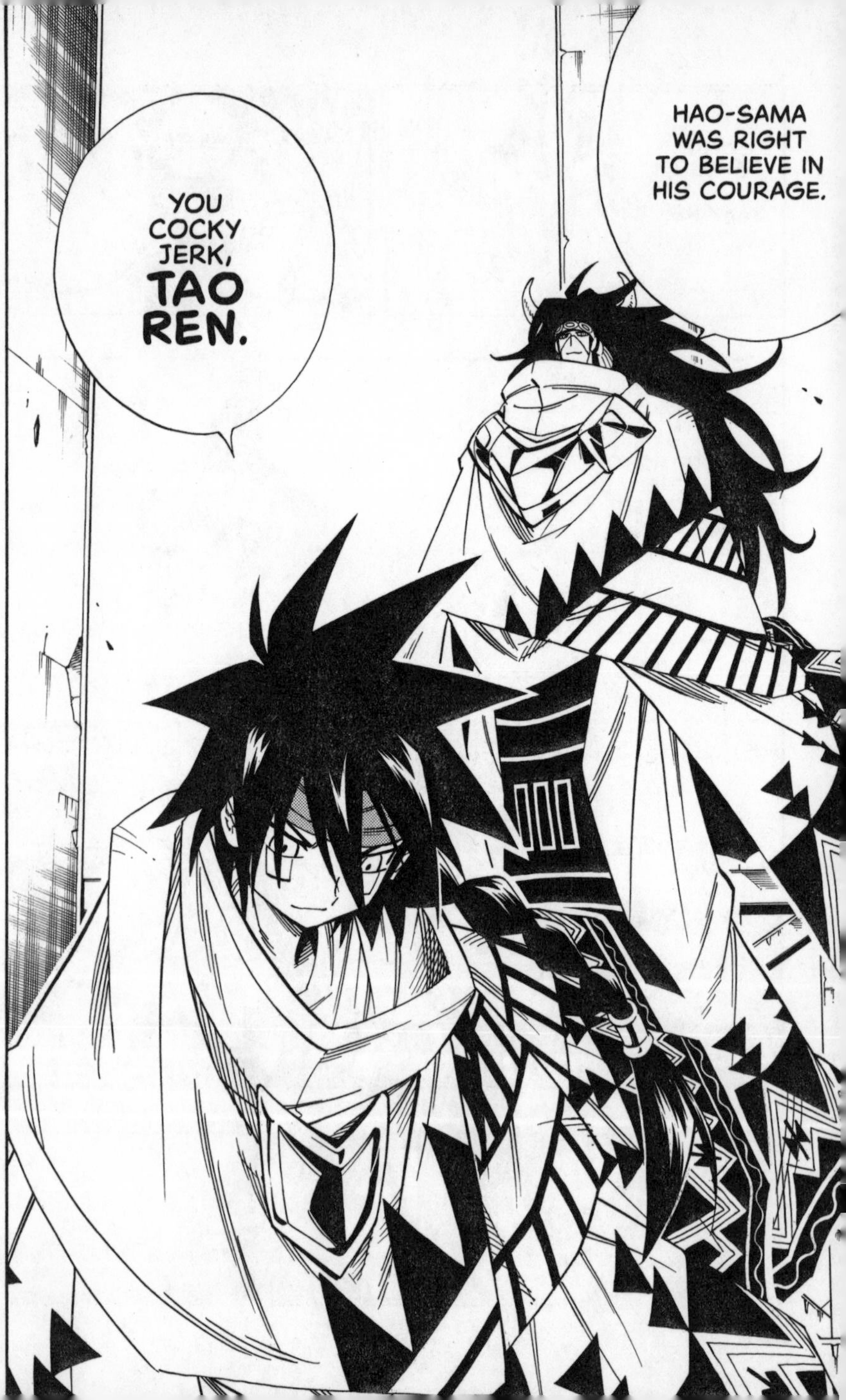
HAO-SAMA WAS RIGHT TO BELIEVE IN HIS COURAGE.
YOU COCKY JERK, TAO REN.

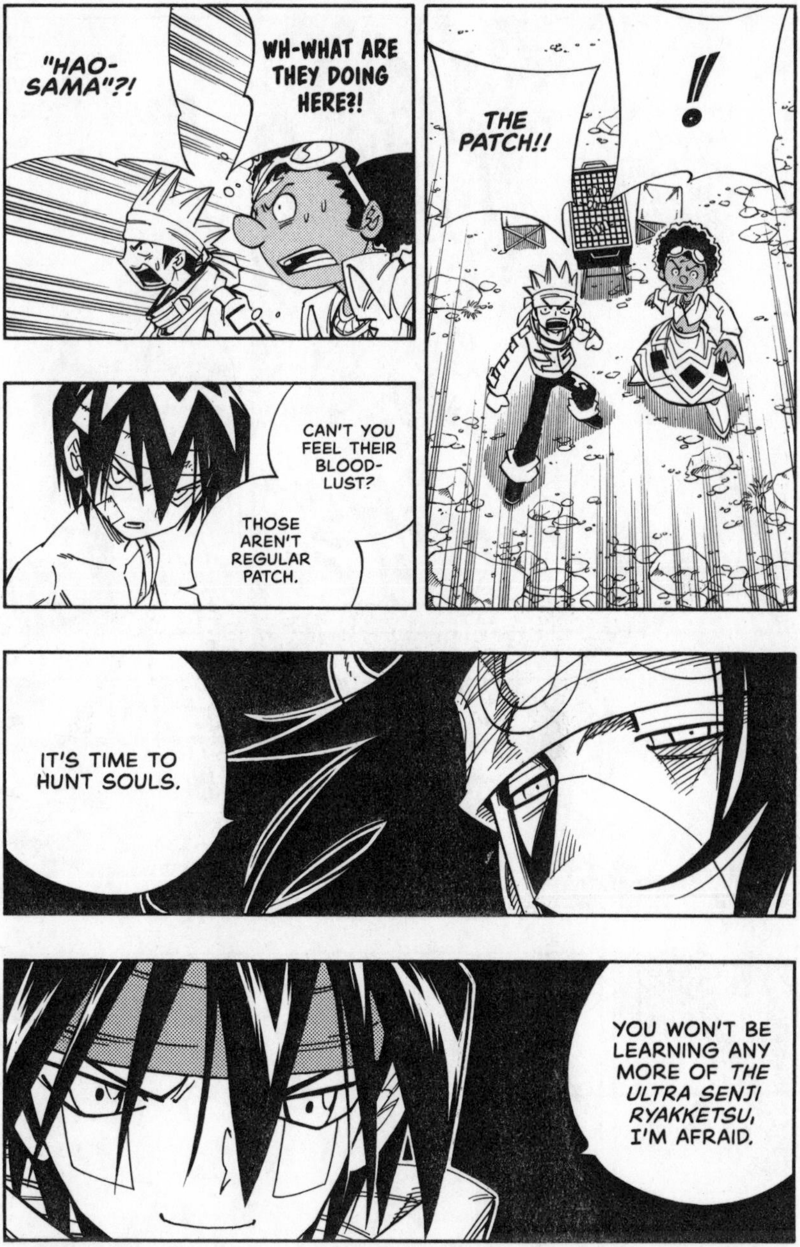
!
THE PATCH!!
WH-WHAT ARE THEY DOING HERE?!
"HAO-SAMA"?!
CAN'T YOU FEEL THEIR BLOOD-LUST?
THOSE AREN'T REGULAR PATCH.
IT'S TIME TO HUNT SOULS.
YOU WON'T BE LEARNING ANY MORE OF *THE ULTRA SENJI RYAKKETSU*, I'M AFRAID.

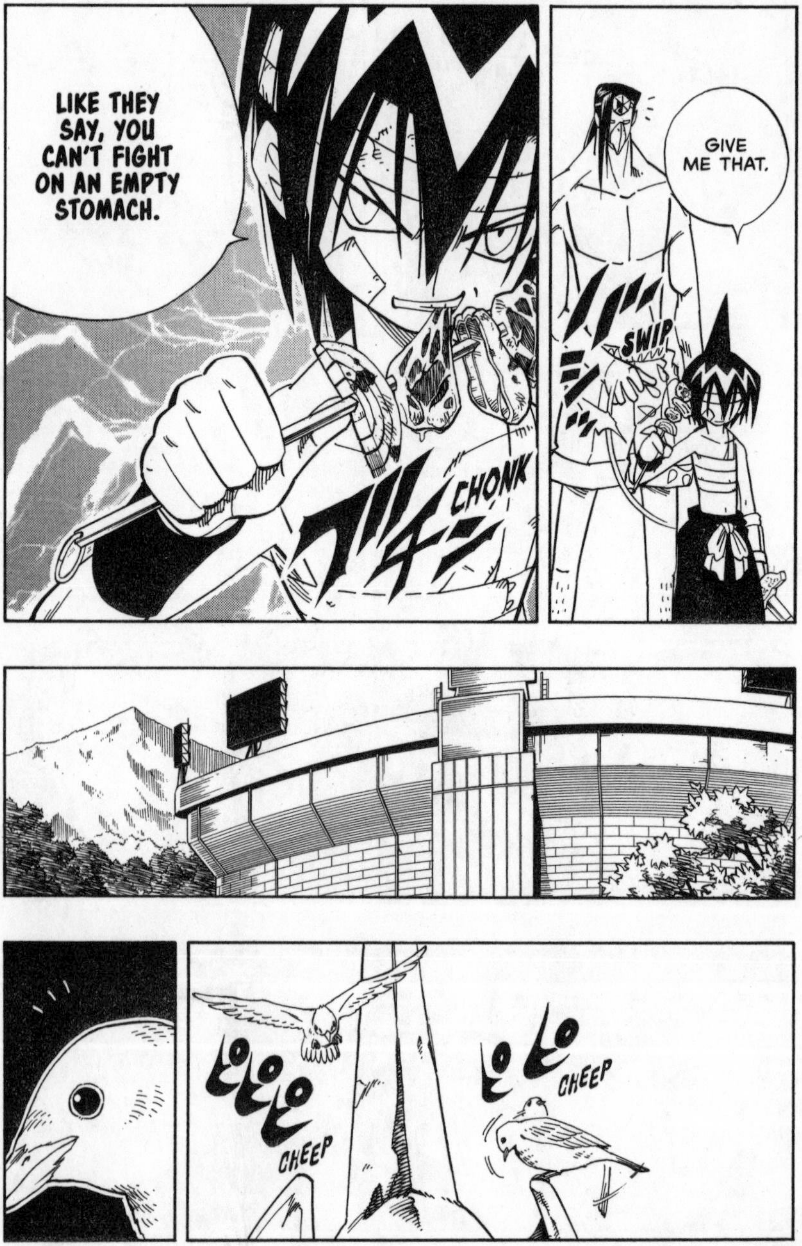
GIVE ME THAT.
SWIP
LIKE THEY SAY, YOU CAN'T FIGHT ON AN EMPTY STOMACH.
CHONK
CHEEP
CHEEP

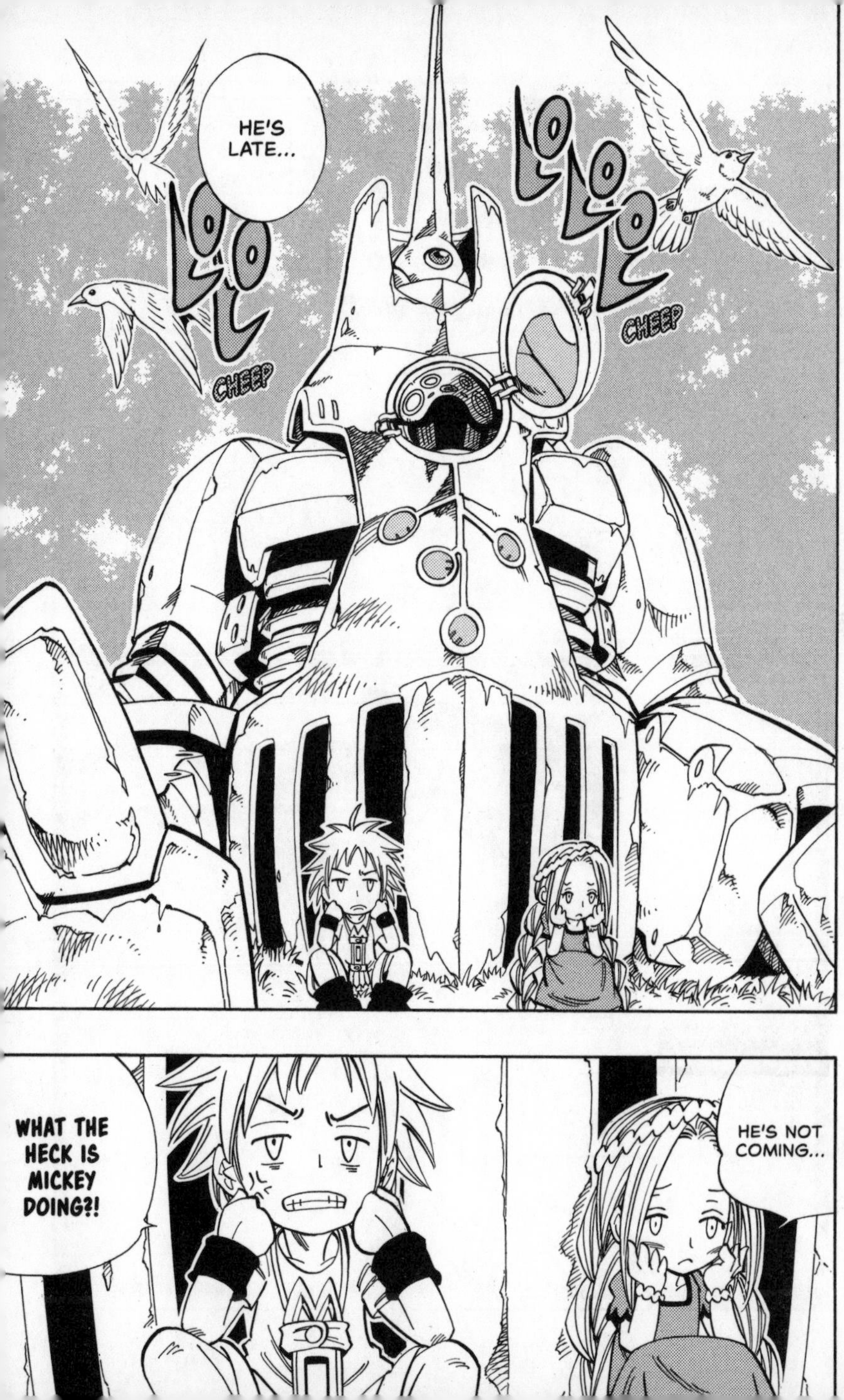
CHEEP
HE'S LATE...
CHEEP
HE'S NOT COMING...
WHAT THE HECK IS MICKEY DOING?!

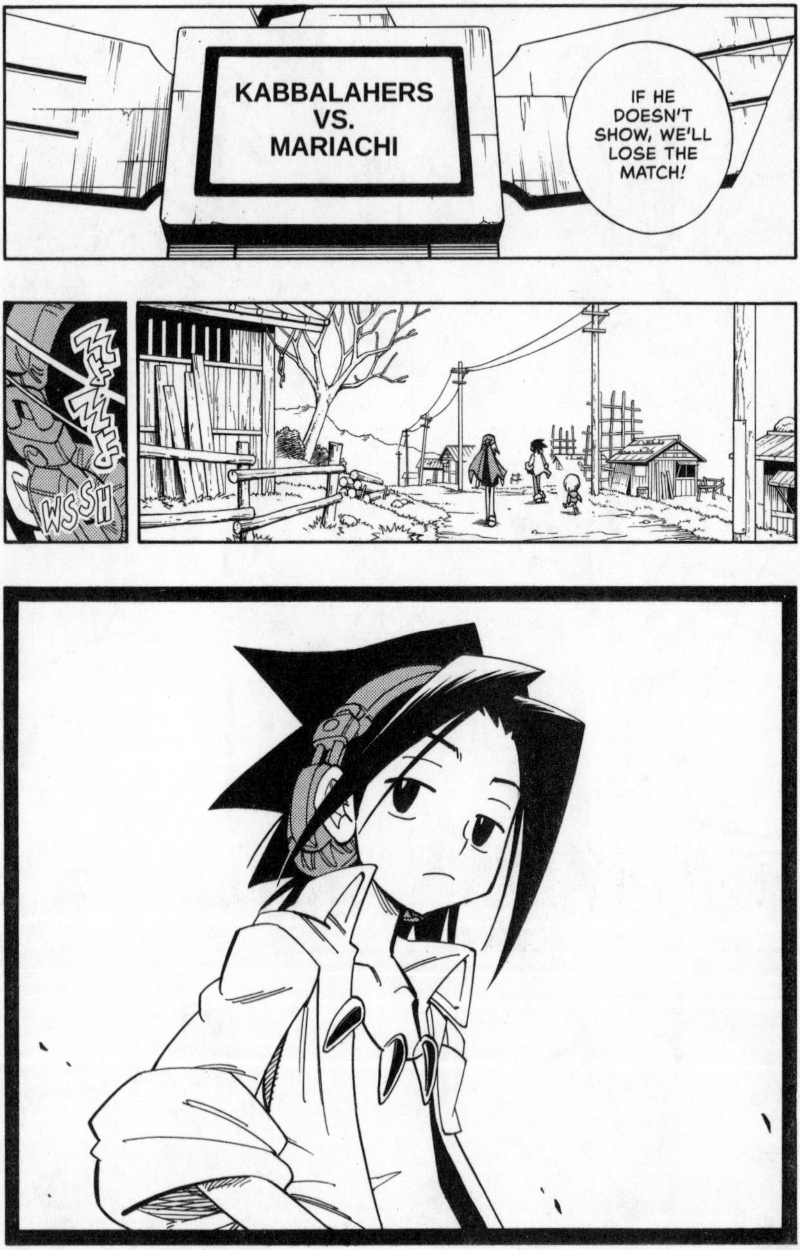
IF HE DOESN'T SHOW, WE'LL LOSE THE MATCH!
KABBALAHERS VS. MARIACHI
WSSH

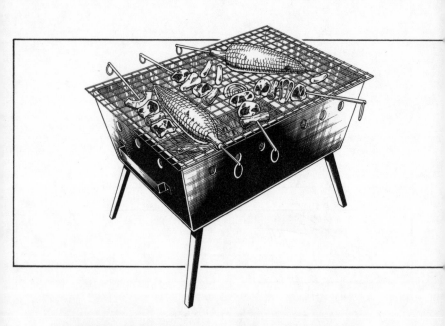

Mickey's Special
Barbecue Set

Chapter 149: Death Clash

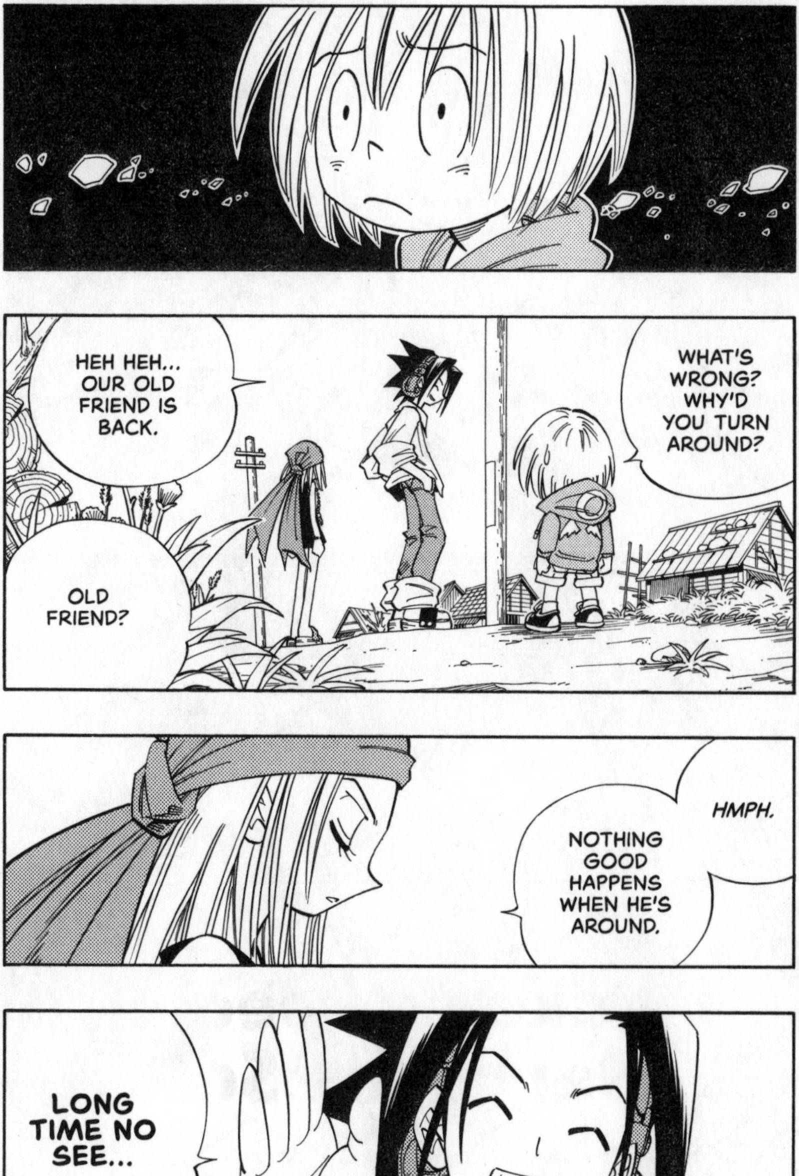
WHAT'S WRONG? WHY'D YOU TURN AROUND?
HEH HEH... OUR OLD FRIEND IS BACK.
OLD FRIEND?
HMPH.
NOTHING GOOD HAPPENS WHEN HE'S AROUND.
LONG TIME NO SEE...

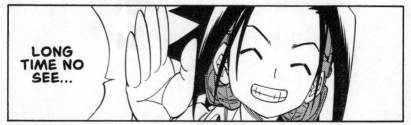

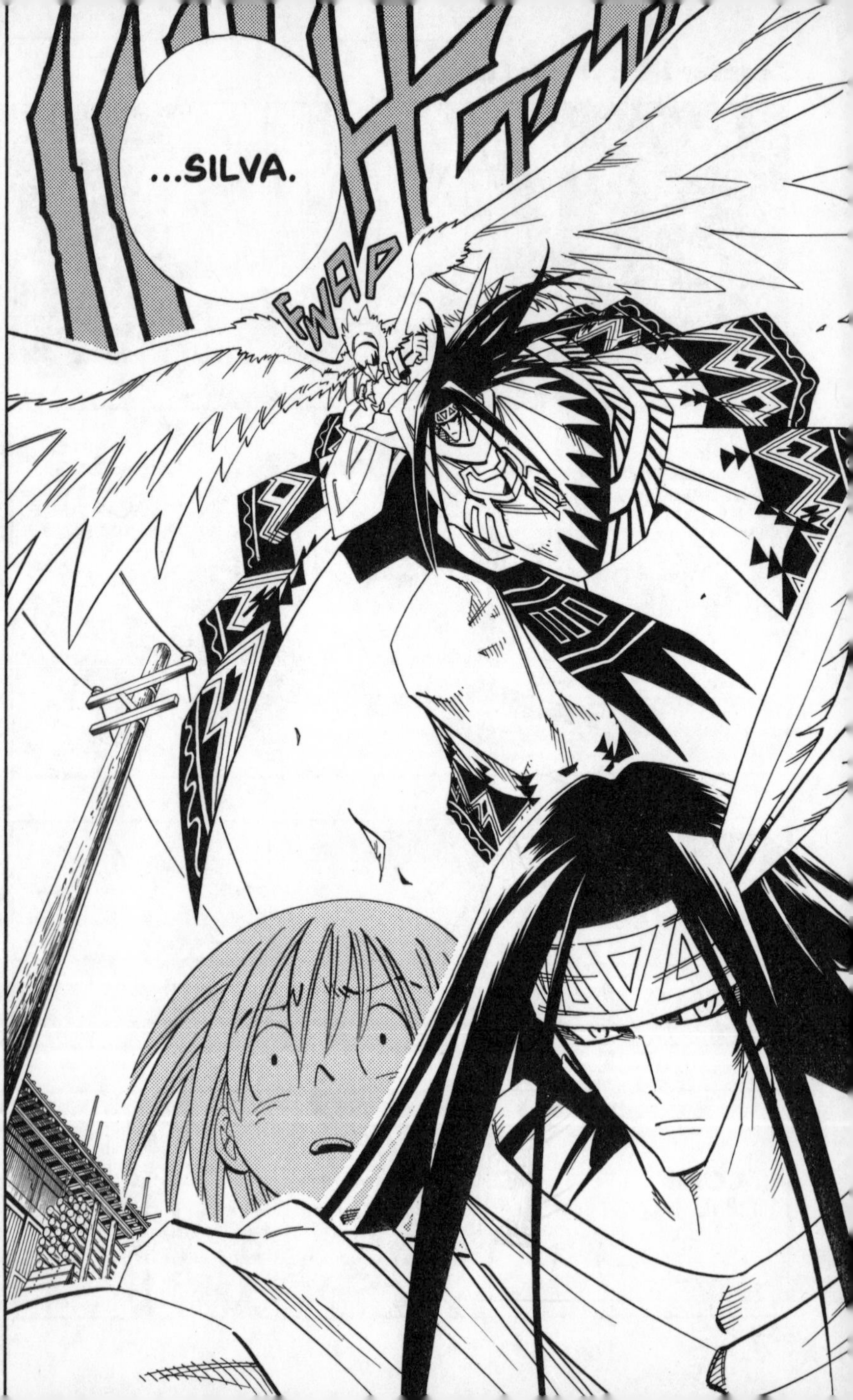
...SILVA.
FWAP

Chapter 149:

Death Clash

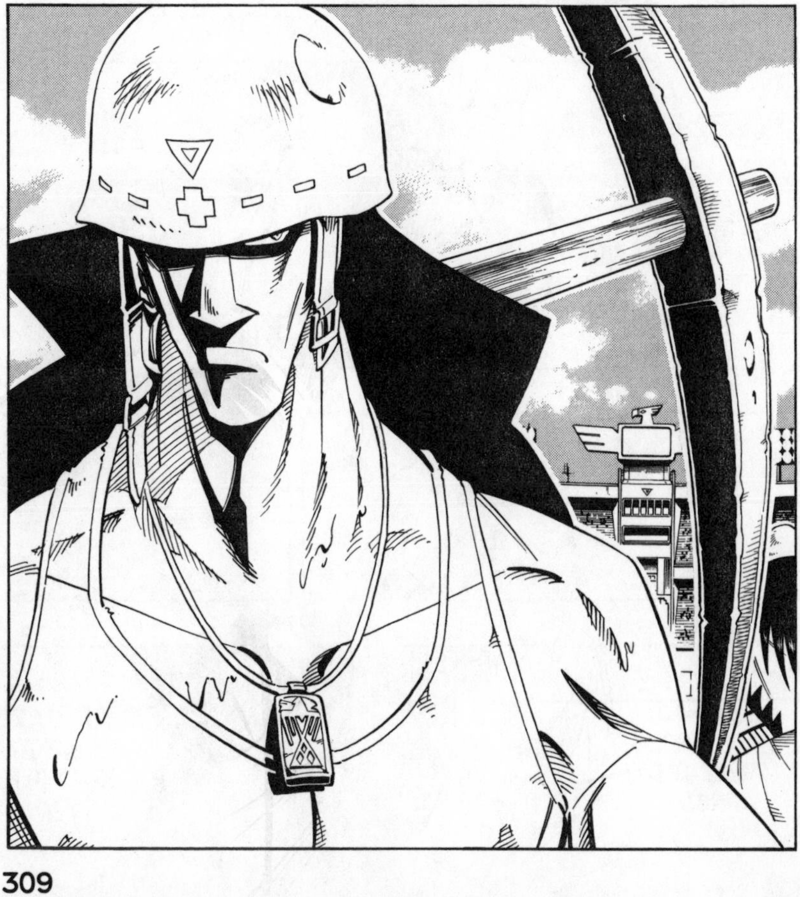

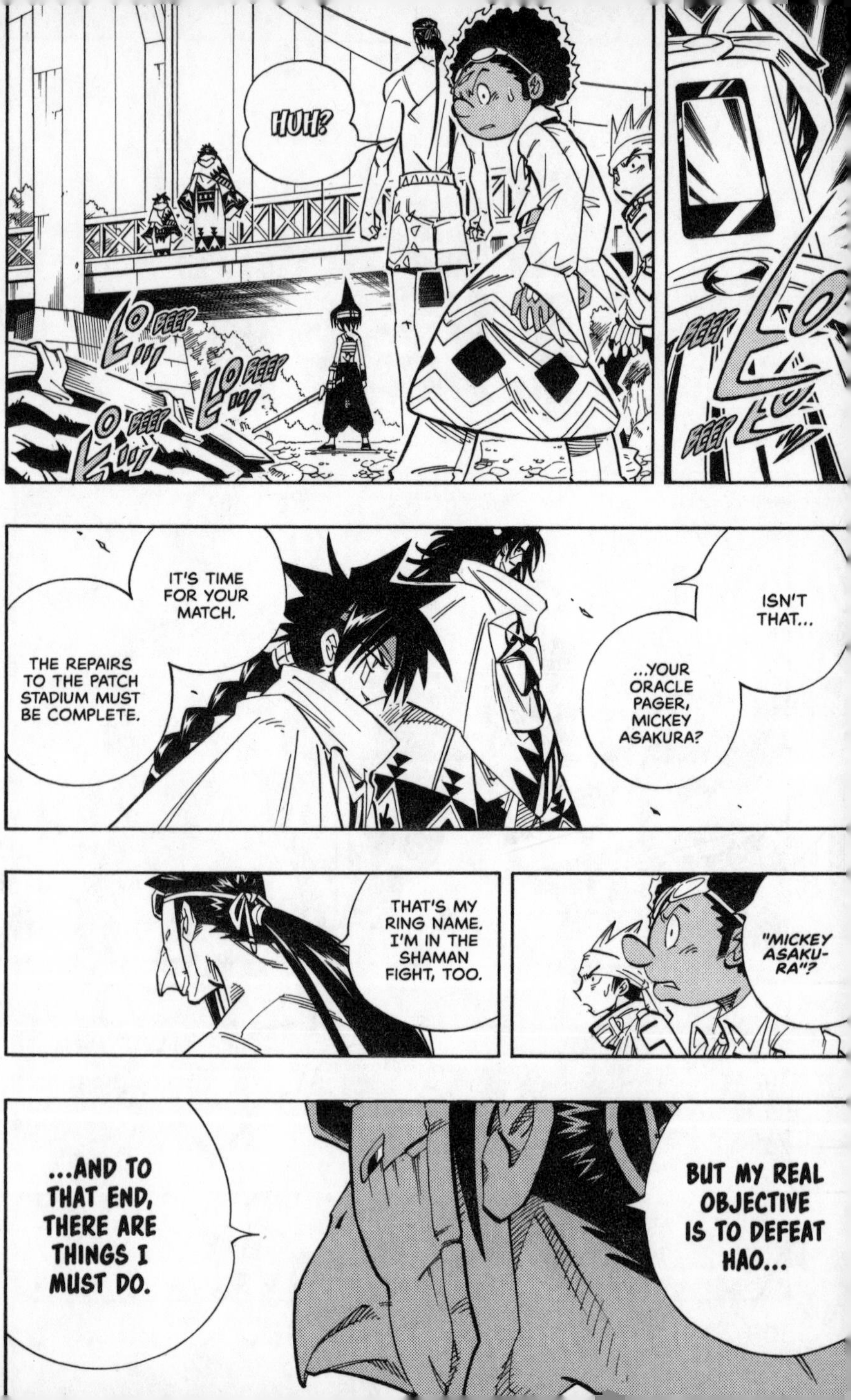
BEEP
BEEP
HUH?
BEEP
BEEP
BEEP
BEEP
ISN'T THAT...
...YOUR ORACLE PAGER, MICKEY ASAKURA?
IT'S TIME FOR YOUR MATCH.
THE REPAIRS TO THE PATCH STADIUM MUST BE COMPLETE.
"MICKEY ASAKU-RA"?
THAT'S MY RING NAME. I'M IN THE SHAMAN FIGHT, TOO.
BUT MY REAL OBJECTIVE IS TO DEFEAT HAO...
...AND TO THAT END, THERE ARE THINGS I MUST DO.

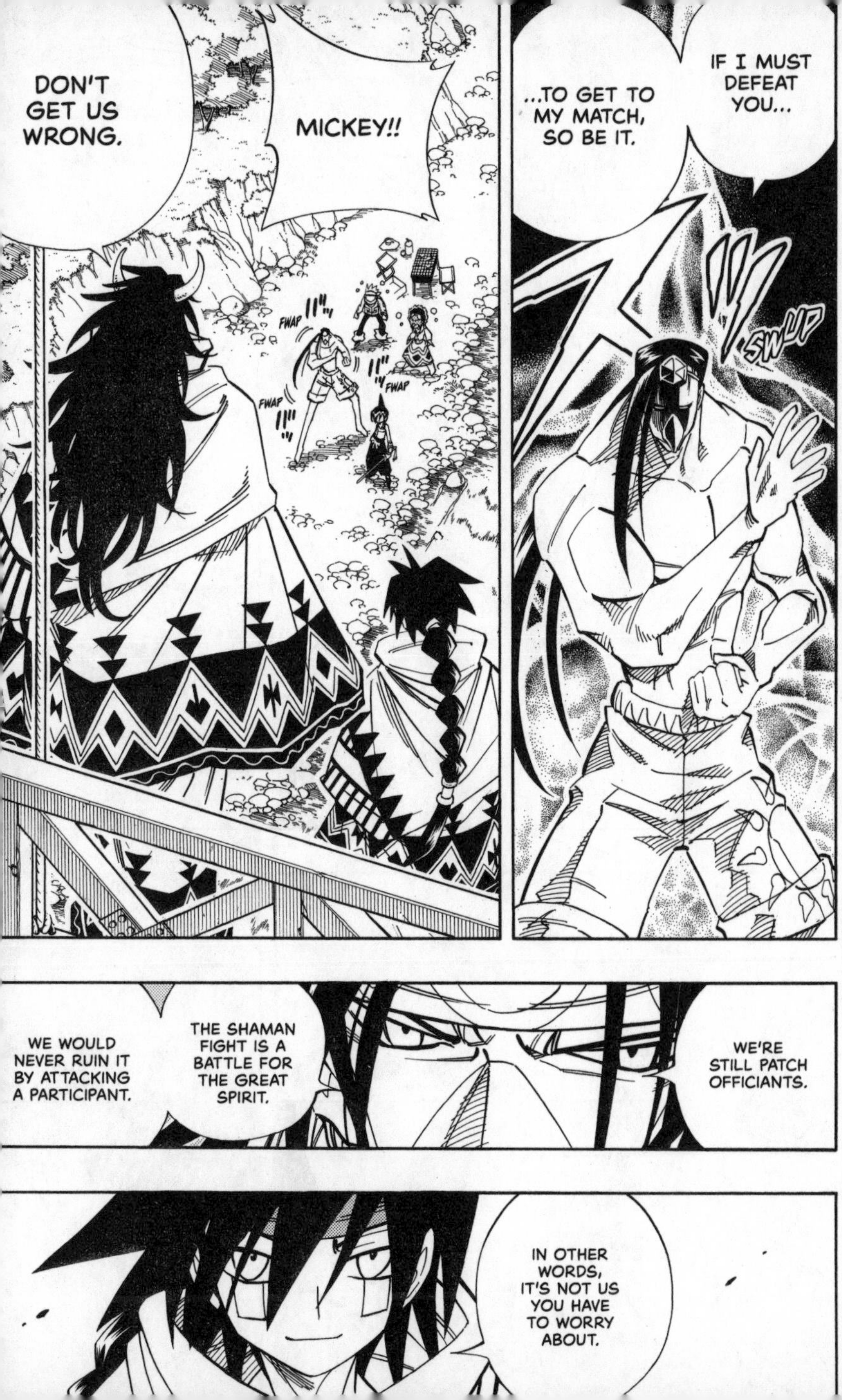
IF I MUST DEFEAT YOU...
...TO GET TO MY MATCH, SO BE IT.
SWUP
MICKEY!!
DON'T GET US WRONG.
FWAP
FWAP
FWAP
WE'RE STILL PATCH OFFICIANTS.
THE SHAMAN FIGHT IS A BATTLE FOR THE GREAT SPIRIT.
WE WOULD NEVER RUIN IT BY ATTACKING A PARTICIPANT.
IN OTHER WORDS, IT'S NOT US YOU HAVE TO WORRY ABOUT.

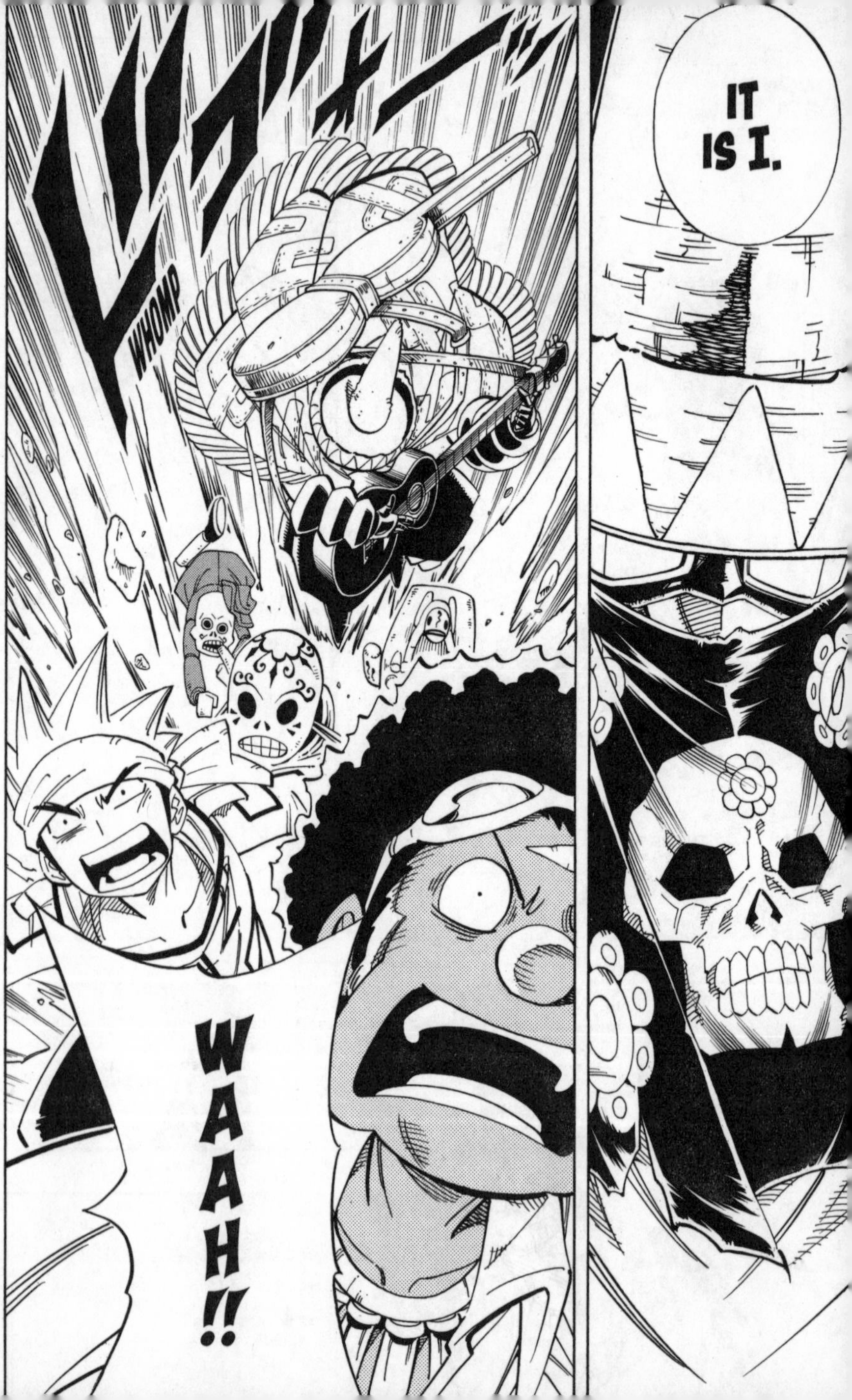
IT IS I.
WHOMP
WAAH!!

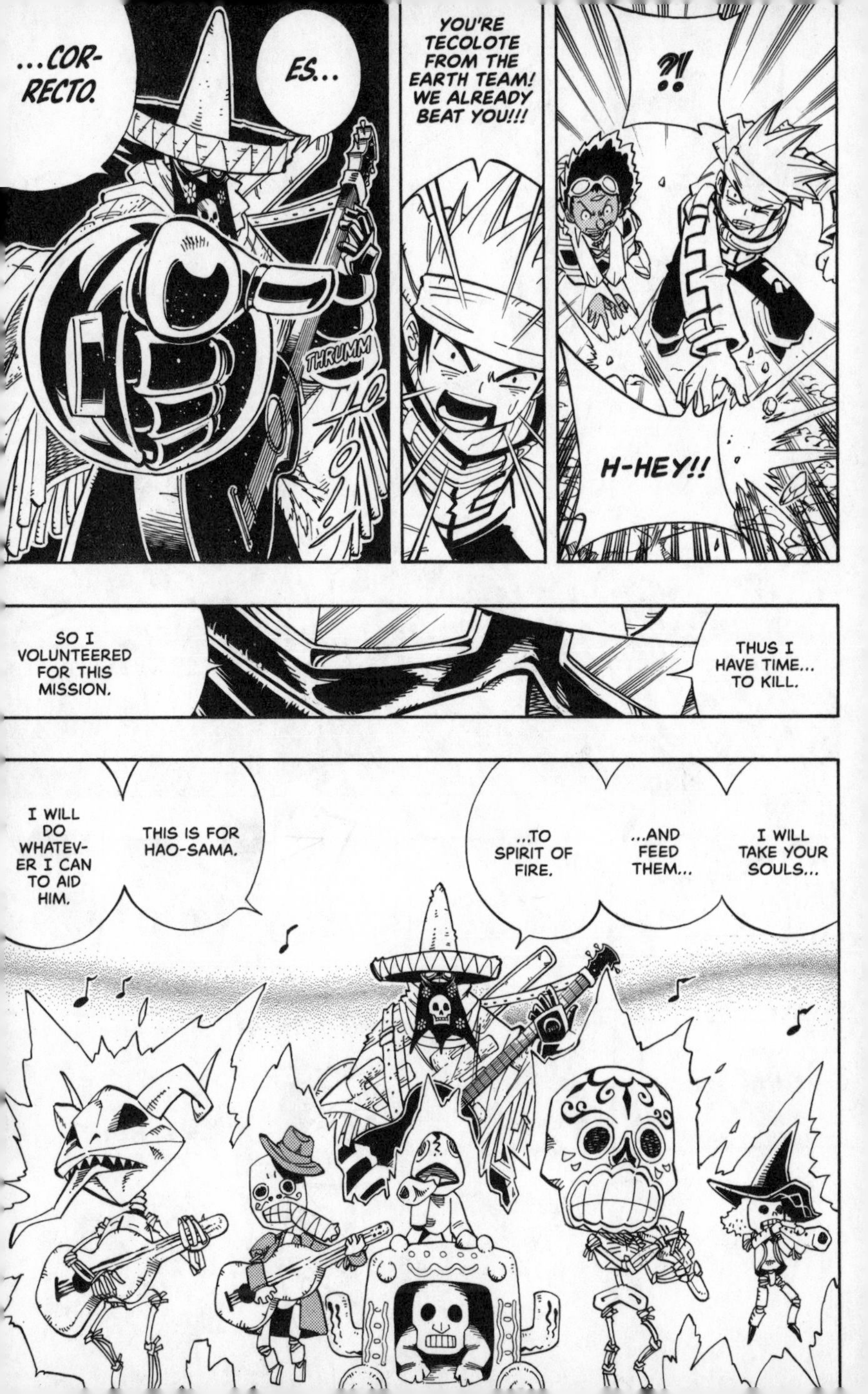
?!
H-HEY!!
YOU'RE TECOLOTE FROM THE EARTH TEAM! WE ALREADY BEAT YOU!!!
ES...
...COR-RECTO.
THRUMM
THUS I HAVE TIME... TO KILL.
SO I VOLUNTEERED FOR THIS MISSION.
I WILL TAKE YOUR SOULS...
...AND FEED THEM...
...TO SPIRIT OF FIRE.
THIS IS FOR HAO-SAMA.
I WILL DO WHATEV-ER I CAN TO AID HIM.

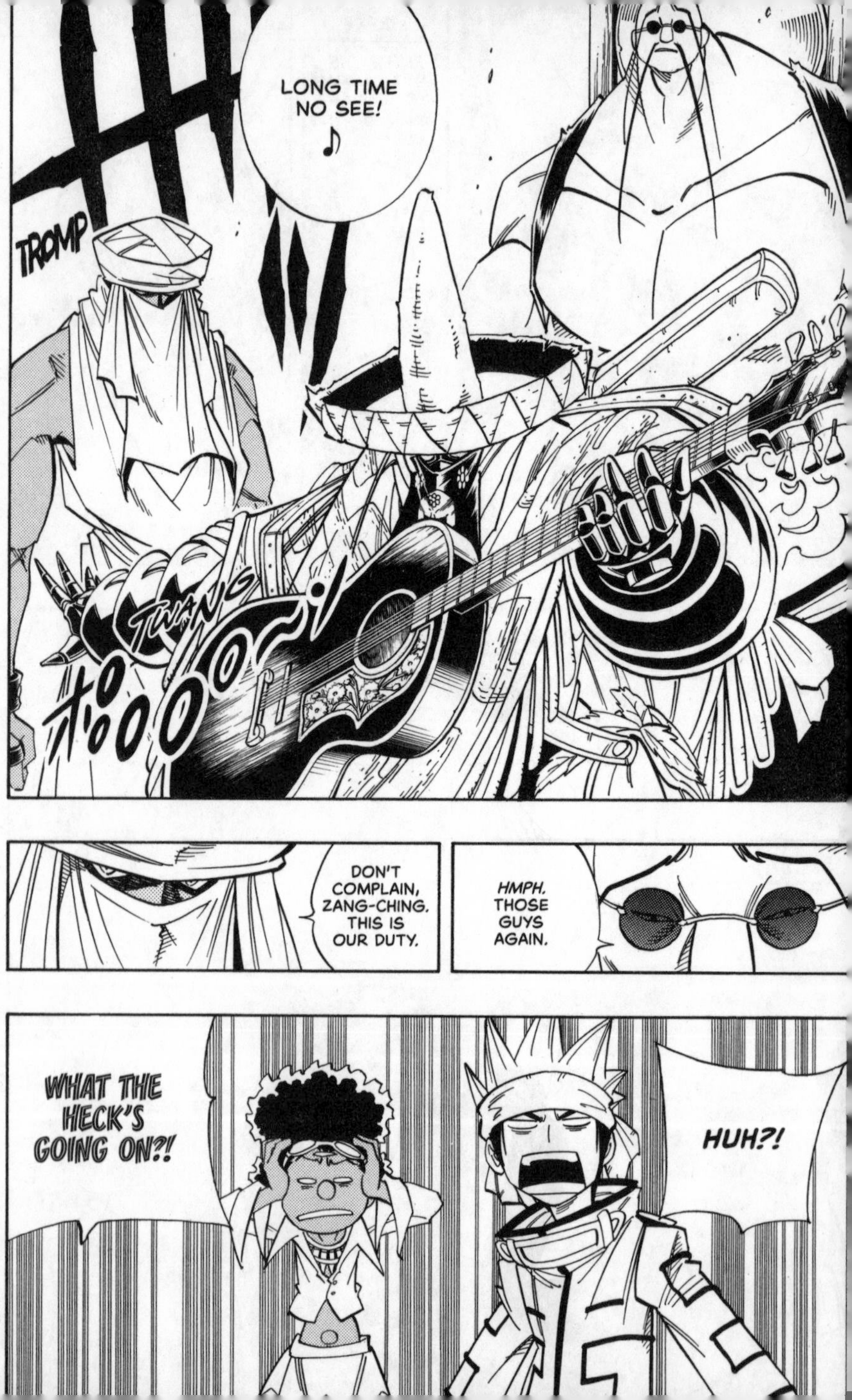
LONG TIME NO SEE! ♪
TROMP
TWANG
HMPH. THOSE GUYS AGAIN.
DON'T COMPLAIN, ZANG-CHING. THIS IS OUR DUTY.
HUH?!
WHAT THE HECK'S GOING ON?!

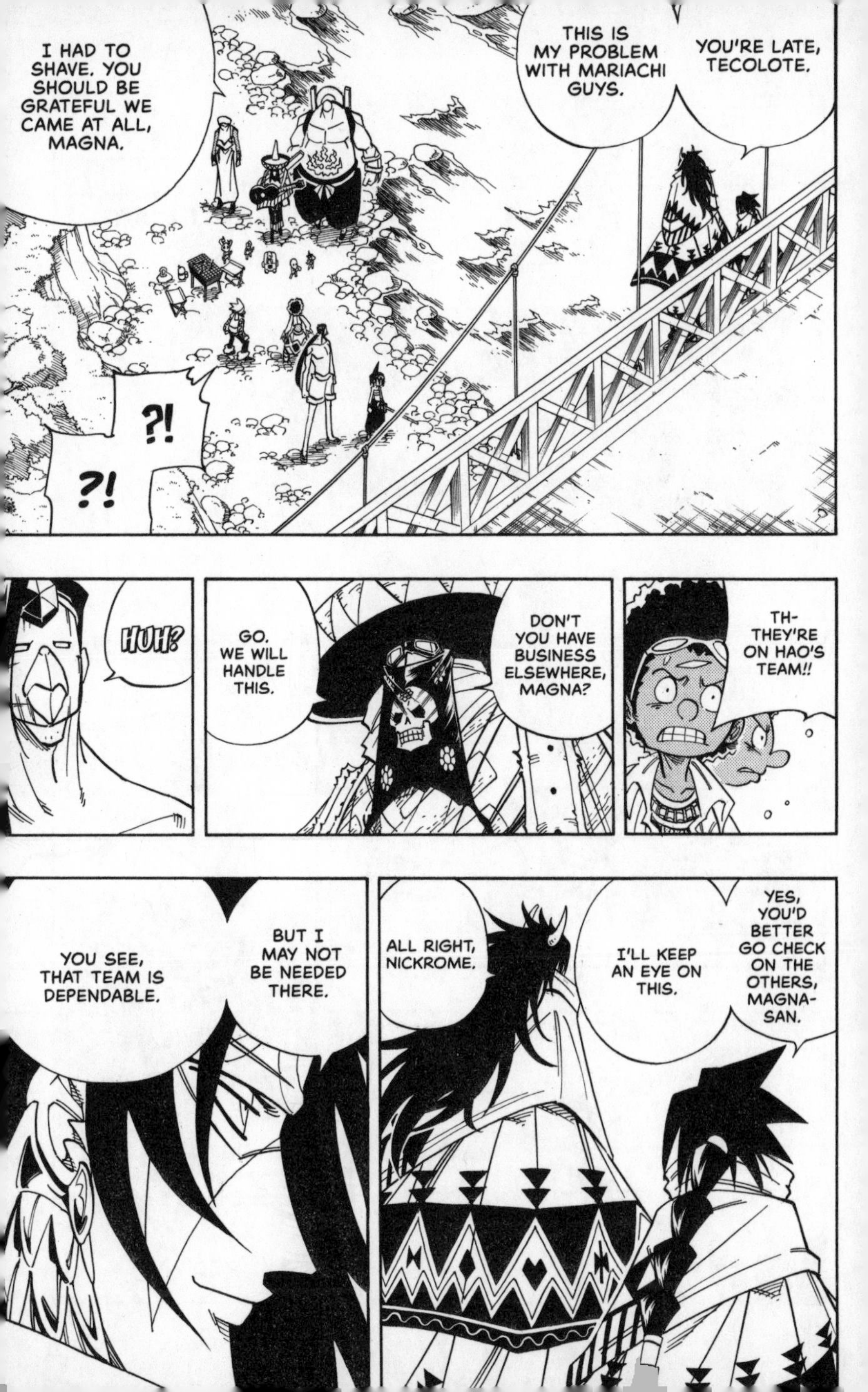
YOU'RE LATE, TECOLOTE.
THIS IS MY PROBLEM WITH MARIACHI GUYS.
I HAD TO SHAVE. YOU SHOULD BE GRATEFUL WE CAME AT ALL, MAGNA.
?!
?!
TH- THEY'RE ON HAO'S TEAM!!
DON'T YOU HAVE BUSINESS ELSEWHERE, MAGNA?
GO. WE WILL HANDLE THIS.
HUH?
YES, YOU'D BETTER GO CHECK ON THE OTHERS, MAGNA-SAN.
I'LL KEEP AN EYE ON THIS.
ALL RIGHT, NICKROME.
BUT I MAY NOT BE NEEDED THERE.
YOU SEE, THAT TEAM IS DEPENDABLE.

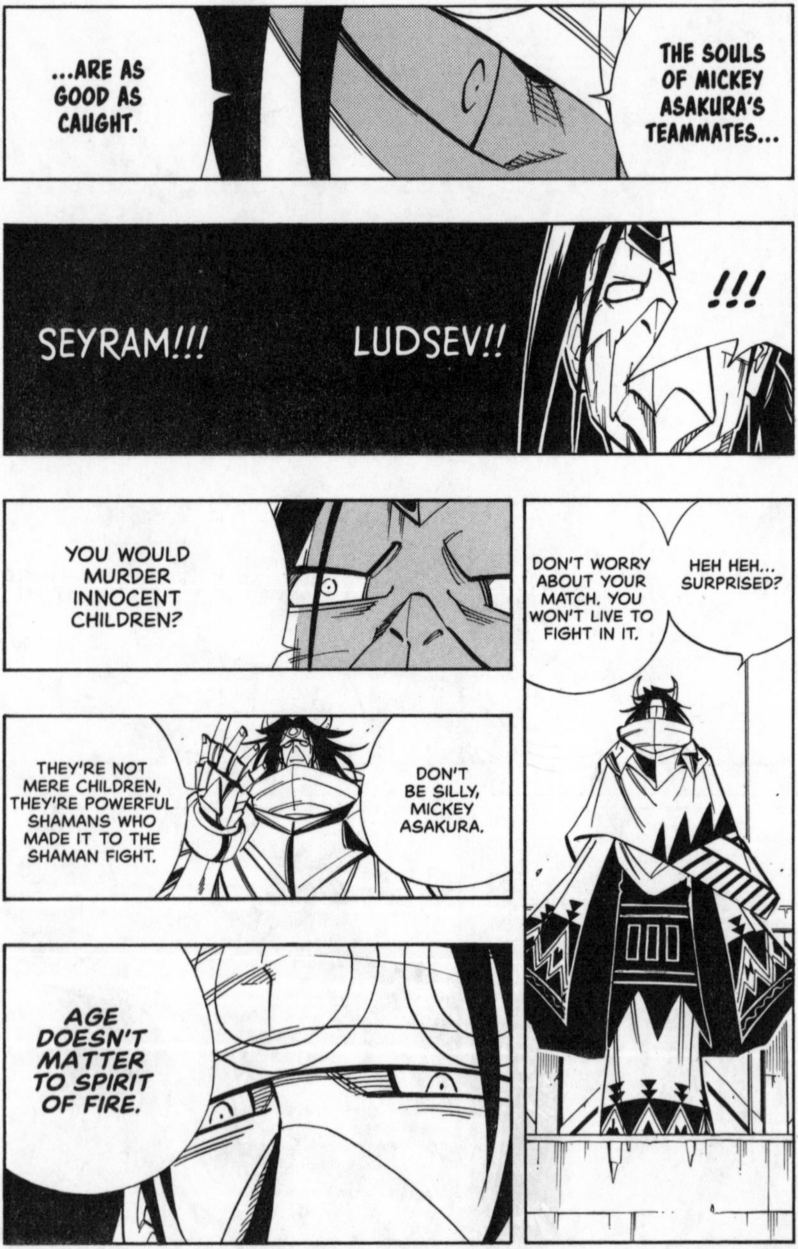
THE SOULS OF MICKEY ASAKURA'S TEAMMATES...
...ARE AS GOOD AS CAUGHT.
!!!
LUDSEV!!
SEYRAM!!!
HEH HEH... SURPRISED?
DON'T WORRY ABOUT YOUR MATCH. YOU WON'T LIVE TO FIGHT IN IT.
YOU WOULD MURDER INNOCENT CHILDREN?
DON'T BE SILLY, MICKEY ASAKURA.
THEY'RE NOT MERE CHILDREN, THEY'RE POWERFUL SHAMANS WHO MADE IT TO THE SHAMAN FIGHT.
AGE DOESN'T MATTER TO SPIRIT OF FIRE.

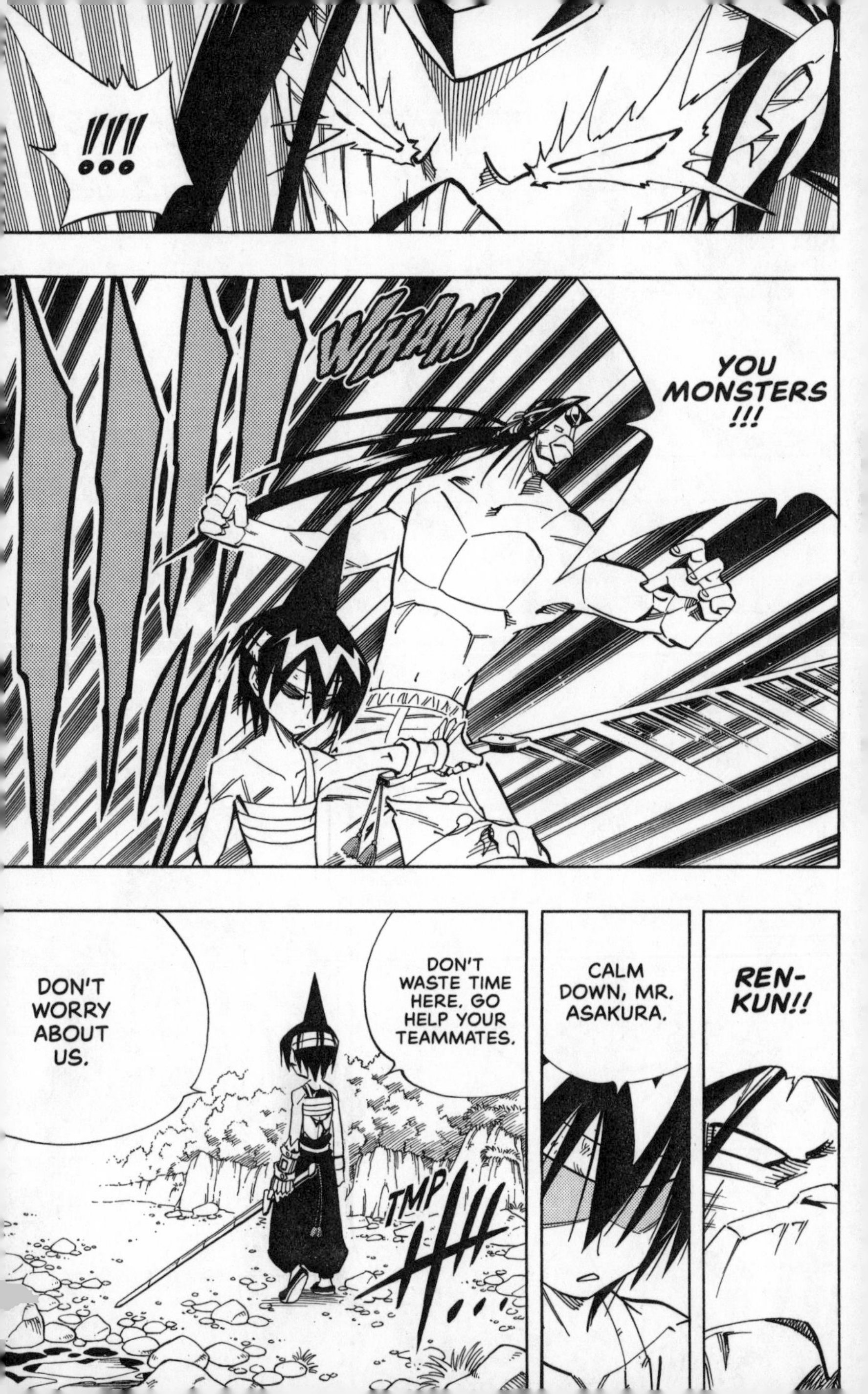
!!!
YOU MONSTERS !!!
WHAM
REN-KUN!!
CALM DOWN, MR. ASAKURA.
DON'T WASTE TIME HERE. GO HELP YOUR TEAMMATES.
DON'T WORRY ABOUT US.
TMP

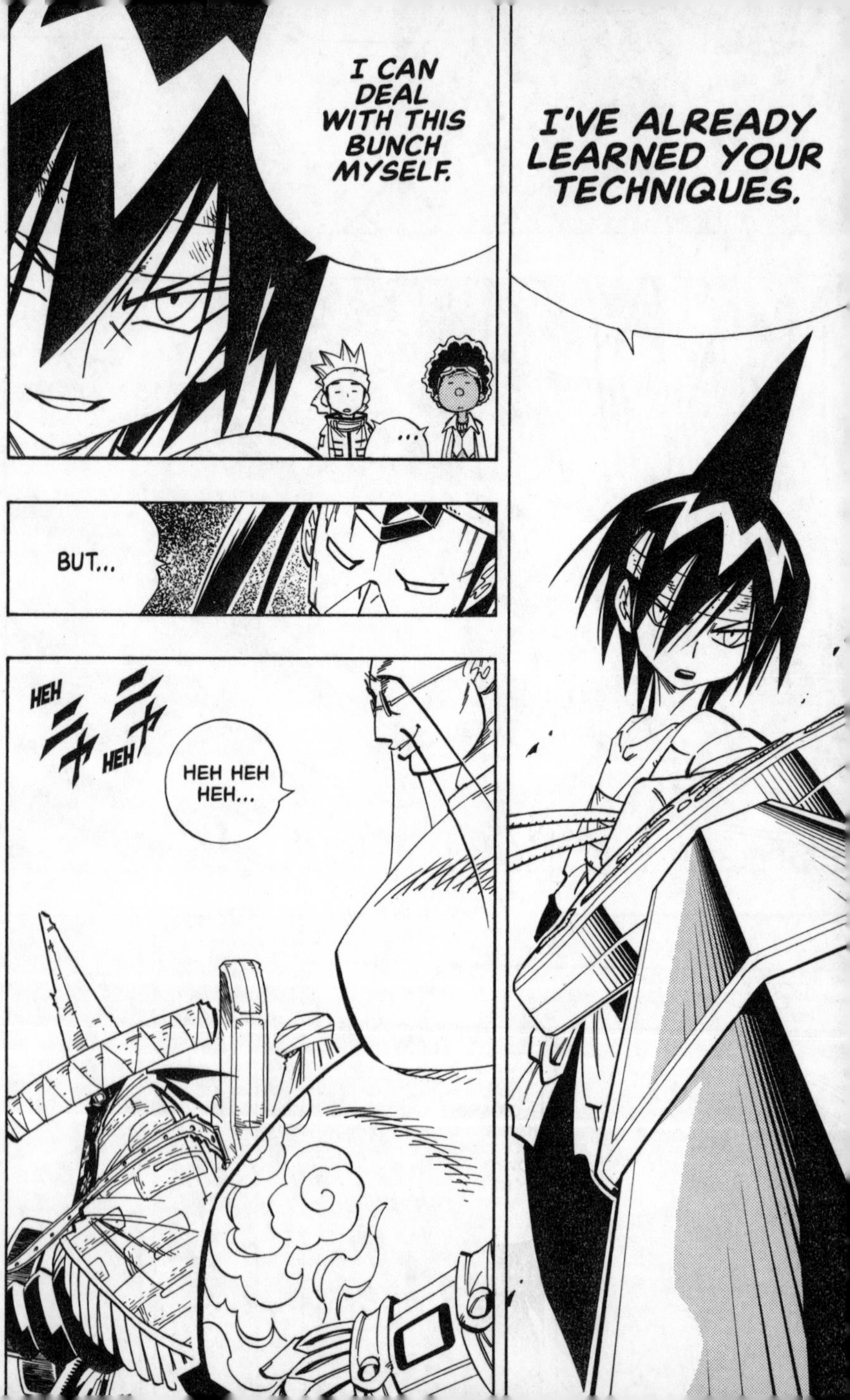
I'VE ALREADY LEARNED YOUR TECHNIQUES.
I CAN DEAL WITH THIS BUNCH MYSELF.
...
BUT...
HEH HEH HEH...
HEH
HEH

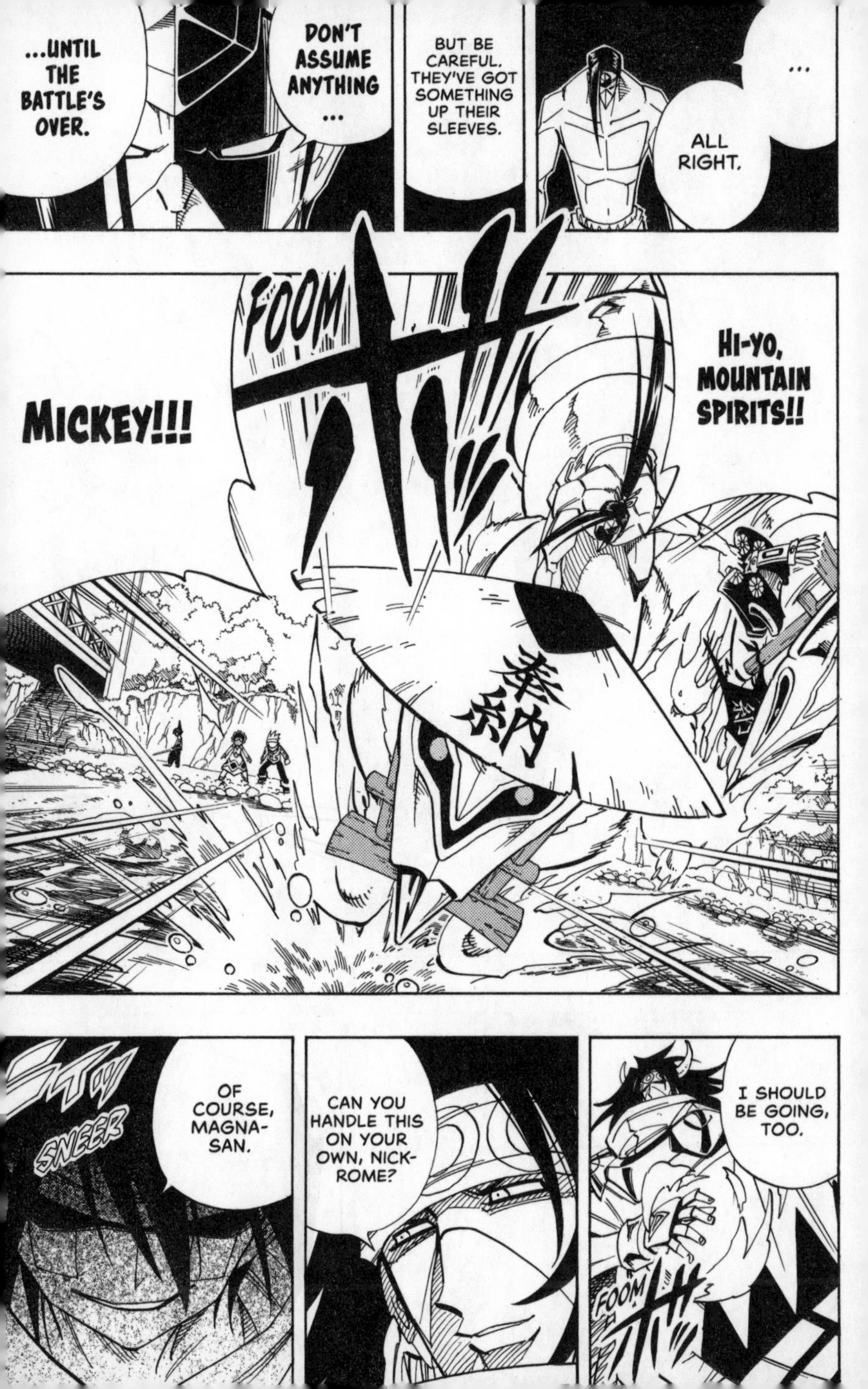
...
ALL RIGHT.
BUT BE CAREFUL. THEY'VE GOT SOMETHING UP THEIR SLEEVES.
DON'T ASSUME ANYTHING ...
...UNTIL THE BATTLE'S OVER.
Hi-yo, MOUNTAIN SPIRITS!!
FOOM
MICKEY!!!
I SHOULD BE GOING, TOO.
FOOM
CAN YOU HANDLE THIS ON YOUR OWN, NICK-ROME?
OF COURSE, MAGNA-SAN.
SNEER

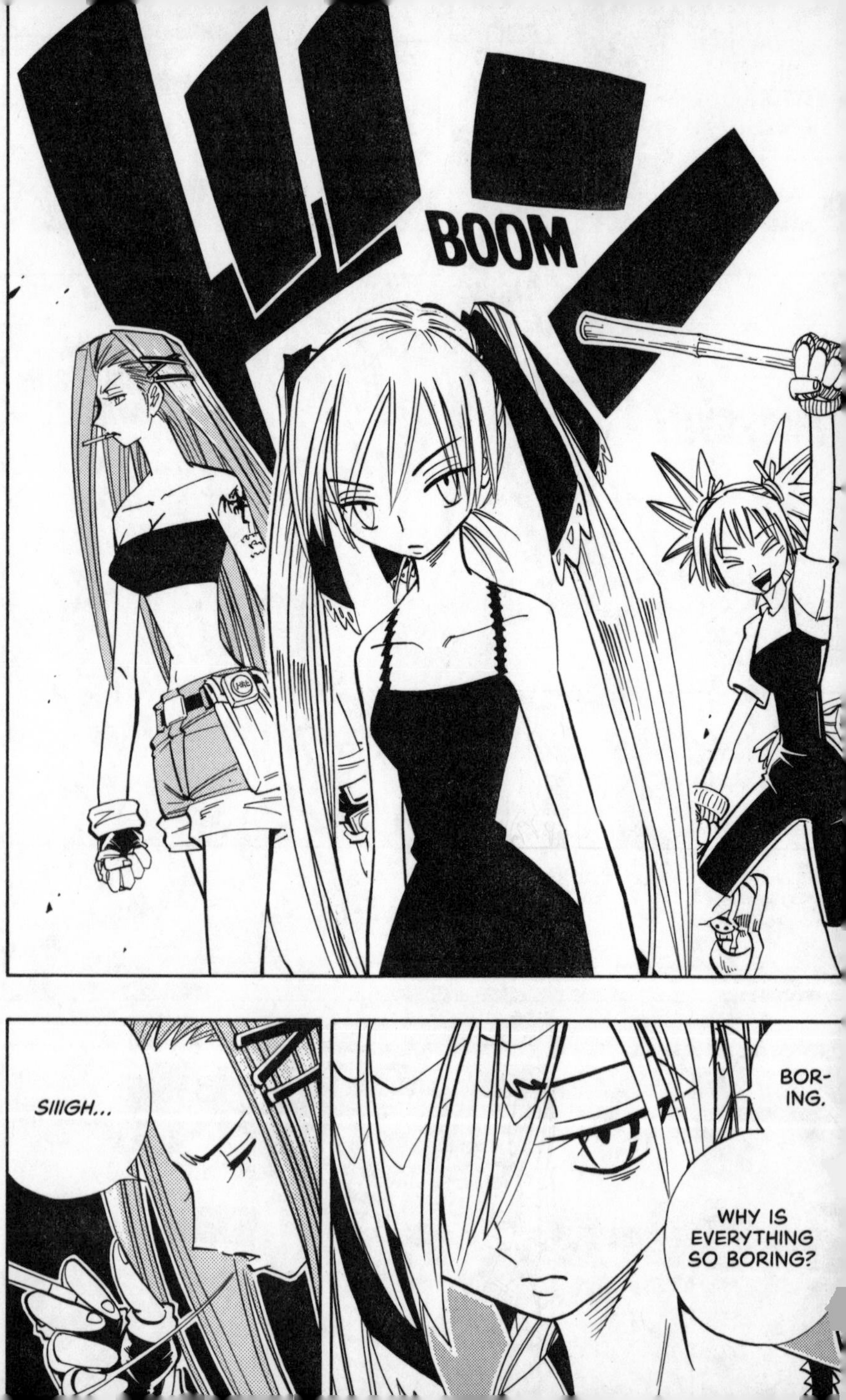
BOOM
BOR-ING.
WHY IS EVERYTHING SO BORING?
SIIIGH...

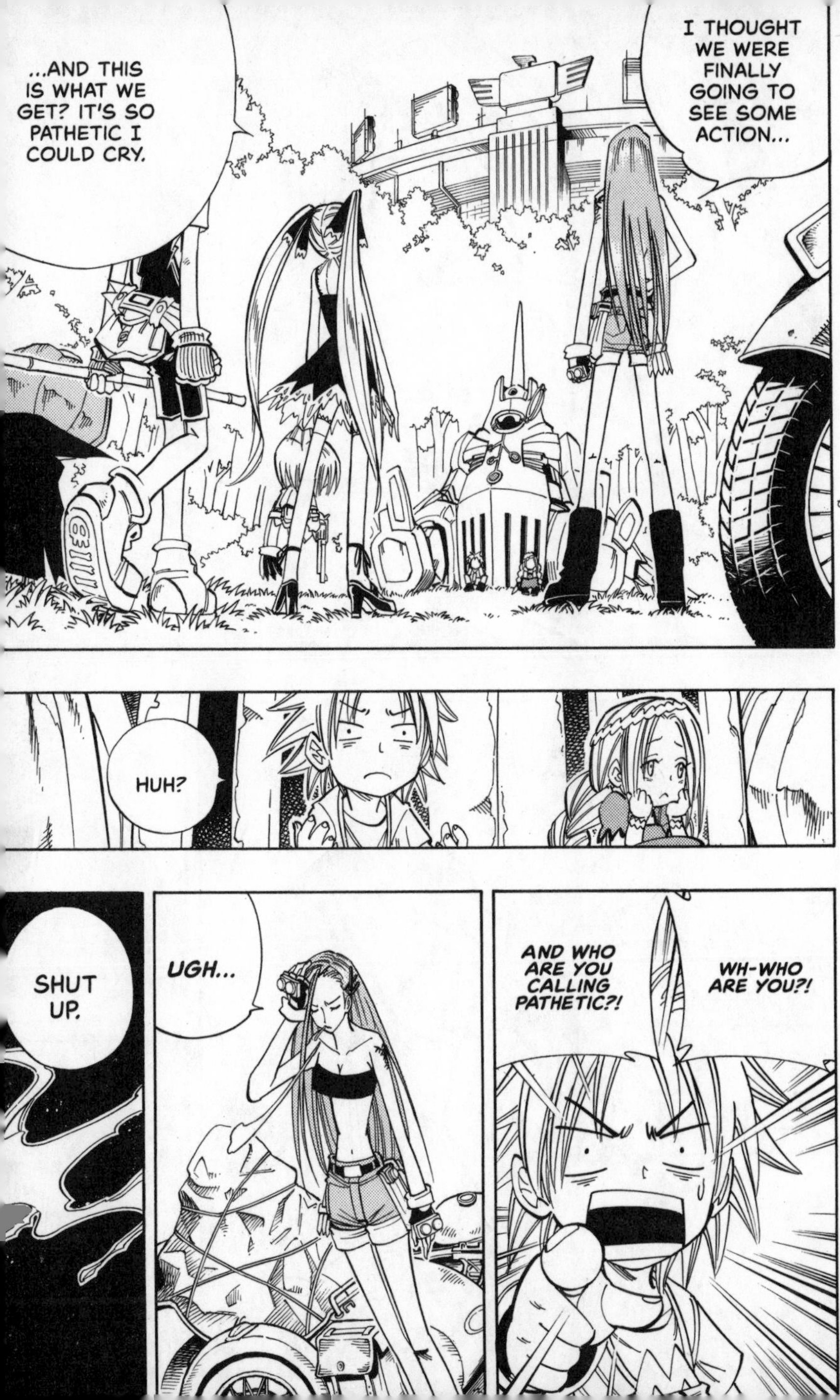
I THOUGHT WE WERE FINALLY GOING TO SEE SOME ACTION...
...AND THIS IS WHAT WE GET? IT'S SO PATHETIC I COULD CRY.
HUH?
WH-WHO ARE YOU?!
AND WHO ARE YOU CALLING PATHETIC?!
UGH...
SHUT UP.

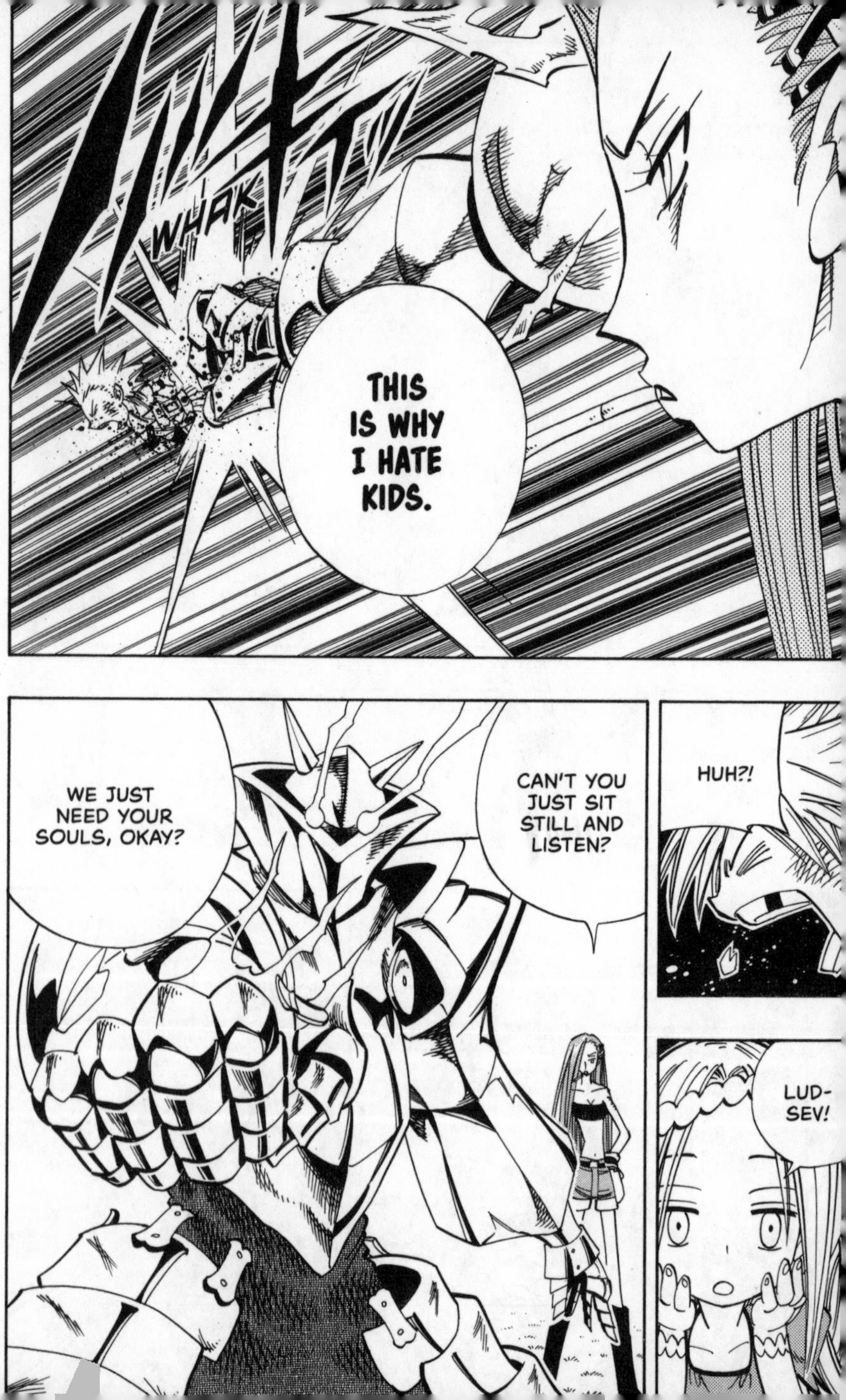
WHAK
THIS IS WHY I HATE KIDS.
HUH?!
LUD-SEV!
CAN'T YOU JUST SIT STILL AND LISTEN?
WE JUST NEED YOUR SOULS, OKAY?

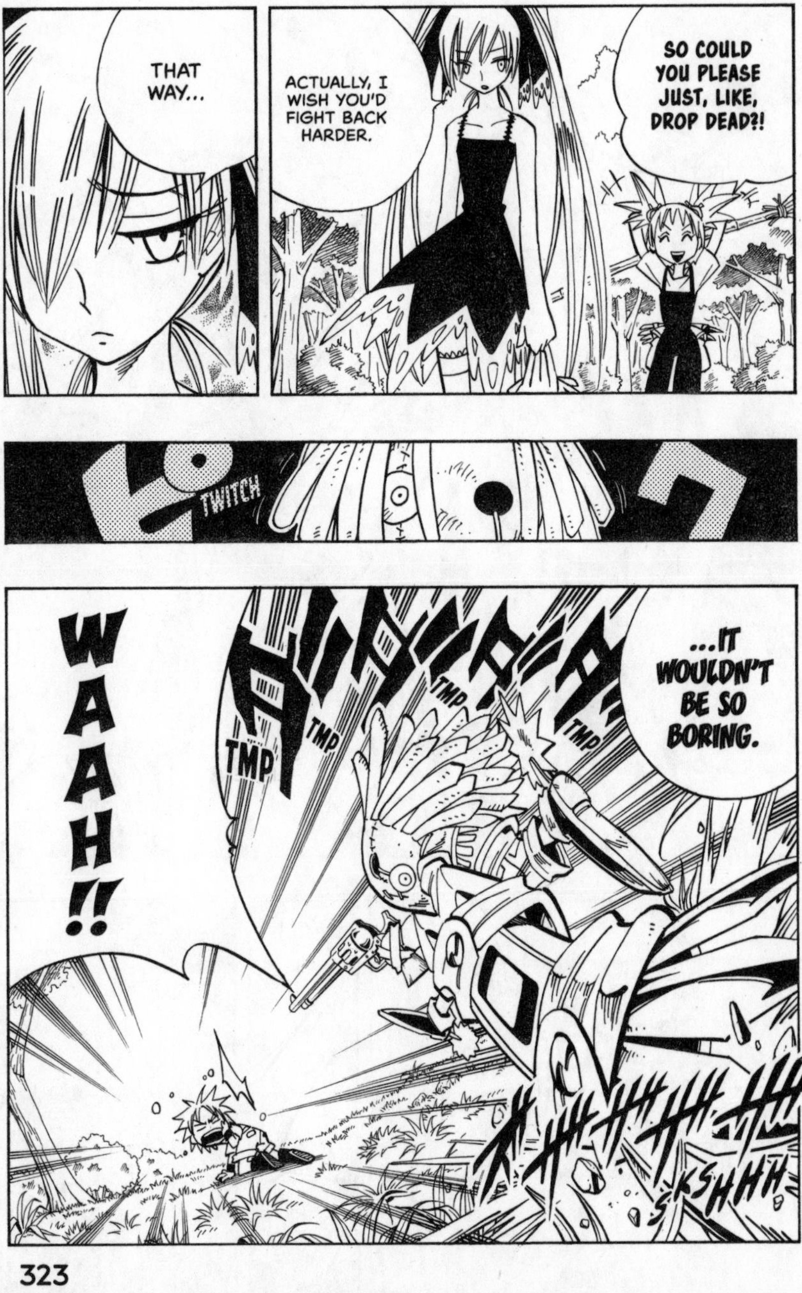
SO COULD YOU PLEASE JUST, LIKE, DROP DEAD?!
ACTUALLY, I WISH YOU'D FIGHT BACK HARDER.
THAT WAY...
TWITCH
...IT WOULDN'T BE SO BORING.
TMP TMP TMP TMP
WAAAH!!
SKSHHH

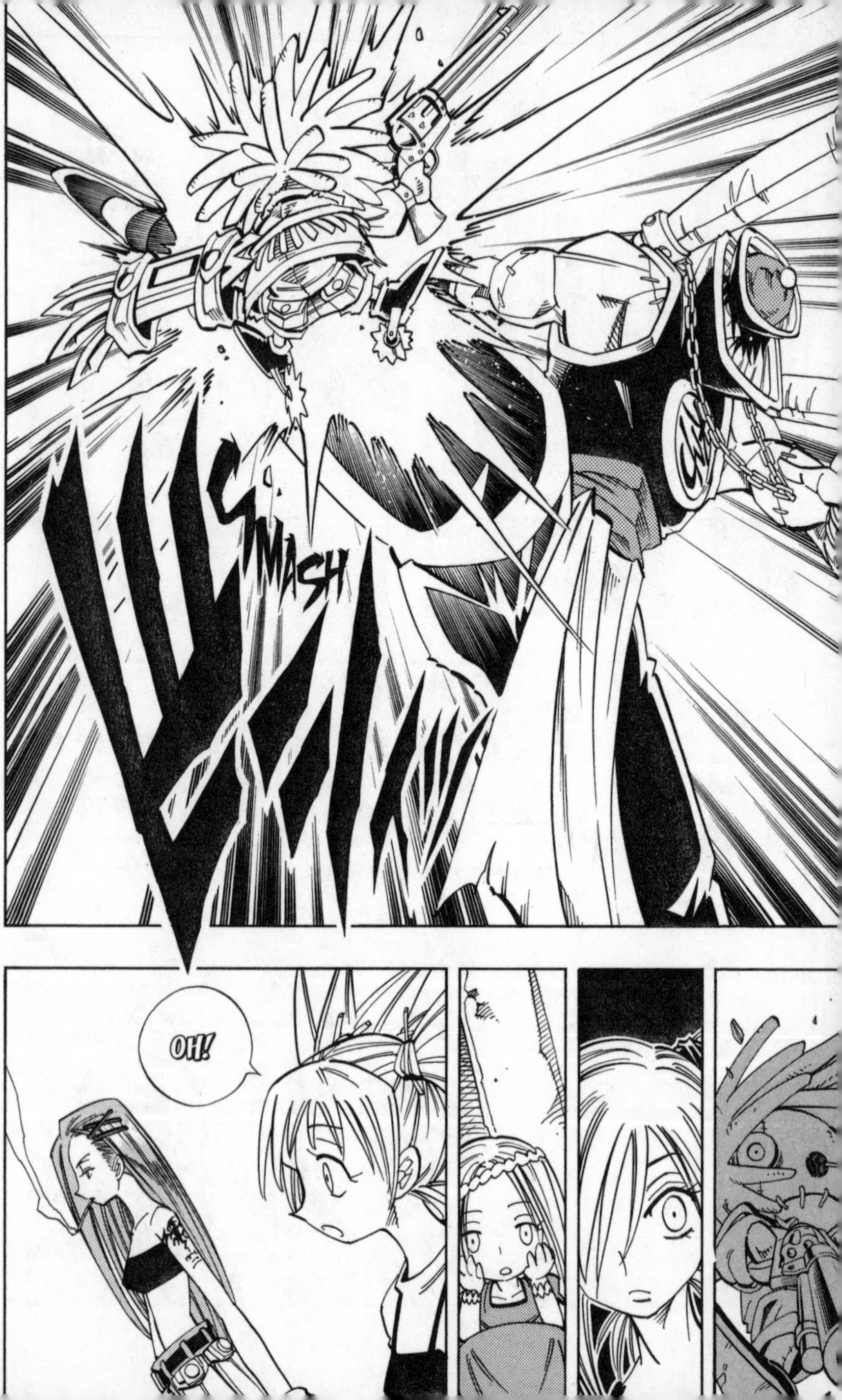
SMASH
OH!

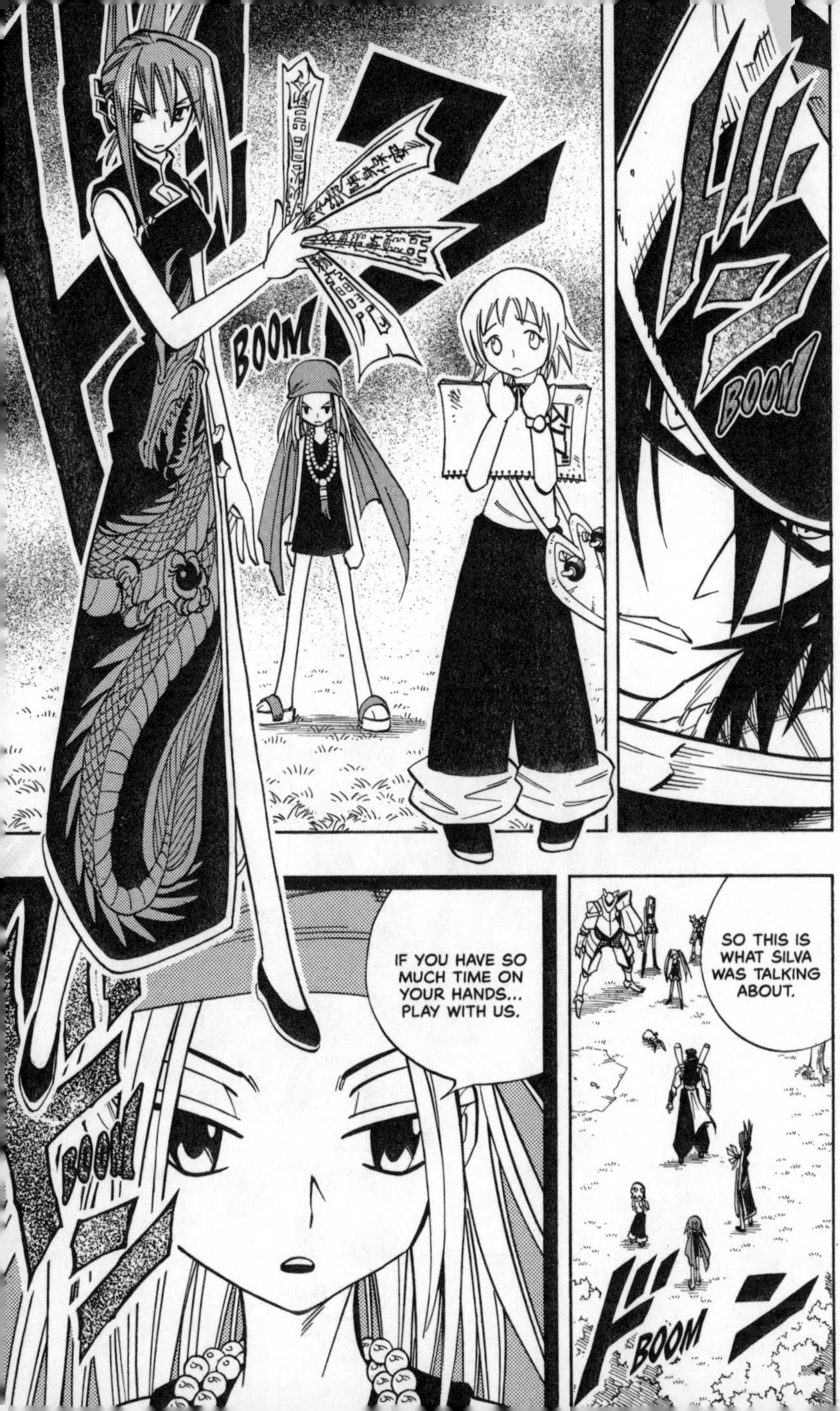
BOOM
BOOM
SO THIS IS WHAT SILVA WAS TALKING ABOUT.
BOOM
IF YOU HAVE SO MUCH TIME ON YOUR HANDS... PLAY WITH US.
BOOM

Zang-Ching

January 2001

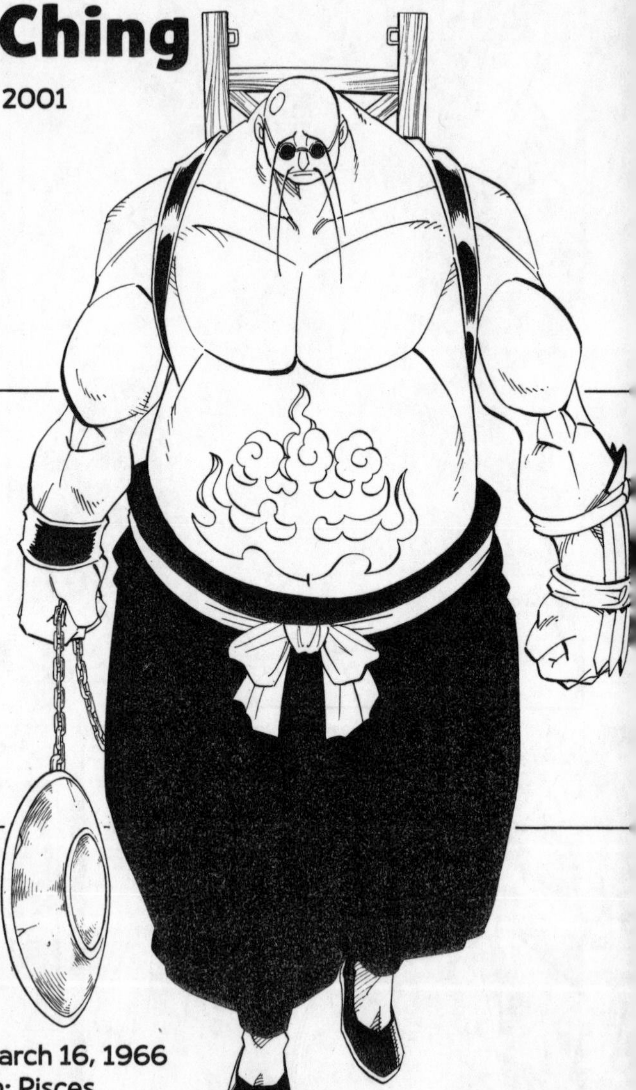

Age: 34
Date of Birth: March 16, 1966
Astrological Sign: Pisces
Blood Type: O

Chapter 150: The Shamanic Oracle

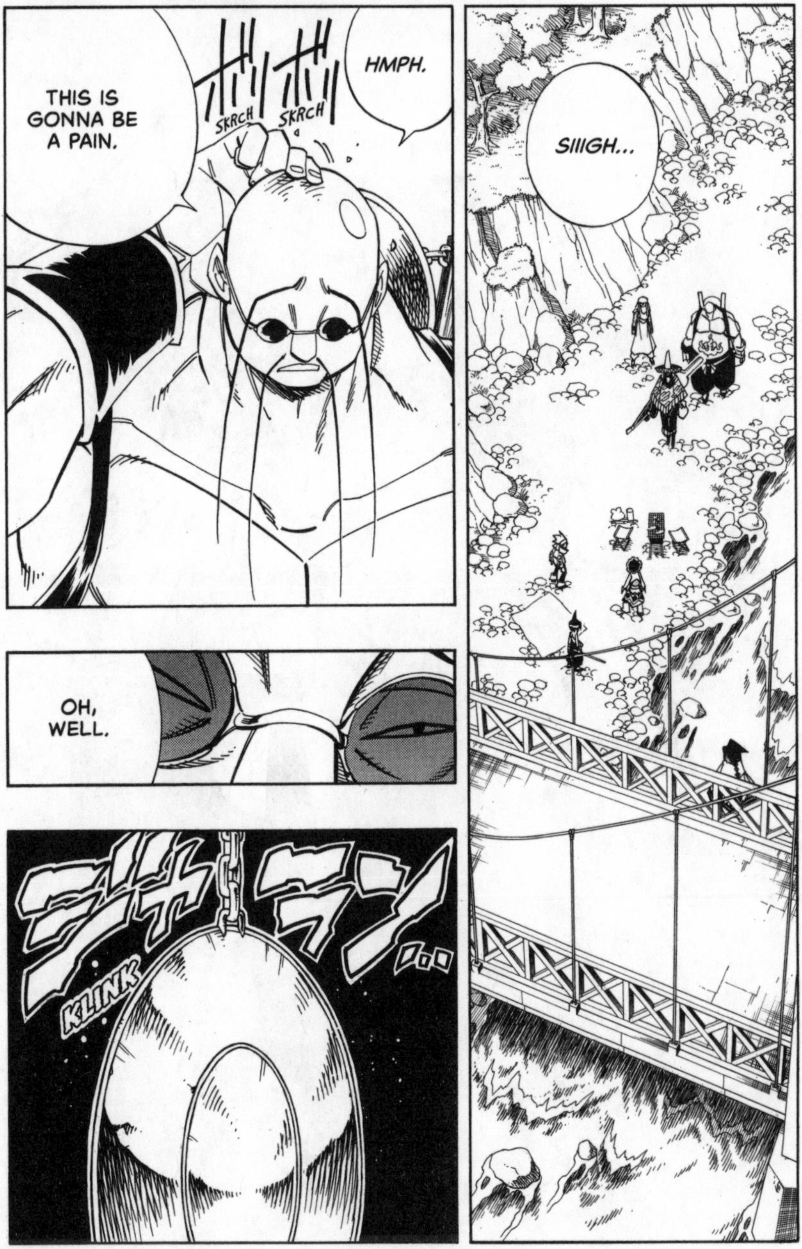
SIIIGH...
HMPH.
SKRCH
SKRCH
THIS IS GONNA BE A PAIN.
OH, WELL.
KLINK

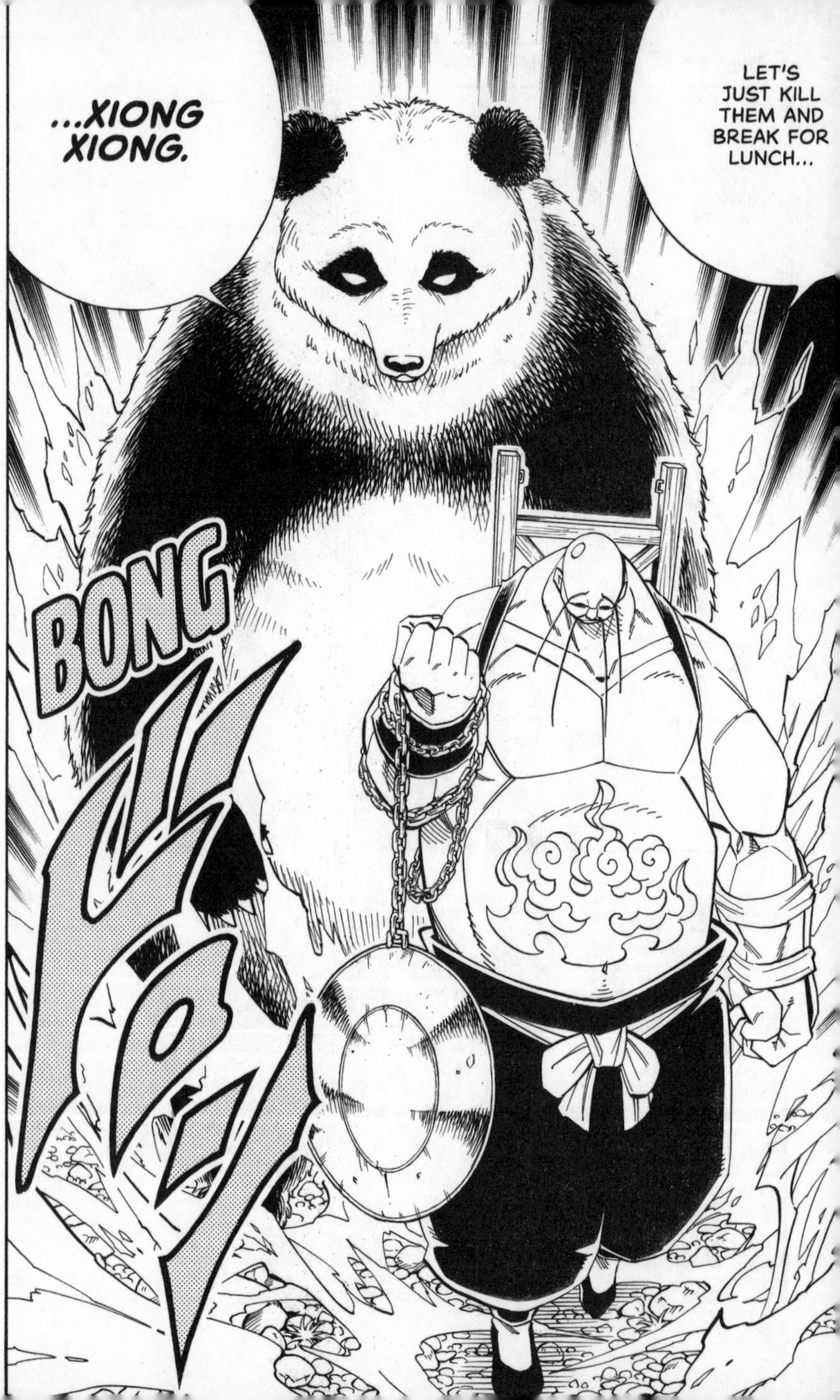
LET'S JUST KILL THEM AND BREAK FOR LUNCH...
...XIONG XIONG.
BONG

Chapter 150:

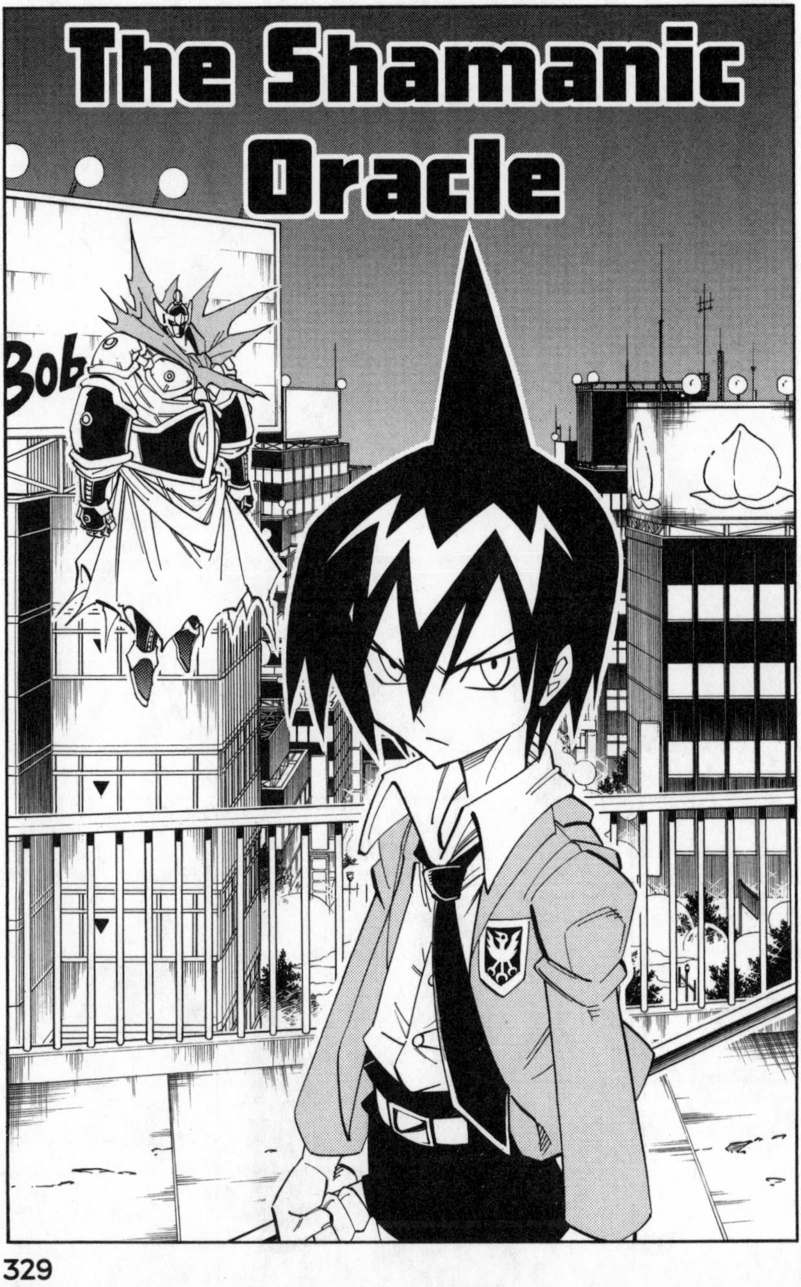
The Shamanic Oracle
Bob

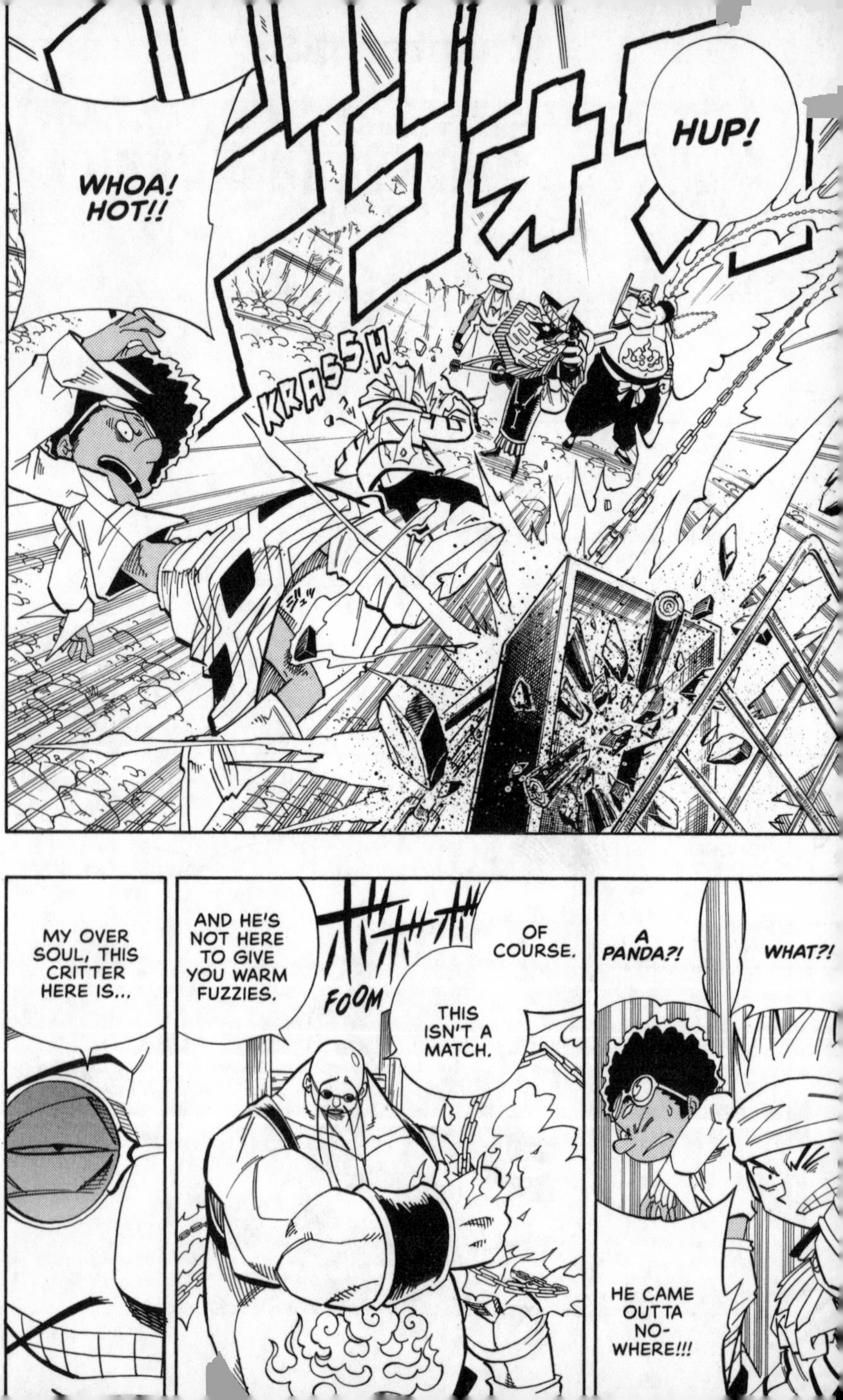
HUP!
WHOA! HOT!!
KRASSH
WHAT?!
A PANDA?!
HE CAME OUTTA NO-WHERE!!!
OF COURSE.
THIS ISN'T A MATCH.
AND HE'S NOT HERE TO GIVE YOU WARM FUZZIES.
FOOM
MY OVER SOUL, THIS CRITTER HERE IS...

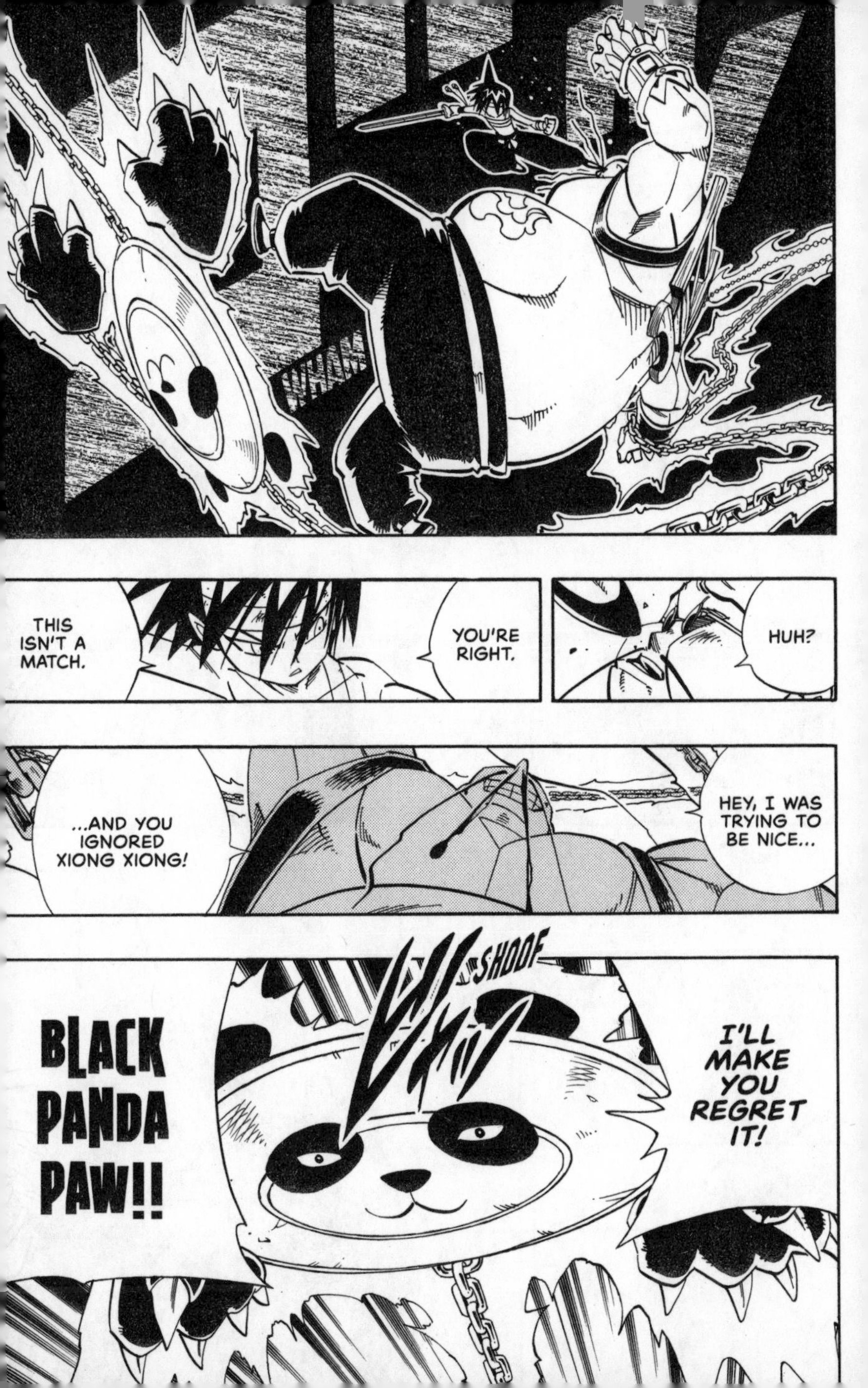
HUH?
YOU'RE RIGHT.
THIS ISN'T A MATCH.
HEY, I WAS TRYING TO BE NICE...
...AND YOU IGNORED XIONG XIONG!
I'LL MAKE YOU REGRET IT!
SHOOF
BLACK PANDA PAW!!

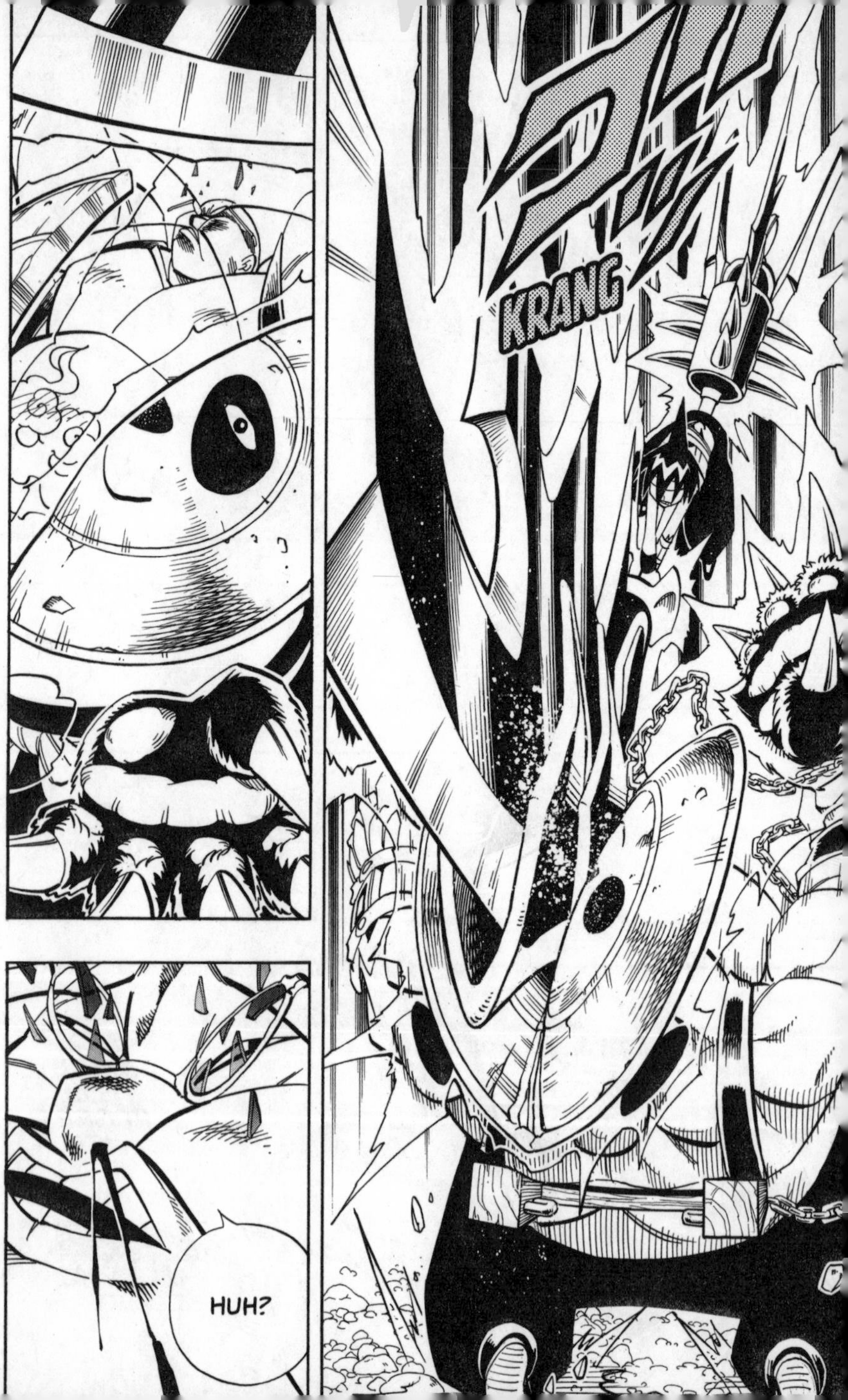
KRANG
HUH?

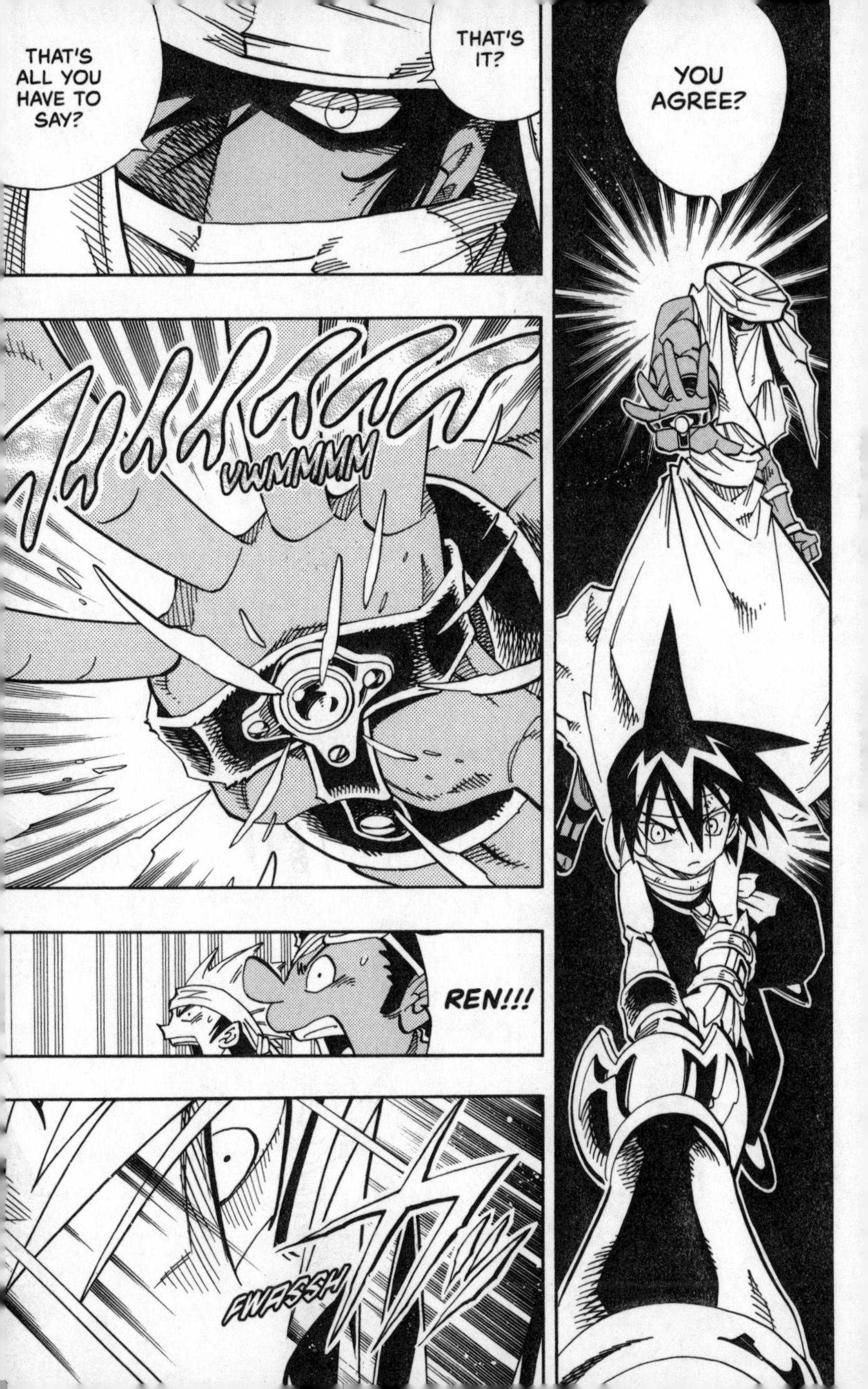
YOU AGREE?
THAT'S IT?
THAT'S ALL YOU HAVE TO SAY?
VWMMMM
REN!!!
FWASSH

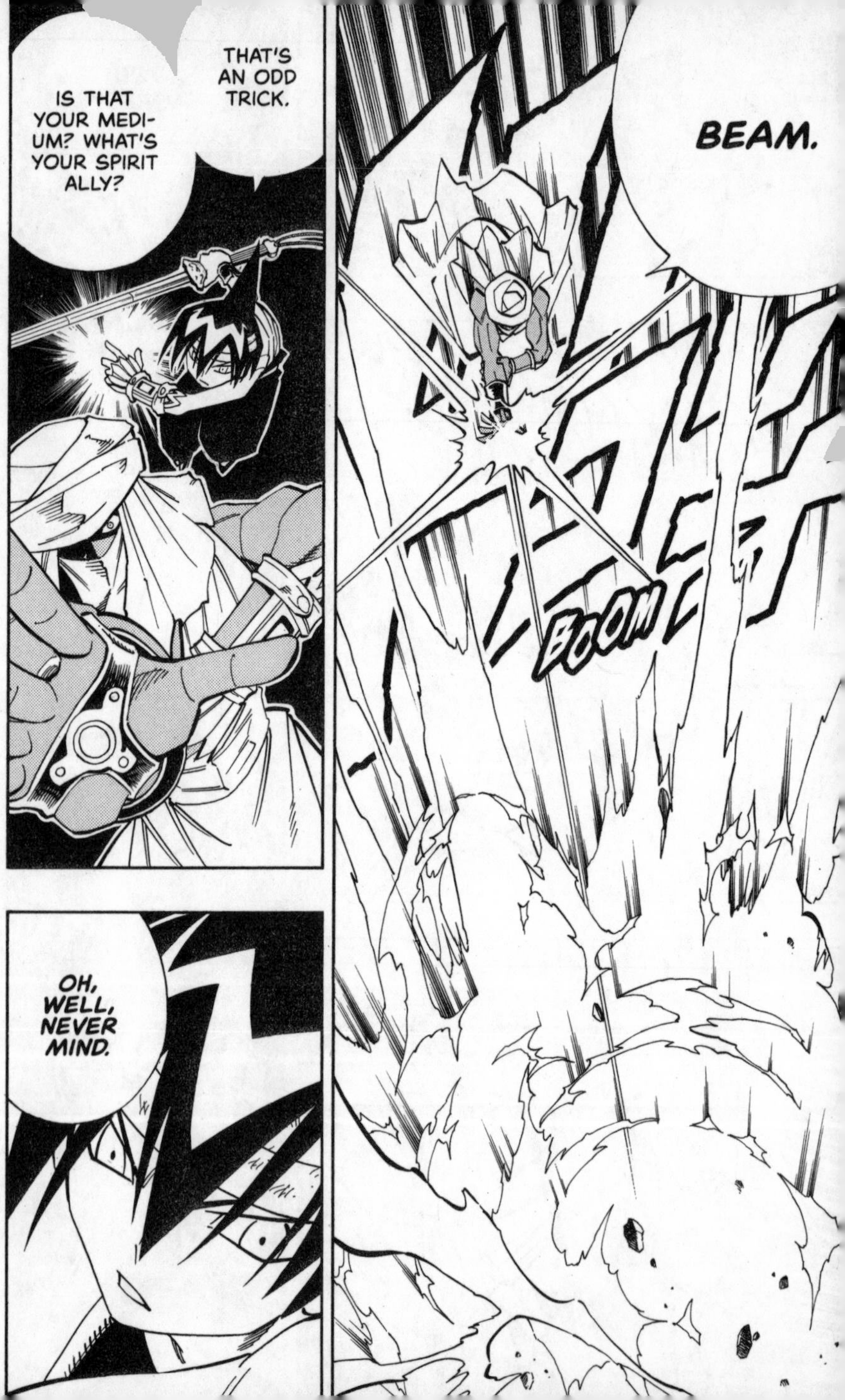
BEAM.
BOOM
THAT'S AN ODD TRICK.
IS THAT YOUR MEDI-UM? WHAT'S YOUR SPIRIT ALLY?
OH, WELL, NEVER MIND.

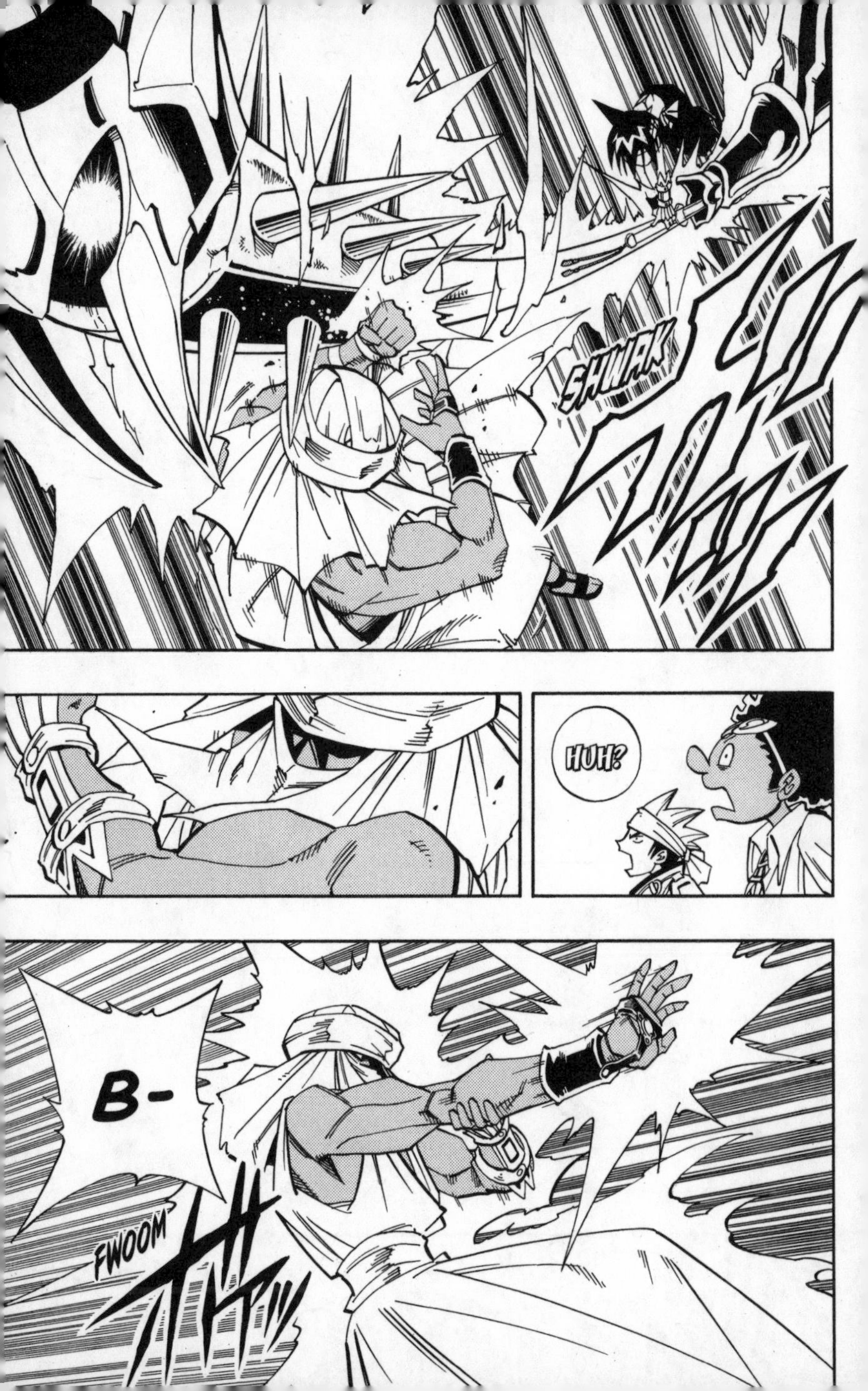
SHWAK
HUH?
B-
FWOOM

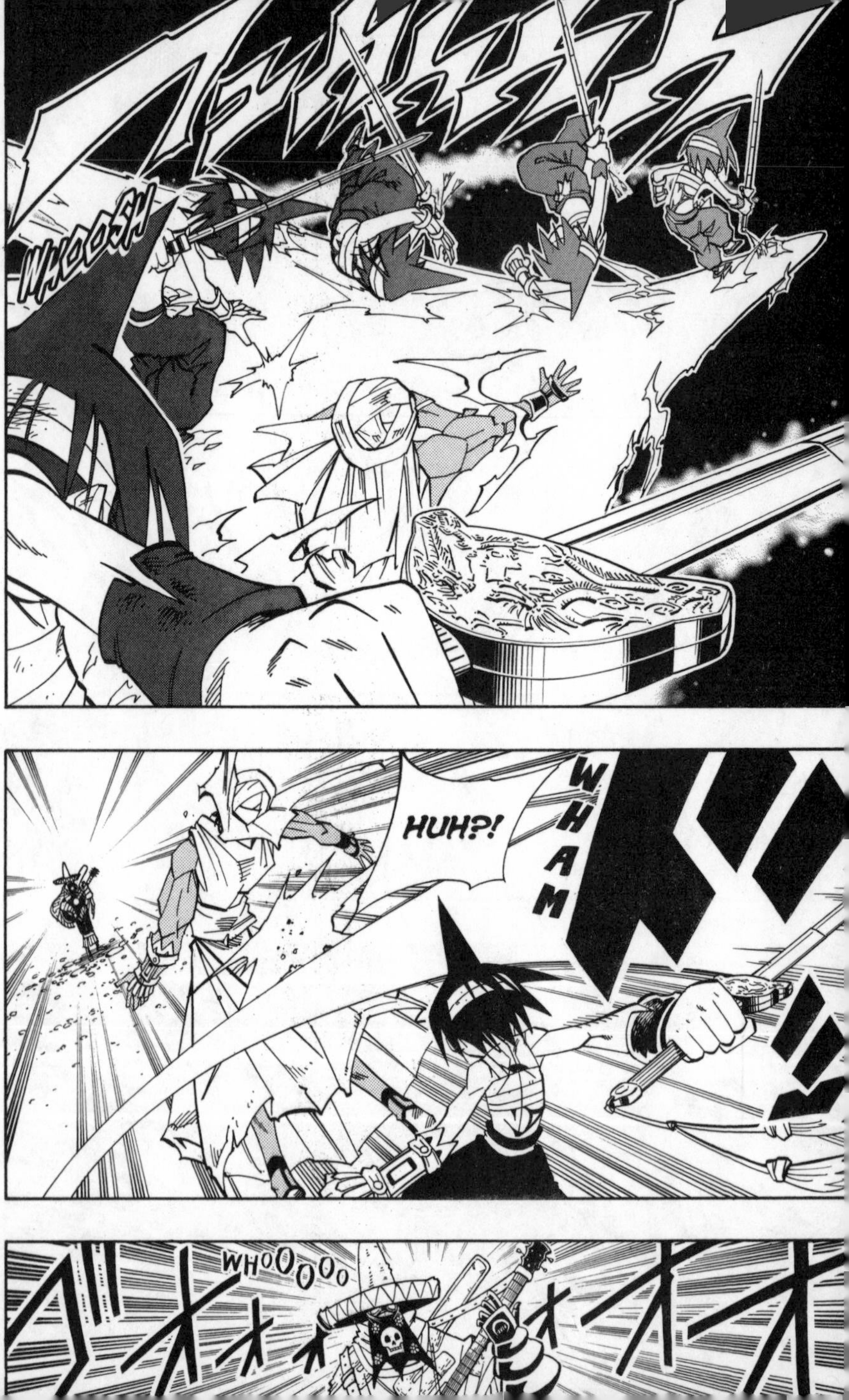
WHOOOSH
WHAM
HUH?!
WHOOOOO

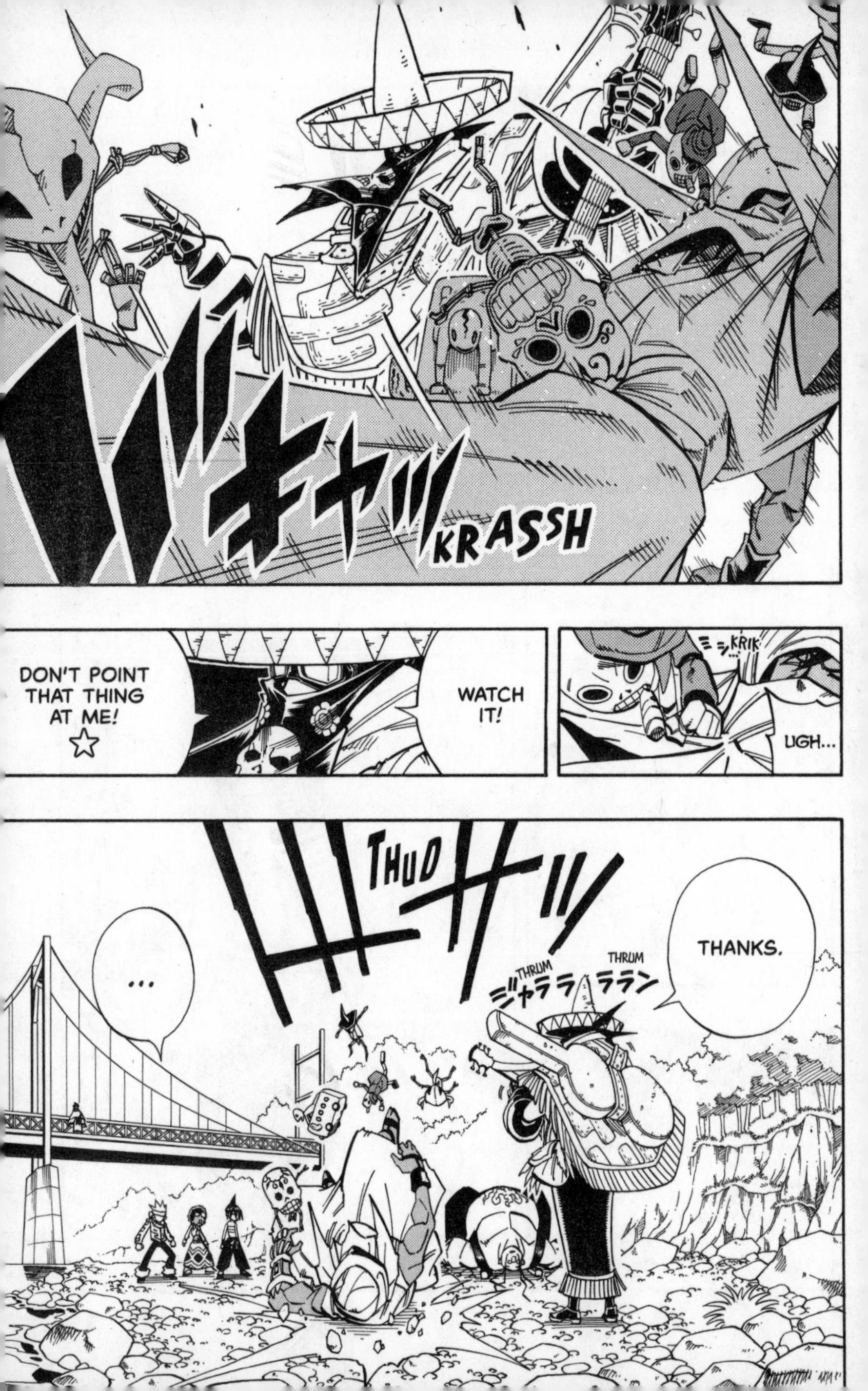

KRASSH
KRIK
UGH...
WATCH IT!
DON'T POINT THAT THING AT ME! ☆
THUD
THANKS.
THRUM THRUM
...

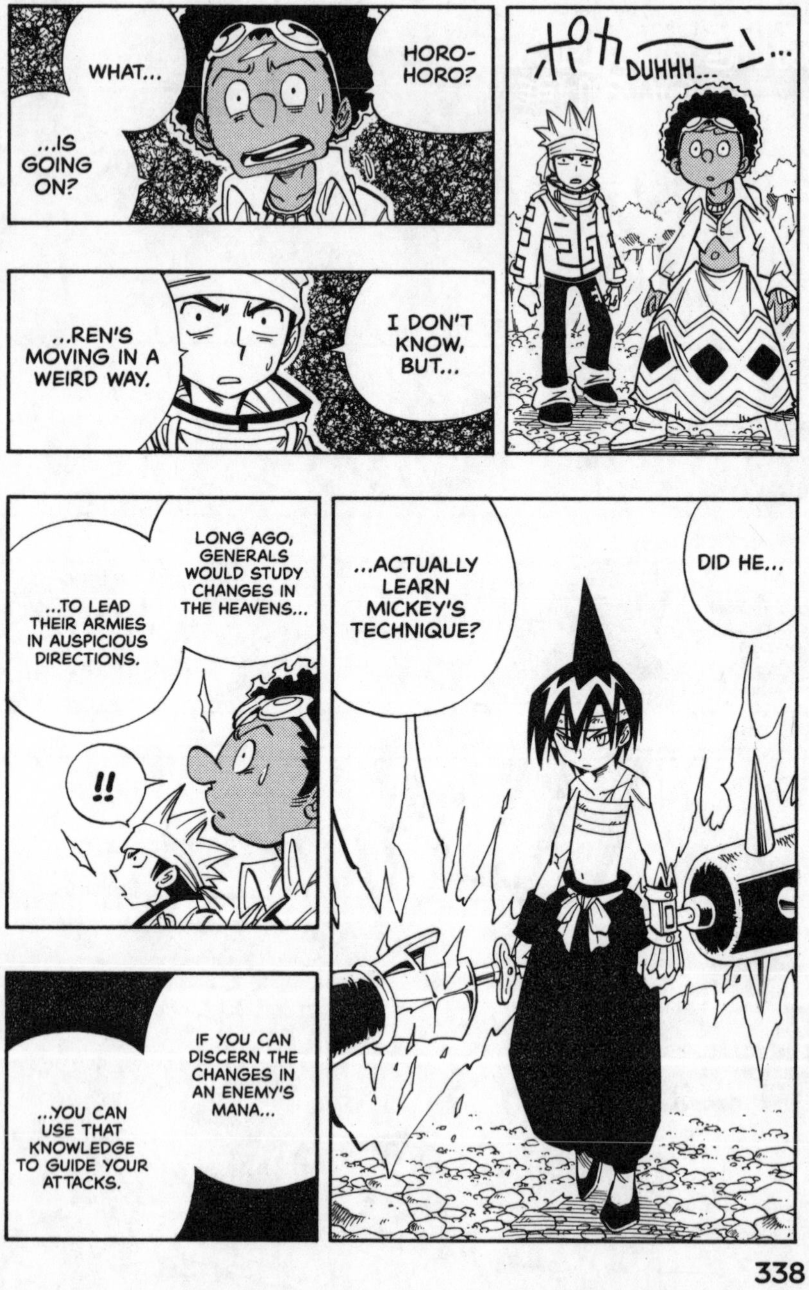
ポカーン...
DUHHH...
HORO-HORO?
WHAT...
...IS GOING ON?
I DON'T KNOW, BUT...
...REN'S MOVING IN A WEIRD WAY.
DID HE...
...ACTUALLY LEARN MICKEY'S TECHNIQUE?
LONG AGO, GENERALS WOULD STUDY CHANGES IN THE HEAVENS...
...TO LEAD THEIR ARMIES IN AUSPICIOUS DIRECTIONS.
!!
IF YOU CAN DISCERN THE CHANGES IN AN ENEMY'S MANA...
...YOU CAN USE THAT KNOWLEDGE TO GUIDE YOUR ATTACKS.

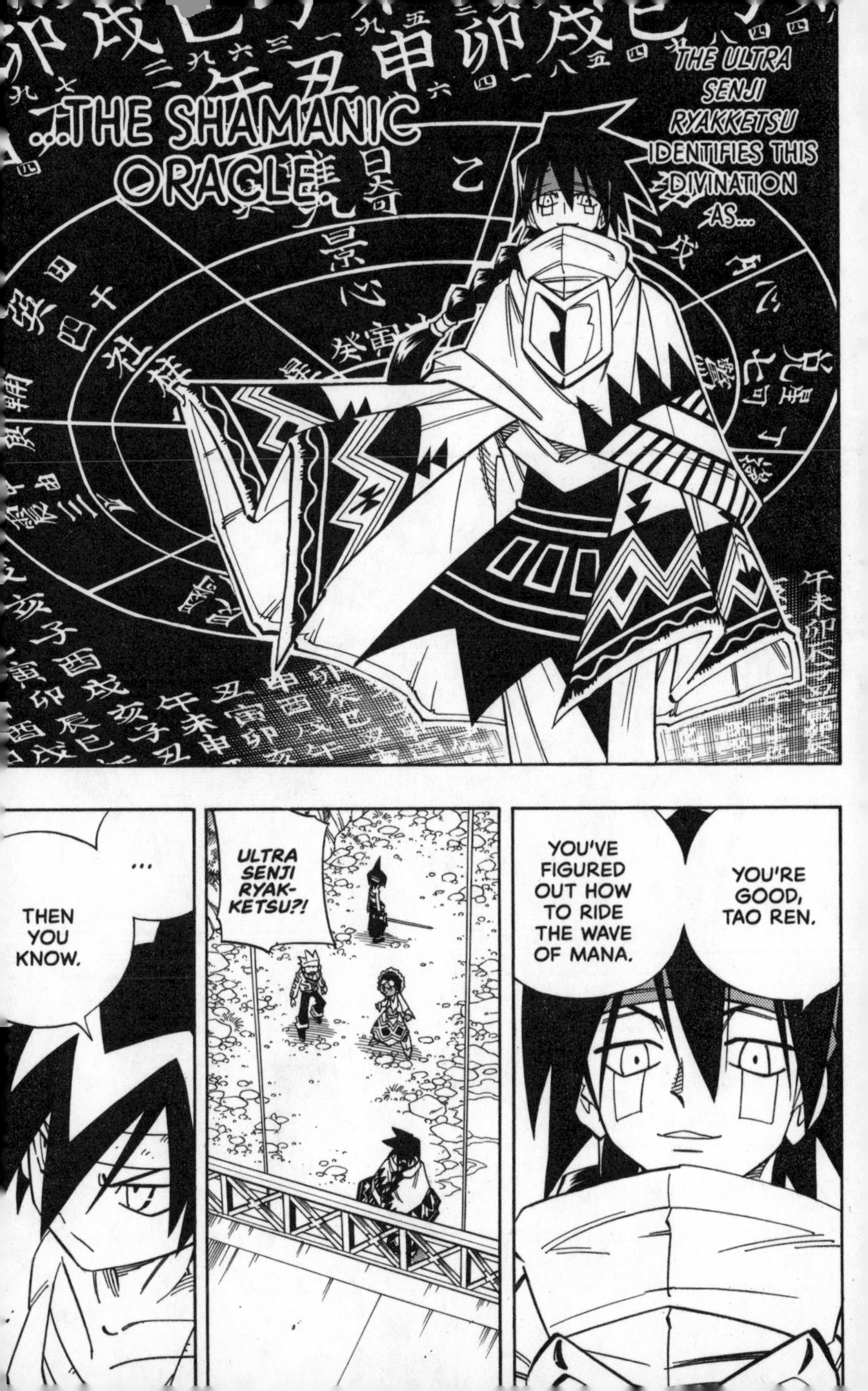
THE ULTRA SENJI RYAKKETSU IDENTIFIES THIS DIVINATION AS...
...THE SHAMANIC ORACLE.
YOU'RE GOOD, TAO REN.
YOU'VE FIGURED OUT HOW TO RIDE THE WAVE OF MANA.
ULTRA SENJI RYAK-KETSU?!
...
THEN YOU KNOW.

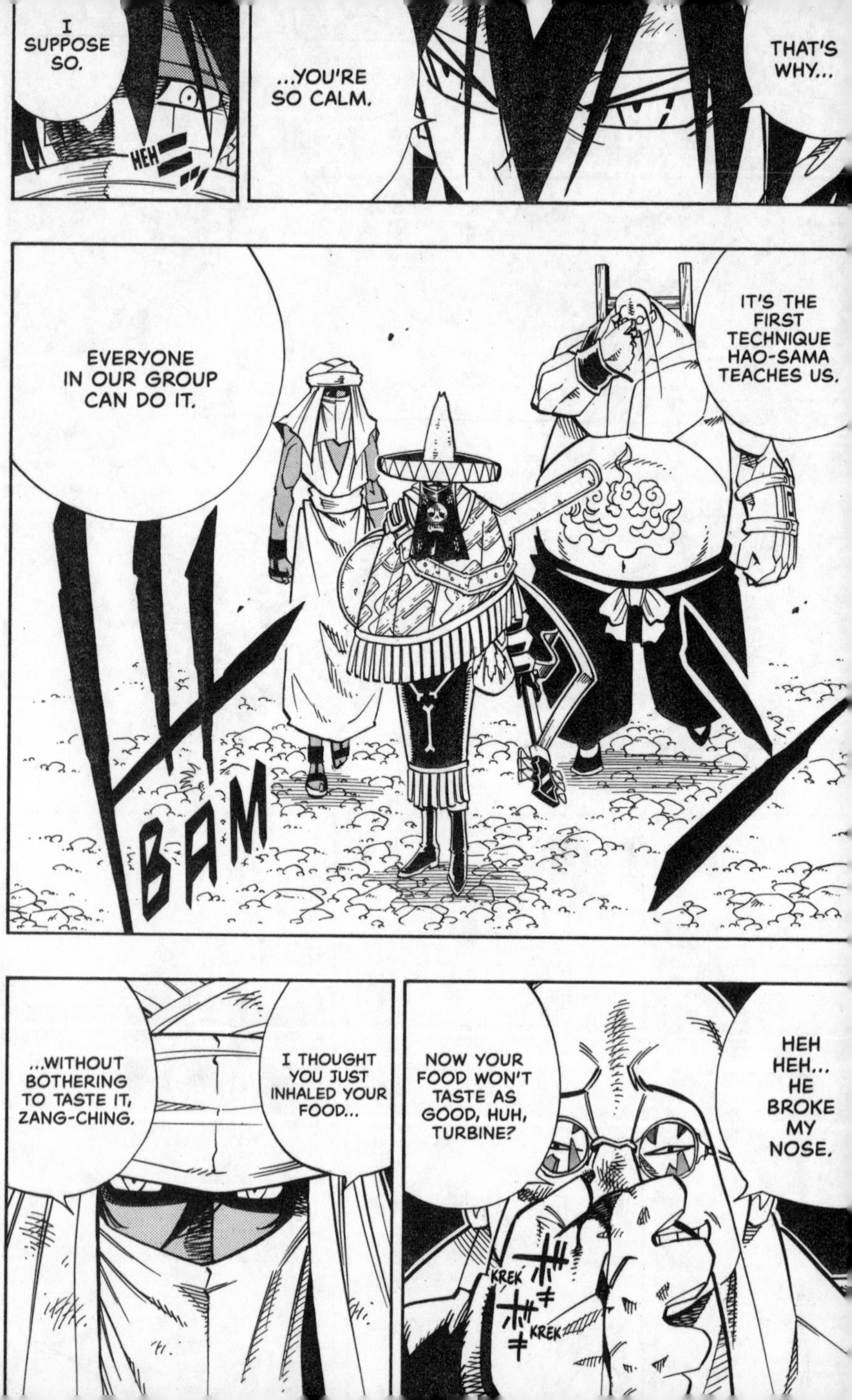
THAT'S WHY...
...YOU'RE SO CALM.
I SUPPOSE SO.
HEH
IT'S THE FIRST TECHNIQUE HAO-SAMA TEACHES US.
EVERYONE IN OUR GROUP CAN DO IT.
BAM
HEH HEH... HE BROKE MY NOSE.
NOW YOUR FOOD WON'T TASTE AS GOOD, HUH, TURBINE?
KREK
KREK
I THOUGHT YOU JUST INHALED YOUR FOOD...
...WITHOUT BOTHERING TO TASTE IT, ZANG-CHING.

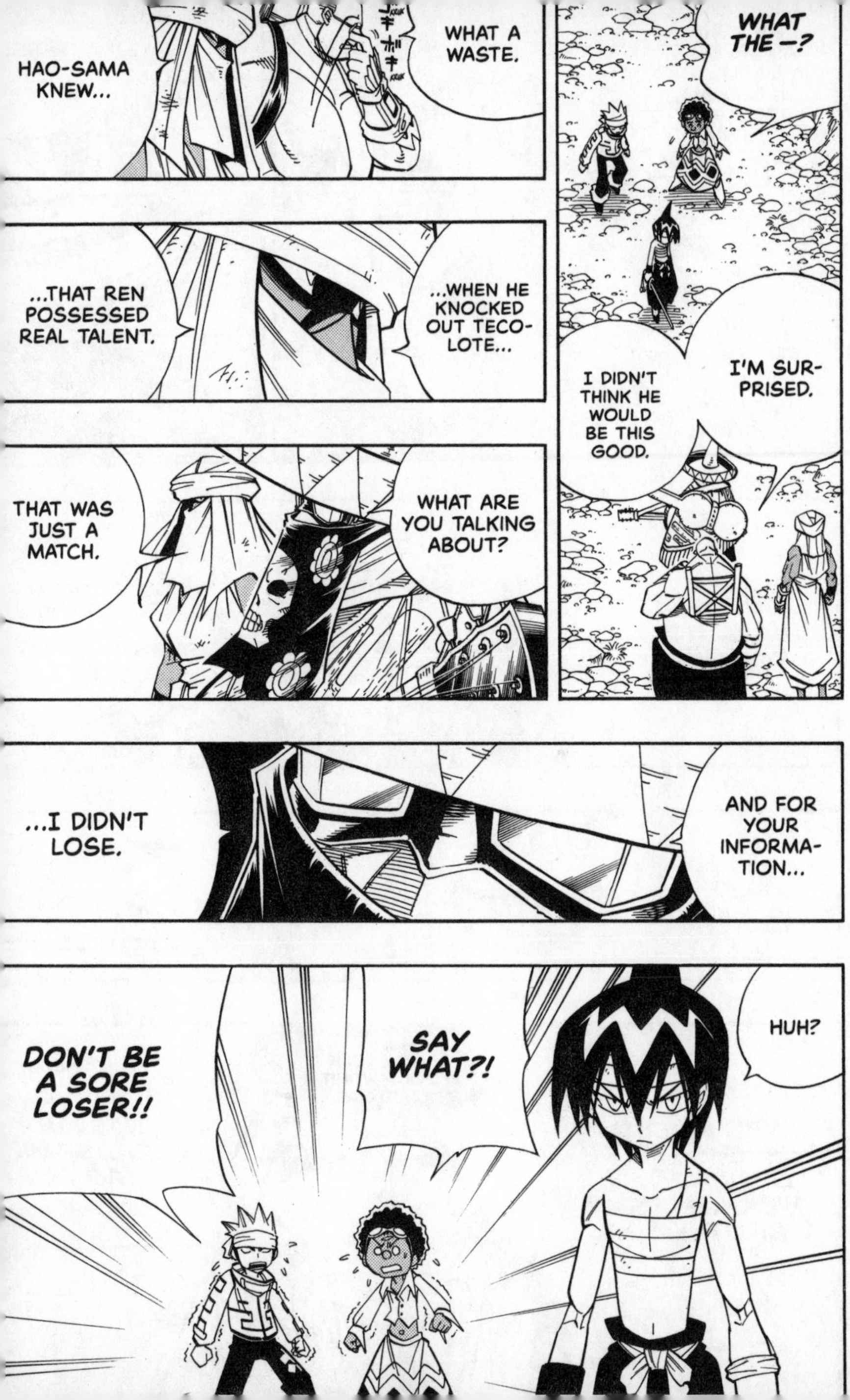
WHAT THE—?
I'M SURPRISED.
I DIDN'T THINK HE WOULD BE THIS GOOD.
WHAT A WASTE.
HAO-SAMA KNEW...
...WHEN HE KNOCKED OUT TECO-LOTE...
...THAT REN POSSESSED REAL TALENT.
WHAT ARE YOU TALKING ABOUT?
THAT WAS JUST A MATCH.
AND FOR YOUR INFORMATION...
...I DIDN'T LOSE.
HUH?
SAY WHAT?!
DON'T BE A SORE LOSER!!

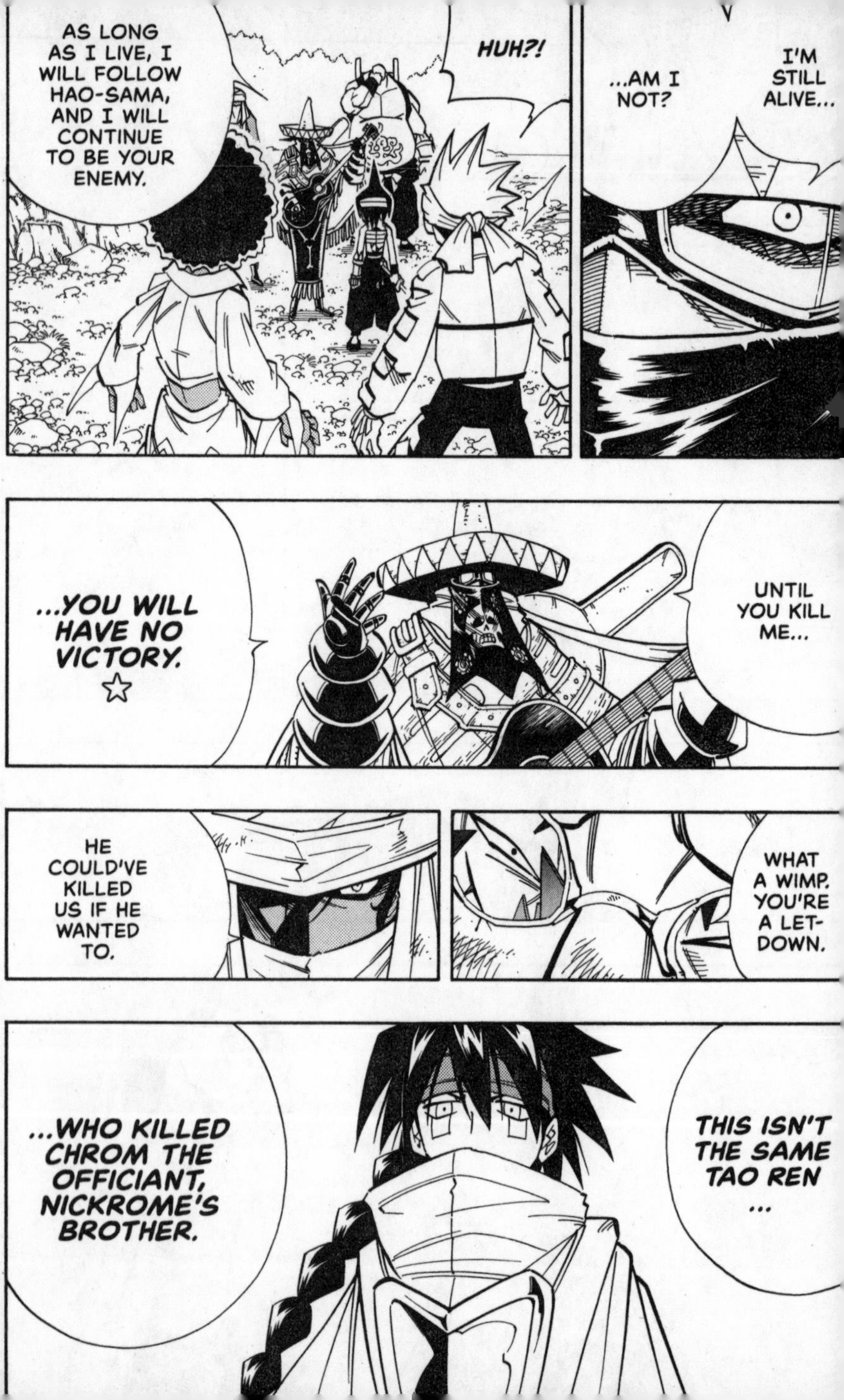
I'M STILL ALIVE...
...AM I NOT?
HUH?!
AS LONG AS I LIVE, I WILL FOLLOW HAO-SAMA, AND I WILL CONTINUE TO BE YOUR ENEMY.
UNTIL YOU KILL ME...
...YOU WILL HAVE NO VICTORY. ☆
WHAT A WIMP. YOU'RE A LET-DOWN.
HE COULD'VE KILLED US IF HE WANTED TO.
THIS ISN'T THE SAME TAO REN ...
...WHO KILLED CHROM THE OFFICIANT, NICKROME'S BROTHER.

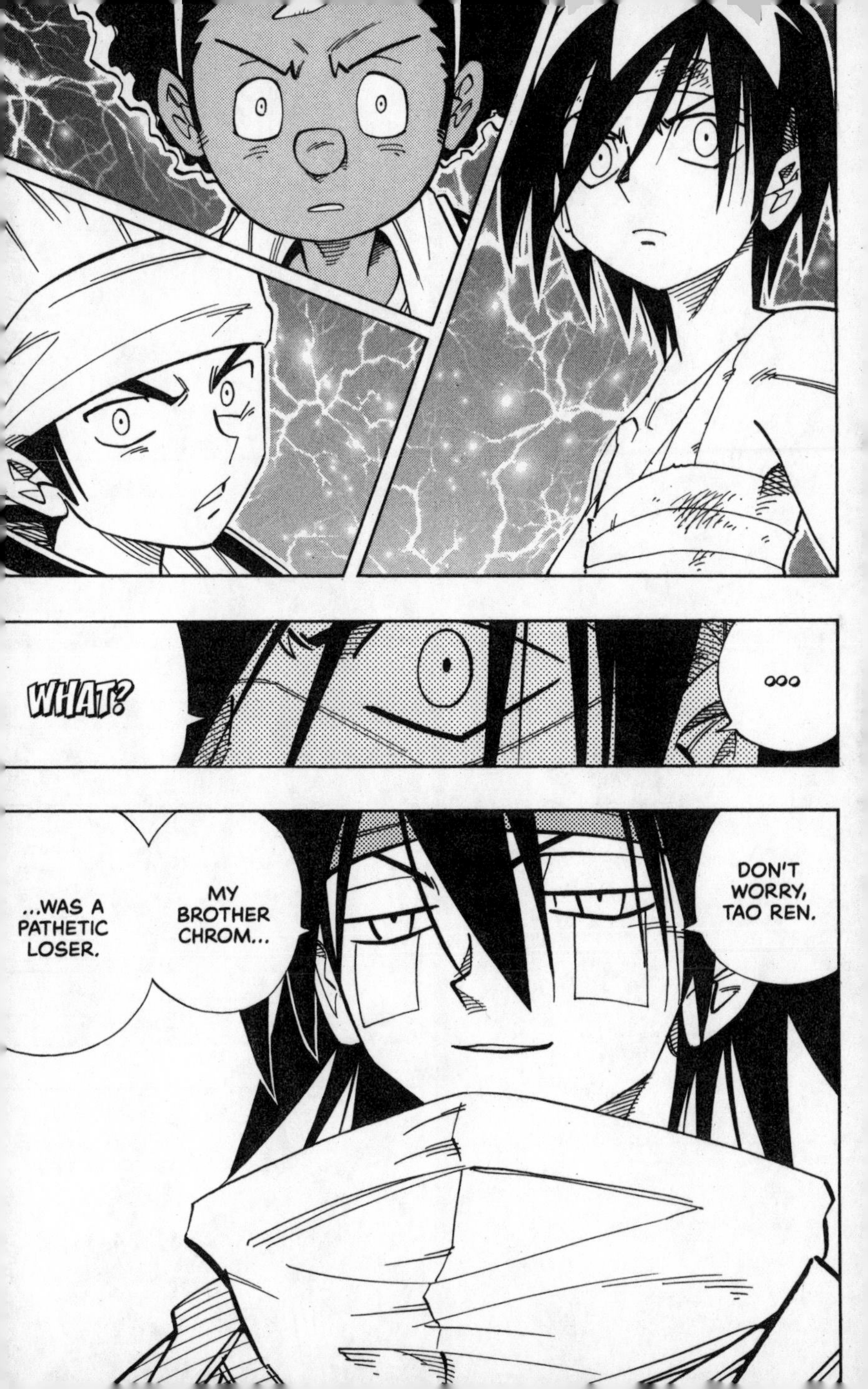

...
WHAT?
DON'T WORRY, TAO REN.
MY BROTHER CHROM...
...WAS A PATHETIC LOSER.

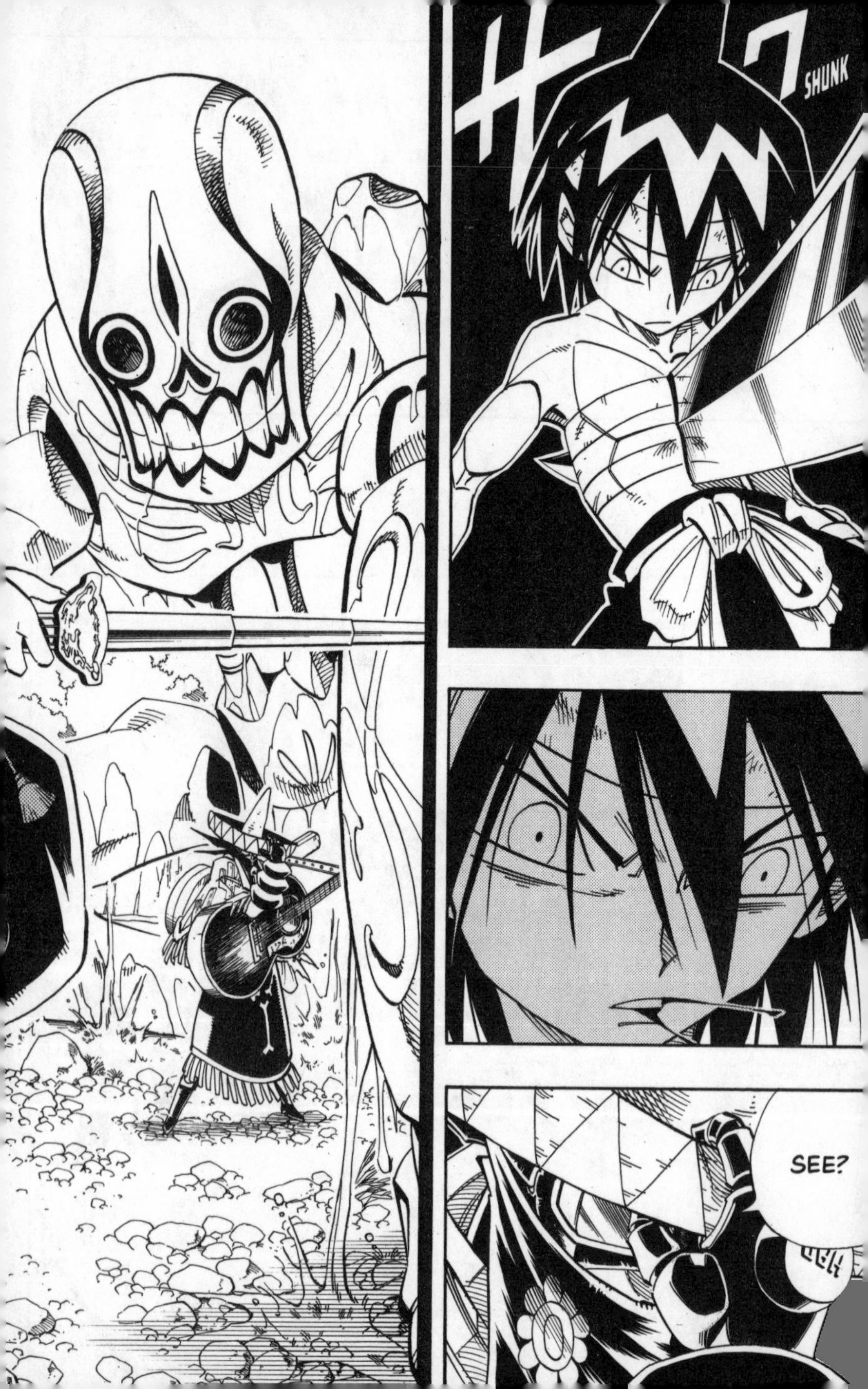
SHUNK
SEE?

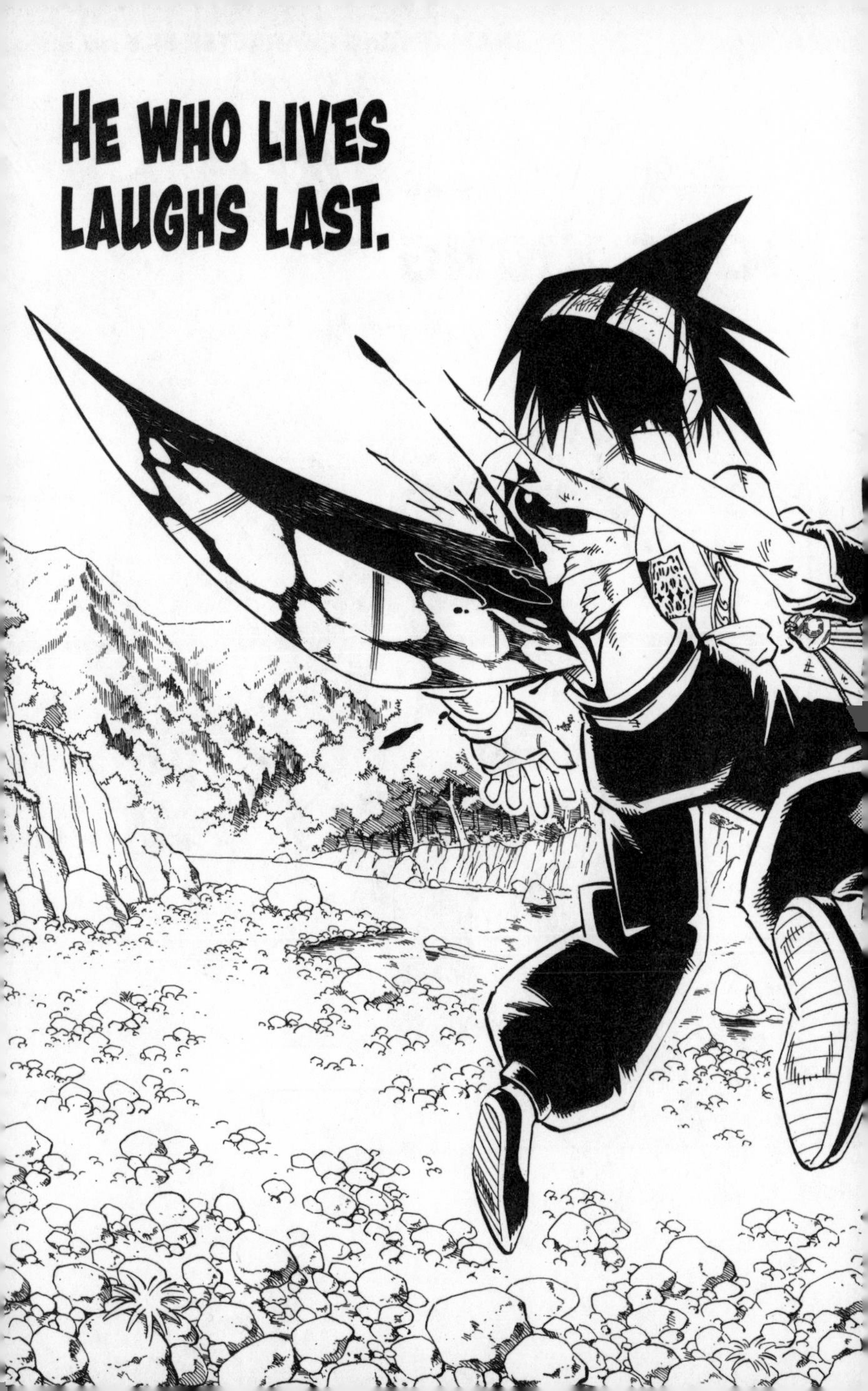
HE WHO LIVES
LAUGHS LAST.

XIONG XIONG

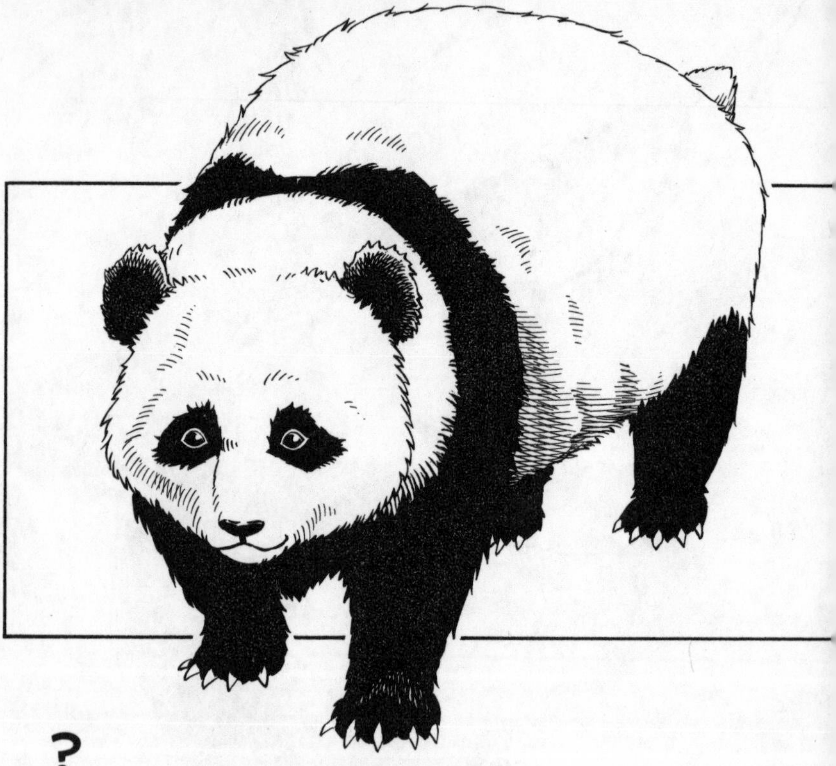

?

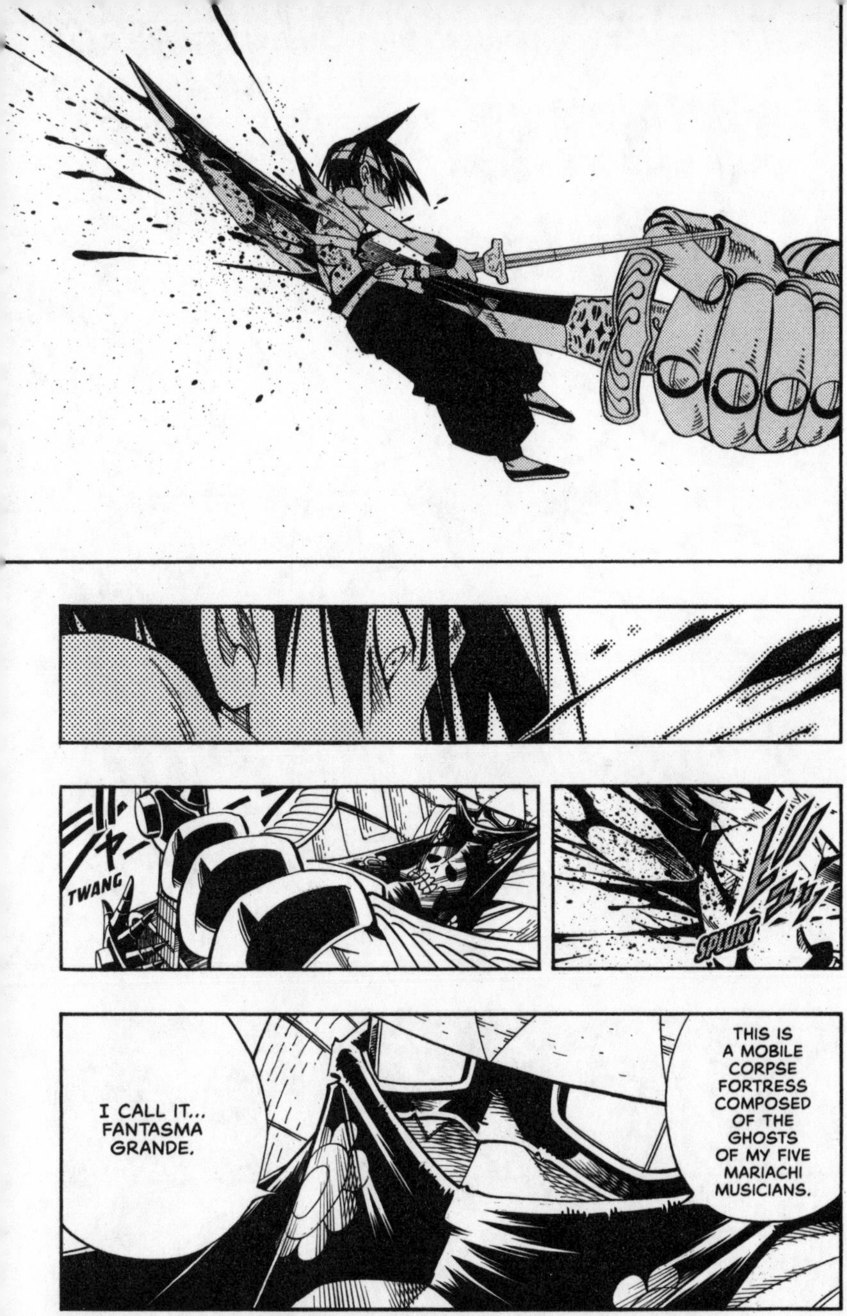
SPLURT
TWANG
THIS IS A MOBILE CORPSE FORTRESS COMPOSED OF THE GHOSTS OF MY FIVE MARIACHI MUSICIANS.
I CALL IT... FANTASMA GRANDE.

Chapter 151: Farewell Forever

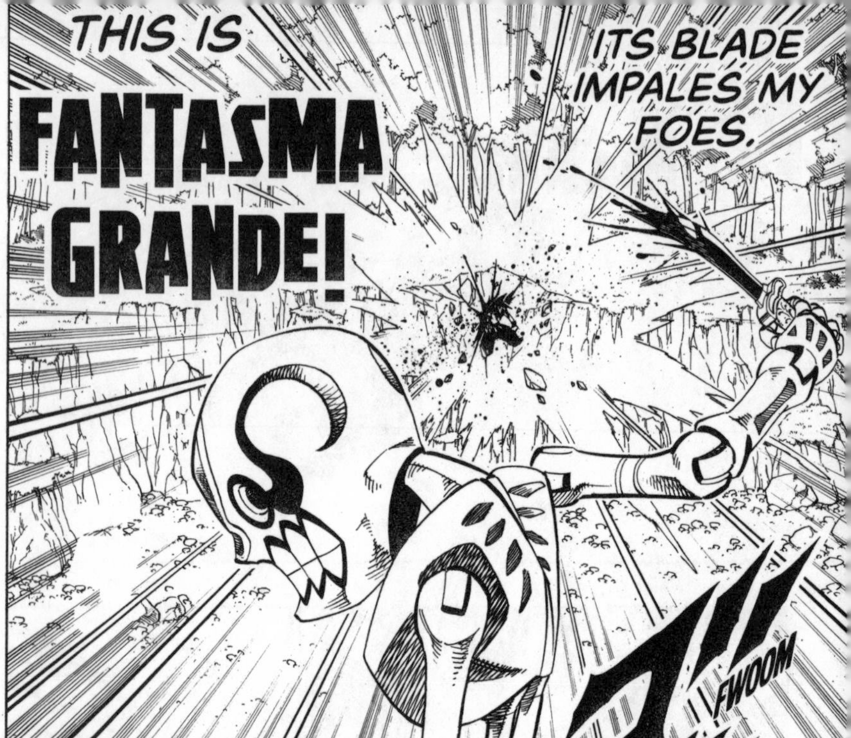
ITS BLADE IMPALES MY FOES.
THIS IS FANTASMA GRANDE!
FWOOM

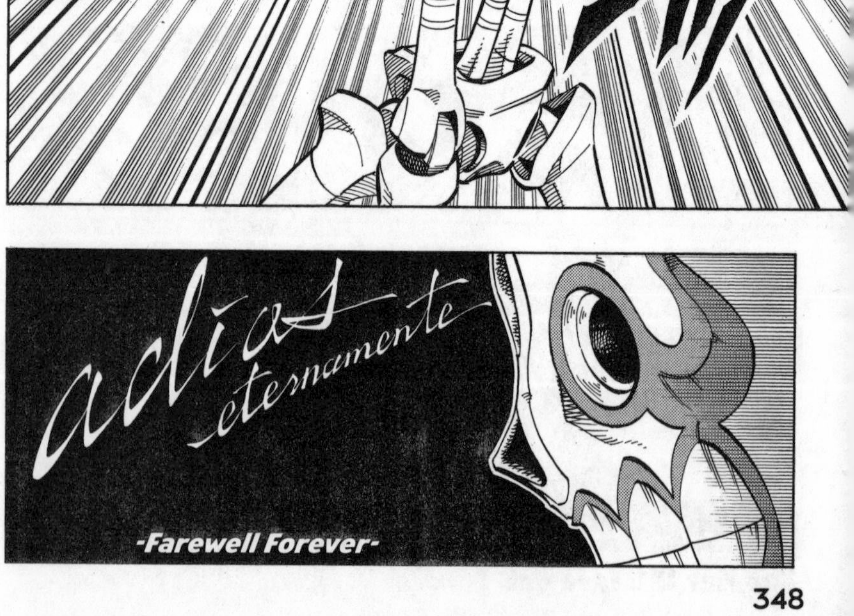
adias eternamente
-Farewell Forever-

Chapter 151:

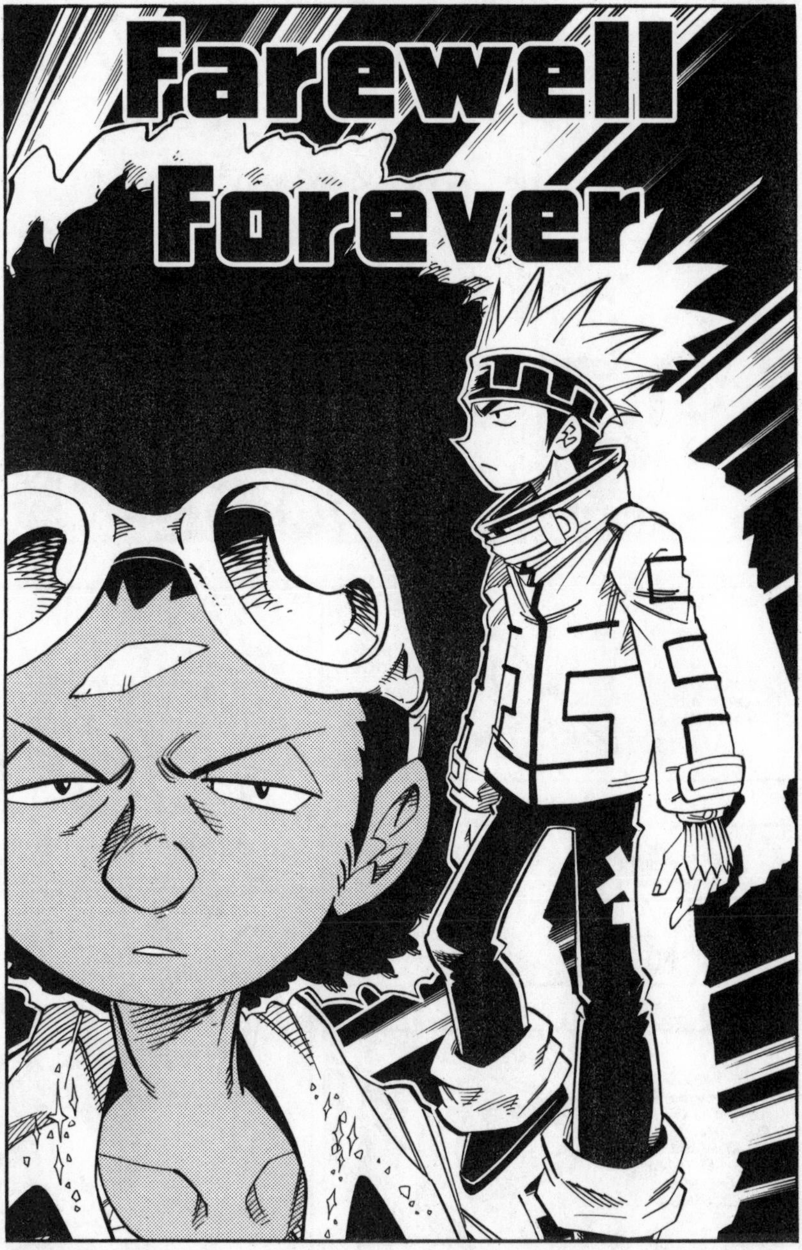
Farewell Forever

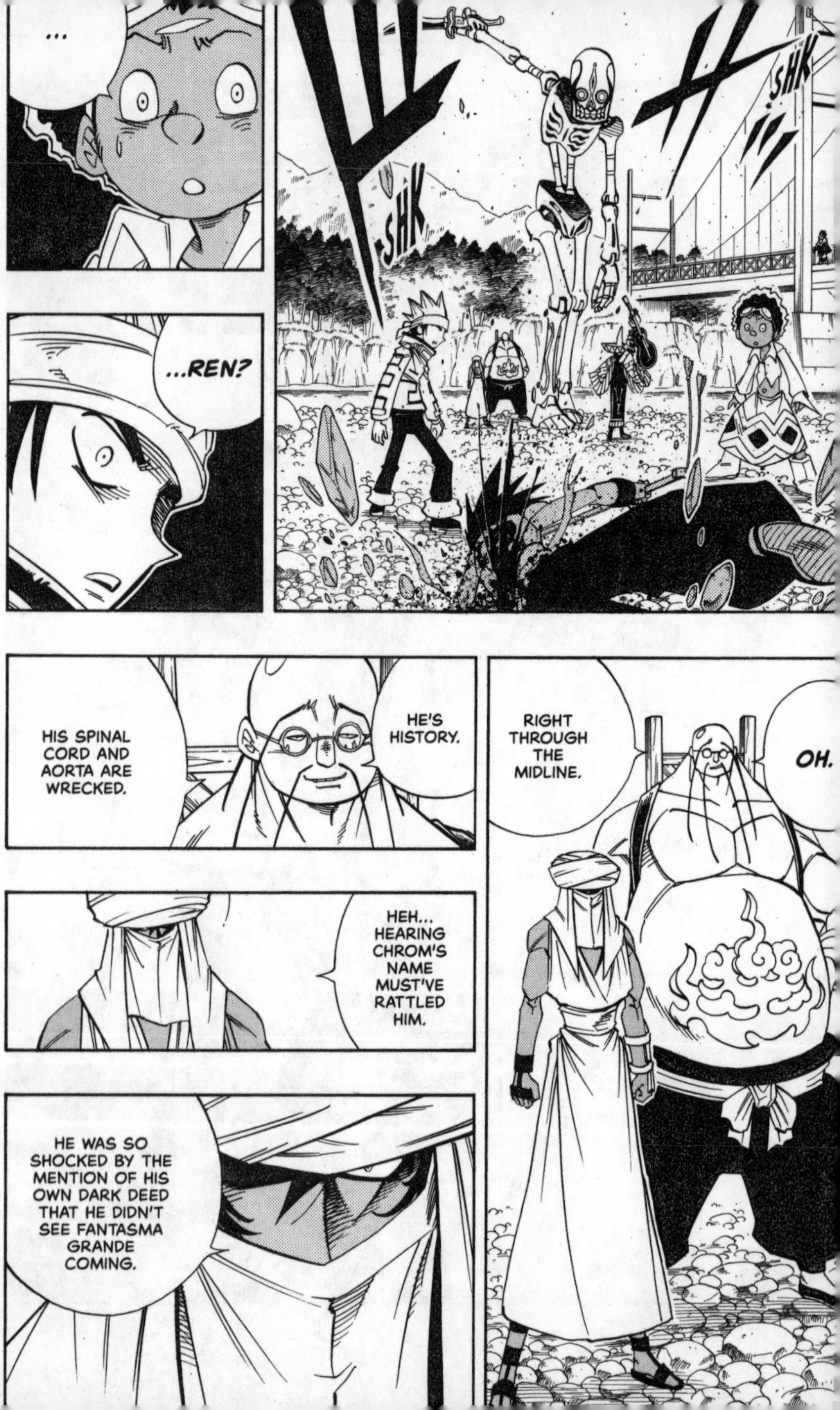
SHK
SHK
...
...REN?
OH.
RIGHT THROUGH THE MIDLINE.
HE'S HISTORY.
HIS SPINAL CORD AND AORTA ARE WRECKED.
HEH... HEARING CHROM'S NAME MUST'VE RATTLED HIM.
HE WAS SO SHOCKED BY THE MENTION OF HIS OWN DARK DEED THAT HE DIDN'T SEE FANTASMA GRANDE COMING.

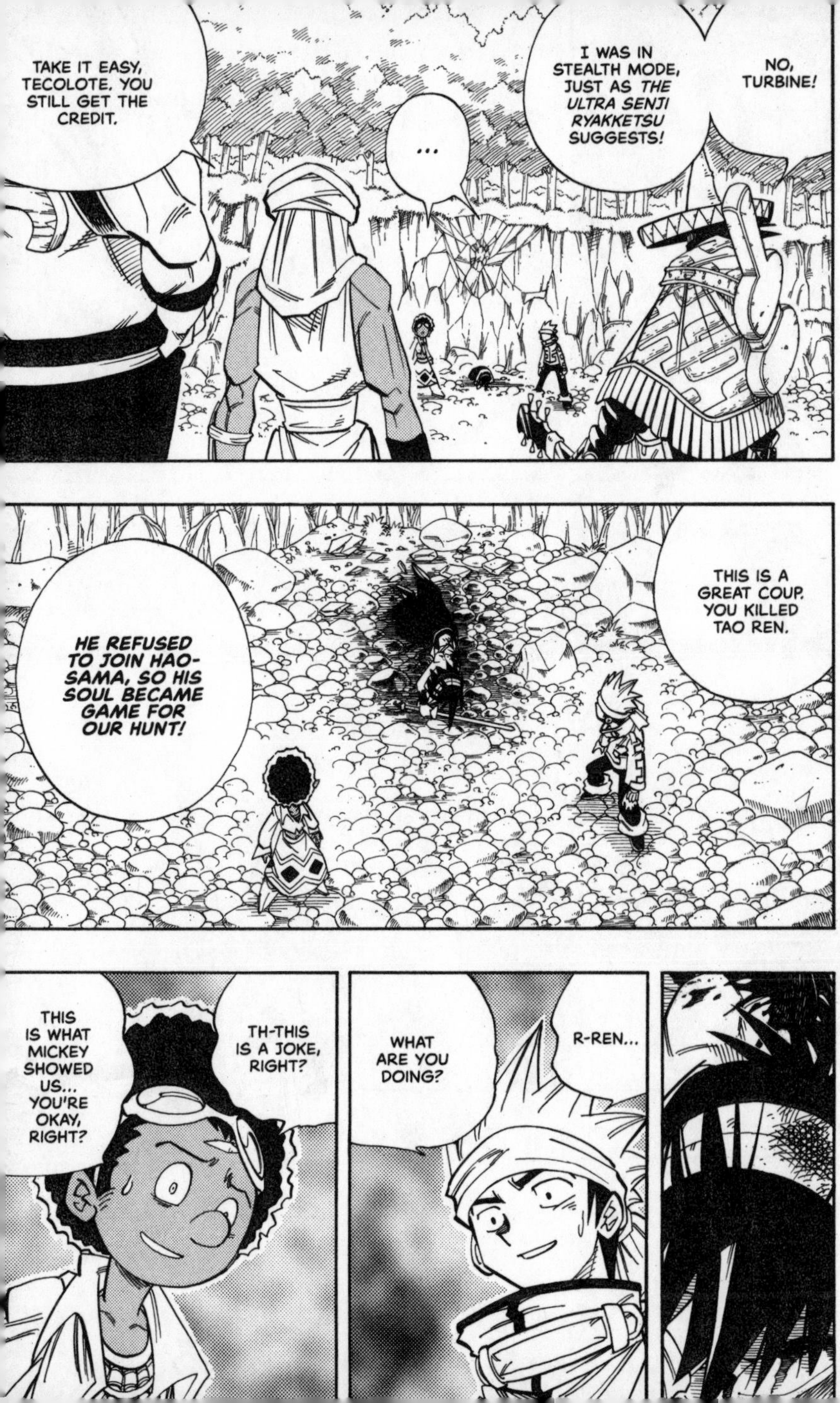
NO, TURBINE!
I WAS IN STEALTH MODE, JUST AS *THE ULTRA SENJI RYAKKETSU* SUGGESTS!
...
TAKE IT EASY, TECOLOTE. YOU STILL GET THE CREDIT.
THIS IS A GREAT COUP. YOU KILLED TAO REN.
HE REFUSED TO JOIN HAO-SAMA, SO HIS SOUL BECAME GAME FOR OUR HUNT!
R-REN...
WHAT ARE YOU DOING?
TH-THIS IS A JOKE, RIGHT?
THIS IS WHAT MICKEY SHOWED US... YOU'RE OKAY, RIGHT?

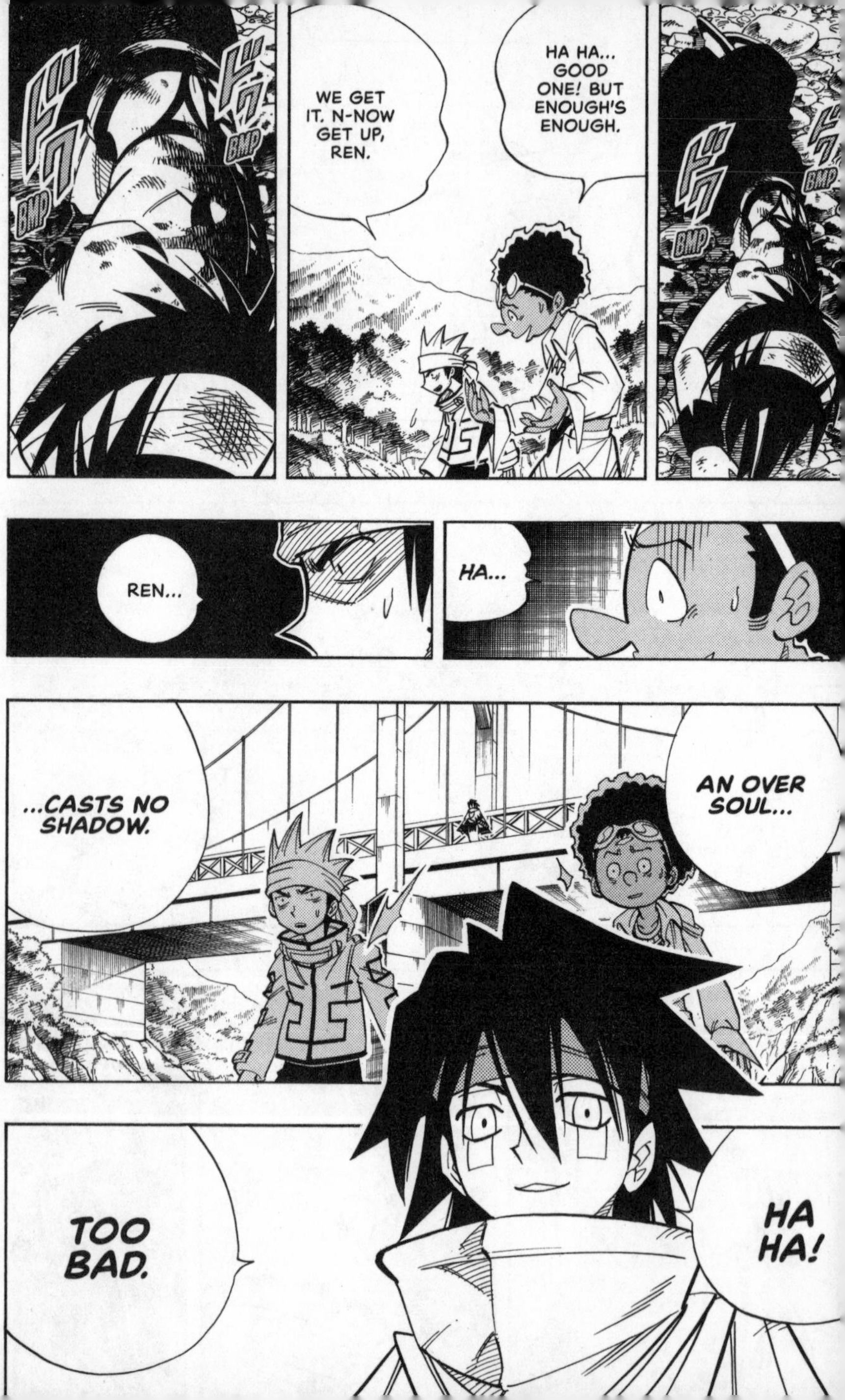
ドク BMP
ドク BMP
HA HA... GOOD ONE! BUT ENOUGH'S ENOUGH.
WE GET IT. N-NOW GET UP, REN.
ドク BMP
ドク BMP
HA...
REN...
AN OVER SOUL...
...CASTS NO SHADOW.
HA HA!
TOO BAD.

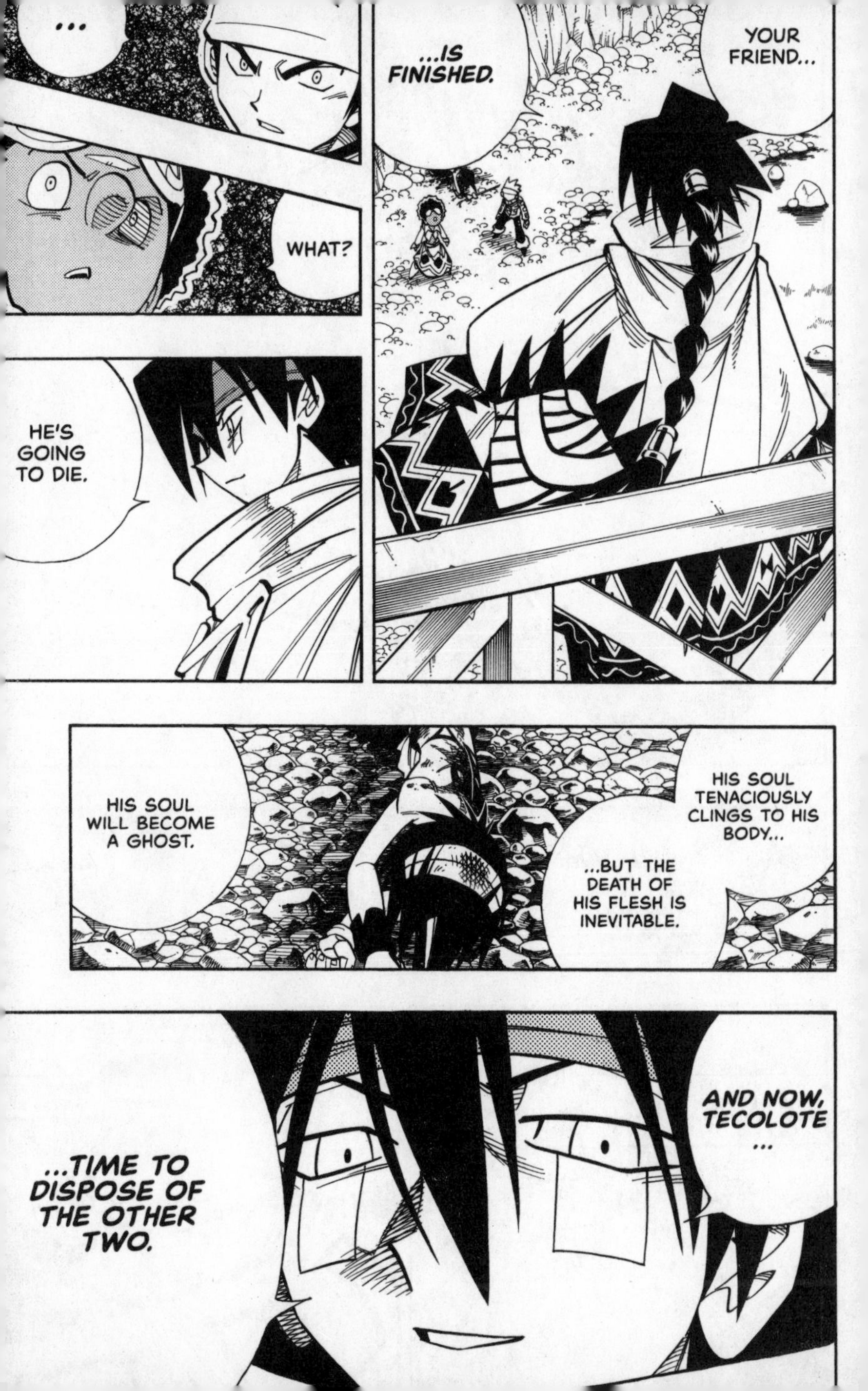
YOUR FRIEND...
...IS FINISHED.
...
WHAT?
HE'S GOING TO DIE.
HIS SOUL TENACIOUSLY CLINGS TO HIS BODY...
...BUT THE DEATH OF HIS FLESH IS INEVITABLE.
HIS SOUL WILL BECOME A GHOST.
AND NOW, TECOLOTE ...
...TIME TO DISPOSE OF THE OTHER TWO.

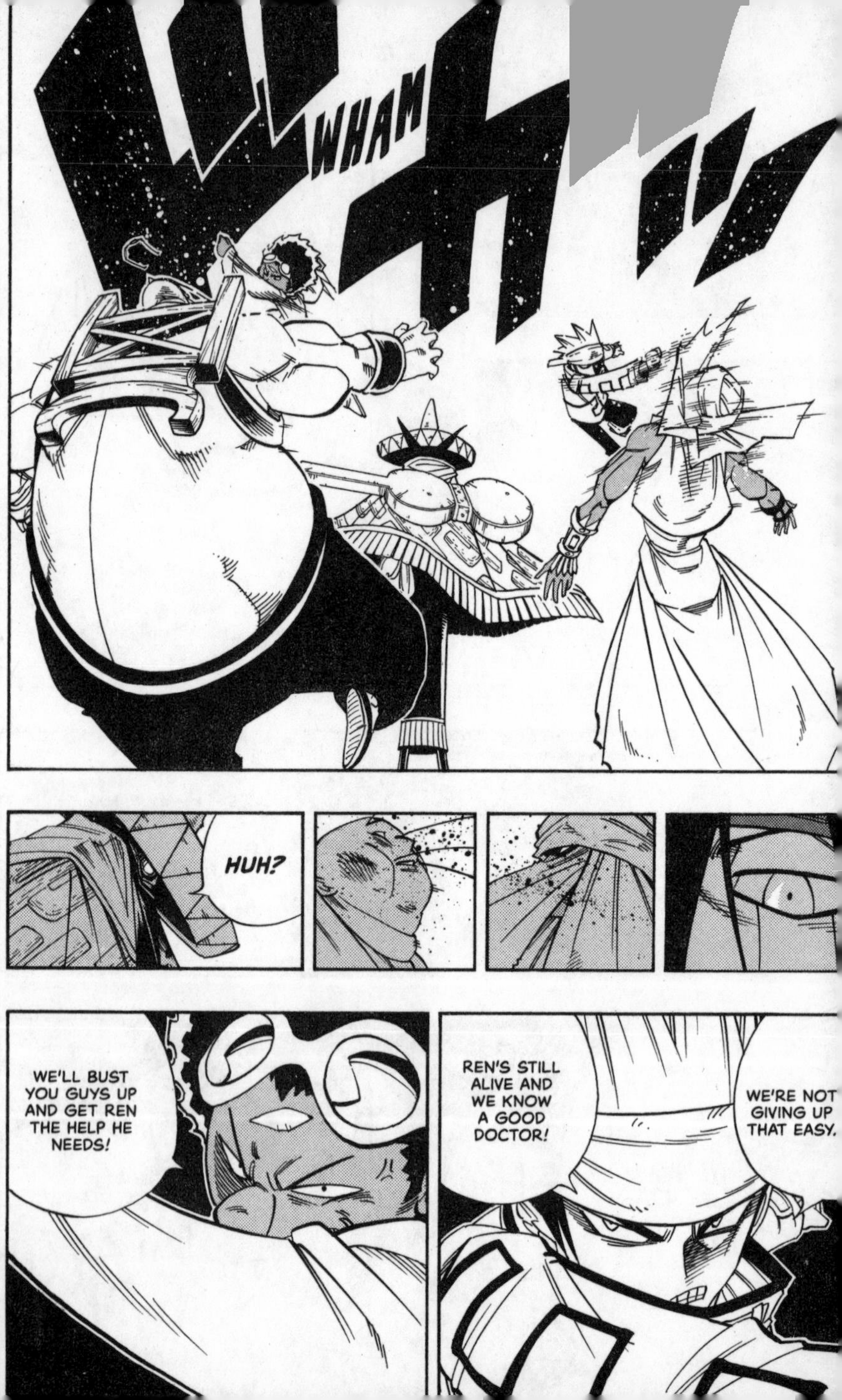
WHAM
HUH?
WE'RE NOT GIVING UP THAT EASY.
REN'S STILL ALIVE AND WE KNOW A GOOD DOCTOR!
WE'LL BUST YOU GUYS UP AND GET REN THE HELP HE NEEDS!

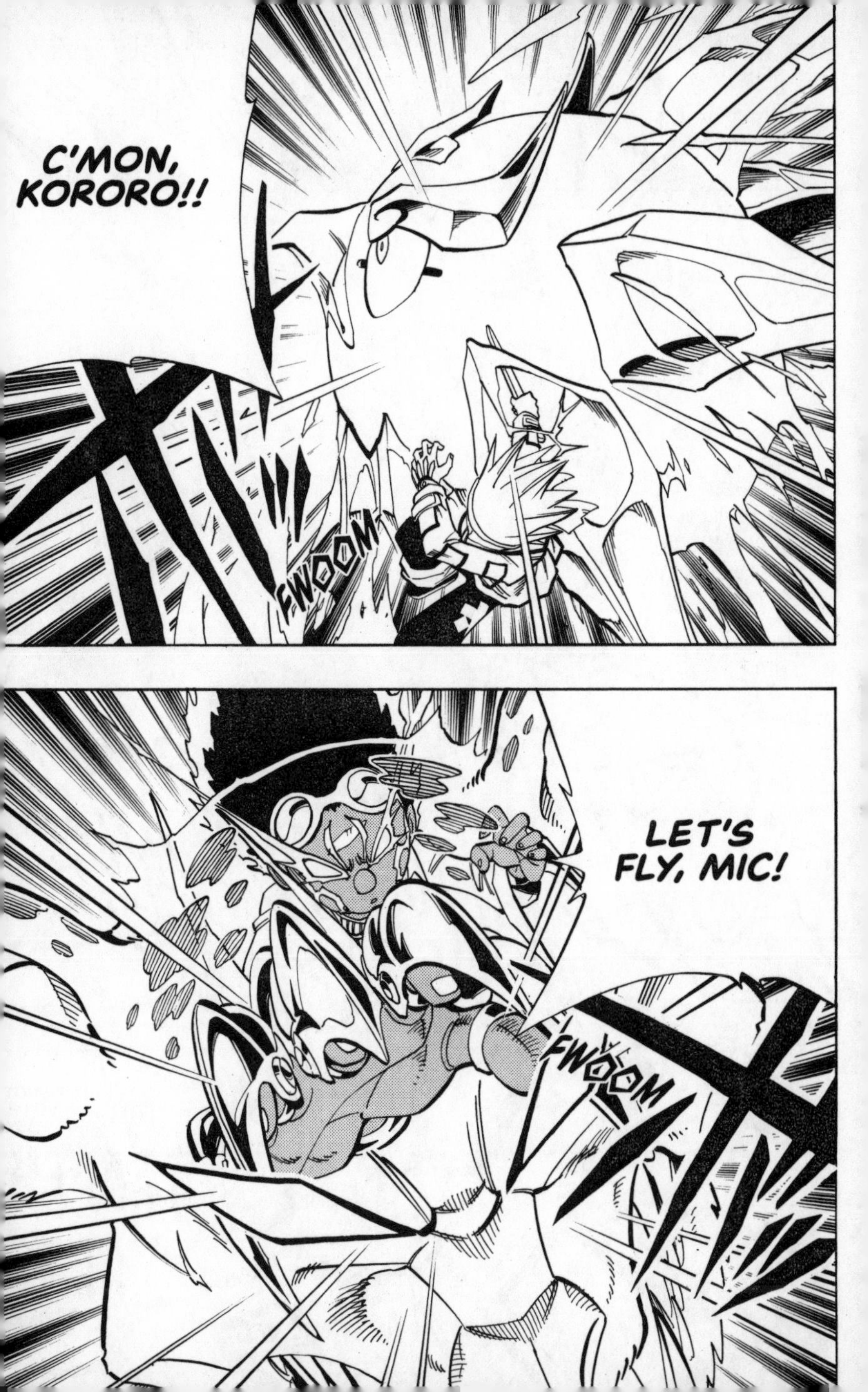
C'MON, KORORO!!
FWOOM
LET'S FLY, MIC!
FWOOM

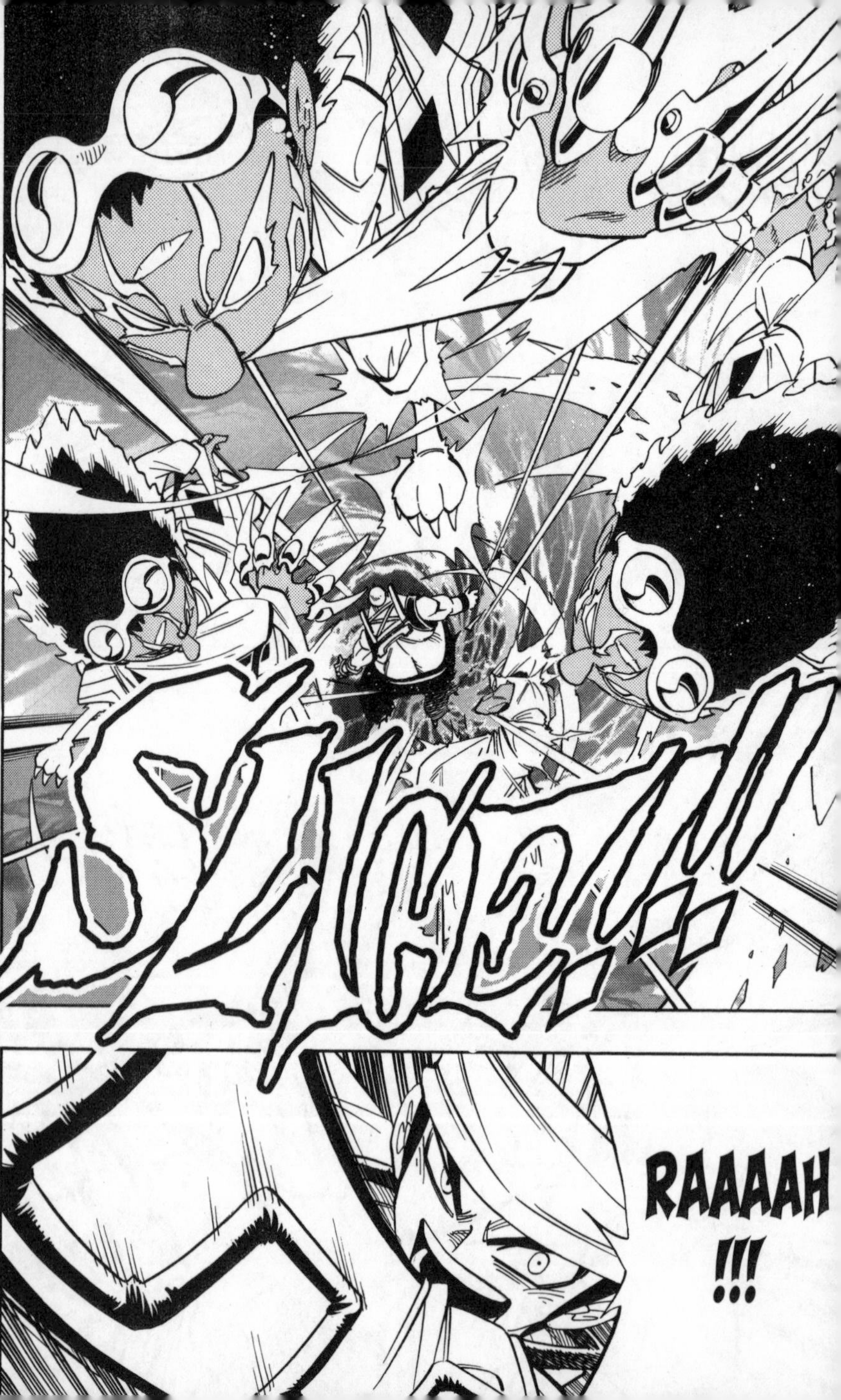
RAAAAH
!!!

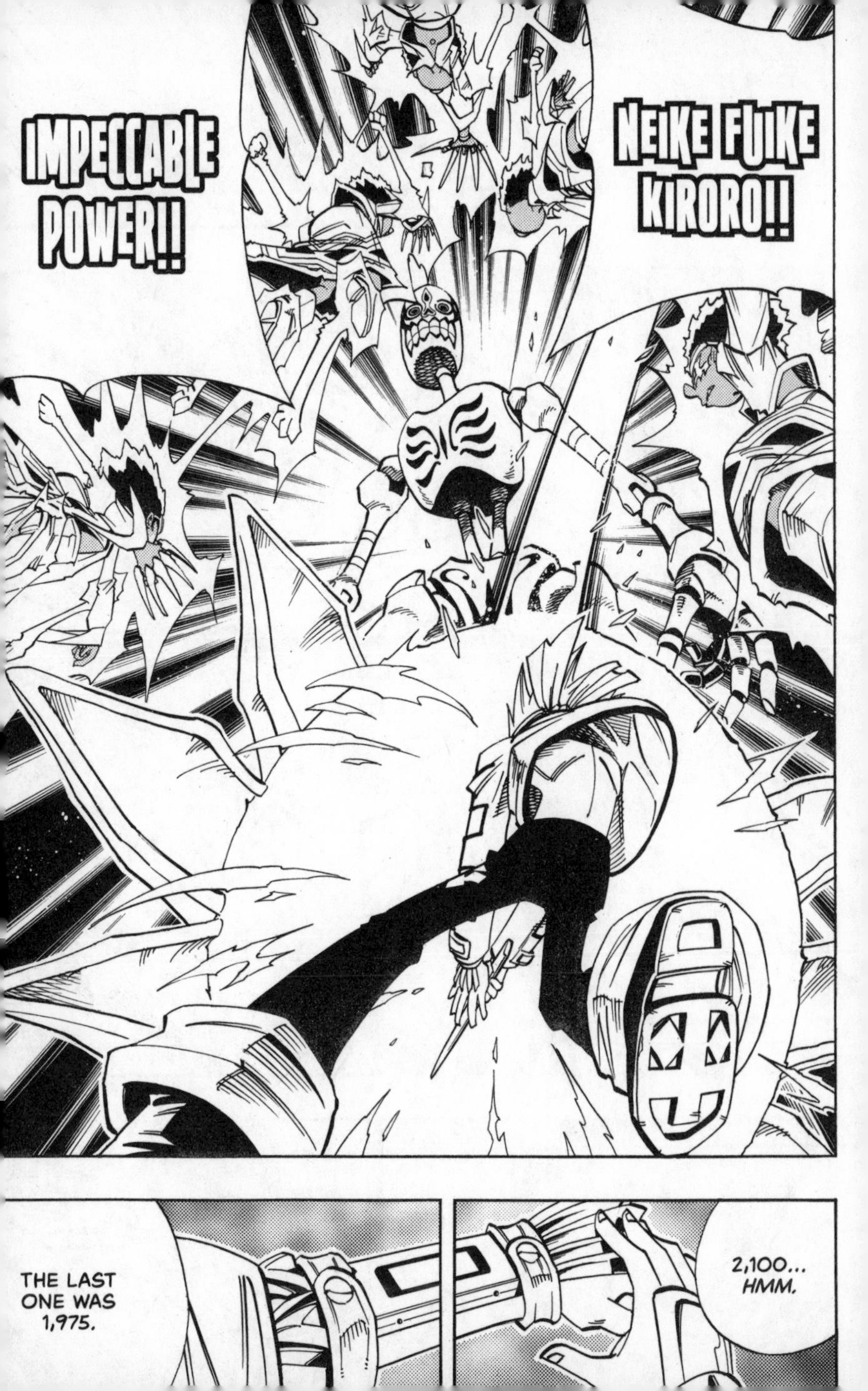
NEIKE FUIKE KIRORO!!
IMPECCABLE POWER!!
2,100... HMM.
THE LAST ONE WAS 1,975.

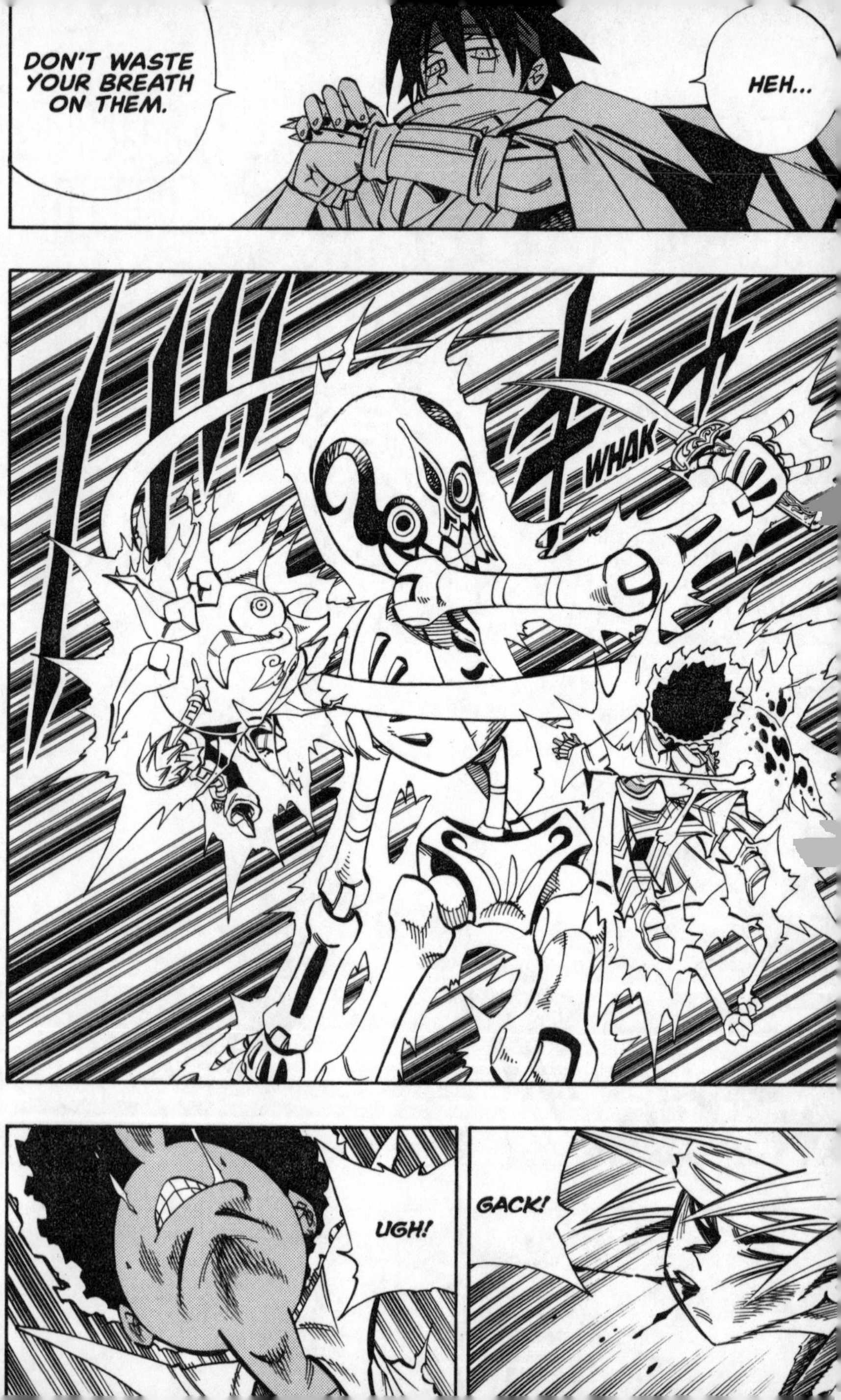
HEH...
DON'T WASTE YOUR BREATH ON THEM.
WHAK
GACK!
UGH!

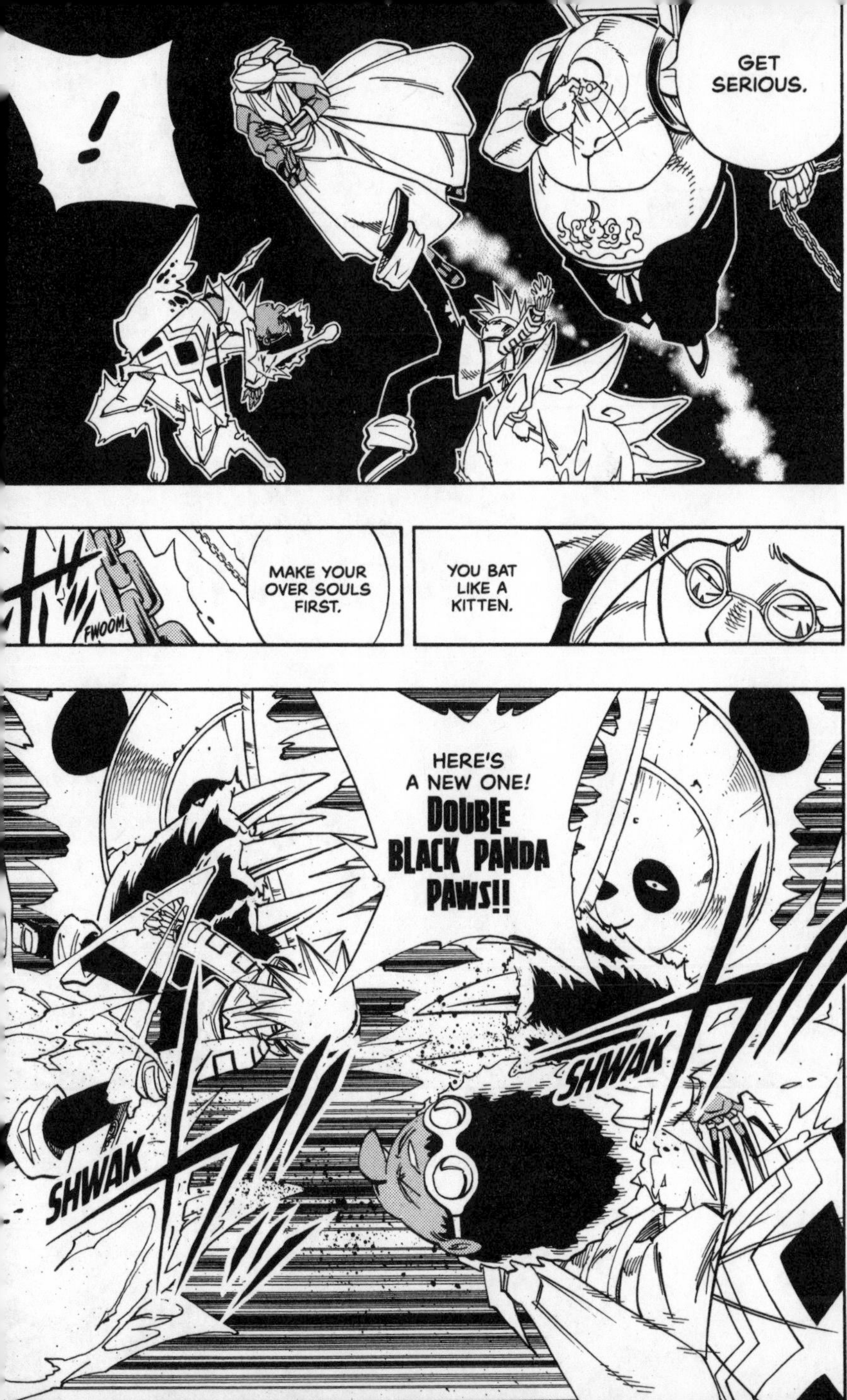
GET SERIOUS.
!
YOU BAT LIKE A KITTEN.
MAKE YOUR OVER SOULS FIRST.
FWOOM
HERE'S A NEW ONE! DOUBLE BLACK PANDA PAWS!!
SHWAK
SHWAK

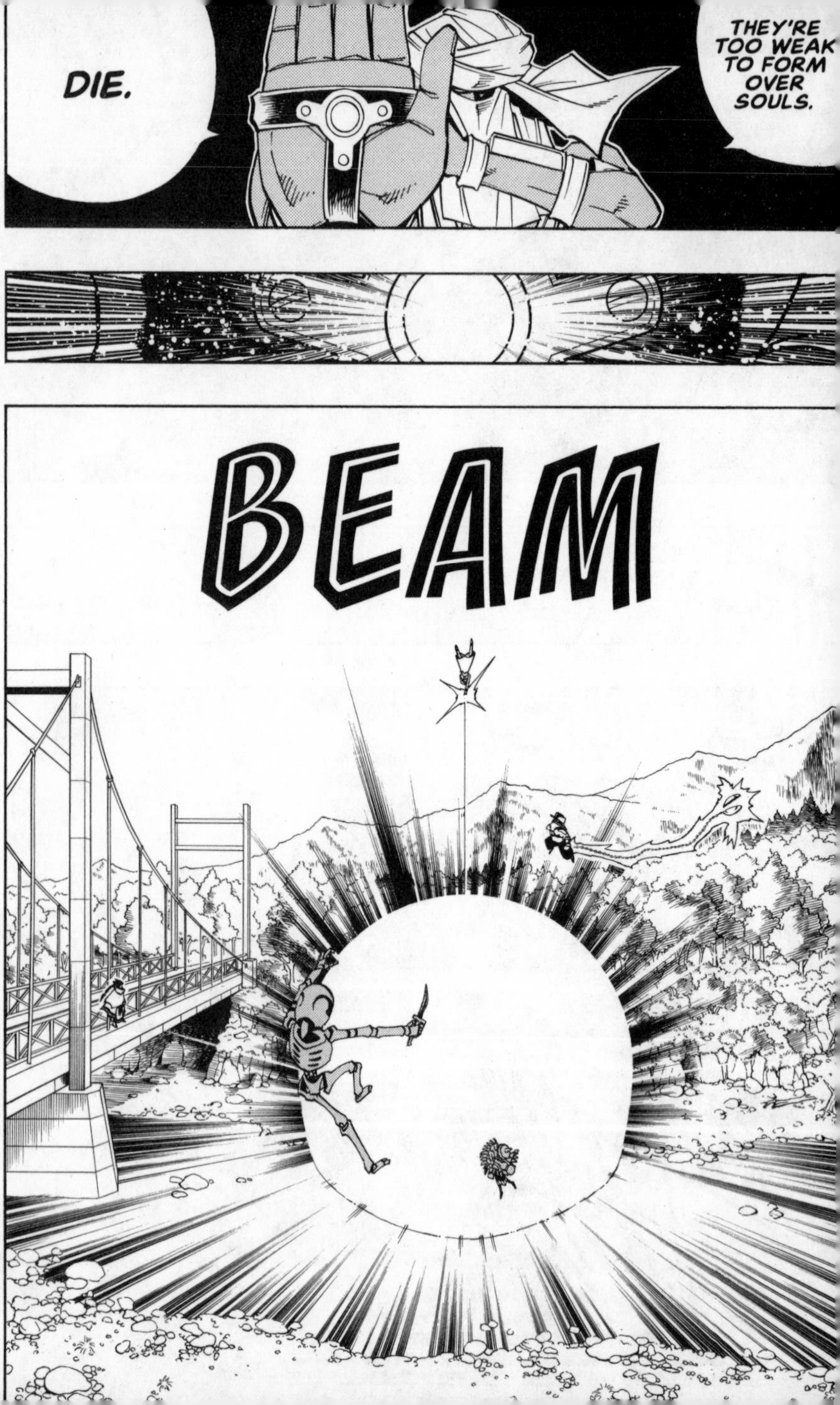
THEY'RE TOO WEAK TO FORM OVER SOULS.
DIE.
BEAM

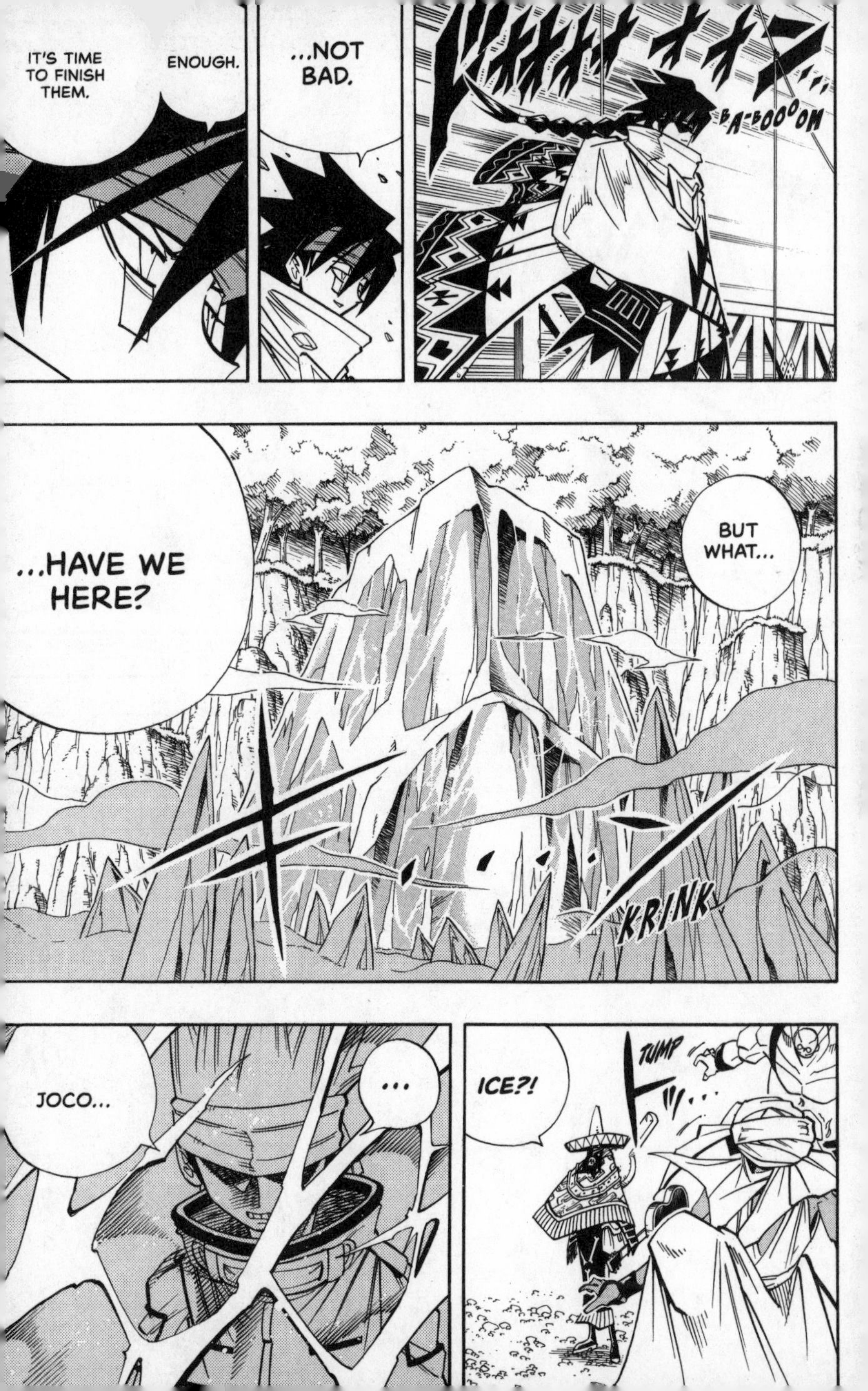
BA-BOOOOM
...NOT BAD.
ENOUGH.
IT'S TIME TO FINISH THEM.
BUT WHAT...
...HAVE WE HERE?
KRINK
TUMP
ICE?!
...
JOCO...

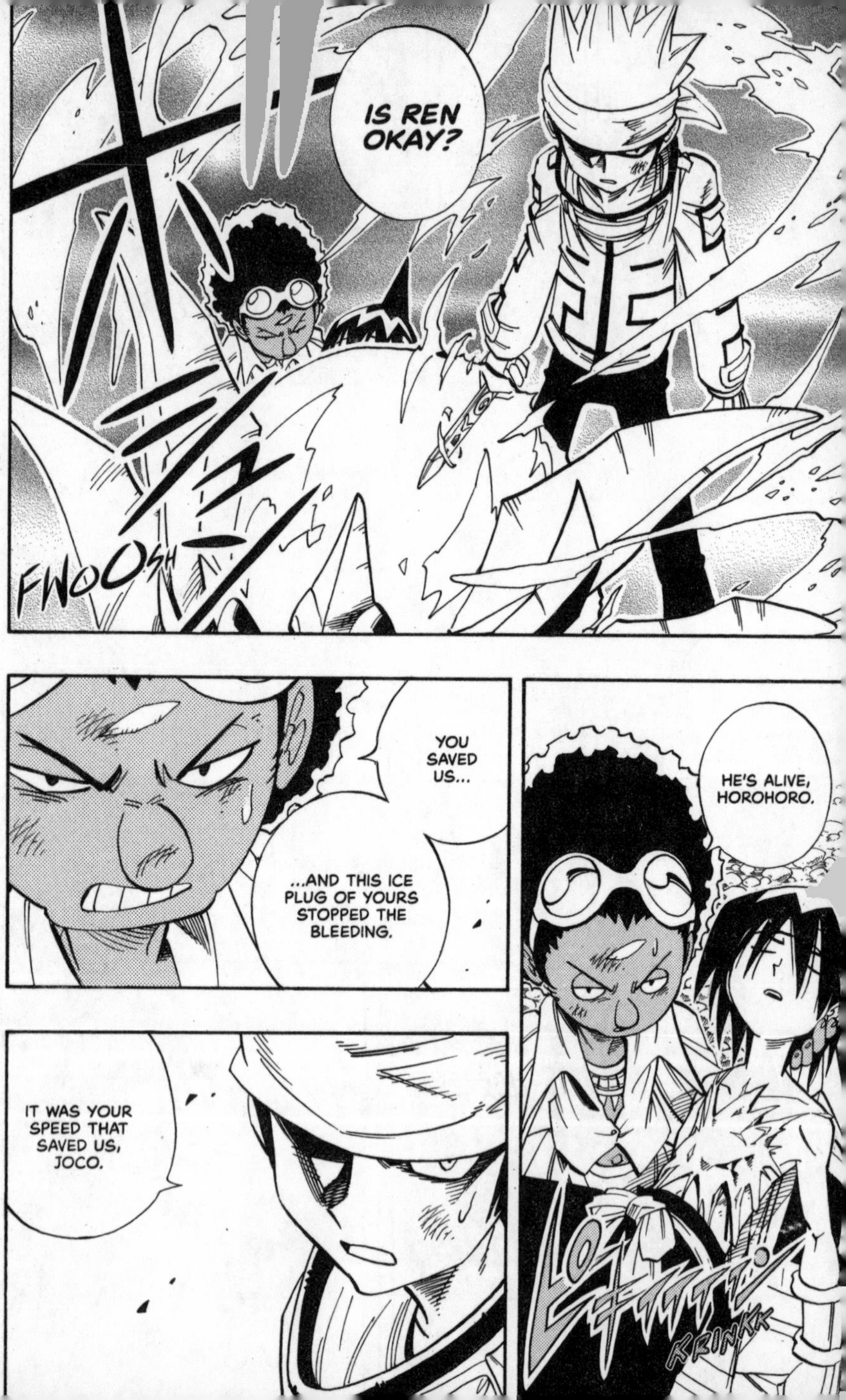
IS REN OKAY?
FWOOSH
HE'S ALIVE, HOROHORO.
KRINKK
YOU SAVED US...
...AND THIS ICE PLUG OF YOURS STOPPED THE BLEEDING.
IT WAS YOUR SPEED THAT SAVED US, JOCO.

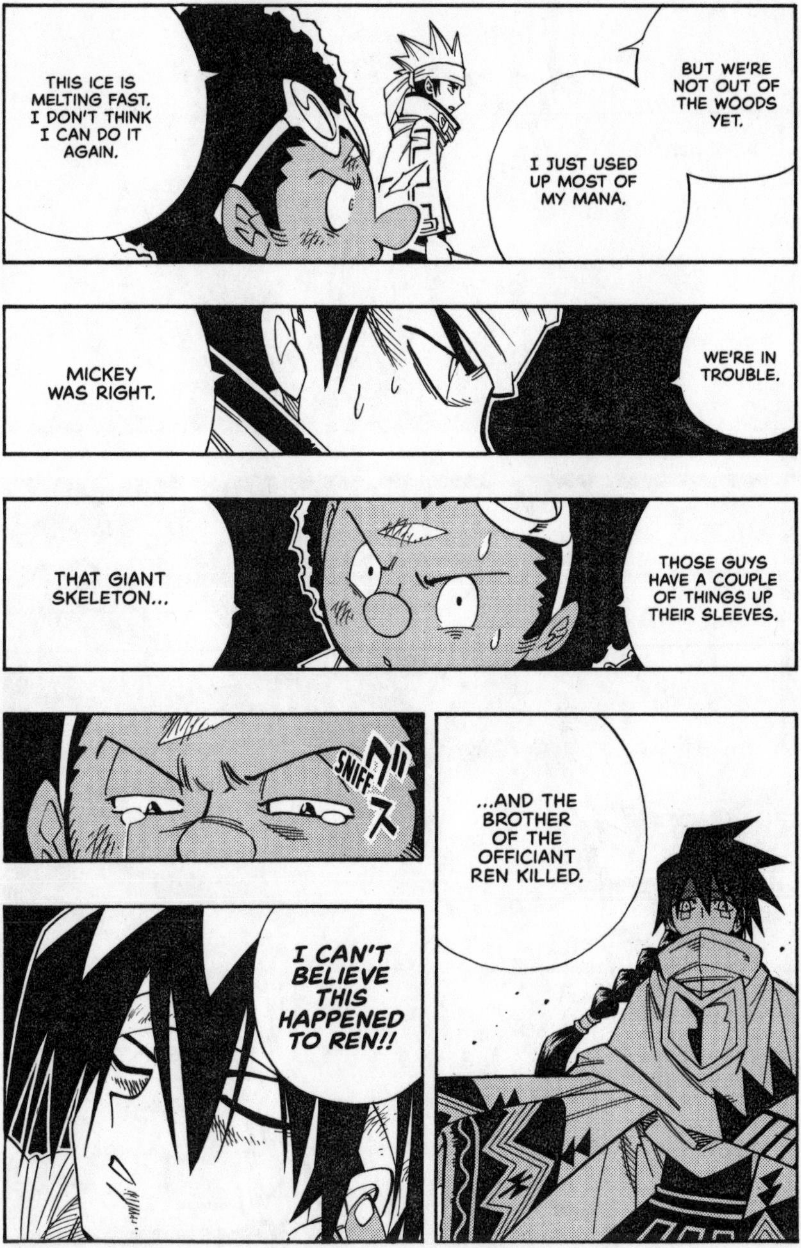
BUT WE'RE NOT OUT OF THE WOODS YET.
I JUST USED UP MOST OF MY MANA.
THIS ICE IS MELTING FAST. I DON'T THINK I CAN DO IT AGAIN.
WE'RE IN TROUBLE.
MICKEY WAS RIGHT.
THOSE GUYS HAVE A COUPLE OF THINGS UP THEIR SLEEVES.
THAT GIANT SKELETON...
...AND THE BROTHER OF THE OFFICIANT REN KILLED.
グス
SNIFF
I CAN'T BELIEVE THIS HAPPENED TO REN!!

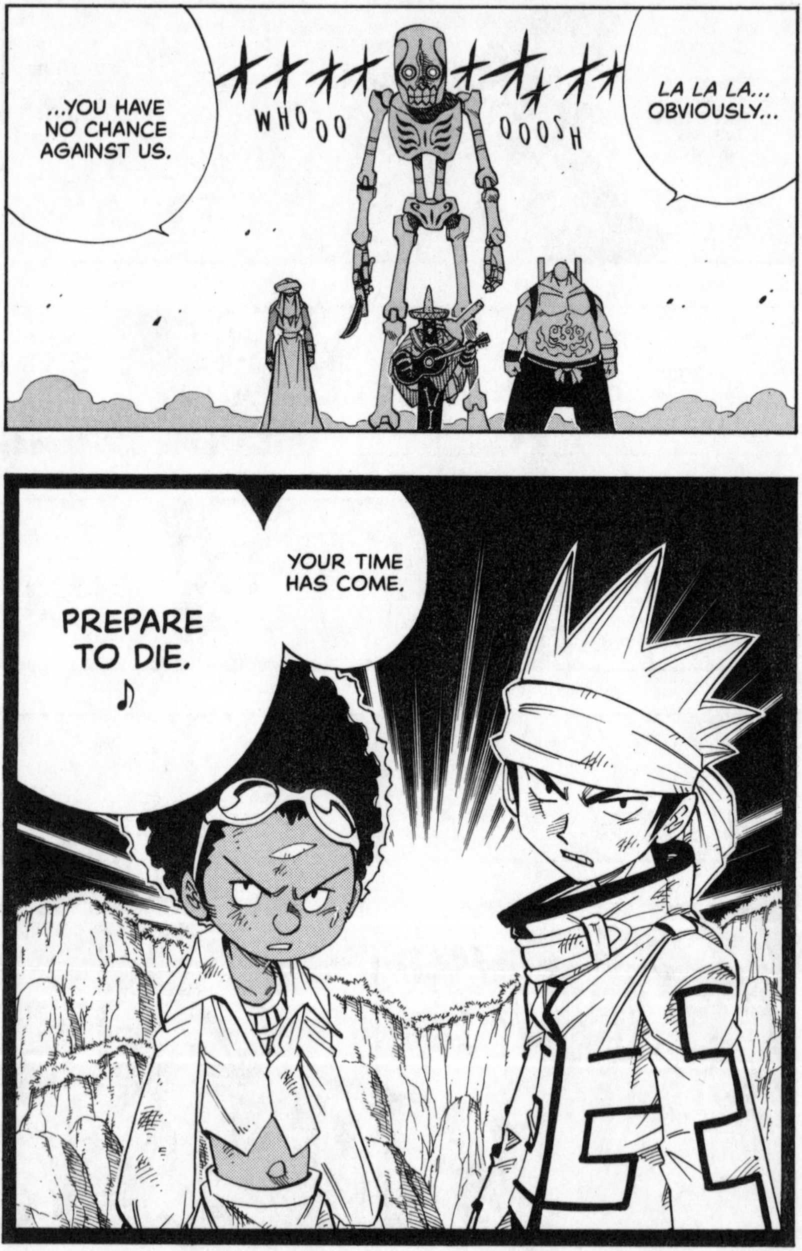
LA LA LA... OBVIOUSLY...
WHOOOOOOSH
...YOU HAVE NO CHANCE AGAINST US.
YOUR TIME HAS COME.
PREPARE TO DIE. ♪

Over Soul: Dorakuma Neko

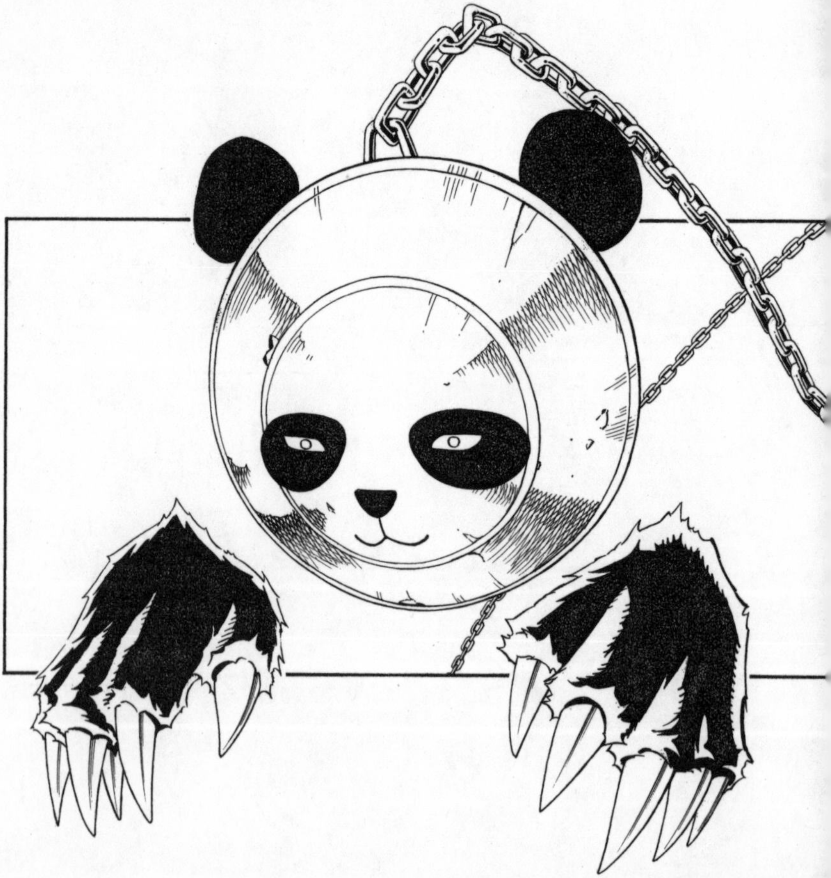

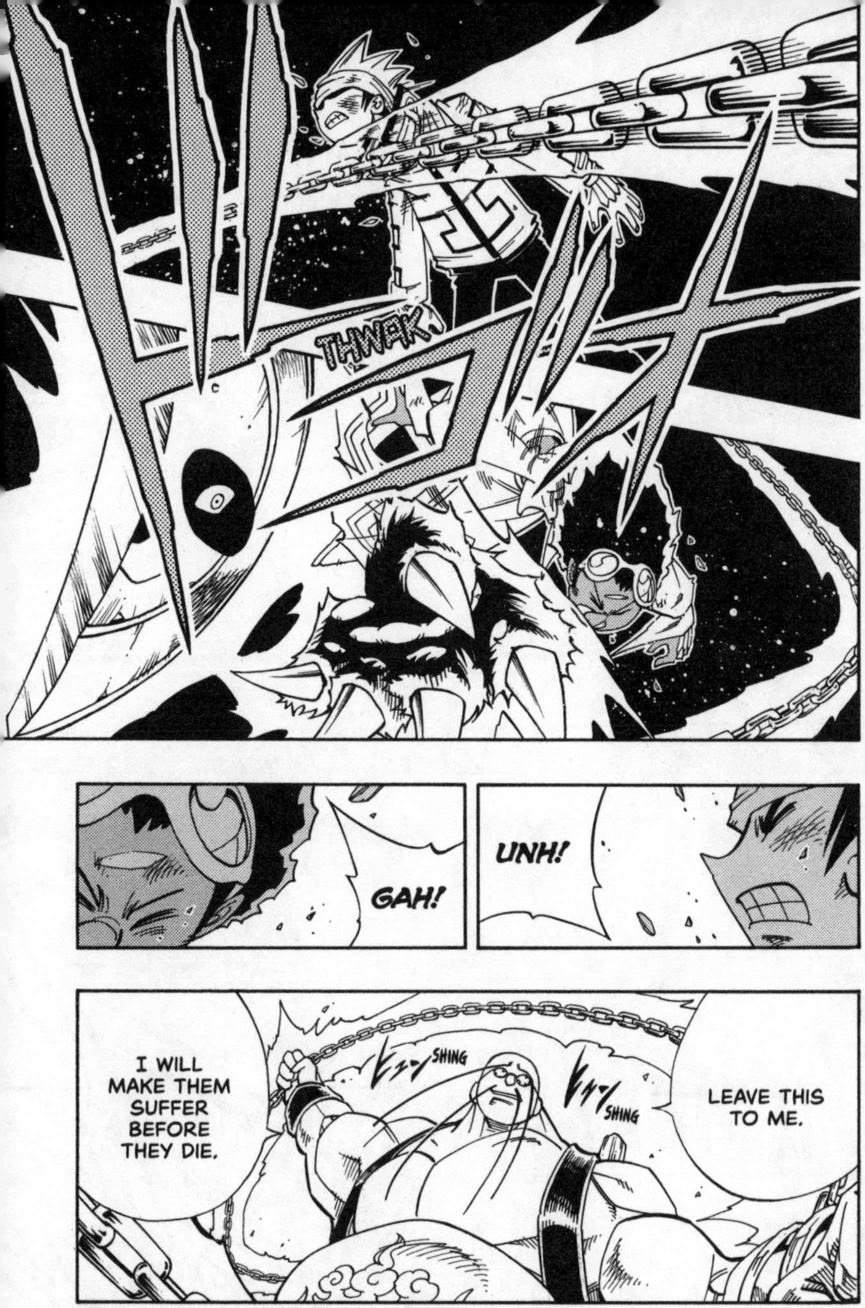
THWAK
UNH!
GAH!
LEAVE THIS TO ME.
SHING
SHING
I WILL MAKE THEM SUFFER BEFORE THEY DIE.

Chapter 152: Secret Mana Value

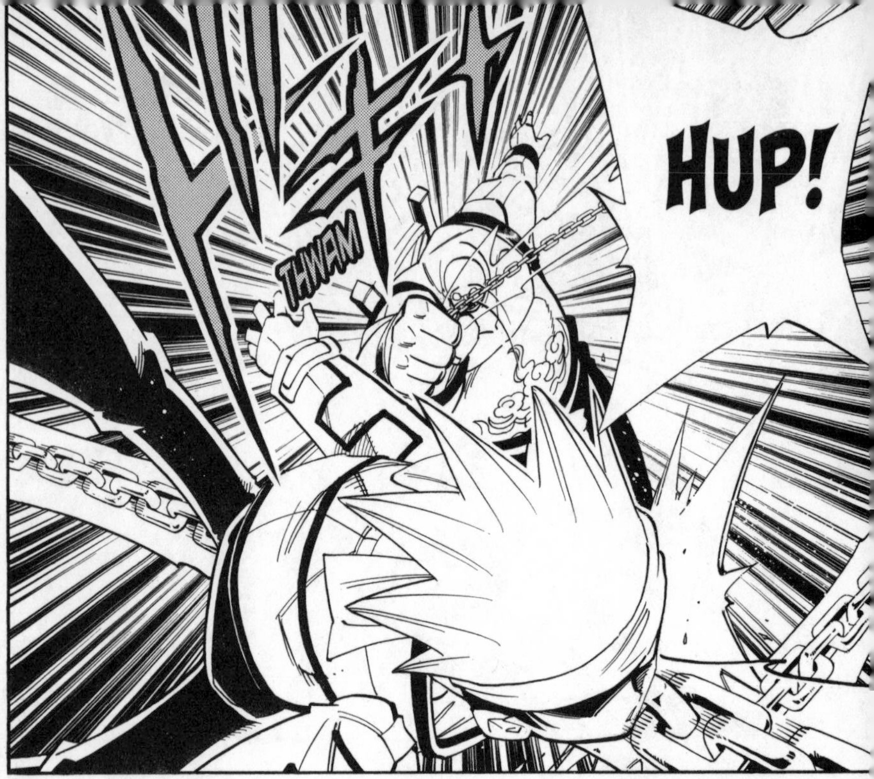
HUP!
THWAM
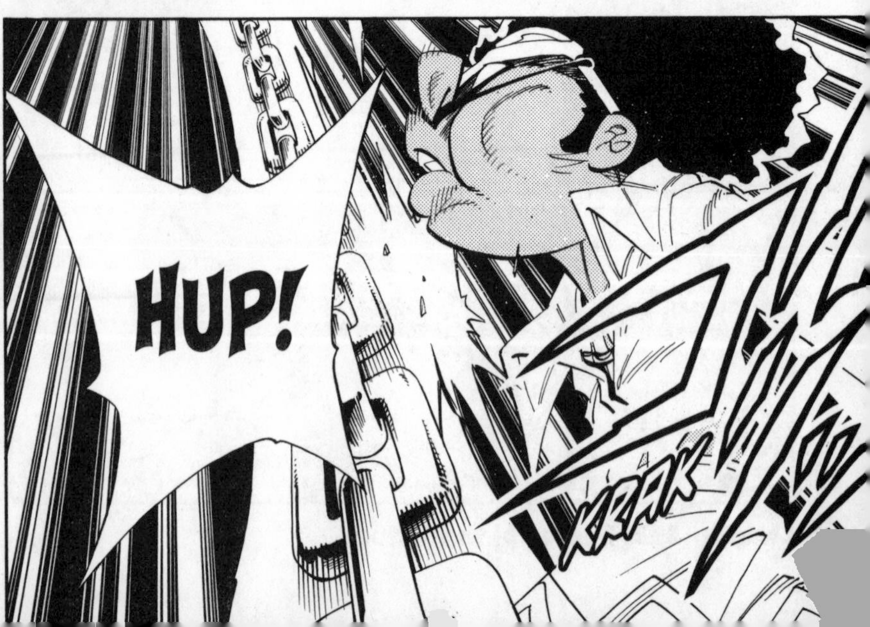
HUP!
KRAK

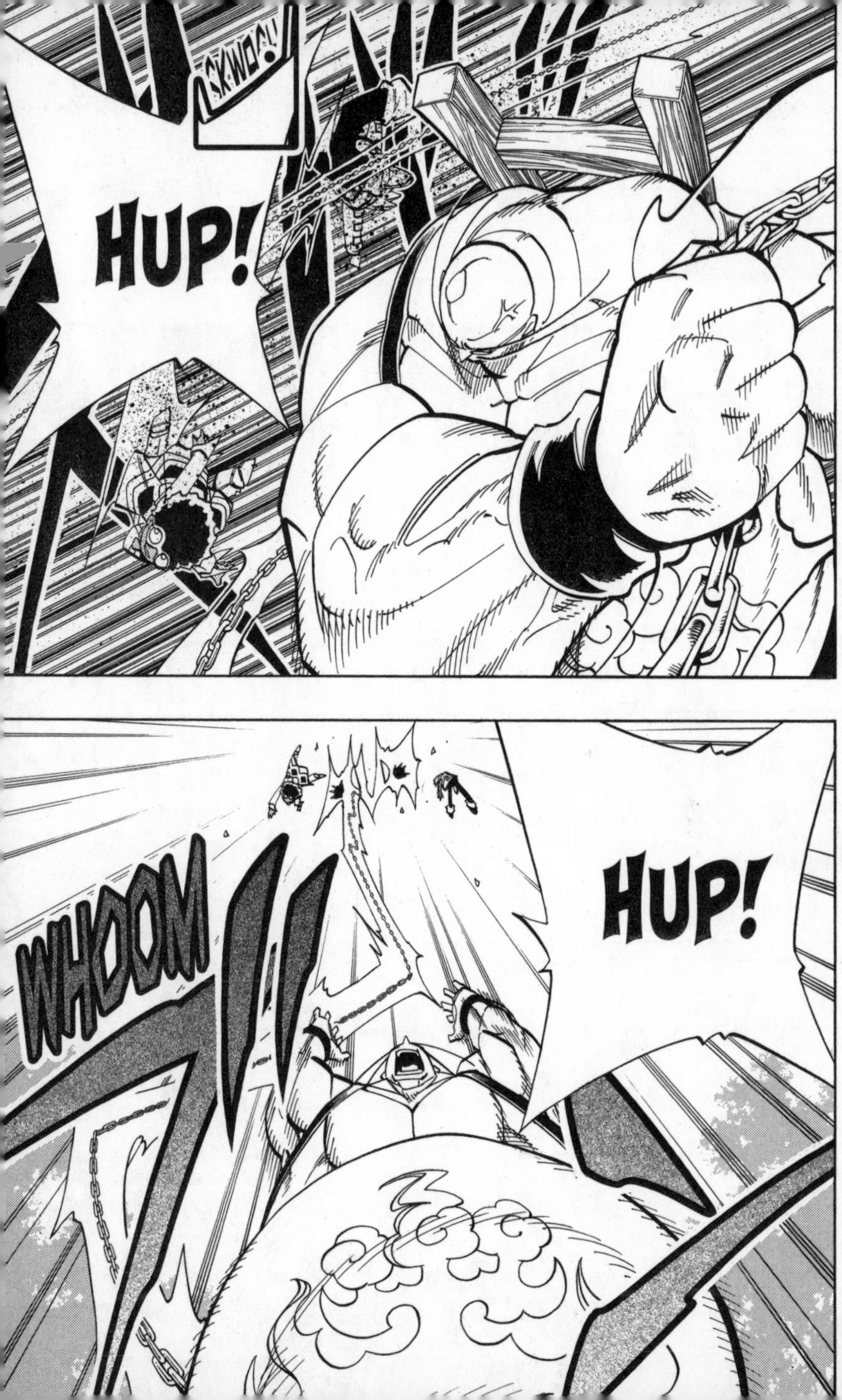
HUP!
HUP!
WHOOM!!

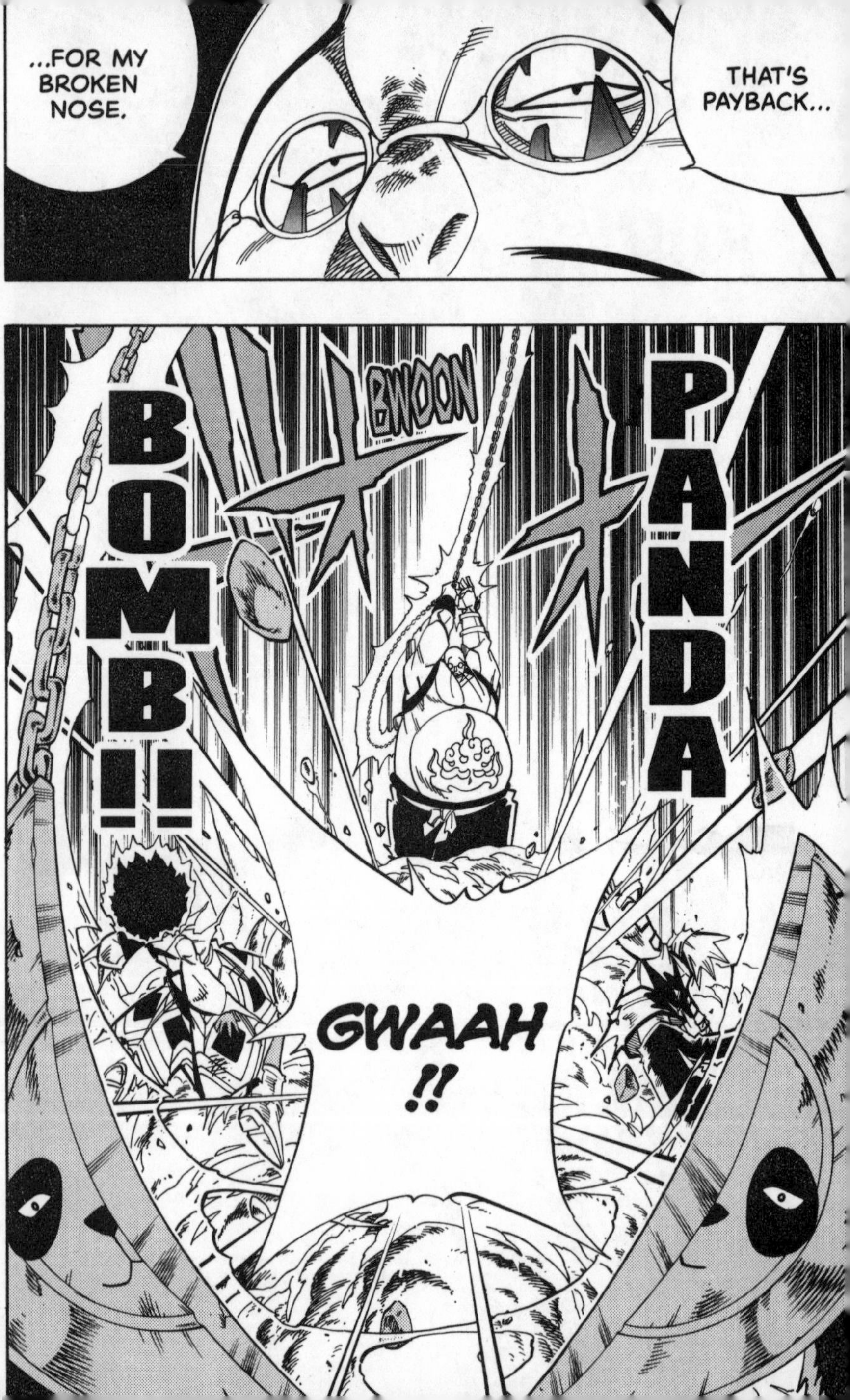
THAT'S PAYBACK...
...FOR MY BROKEN NOSE.
PANDA
BWOON
BOMB!!
GWAAH !!

Chapter 152:

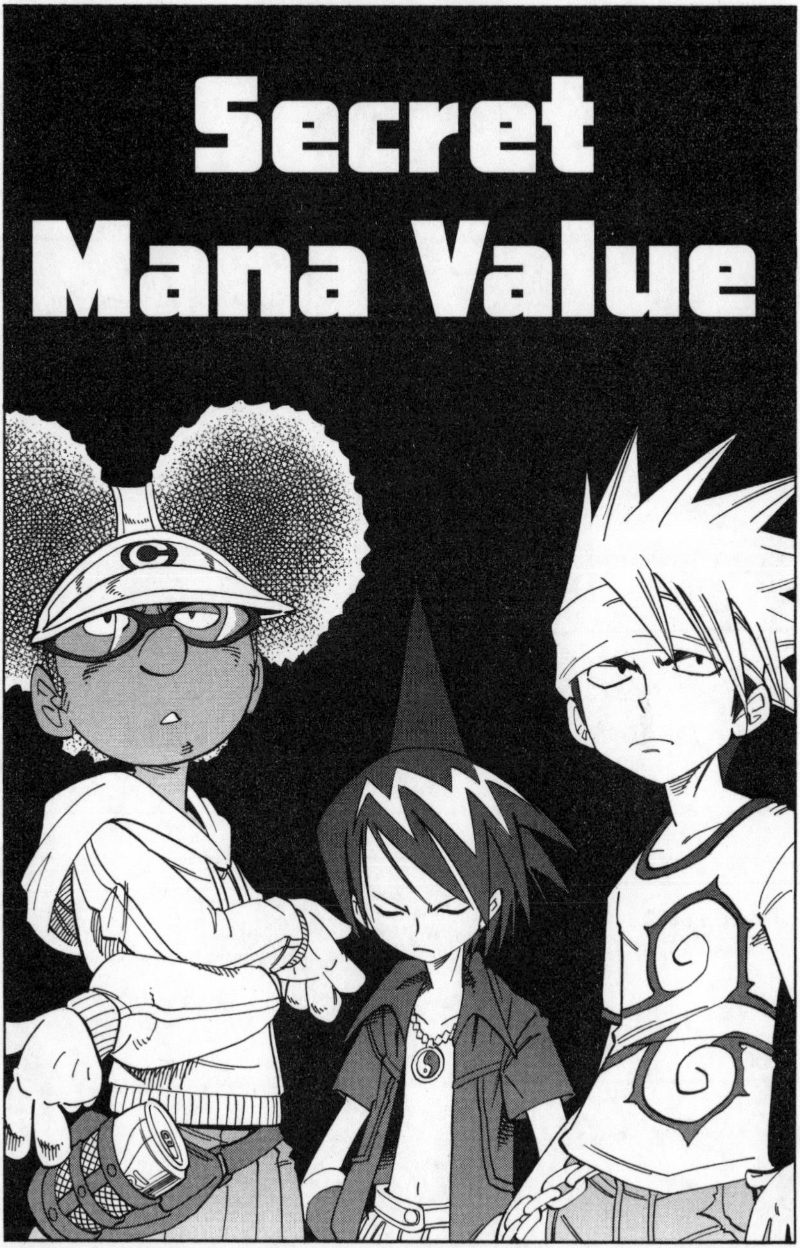
Secret
Mana Value

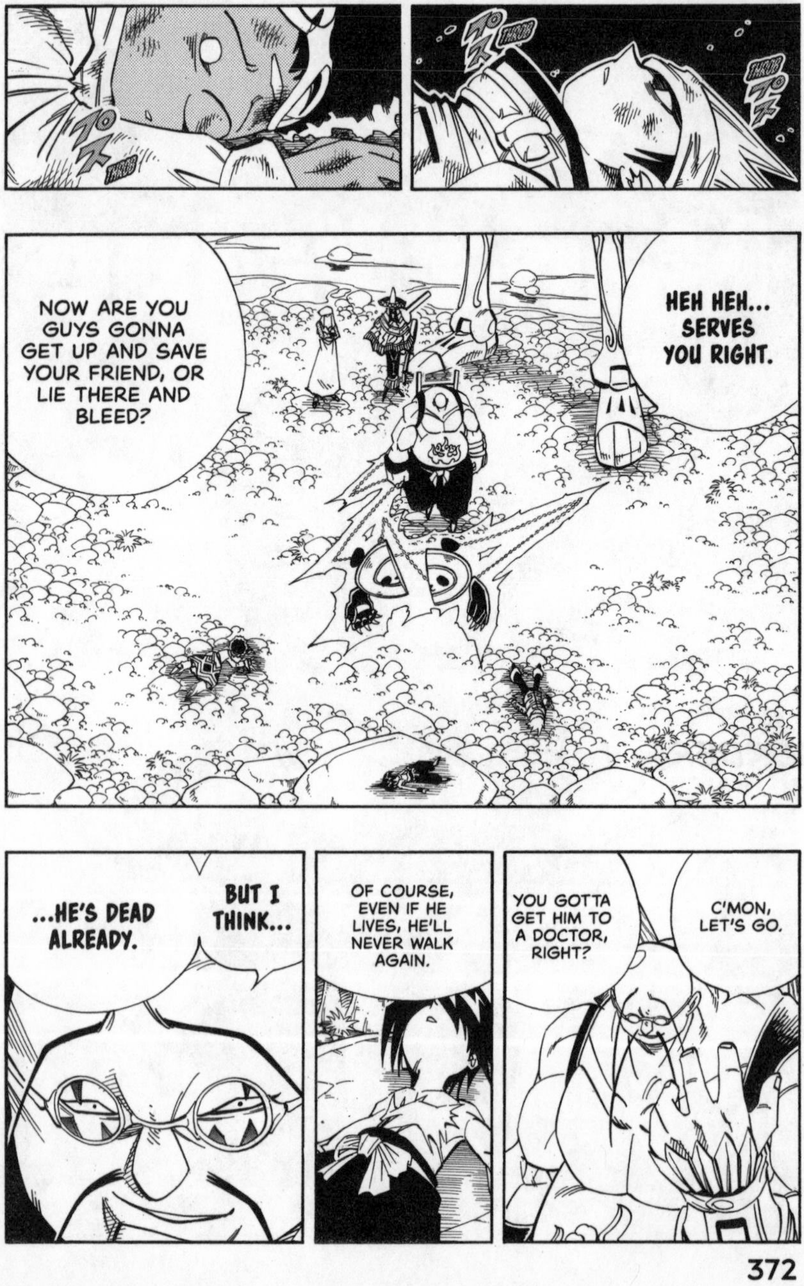
THROB
THROB
THROB
HEH HEH... SERVES YOU RIGHT.
NOW ARE YOU GUYS GONNA GET UP AND SAVE YOUR FRIEND, OR LIE THERE AND BLEED?
C'MON, LET'S GO.
YOU GOTTA GET HIM TO A DOCTOR, RIGHT?
OF COURSE, EVEN IF HE LIVES, HE'LL NEVER WALK AGAIN.
BUT I THINK...
...HE'S DEAD ALREADY.

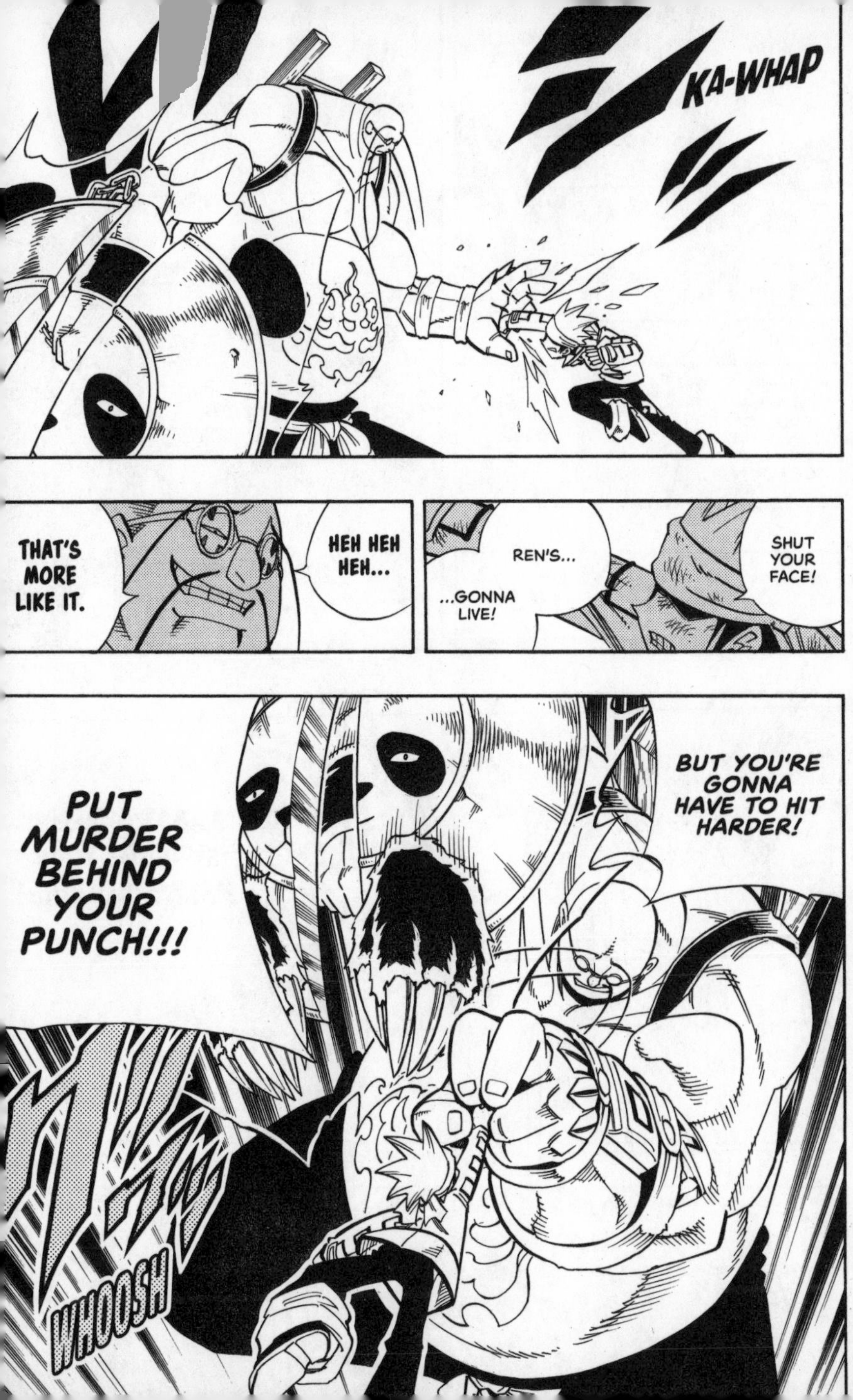
KA-WHAP
SHUT YOUR FACE!
REN'S...
...GONNA LIVE!
HEH HEH HEH...
THAT'S MORE LIKE IT.
BUT YOU'RE GONNA HAVE TO HIT HARDER!
PUT MURDER BEHIND YOUR PUNCH!!!
WHOOSH

STAY BACK.

HUFF

HUFF

HUFF

HORO-HORO...

WHAK

WHO'S GONNA PROTECT REN IF YOU RUN OUT OF MANA?

HUH?

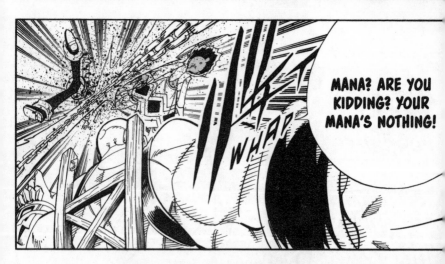

WHAP

MANA? ARE YOU KIDDING? YOUR MANA'S NOTHING!

JOCO!!

UNH ....!

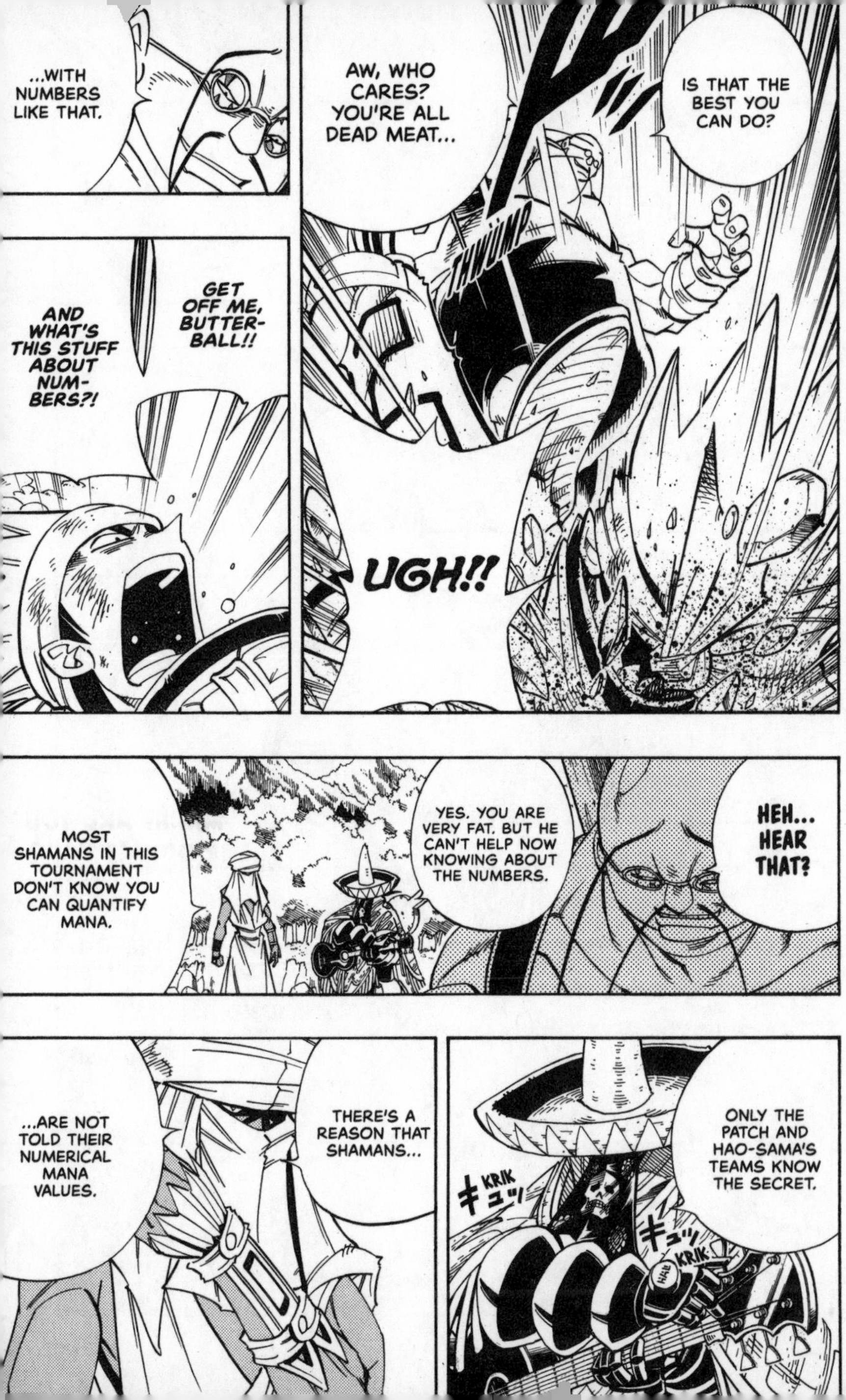
IS THAT THE BEST YOU CAN DO?
AW, WHO CARES? YOU'RE ALL DEAD MEAT...
UGH!!
...WITH NUMBERS LIKE THAT.
GET OFF ME, BUTTER-BALL!!
AND WHAT'S THIS STUFF ABOUT NUM-BERS?!
HEH... HEAR THAT?
YES. YOU ARE VERY FAT. BUT HE CAN'T HELP NOW KNOWING ABOUT THE NUMBERS.
MOST SHAMANS IN THIS TOURNAMENT DON'T KNOW YOU CAN QUANTIFY MANA.
ONLY THE PATCH AND HAO-SAMA'S TEAMS KNOW THE SECRET.
KRIK
KRIK
THERE'S A REASON THAT SHAMANS...
...ARE NOT TOLD THEIR NUMERICAL MANA VALUES.

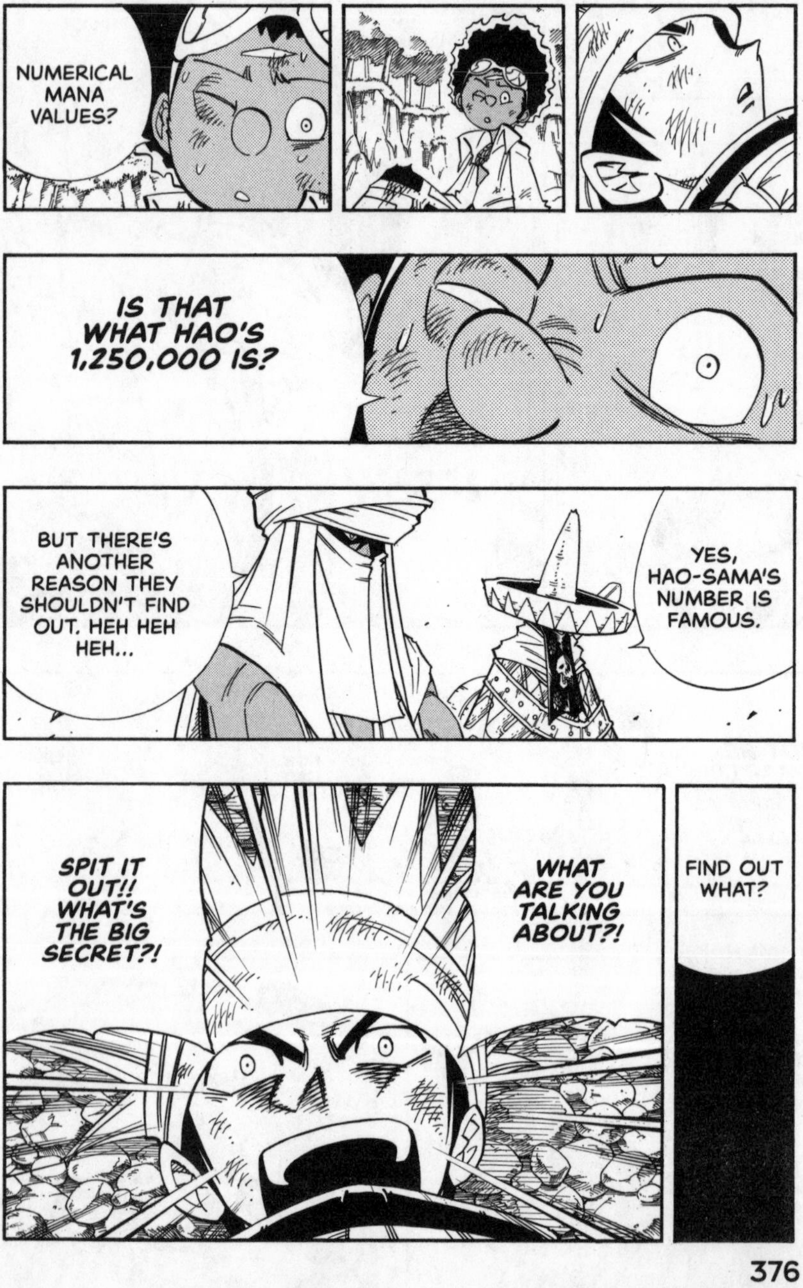
NUMERICAL MANA VALUES?
IS THAT WHAT HAO'S 1,250,000 IS?
YES, HAO-SAMA'S NUMBER IS FAMOUS.
BUT THERE'S ANOTHER REASON THEY SHOULDN'T FIND OUT. HEH HEH HEH...
FIND OUT WHAT?
WHAT ARE YOU TALKING ABOUT?!
SPIT IT OUT!! WHAT'S THE BIG SECRET?!

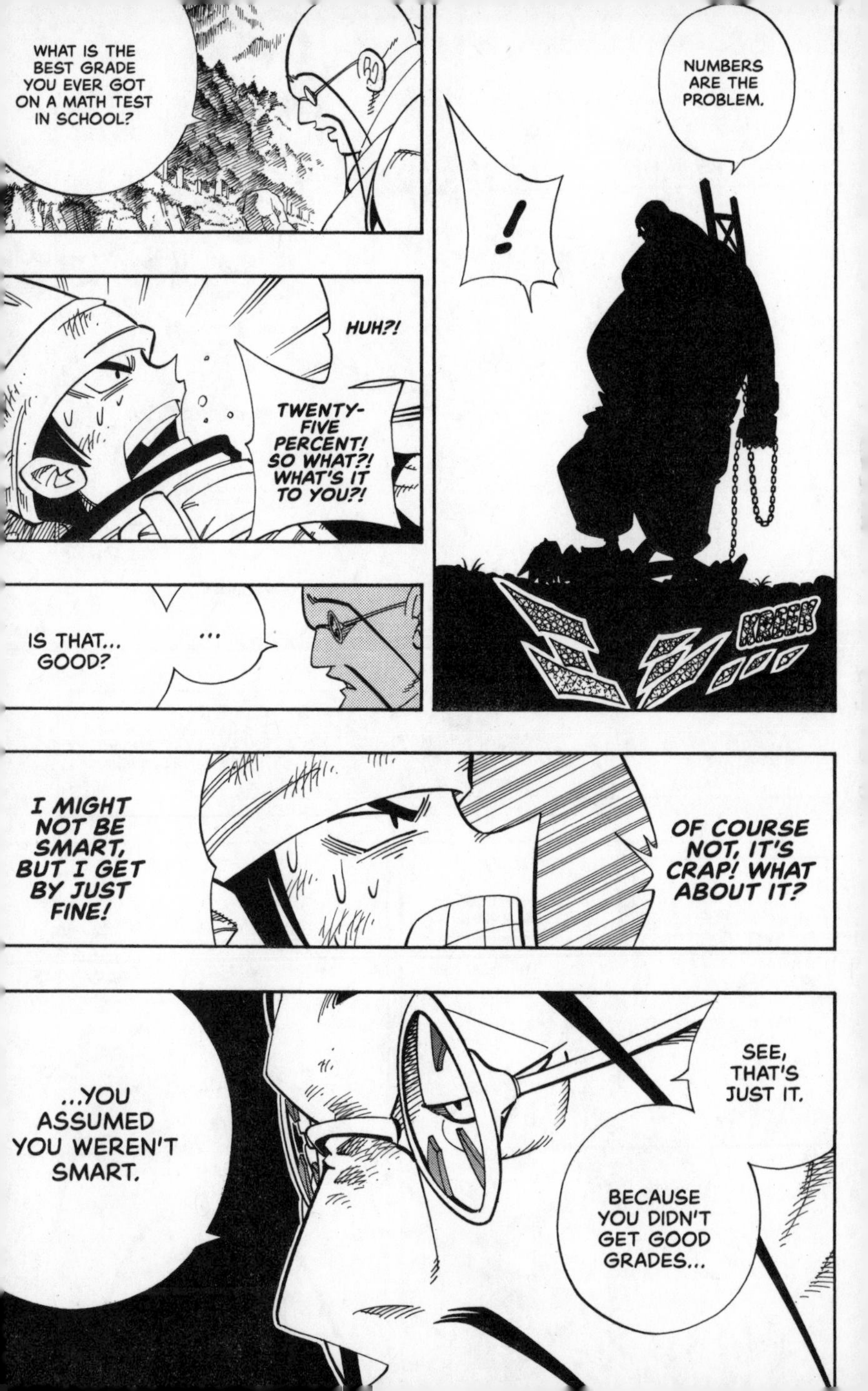
NUMBERS ARE THE PROBLEM.
!
KREEK
WHAT IS THE BEST GRADE YOU EVER GOT ON A MATH TEST IN SCHOOL?
HUH?!
TWENTY-FIVE PERCENT! SO WHAT?! WHAT'S IT TO YOU?!
...
IS THAT... GOOD?
OF COURSE NOT, IT'S CRAP! WHAT ABOUT IT?
I MIGHT NOT BE SMART, BUT I GET BY JUST FINE!
SEE, THAT'S JUST IT.
BECAUSE YOU DIDN'T GET GOOD GRADES...
...YOU ASSUMED YOU WEREN'T SMART.

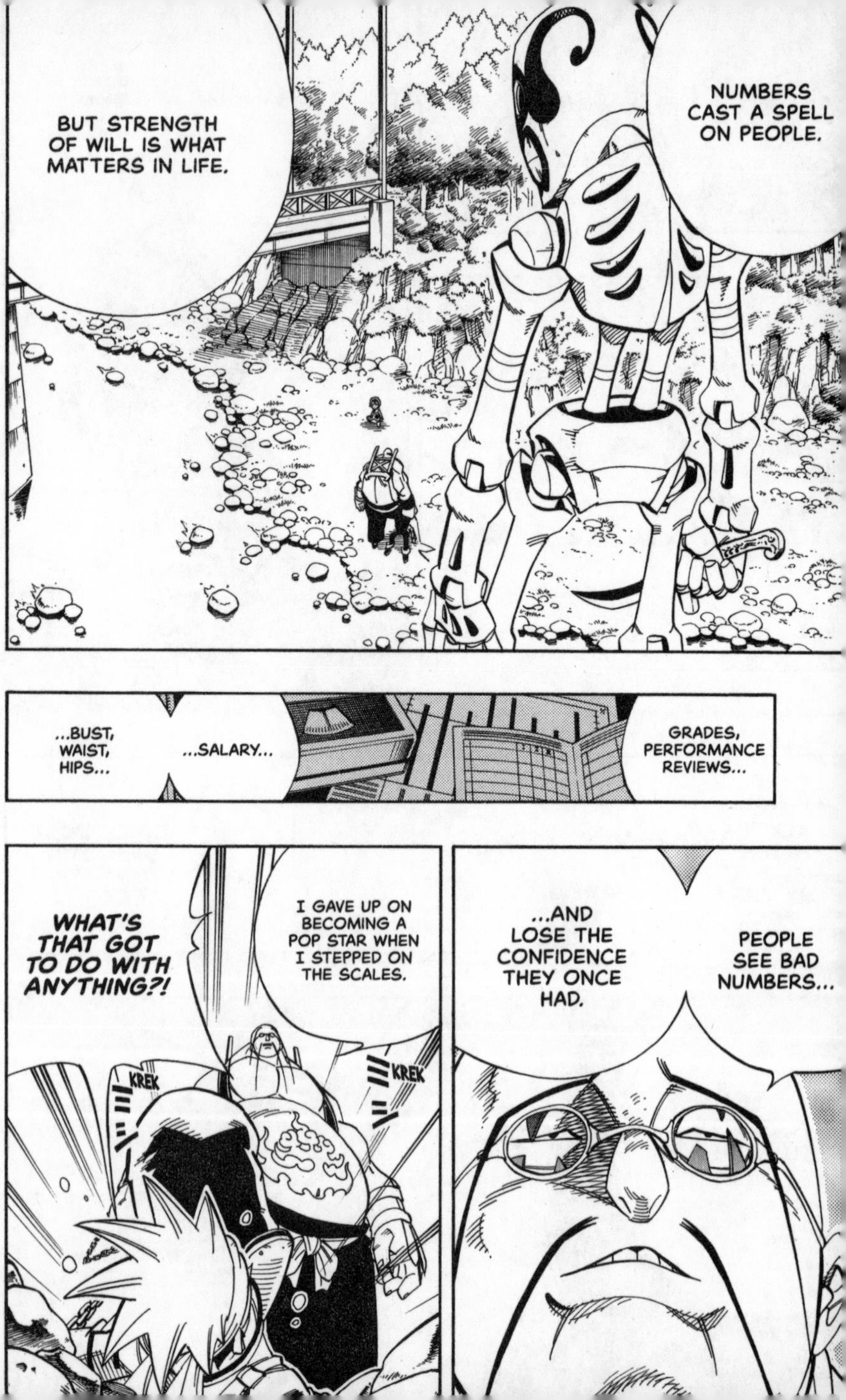
NUMBERS CAST A SPELL ON PEOPLE.
BUT STRENGTH OF WILL IS WHAT MATTERS IN LIFE.
GRADES, PERFORMANCE REVIEWS...
...SALARY...
...BUST, WAIST, HIPS...
PEOPLE SEE BAD NUMBERS...
...AND LOSE THE CONFIDENCE THEY ONCE HAD.
I GAVE UP ON BECOMING A POP STAR WHEN I STEPPED ON THE SCALES.
KREK
KREK
WHAT'S THAT GOT TO DO WITH ANYTHING?!

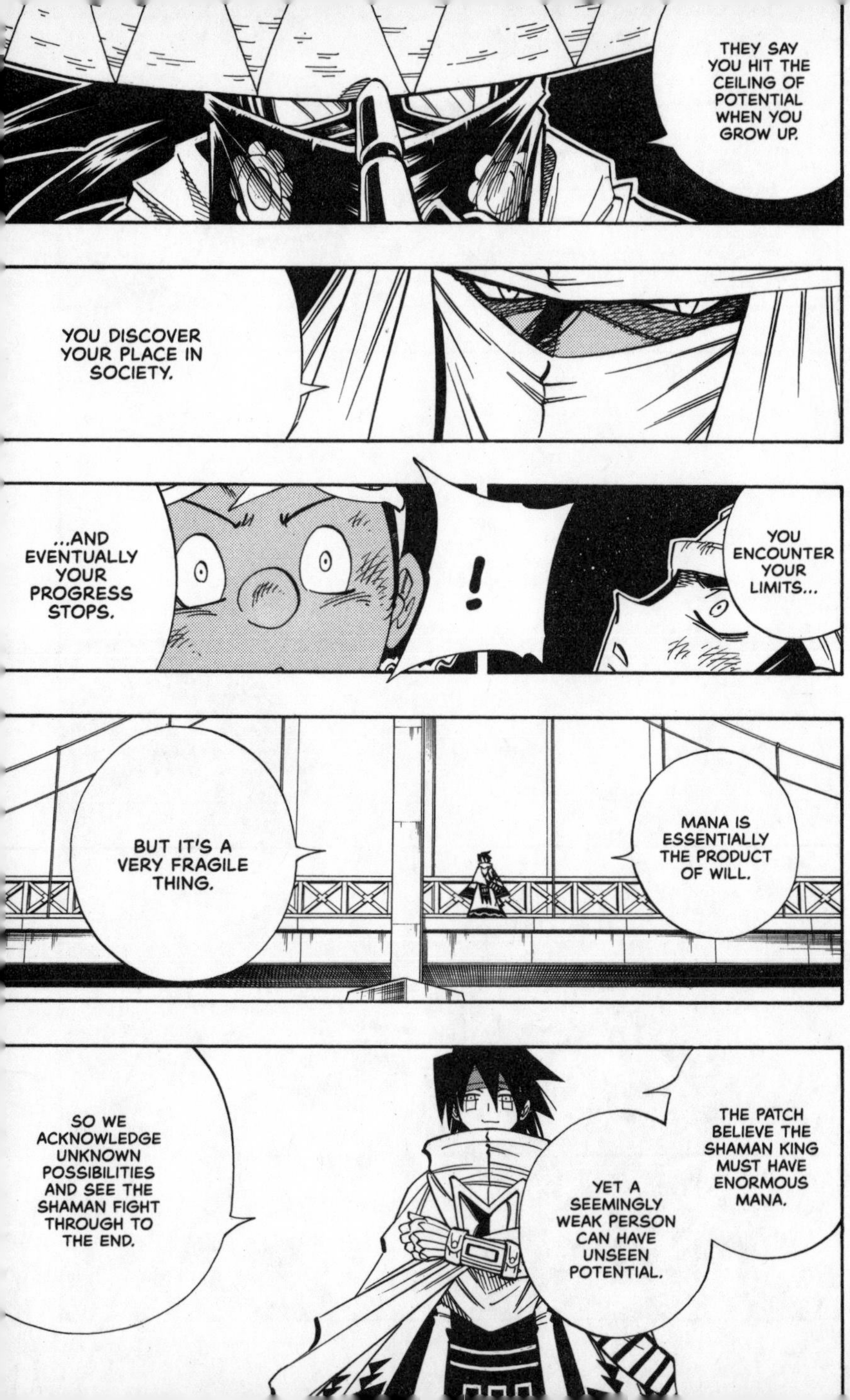
THEY SAY YOU HIT THE CEILING OF POTENTIAL WHEN YOU GROW UP.
YOU DISCOVER YOUR PLACE IN SOCIETY.
YOU ENCOUNTER YOUR LIMITS...
!
...AND EVENTUALLY YOUR PROGRESS STOPS.
MANA IS ESSENTIALLY THE PRODUCT OF WILL.
BUT IT'S A VERY FRAGILE THING.
THE PATCH BELIEVE THE SHAMAN KING MUST HAVE ENORMOUS MANA.
YET A SEEMINGLY WEAK PERSON CAN HAVE UNSEEN POTENTIAL.
SO WE ACKNOWLEDGE UNKNOWN POSSIBILITIES AND SEE THE SHAMAN FIGHT THROUGH TO THE END.

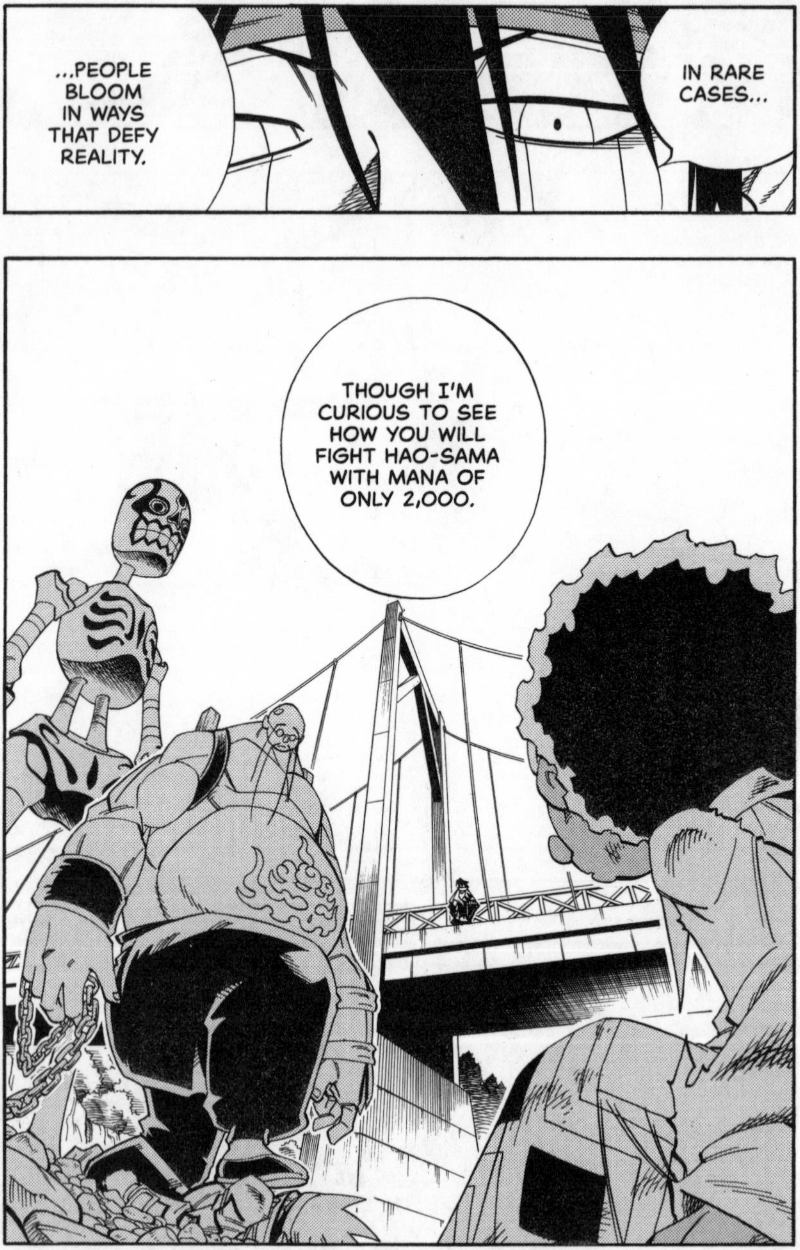
IN RARE CASES...
...PEOPLE BLOOM IN WAYS THAT DEFY REALITY.
THOUGH I'M CURIOUS TO SEE HOW YOU WILL FIGHT HAO-SAMA WITH MANA OF ONLY 2,000.

OUR MANA IS...

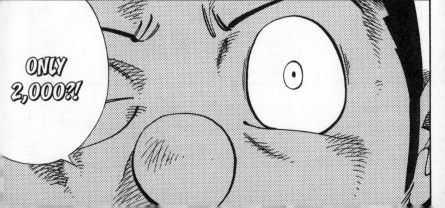

ONLY 2,000?!

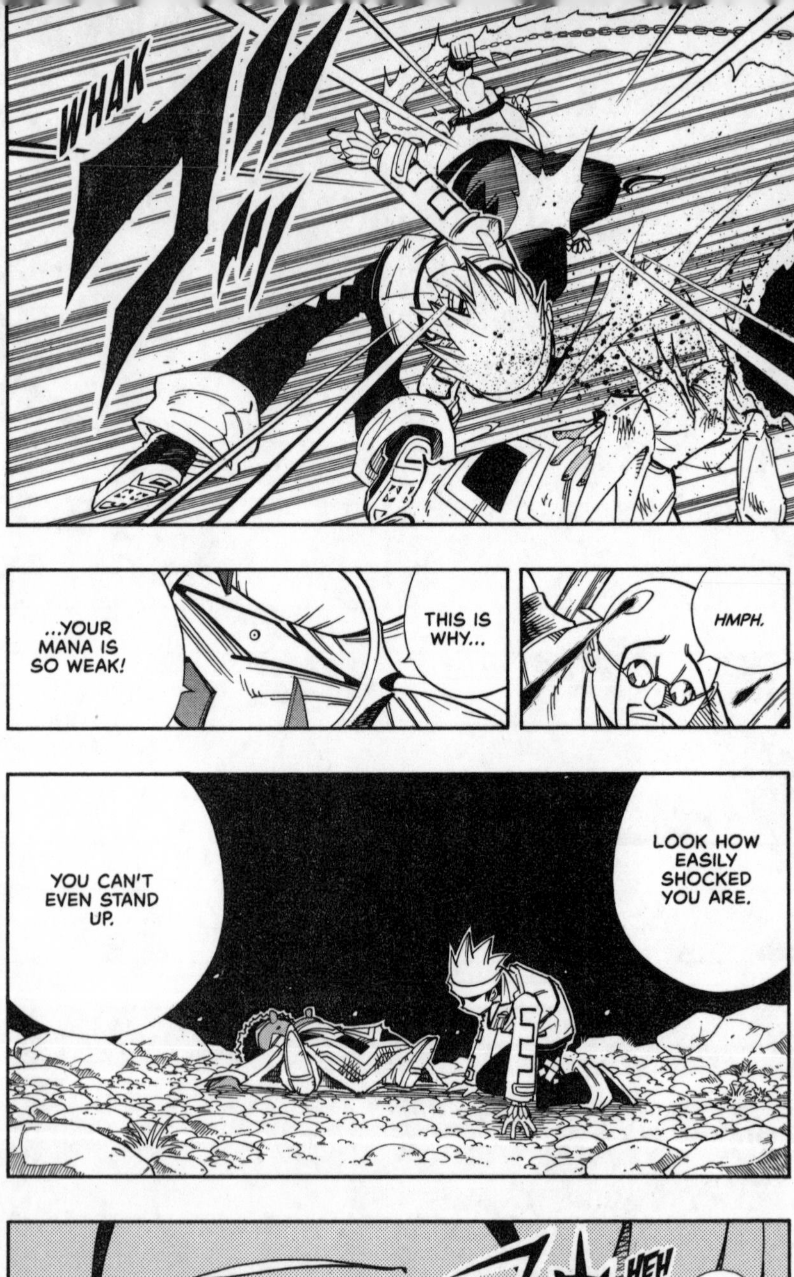
WHAK
HMPH.
THIS IS WHY...
...YOUR MANA IS SO WEAK!
LOOK HOW EASILY SHOCKED YOU ARE.
YOU CAN'T EVEN STAND UP.
HEH

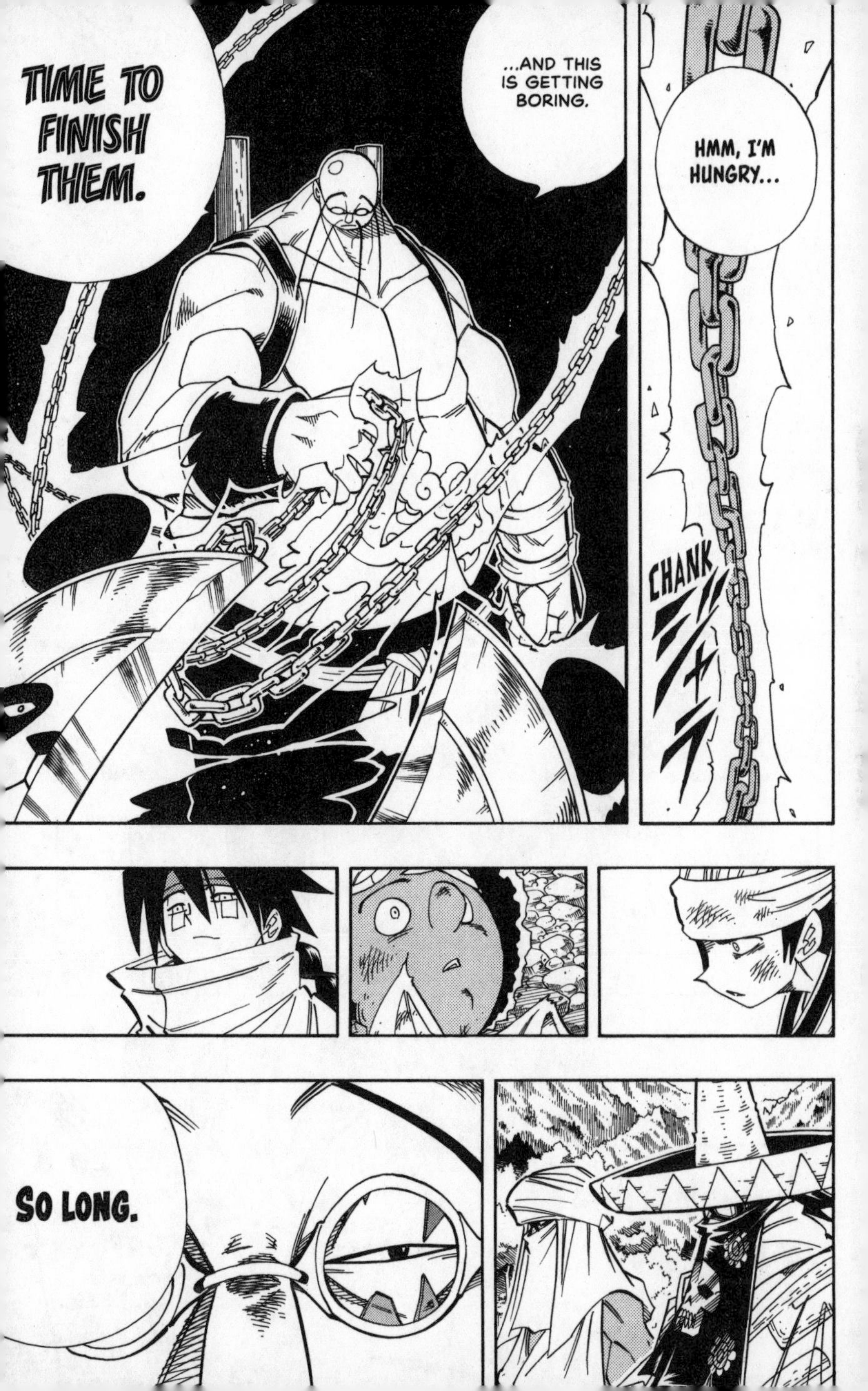
HMM, I'M HUNGRY...
CHANK
...AND THIS IS GETTING BORING.
TIME TO FINISH THEM.
SO LONG.

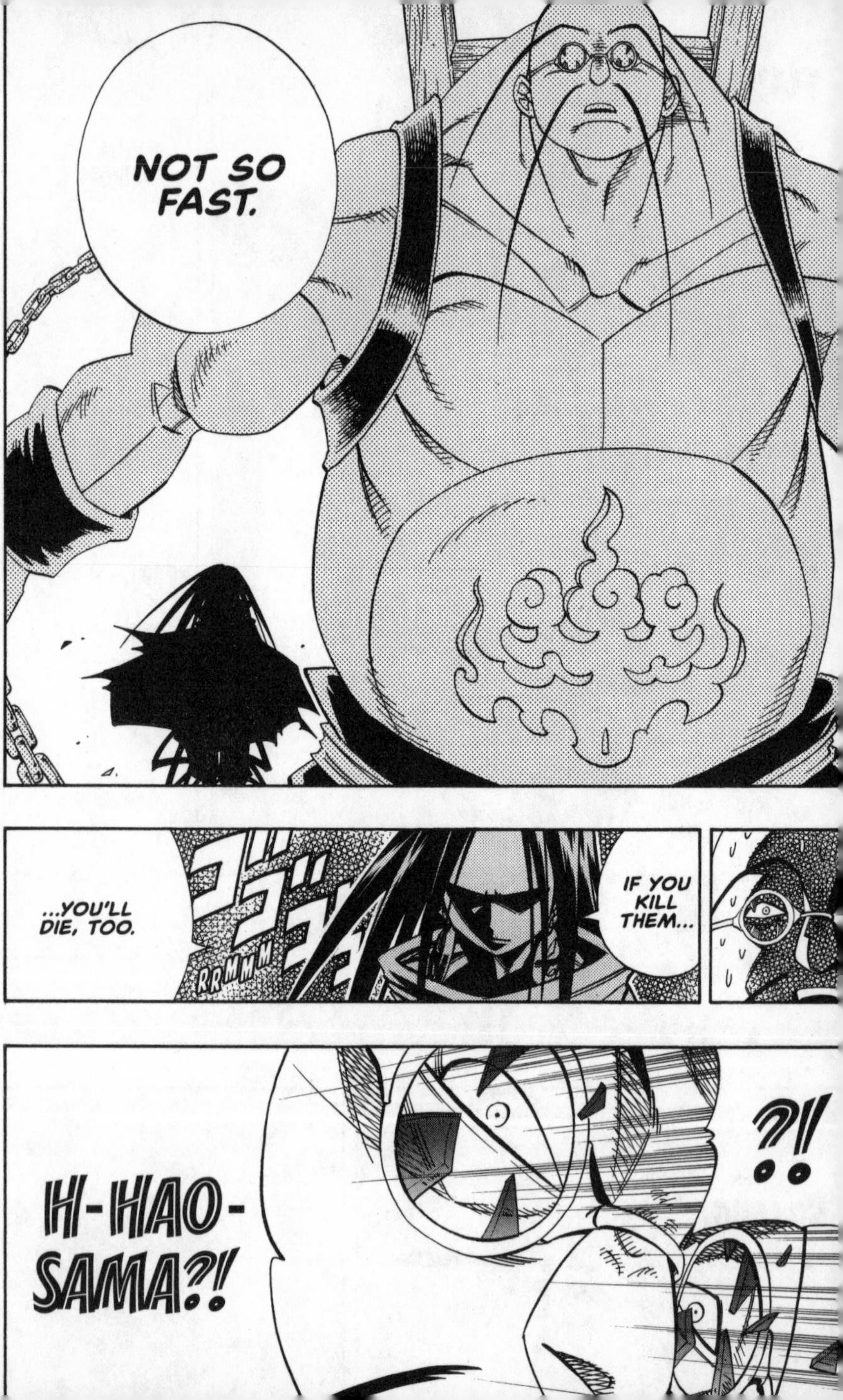
NOT SO FAST.
IF YOU KILL THEM...
...YOU'LL DIE, TOO.
RRMMM
?!
H-HAO-SAMA?!

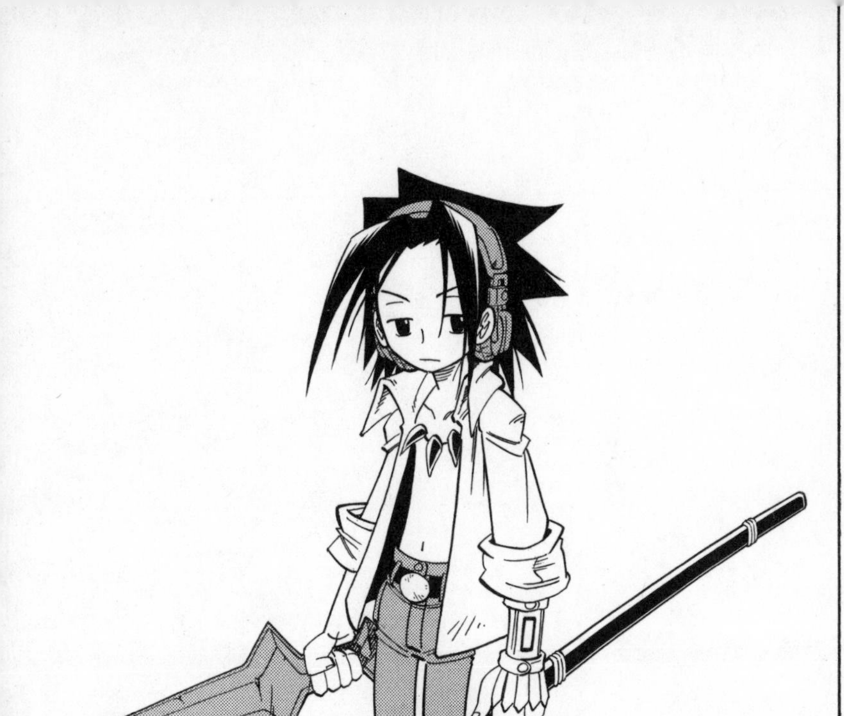

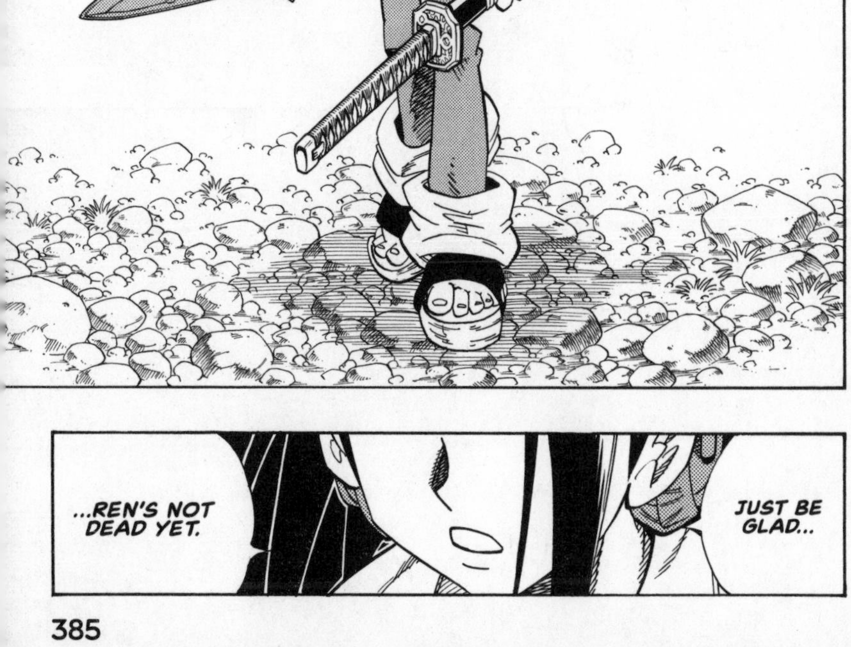
JUST BE GLAD...
...REN'S NOT DEAD YET.

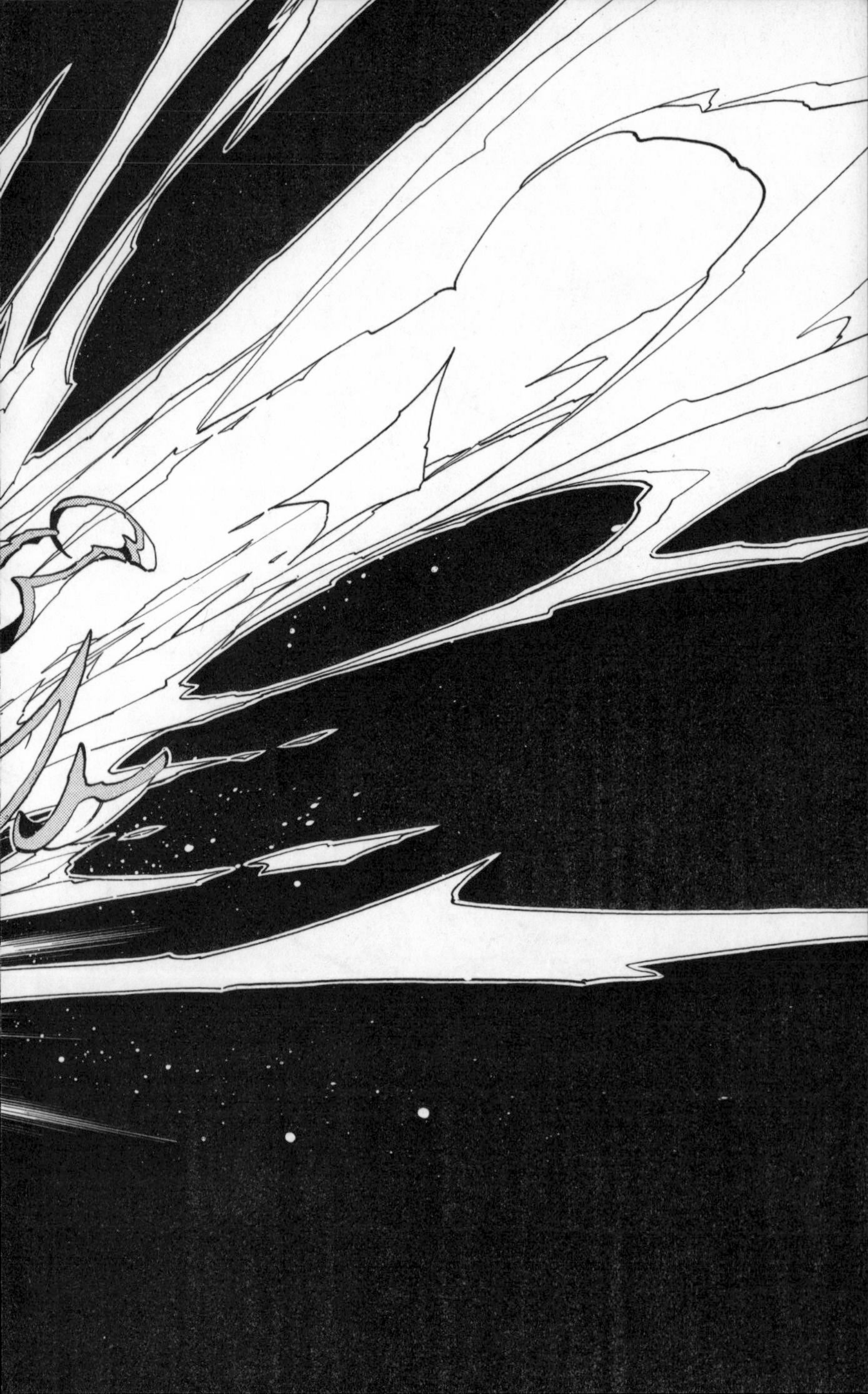

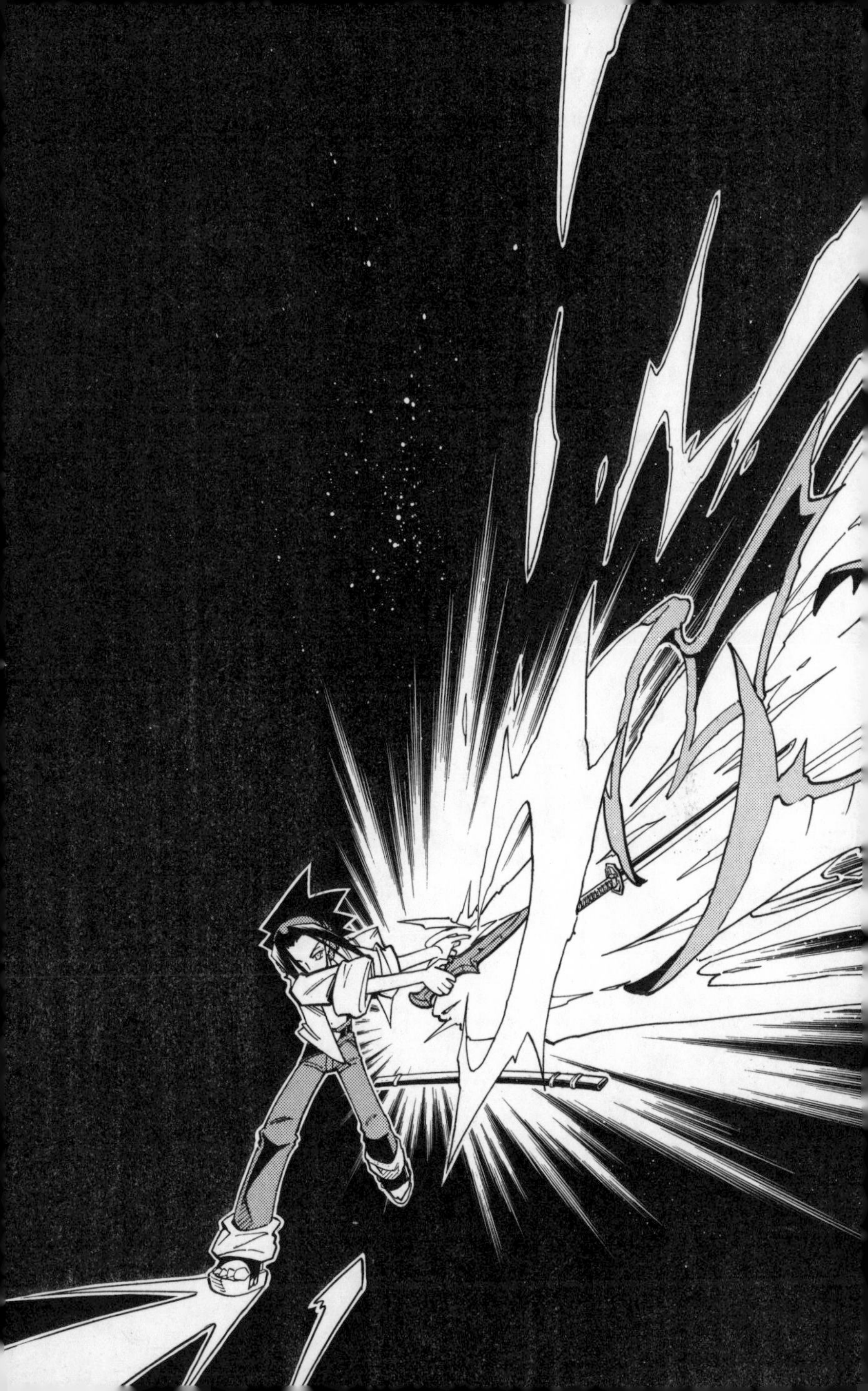

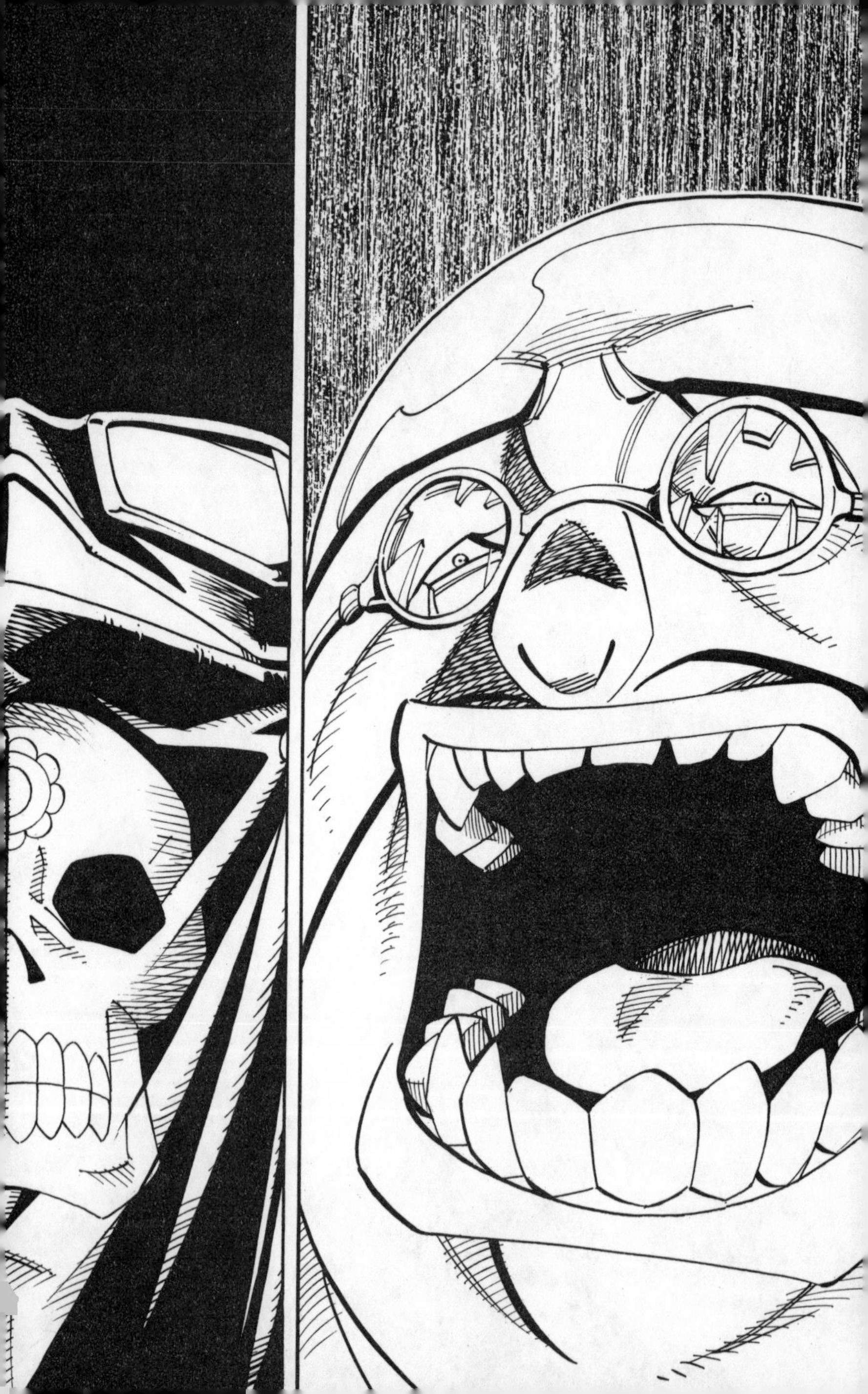

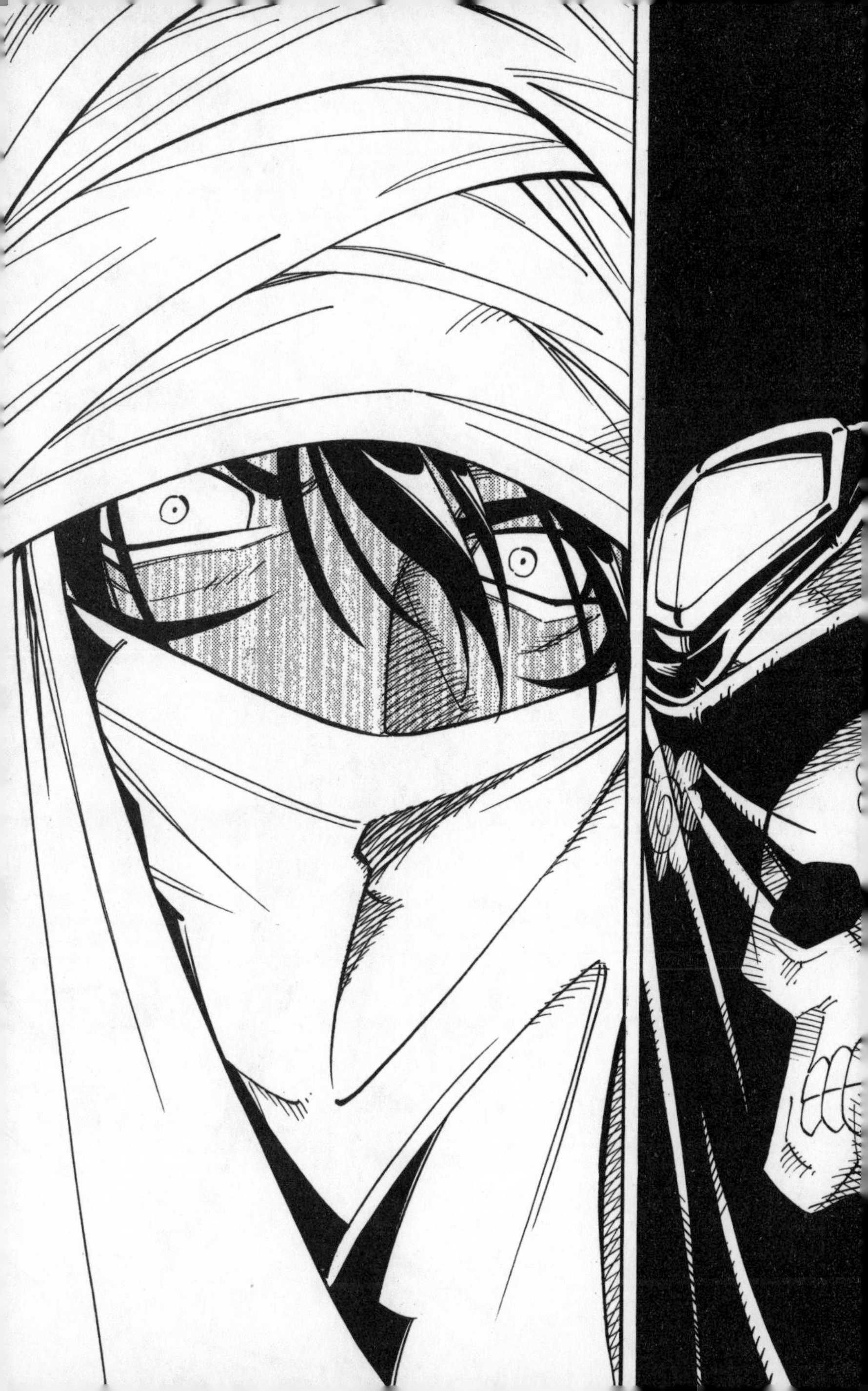

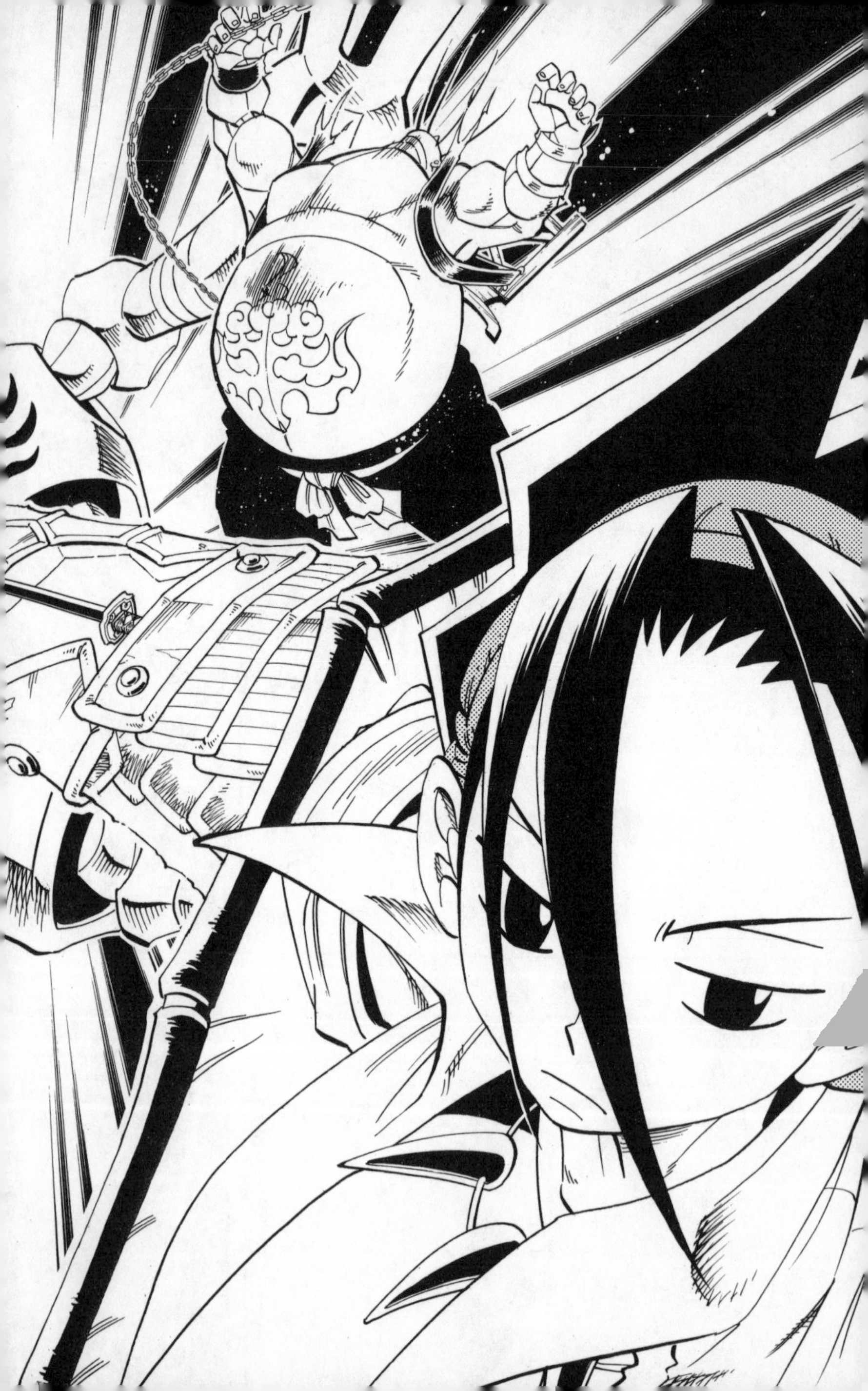

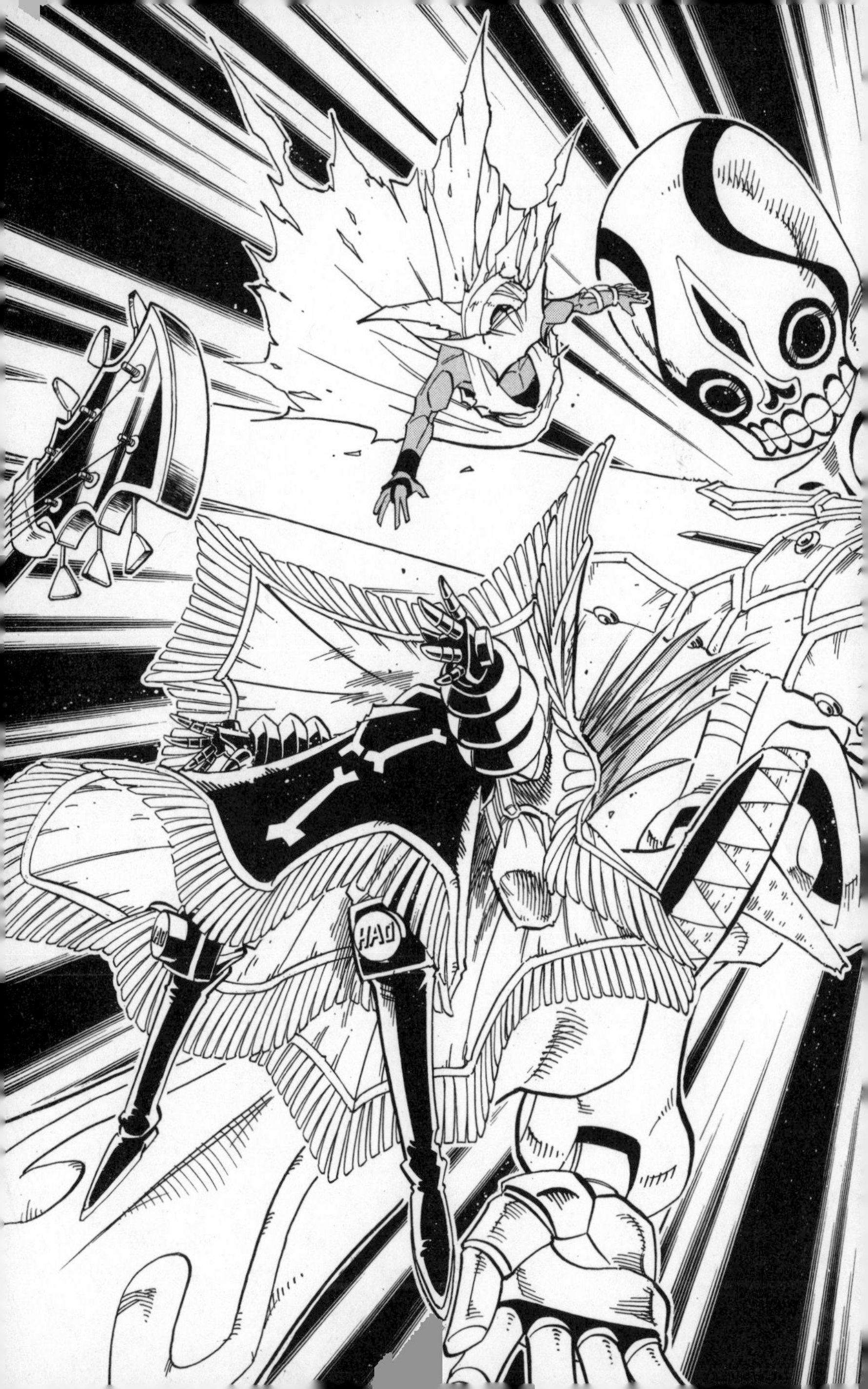

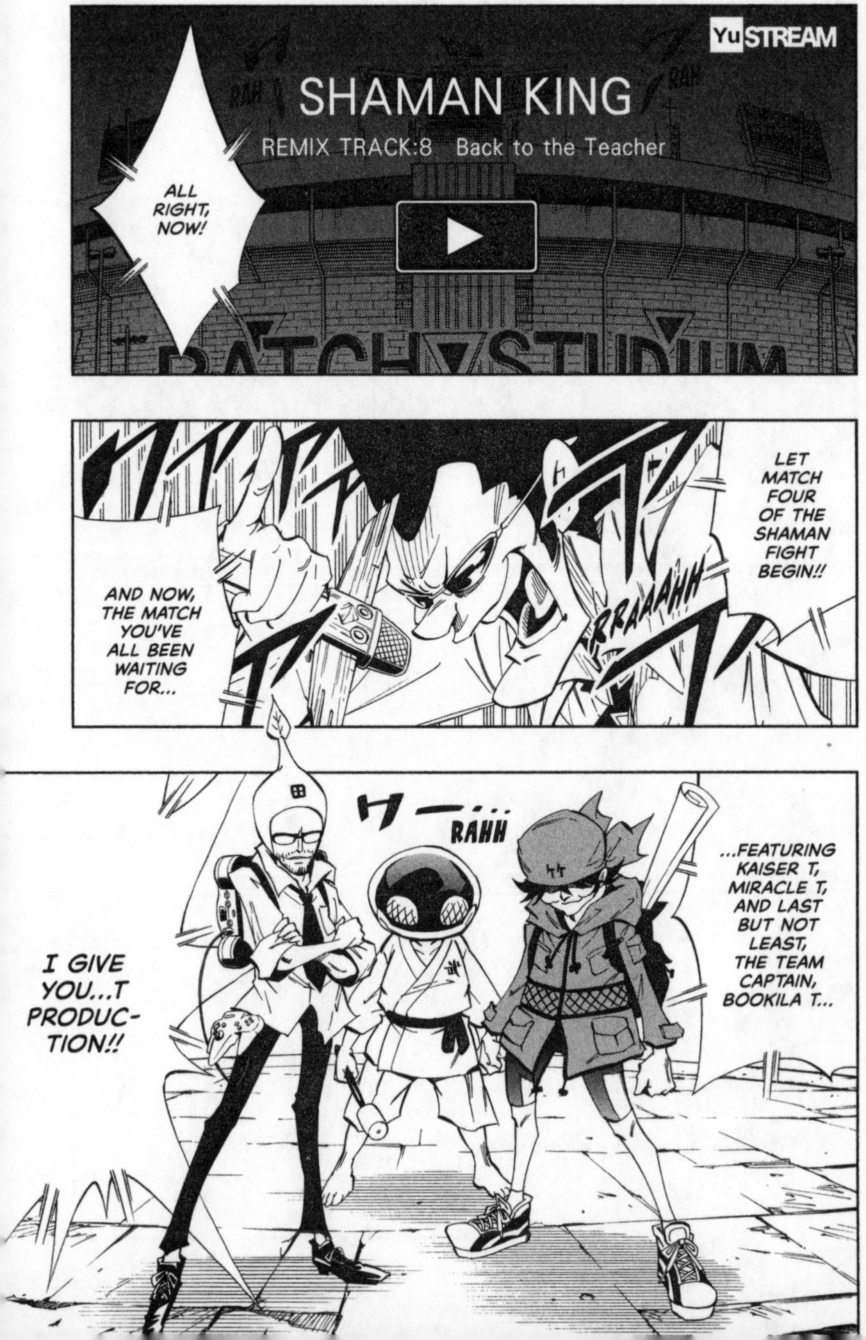
YuSTREAM
SHAMAN KING
REMIX TRACK:8 Back to the Teacher
ALL RIGHT, NOW!
LET MATCH FOUR OF THE SHAMAN FIGHT BEGIN!!
RRAAAHH
AND NOW, THE MATCH YOU'VE ALL BEEN WAITING FOR...
...FEATURING KAISER T, MIRACLE T, AND LAST BUT NOT LEAST, THE TEAM CAPTAIN, BOOKILA T...
ワー...
RAHH
I GIVE YOU...T PRODUCTION!!

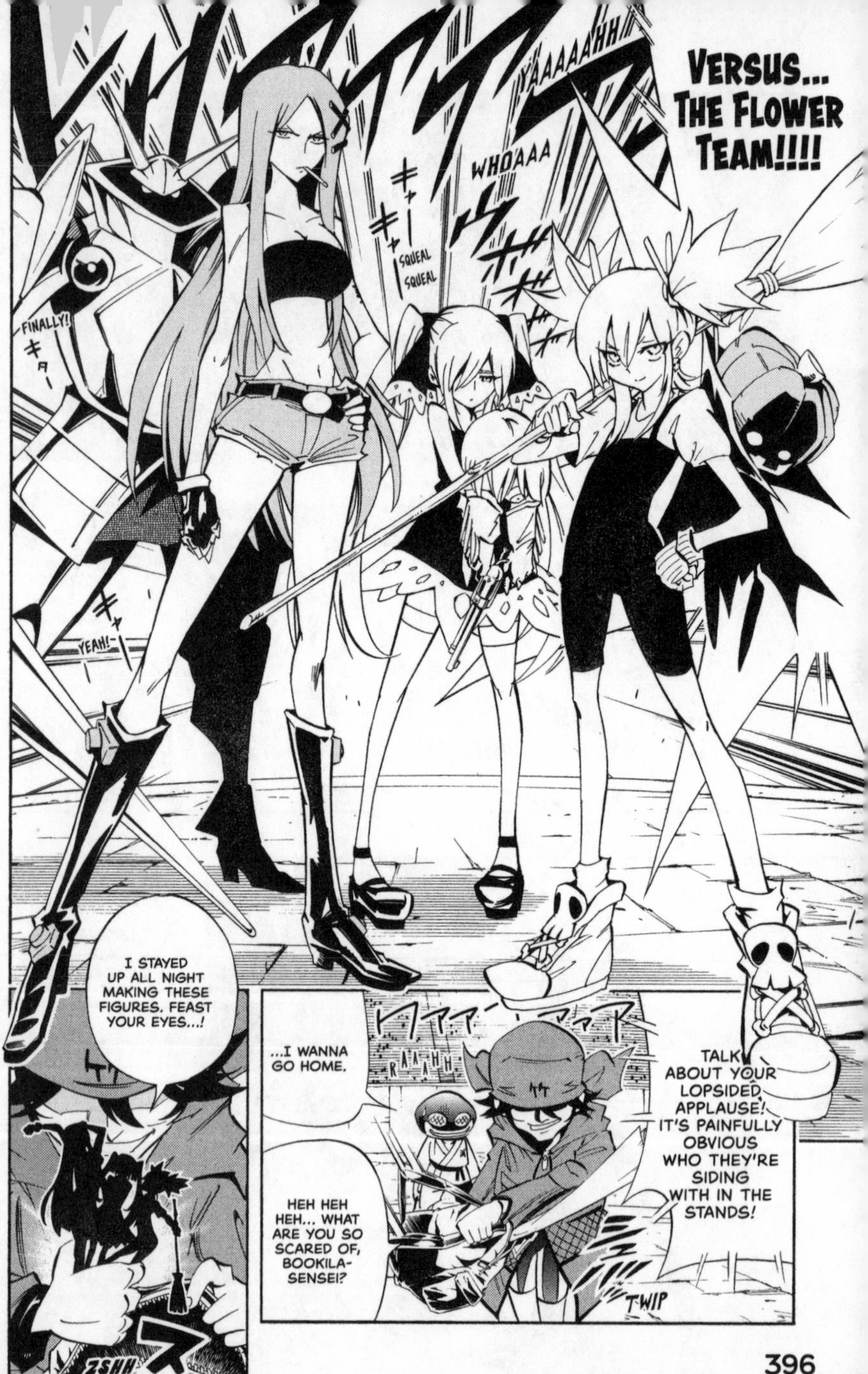
VERSUS... THE FLOWER TEAM!!!!
YAAAAAHH
WHOAAA
SQUEAL SQUEAL
FINALLY!
YEAH!
TALK ABOUT YOUR LOPSIDED APPLAUSE! IT'S PAINFULLY OBVIOUS WHO THEY'RE SIDING WITH IN THE STANDS!
RAAAHH
...I WANNA GO HOME.
HEH HEH HEH... WHAT ARE YOU SO SCARED OF, BOOKILA-SENSEI?
TWIP
I STAYED UP ALL NIGHT MAKING THESE FIGURES. FEAST YOUR EYES...!
ZSHH

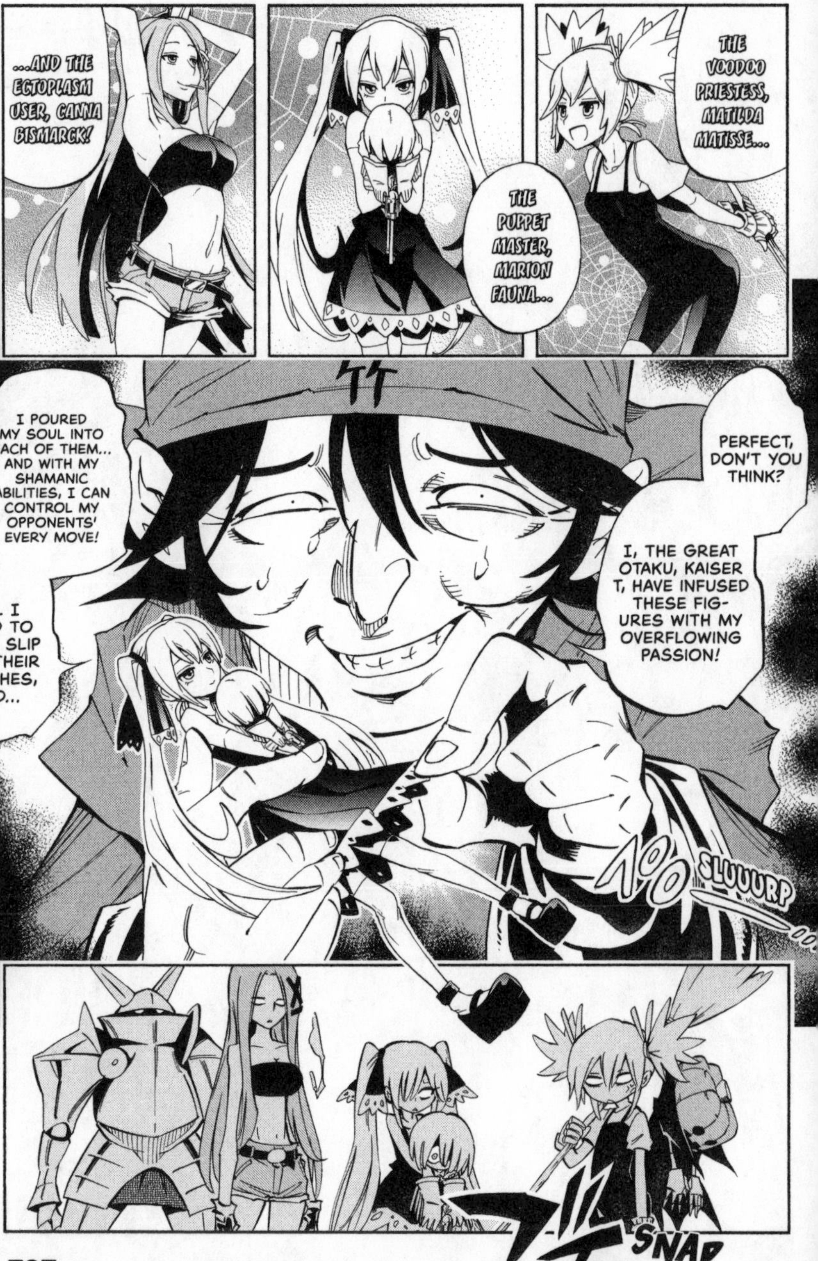
THE VOODOO PRIESTESS, MATILDA MATISSE...
THE PUPPET MASTER, MARION FAUNA...
...AND THE ECTOPLASM USER, CANNA BISMARCK!
PERFECT, DON'T YOU THINK?
I, THE GREAT OTAKU, KAISER T, HAVE INFUSED THESE FIG-URES WITH MY OVERFLOWING PASSION!
I POURED MY SOUL INTO EACH OF THEM... AND WITH MY SHAMANIC ABILITIES, I CAN CONTROL MY OPPONENTS' EVERY MOVE!
ALL I NEED TO DO IS SLIP OFF THEIR CLOTHES, AND...
SLUUURP
SNAP

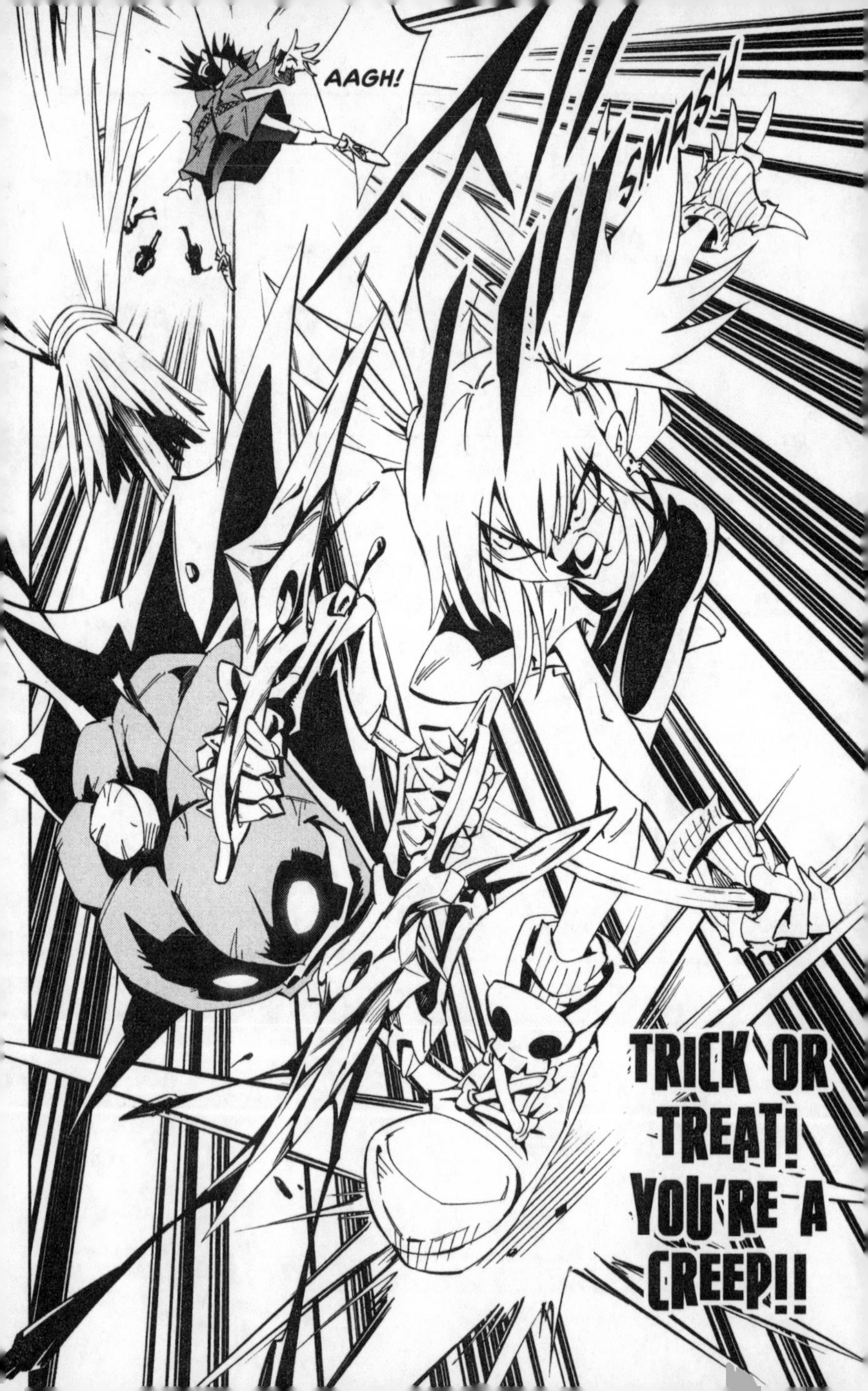
SMASH
AAGH!
TRICK OR TREAT! YOU'RE A CREEP!!

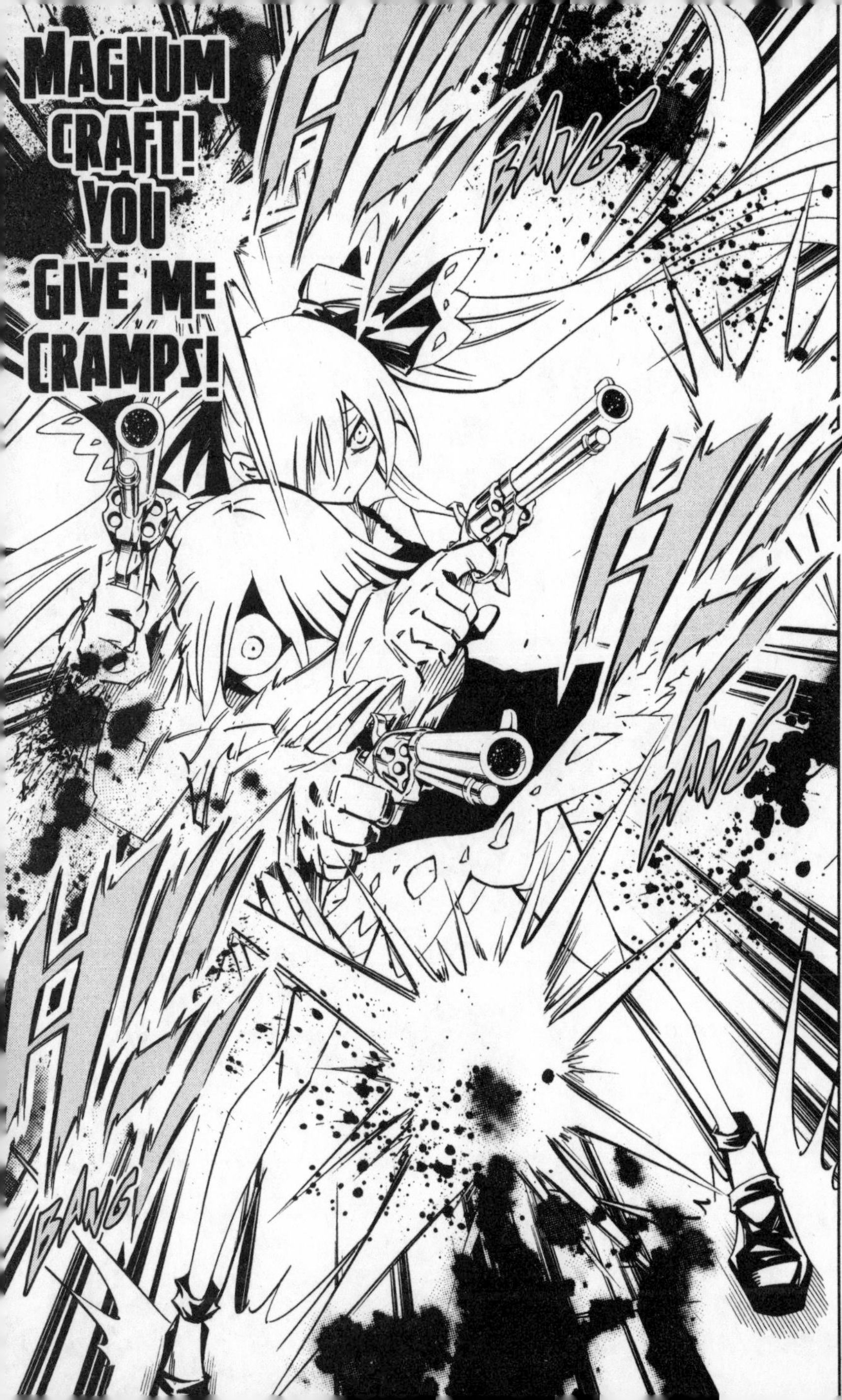
MAGNUM CRAFT! YOU GIVE ME CRAMPS!
BANG
BANG
BANG

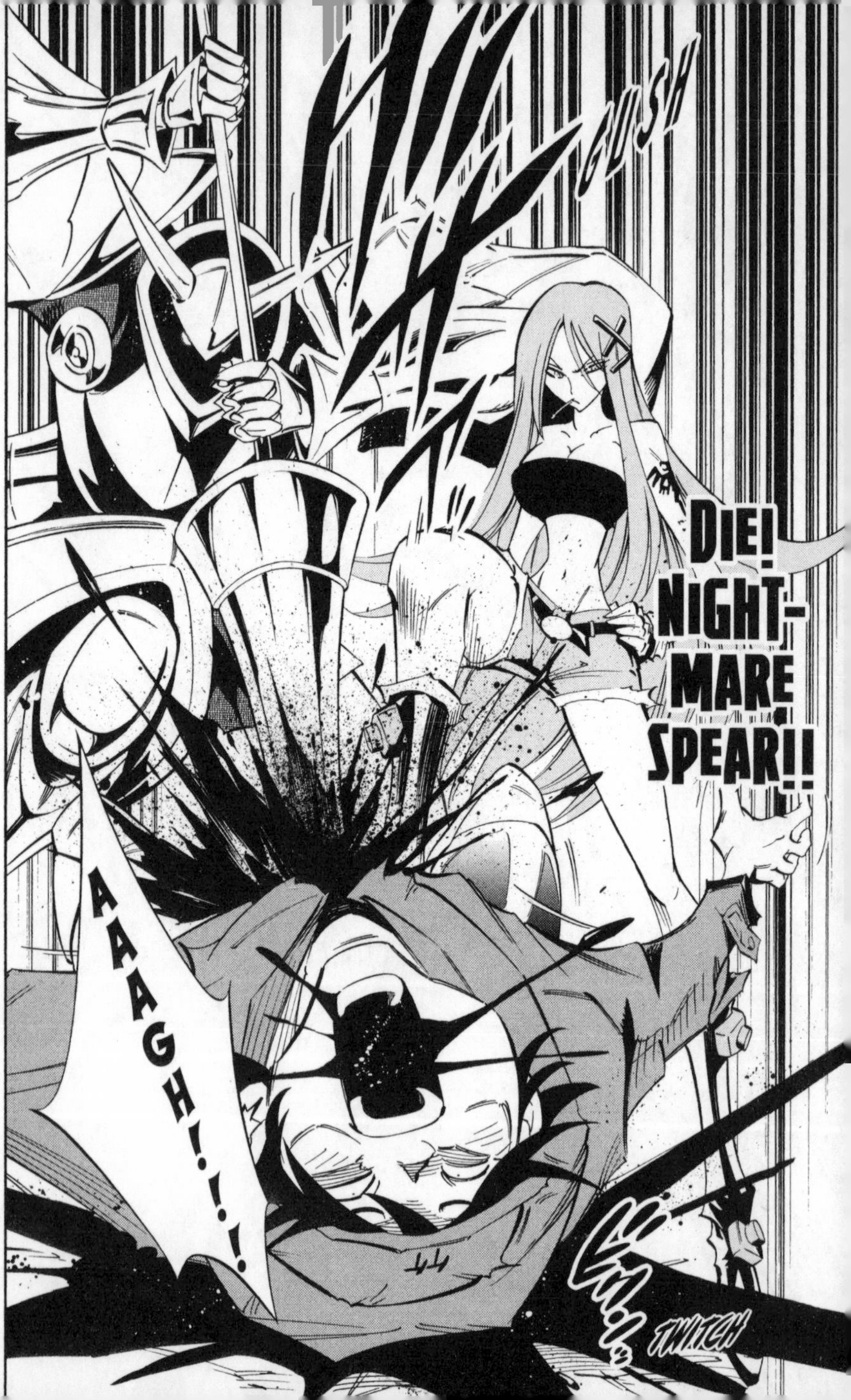
GUSH
DIE! NIGHT-MARE SPEAR!!
AAAGH!!!!
TWITCH

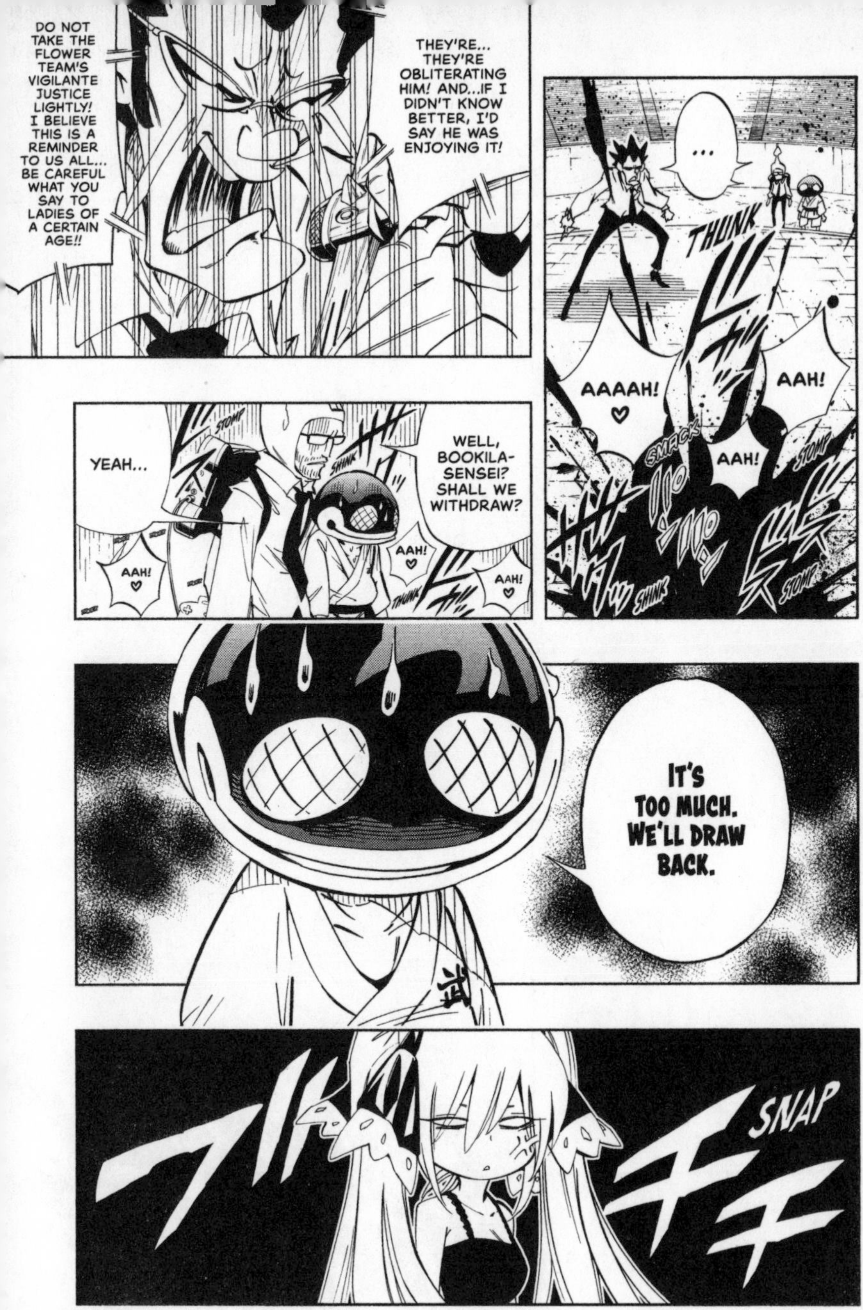
THEY'RE... THEY'RE OBLITERATING HIM! AND...IF I DIDN'T KNOW BETTER, I'D SAY HE WAS ENJOYING IT!
DO NOT TAKE THE FLOWER TEAM'S VIGILANTE JUSTICE LIGHTLY! I BELIEVE THIS IS A REMINDER TO US ALL... BE CAREFUL WHAT YOU SAY TO LADIES OF A CERTAIN AGE!!
...
THUNK
AAH!
AAAAH! ♥
SMACK
AAH!
STOMP
SHINK
STOMP
WELL, BOOKILA-SENSEI? SHALL WE WITHDRAW?
SHINK
STOMP
YEAH...
AAH! ♥
THUNK
AAH! ♥
AAH! ♥
IT'S TOO MUCH. WE'LL DRAW BACK.
SNAP

SHAMAN KING

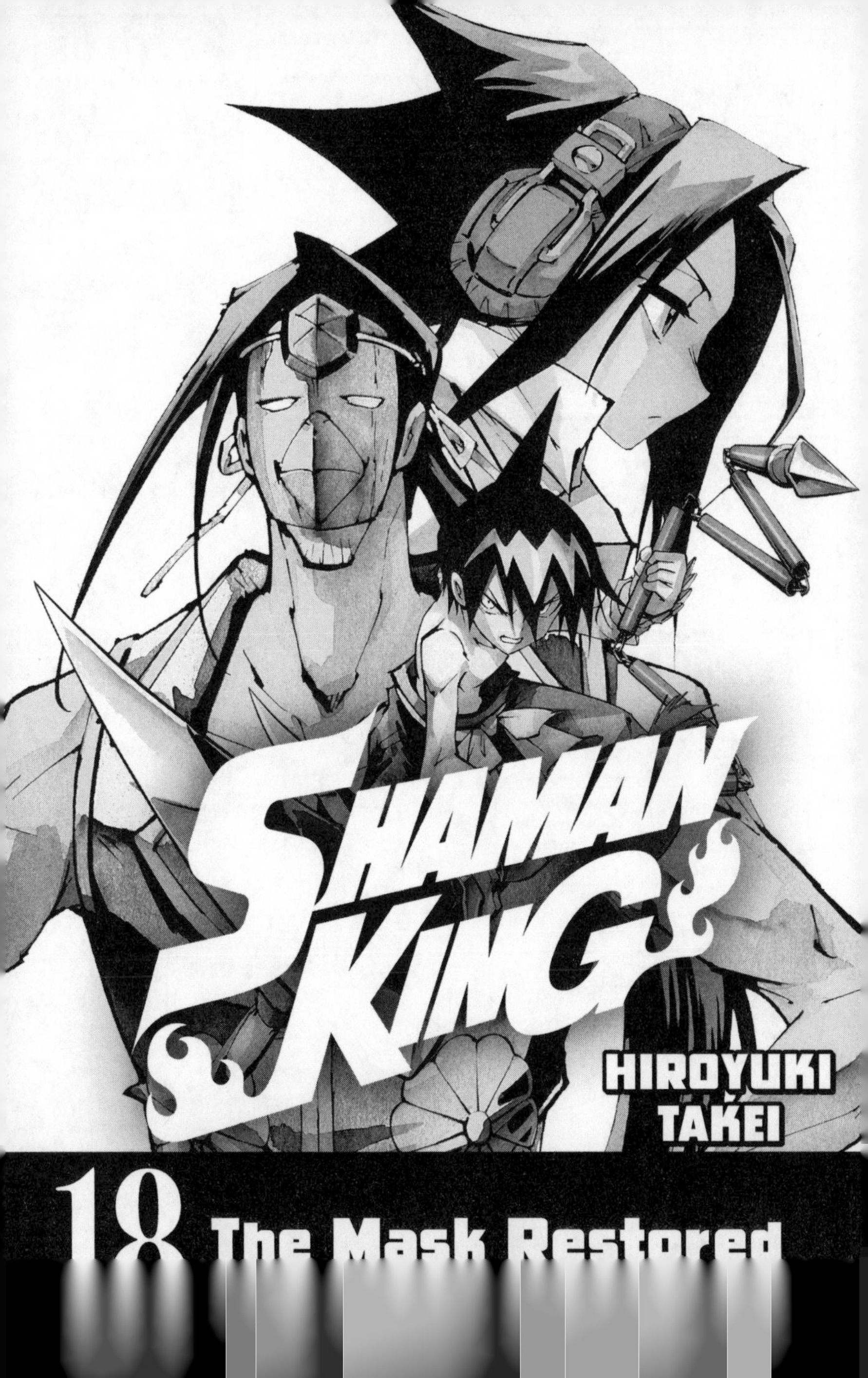
SHAMAN KING
HIROYUKI TAKEI
18 The Mask Restored

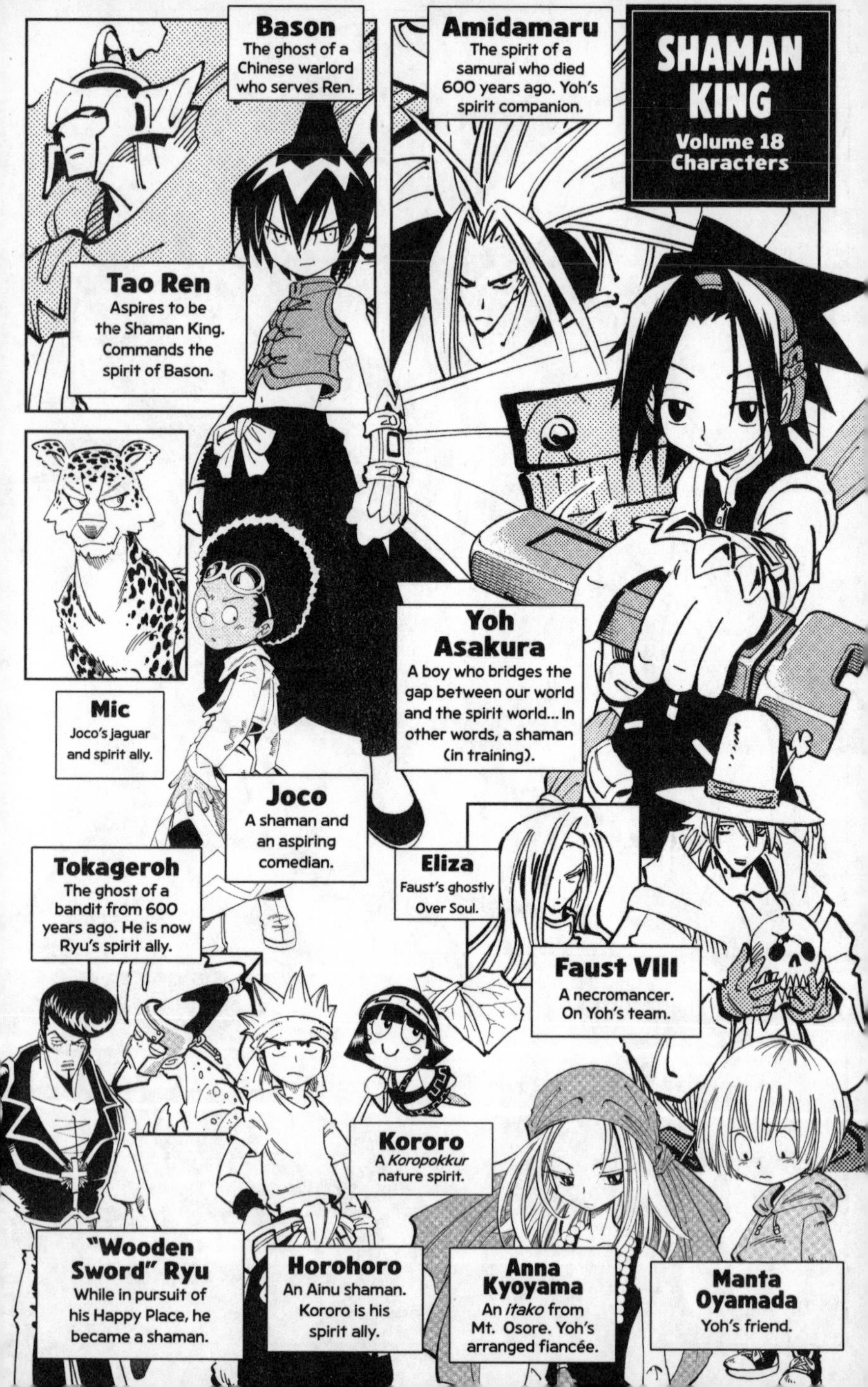
SHAMAN KING
Volume 18 Characters
Amidamaru
The spirit of a samurai who died 600 years ago. Yoh's spirit companion.
Bason
The ghost of a Chinese warlord who serves Ren.
Tao Ren
Aspires to be the Shaman King. Commands the spirit of Bason.
Yoh Asakura
A boy who bridges the gap between our world and the spirit world... In other words, a shaman (in training).
Mic
Joco's jaguar and spirit ally.
Joco
A shaman and an aspiring comedian.
Eliza
Faust's ghostly Over Soul.
Tokageroh
The ghost of a bandit from 600 years ago. He is now Ryu's spirit ally.
Faust VIII
A necromancer. On Yoh's team.
Kororo
A *Koropokkur* nature spirit.
Manta Oyamada
Yoh's friend.
Anna Kyoyama
An *itako* from Mt. Osore. Yoh's arranged fiancée.
Horohoro
An Ainu shaman. Kororo is his spirit ally.
"Wooden Sword" Ryu
While in pursuit of his Happy Place, he became a shaman.

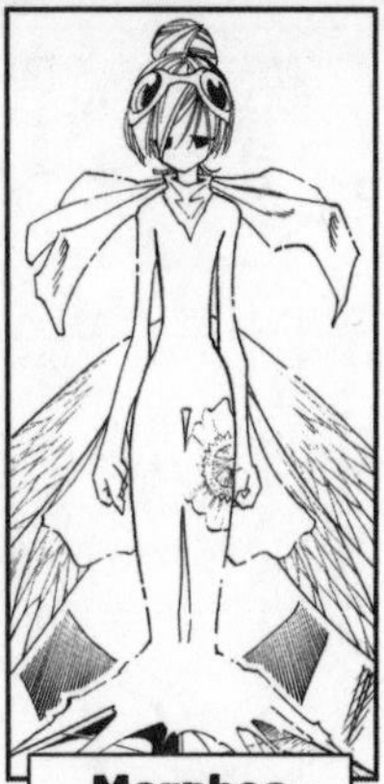

Morphea
Lyserg's spirit ally.
A poppy flower fairy.

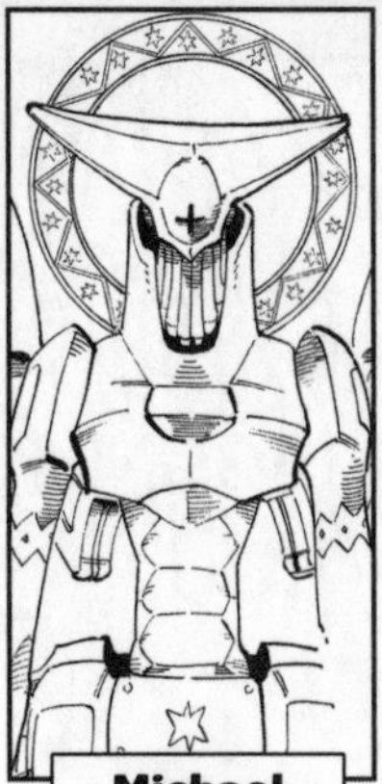

Michael
Marco's spirit ally.
An angel.

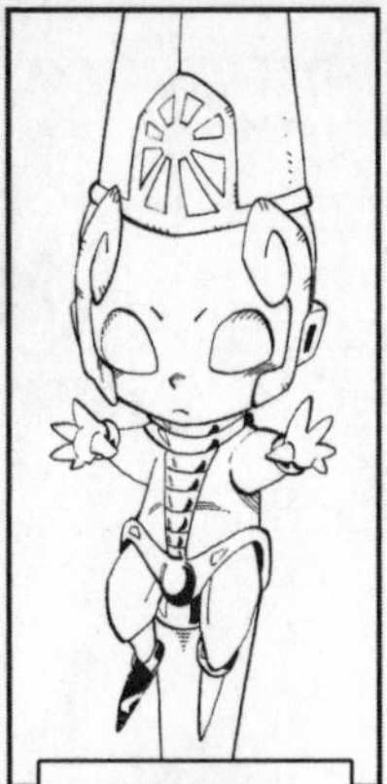

Shamash
Jeanne's spirit ally.
kami class.

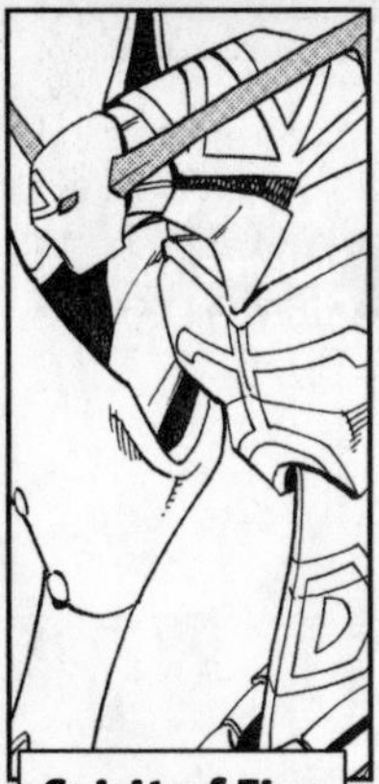

Spirit of Fire
One of the five High Spirits, and Hao's spirit ally.

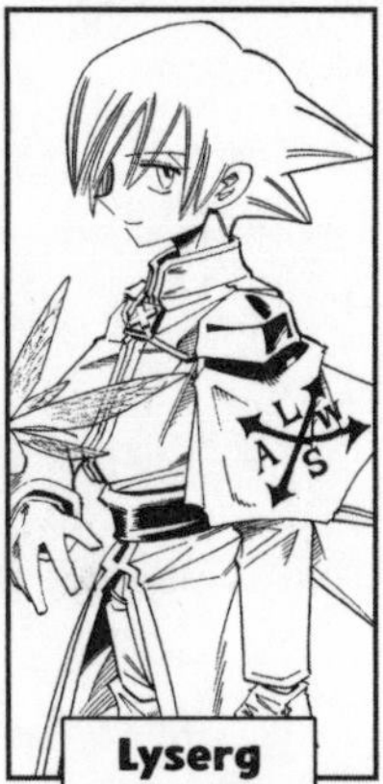

A
L
W
S

Lyserg
A boy who wants revenge against Hao.

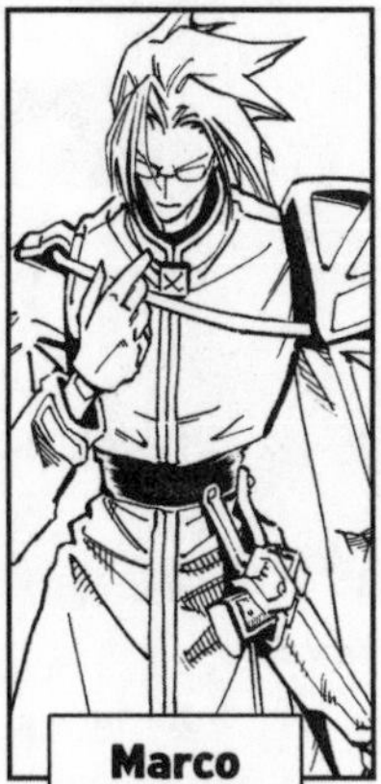

Marco
The leader of the X-Laws.

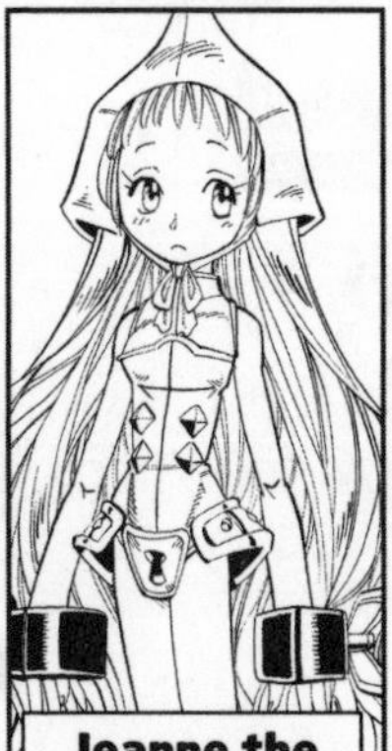

Jeanne the Iron Maiden
The true leader of the X-Laws. Mostly inside an iron maiden.

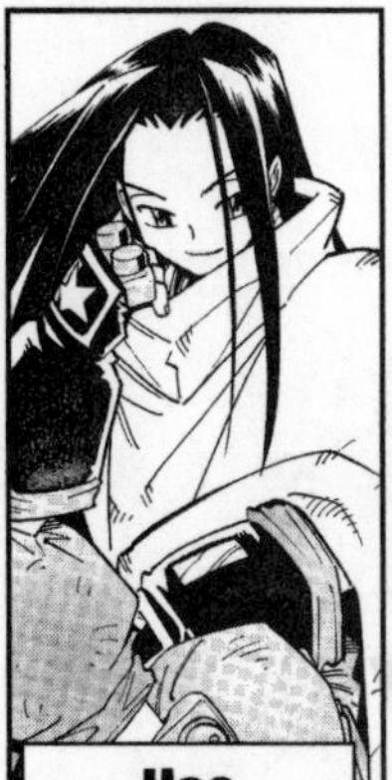

Hao
An enigmatic figure who calls himself the "Future King."

THE STORY SO FAR

This kid named Yoh Asakura-kun transferred to my class from Izumo...and it turns out he's a shaman! The Shaman Fight, which takes place once every 500 years, has begun. Yoh-kun and friends arrived at Patch Village—and experienced the limitless power of the Great Spirit. They formed new teams for the tournament proper. Along with their new ally, Joco, they divided into two teams. As the competition proceeded, Hao's minions confronted Team Ren. They hunted down Ren, who was uncharacteristically caught off guard and left barely clinging to his life. Yoh-kun witnessed the massacre and reacted...

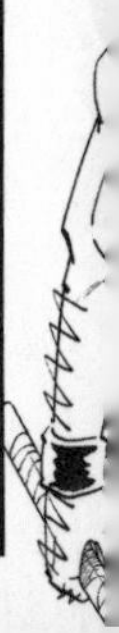

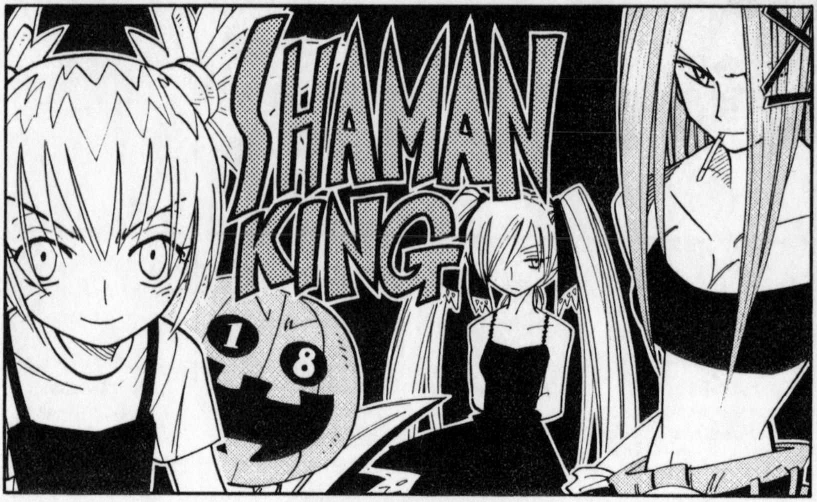
SHAMAN KING
18

The Mask Restored

18

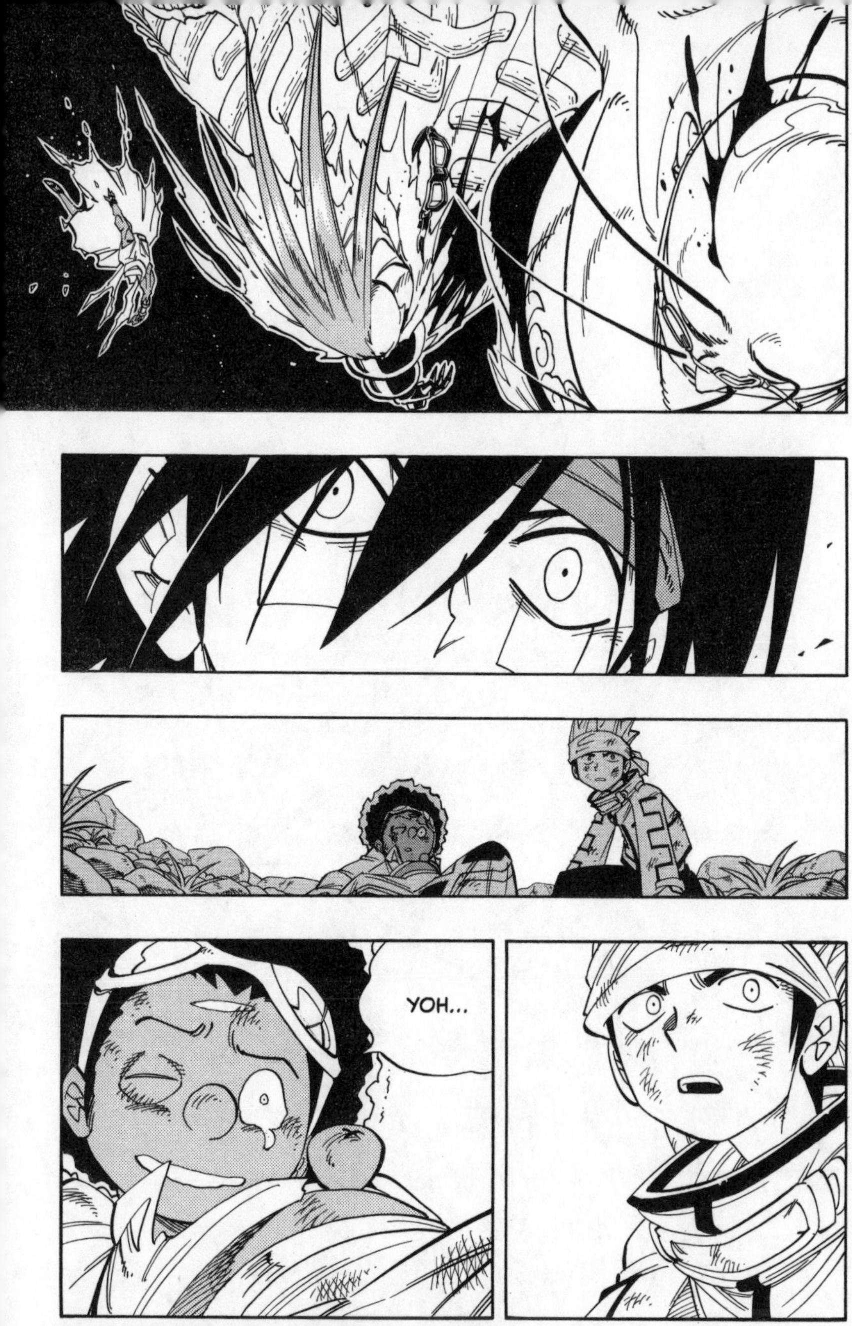
YOH...

Chapter 153: The Old Ren is Gone

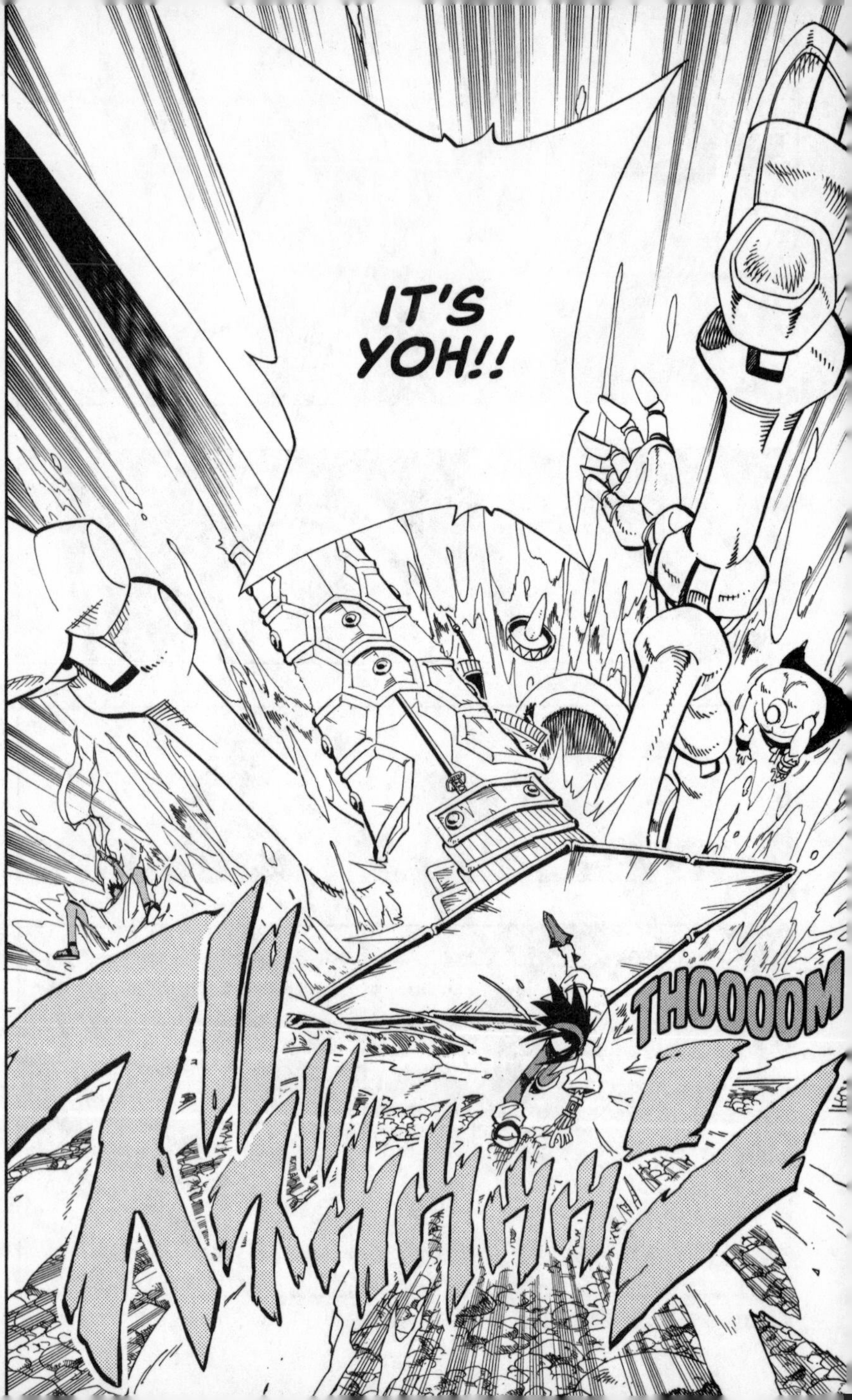
IT'S YOH!!
THOOOOM

Chapter 153: The Old Ren is Gone

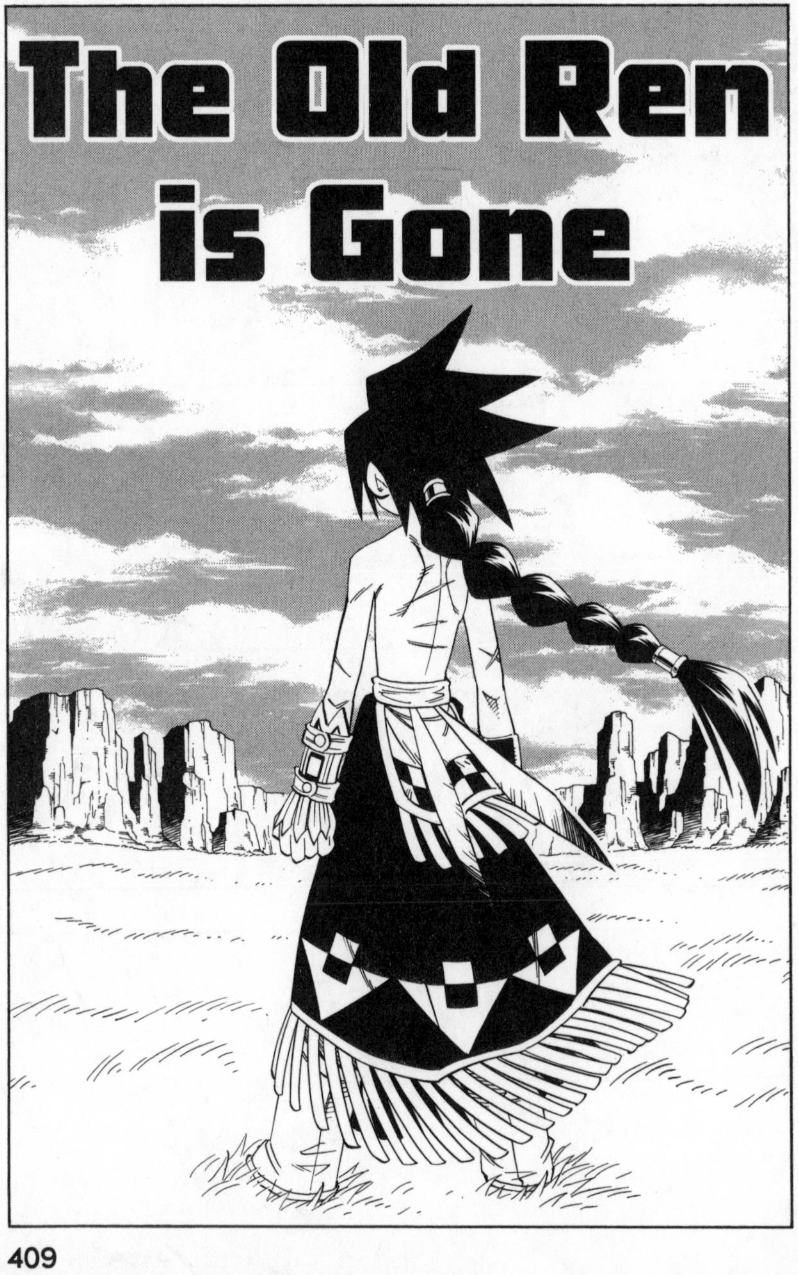

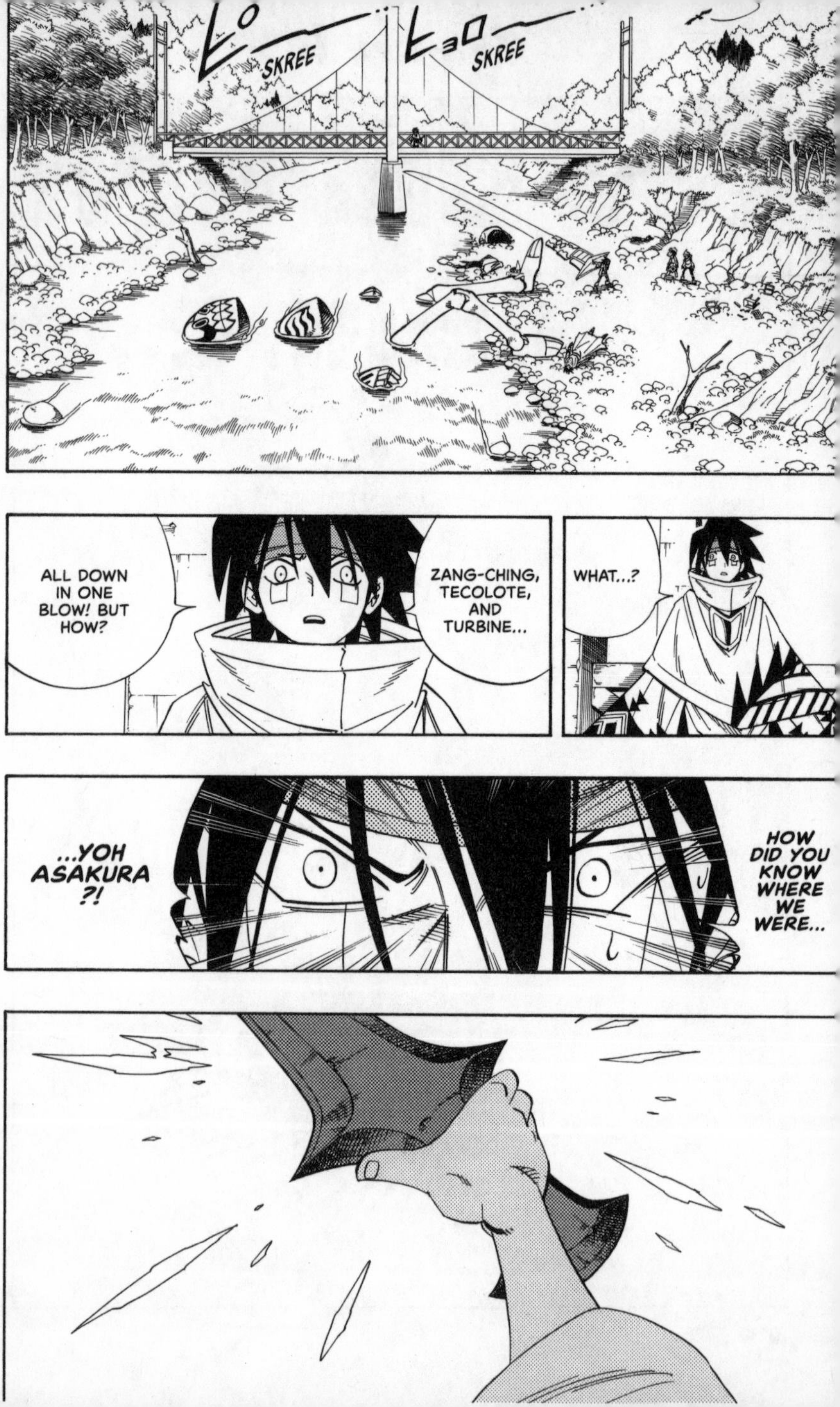
SKREE
SKREE
WHAT...?
ZANG-CHING, TECOLOTE, AND TURBINE...
ALL DOWN IN ONE BLOW! BUT HOW?
HOW DID YOU KNOW WHERE WE WERE...
...YOH ASAKURA ?!

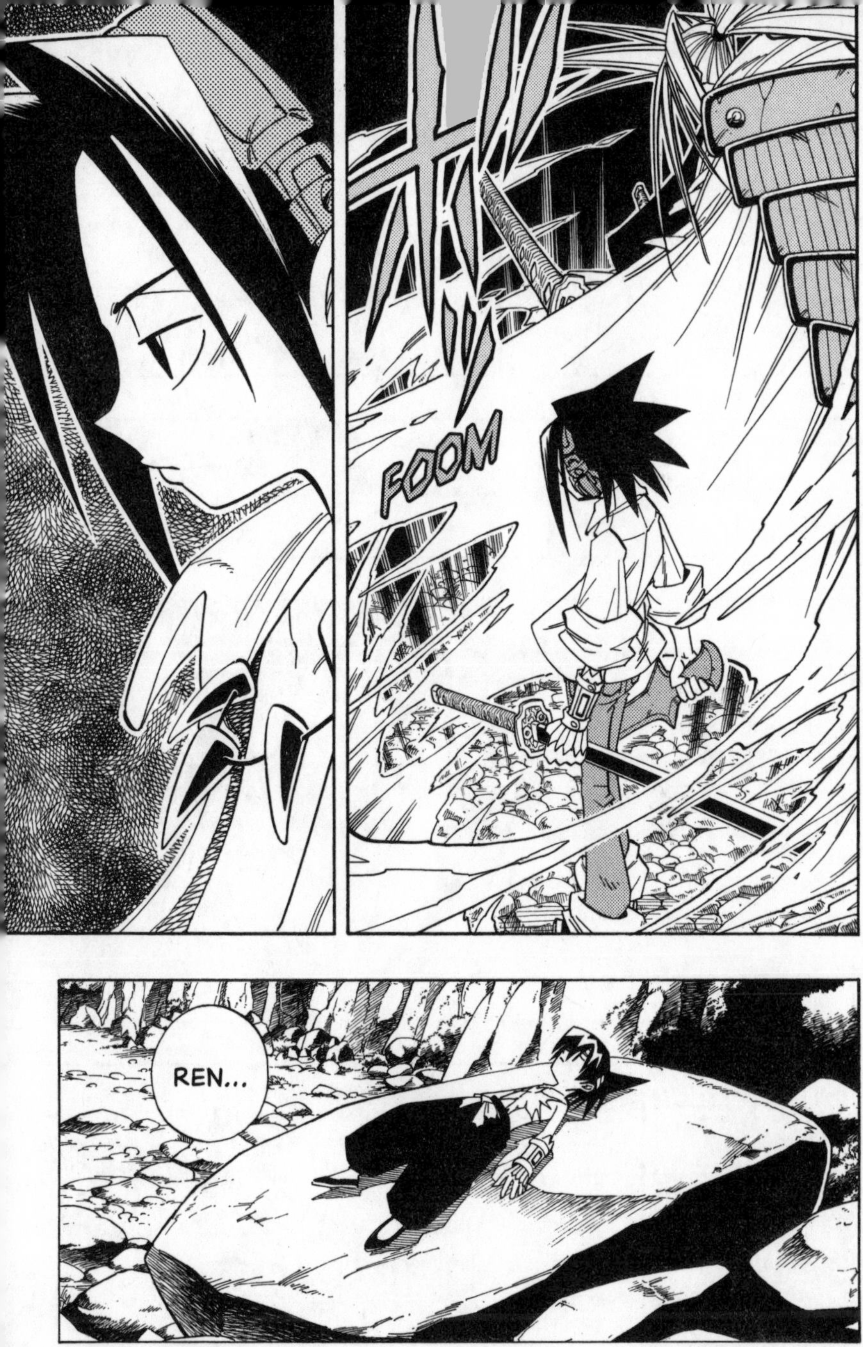
FOOM
REN...

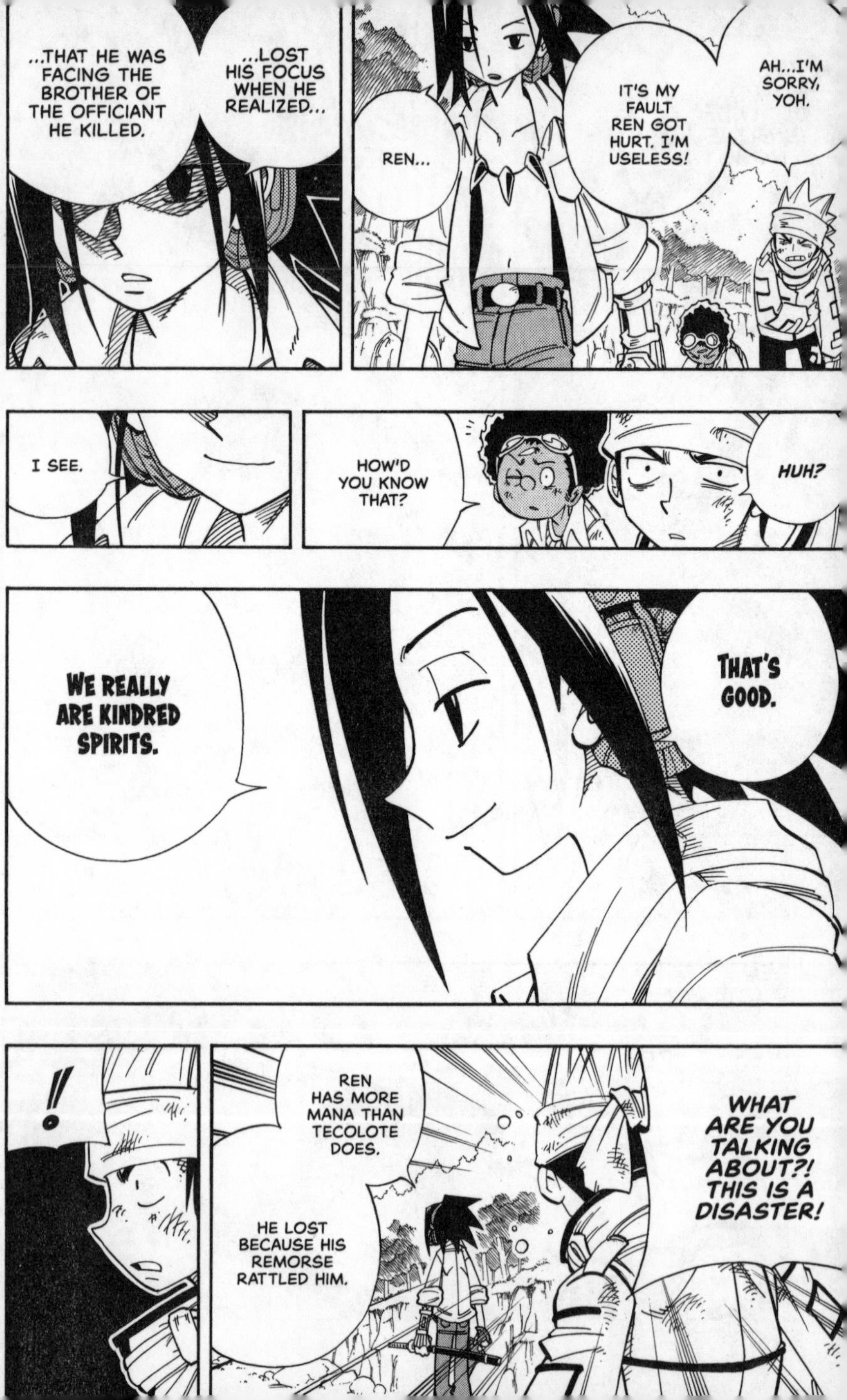
AH...I'M SORRY, YOH.
IT'S MY FAULT REN GOT HURT. I'M USELESS!
REN...
...LOST HIS FOCUS WHEN HE REALIZED...
...THAT HE WAS FACING THE BROTHER OF THE OFFICIANT HE KILLED.
HUH?
HOW'D YOU KNOW THAT?
I SEE.
THAT'S GOOD.
WE REALLY ARE KINDRED SPIRITS.
WHAT ARE YOU TALKING ABOUT?! THIS IS A DISASTER!
REN HAS MORE MANA THAN TECOLOTE DOES.
HE LOST BECAUSE HIS REMORSE RATTLED HIM.
!!

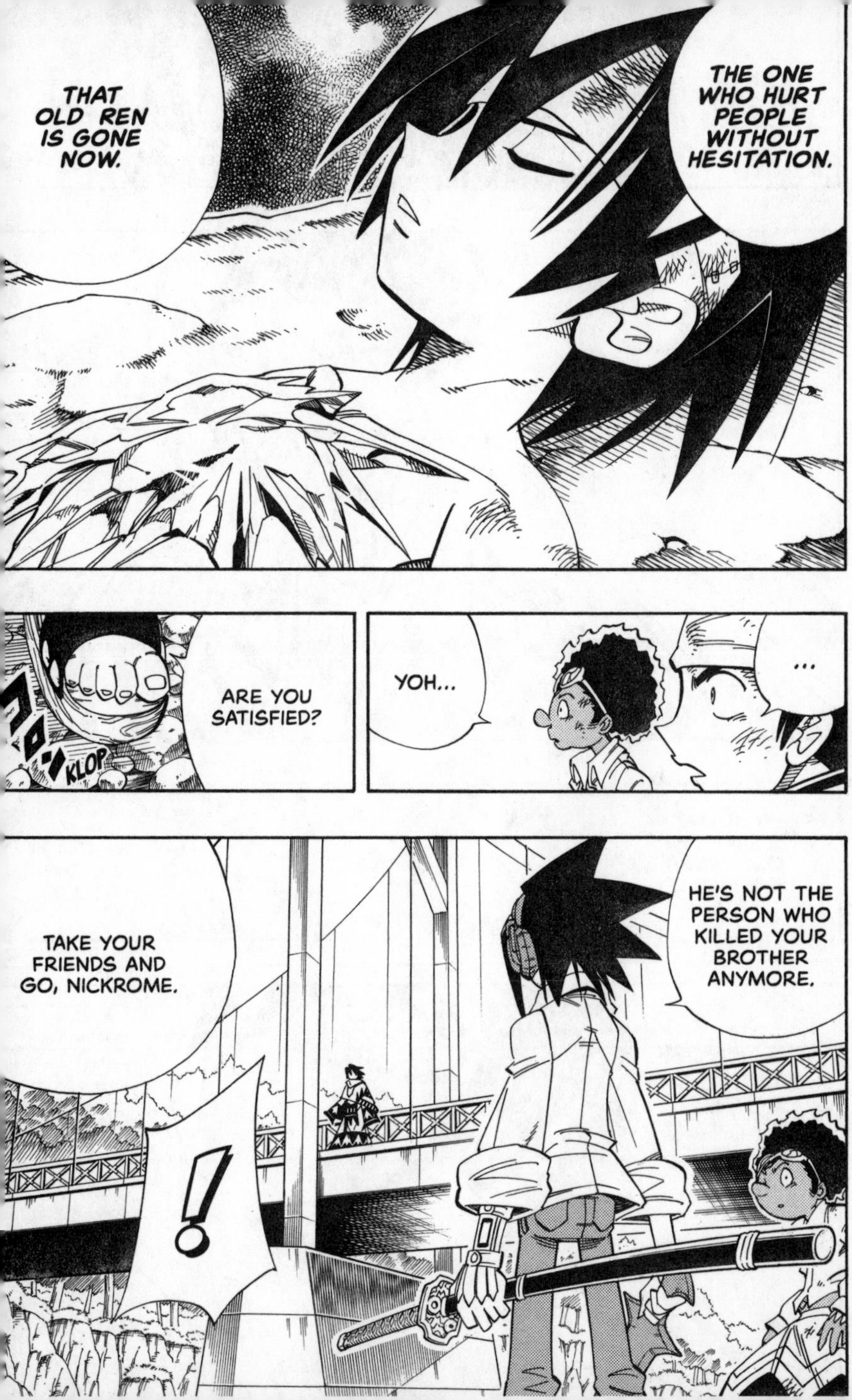
THE ONE WHO HURT PEOPLE WITHOUT HESITATION.
THAT OLD REN IS GONE NOW.
...
YOH...
ARE YOU SATISFIED?
KLOP
HE'S NOT THE PERSON WHO KILLED YOUR BROTHER ANYMORE.
TAKE YOUR FRIENDS AND GO, NICKROME.
!

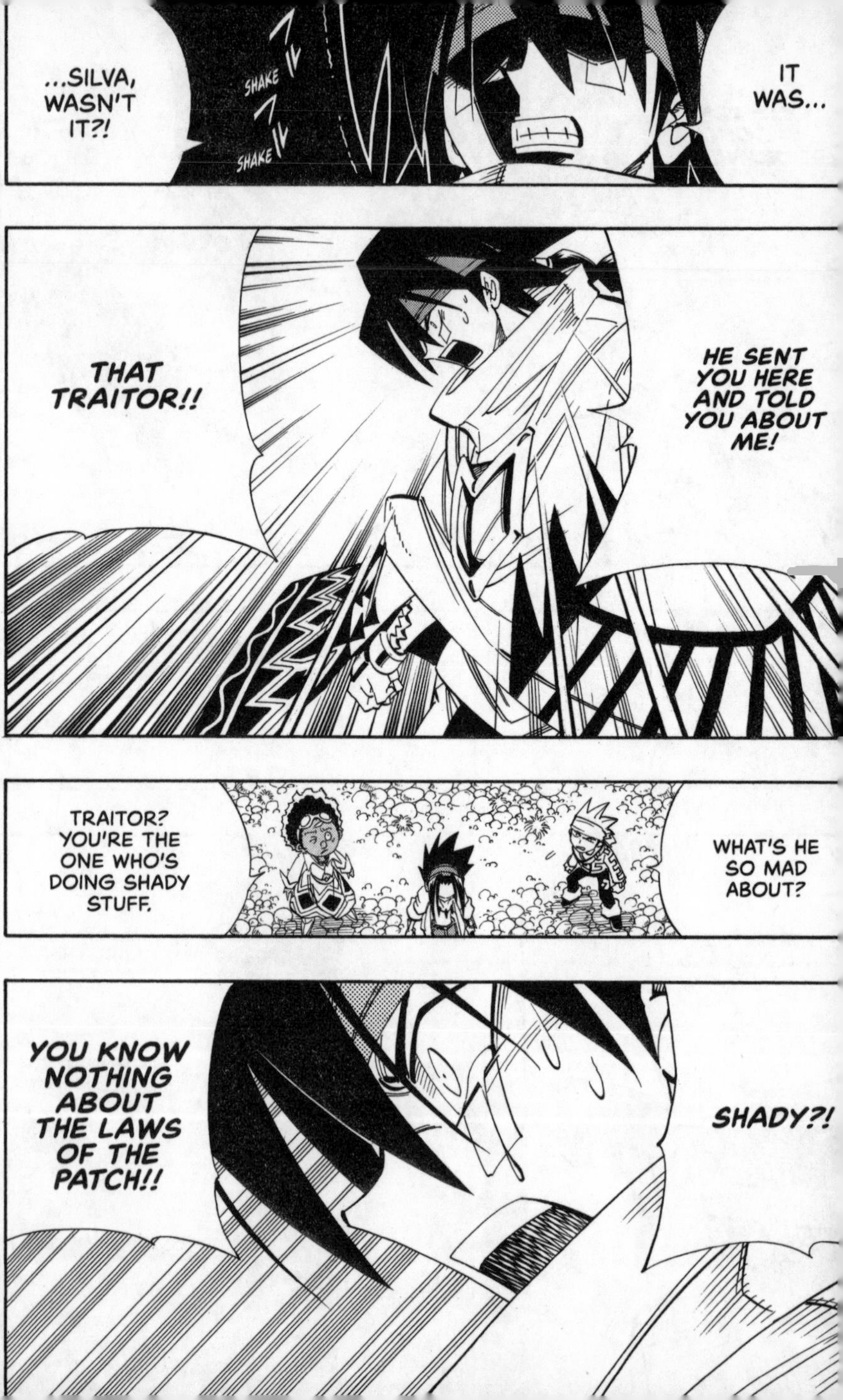
IT WAS...
SHAKE
SHAKE
...SILVA, WASN'T IT?!
HE SENT YOU HERE AND TOLD YOU ABOUT ME!
THAT TRAITOR!!
WHAT'S HE SO MAD ABOUT?
TRAITOR? YOU'RE THE ONE WHO'S DOING SHADY STUFF.
SHADY?!
YOU KNOW NOTHING ABOUT THE LAWS OF THE PATCH!!

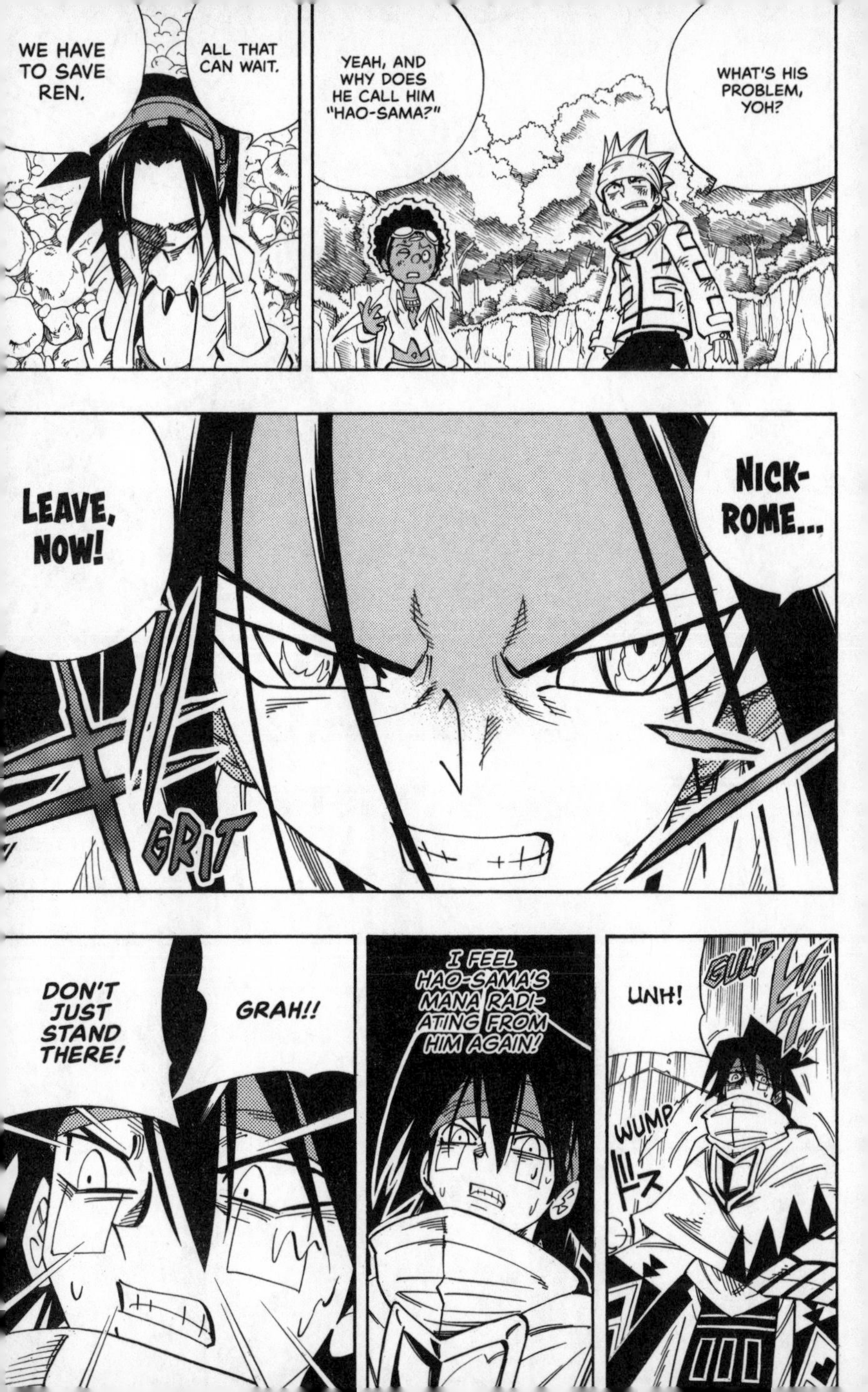
WHAT'S HIS PROBLEM, YOH?
YEAH, AND WHY DOES HE CALL HIM "HAO-SAMA?"
ALL THAT CAN WAIT.
WE HAVE TO SAVE REN.
NICK-ROME...
LEAVE, NOW!
GRIT
GULP
UNH!
WUMP
ドス
I FEEL HAO-SAMA'S MANA RADI-ATING FROM HIM AGAIN!
GRAH!!
DON'T JUST STAND THERE!

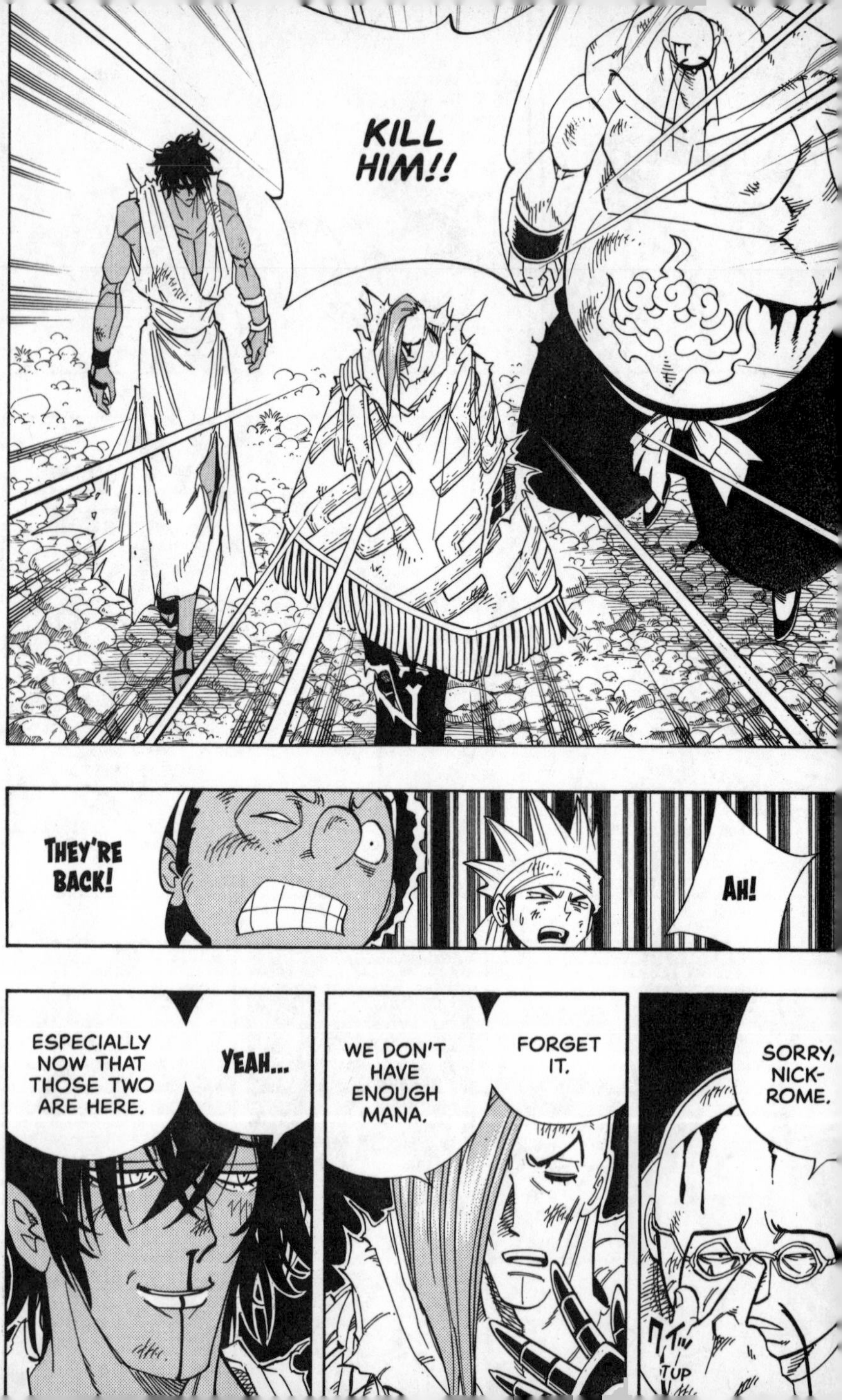
KILL HIM!!
AH!
THEY'RE BACK!
SORRY, NICK-ROME.
TUP
FORGET IT.
WE DON'T HAVE ENOUGH MANA.
YEAH...
ESPECIALLY NOW THAT THOSE TWO ARE HERE.

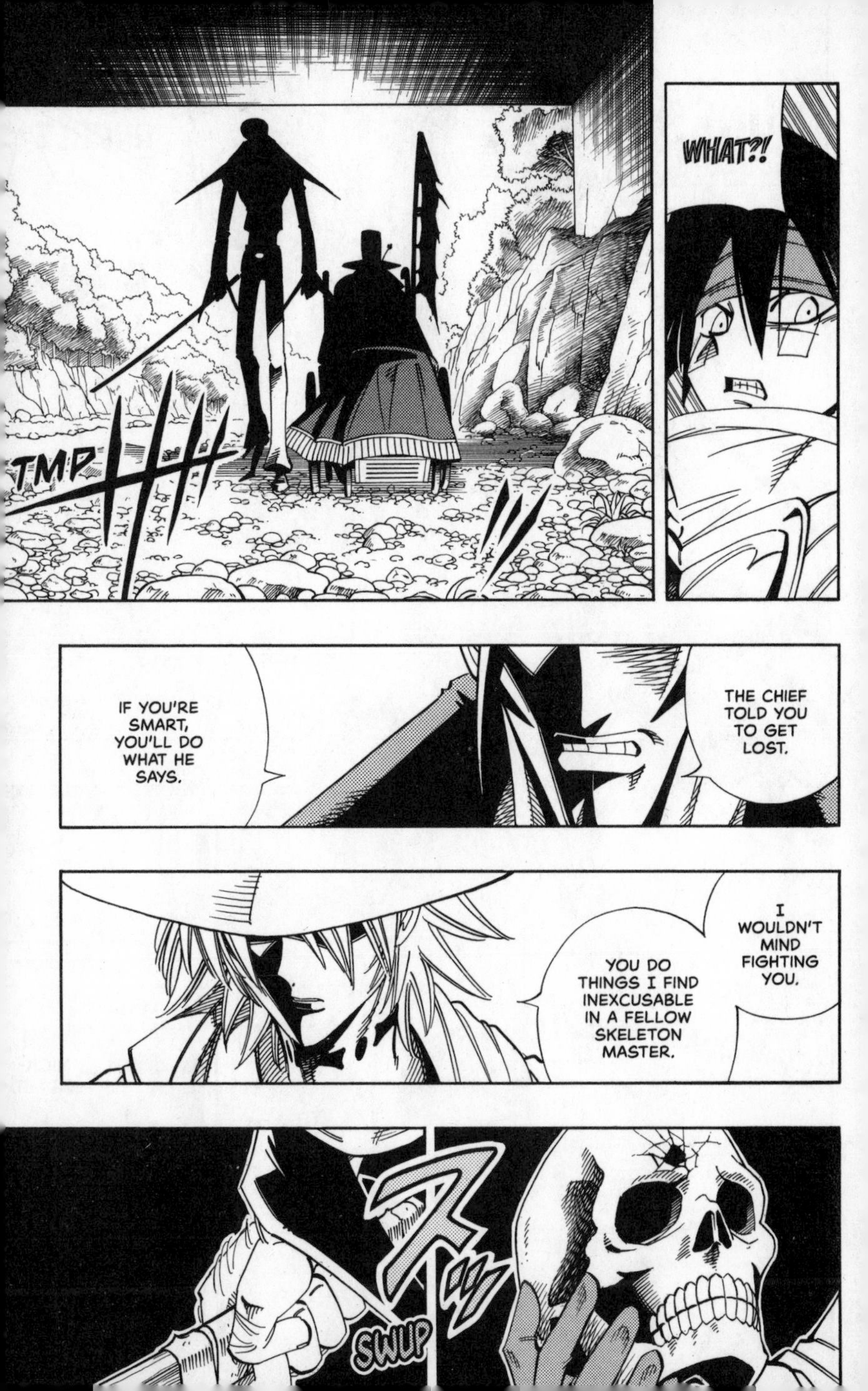

WHAT?!
TMP
THE CHIEF TOLD YOU TO GET LOST.
IF YOU'RE SMART, YOU'LL DO WHAT HE SAYS.
I WOULDN'T MIND FIGHTING YOU.
YOU DO THINGS I FIND INEXCUSABLE IN A FELLOW SKELETON MASTER.
SWUP

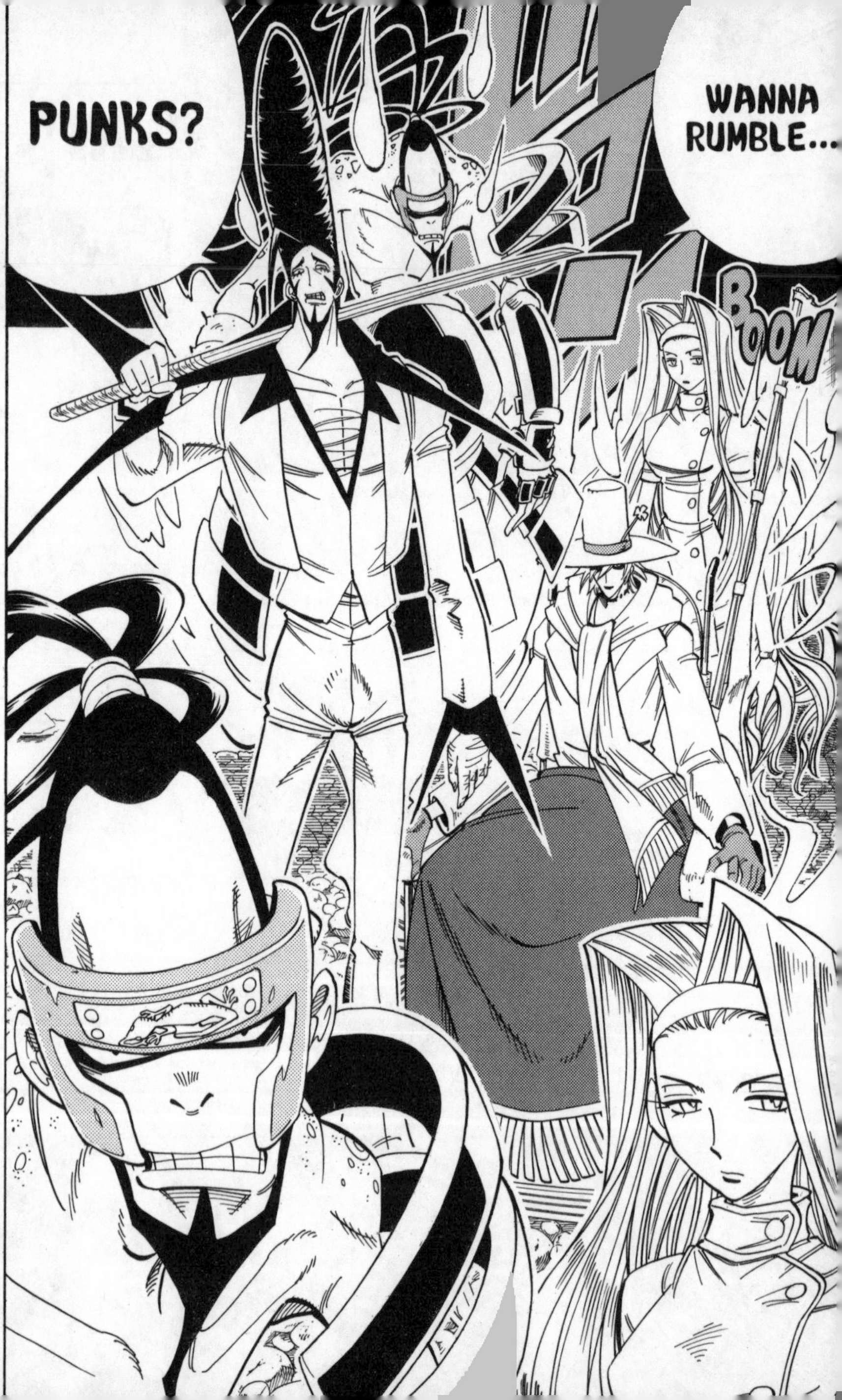
WANNA RUMBLE...
PUNKS?
BOOM

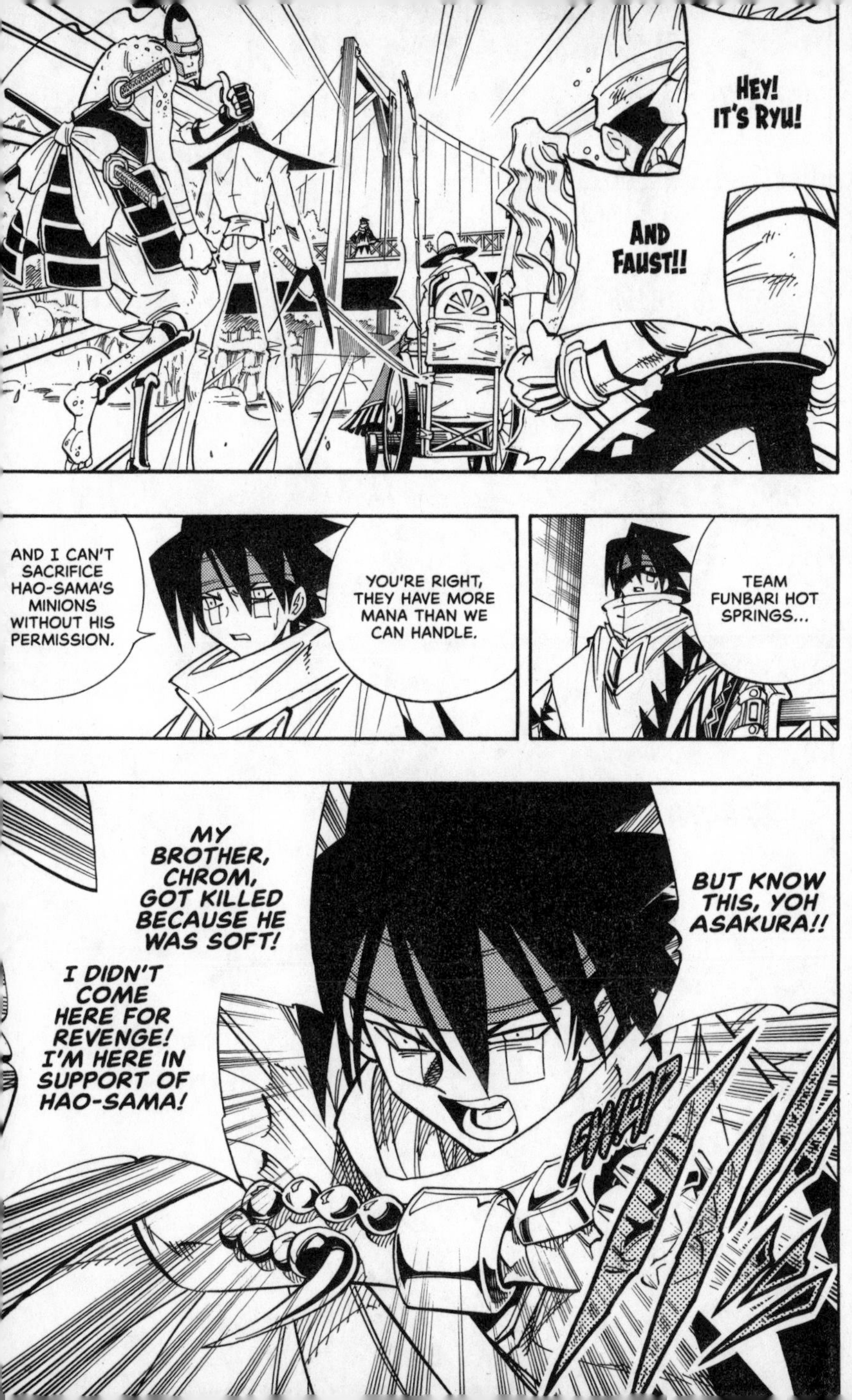
HEY! IT'S RYU!
AND FAUST!!
TEAM FUNBARI HOT SPRINGS...
YOU'RE RIGHT, THEY HAVE MORE MANA THAN WE CAN HANDLE.
AND I CAN'T SACRIFICE HAO-SAMA'S MINIONS WITHOUT HIS PERMISSION.
BUT KNOW THIS, YOH ASAKURA!!
MY BROTHER, CHROM, GOT KILLED BECAUSE HE WAS SOFT!
I DIDN'T COME HERE FOR REVENGE! I'M HERE IN SUPPORT OF HAO-SAMA!

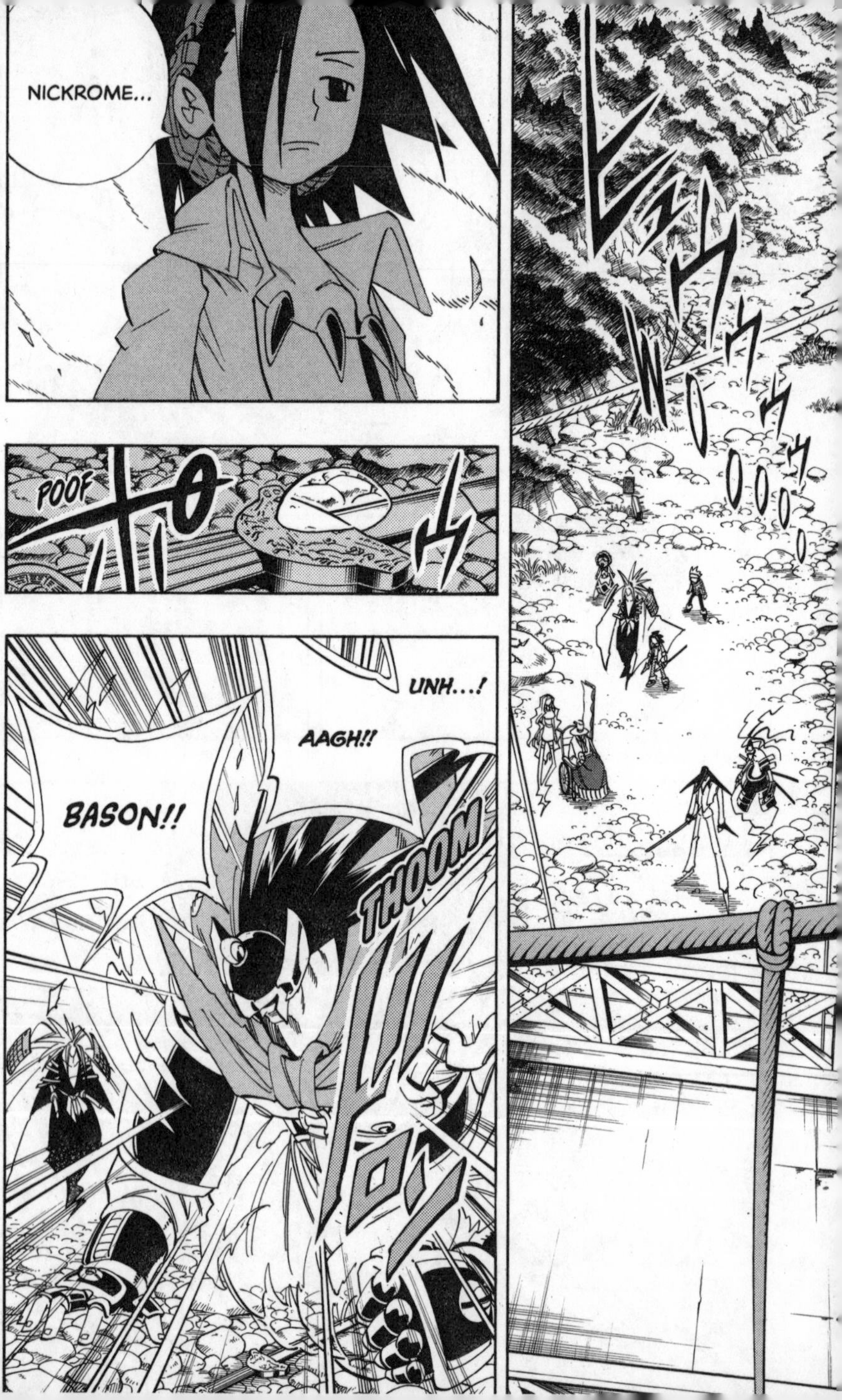
NICKROME...
POOF
UNH...!
AAGH!!
BASON!!
THOOM

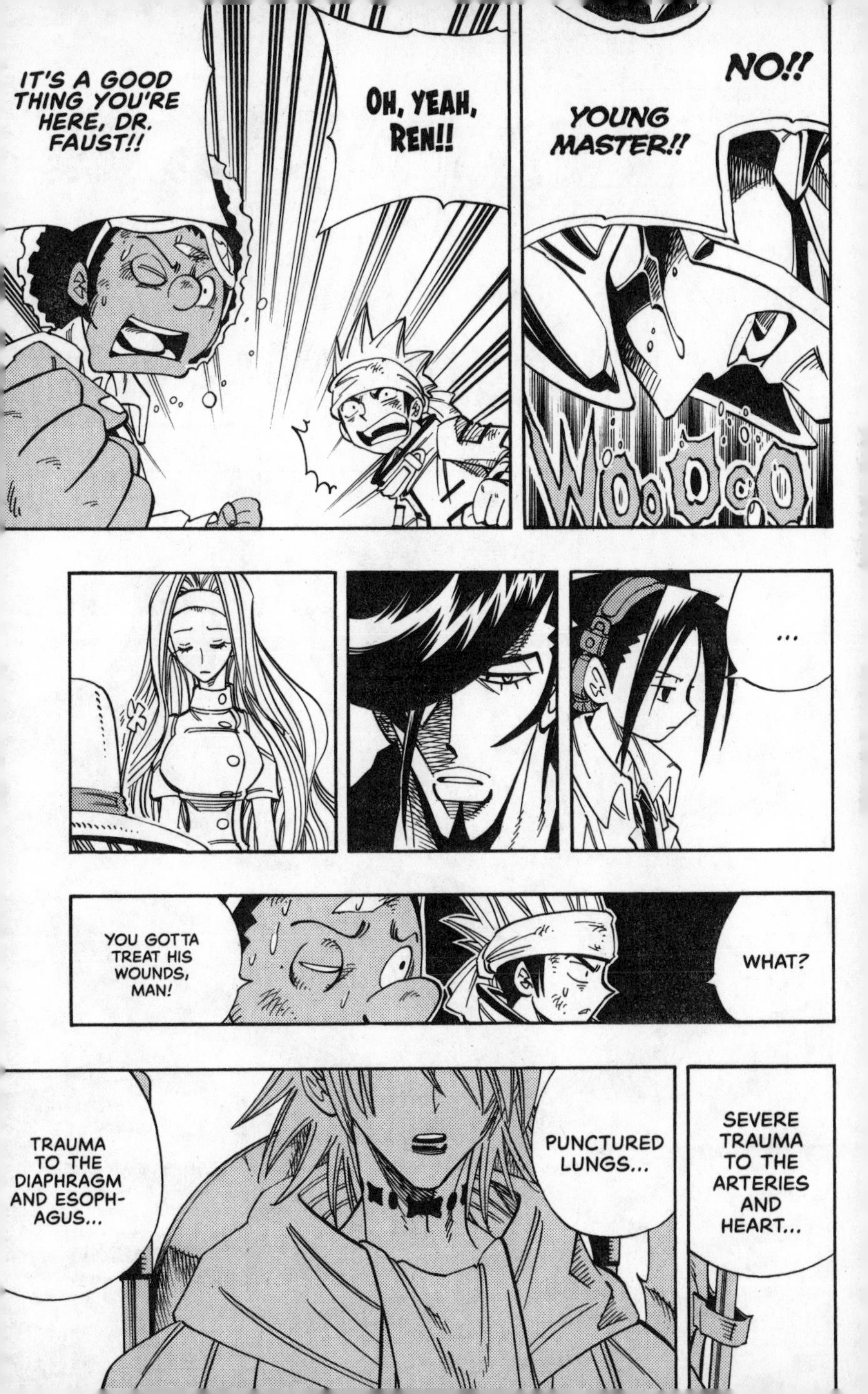
NO!!
YOUNG MASTER!!
OH, YEAH, REN!!
IT'S A GOOD THING YOU'RE HERE, DR. FAUST!!
...
WHAT?
YOU GOTTA TREAT HIS WOUNDS, MAN!
SEVERE TRAUMA TO THE ARTERIES AND HEART...
PUNCTURED LUNGS...
TRAUMA TO THE DIAPHRAGM AND ESOPHAGUS...

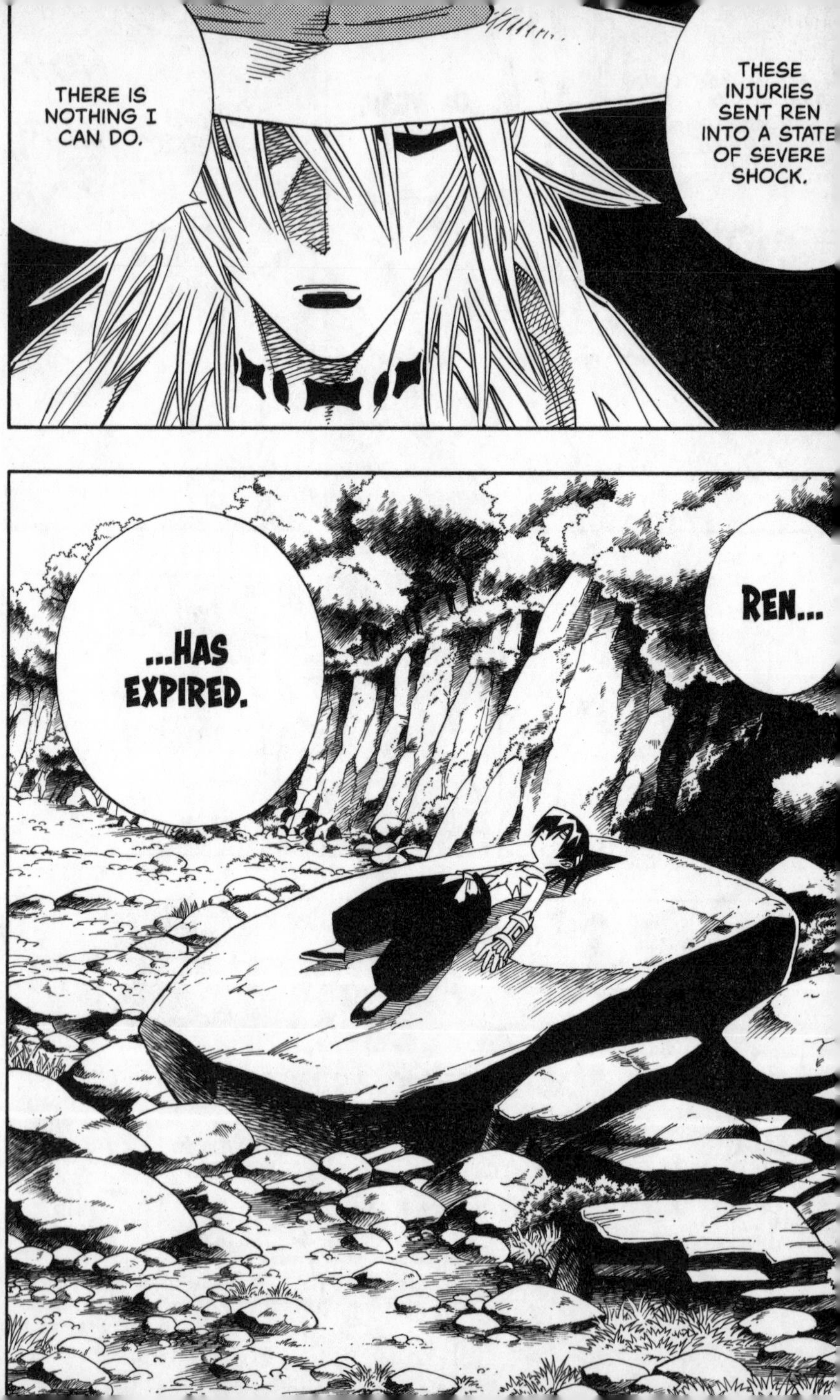
THESE INJURIES SENT REN INTO A STATE OF SEVERE SHOCK.
THERE IS NOTHING I CAN DO.
REN...
...HAS EXPIRED.

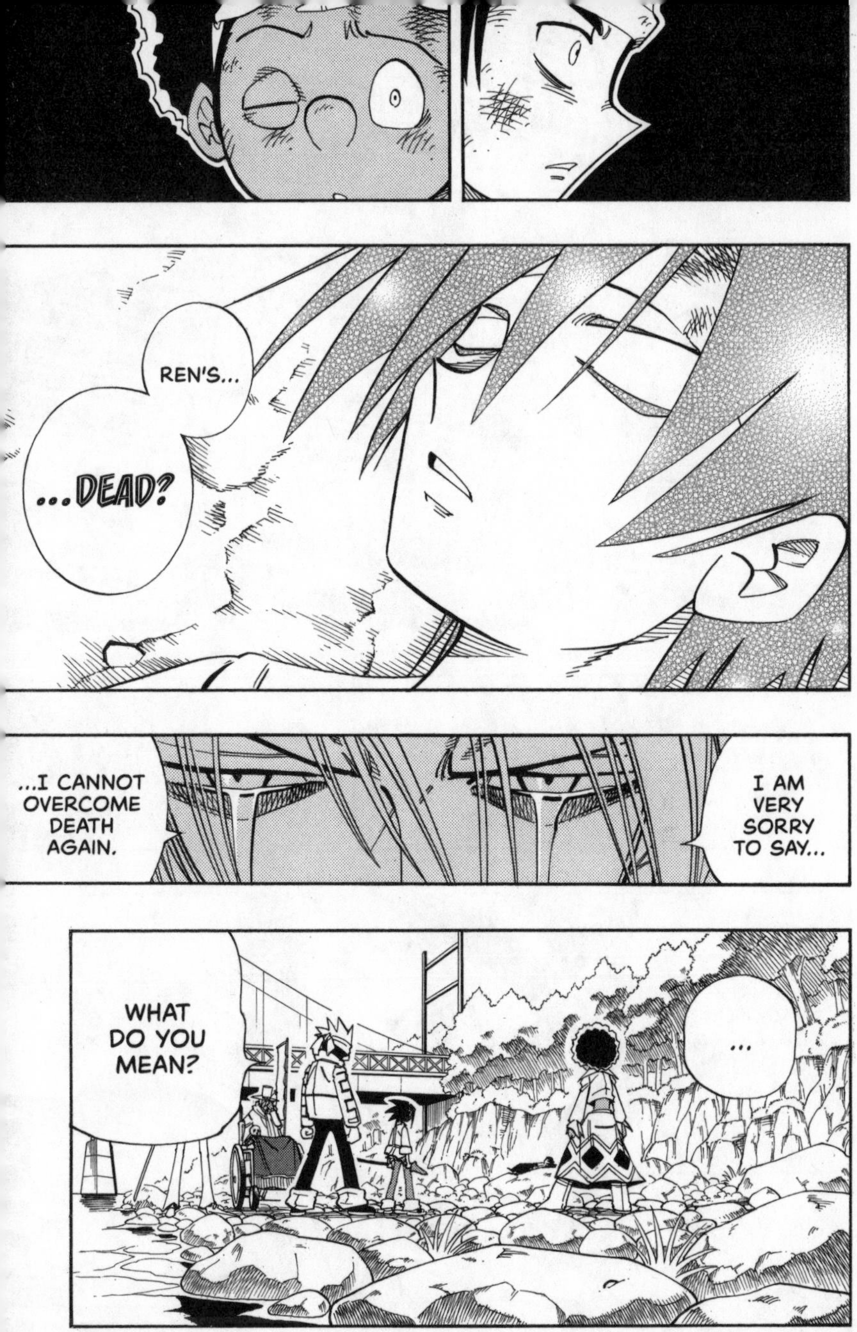
REN'S...
...DEAD?
I AM VERY SORRY TO SAY...
...I CANNOT OVERCOME DEATH AGAIN.
...
WHAT DO YOU MEAN?

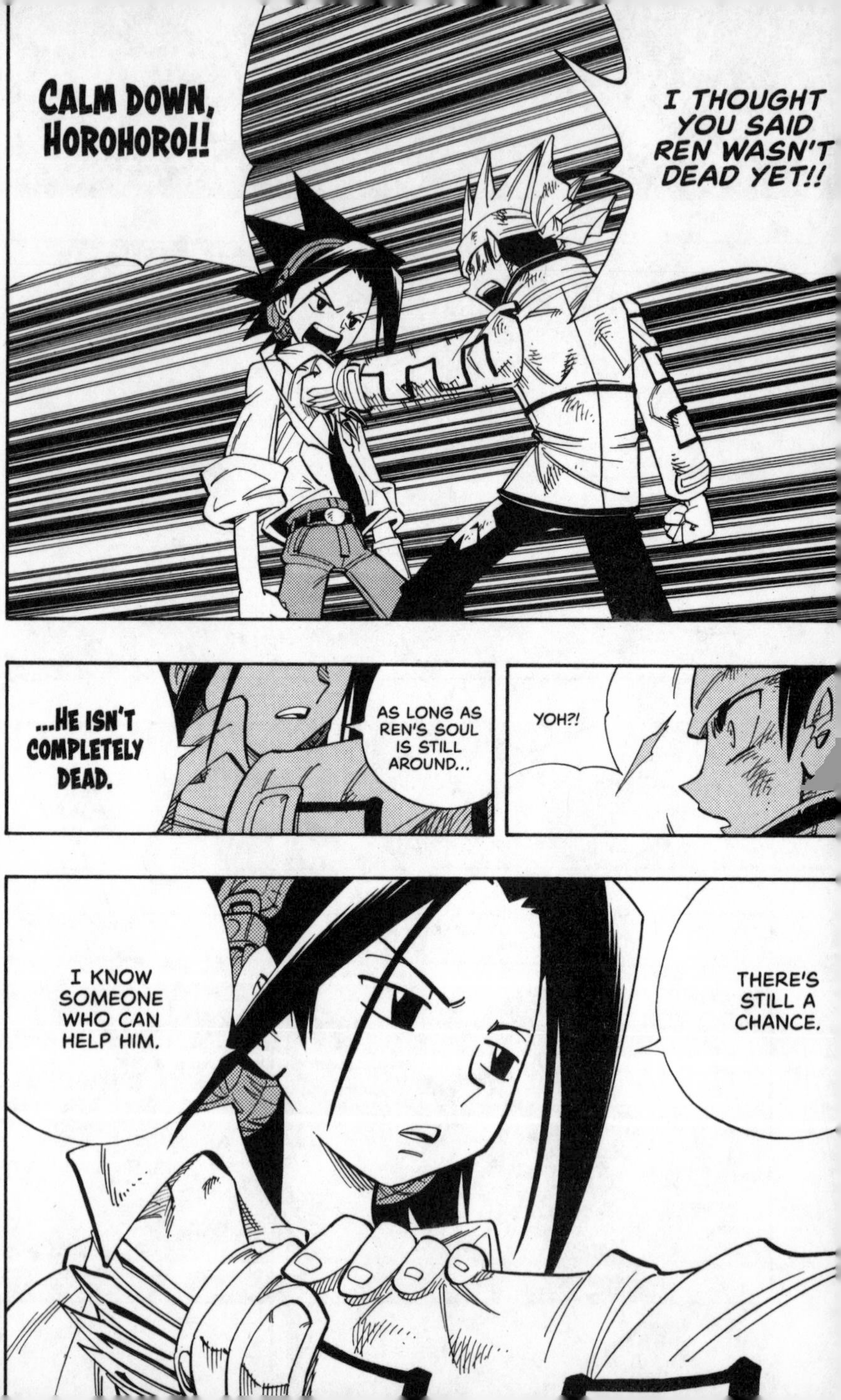
I THOUGHT YOU SAID REN WASN'T DEAD YET!!
CALM DOWN, HOROHORO!!
YOH?!
AS LONG AS REN'S SOUL IS STILL AROUND...
...HE ISN'T COMPLETELY DEAD.
THERE'S STILL A CHANCE.
I KNOW SOMEONE WHO CAN HELP HIM.

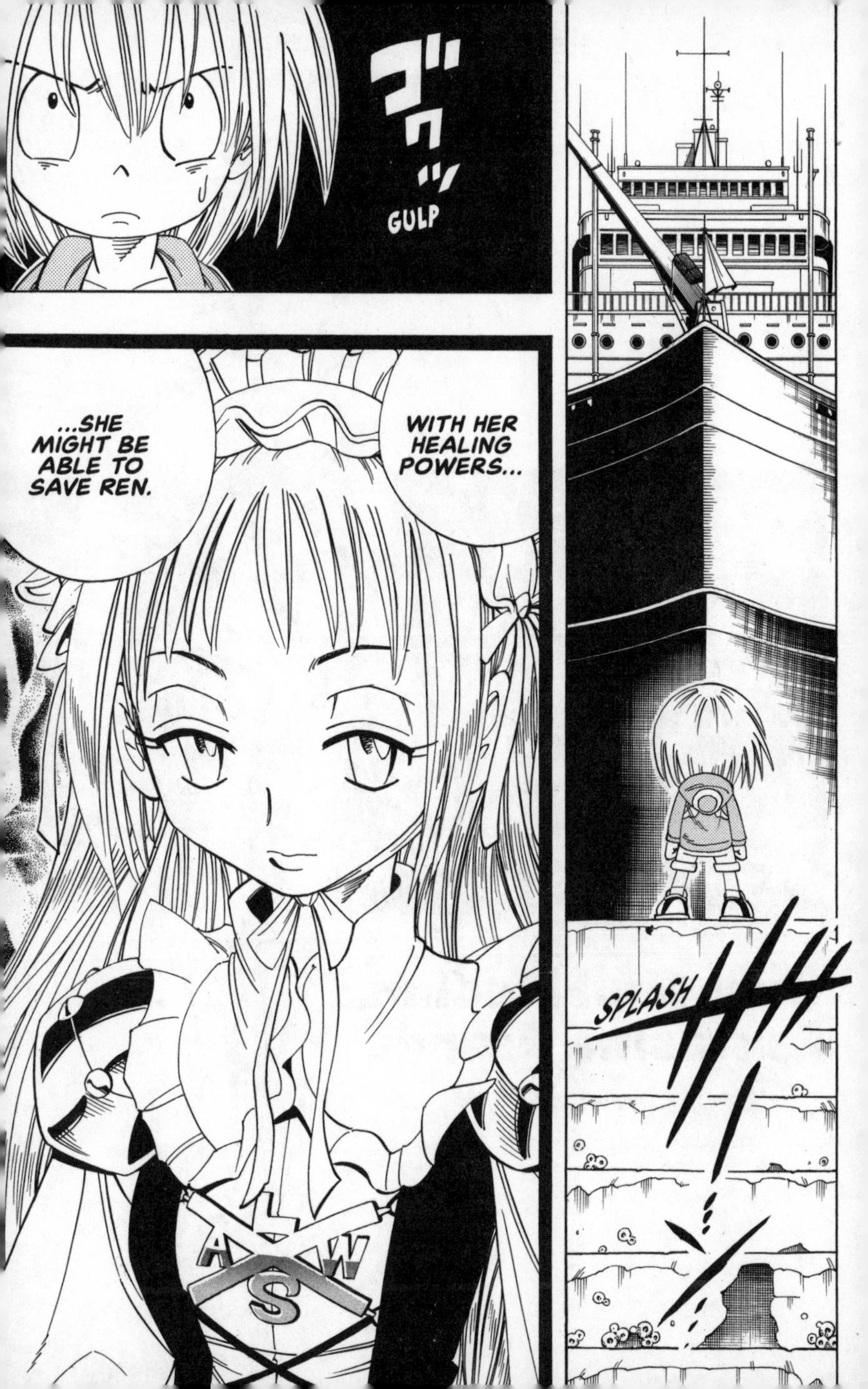
SPLASH
ゴクッ
GULP
WITH HER HEALING POWERS...
...SHE MIGHT BE ABLE TO SAVE REN.

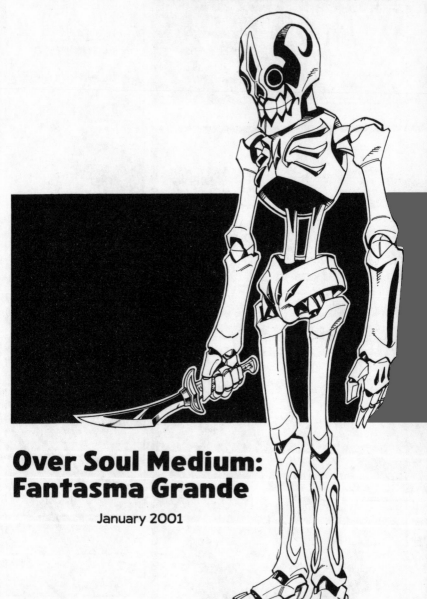

Over Soul Medium:
Fantasma Grande

January 2001

Chapter 154: Who the Hell?

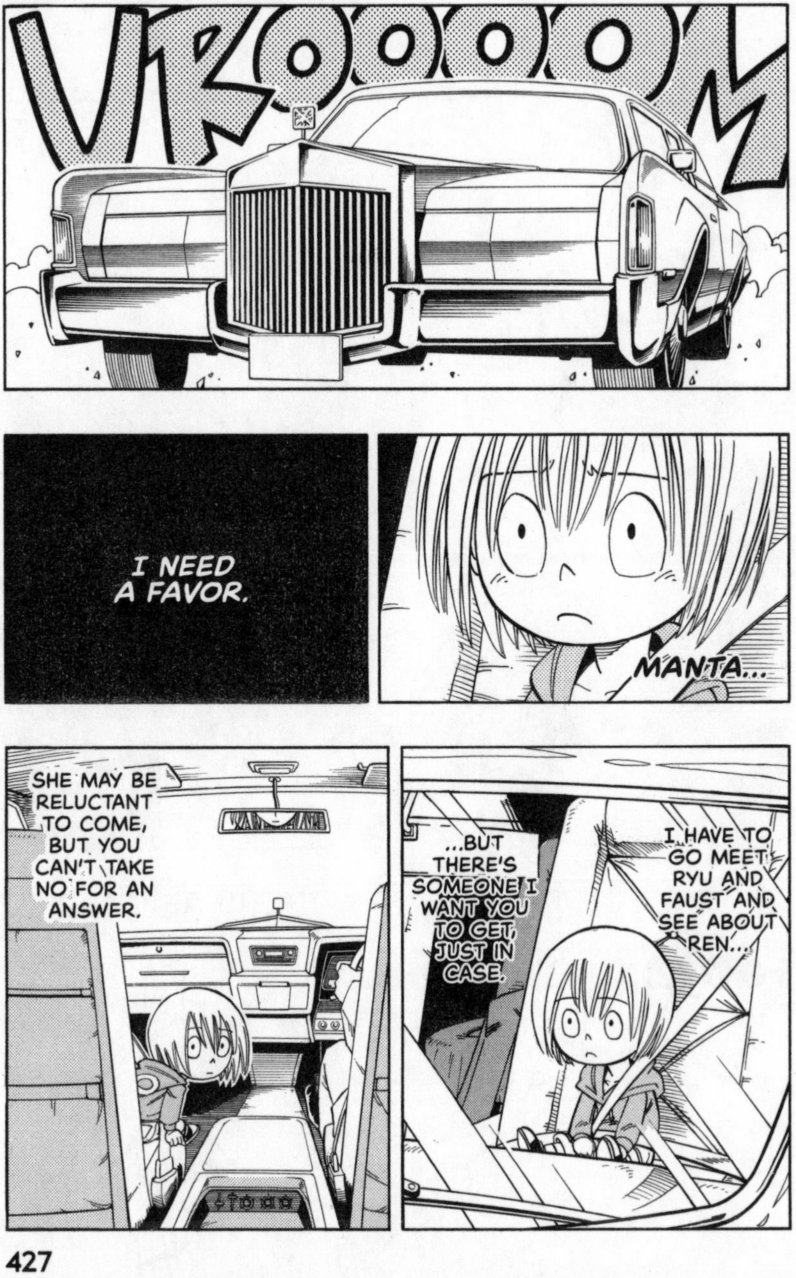
VROOOOOM
MANTA...
I NEED A FAVOR.
I HAVE TO GO MEET RYU AND FAUST AND SEE ABOUT REN...
...BUT THERE'S SOMEONE I WANT YOU TO GET, JUST IN CASE.
SHE MAY BE RELUCTANT TO COME, BUT YOU CAN'T TAKE NO FOR AN ANSWER.

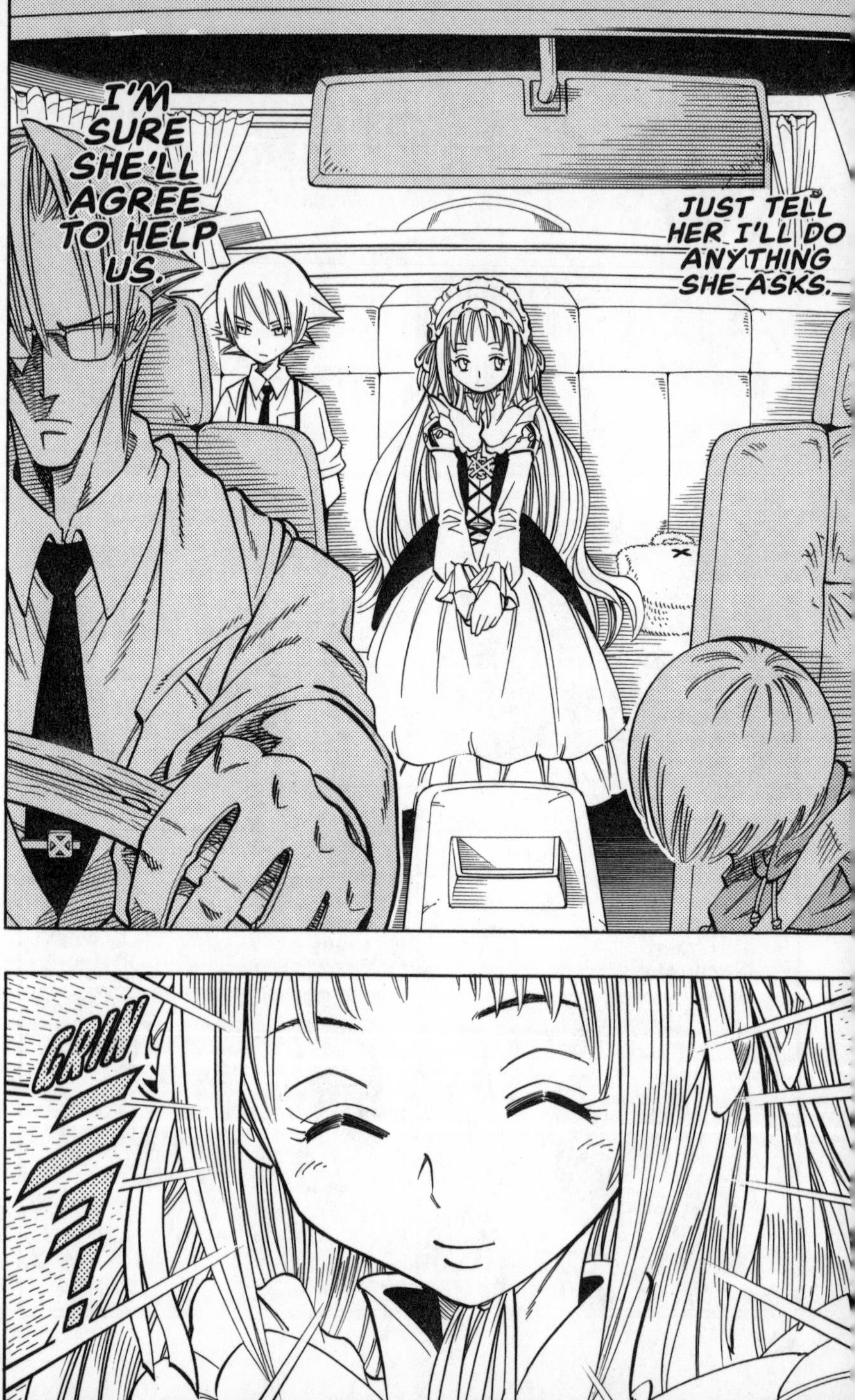
JUST TELL HER I'LL DO ANYTHING SHE ASKS.
I'M SURE SHE'LL AGREE TO HELP US.
GRIN
?!

Chapter 154:

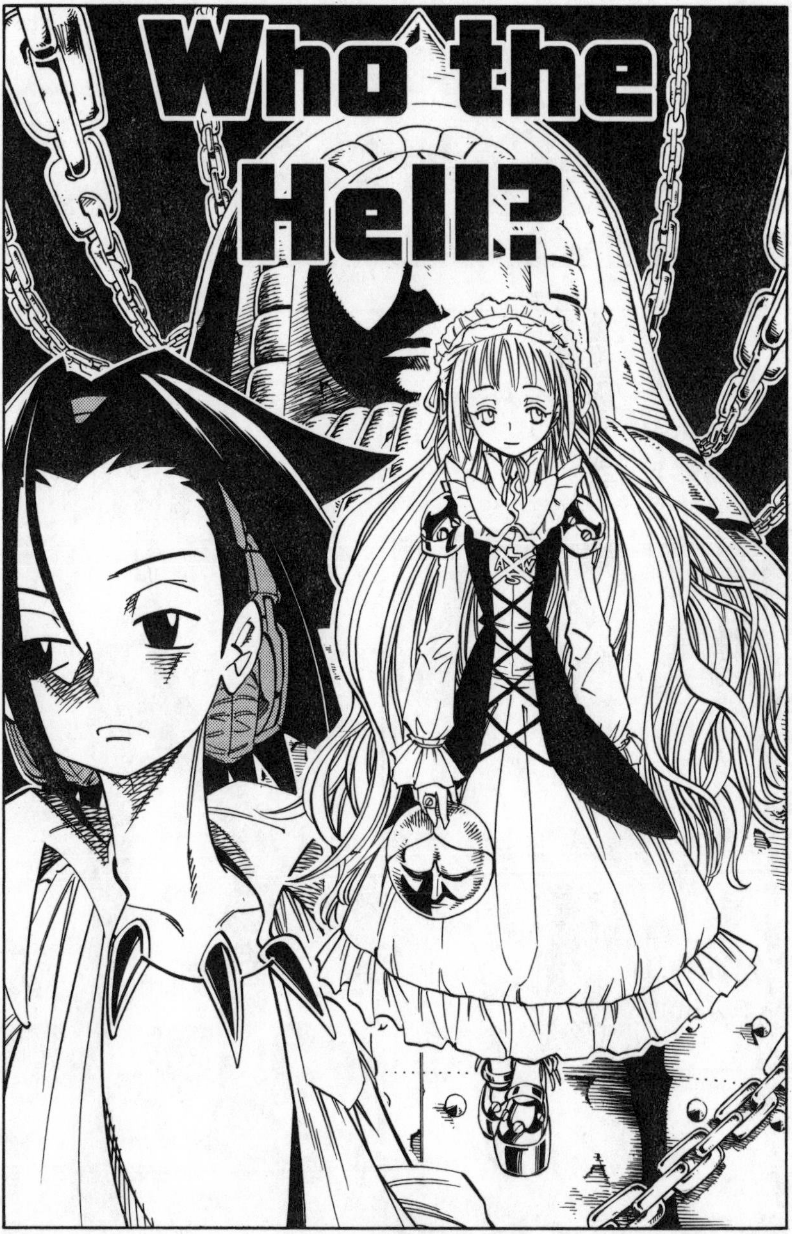
Who the Hell?

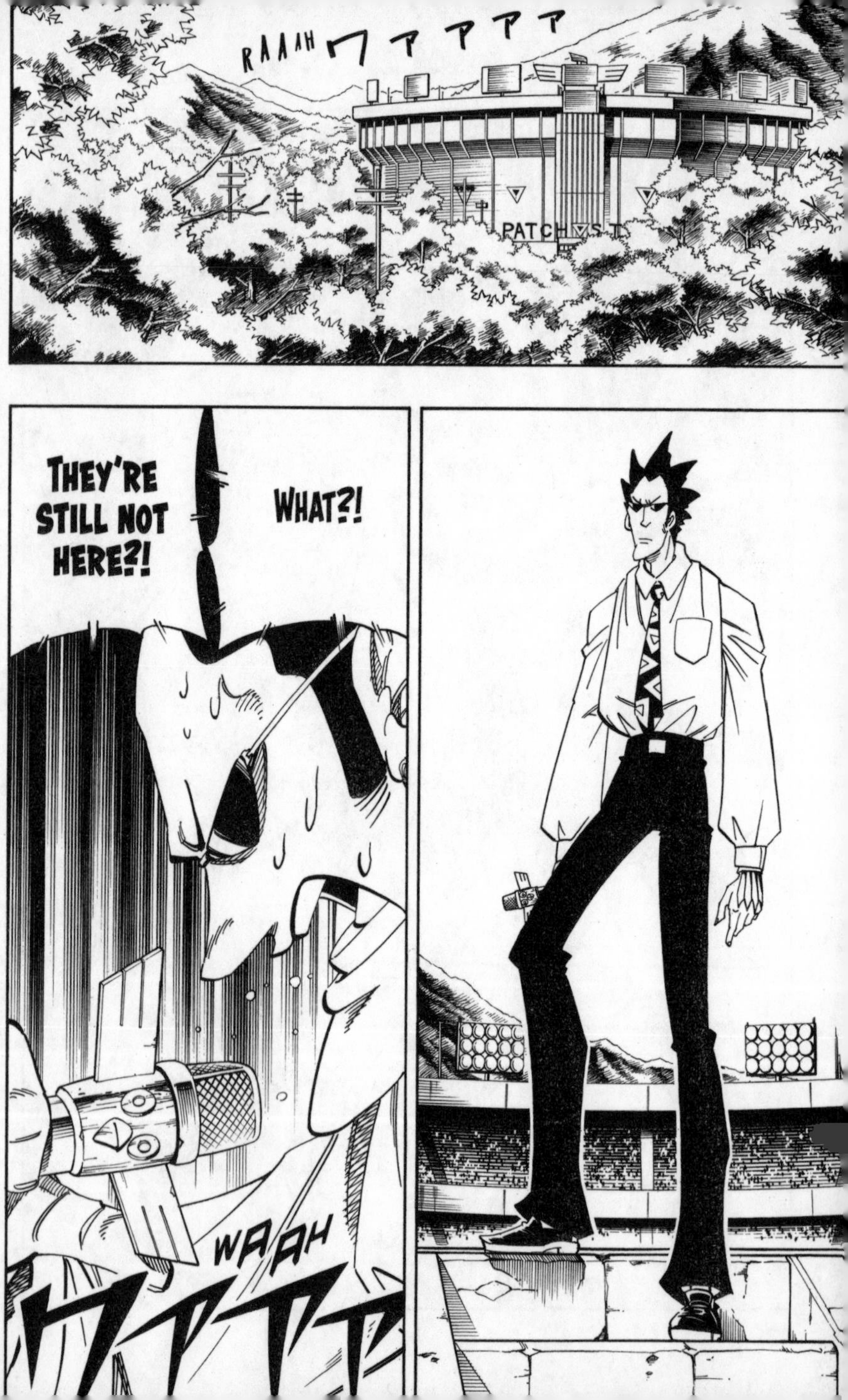
RAAAH ワアアア
PATCH
THEY'RE STILL NOT HERE?!
WHAT?!
WAAH

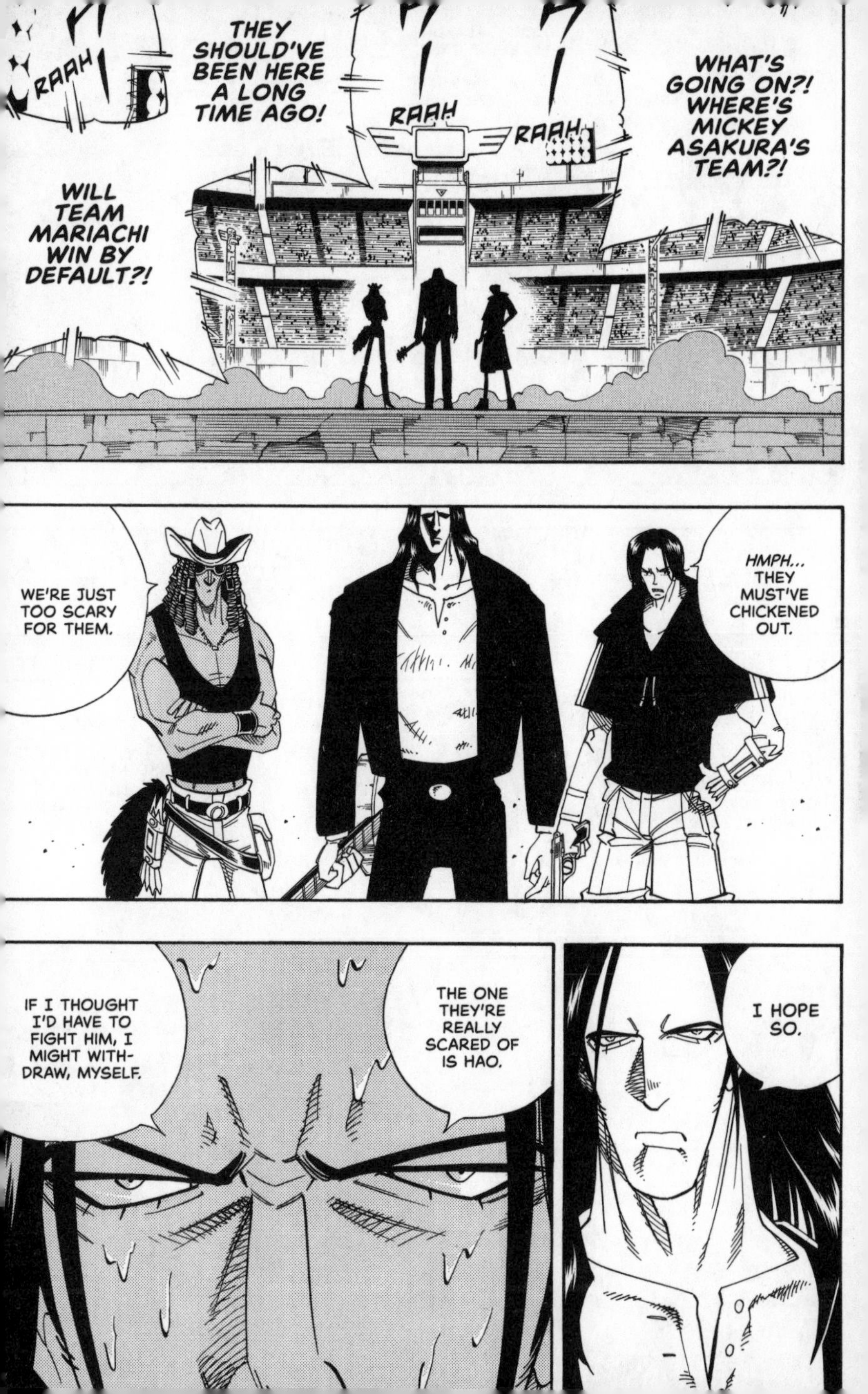
WHAT'S GOING ON?! WHERE'S MICKEY ASAKURA'S TEAM?!
RAAH
RAAH
THEY SHOULD'VE BEEN HERE A LONG TIME AGO!
RAAH
WILL TEAM MARIACHI WIN BY DEFAULT?!
HMPH... THEY MUST'VE CHICKENED OUT.
WE'RE JUST TOO SCARY FOR THEM.
I HOPE SO.
THE ONE THEY'RE REALLY SCARED OF IS HAO.
IF I THOUGHT I'D HAVE TO FIGHT HIM, I MIGHT WITH-DRAW, MYSELF.

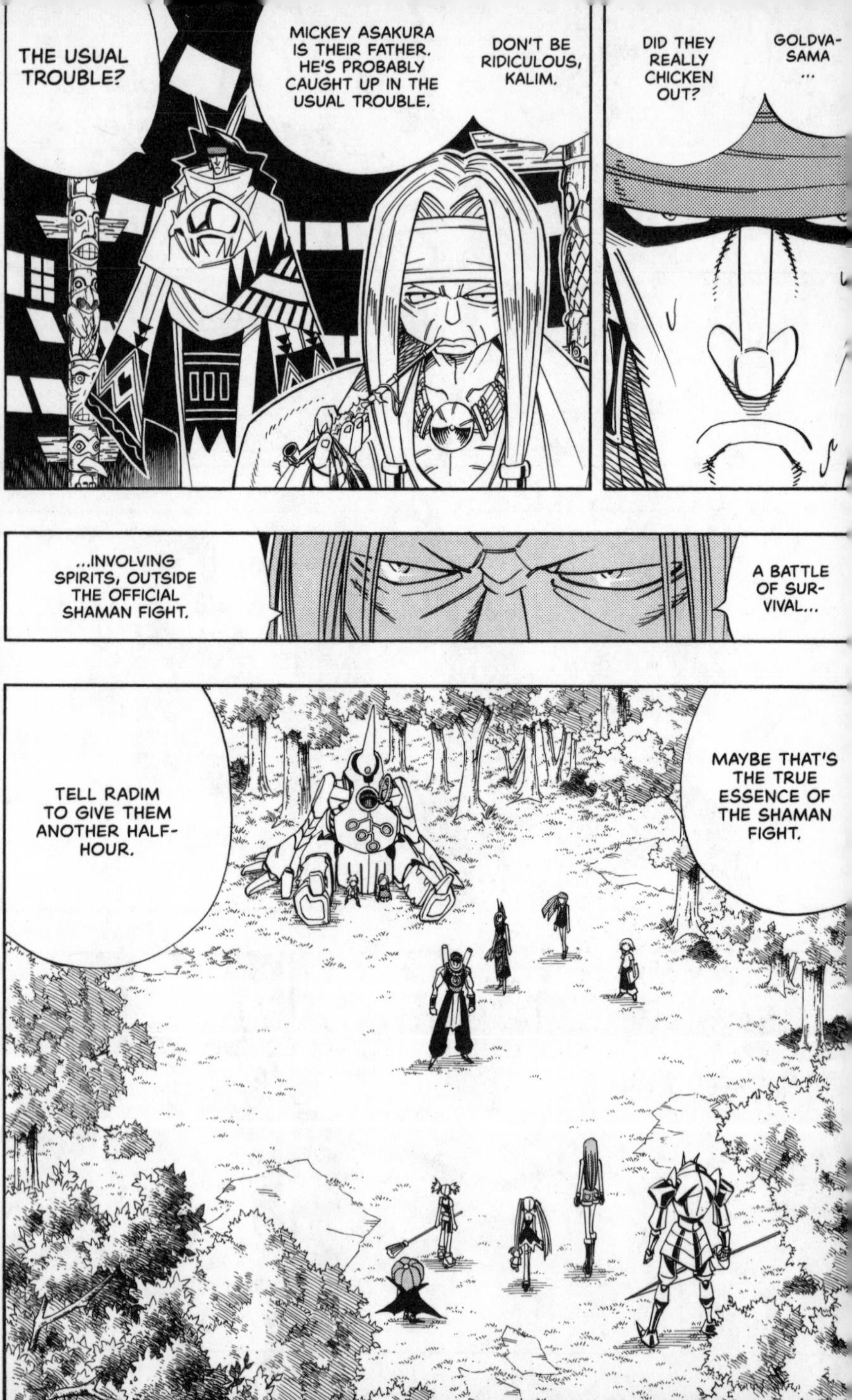
GOLDVA-SAMA ...
DID THEY REALLY CHICKEN OUT?
DON'T BE RIDICULOUS, KALIM.
MICKEY ASAKURA IS THEIR FATHER. HE'S PROBABLY CAUGHT UP IN THE USUAL TROUBLE.
THE USUAL TROUBLE?
A BATTLE OF SURVIVAL...
...INVOLVING SPIRITS, OUTSIDE THE OFFICIAL SHAMAN FIGHT.
MAYBE THAT'S THE TRUE ESSENCE OF THE SHAMAN FIGHT.
TELL RADIM TO GIVE THEM ANOTHER HALF-HOUR.

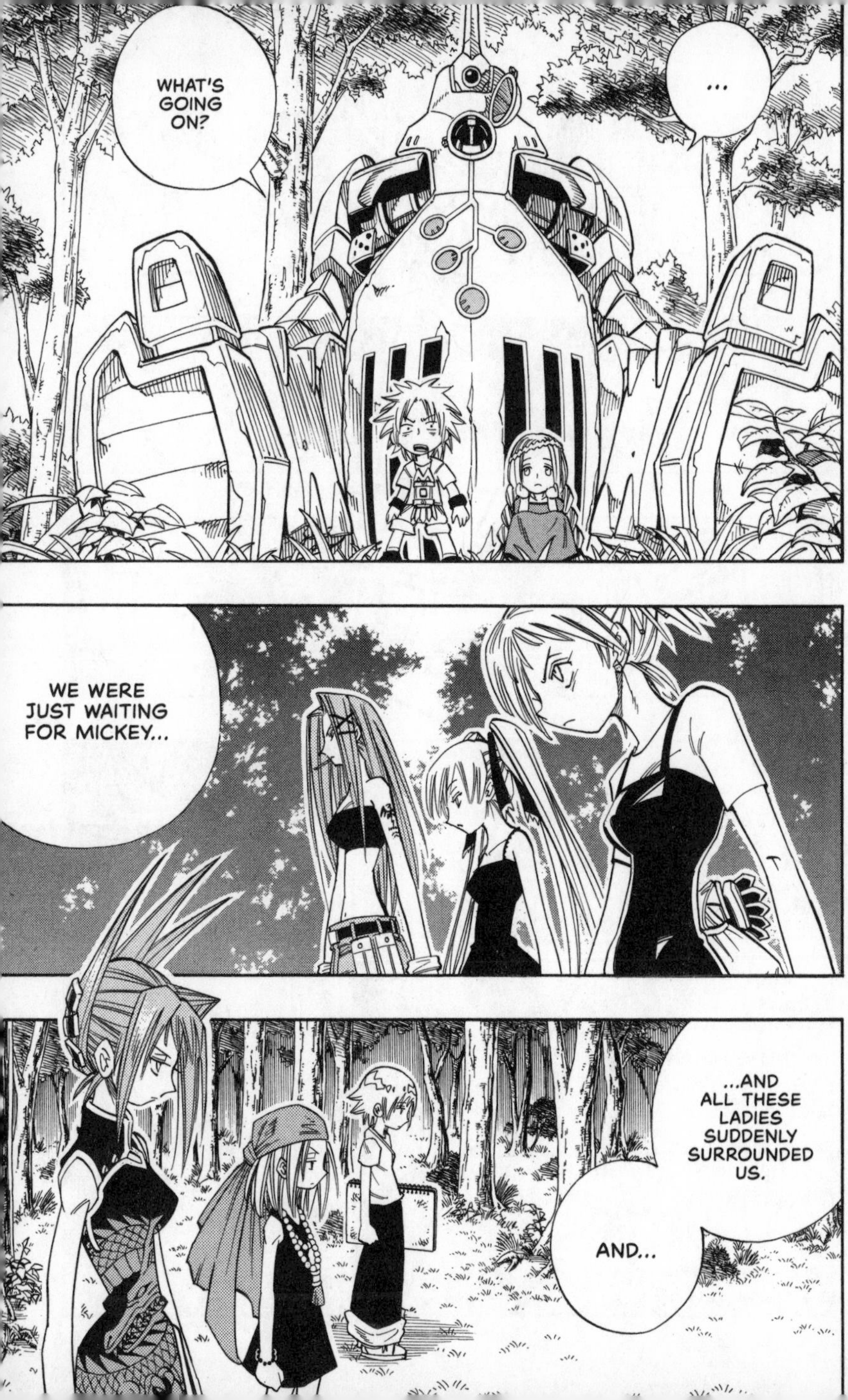
...
WHAT'S GOING ON?
WE WERE JUST WAITING FOR MICKEY...
...AND ALL THESE LADIES SUDDENLY SURROUNDED US.
AND...

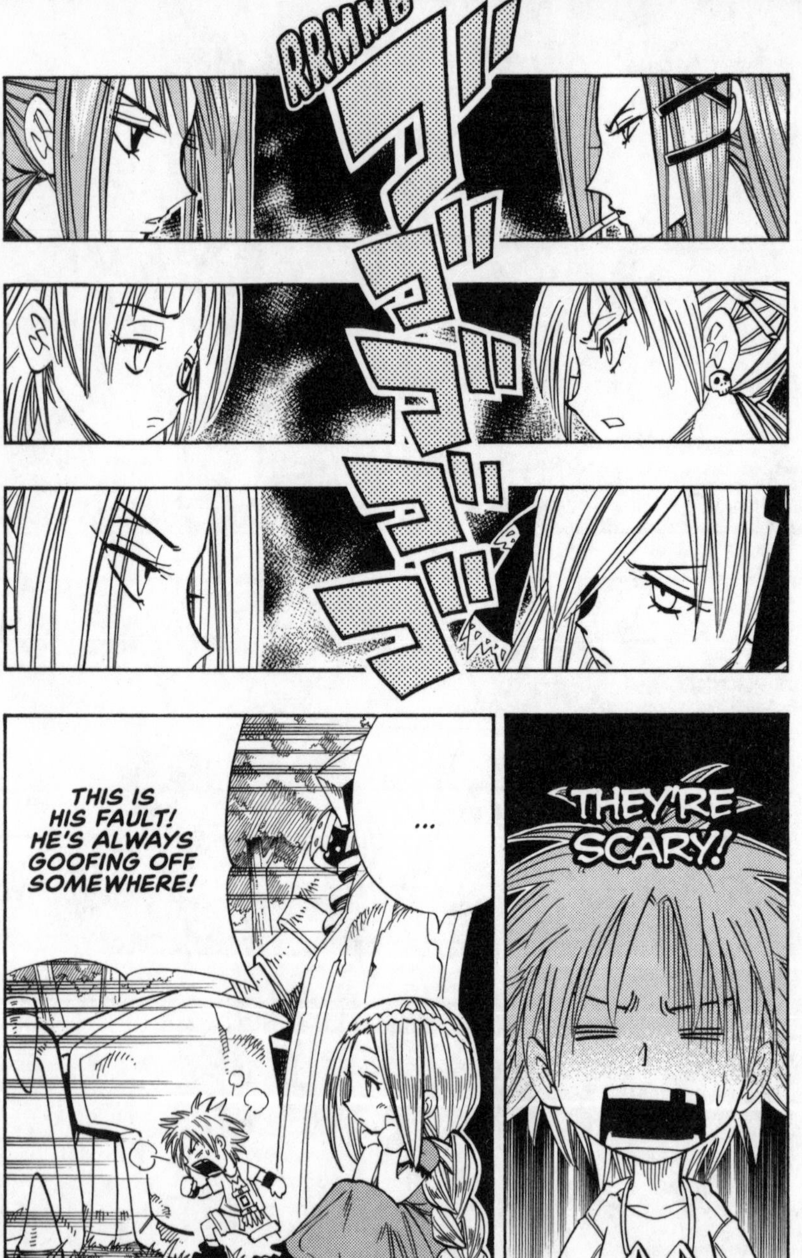
RRMMB
THEY'RE SCARY!
...
THIS IS HIS FAULT! HE'S ALWAYS GOOFING OFF SOMEWHERE!

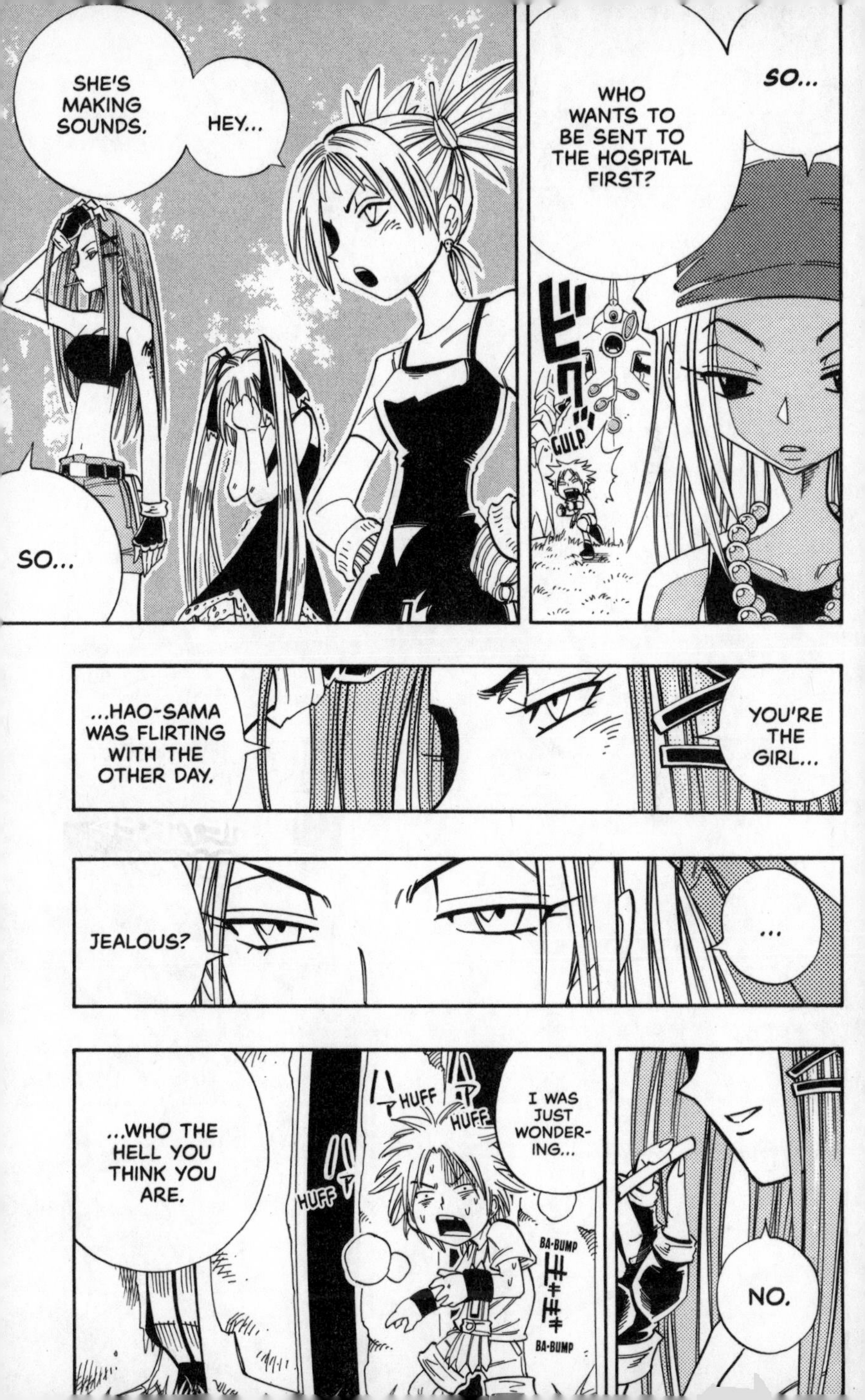
SO...
WHO WANTS TO BE SENT TO THE HOSPITAL FIRST?
GULP
HEY...
SHE'S MAKING SOUNDS.
SO...
YOU'RE THE GIRL...
...HAO-SAMA WAS FLIRTING WITH THE OTHER DAY.
...
JEALOUS?
NO.
I WAS JUST WONDER-ING...
HUFF
HUFF
BA-BUMP
BA-BUMP
HUFF
...WHO THE HELL YOU THINK YOU ARE.

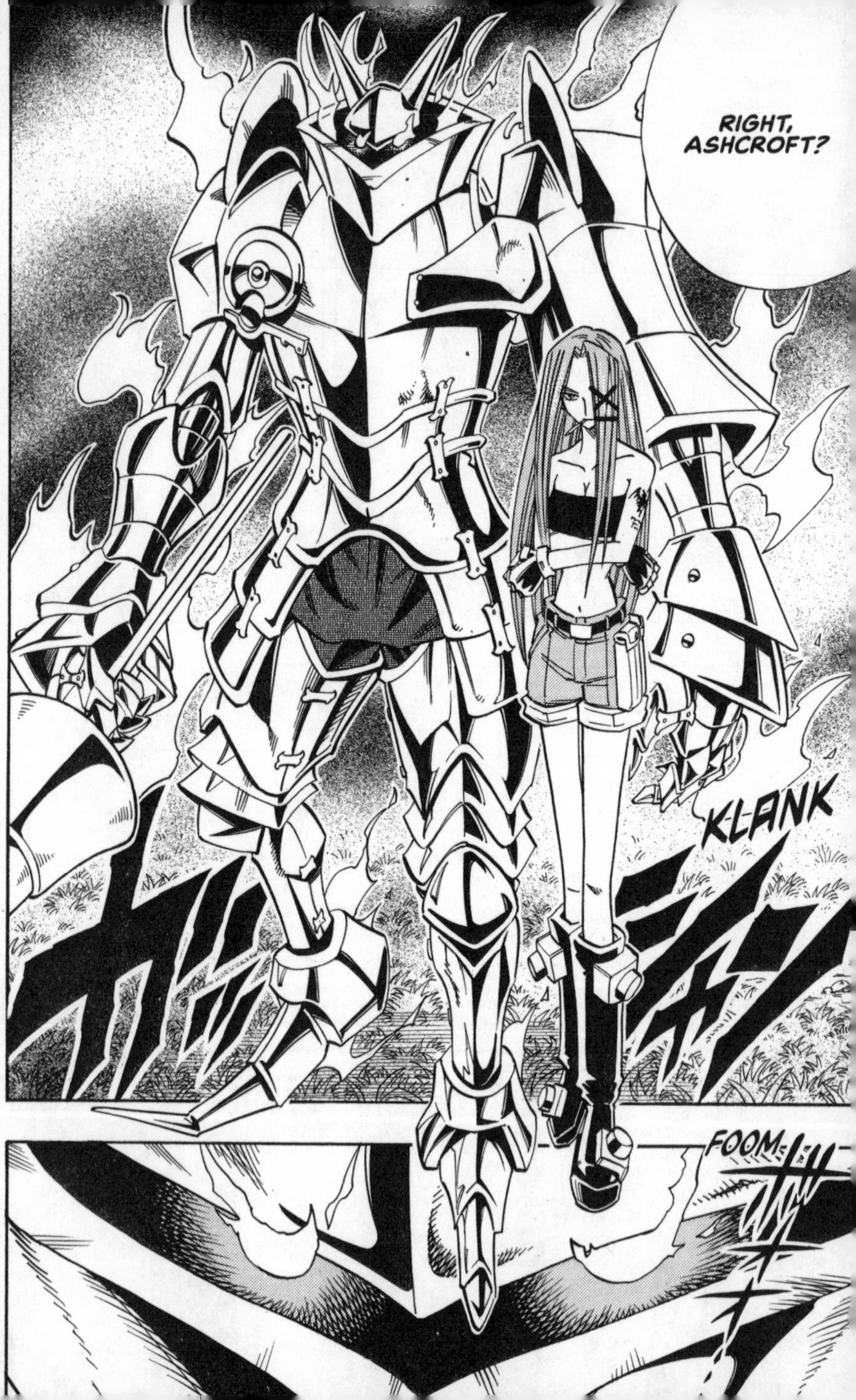
RIGHT, ASHCROFT?
K-LANK
FOOM

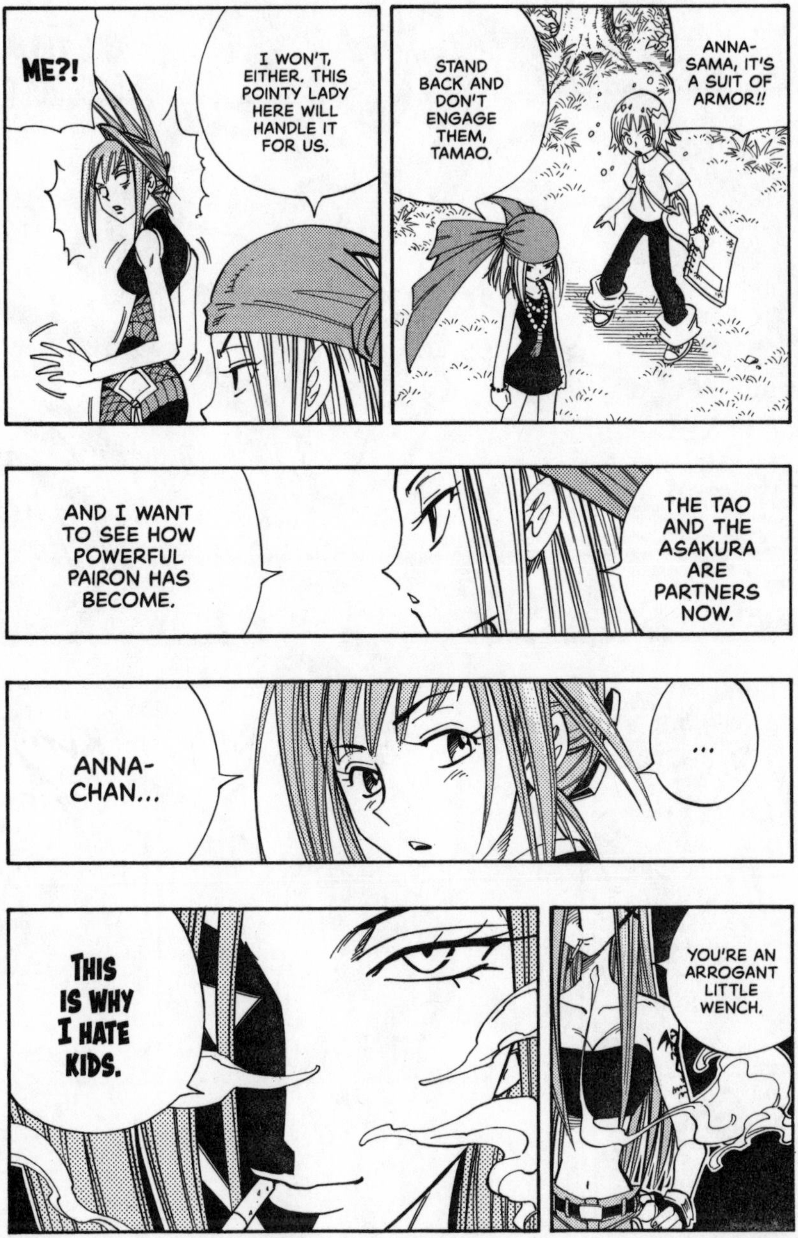
ANNA-SAMA, IT'S A SUIT OF ARMOR!!
STAND BACK AND DON'T ENGAGE THEM, TAMAO.
I WON'T, EITHER. THIS POINTY LADY HERE WILL HANDLE IT FOR US.
ME?!
THE TAO AND THE ASAKURA ARE PARTNERS NOW.
AND I WANT TO SEE HOW POWERFUL PAIRON HAS BECOME.
...
ANNA-CHAN...
YOU'RE AN ARROGANT LITTLE WENCH.
THIS IS WHY I HATE KIDS.

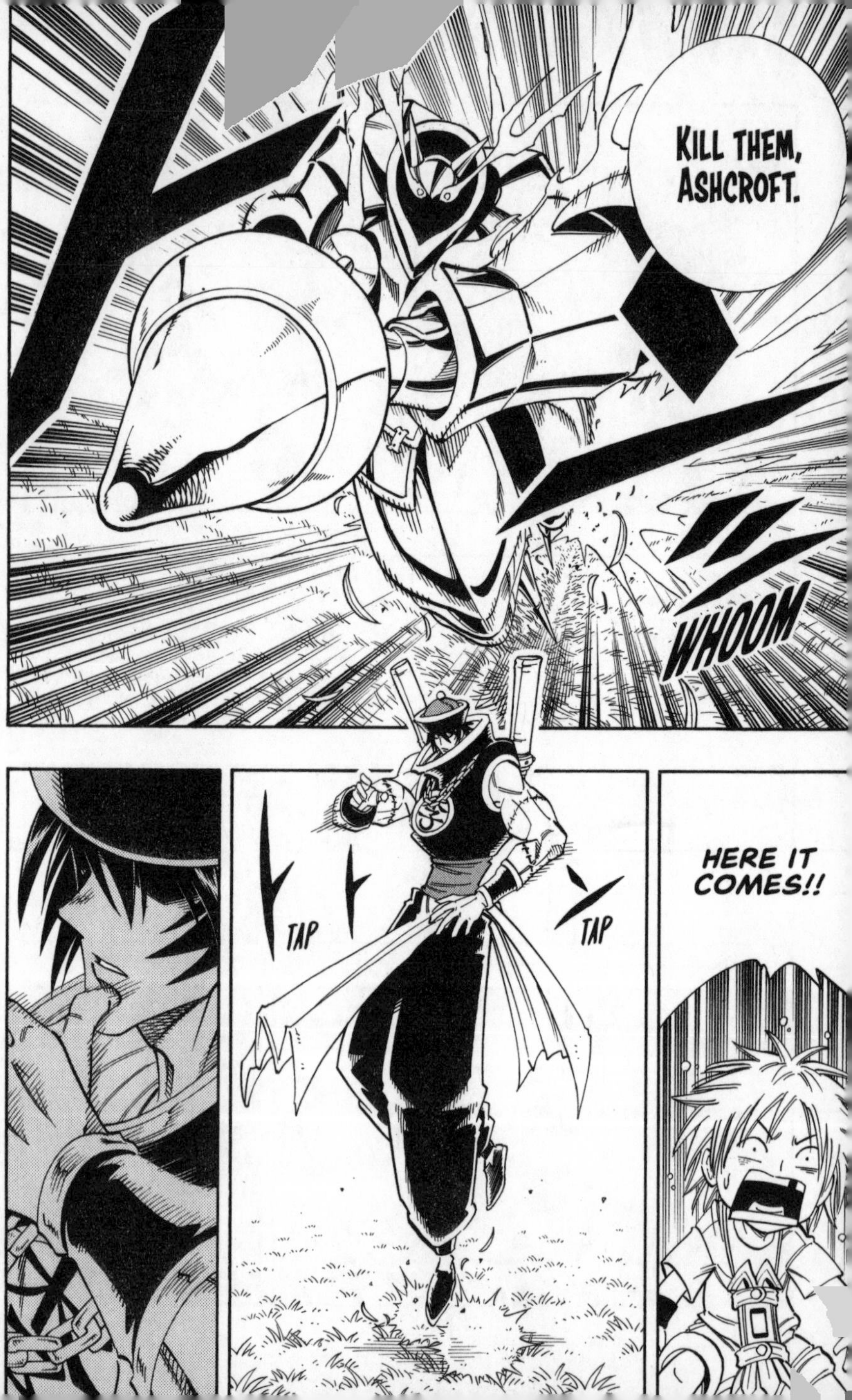
KILL THEM, ASHCROFT.
WHOOM
HERE IT COMES!!
TAP
TAP

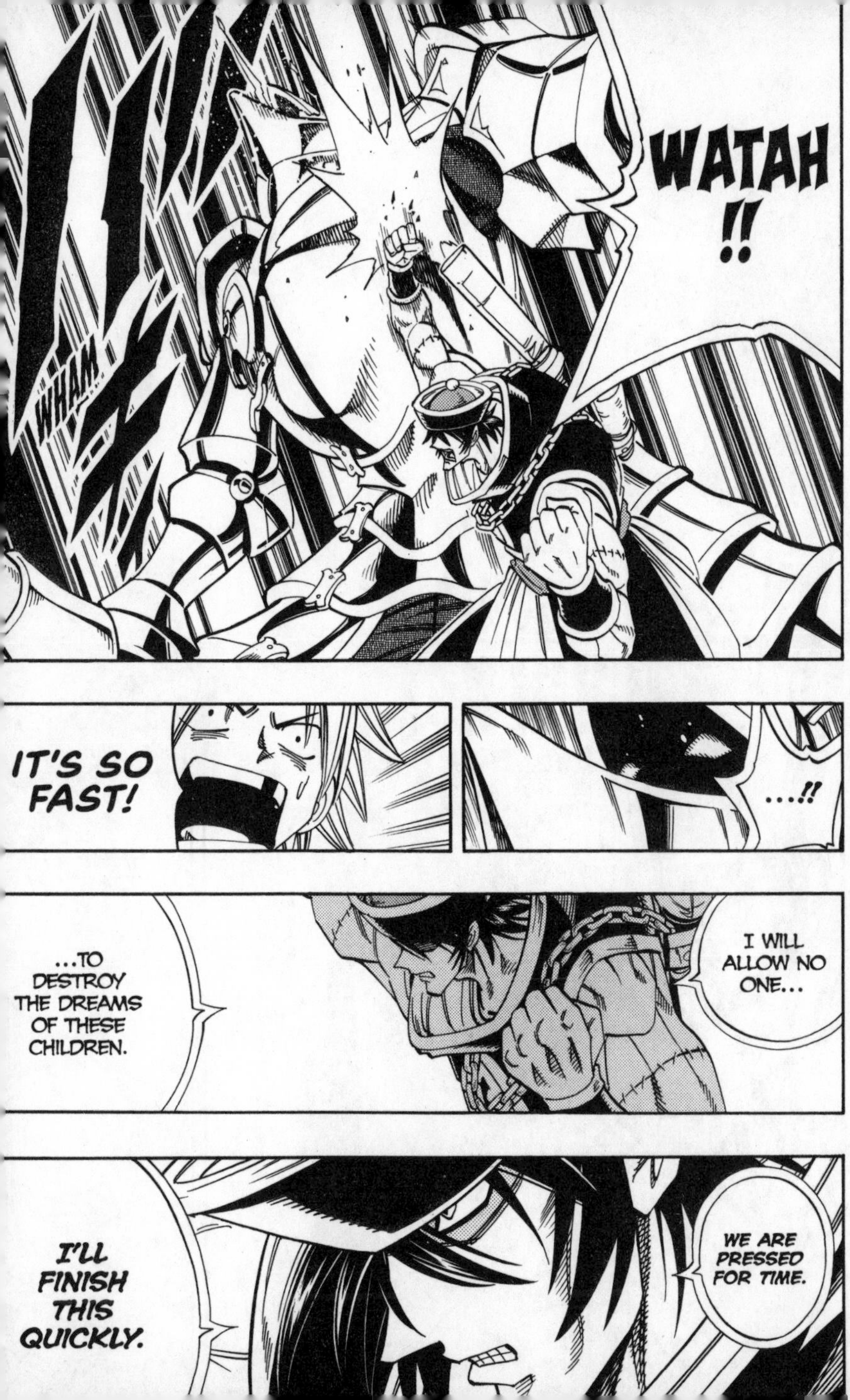
WATAH!!
WHAM
...!!
IT'S SO FAST!
I WILL ALLOW NO ONE...
...TO DESTROY THE DREAMS OF THESE CHILDREN.
WE ARE PRESSED FOR TIME.
I'LL FINISH THIS QUICKLY.

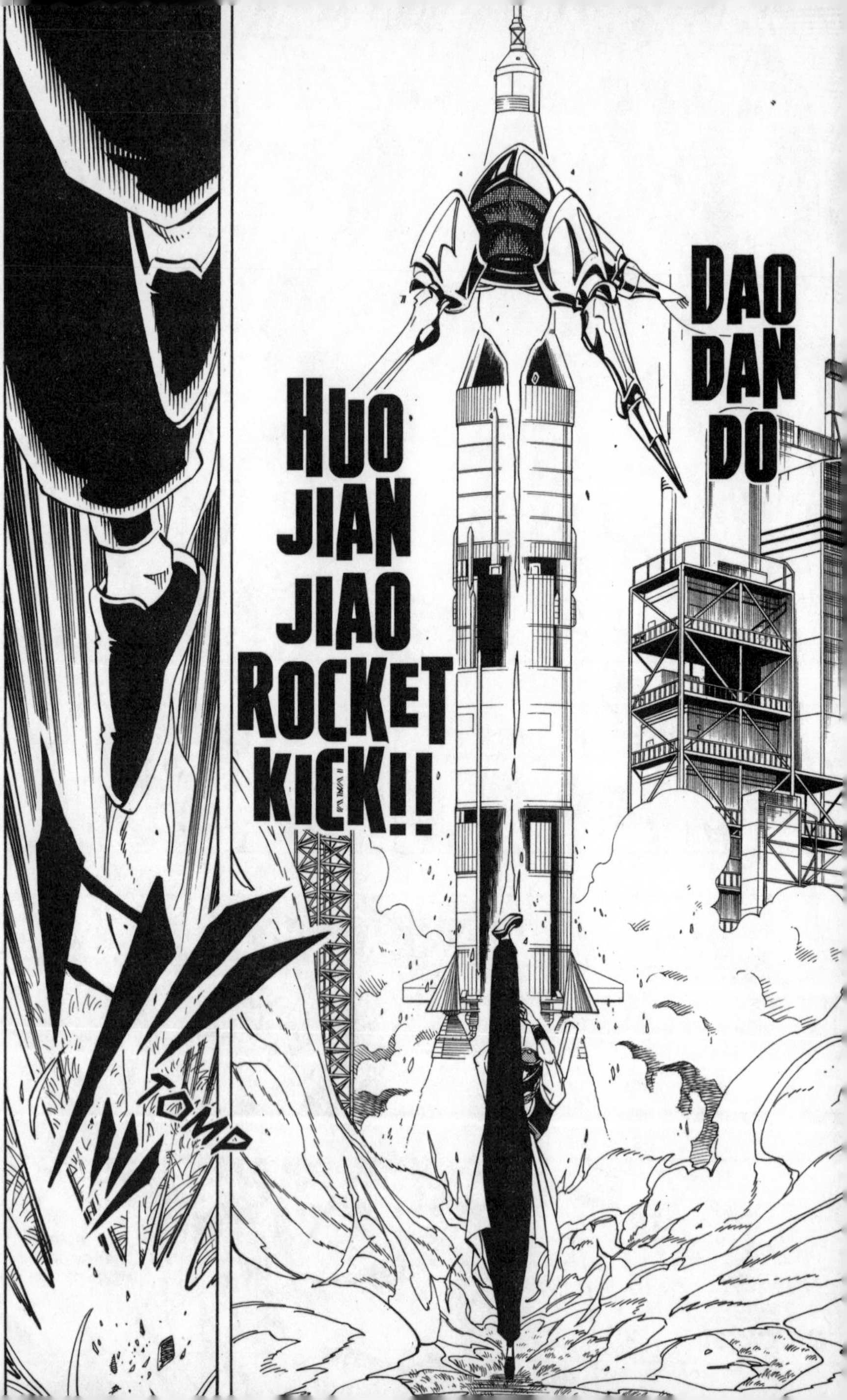
DAO DAN DO
HUO JIAN JIAO ROCKET KICK!!
TOMP

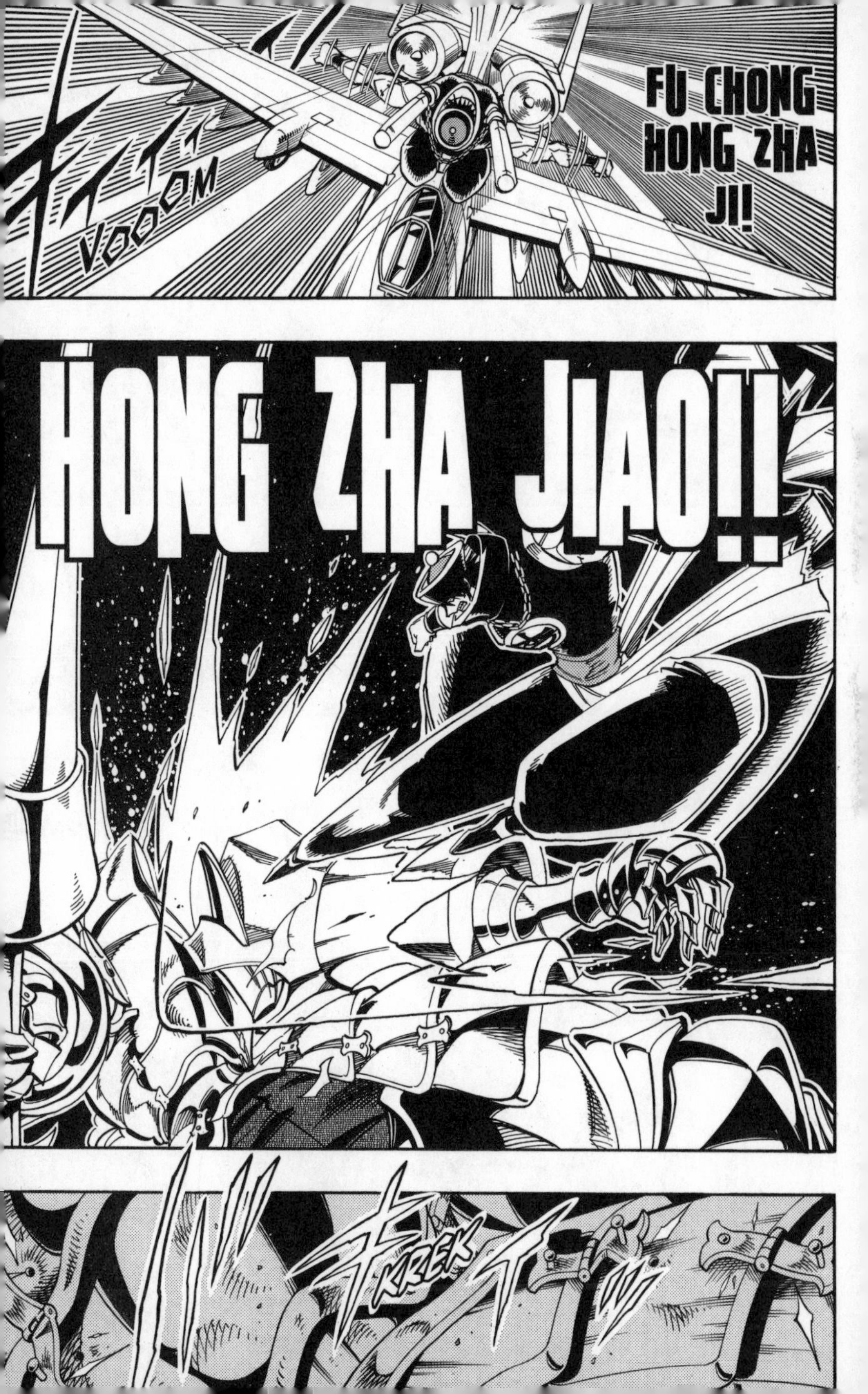
FU CHONG HONG ZHA JI!
VOOOM
HONG ZHA JIAO!!
KRZEK

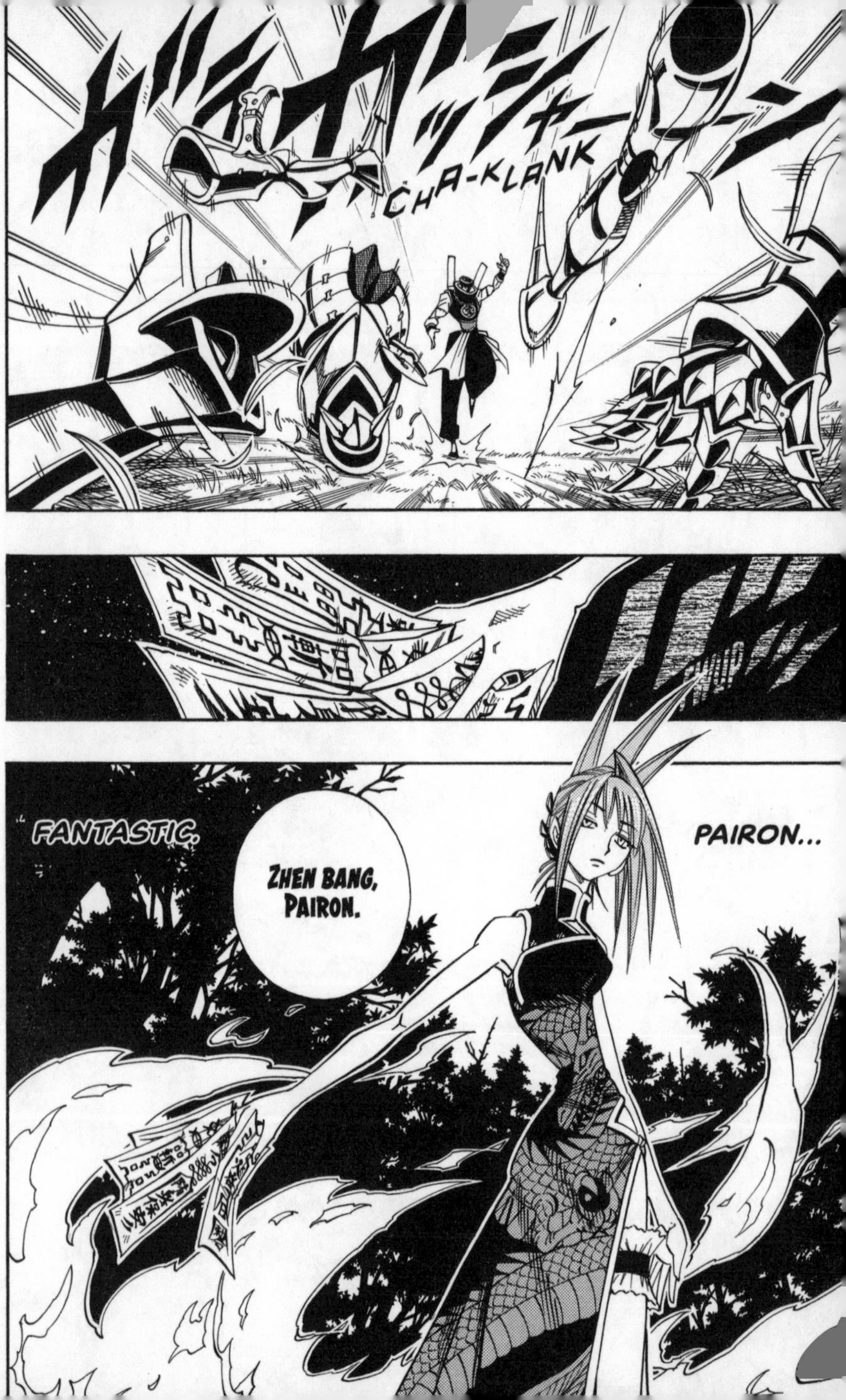
CHA-KLANK
PAIRON...
ZHEN BANG, PAIRON.
"FANTASTIC."

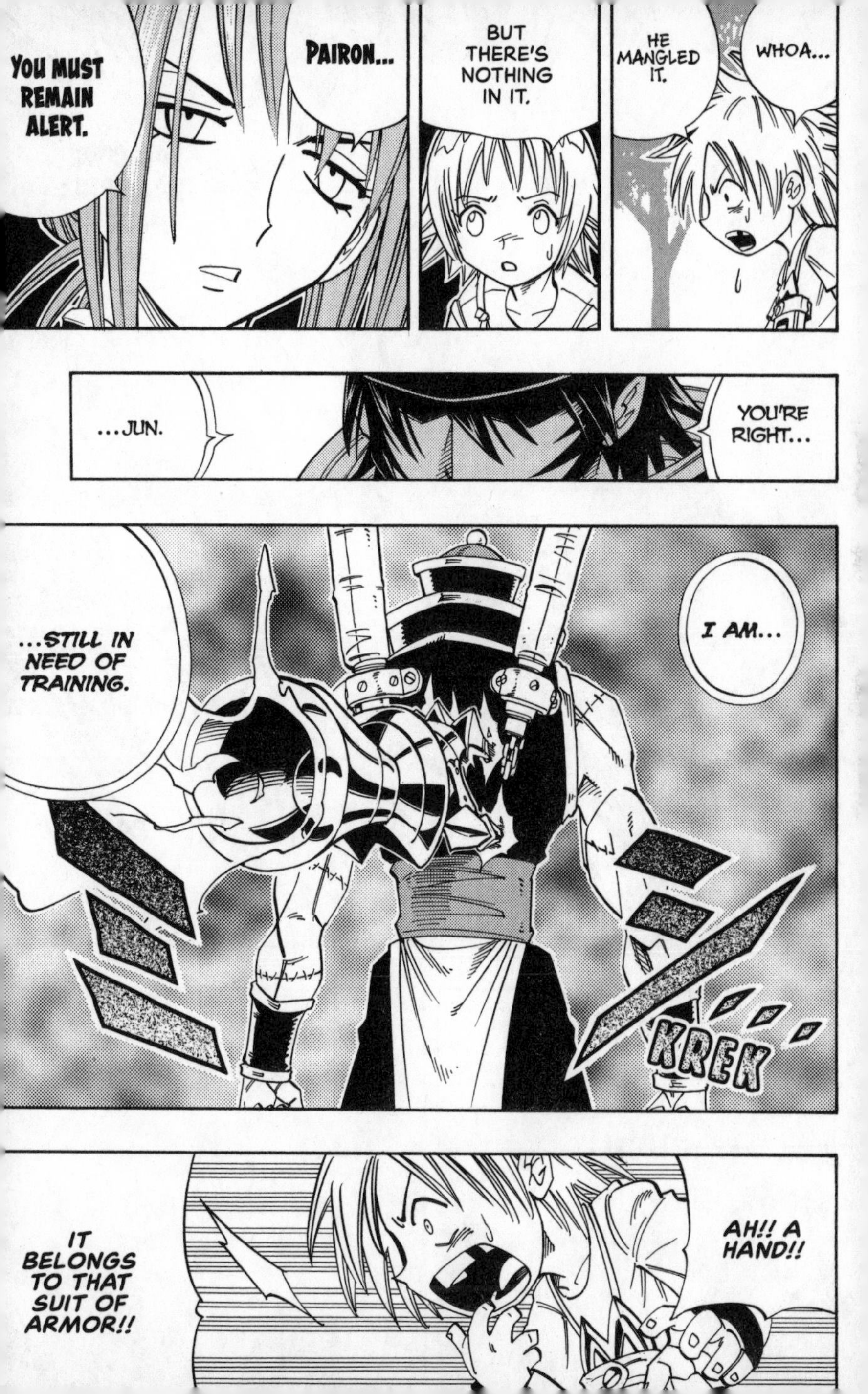
WHOA...
HE MANGLED IT.
BUT THERE'S NOTHING IN IT.
PAIRON...
YOU MUST REMAIN ALERT.
YOU'RE RIGHT...
...JUN.
I AM...
...STILL IN NEED OF TRAINING.
KREK
AH!! A HAND!!
IT BELONGS TO THAT SUIT OF ARMOR!!

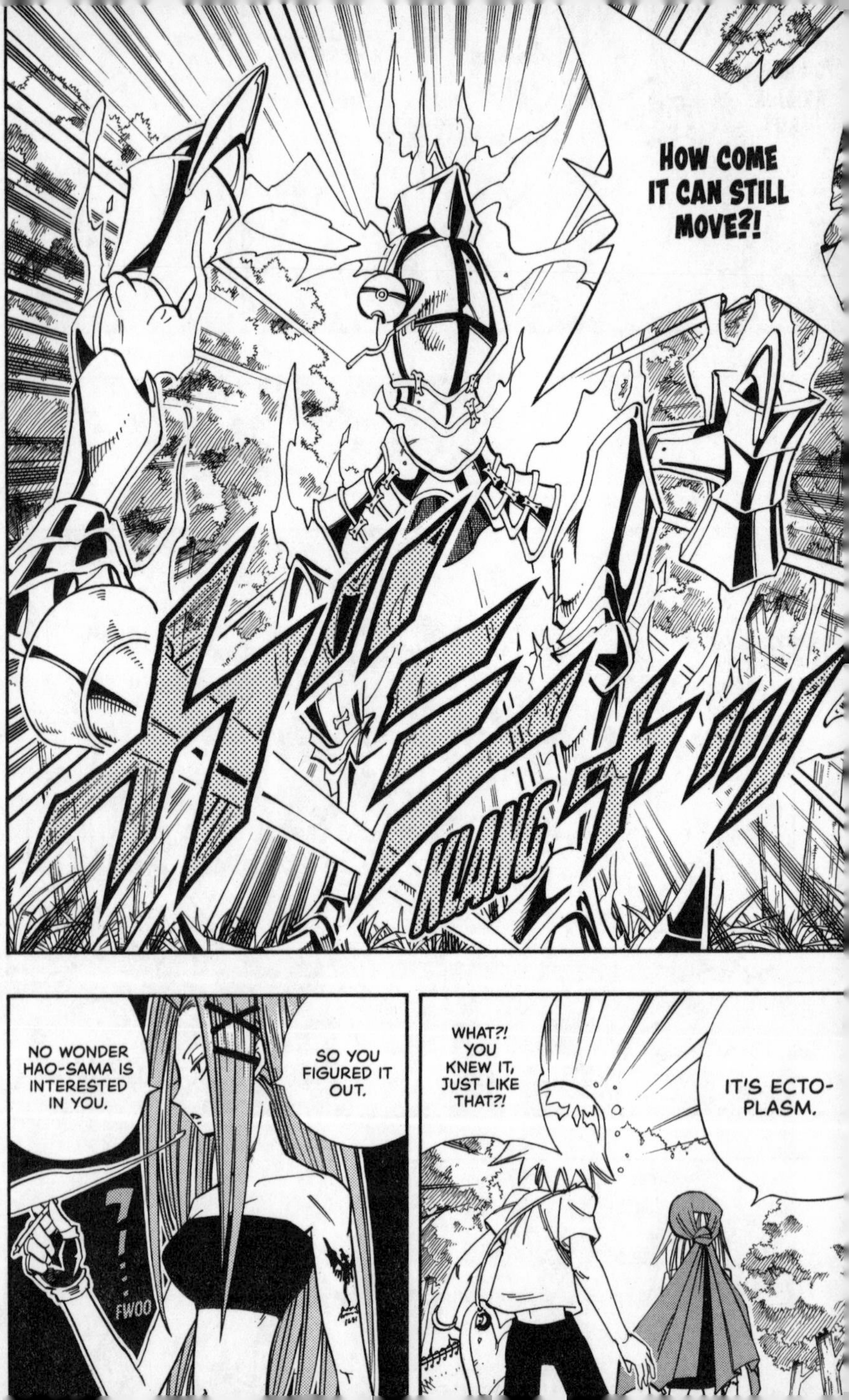
HOW COME IT CAN STILL MOVE?!
KLANG
IT'S ECTO-PLASM.
WHAT?! YOU KNEW IT, JUST LIKE THAT?!
SO YOU FIGURED IT OUT.
NO WONDER HAO-SAMA IS INTERESTED IN YOU.
FWOO

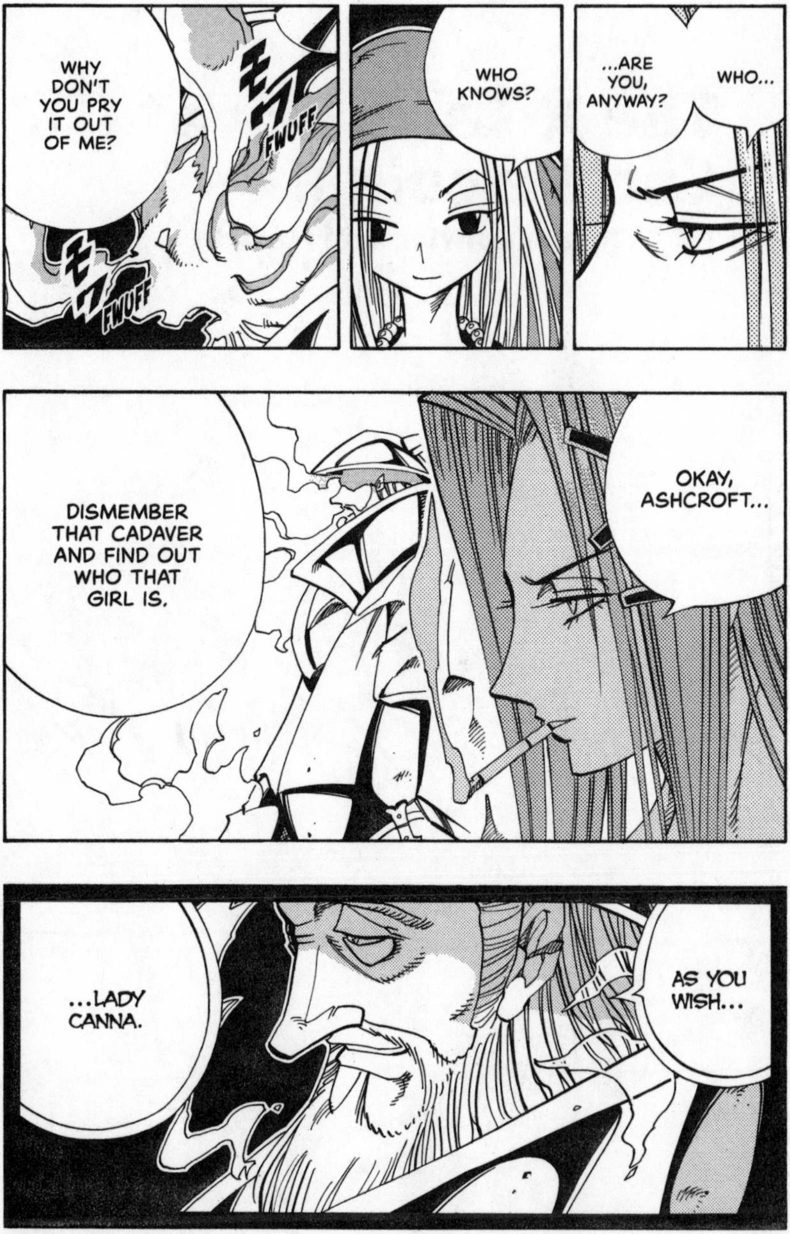
WHO...
...ARE YOU, ANYWAY?
WHO KNOWS?
WHY DON'T YOU PRY IT OUT OF ME?
FWUFF
FWUFF
OKAY, ASHCROFT...
DISMEMBER THAT CADAVER AND FIND OUT WHO THAT GIRL IS.
AS YOU WISH...
...LADY CANNA.

The X-Laws Private Car, Lincoln X

1972 Lincoln Continental Mark IV

January 2001

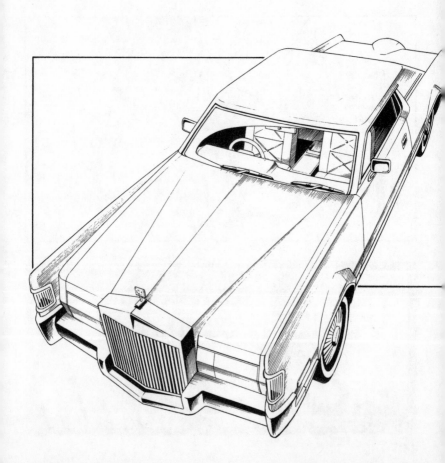

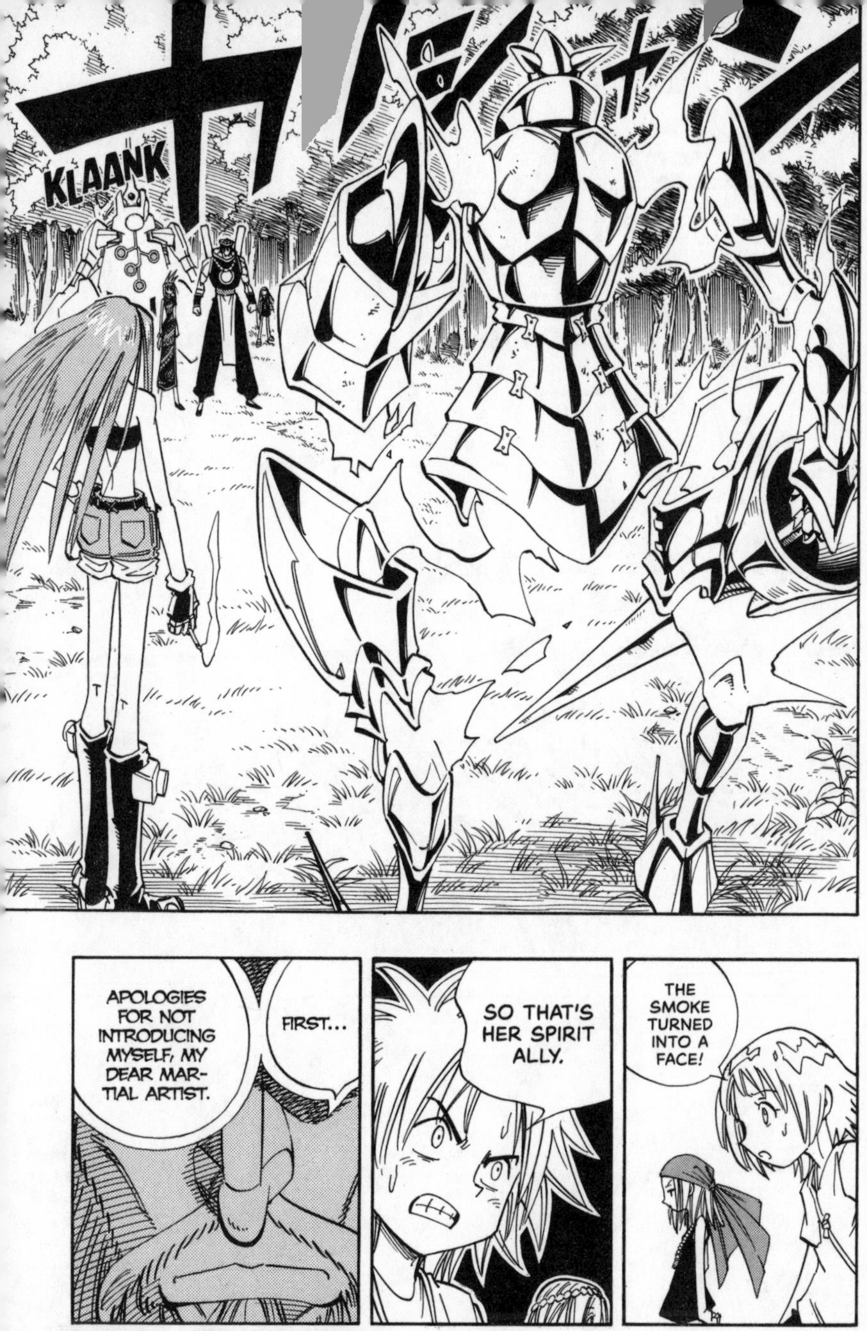
KLAANK
THE SMOKE TURNED INTO A FACE!
SO THAT'S HER SPIRIT ALLY.
FIRST...
APOLOGIES FOR NOT INTRODUCING MYSELF, MY DEAR MAR-TIAL ARTIST.

Chapter 155: My Terms

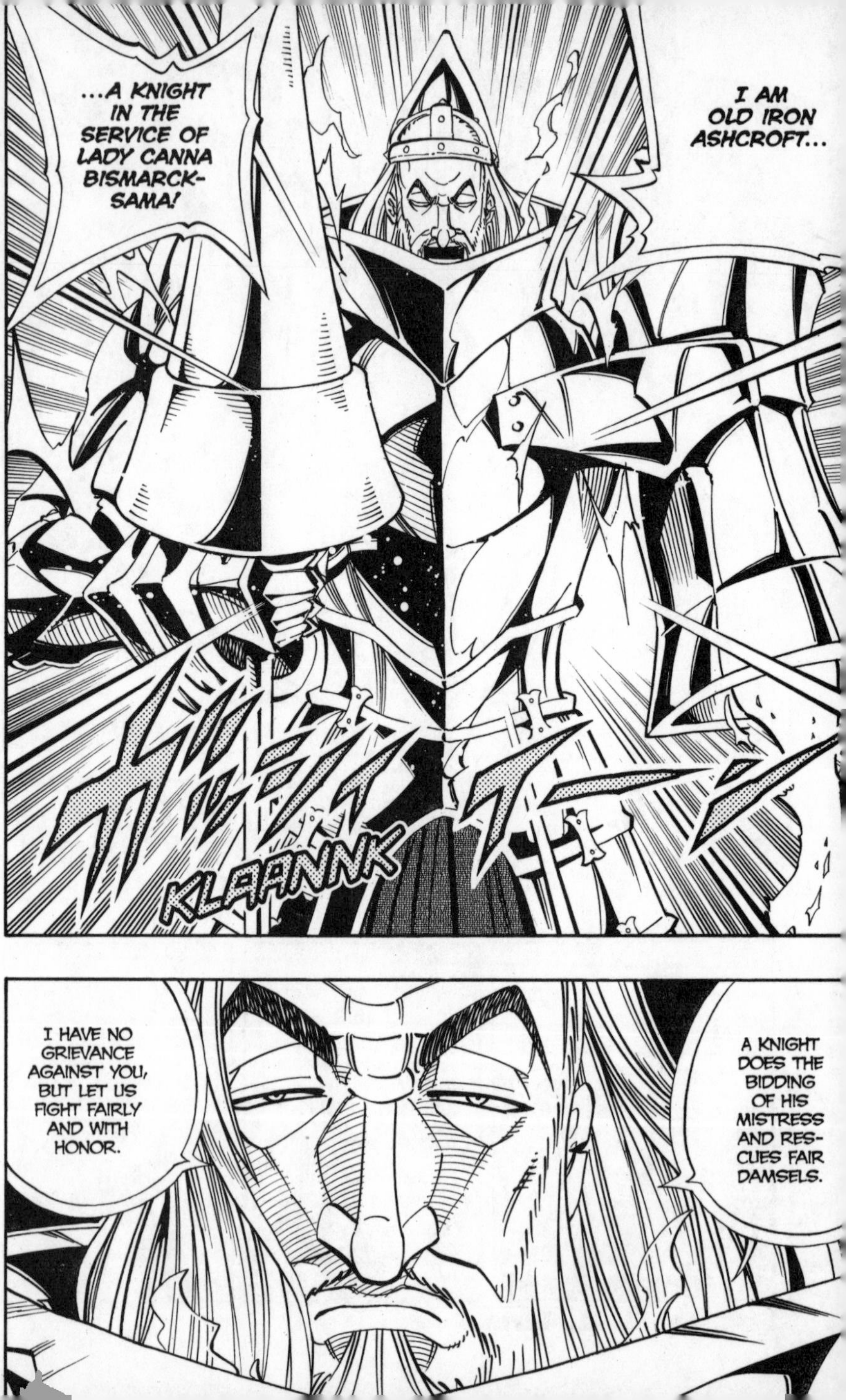
I AM OLD IRON ASHCROFT...
...A KNIGHT IN THE SERVICE OF LADY CANNA BISMARCK-SAMA!
KLAANNK
A KNIGHT DOES THE BIDDING OF HIS MISTRESS AND RESCUES FAIR DAMSELS.
I HAVE NO GRIEVANCE AGAINST YOU, BUT LET US FIGHT FAIRLY AND WITH HONOR.

Chapter 155:

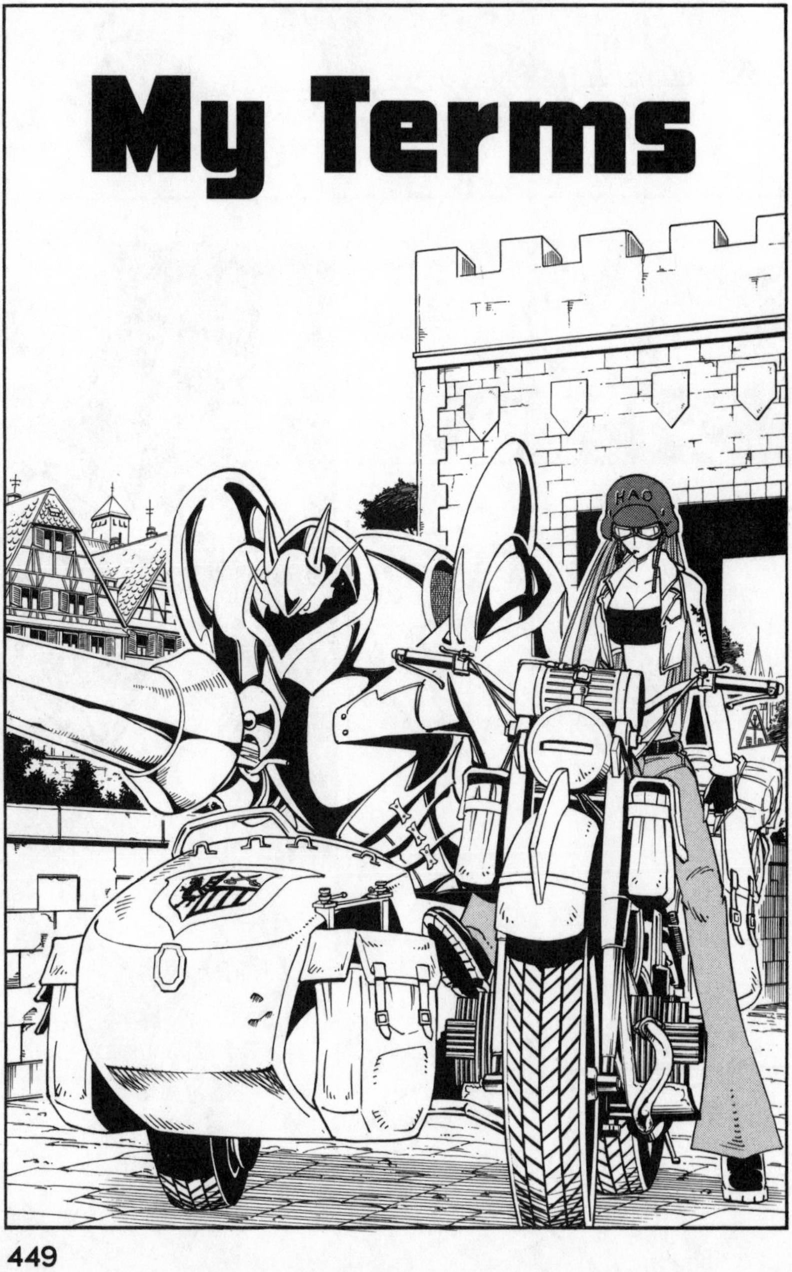
My Terms
HAO

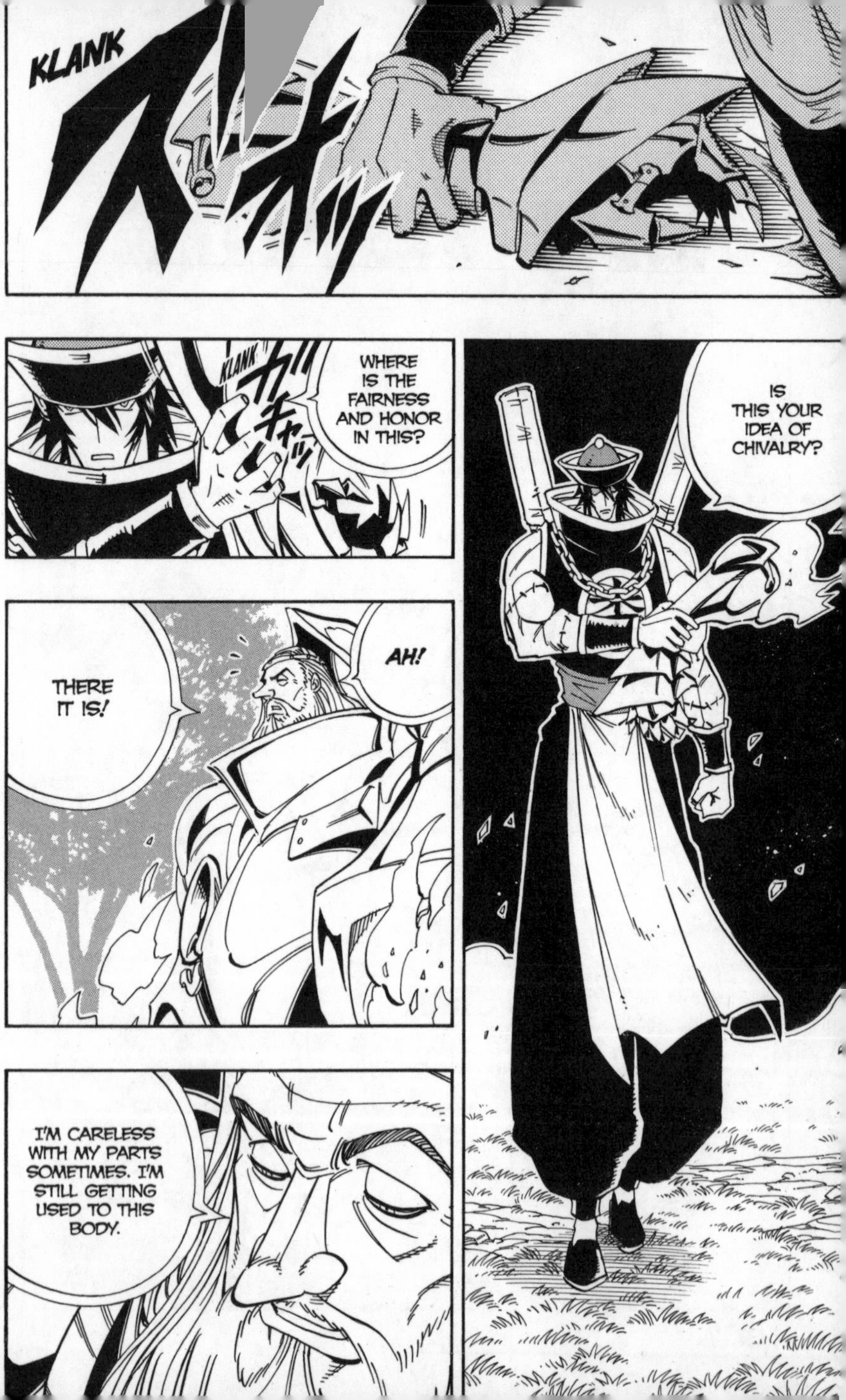
KLANK
IS THIS YOUR IDEA OF CHIVALRY?
KLANK
WHERE IS THE FAIRNESS AND HONOR IN THIS?
AH!
THERE IT IS!
I'M CARELESS WITH MY PARTS SOMETIMES. I'M STILL GETTING USED TO THIS BODY.

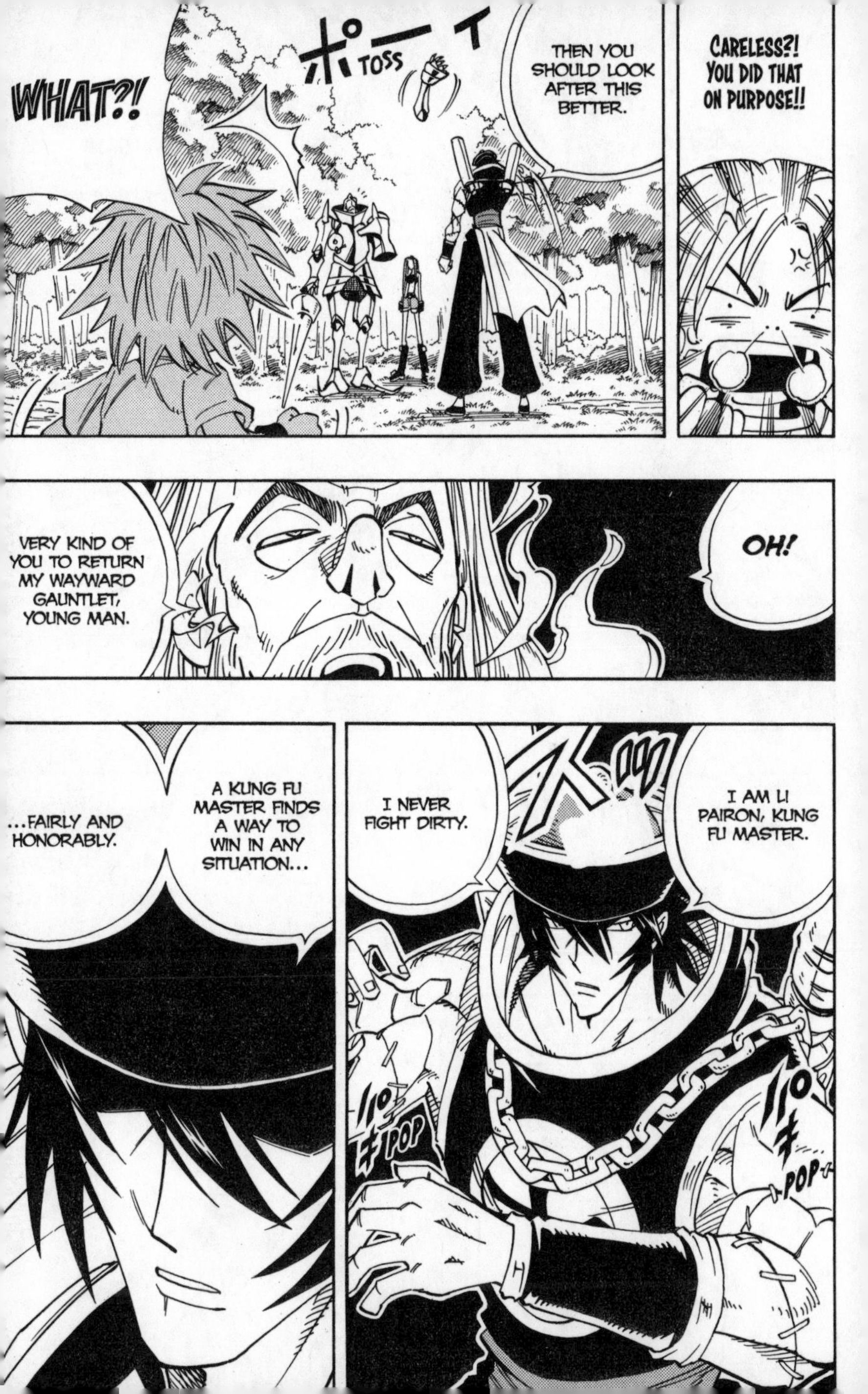
CARELESS?! YOU DID THAT ON PURPOSE!!
THEN YOU SHOULD LOOK AFTER THIS BETTER.
ポーイ
TOSS
WHAT?!
OH!
VERY KIND OF YOU TO RETURN MY WAYWARD GAUNTLET, YOUNG MAN.
I AM LI PAIRON, KUNG FU MASTER.
I NEVER FIGHT DIRTY.
POP
POP
A KUNG FU MASTER FINDS A WAY TO WIN IN ANY SITUATION...
...FAIRLY AND HONORABLY.

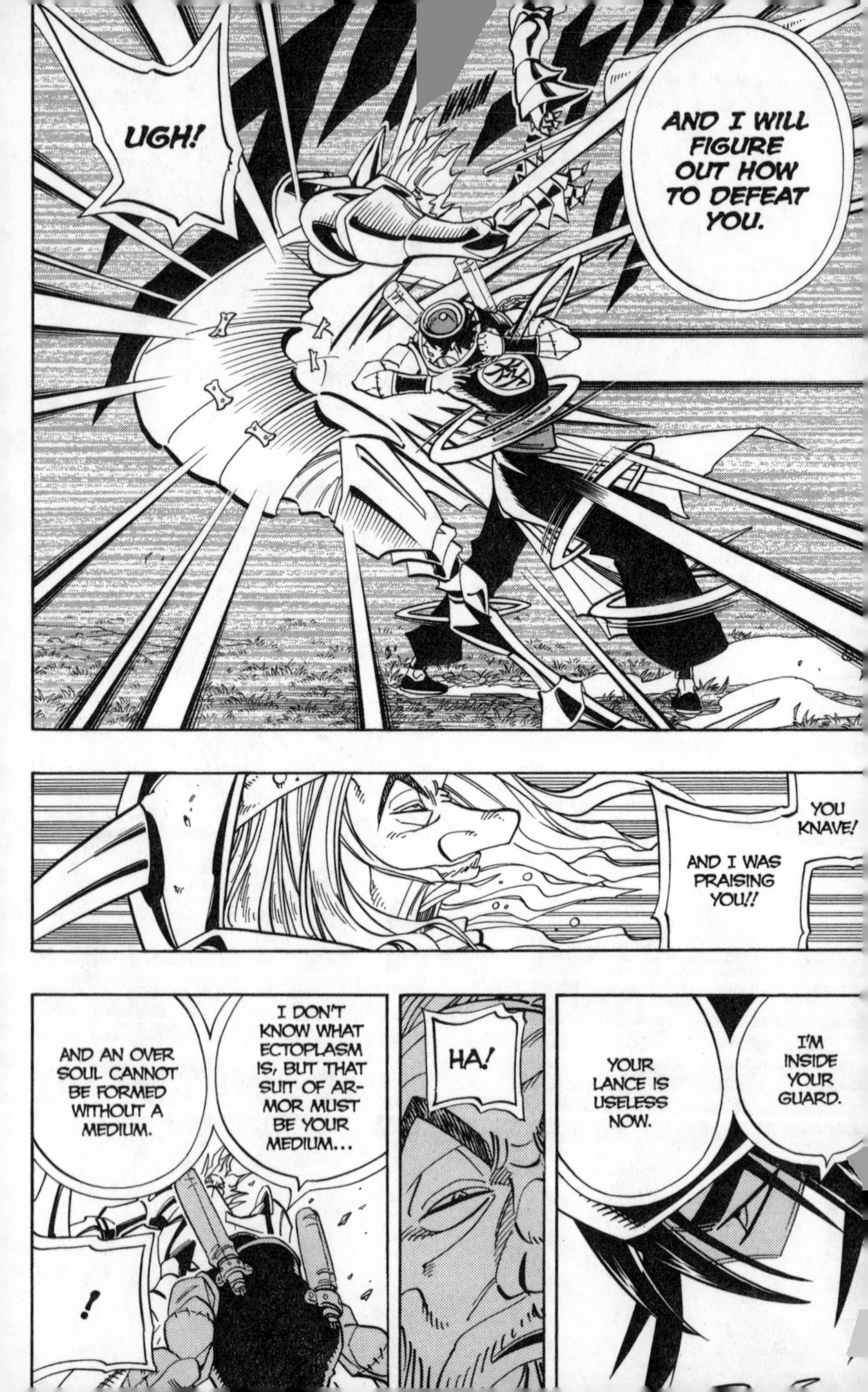
AND I WILL FIGURE OUT HOW TO DEFEAT YOU.
UGH!
YOU KNAVE!
AND I WAS PRAISING YOU!!
I'M INSIDE YOUR GUARD.
YOUR LANCE IS USELESS NOW.
HA!
I DON'T KNOW WHAT ECTOPLASM IS, BUT THAT SUIT OF ARMOR MUST BE YOUR MEDIUM...
AND AN OVER SOUL CANNOT BE FORMED WITHOUT A MEDIUM.
!

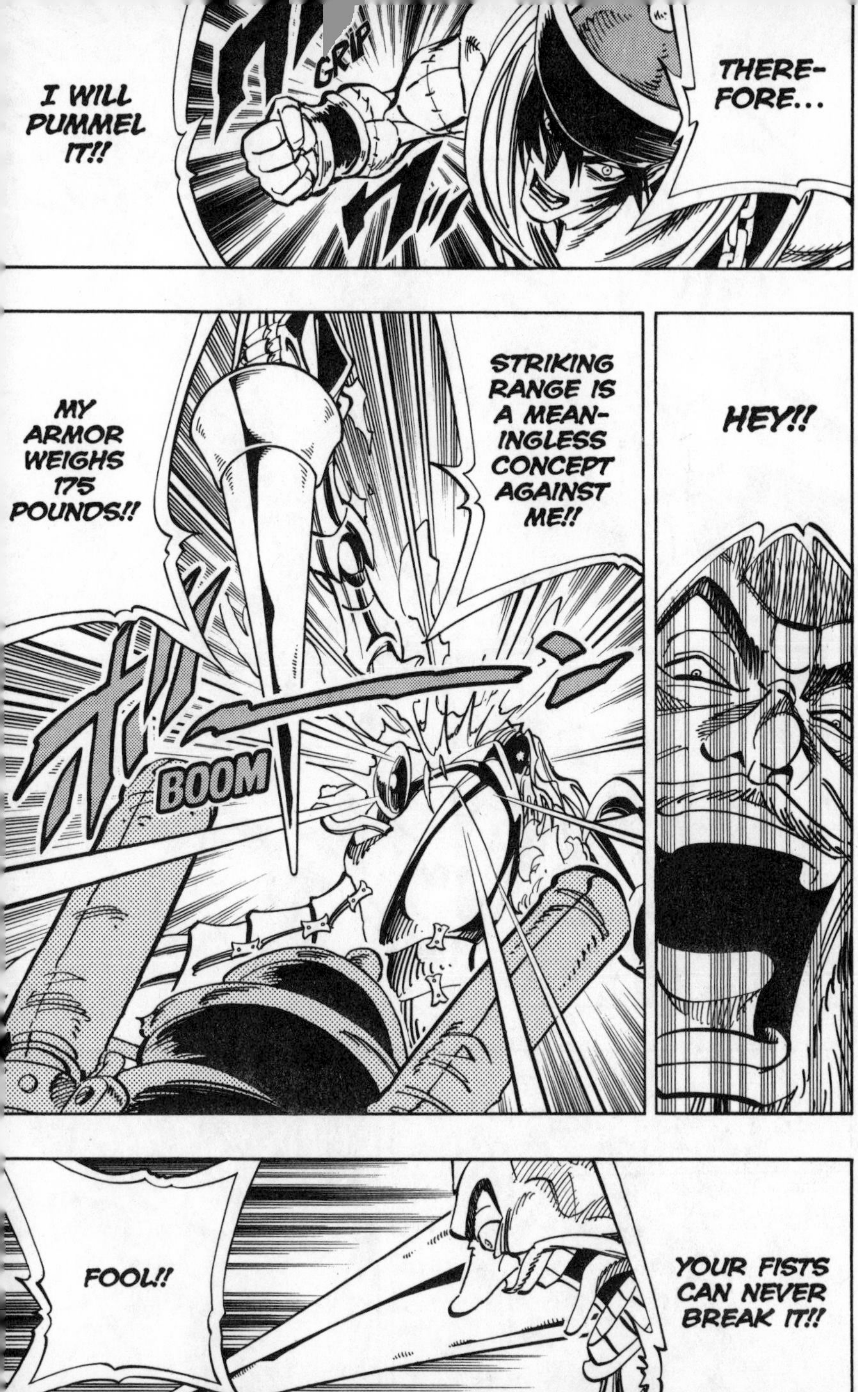
THERE-FORE...
GRIP
I WILL PUMMEL IT!!
HEY!!
STRIKING RANGE IS A MEAN-INGLESS CONCEPT AGAINST ME!!
MY ARMOR WEIGHS 175 POUNDS!!
BOOM
YOUR FISTS CAN NEVER BREAK IT!!
FOOL!!

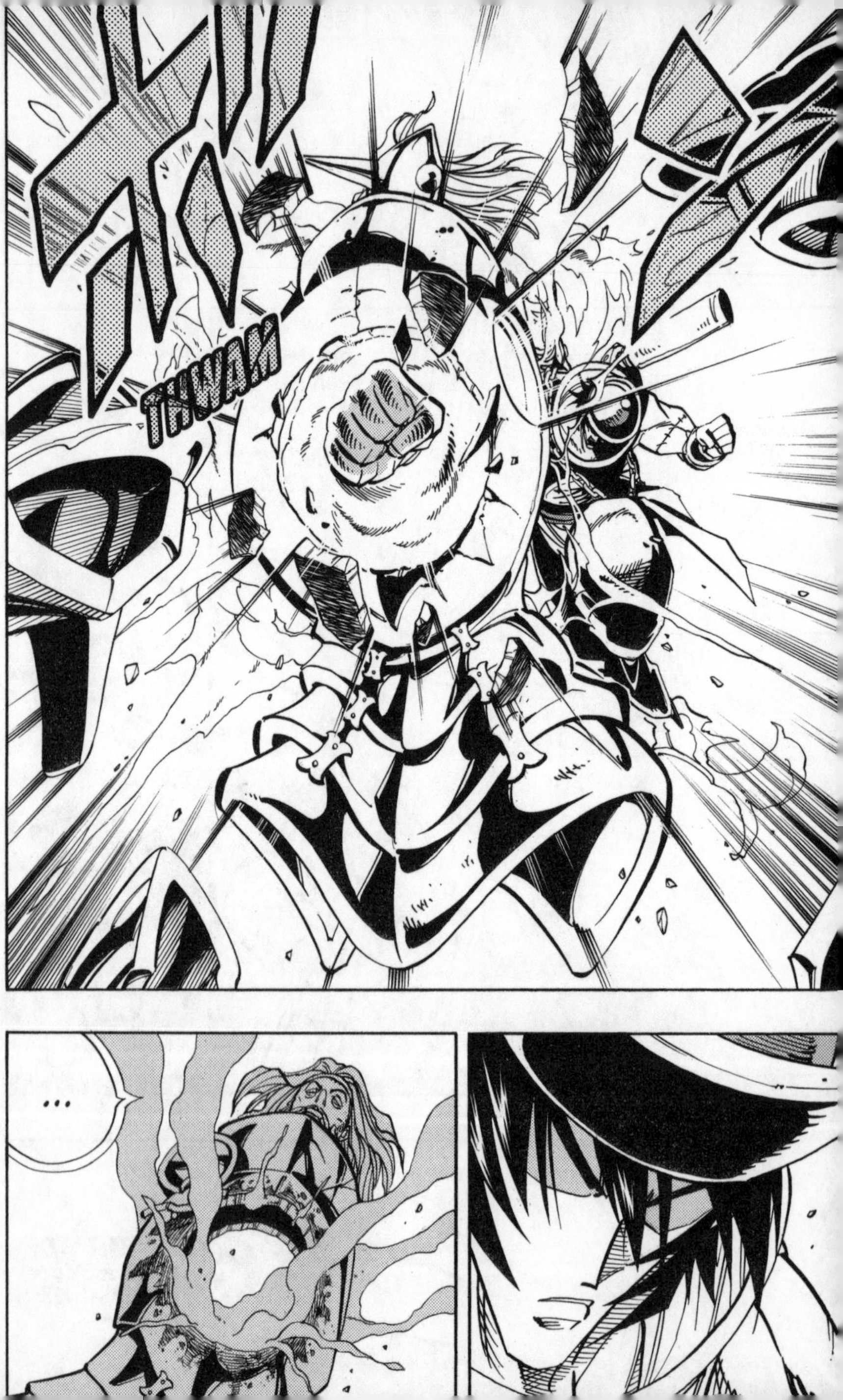
THWAM
...

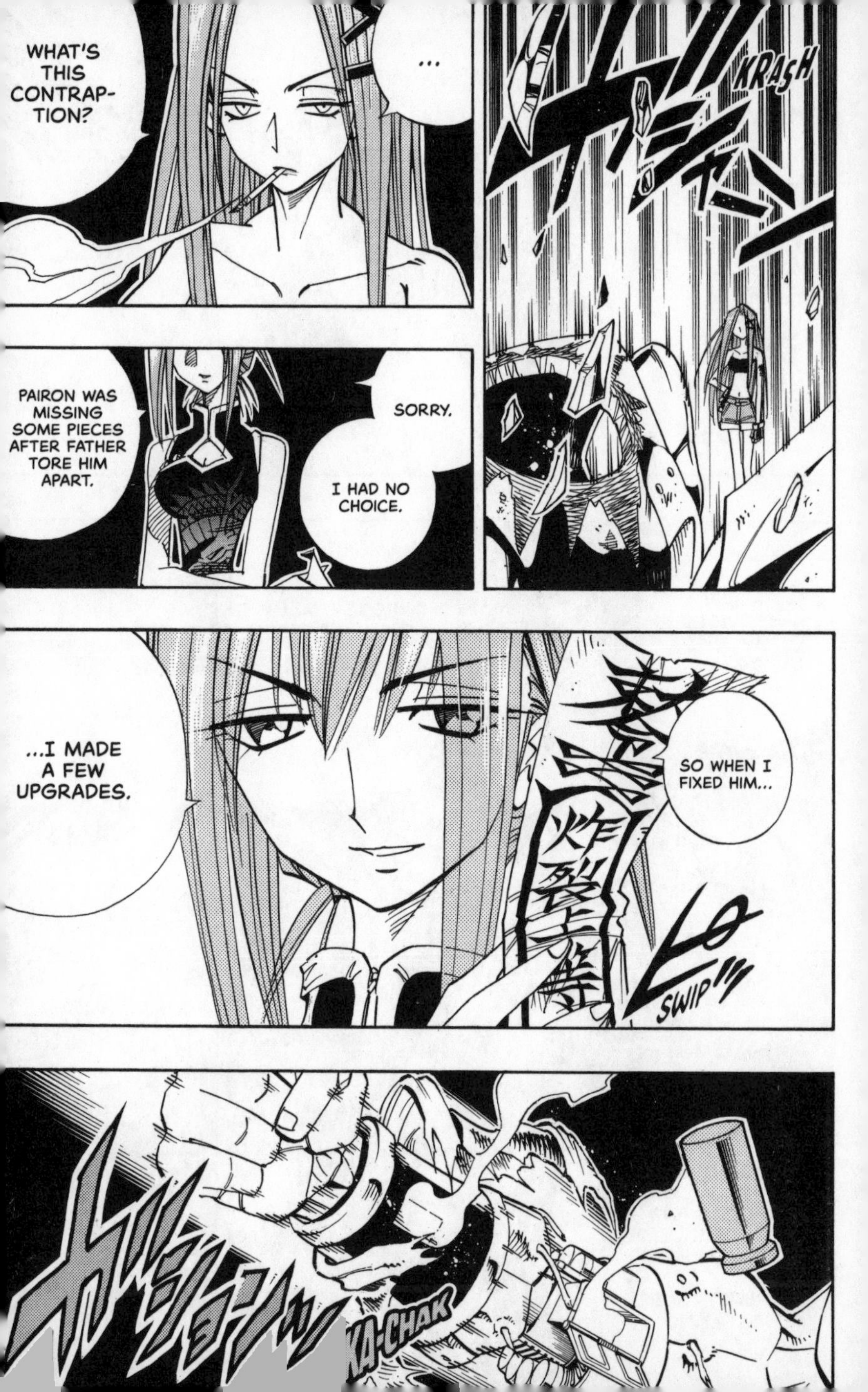
KRASH
...
WHAT'S THIS CONTRAPTION?
SORRY.
I HAD NO CHOICE.
PAIRON WAS MISSING SOME PIECES AFTER FATHER TORE HIM APART.
SO WHEN I FIXED HIM...
SWIP
...I MADE A FEW UPGRADES.
KA-CHAK

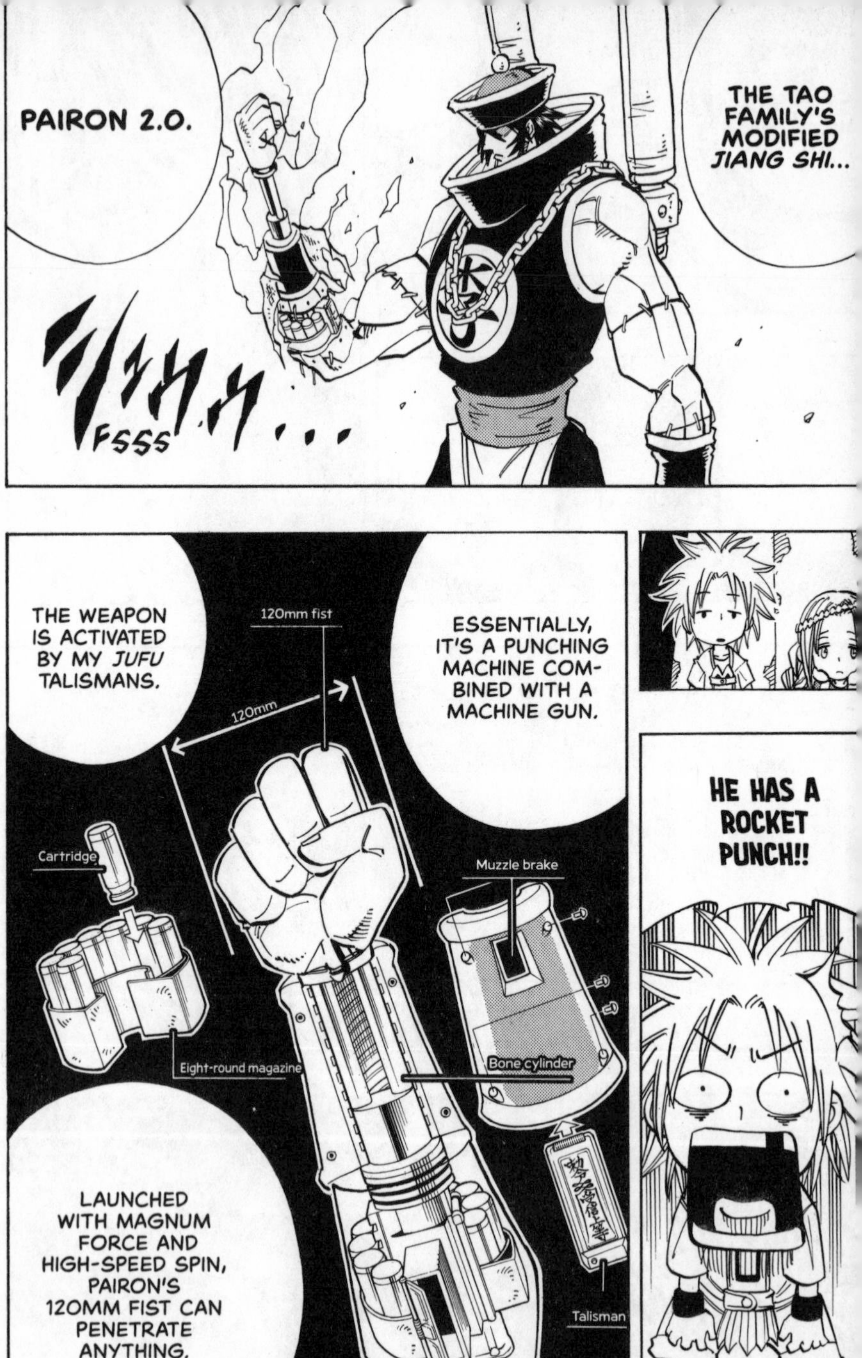
THE TAO FAMILY'S MODIFIED *JIANG SHI*...
PAIRON 2.0.
FSSS
HE HAS A ROCKET PUNCH!!
ESSENTIALLY, IT'S A PUNCHING MACHINE COMBINED WITH A MACHINE GUN.
THE WEAPON IS ACTIVATED BY MY *JUFU* TALISMANS.
120mm fist
120mm
Muzzle brake
Cartridge
Bone cylinder
Eight-round magazine
Talisman
LAUNCHED WITH MAGNUM FORCE AND HIGH-SPEED SPIN, PAIRON'S 120MM FIST CAN PENETRATE ANYTHING.

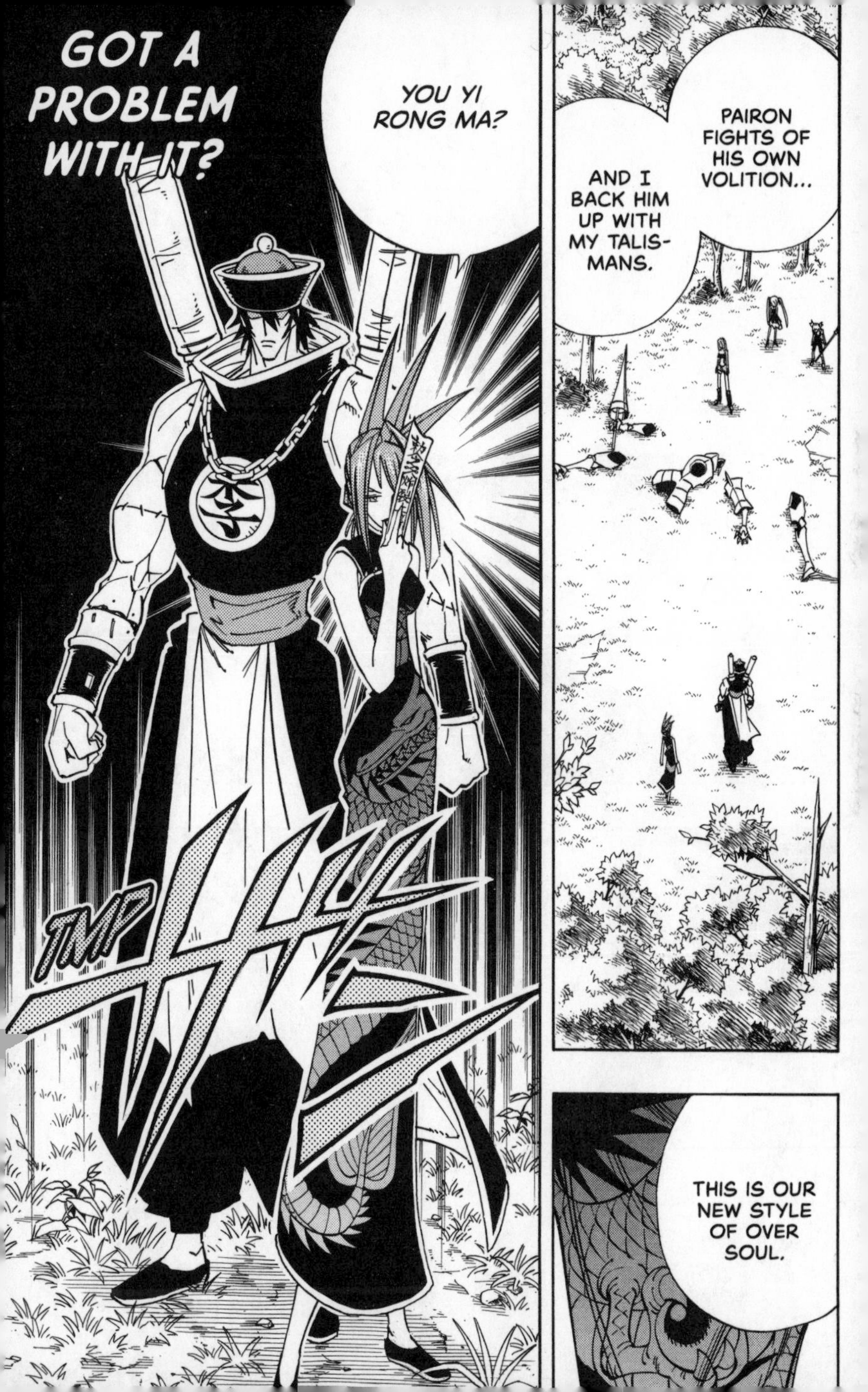
PAIRON FIGHTS OF HIS OWN VOLITION...
AND I BACK HIM UP WITH MY TALIS-MANS.
THIS IS OUR NEW STYLE OF OVER SOUL.
YOU YI RONG MA?
GOT A PROBLEM WITH IT?
TMP

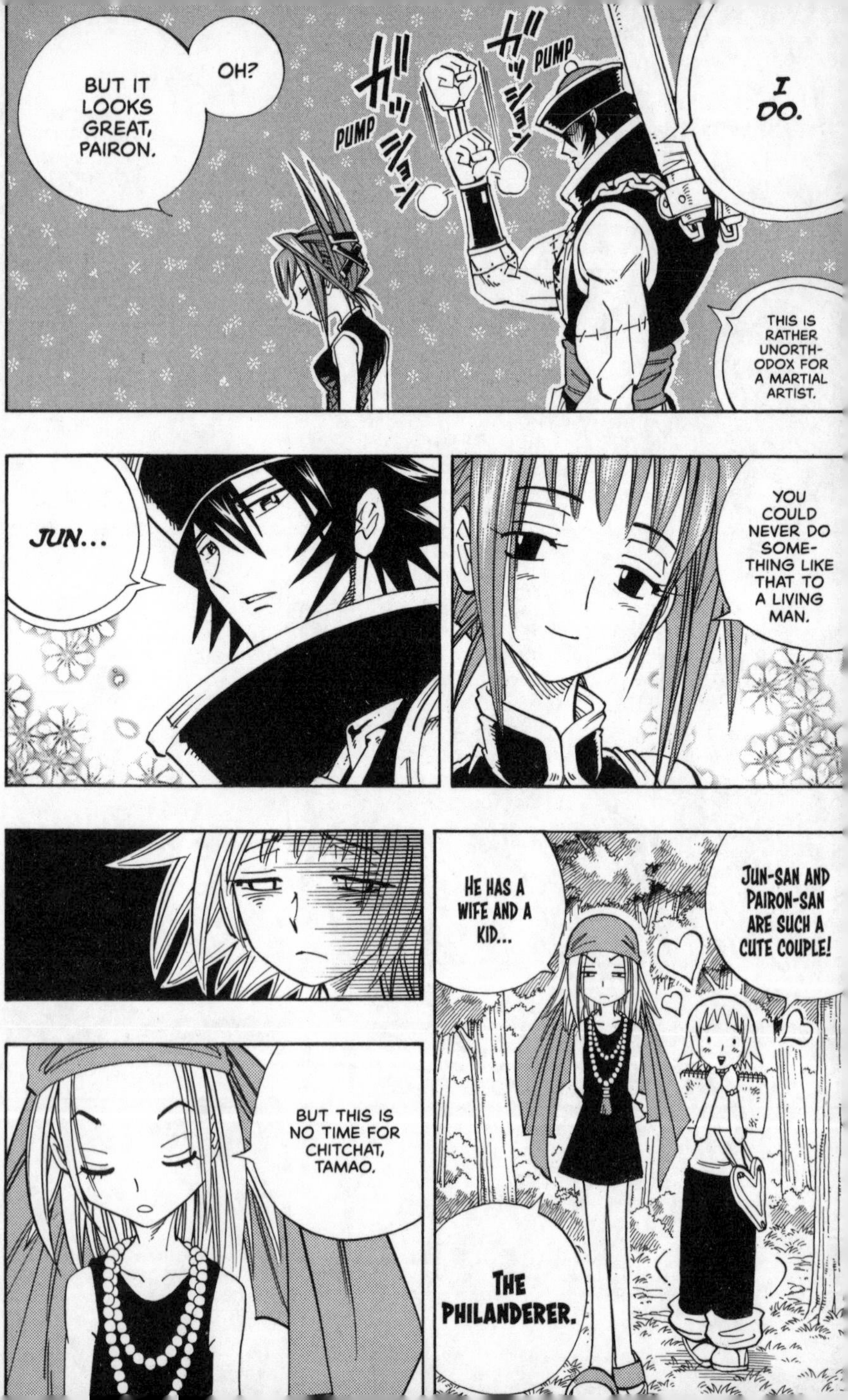
I DO.
PUMP
PUMP
THIS IS RATHER UNORTHODOX FOR A MARTIAL ARTIST.
OH?
BUT IT LOOKS GREAT, PAIRON.
YOU COULD NEVER DO SOMETHING LIKE THAT TO A LIVING MAN.
JUN...
JUN-SAN AND PAIRON-SAN ARE SUCH A CUTE COUPLE!
HE HAS A WIFE AND A KID...
THE PHILANDERER.
BUT THIS IS NO TIME FOR CHITCHAT, TAMAO.

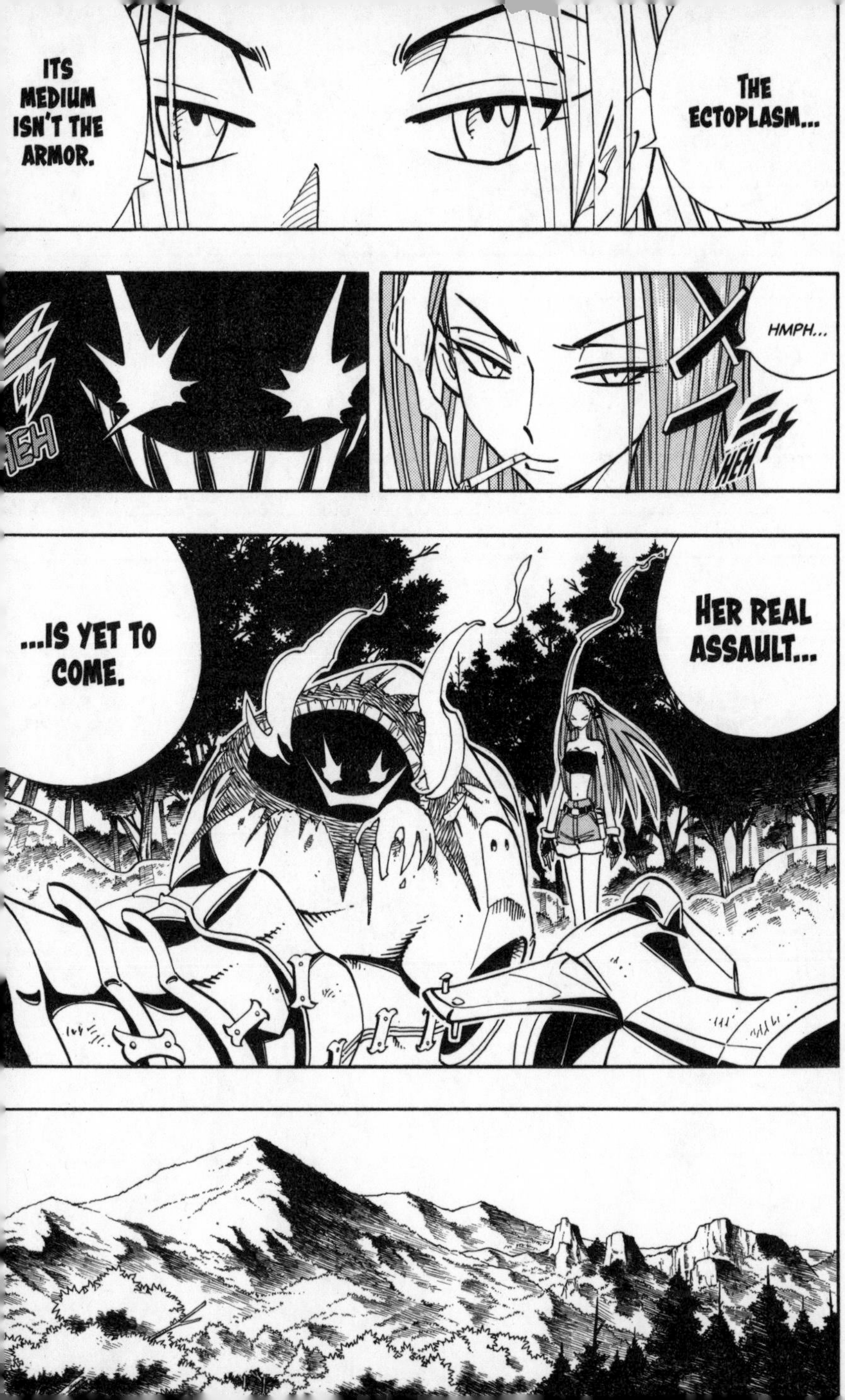
THE ECTOPLASM...
ITS MEDIUM ISN'T THE ARMOR.
HMPH...
HEH
HEH
HER REAL ASSAULT...
...IS YET TO COME.

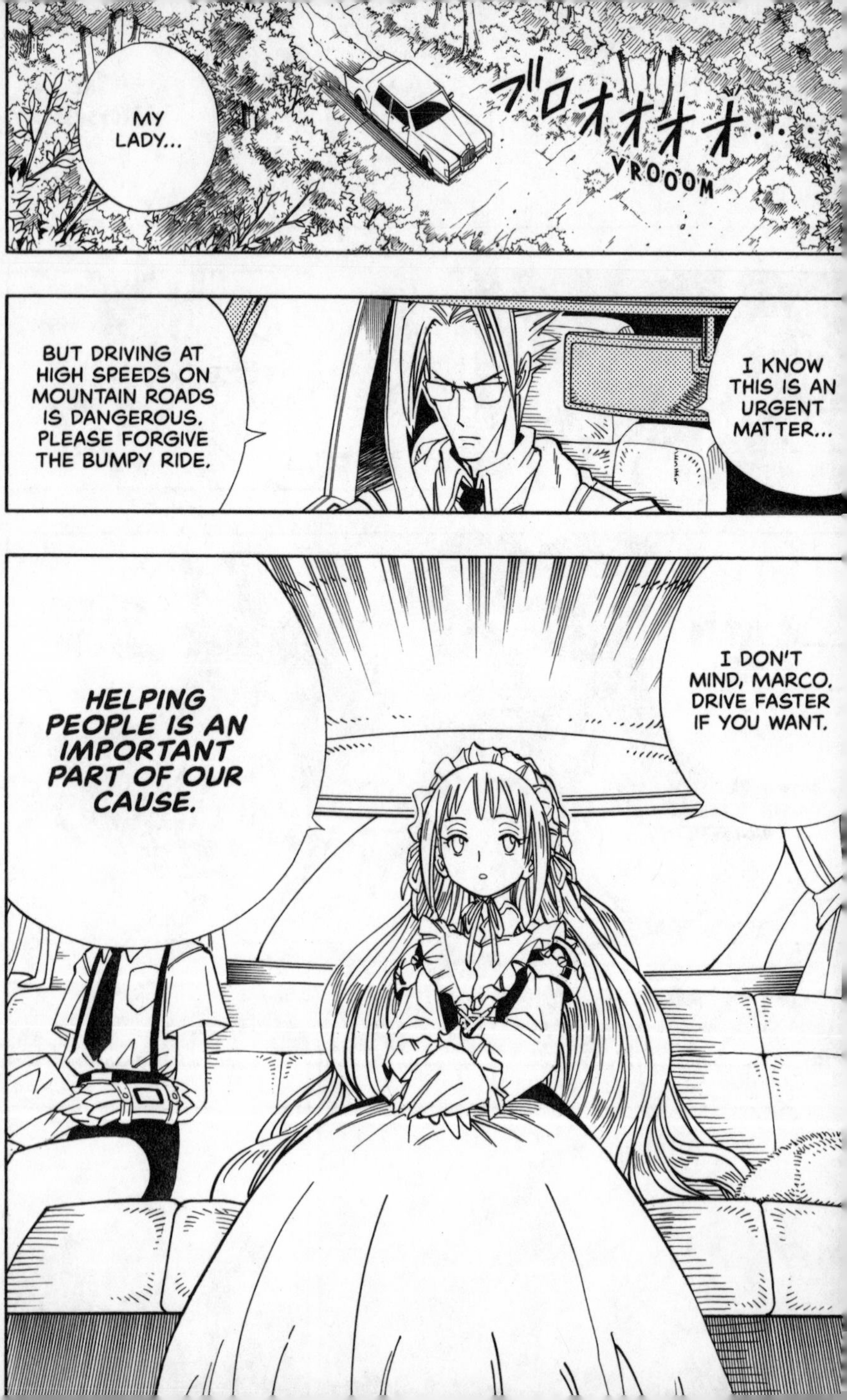
ブロオオオオ・・・
VROOOM
MY LADY...
I KNOW THIS IS AN URGENT MATTER...
BUT DRIVING AT HIGH SPEEDS ON MOUNTAIN ROADS IS DANGEROUS. PLEASE FORGIVE THE BUMPY RIDE.
I DON'T MIND, MARCO. DRIVE FASTER IF YOU WANT.
HELPING PEOPLE IS AN IMPORTANT PART OF OUR CAUSE.

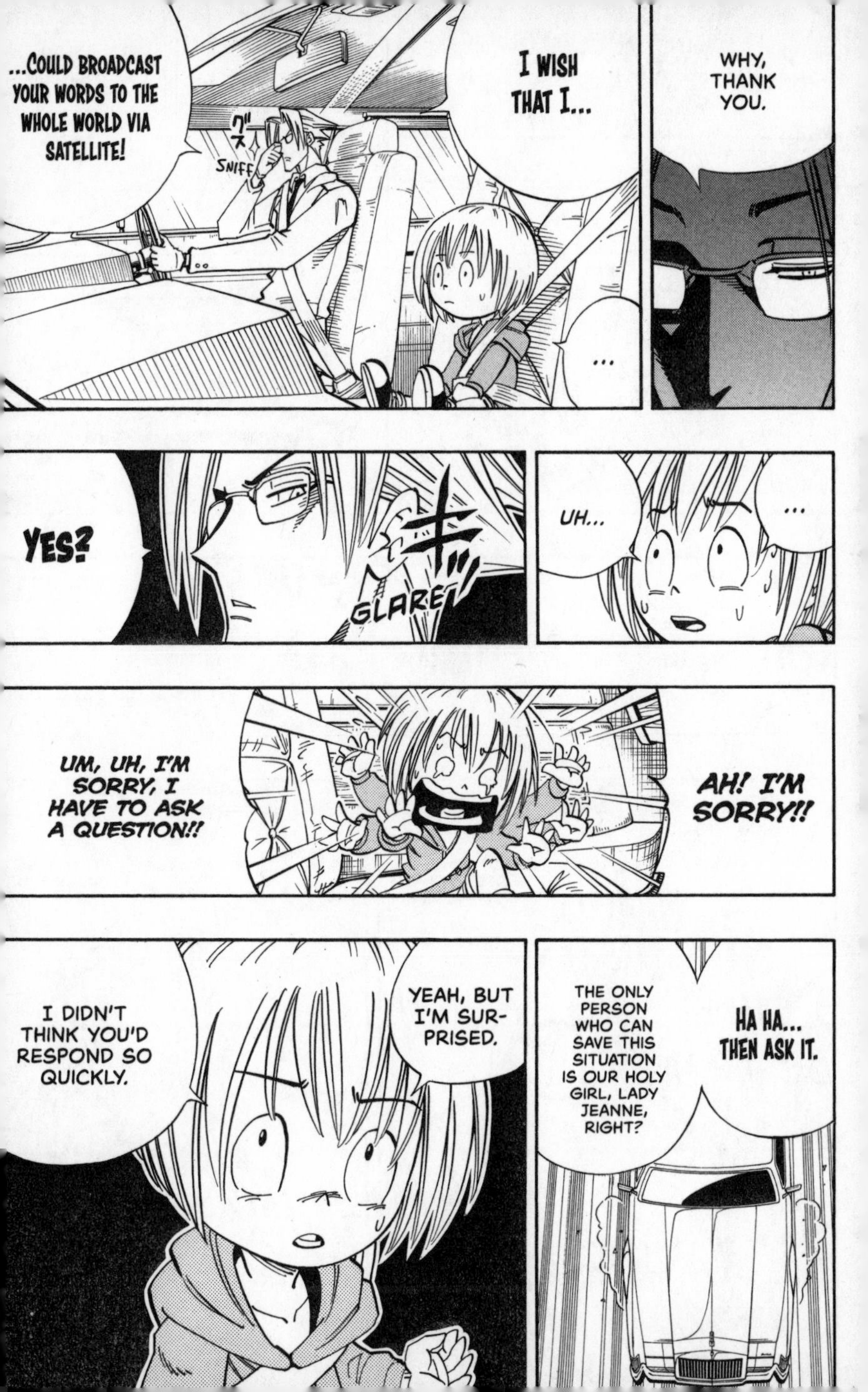
WHY, THANK YOU.
...
I WISH THAT I...
...COULD BROADCAST YOUR WORDS TO THE WHOLE WORLD VIA SATELLITE!
グス
SNIFF
...
UH...
YES?
GLARE
AH! I'M SORRY!!
UM, UH, I'M SORRY, I HAVE TO ASK A QUESTION!!
HA HA... THEN ASK IT.
THE ONLY PERSON WHO CAN SAVE THIS SITUATION IS OUR HOLY GIRL, LADY JEANNE, RIGHT?
YEAH, BUT I'M SUR-PRISED.
I DIDN'T THINK YOU'D RESPOND SO QUICKLY.

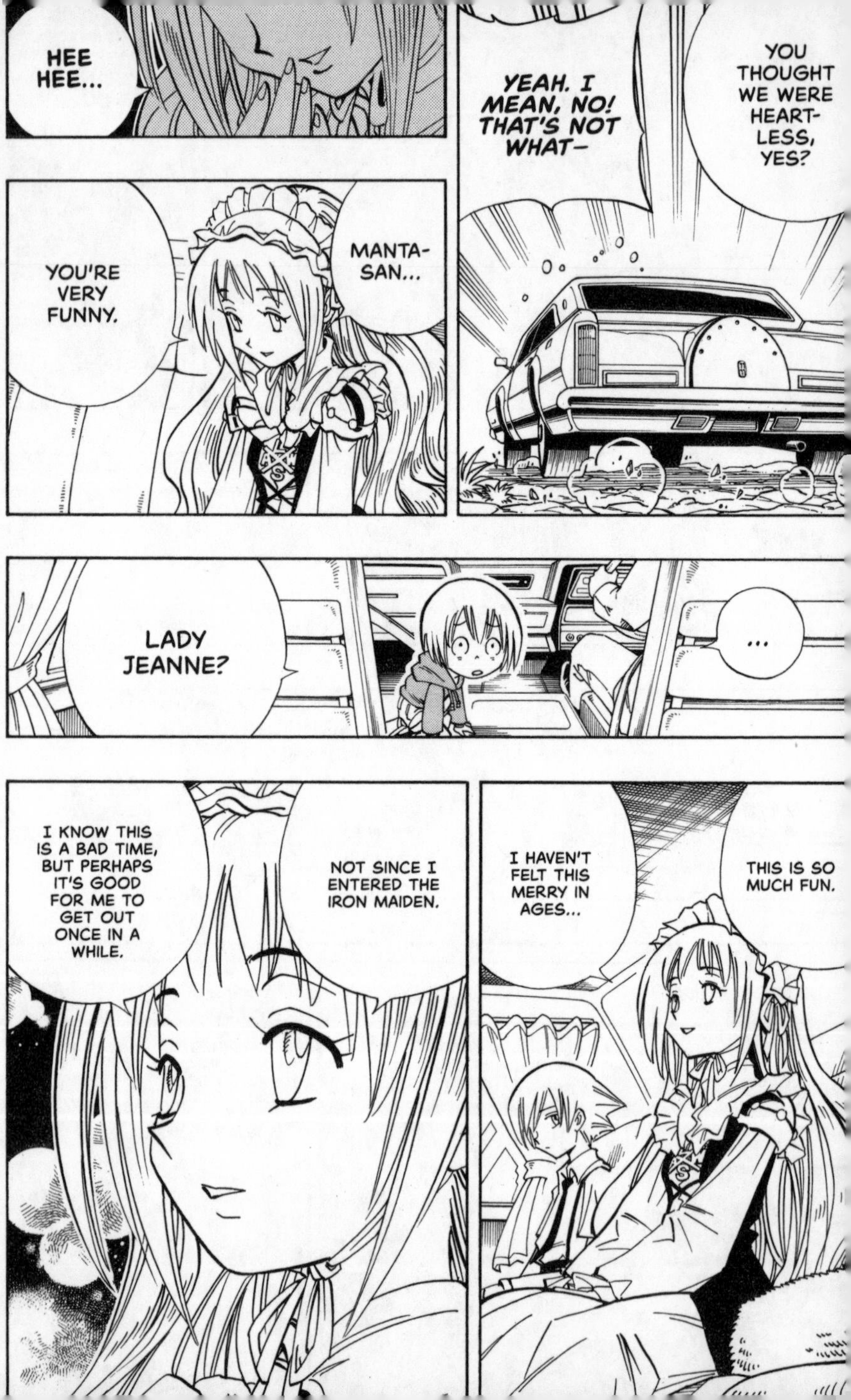
YOU THOUGHT WE WERE HEART-LESS, YES?
YEAH. I MEAN, NO! THAT'S NOT WHAT—
HEE HEE...
MANTA-SAN...
YOU'RE VERY FUNNY.
...
LADY JEANNE?
THIS IS SO MUCH FUN.
I HAVEN'T FELT THIS MERRY IN AGES...
NOT SINCE I ENTERED THE IRON MAIDEN.
I KNOW THIS IS A BAD TIME, BUT PERHAPS IT'S GOOD FOR ME TO GET OUT ONCE IN A WHILE.

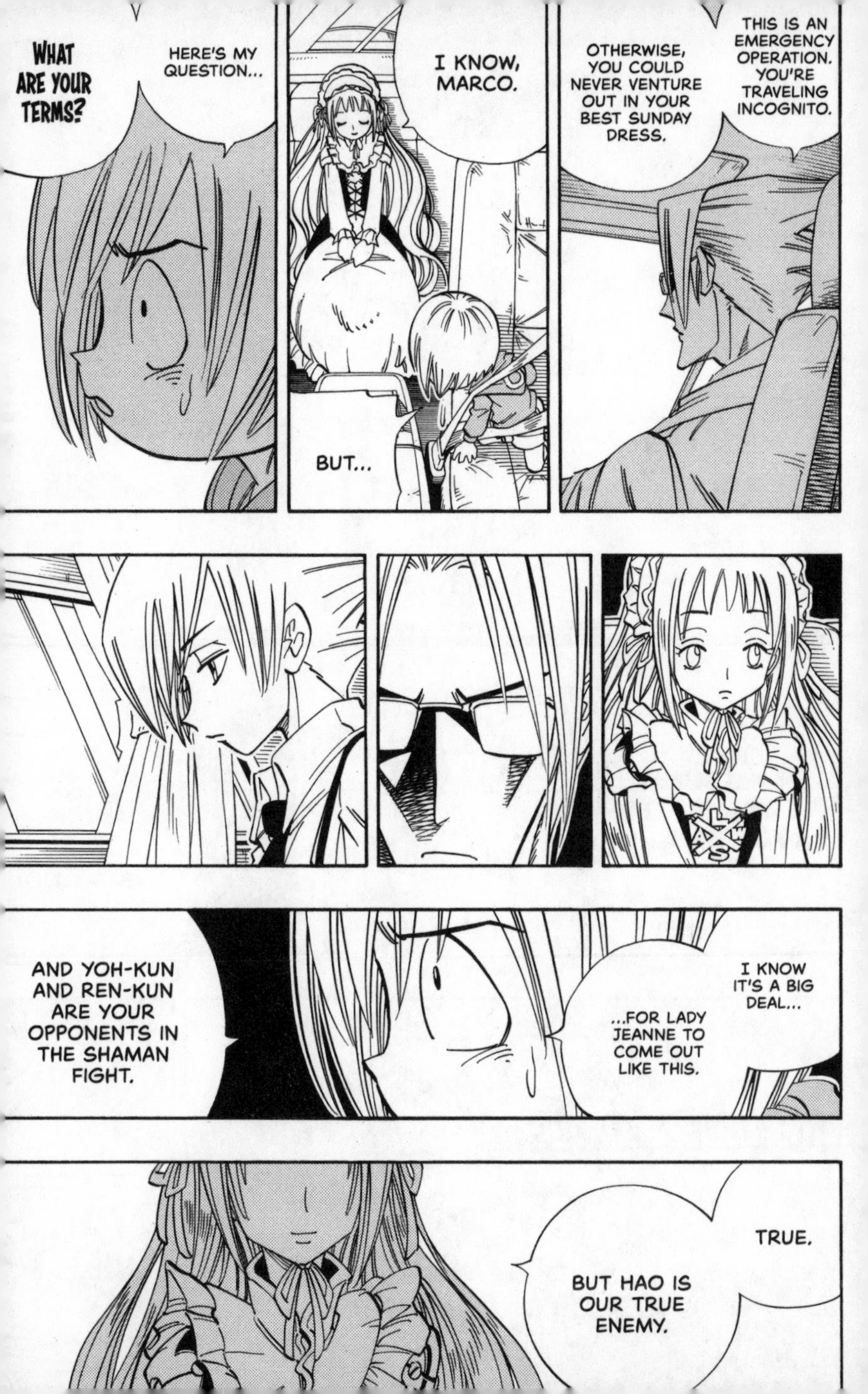
THIS IS AN EMERGENCY OPERATION. YOU'RE TRAVELING INCOGNITO.
OTHERWISE, YOU COULD NEVER VENTURE OUT IN YOUR BEST SUNDAY DRESS.
I KNOW, MARCO.
BUT...
HERE'S MY QUESTION...
WHAT ARE YOUR TERMS?
I KNOW IT'S A BIG DEAL...
...FOR LADY JEANNE TO COME OUT LIKE THIS.
AND YOH-KUN AND REN-KUN ARE YOUR OPPONENTS IN THE SHAMAN FIGHT.
TRUE.
BUT HAO IS OUR TRUE ENEMY.

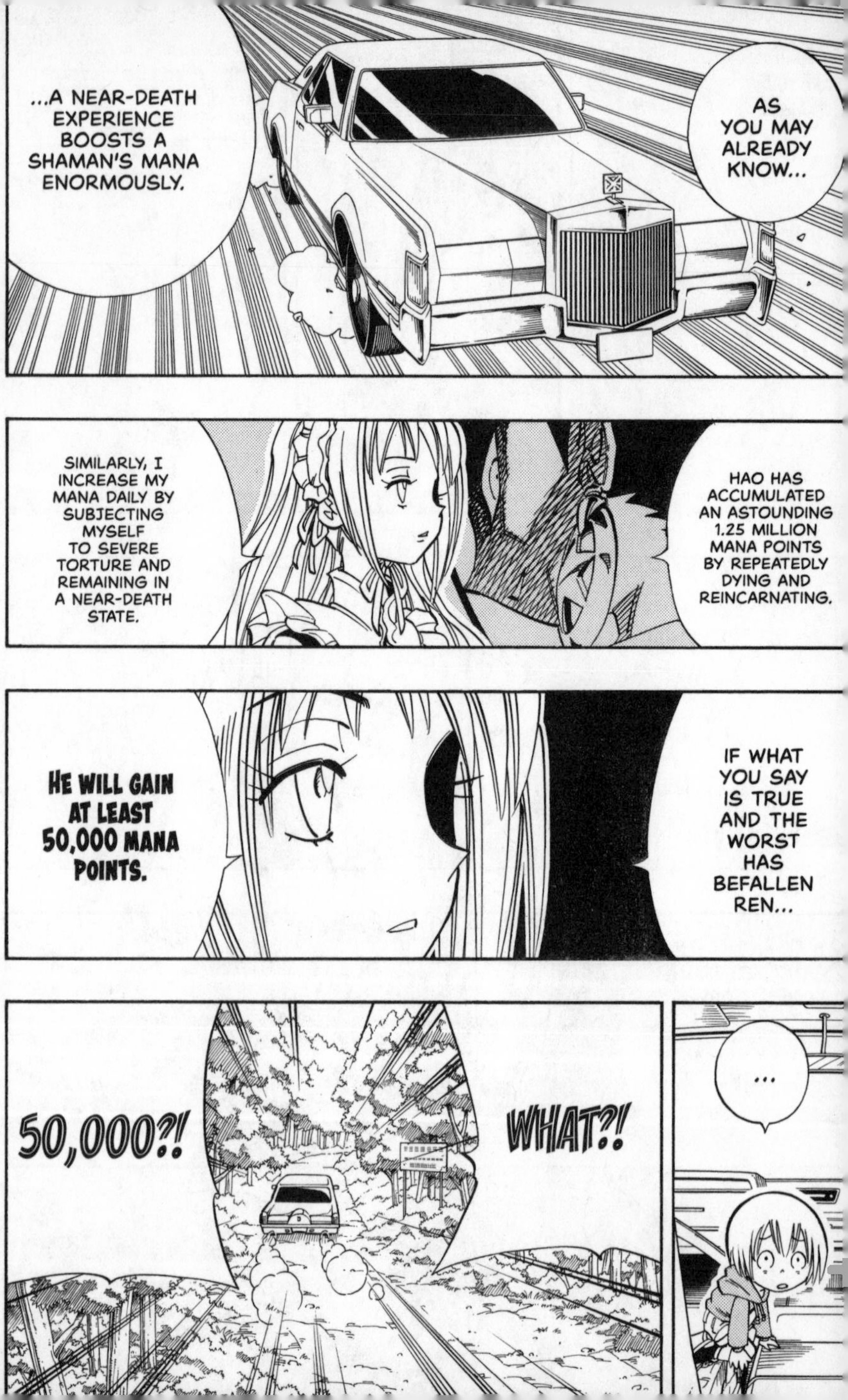
AS YOU MAY ALREADY KNOW...
...A NEAR-DEATH EXPERIENCE BOOSTS A SHAMAN'S MANA ENORMOUSLY.
HAO HAS ACCUMULATED AN ASTOUNDING 1.25 MILLION MANA POINTS BY REPEATEDLY DYING AND REINCARNATING.
SIMILARLY, I INCREASE MY MANA DAILY BY SUBJECTING MYSELF TO SEVERE TORTURE AND REMAINING IN A NEAR-DEATH STATE.
IF WHAT YOU SAY IS TRUE AND THE WORST HAS BEFALLEN REN...
HE WILL GAIN AT LEAST 50,000 MANA POINTS.
...
WHAT?!
50,000?!

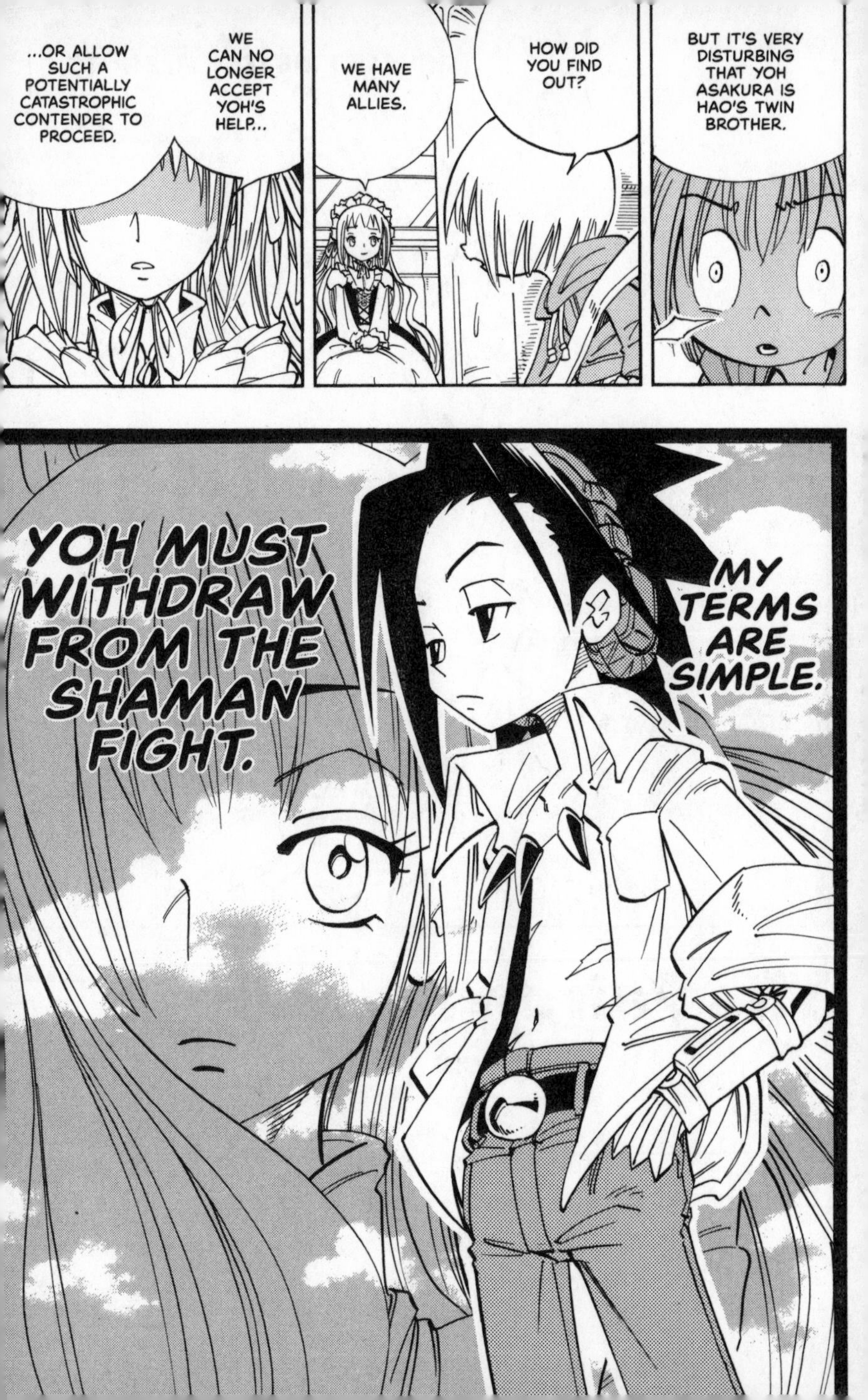
BUT IT'S VERY DISTURBING THAT YOH ASAKURA IS HAO'S TWIN BROTHER.
HOW DID YOU FIND OUT?
WE HAVE MANY ALLIES.
WE CAN NO LONGER ACCEPT YOH'S HELP...
...OR ALLOW SUCH A POTENTIALLY CATASTROPHIC CONTENDER TO PROCEED.
MY TERMS ARE SIMPLE.
YOH MUST WITHDRAW FROM THE SHAMAN FIGHT.

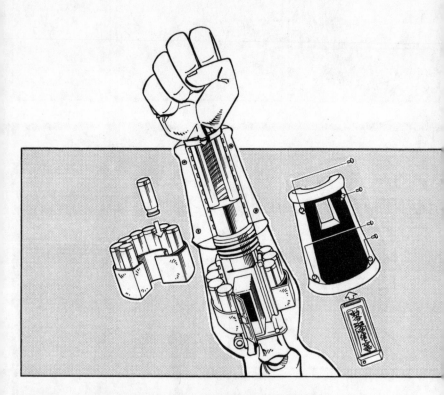

The Pairon Bunker

January 2001

...OR ALLOW SUCH A POTENTIALLY CATASTROPHIC CONTENDER TO PROCEED.

WE CAN NO LONGER ACCEPT YOH'S HELP...

MY TERMS ARE SIMPLE.

YOH MUST WITHDRAW FROM THE SHAMAN FIGHT.

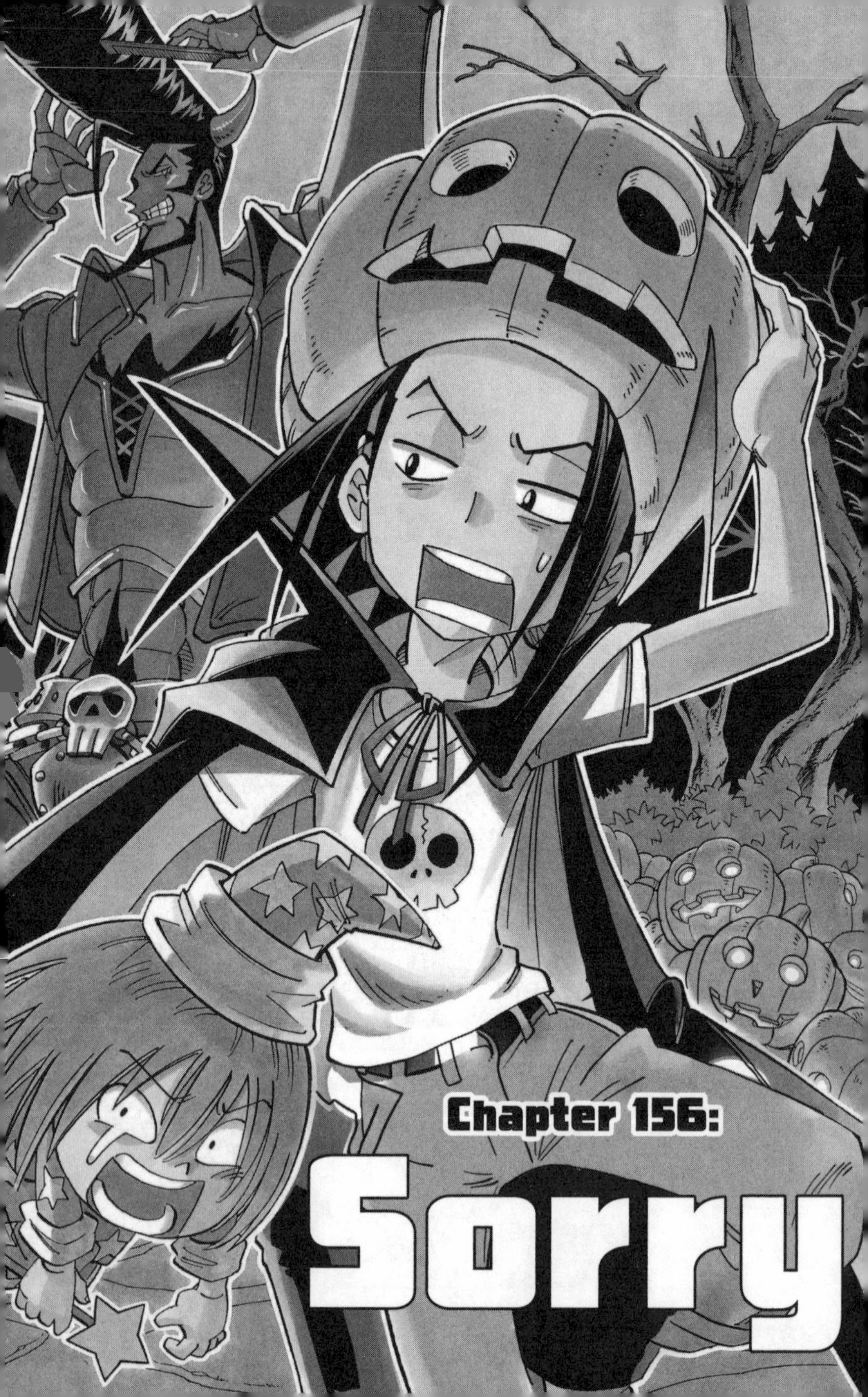
Chapter 156:
Sorry

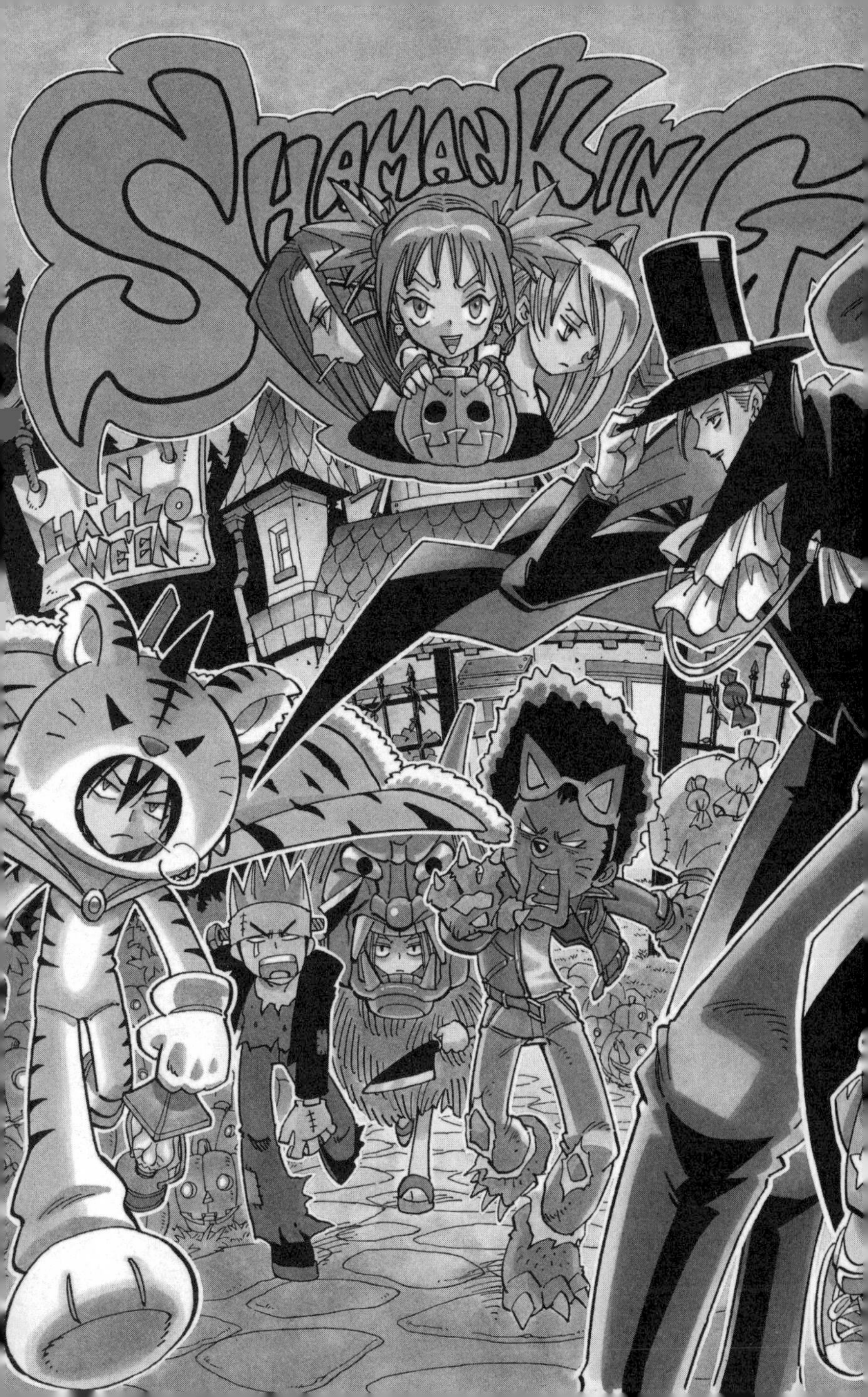
SHAMAN KING
IN HALLOWE'EN

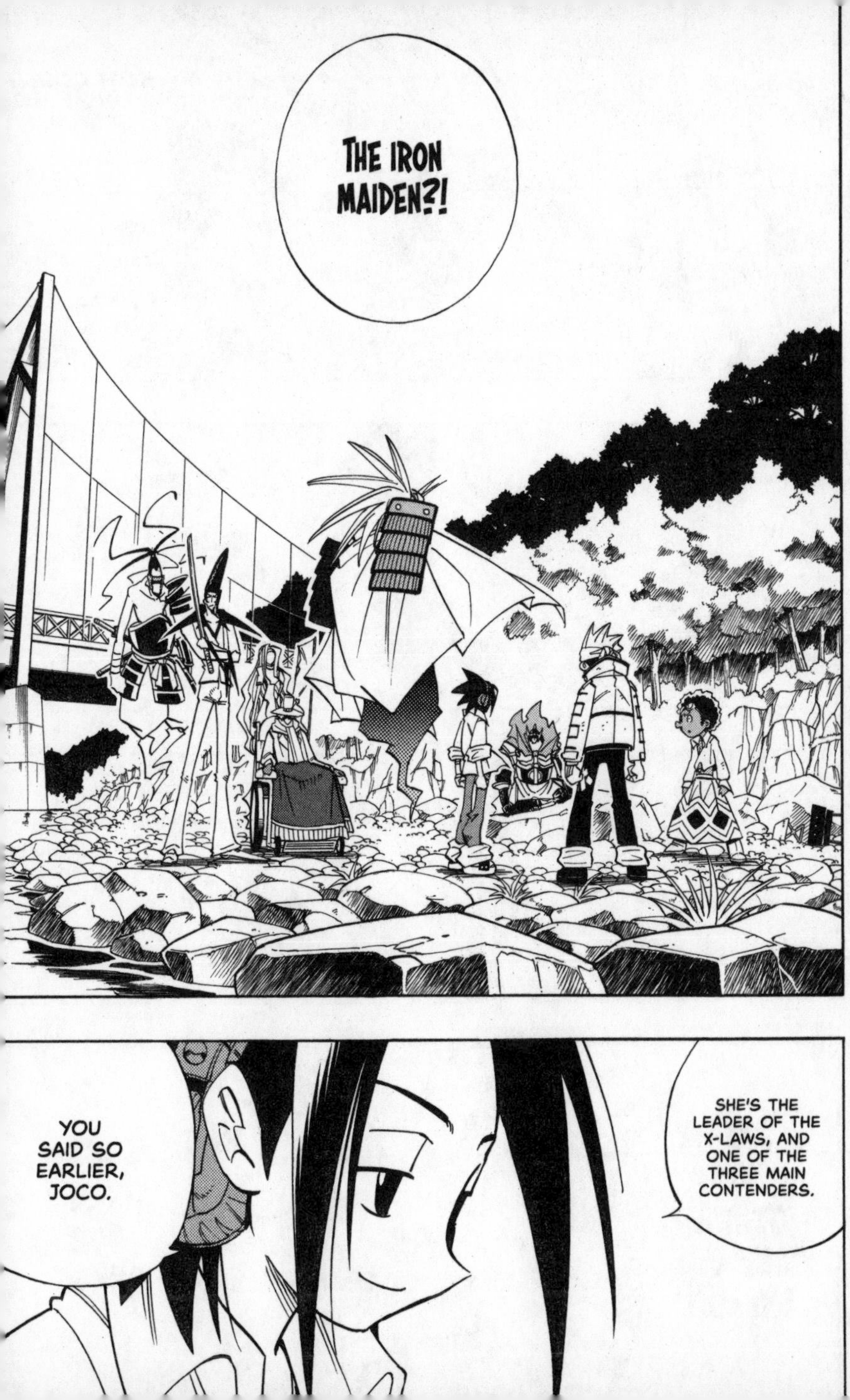
THE IRON MAIDEN?!
SHE'S THE LEADER OF THE X-LAWS, AND ONE OF THE THREE MAIN CONTENDERS.
YOU SAID SO EARLIER, JOCO.

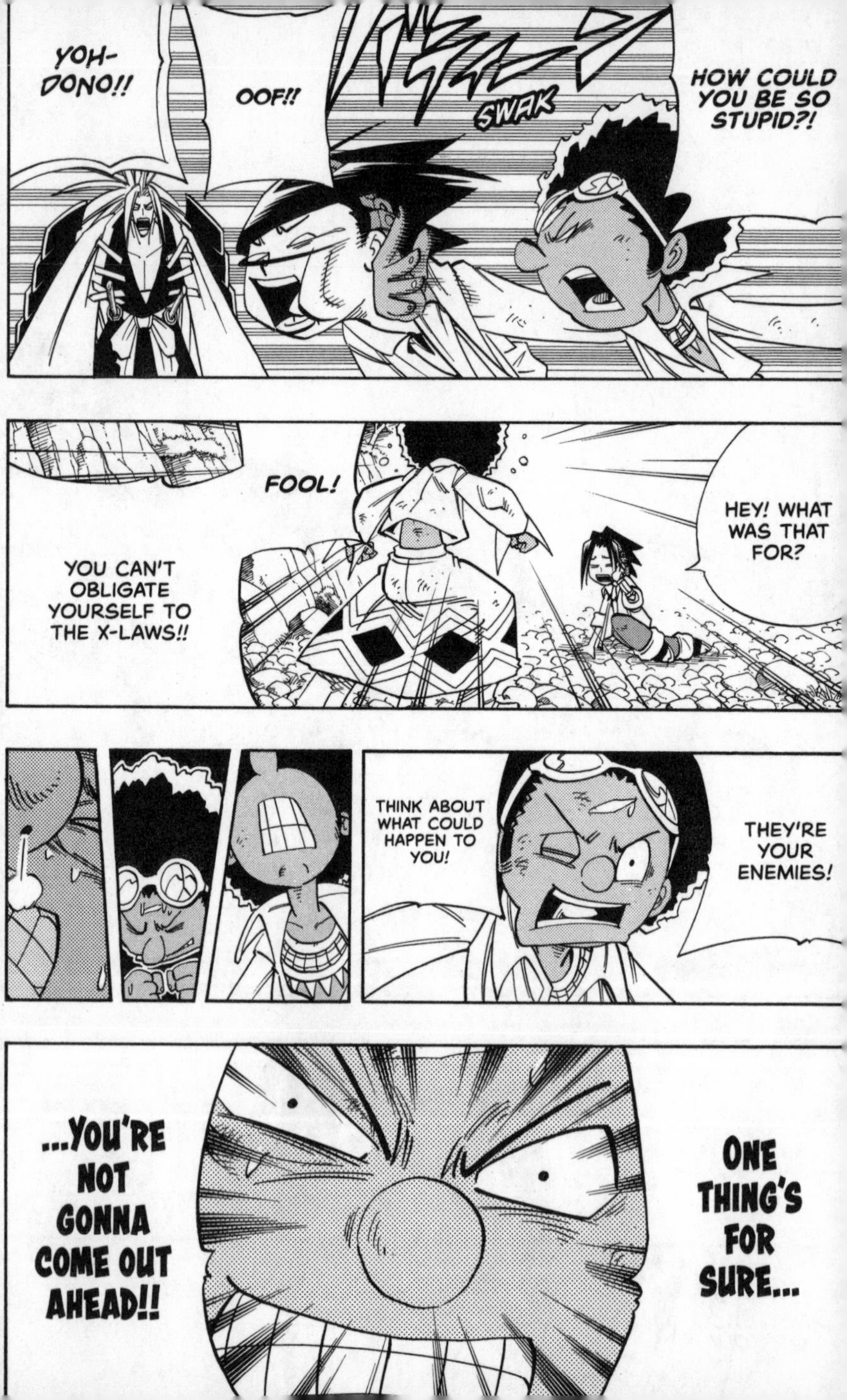
HOW COULD YOU BE SO STUPID?!
SWAK
OOF!!
YOH-DONO!!
HEY! WHAT WAS THAT FOR?
FOOL!
YOU CAN'T OBLIGATE YOURSELF TO THE X-LAWS!!
THEY'RE YOUR ENEMIES!
THINK ABOUT WHAT COULD HAPPEN TO YOU!
ONE THING'S FOR SURE...
...YOU'RE NOT GONNA COME OUT AHEAD!!

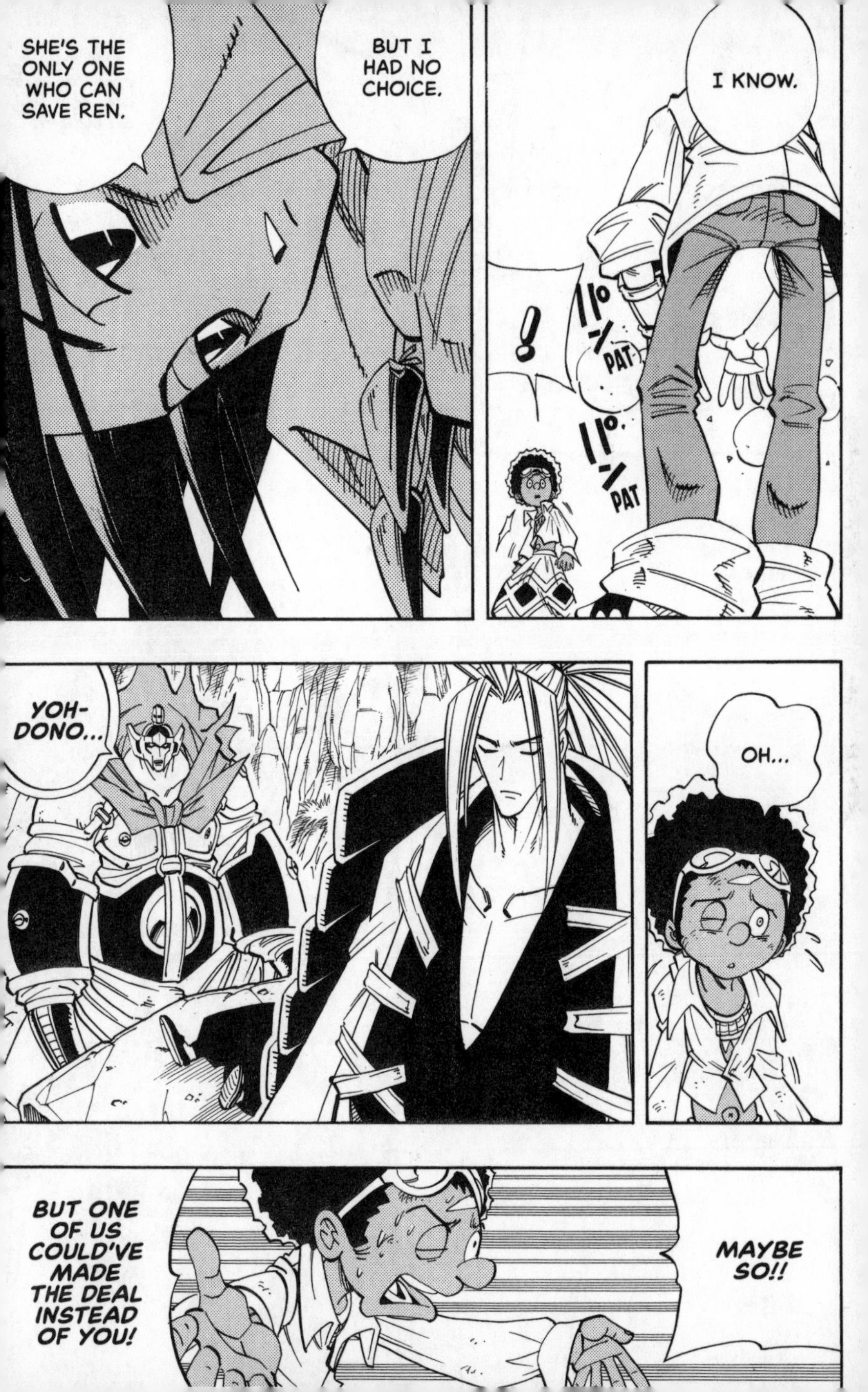
I KNOW.
!
PAT
PAT
BUT I HAD NO CHOICE.
SHE'S THE ONLY ONE WHO CAN SAVE REN.
OH...
YOH-DONO...
MAYBE SO!!
BUT ONE OF US COULD'VE MADE THE DEAL INSTEAD OF YOU!

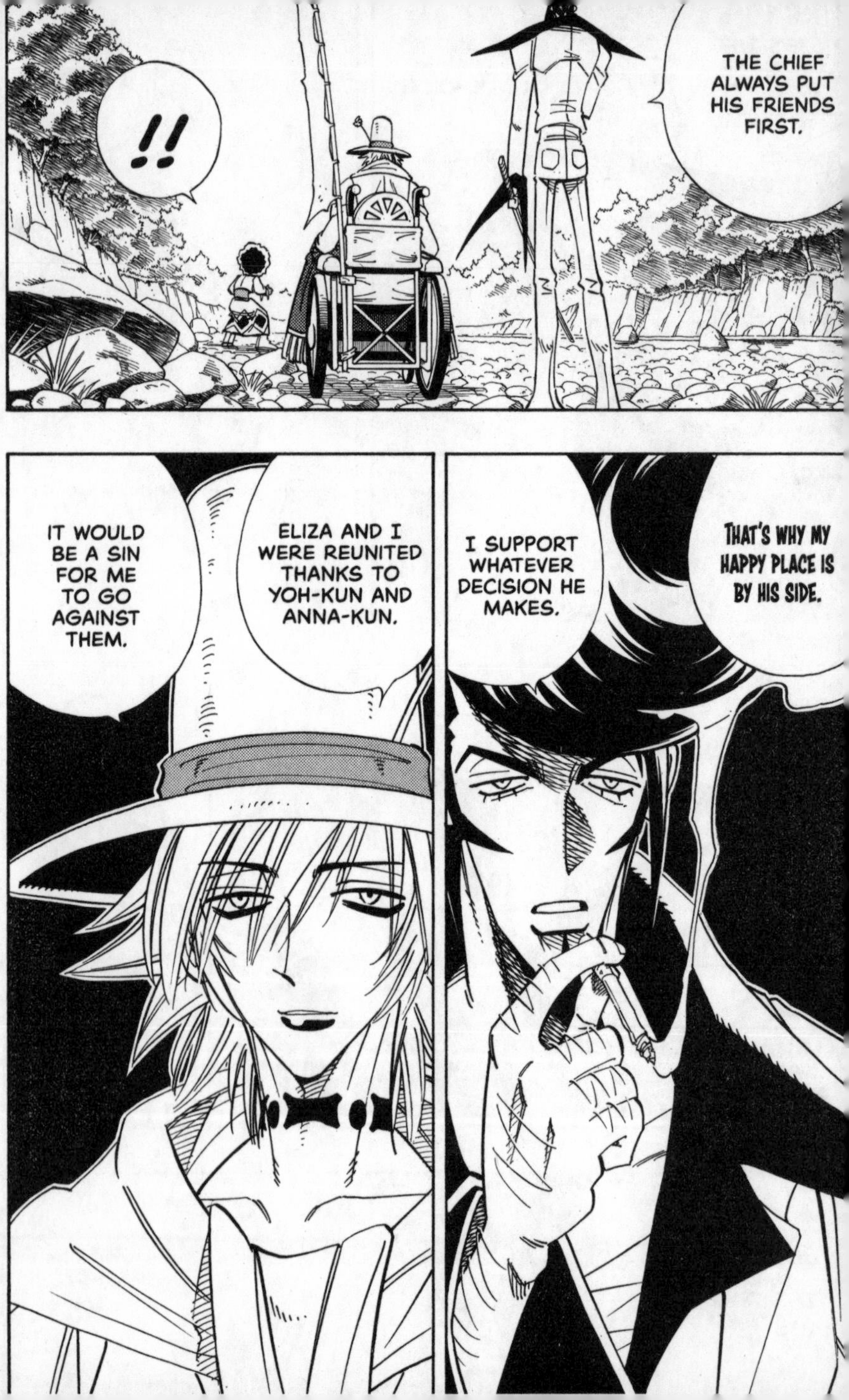
THE CHIEF ALWAYS PUT HIS FRIENDS FIRST.
!!
THAT'S WHY MY HAPPY PLACE IS BY HIS SIDE.
I SUPPORT WHATEVER DECISION HE MAKES.
ELIZA AND I WERE REUNITED THANKS TO YOH-KUN AND ANNA-KUN.
IT WOULD BE A SIN FOR ME TO GO AGAINST THEM.

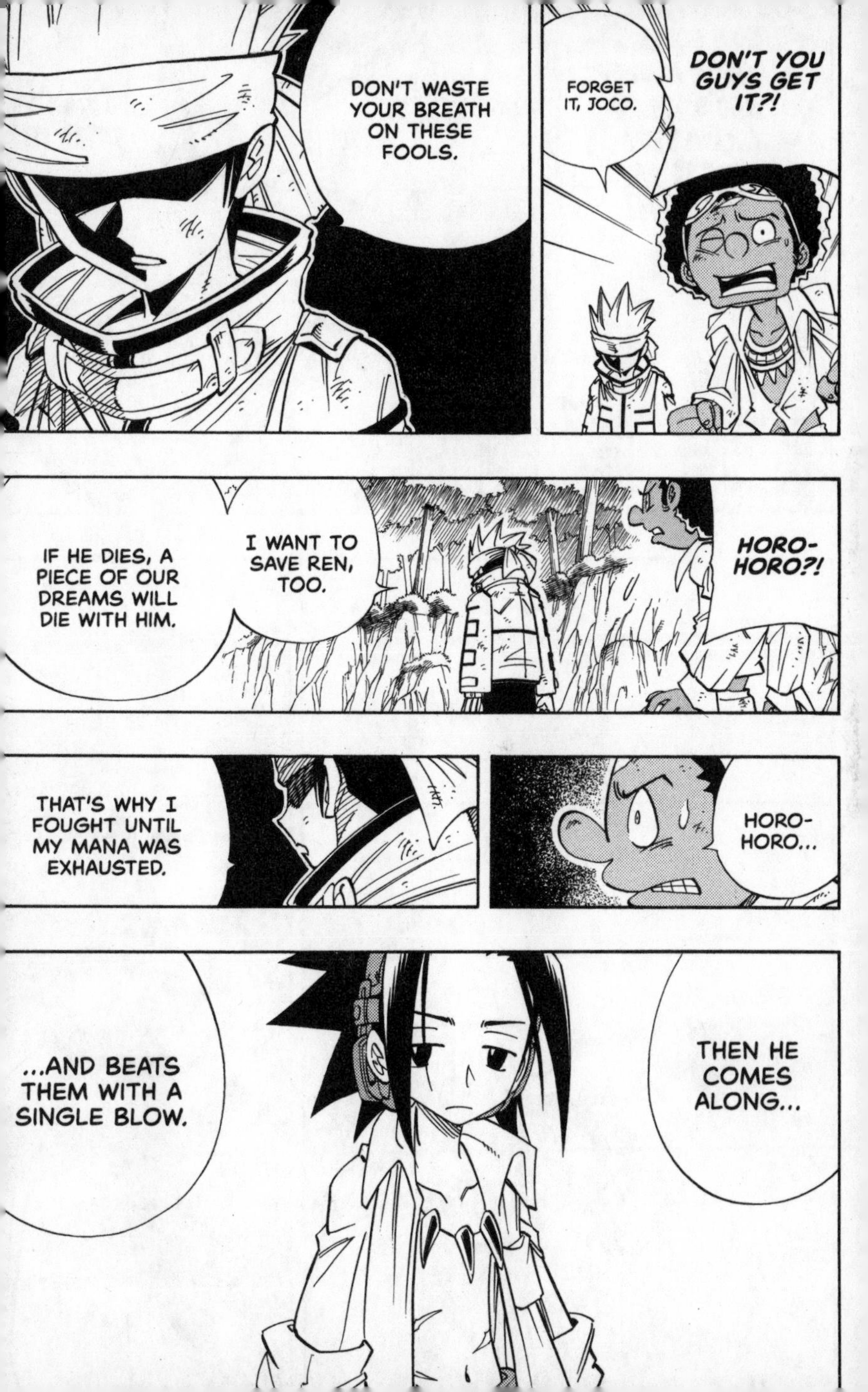
DON'T YOU GUYS GET IT?!
FORGET IT, JOCO.
DON'T WASTE YOUR BREATH ON THESE FOOLS.
HORO-HORO?!
I WANT TO SAVE REN, TOO.
IF HE DIES, A PIECE OF OUR DREAMS WILL DIE WITH HIM.
HORO-HORO...
THAT'S WHY I FOUGHT UNTIL MY MANA WAS EXHAUSTED.
THEN HE COMES ALONG...
...AND BEATS THEM WITH A SINGLE BLOW.

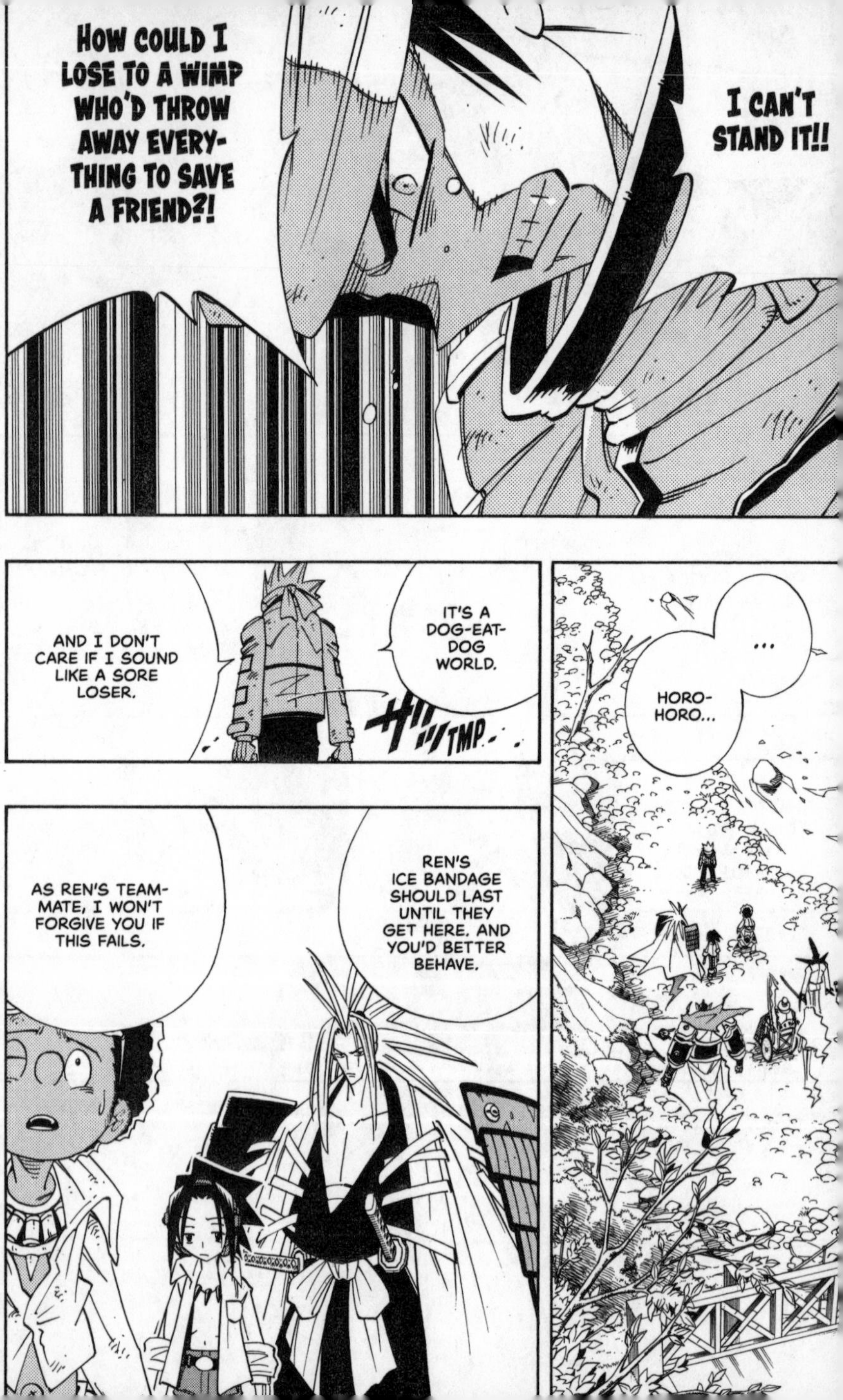
I CAN'T STAND IT!!
HOW COULD I LOSE TO A WIMP WHO'D THROW AWAY EVERY-THING TO SAVE A FRIEND?!
...
HORO-HORO...
IT'S A DOG-EAT-DOG WORLD.
TMP
AND I DON'T CARE IF I SOUND LIKE A SORE LOSER.
REN'S ICE BANDAGE SHOULD LAST UNTIL THEY GET HERE. AND YOU'D BETTER BEHAVE.
AS REN'S TEAM-MATE, I WON'T FORGIVE YOU IF THIS FAILS.

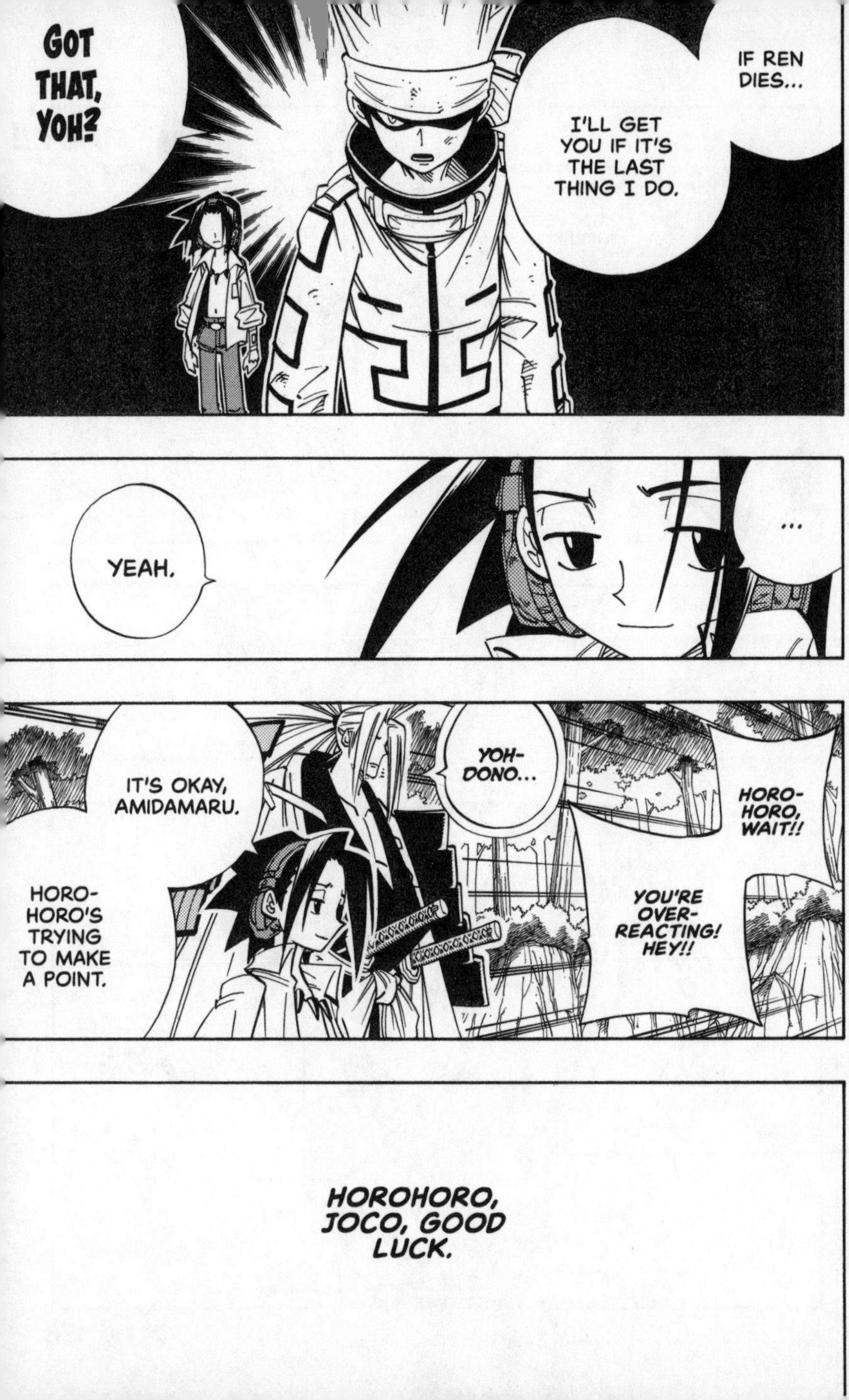
IF REN DIES...
I'LL GET YOU IF IT'S THE LAST THING I DO.
GOT THAT, YOH?
...
YEAH.
HORO-HORO, WAIT!!
YOU'RE OVER-REACTING! HEY!!
YOH-DONO...
IT'S OKAY, AMIDAMARU.
HORO-HORO'S TRYING TO MAKE A POINT.
HOROHORO, JOCO, GOOD LUCK.

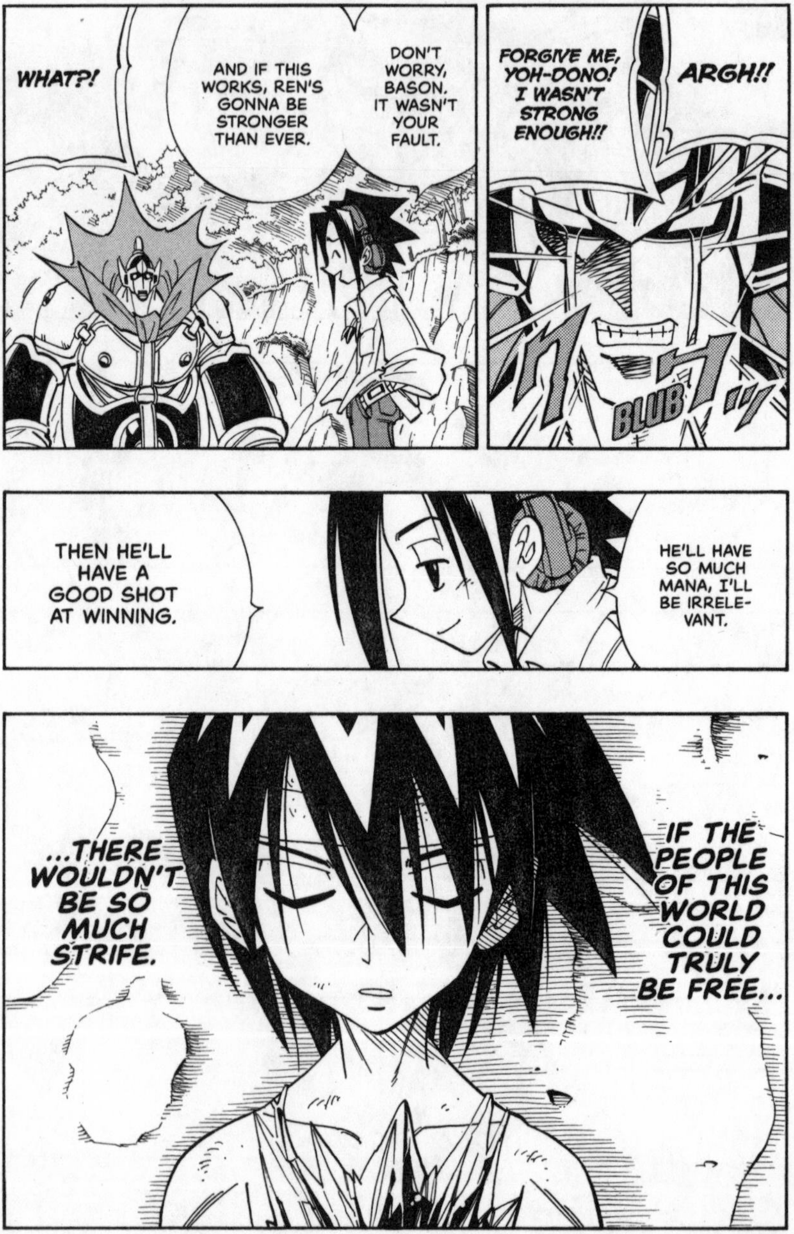
ARGH!!
FORGIVE ME, YOH-DONO! I WASN'T STRONG ENOUGH!!
BLUB
DON'T WORRY, BASON. IT WASN'T YOUR FAULT.
AND IF THIS WORKS, REN'S GONNA BE STRONGER THAN EVER.
WHAT?!
HE'LL HAVE SO MUCH MANA, I'LL BE IRRELE-VANT.
THEN HE'LL HAVE A GOOD SHOT AT WINNING.
IF THE PEOPLE OF THIS WORLD COULD TRULY BE FREE...
...THERE WOULDN'T BE SO MUCH STRIFE.

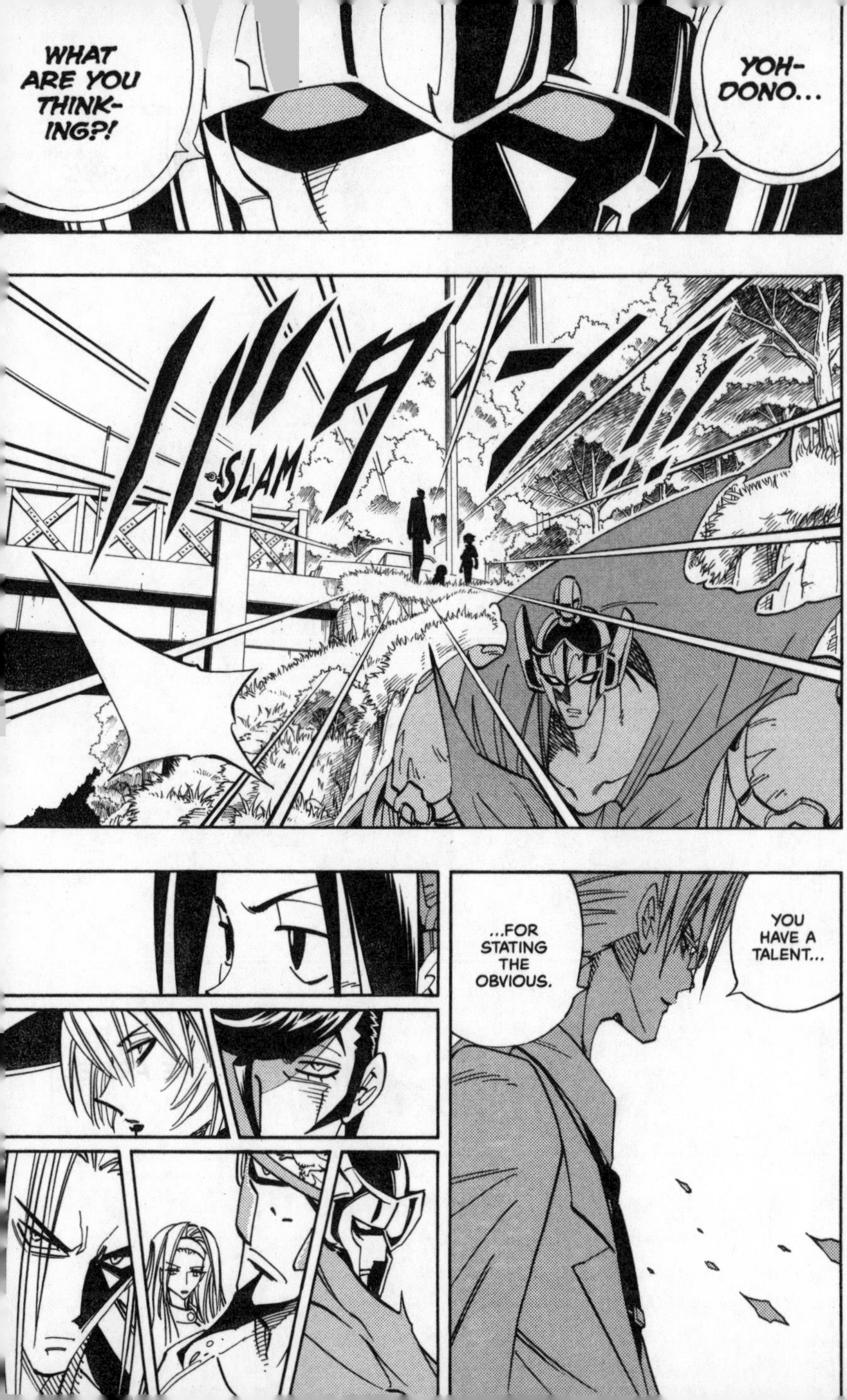
YOH-DONO...
WHAT ARE YOU THINKING?!
SLAM
YOU HAVE A TALENT...
...FOR STATING THE OBVIOUS.

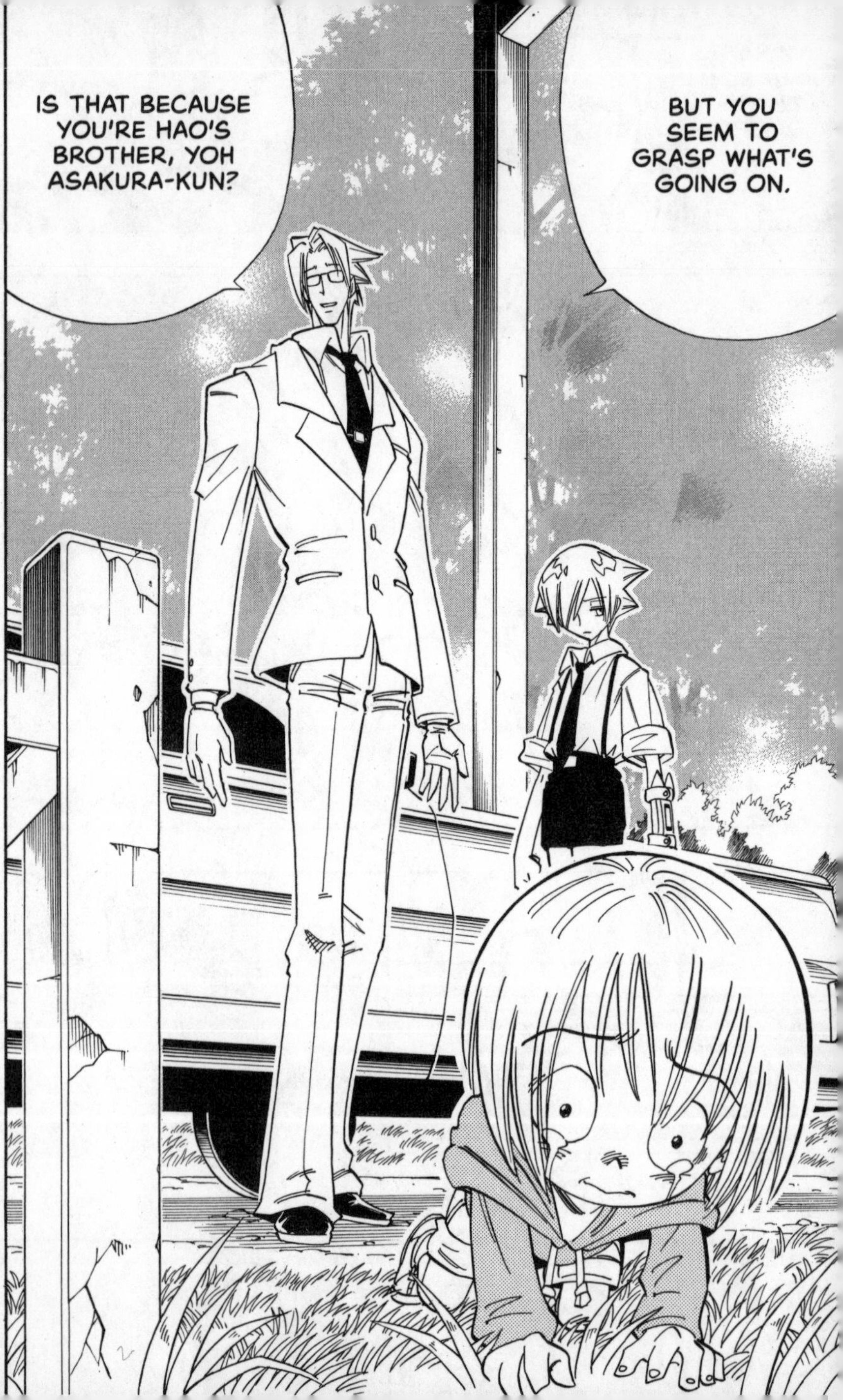
BUT YOU SEEM TO GRASP WHAT'S GOING ON.
IS THAT BECAUSE YOU'RE HAO'S BROTHER, YOH ASAKURA-KUN?

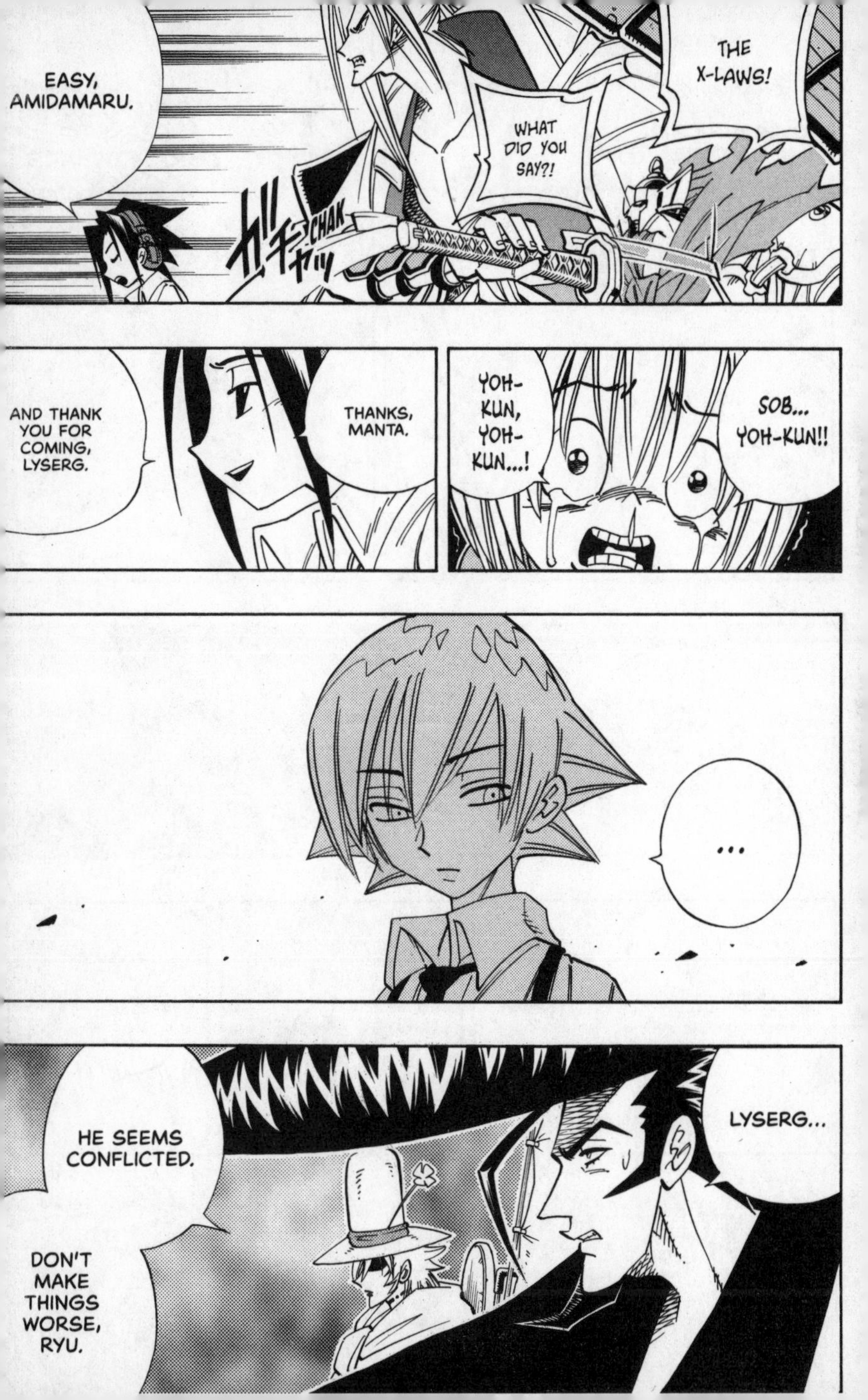
THE X-LAWS!
WHAT DID YOU SAY?!
EASY, AMIDAMARU.
CHAK
SOB... YOH-KUN!!
YOH-KUN, YOH-KUN...!
THANKS, MANTA.
AND THANK YOU FOR COMING, LYSERG.
...
LYSERG...
HE SEEMS CONFLICTED.
DON'T MAKE THINGS WORSE, RYU.

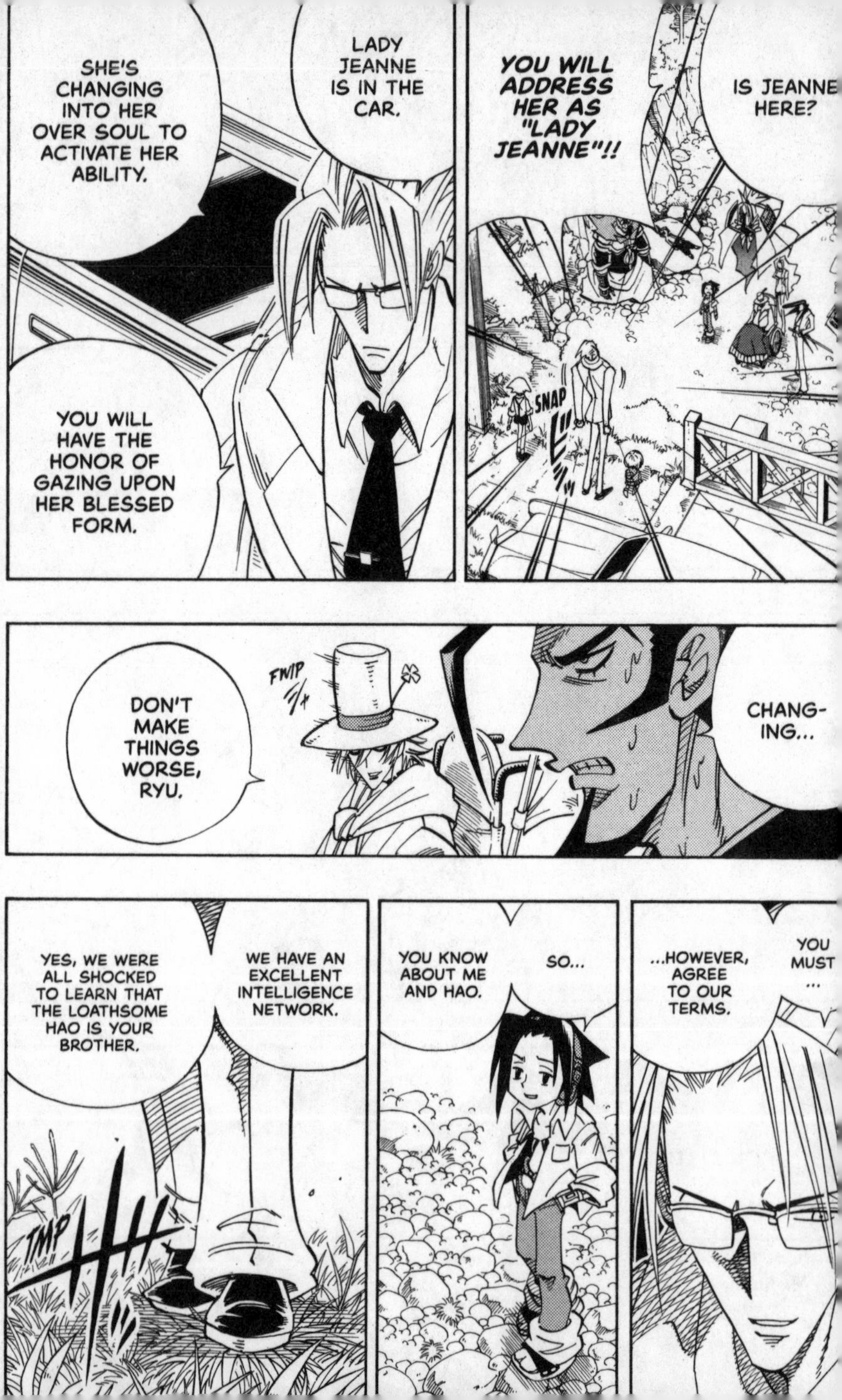
IS JEANNE HERE?
YOU WILL ADDRESS HER AS "LADY JEANNE"!!
SNAP
LADY JEANNE IS IN THE CAR.
SHE'S CHANGING INTO HER OVER SOUL TO ACTIVATE HER ABILITY.
YOU WILL HAVE THE HONOR OF GAZING UPON HER BLESSED FORM.
CHANG-ING...
FWIP
DON'T MAKE THINGS WORSE, RYU.
YOU MUST ...
...HOWEVER, AGREE TO OUR TERMS.
SO...
YOU KNOW ABOUT ME AND HAO.
WE HAVE AN EXCELLENT INTELLIGENCE NETWORK.
YES, WE WERE ALL SHOCKED TO LEARN THAT THE LOATHSOME HAO IS YOUR BROTHER.
TMP

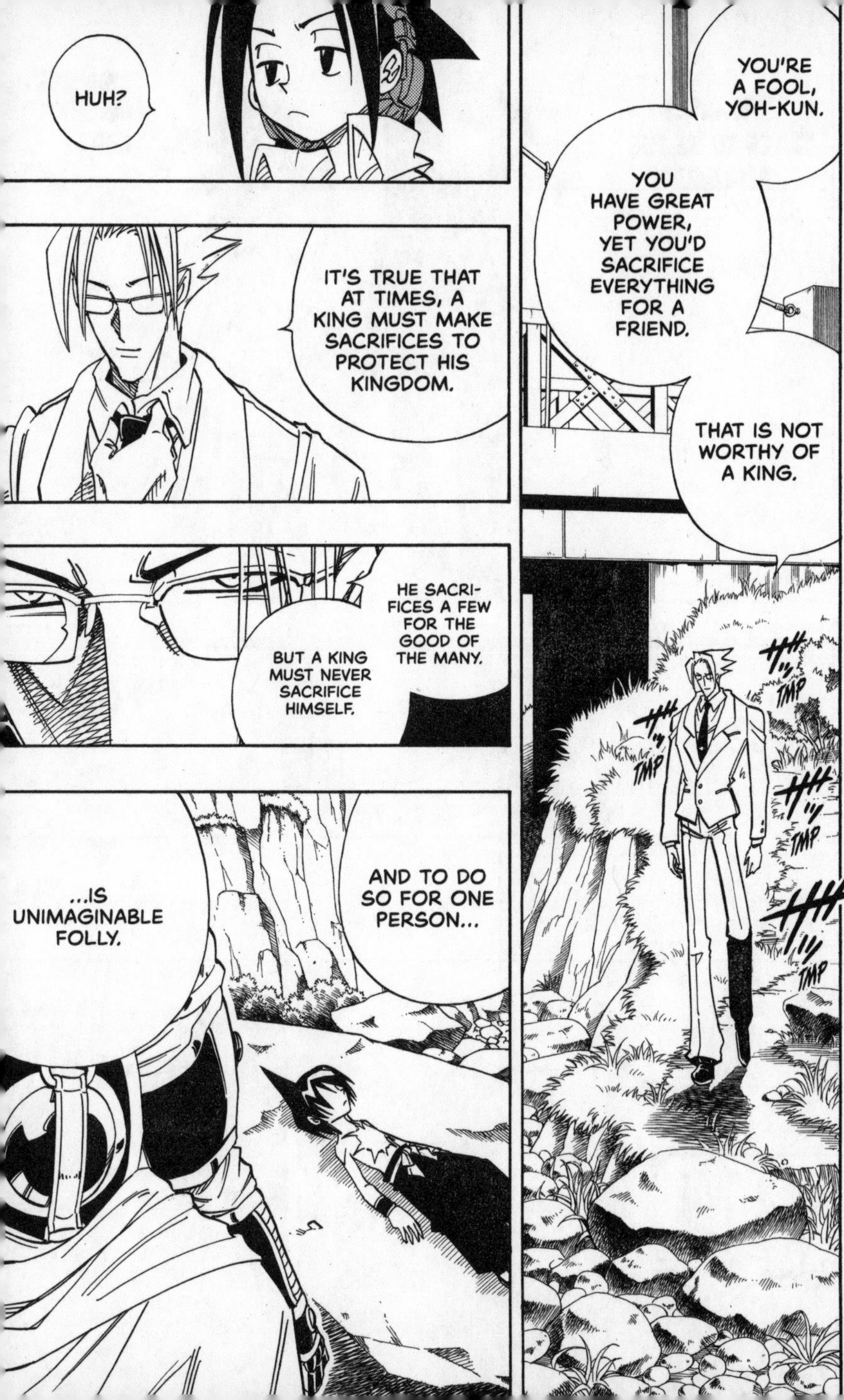

YOU'RE A FOOL, YOH-KUN.
YOU HAVE GREAT POWER, YET YOU'D SACRIFICE EVERYTHING FOR A FRIEND.
THAT IS NOT WORTHY OF A KING.
TMP
TMP
TMP
TMP
HUH?
IT'S TRUE THAT AT TIMES, A KING MUST MAKE SACRIFICES TO PROTECT HIS KINGDOM.
HE SACRIFICES A FEW FOR THE GOOD OF THE MANY.
BUT A KING MUST NEVER SACRIFICE HIMSELF.
AND TO DO SO FOR ONE PERSON...
...IS UNIMAGINABLE FOLLY.

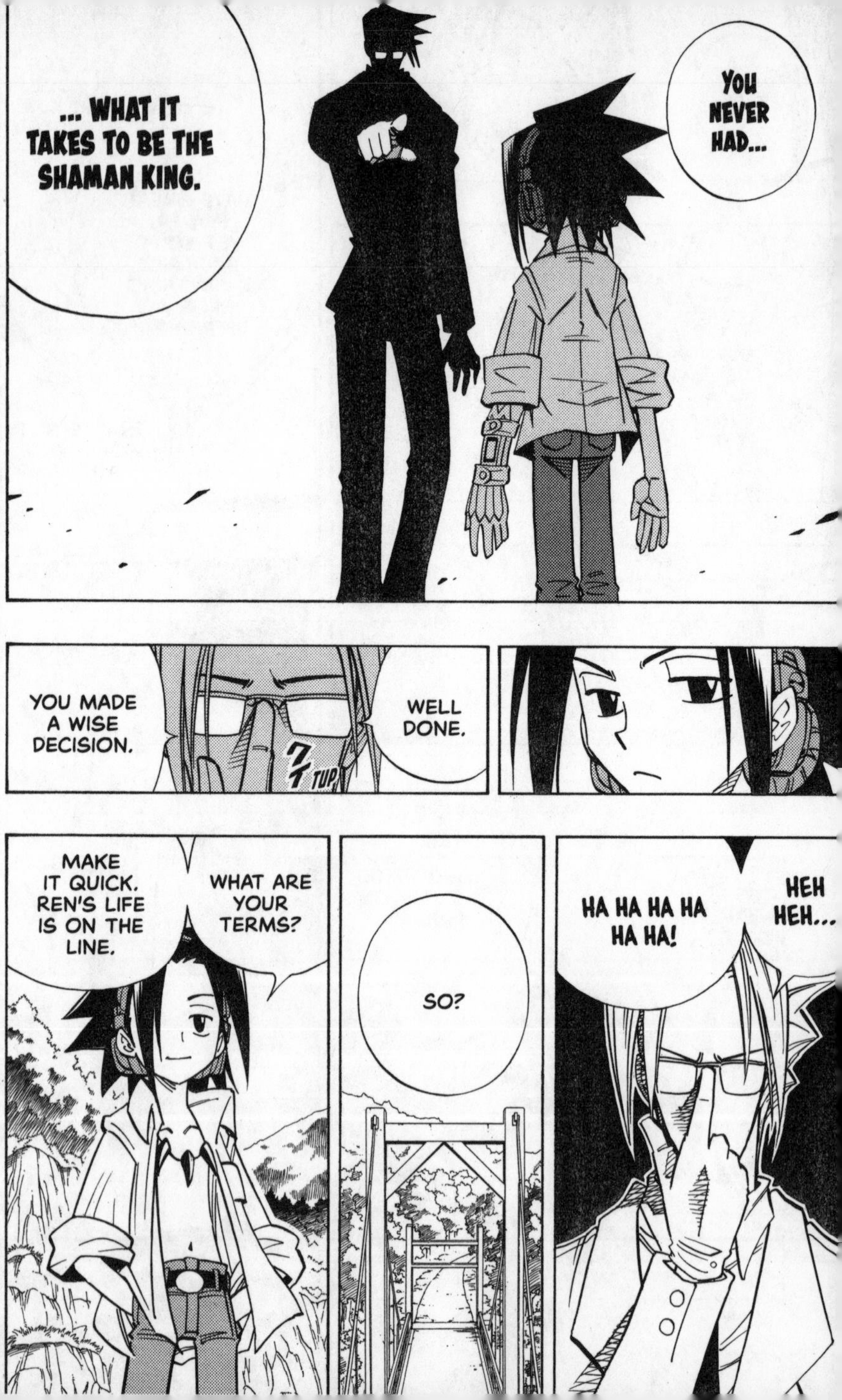
YOU NEVER HAD...
... WHAT IT TAKES TO BE THE SHAMAN KING.
WELL DONE.
TUP
YOU MADE A WISE DECISION.
HEH HEH...
HA HA HA HA HA HA!
SO?
WHAT ARE YOUR TERMS?
MAKE IT QUICK. REN'S LIFE IS ON THE LINE.

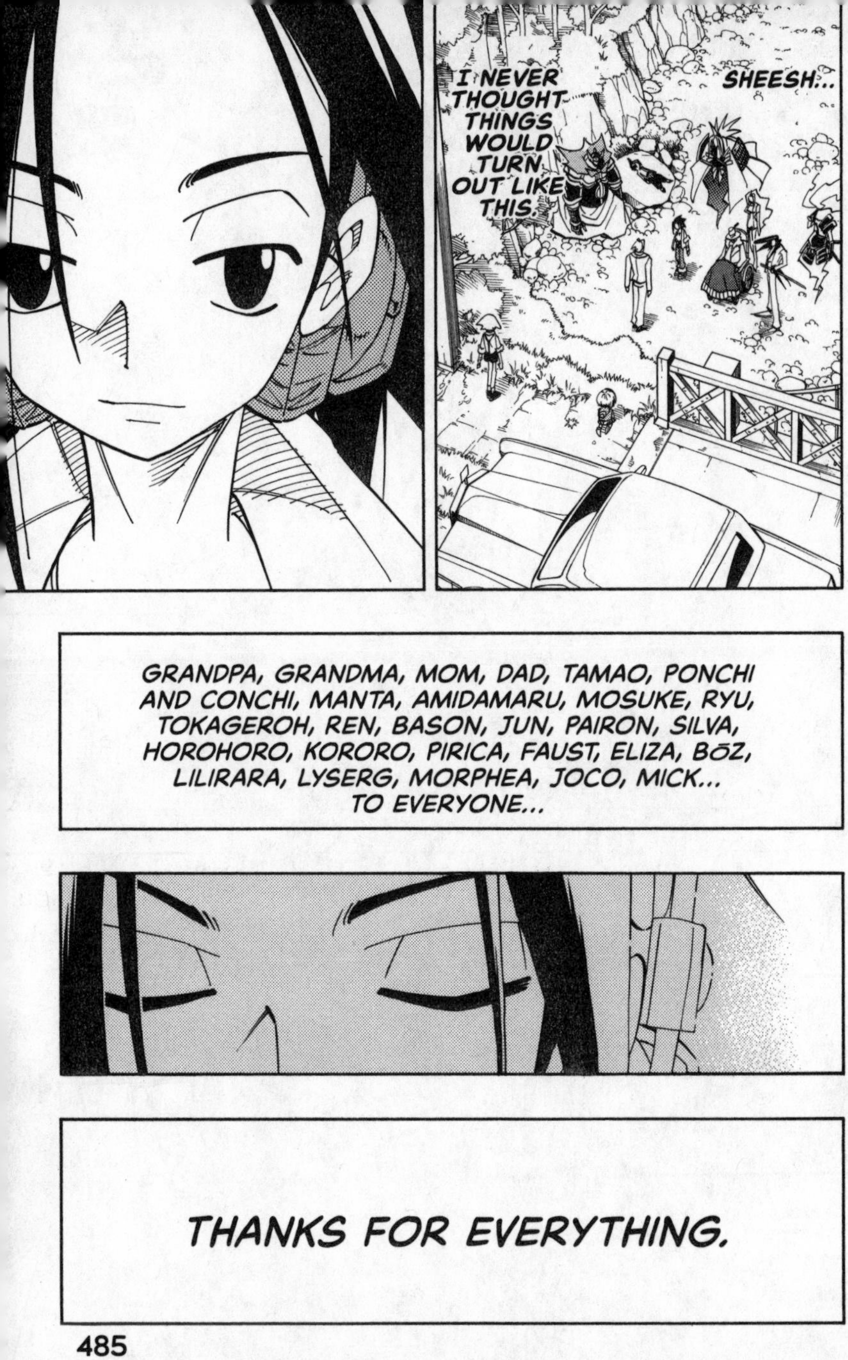
SHEESH...
I NEVER THOUGHT THINGS WOULD TURN OUT LIKE THIS.
GRANDPA, GRANDMA, MOM, DAD, TAMAO, PONCHI AND CONCHI, MANTA, AMIDAMARU, MOSUKE, RYU, TOKAGEROH, REN, BASON, JUN, PAIRON, SILVA, HOROHORO, KORORO, PIRICA, FAUST, ELIZA, BŌZ, LILIRARA, LYSERG, MORPHEA, JOCO, MICK... TO EVERYONE...
THANKS FOR EVERYTHING.

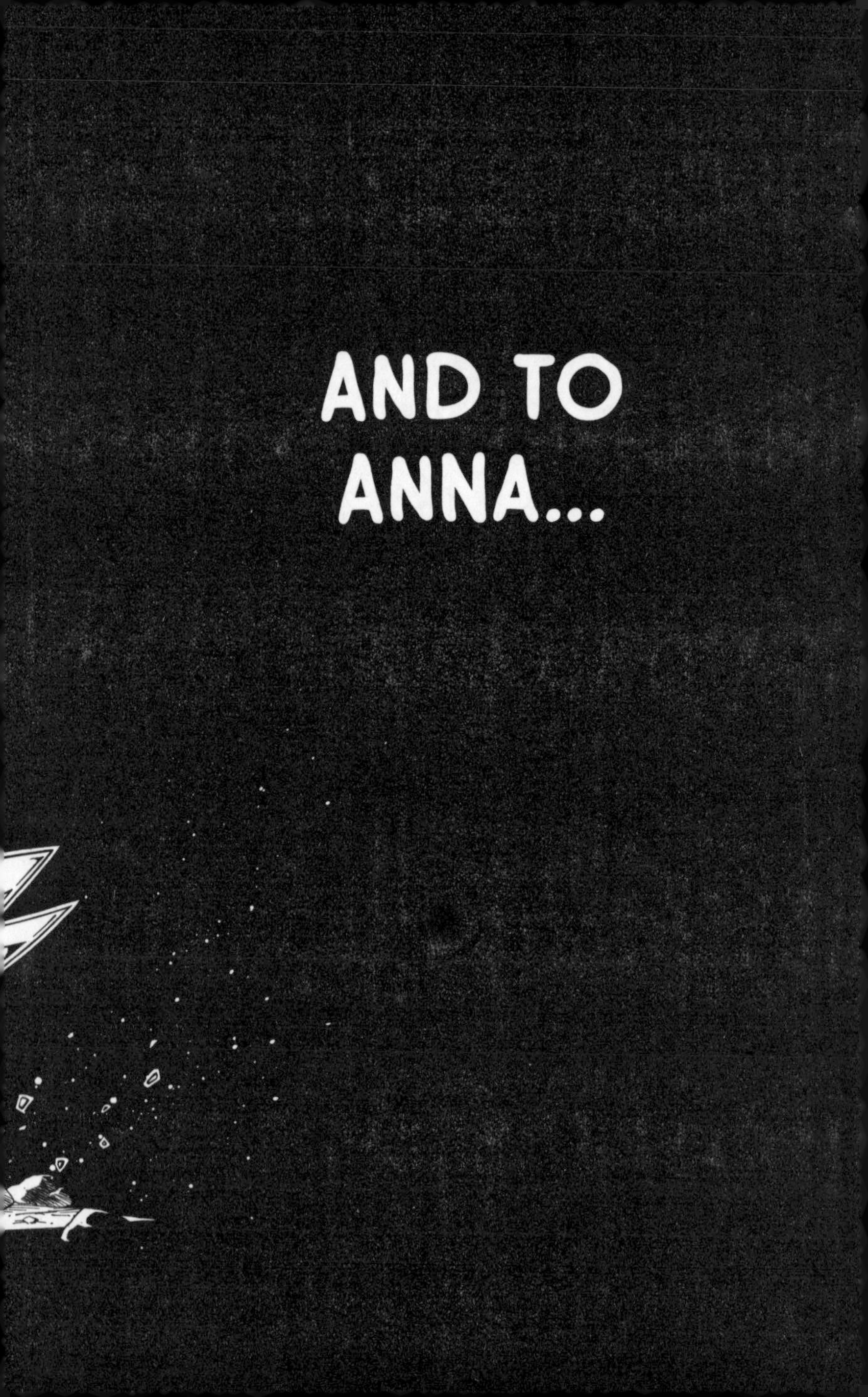
AND TO ANNA...

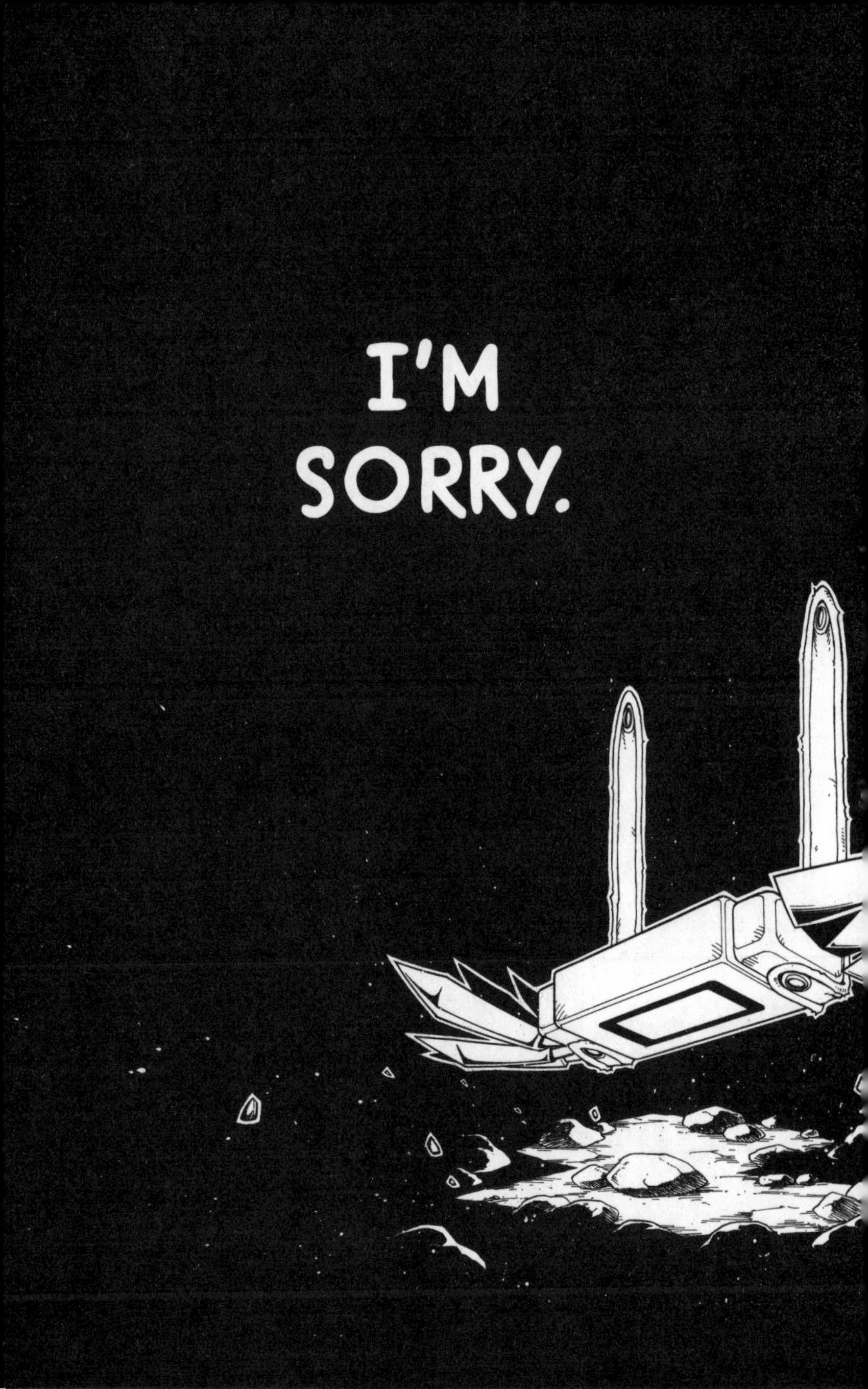
I'M SORRY.

SHAMAN KING CHARACTER FILE No.92

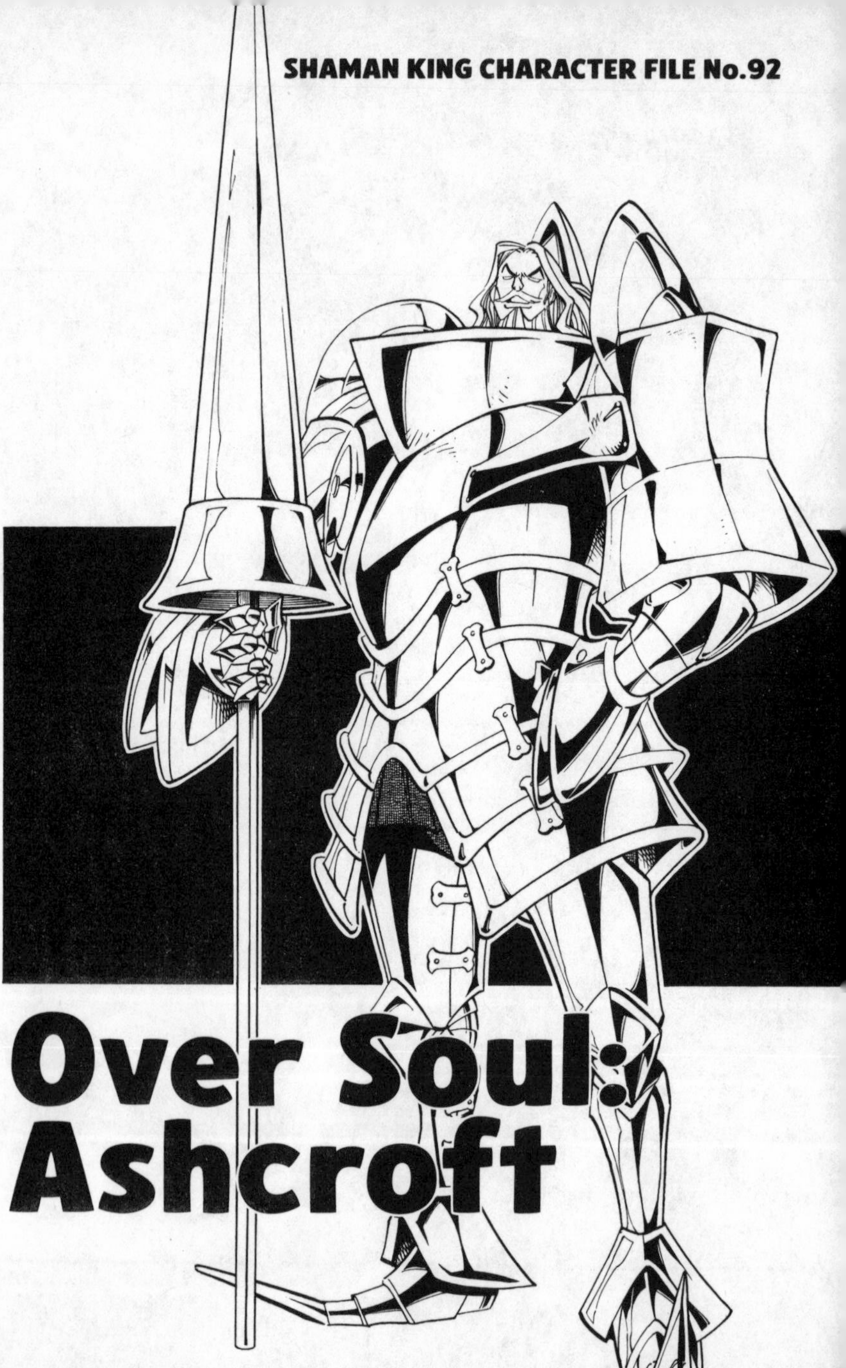

Over Soul: Ashcroft

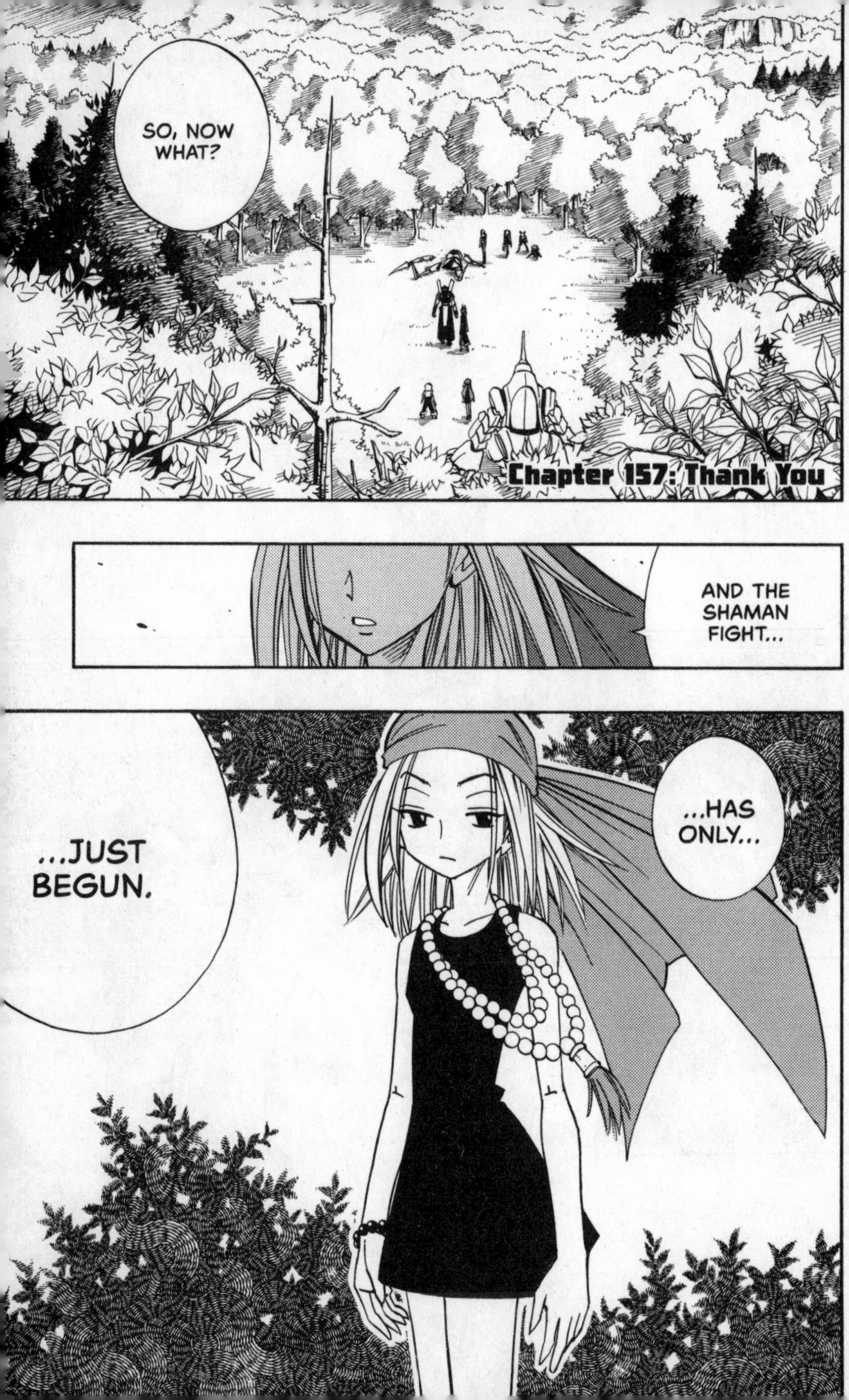
SO, NOW WHAT?
Chapter 157: Thank You
AND THE SHAMAN FIGHT...
...HAS ONLY...
...JUST BEGUN.

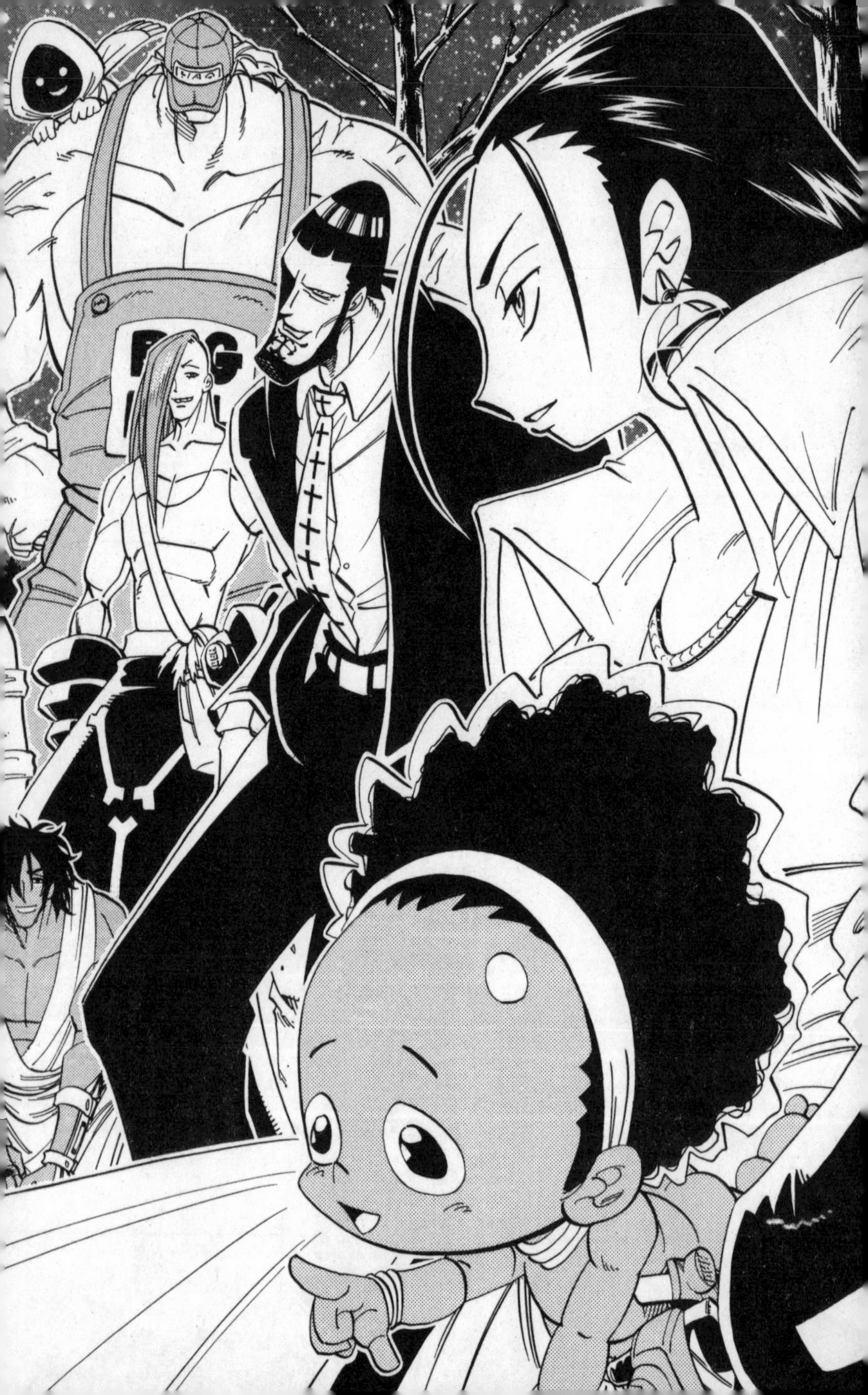

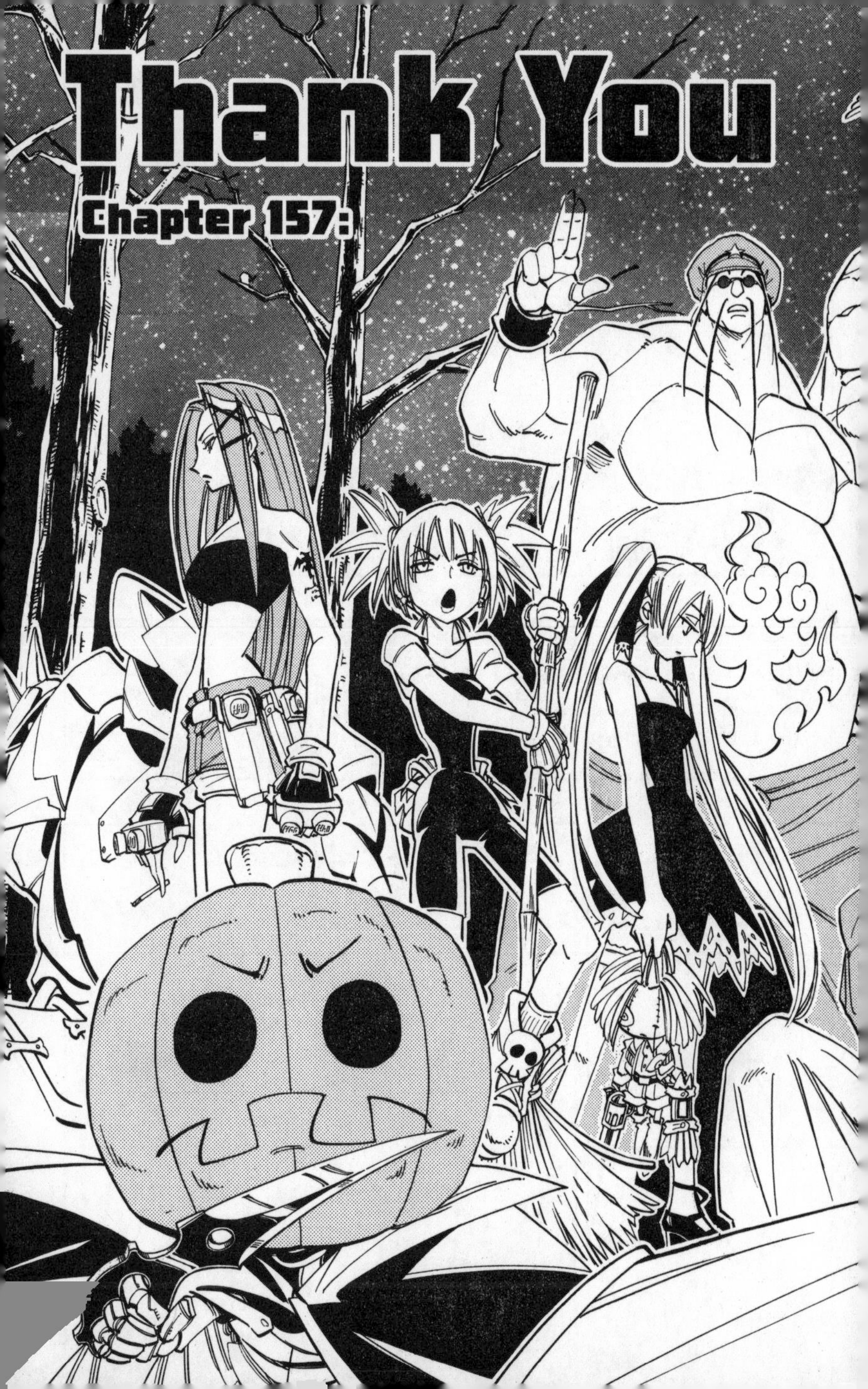
Thank You
Chapter 157:

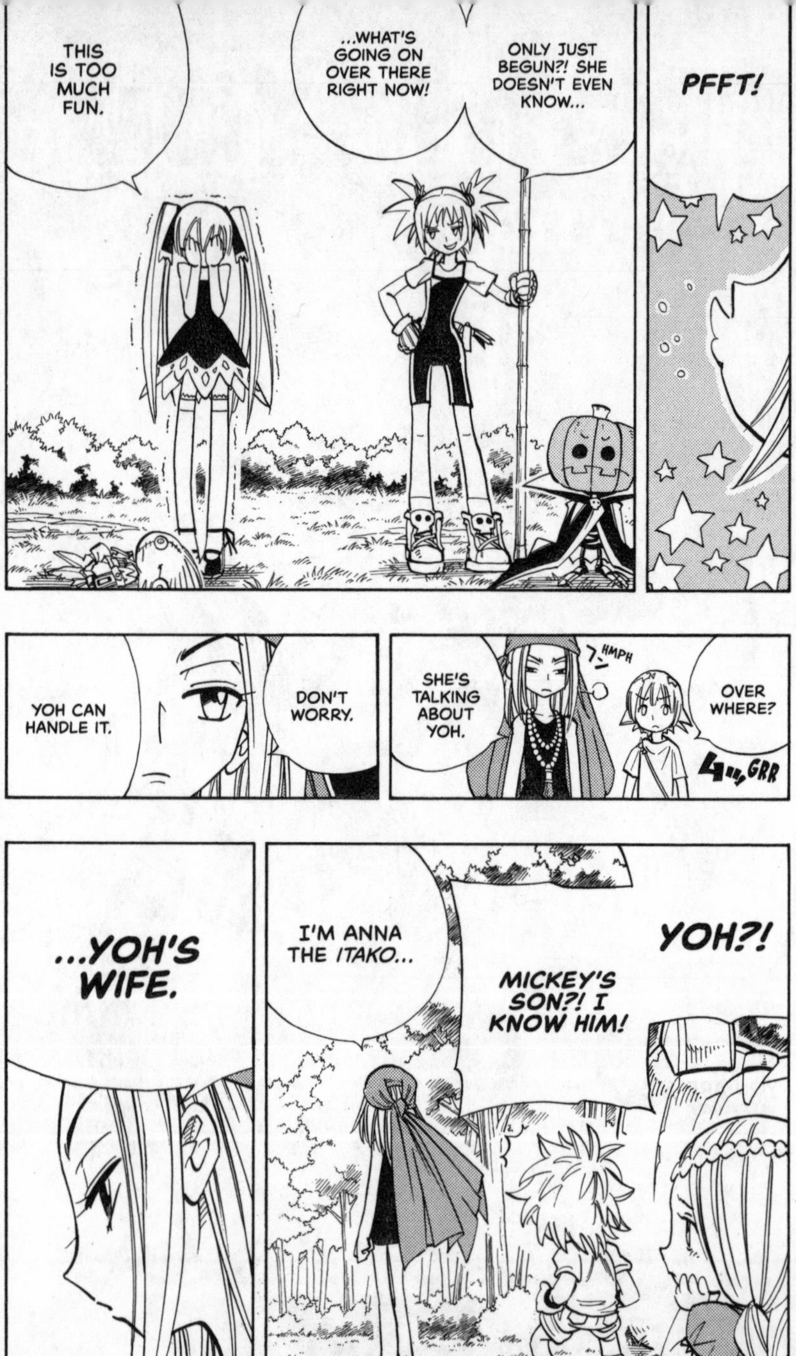
PFFT!
ONLY JUST BEGUN?! SHE DOESN'T EVEN KNOW...
...WHAT'S GOING ON OVER THERE RIGHT NOW!
THIS IS TOO MUCH FUN.
OVER WHERE?
HMPH
GRR
SHE'S TALKING ABOUT YOH.
DON'T WORRY.
YOH CAN HANDLE IT.
YOH?!
MICKEY'S SON?! I KNOW HIM!
I'M ANNA THE ITAKO...
...YOH'S WIFE.

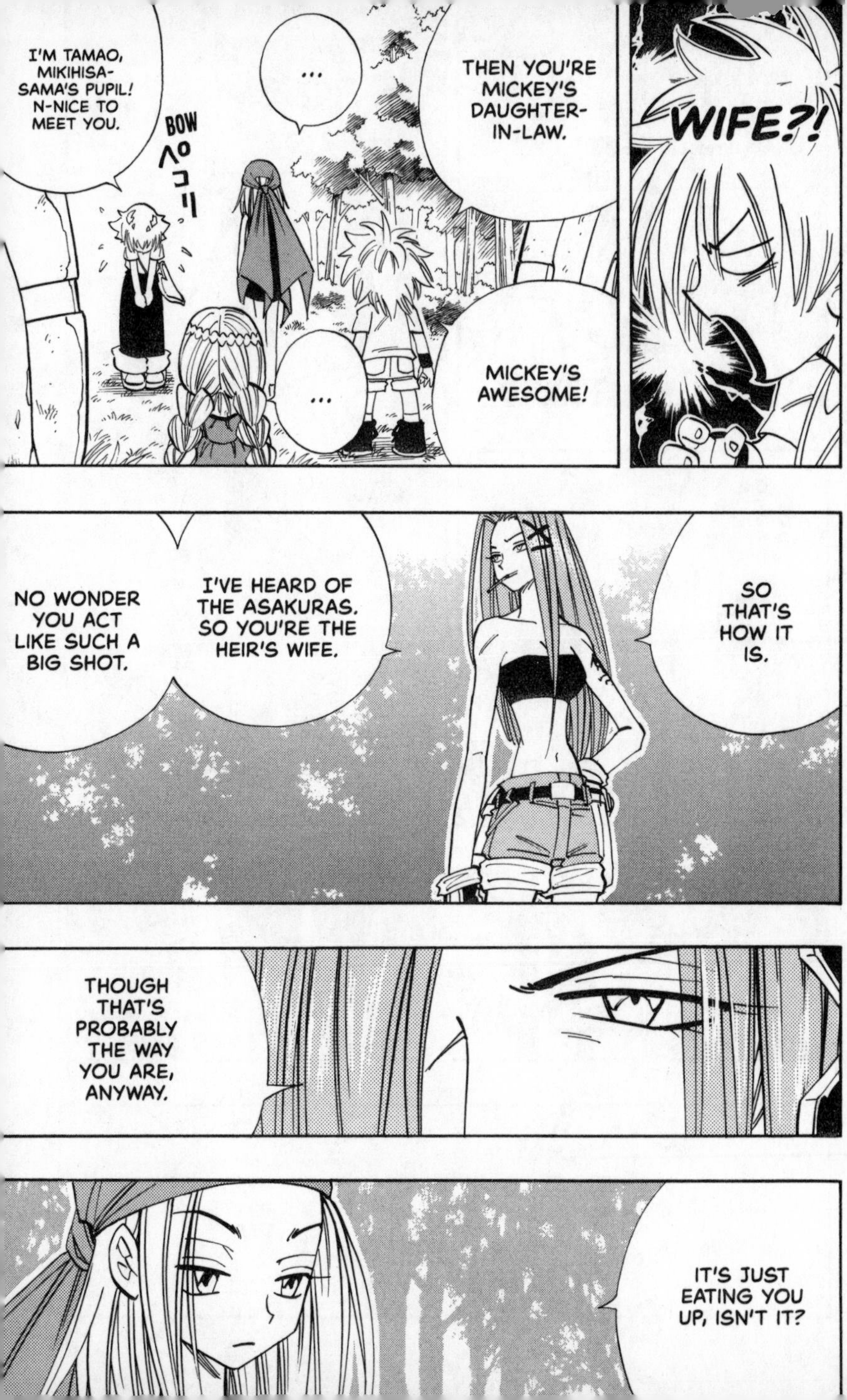
WIFE?!
THEN YOU'RE MICKEY'S DAUGHTER-IN-LAW.
...
I'M TAMAO, MIKIHISA-SAMA'S PUPIL! N-NICE TO MEET YOU.
BOW
ペコリ
MICKEY'S AWESOME!
...
SO THAT'S HOW IT IS.
I'VE HEARD OF THE ASAKURAS. SO YOU'RE THE HEIR'S WIFE.
NO WONDER YOU ACT LIKE SUCH A BIG SHOT.
THOUGH THAT'S PROBABLY THE WAY YOU ARE, ANYWAY.
IT'S JUST EATING YOU UP, ISN'T IT?

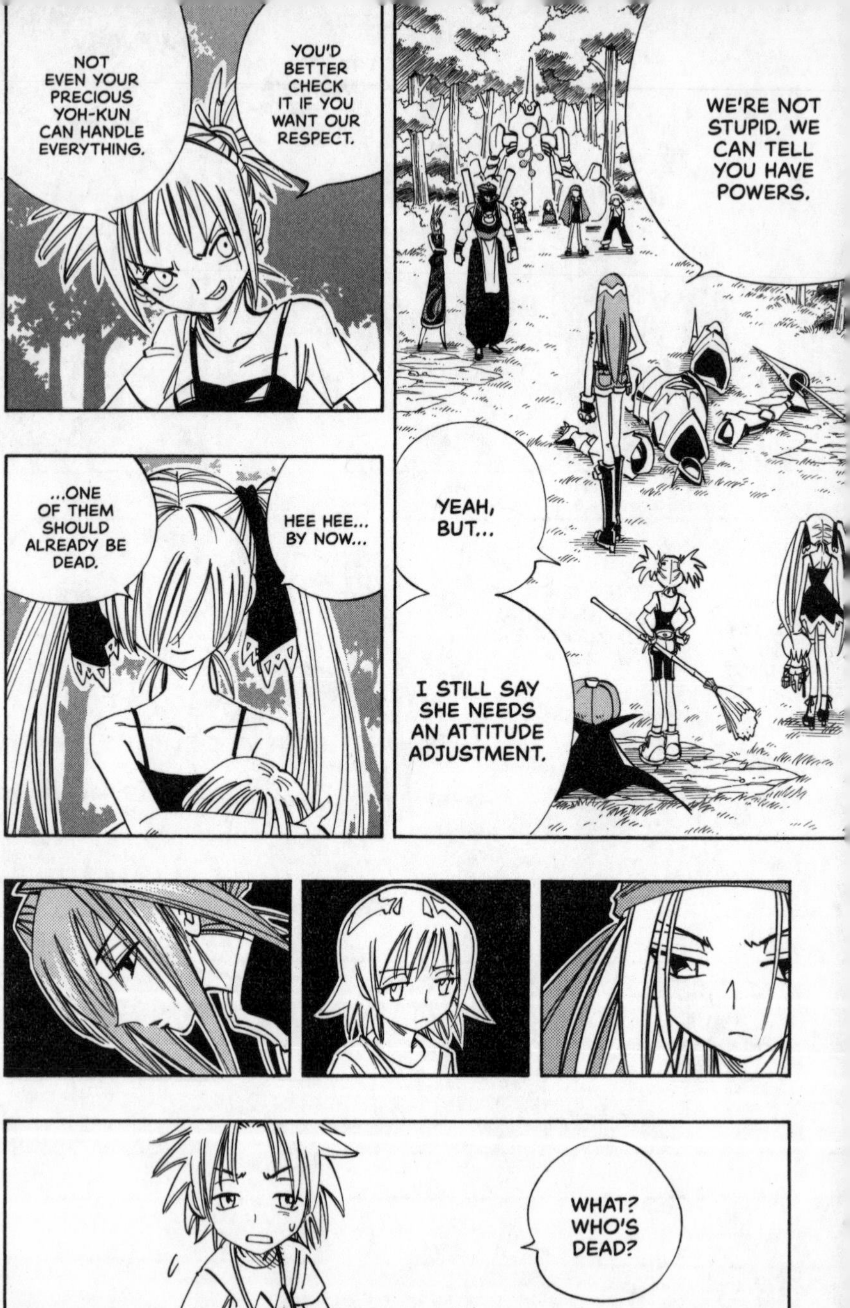
WE'RE NOT STUPID. WE CAN TELL YOU HAVE POWERS.
YEAH, BUT...
I STILL SAY SHE NEEDS AN ATTITUDE ADJUSTMENT.
YOU'D BETTER CHECK IT IF YOU WANT OUR RESPECT.
NOT EVEN YOUR PRECIOUS YOH-KUN CAN HANDLE EVERYTHING.
HEE HEE... BY NOW...
...ONE OF THEM SHOULD ALREADY BE DEAD.
WHAT? WHO'S DEAD?

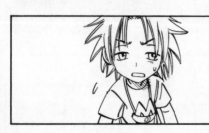

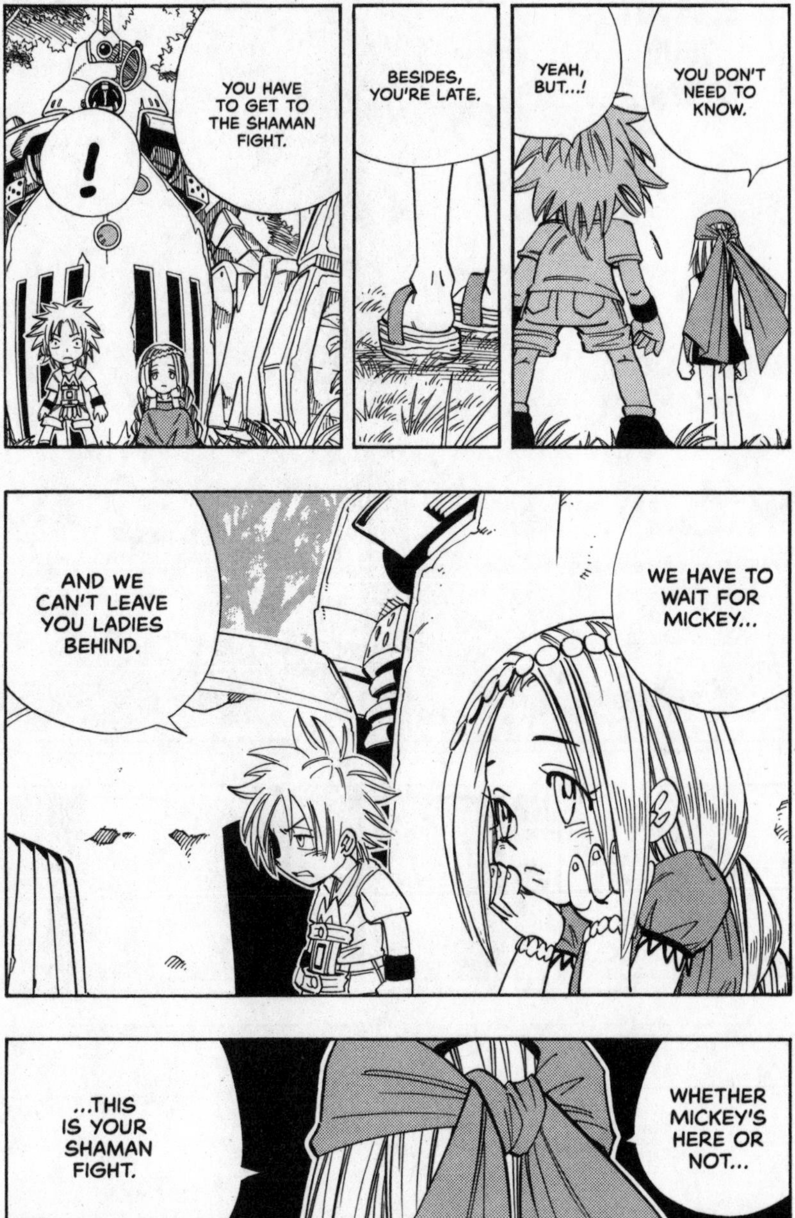
YOU DON'T NEED TO KNOW.
YEAH, BUT...!
BESIDES, YOU'RE LATE.
YOU HAVE TO GET TO THE SHAMAN FIGHT.
!
WE HAVE TO WAIT FOR MICKEY...
AND WE CAN'T LEAVE YOU LADIES BEHIND.
WHETHER MICKEY'S HERE OR NOT...
...THIS IS YOUR SHAMAN FIGHT.

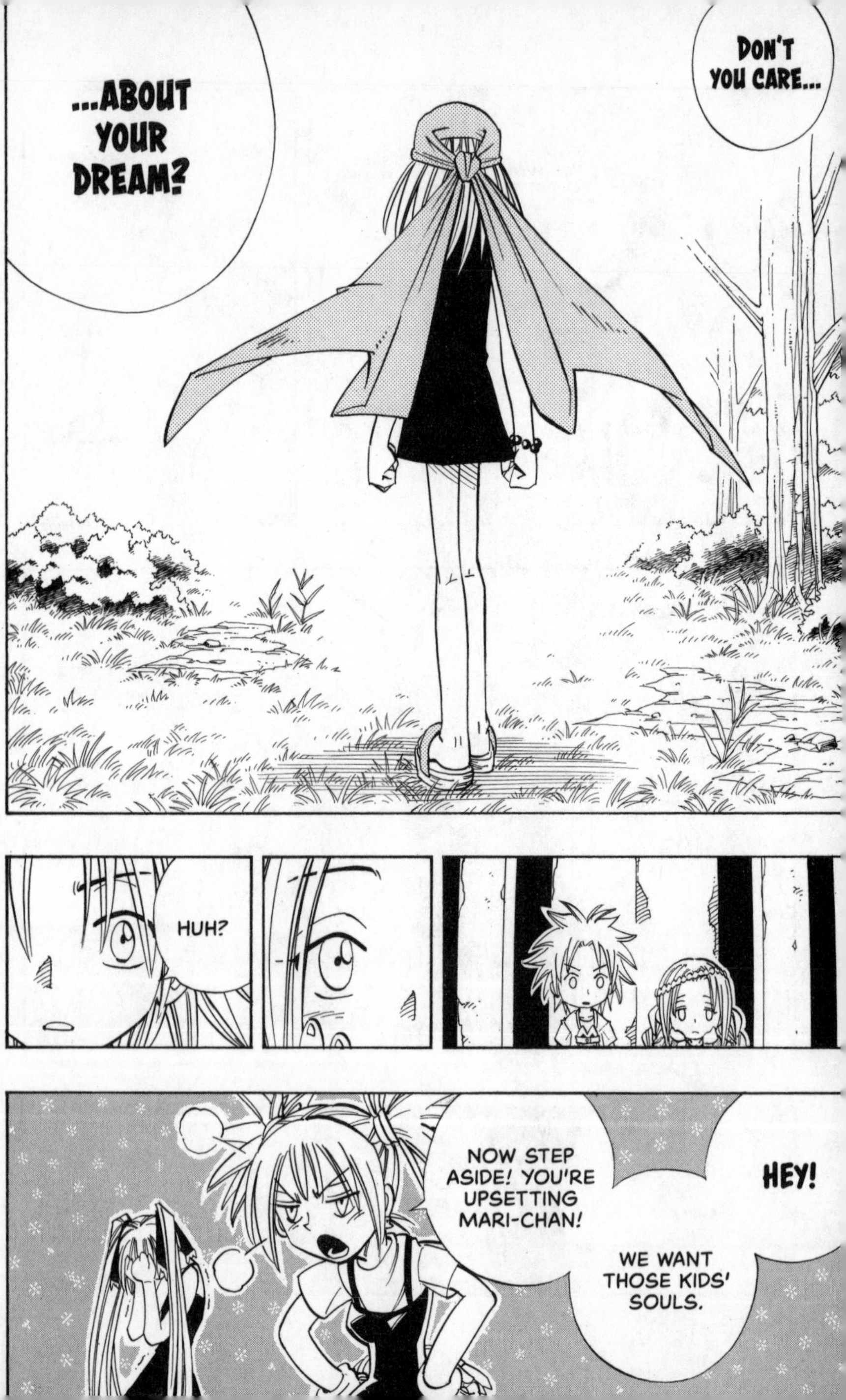
DON'T YOU CARE...
...ABOUT YOUR DREAM?
HUH?
HEY!
WE WANT THOSE KIDS' SOULS.
NOW STEP ASIDE! YOU'RE UPSETTING MARI-CHAN!

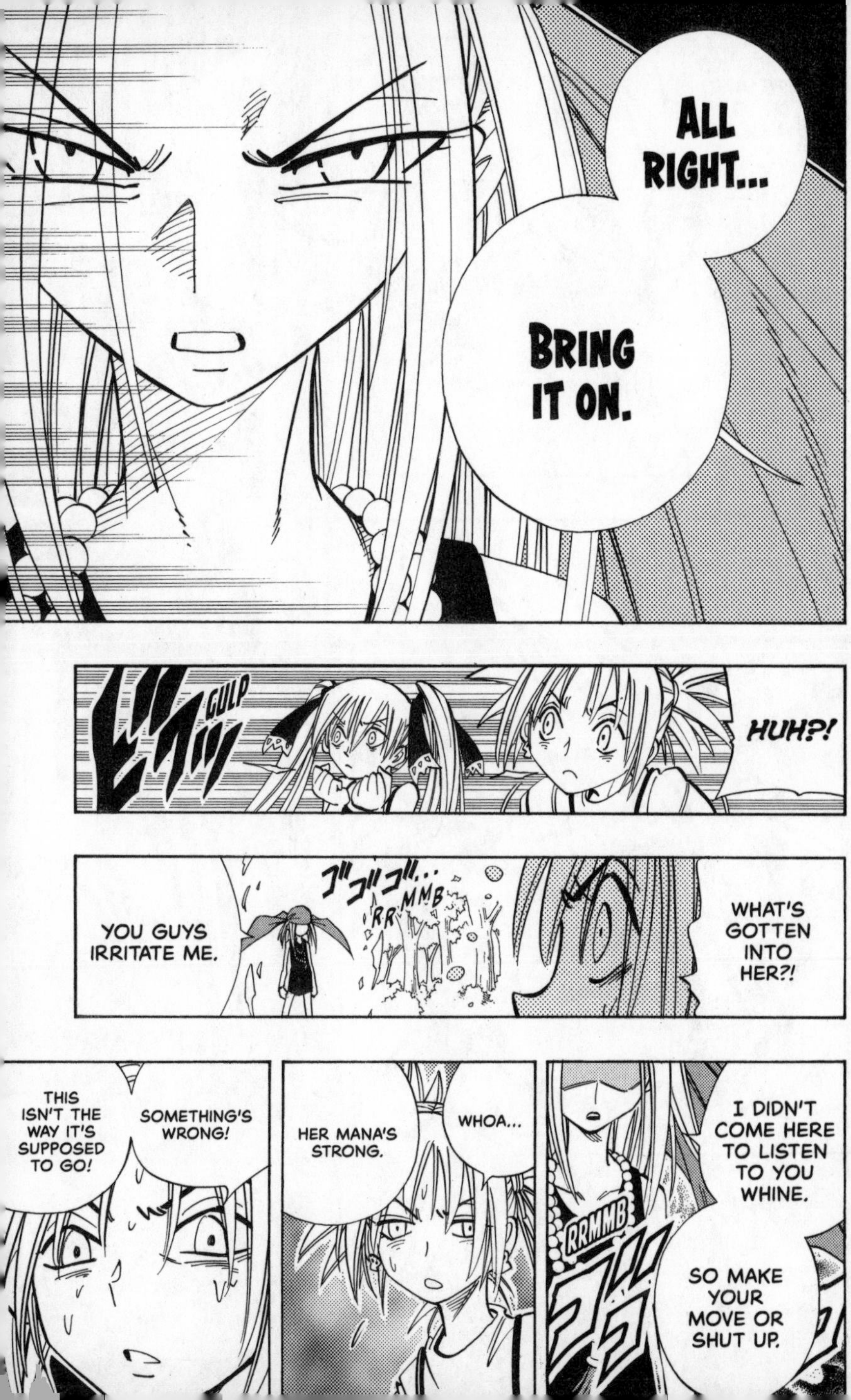
ALL RIGHT...
BRING IT ON.
HUH?!
GULP
WHAT'S GOTTEN INTO HER?!
RRMMB
YOU GUYS IRRITATE ME.
I DIDN'T COME HERE TO LISTEN TO YOU WHINE.
RRMMB
SO MAKE YOUR MOVE OR SHUT UP.
WHOA...
HER MANA'S STRONG.
SOMETHING'S WRONG!
THIS ISN'T THE WAY IT'S SUPPOSED TO GO!

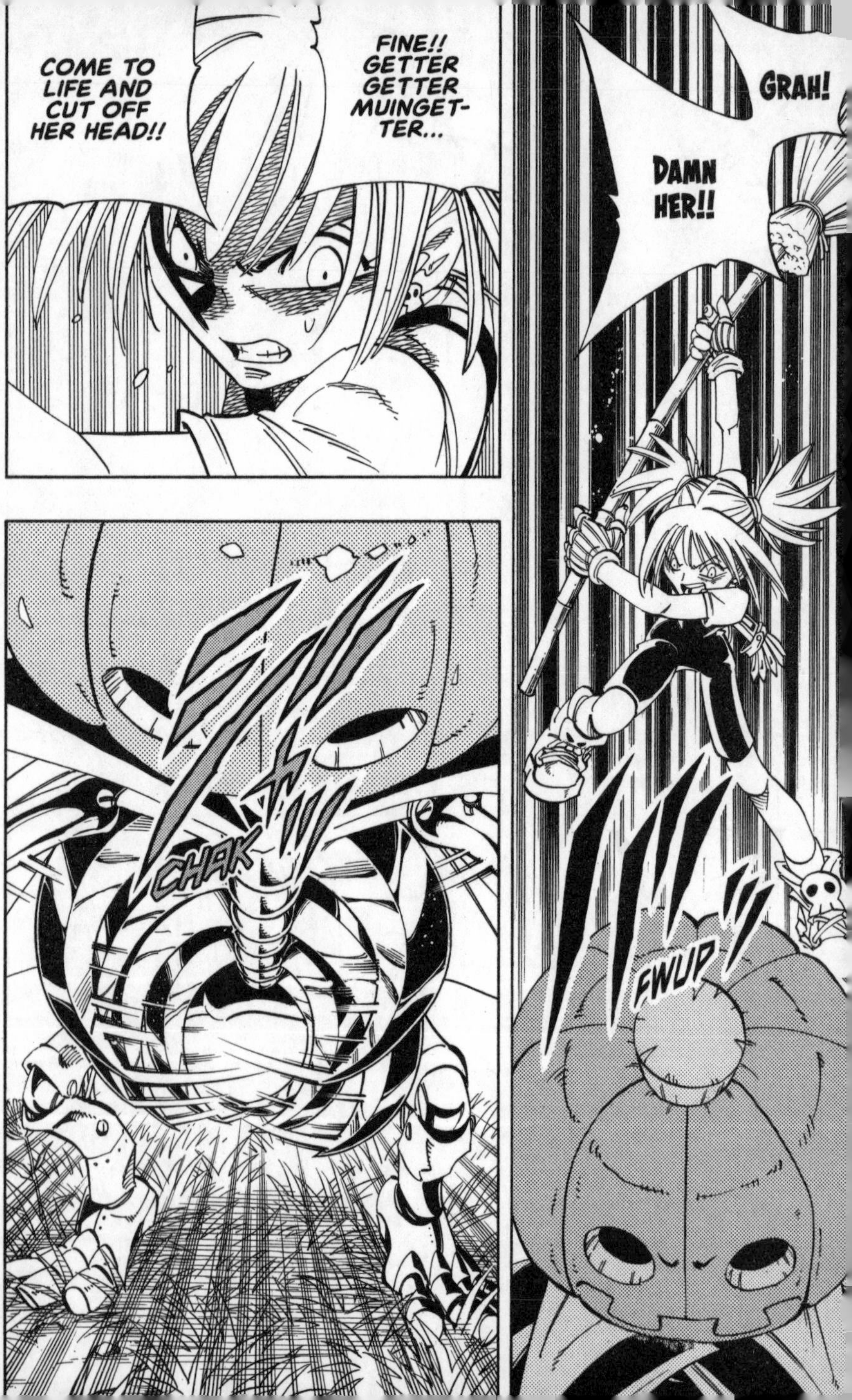
GRAH!
DAMN HER!!
FWUP
FINE!! GETTER GETTER MUINGETTER...
COME TO LIFE AND CUT OFF HER HEAD!!
CHAK

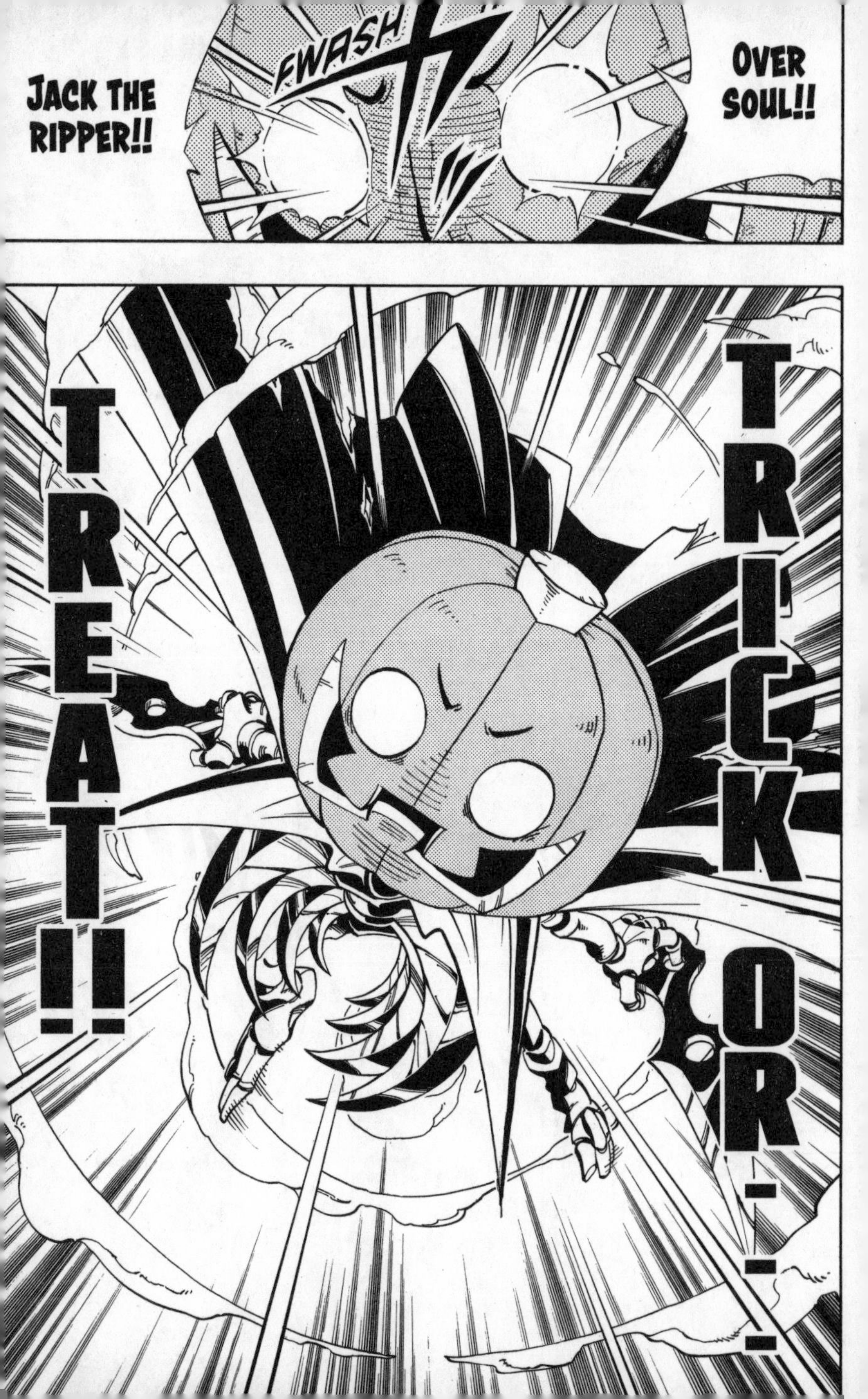
OVER SOUL!!
FWASH
JACK THE RIPPER!!
TRICK OR--
TREAT!!

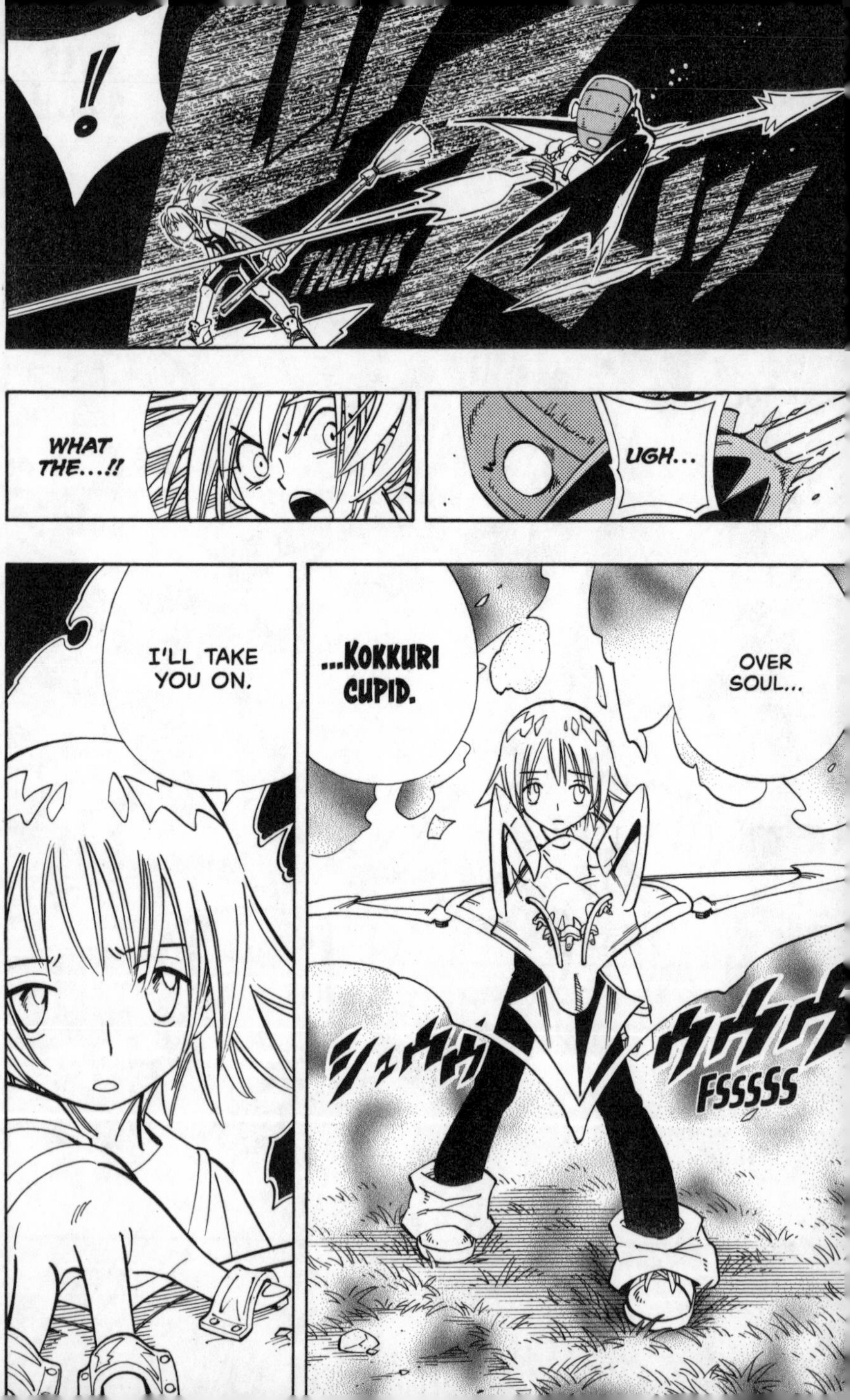
!!
THUNK
UGH...
WHAT THE...!!
OVER SOUL...
...KOKKURI CUPID.
FSSSSS
I'LL TAKE YOU ON.

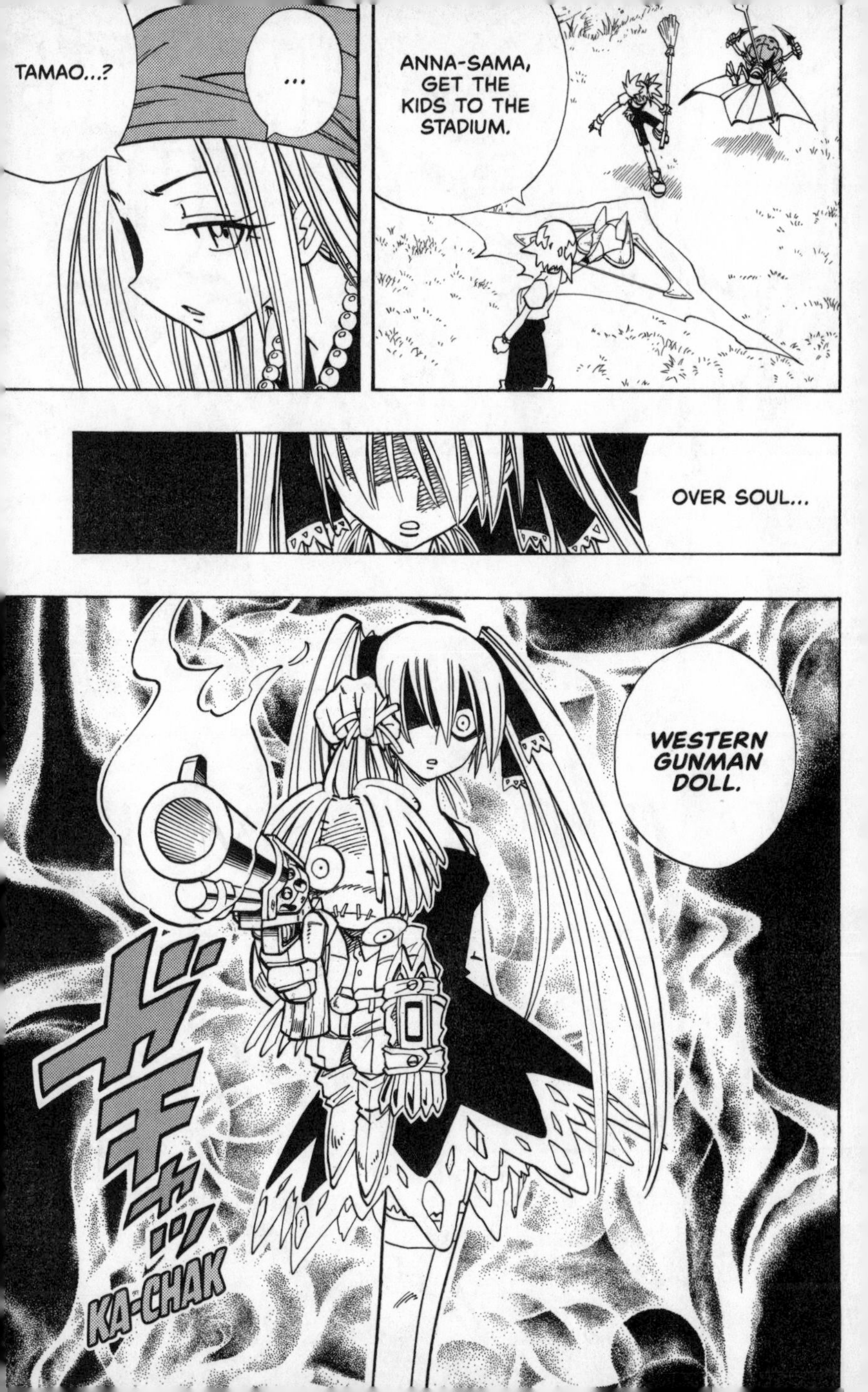
ANNA-SAMA, GET THE KIDS TO THE STADIUM.
...
TAMAO...?
OVER SOUL...
WESTERN GUNMAN DOLL.
KA-CHAK

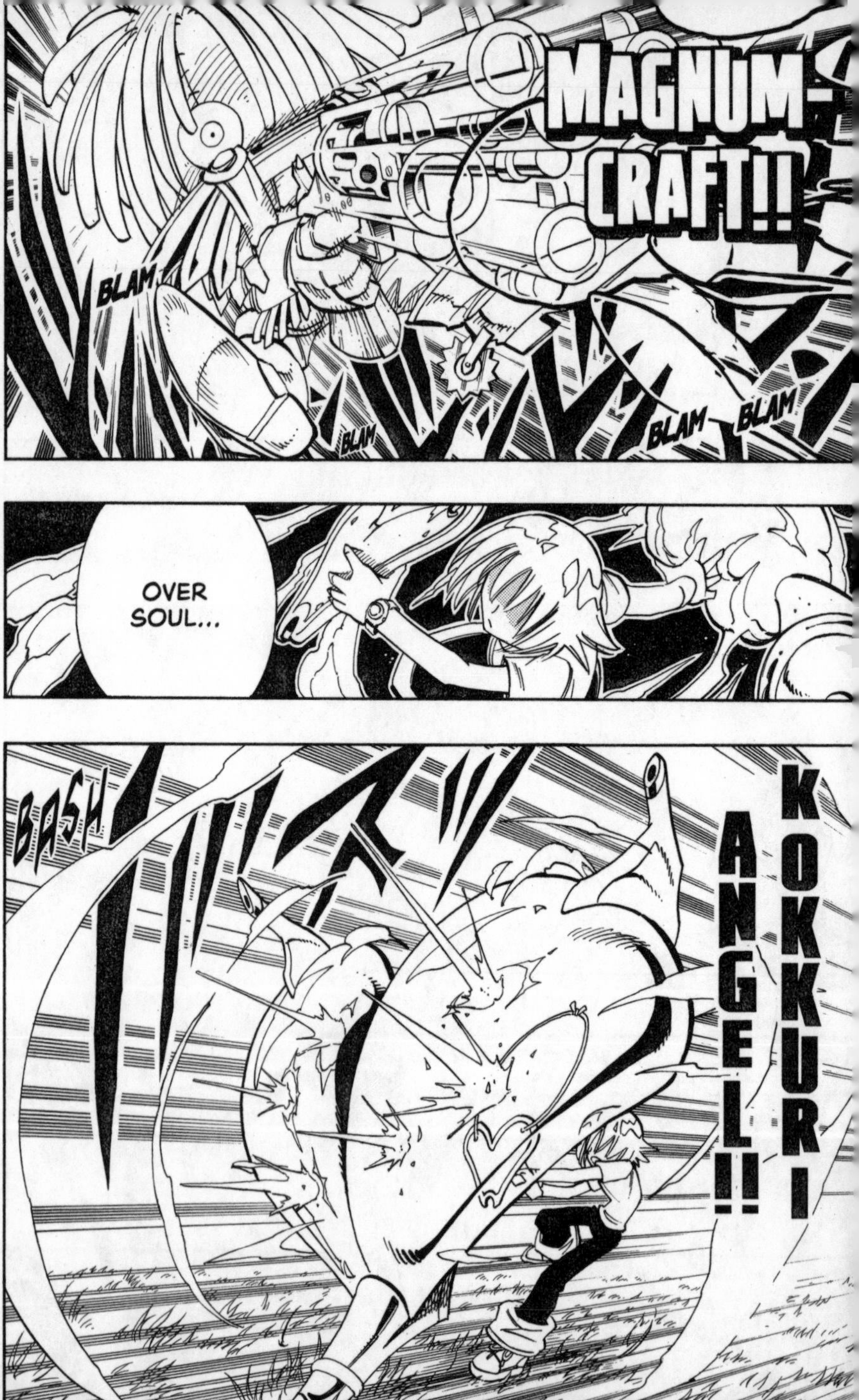
MAGNUM-CRAFT!!
BLAM
BLAM
BLAM
BLAM
OVER SOUL...
KOKKURI ANGEL!!
BASH

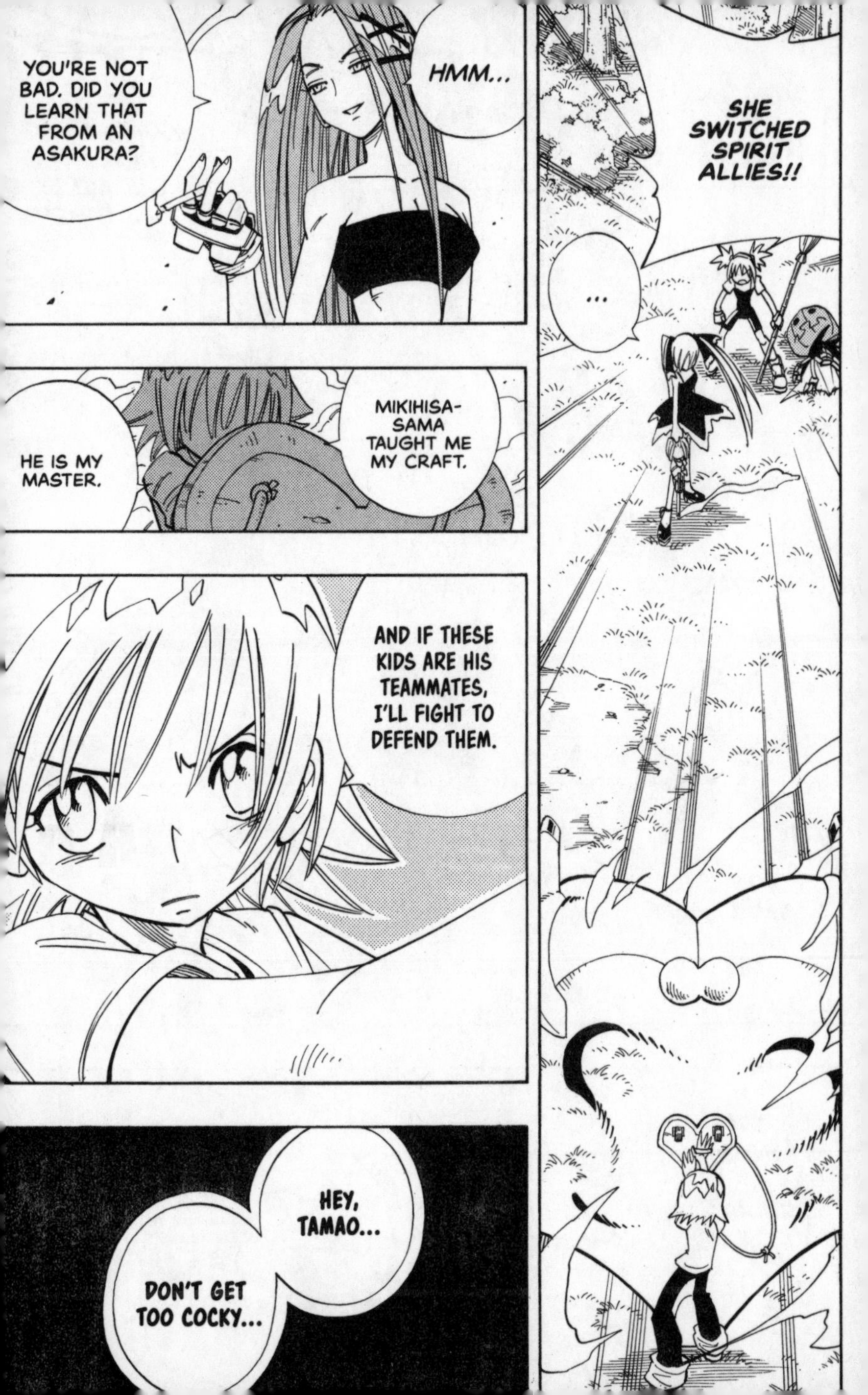
SHE SWITCHED SPIRIT ALLIES!!
...
HMM...
YOU'RE NOT BAD. DID YOU LEARN THAT FROM AN ASAKURA?
MIKIHISA-SAMA TAUGHT ME MY CRAFT.
HE IS MY MASTER.
AND IF THESE KIDS ARE HIS TEAMMATES, I'LL FIGHT TO DEFEND THEM.
HEY, TAMAO...
DON'T GET TOO COCKY...

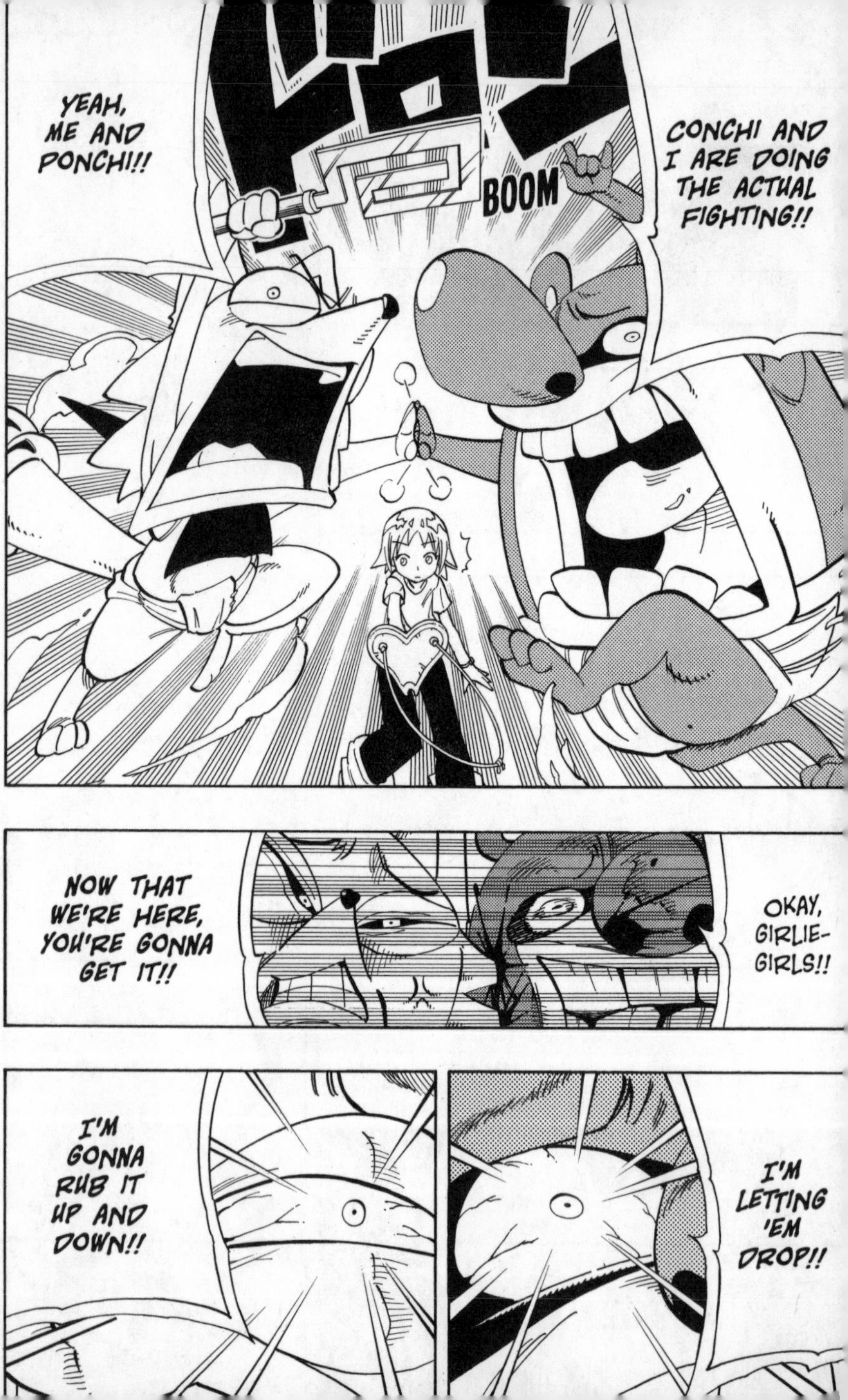
CONCHI AND I ARE DOING THE ACTUAL FIGHTING!!
BOOM
YEAH, ME AND PONCHI!!
OKAY, GIRLIE-GIRLS!!
NOW THAT WE'RE HERE, YOU'RE GONNA GET IT!!
I'M LETTING 'EM DROP!!
I'M GONNA RUB IT UP AND DOWN!!

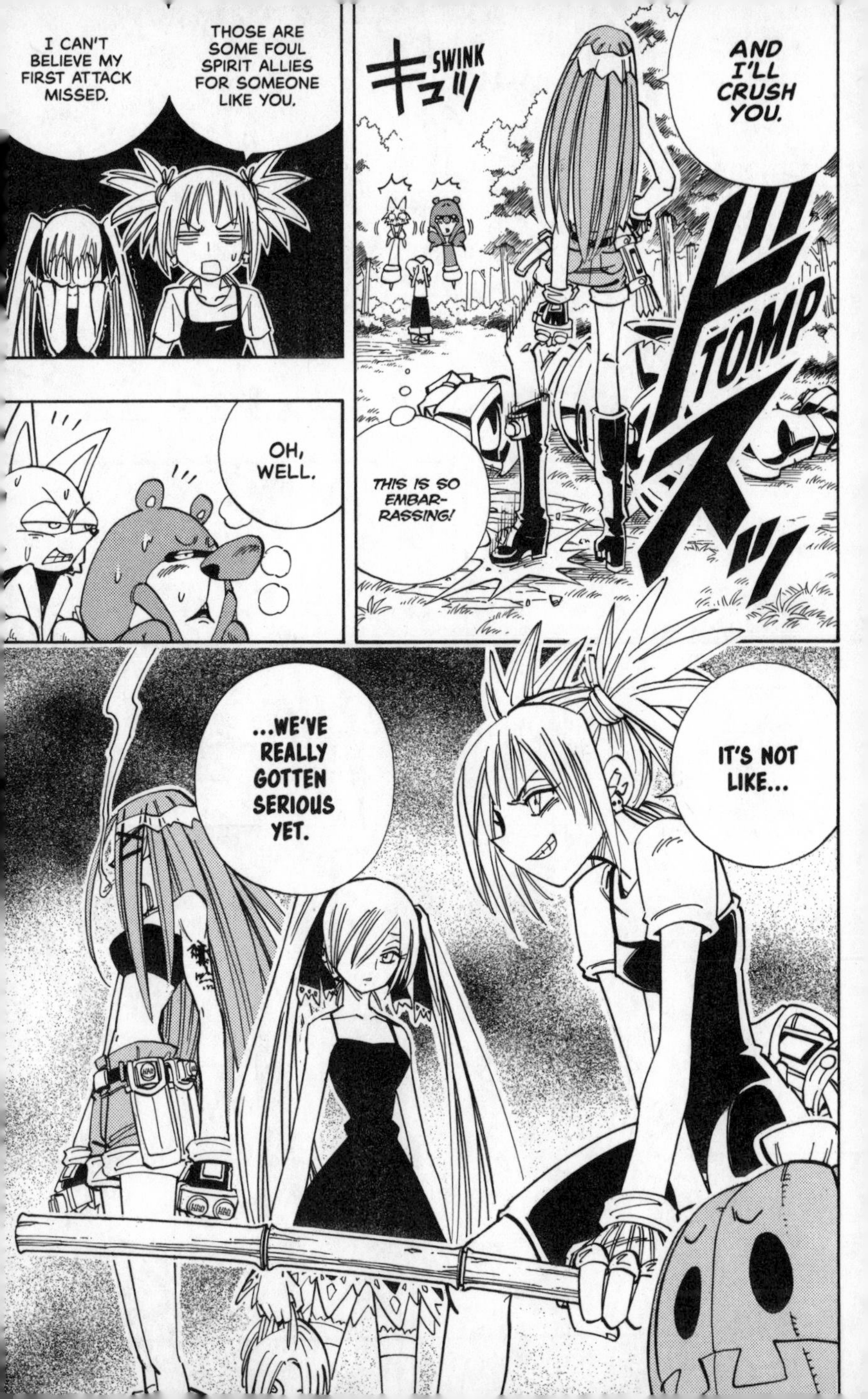
SWINK
AND I'LL CRUSH YOU.
TOMP
THIS IS SO EMBARRASSING!
THOSE ARE SOME FOUL SPIRIT ALLIES FOR SOMEONE LIKE YOU.
I CAN'T BELIEVE MY FIRST ATTACK MISSED.
OH, WELL.
IT'S NOT LIKE...
...WE'VE REALLY GOTTEN SERIOUS YET.

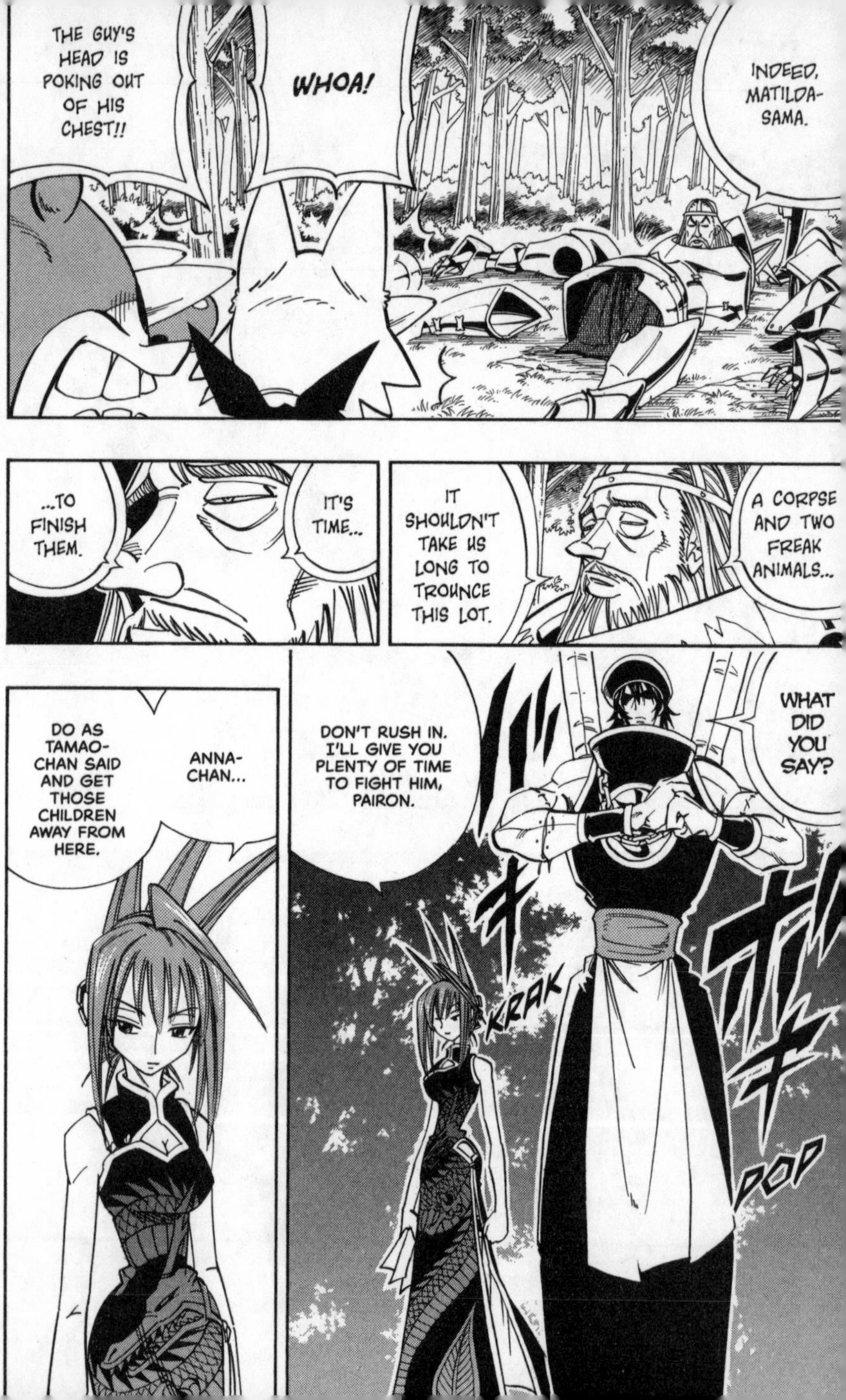
INDEED, MATILDA-SAMA.
WHOA!
THE GUY'S HEAD IS POKING OUT OF HIS CHEST!!
A CORPSE AND TWO FREAK ANIMALS...
IT SHOULDN'T TAKE US LONG TO TROUNCE THIS LOT.
IT'S TIME...
...TO FINISH THEM.
WHAT DID YOU SAY?
DON'T RUSH IN. I'LL GIVE YOU PLENTY OF TIME TO FIGHT HIM, PAIRON.
KRAK
DOP
ANNA-CHAN...
DO AS TAMAO-CHAN SAID AND GET THOSE CHILDREN AWAY FROM HERE.

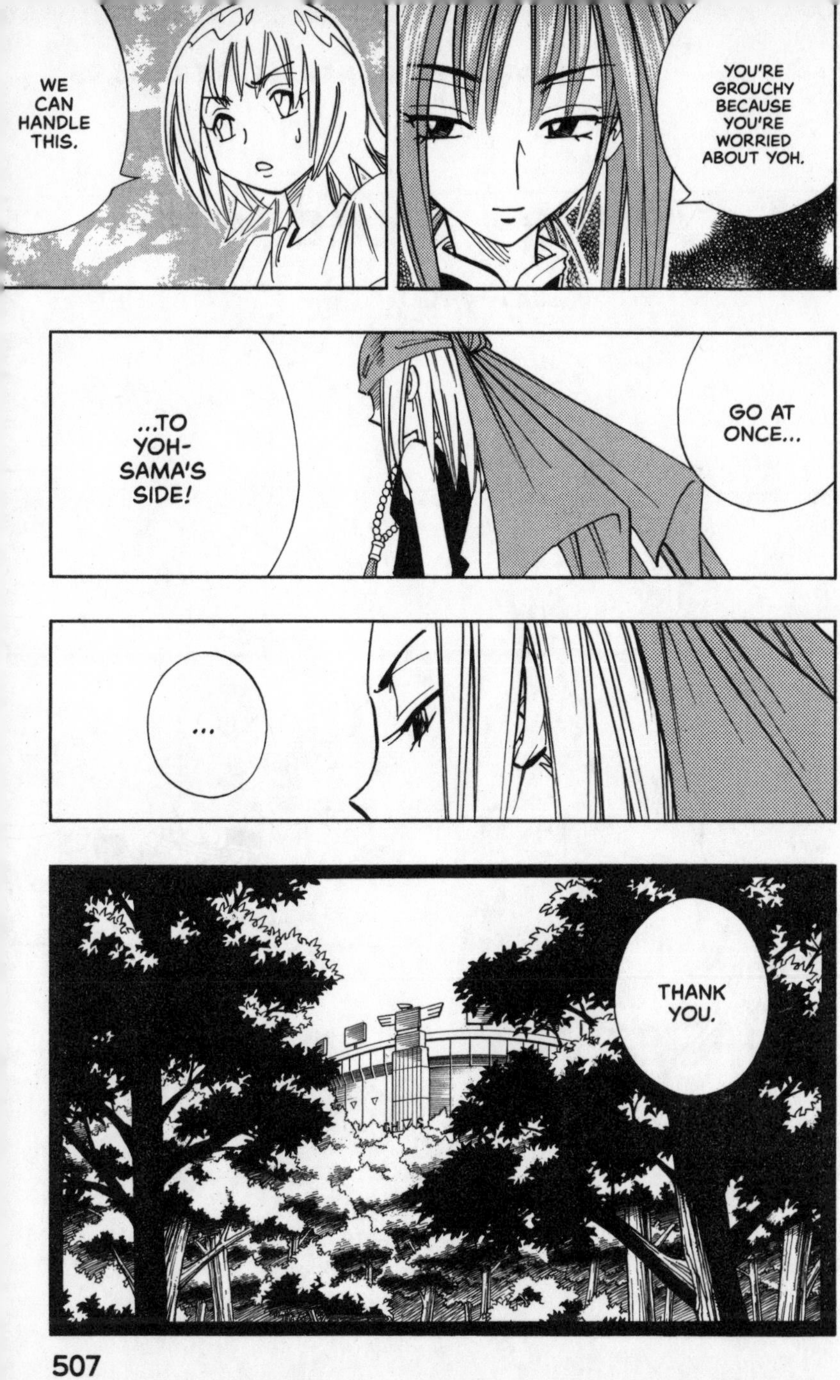
YOU'RE GROUCHY BECAUSE YOU'RE WORRIED ABOUT YOH.
WE CAN HANDLE THIS.
GO AT ONCE...
...TO YOH-SAMA'S SIDE!
...
THANK YOU.

Seyram Ludsev

January 2001

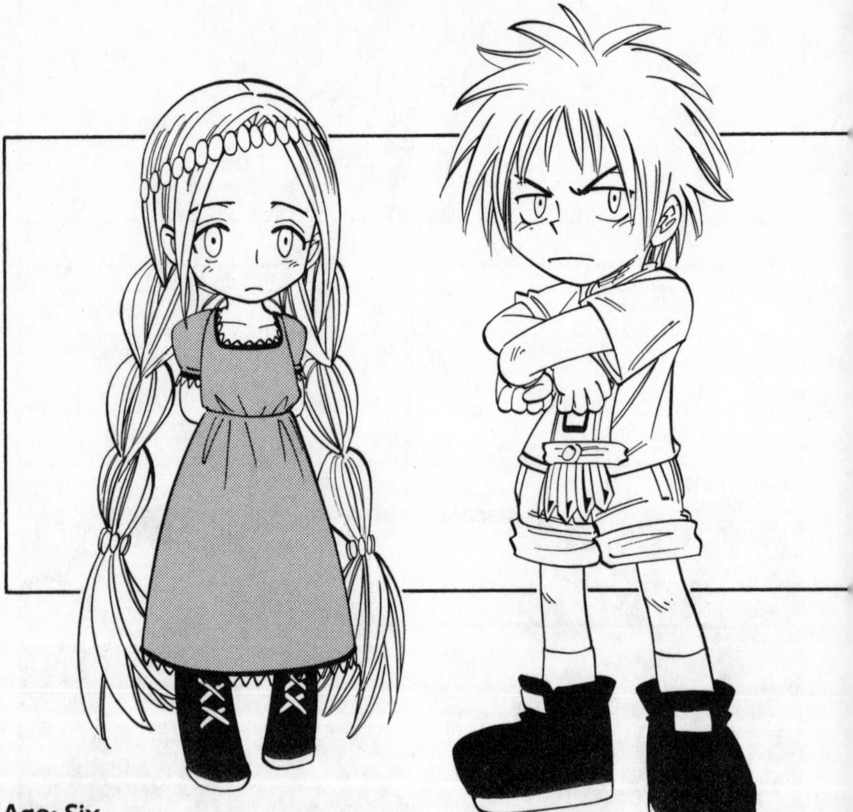

Age: Six
Date of Birth: February 16, 1994
Astrological Sign: Aquarius
Blood Type: O

Age: Eight
Date of Birth: August 15, 1992
Astrological Sign: Leo
Blood Type: O

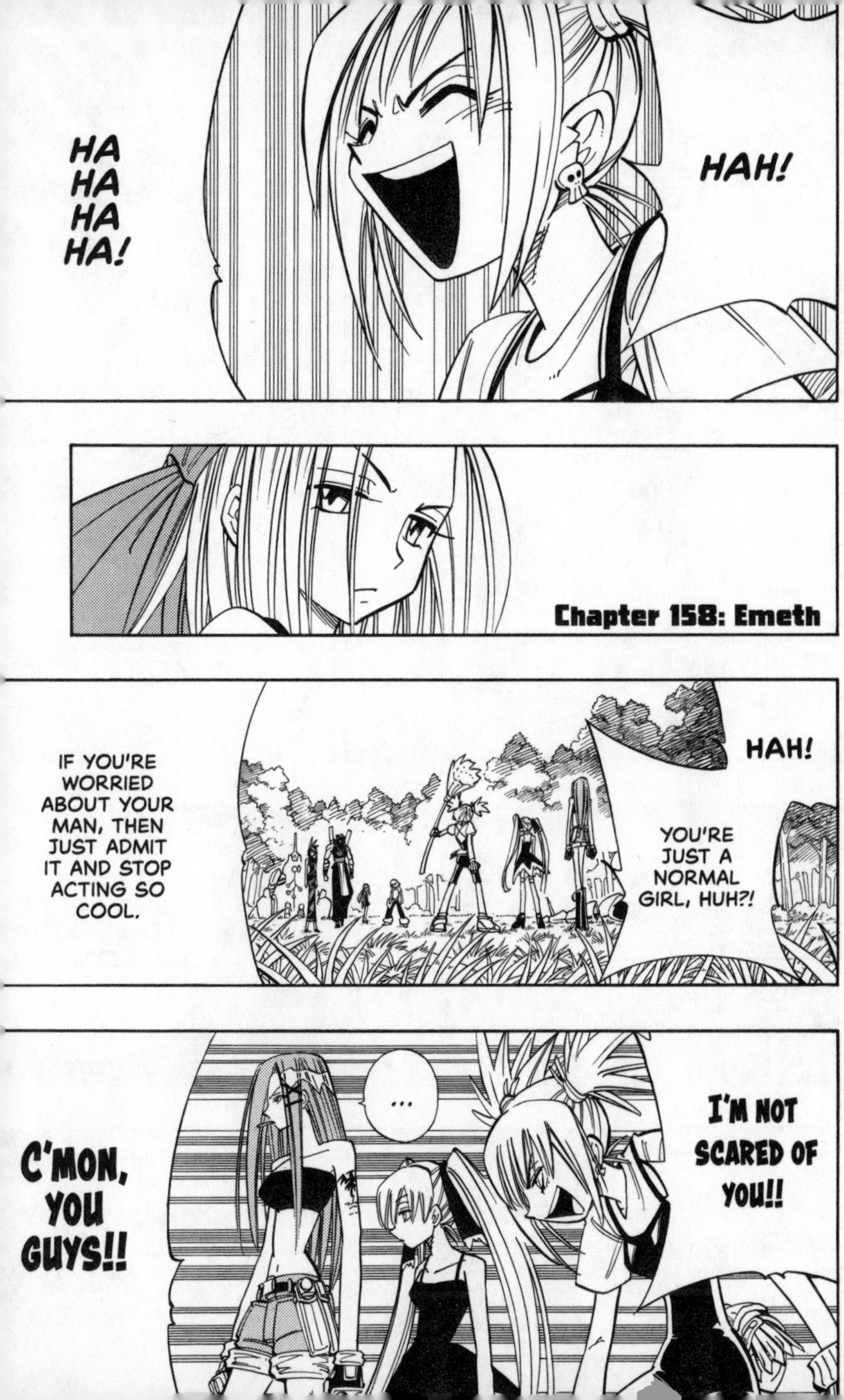
HAH!
HA HA HA HA!
Chapter 158: Emeth
HAH!
YOU'RE JUST A NORMAL GIRL, HUH?!
IF YOU'RE WORRIED ABOUT YOUR MAN, THEN JUST ADMIT IT AND STOP ACTING SO COOL.
I'M NOT SCARED OF YOU!!
...
C'MON, YOU GUYS!!

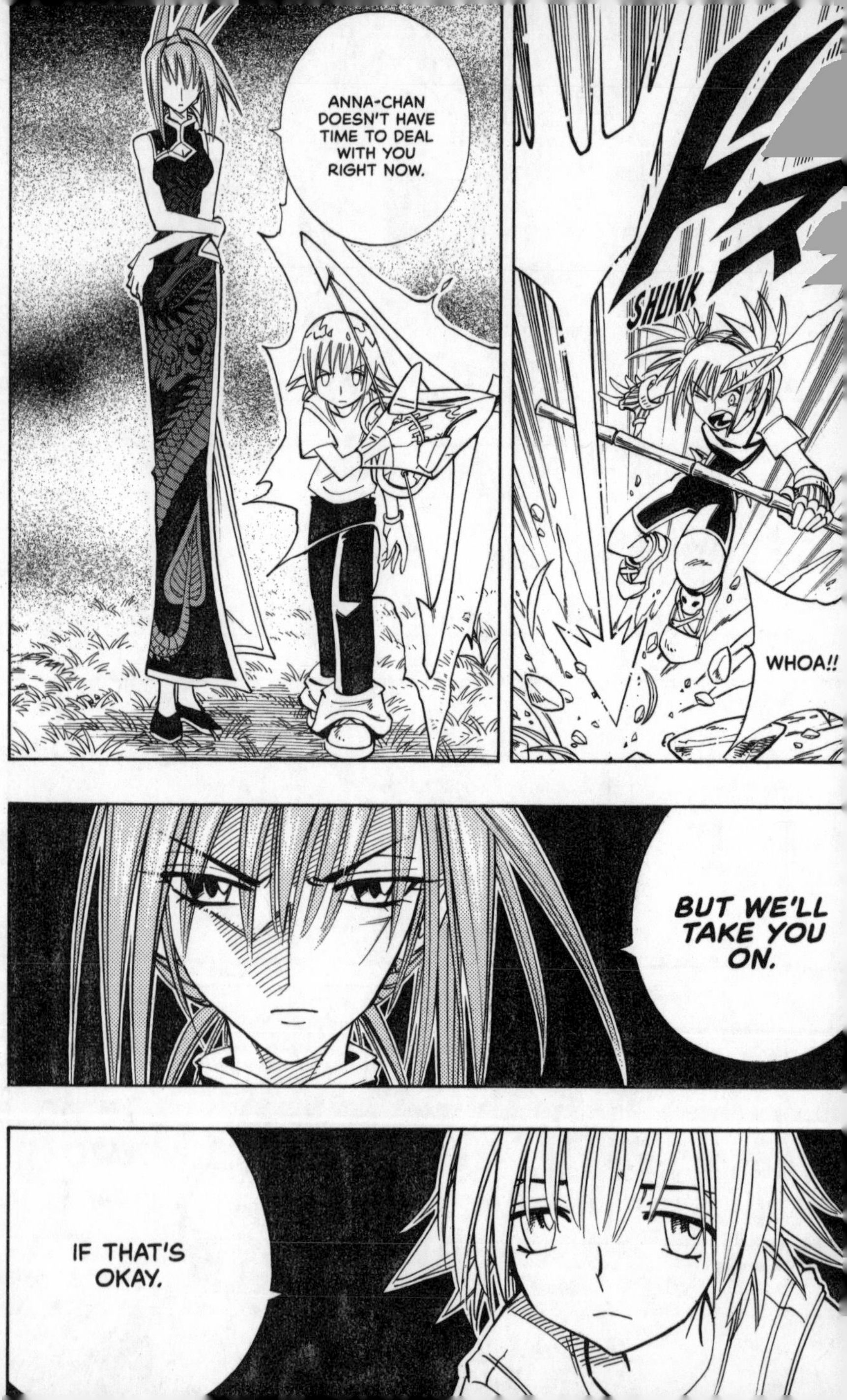
SHUNK
WHOA!!
ANNA-CHAN DOESN'T HAVE TIME TO DEAL WITH YOU RIGHT NOW.
BUT WE'LL TAKE YOU ON.
IF THAT'S OKAY.

Chapter 158: Emeth

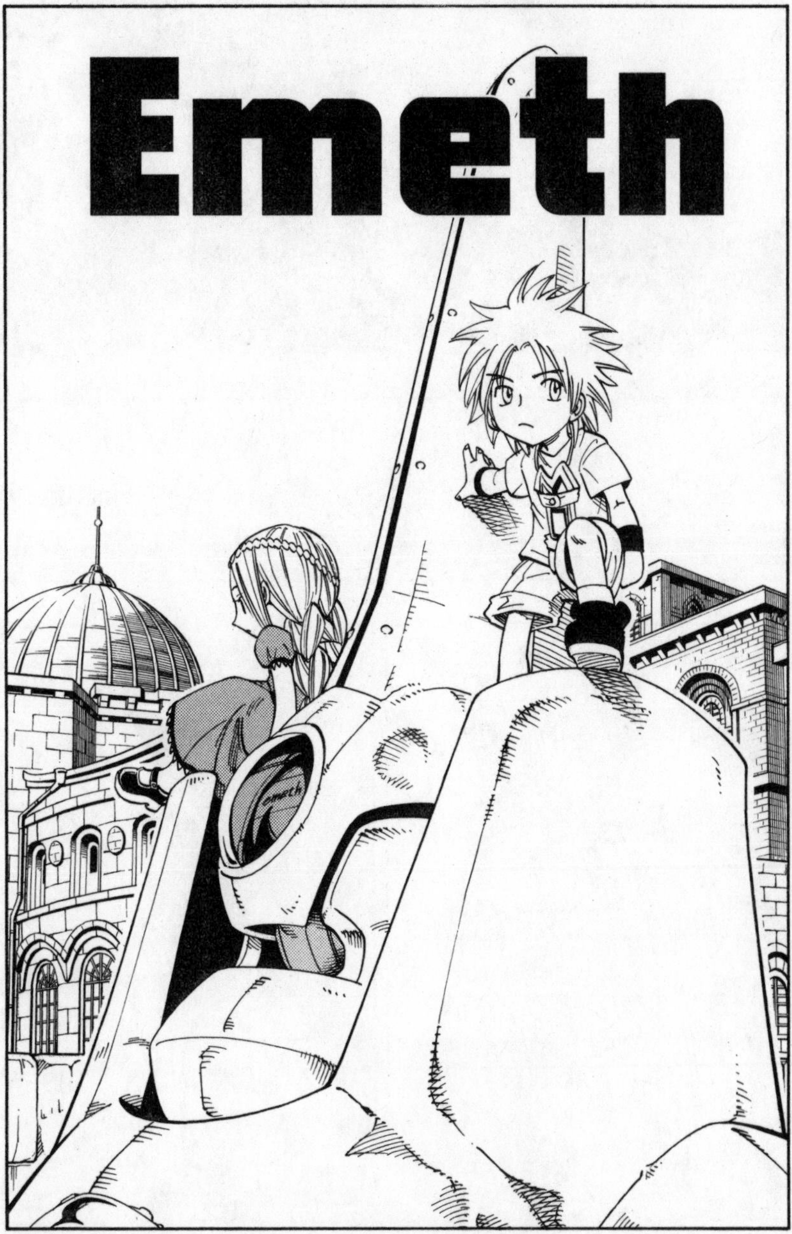
emeth

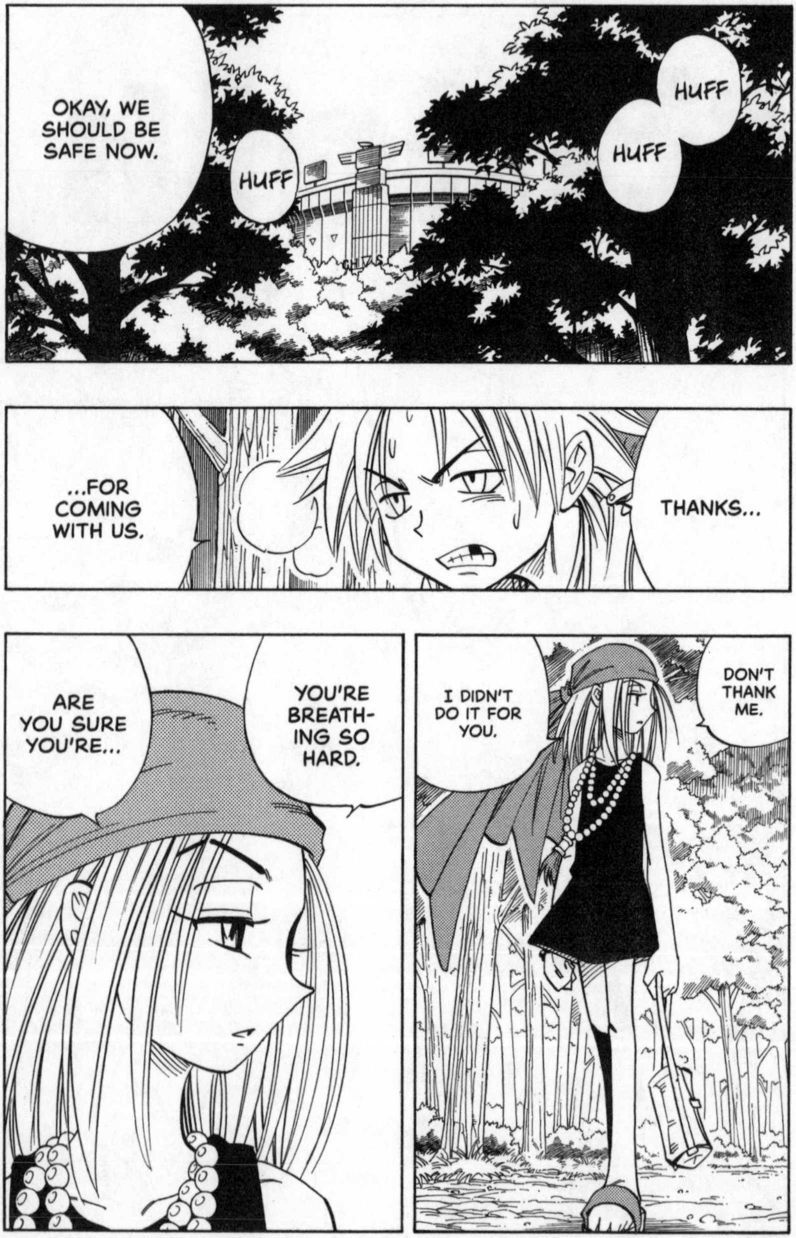
HUFF
HUFF
OKAY, WE SHOULD BE SAFE NOW.
HUFF
THANKS...
...FOR COMING WITH US.
DON'T THANK ME.
I DIDN'T DO IT FOR YOU.
YOU'RE BREATH-ING SO HARD.
ARE YOU SURE YOU'RE...

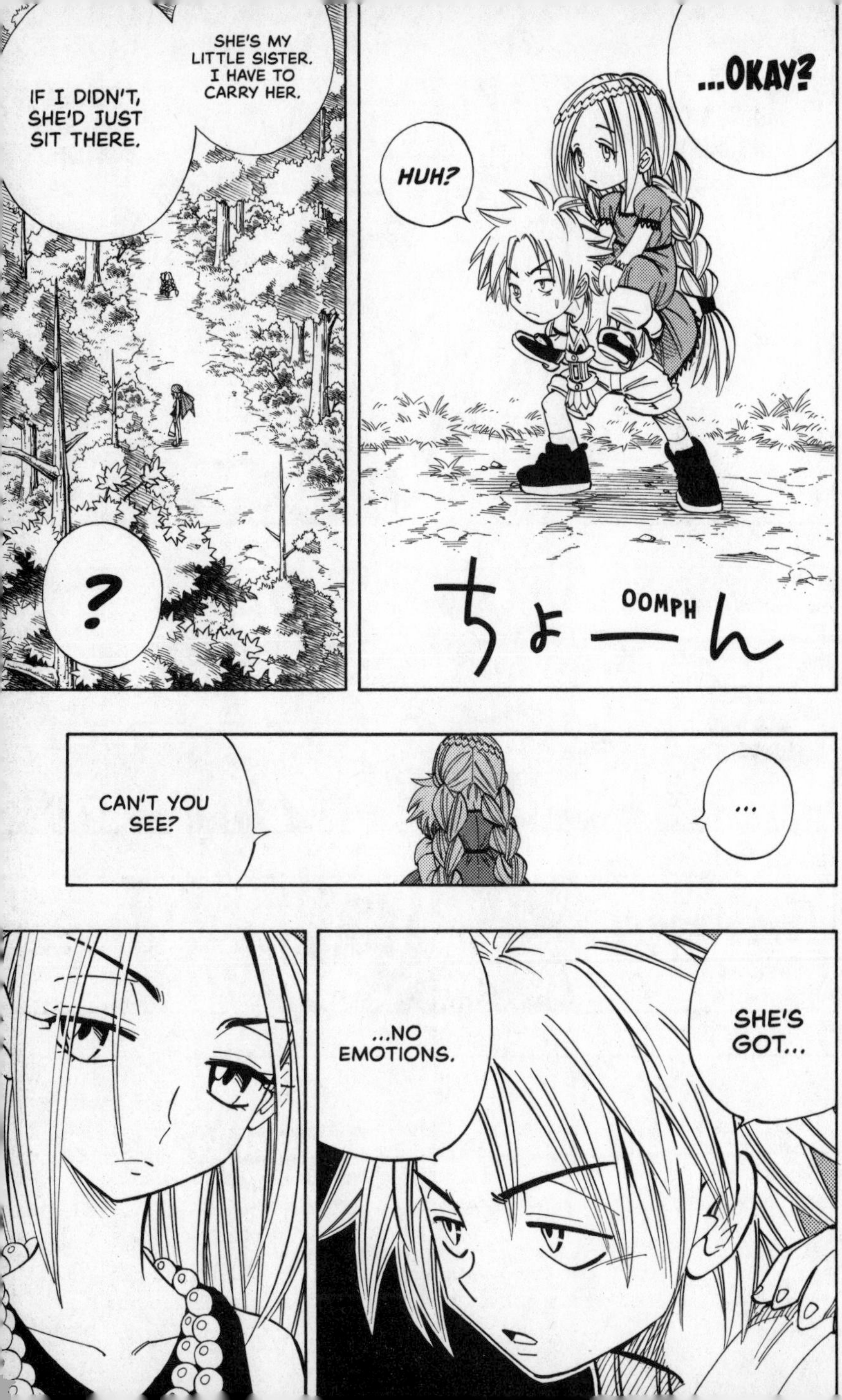
...OKAY?
HUH?
ちょーん
OOMPH
SHE'S MY LITTLE SISTER. I HAVE TO CARRY HER.
IF I DIDN'T, SHE'D JUST SIT THERE.
?
...
CAN'T YOU SEE?
SHE'S GOT...
...NO EMOTIONS.

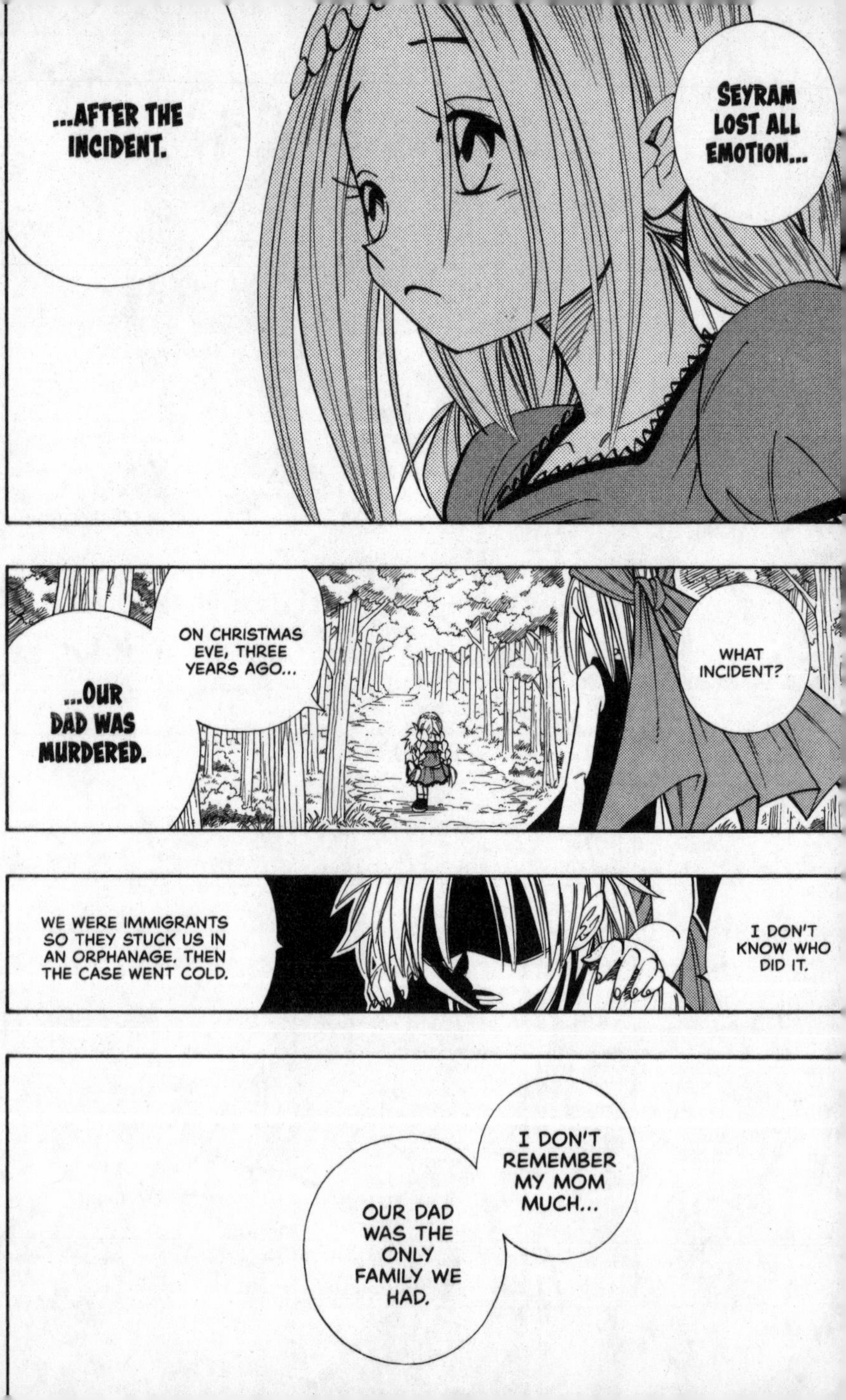
SEYRAM LOST ALL EMOTION...
...AFTER THE INCIDENT.
WHAT INCIDENT?
ON CHRISTMAS EVE, THREE YEARS AGO...
...OUR DAD WAS MURDERED.
I DON'T KNOW WHO DID IT.
WE WERE IMMIGRANTS SO THEY STUCK US IN AN ORPHANAGE. THEN THE CASE WENT COLD.
I DON'T REMEMBER MY MOM MUCH...
OUR DAD WAS THE ONLY FAMILY WE HAD.

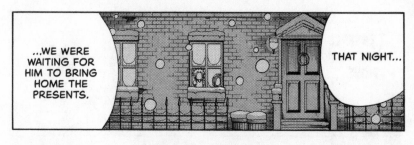

THAT NIGHT...
...WE WERE WAITING FOR HIM TO BRING HOME THE PRESENTS.
NEXT TIME WE SAW HIM...
...HE WAS A COLD, DEAD BODY. SOMEONE HAD TAKEN ALL OUR PRESENTS AND KILLED HIM.
SEYRAM HAD GONE OUT TO LOOK FOR HIM...
...AND FOUND HIM LIKE THAT.
SHE'S BEEN LIKE THIS EVER SINCE.
SO I HAVE TO TAKE CARE OF HER.
BUT I'M GOING TO MAKE HER RIGHT AGAIN SOMEDAY.

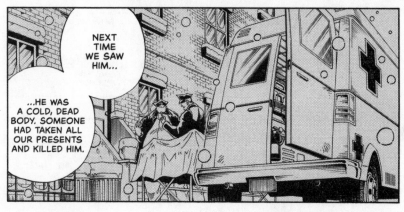

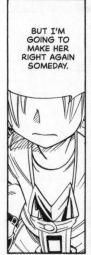

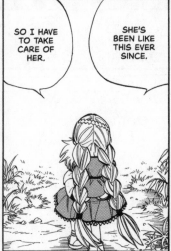

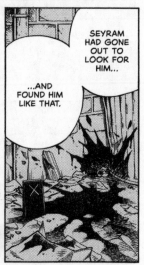

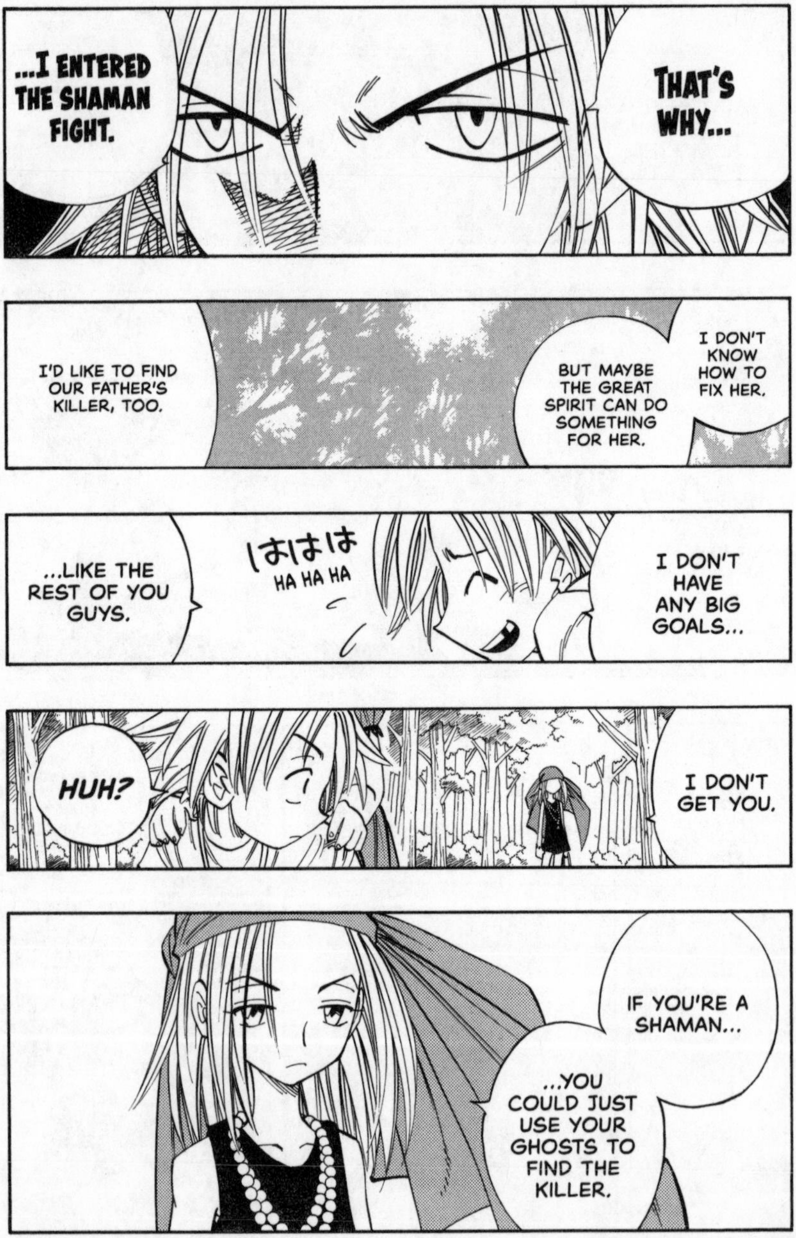
THAT'S WHY...
...I ENTERED THE SHAMAN FIGHT.
I DON'T KNOW HOW TO FIX HER.
BUT MAYBE THE GREAT SPIRIT CAN DO SOMETHING FOR HER.
I'D LIKE TO FIND OUR FATHER'S KILLER, TOO.
I DON'T HAVE ANY BIG GOALS...
ははは
HA HA HA
...LIKE THE REST OF YOU GUYS.
I DON'T GET YOU.
HUH?
IF YOU'RE A SHAMAN...
...YOU COULD JUST USE YOUR GHOSTS TO FIND THE KILLER.

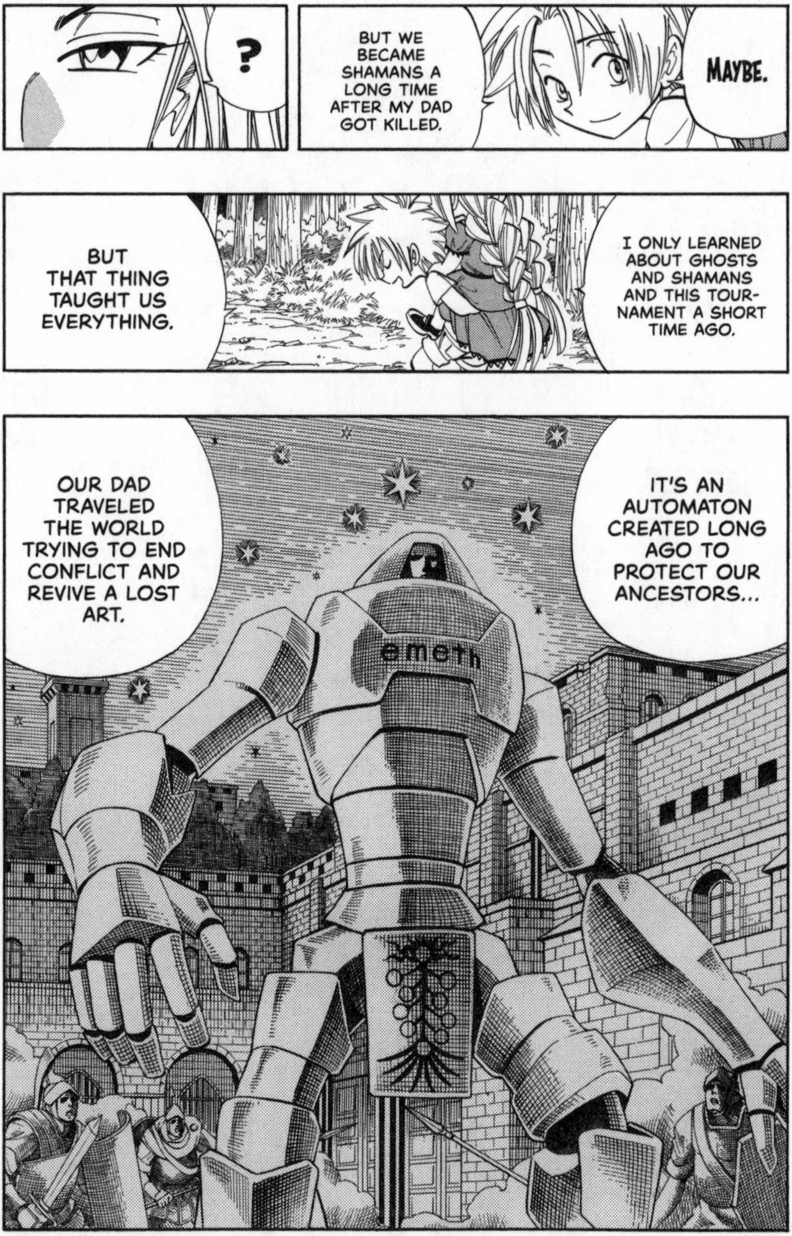
MAYBE.
BUT WE BECAME SHAMANS A LONG TIME AFTER MY DAD GOT KILLED.
?
I ONLY LEARNED ABOUT GHOSTS AND SHAMANS AND THIS TOURNAMENT A SHORT TIME AGO.
BUT THAT THING TAUGHT US EVERYTHING.
IT'S AN AUTOMATON CREATED LONG AGO TO PROTECT OUR ANCESTORS...
OUR DAD TRAVELED THE WORLD TRYING TO END CONFLICT AND REVIVE A LOST ART.
emeth

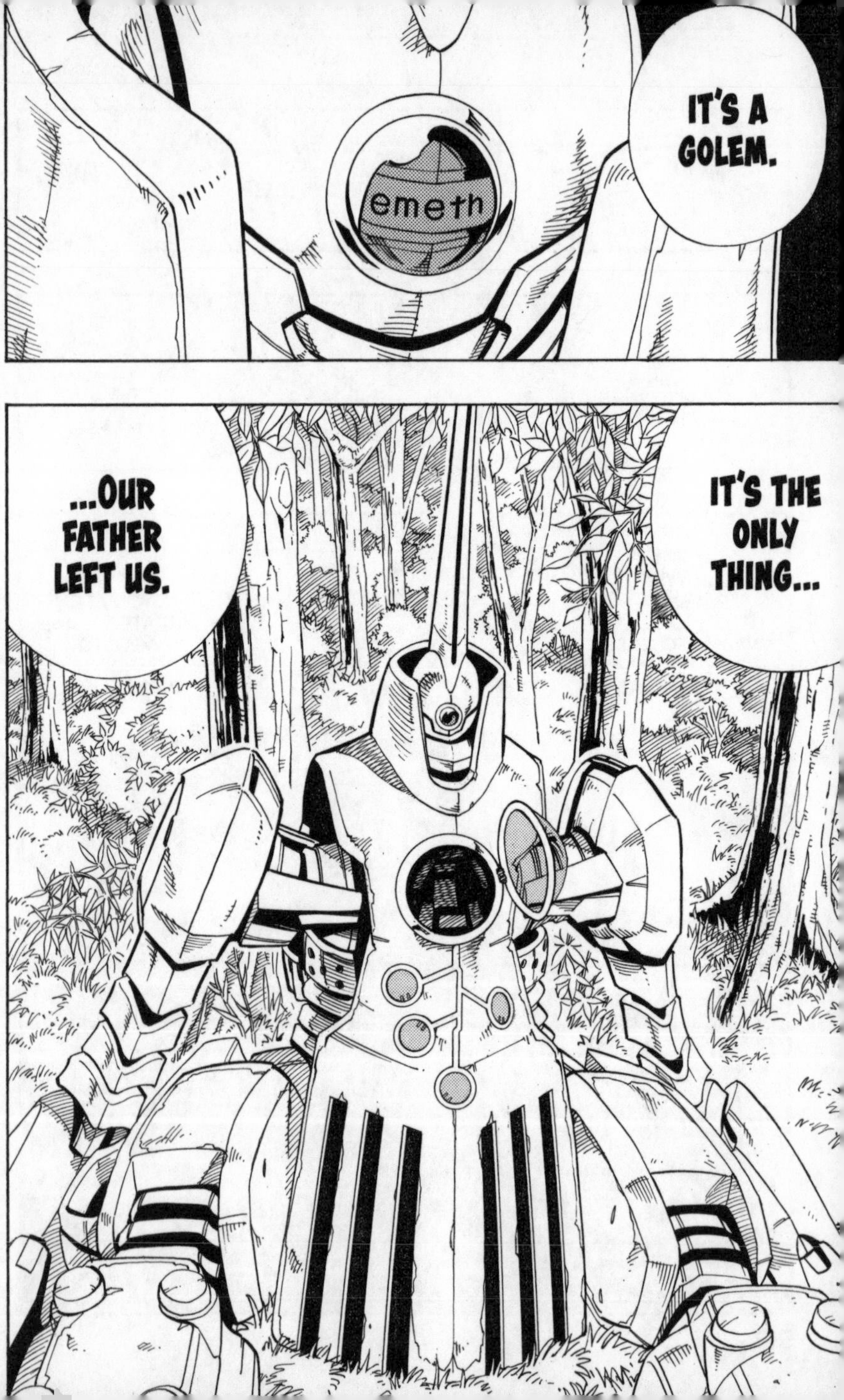
IT'S A GOLEM.
emeth
IT'S THE ONLY THING...
...OUR FATHER LEFT US.

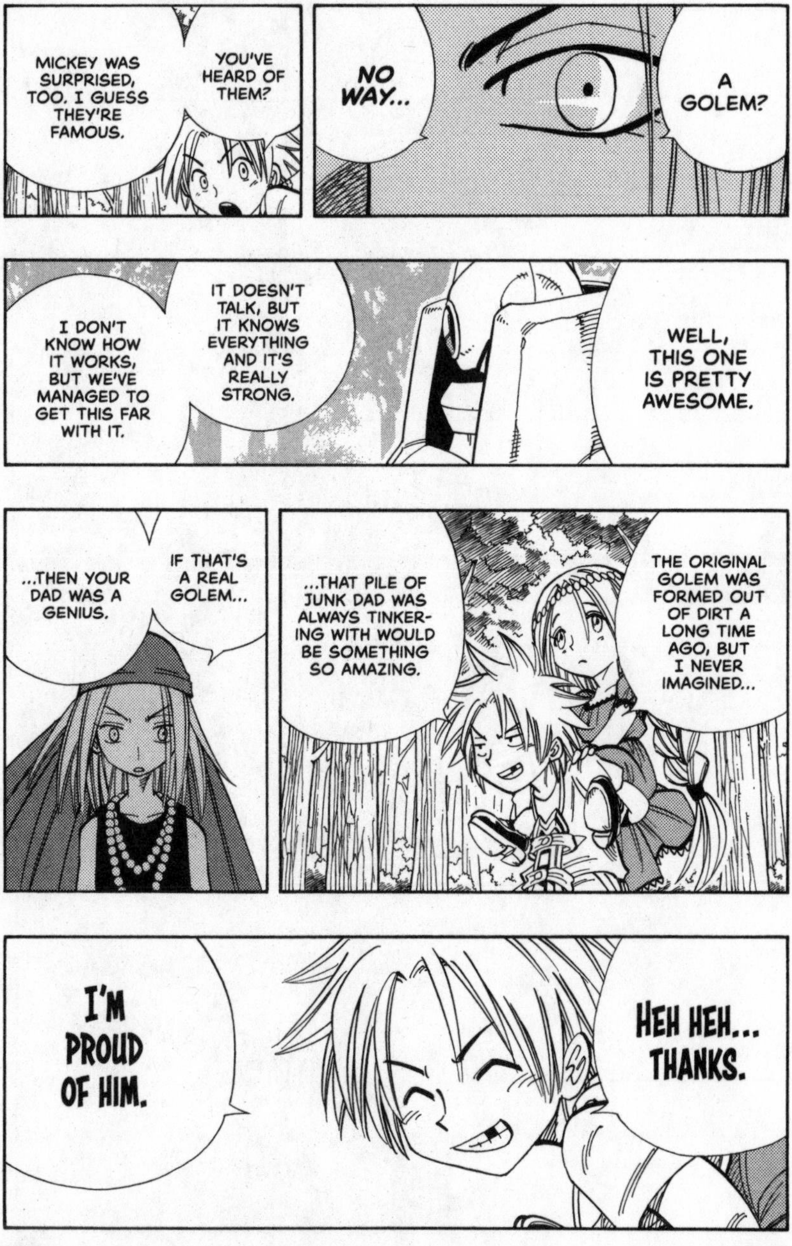
A GOLEM?
NO WAY...
YOU'VE HEARD OF THEM?
MICKEY WAS SURPRISED, TOO. I GUESS THEY'RE FAMOUS.
WELL, THIS ONE IS PRETTY AWESOME.
IT DOESN'T TALK, BUT IT KNOWS EVERYTHING AND IT'S REALLY STRONG.
I DON'T KNOW HOW IT WORKS, BUT WE'VE MANAGED TO GET THIS FAR WITH IT.
THE ORIGINAL GOLEM WAS FORMED OUT OF DIRT A LONG TIME AGO, BUT I NEVER IMAGINED...
...THAT PILE OF JUNK DAD WAS ALWAYS TINKER-ING WITH WOULD BE SOMETHING SO AMAZING.
IF THAT'S A REAL GOLEM...
...THEN YOUR DAD WAS A GENIUS.
HEH HEH... THANKS.
I'M PROUD OF HIM.

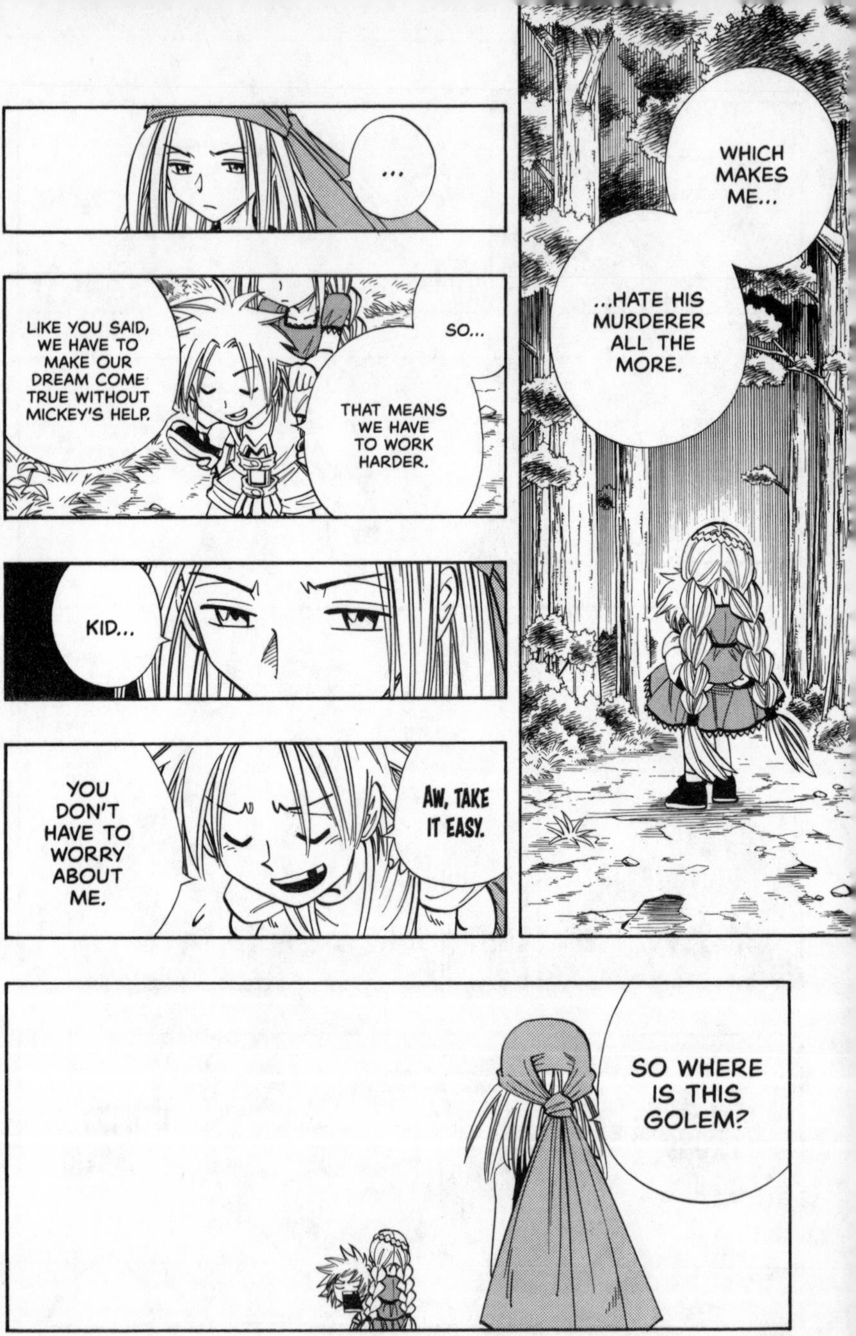
WHICH MAKES ME...
...HATE HIS MURDERER ALL THE MORE.
...
SO...
THAT MEANS WE HAVE TO WORK HARDER.
LIKE YOU SAID, WE HAVE TO MAKE OUR DREAM COME TRUE WITHOUT MICKEY'S HELP.
KID...
AW, TAKE IT EASY.
YOU DON'T HAVE TO WORRY ABOUT ME.
SO WHERE IS THIS GOLEM?

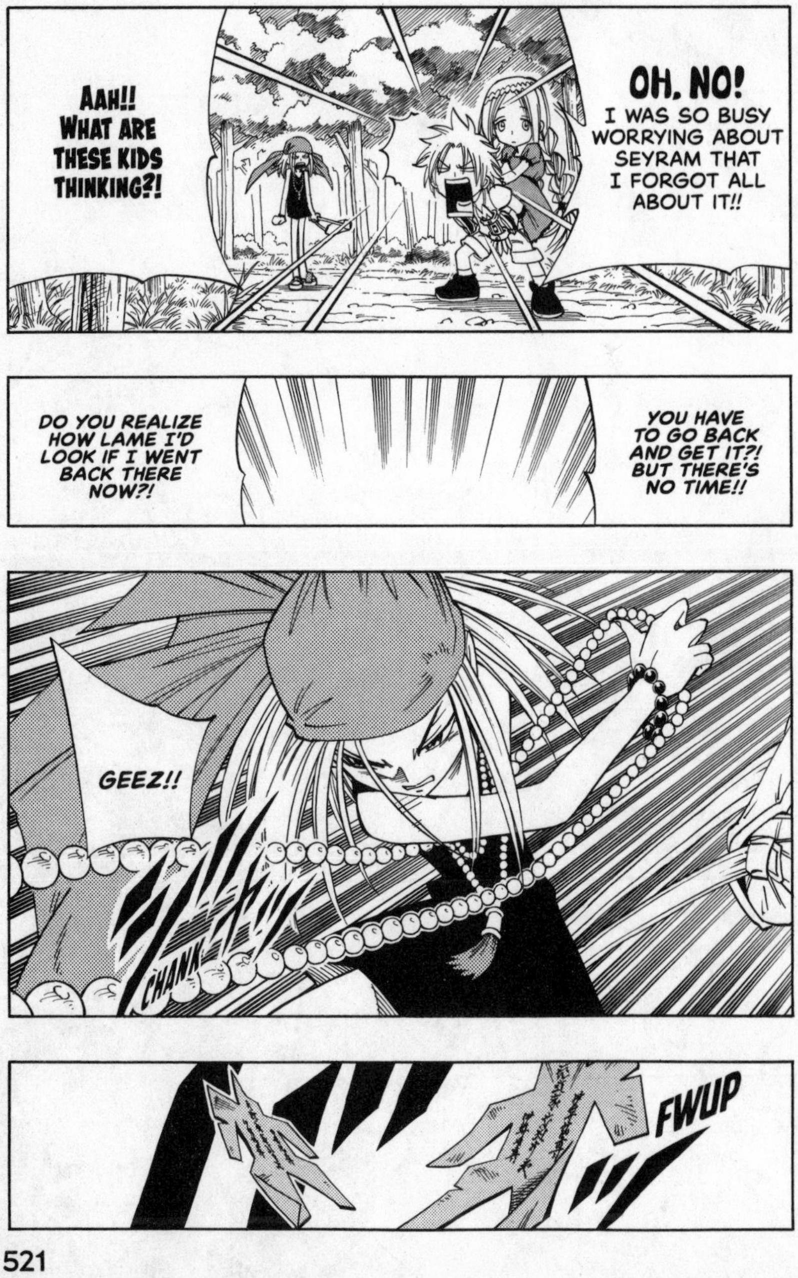
OH, NO!
I WAS SO BUSY WORRYING ABOUT SEYRAM THAT I FORGOT ALL ABOUT IT!!
AAH!! WHAT ARE THESE KIDS THINKING?!
YOU HAVE TO GO BACK AND GET IT?! BUT THERE'S NO TIME!!
DO YOU REALIZE HOW LAME I'D LOOK IF I WENT BACK THERE NOW?!
GEEZ!!
CHANK
FWUP

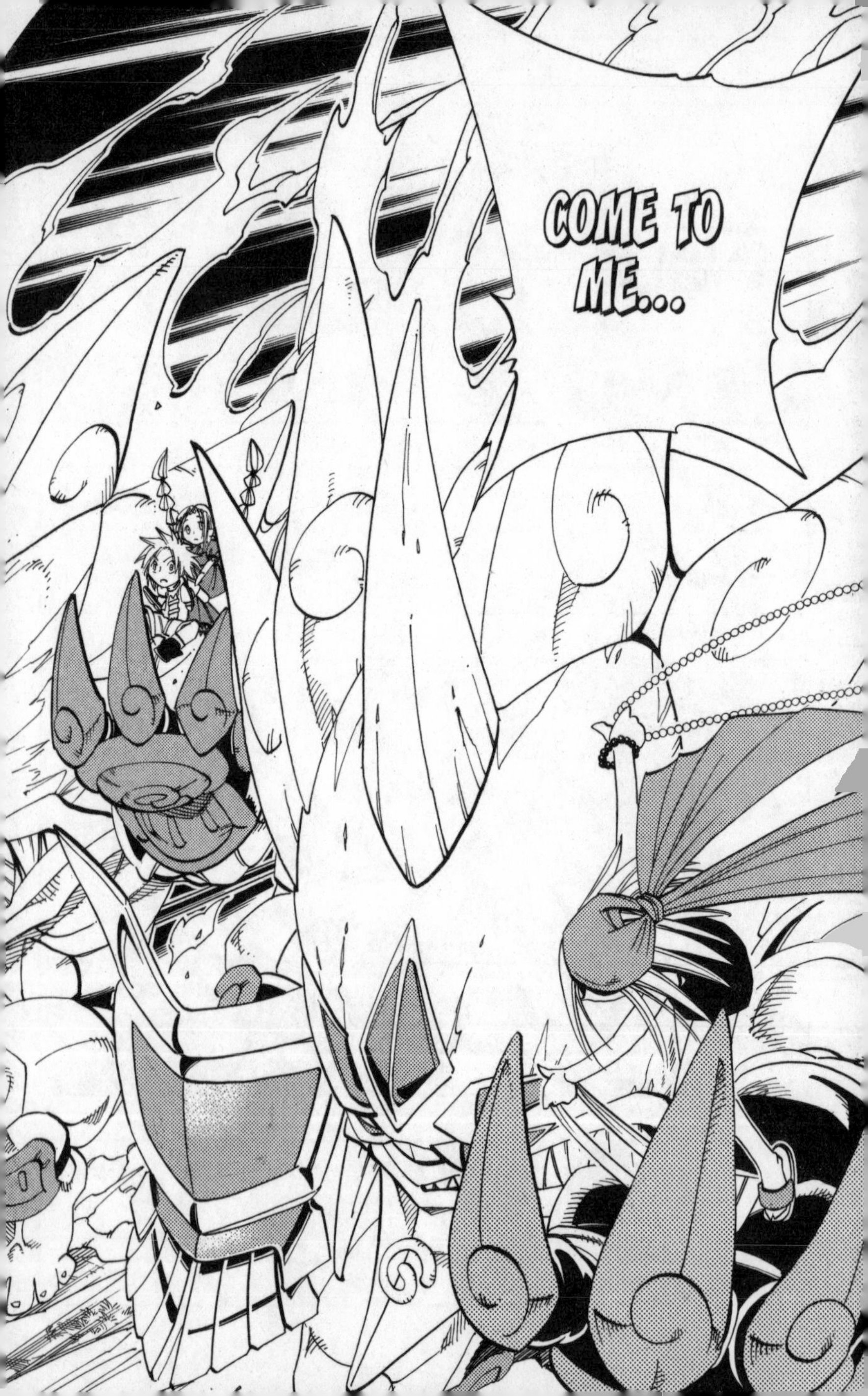
COME TO ME...

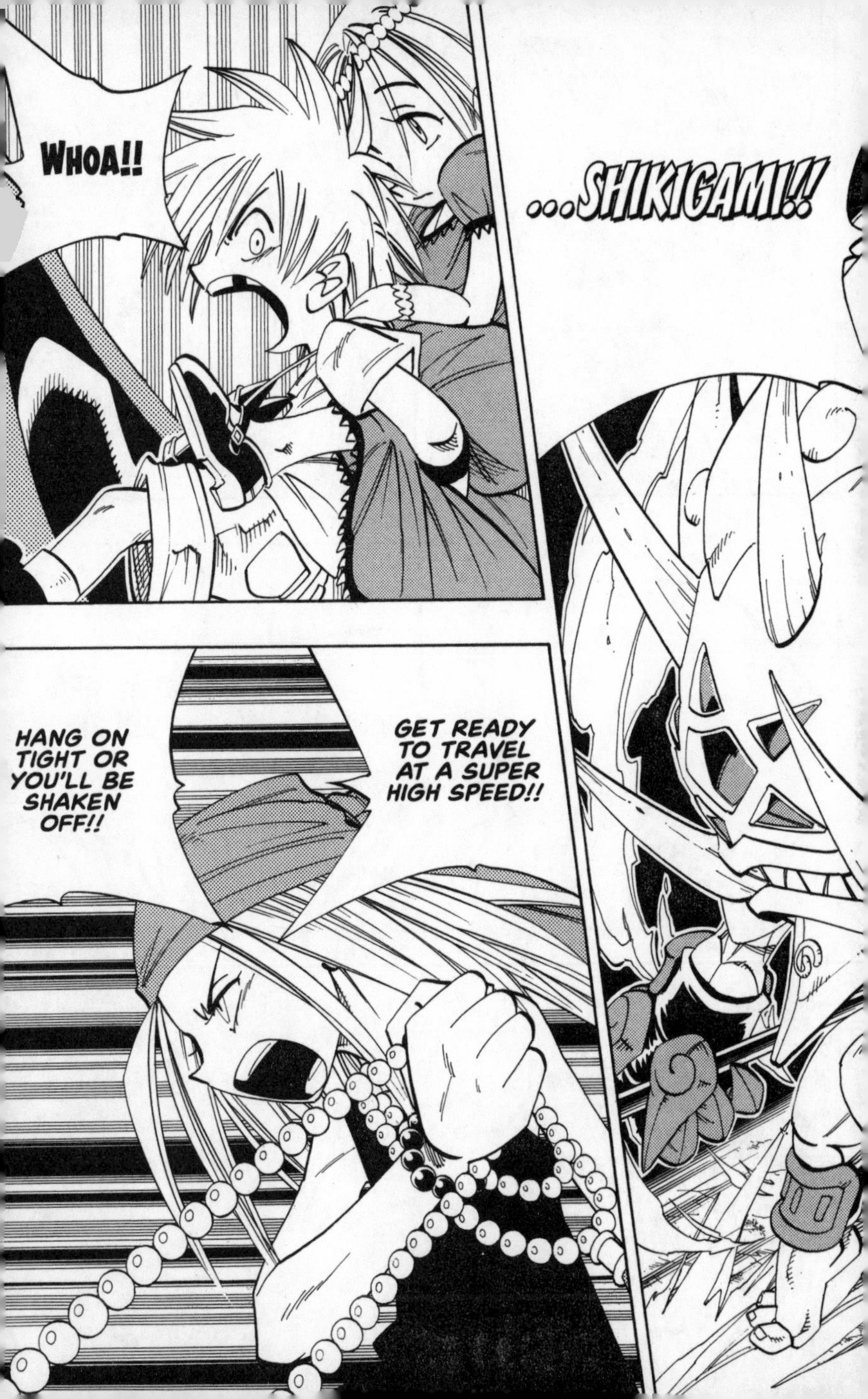
...SHIKIGAMI!!
WHOA!!
GET READY TO TRAVEL AT A SUPER HIGH SPEED!!
HANG ON TIGHT OR YOU'LL BE SHAKEN OFF!!

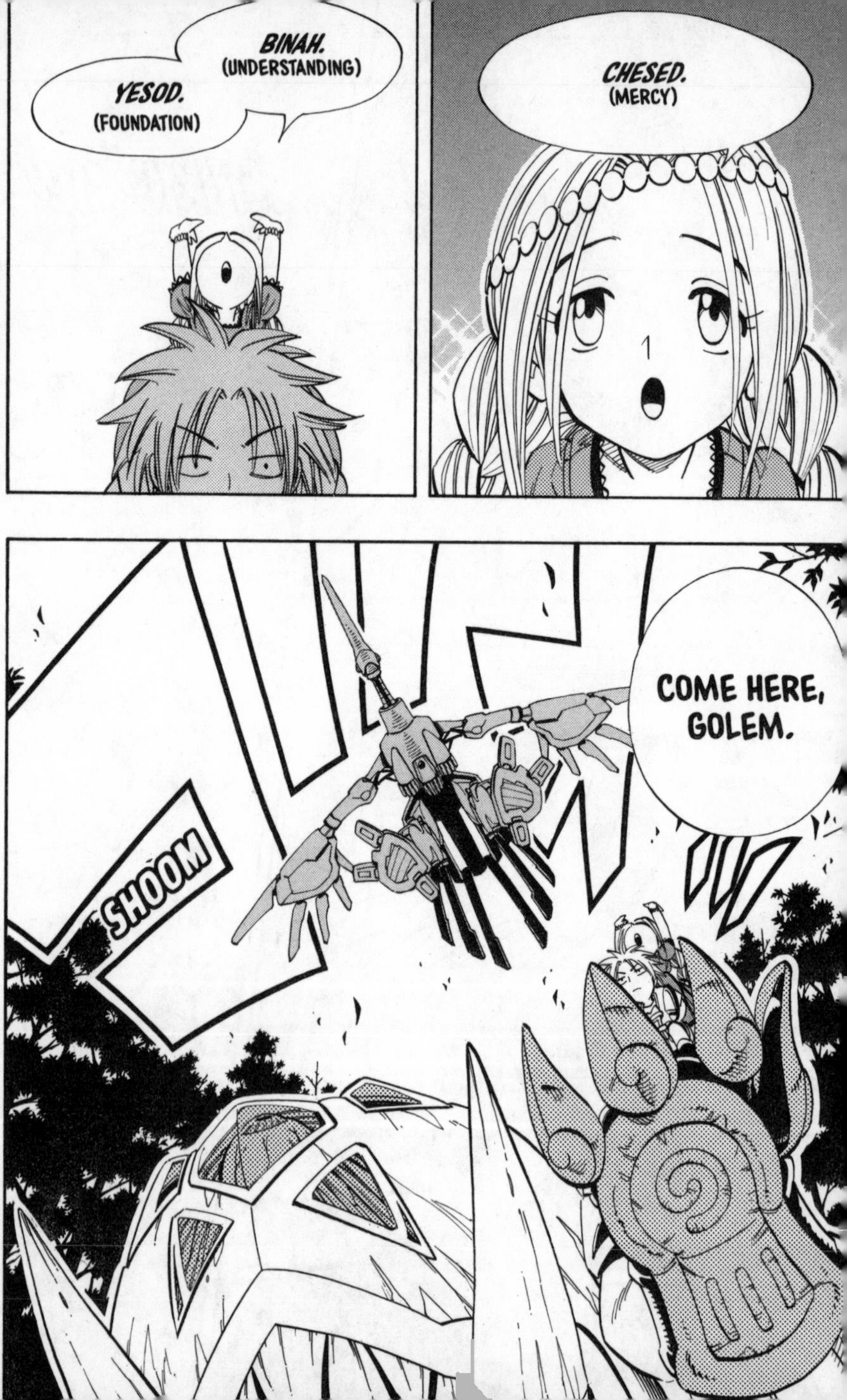
CHESED. (MERCY)
BINAH. (UNDERSTANDING)
YESOD. (FOUNDATION)
COME HERE, GOLEM.
SHOOM

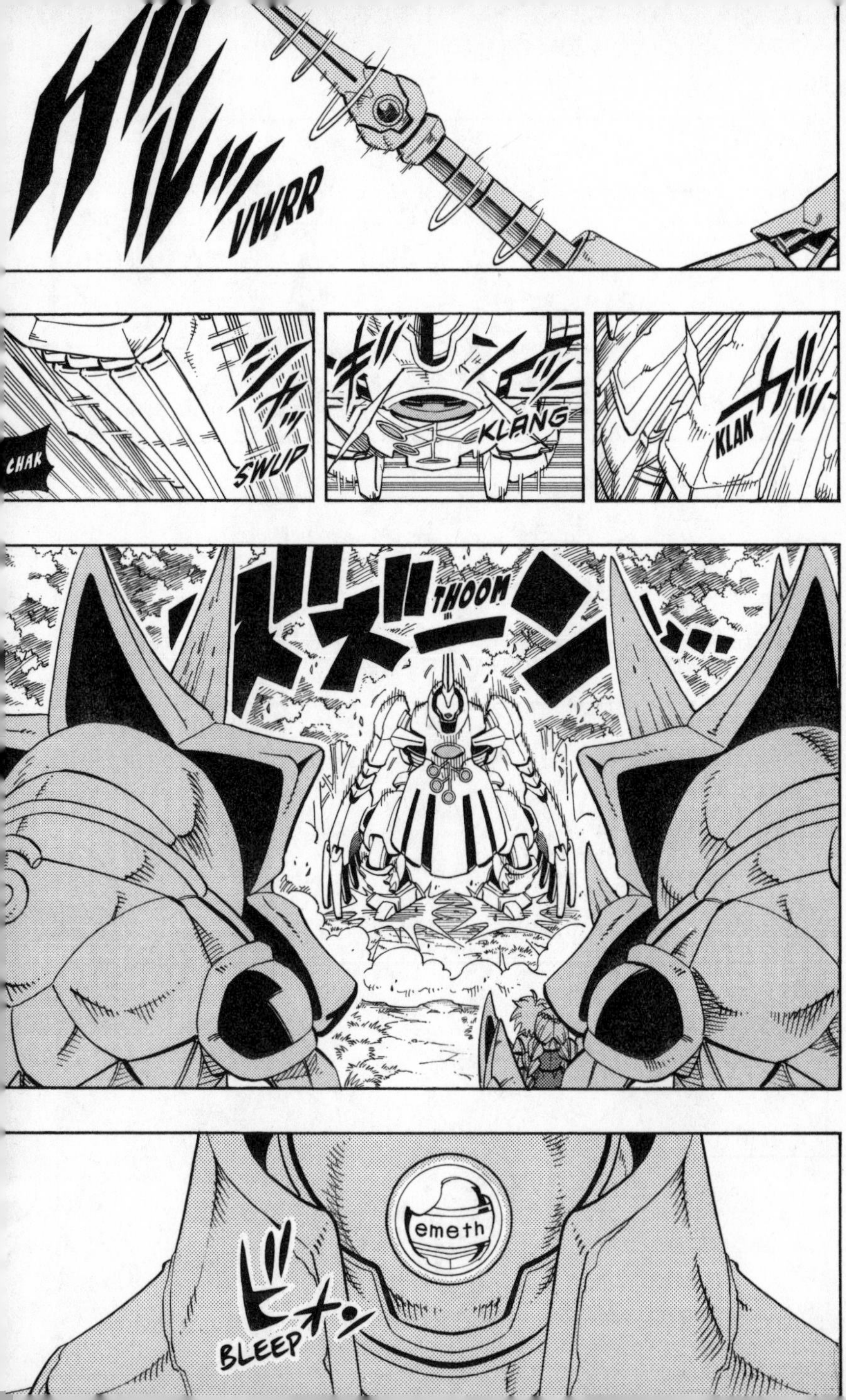
VWRR
KLAK
KLANG
SWUP
CHAK
THOOM
emeth
BLEEP

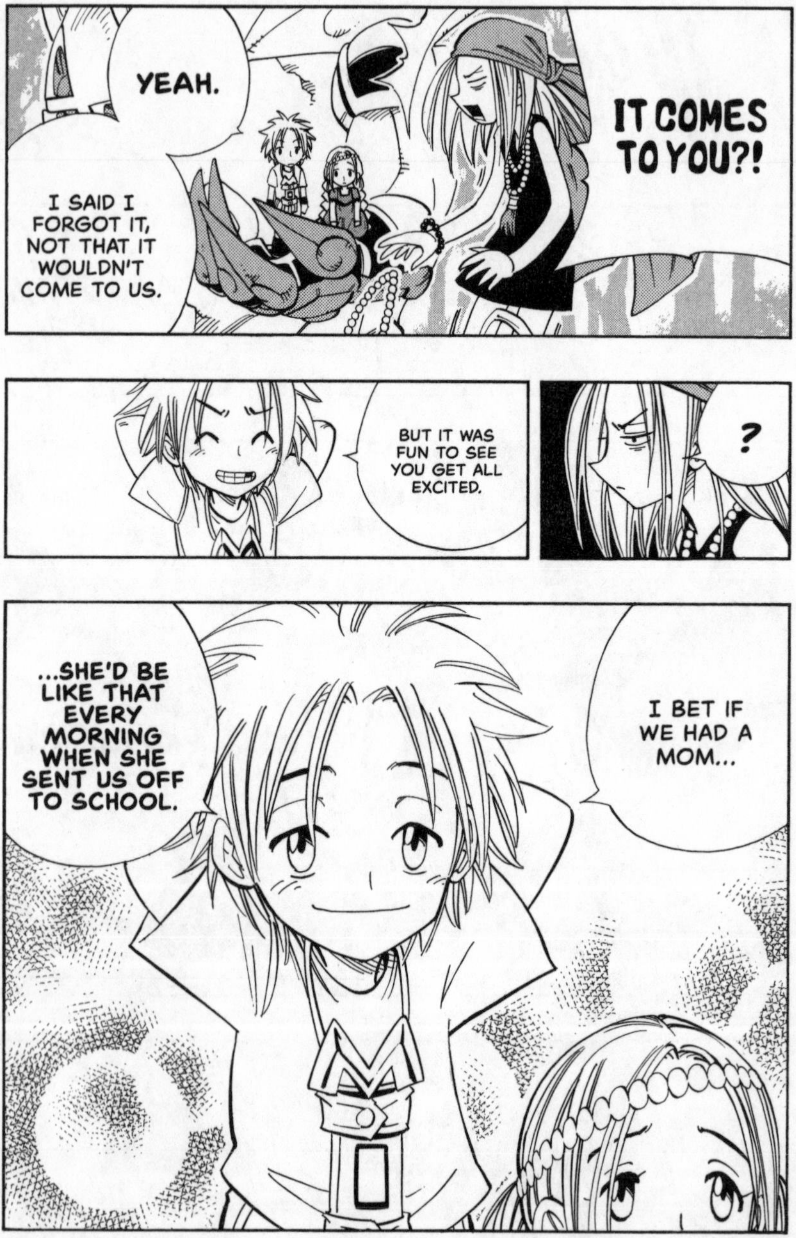
IT COMES TO YOU?!
YEAH.
I SAID I FORGOT IT, NOT THAT IT WOULDN'T COME TO US.
?
BUT IT WAS FUN TO SEE YOU GET ALL EXCITED.
I BET IF WE HAD A MOM...
...SHE'D BE LIKE THAT EVERY MORNING WHEN SHE SENT US OFF TO SCHOOL.

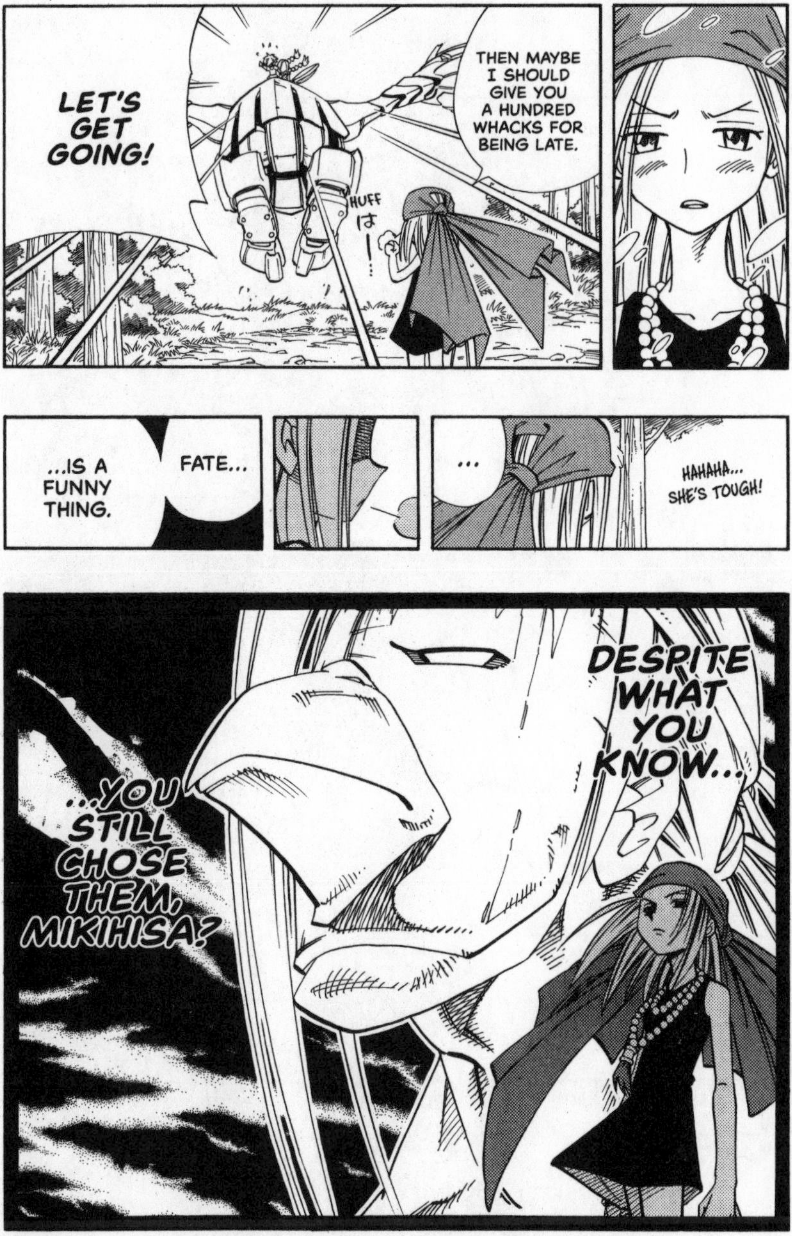
THEN MAYBE I SHOULD GIVE YOU A HUNDRED WHACKS FOR BEING LATE.
LET'S GET GOING!
HUFF
HAHAHA... SHE'S TOUGH!
...
FATE...
...IS A FUNNY THING.
DESPITE WHAT YOU KNOW...
...YOU STILL CHOSE THEM, MIKIHISA?

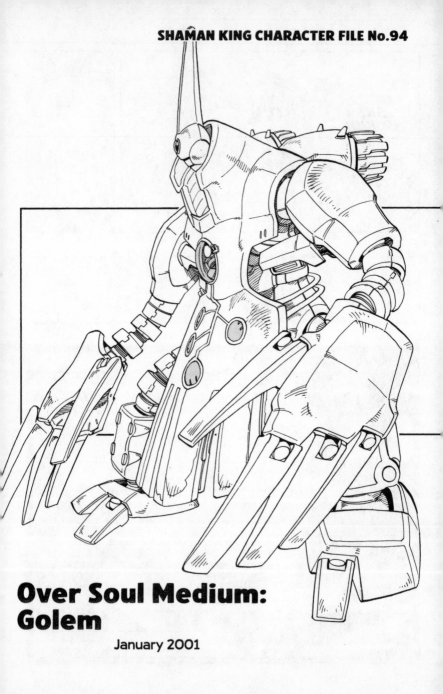

Over Soul Medium:
Golem

January 2001

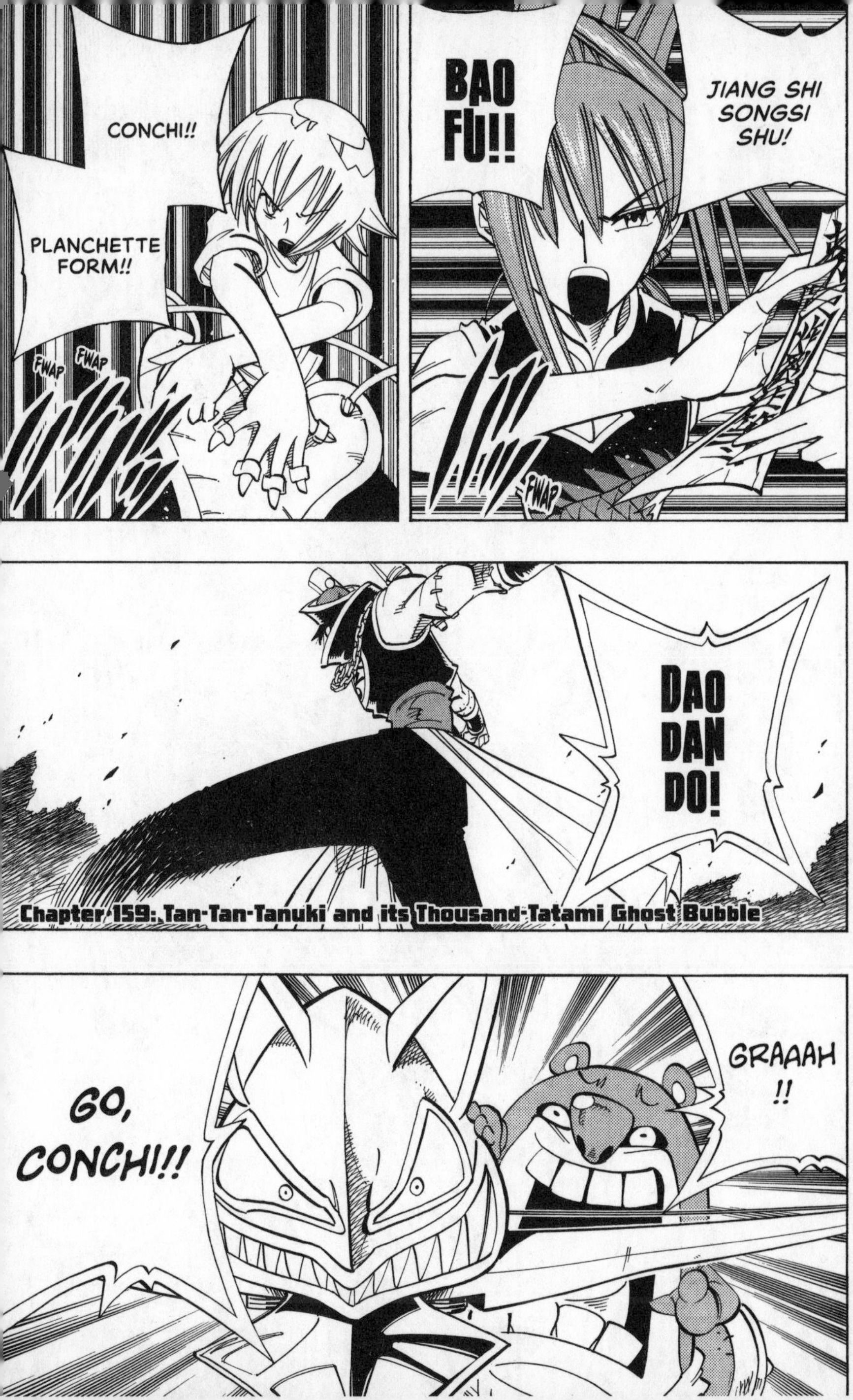
JIANG SHI SONGSI SHU!
BAO FU!!
FWAP
CONCHI!!
PLANCHETTE FORM!!
FWAP
FWAP
DAO DAN DO!
Chapter 159: Tan-Tan-Tanuki and its Thousand-Tatami Ghost Bubble
GRAAAH !!
GO, CONCHI!!

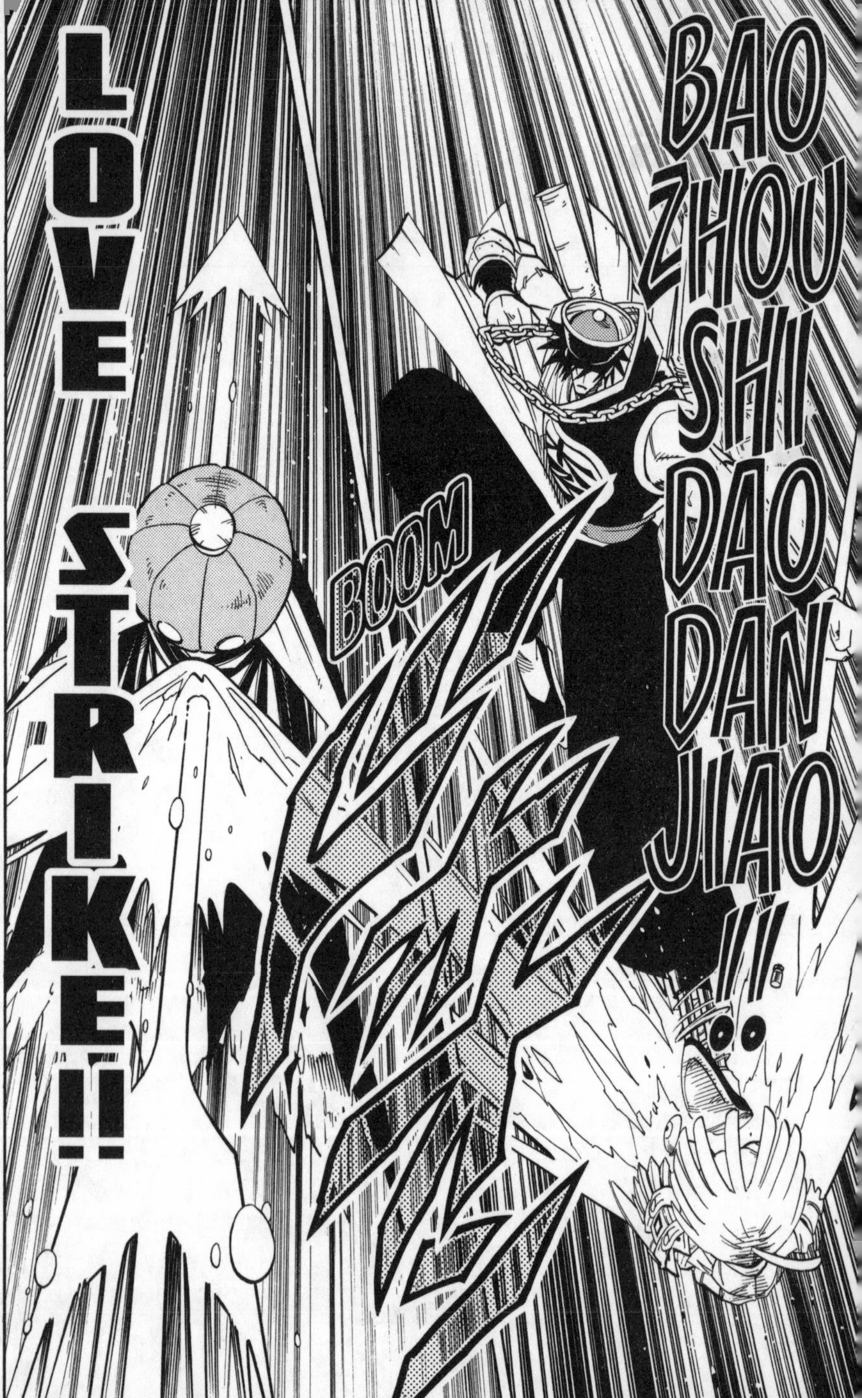
BAO ZHOU SHI DAO DAN JIAO!!
BOOM
LOVE STRIKE!!

Tan-Tan-Tanuki and its Thousand-Tatami Ghost Bubble

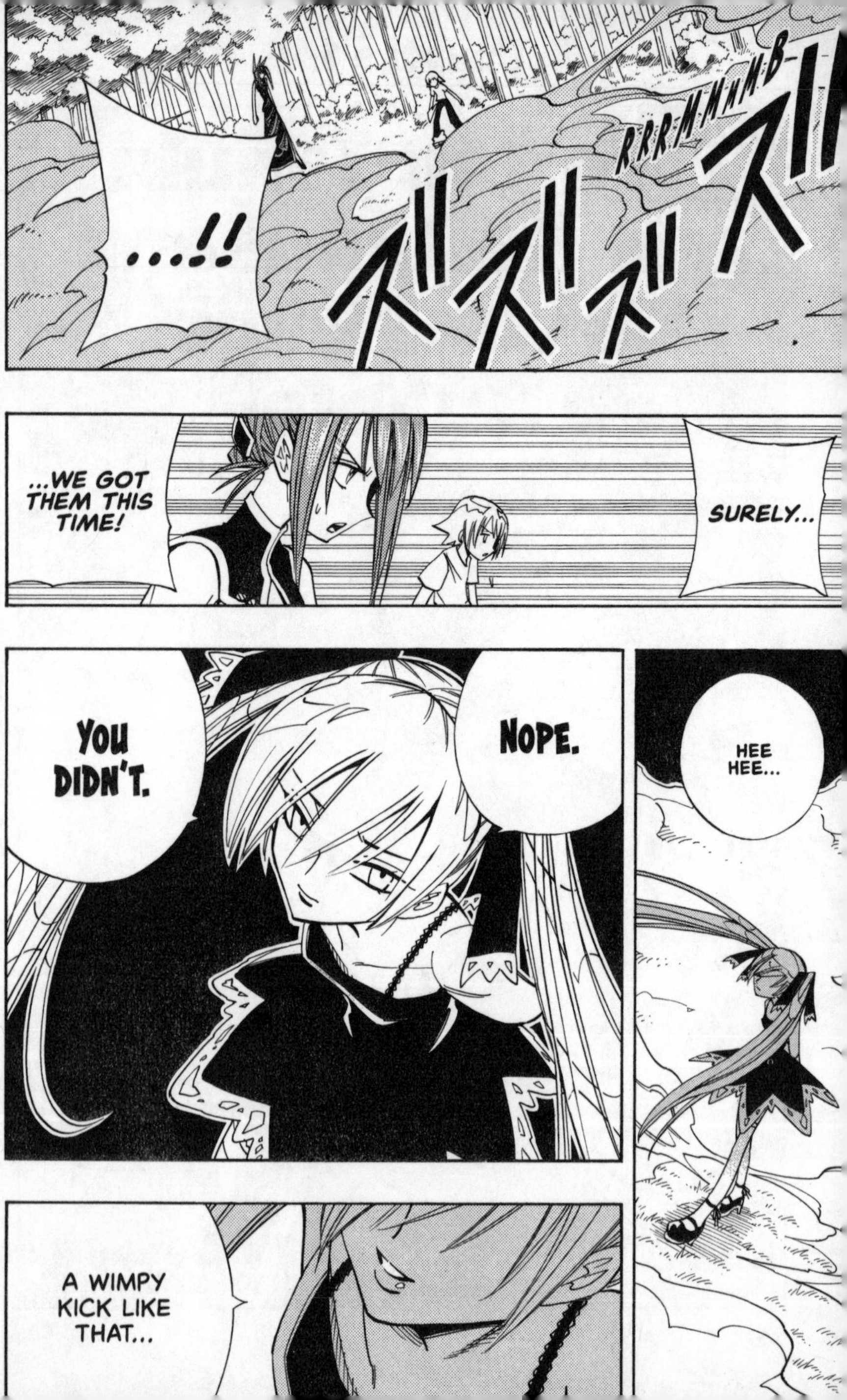
...!!
RRRMMMMMB
ズズズズ
SURELY...
...WE GOT THEM THIS TIME!
HEE HEE...
NOPE.
YOU DIDN'T.
A WIMPY KICK LIKE THAT...

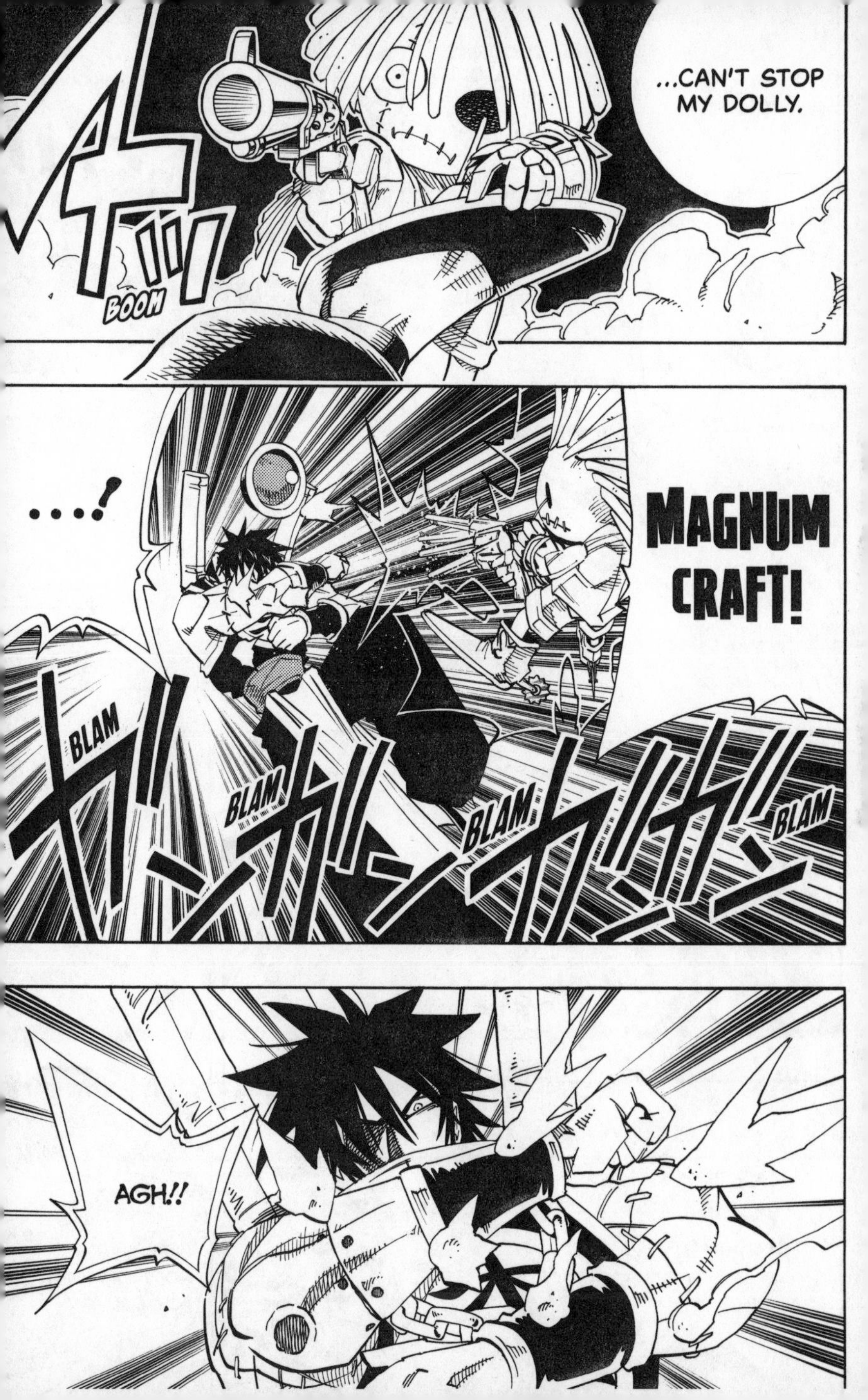
...CAN'T STOP MY DOLLY.
BOOM
MAGNUM CRAFT!
...!
BLAM
BLAM
BLAM
BLAM
AGH!!

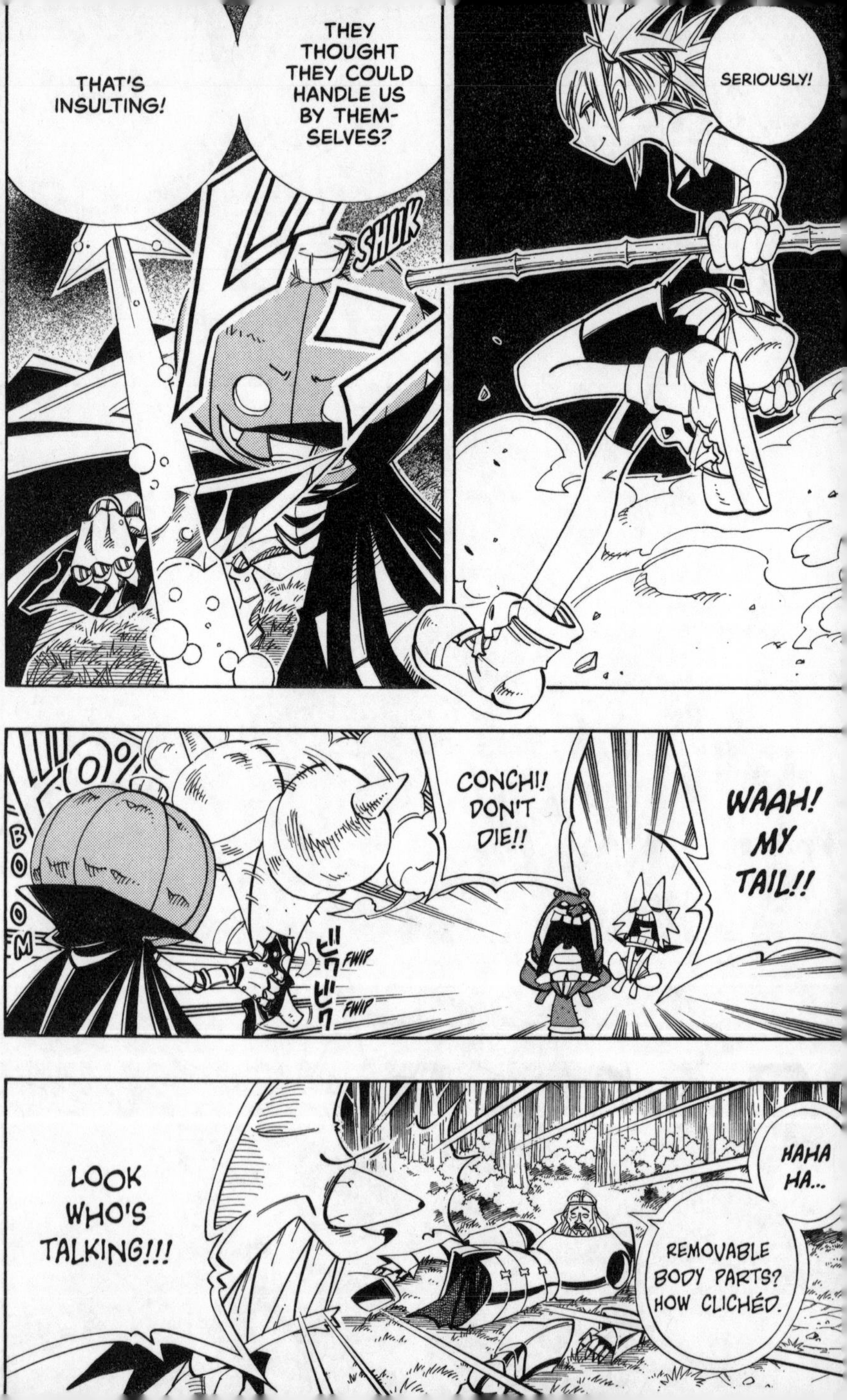
SERIOUSLY!
THEY THOUGHT THEY COULD HANDLE US BY THEM-SELVES?
THAT'S INSULTING!
SHUK
WAAH! MY TAIL!!
CONCHI! DON'T DIE!!
FWIP
FWIP
BOOOM
HAHA HA...
REMOVABLE BODY PARTS? HOW CLICHÉD.
LOOK WHO'S TALKING!!!

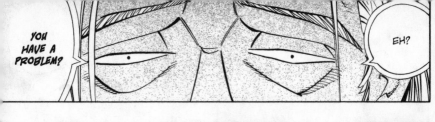

EH?
YOU HAVE A PROBLEM?
GACK!
OH, NO!
WE'RE HAVING ENOUGH TROUBLE WITH THOSE TWO! WE DON'T NEED ANOTHER ENEMY!
PONCHI! CONCHI! GET BACK!
LOWLY ANIMAL SPIRITS...
YOU DARE SPEAK TO ME SO INSOLENT-LY?
I'LL SKEWER YOU!!
KLANG
GWAAH!!

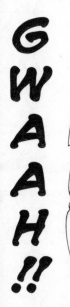

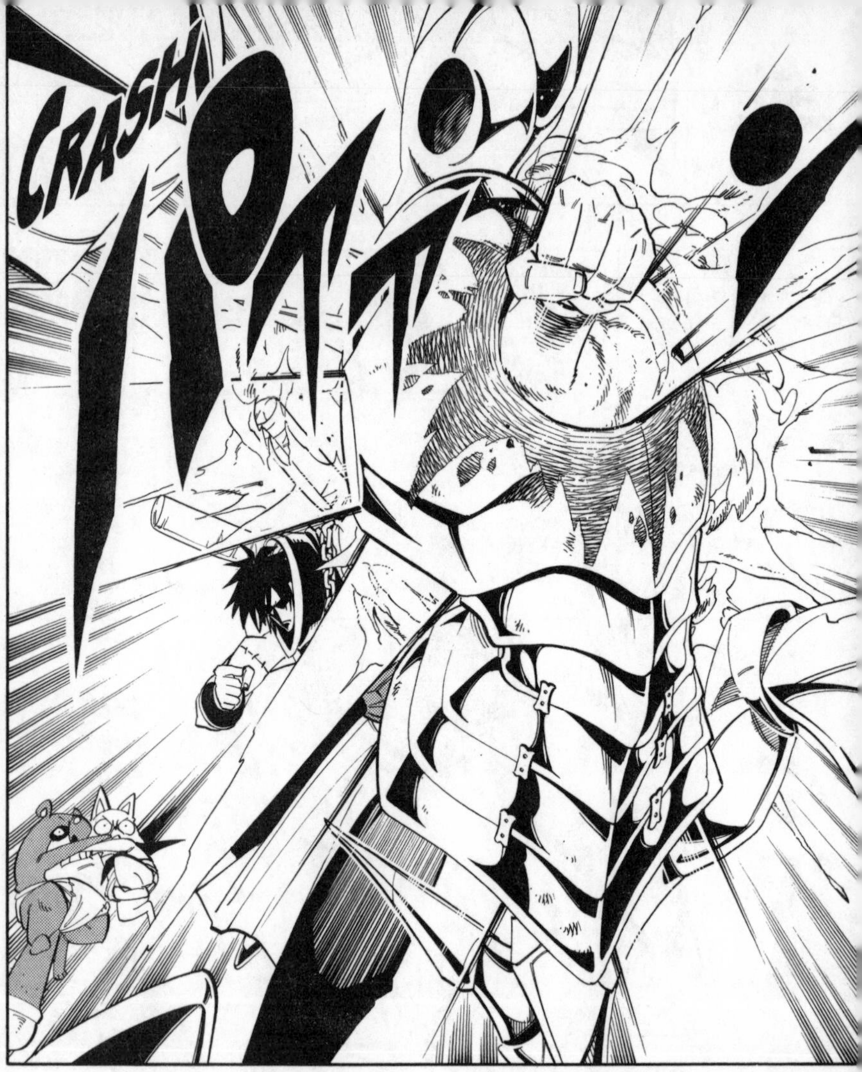
CRASH!
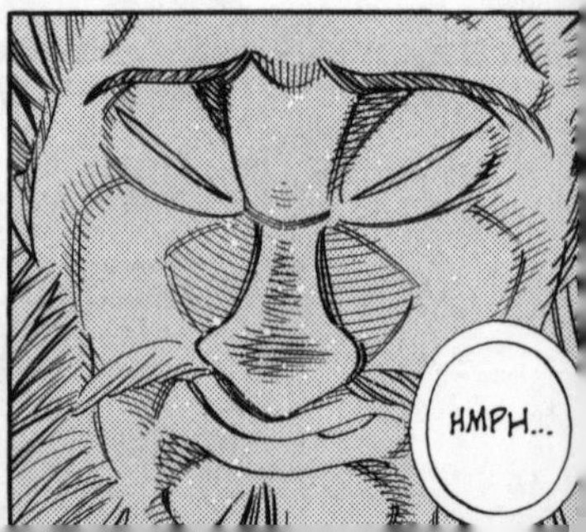
HMPH...
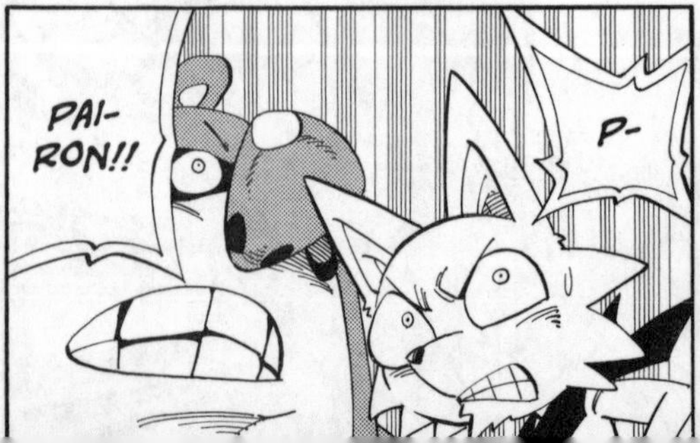
P-
PAI-
RON!!

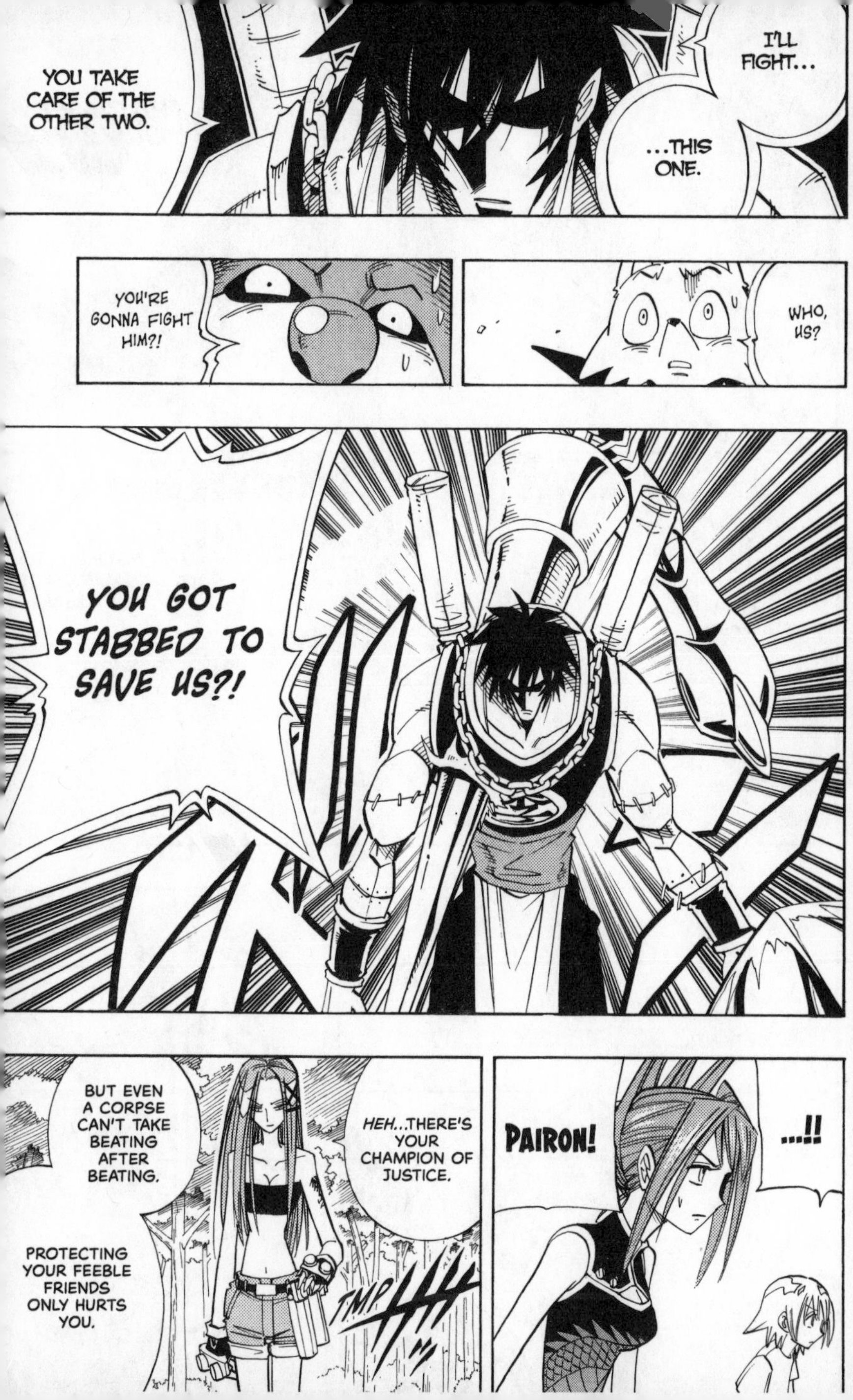
I'LL FIGHT...
...THIS ONE.
YOU TAKE CARE OF THE OTHER TWO.
WHO, US?
YOU'RE GONNA FIGHT HIM?!
YOU GOT STABBED TO SAVE US?!
...!!
PAIRON!
HEH...THERE'S YOUR CHAMPION OF JUSTICE.
BUT EVEN A CORPSE CAN'T TAKE BEATING AFTER BEATING.
PROTECTING YOUR FEEBLE FRIENDS ONLY HURTS YOU.
TMP

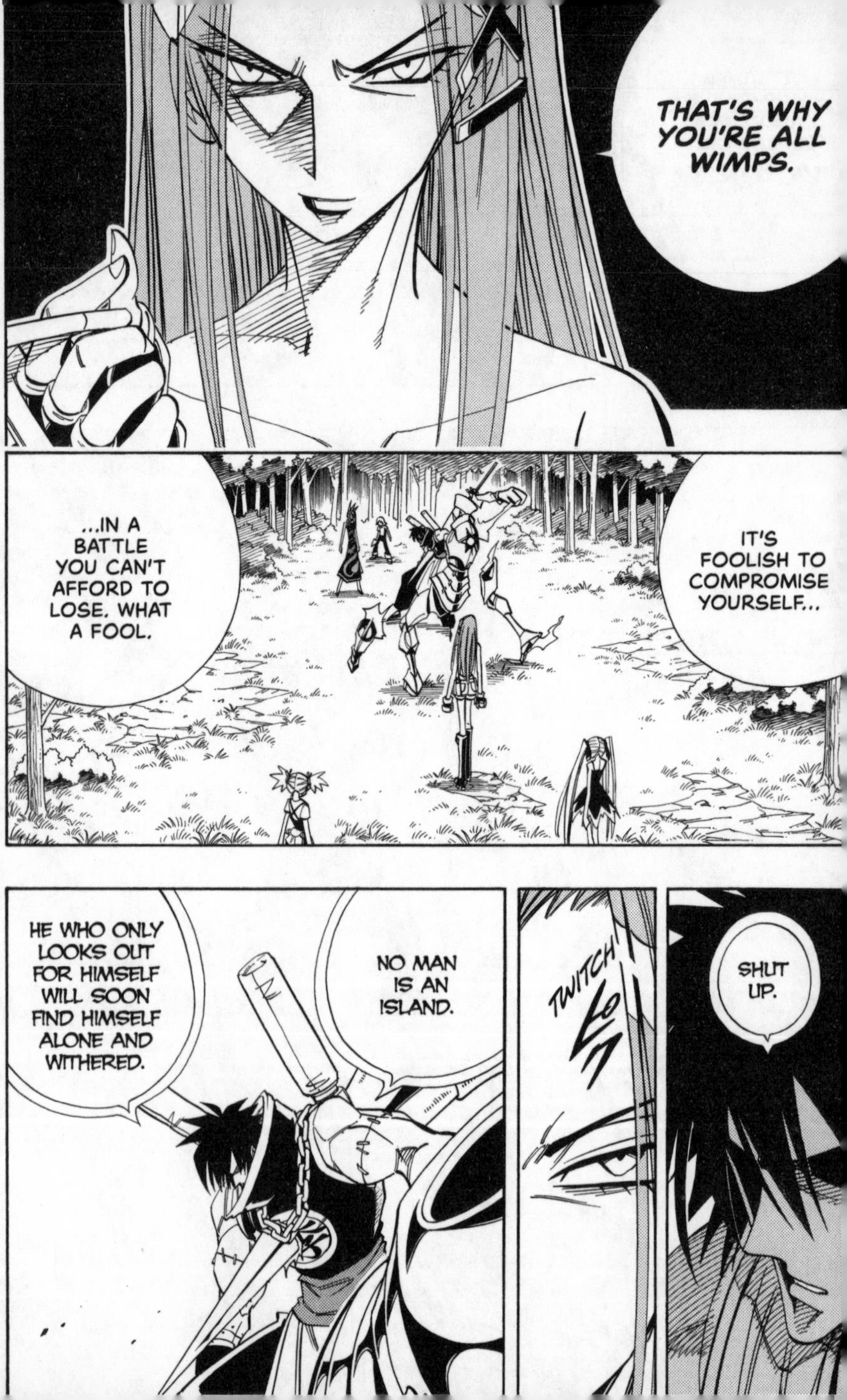
THAT'S WHY YOU'RE ALL WIMPS.
IT'S FOOLISH TO COMPROMISE YOURSELF...
...IN A BATTLE YOU CAN'T AFFORD TO LOSE. WHAT A FOOL.
SHUT UP.
TWITCH
NO MAN IS AN ISLAND.
HE WHO ONLY LOOKS OUT FOR HIMSELF WILL SOON FIND HIMSELF ALONE AND WITHERED.

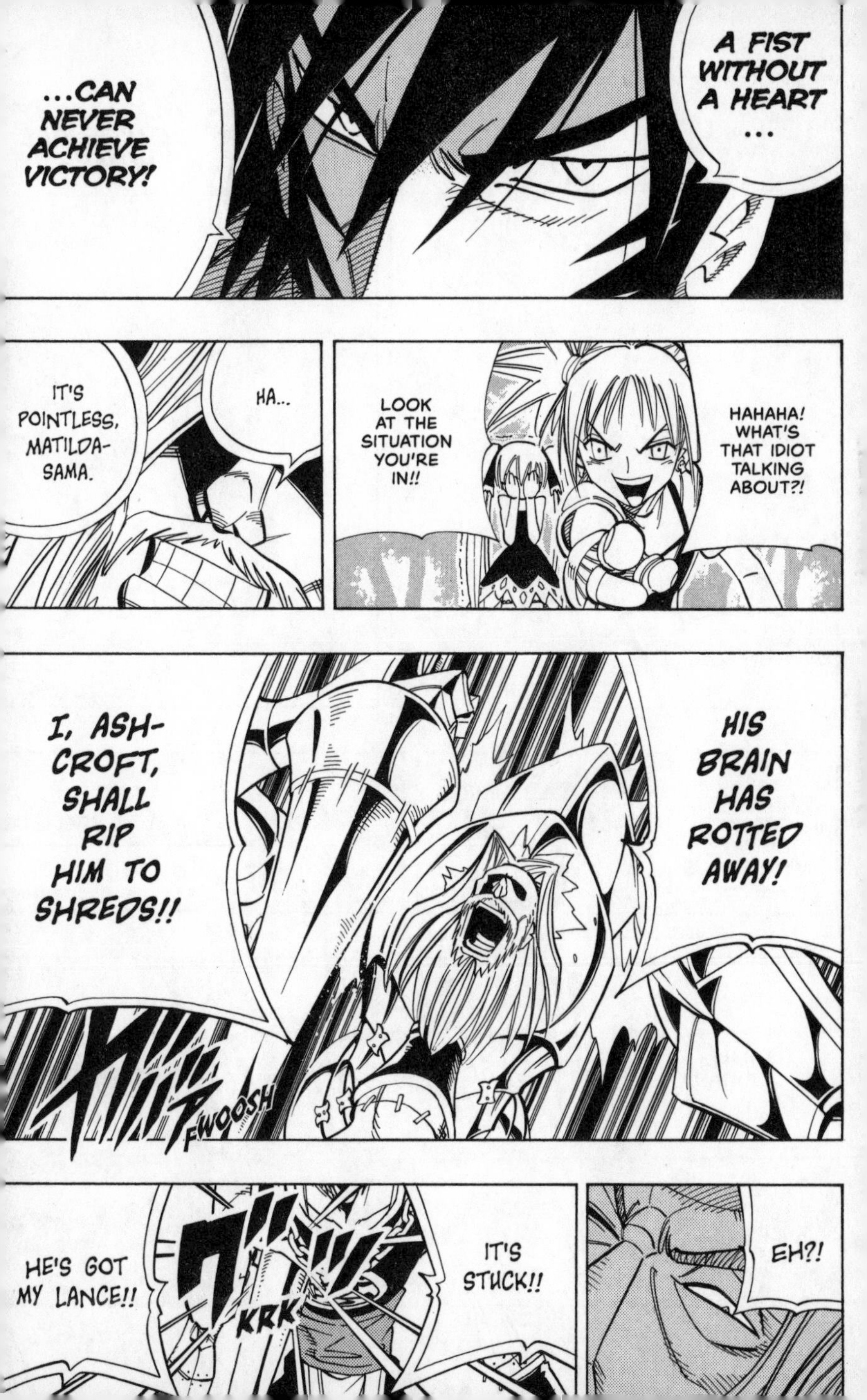
A FIST WITHOUT A HEART ...
...CAN NEVER ACHIEVE VICTORY!
HAHAHA! WHAT'S THAT IDIOT TALKING ABOUT?!
LOOK AT THE SITUATION YOU'RE IN!!
HA...
IT'S POINTLESS, MATILDA-SAMA.
HIS BRAIN HAS ROTTED AWAY!
I, ASH-CROFT, SHALL RIP HIM TO SHREDS!!
FWOOSH
EH?!
IT'S STUCK!!
KRK
HE'S GOT MY LANCE!!

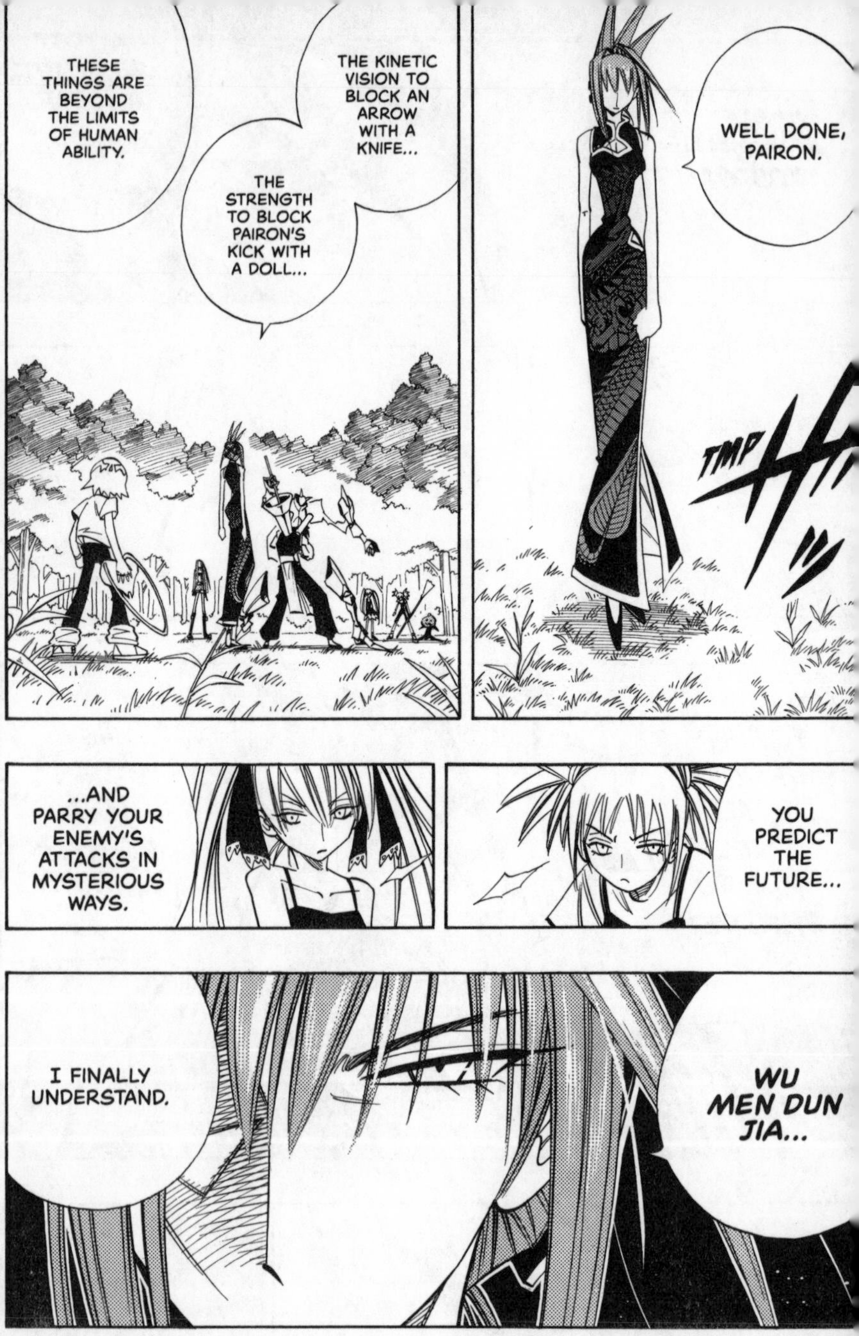
WELL DONE, PAIRON.
TMP
THE KINETIC VISION TO BLOCK AN ARROW WITH A KNIFE...
THE STRENGTH TO BLOCK PAIRON'S KICK WITH A DOLL...
THESE THINGS ARE BEYOND THE LIMITS OF HUMAN ABILITY.
YOU PREDICT THE FUTURE...
...AND PARRY YOUR ENEMY'S ATTACKS IN MYSTERIOUS WAYS.
WU MEN DUN JIA...
I FINALLY UNDERSTAND.

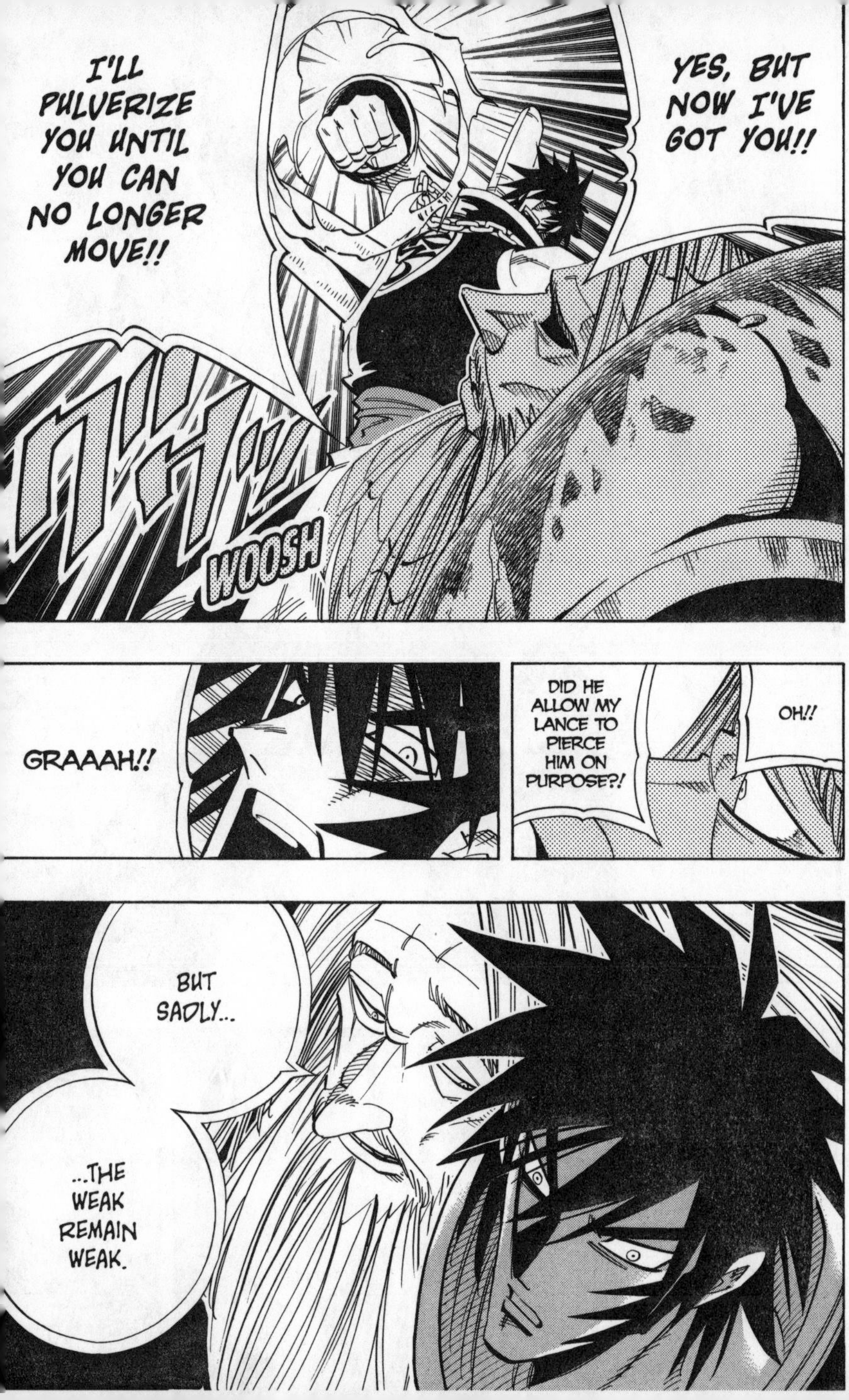
YES, BUT NOW I'VE GOT YOU!!
I'LL PULVERIZE YOU UNTIL YOU CAN NO LONGER MOVE!!
WOOSH
OH!!
DID HE ALLOW MY LANCE TO PIERCE HIM ON PURPOSE?!
GRAAAH!!
BUT SADLY...
...THE WEAK REMAIN WEAK.

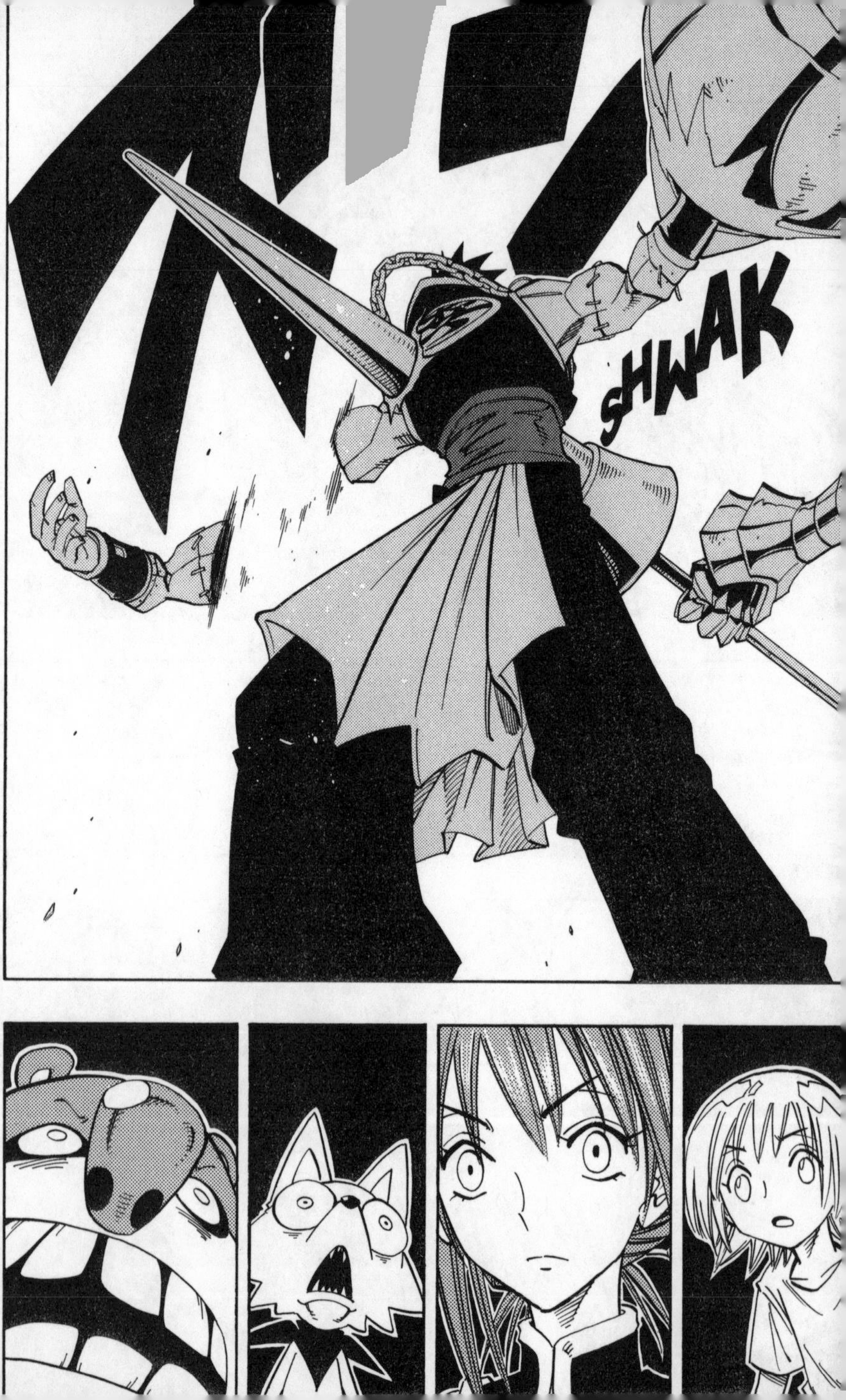
SHWAK

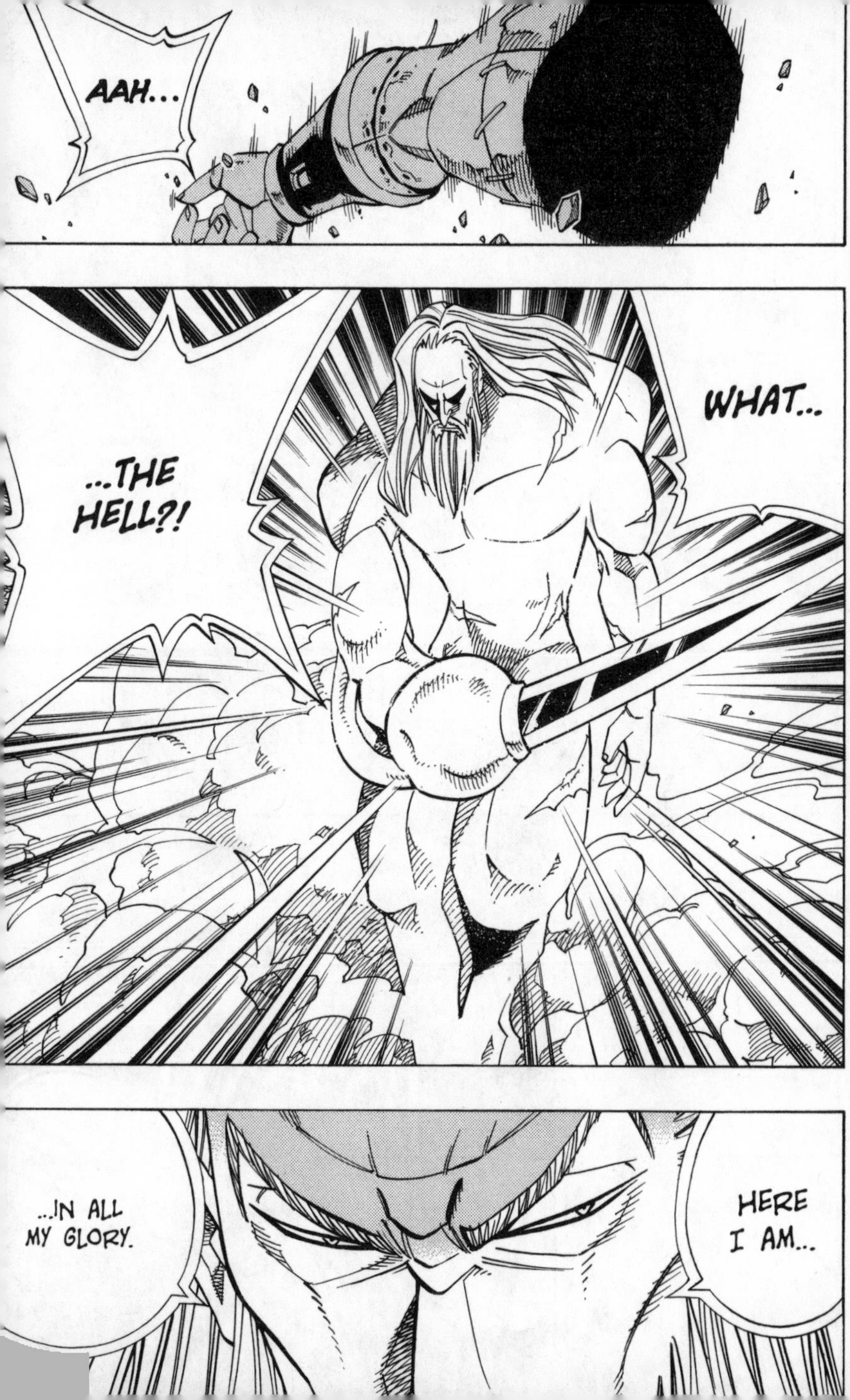
AAH...
WHAT...
...THE HELL?!
HERE I AM...
...IN ALL MY GLORY.

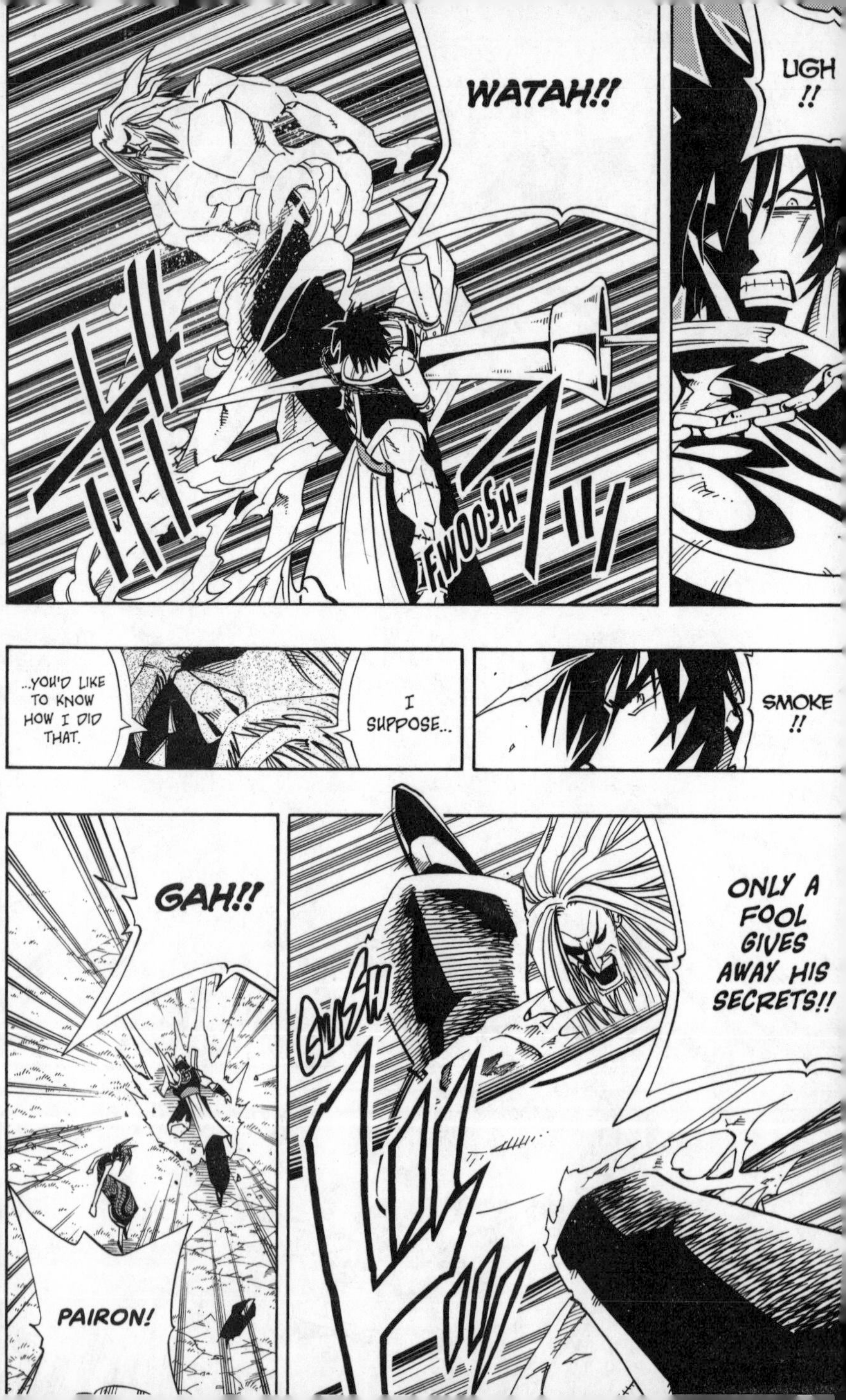
UGH !!
WATAH!!
FWOOSH
SMOKE !!
I SUPPOSE...
...YOU'D LIKE TO KNOW HOW I DID THAT.
ONLY A FOOL GIVES AWAY HIS SECRETS!!
GUSH
GAH!!
PAIRON!

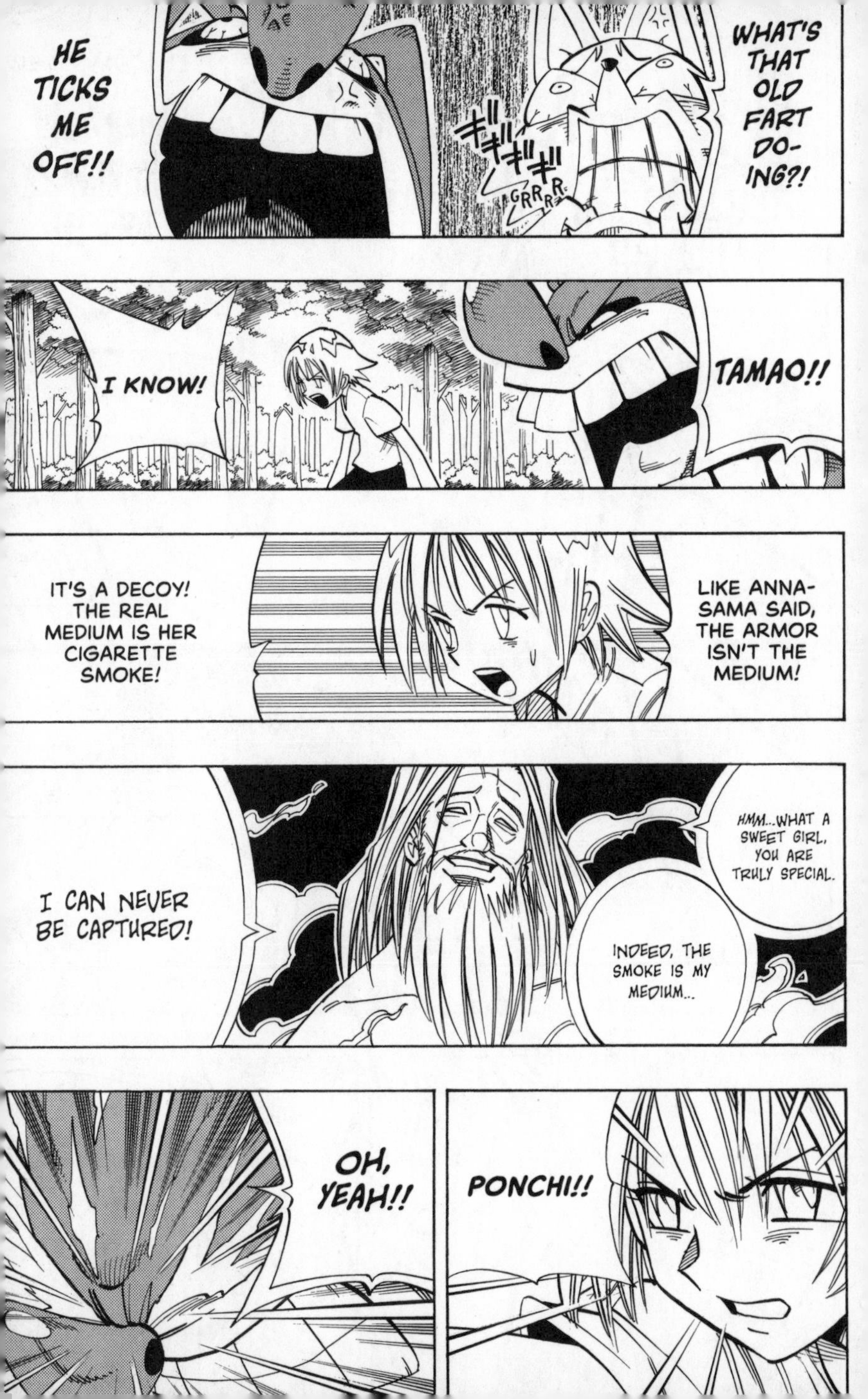
WHAT'S THAT OLD FART DO-ING?!
ギギギギ
GRRRR
HE TICKS ME OFF!!
TAMAO!!
I KNOW!
LIKE ANNA-SAMA SAID, THE ARMOR ISN'T THE MEDIUM!
IT'S A DECOY! THE REAL MEDIUM IS HER CIGARETTE SMOKE!
HMM...WHAT A SWEET GIRL, YOU ARE TRULY SPECIAL.
INDEED, THE SMOKE IS MY MEDIUM...
I CAN NEVER BE CAPTURED!
PONCHI!!
OH, YEAH!!

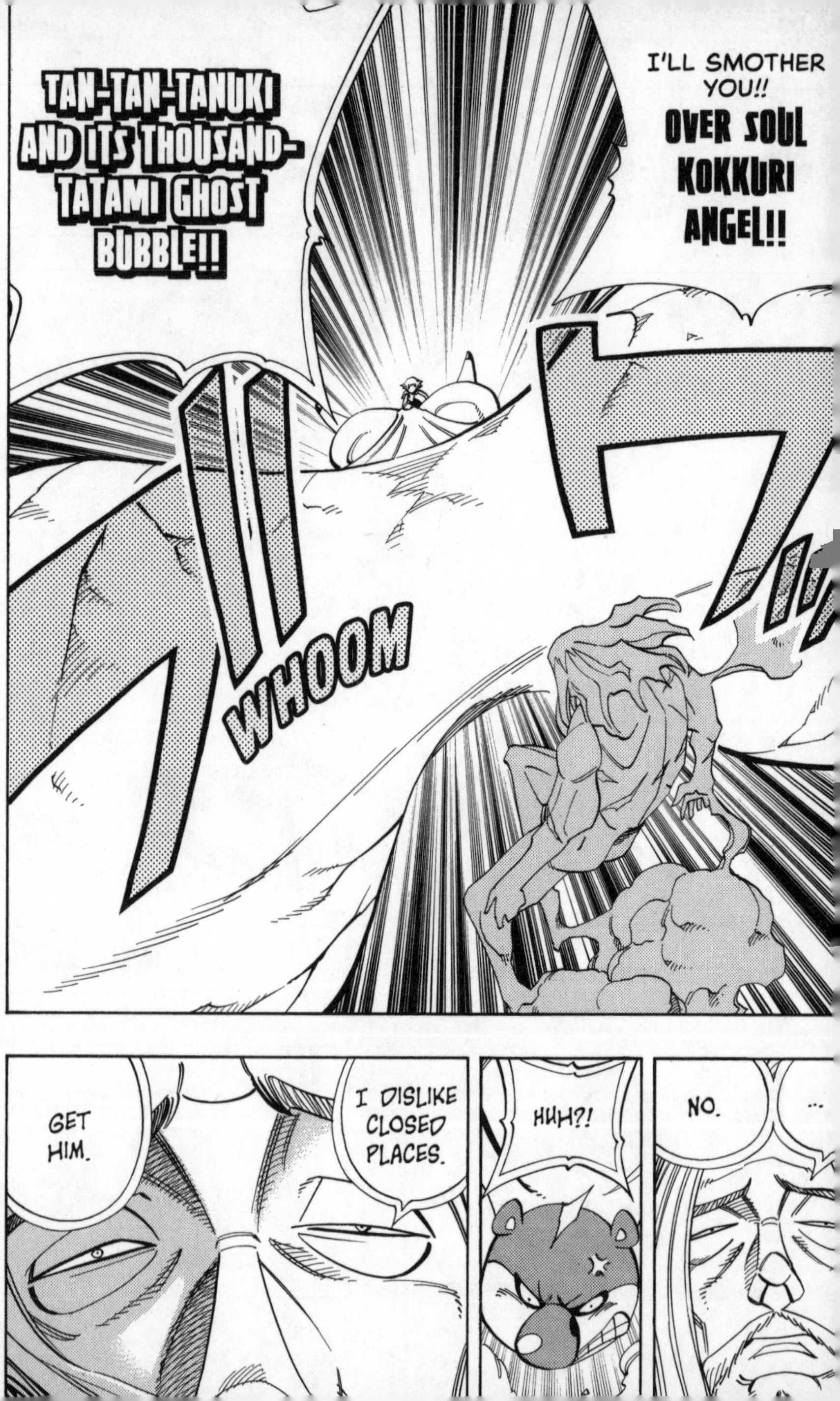
I'LL SMOTHER YOU!!
OVER SOUL KOKKURI ANGEL!!
TAN-TAN-TANUKI AND ITS THOUSAND-TATAMI GHOST BUBBLE!!
WHOOM
...
NO.
HUH?!
I DISLIKE CLOSED PLACES.
GET HIM.

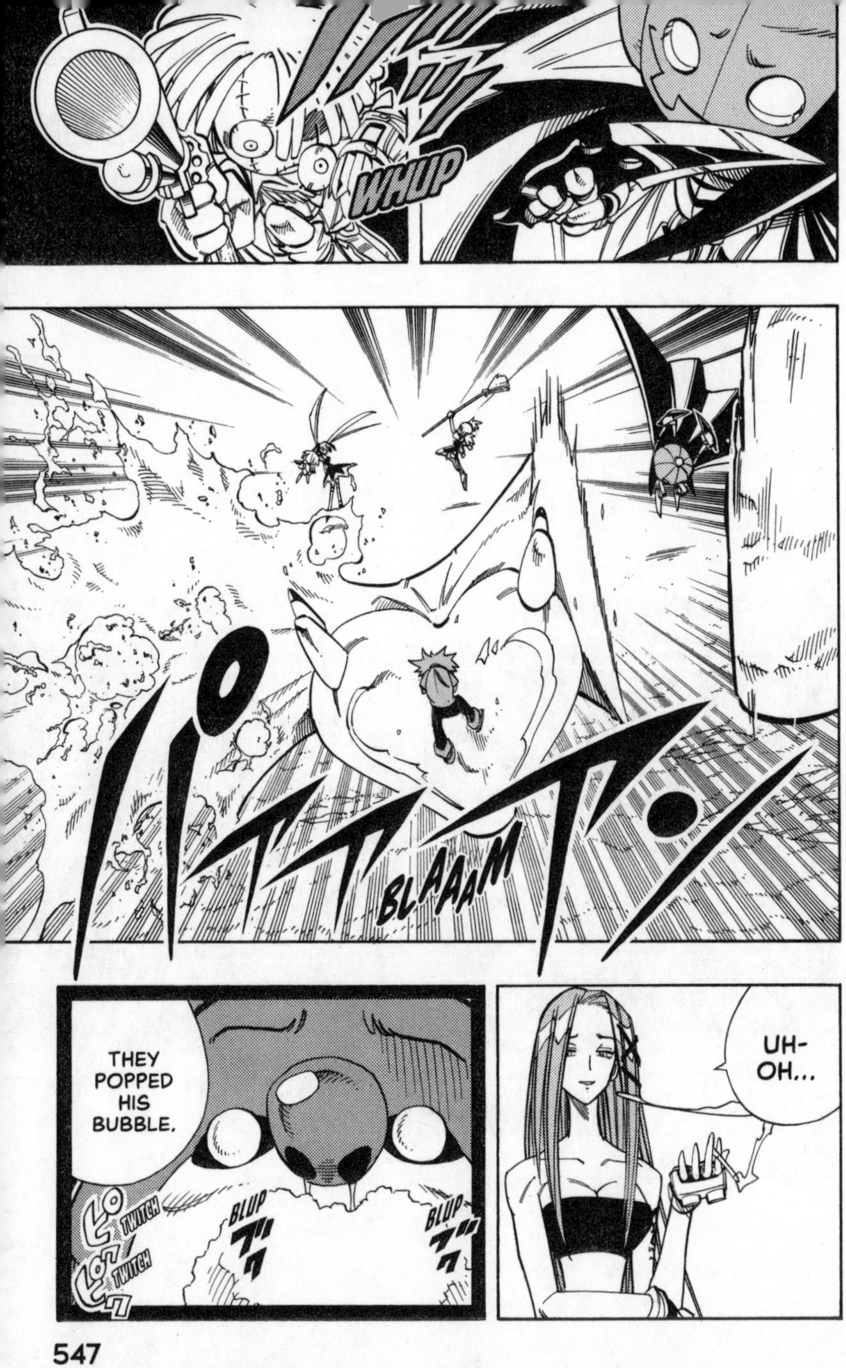
WHUP
BLAAAM
UH-OH...
THEY POPPED HIS BUBBLE.
TWITCH TWITCH
BLUP
BLUP

Over Soul Medium: Chuck

January 2001

Chapter 160: The Mask Restored

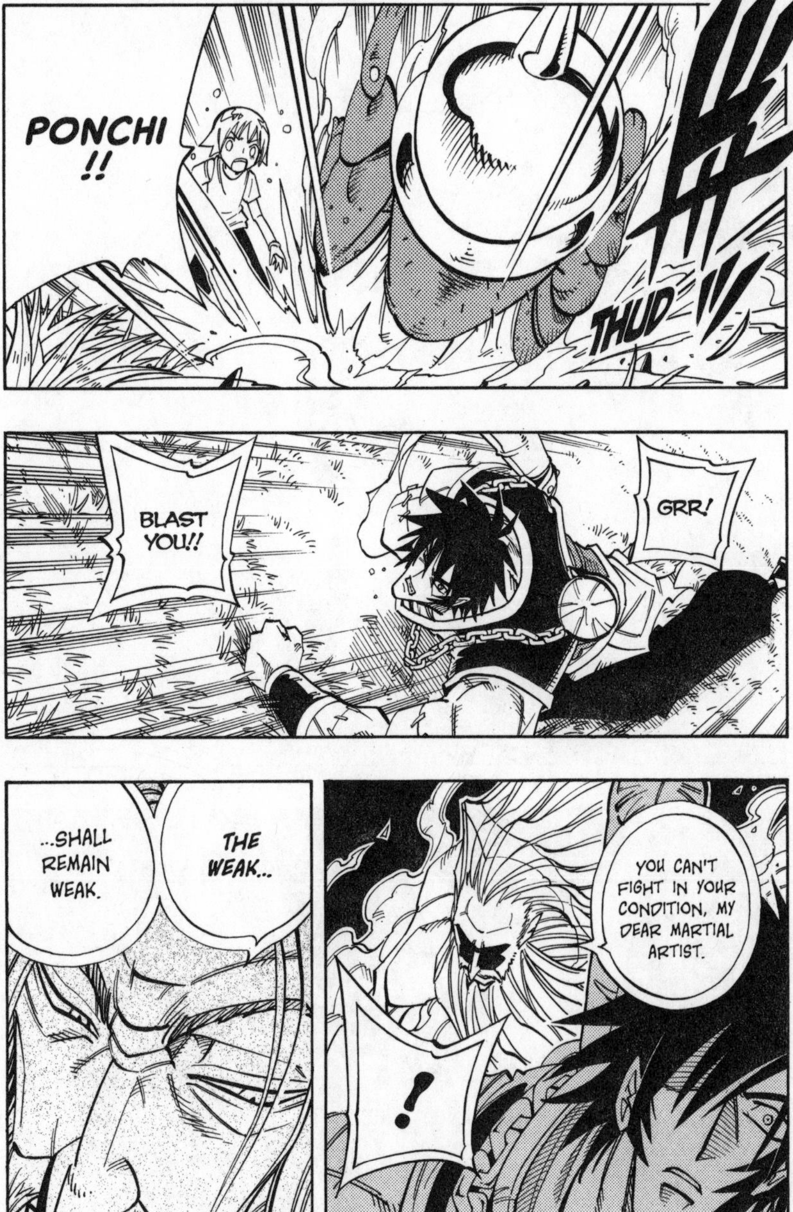
THUD!!
PONCHI!!
GRR!
BLAST YOU!!
YOU CAN'T FIGHT IN YOUR CONDITION, MY DEAR MARTIAL ARTIST.
!
THE WEAK...
...SHALL REMAIN WEAK.

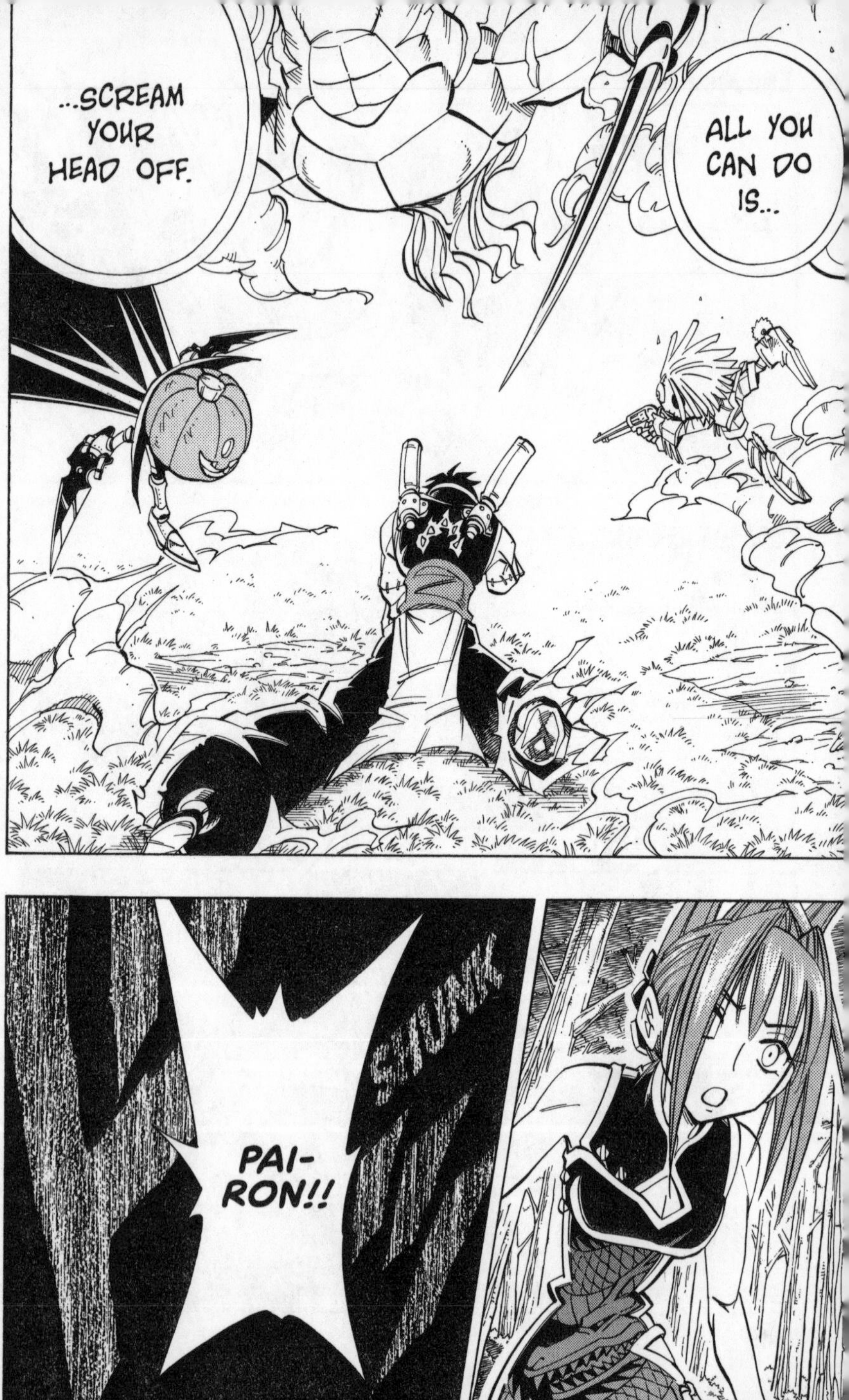
ALL YOU CAN DO IS...
...SCREAM YOUR HEAD OFF.
SHUNK
PAI-RON!!

Chapter 160:

The Mask Restored

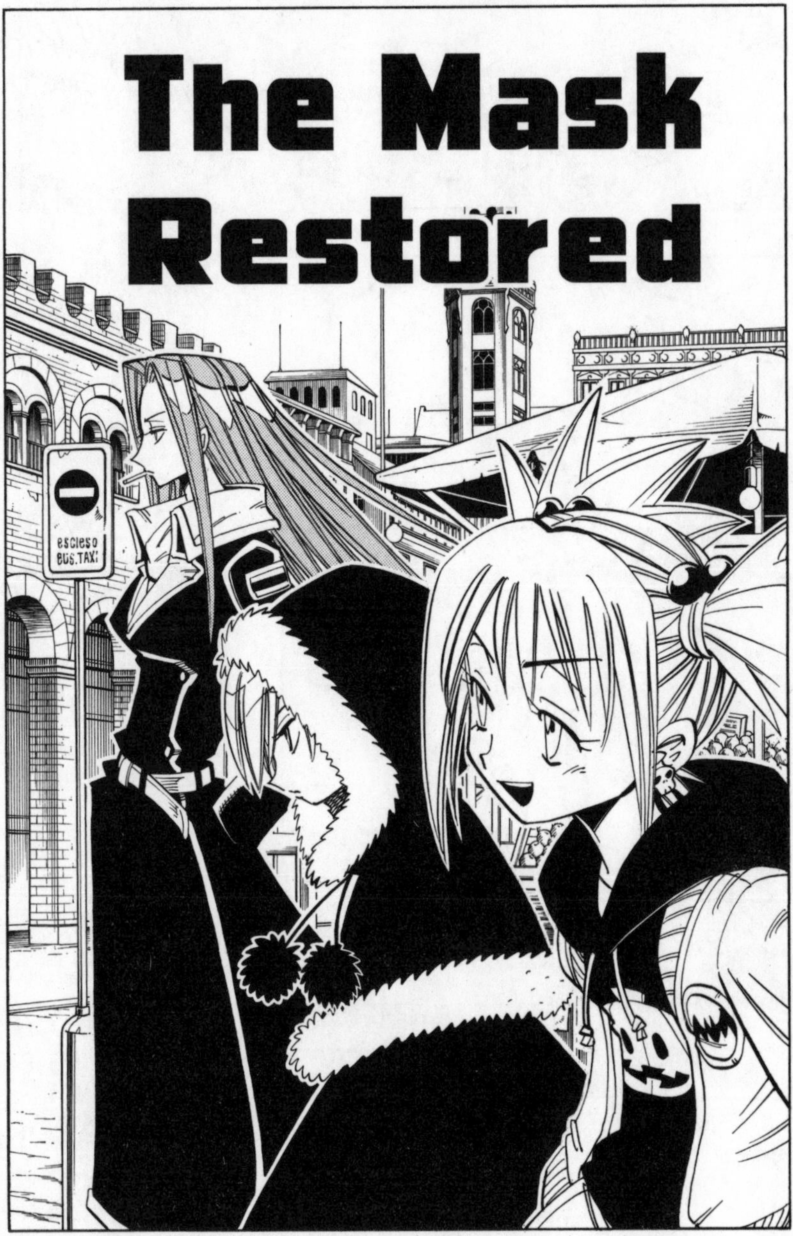
escieso
BUS.TAXI

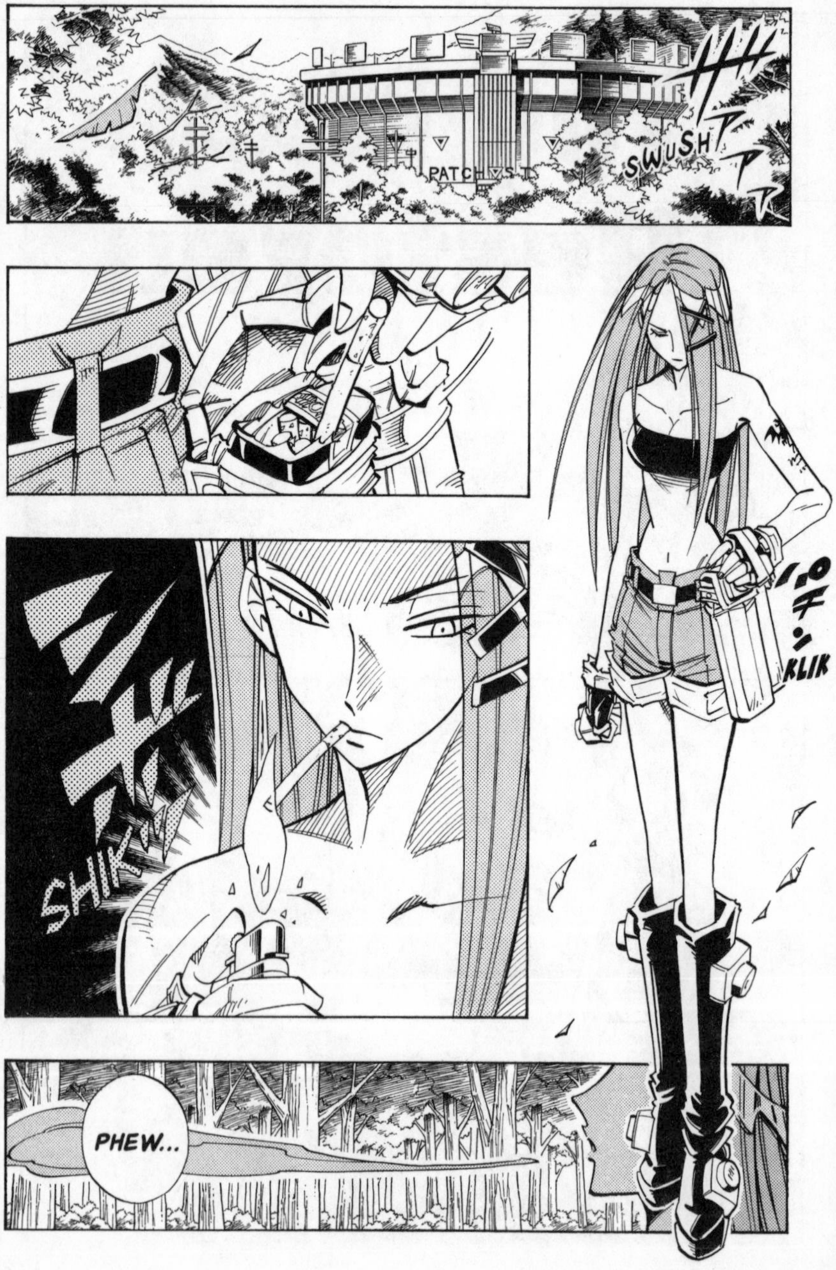
SWUSH
KLIK
SHIK
PHEW...

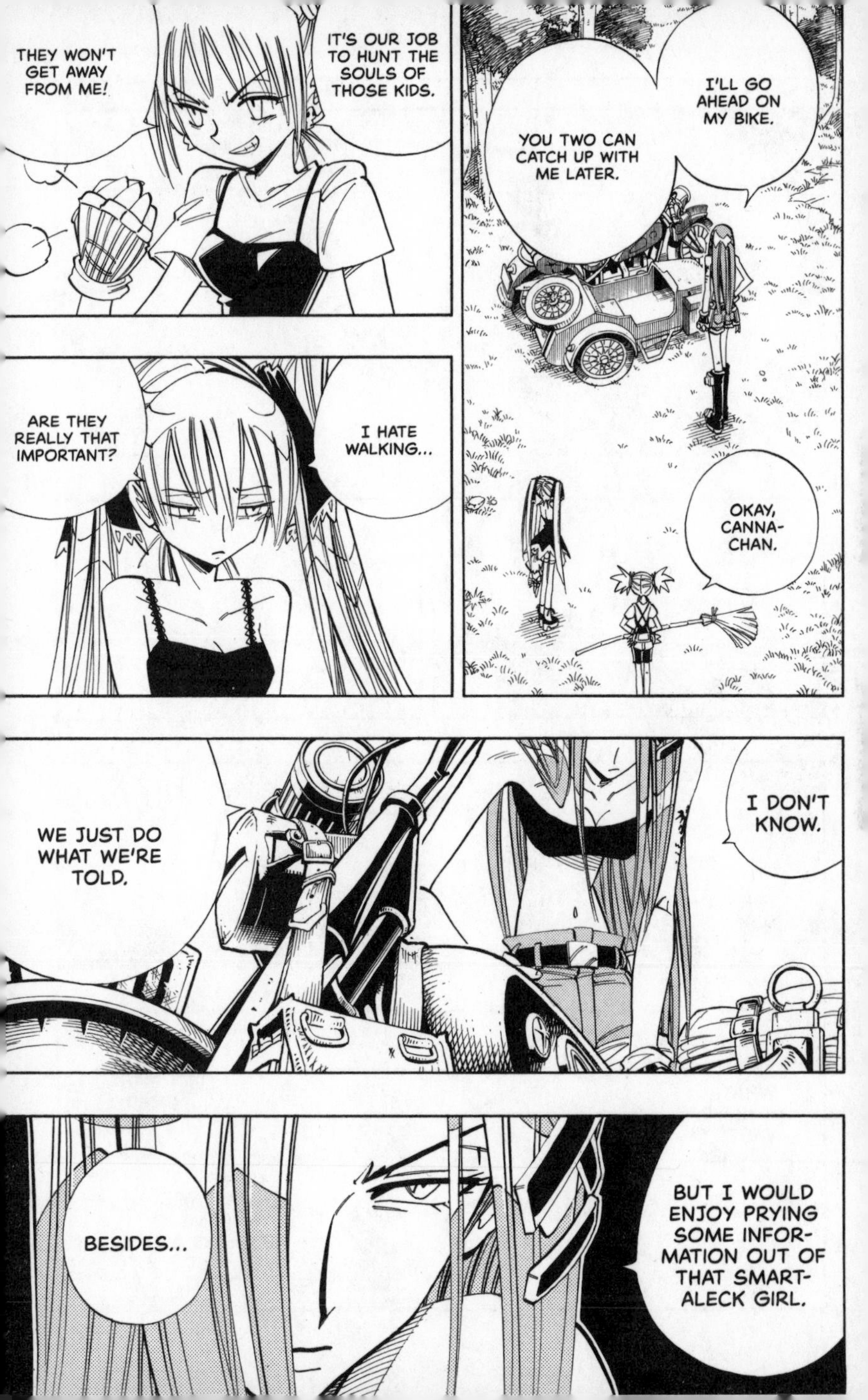
I'LL GO AHEAD ON MY BIKE.
YOU TWO CAN CATCH UP WITH ME LATER.
OKAY, CANNA-CHAN.
IT'S OUR JOB TO HUNT THE SOULS OF THOSE KIDS.
THEY WON'T GET AWAY FROM ME!
I HATE WALKING...
ARE THEY REALLY THAT IMPORTANT?
I DON'T KNOW.
WE JUST DO WHAT WE'RE TOLD.
BUT I WOULD ENJOY PRYING SOME INFORMATION OUT OF THAT SMART-ALECK GIRL.
BESIDES...

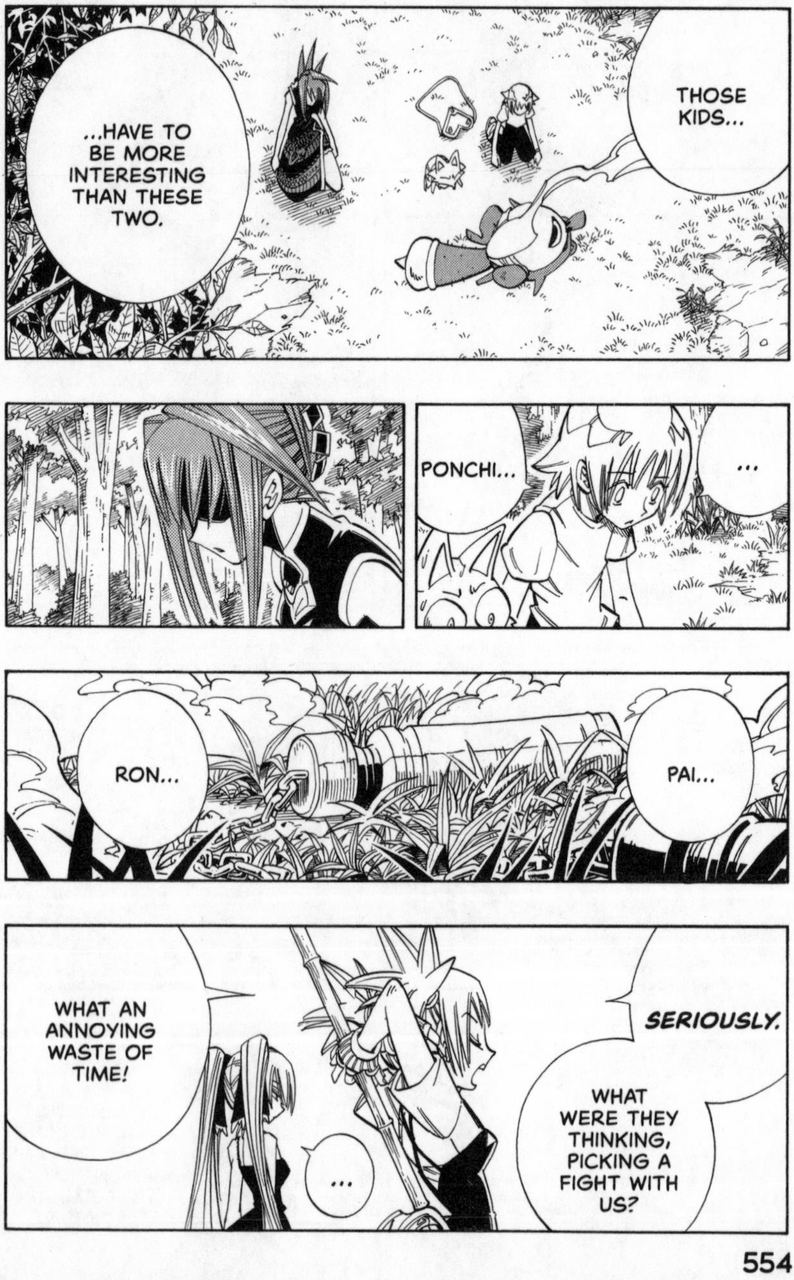
THOSE KIDS...
...HAVE TO BE MORE INTERESTING THAN THESE TWO.
...
PONCHI...
PAI...
RON...
SERIOUSLY.
WHAT WERE THEY THINKING, PICKING A FIGHT WITH US?
WHAT AN ANNOYING WASTE OF TIME!
...

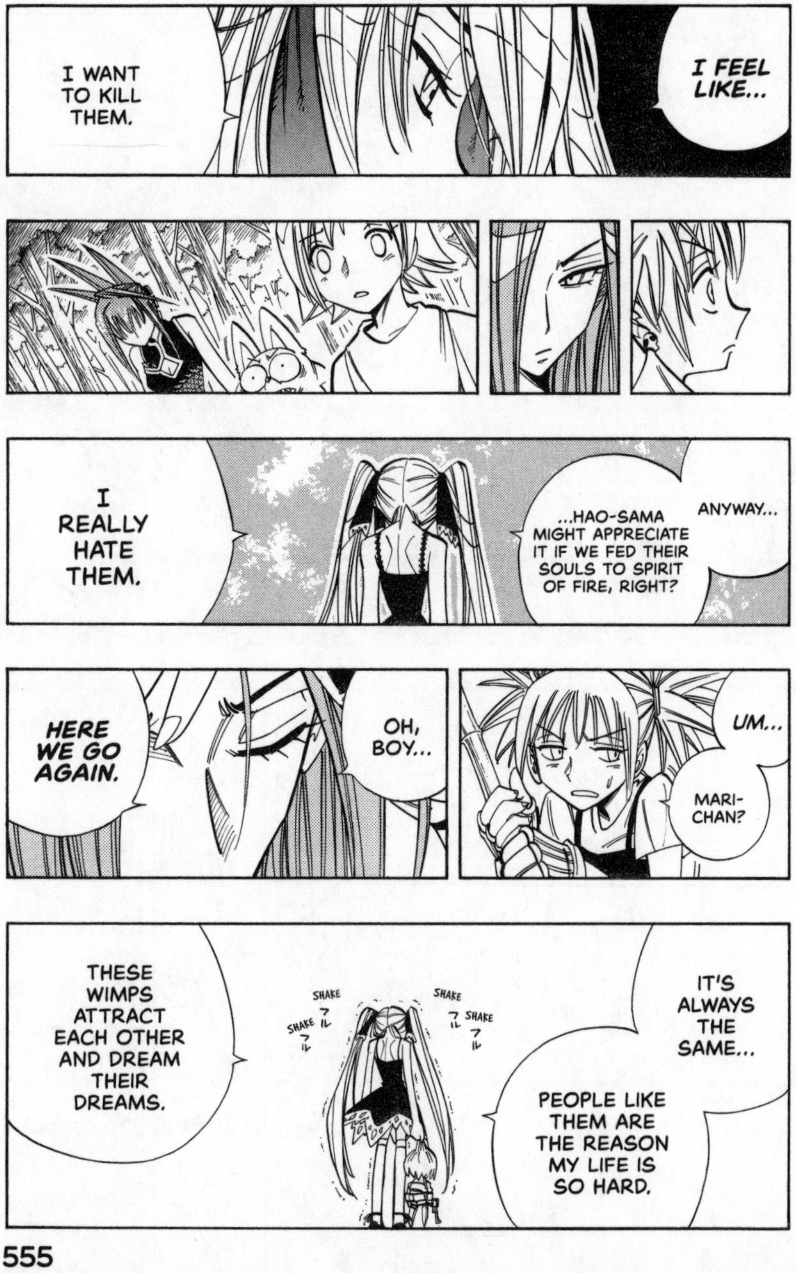
I FEEL LIKE...
I WANT TO KILL THEM.
ANYWAY...
...HAO-SAMA MIGHT APPRECIATE IT IF WE FED THEIR SOULS TO SPIRIT OF FIRE, RIGHT?
I REALLY HATE THEM.
UM...
MARI-CHAN?
OH, BOY...
HERE WE GO AGAIN.
IT'S ALWAYS THE SAME...
PEOPLE LIKE THEM ARE THE REASON MY LIFE IS SO HARD.
SHAKE フル
SHAKE フル
SHAKE フル
SHAKE フル
THESE WIMPS ATTRACT EACH OTHER AND DREAM THEIR DREAMS.

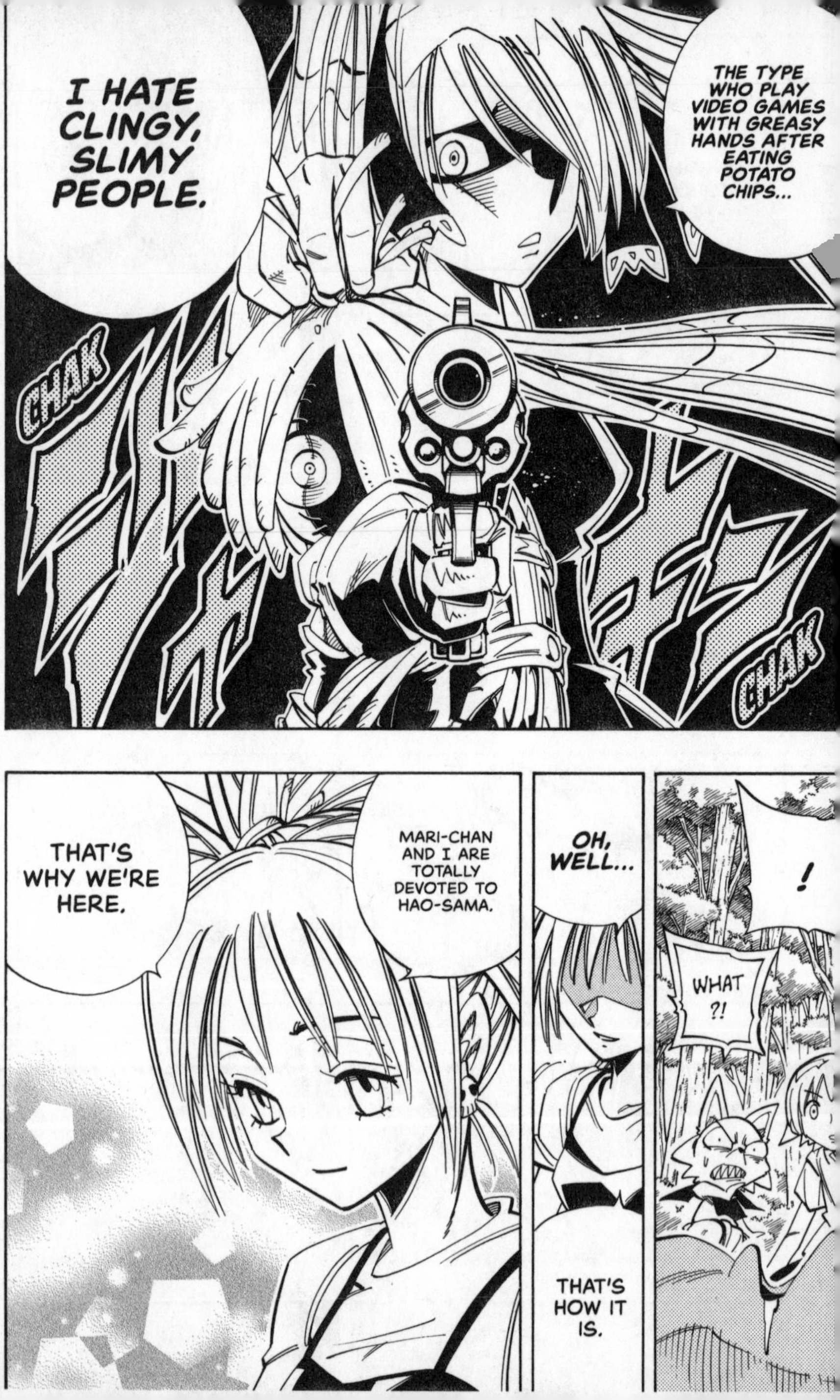
THE TYPE WHO PLAY VIDEO GAMES WITH GREASY HANDS AFTER EATING POTATO CHIPS...
I HATE CLINGY, SLIMY PEOPLE.
CHAK
CHAK
!
WHAT ?!
OH, WELL...
THAT'S HOW IT IS.
MARI-CHAN AND I ARE TOTALLY DEVOTED TO HAO-SAMA.
THAT'S WHY WE'RE HERE.

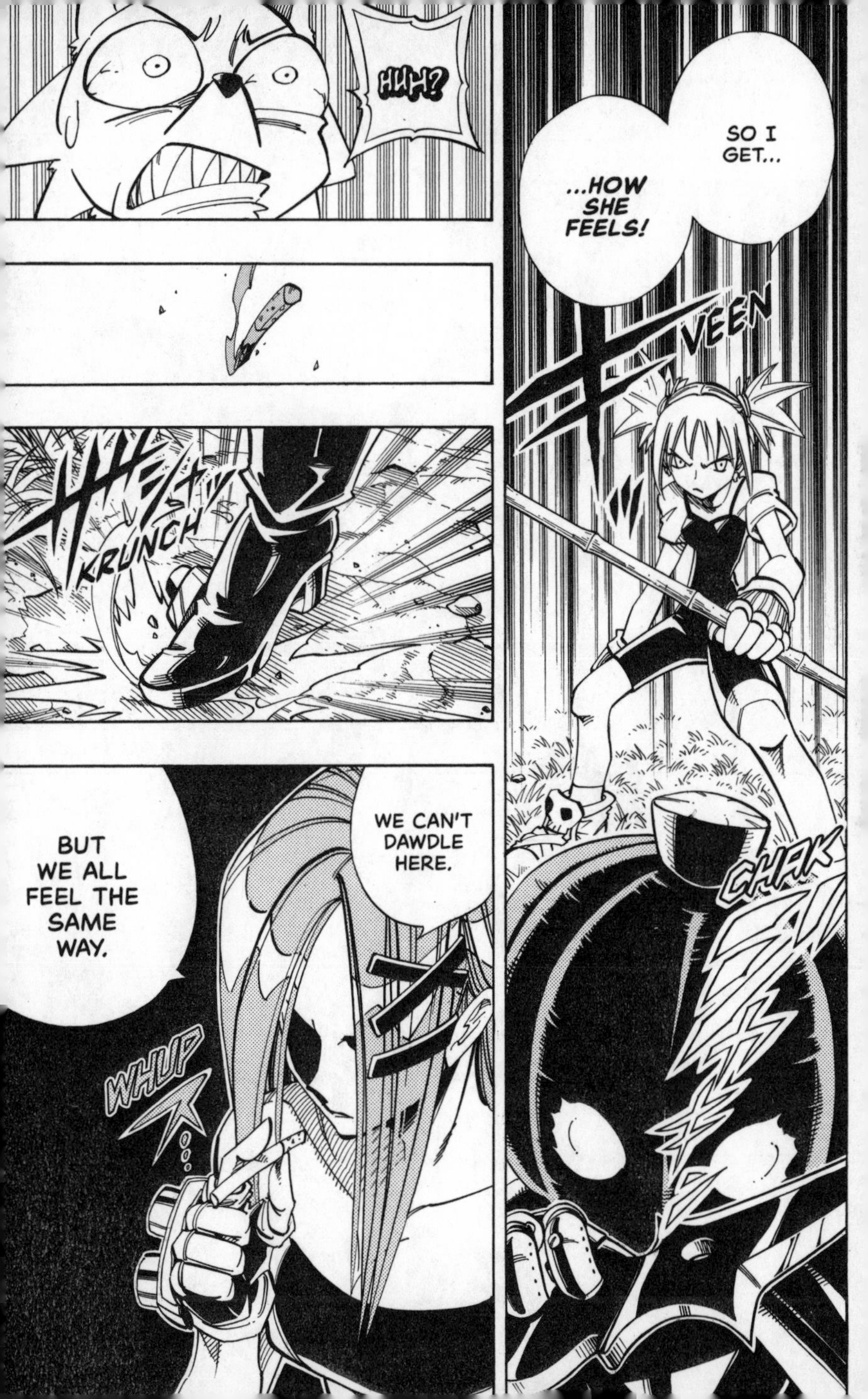
SO I GET...
...HOW SHE FEELS!
VEEN
CHAK
HUH?
KRUNCH
WE CAN'T DAWDLE HERE.
BUT WE ALL FEEL THE SAME WAY.
WHUP

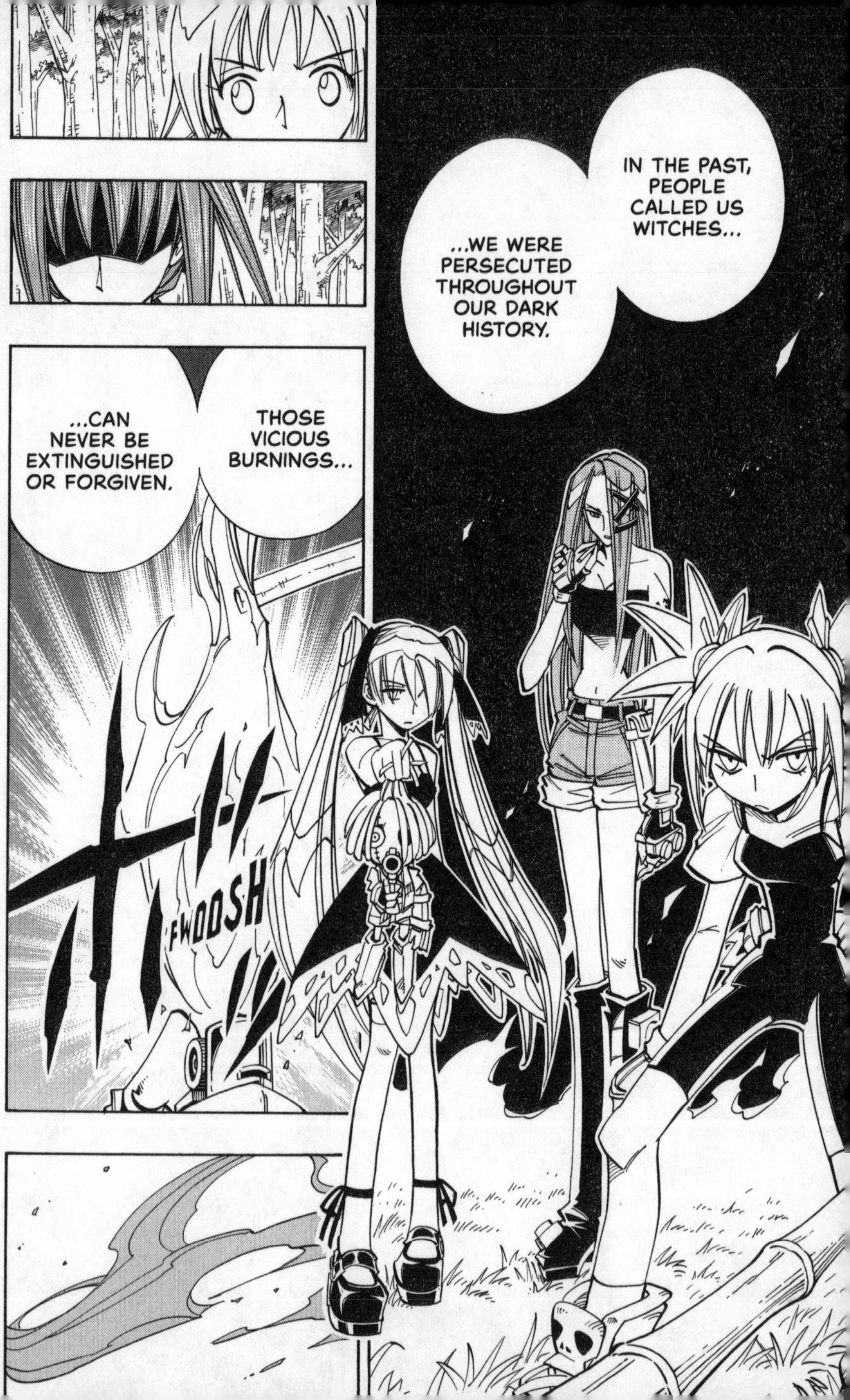
IN THE PAST, PEOPLE CALLED US WITCHES...
...WE WERE PERSECUTED THROUGHOUT OUR DARK HISTORY.
THOSE VICIOUS BURNINGS...
...CAN NEVER BE EXTINGUISHED OR FORGIVEN.
FWOOSH

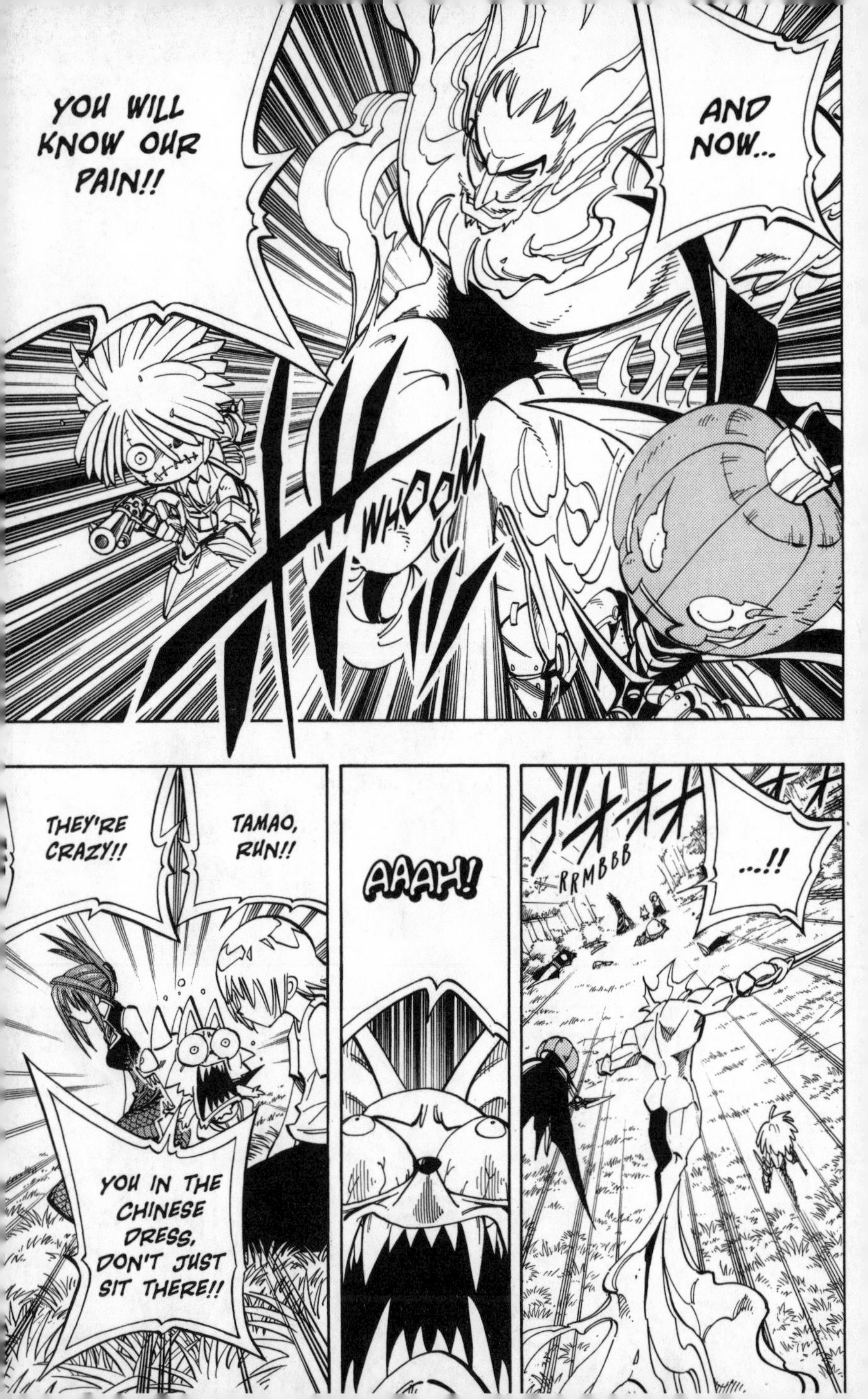
AND NOW...
YOU WILL KNOW OUR PAIN!!
WHOOM
...!!
ゴオオオ
RRMBBB
AAAH!
TAMAO, RUN!!
THEY'RE CRAZY!!
YOU IN THE CHINESE DRESS, DON'T JUST SIT THERE!!

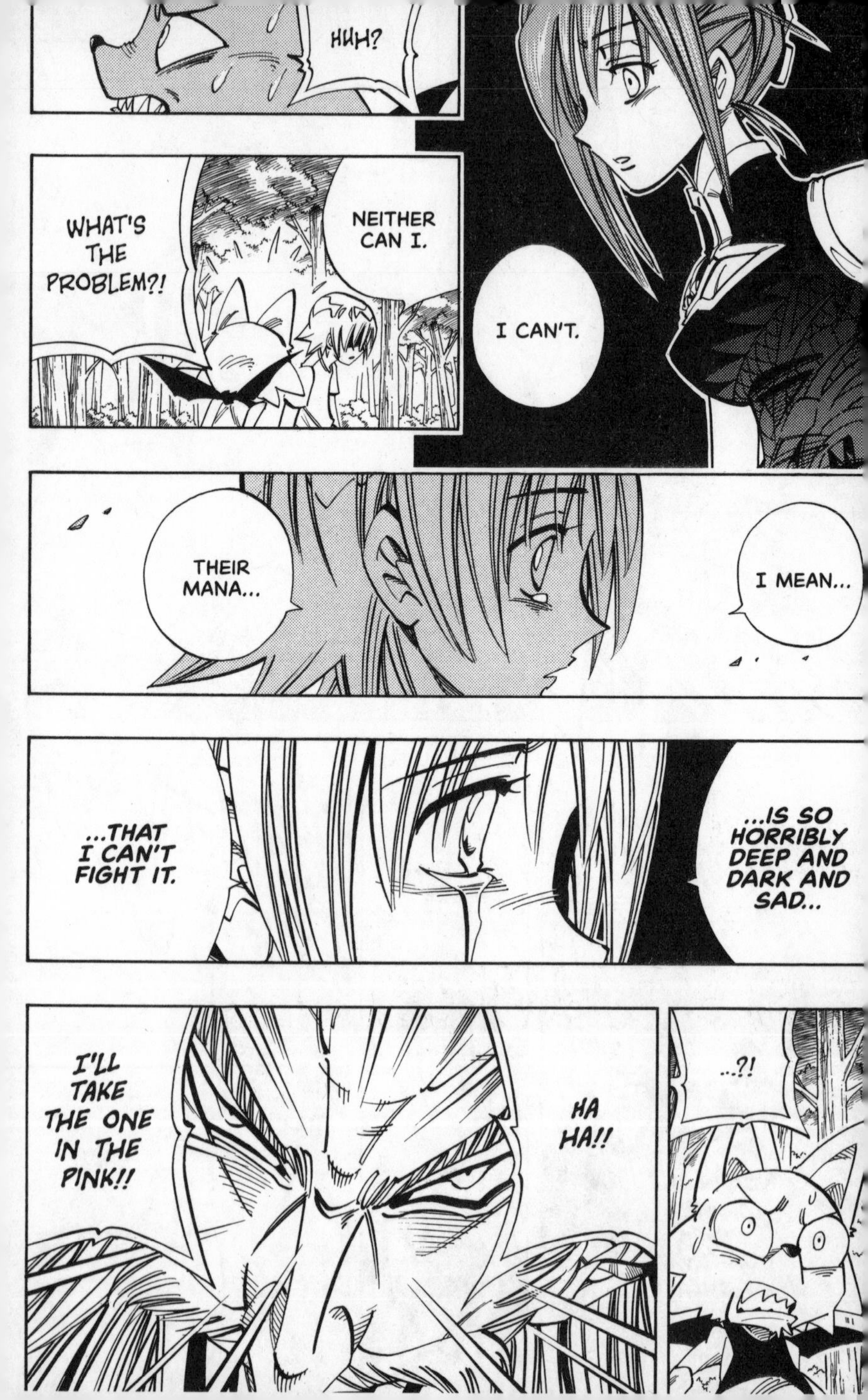
I CAN'T.
HUH?
NEITHER CAN I.
WHAT'S THE PROBLEM?!
I MEAN...
THEIR MANA...
...IS SO HORRIBLY DEEP AND DARK AND SAD...
...THAT I CAN'T FIGHT IT.
..?!
HA HA!!
I'LL TAKE THE ONE IN THE PINK!!

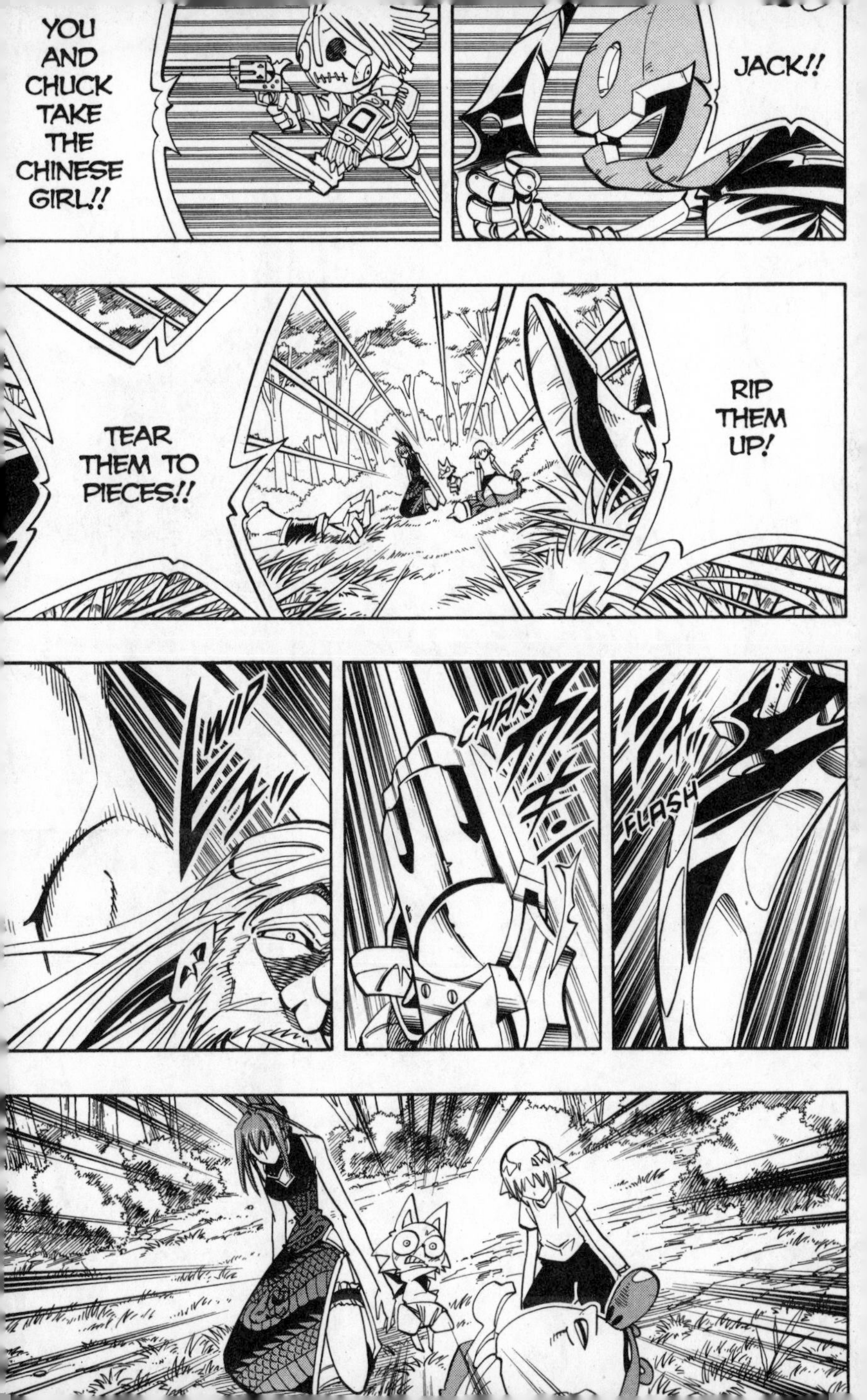
JACK!!
YOU AND CHUCK TAKE THE CHINESE GIRL!!
RIP THEM UP!
TEAR THEM TO PIECES!!
FLASH
CHAK
WIP

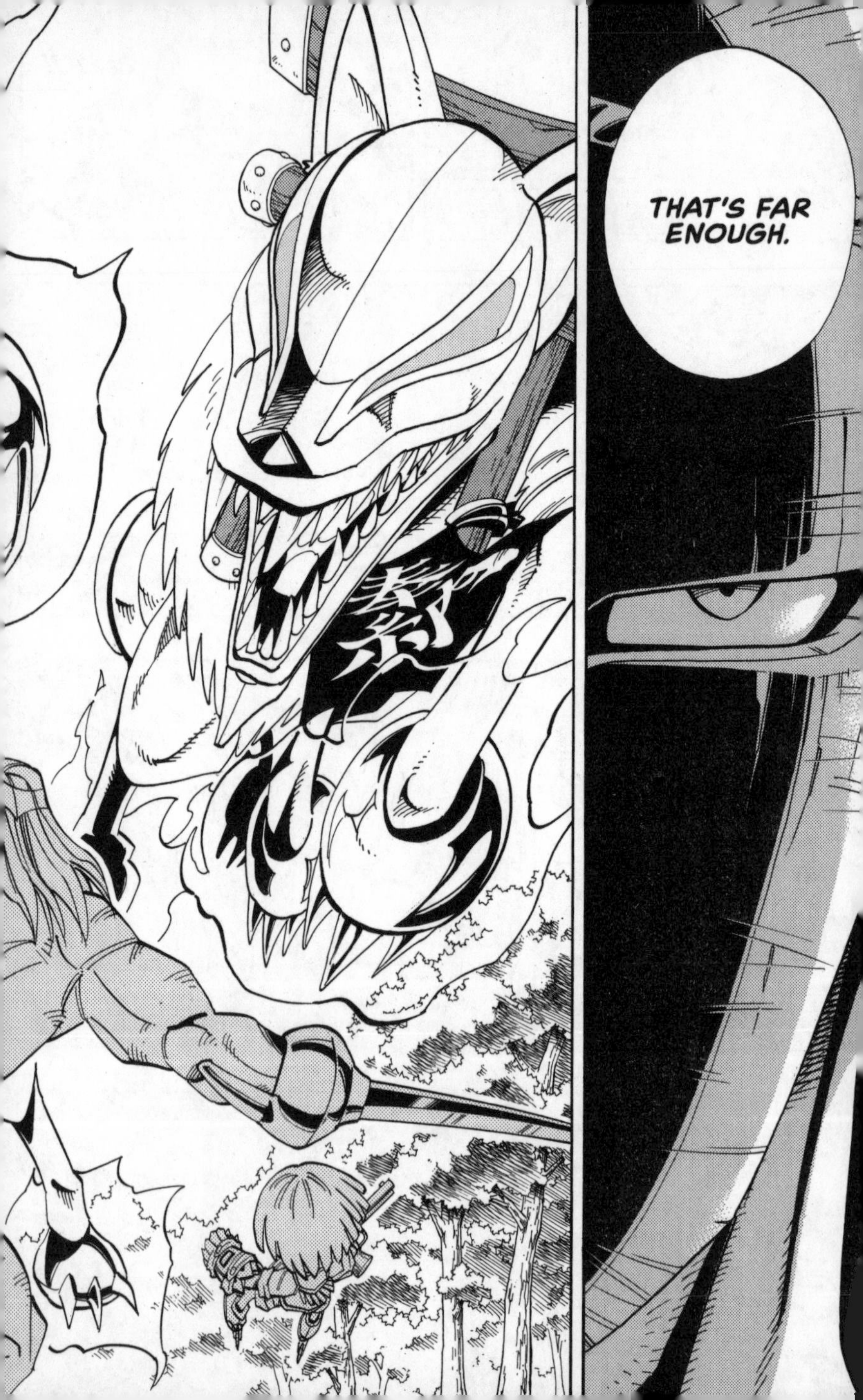
THAT'S FAR ENOUGH.

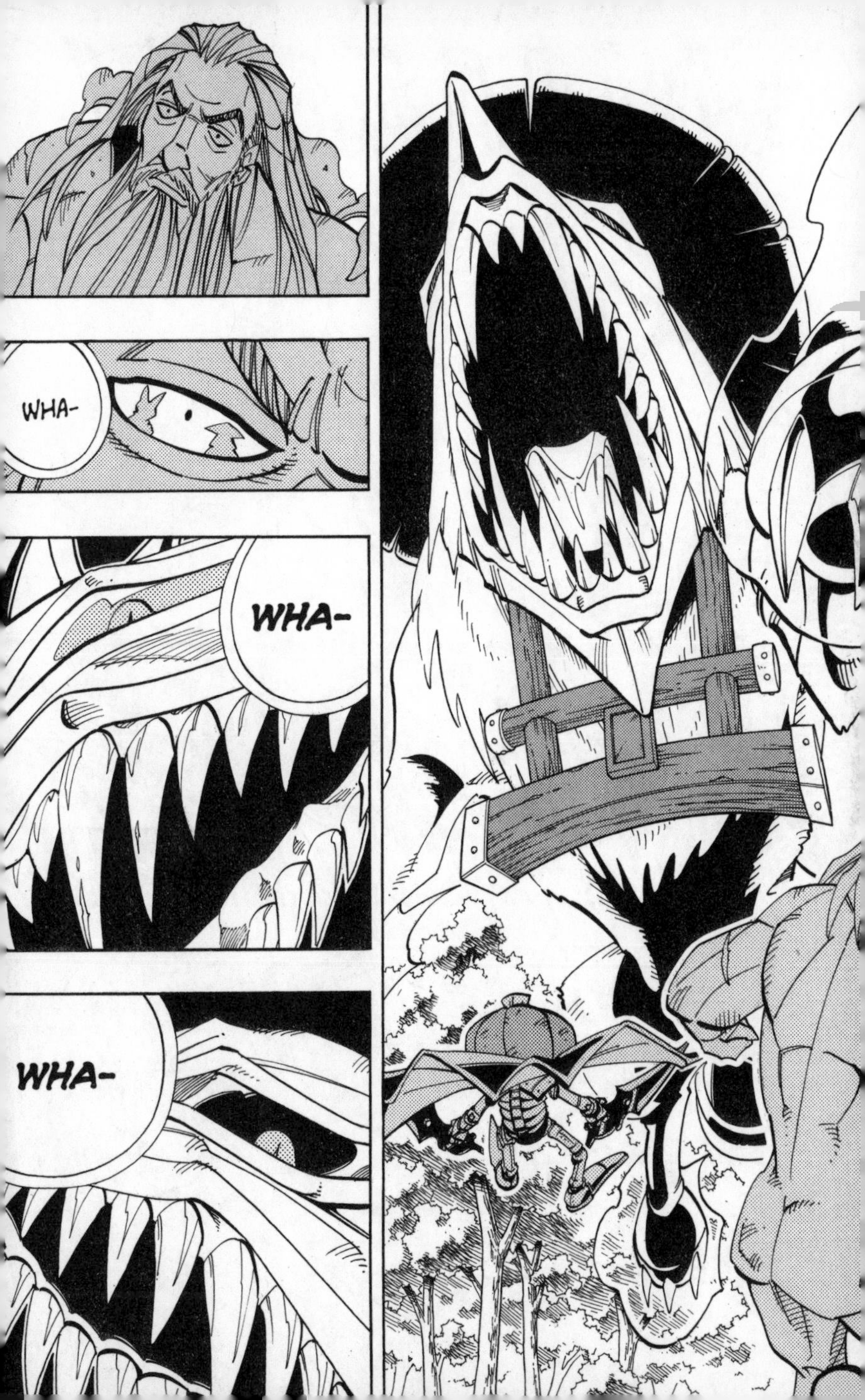
WHA-
WHA-
WHA-

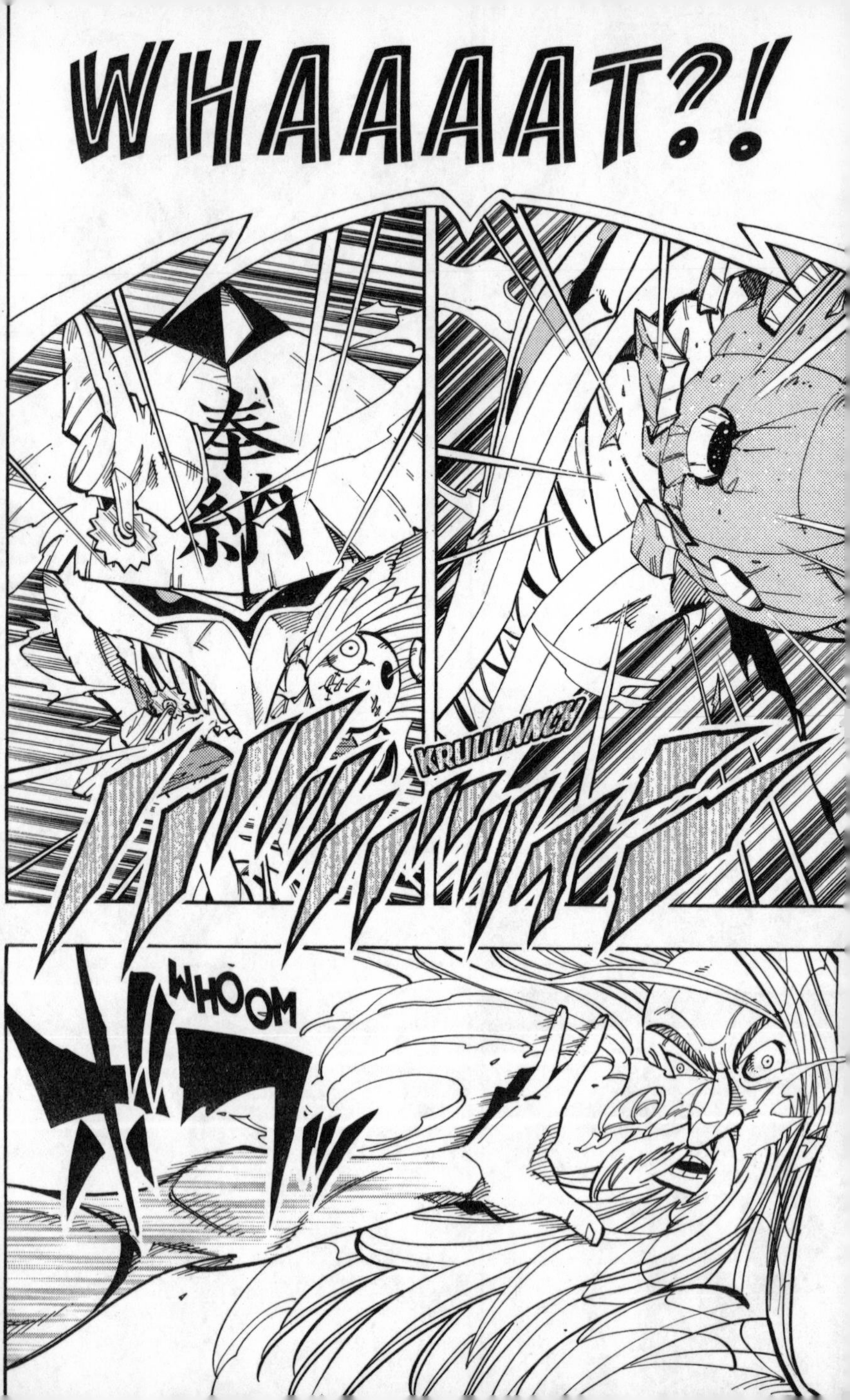
WHAAAAT?!
拳納
KRUUUNNCH
WHOOM

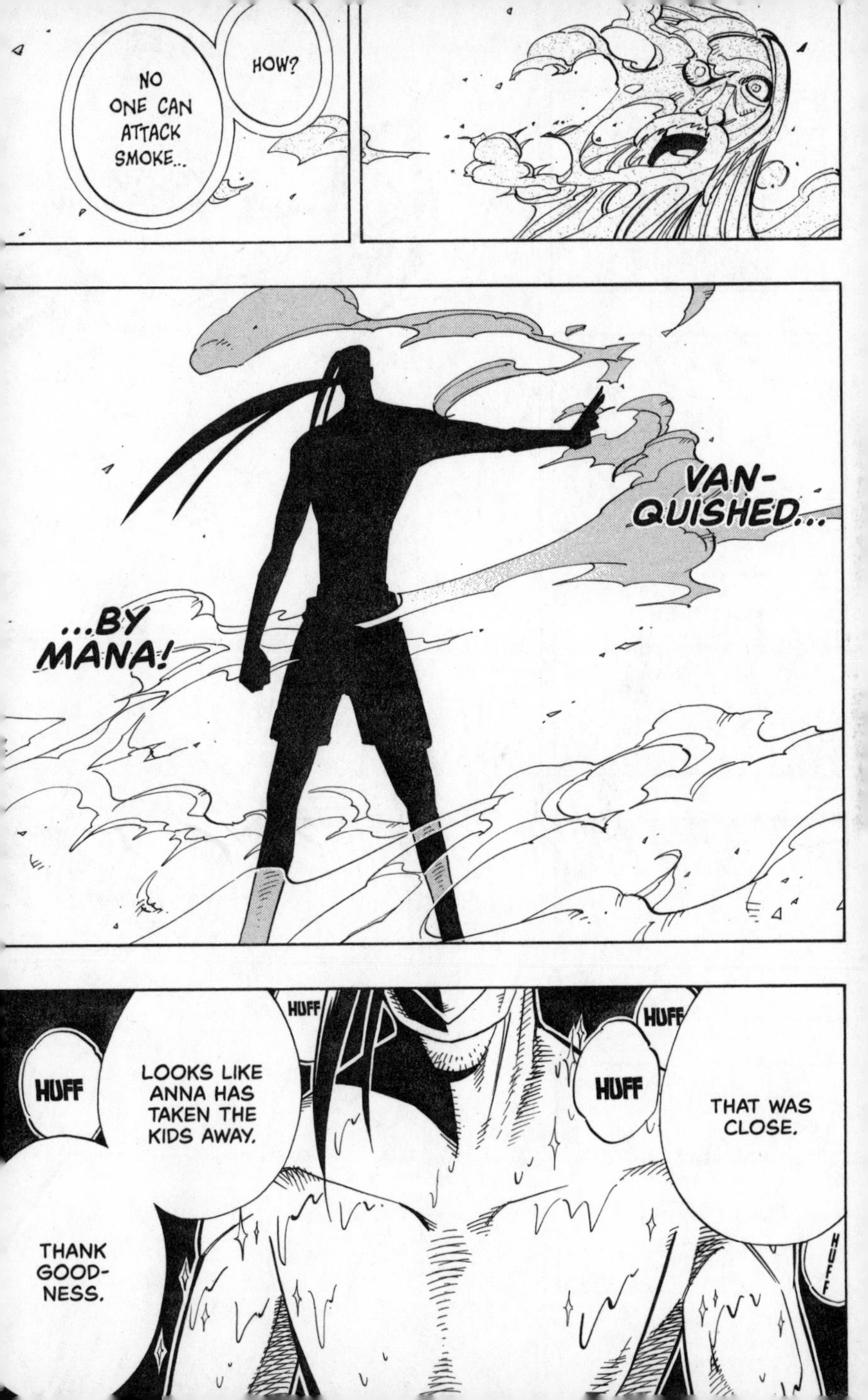
HOW?
NO ONE CAN ATTACK SMOKE...
VAN-QUISHED...
...BY MANA!
HUFF
HUFF
THAT WAS CLOSE.
HUFF
HUFF
HUFF
LOOKS LIKE ANNA HAS TAKEN THE KIDS AWAY.
THANK GOOD-NESS.

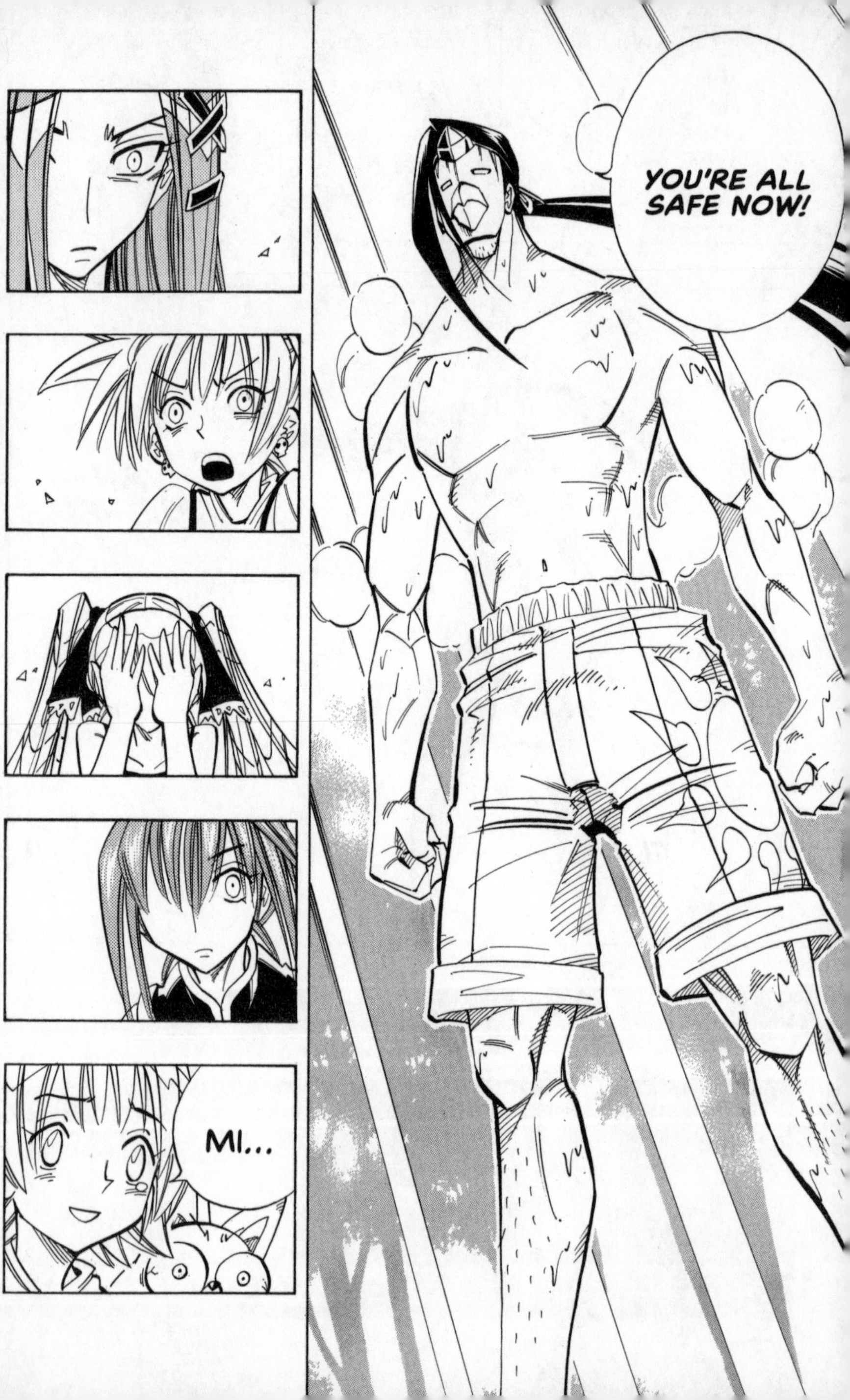
YOU'RE ALL SAFE NOW!
MI...

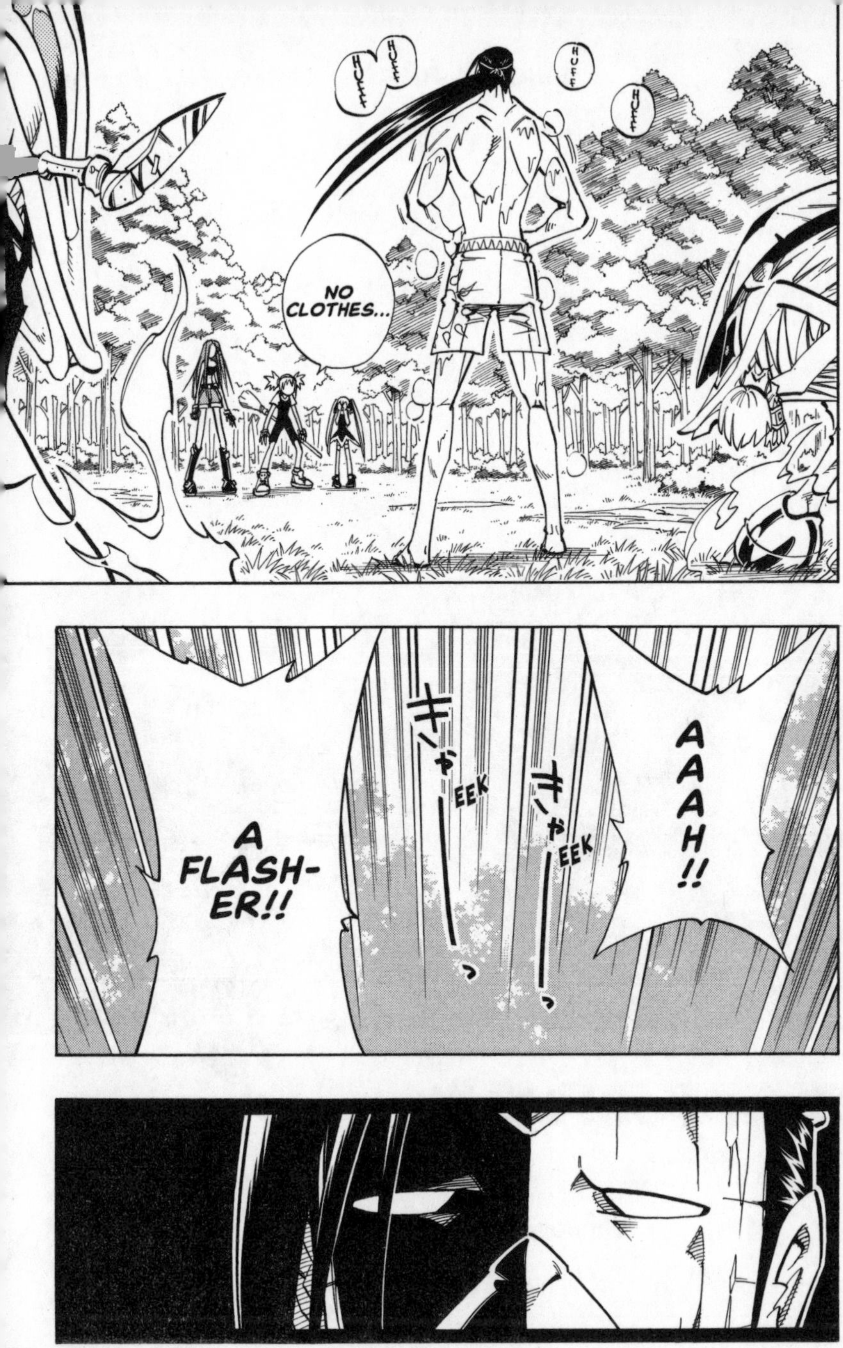
HUFF
HUFF
HUFF
HUFF
NO CLOTHES...
AAAAH!!
きゃーっ
EEK
きゃーっ
EEK
A FLASH-ER!!

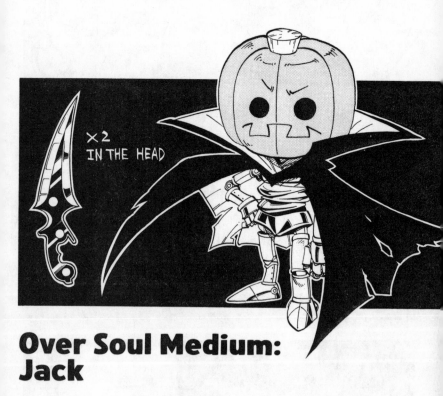

×2
IN THE HEAD

Over Soul Medium: Jack

January 2001

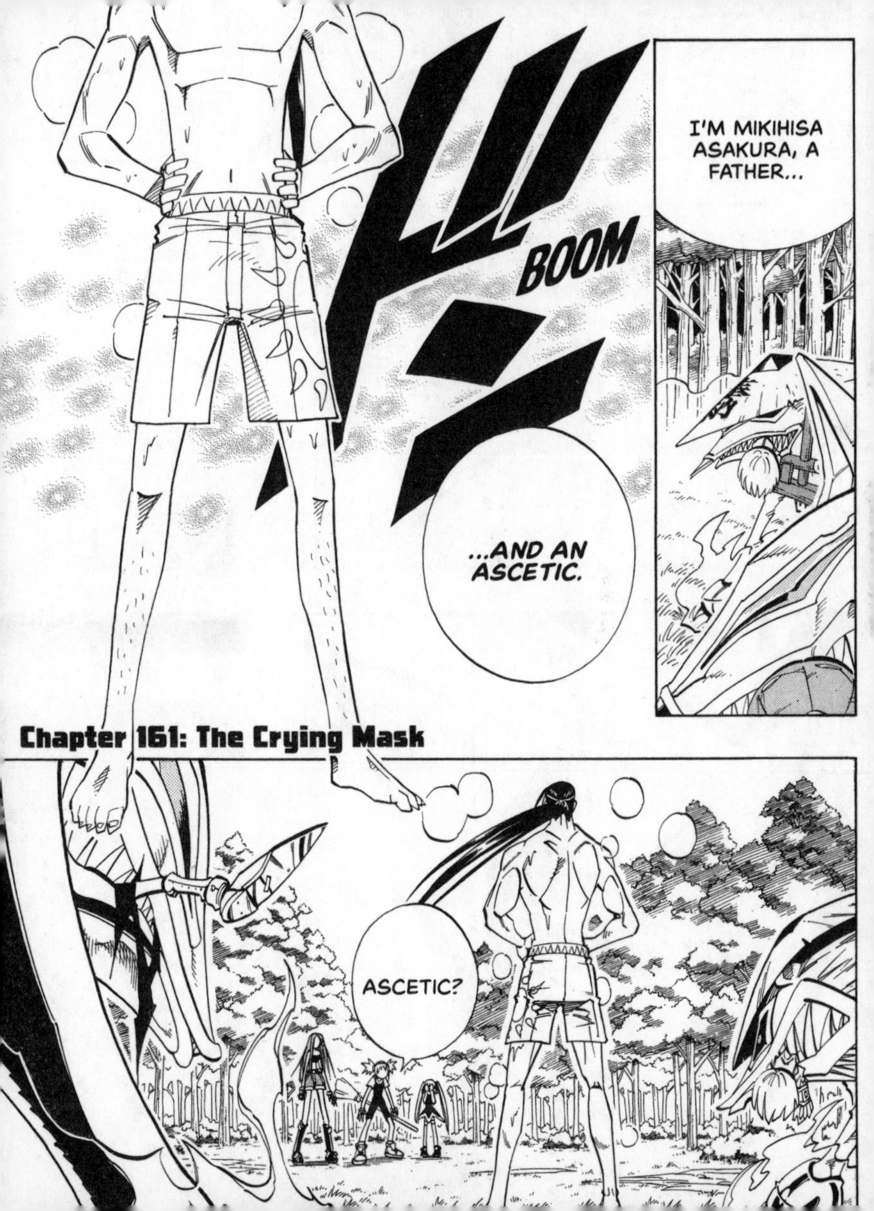
I'M MIKIHISA ASAKURA, A FATHER...
BOOM
...AND AN ASCETIC.
Chapter 161: The Crying Mask
ASCETIC?

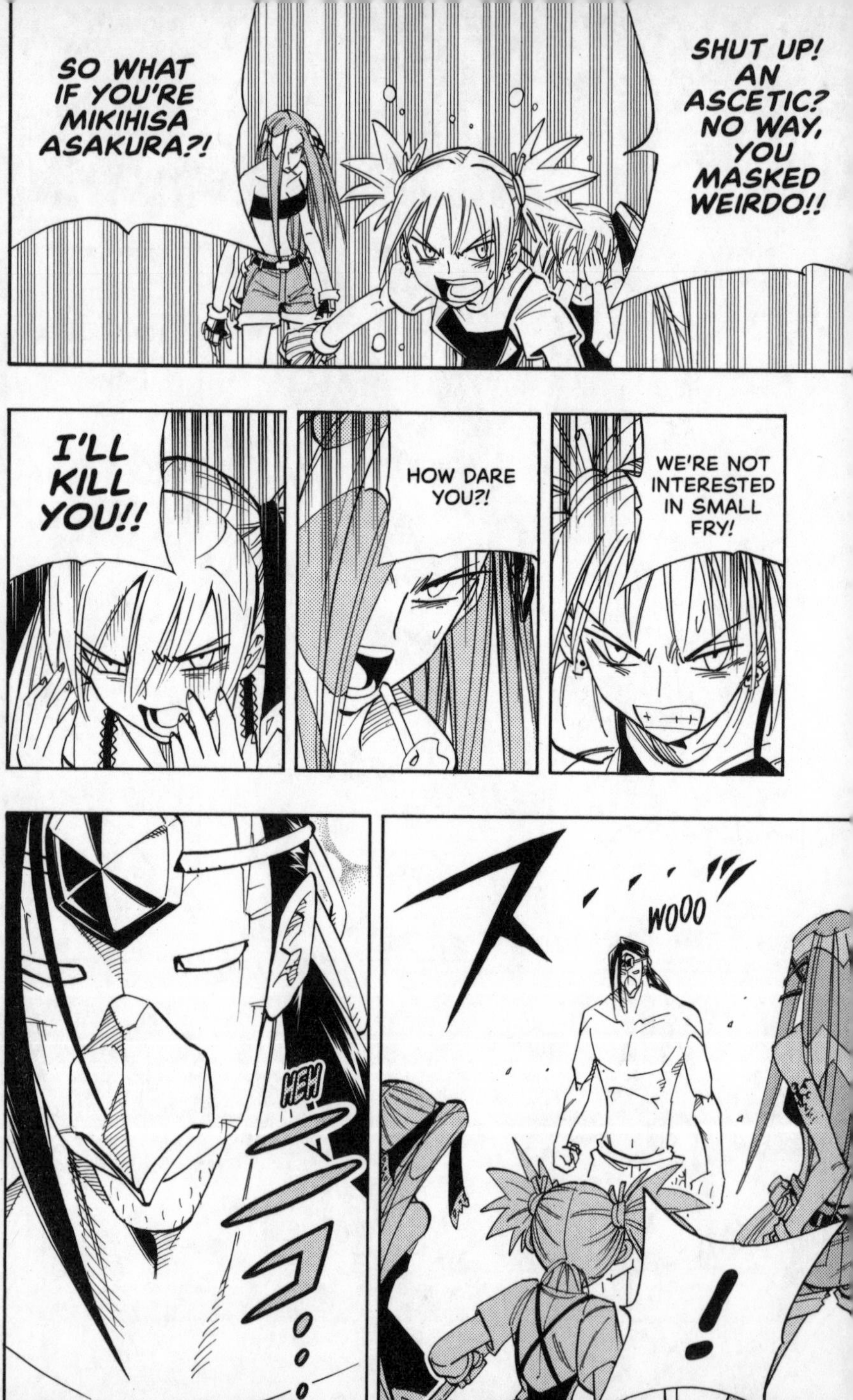
SHUT UP! AN ASCETIC? NO WAY, YOU MASKED WEIRDO!!
SO WHAT IF YOU'RE MIKIHISA ASAKURA?!
WE'RE NOT INTERESTED IN SMALL FRY!
HOW DARE YOU?!
I'LL KILL YOU!!
WOOO
!
HEH

Chapter 161:

The Crying Mask

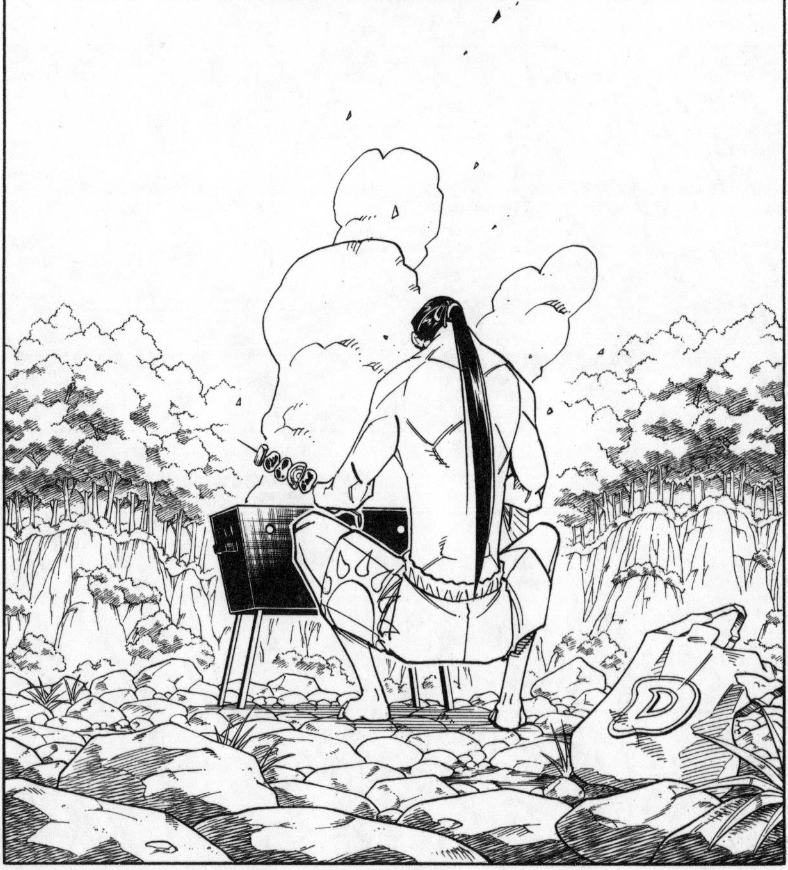

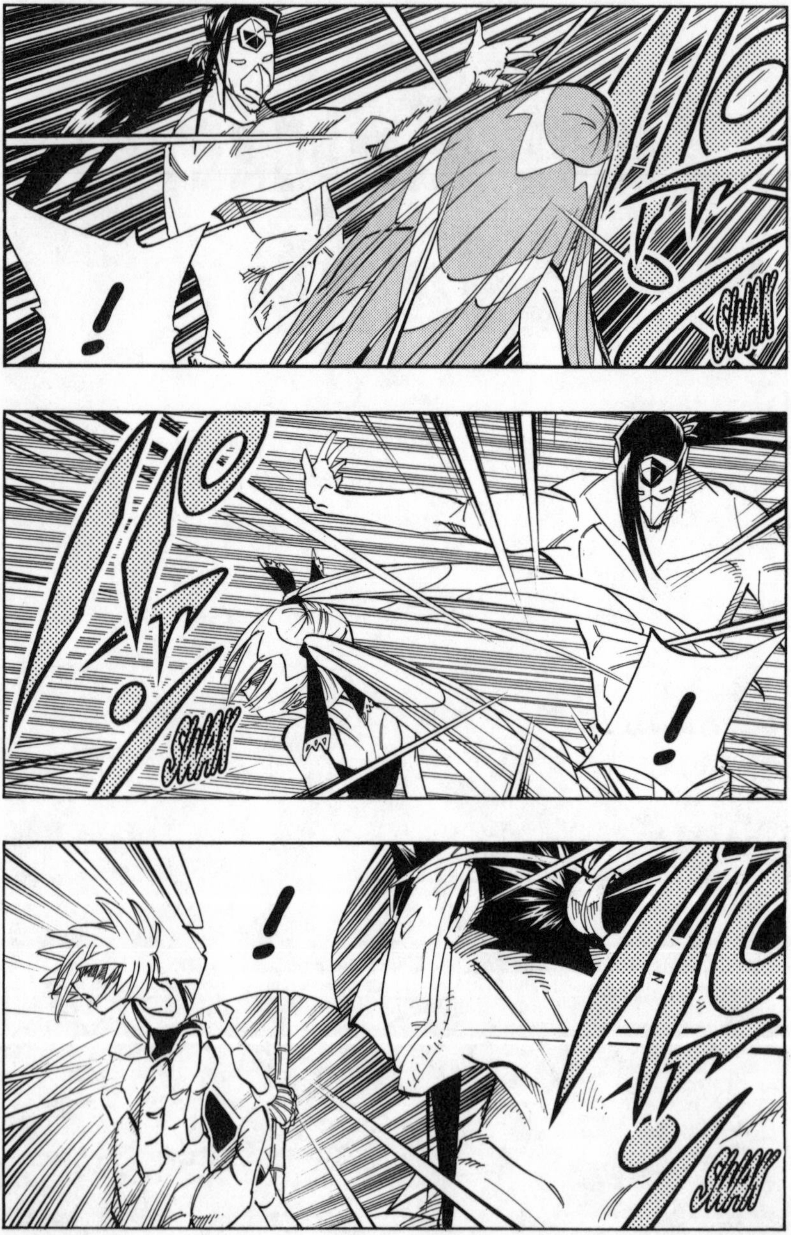
!
!
!

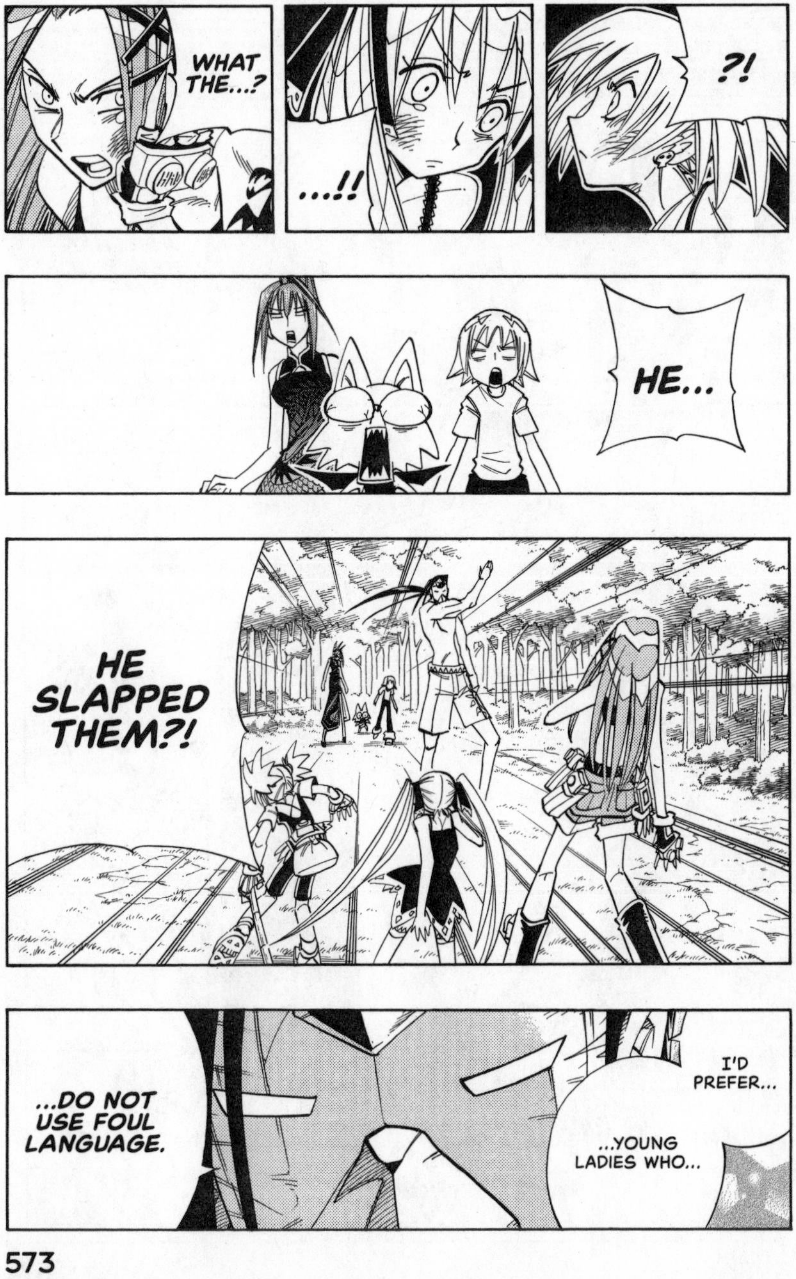
?!
...!!
WHAT THE...?
HE...
HE SLAPPED THEM?!
I'D PREFER...
...YOUNG LADIES WHO...
...DO NOT USE FOUL LANGUAGE.

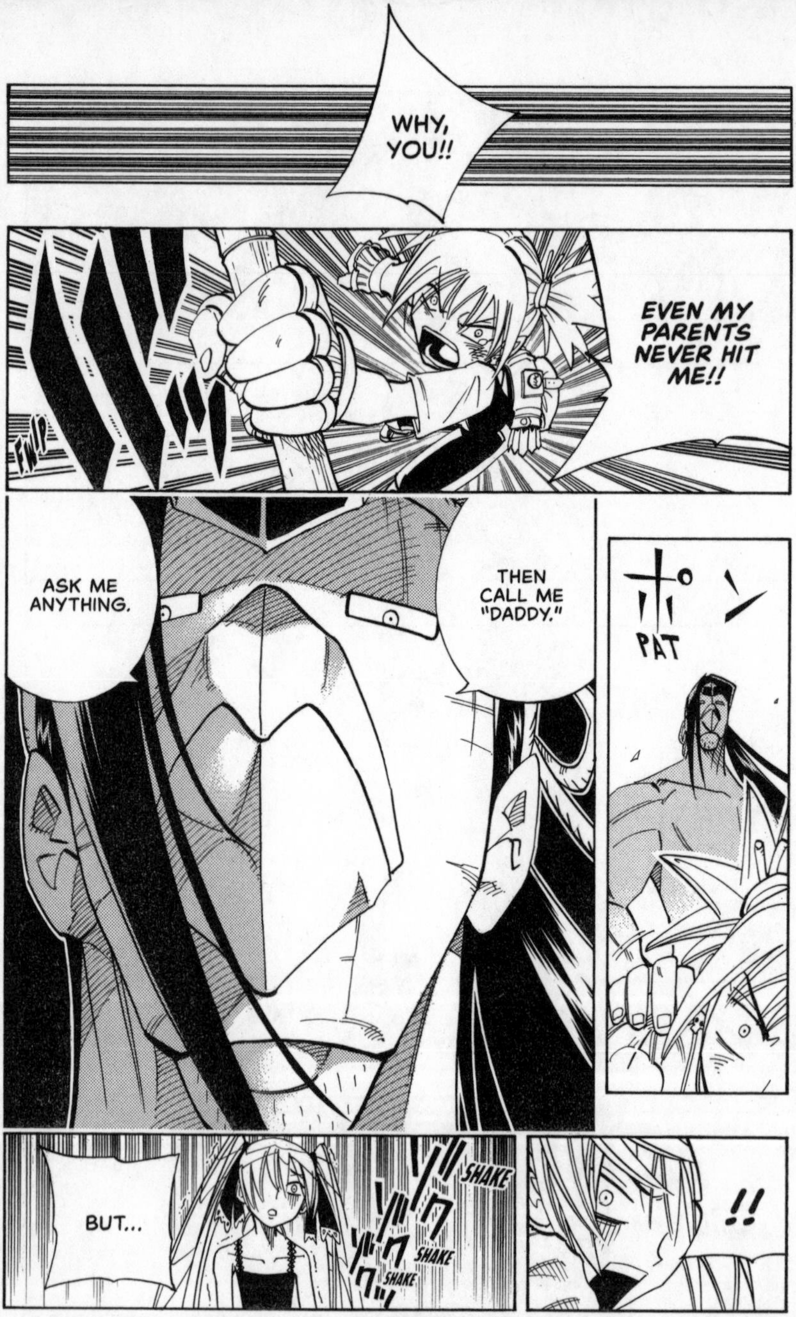
WHY, YOU!!
EVEN MY PARENTS NEVER HIT ME!!
FWIP
PAT
THEN CALL ME "DADDY."
ASK ME ANYTHING.
!!
SHAKE
SHAKE
SHAKE
BUT...

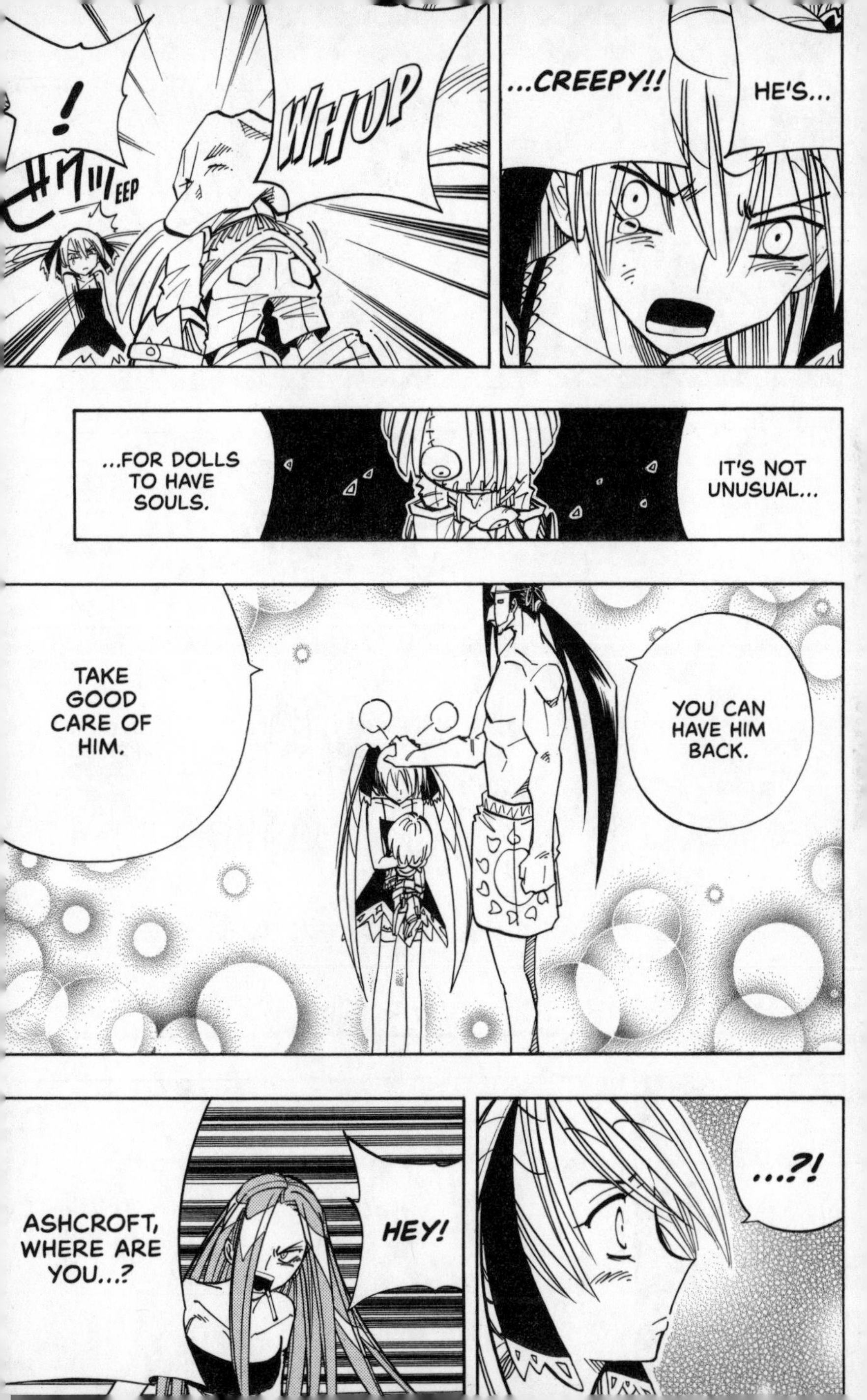
HE'S...
...CREEPY!!
WHUP
!
EEP
IT'S NOT UNUSUAL...
...FOR DOLLS TO HAVE SOULS.
YOU CAN HAVE HIM BACK.
TAKE GOOD CARE OF HIM.
...?!
HEY!
ASHCROFT, WHERE ARE YOU...?

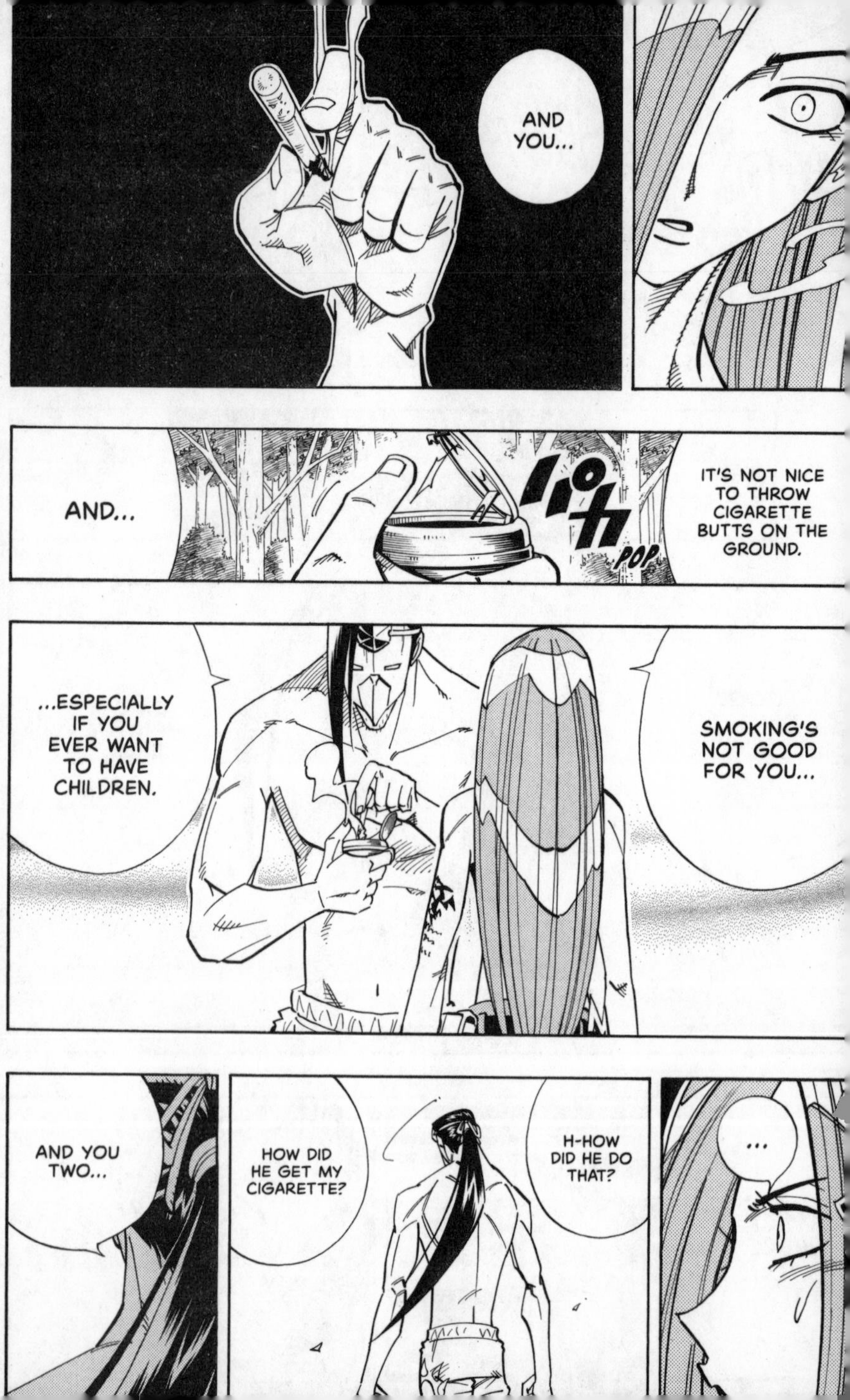
AND YOU...
IT'S NOT NICE TO THROW CIGARETTE BUTTS ON THE GROUND.
パカ
POP
AND...
SMOKING'S NOT GOOD FOR YOU...
...ESPECIALLY IF YOU EVER WANT TO HAVE CHILDREN.
...
H-HOW DID HE DO THAT?
HOW DID HE GET MY CIGARETTE?
AND YOU TWO...

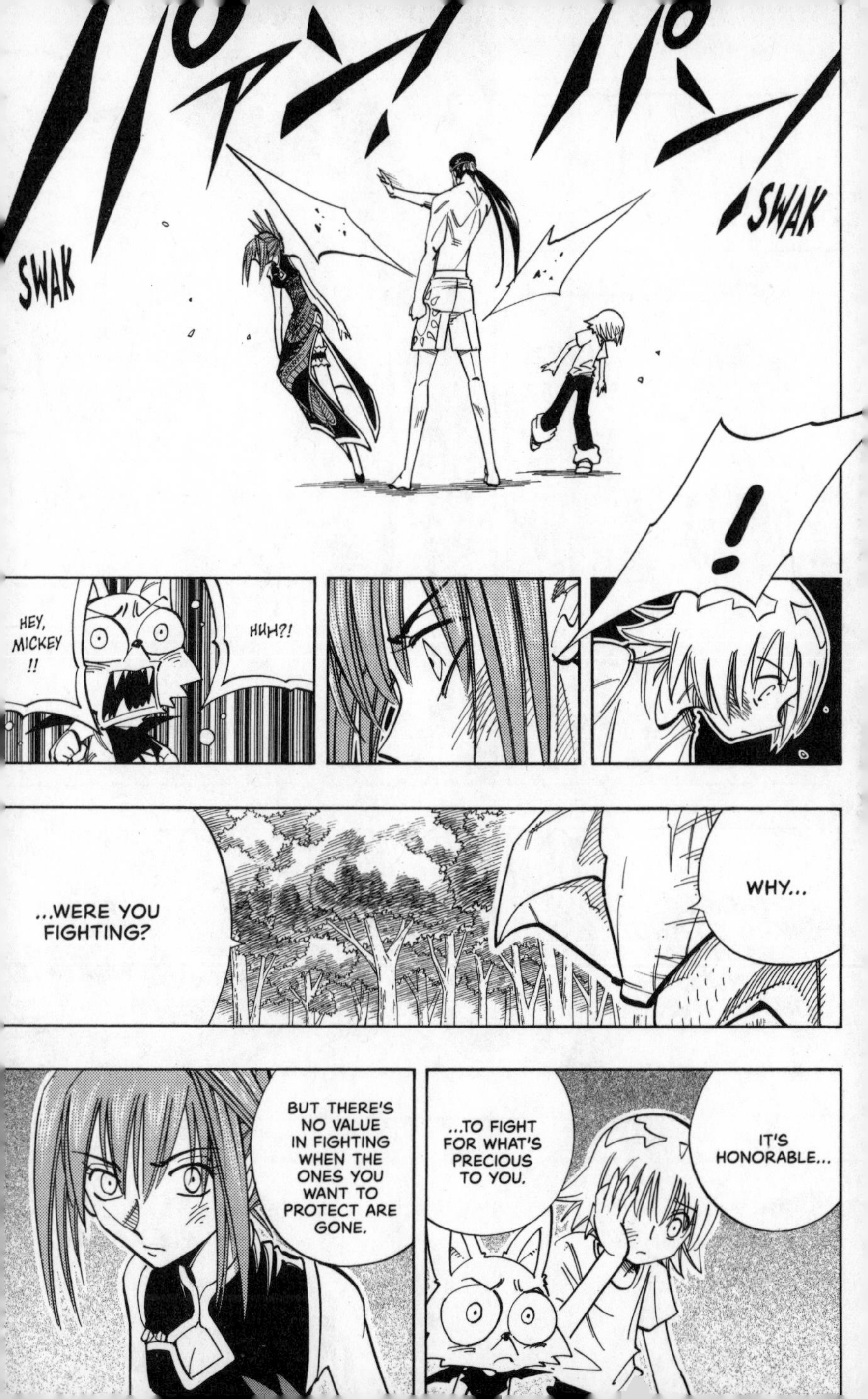

パン!
SWAK
パァン!
SWAK
!
HUH?!
HEY, MICKEY !!
WHY...
...WERE YOU FIGHTING?
IT'S HONORABLE...
...TO FIGHT FOR WHAT'S PRECIOUS TO YOU.
BUT THERE'S NO VALUE IN FIGHTING WHEN THE ONES YOU WANT TO PROTECT ARE GONE.

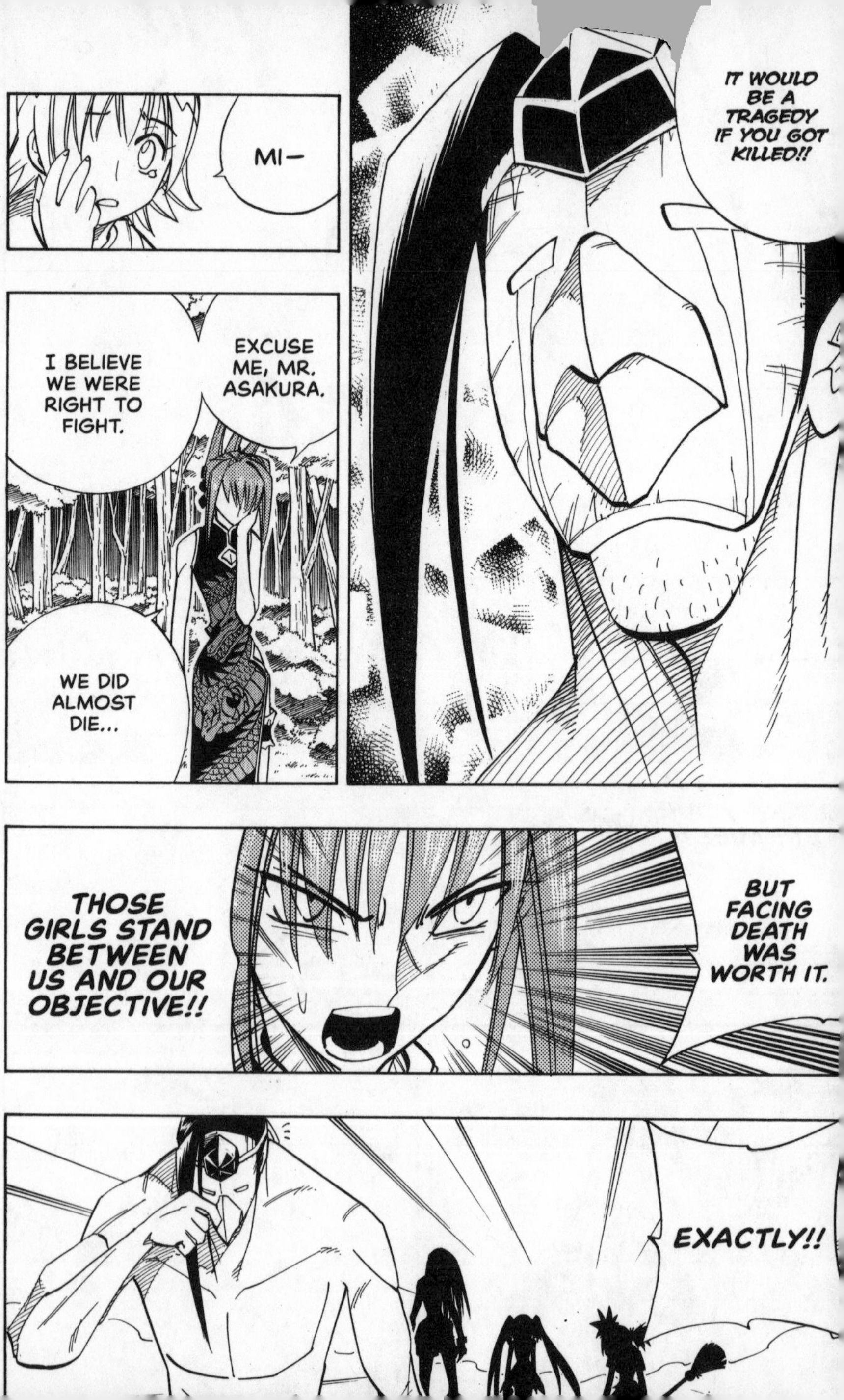
IT WOULD BE A TRAGEDY IF YOU GOT KILLED!!
MI—
EXCUSE ME, MR. ASAKURA.
I BELIEVE WE WERE RIGHT TO FIGHT.
WE DID ALMOST DIE...
BUT FACING DEATH WAS WORTH IT.
THOSE GIRLS STAND BETWEEN US AND OUR OBJECTIVE!!
EXACTLY!!

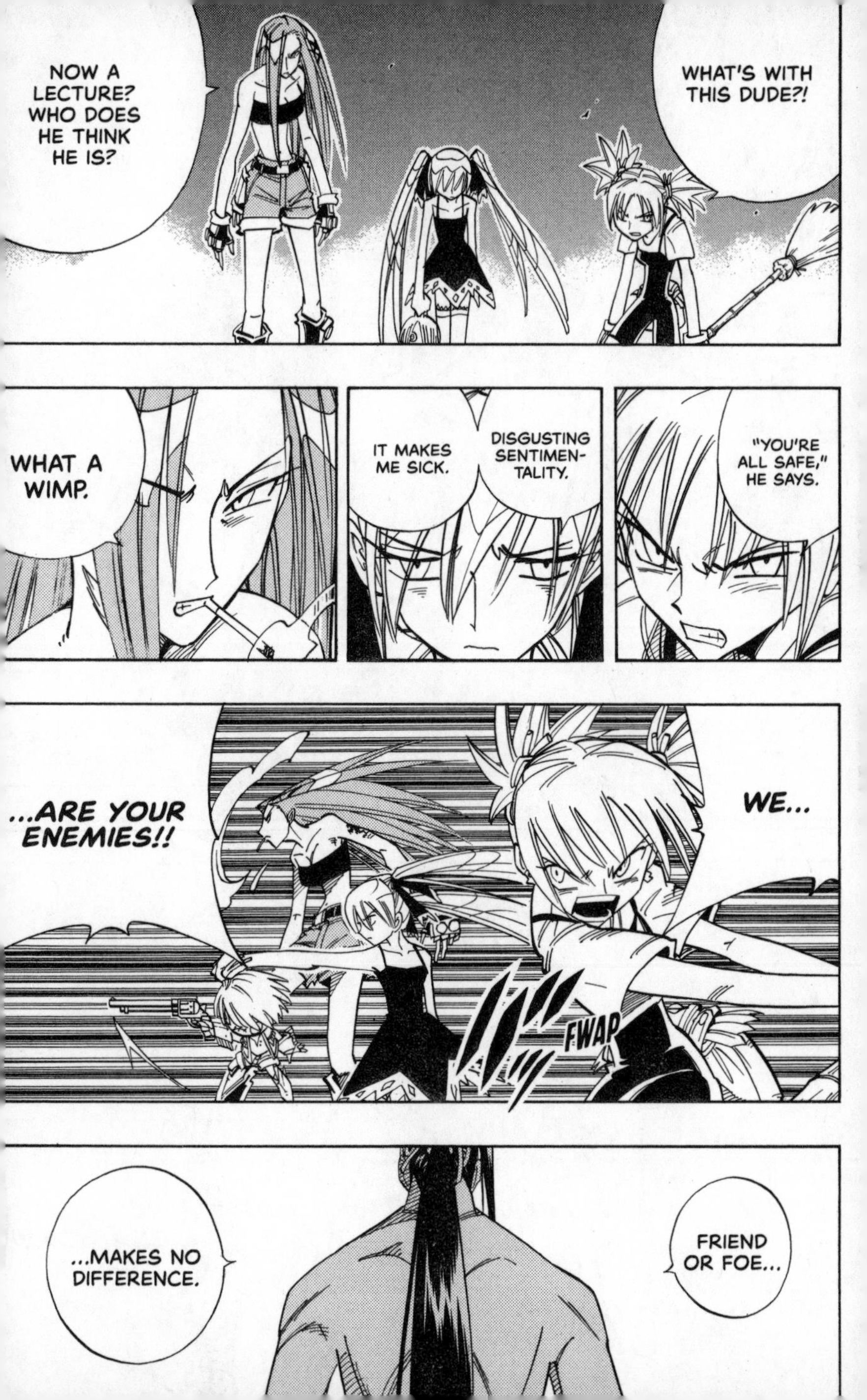
WHAT'S WITH THIS DUDE?!
NOW A LECTURE? WHO DOES HE THINK HE IS?
"YOU'RE ALL SAFE," HE SAYS.
DISGUSTING SENTIMEN-TALITY.
IT MAKES ME SICK.
WHAT A WIMP.
WE...
...ARE YOUR ENEMIES!!
FWAP
FRIEND OR FOE...
...MAKES NO DIFFERENCE.

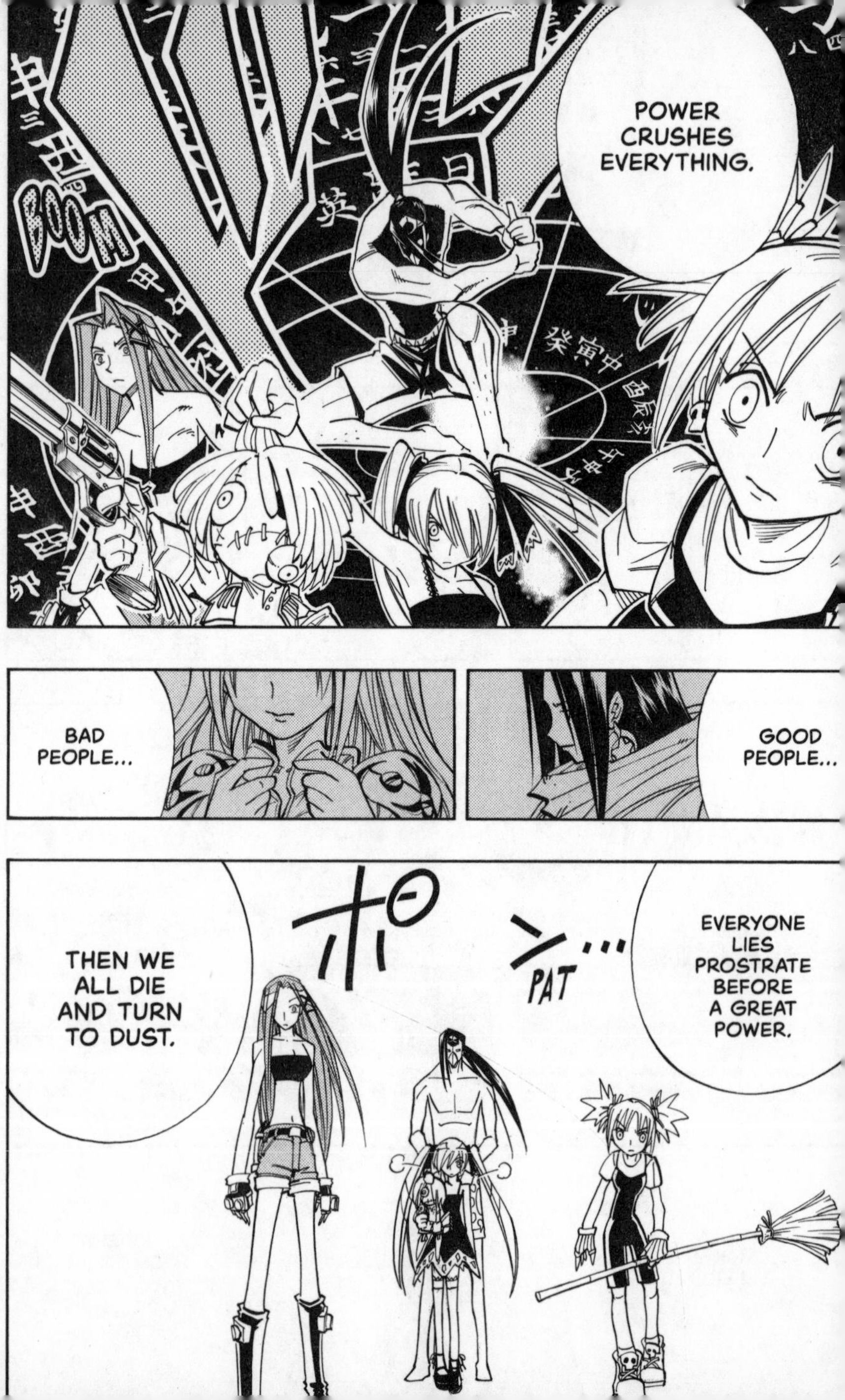
POWER CRUSHES EVERYTHING.
BOOM
GOOD PEOPLE...
BAD PEOPLE...
EVERYONE LIES PROSTRATE BEFORE A GREAT POWER.
ポン…
PAT
THEN WE ALL DIE AND TURN TO DUST.

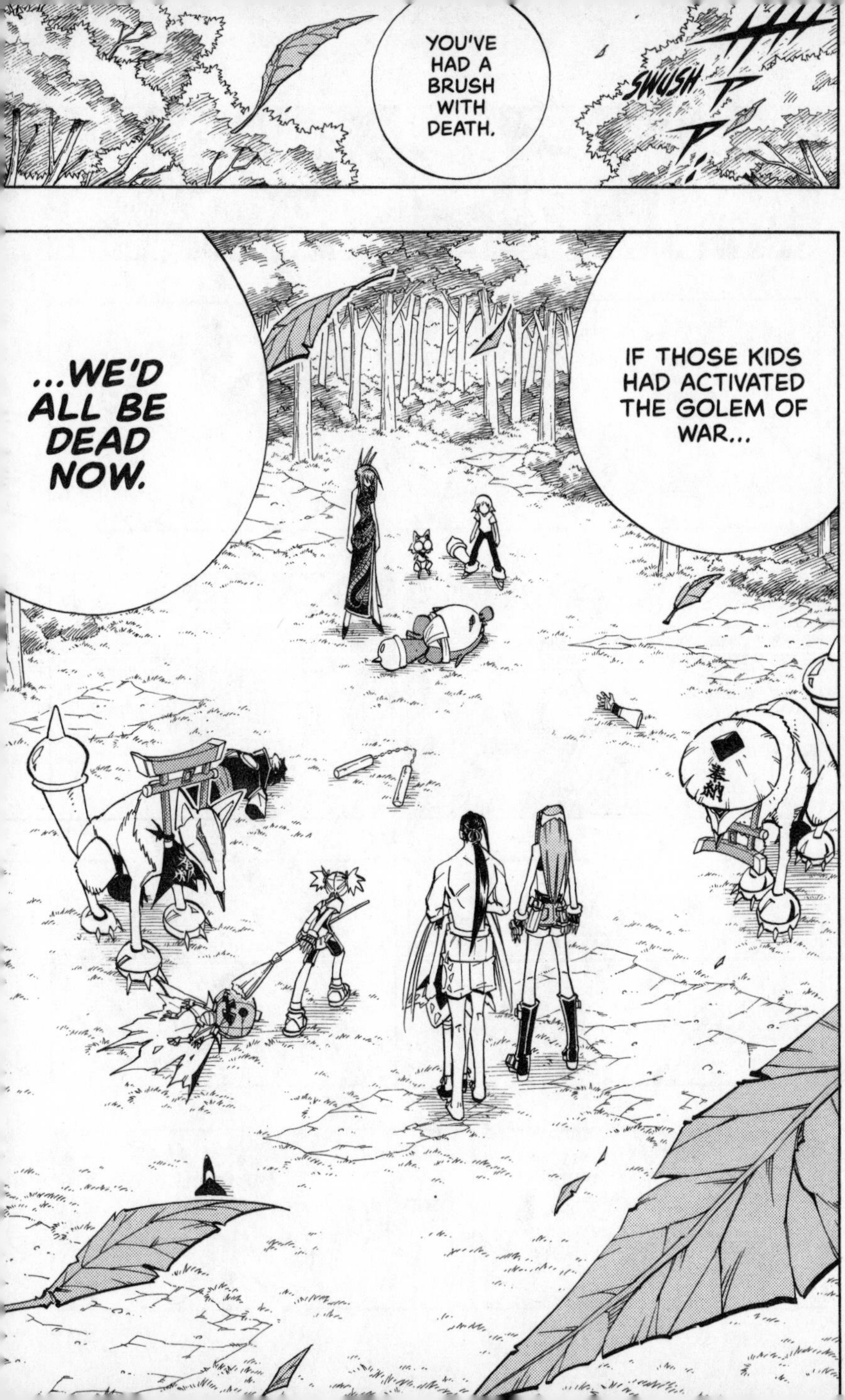
SWUSH
YOU'VE HAD A BRUSH WITH DEATH.
IF THOSE KIDS HAD ACTIVATED THE GOLEM OF WAR...
...WE'D ALL BE DEAD NOW.
奉納

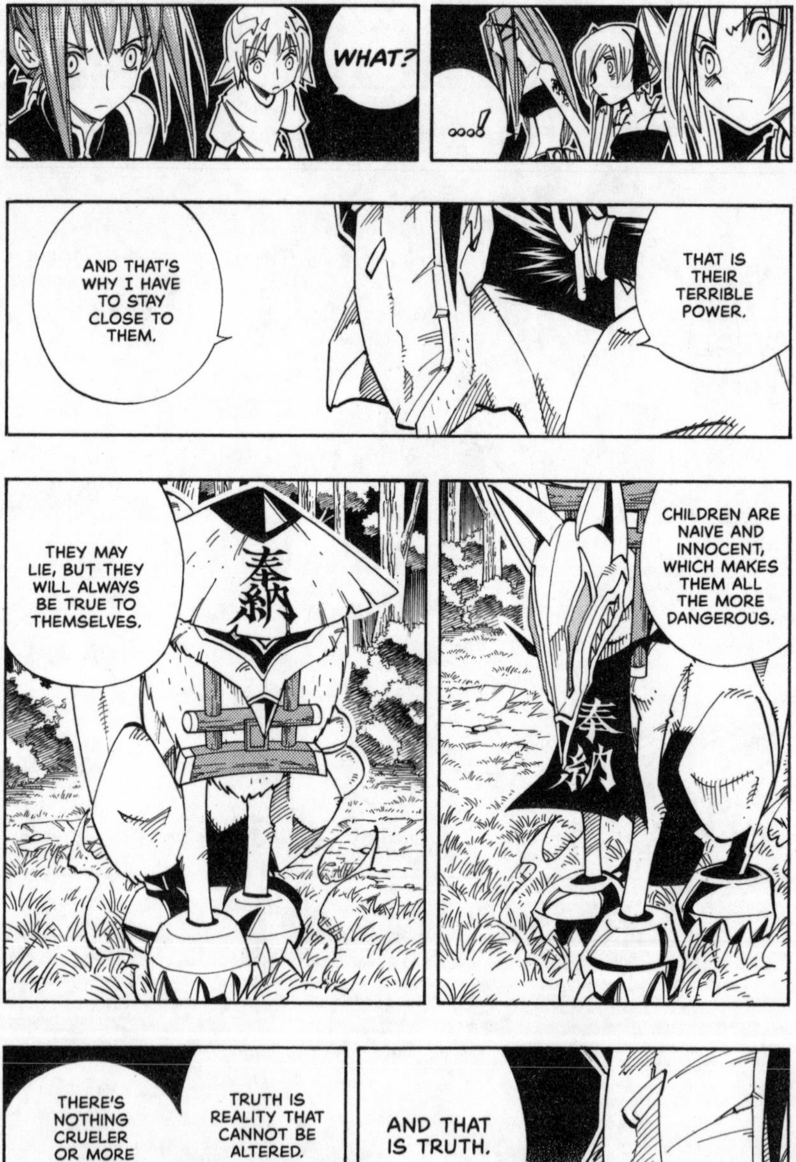
...!
WHAT?
THAT IS THEIR TERRIBLE POWER.
AND THAT'S WHY I HAVE TO STAY CLOSE TO THEM.
CHILDREN ARE NAIVE AND INNOCENT, WHICH MAKES THEM ALL THE MORE DANGEROUS.
THEY MAY LIE, BUT THEY WILL ALWAYS BE TRUE TO THEMSELVES.
AND THAT IS TRUTH.
TRUTH IS REALITY THAT CANNOT BE ALTERED.
THERE'S NOTHING CRUELER OR MORE COMMON-PLACE THAN TRUTH.

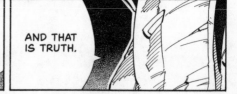

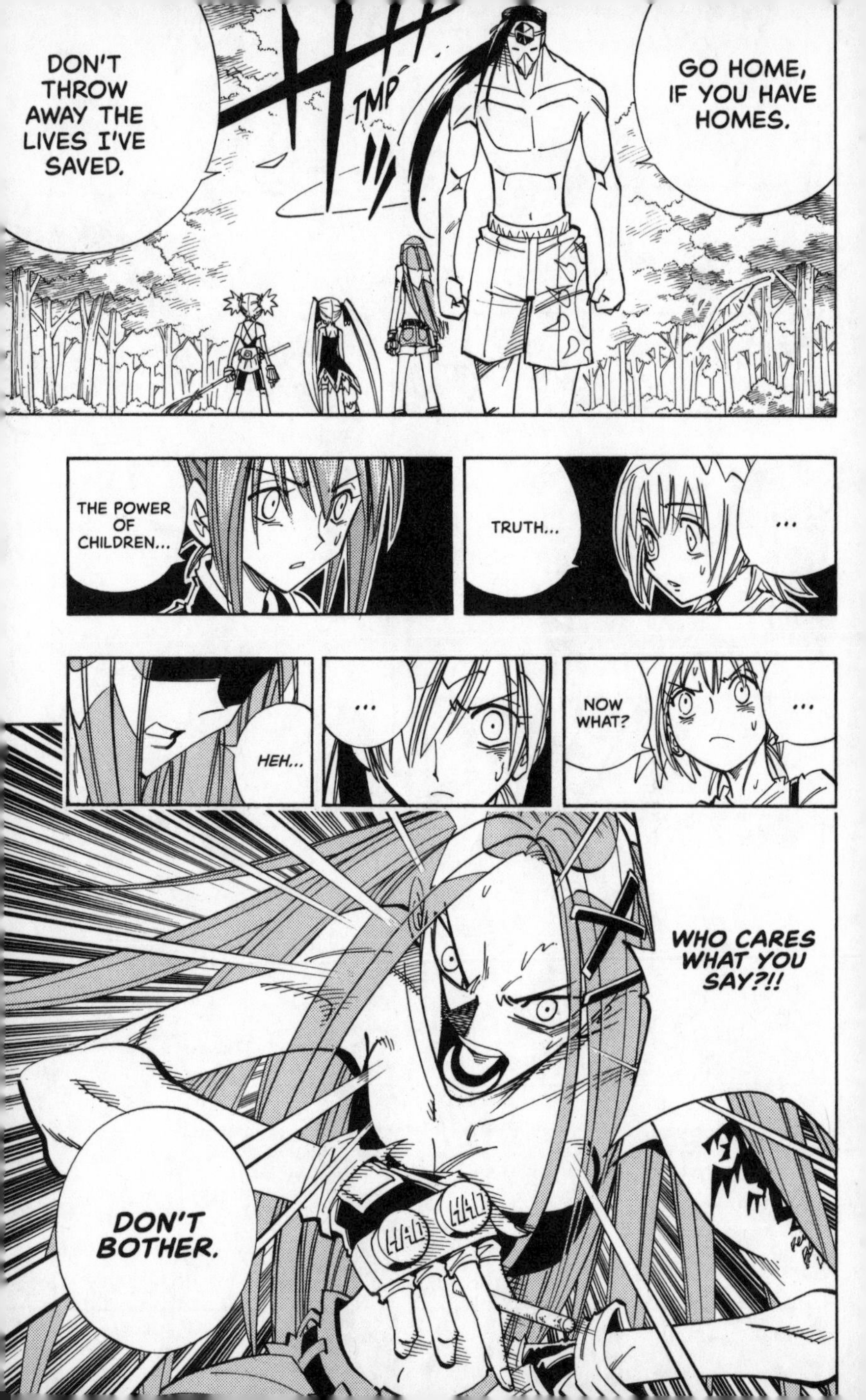
GO HOME, IF YOU HAVE HOMES.
TMP
DON'T THROW AWAY THE LIVES I'VE SAVED.
...
TRUTH...
THE POWER OF CHILDREN...
...
NOW WHAT?
...
HEH...
WHO CARES WHAT YOU SAY?!!
DON'T BOTHER.

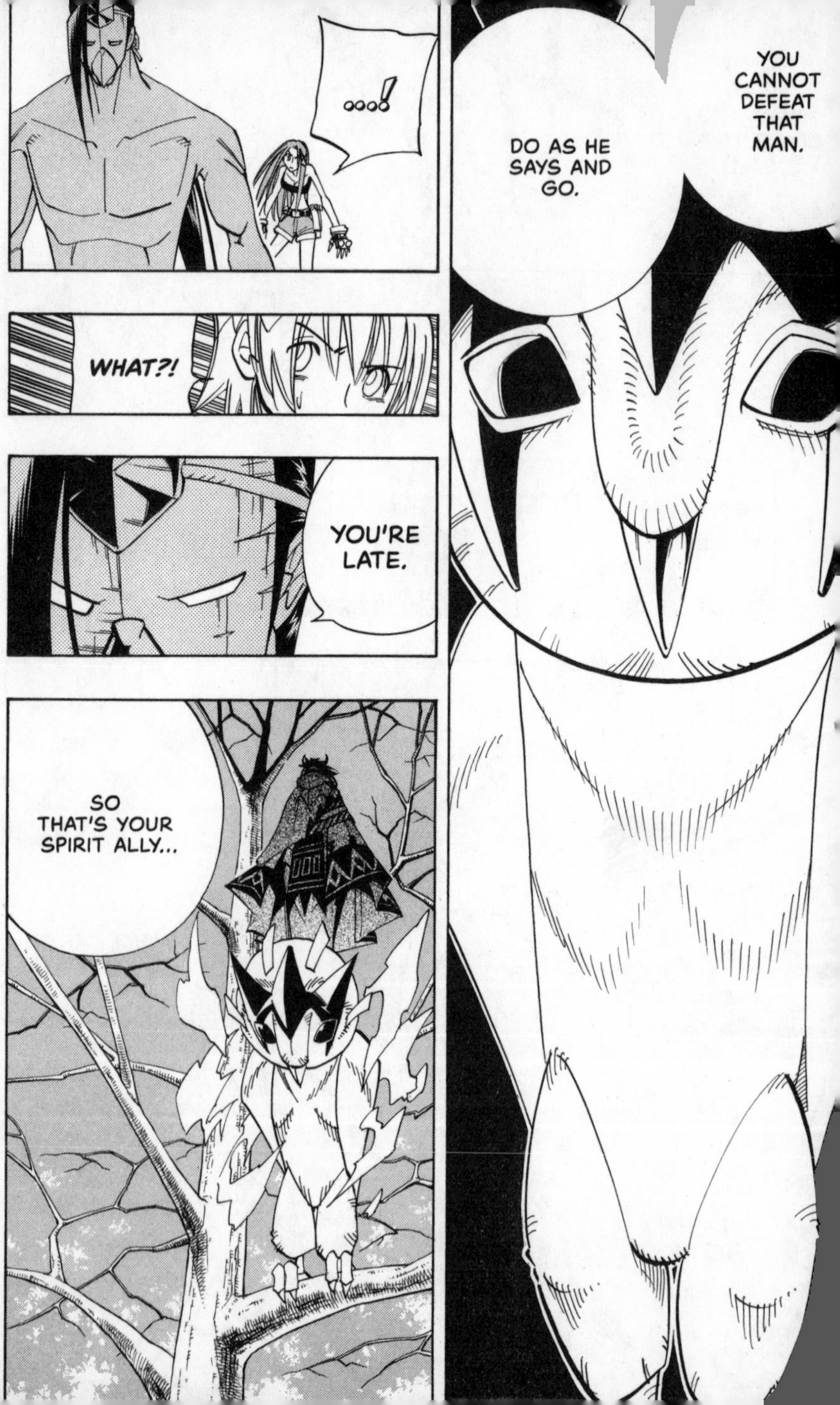
YOU CANNOT DEFEAT THAT MAN.
DO AS HE SAYS AND GO.
...!
WHAT?!
YOU'RE LATE.
SO THAT'S YOUR SPIRIT ALLY...

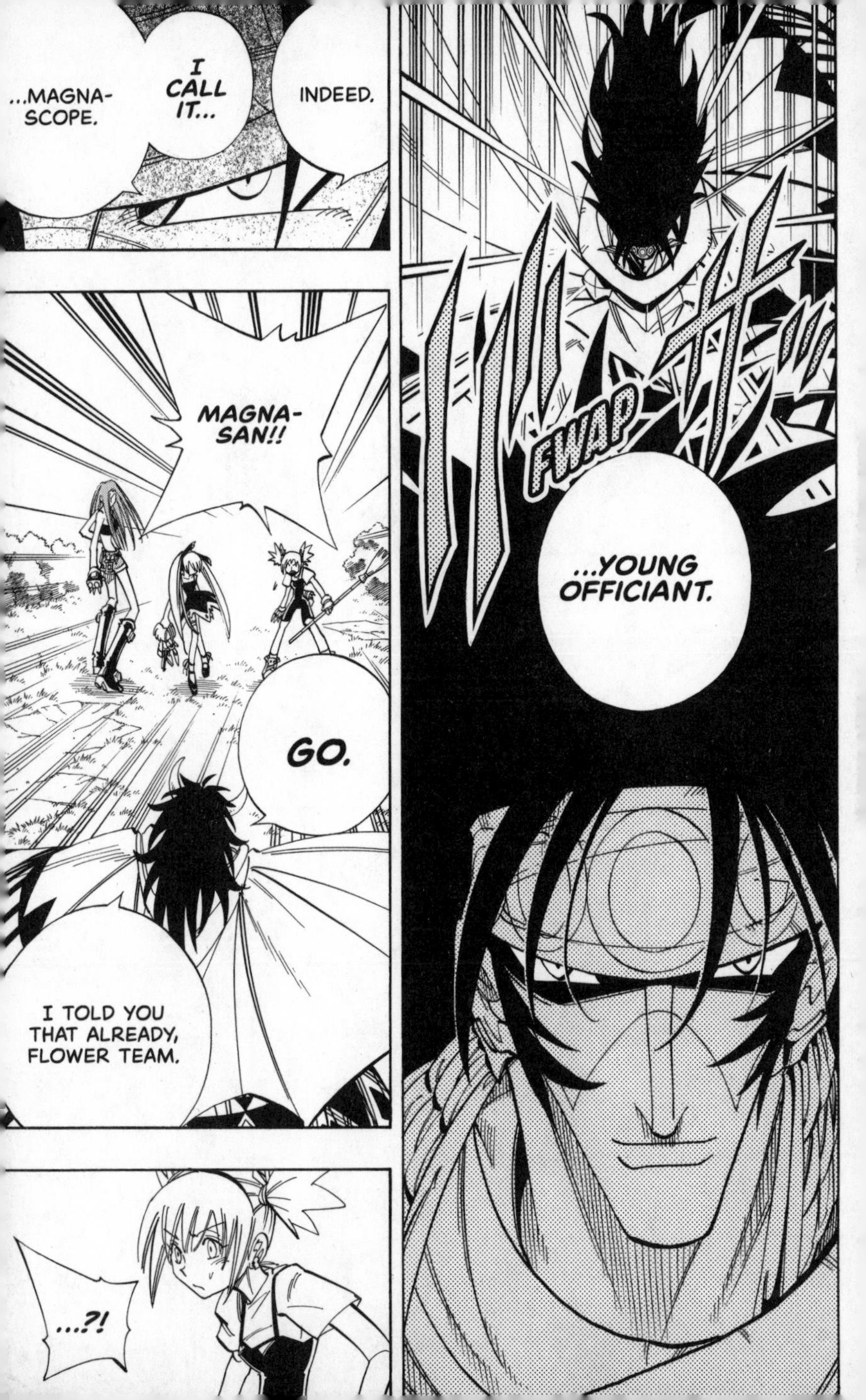
FWAP
...YOUNG OFFICIANT.
INDEED.
I CALL IT...
...MAGNA-SCOPE.
MAGNA-SAN!!
GO.
I TOLD YOU THAT ALREADY, FLOWER TEAM.
...?!

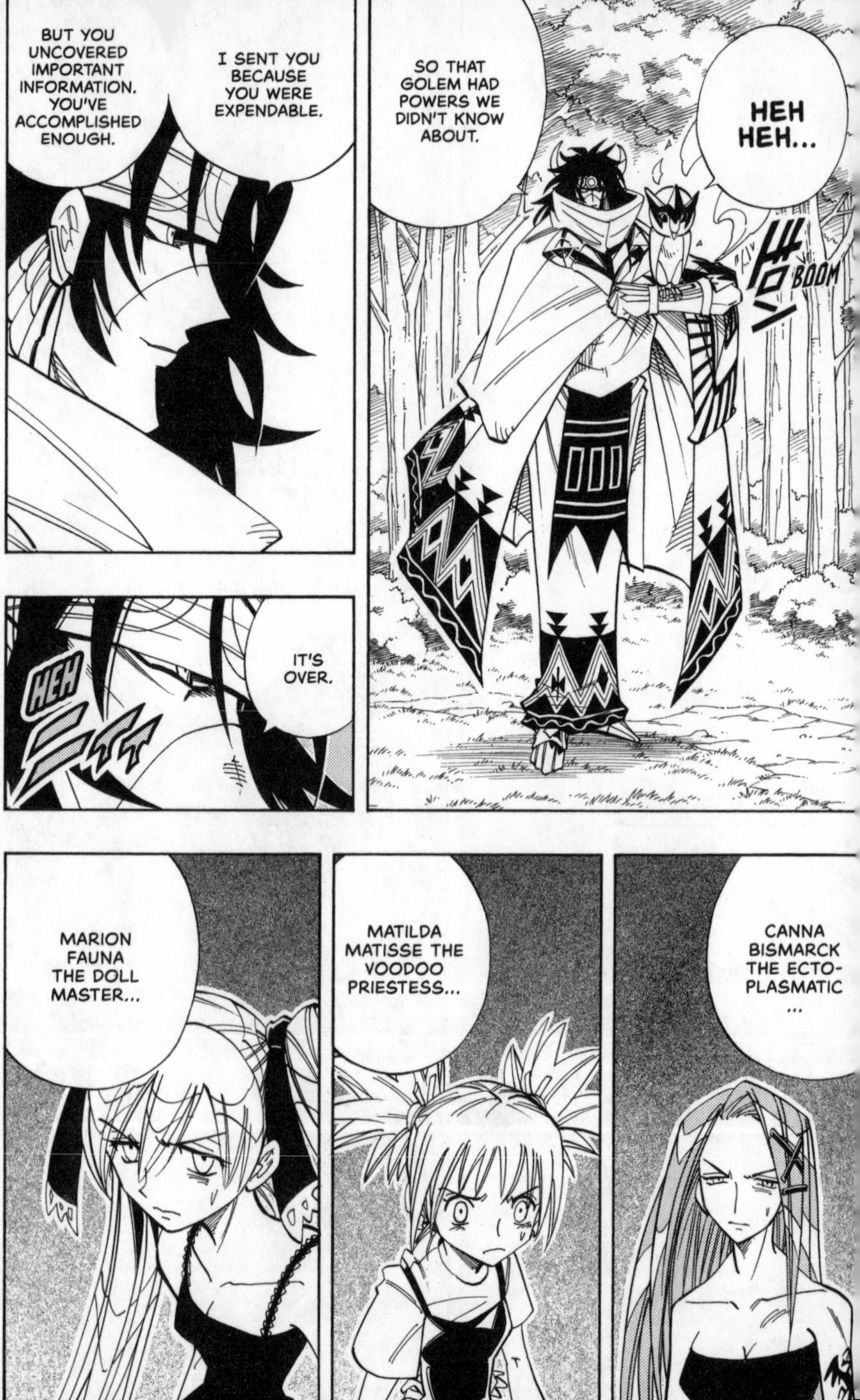
HEH HEH...
BOOM
SO THAT GOLEM HAD POWERS WE DIDN'T KNOW ABOUT.
I SENT YOU BECAUSE YOU WERE EXPENDABLE.
BUT YOU UNCOVERED IMPORTANT INFORMATION. YOU'VE ACCOMPLISHED ENOUGH.
IT'S OVER.
HEH
CANNA BISMARCK THE ECTO-PLASMATIC ...
MATILDA MATISSE THE VOODOO PRIESTESS...
MARION FAUNA THE DOLL MASTER...

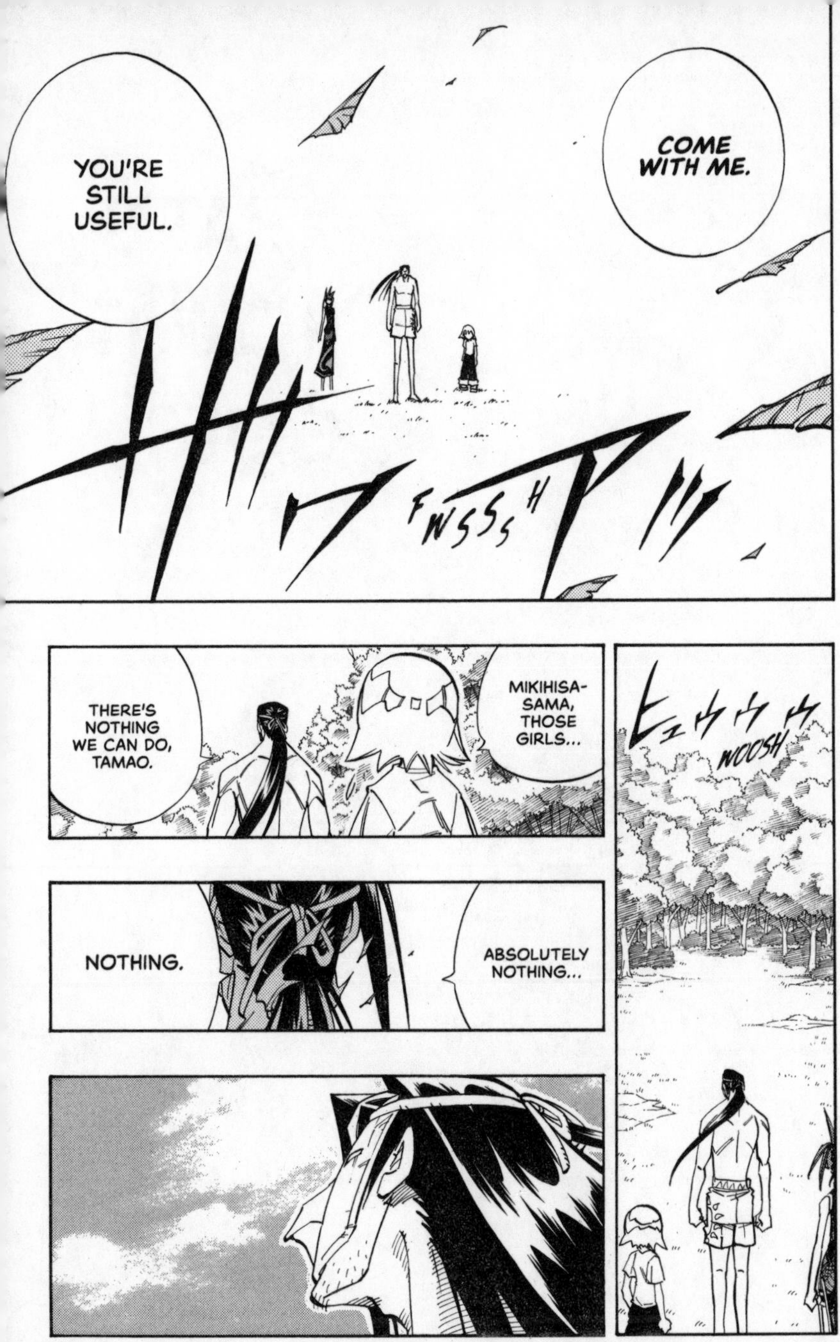
COME WITH ME.
YOU'RE STILL USEFUL.
FWSSSH
ヒュウウウ
WOOSH
MIKIHISA-SAMA, THOSE GIRLS...
THERE'S NOTHING WE CAN DO, TAMAO.
ABSOLUTELY NOTHING...
NOTHING.

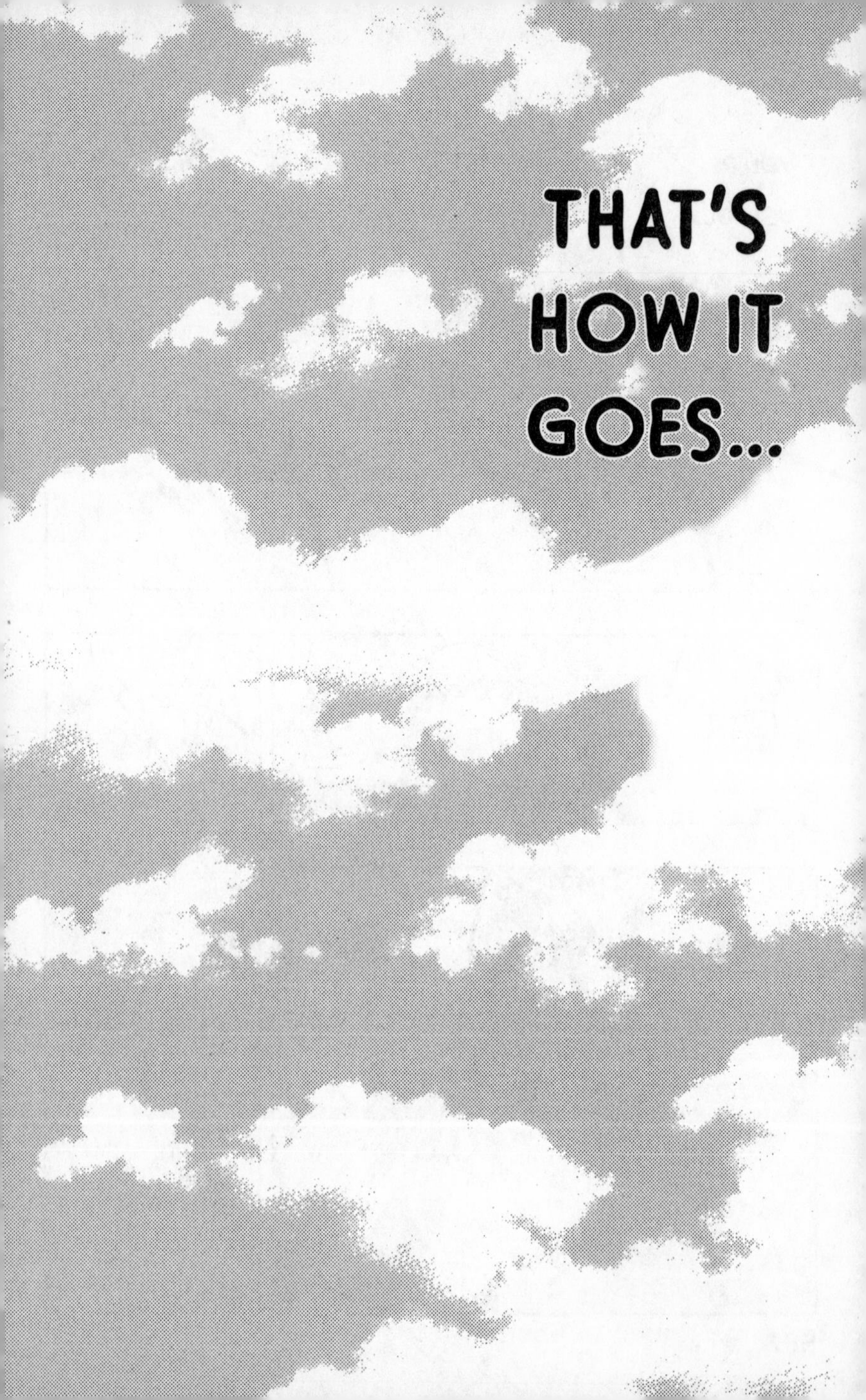
THAT'S HOW IT GOES...

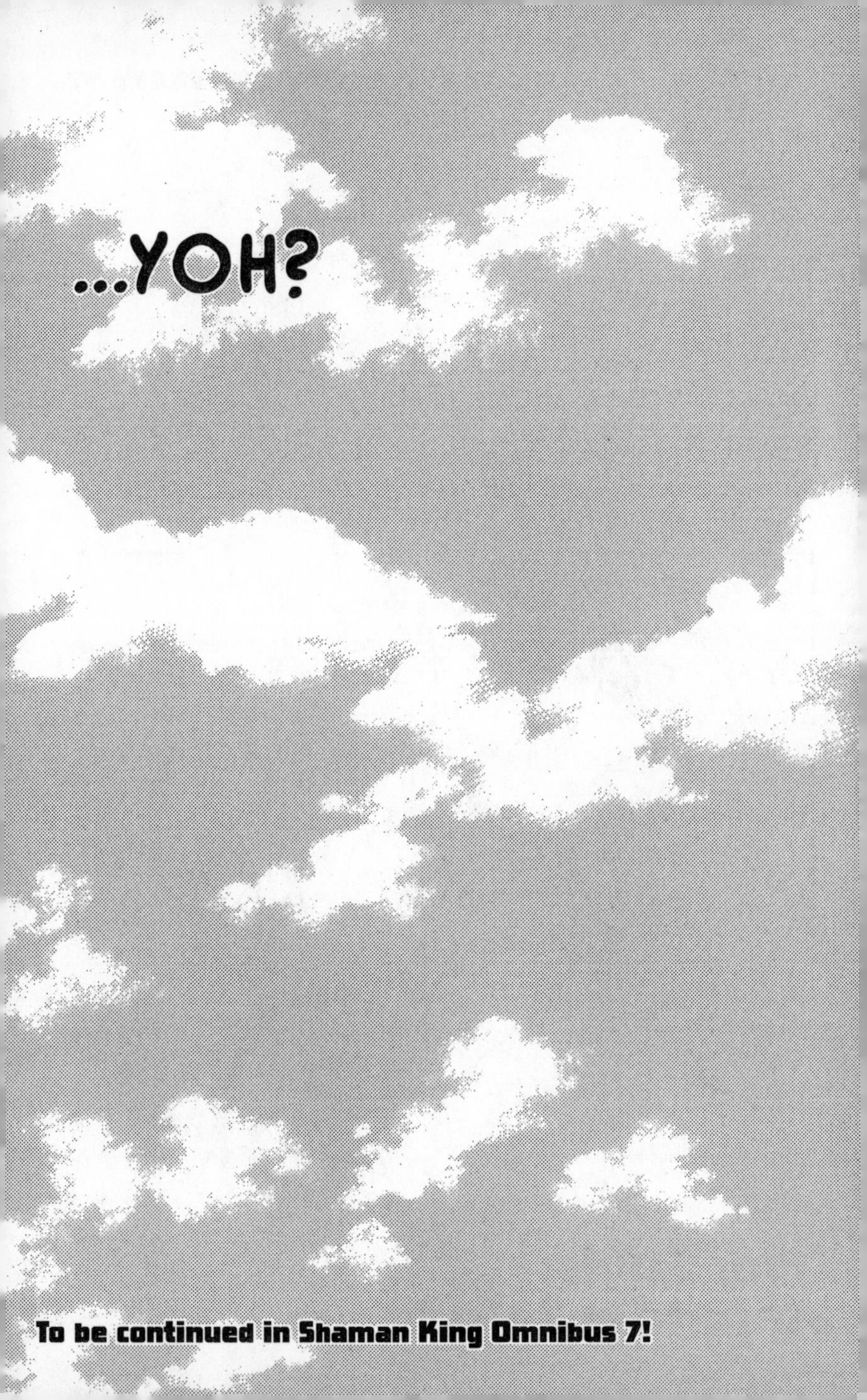
...YOH?
To be continued in Shaman King Omnibus 7!

SHAMAN KING CHARACTER FILE No.97

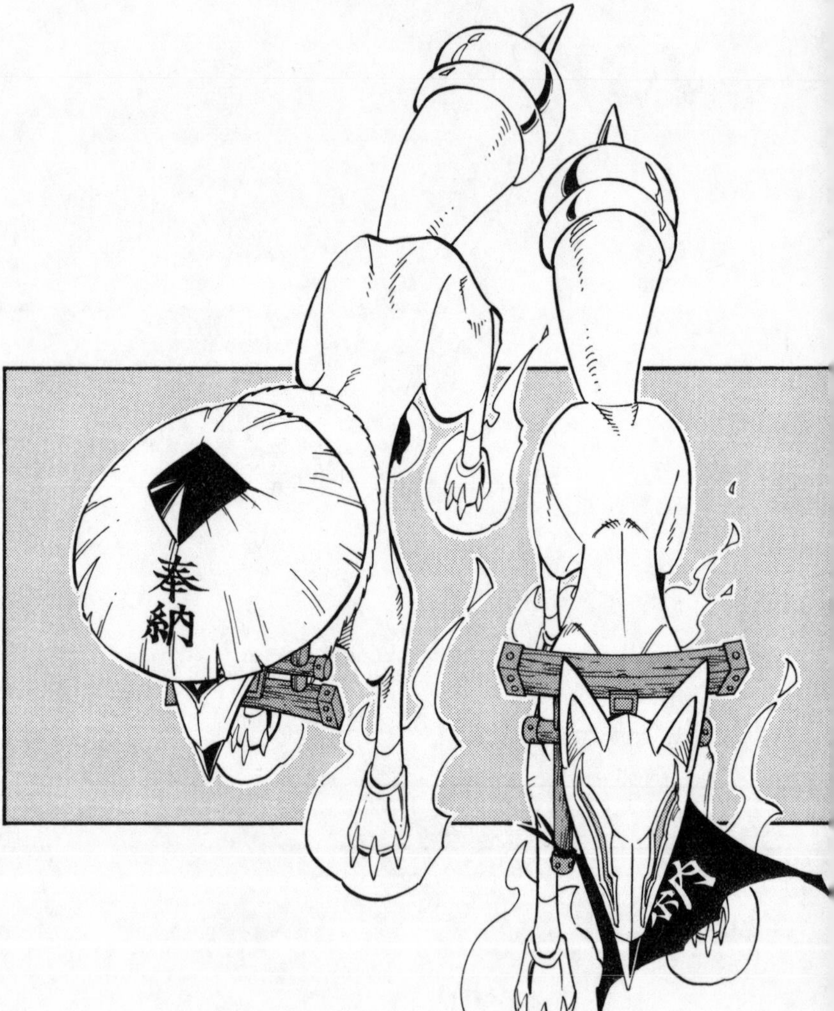
奉納

Over Souls: Mountain Spirits

A Kodansha Comics Trade Paperback Original
Shaman King Omnibus 6 copyright © 2020 Hiroyuki Takei
English translation copyright © 2021 Hiroyuki Takei

All rights reserved.

Published in the United States by Kodansha Comics, an imprint of Kodansha USA Publishing, LLC, New York.

Publication rights for this English edition arranged through Kodansha Ltd., Tokyo.

First published in Japan in 2020 by Kodansha Ltd., Tokyo.

ISBN 978-1-64651-284-3

Original cover design by Toru Fukushima (Smile Studio)

Printed in the United States of America.

www.kodansha.us

1st Printing
Translation: Lillian Olsen, Erin Procter
Lettering: Jan Lan Ivan Concepcion
Retouching: Jan Lan Ivan Concepcion, Nicole Roderick
Additional Lettering: Nicole Roderick
English Adaptation: Lance Caselman
Editing: Tomoko Nagano, Jason Thompson
YKS Services LLC/SKY Japan, INC.
Kodansha Comics edition cover design by Phil Balsman

Publisher: Kiichiro Sugawara

Director of publishing services: Ben Applegate
Associate director, publishing operations: Stephen Pakula
Publishing services managing editors: Madison Salters, Alanna Ruse
Production managers: Emi Lotto, Angela Zurlo
Logo and character art ©Kodansha USA Publishing, LLC

How To Read Manga

YOU READ MANGA ***RIGHT TO LEFT*** JAPANESE STYLE!

FOLLOW THE NUMBERS BELOW STARTING FROM THE **TOP RIGHT PANEL** AND KEEP IT MOVING FROM THERE! YOU MAY FEEL LIKE YOU'RE READING BACKWARDS, BUT YOU'LL GET THE HANG OF IT FASTER THAN YOU THINK! IF YOU GET LOST ALONG THE WAY, JUST TAKE A LOOK AT THE SAMPLE BELOW! HAPPY READING, AND HAVE FUN!

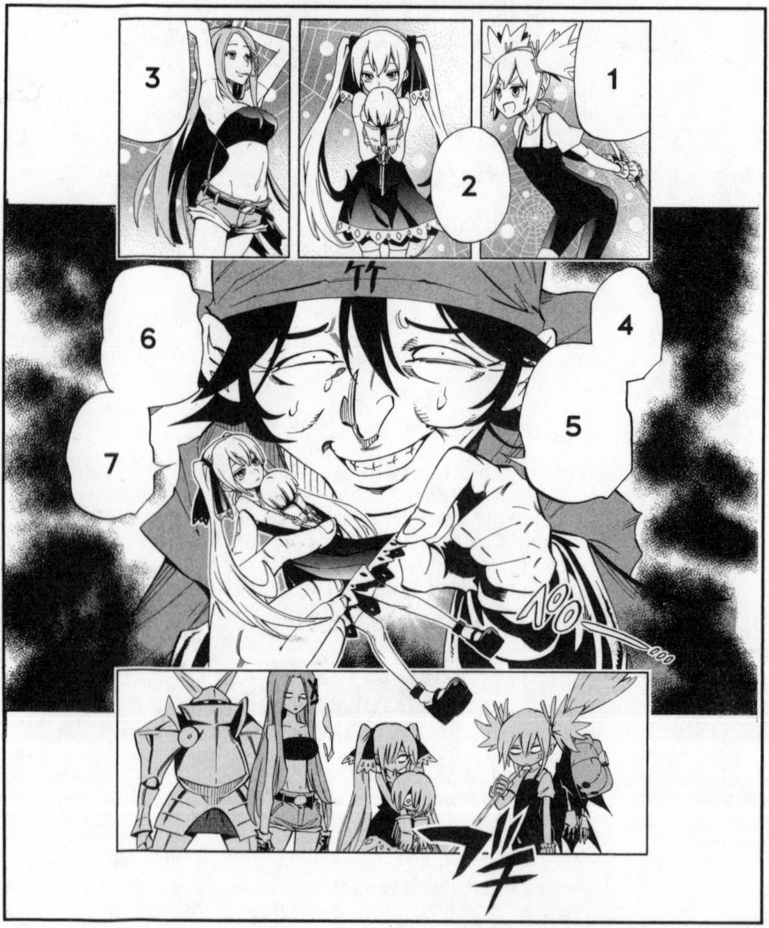
1
2
3
4
5
6
7